Another World

ANOTHER WORLD

Frank Logan

The Book Guild Ltd.
Sussex, England.

This book is sold subject to the condition that it shall not, by way of trade or otherwise, be lent, re-sold, hired out, photocopied or held in any retrieval system or otherwise circulated without the publisher's prior consent in any form of binding or cover other than that in which this is published and without a similar condition including this condition being imposed on the subsequent purchaser.

The Book Guild Ltd.
25 High Street,
Lewes, Sussex.

First published 1992
© Frank Logan 1991
Set in Baskerville
Typesetting by Southern Reproductions (Sussex)
East Grinstead, Sussex
Printed in Great Britain by
Antony Rowe Ltd.
Chippenham, Wiltshire.

British Library Cataloguing in Publication Data
Logan, Frank, 1904-
 Another world.
 1. Social life. History
 909. 82092

ISBN 0 86332 663 3

CONTENTS

1	A small boy in Africa	5
2	Growing up in England	16
3	A hard life at school	29
4	France and my first love affair	37
5	Cambridge – the three best years of my life	47
6	Skiing in Switzerland and getting engaged	56
7	Off to India – alone	81
8	A different life in the Indian Civil Service	89
9	(1) Back to England to get married (2) Our first daughter is born in Allahabad – 'the abode of Allah'	110
10	My father visits us in Roorkhee	127
11	(1) I become a Judge (2) Our second daughter is born 'in the hills'	144
12	A change of life – back to England for good and a new job	152

LIST OF ILLUSTRATIONS

Frank and Brian Logan as small boys in Nakuru	67
Sir Ewen Logan	67
A few zebra	68
Ewshott Cottage	68
Frank and Brian at Weymouth c. 1912	69
The wedding of Frank Logan to Peggy Fass	70
The author and his wife, Allahabad	71
Our unusual cavalcade in Allahabad	72
John Nash with the Pigeons	72
Peggy and Leonora at Foxhill, May 1934	73
Peggy with her parents	73
Christmas camp at Andheri Rau, 1934	74
Nancy and Raymond Vernede	75
The author's Magnificent Tiger	76
The author, the District Officer	77
Peggy and Frank at Cambridge	78
Leonora and Frank at Totland Bay, 1938	78
Sara in her father's hat	79
The first summer after our return from India	79
Grannie Neame with the Children, Totland	80

1

A Small Boy in Africa

'We shall be quite all right if we meet a lion,' I remarked to my brother, 'now that I have my new gun.' It was my sixth birthday, and I had just been given a toy gun that fired a cork attached to a piece of string. I felt perfectly confident that we would indeed be all right if we met a lion, which was not entirely impossible. My brother Brian and I had escaped from our nurse and were walking over the lower slopes of a small extinct volcano that rose behind our parents' bungalow in Nakuru in British East Africa, now Kenya, where my father was the Resident Magistrate. In those far-off days the country teemed with game, and when we drove out in our trap to visit a friend who farmed a few miles from Nakuru, we were sometimes held up by large herds of zebra crossing the road. On one occasion we passed quite close to a pride of lions lolling lazily about in the tawny African grass. They looked lovable, but when I asked my mother if I could have a cub as a pet, she replied with unusual sharpness, 'No.' I knew, of course, from the grown-ups' talk that lions were dangerous., but the word held no meaning for a child of my age.

My father, after leaving Oxford, had been a struggling young barrister for a year or two, and had then enlisted in the Imperial Yeomanry and gone out to South Africa towards the end of the Boer War. Surviving a severe attack of typhoid, he had obtained a temporary post as Magistrate in an obscure little town in the Transvaal called Volksrust. My unfortunate mother, who was about thirty – old for marriage in those days – came out to join him. They were married in Cape Town from a distant relative's house, and then, after the briefest of honeymoons, they made the long journey to Volksrust, which, as old letters show, they both heartily disliked – a dusty, primitive little *dorp*, where they were surrounded by hostile neighbours with whom we had recently been at war. My father – a man of the highest rectitude – fell foul of that distinguished, but to us not very likeable character Lord Milner, because he had refused to allow some traders to filch an area (several 'erwins') of railway land belonging to the Government. Milner, putting politics above law, took the side of the Boers when they lobbied him, and my father's appointment was terminated, being held, in Milner's phrase, 'at pleasure'. I rather think that my mother had returned to England by this time, in order to have her first child (myself) at her parents' home at Ewshott, Surrey.

My father eventually obtained an appointment in the Colonial Judicial Service and was posted to Nairobi as a Resident Magistrate in the newly created Protectorate of British East Africa. My mother, with myself and my brother Brian, joined him there, but I recall nothing of this first visit to Africa.

The very earliest memory I have is of being brought on deck at night as our outward-bound ship passed Stromboli, which had recently erupted. I have a hazy recollection of a steep mountain, with white houses clinging to its side and a red glow in the sky above the summit. Small children for the most part are only capable of taking in what is close to them or relates in some way to their experience – their parents, their toys, their pets, the cracks in the nursery ceiling, a favourite piece of old wood. But when the ship reached Kilindini (still the port for Mombasa) on our way to Nakuru, there was something really to thrill me. We travelled from the harbour to the railway station on a trolley pushed by African 'boys' (first time only) along real railway lines; on the way the trolley stopped, the head boy went to the side of the road and pulled a lever to change the points, and then waved a green flag. It was more exciting than almost anything that has happened to me since.

In Nakuru we lived an ordered life, modelled as closely as possible on an English upbringing, but there were differences. In the afternoons we were taken for a walk by our nurse along a dusty white road which led in one direction into Nakuru and the other out into the bush. On our walks we passed groups of Africans going or coming from market in the little township, and I observed the bare breasts of the women just as I noticed the spears and knobkerries carried by the men. I realized that the women were different from the men, but it was all part of Africa, and I doubt if I made the intellectual jump, at any rate consciously, to connecting this difference with my nurse and my mother. One day we saw a moving cloud of dust in the distance: our nurse turned tail, clutched our hands, and rushed us back to the bungalow at top speed, taking a short cut across some rough scrub which normally she would not have dared to do, for fear of snakes. I gathered from our parents' conversation that nurse had probably seen a hartebeeste – a perfectly harmless, though fairly large animal. I was furious, and remarked to my father, 'If only nurse had allowed me to bring my gun, we needn't have run away.'

This sounds as if I was a brave little boy. Not at all. I merely did not appreciate the dangers, and, like all children, I was frightened of some quite ordinary things. For example, there was a rubbish heap opposite our bungalow, just on the other side of the road, with gourds growing on it, giving out a hot foetid smell. For some reason, I thought this heap was the home of an ogre and that the gourds had grown from the skulls of boys and girls he had devoured. For a time I had terrifying dreams that I was going to be captured and eaten by this ogre.

Occasionally, as a special treat, we would go with friends for a picnic on the shores of Lake Nakuru. I remember the grown-ups pointing towards the lake and saying excitedly, 'Look at the hippos.' I have a faint recollection of seeing some kind of black object moving in the water, but I do recall a huge flock of flamingoes that rose suddenly from the lake and turned into what seemed to be a pink cloud in the sky.

We had a modest establishment of servants consisting of a Goanese cook, a Swahili house-boy, a *sais* for the pony and trap, and an odd-job boy to keep the garden tidy and help generally. My brother and I were very attached to the house-boy, whose name was Gola. One day he gave me a banana: I was thrilled, although I can't think why, as bananas must have been plentiful – perhaps my mother thought they were indigestible for small boys. The *sais*, on the other hand, was surly and refused to run alongside my donkey to make it trot. Probably I was tiresome and dictatorial, but he finally got his revenge one day when we had gone to Nakuru town to buy something at the little shop there. He managed somehow or other to keep the donkey, with me sitting on it, outside the shop for a few minutes until my nurse and brother had gone a little way towards home, then he released the animal which broke into a canter, took a short cut across country, and brushed me off under some trees as it rejoined the road. I was frightened and humiliated by this incident, though only slightly hurt. Nurse must have told my parents, as soon after a new *sais* appeared on the scene. Such an incident would never have happened in India – where I later served – where all the servants from the highest to the lowest were immensely kind and patient with children.

One morning there was a bush fire which swept down the low hill behind us towards the group of five or six European bungalows that lined the road. It so happened that my father had just left on one of his regular visits to Kisumu on Lake Victoria Nyanza, which fell within his jurisdiction, so my mother had to organize our fire-fighting preparations. Everyone – men, women and servants from the half-dozen or so neighbouring bungalows along the road – was mobilized. Even we children were given small brooms, no doubt to give us a feeling that we were helping, and also to keep us occupied. I saw myself at first as a hero, stopping the fire at the last moment. As it came rapidly nearer, I began to feel alarmed at the sight of the flames and smoke; suddenly a hot spark hit me on the cheek, I let out a loud yell, declared that it was not fair, and retreated to a safe distance. Fortunately for all concerned, the wind suddenly changed and the fire roared off in a different direction. When we next took our walk, the African plain was black in every direction. Stopping for a moment to rest, I found myself looking at a large black-topped boulder close to the road, where I noticed some shoots of bright green grass growing up from the charred earth. It seemed extraordinary to me, and I have never forgotten that little incident.

At that early age, my parents were part of the natural order of things, and I don't think I had any conscious feelings towards them. Very young children accept the world as it is, and are not unhappy unless actively ill-treated – perhaps not even then. On Sunday mornings we used to go into our parents' bedroom, and I recall a small tiff between them about whose bed I should get into. I ended up in my father's. We always used to go to church on Sundays, but the service made no mark on my mind. After church there was always a wait as we sat in our trap. The pony, called Lucy, would never start, in spite of much urging from my father, who addressed it as 'you nasty beast', until our *sais* had lifted up its foreleg, held it for a few moments, and then let go, after which Lucy would break into a smart trot, while the *sais* ran alongside and usually managed to scramble on to the back of the vehicle.

In due course we returned to England, travelling in an ancient ship called the *Gemna*, belonging to the Messageries Maritimes line. This line was chosen, partly for cheapness and partly because my parents had met and become engaged while on holiday in Dieppe, and were both devoted to France and the French way of life. A sailor was hired to take us off their hands for a couple of hours in the afternoon. He had pointed waxed moustaches, and even to me he seemed a little man. He used to walk us to the stern of the ship where there was a collection of animals – dogs, monkeys, parrots, and a leopard in a cage which snarled ferociously at us. We were sorry for the leopard, which was being taken to some zoo, but felt no wish to have it as a pet. A powerful smell came from the animals crowded together in the hot sun; the deck vibrated strongly under our feet as the old ship rolled gently in an oily sea – a rather soothing feeling that I sometimes recall when feeling restless.

But things changed when we got into the Red Sea. It was not red, as I had expected, and it became rough for a time. My mother forced us to drink condensed milk, which I have loathed ever since, and I felt aggrieved as well as seasick. I have no recollection of passing through the Suez Canal on this voyage, but I do remember calling at Port Said, with the monotonous chanting of the long lines of workers carrying sacks of coal on their backs up a plank into a hole in the side of the ship, and down another plank in a never-ending procession. More important, our French sailor gave me and my brother a box of Turkish Delight – pink and yellow squares coated with sugar and with nuts in them. It was the most delicious thing I had ever tasted.

We disembarked to Marseilles, to travel overland by train to

England and thus save a week. For some unknown reason, the French Customs officials became suspicious of a box of children's bricks belonging to my brother and myself, and we were held up for a considerable time while the bricks were minutely examined. My father was furious that he, a Magistrate, should be suspected of smuggling, but the angrier he became, the more obstructive were the officials. Finally it was decided to cut open a brick: this was solemnly done under the personal supervision of the *Chef de Douanes* and, needless to say, nothing was revealed. What the French suspected, Heaven only knows: it was, of course, long before the days of drug-trafficking.

At the Marseilles railway station, my brother and I were walked up the platform to see the engine; it looked enormous, hissing and belching steam. What a thrill when the driver invited us to climb into the cabin and allowed us to touch some of the levers. In due course we reached London, where our train was held up for a few minutes outside the station; it was dark by then, and I could just catch a glimpse of the red and green signal lights ahead of us. They seemed dazzlingly beautiful, and I burst into tears when I was not allowed to put my head outside the carriage window to get a better view. From London we had to travel on to Farnham, although I think my father must have remained in London, as it was my mother who told the porter, when we finally arrived there, that we needed a cab to take us to Ewshott. Eventually one was found and, tired and sleepy, we piled in with our luggage. There was a dank smell from the straw on the floor of the cab, then the clip-clop of hooves, and in a few seconds I was sound asleep.

We – my brother and I – lived for two or three years at Ewshott Cottage with my maternal grandparents and an unmarried aunt. We loved them all, but at that stage I think we were most attached to my grandfather, whom we called Mr Bear. He told us fascinating stories about the adventures of a mouse prince, which I later re-told – with newly invented adventures of course – to my own children, with great success. When we had outgrown the mouse stories, my grandfather started to read us *Robinson Crusoe*. Finding the book left on a chair one day and leafing through it, I came on the illustration of Crusoe discovering the footprints of Man Friday in the sand. This terrified me – even now I can see the picture clearly – and as the moment of discovery grew nearer, I was compelled to pretend that I was bored with the story. I think my grandfather was a little hurt. At any rate, he gave up reading the book. My grandfather also provided an element of masculinity in a mainly female household. He had a workshop smelling of paint and oil and sawdust, where we were expected to be useful, mainly sawing up wood for burning in the house. He taught us to make a few simple objects and boxes. When we were hammering in a nail and hit our finger we got no sympathy. 'Next time,' he would remark, 'you'll hit the nail on the head.' We had to be useful in other ways too – going up ladders, for example, which I rather enjoyed. But I was resentful when we were put to the task of collecting stones from a piece of ground he wanted to cultivate, even though we were paid one penny a bucket. This was no work for a gentleman, I thought, and of course we had been brought up to consider being, or rather behaving, like a gentleman as all-important. I had no doubt at all that I was one.

My maternal grandparents were in fact descended from a long line of impoverished Irish gentry, going back, they claimed, to the Princes of the Plains. The family house was Kiltanon in County Clare – burned down during 'the troubles', but I don't think either of them ever lived there. Although they were first cousins, my grandmother had been brought up in England by a wealthy relation or godfather who owned a house called Ashley Court near Bristol. She liked to recall picking warm ripe peaches off the wall as a child, and had expected to be left all or some of his money, but for some reason his fortune went elsewhere. She was musical, and as a young woman had sung in choirs at the Albert Hall; unfortunately I did not inherit her talent, and have never been able to sing a note in tune. When we were still quite young – though after leaving Ewshott – she told us the facts of life, or more precisely the facts of birth, quite plainly. This bit of information led to an embarrassing occurrence later on when I was at my prep school.

My grandfather, on the other hand, had been brought up in Ireland and knew how to tickle a trout and set a snare for a rabbit. Once, when we had been lent a rather grand house near Lechdale for a few weeks in the summer, he captured a large trout swimming in the moat by this means; the trout was duly cooked and enjoyed by all. Later it transpired that the trout had been regarded as a sort of pet by the owners who, we gathered, were not at all pleased when they heard of its fate. My grandfather had started his career in the Royal Irish Constabulary, and then managed to obtain a commission in the Royal Irish Fusiliers. When a young captain, his horse had fallen on him heavily, and he had been obliged to retire from the army. After that he had never held another paid job – partly, I fancy, because with his Irish temperament he didn't particularly like work, and partly because he lacked both training and influence. I remember my mother once remarking rather bitterly that she had had to make do with someone else's dress for her first dance. However, our 'Mr Bear' was a handsome and charming man – there was no doubt that he had kissed the Blarney Stone – and in his old age he did sterling work for the blind in Dorset almost up to his death at the age of eighty five.

Brian and I were not in the least worried, indeed barely conscious of this relative poverty. We were loved; we lived in what seemed to us a nice house (in fact a pretty old cottage that had been enlarged) and we had plenty to eat, though things like porridge, rice pudding, brains and lots of milk were considered the right diet for children in those days. Best of all we had a large garden to play in, and woods at the back with the right sort of trees to climb, but I don't think we ever ventured more than a short way into the woods, half expecting, perhaps with memories of Africa at the back of our minds, that we might encounter something dangerous. At the bottom of the garden there was a line of large old cherry trees, with a swing attached to one of them; in high summer it was fun to swing slowly backwards and forwards while eating the small bitter cherries that fell from the trees. On Sundays we always walked to church with our grandparents, passing on the way the grounds of a large house belonging to a well-to-do stockbroker. My grandmother, who was pious and much attracted by Roman Catholic ritual (as I realized later), used to tell us that the only son of the house, Maurice, was allowed to play on Sundays and did not have the privilege of going to church. My brother and I felt quite sorry for Maurice, although one Sunday in high summer, with the doors of the church open and the sun streaming in, I wished – though knowing it to be wrong – that I too could be out playing in the woods.

As I write this sketch of my life as a small boy at Ewshott – which has grown longer than I intended as almost forgotten incidents re-enact themselves in my mind – I must try and pick out two or three red-letter days. One was my seventh birthday, when I was given a box of tools. For some reason there were no nails with the box. I was disappointed at not being able to set to work immediately, and probably sulked. To put matters right, it was decided that we should drive into Farnham to buy nails, so the old brown pony was harnessed to the governess cart, and off we went down the long hill past Farnham Castle, where my grandparents were occasionally invited to a garden party given by the Bishop. The nails were duly bought, and I made up my mind to start at once on making a new hutch for our two pet rabbits; this, I fear, remained one of numerous unfulfilled resolutions, and I have no recollection of ever making anything.

On the way home we were expected, as usual, to get out and walk from time to time, to relieve the pony as it climbed the hill back to Ewshott. One or two cars passed us on the way – it was the early days of motoring – raising a thick cloud of white dust as they went by. My grandfather cursed heartily, my grandmother remarking that the drivers could not be gentlefolk to behave in such an inconsiderate manner. The hedges were all white with dust in those days before the roads were tarred. That same afternoon, a jolly uncle came to tea, bringing a friend with him. He gave me a miniature cricket bat as a birthday present, and after tea he organized a game of cricket. I batted, my uncle bowled, the friend fielded and my grandfather kept wicket. Every time I managed to make contact with the slowest possible lob and hit the ball a few feet, there was loud applause from the fielders. It was all extremely gratifying, and I went to sleep that night dreaming of the great things I was going to accomplish as a cricketer, an engine driver, a soldier.

It was the following winter that I went to the first children's party that I can recall, and a rather grand one at that, held at Clare Park near Crondell, now a retirement home for the elderly. It was a fancy dress party; I wore a vaguely Turkish costume cobbled up by my aunt, with a fez made out of red cardboard stuck on my head. The daughter of the house was dressed as a fairy; she seemed enchantingly pretty to me, and I immediately fell in love with her, though I am not sure that I even spoke to her. For a night or two afterwards, I had dreams of little girls that might be described as erotic; then they faded, and I had no further interest in girls until the usual age.

One day a visiting governess appeared, and I started lessons – much later than children do nowadays. I began by folding coloured paper into different shapes, and then moved on to the intricate task of constructing 'pot-hooks and hangers'. One winter's afternoon there was snow lying on the ground and we went tobogganing on a slope below what was known as the Queen's Drive (so called, I believe, because Queen Victoria once drove along this short stretch of road, probably after reviewing troops in nearby Aldershot). Tobogganing for the first time was enormous fun, and I felt indignant and rebellious when we were made to return to the house for lessons with our governess. In due course I learned to read and then, for better or worse, entered a new world. In our downstairs 'den', as it was called, there was a collection of bound volumes of the *Boys Own Paper* that had belonged to my mother's brother – at that time an officer in the Connaught Rangers. Before long I was immersed in story after story – mostly in serial form – of thrilling adventures all over the world. One moment I was a midshipman in command of a cutter in the South China Seas, ordering my men to lie low as we approached a pirate junk, before drawing our cutlasses and leaping on board to rescue their captives. In another I was a Russian boyar lashing my horses into a frenzy as we galloped through the snows of a winter forest, pursued by a pack of howling wolves. Or I was a young cadet of the East India Company ordered by Clive to rescue a beautiful English girl who had been abducted by the wicked Rajah of Bognipur. These heroes of an already long-vanished world were, of course, brave, good, and impeccably upright, and were always motivated by the highest moral principles. I suppose all children inhabit a fantasy world to a greater or lesser extent, even in these days of television, but perhaps my *vie intérieure* was more remote from reality than most, owing to the impact of my first reading. At any rate, I suffered a considerable shock when I first started school and found out what boys were really like. I suppose I was a bit too good at that stage, and probably a bit of a prig.

2

Growing up in England

When I was about nine, my grandparents decided to move to Weymouth, probably because they – my grandfather in particular – felt rather isolated living in rural Surrey (as it was then) on a very small income. Weymouth was, at that time, a haven for retired officers from the Armed Forces, the Colonial Services, schoolmasters and the like, all living on modest pensions. At first we shared a tall old house backing on the harbour, close to where the Jersey boats tied up. Their names all began with R – *Reindeer, Roebuck* and so on. My brother and I spent hours watching them loading and unloading, and once or twice managed to hop on board with the connivance of a friendly seaman. After living for several years in a succession of rented houses, my grandparents finally bought an attractive little house, with a small garden, called *La Casita* – a name which suited it rather well – and lived there for the rest of their lives.

I began my education at a local dame's school and then, at about the age of eight, became a pupil at Weymouth College junior school. It must have been the autumn term, as conkers were all the rage; by a stroke of luck, I acquired a particularly hard horse-chestnut which defeated all others in my class, giving a much-needed boost to my self-confidence. My only other achievement of note was to win a prize for mathematics – a subject at which I have never since been the slightest good. The prize was a book on electricity, and at my next prep school in Warwickshire, to which I went afterwards as a boarder, I used to discourse learnedly on this subject to a chum while out on walks, while he told me about the Stock Exchange.

My brother and I lived what today would be considered rather dull lives. As small boys, we often accompanied my grandfather on his regular morning round, walking about two miles into the shopping streets via the cobbler, the blacksmith (who mended tools) and the greengrocer, stopping for frequent and lengthy chats with friends encountered by my grandfather on the way. Occasionally we would go off on our own to explore the harbour area and walk up the backwater to watch the black Australian swans. As we grew older and learned to swim, it became a point of honour to bathe every day throughout the summer, however bad the weather. I still recall the icy sea, the pebbles hurting one's tender feet, and drying and dressing in a windy tent. Sometimes, as a special treat, we saved up enough of our meagre pocket money – sixpence a week, was it? – to hire canoes. This was exciting, and could be quite dangerous if the sea was at all rough – the knack was to keep the canoe head on to the waves and not get caught broadside on while turning. Fortunately, we never capsized. Looking back, it was broadminded of our grandparents, perhaps a little too much so, to allow us to go canoeing on our own. At home, we were content with the usual pastimes of the day – our Meccano, though only the early, less expensive sets, stamp-collecting, draughts, later graduating to chess, and of course reading whatever we could lay our hands on. How lucky children are to be given the right books at the right age. This happened to me when I was given a splendidly illustrated copy of Macaulay's *Lays of Ancient Rome*. Before long, my brother and I knew it by heart, and used to declaim passages from it to each other. I think Winston Churchill might well have encouraged the nation during the war by quoting Horatius (as he quoted other verses):

> 'To every man upon this earth death cometh soon or late
> And how can man die better than facing fearful odds
> For the country of his fathers and the honour of his gods'

In our early teens we became enthusiastic long-distance walkers. Once we walked from Weymouth to Lulworth Cove, following the coast and stopping to bathe at Durdle Door, where the sea flows through a natural arch in the cliffs. We had the little sandy cove entirely to ourselves, and lay in the sun for a bit after swimming. We were very tired by the time we reached Lulworth, but after a cup of tea and a short rest had to plod on for seven miles to Wool to catch a late train back to Weymouth. It was 10 o'clock by the time we got home, pretty well dead-beat. Another long walk was in the opposite direction – from Weymouth to Lyme Regis, again keeping as close to the sea as possible. We passed through Abbotsbury with its famous Swannery, ate our sandwiches at West Bay near Bridport, and then climbed up and over Golden Cap with the gorse which gives it its name in full bloom. The view from the top of Golden Cap was superb – Portland Bill projecting out to sea to the east, and the Devon cliffs just visible to the west on a clear day, while inland the unspoiled Dorset landscape stretched away as far as one could see. By the time we reached Lyme Regis, it was too late to get a train back to Weymouth, and we spent the night there in a small pub. Brian and I were rather pleased with ourselves at having achieved these two quite long walks – we were about twelve and ten at the time and did everything together in those days; indeed, I would have been very lonely without him. Apart from a few jealousies in early adolescence, we remained good friends until our work and careers took us in different directions. In retirement and old age we have come together again.

So far I have only mentioned my maternal grandparents. We also spent a good deal of time staying with my father's family at Bournemouth, though we never regarded this as 'home'. My grandfather, whom we never knew, had been called to the Bar, but never practised and died young. My grandmother apparently never recovered from the shock and was a frail old lady, slightly weak in the head, with a full-time nurse. We hardly ever saw her except briefly, when she appeared for afternoon tea in the drawing room. My Aunt Gracie, the unmarried eldest daughter, ran the house. We were fond of her, and she did her best to make our stays at Cliffe Side enjoyable. She bought us a small tent which my brother and I carried down to the beach every day in the summer, erected it on any vacant spot and used it for bathing – dressing and undressing one at a time. Cliffe Side was a large house, rather hideously furnished in late Victorian style.

There were six indoor servants, in addition to the nurse and a lady's maid. My brother and I adored the house-maid, Alice, who looked after us as small boys. She used to sing to us in our baths and, we gathered, sang in a church choir and sometimes at friends' houses. We decided once to give her the score of a song as a very special birthday present, but were rather puzzled as to what to buy in the Bournemouth music shop; eventually we decided on *The Bing Boys*. She thanked us warmly, but we later found she had changed it for another song.

Life at Cliffe Side was conducted in a fairly formal manner, and the whole household was expected to attend morning prayers before breakfast. All the domestic servants, headed by cook, filed in and sat in a row. Nurse and Hull, the lady's maid, sat separately. My aunt read a short passage from the Bible, and we then knelt for prayers. I suppose morning prayers were still held in a fair number of upper-middle-class homes, though this Victorian practice must have been dying out by then. Breakfast followed immediately; the first course, served by the parlour maid, was always oatmeal porridge, as my aunt attached great importance to the family's descent from a lowland Scottish clan. In her younger days she had travelled quite extensively, including a visit to Sicily (how did she get there, I wonder) and bicycling in the Alps. She still had the same bicycle which was fitted with a back-pedalling footbrake which, she told us, was far more effective than a handbrake in descending Alpine passes. Shortly before the First World War she bought a car – a Renault – with an aluminium body, which was considered the last word in up-to-dateness. It was driven by the former coachman, House, who was clearly very nervous and never exceeded 30 mph. Once, when my aunt was out for the afternoon, she left instructions for House to take Brian and me for a drive, but he sent a message saying he had a headache and could not go. We felt sure it was an excuse, and we were furious at being deprived of this treat. The car was very little used, and was sold by my aunt after being stored throughout the First World War.

As growing-up boys we were expected to amuse ourselves for most of the time. Besides bathing in the summer, we went through the normal 'crazes', an early one being croquet, which is an excellent game played by non-experts on a rather rough lawn: it was very satisfying despatching one's opponent's ball to the furthest corner of the shrubbery. Later, came bicycling. On one occasion, going down a steep hill into the town, my brother passed a tram, then caught his wheel in the line and fell off; the driver just managed to stop in time, the tram rocking and swaying and throwing some passengers out of their seats. For a year or two we were fascinated by the Bournemouth trams clanging their way through the streets, and occasionally saved up enough pocket money to make a trip to the end of the line – Christchurch in one direction and Poole in the other – sitting in the front seat on the open top deck. Once, through the gardener who had a friend who was a tram driver, we were allowed in the driver's compartment on condition we sat on the floor for most of the time, but we were each allowed for a brief spell to put our hands on the controls and believe we were driving the powerful clumsy vehicle.

During our bicycling days we sometimes rode quite long distances. Once we had gone blackberrying, and found a suitable common a little beyond New Milton. I was picking on one side of a large bush and Brian on the other. Suddenly he let out a loud yell, and I saw him rushing away at top speed, pursued by a swarm of angry wasps. He had trodden on a nest. I was quite untouched on the other side of the bush. When I rejoined Brian, I found he had been badly stung all over the face, arms and legs. On getting back to Cliffe Side, he was put to bed and the doctor sent for, but within a couple of days he was nearly recovered. Fortunately for me it was that way round as I am allergic to wasps; even one sting gives me a high temperature and makes me feel thoroughly ill.

As we grew older, we learnt to play tennis; there was just room for a court with not quite enough run-back. Once, as teenagers who were beginning to be interested in girls, we organized a small American tournament, with about six couples playing; as a very special concession we were allowed to ask one couple to lunch, the rest only to a very simple tea. Tennis in those days was an essential social accomplishment: in the country it was the main, almost the only way of bringing young people together. My brother and I became reasonably good, playing occasionally in small seaside tournaments, and continued to play for many years as adults.

From time to time, one aunt, Aunt Ellie, used to come bathing with us. She was a tiny person, swam rather well, and had a sense of humour that appealed to us. We nicknamed her 'Sardine', something we would never have dreamed of doing to Aunt Gracie. Poor thing, she had a sad life. Her husband, a Church of England parson in a London parish, was converted to Roman Catholicism, then reverted to Protestantism, and finally, in his last moments, changed again to die a Catholic. I believe it was a *cause célèbre* in ecclesiastical circles at the time (his name was The Rev. H. Ley).

My father's elder brother, Uncle Car (Carleton – my grandmother's maiden name), was a horse of a very different colour – a retired Colonel who enjoyed the good things of life, particularly sport and, I fancy, women when he was younger. He had an endless fund of (in retrospect) slightly juvenile funny stories and jokes. He was good with young people, though we were slightly in awe of him. One Christmas he organized and probably paid for a sizeable children's party – the first we had ever had, apart from very small affairs – when he dressed up as Father Christmas and distributed the presents from a rather splendid tree. He played the part so well that it was some time before we cottoned on to who he was. He always brought his two greyhounds with him when he came to stay and, rather surprisingly for a strict disciplinarian, they were not made to lie down at mealtimes, but from time to time were admonished 'Faces off the table, chaps'. At that time Uncle Car owned a small country estate called Royden in the New Forest, and I used to stay there occasionally. My father's twin sister, Aunt Isabel, was married to a Major John Burbey, who was a master at Clifton College; she seldom came to Bournemouth, probably because she was too busy, even during the school holidays, but my brother and I often stayed with them in Clifton. We were very fond of Uncle Jack, who taught us to play golf and gave us our first interest in architecture when bicycling round the countryside with him.

During the Christmas holidays, Aunt Gracie always took us to the pantomime. For a brief period, one was transported to a different world that we knew was not real, though it seemed more interesting and exciting than the real one. I was mildly amused by the antics of the Dame, but it was the love passages between the principal boy and girl that really appealed to me. It seemed quite right and proper that the 'boy' should be played by a girl, always with shapely legs that I did not fail to notice, but it was the 'girl' that enthralled me: beautiful, charming and good – that was how I thought in my innocence girls were and should be. If I had had a sister I would, no doubt, have known better, and avoided the fatal mistake of putting real girls on a pedestal when I reached adolescence. Even at Cambridge – still a semi-monastic society in my time – I doubt if more than a tiny proportion of my contemporaries had had sexual relations with women, and even fewer with girls of their own class. No doubt today's attitudes are more natural and sensible in many ways, though one wonders sometimes about the emotional effects, particularly on girls, of starting sexual relations at sixteen or earlier, and also about how the contemporary young will feel about sex by the time they reach their late twenties. Maybe it is a case of *plus ça change, plus c'est la même chose.*

As Brian and I began to grow up – he a naval cadet at Dartmouth, I a schoolboy at Haileybury – Aunt Gracie must have made great efforts to contact old friends and get us invited to a few parties and dances. At one party, playing hide and seek, I was lucky enough to find myself hiding with the prettiest girl in the room. I still remember her name, Cissie Simmons. We hid in the corner of an empty room behind a screen and, greatly daring, I put my arm round her waist for about two seconds – what a thrill – and then we had to make a dash for 'home'. I never saw her again. Most of these parties were very simple affairs, and of course we all behaved impeccably – today's young would consider then intensely boring, though boredom in reality is in the mind of the beholder. Once or twice we were invited to rather grander dances, for example, the annual dance given by the Malmesburys, who lived (I think) somewhere near Christchurch. Once I danced with my hostess, Lady Malmesbury. I was anything but a good performer, and I fancy she was not either; at any rate we spent most of the time treading on each other's feet, but she evidently forgave my clumsiness as I was invited again the following year.

As Brian and I grew up and made our own friends, we naturally enough stayed less and less at Cliffe Side. Eventually my grandmother died, during my first year at Cambridge; Cliffe Side was sold, and Aunt Gracie moved to Parkstone. We always remained fond of her and saw her whenever we could until she died in her turn in 1948. Cliffe Side is now a large hotel, and quite unrecognisable as it used to be.

There was a mystery about how the family came to live in Bournemouth. We were never told anything by Aunt Gracie, but later I gleaned a few facts from Uncle Car, though I doubt if even he knew the full story. It seems that my grandparents had lived in Clifford Street, off Bond Street, and then, sometime in the early 1860s, they decided to leave London with a group of friends and move to Bournemouth. At that time Bournemouth was little more than a small village clustering round the little river Bourne, while the East and West Cliffs were mainly covered with pine woods. The move seems to have occurred because the group were extremely religious and wanted to live near each other. My grandparents, and no doubt others in the group, contributed much of the money for building the church of Holy Trinity, and we had a reserved pew for the family immediately behind the churchwardens' seats. Aunt Gracie always knew the vicar well and remained active in church circles for many years, and I remember the Bishop of Winchester coming to tea on one occasion. One family she knew were the Earl and Countess of Cairns, who had a large house and garden immediately behind Cliffe Side; we had permission to go through their garden, and often did, as a short-cut to Bournemouth Central Station, while the Cairns could do the same at Cliffe Side to reach the walk along the East Cliff. I believe Lord Cairns had held a post in one of Balfour's administrations.

Uncle Car, while confirming this picture, had a footnote to add. Apparently his Uncle, a parson, who lived next door at East Cliffe House, was somewhat unorthodox, to say the least, and while prayer meetings were going on on the lawn at Cliffe Side, Uncle Fred the parson, was giving gay parties in the adjoining garden. At any rate, he got through all his money and his family were left more or less penniless, one son being shipped off to Australia and another adopted by the Burbeys.

The other family mystery goes back much further. My great-great-grandfather, Robert Logan (1746-1826), whose portrait hangs in my dining room at Rusham End – he looks a benevolent old gentleman – lived in Jamaica and evidently amassed a fortune there from sugar. At some point he returned to England and settled at Egham Lodge in Surrey. In his Will, of which I have a copy, he refers to 'my plantation or sugar works called Arcadia and Cedar Grove and mansion house and lands called Airey Mount in the parish of St Thomas in the East, Jamaica, the lands, shares, cattle etc. thereto belonging. . .' He also refers to his house 'Egham Lodge and the land called Runnymede'. The Will is extremely difficult to interpret, but it seems that, after leaving a life interest to his wife, the bulk of his estate went to his only daughter, Isabella, wife of Joseph Dobinson, and then to his second granddaughter, also named Isabella. His other seven grandchildren appear only to have inherited £1000 on marriage, except for a 'contingent remainder' to his eldest grandson. In a codicil he also bequeathed £2000 – then a sizable sum – to his 'natural son, Robert Logan, living near Red River in America, in the service of the Hudson Bay Company'. In a second codicil, he gives their freedom to eight slaves by name, and asks that they should be allowed to continue to work on the plantation if they so wished. As his granddaughter, Isabella, died without issue and no Will survives, it is impossible to say what happened to what must have been a large fortune. But I do not think my grandfather Francis can have inherited any substantial amount, as we always understood that my grandmother, Louisa Carleton, had been an heiress of a sort, and that the family money – such as it was – came from her. Even this seems to have seeped away – as adolescents we gathered that the family solicitors were incompetent or worse – and my father was certainly not a rich man.

However, most families have these sort of stories of how their ancestors behaved. What my brother and I now regret is that we were not told more about the family as boys. Brian, early in his naval career, was stationed in the West Indies, and his ship called at Jamaica several times. It is just possible that he might have tried to locate Airey Mount and the sugar plantations, although I must admit that young people are seldom interested in their family history. Again we both regret that we did not try and discover what 'lands at Runnymede' my great-great-grandfather had owned; all we know is that Egham Lodge has long since been pulled down, and its grounds built over. Here I ought to mention that in 1865 all the Dobinsons, that is Robert Logan's grandchildren, changed their name back to Logan, probably a piece of Victorian snobbery. Nothing is known about Joseph Dobinson or his ancestors; Dobinson sounds an old, if undistinguished, name (I cannot find a single one in the London telephone directory).

I have already mentioned that we used to stay with various uncles and aunts from time to time. I think Brian and I most enjoyed our visits to Clifton. As small boys it was always exciting and slightly alarming to walk across Clifton suspension bridge above the Avon – a still impressive achievement of Victorian engineering. In a high wind the bridge used to sway slightly, and I remember being told that in earlier days a lady wearing a crinoline had jumped off the bridge with the intention of committing suicide. However, the wind blew out her crinoline, which acted as a sort of parachute in reverse, and she landed more or less unharmed in the river mud. Uncle Jack sometimes used to take us bicycling in the country, then easily accessible from Clifton. On one occasion we had a bread and cheese lunch in a small country pub near Frome, and for the first time tasted alcohol; this consisted of half a glass of rough country cider, topped up with fizzy lemonade. We did not enjoy it much but felt very grown-up at having a real man's drink. What a sensible introduction to alcohol! Later in life we both drank moderately, but never, or hardly ever, to excess. Rugger night supper at Cambridge might have been an exception in my case. Now a glass of good Claret or Burgundy is one of the few pleasures left.

As well as bicycling and walking, we also learned to play golf, first of all knocking a ball about on Clifton Downs, and later graduating to Uncle Jack's club at Fayland on the other side of the Avon. Our Aunt Isabel, my father's twin sister, had a certain sense of humour and was used to dealing with boys; she looked after us well and we were quite fond of her. Sadly, in later years, she became highly eccentric and a trial to everyone. But all in all, I have pleasant memories of our visits to Clifton.

Staying with Uncle Car at Royden, where I went on my own,

was quite a different kind of life. Having retired from the Regular Army, he and my Aunt Mabel lived in a pleasant, rambling old house in the depths of the New Forest. He had an only son, Vere, whom I did not particularly like at that age (in later life we were on friendly terms); he seemed to me rather bumptious and inclined to be patronizing. However, for the most part we played together fairly amicably. The upper reaches of the Beaulieu River ran through the grounds, and on summer days we used to paddle in it, sail paper boats, collect objects of interest and generally muddle around. Once Vere dared me to climb out along a branch that hung over the stream; I accepted the dare, started to climb out and promptly fell in. Fortunately, the kind housekeeper, known as Clark, gave me some dry clothes to change into, and did not report me to Aunt Mabel. On wet days we often played in an open-sided barn filled with large blocks of wood for burning in the house; Vere and I used to make our own make-believe 'motor cars' out of these blocks of wood, and then drive them around, uttering appropriate noises. On one occasion my car was in a higher position than his, and I managed to dislodge a block of wood which fell into Vere's and slightly bruised one of his legs. I said I was sorry, but I really could not help it if a wheel came off my car when I was driving at the terrific speed of 60 mph. So on the whole, honours between us were even.

Uncle Car owned two cars – one a Daracq, which was considered rather dashing. From time to time we drove into Lymington (driven by a chauffeur); I anxiously watched the speedometer to see if the car ever reached 40 mph, but it never quite did, to my disappointment. In Lymington, we bathed in the large salt-water swimming pool, which then had a section for non-swimmers and children. Once a large fish, probably a mackerel, somehow managed to get into this section, or perhaps was thrown in by a naughty boy. The fish darted around trying to escape, and I remember the shrieks uttered by some of the women and girls who seemed to think they were being pursued by a shark.

Uncle Car was a founder member of the Lymington Sailing (now Royal Yacht) Club – a very modest affair in those days. His name (Lt-Col F C Logan) still appears on the Club board. He owned a small yacht and also a tiny single-seater craft known as a 'pram' for beginners to learn to sail. Although a hunting, shooting and fishing man, he had not taken to sailing until fairly late in his life when he came to live at Royden and was not, I think, very experienced. He had a retired seaman as a paid crew, but liked to take the helm himself as much as possible. In good weather we made short trips across the Solent to Yarmouth in the Isle of Wight, or along the coast to Beaulieu. That was about the limit of our voyages. Once, coming up the Lymington River with Uncle Car at the helm, we managed to get in the way of the Lymington-Yarmouth paddle steamer; there was much shouting and yelling, and we finally went aground on a mud flat, where we had to wait ignominiously for at least an hour until a rescue boat arrived to pull us off. Uncle Car was considerably put out by this incident and fulminated against the ferry company, threatening to sue them. I enjoyed the sailing more than the swimming pool, and years later, after leaving Cambridge, I had a small boat myself at Lymington for a short time before I went to India.

The popular game for boys in those days, before tennis caught on, was cricket. We were invited to play during the summer holiday in neighbouring country houses; I can't say I enjoyed these occasions very much, as I was not much good at the game, hadn't the right clothes, and didn't know the other boys, who were mostly older and more sophisticated. However, I remember once, when there was a return match at Royden, amassing the large score of ten runs and actually holding a catch. Very gratifying, especially as Vere, who was no good at games, was out for a duck. These visits to Royden continued until the outbreak of the First World War, when Uncle Car was recalled to the Army to command a training battalion of his regiment, the Loyal North Lancs, at Seaford in Sussex. My Uncle Jack got the job of second-in-command, and thus acquired his rank of Major (probably he had been a Territorial Officer in the Clifton Cadet Corps).

From time to time, Brian and I stayed in Seaford with one or other of these uncles. The Downs all around became one vast military camp. As soon as a contingent was trained, it was marched down to Seaford station, band playing, and from there set off for Flanders via Newhaven and Dieppe. That is why Seaford still has one of the longest station platforms in England. Once or twice we boys went to the station to see a unit from the regiment depart. It was a stirring sight. We did not realize, of course, that few of those who set out would ever return. uncle Car, I was told later, had a set speech for use on these occasions. It went as follows: 'Now men, when you get to the trenches, you must uphold the honour of the regiment. When the order comes to go over the top and attack the enemy, over the top you will go. Probably you will be shot, but if you disobey the order you certainly will be shot.' I can't vouch for the exact words of this address, but it certainly was in accord with the spirit of the times and the sort of training young men had to receive before facing the horrors of the trenches. Years later, an uncle on my mother's side, who had fought in the battle of the Somme, told me how his entire battalion had almost been wiped out in trying to gain a hundred yards or so of ground; even then he could hardly bear to speak about it.

Occasionally, we were taken to camp concerts and enjoyed joining in the choruses sung by the men, which of course always included *It's a long Way to Tipperary* (odd that the Second World War produced no comparable song that really caught on). Once a visiting politician, a member of the Government (was his name McNamara?) came down and addressed the troops, haranguing them in a highly emotional and, I suspect, ranting way. The speech was received with enthusiasm, and Uncle Car quoted passages from it for days afterwards. He particularly liked to declaim one phrase which still sticks in my mind – '*You* do not call your King a Warlord'. Of course, in those days few of the men, or even the officers, would have heard a speech from an accomplished, if bombastic, orator. Although I was just ten by the time war broke out, I remember little of day-to-day life at Seaford – probably because the grown-ups were too busy coping with the war, and we were left mostly to amuse ourselves as best we could. Certainly there were no longer any car rides or cricket or even bathing – perhaps because I was never at Seaford in the summer. I do remember climbing over the breakwaters and playing hop-scotch with Vere and a boy in a kilt called Ludovic somewhere behind the old Beach Hotel, now pulled down. As I shall recount later, my wife also had an early association with Seaford, and in late middle-age we had a little holiday house there for about ten years.

3

A Hard Life at School

At eleven I was sent as a boarder to a preparatory school in Warwickshire called Packwood Haugh. I think it was quite a good school, though the masters were a mixed lot owing to the war. My first form-master had a caustic tongue and enjoyed embarrassing the shyer boys, including myself. Once he remarked to a boy who had had an accident, 'Just because you were stupid enough to fall out of a tree, Walker, and break an arm, that's no excuse for making such gross errors of punctuation. Write out the passage correctly one hundred times' (this, when the unfortunate boy could hardly write without pain). He also had favourites, who were allowed the privilege of holding his arm, one on either side, during school walks. Fortunately, after about a year, a young woman teacher called Miss Potter arrived straight from Oxford. Dear Miss Potter, she taught us English, and gave me a real interest in the subject. She sometimes read us poetry from the modern poets then in vogue (she must have read English at Oxford), set us interesting subjects for essays and gave praise whenever possible. For one end of term entertainment before Christmas, I was allotted *Quinquereme of Nineveh* to recite, and another time played Brutus in a short extract from *Julius Caesar*. Once, the conversation in class somehow got on to the subject of childbirth. Most of the boys believed in the gooseberry bush theory or something similar, and when I trotted out the real facts as told me by my grandmother (only in broad outline, of course) Miss Potter turned bright puce and the class laughed me to scorn. The headmaster's wife, Mrs Bradshaw, kept a close eye on our health, and there was a tiny but jolly matron called Letty who, amongst other things, supervised our baths, which we greatly enjoyed, splashing each other and throwing sponges around. There was one bath in a closed compartment, used only by a swarthy older boy. One day the door happened to be open just as he was getting out, and to my surprise I saw that he had a thick bush of hair round his private parts. Perhaps this was a good thing for me to see, and saved me from a greater shock when I got to my public school.

On the whole, I was not unhappy at prep school, and did reasonably well at work and games. I still remember lying under the elms that lined the cricket ground on a hot summer's day, and exploring the still unspoiled Warwickshire countryside in search of birds' eggs, or butterflies, or wildflowers or whatever happened to be the collecting craze of the moment. In due course I passed the Common Entrance examination required for public school entry, but did not attempt a scholarship. Just before the end of my last term, the headmaster gave me and other leavers a talk on sex, couched in discreet and opaque language, that meant absolutely nothing to me. We were an innocent lot, at least at that prep school, but I was in for a rude shock when I got to public school.

During the whole of my time at Packwood Haugh, my parents were marooned in the Seychelles, where my father was Chief Justice and once or twice Acting Governor. Owing to the war, it was impossible for them to get home leave, and letters took an interminable time. They had a delightful house there, and my mother, in particular, liked the place because it had originally been a French possession and the people – very poor in those days – spoke a sort of French *patois*, so she was able to natter away to them to her heart's content in her fluent but ungrammatical French. My father often used to illustrate his letters to me with little drawings of local scenes; I still have one, showing a small boy sitting on the back of one of the giant tortoises indigenous to the islands. I don't believe there was a single car there in those days; my father used to ride to his office on horseback as I sometimes did twenty years later in India, though in my case I did so as a matter of choice rather than necessity. The Seychelles or, to be more precise, the main island of Mahé, must be one of the most beautiful places in the world. My parents always spoke of the island and its people with affection, and my father left a small sum in his Will to assist with the education of a poor Seychelles boy. Recently it has become a holiday resort for the rich, although ruled by a left-wing dictator. I hope that some of the beauty of the island has survived, and that the people are better off (though are they happier? I rather doubt it, from what one reads in the press).

Owing to my parents being so far away, the choice of a public school was left mainly to my grandparents. My father had been at Charterhouse, but I have the impression that he had not been happy there – I never remember him mentioning his schooldays. It so happened that my grandparents knew a boy called Tom Tennant, who often came to stay with an uncle living in Weymouth and was already at Haileybury. They thought he had particularly good manners as well as being unusually good-looking, and so it was decided that I should go to Haileybury (no doubt they made enquiries as well and probably consulted my schoolmaster Uncle Jack). I shall pass rather briefly over my time at public school, but I cannot omit it entirely, as it is a period of life that indelibly marks the mind and character for better or worse.

First, my arrival. My mother's brother – the soldier uncle – had agreed to escort me to Haileybury, but at the last moment he cried off for some reason, and was only able to take me by taxi from Waterloo to Liverpool Street. I still remember the short train journey to Broxbourne in a carriage packed with homing businessmen, the anxiety of not getting out at the right station and acute apprehension of what lay ahead. Even looking back a long way, I think it was a cruel ordeal for a nervous boy to have to face. However, I did get out at the right station, took a cab and arrived at the porter's lodge at Haileybury. I was advised by someone to go to my house, Edmonstone, on the other side of the very large quadrangle, and started to make my way across. Halfway, I passed a boy and asked him if one was supposed to go to one's house. He replied snootily, 'I suppose so' and walked on. I didn't know who he was, but I shall never forgive him (I am surprised to find that I still feel indignant on recalling this small and unimportant incident!). Soon after, I found my house and was greeted by a few new boys who had already arrived and were anxiously awaiting developments.

Before long the other boys began to appear, and my public

school life had begun. I went to bed dog-tired, and awoke abruptly to the sound of a clanging bell; I saw the younger boys jumping out of bed, throwing off their pyjamas and rushing naked down the bare boards of the long dormitory to the bathroom. When I arrived there, I found that we had to wash in a basin and then take a quick dip in a cold bath – the limited supply of hot water was reserved for the prefects and senior boys. The first few days were a nightmare. Everything was new, and everything had to be found out; one's form room, one's place in chapel, one's place in hall, the angle to wear one's cap, how to recognize a prefect, and a myriad of other details. Then gradually things became a little easier, one began to know what to do and, more importantly, what not to do. People assumed identities, and one quickly discovered whom one liked and whom one did not. I took the first tentative steps towards forming a friendship with a boy called Ronald Russell (later Sir Ronald Russell MP), and remember a walk with him around Hertford Heath on a sunny Sunday afternoon; he was quiet, clever (it turned out later), and I felt at ease in his company. But for most of the time one was with the other boys, trying to fight one's corner. For those who were good at games, life was relatively easier. To be good at games and to be popular – that was what nearly everyone wanted. Work was no more than a necessary evil, except perhaps for a few boys in their last year aiming at Oxford or Cambridge scholarships.

 I suppose all public schools at that time were harsh places, and Haileybury was certainly no exception. Discipline was extremely severe; even house prefects could cane boys for quite minor offences. Fagging was still the order of the day. There were no comforts of any kind. The dormitories and classrooms were freezing in winter; one had (until senior) to wash in cold water, even after coming in covered in mud after rugger, and the food was appalling.

 The whole school of over 500 boys ate together in a very large dining hall, and at each table a master or senior prefect put a helping on a plate which was then passed rapidly along to everyone in turn. On weekdays, breakfast consisted of lumpy porridge and bread and margarine, plus marmalade or jam for those lucky enough to have it (my meagre supply was always finished within a fortnight). On Sundays there were sausages, and one anxiously watched one's plate approaching to see what was coming; one Sunday, as my sausage got near I saw that it was unusually small, and I had considerable difficulty in not dissolving into tears. A social worker today would, I am sure, have been appalled at the conditions in which we lived.

The teaching too was dull and pedestrian, and few masters made any effort to create an interest in their subject – just to cram in the necessary quota of knowledge. Here I must admit that they were up against a real difficulty – few boys wanted to learn, and those who did were regarded as 'swots'. But was it really the boys' fault? Once, I remember, the school chaplain – a peculiar and, I suspect, sadistic character – instead of giving us the prescribed scripture lesson, suddenly launched into an eloquent tirade about the dangers of the 'yellow peril' (ie. the Chinese). We were enthralled, though of course, as I realized later, it was all a lot of nonsense. But the point is that if the 'yellow peril' could be made interesting, so could other subjects, at least occasionally. Indeed, one master did succeed in doing this, when I finally got as far as the Lower Sixth in my last year. He was Charles Carrington, one of the first new masters to arrive after the end of the war; he had served in the trenches and was young, handsome and elegant, having evidently spent much of his gratuity on expensive suits. He taught history, and for the first time gave me an interest in a subject. We all admired him immensely. Many years later, Charles and I found ourselves colleagues at Chatham House (the Royal Institute of International Affairs), where he was Stevenson Professor of International History.

Haileybury had once been the training college for the old East India Company until the Mutiny, after which the government of the country was taken over by the British Crown. All the school houses at Haileybury were named after distinguished Indian administrators, and the handsome neo-classical facade (the 'Terrace') of the Company college still remained and remains today. At that time, the British Empire seemed to be at its height (though in fact beginning to decline) and needed competent people for its numerous services. One would have thought that the harsh regime of the school was aimed, at least in part, at producing the right sort of people for the services, and it would have been easy to get Indian and

Colonial officials home on leave to come and give talks to the boys. Yet we were never told a single thing about the past history of the school, or about the distinguished men after whom the houses had been named (one, for example, was called 'Lawrence' – the hero of the Indian Mutiny – what a fascinating story for boys an account of his life would have made). I find it difficult to forgive the then Headmaster for this total lack of imagination. Later, I myself entered the Indian Civil Service, though this had nothing to do with my time at Haileybury.

Having made these criticisms (and I don't doubt that much the same applies to other public schools of the period), I must now turn to the good side. Loyalty, stoicism, physical courage and determination were perhaps the qualities that public school life tended to develop, though it was very much a matter of kill or cure. Certainly one felt an intense loyalty to one's house, and longed for it to be 'cock-house' at cricket or rugger. Equally it seemed all-important that the school should win its matches against other schools; when E B Wakefield (brother of the famous 'W W' and later Sir Edward Wakefield MP, and then High Commissioner in Malta), scored the winning try in the annual match against our chief rival, Uppingham, he was indeed a hero. He happened to be the head of my house at the time and, although he weighed a ton, I remember we carried him in triumph up and down the long dormitory at full tilt. Next to games, I think chapel was the most important influence, not, I am afraid, for religious services, but because it brought the whole school together in one body for a common purpose, and the singing of hymns by five hundred boys was both enjoyable and inspiring. Much the same can be said of 'Big School', which was a very large hall used for various purposes, such as morning prayers on certain days, sing-songs (when the Headmaster invariably sang *Over the Sea to Skye* in a nasal, tuneless voice), and occasional talks by visiting speakers. I recall an absolutely thrilling one about Scott's expedition to the South Pole and the journey back in appalling conditions, when Oates – 'a very gallant gentleman' – walked out of their tent into the blizzard to try and save his comrades, and of course never came back. Once a few of the younger masters, their wives and some boys from the choir, put on *HMS Pinafore*. We all enjoyed it hugely.

I had one unusual adventure, which might have ended badly. My parents or grandparents decided that I should learn riding. The horses were provided by a local riding-school, and one of the masters then took us for a ride round the countryside. One day there was a horse short, but a local 'plater' had been sent along, probably to get it out of the stable after being lame, but not intended to be ridden. I was the last boy to arrive – punctuality was not my strong suit – and, owing to a mistake, I was allotted this horse. By the time I had managed to mount, the horse broke into a canter to catch up, and then into a gallop. I was quite unable to stop it, and we galloped down the main road towards Hertford, narrowly missing several vehicles on the way. I though of throwing myself off, but could not nerve myself to do it. Finally, the horse galloped up the main street of Hertford and ended by trying to jump a large dray that had just emerged from a yard. I was thrown off, and some kindly shopkeepers took me into their house and made me lie down. A little later the master arrived, expecting to find me badly injured or dead, but by some miracle I was completely unhurt, though naturally a bit shocked. My horse, I learned later, had been killed. It was a lucky escape. Someone later gave me a cutting from a local newspaper, reporting this adventure.

I was, I suppose, an average boy at this stage, not particularly good at either work or games. I moved slowly up the school, became a house prefect, then a school prefect, and, as I have already mentioned, scraped into the Lower Sixth in my last year, when for the first time I developed some interest in an academic subject – history. At games I was no cricketer, but reasonably good at rugger, though not good enough to get into the school fifteen. However, I did have a small triumph in my last year, when I played particularly well in the rugger finals for 'cock-house' and scored the winning try. I was secretly highly gratified when a rather sophisticated boy told me that his pretty sister, who had been watching the game, asked 'Who was that fair-haired boy who played so well?' Eventually the last day of term arrived. It seemed like the end of the world; I simply could not believe that I would not be returning to a place that had been the centre of my life – almost my whole life – for three years. Never again would one feel so closely involved in a community, and know its members so intimately.

I must now say something about my parents. They returned to England from the Seychelles towards the beginning of my third term at Haileybury, the war having ended the previous November. It was a bitterly cold winter with deep snow everywhere; some of the school, including myself, had been tobogganing on a nearby hill. On the last run, I decided to go down alone instead of with one or two other boys. The toboggan went much faster than I had expected, I was unable to stop, and shot into a deep ditch. I clambered out badly shaken, was put on a toboggan and hauled back straight to the 'sick-house', where I was put to bed suffering from mild concussion, though not otherwise injured. I had almost recovered, when my parents arrived quite unexpectedly to find me in bed. They were total strangers. My mother had brought a bag of oranges all the way from Port Said, and I think I was also given a cake, but no tip, from my father – not that I expected one. They were only able to stay a few hours before returning to London. However, shortly afterwards my father arranged for me to be given an 'Exeat' to spend a few days with him in London, my mother having gone to Weymouth by that time to visit her parents. We stayed in a small hotel in South Kensington, and I remember accompanying my father to his tailor and bootmaker, but he was so horrified by the staggering increase in prices that he ordered nothing (£4 was the price, if my recollection is correct, for a made-to-measure pair of boots). He took me to the Zoo, to a show at Maskelyne and Devant's (conjurers), which I much enjoyed, and to a Sunday concert at the Wigmore Hall, which I enjoyed less. What I really wanted to see was a musical comedy, but my father would have considered this highly unsuitable. Anyway, it was a most welcome break from school life. One aspect of the times that comes back to me as I write was the number of beggars, even in the West End; I particularly remember a ragged boy who pestered my father for a penny, but he refused to give him anything as a matter of principle. There were also shoe-shine men working in the streets, however bad the weather, or in an arcade, if they could find a place. Happily, that sort of poverty has been abolished.

4

France and My First Love Affair

I think it was the following summer that we had our first real holiday, apart from visits to relatives, when our parents took us to stay in a pleasant hotel at Lydford in Devon. Brian and I spent a large part of our time learning to play tennis on a rather rough grass court; there was another boy who often played with us, and my father occasionally made up a four and gave us a bit of tuition – he was a moderately good player. The deep wooded gorge of the River Lyd ran through the hotel grounds, and we – my brother and I – spent a lot of energy piling up boulders to make a small pool for swimming; the river water was icy. The hotel was on the edge of Dartmoor, and once my father and I walked quite a long way to find some beauty spot where there was a small lake with a miniature waterfall at one end; I remember sitting happily under the waterfall on a perfect summer's day, with the moor stretching away in all directions and not a soul to be seen. After Lydford, we went on to stay at the Greenbank Hotel in Falmouth – I believe it still exists – but did not enjoy this part of our holiday so much, as there was no tennis and no swimming from the hotel. We went on various trips by small steamers to St Mawes and other places, and three men friends staying in the hotel for the fishing took us out with them in their boat a few times; I once managed to hook a good-sized mackerel, and was quite pleased with myself.

At the end of the summer holidays, I returned to Haileybury and Brian to Dartmouth as a naval cadet. My parents must have left England about the same time, for the Gold Coast (now Ghana) where my father had been appointed a judge. Owing to the bad climate there and the end of the war, he got home leave much more frequently, but I rather think my mother remained behind in England for some of the time as we went with her to stay at Seaton in Devonshire during the summer holidays.

When my father came on leave he always took us to France, and I remember every detail of our first visit. We crossed by the night boat to St Malo, arriving in the early morning, when hordes of French porters dressed in blue overalls rushed on board shouting *'porteur'* loudly, and competing to grab our luggage and carry it through the Customs. Then we had *petit déjeuner* outside a café in the main square – my first taste of petits pains, croissants and good coffee, and watched the bustle and strange sights of a busy French port. St Malo was a delightful old town in those days. Everything was a bit different – the language of course, the clothes and appearance of the men and women (many of the former with beards), the formal salutations, the peasants bringing in their produce, the goods in the shops and a hundred other things.

Some time in the late afternoon we caught the *rapide* to Brest. As my mother was recovering from an illness, Brian and I were allowed to go off to the restaurant car on our own for dinner, and I recall not so much the meal, but walking for what seemed miles along the corridor as the almost empty train thundered through the darkening landscape of the Breton countryside. By the time we arrived at Brest, it was late in the evening, and an outside porter pushed our luggage through the streets, while we followed on foot, to a modest hotel that he must have recommended. Next morning we embarked on a small steamer and arrived at Morgat – our destination – in a few hours.

We were the only English staying in the one hotel there. Brian and I spent most of our time playing tennis, sometimes with two French boys; one called Guy (odd that I should remember his name) was tiny but a remarkably good player, and to our chagrin we were usually beaten. We bathed a bit – the weather was not good – and went on a number of expeditions, which my father always liked to do. One was to the Pointe du Raze – a long, rocky peninsular that stretched far out to sea, on which many ships, including British ships, have been wrecked. After a fortnight, we moved on to Treuberden on the north coast of Brittany for the second part of our holiday. My mother went alone by train, while my father, Brian and I embarked on a more adventurous journey.

The first stage was by train to Roscoff. There we hired bicycles and bicycled along the coast as far as a deep inlet, where we sent the bicycles back and got a fisherman to take us across the estuary in his boat. Then we walked for some hours through the wildest and least populated part of Brittany – and it really was remote in those days – until we reached a small village at nightfall. There were two tiny *auberges*; the first could offer us only two beds, so we went on to the second, with the same results. For some reason we decided to sleep at the first inn, but eat at the second. However, when we told the madame this, she was furious and shouted out, *'Si vous ne mangez pas ici, vous ne couchez pas.'* We beat a hurried retreat, my father muttering, 'Horrid old cat.' We had a good meal at the second auberge, sitting at a long table with about a dozen or so of the local people, who were friendly, and we exchanged reciprocal toasts of *'a votre santé'* in the very strong Breton cider. Next day we continued our journey, and arrived at Treuberden late in the evening and pretty tired.

Here there was less to do than at Morgat; no tennis, but swimming, walking and one or two expeditions. The hotel was very simple, and the loo smelt appalling, French sanitation in those days being pretty primitive. The neighbouring villages were bleak by English standards, though most had an *épicerie* with very limited stocks, and a *buvette* or two for the men to drink in; the only chocolate available, which I craved, was coarse and grainy, and intended for making drinking chocolate, not for eating.

We went to Mass one Sunday in the local church as my father was a stickler for Sunday observance, even if it had to be a Catholic church. At some stage in the service, a basket of bread was passed round the congregation and each person took a sizable chunk; there was no wine accompanying it, and probably this was only given at the altar to those who wished to observe the full rites of Holy Communion. In those days, Brittany was difficult to reach, with few holiday-makers, even French, in the smaller places. Now, I suppose, it is swarming with tourists of all nationalities.

In the summer I left Haileybury, we went to stay at Ambleteuse near Boulogne for a few weeks. My father, who was mean in small ways though generous in giving to charities, always undertipped, and had apparently not realized how much the franc had fallen in value since his days in Paris, nor that French porters and waiters relied largely on tips for their livelihood. When we left Boulogne station by car for Ambleteuse, we departed to shouts of execration from the porters, who had evidently been grossly undertipped, and much the same thing happened on other occasions, to the extreme embarrassment of my brother and myself. At Ambleteuse we stayed in the only *auberge* – no hotel at that time – and, as usual, Brian and I spent most of our time playing tennis and swimming. There was a *parc aux huitres* close by, which sounded exciting, and we persuaded our father to take us there, but all we got was six oysters, with nothing to eat or drink with them – a big disappointment. Brian and I went into Boulogne by bus once or twice, and greatly daring, had a glass of *bière aux champignons* (that was how it was advertised) in a café – again a disappointment as the beer tasted of beer and not in any way of mushrooms, as we had expected.

On one of these occasions we found our way to the tennis club, somewhere up on the ramparts, to watch the finals of the men's singles, followed by an exhibition match. The players in this match were three men and one woman. Two of the men were Borotra and Cochet, and the woman Suzanne Lenglen, later of course a world-famous champion and several times winner of the Ladies' Singles at Wimbledon. We had never seen tennis anywhere near this standard, and we were absolutely thrilled. In due course the holiday came to an end. On the last evening there was a special dinner in my honour, my father made a short speech wishing me good luck in my new life, and I mumbled a few words in reply, in not a very good temper as the dinner had contained none of the dishes that I had specially wanted. Next day, the other members of the family returned to England – I think Uncle Jack and Aunt Beryl had joined us for part of the time – and my father and I travelled to Lille, where I was to stay with a family to improve my French.

It was not a good choice. The family were very badly off and I lived in an uncomfortable and sparsely furnished flat with one loo only, embarrassingly situated between the single living room and the kitchen. The *père de famille* was an overworked teacher in a large Catholic school, and could only spare a short time to give me a brief lesson before *déjeuner*. There were three children – a boy of about sixteen, who was a pupil at the school where his father taught, a crippled girl, and a bright little boy known as *petit Pierre*. Talk at meals was too fast for me to follow, and by the time I had thought out a suitable remark, the conversation had passed on to something else. I suppose I did gradually pick up a certain amount of French and learn a bit about French attitudes and customs, but for the first month or so I was abysmally bored, and spent most of the time doing nothing much in my room when I should have been studying, or going for endless lonely walks down the long, straight streets of Lille.

Occasionally, when I could afford it, I took one of the super-rapid electric trams that ran from Lille to Roubaix and Tourcoing along a special track parallel with the main road; they went faster than most of the cars, and it was quite an exciting form of travel and at least made a change from my lonely walks. Then by a lucky chance I met the British Consul (how did it happen – I can't remember), and thanks to his kindness became a member of the Lille golf club. Gradually I began to get to know a few people – nearly all English and connected in some way with the textile industry. I remain grateful to the families who showed me hospitality, even though I have long since forgotten most of their names. One was called Tongue, and I became friendly with their only son Jack, a young man slightly older than myself, who had just started out on his own account selling some kind of device connected with textile machinery. His parents lived in a pleasant house and garden a few miles outside Lille, which formed a sort of oasis in the hideous, flat muddy countryside that surrounded the city in all directions. They had a tennis court on which we played frequently, and Jack was allowed to drive (I was very envious) one of the family cars called a Delahaye. We went to cafés together, and sometimes after playing tennis, when we were hungry, to a patisserie where they had a particularly luscious pastry called a *hongrois* that we thoroughly enjoyed, though I couldn't always afford it on my meagre allowance. Once, greatly daring, we went to a *boîte de nuit*, and were both shocked and excited by what we saw, but it never occurred to us to do anything more than chat to one or

41

two of the hostesses who, seeing our naïveté, were rather nice to us.

I tried to join the local rugger club, but was shoved into the scrum, when I had always played as a three-quarter, and also found the other players older, heavier and stronger, so soon gave up. Another venture was to join a class in French language and literature run by Lille University for foreign students. Here I really did begin to improve my knowledge of the language, and also made a few acquaintances of different nationalities. One was a rather pretty English girl who had just come down from Oxford, called Margaret; I fell for her in a mild way and she seemed to like me, though of course I was too much her junior for anything serious to develop. Once, when a few of us were returning from a class, I was challenged or decided to show off and lift Margaret in my arms and carry her a few yards, which I just about managed to do. She then said I must do the same thing with another girl in the party, who seemed even heavier, and I let her down with rather a bump on her backside. She was not at all pleased. I somehow got to know one or two better class French families, and went once to a dance for young people in a rather luxurious apartment; it was a very formal affair – the French were very formal in those days – and we young men all carried white gloves. The daughter of the house wore an elegant dress with a very long tight corsage right down to the buttocks (not a word I would have dreamed of using or even thinking about in connection with a girl at that time), with a full skirt – no doubt in the current fashion. Why on earth should I remember that tiny detail when I am far from being observant in such matters – very unobservant my wife would say! Another acquaintance I made through the University was a French professor who taught phonetics; he occasionally asked me back to his house for an apéritif, and allowed me to browse in his library and borrow a book. Talking and listening to him – he was extremely voluble – helped considerably to improve my French. Once, when we were discussing the possibility of a future life – which he didn't believe in – I remember him remarking *'Vous savez, mon vieux, que l'homme est un tube digestif percé aux deux bouts. C'est vrai, n'est-ce pas?'*

After about seven months, I had to leave Lille and travel to Cambridge to take the entrance examination for Corpus

Christi College, for which my name had been put down. I suppose my stay at Lille had done me some good, apart from the language aspect; it opened my eyes to a different culture and way of life, it taught me to stand on my own feet, put up with boredom and cope unaided with difficulties, but I can't pretend that I enjoyed the process. I was determined not to return there, and before leaving I had written to Gabbitas Thring, the well-known scholastic agents to find me a new family; this turned out to be a good move.

I arrived at Cambridge, after a rough crossing, rather late in the evening. I was fascinated by the lighted colleges and other buildings that we passed in the taxi, the crowded streets and the young men, a few in cap and gown, that we passed on the way. On arrival at the quite imposing entrance to Corpus, the Head Porter, wearing a top hat, received me with the utmost politeness and directed someone to show me to my rooms, mentioning that dinner had already started in the Hall, but that it would be perfectly in order for me to go in. However, I had not the nerve to do so, and went to bed supperless. The entrance examination, which was not difficult, started next morning; at some point I visited the College library and happened by chance on an article by Lionel Curtis in the *Round Table,* advocating a much more lenient policy towards defeated Germany, which I read with interest – probably the first article on foreign affairs that had come my way. By good luck, there was a question on the subject in the last examination paper, and I practically reproduced a shorter version of the *Round Table* article. Later, I heard that my answer had caused quite a bit of favourable comment, none of the dons concerned having read the article. By an even better piece of good luck, I made my first friend – Jim Bourne (the youngest son of the Bourne family of Bourne and Hollingworth), who later had a most interesting career as a doctor. He told me recently that I introduced him to smoking by giving him a cigarette – it must, I think, have been a French cigarette. All in all, I much enjoyed my first brief visit to Corpus – how different the atmosphere from one's public school – and looked forward eagerly to my first term. But for the moment I had to return to France after a brief visit to Weymouth.

I had arranged, through Gabbitas Thring, to stay with a

family at Melun, a small town on the Seine, 45 kilometres south of Paris, but decided to spend a few days in the capital on the way there. I stayed in a small bed and breakfast hotel near the Opera, recommended by someone in Lille, and explored the city on my own. I went everywhere on foot, by bus or by *métro,* including a long walk in the Bois de Boulogne. Of course it would have been more fun to have had a friend with me, or better still a girl, but nonetheless it was an exciting new experience. Paris remains today, after Venice, my favourite city. I ate in cheap restaurants, and had numerous cups of coffee and glasses of beer in cafés, my favourite being the *Café de la Paix* where one could watch the whole world go by. Inevitably one was accosted by prostitutes, but it never occurred to me to go with one – not that I could have afforded to do so. I had been in contact by letter with Margaret, who was passing through Paris, and on my last day there I invited her to lunch at Ledoyen in the Champs Elysees. We had a delicious *déjeuner,* but when the bill came I was staggered by the amount, not having realized that I had picked a very expensive restaurant. Margaret must have seen my consternation, and offered to lend me some money, but I was too proud to accept. When I got to the Gare de Lyon later in the afternoon, I had just enough francs left to buy a third-class ticket to Melun. What would have happened if I had not, I really don't know.

At Melun I was met by Monsieur Tourneur, and walked with him to where he lived with his wife – there were no children – about a mile outside the town. They rented an upper floor of a small farmhouse, and I was allotted a room on the ground floor which gave directly onto a quiet country road, with shutters to close at night. I immediately felt at ease. Madame Tourneur, who was Russian by birth, was charming and extremely kind to me; she even went to the trouble of cooking me an English breakfast. Monsieur Tourneur was a schoolmaster, like my previous host, but a different type – younger, keen on fishing, and not, I fancy, very enthusiastic about his profession. We went swimming together in the Seine – it was a superb summer – bicycled around the countryside, once or twice with boys from his school, and visited several *chateaux* and places of interest like Fontainbleau. The house had a pleasant garden with a summerhouse where I worked spasmodically. M. Tourneur started by giving me brief lessons, but when he found that I had begun to read Lanson's massive history of French literature, he said that he could not teach me better, and the lessons faded out. But I found the conversation so much easier, talking with one or two people rather than the rapid-fire conversation of a family, that my French really did begin to improve. Mme. Tourneur had a young niece called Lili Arabey who used to come and stay at weekends. She was petite, not pretty but lively, and for her *l'amour* was the most important thing in the world. I was asked to escort her back to the station the first Sunday evening, as M. Tourneur was a little unwell, and it was not long before we were walking in a close embrace and pausing at intervals to kiss. I must admit that the initiative was taken by Lili, and that the kisses she gave me were quite different from anything I had hitherto experienced or indeed imagined. These weekly walks to the station soon became a regular habit, and often we arrived only just in time for Lili to catch the last train back to Paris. On the way, sometimes sitting on a bench by the Seine, she used to hum a popular tune of the day, one of which began:

Nuit de Chine
Nuit caline
Nuit d'amour

Once, we did miss the last train, and had no option but to return to the house. Lili was afraid to waken her uncle and aunt, so we climbed into my room through the window giving on the road. After our embraces had continued for some time, I took fright, partly because I genuinely felt that it was wrong to seduce the niece of my kind hosts, and partly because I didn't know what to do. I left Lili in my room, to her annoyance I fear, then grabbed a blanket and sat in the garden summerhouse, cold and uncomfortable, until it was time to take Lili to the station to catch a very early train to Paris. Later that morning, Madame Tourneur had to knock loudly on my door to wake me, as I had not appeared for breakfast at the usual time. Once I went to Paris to take Lili out in the evening. We found a small *boîte de nuit* in Montmartre which did not look too expensive, and sat there drinking slowly. There was a door at one end of the room and I kept expecting an exciting *spectacle* to emerge. But absolutely nothing happened. We sat there for hours, and eventually it was time to take Lili home, as she had to go to work. We travelled by *métro*, and for part of the way the line ran high above the streets, so I saw what perhaps not many people have seen – the dawn breaking over the *toits de Paris*. Once or twice M. Tourneur hired a rowing boat, Madame prepared a *pique-nique*, and the four of us rowed slowly down the Seine on a summer's afternoon. Lili always bathed, showing off her neat little figure, but for some reason I did not. In due course, the time arrived for me to return to England to prepare for Cambridge. It had been, in many ways, an idyllic summer. I had liked my hosts, improved my French, seen a little of both Paris and the countryside, and had my first love affair. I left France with real regrets.

5

Cambridge – the Three Best Years of my Life

In October 1923, I began my first term at Cambridge. Corpus followed the Oxford pattern, and undergraduates spent their first two years in college and only their last year in 'digs' – an excellent arrangement, as it made it much easier to make friends. I was fortunate in being allotted a very pleasant set of rooms on the ground floor of the Old Court – the oldest Court in Cambridge. The tutor in my time was Will Spens, later Master of the College for many years and twice Vice-Chancellor of the University (as Sir Will Spens). He was a man of great ability, and completely changed the ethos of the college, which for generations had been a small sleepy place, with many of the undergraduates designated for the church. Although nominally a theologian (though, I don't believe he ever taught the subject), Spens was really a brilliant administrator and diplomat. Under his regime the academic standard of Corpus rose sharply; in one year while I was 'up', it attained the highest percentage of 'firsts' of any college. We had two rugger blues, one of whom, Tom Devitt (Sir Thomas Devitt), later played wing-threequarter for England and also the captain of the University hockey team – not bad for one of the smallest colleges in Cambridge. The aspirations of the undergraduates had also changed, and a number of my contemporaries subsequently had successful careers in various fields. For example, (Sir) Humphrey Mynors became Deputy Director of the Bank of England, and EJD (Jackie) Whitcroft, Chairman of Imperial Tobacco. More unusually, Christopher Isherwood was at Corpus in my time, though I don't remember him at all; I think he wrote somewhere that he hated his time at Cambridge. I felt the exact opposite – it was the best three years of my life.

Friendship, games and, to a varying extent, work, were the

things that mattered to most people. I did reasonably well at games, playing rugger for the College and getting my tennis 'colours' in my last year. At work, I was extremely idle in my first year, but pulled myself together and achieved an Upper Second in Part 2 of the History Tripos. I had, I think, absorbed almost unconsciously the feeling that intellectual things were both important and interesting, and that it was of some value to be able, for example, to recall passages from Corneille or Racine or to have read Don Quixote in the original Spanish. I was aware, too, by this time that I had no ready-made job awaiting me, and that my father had more or less decided I should try and get into the Consular Service, for which, of course, a good standard in languages was a prerequisite.

During my first long vacation, I went to stay with a family in San Sebastian to improve my Spanish. They were the Comte and Comtesse de la Vallée: he was a small, rather cynical Frenchman, she a charming woman born in Mexico. They had two daughters, one away at the time; the younger girl, Micheline, about fifteen and more Spanish than French, was difficult, and clearly resented her parents having to take paying guests, though she could be lively and amusing when in a good mood. There were two other young English men staying there that summer, and we spent most of our time together enjoying the gay panorama of San Sebastian, at that time one of the most fashionable resorts in Europe. Through the de la Vallées we were able to join the Club Nautico – a highly select club – and so had excellent opportunities for swimming and sailing, as well as getting to know a few of the younger Spaniards belonging to the club. In the evening we usually took part in the *paseo*, that is, parading up and down a suitable street – in this case the sea front lined by elegant hotels and villas – with everyone dressed in their best clothes; in those days (I don't know if things have changed), the girls and men walked in separate groups, with little or no conversation between the two, but the men making comments in a loud voice and paying lavish compliments (*que chica mas guapa* – what a very lovely girl) to the ones they fancied. We also went occasionally to the casino, perhaps for a *thé dansant* or to gamble mildly with a few pesetas. By way of a change, we found a simple taberna used by fishermen in an old part of the town, where we consumed large quantities of anchovies washed down with a strong spirit whose name I forget. It was, on the whole, an enjoyable summer holiday, though at times I felt lonely and longed for English scenes and pastimes.

After a few weeks, one of the young English boys left and was replaced by another slightly older man, who had just embarked on a business career somewhere in the North of England, and needed to improve his Spanish. We both went to have lessons with a rather impoverished though likeable Spaniard named Satorres, with a wife and daughter whom we barely glimpsed – they seemed to be in purdah. The young business man was keen to see Lourdes, and persuaded me to take Satorres with us, paying his expenses between us, which I could ill afford to do. On arrival at Lourdes, I was somewhat shocked by the shoddy religious objects in the shops, then interested by the grotto, where those who had been cured of their illnesses had left their crutches and other similar objects piled high in heaps. But at night the whole scene changed, when the pilgrims, all carrying a lighted candle in their hands, moved slowly in a long procession up the steps on one side of the great church and then down the other, chanting *Ave Maria* in unison. It was a moving and impressive sight, and I can well believe that many people were, and are, cured of their infirmities by a visit to Lourdes.

In due course I returned to Cambridge, having improved my Spanish to a certain extent and learned a little about an ancient and quite different country.

The following Lent vacation I again went to Spain, this time with an undergraduate from another college, called Alistair Blair, whom I only knew slightly. Our aim was to see as much of the country as we could manage in a fortnight. We travelled of course by train, thundering for hours across the arid plains of Castille. We stopped briefly in Burgos to visit the magnificent cathedral, and then on to Madrid for a brief stay of five days. We went at least twice to the Prado, primarily to see the Velasquez; for years afterwards I had a treasured picture postcard of *Las Meninas* – one of my four or five favourite paintings. The El Grecos were a bit too austere for me to appreciate at that stage. We walked for miles in both the fashionable and unfashionable parts of the city, and I remember having a coffee watching the lively crowds in the rather ugly and misnamed Puerta del Sol (it may well have changed since those days). We made two short expeditions from Madrid: the first was to the vast, austere palace of the *Escorial*, set in a bleak landscape; the guide showed us the small room where King Philip II – who despatched the Armada – had died lying on a heap of filth, but able to see through a peep-hole the figure of the Madonna in his private chapel. Our other expedition was to Toledo – a superb town, then approachable only by one narrow bridge across a deep gorge. There was not a tourist to be seen, but instead we were followed everywhere by a crowd of small boys begging for money; finally, in desperation, we decided to throw all our loose change into the crowd, and dashed up a narrow side-street to escape while they were picking up the money. Unfortunately, the street ended in a blank wall, we were forced to return, and as we emerged, there came the pack in full cry after us. So my recollections of Toledo are somewhat mixed, though I am very glad to have seen it before the days of mass tourism.

One evening, while still in Madrid, I managed to persuade my rather straight-laced companion to come to a night-club where we watched, and I at least, enjoyed the singing and especially the dancing; in the genuine thing there is no prancing about on stage, and it is a matter of the right expressive movements of the body, the head, the arms and of course the rhythmic stamping and playing of the castanets.

From Madrid we went on to Granada and Cordoba. Both were superb in their different ways. I knew of course that the Moors had been a talented and highly civilized people, but I was overwhelmed by the beauty and peace of the Alhambra – so utterly different from anything I had seen before – with its symmetrical courtyards, shaded by myrtles and other trees, and its elegant pools open to the sky. Cordoba was equally impressive in a different way. After the expulsion of the Moors in 1236, the Christians mistakenly constructed a cathedral inside the enormous mosque. It still remains, as I recollect it, giving the impression of a mosque rather than a cathedral, with a low ceiling and forests of highly ornate columns. There is nothing like it, I think, anywhere else in the world. At that time, Cordoba was utterly different from sophisticated

Madrid – narrow streets, ancient buildings, virtually no motor traffic, and in some streets only people on foot. One seemed to go back in time for hundreds of years; I wonder what it is like today?

In due course we arrived in Seville for the last few days of Holy Week. Something had gone wrong with our bookings, and there were no rooms available at the hotel where we had intended to stay; after various fruitless enquiries, we hired a horse-drawn cab and drove around trying to find somewhere to go. Finally, in desperation, we were forced to take a room at a horrible dirty little *fonda*. We went to bed late after wandering for hours round the narrow crowded streets of the city; during the night I woke up feeling itchy and uncomfortable, and, on lighting a candle – no electricity of course – saw that the bed and even the walls were covered with lice. I also developed an acute attack of diarrhoea, but an English doctor, to whom I am eternally grateful, managed to get me more or less right by Easter Sunday – our last full day. In the morning we went to Mass in the great cathedral, which was ablaze with lights after the end of Lent, and in the afternoon to see our first bullfight. We hired a carriage to take us to the Plaza de Toros, and as it made its way through the crowds we passed several groups of young men on horseback, with their girls sitting pillion-fashion behind them. I had mixed feelings about the bullfight. At first I admired the pageantry and the early stages of playing the bull with cloaks, but the deliberate slaughter of old broken-down horses to tire the bull was sickening, and, as bull after bull was killed by the Matadors, I became more and more repelled by the proceedings. That was our last event of note in Seville. Next day we returned to England.

The summer term at Cambridge passed pleasantly enough, though I had to get down to work in preparation for Part 1 of the Tripos examination at the end of it. Still, this did not prevent me from playing tennis and bridge, going punting on the river from time to time, and leading a fairly active social life. By now I had a circle of friends, several of whom I have already mentioned. My closest friend was Pat (Patrice) Charvet, whose French father had been killed in the First World War while still a young man, after which he (Pat) was brought up in England by his English mother. Pat was clever as well as charming, and had the advantage of being virtually bilingual in French and English, so he had no difficulty in getting a First in Modern Languages. Later, after a short period teaching at Rugby, he became a Fellow of Corpus and University Reader in French language and literature. We have remained close friends throughout our lives. By way of a small footnote, he happened to mention many years later that his father had owned a 25 hp Peugeot – a luxury car – and that their chauffeur, whom he clearly remembered, had been called Maigret.

I have already said that my first friend was Jim Bourne, and again we have remained friends for life, though our very different careers have prevented us from seeing as much of each other as we both would have liked. Jim was the youngest son of the founder of Bourne and Hollingsworth's department store, and, after leaving Cambridge, went into the family business for a short time – indeed I remember calling on him there, when he popped out of a small office dressed in a morning coat. He soon grew tired of selling ladies' underwear, returned to Cambridge for a second spell to read medicine, and qualified as a doctor, ending up, I believe, as Head Anaesthetist at St Thomas' Hospital, a most unusual career. Another friend was (Sir) Basil Bartlett, who later held a senior post at the BBC and became well-known in London literary circles. Naturally, I had some friends outside Corpus; one was Edward Wakefield, who had been Head of School, Captain of rugby football and Head of my House at Haileybury. He was two years older than I, and had already decided to enter the Indian Civil Service; I remember him telling me, sitting in his rooms at Trinity, what a splendid career it offered, but at that moment I was not interested, being destined, as I thought, for the Consular Service. Later, after the end of British rule in India, he became an MP, a Whip, and finally, as Sir Edward Wakefield, British High Commissioner in Malta. This last paragraph sounds a bit like name-dropping, but, of course, I also had a number of friends who afterwards led lives of no particular distinction; one, indeed, whom I liked particularly, had a sad life and died a young man.

By this time, my father had progressed in his career and, after a period as Chief Justice of Northern Rhodesia (now Zambia), had become Chief Justice of the Bahamas, where he had a beautiful house on the sea with its own private landing-stage. It had been proposed that I should spend part of the long vacation staying with him, but at the last moment the plan was cancelled, for some reason I have forgotten. I was bitterly disappointed. Instead, I had to make the usual round of visits to relatives – by this time I was thoroughly bored with Weymouth, where there were no young people of my age – since there was no longer any compelling reason for me to go abroad.

My mother happened to be in England that summer, and I went with her to spend a fortnight or so at Totland Bay in the Isle of Wight. Through the local tennis club I made a few temporary friends. One was Peter Gladstone, also up at Cambridge at the time, who had just been given a new car, and drove me at high speed round the narrow roads of the Island. I was asked to play tennis once or twice by the Leveson Gowers – a well known Island family – and also met another family with two cheerful young daughters who first introduced me to the game of 'sardines'. It was my first, but by no means my last, visit to Totland Bay, as I shall recount later.

My final year at Cambridge arrived all too soon. I had 'digs' in Silver Street, which gave me a little extra freedom, though I really preferred the more intimate atmosphere of life 'in college'. Reading Part 2 of the History Tripos, my supervisor was Sir Geoffrey Butler, uncle of RAB Butler (later a Minster of Education and Chancellor of the Exchequer); he was an authentic Cambridge 'character' – a hunchback with a high squeaky voice, but a brilliant mind and great sense of humour. He was once heard to remark 'Why have they painted the walls that horrid shit colour?' He didn't think much of the first few weekly essays I wrote, but I gradually improved under his tuition and in the end, as I have mentioned, achieved an Upper Second. I belonged, of course, to various College societies, of which the most select was the Chess Club – reputedly one of the oldest clubs in Cambridge. Chess may once have been played, but in my day it was purely a social club; we wore embroidered dinner jackets, drank mulled claret made according to an ancient recipe, and at each meeting two members had to sing a song or tell a story. I was a member also of several University societies, including the Union, though I regret to say I never spoke there –

unfortunately, we had no College debating society in which to make a start.

In April 1926, near the beginning of my last term at Cambridge, the General Strike in support of the miners broke out, involving virtually the whole country. With hindsight, I think the miners of those days had received a pretty raw deal from the owners, but equally any responsible Government was bound to resist a General Strike called by the Trade Unions. Corpus was, as I have said, a conservative college in every sense of the word, and with very few exceptions we all wanted to respond to the call of the Prime Minister, Stanley Baldwin, and play a part in defeating the strike. Someone from another college – I think Magdalen – with great enterprize organized a large convoy of cars to drive volunteers to London, where we were assigned to a wide variety of different jobs. The lucky ones became bus drivers or bus conductors, the former, in particular, having great fun; my wife, then a very pretty girl of eighteen, remembers being given a ride in the front seat of a bus driven by an undergraduate boy friend who soon managed to take a wrong turning and lose his way temporarily until put right by the passengers. I, myself, became a platform worker at Euston tube station. The only interesting part of the job was to operate the entry and exit gates of the lift by means of an electric control, and once, on my first day, I managed to press the wrong switch and the gate on the side people were leaving by began to close with considerable force; fortunately, I reacted quickly to the shouts of the passengers and reversed the gates before anyone was injured. Very soon I was promoted to be a signalman, and, after the briefest period of instruction, I and another undergraduate from Oxford were put in charge of the signal cabin at Euston. There were, of course, very few trains running, but even so it was a responsible job that required all my attention. But I thoroughly enjoyed it, in spite of being shut up all day underground.

At night we were taken by tube to a depot – at Bethnal Green I think – to sleep in pretty rough conditions; there we were fed and looked after by girls who too had volunteered to oppose the strike. One, whom I got to know slightly, turned out to be the daughter of a Duke, and my suggestion that we should have lunch together was politely declined. The General Strike did not last long and of course failed, though the miners struggled on alone for some time. It had been an exciting experience for me, and I was highly gratified to receive my pay – about £6 if I remember rightly – which seemed a large sum. It was the first money I had earned. It is perhaps worth adding that, so far as I know, there was little or no violence during the General Strike; the few strikers I saw in London looked depressed and seemed aware that they were going to lose, while many ordinary people appeared rather to enjoy the occasion. I suppose it made a break from their normal routine.

Sadly, the summer term drew to a close, and I had to begin the process of saying goodbye to dons, college servants and one's friends. We all swore to keep in touch, though knowing well that it would often not be possible. The final break was slightly eased by the May Week Balls. That year I had invited a pretty, though rather reserved, girl called Brownie Mullens as my guest; she lived in Weymouth, where she taught dancing – not my strongest point, as my wife would confirm. After the last ball, we – that is the Corpus undergraduates and their girl friends who had stayed on for May Week – were photographed in the Old Court, and then Jim Bourne drove a few of us in an ancient open Rolls-Royce – still wearing our tails – to Huntingdon for an early breakfast. So ended three of the best years of my life.

6

Skiing in Switzerland and Getting Engaged

After going down from Cambridge for the last time, it was decided that I should spend part of the next year preparing for the Higher Civil Service examinations, with my eye fixed primarily on the Consular Service. This meant, of course, that I had to maintain, and improve, my knowledge of modern languages. I therefore found, through an agency, a family in Santander (on the north coast of Spain) that was willing to take me. In those days it was much harder to find suitable families, and there was no system of 'if you'll take my boy, I'll take yours'. My choice – not my fault, but the agency's – turned out to be a disaster. The family were very badly off, living in conditions not far from squalid. I had nothing in common with any of them. The season was over, there was nothing to do, and I was bored to tears. After sticking it out for two or three weeks, I ascertained that the de la Vallées were still in San Sebastion – not very far away – and decided to transfer myself there. This was a considerable improvement, though less enjoyable than on my previous visit. Here too the season was over, the academic year had started again, and there were no other young men staying with the family. Fortunately, after a short time the Comte de la Vallée was suddenly offered a job with a leading Paris couturier – I think it was Lanvin – who wished to add a *parfumerie* to their main activities – a new vogue then just beginning. The Comte was an expert on perfumes ('scent' was the word I had been brought up to use, not 'perfume'), though how he acquired this unusual knowledge I have no idea. Anyway, he accepted the offer, and the whole family moved to Paris. They offered to take me along and, having nothing else in view, I decided to accept.

We were soon installed in a fairly comfortable apartment in

the Rue César Frank, not very far from the Invalides on the left bank of the Seine. The flat was furnished in imitation Louis XVI style, and although I had my own bedroom, there was only one bathroom with one loo for everyone – pretty normal at that time. The bathwater was heated by an ancient geyser that always seemed on the point of exploding – indeed it did once, though luckily no-one was in the bathroom at that moment, and not much damage was done.

The de la Vallées soon got to know a family living in an adjoining apartment. The *père de famille* was a journalist and a highly intelligent man with a fund of amusing stories. I have forgotten these, but I remember him remarking on one occasion when we had got on to the subject of women, *'N'oubliez pas que la femme ne voit jamais ce que l'on fait pour elle; elle ne voit que ce qu'on ne fait pas?'* He was kind to me and lent me several books to read, including one or two by Jean Cocteau, who was then very much in vogue. I didn't know a soul in Paris at that time, apart from the de la Vallées, and had to set to to develop a life of some sort for myself, keeping in mind that my father was paying fairly heavily to continue my education. Through the British Embassy I was put in touch with a young French diplomat working at the Quai d'Orsay, who agreed to give me a weekly lesson – presumably the small amount I paid him provided a little extra pocket money. I wrote an essay, he corrected it, and we chatted a bit about the subject of the day. It did help to improve my French, but socially it led nowhere – he never introduced me to anyone or invited me to anything, so after a bit I decided to explore the possibilities of the Sorbonne. First of all, I joined a class of foreigners – mostly older than myself – attending a course on French literature. It was conducted with extreme formality. The lecture room – quite unlike anything at Cambridge – resembled a small section of a theatre upper circle, with rows of benches rising steeply one behind the other. The lecturer, a senior Professor, reached the dais through a separate door, gave his lecture and departed. There were no questions and no contact with the audience, who, in their turn, soon melted away. I found it extremely boring and not much help except for the pleasure, such as it was, of listening to beautifully enunciated French. This was not at all what I was looking for, and after some further digging around I managed to attach myself to a group of young foreign students working for a diploma in French language, history and literature; here, I fear I cheated as the course lasted a year, and I had to pretend I was enrolling for that period. The group were all from various European countries, and I soon made friends with several of them, in particular a young Dutchman called Vanderveld.

We had younger and livelier lecturers for these classes, but the great advantage was that, all of us being foreigners and much the same age, we had to talk to each other in French, and it didn't matter much if one made mistakes. Indeed, I remember one of the lecturers remarking to a senior official who came round to inspect the class, *'Ici on parle français dans toutes les langues'*. So we chatted away to each other without inhibitions in a wide variety of accents, and often, I have no doubt, in a way that a Frenchman would have found hard to understand. Having plenty of leisure, we frequented cafés in and around the Boulevard St Michel, drinking whatever we could afford – usually coffee, beer or a glass of *vin ordinaire*. The café proprietors were very tolerant to students, and provided one ordered a drink of some kind, one could stay for as long as one wanted. Apart from talking, we played various card games (not bridge), draughts, bezique, and a few of us chess. One could also read the newspapers, which in those days were attached to heavy pieces of wood so that they could not be removed from the café. Sometimes we would walk in the Luxembourg Gardens or take the *Métro* or bus to the Bois de Boulogne. The buses in those days, and for a good many years afterwards, had platforms at the rear on which one could stand if the inside was full, or if one wanted to see more of the passing scene – rather enjoyable, we thought. Occasionally a few of us ventured further afield, and I remember walking in the Forest of Marly le Roi on a beautiful day in early spring, and seeing a deer jump across the path.

There were no girls taking the Sorbonne course, but a few had attached themselves to one or other member of our group. They were a pretty mixed bunch; ranging from serious students to near-tarts. I gradually became friendly with a rather pretty Danish girl called Anna, who was studying art. After a time, I got to the point of asking her to have a drink with me alone from time to time, our favourite place being the Coupole in the Boulevard Montparnasse, from where one could watch the left-bank life of Paris flowing past. One day she invited me to come to her apartment for an evening omelette, mentioning casually that the friend with whom she shared it would be out. I was thrilled, wondering how far I could go, and determined that at least I would try to kiss and hug her. But when I got to the apartment I found to my great disappointment a piece of paper pinned to the door saying (in French), 'My mother has been taken ill, have had to leave for home. Hope to see you later.' Soon after, my time in France was over and I had to say goodbye, not without regrets, to what we grandly called our *meute de lions* (pack of lions).

Perhaps I ought to mention that while in Paris, I had not failed to do the usual sightseeing, mainly during the early part of my stay before I joined the Sorbonne group, when we had other things to interest us. Among other 'monuments', I visited the Louvre a number of times – superb but overpowering – Notre Dame, the exquisite Sainte-Chapelle, the Invalides, Versailles, numerous museums, of which my favourite was the Musée Carnavalet, as I had happened to read a book about Madame de Sévigné, and then a collection of her letters. Of course I went to the Eiffel Tower, the first time only up to the first platform, but the second time I screwed up my courage to go to the top, which was quite frightening if one lacked a good head for heights; luckily it was a fine day, and the view was superb, with the whole of Paris laid out below like a map. I also wandered about the streets, especially the less fashionable areas like the Marais, Montparnasse, Place du Tertre (then unspoiled), Montmartre (by day), and so on. But this is not intended to be a guide to Paris, and I will merely say that at that time I knew some parts of the city quite well.

On getting back to England, I spent the last few months before the dreaded examination at Scoone's, a very well-known crammers, specializing in candidates for the Diplomatic and Consular Services. It was run by an eccentric Frenchman, who explained to new arrivals that the heavy fees required were fixed by his partner who, I soon discovered, was a non-existent person. On the whole I found the place very little use. All the attention was given to the Diplomatic candidates, most of whom had relations already in the Service and who hoped, if they failed the examination, to get in by the back door – which was still sometimes possible at that time if one had the right connections, usually by becoming an Honorary Attaché. I remember one of the diplomatic students deliberately enraging our rather choleric history teacher by arguing that the title 'Czar' did not derive from 'Caesar', but from some ancient Slavonic word.

In due course the date for the examination arrived, about mid-July, I think. It was held at Burlington House – in the rear section, now used for specialist exhibitions. I was unlucky over the questions, especially in history, and was forced, I remember, to answer several questions about Germany and Austria, including some aspects of Bismark's foreign policy, about which I knew little, whereas I was quite well informed about French and Spanish affairs. I was more fortunate over the interview – a formidable affair as one had to appear alone before a board of some fifteen or more elderly (to me) gentlemen. One of them asked me the name of my favourite author; I replied 'Galsworthy'. He seemed to agree, and I was able to spend about five minutes of the interview chatting about *The Forsyte Saga* and other Galsworthy novels. When the results of the examination were announced, about a month later, I found I had done reasonably well, being placed sixteenth out of a total of some two hundred candidates. In the interview I had received 275 marks out of 300, which helped my placing considerably and was bettered by only a handful of people, one being Philip Mason, later a friend of mine in India, and subsequently a well-known writer.

I then had to decide on my future career. I had not passed for the Diplomatic Service, for which there were precisely two vacancies (nowadays there are 30 to 40), nor had any of my Scoone's contemporaries, though I believe one or two of them did get in by a back door, as mentioned above. But I had passed for all the other Services, including the Home Civil, Indian Civil, Consular and Far Eastern cadetships. Perhaps influenced by what my Haileybury and Cambridge friend, Edward Wakefield, had told me, I decided to choose the Indian Civil Service. Who could foresee that within twenty years the British would have left India for good, and that in a considerably shorter time the Consular Service would be merged with the Diplomatic? One sometimes wonders how much control people really have over their lives, and it is not surprising that the doctrine of predestination has had many adherents over the centuries.

Anyway, having opted for the Indian Civil Service (in future I shall refer to it as the ICS), the new recruits had to undergo a year's training in England, studying Indian languages, history and law. One could do this either at Oxford, Cambridge or the School of Oriental Studies in London. I felt it would be a mistake to return to Cambridge, and decided to spend my year in London. By this time I was living as a paying guest with an elderly friend of one of my aunts, a Miss Raleigh King, who had a pleasant house in Tedworth Square, just off the Kings Road in Chelsea. Before long I was being treated like a favourite nephew and rather spoiled by my hostess, who I christened 'Tantine'. The house was crammed with furniture, much of it old and valuable. There was a huge portrait of Tantine's mother painted as a young woman; she seemed to me incomparably beautiful, and I liked to fancy myself in love with her. Tantine had a sealyham dog called Banshee, that I quickly became very fond of and for some reason nicknamed 'Poot'. I used to take her for walks in the Royal Hospital Gardens or Kensington Gardens, and before long for drives in the car that I soon managed to acquire, though not really able to afford it. I came to regard Poot almost as my own dog – the first in a long succession that I have had throughout my life. Indeed, for me life would hardly be worth living without the companionship of dogs and, to a lesser extent, other animals.

I regret to say that. during the whole of my year at the School of Oriental Studies, I did the absolute minimum of work, partly perhaps as a reaction to the sweat of getting a good degree and then passing the Civil Service examination, but I was also determined to make the most of my last year in England and have as enjoyable a time as possible. Naturally, I had to attend the School – then located in Finsbury Circus – on most weekdays. There I soon made friends with two other young ICS probationers, and we used to lunch together regularly at various local pubs where one could get a good hot meal and a pint of beer for around half-a-crown (2/6d) – about 12p in today's currency. There were also several Indian probationers, but I never got to know any of them socially as I should have done, though we were all on quite friendly terms.

At that point I think few, if any, of the English probationers realized that Indianisation of the various Government Services was already well under way, and that we would soon have to adjust ourselves to it.

Apart from the School of Oriental Studies and my life in Tedworth Square, I found plenty to occupy my leisure time. Through some distant relatives, I got on the lists of one or two London hostesses and was invited to a few of the numerous balls and dances that were given at that period. Unfortunately, it was then the custom to take, or be taken by, a girl to these affairs; there were no introductions, and one danced with the same partner for most of the evening, a thoroughly bad arrangement. Consequently, there was little opportunity to make new friends. I also went to some of the regular sporting and social occasions – Twickenham, of course, for the varsity rugger match, the Derby, Lords, Henley and so on. But I can't say that I was ever more than on the fringes of London 'Society', as it used to be called. I had, however, a small number of men and women friends, one of the former having been at Haileybury with me. I don't think he had even got into the Sixth Form there, but he suddenly emerged as the dramatic critic of a leading Sunday newspaper with a whole page to himself headed 'Dudley Leslie Says'. He invited me once or twice – for free – to the opening night of a new play, and I remember on one of these occasions going on afterwards with two other critics – very scruffy they seemed to me – for a snack at the Savoy. There, to my surprise, they all ordered milk to drink and, rather unwillingly, I felt obliged to do the same. I also kept in touch with several of my Cambridge friends who were working in London, including Jim Bourne and Basil Bartlett. Of my girl friends – a pretty mixed lot – my 'steady' for some time was a young woman called Molly Shaw, whom I met when I went to have some much-needed dancing lessons. She was pretty, a little older than me and recently divorced. I think she had once worked in a dress shop and had had to earn her own living. I used to take her for drives at weekends in my ancient Riley car, often down the Great West Road to Maidenhead or somewhere else on the river. One sunny day in early summer, we were in a punt moored to the bank, when a motor boat came by much too fast. Just at that moment Molly had got up for some reason, and the wash from the motor boat made the punt sway sharply, and she fell into the water. I was able to fish her out unharmed but, of course, soaked, and had to drive her straight back to London sitting on the floor to keep out of the wind. Although I was very fond of her, the idea of marriage never entered my head, and it came as quite a shock when she told me the following spring that she herself was about to remarry. In fact, this end to our relationship came at just the right time for me.

The previous winter, I was asked by a girl I knew slightly called Barbara Chetwyn-Stapleton – I think I met her through Tantine – if I would care to join a party to go skiing at Wengen in Switzerland. This seemed an excellent idea, and I accepted. I liked Barbara, who was tall, slim and pretty, and I felt sure that she would have nice friends. The organizers of the party were a Mr and Mrs Topham. He was a well-known KC and they had a young family consisting of a boy called Romer, then at Cambridge, and two girls. They were all keen on winter sports, and the family liked to rent a large chalet and fill it with their own party. To make up the necessary numbers, some of their young friends were asked to bring a partner, which was the reason why I was invited. On arrival at Waterloo one day in early January I was introduced to the Tophams, found my seat, and then walked once or twice up and down the platform, passing a strikingly beautiful blonde girl talking animatedly to the young men on either side of her. When I took my seat in the train, I found to my surprise and pleasure that she was a member of our party. Her name was Peggy Fass. On arrival at Calais after the Channel crossing, I managed to get a seat next to her in the train to Switzerland. We were travelling second class, and had to sit up for the whole night, four or five on each side of the carriage. Peggy seemed to like me, and, as one dozed fitfully while the train roared through the night, her head fell on my shoulders and appeared to rest there contentedly.

In due course we arrived at Wengen, where Romer Topham and one or two others who had already arrived, met us at the station. Peggy and Romer greeted each other affectionately, and I was dropped like a hot brick – somewhat to my annoyance. It soon became clear that they were in love, so that was that for the time being. Unfortunately, I was not attracted by any of the other girls, and the men were mostly a little younger than me and still at university, which made a difference, and also a little on the 'hearty' side (to use a word then in vogue). That year there had been almost no snow, and the ground was iron-hard. As a complete beginner, skiing was a painful process; the longer one stayed on one's feet, the faster one went and the harder one fell. I don't remember if it was possible to have lessons, but none of us did, only a little advice from Mr Topham who was a good skier. On one occasion we all went up by the funicular railway to Scheidegg, ate our sandwiches there in glorious sunshine, with a marvellous view of the Alps spread out before us; and then skied down. I fell every few hundred yards, ran into at least one tree, and arrived back at the chalet battered, bruised and exhausted. Peggy, who had spent a year at a finishing school near Geneva, could ski a bit; she had Romer Topham and another man to help her, and got back long before me, quite pleased with herself. She was, as I have said, an extremely pretty girl who had great self-confidence, and I remember one breakfast at the chalet, when she recounted a not very interesting dream she had had the previous night to the whole party, which included not only Mr and Mrs Topham but a friend of theirs, Wilfred Green, who later became Lord Chief Justice of England. Once, greatly daring, I took a luge down the ski run, about halfway misjudged a corner and went over the side. I shot a long way down the steep slope before I could stop, and it took me half an hour or more to scramble back to the foot of the run, fortunately unhurt. At night, after dinner, we used to go dancing in one or other of the hotels; I didn't much enjoy these occasions at first, as the only girl in our party I wanted to dance with was Peggy, who was a very good performer and much in demand. However, after a few days, I met by chance a good-looking French girl with black hair and a sallow complexion, who told me she came from Carcassone but worked in a *parfumerie* in Paris. So we had a bit in common and were getting on rather well, when she suddenly disappeared, much to my disappointment.

This holiday in Wengen turned out to be my first and last attempt at winter sports, though in my middle years I had several enjoyable holidays in Switzerland, either walking in the mountains or relaxing by a lake.

On getting back to London, my life resumed its normal pattern for several months. Then, one day in early summer, I needed a partner for tennis and decided to take a chance and ring up Peggy Fass, whom I had not forgotten, though by no means sure whether she would want to see me again. Rather to my surprise, she seemed delighted to hear from me, and we not only enjoyed our game of tennis but seemed to get on well. I gradually began to see more of her, and soon discovered that she was no longer so much in love with Romer Topham, who was still at Cambridge. No doubt too, it was convenient to have another boyfriend in London as a partner for dances or tennis. Anyway, our relationship developed rapidly, and we were soon meeting frequently. One day she and her sister Mary came down to sail with me at Lymington, where I had a small boat; it was a windy day, and quite rough once one got outside the estuary. Peggy insisted on taking the helm, though knowing nothing about sailing, and we very nearly capsized in a sudden gust; I was just able to grab the tiller in time and avert a disaster. A week of two later I was invited to spend a night at her parents' country cottage at Inkpen near Newbury, and just as I turned into their drive, my ancient Riley burst a tyre, and I had the dirty and rather embarrassing job of changing the wheel in front of a family I hardly knew. Not long afterwards I decided to go a bust (in the expression of the day), and took Peggy to dinner at the very expensive and fashionable Hotel de Paris at Bray. It was a beautiful evening in late summer, and after an excellent meal we lay in one of the hotel's punts moored to the bank of the Thames. Inevitably we cuddled and kissed – no more – and when we got back on dry land I found, rather to my surprise, that we were engaged.

The news was greeted next day by Peggy's parents – understandably enough – with a marked lack of enthusiasm, her mother remarking 'Poor Peggy, having to go and live amongst those blacks.' Nonetheless, an announcement of our engagement appeared shortly afterwards in *The Times* – at the head of the day's list – and this was followed by a sherry party – then the current vogue – at the family's London home at 19 Chelsea Park Gardens.

Soon afterwards, my parents returned from the Bahamas, where my father had been Chief Justice, and Miss Raleigh

King very kindly lent them her house in Tedworth Square, where I continued to live. I found myself in an extremely difficult position. I was just engaged and in love; my parents naturally wanted to see something of me before I left for India, and so did Miss Raleigh King. On top of all this, I had a lot of essential business to see to before my departure in mid-October, and one was not going for a brief visit but probably for the normal span of three-and-a-half years. There were travel arrangements to be made, clothes and equipment, including a gun, to be bought, and official visits to be paid. I had to have a typhoid inoculation the day before a farewell dinner dance at the Berkeley; I reacted badly, felt very unwell at the party, and Peggy and I had to leave first before our guests. On getting back to Tedworth Square, I was shivering violently and my hand was so unsteady that I couldn't get the key into the door. Peggy was naturally somewhat put out at this dismal ending to our farewell party, not realizing what an enormous amount I had to fit in. At any rate, life was certainly not dull at that point!

Before long the day of departure arrived. Peggy and I had spent the last evening together, vowing to be true to each other and to get married as soon as my first leave arrived, but she was too upset to come to the station to say a final goodbye. My parents, her father and various relations and friends were there to wish me well. I myself had mixed feelings. On the one hand, I was setting out on a big adventure; on the other, I was leaving all my friends and familiar surroundings for a far-distant country where I literally didn't know a soul. I think I piped a tear or two as the train pulled out of the station, but soon recovered and eagerly looked out for my ship as we approached Tilbury. She was the *Kaiser-i-Hind* (Emperor of India), one of the oldest P & O liners still in service, but I found after going on board that I had been allotted a comfortable first-class cabin to share with another newly-joined ICS officer, though he had been posted to a different Province.

Frank and Brian Logan as small boys in Nakuru, British East Africa (now Kenya).

Sir Ewen Logan as a young man, father of Frank and Brian.

A few Zebra photographed by my father.

Ewshott Cottage, near Farnham, 1904

Frank and Brian at Weymouth, Dorset, c.1912

The wedding of Frank Logan to Peggy Fass
on 17th June 1931 at
Holy Trinity, Kensington Gore, London.

The author and his wife outside their house in Allahabad.

Our unusual *cavalcade* in Allahabad.

John Nash
with the pigeons.

Peggy and Leonora at Foxhill, May 1934.

Peggy with her parents Sir Ernest and Lady Fass.

Christmas camp at Andheri Rau, 1934.
Left to right: Stuart, Frank and Jean.

Nancy and Raymond Vernede.

The author's magnificent tiger photographed where he fell.

The author, the District Officer,
on tour in the United Provinces, India.

Peggy and Frank at the Charvet's, Cambridge

Leonora and Frank at Totland Bay, Isle of Wight, 1938.

Sara in her father's hat.

The first summer after our return from India.

Grannie Neame with the children. Totland.

7

Off to India – Alone

There was plenty to do on the long three weeks' voyage. One could read in a deckchair sitting in the open, with one's feet on the ship's bulwarks, play the usual games, walk round the deck a number of times for exercise, socialize in the bar, and in the evenings dance under the stars once the ship got into warmer waters. A large group of us – all young men in the various Indian Services – sat together at one table. One evening, a slightly bumptious young Indian Army officer insisted that we should all pretend to be clergymen by reversing our collars and leaving off our ties; we then trooped into dinner after everyone else was seated, causing some mild amusement. I thought it extremely childish, but had to comply. By this time I had begun to realize that I was moving back in time into a strictly conformist society. On the civilian side, the Indian Civil Service ranked first, and its members were sometimes referred to with a touch of irony as 'the Heaven-born'. In the Army the cavalry regarded themselves as socially superior to the infantry, and so on. One was expected, I soon found out, to defer to the views of a more senior officer, not only in one's own Service, but in other Services as well; there was no question of calling him by his Christian name, as I had been accustomed to do with some of the younger Dons at Cambridge.

The ship made a number of brief stops on the way. At Gibraltar, I just had time to have lunch with Sir Sydney and Lady Nettleton – he was the Chief Justice at that time – who were friends of my parents. I also knew their daughter Cynthia who later married Rab Butler, but died young before he became a famous Chancellor of the Exchequer. The Nettletons had a house high up on the Rock, with the most glorious views across the Straits to the Spanish coast beyond.

It must have been a perfect job, with not much work, an agreeable social life and interesting places to visit. At Malta my brother, whose ship was based there, came on board for a brief visit, as the *Kaiser-i-Hind* only stayed for a short time; he later remarked in a letter to my father on the state of 'Frank's hair' (much too long in his opinion). Odd how fashions go round and round!

In due course the ship arrived at Port Said, and proceeded to coal in much the same way as the *Gemna* had when we were on our way back from East Africa as small boys. One or two of the usual *gulli gulli* men – conjurors – came on board and performed some of their tricks. One I was watching waved his hands, and suddenly a nasty-looking snake appeared crawling about on the deck; after a second or two he waved them again and the snake vanished. I suppose the *gulli gulli* man distracted attention by carrying on a flow of conversation, and gesticulating with the hand he wasn't using to hold the snakes. It was certainly a clever trick that I never saw before or since. Most of the passengers took the opportunity of going ashore, nearly everyone making for Simon Artz, a famous shop in those days where one could buy all kinds of duty free goods at low prices. I bought a few oddments, including a small dagger which I thought might come in useful as a defensive weapon in India. Needless to say, I never used it.

Coaling completed, the ship entered the Suez Canal, and I spent several hours on deck watching the passing scene. On the port side there was little but desert stretching away to the horizon. On the starboard side a neat road bordered with trees ran parallel with the Canal. Although not much used, one saw enough people – either on foot, on donkeys, on bicycles or the occasional car – to get a rough idea of what Egyptians looked like and their way of life. I suppose we must have passed a few small towns or villages, though I don't remember them clearly. At one point the Canal widened for a short stretch to allow ships to pass; we waited at anchor for a bit, and before long a much larger P & O liner appeared from the opposite direction and steamed slowly past us, the passengers on both ships waving vigorously to each other. How I wished I could jump on board the other liner and return to England! Soon after we had resumed our journey, it became dark very quickly, and I went below to change for dinner. That was all I saw of the Suez Canal on my first voyage, with one small exception. Soon after going to bed, I was woken up by a lot of noise and shouting. Looking out through the cabin porthole, I saw the bright lights of a sizable town – which turned out to be Ismailia (at the entrance to the Bitter Lake). It seemed that supplies were being brought on board, as a large rowing boat heavily loaded with vegetables and fruit was approaching the ship just at that moment. Before long I was asleep again. We reached Suez very early in the morning, but I don't think anyone went ashore and doubt if there was anything worth seeing anyway. By the time I had breakfasted and got up on deck, we were well into the Red Sea, with the coast still just visible on either side. I remembered my disappointment, as a child returning from East Africa, that the Red Sea was not red! The coast soon disappeared, and we did not see it again until our arrival at Aden about four days later.

Here I made the standard but none the less interesting trip by car to see an Arab garden with a small lake or 'tank' close to it. It was stiflingly hot – the first real heat I had encountered. On the way we had to cross a short stretch of desert, where I was fascinated to pass two or three strings of heavily-loaded camels plodding through the burning sand, urged on by the cries of their drivers wearing long white robes. Aden itself – 'the barren rocks of Aden' – was not of much interest, a shabby little town whose *raison d'être* was that it provided a convenient port about half way between Egypt and India, and I imagine that it has now lapsed into its original obscurity. One day out from Aden, there was a rather unusual incident. The ship unexpectedly came to a stop and, looking over the side, we saw an Arab dhow with three or four exhausted men sitting or lying in it. They had been becalmed for several days, and had run out of food and water. Our captain ordered some supplies to be lowered into the dhow and, after half an hour or so, we continued on our way. I hope the Arabs got back to their harbour safely. Then at last, after four days steaming across the Indian Ocean in a dead calm, and by now pretty hot, we arrived at Bombay very early in the morning.

On coming up on deck, I had my first sight of India. A large crowd was milling about on the quay-side; most were obviously coolies or workers of one kind or another, but among them were a few Indians of better class, though at that point I could not distinguish between a Hindu and a Muslim, much less between different castes and ranks. Near the ship stood two good-looking men wearing white jodhpurs, who had evidently come to meet a passenger; I asked a young Indian Army officer standing near me who they were. He replied, '*Rajputs,* they are officers from my regiment' (at that time Indians were beginning to be appointed as officers, though few, if any, had risen above the rank of captain).

The ship itself was crowded, as a number of Europeans and Indians had been allowed on board to meet relatives or friends or help with travel arrangements. Before long, I made contact with Grindlays' representative – a distinguished looking Parsee wearing – I still remember – a strange-looking hat with two sharp ridges ornamented with gilt. He turned out to be extremely efficient and helpful, and said he would call on me later in the day at the Taj Mahal hotel – where he advised me to go – by which time I would know the District to which I had been posted. In the meantime, he would take charge of all my heavy luggage and get it to the station in due course. Almost as soon as I had gone down the gangway, a tall Indian with a beard *salaamed* to me and presented a letter. It was from Mr Justice Moss-King of the Allahabad High Court – a relation of Miss Raleigh King's – to whom she had written on my behalf. He had engaged the Indian – a Muslim named Mahommed Khan – as my 'bearer' (personal servant) and sent him down to Bombay to meet me – a normal practice in those days.

I went first to the Taj Mahal hotel to book a room for the day, and then to the Bombay Secretariat (headquarters of the Government), where a rather off-hand official read out to our small group of first-time arrivals the names of the Districts (roughly equivalent to an English County) to which we had been posted. Mine was Jhansi in the United Provinces (now Uttar Pradesh). He advised us to send a telegram to the District Officer, giving the time of our arrival. So I went first to the railway station, to buy a ticket to a place I had never heard of and ascertain the time of departure of my train and its arrival at Jhansi, then to the Post Office to send a telegram to the District Officer, hoping it would reach the right person, next to Grindlays, to arrange for a bank account to be opened for me at the appropriate branch of the Imperial Bank of India, and finally to the Army & Navy Stores – a famous shop in those days – where I bought, amongst other things, an expensive saddle for the horse I didn't yet own.

I got back to the Taj Mahal hotel just in time for my first Indian *tiffin* (lunch), where I enjoyed an excellent curry accompanied by an array of little saucers filled with all kinds of chutney and spices (the East India Club in London still provides almost as good a curry). By this time it was very hot and sticky, and, having nothing further to do, I retired to my large dark room for a rest, lying on the bed in pyjamas with a fan rotating slowly overhead. I dozed off and was awakened at about 5 o'clock by my bearer carrying a tray with tea, toast, sandwiches and cake on it. To my astonishment, he was dressed in immaculate white clothes, including a white *pagri* (turban). How on earth did he achieve it?

In the early evening the time came to leave for the station. On arriving there, we were met by the Parsee representative of Grindlays, who led us up the platform which was packed with Indians, both men and women – the latter usually with their faces covered up – pushing and shoving to get into the wooden-seated and extremely uncomfortable third-class carriages. A second-class compartment near the front of the train had been reserved for me (first-class would have been too expensive for a new recruit – a mean Government requiring us to pay our own railway fares, whatever the distance). I said goodbye to the Grindlays' representative, my servant paid off the porters who had carried my luggage – not without the usual wrangle – and then proceeded to prepare for the night, laying out my bedding roll on one of the long seats the carriage contained, and unpacking my pyjamas. Finally, he *salaamed* and departed. After watching the crowded platform for a bit through an outer wire-mesh grill, and listening to the cries of sellers of various goods – *pan, char, biri* (which I then didn't understand), I pulled up first a wooden shutter and then a normal glass window, undressed and was soon asleep.

When I awoke it was just after dawn, and the train was moving slowly through a deep cutting with thick scrub growing up the side. To my delight and amazement, I suddenly saw a small group of monkeys looking down on the train and gesticulating to one another. Soon after, the train emerged on to a very long high bridge over a wide river, though with more sandbanks than water at that time of year. As we crawled slowly over the bridge, I was reminded of Kipling's story, *The Bridge Builders*, and felt a touch of pride over what the British had achieved in India. Not long afterwards – still in the very early morning – the train stopped at a station; immediately opposite, a group of men were washing themselves and their clothes – *dhotis* I would have called them later – at a water pump for refilling the engine boilers. I was considerably impressed by this attention to cleanliness, which I never quite forgot in spite of what one saw later in the teeming cities and towns and impoverished villages of Northern India. After another hour or so, the train stopped at a much larger station – I think it was Itarsi – and my bearer appeared and indicated that I should get out of my carriage and walk down the platform for *hazri* (breakfast). Somewhat to my surprise, I soon saw some tables outside the stationmaster's office laid with white cloths and cutlery, where the few Europeans on the train – mostly travelling first-class – proceeded to enjoy an English-style meal – half breakfast, half lunch – waited on by dignified-looking *Khitmagars*. Meanwhile, the Indian passengers, who were kept away from our tables, had the chance of stretching their legs and relieving themselves as best they could, after what must have been an appallingly uncomfortable night. After half-an-hour or so, a new engine was attached, everyone climbed back into their carriages, and the train started off again. Then, for hour after hour, we thundered across the endless plains of India, from time to time crossing a dusty white road where nearly always a row of bullock carts were waiting on their way to a village or small town. These were few and far between as we were passing through an arid and thinly populated area of the Central Provinces (now Madyha Pradesh), but I do recall seeing a group of women walking away from a well with earthenware pots gracefully balanced on their heads, and a cow wandering on its own through a small bazaar munching at anything edible it saw before being driven away (cows are of course sacred to the Hindu, but that does not mean that they are well-treated). At one point the train slowed almost to a crawl before going through a station, and I looked down on a group of men carrying a rough sort of stretcher, with a figure clothed in white – the face visible – lying on it. I realized with a bit of a shock that the man was dead. I suppose he was being taken to a suitable river, perhaps a tributary of the Jumna, to be burnt and his ashes then cast on the water.

Having no family connection with India (other than my uncle Carleton Logan, who had served there for a year or two with his regiment as a young man), I was surprised, indeed shocked, by the primitive nature of the villages, with nearly all the 'houses' built out of a sort of sticky mud with thatched roofs. Usually there was a small white temple and one or two slightly larger brick-built houses. Most of the villages were surrounded by thorn hedges and half-concealed by a grove of trees (usually mango trees, I later learned). This was all very different from what I had expected, my ideas having largely been taken from photographs and paintings of the Taj Mahal, the Viceroy's house in Delhi or Maharaja's palaces. The reality was very different.

Suddenly, and rather early, the sun went down, and it quickly became dark. I knew that we must be approaching Jhansi, and before long my bearer appeared and began to get my things together. I was both excited and nervous, and wondered what I would do on arrival. Soon the train drew into a large station and stopped. I got out, and was immediately greeted by a short, stocky man, who told me that he was the Collector (District Officer) and that his name was Darling (Kenneth, though I never called him by his Christian name). He immediately barked out a series of sharp orders to his *chuprassis* (orderlies) and my bearer in Hindustani, and my luggage was quickly removed from the carriage. We then proceeded down the crowded platform with two *chuprassis* clearing the way for us. We got into Mr Darling's large Buick car, with him driving and the chauffeur sitting behind. My luggage followed in a *tonga* (horse-drawn trap), with my bearer and a *chuprassi* accompanying him.

I shall always remember that drive and the smell of the night air – it was the beginning of the 'cold weather' – compounded of dust, smoke, dung and an indefinable tang that I can neither describe nor forget. We passed several clusters of Indian houses, and then drove through the 'civil lines' – the residential area for Europeans – before finally reaching the Collector's bungalow. It was a large, white, impressive building with a covered portico for the car to stop in – not in any way a bungalow in the usual English sense, except that it had only one storey. I was greeted by Mrs Darling, but offered no meal, though I was starving – it was late by then – and soon shown my bedroom. This was large, with a very high ceiling that I could hardly see, as the house was lit by lamps (electricity came soon after); the walls were whitewashed, and the floor covered with fine matting. The furniture was minimal – bed with mosquito netting, dressing table, large wardrobe and a few odd tables and chairs. It was impressive in its way, but certainly not comfortable or luxurious in a European sense. What astonished me most was the bathroom – large, dark, lit only by a tiny *bhatti* (lamp) – with a washbasin and jug, a commode (known colloquially as a 'thunder box') and a tin bath in one corner with a hole in the wall for the water to run out of (and the occasional snake to get in by). I wanted to use the commode, but could not bring myself to do so at that point, as I had no idea that there was a servant known as a 'sweeper' – the lowest of the low in the hierarchy of servants – whose main duty was to empty and clean these receptacles. My bearer had by now unpacked my night things, and before long I was in bed and asleep. Just before I dozed off, I heard the howling of an animal not very far away – it was, I realized, a jackal.

8

A Different Life in the Indian Civil Service

I was woken early in the morning by my bearer with a cup of tea. By the time I was dressed, both Mr and Mrs Darling were up and about. He told me that he had to see his *mulaqatis* or visitors before breakfast, and Mrs Darling offered to take me round the garden. There were dozens of flower pots ranged around the verandah and down the drive for some way, including freesias, carnations, lilies, pinks, chrysanthemums, though many were not yet out, as it was still the beginning of the cold weather – cool in the early morning, though still quite warm by midday. Some English-style lawns had been created near the house by constant cutting and watering, and there were a few large beds, filled mainly with canna lilies and roses not yet in flower. Beyond the watered lawns, the arid brown grass stretched away to the walls of the 'compound'. However, we had hardly left the verandah when a young man trotted up the drive on a tall gaunt horse. He was Johnnie Johnstone, my predecessor by a year, who had just been transferred to another District. We chatted amicably for a few minutes and he told me one or two of the things I needed to know. I admired his horse, even though it was no beauty; he mentioned that it was a fast trotter and good for getting about on, and I rather think he regarded it as a superior sort of bicycle that could be used where there were no roads or paths. Before leaving, he told me that on Kenneth Darling's instructions I would be coming to his Court that morning, and then every day for a week, to get a first impression of the Indian criminal system.

Before long it was time for breakfast, and soon afterwards I left in Mr Darling's car for the *Kacheri* or Court House. With us came two *chuprassis,* dressed in red robes, and carrying a load of papers. The *Kacheri* really fulfilled two functions; it contained most of the Courts falling under the jurisdiction of the District Magistrate, and was also the centre for the District administration. On arriving there, I saw a jumble of buildings in the middle of a large bare compound surrounded by trees. JJ appeared almost at once, and as I walked along with him, I enquired who were the groups of peasants sitting round the compound, usually with a better dressed man, perhaps wearing a black coat, talking to them. 'Litigants, being tutored by their lawyers,' he replied. We soon reached JJ's Court, and I was much impressed by his competence. He appeared to understand most of what the witnesses said – pretty good after a year – and took down their evidence in English on his typewriter (I didn't own one), while his chief *peshkar* (assistant) recorded the evidence verbatim in Urdu. After a couple of hours or so, I was beginning to get a bit bored, when suddenly there were loud shouts from outside. JJ rushed out with his staff, collected one or two policemen and proceeded to arrest a man who was shouting and yelling and trying to hit another man with his *lathi* (long pole). On getting back to Court, JJ recorded the statement of this man and one or two witnesses, before transferring the case to another Magistrate. It transpired that the man had been promised a bribe if he gave false evidence in a case, but after making the long journey from his village to Jhansi, he had been told that he would get only half the promised amount. He was most indignant!

After a week, JJ left for his new District and I had to try my first case. It so happened that it was a case under a little-used section of the Indian Penal Code (admirably composed by Lord Macaulay, though becoming a little out of date here and there, as in the particular case I was hearing). A middle-aged husband had prosecuted a much younger man for enticing away his wife. The section empowered the Magistrate to imprison the accused, if found guilty, or to fine him and – here is the point – award a certain amount of compensation to the abandoned husband. It was quite clear to me, after seeing the parties and hearing the evidence, that the wife had willingly left her husband (it was, of course, an arranged marriage) and did not wish to return to him. I saw no reason why she should, and acquitted the young man – clearly no villain. There were some raised eyebrows among the lawyers and Court staff. Strictly, what I should have done was to find the young man guilty, fine him a modest amount, and award some compensation to the aggrieved husband – that was what he was after – money, not getting his wife back. Still, I have no great regrets over this incorrect decision. I still remember the look of relief exchanged between the young man and his new woman.

Apart from court work, I was also allotted various miscellaneous jobs to give me a little insight into Indian civil administration. One was to supervise the accounts of the Nazir. He was the official responsible for maintaining the buildings, paying a large part of the staff and generally keeping the administrative machinery running. He produced his accounts books daily, I looked at them briefly, perhaps asked on or two questions and then signed. I suppose this served a useful purpose, as after a few weeks I think I would have spotted any marked change or deviation. But I had no idea whether the hundreds of sums paid out were correct or incorrect. My strong feeling is that nearly all Nazirs were honest men in the Indian sense, that is, they accepted small commissions on sales and purchases – indeed, they needed to do so in view of the miserly salary paid them by the Government and the demands they had to meet – but were seldom bribed into wrong decisions. I recall a story I heard later about a young District Officer who sent a note to his Nazir saying, 'I need an alligator. Please arrange (he wanted one to make some shoes and gaiters out of the skin)'. He received a note back, 'Sir, I will carry out your instructions. An alligator will be placed in your bathroom tomorrow. It should still be quite strong. Nazir.'

Another job I was assigned to do was to help Kenneth Darling check the funds in the District Treasury. It was a boring and lengthy task that had to be carried out at regular intervals. The Treasury was a small, strong, separate building, guarded by police at night. Inside, it contained rows of shelves filled with large quantities of rupee notes of various denominations. We each picked out a batch to count. It took us about an hour to do so. Both were correct. It would have needed at least a week to count the whole amount, probably longer, so it would not have been difficult for a dishonest official to replace a quantity of larger notes with smaller ones. But I never heard of this happening.

In my view, the standard of honesty among Indian officials was surprisingly high, given the customs of the country and the temptations to which they were exposed. But I am running ahead of my experience, and will return to this subject later.

Life was not all work at this stage, far from it. I had been lent, early on, a quiet elderly horse and asked to exercise it. So in the morning before breakfast I went for short rides, either along the avenues that constituted the 'Civil Lines' (where the civilian officials lived) or into the *mofussil* (countryside), which was arid and stony in that part of the District. I soon found a track leading to a small village, and after riding through it a few times, the villagers and I got to know each other by sight. I was quite flattered when one day the *mukhia* (headman) invited me to dismount and drink some milk out of a brass *lotah*. I knew I was running a risk of getting typhoid, but felt I could not refuse. Sitting on the rim of a well, I was watched by a group of villagers as I drank the milk, while the *mukhia* and one or two other elderly men talked to me at length about some local problem that I could not really grasp. However, I made a few sympathetic signs and indicated that the matter would be looked into. In due course I remounted, the villagers made respectful *salaams* to me, and I rode off, feeling that perhaps I had helped them a little by listening to their grievances, but realizing too the immense amount I would have to learn.

In the afternoon, I usually went to play tennis at the club. Jhansi was not only a civil headquarters but also an important military station, so I had plenty of people to play with, including at that time of the year a number of young women. Some had come out to stay with relations or friends, and were referred to generically – and not very politely – as the 'fishing fleet', ie. looking for a husband. After tennis we would sit around in groups drinking *chota pegs* – tots of whisky – too many, and for too long. Then I had to get back to the Darlings' house for dinner. As I had no car, I was obliged to hire a *tonga* – a kind of small two-wheeled trap in which the one or two passengers sat facing rearwards; it was rather fun trotting fast through the night with only the dimmest of dim lights, passing groups of Indians on foot, rows of unlit bullock carts and the occasional motor car.

Before long Christmas was approaching, a time of year

when everyone who could, got away – ideally to a camp in the jungle, or perhaps close to a lake with good duck shooting. I had been invited by a favourite aunt of Peggy's, Aunt Gracie, who was married to a Colonel Neale, at that time Political Agent to the State of Bhopal, to accompany them to a Christmas camp in the north of the United Province.

Here I must digress for a moment to mention that I had been asked a few weeks earlier to spend a weekend with the Neales in Bhopal. The main event had been a dinner party given by the Maharajah in his palace. It was a grand affair, with fifty or more guests and innumerable servants. The room was huge, the table loaded with gold and silver ornaments, including polo cups won by the Maharajah (who was a famous player), and the guests – nearly all Indians – dressed in the most elegant and lavish clothes. But, rather to my surprise, here and there on the floor were the cheapest of cheap tin spittoons, and behind small screens receptacles for the men to urinate into. Later, I realized that the latter arrangement was a highly practical one, since at a normal up-country English dinner party, the men would retire into the garden after the meal for the same purpose.

But I must return to my first Christmas in India. I joined the Neales in their train at Jhansi railway station, and travelled with them across the fertile plains of the United Provinces, to Saharanpur in the north. The Neales were extremely kind, and Colonel Neale – Uncle Gordon as he later became – was able to give me quite a lot of useful information about Indian customs and habits. At Saharanpur we were met by a car and driven to the camp of our host, Michael (later Sir Michael) Keane, then Commissioner of Meerut, later Governor of Assam. The camp was in the Siwaliks, a range of hills running parallel and close to the Himalayas for a hundred miles or so. On leaving the main road, our track ran for some way through high brown grass, with the hills rising on one side and the distant plains just visible on the other. At one point, a herd of Chital (small spotted deer) suddenly darted across the track in front of the car, and Uncle Gordon told me that deer and other animals grazed in the grassland at certain times of the year, where they were often preyed on by panthers. Sometimes a hungry panther would leave the jungle and kill a goat or dog or other small animals in a nearby village. Very occasionally, a panther would become a man-eater.

After some miles we entered the jungle proper. It was not the dense, lush, luxuriant forest I had expected, but dry at that time of year, with well-spaced out trees and little or no undergrowth, so that one could move through it fairly easily on foot or on an elephant, and usually see some way ahead through the trees. At intervals we crossed wide, stony river beds, almost empty of water in the middle of the cold weather, though raging torrents during the monsoon. Suddenly we rounded a bend and there was the Christmas camp in front of us. It consisted of a dozen or so white tents of varying sizes with improvised shelters on the opposite side of the clearing for the numerous servants, and a sort of cooking stand made mainly of mud. How we were so well-looked-after and well-fed in such primitive circumstances was little short of a miracle. Michael Keane greeted us warmly and introduced us to his other five guests, who had already arrived. They included a young officer from a cavalry regiment in Meerut and his recently-married wife; both were charming, and we were soon on friendly terms. Before long a servant took us to our tents, and I was pleasantly surprised that mine was quite large by English standards and included a tiny, draughty extension where there was just room for a small tin bath and commode. Leaving the bearer to unpack, I went for a stroll round the camp and was delighted to find a group of four elephants and their mahouts who had been loaned by local landowners. Indian elephants are the most attractive animals – friendly (except when 'must'), intelligent and capable of many heavy and dangerous tasks. I always wished I could have owned one, but that, of course, was impossible – one could hardly have taken them by train when one was transferred to another District.

On the way back from my stroll, I met another young man standing outside his tent. It was Philip Mason, who had entered the ICS the same year as myself. We had not met, as he had been at Baliol and then back to Oxford for his year's probation. He later had a highly successful career in India, during the war being Secretary to the Chiefs of Staff Committee, and later, after the transfer of power, making a second reputation as a writer. He had recently arrived at Saharanpur, his first station, as I had at Jhansi. We had, of course, plenty in common.

I soon discovered that this rather large Christmas camp was a joint affair, our hosts being Michael Keane and Charles Grant, the Collector and District Magistrate of Saharanpur. Here I had better explain that a Collector was the head of a District, roughly comparable in size to an English county, and with perhaps a million inhabitants. The Commissioner was in charge of a group of four or five Districts, though he had less direct authority – at least in my day – than the Collector, who could order almost anything to be done.

Our two parties were separately organized, but we joined up for shooting during the day, and after dinner in the evening we all sat round an enormous bonfire – the biggest I have ever seen. Usually we chatted and told stories, but on Christmas Eve someone started to hum a carol, we all joined in, and before long were singing loudly. It must have been a surprise for the Indians, and was the only time I recall such a thing happening outside a church.

Before going to bed, I was asked if I would like to go 'grooming' on an elephant the next morning. I said yes, not really knowing what was involved. I was woken very early and, on emerging from my tent, found an elephant waiting for me. It was made to kneel, I climbed onto its back via the tail (no *howdah* of course) and we set off into the jungle – just the mahout and myself. Any animals we encountered would, of course, see the elephant of which they were mostly not afraid, but, curiously enough, would not see the human beings on the elephant's back. It was delightful just wandering about soon after dawn, mostly through trees, but occasionally going through an open patch of grass or crossing a *nullah* (ravine). We didn't see a tiger, as I had hoped – in fact they were rare in the Siwaliks – but we got quite close to one or two herds of deer, one of sambhur – large brown animals – the other chital, which I have mentioned; they didn't seem afraid of us, and just moved a little further away. I was also lucky enough to catch a glimpse of a panther sitting near the foot of a large tree; as we got nearer, it must have smelt something ominous as it got to its feet and moved off quickly, disappearing almost at once. In due course I got back to the camp in time for breakfast after an enjoyable and exciting 'groom'.

During the day we spent most of the time bird-shooting –

either jungle fowl or peafowl. The former – not unlike the domestic variety – flew fast and low as they were driven towards us by the beaters, and were quite difficult to hit; the latter flew higher and more slowly. I must admit I was rather shocked when I saw our first day's bag laid out for us to inspect, including a number of peacocks with their beautiful plumage. But they were plentiful in those days, and not more were shot than the Forestry Department permitted; they were also, I might add, excellent for eating, rather like turkey, and provided a useful addition to our menu. I only hope they have survived the cutting down of so much of the Indian jungles, though, to be fair, they will not have been deliberately harmed by the Hindu population, who regard them as sacred.

In due course I returned to Jhansi, spending a couple of nights in Delhi on the way, where I remember buying a white dinner jacket from the best shop – Rankin's – situated near the Kashmir Gate. It was a long time before there was any opportunity to wear it! I had already been instructed by Kenneth Darling to proceed to the Lalitpur Sub-Division of the Jhansi District for my first cold weather 'tour'. On arriving at the Jhansi Club, I found a letter from the Sub-Divisional Officer in question – a Captain Jameson (not his real name) – saying that he had already started his tour and would be in camp at a village about ten miles from a small railway halt; I must catch the only train that stopped at this halt the following afternoon, spend the night in a tent he would provide, and get to his camp on foot next morning. So I duly set off with my bearer, and after about an hour arrived at the halt in question. We just had time to scramble out before the train moved off. As I watched it disappear in the distance, I have never felt more lonely in my life. There was no station, no village, no people, nothing! We seemed to be totally alone in an endless arid plain. Pulling myself together, I looked around and saw that a few hundred yards away a very small tent had been pitched close to the railway line, As we approached it, a man appeared and handed me a note from Jameson, saying that he had sent me some sandwiches as he could not spare a cook, and giving me a few directions for finding his camp.

After an uncomfortable night, I ate the remaining sandwich for breakfast, and set off alone, leaving my bearer to follow with the other servant, the tent, and such luggage as I had brought with me. It was a cool, still, sunny morning, and I quite enjoyed the first part of my walk along a sandy track with scrubby jungle stretching away in all directions. Stopping at one point to look at a shrub that faintly resembled a buddleia, a large black snake suddenly emerged and slithered away into the grass. I think it was a cobra. After walking for nearly two hours, the track divided, and I had to decide which fork to take. I began to think I had made the wrong choice when nothing appeared after another half hour or so, and that I was lost in the wilderness. Then, suddenly, to my great relief, I saw a small village round a bend, with a large 'tank' (reservoir for water) in front of it and a few white tents pitched at one end.

Jameson, who had his sister camping with him – a plain but quite pleasant girl – greeted me briefly and showed me the small tent I had been allotted before going back to his work. He had served in the Indian Army during the war, and had somehow managed to get into the Indian Civil Service after it was over. In my opinion he was quite unsuitable, and I disapproved strongly of some of his methods of dealing with Indians. The Jamesons were clearly badly off, and had brought the minimum of everything – from tents to food – with them. I was told I had too much luggage, and that some of it must be sent back to headquarters. In a normal District I would have been entitled under the regulations, as a very junior officer, to one bullock cart to carry my luggage, but in Lalitpur, owing to the very rough nature of the country, camels were used instead of bullock carts. I later worked out that my entitlement – not covered by the regulations – would have been one-and-a-half camels!

The standard practice in touring a District or Sub-Division was to spend one or two nights at each camp, inspect the neighbouring villages and their relevant land records, and then move on about six to ten miles to the next camp, usually doing some inspections on the way. The Jamesons each had a very second-rate 'country' pony to ride, but I had not yet acquired a horse and so was lent a bicycle to get from camp to camp. I found this extremely uncomfortable and undignified, and inevitably one had at least one puncture to mend. I soon gave up the bicycle and instead walked, accompanied by a *chuprassi*. I found this much more agreeable as I was able to look at the countryside instead of the bicycle wheels, pause in villages for a rest and chat (aided by my *chuprassi*), and occasionally do a small bit of shooting. This was the only tour I did on foot; in future I always had horses, and quite often one or two elephants loaned by a local landowner.

One of the jobs a touring officer had to do was to check the land records. These were maintained by a local village clerk known as the *Patwari*. They were surprisingly complicated, and must have evolved over a very long period, going back to the days before British rule. They included a cloth map showing every cultivated plot, however small, all carefully numbered; a list of every cultivator, his status, the crops grown and the rent payable; a list of the landowners or, more precisely, those entitled to receive a share of the rents, which could range from a single *zemindar* (landowner) in some villages to a hundred or more in another. The primary purpose of the system was to assess and collect the Land Revenue payable to the Government – which provided its main source of income – though over the years much had been done to provide a fairer and more stable rural economy.

Looking back, I think it was remarkable how reliably the *Patwaris* maintained their records, given their slight education, the conditions in which they lived and the primitive equipment they had to make do with; they must also have been subject to pressure and bribery in Court cases relating to land, when they were usually the most important witness. But it was rare in my recollection for a *Patwari* to have been found guilty of giving false evidence, though of course some may have done so without being discovered.

The normal practice was for the touring officer to go out early in the morning, accompanied by a *Patwari* and a group of villagers, to a place of his choice, when the *Patwari* would be required to read out some of the above-mentioned details from his records, and any villagers could object. This rarely happened in my experience.

Jameson clearly did not understand the system, though he had no hesitation in shouting at the *Patwaris* and frightening them out of their wits. To be fair, I should add that I heard later that an Indian colleague who had been at the School of Oriental Studies with me was even worse in this way, but as he understood the records he, at least, did detect errors from time to time.

Perhaps this provides an opportunity to contradict the nonsense one reads these days about the alleged bad behaviour of the British. It is undeniable, of course, that we kept ourselves to ourselves, but how could it be otherwise in a huge country where a few thousand British had to rule countless millions of Indians, who were themselves divided by race, religion, caste and innumerable other differences? I think it is true to say that we introduced over the years the first reasonably fair and efficient system of government that India had enjoyed. Even in my day, some of the rulers of the independent states could act in a highly capricious and cruel manner. Certainly it is arguable that we hung on a bit too long, as more and more educated Indians emerged – educated under a system we ourselves had introduced – on the ground that still more training in the art of government was necessary. I feel sure that Clement Attlee and Lord Mountbatten were right in their decision to hand over power without further delay, though the latter may have acted a bit too quickly.

But I have jumped much too far ahead, and must return to my first cold weather tour. I used to have my evening meal with the Jamesons – very bad it was, too – and then retire to my tent, which was lit by a small oil lamp. I spent the time writing long letters to Peggy, to my parents and relations, and to friends. After a week or so, I felt that I was learning nothing, and managed to get a junior clerk to come in for an hour or so and teach me a little Urdu and also a bit about the land records. In exchange I gave him a few lessons in English, which I hope may have helped him in his career. The tour seemed to go on and on for ever, with every day like every other day. There was nothing to do apart from the standard routine. I learned little from Jameson, and one had not the responsibility that later made touring one's own Sub-Division or District a worthwhile task. I began to think I had made a disastrous mistake in joining the Indian Civil Service, and that I would have been better off in the Consular Service or the Foreign Service.

In due course we arrived back at Lalitpur, where Jameson, as Sub-Divisional Officer, had a pleasant little bungalow.

After a few days there doing little or nothing, I returned to Jhansi, where a totally different life awaited me. Kenneth Darling had arranged – greatly to my surprise – that I was to live with a famous Indian foot regiment called the 45th Rattray's Sikhs. The officers were extremely kind to me, though in some ways I was evidently regarded as a newly-joined subaltern. One evening after dinner in the Mess, a rather wild young Scotsman called Sandy Macpherson, with whom I had become friendly challenged me to a wrestling match, with the intention of 'debagging' me, if successful. Fortunately, I remembered a trick or two from my Haileybury days and, by giving way and then twisting abruptly, I managed to fall on top of him, and the 'debagging' was abandoned. Sandy was very kind in many ways, particularly in helping me to school a beastly horse I had bought from a friend of the Jamesons. Going for a ride in the evening along a sandy track that led away from the cantonment, I had the greatest difficulty in getting the animal to canter, but as soon as I turned for 'home' (not a very appropriate word) it lowered its head, got the bit between its teeth and broke into a gallop. I was quite unable to stop it, and several times had near-misses with other riders. On getting back to the bungalow, the horse stopped outside its stable – fortunately for me – stood there quietly, and allowed me to dismount. Thanks to help from Sandy, I was able to get the horse accepted by an Indian cavalry regiment (whose name I forget) for schooling, and in due course it became rideable, and later I even played polo on it.

For several months, while living with the 45th Sikhs, I shared a bungalow with two English subalterns and an Indian officer. I became quite friendly with the latter, and learnt a little about Sikh habits and customs from him. The bungalow was primitive to a degree, and contained the absolute minimum of furniture; instead of a proper ceiling it had a 'ceiling cloth' – still fairly common in those days – and lying in bed I could see various small animals such as lizards scuttling about on the cloth. One morning, just after I had got up, a small snake fell through a hole in the cloth onto my bed; my bearer, who happened to be in the room at the time, said it was a krite – a highly poisonous snake – so I probably had a lucky escape.

Once I had settled down and been accepted, I had a much better time than I would have done living on my own. I used to go shooting with Sandy or one or two of the other young officers, just wandering through the countryside shooting whatever birds came to hand. Much of Jhansi was quite different from the endless flat cultivated plains of most of the United Provinces; it was much less thickly populated, there were areas of semi-jungle between many of the villages, and here and there low hills often with red soil and rocky red outcrops. Best of all, some of the hills had clear streams running down them with pools in which one could swim. Swim we did, and thoroughly enjoyed it – almost as if we had been on Dartmoor or in the Lake District. This would have been possible nowhere else in the United Provinces where the rivers were wide, slow and far from clean, with muddy banks, often containing alligators. I never swam again in a stream or river in India.

It was soon May, and the hot weather had begun, with a shade temperature at midday of 105 degrees F or so, rising by June to 110 degrees or higher. Being very fair, I did not stand this burning heat well. I had, of course, to continue with my work, which involved bicycling three miles or so to the *Kacheri* every day and then sitting in a stifling court-room. I also continued with riding and tennis. It was the latter that finally got me down. There was a new acting District Officer for the hot weather – much younger than Kenneth Darling – who was a keen tennis player and liked to play singles with me. After two or three sets in a temperature of 90 degrees or so, I was pretty exhausted and began to feel unwell. By this time, the Mess dinner was being held out of doors on a stone platform about three feet high known as a *Chabutra*. One evening I felt sick, got up from my chair to leave the dinner table, and fell off the *chabutra,* knocking myself out. When I awoke the next morning, I found I was in hospital, and was informed that I had developed jaundice. In the burning heat of May, it took me about three weeks to recover, and I was then told that a kindly administration had transferred me to Naini Tal – the summer headquarters of the Government – located in 'the hills', that is, the lower Himalayas.

After a night in the train, crossing the United Provinces from south to north, the final lap was a short section on a line running from Bareilly to the last station (Kathgodam) below the Himalayas. Looking out of the window at – compared to Jhansi – the richer and more thickly populated countryside, I suddenly saw through the hot weather haze the outline of the foothills rising from the plains. It was a marvellous sight. Before long the train stopped for the last time, and I hired a car to drive me up a steep Alpine-type road to Naini Tal. We stopped at the bazaar-end of the town – cars not being allowed further – and before me stretched a beautiful lake, with steep hills rising all around it, dotted with houses. It might have been Austria or Switzerland. I was quickly trundled along the lakeside in a rickshaw to reach the Deputy Commissioner's house a little way up the hill at the far end. His name was Vyvyan, a short, tough, highly intelligent man known to his friends as Ham; his wife was a good-looking woman with a talent for drawing and painting. They welcomed me in kindly fashion and allowed me to relax for a few days after my rather gruelling time in Jhansi. I think I should say here that I have gone into greater detail than I had originally intended about my early days in India, partly because they were a little unusual, but mainly because people who have written about their Indian careers have tended to concentrate on the period when they had attained positions of some importance and influence, or were involved in an unusual activity. I may be wrong, but I think that young Indian Civil Servants often had an exceptionally tough time, even for those days.

After a fortnight I moved to the Naini Tal club and was lucky to secure a tiny separate bungalow with my own sitting room where I could work in peace or relax if not feeling sociable. Inevitably I felt lonely at times, especially at night during the monsoon, with the rain deluging down for hours on end. Once there was a very small landslide and a boulder ended up with a crash against the wall of my bedroom. Fortunately, no serious damage was done. Unlike a London club, the Naini Tal club also acted as a social centre for the hill station, and there were frequent dinners, dances and even an occasional theatrical show. I remember a performance of the *Mikado* soon after I arrived – really quite well done, or so it seemed to me at the time. One of the women in the cast, whom I got to know and fell mildly in love with, had been a professional singer before her marriage.

I was also lucky over my job, being appointed Assistant Judicial Secretary and Legal Remembrancer to the Government. This suited me admirably, as I had inherited my father's legal talents, and I feel pretty sure I would have become either Judicial Secretary or a High Court judge if British rule had continued in India for a bit longer, and I had remained there to the end. One of my duties was to recommend whether or not there should be an appeal to the High Court or a retrial in a case where the prosecuting counsel considered that the accused had either been wrongly acquitted, or had received too lenient a sentence. These were, of course, important cases such as murder, riot or serious robbery, and it was seldom that an appeal was undertaken. I recall one case where a young woman, kept with other women by a wealthy landowner in his *zenana*, had been murdered. There was no doubt who had done the deed; the question was whether he had been ordered to do it by the *zemindar* for whom he worked. The District Judge had convicted the actual murderer, but acquitted the *zemindar*. I felt sure that this was a wrong decision, and on my advice the case was sent back for retrial, with new evidence to be taken on a vital point, namely the nature of the relatively large sum of money found in possession of the actual murderer. It turned out that it could not have been money collected in the normal way as rents, but included a number of coins that only a fairly wealthy man could have inherited from his forbears. On the re-hearing, the *zemindar* was convicted as an 'accomplice before the fact'.

A lot has been written about life in Indian hill stations, particularly Simla, so I will mention only one or two points peculiar to Naini Tal. One was the lake. So far as I know, it was the only lake in the Himalayan foothills on which sailing was possible. There was a Yacht Club with about a dozen small yachts for use by members, and a 'boathouse' which also served as a social centre; dances were held there from time to time, and it could be rather romantic dancing close to the lake with a full moon shining down on the calm water. I joined the yacht club, but owing to my work could only sail at weekends or on holidays. The sailing varied from being rather dull, with the yacht hardly moving in a flat calm, to over-exciting when a wind got up, blowing in sudden violent gusts. I once had to help rescue a young couple whose yacht had overturned, but who had fortunately been able to extricate themselves and cling to the sides of the boat until we arrived.

Two or three times during the 'season', the Governor, Sir Malcolm Hailey (later Lord Hailey) and his wife would give a ball at Government House. This was a large, impressive (though architecturally undistinguished) building, standing near the southern end of the lake high above the bazaar. As everyone was, of course, in evening dress, all the women and most of the men were carried to the ball in a 'dandy' – a sort of portable bathchair without wheels supported by poles from which a single seat was suspended; the poles were carried by four men, two in front and two behind, with a fifth man walking alongside, and all changing places frequently. At night, the fifth man always had a lantern, and on the way to the ball it was a fascinating sight to see the hundreds of twinkling lights from the dandies as they moved along the numerous narrow paths above the lake towards Government House. The ball itself was a grand affair, the Governor and his wife – the former splendidly dressed with rows of medals – receiving the guests, and many of the dancers in full dress uniform, as Naini Tal was the summer headquarters of the Army Eastern Command as well as of the provincial government. We junior civilians had only tail coats to wear, and felt a little envious of the military, as their uniforms certainly made them look handsomer and more attractive to the women. Still, I enjoyed these balls, as they were occasions one would probably never have encountered in England, and by now I had a circle of men and women friends with whom to link up.

It was rather like being back at Cambridge again to be sure of meeting a few people one liked if one looked in at the club, the boathouse, or one of the hotels, and of course at the dances. Our group, which was quite informal and varied according to who happened to be on leave, included several women – mostly wives of army or civilian officers. One – rather surprisingly the wife of a very conventional Forest Officer – was perhaps the most amusing woman I have met; she was only moderately good-looking, but had the talent of making almost every man think that she was in love with him, and that he was unusually interesting and attractive.

In due course the hot weather and monsoon came to an end in the plains, and the Government returned to its headquarters in Lucknow about the middle of September. I was posted to a District called Moradabad – a little to the east of Delhi – to attend along with my contemporaries a training course after our first year of service in India. This turned out to be largely a waste of time, mainly due to the fact that the officer in charge, though a kindly and learned man, could not make up his mind about important matters, but niggled about trifles. Philip Mason (whom I have already mentioned), Raymond Vernède (later the Bursar and Fellow of an Oxford College) and I myself decided, contrary to the usual practice, to live together in a small camp of our own, instead of in the Police Headquarters of the Province located in Moradabad. I am afraid we behaved badly. Irritated in particular by being required to debate in Urdu at large gatherings attended by many Indian officials of a lower rank than ourselves, we bribed a servant to drop a jackal through a hole in the ceiling during one of the debates. This created complete confusion, though the jackal soon managed to escape from the room. We did at least apologise afterwards to the Director.

When the course ended, I took a few days leave to go to Delhi, staying with the young couple I had met in Christmas camp. The wife, Patricia, who was charming, acted as a guide and showed me around both Old and New Delhi, though on this occasion I saw only the exterior of the magnificent Viceroy's House (designed by Sir Edward Lutyens). It was a gay and enjoyable few days – the last for a long time – as, in addition to sightseeing, we went to several lunch and dinner parties and a dance at the best hotel. But it soon came to an end, and I had to set out for my new District – Gonda – to which I had been posted. This lay at the other end of the Province, some 600 miles away, not far from the Nepalese border. Before leaving, I had to collect the new car I had bought – an Austin 16. I had had it fitted with very large low-pressure tyres, which turned out to be a mixed blessing; it made it possible to drive the car on very rough tracks, but reduced the maximum speed to 50 mph. So it took me a long time to cover the 400 miles or so to Lucknow, especially as one inevitably had to pass endless streams of bullock carts which stuck to the middle of the narrow road and forced one on to the rough, dusty side-tracks.

I spent the night at the Lucknow Club, and early the next

morning started on the last leg of my journey, which turned out to be the most difficult. About halfway, I had to cross the very large Gogra river near Faizabad; there was a primitive pontoon bridge over most of it, but at one point it was necessary to get my car onto a boat to cross a gap in the bridge. Something went wrong, the boat was swept down stream, and the crew had great difficulty in getting it to the bank. There a gang of peasants had to be collected to get the car ashore – not without some minor damage – and then bullocks were tied to it to lug the car back onto the road. But everyone did their best to help, amid much shouting and yelling. The mishap cost me a bit of money, as I felt obliged to give the numerous helpers some small tips, even though I was now in my own District. Eventually, long after dark, I got to Gonda where I was warmly welcomed by the Deputy Commissioner, BJK Hallowes, and his wife, who were both a bit worried about my late arrival and what might have happened to me. After a quick meal I was soon in bed and asleep.

Before long I was on good terms with the Hallowes', and they kindly asked me to spend the hot weather in their house, instead of living alone in a primitive bungalow that had been empty for several years. Of course I accepted, and was allotted a pleasant room in the large rambling Deputy Commissioner's house (Deputy Commissioner, not Collector, was the title of the head of the District as Gonda was in the Province of Oudh). I often used to go for a ride in the early morning – now having two horses – and once, having gone a bit further than usual, I came quite by chance on the remains of a small British military cemetery in the middle of nowhere. The surrounding walls were more or less intact, and many of the gravestones still standing; I was able to decipher a few of the inscriptions – most evidently relating to men who had been killed in the Indian Mutiny. I expect that by now the cemetery has totally vanished and become cultivated land. *'Tout lasse, tout casse, tout passe'*.

The hot weather soon arrived, but this time I survived it, living as I was in relative comfort with the Hallowes. In the evenings BJK, as he was always known, and I sometimes used to knock a polo ball about on what had been the parade ground in the far-off days when Gonda was a small military 'cantonment'. More often we would go to the club to play tennis. For part of the way there were a few bungalows on one side of the dusty road, while on the other the plains stretched away to the horizon, with here and there a village or two just visible in the distance. It was an unusual way to reach a club! After tennis, some of us would play bridge or snooker, and others just sat around drinking the inevitable *chota peg*. I suppose there were about fifteen or so members of the club – all British or near British, and of course always the same people every evening. I can't say that I would have chosen any of them as my friends, but we managed to get on well enough. The man I liked best was a Scottish engineer in the East India Railway, still a private company running through some of the remoter areas of Bengal and the United Provinces. He had a fund of amusing stories, both about his home-town of Glasgow and the railway workers in India, nearly all of whom were Eurasians of various shades of colour living in their own communities and looked down upon – very unfairly – by both British and Indians. One story I recall was about a railway worker who met a pretty girl he knew slightly on the way to work and enquired, 'How you feel this morning, Miss?' to which she replied, 'Feel me and see'.

I was invited once or twice to play tennis at the Indian Club – a courtesy I much appreciated. I though it essential that the invitation should be returned, and with considerable difficulty I managed to persuade the members of our club to allow me to do so. In due course the Indian chairman and his secretary came along, suitable fours were arranged, and all went smoothly. It was, in its way and on a tiny scale, a unique occasion.

By the end of the hot weather and monsoon, I had completed all my training and was put in charge of my own Sub-Division that ran northwards from Gonda to a small independent state called Balrampur. I have already described some of the work of an SDO – the usual expression – and will not repeat it. However, this time I was in charge and could do things in my own way, which made all the difference. I had been lent an elephant by a local landowner and, as I also had my two horses, I was able to see quite a lot of the countryside and its villages. One morning, as I was sitting outside my office tent listening to petitioners and litigants, a rather wild-looking man pushed his way forward and threw a bundle on to the table in front of me, calling out in a loud voice, 'My wife has been unfaithful to me – here is her head.' It was indeed the bloody head of a woman that appeared as the cloth bundle unrolled. I had, of course, no option but to arrest the man and send him in to Gonda for trial. It was an unpleasant experience, though I must admit I felt a certain respect for the murderer's courage in admitting to his crime – a most unusual event in India.

While camping near the Balrampur border, I made a point of contacting the Administrator of the State, the Rajah still being a young man under tutelage. I was invited to play polo, and was provided with two or three excellent ponies. The game was enjoyable, but I soon noticed that when the Rajah got the ball, no-one liked to get in his way, though sometimes pretending to do so. He seemed quite surprised when I rode him off on one occasion. But at a reception afterwards he was most affable, and said he must instruct his retainers who played polo with him to treat him in the same way as everyone else, as he hoped to become a good player some day. I do not know whether he had time to do so before the handover of power. Balrampur is no longer an independent state, but part of Uttar Pradesh.

A little days later I managed to catch an intestinal bug, and was forced to lie up in camp for a few days. Fortunately for me, the trouble cleared up of its own accord, as I was at least three days march from the nearest doctor. My bearer, who was more outspoken than most Indian servants, remarked, 'Master, if you will run about your district without stopping, you are bound to get ill.' He was probably right.

In due course my tour came to an end, and I returned to headquarters. It had been a lonely journey in some ways, as I had no-one to talk to except my servants and officials. But I had been busy from morning to night, and as soon as I got into bed I was quickly asleep. I can't say that I enjoyed the tour, but I felt that I had achieved something useful and learnt quite a lot. I am sure that the most important thing in life is to have a purpose. Merely to have money is not enough.

On getting back to Gonda, I had a mass of work to catch up with, but my great excitement was to find a letter waiting for me from the Chief Secretary to Government, saying that I had been granted six months' leave that summer. I had written earlier, explaining that I was engaged to be married, that my fiancée had already waited two-and-a-half years, and could I be allowed leave earlier than the usual period of three-and-a-half years' service. On getting the Chief Secretary's reply, I immediately sent off a cable to Peggy, and wrote to Grindlays to book a passage. The last month passed quickly. I completed my work, made arrangements for my servants and horses, and said goodbye to the friends I had made, both English and Indian. Then, in mid-March, the day came for me to leave. I was, of course, delighted to be returning to England, to be getting married (I hoped), to see my relations and friends again and, I must admit, to escape the oncoming hot weather. But it was not without some regrets that I left Gonda – the first District where I had exercised real authority, and for whose people I had developed a sort of paternal affection. I shall always remember it.

I enjoyed the voyage home – my last as a bachelor. At Suez I made a trip that was possible in those days, catching a train to Cairo, spending a brief period in that marvellous city, having a glimpse of the Pyramids, and rejoining my liner at Port Said. I always intended to visit Egypt again, perhaps making a journey up the Nile, but unfortunately I never managed it. In due course the ship arrived at Marseilles, where I left it to catch the train across France, and arrived at Dover the following afternoon – tired and scruffy, having sat up all night, but overjoyed to be back in England again.

9

Back to England to get Married
Our First Daughter is Born in Allahabad

I quickly spotted Peggy and Uncle Gordon on the quay, and it was not long before I was down the gangway, and Peggy and I in each other's arms. Uncle Gordon's car was parked nearby, and we were soon in it, he sitting in front to drive, tactfully leaving Peggy and me to sit together behind. She seemed delighted to see me again after two and a half years and we held hands as we drove along the cliffs to Folkestone and then a short distance inland to the Neale's house, Kench Hill near Tenterden. The English countryside seemed unbelievably green and lovely after the arid plains of India. Aunt Gracie Neale greeted me warmly, and told me that she and her husband were going out to dinner that night – another tactful gesture. I had a much-needed bath after my rail journey across France, and remember putting on a dinner jacket, while Peggy looked very beautiful in her evening dress. We were, of course, waited on at dinner, as was usual in those days. It all seemed too good to be true! After a few days with the Neales, Peggy and I took the train to London. It was a short but enjoyable journey, looking out of the windows at the Kentish hopfields and meadows, the fat cattle and sheep, the neat and tidy stations – everything was familiar, but somehow more vivid than one remembered it. Perhaps it could be compared to looking at a picture by Constable of a country scene that one had once known but not seen for a long time.

On arrival in London, Peggy went to her parents' house in Chelsea Park Gardens, and I to stay with my parents, who had taken a rather nice flat in Elm Park House, just off the Fulham Road, my father having retired from the Colonial Service about a year earlier. He had been knighted shortly before his retirement – too late to give him much satisfaction – and both he and my mother felt strangers in London after nearly forty years abroad.

It was soon decided that Peggy and I would be married on 17th June at Holy Trinity Church, Kensington Gore. We chose this church mainly because it was close to 64 Queen's Gate, where our wedding reception was to be held in a large house belonging to the Dowager Lady Boyle, the grandmother of Peggy's closest girl friend, Maureen Hallahan. For the next two months or so, I was kept pretty busy. I had arrangements to make for the wedding and our honeymoon, letters of thanks to write for wedding presents, friends and relations to see, as well as spending some time with my parents, whom I am afraid I rather neglected (who does not at some stage?).

But much of my time was, of course, spent in meeting and doing things with Peggy. We were in love, we were about to get married, and we had been separated for a long time. In London we quite often met, and met our friends, in Harrods' banking hall – then on the ground floor – which in those days was almost like a club. Sadly, it has long since disappeared. I was far from well off, and needed to save as much money as possible for the remainder of my leave after marriage, so Peggy and I had to content ourselves with simple pleasures – walking in Kensington Gardens, going for trips on a bus, tea or lunch with relations, and an occasional sherry party – cocktails were only just beginning to come in. However, before long I spent more than I ought to have done on buying a second-hand 4.5-litre Invicta car, which in those days ranked next to a Bentley, so we were then able to drive to places like Richmond Park to walk, or further afield to visit friends and relations.

In due course, our wedding day arrived. My best man was my brother, Brian, who by that time was a lieutenant in the Navy, and luckily able to get leave. Peggy had six bridesmaids, including her two sisters, and also a small girl cousin to hold up her train. A cousin of mine, Vere Logan, son of my Uncle Car, was one of the three priests conducting the service. The church was full on the bride's side, less so on the bridegroom's, but enough of my relations and friends had turned up to make a reasonable showing. Both the wedding and subsequent reception at Lady Boyle's house went off smoothly. I was a nervous speaker in those days, but managed to say a few words without breaking down. Peggy looked beautiful in her wedding dress. After the reception we drove to the Mayfair Hotel and spent our first night together there.

Next day we drove down to Weymouth in my Invicta, had supper with my grandfather, who had been unable to attend the wedding, and then caught the night boat to Guernsey. I had decided on Sark for the first fortnight of our honeymoon – partly because I felt sure it was a beautiful little island, and partly because it was inexpensive. Next morning we had a rather rough trip in a motor boat – Peggy turned green – from St Peter Port, Guernsey, to Sark's tiny but delightful little harbour. I believe it still exists, though there is now another larger harbour, capable of accommodating ships filled with tourists.

On landing – rather thankful to be on dry land again – we took a very old-fashioned open carriage drawn by one horse, first up a steep hill to the top of the island, then along the central ridge until we reached a narrow path with a sheer drop on either side to the sea, connecting Sark with Little Sark. Here the carriage had to stop; we crossed the short link between the two 'islands' a little nervously (nowadays I believe there is a fence or railings of some kind), and in a few minutes reached the simple little house where I had arranged for us to stay.

It turned out to be a great success. The owner of the house – a widow – looked after us very well and produced excellent simple food, including lots of lobster and crab. The weather was perfect, and the coast of Little Sark quite superb and completely unspoiled. We managed to find a point where we were able to scramble down the cliff to a flat platform of rock, where we could lie in the sun, dive into a tiny inlet and swim safely. It was sheer bliss. Occasionally, we would walk across the 'bridge' into Sark, and explore other parts of the island. We even had a little social life, as somehow or other we got to know 'La Dame de Sark', a Mrs Hathaway, who invited us once or twice to lunch or tea in her beautiful house. We went swimming with her daughter, Diana, and one or two friends, and once, as a sort of joke, she asked if anyone would like to buy a tiny island that belonged to her – little more than a large rock – off the Sark coast. I offered £5 (about £100 today); she accepted the offer, but the deal was never finalised and I never saw my island. Perhaps I might have done so if I had not had to return to India a few months later.

Before long our real honeymoon came to an end, and we went first to stay for a few days on our own at Foxhill and then on a round of visits. Being constantly on the move was not without its difficulties, and inevitably we had our ups and downs. Towards the end of my leave, in September, we went to stay with my father and mother at a little resort near Dieppe called Veules-les-Roses. The weather was appalling – much too cold to swim – and Peggy and I spent much of the morning in bed – somewhat to my parents' annoyance. We were able to make a few excursions – my father's favourite occupation when on holiday – the most interesting one being to Rouen, where, by a lucky chance, we visited the magnificent cathedral while a choral mass was in progress.

Another time Peggy and I went into Dieppe by bus, pottered about the old part of the town and the quayside, and had an excellent lunch for what nowadays would be regarded as practically nothing. On the way back to Veules-les-Roses our bus broke down, and we had to sit for more than an hour looking at the flat, dull countryside that stretches inland from the top of the cliffs – how different from the Kent and Sussex fields and downs.

Before long my leave drew to a close, and one morning in early October Peggy and I were seen off from Victoria Station by a small gathering of relations and friends, including both our parents. Peggy left in tears, but soon cheered up and quite enjoyed our journey across France.

On arrival at Marseilles we took a taxi straight to the harbour, and there saw the black sides of our P & O liner – it must have been high tide – rising above us in a rather sinister way. We went straight on board, found our cabin – quite a nice one – left our hand luggage and then took a taxi back to a large café in the Cannebière – the main street of Marseilles – where we sat watching the lively crowds passing up and down. After an excellent *déjeuner*, we made our way to the pilgrim church of Notre Dame de la Garde, standing high on the cliffs above Marseilles and filled with interesting relics and gifts, including hand-made model ships, made by seafarers saved from wreckage or drowning in the Mediterranean. Then it was back to our liner, dinner and into our bunks for the first time. The ship sailed during the night, and next morning we sat on deck in warm sunshine watching the coast of France glide by. Peggy soon became accustomed to ship-board life, and enjoyed her first glimpse of the East, as I had done, on reaching Port Said and going through the Suez Canal. At Aden we went ashore and hired a car for the usual short trip across the desert; Peggy went puce in the face from the heat and gasped out, 'I can't stand it, it's unbearable,' to which I replied a little unkindly, 'Calm down, darling, it's nothing compared to the hot weather in India.'

Eventually we arrived at Bombay, where we were met by my bearer, and went as usual to the Taj Mahal hotel to stay briefly while waiting for our train. I got a nasty shock on calling at the Secretariat to ascertain my new District, to find that we had been posted to Gorakhpur in the extreme East of the United Provinces – about the last place I would have chosen. Peggy stood up quite well to the long journey. This time we travelled first class. In those days a first-class compartment consisted of two long leather-covered seats on either side of the carriage, on which one sat or lay during the day; at night the bearer laid out one's bedding, even sheets, on each 'bunk', and there was a private lavatory, so one travelled in relative comfort. At Lucknow we had to leave the main line and, as there were a few hours to fill in, I took Peggy by tonga – a bit of a shock for her – to the Chattarmunzil Club for breakfast. The club was impressive, having once been a Maharajah's palace, the food excellent by Indian standards, with numerous immaculately-dressed servants to wait on us. Then it was time to catch the train that ran along the line I knew, first to Gonda and then on to Gorakhpur. We stopped for a couple of nights with the Hallowes, who were still in Gonda; it was Peggy's first stay in an Indian bungalow, and she was terrified by the dark, primitive bathroom, fearing that a snake would creep in through the bath-water outlet.

Gorakhpur, when we arrived there, had even more disadvantages than I expected. The Deputy Commissioner, Hewdish Edye, had just arrived from England, having been on leave himself, without his wife, and wanted us to share the vast official house with him; Peggy was to manage the servants and order the food. This would have been almost impossible for her, never having been to India before, and in any case she wanted to be with me. So we had no choice but to occupy a sort of annexe that had only one large room for us to live in, have our meals in and sleep in at night – the beds having to be carried in. Socially, too, we found the place uncongenial, Gorakhpur being the headquarters of the East India Railway Company, with a largely Scottish staff with whom we had little in common. But it was better from the work aspect. I had a large Sub-Division which stretched northwards to the border with Nepal – then a virtually independent and isolated state (the Gurkhas being its main inhabitants), with no foreigners allowed to enter, except for a few British officials in the capital, Katmandu. There happened to be a minor boundary dispute going on at the time with the Nepalese Government, and I was ordered to go to the area and settle it. The boundary with Nepal runs through flat, thickly wooded country known as the Terai, with the Himalayan foothills to the north. We were able to camp in delightful jungle, with excellent shooting and much less work than usual. After three days, the Nepalese delegation I was supposed to meet had not arrived, so, against all the rules, I made a short march into Nepal to make enquiries. There was no sign of the delegation, and no-one had heard of it, so I gave up waiting and continued the tour of my Sub-Division. I rather think that the dispute was eventually forgotten by both sides.

During my tour we were able to see at Bodh Gaya a tree said to be exactly similar to, and in exactly the same place as, the 'tree of enlightenment' under which Buddha had sat. I was interested even at that age in the many appealing qualities of Buddhism which, strangely, has long since disappeared from India, but is still practised by millions of people in Sri Lanka, Burma, Thailand and even Tibet. I still like to remember occasionally that I have sat where Buddha sat, under a similar tree.

Peggy soon got used to 'touring' in an Indian district – more than a little different from the life of a young woman in London – and enjoyed riding from camp to camp on the well-behaved horse named 'Conceit' that had been allotted to her. I had, as usual, been able to borrow an elephant for part of my tour, and I have an amusing photograph of Peggy being lifted on to it from in front by means of its trunk, and looking as if she was on the point of falling off. Having some talent for drawing and painting, she made a lot of sketches of our camp and animals, and also scenes of life in Indian villages. Most unfortunately, the sketch book was later lost. All I have are some photographs, and many of these have faded badly owing to the effect of the 'hot weather'.

About mid-February we were asked by some friends of mine called Robertson to stay with them for Lucknow 'week' – racing, polo, dances and so on. I could not get away, so Peggy went on her own as I thought she ought to have a change of scene after the rigours of camping. She and the Robertsons were invited to dinner at Government House, and Peggy found herself sitting on the left side of Sir Malcolm Hailey, the Governor. As a result – I am quite sure this was the reason – we soon afterwards found ourselves transferred – much to our delight – from Gorakhpur to Allahabad, where I was to be the City Magistrate.

Allahabad – 'the abode of Allah' – lies close to the junction of the Ganges and Jumna, and is a holy city for both Hindus and Muslims. The fort overlooking the Ganges bears the inscriptions called the Edicts of Asoka. The Muslims have their Jamma Masjid (great Mosque) near the centre of the city, and not far away are the remains of a palace built by Akbar, the greatest of the Mogul Emperors. In my day there was a large population of both Hindus and Muslims, with continuing tension between them, which occasionally burst into flames. An important function of the District Officer and his staff was to keep the peace between the adherents of the two religions.

Allahabad was also the seat of the High Court, with most of the judges living in handsome houses with beautifully-kept gardens. We became friendly with Mr Justice and Mrs Kendal and their two daughters, Barbara and Nancy. About two years later, Nancy met my friend Raymond Vernède, whom I have already mentioned, at a Christmas camp I organized (Peggy and I being the hosts), became engaged and married soon after. We have been friends ever since.

On arrival at Allahabad, Peggy and I stayed briefly with the then District Officer, but were soon lucky enough to find a bungalow that suited us admirably – just the right size, with a large garden and tennis court, and a view across some cultivated fields to the Ganges, about a mile or so away. We were lucky too to find an excellent Indian carpenter to make us the furniture we needed having almost none at this point. I remember in particular a large round teak table with teak chairs, that would seat eight people comfortably for dinner. This furniture remained with us for the rest of our time in India.

Socially, Allahabad was a great improvement on Gorakhpur. In addition to the High Court judges and their families, there was a fair sprinkling of 'civilians' in various jobs, and also three regiments, one British and two Indian. The British regiment was the Cheshires, and we soon became close friends with a young couple called Captain and Mrs Simpson. We played a lot of tennis, there were just enough people for me to play polo of a sort, we went to numerous dinner parties and an occasional dance at the club. I should add that these activities took place mainly in the cold weather and the early part of the hot weather. By mid-April, the temperature was over 100 degrees F in the shade in the hottest part of the day, and by the end of June, about 112 or even 115 degrees F occasionally. Most women went to the hills in the hot weather, but Peggy bravely decided to stay with me, not wanting to be alone in a strange hill station. It was a pretty grim ordeal – worse for her than for me, as I was kept busy with my work, while she was shut up in the house for most of the day with little to do. At night we slept in the garden, being guarded in theory by a special policeman, who in practice slept much better than we did. Once, when I asked him to pull out his revolver and aim it, it took him several minutes to disentangle it from his clothes, by which time we would have been dead if anyone had been trying to shoot us. As soon as the sun rose, we got up and our beds were carried into the bungalow. The doors and windows were then closed and screened for the day. We had electric light but at that date no electric fans (they were gradually being introduced, already being in use in large cities like Bombay and Calcutta). Instead, we had to rely on 'punkahs' – a long beam with a piece of cloth below it, which was pulled backwards and forwards by means of a rope in order to create a draught. The puller was the 'punkah wallah' – a low-grade servant who had to sit outside the house pulling the rope. Poor man, he would occasionally fall asleep in the burning heat, and a senior servant would shout at him to get going again.

We did manage to escape very briefly from the hot weather when we were invited to stay for a few days at Government House, Naini Tal. Life there was a combination of the formal and informal. Before lunch and dinner, all the numerous guests were arranged in a large semi-circle; the Governor, accompanied by an ADC, then went round saying a brief word to everyone in turn. Each guest received a printed menu and table plan showing where he was to sit (the placing of guests was considered – perhaps rather absurdly – to be an important matter, and the ADCs spent quite a lot of time preparing the table plans). Apart from meals and the occasional dance, life for the guests was quite informal. There was a delightful swimming pool where we spent a lot of time just sitting, talking and drinking, or one could play tennis, golf, or sail on the lake. The first hole on the golf course was rather unusual – one had to drive over a dense patch of trees to an invisible green some 200 feet lower down. I once hit a good shot, and after scrambling down through the trees found that my ball was on the green. Very satisfying!

Peggy was much the prettiest girl staying at Government House at the time, and soon had a number of admirers, including the senior ADC, nicknamed Lamb as he had the initials L A M. He was a good-looking, attractive man and in the evening, dressed in his military uniform, he looked extremely handsome. Peggy, after her dull life in the plains, was not unnaturally affected by all this attention and glamour, and for a few days lived in a romantic world of her own. I was, I must admit, a bit upset, but it was soon all over, and we left Government House to spend a week or so in one of the Naini Tal hotels. Then it was time to return to Allahabad for the rest of the hot weather.

At last, towards the end of June, when we felt at the end of our tether, black clouds began to pile up from the East. Then, suddenly, one afternoon – it was a Sunday – there was a flash of lightning and heavy rain began to pour down. We rushed on to the verandah and, between showers, into the garden. It seemed quite marvellously cool as we breathed in the air and let raindrops fall on our faces. When we went back into the house after a bit, it was unbearably hot – a complete reversal of temperatures in less than an hour. The monsoon went on for about two months, mostly humid, sticky and hot, but not too bad when there were thick clouds or when it was raining. This was the time of year when one had to have boards fixed across the entrances to the house, to avoid the risk of snakes slithering in. It was too wet to play tennis or polo, and our only form of exercise was to ride our horses, sometimes managing to get out into the surrounding countryside, and once riding through part of the city – a bit daunting for Peggy – to see an ancient Hindu temple close to the Ganges. By the beginning of October, the monsoon was over and the next 'cold weather' had begun. By now we had plenty of friends, and were able to enjoy all the social life we wanted. One day. to make a change, a dozen or so of us dressed up in vaguely Victorian/Edwardian clothes and managed to borrow or hire a number of pony traps or similar vehicles, and then drove in a row into the countryside for a picnic. I have a snapshot of our little cavalcade. I was lucky to have a horse that was easy to control, but another couple were less fortunate – their horse bolted and went off down a side-track at full gallop, though fortunately it stopped after a time without overturning the trap, and they were able to rejoin the party in due course.

A few of us also occasionally hired a large, heavy, extremely primitive rowing boat, together with crew, and made trips either up the Ganges or, more interestedly, down the river past the city, though this involved a bit of planning in advance, so as to avoid Hindu festival days and so on.

Now I must say a little about my work as City Magistrate. Broadly speaking, it fell into two main categories; first the judicial side which took up the greater part of my time, when I had to try most of the more important cases brought by the police (King Emperor versus Jagdish Pershad, or whatever happened to be the name of the accused). Reaching the right decision was often far from easy, as much of the evidence was highly unreliable, and 'false witnesses' were easy to get hold of. I think an English Magistrate has an easy job by comparison. The most difficult cases to decide were perhaps affrays between different groups of people, usually of different castes, standing and sometimes religion. In one case, the police prosecuted a group who were alleged to have attacked, beaten up and seriously injured several members of another group in a dispute over a house and piece of land. The second group filed a counter-case, saying it was they who had been attacked and that one of their party – a very old man – had had his legs broken. After hearing the evidence, I found in favour of the police, and imposed sentences of imprisonment on those found guilty. Later, I was relieved to hear from a reliable confidential source that the decision was the right one, and that the convicted group had deliberately broken the legs of the old man – a member of their own caste – in order to support a counter-case. My other duties were numerous and varied, ranging from the issuing of firearms licences to supervising the running of a sort of temporary hostel for wandering down-and-out Europeans. By careful checking of the hostel accounts, I was able to find a little extra money to improve the quite appalling food, and once or twice to give a little help to an honest man – most of them were rogues – who had fallen on hard times through bad luck or bad judgment. But it was not an agreeable sight to see Europeans living in these highly unpleasant conditions.

However, my more important duties related to rather vaguely-defined responsibilities for law and order – indeed I think I am right in saying that they were not defined anywhere, but rested on a long-established practice. For instance, in the case of a serious riot, a senior Magistrate would normally be present, and the police could not open fire without his permission. Once during the Muslim festival of Moharram, a *tazia* (representing the symbolic tomb of the Prophet and his grandson Husain) was, as usual, being carried through the streets followed by a large crowd of Muslims, when it stopped opposite a Hindu temple because of an overhanging branch from a sacred pipal tree. The Hindus would do nothing about the tree. The Muslims would not lower the *tazia* an inch. There was every danger of a riot. With the help of the senior police officer, I managed to persuade the Hindus to pull the branch up a foot or two, and the Muslims to take their procession to the opposite side of the street. The *tazia* would then just pass under the tree without being lowered, and all was well.

As I have already mentioned, the confluence of the rivers Ganges and Jumna lay just outside the city walls, and it was therefore a place of great holiness for Hindus. At the annual festival of the Magh-Mela, pilgrims would come, often from long distances, in very large numbers to bathe in the sacred waters; among them would be some dying men carried there to purify their souls for the last time. Fortunately, it was a peaceful procession, and I remember taking Peggy there once and walking almost unnoticed through the crowds as we watched the bathing going on, the men in *dhotis* and the women usually in long white garments. I gather that these Hindu and Muslim festivals still continue today, though of course a great many Muslims have left India for Pakistan. Every twelve years there would be a much larger festival called the Kumbh Mela; according to a recent *Times* article three million people attended it in 1989.

About the middle of my time in Allahabad, the Congress Party began an agitation against British rule in India. That remarkable man, Mahatma Gandhi was the leader of the Party – in some ways almost a saint, in others an extremely astute politician. This is not the place to go into the political pros and cons, and I will merely say that the British Government, and therefore the Indian Government, were at that stage utterly opposed to the demands of Congress since – in theory at least – we were preparing India for the orderly hand-over of power in the not too distant future. All officials, from the highest to the lowest – both British and Indian – were therefore required to oppose and suppress Congress' demands. I doubt if there was a single British official, and not many Indian officials, who would have taken a different view in those days.

The trouble began with the Congress Party leaders haranguing small groups which quickly grew larger; then processions through the streets were started, and before long several thousand people had become involved, including most of the city's rogues and vagabonds. Late one evening, a huge crowd poured out of the town with the intention of 'invading' the residential area, which included the houses of the High Court judges and of most officials, both British and Indian, and of buildings like the High Court itself, the European church and club, the *kacheri*, and so on. Briefly, it was – as everywhere in India – the area where those who ruled the country lived. If the rioters had been allowed to proceed, not only would a lot of damage have been done and probably some people killed, but it would also have resulted in the complete breakdown of law and order. The riot, therefore, had to be stopped. For this purpose, substantial numbers of police were posted at critical points, mainly where the roads emerged from the city. The military had been alerted by the District Magistrate, but it had not been thought necessary to call them out at this point. Before long we were confronted by a large threatening crowd. I was at one important road junction, the District Magistrate at another. I ordered the crowd to disperse, as was my duty, and had the order repeated several times by an Indian assistant. No notice was taken, so the order to advance was given. The crowd immediately turned tail and began to retreat. We followed them towards the city, meeting little resistance. At one point, the very senior police officer whom I was accompanying asked for permission to open fire. I refused, as it was clear that the mob were going to offer no serious resistance. I am sure my decision was the right one. Before long most of the crowd had dispersed, except for a relatively small group that we followed into the city. The District Magistrate, with whom I had now joined up, after giving all possible warning, ordered the police to fire a limited number of single shots. It was now dusk, so we could not see the results, but as we advanced and the rioters retreated, we found that one man had been killed and two badly wounded (both recovered). It turned out that none of them had any connection with the Congress Party or politics, two being low caste manual workers, and the third (the one killed) a local *badmash* (bad character) who had come into the street to urinate. That was virtually the end of the rioting. The Congress Party leaders were either arrested or left the city, and in a day or two things had returned to normal. Shortly afterwards I had to try the arrested men, and I am bound to say that they behaved with some dignity. I am sure that they did not deliberately sct out to incite violence, though they must have known that violence was the inevitable result of their activities.

Well, that is enough about my duties as a City Magistrate. I have one other thing to mention before my departure from Allahabad. Towards the beginning of our second hot weather, Peggy became pregnant. It was obviously impossible for her to remain in the plains during the hot weather, and, for reasons that we have both forgotten, it was arranged that she should go and stay as a paying guest with a family living in a remote village in the hills some ten miles from Naini Tal (very unusual in those days, as practically all British people lived or stayed in sizable hill stations). Peggy soon became extremely bored as there was nothing to do except walk, but at least it was cool and healthy, whereas I had to continue to slog away at my work – living alone in our bungalow – throughout the burning heat of the hot weather. Towards the end of June I went up to Naini Tal for my leave, and Peggy joined me there. This time she was not the favourite girl of the Government House staff and young men on leave! However, we had a pleasant, restful time staying in a superior sort of boarding house called 'The Manor House'. When my leave came to an end, Peggy did not want to remain alone in the hills, and bravely decided to return with me to Allahabad. BY then the monsoon had broken; as I have said, it could be extremely hot and humid at times, but was bearable compared to the hot weather.

Peggy stuck it out very well, but we had one unpleasant experience. We had agreed to look after the dog belonging to the Brigadier who commanded the local regiments, having become friendly with him and his wife, while they were on leave in Kashmir. After a week or two the dog began to behave oddly. We suspected that it might be developing rabies – very common in India. A blood sample was taken and sent for analysis to the laboratory in Kasauli established for this particular purpose. The result was positive (later I learned that the laboratory took no risks, and practically always gave a positive answer). We both, therefore, had to have a long series of highly unpleasant anti-rabies inoculations in case we had been licked and infected by the dog – much worse for Peggy in her condition than for me. After some time, our doctor (the District Medical Officer) advised that she should give up the inoculations, in view of the dangerous effect they might have on a pregnant woman. I gave up too soon afterwards, unable to stand it any longer. Neither of us developed rabies, nor did the servants who looked after the dog. Whether the dog had the disease or not we shall never know, as it had to be put down.

By the beginning of November, Peggy was clearly near to giving birth, and was told by the doctor that she should go into the local hospital for Europeans. This she did. It was a pretty primitive place, with mainly Anglo-Indian nurses. It so happened at this juncture that the Governor, Sir Malcolm Hailey, came on a visit to Allahabad. As City Magistrate, I had to dance attendance in various ways. One evening the Governor gave a large ball. I had various duties to perform, though I can't remember what they were. I rather think that seating people in order of precedence for an opening address by Sir Malcolm Hailey was one of them. Anyway, I was there throughout the ball, and so was the District Medical Officer. I was woken very early, to be told that Peggy had given birth to a baby girl. It had happened in the early hours of the morning, when both I, and more importantly, the DMO had been at the Governor's ball. Fortunately all had gone well, and the hospital nurses had coped satisfactorily. Of course, I got dressed and rushed off as quickly as possible to the hospital, where I found Peggy, weak but proud. Poor thing, she had had to go through the ordeal without any anaesthetic, owing to the absence of the doctor. Soon after he appeared, and after making an examination assured me, much to my relief, that mother and child were both doing well.

In about a week, Peggy and her baby were well enough to return to our bungalow, where we had had two small rooms redecorated and turned into a nice little nursery. We had also engaged an *ayah* (Indian nurse) who turned out to be competent and reliable – most people with small children had *ayahs* rather than English nurses, who were hard to come by. All was proceeding normally when, about a fortnight later, I received a letter from the Chief Secretary, saying that I had been transferred to the Roorkhee Sub-Division of the Saharanpur District. This was promotion, as Roorkhee was an Independent Sub-Division, and had a good reputation in other ways. I could not have refused the appointment, even if I had wanted to – which I did not – but it presented a real problem for Peggy and our new baby. Fortunately, the Kendalls came to our rescue and most kindly invited Peggy to stay with her baby and the *ayah*, until she was fit to travel.

I had a pretty hectic last fortnight, completing my work, saying goodbye to numerous Indian visitors as well as our English friends, and arranging for the transfer of our goods and chattels. Rather unusually – I think I can say that – a group of *vaqils* (lawyers) gave a farewell party for me, attended by about fifty or sixty people; one of the *vaqils* made the inevitable lengthy speech, and I replied briefly. He also read out and presented me with a copy of a poem he had written in my honour, in English of a sort. It was a kind and rather touching gesture (he had nothing to gain by it as I was leaving). I still have the poem and, albeit with some hesitation, will quote it:

To: F H Logan Esq Indian Civil Service

> Johnson said, better that ten guilty men escape
> Than one innocent person suffer disgrace.
>   This wholesome principle judges must keep in mind
>   When administering criminal justice to mankind.
>
> This noble principle you followed throughout,
> To accused always gave the benefit of doubt;
>   And more, a good cause ever did you help
>   At great inconvenience to yourself.
>
> Never did you hurry through a case,
> But administered justice with a heavenly grace;
>   So both the accuser and the accused
>   Came in, and left your Court amused.
>
> To appear in your Court was a great delight,
> For you were kind and gentle and polite;
>   A junior's inartistic task you did not hamper
>   And above all never did you lose your temper.
>
> After a stay of one and a half year,
> You are going away from here;
>   I'm told that you will leave by earliest train,
>   And Allahabad's loss will be Roorkhee's gain.
>
> Officers come and officers go,
> But your departure is full of woe,
>   For you had won the hearts of all of us
>   In the short space of eighteen months.

With our sincerest wishes you must go,
To Government's order all of us must bow;
   For your welfare ever shall we pray,
   But now our throats are choked and no more can we say.

Anand Swarup

Allahabad
December 5 1933

10

My Father Visits Us in Roorkhee

In due course the day of my departure arrived. I said goodbye to Peggy and my new daughter, thankful that they were in safe hands and would be well looked after. I did indeed leave by 'earliest train', and after a long day's journey across the United Provinces from south to north – endless flat plains dotted with innumerable villages – I arrived at Roorkhee after dark, and was relieved to be met by a small party of officials, including the senior local police officer. On reaching my new home, I went to bed as soon as possible, and it was not until next morning that I was able to have a look around. It turned out to be a pleasant little bungalow, though with rather a small garden and no room for a tennis court. Being an independent Sub-Division, it had the usual official buildings of a District headquarters (though on a slightly smaller scale), including a *Kacheri*, a police station, a Treasury, and a lock-up for criminals. All these were conveniently located just across a road at the end of my garden. My work was much as I have already described it, except that I was in charge of the area and had to take most decisions myself, reporting only matters of special importance to the District Officer in Saharanpur.

But Roorkhee had some characteristics of its own. For one thing it was the Headquarters of the Bengal Sappers and Miners, going back, I suppose, to the days when Bengal extended far into Northern India. All the officers were Royal Engineers who had been trained at Woolwich (where I had once played rugger), and it was not long before we were on friendly terms with most of them and their wives.

Peggy had arrived after about ten days staying with the Kendalls. I had not been able to go to Allahabad myself, but had sent my bearer to accompany her, our baby and the *ayah* on the journey to Roorkhee. Before long, we had settled down in our new home and made a number of friends, mainly among the Sappers. I remember two in particular, both young Captains and bachelors. One was Eddie Cobb - extremely able and likeable - who would certainly have become a General if he had not, sadly, been killed in a motor accident during the 1939-45 War. The other was Stuart Battye, who did become a General. He was good-looking, religious - I remember him saying his prayers by his bedside in a tent in the jungle - though that did not prevent him from developing a certain *tendresse* for Peggy. Naturally we got to know a number of married couples, and led quite a social life with people who were on the whole more congenial than most of those we had met in our previous stations. I was soon playing polo - the highest standard I ever attained - went shooting fairly often, and even took up fly fishing for the first time with the help of Eddie Cobb, who was an expert.

I must say a word about the outstanding feature of the Roorkhee Sub-Division - it contained the holy city of Hardwar, in the extreme north, close to where the Ganges emerges from the foothills of the Himalayas. To reach it was easy - one simply drove about twenty miles up a track alongside the Ganges Canal which ran close behind our bungalow. We were fortunate in having the use of a large house situated exactly at the point where the Ganges Canal - constructed by the British - broke away from the Ganges River and ran for a long way southwards to irrigate some of the areas that most needed it. One could relax in the garden looking up the river towards the hills, with the city of Hardwar on the left and the divided river flowing past on either side. It was delightful in the cold weather. Strange to think that Leonora should once have lain there in her pram and perhaps crawled about on the grass!

Like at Allahabad, there was an annual pilgrimage of Hindus to Hardwar to bathe in the holy pool - the *Har Ki Pari* - and every twelve years there was a festival of special importance, when huge crowds poured in from all over India for the occasion. Undoubtedly it was a very difficult problem to control these vast numbers of people, but in my view it had been dealt with in the wrong way. A ten-year plan - which I was unable to alter - had been approved, which involved the pulling down of many of the ancient buildings in what had been a place of pilgrimage from time immemorial, and also the construction of cement platforms round the pool for the bathers to use. The latter had already been built – ugly, and completely out of character. I am sure that someone like Sir Edward Lutyens could have devised a better plan. But safety, convenience and cost were the criteria of most officials, particularly the Public Works Department, in those days. From what I hear, I am very much afraid that things have got a lot worse since Independence.

Until shortly before my time, the District Officer had been Chairman of the District Board and of the Board of any large town in his area, but as a move towards independence, these jobs had been handed over to elected Indians. In Hardwar, however, because of its importance as a place of pilgrimage, the SDO had remained Chairman of the Town Council. In fact, it was run by its extremely efficient Indian secretary, who had held the job for years (whereas the SDOs were constantly changing), and had most of the Committee members under his influence. I was unable, as I have said, to change the policy of reconstruction that had been laid down for years ahead, though I did succeed in preventing a few interesting old buildings from being demolished, and one small street retained. But I have mentioned this Committee only because it was the most extraordinary one to which I have ever belonged. Its members included not only the usual notability, but also several holy men from the temples of Hardwar and Rikhikesh. The latter could be described as a Hindu monastery, and lay some miles further up the Ganges before it had fully emerged from the Himalayan foothills. The holy men, wearing the garments of their order, turned out to be surprisingly sharp when it came to discussing matters relating to their property, though quite often I found myself holding the same views.

I was once invited to visit Rikhikesh, and spent a most interesting few hours there. First of all I removed my boots and was then taken to various parts of the temple that a normal visitor would not have seen. It was a delightful place, with the Ganges flowing past, low hills rising all around, and glimpses of the high peaks of the Himalayas visible in the distance. In those days, very few British would have visited Rikhikesh, so I was astonished to read in the papers a few years ago that the Beatles had stayed there. I fervently hope that it has not become a tourist attraction.

We spent our first Christmas in Roorkhee in our own house, since it was of course impossible to take a tiny baby to camp in the jungle. What I chiefly remember is the large number of Indian visitors who called on me, all bringing presents of flowers, garlands, fruit, delicacies of various kinds, and so on (we were not allowed to accept gifts of any value, and were required to refuse them if offered, as occasionally happened). I appreciated these visits (perhaps not always entirely without motive), though they took up a great deal of my time. Indians undoubtedly have a talent for showing their respect, liking, affection, or gratitude, which is something that many Europeans lack.

I had, of course, to tour my Sub-Division during the cold weather. Peggy could not come with me except once when my first stop was near a small town where there was a *dak bungalow* (rest house) that could be reached by car. It so happened that we needed an extra servant to do the washing-up. A local man offered himself for the humble job and we took him on temporarily, knowing little about him. His name was Din Muhammad. He turned out to be the best servant we ever had – loyal, competent, brave. A year later, when he had become our *Khitmagar* (table servant), he saved us from what might have been a very bad accident, when the lamp hanging from the roof of our tent caught fire: he dashed in and took the lamp outside before the tent itself ignited. His hands were badly burnt, but he said nothing until my wife noticed what had happened and did what she could to help.

I have already described what an officer's duties were while on tour and will not repeat it. As Peggy could not come with me, I had to arrange things rather differently, going for shorter but more frequent visits of inspection, and returning briefly to Roorkhee in between. One day I arrived late in the afternoon at my next camp – having been delayed for some reason – and when I went out of my tent the next morning, I suddenly saw the distant peaks of the Himalayas running across the horizon looking like icy white stilettos pointing upwards into the sky. It was a marvellous sight.

In due course, I completed my tour and arrived back at headquarters. Peggy and I had agreed that she should return to England with Leonora – neither of us can remember exactly when we decided to call her that – before the beginning of the hot weather. So we said goodbye about the middle of March, and she left for Bombay, accompanied by our *ayah* and bearer. But once on board the *SS Mooltan*, she had to cope alone. By a lucky chance, the captain of the ship – Captain Harrison (later Commander of the P & O fleet) – noticed her coming up the gangway, tired and dishevelled after the long train journey, and took a liking to her. She was given a better cabin almost at once, and before long Leonora was being carried up every day in her cot by a sailor to the Captain's private deck, much to the envy of the other women with children. It was a voyage Peggy has never forgotten.

At Port Said, Peggy was joined by her mother and two sisters, returning to England from the Sudan, where her father had been appointed Financial Adviser; not long afterwards he became the Public Trustee. Rather ironically, Peggy's mother, whose remark when we became engaged, 'Poor Peggy, having to go and live amongst the blacks', enjoyed her few years in the Sudan enormously.

On arrival in England, Peggy spent most of the time staying at her parents' home at Inkpen or with her favourite aunt, Aunt Marge, who had a delightful house on the Downs between Seaford and Eastbourne. Leonora was christened at Inkpen Church on 16 May 1934 – sadly I could not be there. She was given the names Leonora Felicity. The first, as I have said, we had decided on at an early stage; the latter was chosen by my mother. By this time Peggy had been fortunate in finding an excellent young Nanny, who stayed with us for a number of years until she eventually married a soldier (neither of us can remember her surname, and always refer to her as old Nanny). When October arrived, it was time for Peggy to return to India, but we had decided, for health reasons, that Leonora should, if possible, remain in England for the winter, as I was due for leave the following spring. Fortunately, an aunt on my mother's side – Aunt Beryl, who had looked after Brian and me as children – agreed to have her and Nanny in the small house she still had in Weymouth.

Soon after Peggy left for England, I was appointed to officiate as Collector and District Magistrate of Saharanpur for the hot weather. I was pleased to have the job. Even in those far-off days, not many people had the opportunity and responsibility of virtually ruling a million people. I am glad to say that during the seven months I was there nothing went seriously wrong in the District – luck rather than merit, let me add. But I was extremely lonely, living in a vast gloomy house with no-one to talk to except the servants. Fortunately, there was a large swimming pool in my grounds, which became a sort of meeting-place in the late afternoon for the few English people in Saharanpur. Among them were four or five officers from the Remount Depot, who bought and trained horses for the Indian cavalry regiments. One of them had a pretty young cousin staying with him for a few weeks. I soon got to know her, and she certainly helped to make life a little more lively during her visit.

There was an English Superintendent of Police and a senior Forest Officer with whom I was beginning to become friendly – he was away a lot – when he suddenly died from cholera. Since it was in the middle of the hot weather, the burial had to take place without delay, and there was no time to get a priest from Meerut or Delhi to conduct the funeral service. As District Officer, it fell on me to make the necessary arrangements and to lead the prayers that about a dozen of us said over the coffin before it was interred. It was a sad occasion.

In the middle of June I felt I could stand the heat of the plains no longer, and decided to take a week's leave in Mussourie – the nearest hill station and only a few hours' drive from Saharanpur, so that I could get back quickly in case of need. Mussourie was very different from Naini Tal – no Governor, no Secretariat, no Army headquarters, no formalities – just a place where people of all sorts – mostly not the *burra sahibs* and their wives – came to escape from the hot weather and relax in beautiful surroundings. I did very little, just sitting in the hotel garden having a drink while listening to a military band playing on the Maidan, or going for short walks along the narrow paths that wandered about the steep hillsides with occasional glimpses of the burning plains below. In the evening the hotel put on some kind of entertainment for its guests. While I was there, it was provided by a young couple; the man played the piano and sang, while the girl danced – neither very well. I got to know them as they were staying at the hotel. The man was homosexual, the girl a very pretty and very sexy Eurasian. But it was soon time to return to Saharanpur.

Before long the monsoon began, and there was even less to do than before – walking or riding along the same tracks, and golf of a sort. So I concentrated on my work, and even made a few visits to different parts of the District – usually a matter for the cold weather. One was in connection with a dispute about land ownership that might have ended in serious trouble. I decided to see things for myself, but found that the only way of getting to the place was by train to a nearby small town. On arrival, I was met by the usual crowd, and provided with a horse to take me to the village in question. I got there without difficulty, inspected the disputed land, took evidence and made notes. It was then time to ride back and catch the return train to Saharanpur. The horse immediately broke into a gallop, and I could not stop it – rather like my ride from Haileybury to Hertford – though I was now an experienced rider and my only worry was that I had to cross the railway line at a point where there were gates. Fortunately, they were open – there were not many trains on that line – and I galloped safely into the owner's courtyard without hurting myself, the horse or any of the inhabitants.

By the beginning of October the cold weather had begun, my period as acting District Officer of Saharanpur was over, and I returned to Roorkhee Sub-Division. Soon after, Peggy arrived from England, without Leonora, but full of stories of her christening at Inkpen, her baby talk, how she had grown and so on. It was sad for her to be without her first-born child, but she was now in good health and we had an enjoyable winter.

That year we had our own Christmas camp – in a section of jungle called Andheri Rao, lying to the north of Hardwar and Rikhikesh. All the people who came were friends of ours. They included Nancy Kendall, Raymond Vernède, Stuart Battye, and a close girl friend of Peggy's called Jean Crosthwaite, who was visiting India and spent some time staying with us. Organizing the camp involved quite a lot of work for me. I had to arrange for the necessary number of tents to be sent in advance by bullock cart, food and drink for a week to be available, the right servants to be there at the right time, and many other things. Happily all went well, and the camp was a great success. I shall mention two things only. Firstly, Raymond Vernède and Nancy Kendall, who only knew each other slightly before, fell in love and before long became engaged, and about a year later got married. We have been close friends ever since. Years later, Raymond and I had several enjoyable expeditions together, walking in Switzerland and motoring in France and Crete.

Secondly, I shot my first tiger. This happened near the end of our 'camp', by which time several of our guests had left. There was a tiger kill one night, a beat was quickly organized the next morning, and five or six of us sat up in *machans*. Peggy climbed up off an elephant's back to reach ours and sat with me. After a time we heard the noise of the beaters' sticks as they approached, and then suddenly a tiger emerged almost opposite our tree, moving slowly and cautiously at a slight angle. I waited for a few seconds and then fired; the tiger fell, but then struggled to its feet. I fired again, and this time it fell and lay motionless. We scrambled down the tree, and Peggy rushed forward to look at the animal – a dangerous act, as the tiger might have just had the energy to rise and make one more kill. But he – it was a male – was dead. It was a beautiful animal, and for the moment I felt proud. But I now wish I had photographed it rather than shot it.

Soon after Christmas my father came on a visit, mainly to see us but also to have a glimpse of India. His train was due to arrive at Saharanpur from Bombay in the middle of the night, and in order to save him an uncomfortable time alone in the station, I drove my car to Saharanpur to meet him. He arrived more or less on time, we greeted each other warmly – it was good to see him – and started the drive back to Roorkhee. Suddenly, about half-way home, my car gave a splutter or two and then stopped. Nothing would make it start. It was not a pleasant situation – stranded in the night far from anywhere in a remote part of an Indian district. Eventually my *chuprassi* and I walked some way across the fields to the nearest village and roused the inhabitants. At first they thought we were robbers, and we were almost attacked! Eventually a bullock cart was yoked up and driven to the road, where my father was waiting rather anxiously. By this time he was pretty tired and got into the cart for the remainder of the way, highly uncomfortable though it was. At about 7.30 we arrived at our bungalow. Peggy had just come into the verandah, wondering rather anxiously what had happened to us, when she was amazed to see a bullock cart drawing up in front of the house, with my father sitting in it, wearing an English felt hat!

He soon recovered from this adventure, and quite enjoyed the fortnight or so he spent in Roorkhee, particularly visits to Hardwar and Rikhikesh and a few days in the jungle. Then I had to go on tour, and he set off to see some of the more interesting cities of that part of India, including Delhi – where he was invited to a lunch party given by the Viceroy-Agra (to see the Taj Mahal), Lucknow, Benares and finally Allahabad, where the Kendalls had him to stay. Mr Justice Kendall very kindly took him to the High Court to listen to a case; my father told me afterwards that the Indian lawyers appeared to be very able, compared to those he had to deal with in Africa. In due course he returned to Roorkhee for the last part of his stay in India. This time I took him with me for a short tour of part of my Sub-Division. One day, while I was hearing cases sitting outside a tent, he said he was going for a short walk. When I had finished my work he was not to be seen, and as he had not returned after another half-hour, I became a bit worried, and before long decided to organize a search party, which included a number of people from the local village. We had gone several miles in a long line, when a *chuprassi* came running up to me to say that my father had been found walking steadily in the wrong direction away from our camp! He had little sense of direction, the country all looked much the same, and of course he could not ask the way from any Indian he met. It was very lucky that we found him before nightfall. Soon after, it was time for him to return to England. I think he had, on the whole, enjoyed his visit.

Peggy and I had another two months to spend in India before my leave became due. The time passed pleasantly enough. In the last week, the police officers of the Sub-Division paid a formal farewell call on me, and I have a photograph of myself, well garlanded, standing in a line with them. I gave a farewell party to about forty Indians – officials, local dignitaries of various kinds, and people who had helped me in one way or another. This was a pretty unusual gesture for an English officer, but I had received so much support and kindness from so many people that I felt I ought to do something about it. I think the occasion was much appreciated and remembered for a time.

Then the day came to say goodbye to Roorkhee and leave for England, home and daughter. I remember very little about the voyage, but I think we went the whole way by sea to Southampton and then straight on to Inkpen, where Nanny and Leonora had already arrived. Peggy was, of course, absolutely thrilled to have her baby again. I was pleased too but not, I must admit, to the same extent. In those days, fathers had very little to do with their children when they were babies, but I was occasionally allowed or encouraged to hold Leonora in my arms, and I recall the strange sensation it gave me to realize that this tiny object belonged to me. Gradually, as she grew older, I became fonder and fonder of her, and by the time we were back in England for good, just before the outbreak of the Second World War, the two of us much enjoyed doing things together and were happy in each other's company. In fact, I was more than once accused by my wife of thoroughly spoiling her.

As we now had a daughter and nurse, we were a lot less mobile than in the past. Peggy spent much of her time staying at Foxhill with her parents, who kindly provided a base for our family. I divided my time between Foxhill and staying with my own parents in London. I was able to contact one or two old friends, play squash and swim at my club, and generally enjoy a few aspects of London life. One friend – sophisticated and unmarried – persuaded me, though I must admit I did not need much persuasion, to accompany him a few times to the Four Hundred Club – then the most fashionable night club in London – and to one or two other parties. I should not have done this, but it was, I suppose, partly a reaction to the utterly different life in India, and partly a last fling before settling down to a stable married life.

But I did not spend all my time in a frivolous way. Through my father, who had now become a Justice of the Peace, I was able to attend the court of an excellent Stipendiary Magistrate in the West End of London, listen to interesting cases and afterwards discuss a few points briefly with the very helpful Clerk of the Court. The day usually began with a string of minor cases where the accused were likely to plead guilty, and often included a number of prostitutes. The girls looked perfectly normal, were soberly dressed and not unduly made up; they invariably pleaded guilty – there was only a small fine – and I recall only one girl who made a bit of a scene. I suppose the police accepted that prostitution could not be wiped out but needed to be kept under control by the regular prosecution of a few girls in different areas of London.

But these were minor prosecutions, and not what I had come to hear. I did, in fact, listen to several very interesting cases, though it would take too long to describe them. Very briefly, one related to a personable young man with wealthy parents, who had lost all his money gambling and been forced to live in cheap lodgings in the East End. There he had been contacted somehow or other by a notorious robber, and persuaded or forced to show where some of his parents' friends lived, and how best to break into their houses. Before long he was caught taking part in a burglary, brought before the Magistrates' court and eventually sentenced to a long term of imprisonment (by a higher court). I felt a little sorry for him as he was a bit like someone I had known at Cambridge and was, I think, weak rather than criminal.

After a few weeks, I had had enough of listening to cases. But my time had not been wasted; I had learned quite a lot about how a Magistrate should conduct cases and deal with lawyers, and various matters of procedure. There was, of course, a great deal of difference between English and Indian criminal law, the latter being codified (Indian Penal Code, Criminal Procedure Code, etc.) and in some ways easier to administer. On the other hand, I felt we in India had a much harder task in judging the truth or otherwise of evidence. I doubt if a completely fabricated case has ever been brought in an English court. It certainly has in India.

Peggy and I joined up whenever we could and made a number of brief visits to relations and friends. One was to stay with a former boyfriend of hers, Robert Buxton, now married, who lived in a delightful house in the depths of the country in Somerset. Rather like my friend Jim Bourne, he had decided not to go into one of the businesses belonging to the wealthy Buxton tribe, but to become a doctor, and had qualified as an eye-specialist and, at the time we went to stay, had a practice in the nearby town of Yeovil. I mention him because, not very long afterwards he came out to India for an unusually interesting purpose. Among the guests was a very good-looking, very athletic, very wealthy and very stupid man who was a keen polo player. When he heard I had played in India, he offered to lend me a pony or two to play at Hurlingham or Windsor, but nothing came of it – just as well, since the standard would have been too high for me. The main thing I remember about this visit, apart from the Buxtons' hospitality and the pleasant surroundings, was going for a swim in the nearby lake, when one of the girls got caught up in some weeds; she yelled and shouted, but at first none of us paid any attention, then Robert and I realized she was in difficulties and managed to extricate her just in time.

In July, my parents asked us all to come and stay with them for a month at the Whitesand Bay Hotel, not very far from Plymouth, where they had booked rooms, including one for Nanny and Leonora. This leave I had bought a large second-hand Buick and a small trailer for our luggage. When we set off on the long drive to Devon, the trailer was piled high with nearly all our goods and chattels, including Leonora's pram. Unfortunately, fairly soon after setting off, I made a mistake and took the wrong turning. To have gone on would have added about twenty miles to our journey, so I decided to go back the short way necessary to take the right road. I thought there was just room to turn, but there wasn't owing to the trailer. After getting more than three-quarters way round, I was stuck – to go forward meant leaving the road and sinking into mushy grass, to go back was impossible. Before long, cars began to pile up and start hooting. I simply didn't know what to do. Then, fortunately, two men from a lorry walked up to see what was happening, and very kindly came to my aid; between us we managed to lift the trailer a few feet to the left, and this made it possible for me to complete the turn. I am still grateful to the two men.

We got to Exeter in time for lunch and went to the best hotel – the Royal Clarence – to have it (in those days one seemed able to afford this sort of thing even as a young man; now, more often than not my wife and I go to a pub). The four of us had lunch together. Leonora, who had been provided with a suitable high chair, behaved impeccably; I felt quite proud to be a father! We then went on to Plymouth, where the car and trailer had to be driven on to a ferry to cross a stretch of water which was, I suppose, part of Plymouth Sound. I had a row with a disagreeable man who refused to move his car a few yards forward to make room for mine. Finally, I told him in as commanding a way as possible that I was a Magistrate and would have him prosecuted if he didn't make room for me. This worked, and he moved forward the necessary distance – it was no problem at all for him – and I got my car and trailer safely on to the ferry. After crossing the small bit of water, we had only a short distance to drive to reach the hotel where my parents were waiting to greet us. Leonora, who had stood the long journey very well, was put to bed immediately, and next morning was her usual lively self.

We had an enjoyable time at Whitesand Bay. The weather was perfect, the hotel comfortable, and not another house in sight for miles. The beach was just right, with rocks, pools and plenty of sandy patches. Leonora thoroughly enjoyed digging in the sand, building castles with a bit of help, and paddling in one of the shallow pools. Peggy and I, and sometimes my father, used to swim in the morning and then lie in the sun. My mother had given up swimming, but liked to sit on the beach watching us while she knitted. My father, as usual, wanted to go to church on Sundays, and naturally I agreed to drive him and my mother to the nearest village church, which was quite a long way from the hotel. One Sunday the car broke down about half-way there, and I couldn't get it started. My father insisted on walking the rest of the way, which would have been much too far for him at his age. I was still fiddling with the engine when, very luckily, a local car came by, very kindly picked up my mother and myself, and then my father, who we found sitting exhausted by the roadside. The driver dropped my parents at the church and then took me on to the village, where a local blacksmith with some knowledge of cars agreed to come to the rescue. He managed to put my car right – it was something to do with the carburettor – and I got back to the church just as the service was ending. My father was quite put out 'Couldn't you have got here before the end of the service?' he asked me rather crossly. I should say here that I liked and got on well with my father once I had got to re-know him after his war-time exile in the Seychelles. Of course we had different views on many things, and I remember being highly embarrassed when he gave me a religious lecture standing on the platform at Liverpool Street Station while waiting to catch a train back to Cambridge. He smoked moderately, and when I got to the age to smoke he used to ask, 'Like a cig, Bun?' I had been nicknamed 'Bunny' as a small child, and the name stuck; I continued to be called it by the family until I went up to Cambridge, when I put my foot down and said the nickname must be dropped.

While at Whitesand Bay, I developed an urge to write a play. The story was based on events in the London Underground Railway – about which I knew a little owing to the General Strike – and described what happened in a crash when a group of people were trapped in a carriage after a collision, not knowing whether or not they would be rescued. I worked at the play very hard, and managed to get it finished and typed just before the end of my leave. The play was accepted by one of the best agencies of the day, who said they liked it and thought there was a good chance of getting it produced. Shortly afterwards, I had to return to India and heard no more. Whether or not I would have had better luck if I had remained in London, I shall never know.

After the end of our enjoyable holiday at Whitesand Bay, we drove slowly back to Berkshire, stopping once or twice for brief visits to friends; this time Peggy's parents were unable to put us up, and we had to rent a small house in the depths of the countryside. I needed to go to London from time to time for business reasons, and quite enjoyed staying in this remote spot, but it was boring for Peggy being stuck there for more than a month. One morning, I was in charge of Leonora for some reason, and sitting with her at the end of the garden close to a large wood, when two rabbits suddenly hopped out and stood quite close to us for a second or two. Leonora was absolutely thrilled and realized, I am sure, that they were live creatures and not toys. Perhaps it was the beginning of her love of animals which has become her great interest and activity, almost an obsession.

Not long before my leave came to an end, I had a difficult decision to make. I received a letter from the Chief Secretary, offering me the post of Assistant District and Sessions Judge in Meerut, which involved moving over to the judicial side of the Service. For a variety of reasons I decided to accept, and shortly afterwards we set sail for India. Leonora slept in a cot, with Peggy and me in our cabin, but Nanny appeared fairly early in the morning to take her away to have breakfast with the other children on board. Peggy of course did her share, and soon got to know and like several of the other mothers. From time to time I had to take charge, and once Leonora escaped from me while I was talking to another man; I rushed down the deck, afraid that she might have managed to fall over something or down a staircase or even overboard, but soon found her with a group of other children playing 'Ring a Ring of Roses'.

On arrival at Bombay we were met by our bearer Moti, who had some sad news for us. Din Mahommed had been killed by a car while bicycling round the bazaar, collecting supplies for our new house. Peggy was very upset and burst into tears. I was sad, too. We still remember him with affection.

Leonora and Nanny stood the long journey to Meerut very well, and we were pleased to find that we had been allotted a pleasant house close to the racecourse. Meerut – where the Indian Mutiny had broken out – was an important place. It had a large Indian city, it was the headquarters of a Civil Division (roughly the size of Wales), and an important military cantonment with, in our day, three cavalry regiments and two or three infantry regiments stationed there. I became friendly with a young officer called Edward Collins in the Central Indian Horse, and we used to go fishing and snipe shooting together. I also played polo. though only on days when cavalry officers were schooling their ponies or practising; I had neither the horses nor the experience to play first-class polo. About the middle of the cold weather, Robert Buxton arrived to stay; he had come out to India to perform an eye operation on the Wali of Swat – splendid name! – who was the ruler of a small state in the extreme north-west of India. The operation had been a success and Robert had then gone on, recommended by the Wali, to perform operations on other important people. Peggy remembers that Robert had with him a small bag filled with dried-up eyeballs and skins from these operations. He liked riding, and used to enjoy having a brisk canter with me round the racecourse in the early morning. Once or twice I took him a bit further afield to see some Indian villages, which interested him greatly; once he noticed that there was something wrong with the eye of a village headman, and managed to put it right by some very simple manipulation. The *Mukhia* was immensely grateful; a day or two later he came into Meerut to pay his respects to Robert, and put two or three garlands of flowers around his neck – a novel experience for him.

We also took Robert with us to a Christmas camp, organized this time by two or three of us stationed in Meerut. I have described these camps already, and will mention only two incidents, one rather absurd. Our tents were pitched round a Forest Bungalow in which we had our evening meal. One night we were playing a game in which Robert was crawling about on the floor pretending to be a tiger, when he managed, entirely by accident, to knock his head against a sharp *kukri* (large knife) someone was holding in self-defence against the fierce animal. His forehead was badly cut and bleeding; he could not of course deal with it himself, and Peggy had to put in four or five stitches under his instructions. She did it successfully, and the wound healed up. She has always remained proud – with reason – of performing this operation, which required both skill and nerve.

The other event concerned a real tiger. I had taken Robert 'gooming' on an elephant early one morning. In crossing a *nullah* – a small stream in the cold weather, a roaring torrent in the monsoon – our mahout noticed some tiger footprints in the sand. Robert insisted on getting off the elephant, and took an excellent photograph – which I still have – of one of the footprints. The mahout happened to be a man who knew a lot about this part of the jungle, and on getting going again, he followed the line he thought the tiger would have taken. He turned out to be right. Suddenly he stopped the elephant, and we saw the tiger clearly not more than fifty yards away, slightly on my side. I fired – it was an awkward position, with Robert and me sitting back to back – and hit the animal, but not fatally. It turned and came bounding towards us. We both fired again, but that did not stop the tiger from leaping on to the top of the elephant's trunk. It hung there for a second or two, and then dropped to the ground – dead. The poor elephant had been badly clawed, but fortunately its eyes had escaped. It was an exciting experience, but it was the last tiger I shot or wanted to shoot. Incidentally, I have four large coloured prints hanging in my room all 'published and sold, June 4th 1806, by Edward Orme', of young men – presumably British officers – hunting tigers on elephants. In one, the tiger had leapt on to the side of one of the four elephants depicted, which had its mouth open, obviously bellowing with pain. In another, a tiger is swimming across a wide river, with a Hindu temple in the distance, again pursued by young men on elephants, one of which is completely submerged except for the end of its trunk. I have been told by an expert that this was possible – elephants can swim – though I never saw such a thing myself. But they certainly do like lying by the side of a stream or river, being heavily scrubbed by the mahouts.

Now I must get back to our more mundane life in Meerut. Soon after we arrived there, or perhaps before, Peggy realized that she was pregnant again, though this did not prevent her from enjoying an active social life for some time. It was impossible, of course, for her to return to England so soon after getting back to India, so we decided that she should have the baby – due in May – in Naini Tal, where there was a good hospital with English doctors in charge. So, at the beginning of the hot weather, I took the three of them – Peggy, Leonora and Nanny – to stay there in a comfortable guest house called the Manor House, close to the quite large church. I returned to Meerut expecting to have to spend the hot weather there, but by a stroke of good fortune (or perhaps a sympathetic Chief Secretary), I was soon afterwards appointed acting District and Sessions Judge of Kumaon. This included the three hill districts of Naini Tal, Ranikhet and Garwhal, and covered quite a large area of the lower Himalayas. The headquarters were in Naini Tal.

11

I Become a Judge
Our Second Daughter is Born 'in the hills'

For some reason the Judge's bungalow was not immediately available, so we all stayed at the Manor House for a few weeks. I had a long ride to reach my Court and Office at the other end of the lake, but Peggy had a far worse time; she was now near the point of giving birth, and had to be carried about two miles in a *dandy* to reach the hospital – no joke for a woman in her state. Twice she was sent back, but the third time she was kept in hospital and on 20 May our second daughter was safely delivered. Not long afterwards she was baptised by the Rev Henry Stapleton-Cotton at Naini Tal church, and named Sara Francis Jean. Henry's wife Elaine was one of her godparents, and the Stapleton-Cottons became close friends, finally living not very far away from us in Surrey.

Before long, I was able to obtain possession of my official house, which had a marvellous position, high above the lake with glimpses of some of the Himalayan peaks in the far distance. We were a long way from the social centre of Naini Tal – the club, the boat house, the polo ground – but that did not matter now, as we had two small children to keep us fully occupied, and of course my work as well. Leonora had been lent a tiny tricycle to ride in our small garden – she was now very active – and once somehow managed to get out on to the path outside the house; fortunately I was in the garden at the time, rushed after her and caught her just before the path sloped steeply downwards towards the lake. It was a miraculous escape, as she would almost certainly have shot over the steep hillside and been killed if she had got a few yards further.

After about a month, I had to go to Ranikhet to hear a number of cases awaiting trial. It was not too difficult to get there by car – rather like driving from one ski resort in

Switzerland to another – and we decided to take the children. The drive of thirty miles or so must have gone off without incident, as I remember nothing about it. There was a very pleasant official bungalow for the Judge, with a small court house immediately adjoining it. To reach the latter, handcuffed prisoners had to be marched past our verandah while the children were playing on it; Peggy and Nanny didn't like this much, but I am sure it had no effect on Leonora and Sara at their early age. It was at Ranikhet that Leonora had her first ride. I managed to get hold of a rather decrepit elderly pony with a reliable *sais*, who took her for short rides, leading the pony along one or two safe footpaths and making sure that she didn't fall off. I think I nearly always went too, certainly to start with. Leonora absolutely adored the old pony, and was very proud to be riding it. She longed to own it, but that of course would have been absurd. Sadly, we had no dogs at that time – it was too dangerous with children because of the risk of rabies, and as far as I remember no-one in India ever had a pet cat.

Ranikhet was quite an important military station, mainly because it provided a cool healthy climate for British troops during the hot weather, and at the same time it was possible to move quickly down into the plains if an emergency developed in one of the big northern cities like Lucknow or Cawnpore. We soon had a number of friends, and one very nice couple kindly offered to look after Nanny and the children while Peggy came with me to Almora – the last small town in that part of the Himalayas, beyond which the country became wild and uninhabitable. As I hadn't got my car with me (we had come to Ranikhet in a hired car), I decided we must go by a local bus. When Peggy saw the bus, she almost refused to get in. Apart from being packed with local hill-men and women, it was grossly overloaded, the roof being covered with every kind of object, including a trussed-up goat. However, I got her into a seat in the front, and off we went down a steep winding road; the bus swayed about in a rather alarming manner, but fortunately we had a good careful driver. After several miles we got to the bottom of the hill – I might almost say mountain – where there was a narrow valley before the road went up again steeply to Almora. Here we got off the bus and started to walk up the valley to reach a small rest-house about ten miles away. I had been advised by a Forest Officer friend that this was a walk worth doing; he was quite right. The narrow path followed a crystal-clear stream, the hills covered with trees rose steeply on either side of us, and there was not a soul to be seen. Here and there the stream widened into pools, and about half way we decided to have a swim. The water was cold, but the sun warm and there was no wind. It was gorgeous!

We had just got out – Peggy was wearing a bra and knickers, having no swimsuit with her – when there was a sort of scuffling noise from the nearest trees. Peggy was highly alarmed, thinking a group of villagers were about to emerge, but suddenly we saw that it was two of the large blue-grey hill monkeys – *langurs* – that had come down the hillside to see what was going on; they were quite harmless if left alone. Having got dressed, we continued our walk and arrived at the little rest-house just before dark. A servant of ours was already there, and had somehow managed to prepare quite a reasonable meal for us. We spent the next day there – it was the end of the path – resting and sitting in the verandah, and enjoying the superb view into the hills. Then we had to walk back to the main road, where another crowded bus was waiting to take us on to Almora. (I had arranged this in advance, and in those days the bus driver would have waited for hours, if necessary, to pick up the *Judge Sahib* if he had been ordered to do so.)

Almora was a remote and delightful hill station, quite different from Ranikhet and Naini Tal, as there were no troops stationed there and only the usual District official, plus a small number of people who had come there to escape the hot weather in the Plains and didn't want a social life. I again had a very pleasant bungalow and less work than usual, so I was able to relax a bit and enjoy the beautiful scenery and walk along the narrow hill paths. Once, on a friend's recommendation, I followed a path that became very narrow at one point with an almost sheer drop of hundreds of feet. I nearly turned back, not having a very good head for heights, but screwed up my courage and continued; rounding a bend I suddenly had the most superb view of the distant Himalayan peaks, rising like white icicles into the clear blue sky. One, higher than the rest, was Nanda Devi – more beautiful, though not quite as high as Mount Everest. Before long, it was time to return to Naini Tal and not long afterwards to the Plains. We had all enjoyed our stay in Almora, including the children who looked fit and well. It was the most relaxed three weeks I had anywhere during my ten years in India. I still remember Almora as my favourite hill station.

I have given some idea of the early life of an official in the Indian Civil Service and will now jump to my last six months, just mentioning that during part of the time I held the post of Deputy Judicial Secretary to Government. Then in October 1937, I was appointed District and Sessions Judge of Gonda – the District where I had completed my training and run my first Sub-Division. It was odd to be back there. This time I had a big, rambling, rather ugly house with a large garden and trees through which monkeys used to jump and occasionally skip along the ground. I was a little nervous on account of the children, but there was nothing I could do about it, as monkeys are sacred to the Hindu, and even firing a shot into the air would have caused offence. However, the risk was slight. Another more dangerous incident occurred in connection with a sandpit I had had constructed for the children to play in. I went out one morning for a stroll around the garden, and as I passed the sandpit I saw there was a snake in it; on going a little nearer, the snake rose and hissed at me – it was a large cobra! I rushed back to the house to fetch a gun, but by the time I returned, the cobra had disappeared. It was lucky that I had been a little earlier than usual that morning, as the children were due to come out about that time, and Leonora might have rushed ahead to the sandpit, seen the snake, not realized that it was dangerous and got close enough for it to bite her – fatally, if it had happened.

Life in Gonda had not changed much except for the officials; there was now an Indian Deputy Commissioner living in the house where I had lived with the Hallowes. I was soon on good terms with him officially, but never got beyond that, as his wife or wives were in purdah and he belonged to neither of the two little clubs. The Superintendent of Police was English and had a charming and attractive wife, Phyl Bolam, with whom Peggy became friendly. I quite liked the Forest Officer called Bill (I have forgotten his surname), and he, Jack Bolam and I sometimes went duck or snipe shooting together. But I was kept pretty busy with my work, as there had been a gap between the departure of the previous judge owing to illness and my appointment, and as a result a lot of cases were waiting to be tried.

When Christmas arrived, we had of course to spend it in our house – home would have been the wrong word – as it would not have been feasible to take two small children camping in the distant forest. Several of the numerous visitors I had to receive were kind enough to bring presents, not only for Peggy and me but also for the small girls. One I recall consisted of little animals ingeniously made of wood and leather, whose head, legs and tails, could be moved into different positions. Leonora was thrilled with hers, especially a miniature crocodile, and played with them for hours. I am afraid they have long since disappeared.

After Christmas, I decided to accept an invitation from the Forest Officer to spend a few days with him in the jungle, leaving Peggy and the children to stay with the Bolams. After accompanying Bill on some of his jobs and doing a little bird shooting for the pot – Bill had shot all the big game he wanted – he had to go off from our camp to inspect another part of his territory, leaving me to be looked after by his head *shikari*. Next day, the *shikari* told me that a tiger in his area often took a particular way through the jungle to reach a pool of water, and that if I sat in a *machan* in a tree he would select, I would have a good chance of shooting the animal. I agreed, though I had no intention of shooting another tiger. Early next morning, I went on the back of an elephant to reach the place selected by the *shikari*, situated in a rather dense patch of jungle, and climbed with some difficulty into the *macham* – very small and rather high in the tree. After sitting there for a couple of hours, I was feeling extremely cramped and wondering how much longer I would have to stick it out, when I suddenly saw a tiger moving slowly and cautiously directly towards my tree. I remained absolutely motionless in spite of the cramp, and kept my head well down. The tiger, a most beautiful creature, passed within twenty yards of my tree and even sat down for a moment to lick a rear paw – it would have been easy to shoot him – before moving slowly away. It was a marvellous experience, and I am thankful I didn't shoot. About half an hour later, the *shikari* arrived to take me back on our elephant, and asked me if I had seen the tiger. I replied that I had, but that *Vishnu the Preserver* in my religion had told me that I should not kill this particular animal for reasons that I could not explain. He was a little puzzled, but *sahibs* were of course difficult to understand. Later I saw that he and the other men who worked under him were all well paid.

In February, Phyl Bolam was taken ill. Peggy did her best to look after her, but she soon got rapidly worse and it became clear that she had contracted typhoid. There was no hospital in Gonda, and it was necessary to get her into Lucknow as soon as possible. I remember walking with her and her husband as she was carried on a home-made stretcher to our little station. She looked extremely ill and, I was afraid, dying. But I am glad to say that she recovered.

Soon afterwards I began to feel ill myself, and thought that perhaps I had got typhoid too. But it turned out to be something quite different. My temperature went up and down, I was totally devoid of energy and unable to work, but had no specific symptoms. The local doctor was unable to make any diagnosis. After this had gone on for a fortnight or so, he suggested that, as I was going on leave anyway in April, I should try and get permission to go earlier. I managed to write a letter to the Chief Secretary, and soon had a reply saying I could start my leave whenever I wished. After a good deal of correspondence, mainly conducted by Peggy, we managed to get accommodation of a sort on a second-class ship called *The City of London,* cancelling the excellent cabin we had booked on a P & O Liner a month later.

I left Gonda with no ceremony, owing to my illness, and little regret, thinking of course that I would be returning to India after my leave. We had a pretty grim journey down to Bombay, as our compartment was immediately behind the engine and the hot weather had just begun. Peggy had a brilliant idea, and managed to get a large box of ice put on the floor of the carriage; by directing one of the fans on the ice, the temperature was brought down a few degrees, which made a big difference. How primitive this must sound to tourists who visit India these days! On going on board our ship in Bombay, we found that Peggy had a rather small single cabin for herself and the two children, while I had an even smaller one without a porthole to myself – certainly not what we would have chosen. But it turned out that our early departure had been well worthwhile. Within a couple of days, while our ship was still in the Indian Ocean, I began to feel better, and by the time we got into the Mediterranean I was walking around the deck, and before we arrived at Liverpool I was even playing ship games and dancing a little in the evening. It was little short of a miracle!

Looking out of the carriage window on the journey from Liverpool to London, the English countryside looked unbelievably green and beautiful, and I suddenly made up my mind that I would not return to India if I could somehow or other get a reasonable job in England. It was not that I disliked either India or the Indians; on the contrary, I still have a feeling of affection for both. Nor did I dislike my work, which was much more varied and responsible than most young men would have had in England. But Peggy and I stood the climate badly – we were both very fair when young. More importantly, we now had two small girls and knew that for a good many years we would be separated during the hot weather, with Peggy either in England or the hills with the children while I sweated away in the Plains. I must admit that I also did not like the idea of following my father's example, and returning a stranger to my own country in what then seemed to me like old age.

We spent the first part of our leave in much the same way as I have described previous leaves, including a stay with my parents in a pleasant little hotel they had found at Walmer on the Kent coast. Then Peggy and the children, together with an extremely nice young nurse – Nanny Wind – that we had been lucky enough to engage, went as usual to Foxhill while I rented a very small flat just off the Embankment – not far from Tedworth Square – as I wanted to get down to the task of looking for a suitable job. Over this my father was extremely helpful, and so, to a lesser extent, was Peggy's father. After turning down one or two offers that didn't seem quite right for me – one was in the City, another was a branch of the Secret Service – I was offered the post of Administrative Officer in the Air Raids Precautions Department of the Home Office, which not long afterwards became the Ministry of Home Security. I accepted. At this point in 1938, war with Germany seemed to be inevitable. Under Adolf Hitler, Germany had become virtually an armed camp, the Rhineland had been taken back, in 1937 an alliance formed with Mussolini, and the following year Austria was annexed and the Sudentenland ceded to Germany. Hitler's ranting and raving could no longer be treated as a joke and when, soon after I had joined my new Department, he declared in the course of a speech, 'My patience is now exhausted', we all felt that war was inevitable.

12

A Change of Life – Back to England for Good and a New Job

The ARP Department, which had been in existence for about a year, consisted of a few Home Office officials, a number of Civil Servants from other Departments, and a collection of retired officials from the Colonial Services – a very mixed bunch. As the Department was a new one and there were virtually no precedents, we were all on much the same footing, and I found myself fully able to deal with the subjects allotted to me. These were the provision of transport for the local authority ARP Services falling under the Home Office and, a little later, the question of providing barrage balloons to protect places like docks, important railway junctions, certain factories and so on from low-level attack by German aircraft. There were, of course, expert advisers, but I had to take decisions on whether proposals regarding transport should be approved and money made available up to a certain level; above that, the matter had to be referred to the Assistant Secretary (a quite senior official) in charge of my Division.

He was a charming, intelligent man from the Home Office, but quite incapable of making up his mind about matters he had never dealt with before, and his desk was piled high with unanswered files. I soon found that the best way of dealing with him was to take in a file, explain it briefly, and say that I was sure he would agree that such and such a decision was the right one. He nearly always did. Occasionally I adopted the same method when an important matter had to be referred on to the Assistant Under-Secretary of State, who happened to be one of the three men who had appointed me, and who evidently understood why I was acting in a rather unorthodox way. One of the things I played a part in was to get an increase in the miserly sum allowed by the Treasury for the purchase of vehicles for civil defence, and perhaps in this way made a small contribution to creating a more efficient service by the time war broke out.

My other job – the provision of barrage balloons for protecting certain key areas – was quite a different one. Here I was the joint secretary of a high-powered committee chaired by an eminent scientist. Fortunately I got on well with him, and also with my colleague, an RAF officer. He was able to help with the technical matters that the committee had to consider, while I was perhaps better at preparing memoranda, writing the Minutes and so on. From time to time, we were instructed by the Committee to visit a particular site and report back; this made a nice change from the usual routine, and there were often interesting things to see and interesting people to meet from organizations with which I had never previously had any connection. Once I had the unusual experience – for me – of being flown round an area not very far from Sheffield where there were several important specialist factories, so that my colleague and I could get some idea of the lie of the land and of what was needed. Quite often we were given a good lunch by the officials we were visiting, and sometimes one or other of us had to make a little speech. The Committee had decided in favour of providing these protective balloons for vital civilian areas, and by the time the Second World War broke out, a certain number were available for use. As the war went on and German air-raids started, their value became more and more evident, and before very long they were even protecting the railway junction at Woking near where we had come to live.

Having resigned from the ICS and obtained a regular job in London, I had to find somewhere to put the family. We were far from well-off at that stage, and had two small children and a Nanny – Nanny Wind. After a lot of searching, we ended up renting a small house in Horsell, a sort of residential suburb about two miles from Woking station, from where there was an excellent train service to London. It seemed a bit odd at first sitting in a carriage with a number of other men, all reading their newspapers or business papers, with usually no conversation at all. But I soon got used to it.

Our house at Horsell was adequate but not at all what we wanted, and in any case rented for only a short period. Reading *The Times* in the train one morning, I noticed an advertisement for a house that sounded just right – an enlarged old cottage with an attractive garden, within daily reach of London, to be rented unfurnished for five years. No indication of the whereabouts of the cottage was given. I wrote off immediately to the box number and could hardly believe my eyes when the reply came saying that the house was situated on the outskirts of Woking, less than half a mile from where we were living. Peggy and I rushed round to see it that same morning – the house was called Bridge Barn – and were delighted with it. There were five bedrooms – three very small ones in the old cottage and two larger ones in the well-designed extension – just right for our family. The drawing room – two rooms in the old cottage knocked into one – was particularly attractive with a low-beamed ceiling against which I occasionally knocked my head. The worst feature was the rather primitive kitchen with a coal-fired range, but one didn't bother much about kitchens in those days when one expected to have a cook; two years later, after our best cook had left to become an Army nurse, we, or rather Peggy, paid the penalty. But we never felt that we had made a wrong decision in renting the house, and we still remember our time there with pleasure.

I don't want these recollections to sound like a house-agent's ad., but I must say a brief word about the Bridge Barn garden. It was surrounded on two sides by a very large nursery garden with pretty country beyond; the house itself stood well back from a quiet road, and – special feature – the Woking to Basingstoke canal ran along one side. So we had complete seclusion, though within walking distance, say two miles, of Woking station. By this time Leonora had become an active, lively, and at times rather naughty little girl. Of course the brunt of dealing with her fell on Peggy, while I only saw her briefly in the evening and at weekends. We now got on very well, playing hide and seek, climbing trees and exploring the nursery garden and nearby country. Once we found a decaying old barge by the side of the canal; Leonora got into it, slipped and fell into a deep pool of filthy water at the bottom. When I pulled her out, she was absolutely black from head to toe as well as soaking wet. On getting back home we were both severely reprimanded by mama.

On 3rd September, 1939, the Second World War broke out.

We had gathered in the nursery to hear Neville Chamberlain's sombre announcement on the radio which ended (I seem to remember) with the words, 'This country is now at war with Germany'. For some time, life went on much as before. There were plenty of goods in the shops, including food, we had a nurse and cook, the trains ran normally, though gradually more and more crowded with men in uniforms as people got called up. Then things began to change: food became scarce, and before long rationing began; our car had to be laid up, and I recall having to walk back from the station in pitch darkness and once bumping into a lamp post and nearly breaking my nose. One of the things we felt most was when our very nice Nanny Wind was called up; she came to say goodbye dressed in her WRAF uniform, looking very pretty and smart. After that we had a series of older nurses, none satisfactory and one, we discovered afterwards, who bullied the children when she had them alone, particularly when putting them to bed at night. They were both too frightened to say anything to us at the time; Leonora recovered quickly, but Sara was more badly affected. She was a very pretty, rather shy little girl, who adored her mother, and I can still see them walking together hand in hand round the garden.

Before very long, I myself became the gardener – just as Peggy became the cook – and it was soon my favourite occupation. There is always something to look at, something to do, and something to think about in a garden. The toughest job was mowing the lawns, as in those days there were no motor mowers (or perhaps they were too expensive for me to buy), but fortunately I was able to get the help on Saturdays of a man called Barney, who worked in the nursery garden. He was a real old-fashioned countryman – strong, hard-working and extremely good-natured, with what was, I suppose, a Surrey country accent (long since disappeared). He worked for us until we left Bridge Barn and we all, including the children, became very fond of him.

Having laid up our car, we took to bicycling. Peggy and I bought secondhand bicycles, we gave Leonora a new one as a special present, and Sara sat on the back of mine (later, when we moved to Shalford, she used to bicycle daily to school along quite a busy main road). One beautiful Sunday afternoon, we set out to find a place for a swim. This involved pushing our bicycles up a fairly steep hill; then we mounted and started down the other side. Almost at once the brakes of my old bicycle gave way, and Sara and I shot down the narrow winding road, going faster and faster; I managed to get round the curves, but didn't know what would happen when we joined a main road at the bottom. Fortunately we came in at a bit of an angle, and I just managed to avoid what would have been a pretty nasty crash. Sara took it bravely, though she naturally didn't realize fully what was happening, sitting with her face against my back. After bicycling on for a bit, we were able to find the small lake we were looking for, and the children thoroughly enjoyed themselves, splashing about in shallow water, with Peggy in charge, while I watched from the bank. So our little expedition, after a bad start, ended well.

Our first winter at Bridge Barn was a very cold one, with heavy snow after Christmas. We all got together one weekend and built quite a large snowman (of whom I still have a photo) outside the front door. He remained there for some time, thanks to the cold weather. The canal was frozen solid and covered with snow, but we managed to clear a small bit and then Peggy and I skated after a fashion – she was much better than me – while the children enjoyed themselves sliding about on the rough ice. So there were some compensations for the harsh winter. That spring Leonora started attending the local school, St Mary's, Horsell, as a day girl – the school was only about half a mile from Bridge Barn – and Sara followed in due course. My impression is that the teaching was quite good, though Leonora learned very little – she was far more interested in hearing what the other girls were doing than in her work.

When the war started, the Air Raid Precautions Department became the Ministry of Home Security, more or less independent of the Home Office. One of the first major acts of the new Ministry was to issue gas masks to the whole population, right down to very small children. Both Leonora and Sara got them, and Sara still remembers the pink container her mother gave her to carry hers in. When I joined the ARP Department, the danger of gas was one of the main problems under discussion, and gas masks were designed and arrangements made for their manufacture. I think the masks were issued partly because the Germans might well have used gas – in fact they never did – and partly because they were ready and available, and were a gesture the Ministry could make. As gas had, of course, been used during the First World War, the possession of masks did help to give people confidence. Although the war was going disastrously for Britain, it was not until August that the bombing of England began – the Battle of Britain – starting with extremely damaging attacks on airfields. But the German losses were so heavy, owing to the skill and bravery of the RAF, that on 7 September Hitler ordered the Luftwaffe to change its tactics and bomb London instead. From then until November, London was bombed almost nightly, and places near it were often hit, either intentionally or by accident.* Occasionally, a German pilot who was afraid to cross London owing to the heavy gunfire would drop his bombs before getting there and then return home. This happened at least once close to Woking. By the time the bombing started, we had acquired an indoor shelter; it had a strong steel top with solid steel supports and steel meshing in between. We set it up in the dining room and at night the four of us – and our dog Nicky – crawled in – first the two children, and then Peggy and me. There was just room for us, though very uncomfortable (by that time we had no residential help), but the children rather enjoyed it as an unusual way of spending the night. We frequently heard the drone of German bombers making their way to London, and the crash of anti-aircraft fire. Bombs were dropped from time to time on or near Woking – probably aimed at the railway junction – and early on several fell on Horsell, not very far from us. I am not at all sure that our shelter was a good idea; it would not have resisted a direct hit, and if the house had collapsed on top of us we would probably have been suffocated. But at the time it gave us confidence. The bombing was totally indiscriminate, even Buckingham Palace being hit. It became so bad at one point that I managed to get ten days leave, and took the family to stay for a while in a farmhouse on the north coast of Wales that I had heard of from a friend.

At the London station, the train was so crowded with people

---

* A little later, other cities were also bombed, Coventry being almost completely destroyed.

trying to get away, that we had to push the children through a window into a carriage and then more or less fight our way along the corridor to join them. After a long slow journey to Caernavon, we hired an old car and drove about fifteen miles or so to the little coastal village where we were to stay. The farmhouse turned out to be a disaster. On arriving there tired and hungry after our long journey, we were not even offered a cup of tea. The owners were surly and unhelpful; we had to live entirely on our rations – very difficult – though they could easily have given us a few eggs, a little bacon and perhaps an occasional piece of chicken (the farm having both hens and pigs). To cap it all, the weather was so bad we could not swim and had nothing to do except walk, usually in the rain. I had intended to leave the family there when my leave was up, but towards the end of our time there, Peggy had the very sad news that her brother John had been killed in Normandy. She said that she could not possibly stay on there alone with the children, so we all returned to Bridge Barn. I have never been to Wales again. Fortunately, by the time we got home, the bombing of the Woking area was dying down, though it continued on London for some time.

I must now say a little about my job. I had, like many other people, a dull, though at times fairly dangerous, war. For about a year I continued with my work at the Ministry of Home Security. It was, of course, during this period that the Germans attacked and defeated the French, capturing Paris on 14 June, while the British – who had fought extremely well – retreated to Dunkirk, from where most of them were rescued by ships of all kinds and sizes, ranging from passenger ships to fishing boats. Standing one morning on the platform at Woking station, I saw two trains go by packed with exhausted, dirty-looking soldiers, mostly without arms – survivors of the Dunkirk rescue.

Before long the Home Guard was started, and I joined up promptly. This involved a parade every Sunday morning, followed by an exercise of some kind, and once every week I had to walk at night through the 'blacked-out' streets of Woking to reach a hall where we were given instructions of various kinds. One detail I remember was being taught how to throw a bomb. After being shown what to do with an empty bomb (they varied a bit), one was taken to a special site and had to throw one or two live ones. This required a little nerve, as, once a particular catch had been released, the bomb, if dropped, or thrown too near, would have exploded with disastrous results. But I don't recall this ever happening in our area. I have sometimes wondered how useful the Home Guard would have been if the Germans had invaded Britain. Clearly they could not have resisted a direct attack by trained German troops, but they could have done a lot to delay the Germans by planting bombs or digging holes in roads, by throwing bombs from points close to a road, by firing from a nearby field or wood, and by harassing supply columns. And as soon as the Germans had wiped out one lot, they would find another group in the next town or village. My guess is – though of course no one can say – that the Home Guard might just have made the difference in helping the British Army to repel the German invaders.

By the summer of 1940, Britain stood alone against Germany. There was every reason to suppose that bombing would soon begin and, if successful, that invasion would follow. The country had been divided up into a number of Civil Defence regions, of which London was the most important. I had by then done about two years at Headquarters, and felt that I ought to take on something more active than deal with files and write letters for Ministers to sign. After a considerable amount of effort, I managed to get myself transferred to the London Region; for a time we occupied part of the Science Museum; then a massive concrete building was quickly built, partly underground, between the Museum and the Cromwell Road. Its most important feature was a large operational room where, once the bombing started, information was received from all the London Boroughs throughout the night about the extent of the bombing in their area, the damage done, whether their services were able to cope or whether help was needed from a neighbouring Borough (which we had to arrange), and so on. At the end of the night a report had to be written and sent to the Ministry of Home Security; then one slept for a bit in one of the small dormitories provided.

During the day, one reverted to administrative work or civil defence, dealing with most of the matters that concerned the local authorities, but acting as a go-between with the Ministry on important questions, particularly those that involved substantial expenditure. I also had to visit some of the London Boroughs from time to time to discuss their problems, say the construction of new shelters or the purchase of vehicles. One rather curious development was that the London tube stations became night shelters for a great many people during the blitz; the platforms were sometimes so crowded – and so dirty – that it was quite difficult to get in and out of a train. Once I had to take shelter there myself on the way back from a night-club with a girlfriend; after a couple of hours or so, it became essential for me to get back to my Headquarters, so we had to leave Leicester Square tube station and walk for about three miles through the blacked-out streets, with a certain amount of bombing still going on. Incidentally, the night-club where we had been dining and dancing – the Café de Paris – was later destroyed by a bomb.

In due course the bombing of London came to an end. The Germans switched their attacks to other cities, Coventry suffering the worst damage (though its vital engineering factories were working again in a surprisingly short time). The bombing of England gradually petered out, and by May had virtually ceased. Soon after this, I felt that I had completed my stint at the London Civil Defence Region, and was able to get myself transferred back to the Ministry of Home Security – this time to a Division located in the old Home Office building opposite the Cenotaph. The work was important and reasonably interesting. I joined the Home Office platoon of the Home Guard, and had also to spend one night a week as a 'fire-watcher' to deal with incendiary bombs if they were dropped on the roof of the building. Fortunately they were not – it would have been a dangerous and unpleasant job trying to extinguish one, as they were explosive as well as incendiary.

For a year and a half, after the defeat of France, Britain and the Commonwealth stood alone in the West. We would not have survived if we had not been able to obtain supplies from the USA, first on a 'cash and carry' basis and then, when that great man and friend of Britain, President Roosevelt, obtained office for a third time, on 'lend-lease', with transport ships protected by the American Navy during the 'Battle of the

Atlantic'. On 7 December, 1941, the Japanese attacked Pearl Harbour, and a few days later Germany and Italy declared war on the USA in support of their ally. The world was now at war.

Before long, American staff and their troops began to arrive in England. London was soon full of them, their main aim seemed to be to acquire a girlfriend, and as they had plenty of money and knew how to deal with women, it was not long before practically every unattached girl, from the daughter of a Peer to a tart, had an American soldier boyfriend. It was the same, whether one went to the Dorchester or to a pub – nearly all the girls were with Americans. Quite a lot of them got married and at the end of the war went to live in the USA. One was Peggy's youngest sister – she still had pigtails when I first knew her – who became engaged to and eventually married an American naval officer, who in due course became a Vice-Admiral.

At an early stage, a joint headquarters with the British was established in St James's Square, close to my club and close also to Chatham House (the Royal Institute of International Affairs), where I later worked. Peggy's brother, John Fass, by then a Captain, who had joined the Berkshire Regiment on leaving Sandhurst and later transferred to the Welsh Guards, worked at this headquarters for a time, and we used to lunch together occasionally.Shortly before we and the Americans invaded France, John felt that he – as a regular soldier – ought to be playing a more active role, and rejoined his regiment. He was shot and killed soon afterwards as the British Army fought to capture Caen from the Germans. A sad but brave death.

My own job went on much as I have described it until the end of the war – necessary, unexciting and at times moderately dangerous. I have already mentioned the V1 and V2 bombing that we had at Woking. In London it was, of course, much worse. I can't pretend that I enjoyed sitting at my desk, hearing the noise of a flying bomb approaching nearer and nearer, then a sudden silence, followed by a loud bang as the bomb exploded. Once, when I was visiting someone in an office off Victoria Street, a bomb fell within fifty yards, shaking the building violently and bringing down part of the ceiling. But I was lucky, and was never injured.

On 6 June, 1944, the British and American Armies invaded Normandy. I had no part at all in this, but we were all immensely excited, and most of us felt sure that we were going to succeed. After a difficult but successful landing, both our Armies were pinned down for a bit. Montgomery, who was in full command, concentrated the British in front of Caen – which we just failed to capture on the first day – in order to reduce the forces facing the American army. On 27 June they entered Cherbourg, and the Allies had gained their first port. After six and a half weeks, the Americans broke out of the *Bocage* (wooded country) and under General Patton advanced across France at great speed. Soon afterwards, the British captured Caen and advanced with equal rapidity. The French, under General de Gaulle, entered Paris on 25 August. Before long, the Allied Armies had reached the Rhine. I still remember Montgomery's attempt to outflank the Germans and cross the Rhine at Arnhem – it failed, but it failed with the utmost bravery on the part of the Parachute Division.

By the winter of 1944-45, it was certain that the Allies were going to win the war. This is not a history, so I will not go into further details except for one vital point – Berlin. The Americans and British had tentatively decided in the late autumn of 1944 to march on Berlin. Churchill wanted to do it, but by April 1945 we were further from Berlin than we expected, while the Russians were very close to it. Eisenhower decided to give priority to a drive through Western Germany and leave the Russians to capture Berlin. They did so on 2 May – to our great disadvantage. Two days before, Hitler and his mistress, Eva Braun, committed suicide. The war with Germany was almost over.

It went on for a little longer with Japan. After rejecting an ultimatum from the Allies, President Truman ordered an atomic bomb to be dropped on Hiroshima. Three days later, a second atomic bomb was dropped on Nagasaki. Both cities were almost completely destroyed. On 2 September, the Japanese surrendered.

Not long afterwards – I can't remember the date – there was a Victory March through London. By this time, I had changed my job and was in a Home Office division dealing with what were known as the 'nasty traffics' – dangerous drugs, poisons, and traffic in women and children. My office was in a building on the Embankment, close to Westminster Bridge and the Houses of Parliament. As the troops were to march along the Embankment and then turn into Parliament Square, this made an excellent place from which to watch. I arranged for my family to come up to London for the occasion, and also invited my brother (who must have been on leave) and his wife and daughter, and a close friend of my wife's.

The march-past was a splendid sight, and I think we all had a feeling of relief and happiness that Britain had won the war, after so much hardship and loss. When the march-past was over, we needed – with the exception of Peggy's friend, Pamela Poole – to get to Ebury Street, where we were staying the night in a small hotel. It had been agreed that I would accompany Pamela for a short way and then rejoin the family at Westminster underground station. Having got her safely started by back ways in the direction of a ladies' club in Pall Mall, I returned to find the most appalling crowds milling around Westminster – some trying to cross the bridge to get to Waterloo, others to reach the underground station or to get up or down Whitehall or wherever they wanted to go. I almost had to fight my way through the crowd, wondering anxiously where the family would be. Then I saw them, jammed against a hoarding close to the station, Brian with his daughter on his shoulders, and Peggy with the two children sheltering in front of her. They had had a difficult and dangerous time getting the short distance to where they were; if one of the children had fallen, they might easily have been trampled underfoot. After waiting for some time, praying that the crowd would not suddenly sway in our direction, people began to disperse, and we decided to risk taking an underground train to Victoria – it was too far to walk, and there was no chance of getting a taxi. We were lucky this time; just as we reached the platform a train came in, most of the people waiting managed to force their way into it, but a few others, myself included, did not attempt to do so. Then, a minute or so later, another train came in, not heavily overcrowded this time, and before long we were at the Ebury Court Hotel, which was run by Peggy's former boy friend, Romer Topham, and his wife. Having put the children to bed, we had a pleasant evening in the bar, drinking with the Tophams and their friends in celebration of the Allied victory.

After the end of the war, we remained at Bridge Barn for a few months. Although the fighting and bombing was over, ordinary living conditions got worse for some time. In particular, the shortage of food intensified, and I think we would have nearly starved if we had still not had our hens, and Peggy had not been able to go on making jam from our own fruit. But we were happy at Bridge Barn, and would have liked to stay on there. We loved the house and its surroundings; it was easy for me to get to London, and the children were now doing quite well at their school.

Unfortunately for us, the retired naval officer from whom I had sub-rented the house – he didn't own it – wanted to return and couldn't be dissuaded. So, sadly, we had to decide to leave.

It was not at all easy at that time to find a house; none had been built during the war, and many people were wanting them. Moreover, I then had very little capital. After a lot of fruitless searching round, we heard of a house in Guildford that sounded interesting. Leonora, then aged twelve, and I went over by bus to see it. It was called Mount Manor House, and was in a street, The Mount, that ran steeply up immediately opposite Guildford High Street. We both fell in love with it. The date 1687 was marked above the front door and – we heard later – James II had used it as a hunting lodge. Since those days it had been pulled about a lot, and during the war had fallen into a state of disrepair, with a very old man living there alone. There were some charming rooms – all badly in need of redecoration – and an appallingly primitive kitchen. It had a pretty little garden, with mulberry trees that we loved, and from the top one looked over a wall onto the railway line just outside Guildford Station. It was a combination of the beautiful and the primitive, the convenient and the inconvenient. When Leonora and I returned to Bridge Barn, we told Peggy that we had found the right house for us. I suppose she must have seen it before I bought it – at a very modest price – and agreed to put up with the primitive kitchen and other drawbacks.

In due course, on a cold winter's day, we said goodbye to Bridge Barn with deep regret, and set off for Guildford in a van loaded up with most of our furniture and all our luggage. The children were quite excited, Peggy and I were not.

But once we had got settled in, our new house offered many advantages. It was a short walk to the station for me, the girls could get a bus at the bottom of The Mount to take them to an excellent school – St Catherine's, Bramley – and Peggy was well placed to shop. Guildford was still a delightful old country town with many interesting buildings. On Sundays we used to go to church at St Mary's, Quarry Street – the oldest church, part of it going back to Saxon times. I can still remember attending services there with Peggy and the two little girls.

I won't say much more about Mount Manor House. We had the drawing room redecorated, and with our own furniture it became a pleasant room; there was a bow window at one end from which one could look down The Mount and up the High Street. Upstairs, Leonora had a tiny bedroom and had got to the stage when she spent a lot of time looking out of her window watching people walking up and down, including loving couples wanting to get out of the town. Sara had a larger room on the garden side, and we had a small wooden platform fixed outside her window to enable a beautiful cat we had just acquired to get in and out of the house. The cat, called Landy (Orlando), remained with us for years, and we were all devoted to him. One other small point: upstairs above the bedrooms were several dusty old attics and passages, and the girls had great fun playing hide and seek, first of all with me and later with some of their school friends.

Sadly, soon after getting to our new home, my father died. He and my mother had been obliged to leave their flat in Kensington after it had been damaged by bombing. Although not injured, he had been badly shaken up, and after a spell in hospital I took him down – by train, of course, as the war was still on – to Parkstone (Bournemouth), where his sister (my Aunt Gracie) was able to rent him a couple of rooms in a house immediately opposite her own. But he went downhill steadily, and died not long after the end of the war. I was there at the time.

The funeral took place at Brookwood Cemetery, where the family owned – and still own – a sizable plot. Afterwards we had a family gathering, with food and drinks, at Mount Manor House for all who could get there, including, of course, my mother, who stayed on afterwards with us for a week, my brother Brian, Aunt Gracie, and Uncle Jack, my father's oldest and best friend.

Somehow, as the garden door from the Mount was being frequently opened and shut, our little dog Nicky managed to get out and disappear. I rushed down the street after her – fortunately she was not run over at the bottom – and I found her a short way up the river resisting the advances of a large Alsatian (Nicky was about to come on heat). I rescued her just in time – a fight might have easily occurred with fatal results for her – and I carried her back to the house. No one seemed to have noticed my absence – probably they thought I was doing something in the kitchen.

After a year and a half in Guildford, during which time I continued to work at the Home Office, I was unexpectedly offered the post of Deputy Director of the Narcotics Division of the United Nations Secretariat. This was because the Director of the new Division (the United Nations was, of course, itself a new body) was an extremely astute Austrian of Jewish descent, named Leon Steinig. While on a visit to Europe, he had called at the Home Office for a discussion on the subject of dangerous drugs, and I think I can say that I impressed him favourably since, not long afterwards, the offer of the UN job came along. The salary was high, the work sounded interesting, and I wanted a change. I decided to accept.

At the end of January 1947, I said goodbye to the family (who joined me six months later), caught a special train from Waterloo to Southampton, and there boarded the *Queen Elizabeth* – the largest liner in the world. Lunch was ready immediately, and I found myself sitting at a large round table with Noel Coward and Gertie Lawrence opposite me. Neither seemed to have much to say.

At future meals things were rearranged, and a group of us connected with the Diplomatic Services and the UN Secretariat sat together. I can't say I enjoyed the voyage very much. It was extremely rough and windy and there was neither time nor opportunity to get to know people – rather like staying at an expensive hotel. After the short voyage, we passed the Statue of Liberty and then suddenly saw the skyscrapers of New York rising ahead of us – even more impressive than I had expected. I felt both excited and a bit nervous, hoping that my new job in a new country would turn out well.

* 1,000,000 *
Free E-Books
@
www.ForgottenBooks.org

* Alchemy *
The Secret is Revealed
@
www.TheBookofAquarius.com

Forgotten Books

A Comparative Grammar of the Teutonic Languages

By

Jacob Helfenstein

Published by Forgotten Books 2012
Originally Published 1870

PIBN 1000163095

Copyright © 2012 Forgotten Books
www.forgottenbooks.org

A

COMPARATIVE GRAMMAR

OF THE

TEUTONIC LANGUAGES.

BEING AT THE SAME TIME

A HISTORICAL GRAMMAR OF THE ENGLISH LANGUAGE.

And comprising

GOTHIC, ANGLO-SAXON, EARLY ENGLISH, MODERN ENGLISH,
ICELANDIC (OLD NORSE), DANISH, SWEDISH,
OLD HIGH GERMAN, MIDDLE HIGH GERMAN, MODERN GERMAN, OLD SAXON,
OLD FRISIAN, DUTCH.

BY

JAMES HELFENSTEIN, Ph. D.

BOOKSELLERS & STATIONERS
VANNEVAR & CO.
440 YONGE STREET, · · TORONTO.

London
MACMILLAN AND CO.
1870

[*All rights reserved*]

OXFORD:

BY T. COMBE, M.A., E. B. GARDNER, AND E. PICKARD HALL,
PRINTERS TO THE UNIVERSITY.

PREFACE.

The advantages of a systematic study of our own language are now so generally understood that it will hardly require an apology for any attempt to promote and facilitate research in this direction. By offering my Grammar to the kind consideration of the public, I intend above all to offer the student of English a guide which may lead him through its different stages of development, and show how it arrived at its present grammatical structure. Thus then my volume may be used as an Historical Grammar of the English language.

In order to gain a clear insight into the development of the English, or any other idiom, it is absolutely necessary to pay attention to the historical course of its sister dialects, as the German, the Dutch, the Danish — to compare the different phenomena they present, and thus to arrive at the laws which directed the growth of each. I have therefore placed the Teutonic languages in their different phases of development side by side, so that they may be studied in the relation they bear to one another and to the English language in particular; and I hope I have given all the necessary data for the study of Comparative Grammar. Thus far I have had in view the educated classes in general, who are perfectly alive to the interest and importance attached to the study of their own language.

In working out the chapters on the Ancient and Middle Teutonic languages I took care not to omit any grammatical form the knowledge of which is required for the study of ancient literature, whether Gothic, or Anglo-Saxon, or Early English. The reader will find the grammar of each dialect sufficiently complete to enable him who has mastered the details contained therein to proceed at once to the study of the literature of his chosen dialect.

In order not to stop short in our studies at a point where they promise to become most interesting, I have added at the opening of each chapter a sketch showing the relation of the Teutonic to the cognate languages, Greek, Latin, and Sanskrit. Thus then the student of English is enabled to follow up certain parts of his language, such as numerals, pronouns, &c., to their most ancient forms — forms which in antiquity reach back to the very dawn of civilization.

If on the one hand I have endeavoured to enter as far as possible into the details of Ancient and Middle Teutonic Grammar, I have abstained on the other from giving a detailed account of the Grammar of Modern English, German, or Danish. These languages were treated only so far as is required to show the peculiarities of their grammatical structure and the way by which they arrived at the same. Those who wish to acquire any of these languages for practical purposes must apply to the respective Grammars.

Another object (last not least) I had in view, was to supply

PREFACE.

a preparatory manual for those students who intend to make Teutonic language and literature a special study, and who must have recourse to the works of Grimm, Bopp, Pott, Schleicher, and others, celebrated on the field of Teutonic and Comparative Grammar. He who has been obliged to pass directly to the study of Grimm's works will be able to acknowledge the desirableness of an introductory text-book.

I have tried to consult the best authorities and to convey to the reader's mind the established results of modern research. In the chapters which treat on the Science of Language and Comparative Grammar in general I have made use of the works of Bopp, Schleicher, and Max Müller. Those on the ancient Teutonic languages owe the greater part of their materials to Grimm; while Heyne's volume on the same subject has supplied much valuable information. As to the English language in particular I have chiefly consulted Koch's Grammar and Marsh's Lectures. All these authors and their respective works are enumerated on a separate list.

I have every reason to feel anxious about the fate of my book. Comparing the magnitude of the subject with the smallness of my abilities and the limitedness of my knowledge, I might quail before the censure of the public, if there were not some points redeeming the rashness of my enterprise. The first lies in the fact that there are many educated men in England and America who apply themselves to the study of Early English, Anglo-Saxon, and the Teutonic languages in general, while no work exists as yet in English treating on the Teutonic languages collectively. Further I may plead the earnestness and diligence with which I pursued my work, endeavouring by this means to supply the deficiency in knowledge and abilities. But even these considerations would fail to set my mind at rest, if I were not penetrated with the conviction that the English public are always ready to promote every work which aims at the advancement of science and art, if conducted with perseverance and earnestness of purpose and which promises to be useful, on however limited a scale, to some one or other.

Thus, then, I take leave of my work, which for six years has been my constant companion in trials and sorrows; and I dare to hope that it may not be altogether rejected by those for whom it is intended.

THE AUTHOR.

WHITSUNTIDE, 1870.

CONTENTS.

	PAGE
INTRODUCTION	1
Languages and Dialects	4
Tribes of Teutonic Languages—Gothic, Old High German, Middle High German, New High German	5
Languages spoken in Britain—Celtic, Latin, Anglo-Saxon	8
Southern and Northern Dialect	10
Old Norse and Anglo-Saxon. Norman and French, reaction against its use	11
Late Saxon (Semi-Saxon), Old and Middle English	12
Modern English	13
Old Norse, Icelandic	14
Swedish, Danish, Low German, Old Frisian, Old Saxon	15
Tribes of Aryan languages—the Indian class, the Iranic, Greek, Italic, Slavonic, Lithuanian, Celtic	16
The Primitive language (Ursprache). Relationship of the Aryan languages	18
DIAGRAMS SHOWING THE RELATION OF THE ARYAN AND OF THE TEUTONIC LANGUAGES	20

VOWEL SOUNDS.

Pitch of the Vowels	21
Primitive Vowels; Gradation of Vowels (Steigerung)	22
Degradation or Weakening (Schwachung)	23
Table of Gradations	24

I. OLD TEUTONIC VOWELS.

Short Vowels:—

The Vowel *a* in Gothic and Old High German	26
Umlaut in Old High German; *a* in Old Saxon and Anglo-Saxon	26
ä for *a* in Anglo-Saxon; Umlaut of *a* in Anglo-Saxon	27
a in Old Frisian and Old Norse; Umlaut in Old Norse	28
The Vowel *i* in Gothic, Old High German, Old Saxon, Anglo-Saxon, Old Frisian, Old Norse	29

CONTENTS.

	PAGE
The Vowel u in Gothic and Old High German. Weakening of the u into o.	31
The Vowel $\breve{u}$ (and its weakened form o) in Old Saxon, Anglo-Saxon, Old Frisian, Old Norse; its Umlaut y in Old Norse.	32
The Vowels $e, \breve{o}, y$.	33
Brechung (breaking) of Vowels in Gothic, Old High German, Anglo-Saxon, Old Norse	33
Assimilation.	37

Long Vowels:—

The Vowel a in Old High German.	38
The Vowel $\bar{a}$ in the different Dialects; $æ$ the Umlaut of a	39
$æ$ supplanting a in Anglo-Saxon. The Vowel e	40
$e = ei$ (Gothic ai). The Reduplicational e	41
e, Umlaut of $\hat{o}$ (u) in Anglo-Saxon and Old Frisian. The Production of e.	42
The Vowels $\hat{i}, \hat{o}$	43
The Vowel u; $\acute{y}$ Umlaut of u.	45

Diphthongs:—

ai, ei	47
iu and its weakened form io	48
io (ie, ia) for the ancient Reduplication	49
$e\acute{o}$ in Anglo-Saxon for Gothic iu	50
au in different Dialects.	51
ou, Old High German for Gothic au	52
ea, Anglo-Saxon for Gothic au. uo, Old High German for $\hat{o}$. ey, Old Norse Umlaut of au	53

II. MIDDLE TEUTONIC VOWELS.

Short Vowels:—

The Vowel a in Middle High German, Old and Middle English	54
The Vowel e in Middle High German, Old English and Middle English	55
The Vowel i in Middle High German, Old English and Middle English	57
The Vowel o in Middle High German	58
o Umlaut of o in Middle High German	59
o in Old English and Middle English	60
The Vowel u in Middle High German. $\ddot{u}$ Umlaut of u	60
The Vowel u in Old English and Middle English	61
The Vowel y in Middle High German, Old English and Middle English	61
Brechung of Vowels in Middle Teutonic.	62

Long Vowels:—

| The Vowel a in Middle High German, Old English and Middle English | 63 |

CONTENTS.

	PAGE
The Vowel *æ* Umlaut of *a* in Middle High German; the Vowel *æ* in Old English and Middle English	64
The Vowel *e* in Middle High German, Old English and Middle English	64
The Vowel *i* in Middle High German, Old English and Middle English	64
The Vowel *ô* in Middle High German, Old English and Middle English	65
The Vowel *û* in Middle High German, Old English and Middle English; *y* and *u* in Old English and Middle English	66

Diphthongs:—

ei in Middle High German	66
ie, iu, ou in Middle High German	67
uo, ai, au, ey, oi, oy, ai, au, eu, öi in Middle High German	68
ou, eó, eá in Old English and Middle English	69

III. NEW TEUTONIC VOWELS.

The Vowel *a* in German, English, Dutch, Swedish and Danish	70
The Vowel *a* (*æ*) in German, Swedish and Danish	73
The Vowel *e* in German, English, Dutch, Swedish and Danish	74
The Vowel *i* in German and English	76
The Vowel *i*, in Dutch *ij* (Flemish *y*), the long *i*	77
The Vowel *i* in Swedish and Danish	78
The Vowel *o* in German, English, Dutch, Swedish and Danish	78
The Vowel *o* in German, Swedish and Danish	81
The Vowel *u* in German, English, Dutch, Swedish and Danish	82
The Vowels *u* (*ue*), *y*, in German	84
The Vowel *y* in English, Swedish and Danish	85

Diphthongs:—

The German *ai, au*	86
äu Umlaut of the German *au*; the German *ei*; *ei* and *eu*	87
The German *eu, ie*; the English *ai*	88
The English *au, aw, ea, ei, ew, ey, ie, oa, oe, ou, ow, ue*	89
The Diphthongs in Romance words	90
The Dutch *ai, au, ei, eu, ie, oe, ou, ue, ui*	91
Diphthongs in Swedish and Danish	93
The Danish *au, ei, oi, ju, ou*	94

Triphthongs:—

The Insertion of *j* in Danish	95

CONSONANTS.

Physiological Alphabet	97
Table of Consonants in Sanskrit, in the Primitive Languages, and in Gothic	98
Grimm's Law	99
General Table of Grimm's Law	103

CONTENTS

	PAGE
OLD TEUTONIC CONSONANTS	104

Liquids :—

The *r* in Gothic	105
Rhotacism (*s* changed into *r*)	106
The *m* and *n* in different Dialects	107

Spirants :—

v and *w* in Gothic and Old High German	109
w in Old Saxon and Anglo-Saxon	110
v and *w* in Old Frisian and Old Norse	112
s and *z* in Gothic ; *s* in Old High German and Old Saxon	113
The combination *sc* in Anglo-Saxon; the *s* in Old Frisian and Old Norse	114
The spirant *j* in Gothic, Old High German, Old Saxon, Anglo-Saxon, Old Frisian and Old Norse	115
The *h* in Gothic, Old High German, Old Saxon, Anglo-Saxon, Old Frisian and Old Norse	116

Mutes (Labials) :—

b, *p*, *f* in Gothic, *c* and *p* in Old High German	119
The Labial Aspirates *ph*, *pf*, *f*, *v* in Old High German	120
Table of Labials in Old High German	120
b and *p* in Old Saxon	120
The Aspirates *ƀ*, *v*, *f*, *ph* in Old Saxon	120
The Labials *b*, *p*, *f* in Anglo-Saxon, Old Frisian, and Old Norse	121

——— (Dentals) :—

The Gothic *d*, *t*, þ	123
The Old High German *d*, *t*, *z*, ʒ	123
Table of Dentals in Old High German	125
The Old Saxon Dentals, *d*, *t*, *f*, *th*. The Anglo-Saxon *d*, *t*, ð, þ	125
The Dentals *d*, *t*, *th* in Old Frisian	126
The Dentals *d*, *t*, ð, þ in Old Norse	127

——— (Gutturals) :—

The Gothic *g*, *k*, *q*	128
The Old High German *g*, *k*, *ch* (*hh*, *h*)	128
Table of Gutturals in Old High German	129
The Old Saxon *q*, *c* (*k*)	129
The Anglo-Saxon *g*, *c* (*k*)	130
The Old Frisian *g*, *k*	130
Change of Gutturals into Palatals	131
The Old Norse *g*, *k*	132

MIDDLE TEUTONIC CONSONANTS.

Liquids in Middle High German, Old English and Middle English	132
Spirants in Middle High German, Old English and Middle English	134

CONTENTS.

Mutes:—
    Labials in Middle High German, Old English and Middle English . 138
    Dentals in Middle High German, Old English and Middle English . 141
    Gutturals in Middle High German, Old English and Middle English . 143

NEW TEUTONIC CONSONANTS.
  Liquids in German, English, Dutch, Swedish and Danish . 147
  Spirants in German, English, Dutch, Swedish and Danish . 149
  Mutes:—
    Labials in German, English, Dutch, Swedish and Danish . 153
    Dentals in German, English, Dutch, Swedish and Danish . 156
    Gutturals in German, English, Dutch, Swedish and Danish . 160

ROOTS AND THEMES . 166
  SUFFIXES USED IN THE FORMATION OF THEMES.
    (1) Verbal Themes:—
      ya (a-ya) . 168
    (2) Nominal Themes:—
      a, i . 169
      u, ya . 170
      ra (van) . 171
      ma (man), ra (la) . 172
      an, ana, na . 173
      ni, nu, ta . 174
      tar, tra . 175
      ti, tu . 176
      ant (nt), as . 177
      ka . 178

PRONOUNS.
  PERSONAL PRONOUNS.
    Table of Personal Pronouns in the Cognate Languages . 179
    Remarks on the Personal Pronouns of the Cognate Languages . 180
    Table of the Old Teutonic Personal Pronouns . 186
    Remarks on the Pronouns in the Old Teutonic Languages . 187
    Table of Personal Pronouns in the Middle and New Teutonic Languages . 188
  ADJECTIVE PRONOUNS.
    Pronominal Bases . 190
    Table of Old Teutonic Pronouns of the 3rd person . 193
    Remarks on the Pronouns of the 3rd person . 194
    Table of Middle and New Teutonic Pronouns of the 3rd person . 195
    Remarks on the Middle and New Teutonic Pronouns of the 3rd person . 196

POSSESSIVE PRONOUNS.

	PAGE
Table of Old Teutonic Possessive Pronouns	197
Table of Middle and New Teutonic Possessive Pronouns	198
Remarks on the Possessive Pronouns (APPENDIX)	527

DEMONSTRATIVE PRONOUNS.

First Demonstrative (is)	199
Table of Demonstrative Pronouns in the Middle and New Teutonic Dialects	201
Remarks on the New Teutonic Demonstratives	202
Second Demonstrative (hic)	204
Third Demonstrative (ille)	206
The Suffixed Article in the Scandinavian Languages	207
Other Demonstratives	208

INTERROGATIVE PRONOUNS.

Table of Interrogative Pronouns	210
(1) *Quis?*	210
(2) *Uter?*	211
(3) *Quis eorum?*	211
(4) *Qualis?*	211

RELATIVE PRONOUNS . . . 212

INDEFINITE PRONOUNS . . . 213

NUMERALS.

CARDINALS.

Table of Cardinal Numerals in the Cognate Languages	215
Remarks on the Cardinal Numerals in the Cognate Languages	216
Table of Cardinals in the Old Teutonic Languages	222
Table of Cardinals in the Middle Teutonic Languages	222
Table of Cardinals in the New Teutonic Languages	223
Remarks on the Teutonic Cardinals	224
Declension of Cardinals:—	
Old Teutonic Languages	232
Middle and New Teutonic Languages	234

ORDINALS.

Table of Ordinals in the Cognate Languages	237
Table of Ordinals in the Teutonic Languages	240
Remarks on the Teutonic Ordinals	241

OTHER NUMERALS.

Old Teutonic Languages	244
Middle and Modern Teutonic Languages	246

CONTENTS.

COMPARISONS.

COMPARATIVE BASES IN THE COGNATE LANGUAGES.

(1) Formations with the Suffix *yans* 248
(2) Formations with the Suffix *tara* and *ra* 249

SUPERLATIVE BASES IN THE COGNATE LANGUAGES.

(1) Formations with the Suffix *-ta* 250
(2) Formations with the Suffix *-ma* 251
(3) Formations with the Suffix *ta-ma* 251

OLD TEUTONIC LANGUAGES.

(1) The Comparative 252
    Remarks on the Comparative Form in the Different Dialects . 253
(2) The Superlative 254
    Table of Comparisons 255
(3) Anomalous Forms 255
(4) Defective Comparisons 256
(5) Comparison of the Adverbs 259

MIDDLE AND NEW TEUTONIC LANGUAGES.

Formations in *ir* 260
Formations in *or* 261
Anomalous and Defective Comparisons 263

DECLENSIONS.

THE COGNATE LANGUAGES.

Numbers, Cases, Genders. 265
The Terminations of Nominal Themes 267
    (1) Consonantal Themes 268
    (2) Vocalic Themes 268
Formation of the Cases 269

THE OLD TEUTONIC LANGUAGES.

Strong Declension 281
Formation of the Cases 281
The Plural Neuter with the Suffix *ir* 286
The Umlaut 286

PARADIGMS.

Vocal Themes (Strong Declension) :—
    Themes in *a* in Gothic, Old High German, Old Saxon,
      Anglo-Saxon, Old Frisian, Old Norse . . . 289
    Notes to the Declension in *a* 292
    Themes in *ja* (*ya*), in Gothic, Old High German, Old Saxon,
      Anglo-Saxon, Old Norse 297
    Notes to the Declension in *ja* 299

CONTENTS.

	PAGE
Themes in *va*, in Gothic, Old High German, Old Saxon, Old Norse	302
Notes to the Declension in *va*	303
Themes in *i* in Gothic, Old High German, Old Saxon, Anglo-Saxon, Old Frisian, Old Norse	304
Examples and Remarks to the Declension in *i*	306
Themes in *u* in Gothic, Old High German, Old Saxon, Anglo-Saxon, Old Frisian and Old Norse	311
Notes and examples to the Declension in *u*	312

Consonantal Themes (Weak Declension):—

Themes in *n* in Gothic, Old High German, Old Saxon, Anglo-Saxon, Old Frisian, Old Norse	315
Remarks on the Weak Declensions	317
Words belonging to the Weak Declension in Gothic, Old High German, Old Saxon, Anglo-Saxon, Old Frisian, and Old Norse	320

Other Consonantal Themes:—

Declension of Themes in *tar* in Gothic, Old High German, Old Saxon, Anglo-Saxon, Old Frisian, Old Norse	322
Themes in *nd* in Gothic, Old High German, Old Saxon, Old Frisian, Old Norse	324
Themes ending in a Guttural or Dental in Gothic, Old High German, Old Saxon, Anglo-Saxon, Old Frisian and Old Norse	325
Anomalous Declensions in Gothic, Old High German, Old Saxon, Anglo-Saxon, Old Frisian and Old Norse	327

DECLENSION OF PROPER NAMES in Gothic, Old High German, Old Saxon, Anglo-Saxon, Old Frisian and Old Norse . . 329

DECLENSION OF ADJECTIVES.

Strong Declension in Gothic, Old High German, Old Saxon, Anglo-Saxon, Old Frisian and Old Norse	331
Remarks on the Strong Declension of Adjectives	334
Weak Declension in Gothic, Old High German, Old Saxon, Anglo-Saxon, Old Frisian and Old Norse	339
Remarks on the Weak Declensions	340
Declension of the Participles:—	
Present Participle	341
Preterite Participle	342
Declension of the Infinitive	342

MIDDLE TEUTONIC DECLENSIONS 343

Declensions in Old and Middle English, Middle High German, and Middle Dutch 344

CONTENTS.

xvii

	PAGE
MODERN TEUTONIC DECLENSIONS	
Declensions in English, German, Dutch, Swedish, and Danish	349
DECLENSION OF THE ADJECTIVE IN THE MIDDLE AND NEW TEUTONIC DIALECTS.	
Declension of the Adjective in Old English, Middle English, Middle High German, Middle Dutch, German, Dutch, Swedish, Danish	359

THE VERB.

Stem Verbs and Derivative Verbs—Verbal Roots and Themes	365
Personal Terminations—Modi, Tenses	366
Formation of the Persons in the Cognate Languages	367
Formation of the Persons in the Teutonic Languages	372
The Persons of the Medium or Middle Voice	376
Formation of the Modi (Moods)	377
The Modi in the Teutonic Languages	378
Tempora (Tenses)—Formation of the Present Theme	380
Formation of the Present Theme in the Teutonic Languages	388
Themes in *ja*, in *o*, in *ai*	389
Formation of the Perfect Theme in the Cognate Languages	392
Perfect in -s-	401
The Compound (Weak) Perfect in the Teutonic Dialects	401
The Infinitive	403
Participles:—	
Present Participle Active	404
Perfect Participle Passive of Stem Verbs	406
Perfect Participle Passive of Derivative Verbs	406
The Perfect in the Teutonic Languages—Reduplication (Ablaut)—Classification of Strong Verbs	408
Conjugation—General Remarks	423
I. Paradigm to the Strong Conjugation in the Old Teutonic Dialects	426
II. Paradigm to the Strong Conjugation in the Old Teutonic Dialects	428
Remarks on the Strong Conjugation	429
Middle and New Teutonic Conjugations	439
Classification of Strong Verbs	445
Paradigms to the Middle and New Teutonic Strong Conjugations	459
Remarks on the Conjugation in Middle and New Teutonic	462
Weak Conjugations:—	
First conjugation (Connective *ja*)	475
Second Conjugation (Connective *ô*)	478
Third Conjugation (Connective *ai*)	479
Remarks on the Weak Conjugations:—	
First Conjugation	480
Second and Third Conjugations	484
Verbs belonging to the Weak Conjugations	487
Varbs belonging to the Second and Third Conjugation	489

CONTENTS.

	PAGE
Weak Conjugation in the Middle and New Teutonic Languages	491
Anomalous Verbs	499
Verbs without a Connective or Thematic Vowel	500
The Verb 'to be'	504
Remarks on the Paradigm	508
Præterito-Præsentia in the Old Teutonic Languages	515
Remarks on the Paradigms of the Præterito-Præsentia	518
Verbs following the analogy of Præterito-Præsentia	519
Præterito-Præsentia in the Middle and New Teutonic Languages	521
Verbs following the analogy of Præterito-Præsentia	524

APPENDIX.

   Remarks on the Possessive Pronouns (*omitted in proper place*) . . 527

TECHNICAL TERMS.

Ablaut. The modification of the radical vowel of the verb in the preterite tense and preterite participle; e. g. English wr*i*te, wr*o*te, wr*i*tten, s*i*ng, s*a*ng, s*u*ng; German g*e*lten, galt, geg*o*lten, s*i*ngen, s*a*ng, ges*u*ngen.

Umlaut. The modification of a vowel caused by another vowel in the succeeding syllable; e. g. Old Norse g*i*afa, dative gi*o*fu, where *o*, the Umlaut of *a*, is caused by the *u* in the succeeding syllable; Old High German palc, plural p*e*lkî, where the *a* of the root is changed into *e* under the influence of a succeeding *i*. The same changes take place in German inflexions; e. g. v*a*ter, plur. v*a*ter; hoch, comparative *höher;* kl*u*g, kl*ü*glich.

Trübung, Schwachung. *Darkening, Weakening (Degradation),* of vowels; e. g. Gothic h*i*lpa, Anglo-Saxon h*e*lpe, *i* weakened into *e*; Gothic st*u*lans, Anglo-Saxon st*o*len, *u* weakened into *o*; Gothic stal, Anglo-Saxon stal, *a* weakened into *a*. Compare Latin corp*u*s, corp*o*r-is; pulv*i*s, pulv*e*r-is; f*a*cio, conf*i*cio.

Brechung. *Breaking* of vowels takes place in Gothic, where an *i* or *u*, under the influence of a succeeding *h* or *r*, is changed into *ai*, *au*, respectively—*broken*, as it were, in two vowels; e. g. Latin vir, Gothic v*ai*r; Latin d*u*ximus, Gothic ta*u*hum.

Metathesis. The transposition of certain letters in the same word; e. g. Anglo-Saxon g*ä*rs and gr*a*s; English h*o*rse, German (h)r*o*ss. Compare Latin sp*e*rno, spr*e*vi.

Rhotacism. The change of *s* into *r*, e. g. Old High German ro*r*, Gothic rau*s*, English wa*s*, German wa*r*. Compare Latin hono*r* and hono*s*, ru*s*, ru*r*-is.

Gradation. The combination of a primitive vowel (*a*, *i*, *u*) with the vowel *a*, whence result $a + a, a + i, a + u$; which combinations occur in the different languages under various modifications, as the Grammar will show. (See Introduction.)

All other terms are used in the same sense as in Latin Grammar, or they will find their special explanation in their proper places.

WORKS PRINCIPALLY USED.

A Comparative Grammar of the Sanskrit, Zend, Greek, Latin, Lithuanian, Gothic, German, and Slavonic Languages, by Professor F. BOPP. Translated from the German by EDWARD B. EASTWICK, F.R.S., F.S.A. London: Williams and Norgate, 1862.

Compendium der Vergleichenden Grammatik der Indogermanischen Sprachen, von AUGUST SCHLEICHER. Zweite Auflage. Weimar: Hermann Bohlau, 1866.

Lectures on the Science of Language, by MAX MULLER. First Series. Fourth edition. London: Longmans, 1864.

Lectures on the Science of Language, by MAX MULLER. Second Series. London, 1864.

Deutsche Grammatik, von JACOB GRIMM. Erster Theil. Dritte Ausgabe. Gottingen: Dietrichsche Buchhandlung, 1840.

Deutsche Grammatik, von JACOB GRIMM. Erster Theil. Zweite Ausgabe. Gottingen, 1822.

Deutsche Grammatik, von JACOB GRIMM. Zweiter, Dritter, Vierter Theil: Gottingen, 1831–37.

Grammatik der Altgermanischen Sprachstämme, von M. HEYNE. Paderborn, 1862.

Die Laut- und Flexionslehre der Englischen Sprache, von C. FRIEDRICH KOCH. Weimar: Hermann Bohlau, 1863.

Lectures on the English Language, by MARSH. London, 1861.

The Origin and History of the English Language and of the Early Literature it embodies, by MARSH. London, 1862.

TEUTONIC GRAMMAR.

INTRODUCTION.

GRAMMAR describes the organisms of languages as natural history describes the organisms of natural objects. What plants and animals are to the natural philosopher, words are to the grammarian. The naturalist may satisfy himself with taking notice merely of the outward characteristics represented by any particular object; or he may enter upon a dissection of its organism, lay open the peculiar structure of each organ, show its connection with the whole and the functions it has to perform in this connection. Thus then one and the same object may receive a different treatment, viewed either from the standpoint of natural history or from that of anatomy and physiology. Thus again the grammarian may view the particular word laid before him in its merely outward garb, classify it to its proper sphere, record the changes it may incur under certain conditions—in short, give the natural history of the word; this is ' Descriptive Grammar.' Or he may dissect the word into its component parts, or let us boldly say its organs, show the structure of these organs and their functions in the whole, trace the word back to its first origin, show how it grew and gave birth to a progeny, which, though displaying all the diversity of varieties, nevertheless preserve 'the type of the species.' This anatomical and physiological handling of the word belongs to the sphere of the 'science of language.'

We give a few examples, taken at random; say the word *foot*. Descriptive Grammar teaches us that it belongs to the class 'noun,' the order 'concrete,' the genus 'common;' that this word as it stands has the form of the singular, but that as soon as it has to perform another function, that is, to denote the plurality of the thing called 'foot,' it adopts the form *feet*. Having told us this, Descriptive Grammar has performed its task. Now it is just here that the science of grammar takes it up and explains to us the phænomenon which Descriptive Grammar simply mentions as a fact. The English *foot*, plural *feet*, we can trace to the Anglo-Saxon *fot, fét;* here then the change of *ó* into *é* had already taken place. We must therefore make our way still further back, to a still more ancient form, and thus we arrive at the Gothic *fotus*. This has in the plural *fotjus*, a form in which the modification of the vowel has not yet taken place. How then did it take place? To learn this we may best turn to the nearest relative of Anglo-Saxon, i.e. Old Saxon. There we learn the following facts. The word 'foot,' which in Gothic belonged to the declension in *u* (*fotus*, plural *fotjus*) took in Old Saxon the plural in *i*, hence *fot*, plural *foti*. Now this terminational *i* had in the old Teutonic dialects, Gothic excepted, a peculiar influence under which the vowel *a*, or sometimes *o*, of the root was changed into *e*. This modification occurs so regularly under certain given conditions that we may look upon it as a law, and this law is known under the German name of 'Umlaut' (mutation of sound). According to this law then the Old Saxon *foti* appears in Anglo-Saxon as *feti*, and then as *fet*, the phænomenon of the 'Umlaut' remaining, though the final *i*, the cause that gave it birth, had disappeared. This 'Umlaut,' which originally had nothing whatever to do with the plural, but was merely the result of the modifying influence of the *i*, came later on to be looked upon as the sign of the plural.

Let us take another example. Descriptive Grammar tells us that the imperfect of *I love* is *I loved;* but how it is that by the addition of *ed* the present is changed into a past act, it does not teach. If we apply to the science of language, we are first referred to the Anglo-Saxon *lufode*, which still leaves us in the dark as to the force and meaning of that preterite suffix. We consequently apply to Gothic. Here we find the preterite of the weak verb, say *nasjan* (salvare) for instance, is *nas-i-da* in the singular, a form from which we derive no information as yet; but the plural *nas-i-dedum* shows us in its suffix most distinctly the plural *dedum* of *dad* (did), which is the preterite of *didan* (to do). The English *I lov-ed* consequently means *I love-did*, *I did love*.

If we wish to trace a word to its first origin, to observe how it grew and had offspring, and how these offspring developed themselves, the science of language again, laying open the laws by which all development was regulated, guides us in our researches. Take the words *father*, *mother*, for examples. Looking around us in the modern sister languages we meet the German *vater, mutter*, the Dutch *vader, moeder*, the Danish and Swedish *fader, moder*, the same words everywhere, but all equally obscure as to origin and meaning. Their Old Teutonic ancestors, as the Anglo-Saxon *fader, móder*, Old High German *fater, moter*, reveal no more, and consequently we turn to the cognate languages where we find the Greek πατήρ, μητηρ, the Latin *pater, mater*, the Sanskrit *patri, matri*—forms which refer us back to a primitive *patar, mátar*. In these words we have to deal with two distinct elements—the roots *pa* and *ma*, and the suffix *tar*. The root *pa* means 'to protect,' the root *ma* 'to bear,' 'to bring forth,' the suffix *tar, tara* indicates personal agency, whence the Latin *tor* in *actor, genitor*, &c. Thus then 'father' means 'he who protects,' 'protector;' 'mother,' 'she who brings forth,' 'genitrix.' Casting a glance at the development of this word in the different languages we have mentioned, we find that not only the root, but even the very suffix, is preserved intact, as Latin *pa-ter*, Greek πα-τηρ, German *va-ter*, English *fa-ther*. But then we observe that the Teutonic dialects substitute *f* for the initial *p* of the root. Now this is quite in accordance with a certain law which directs that wherever a word in Sanskrit (or Greek or Latin) uses *p*, that is the tenuis, the Low German languages, as English for instance, must use *f*, the aspirate, and High German *ought* to use the media. Where Sanskrit has the media, the Low German dialects have the tenuis, the High German the aspirate, and so forth. This law, which is known as Grimm's law, shall find a detailed exposition hereafter.

As another and more faithful instance of the application of this law we mention the word we have examined already: now let us trace it to its origin. The English *foot*, the German *fuß*, have their relatives in the Latin *pes, ped-is*, Greek πους, ποδ-ος, Sanskrit *pad-a*, and these we refer to the root *pad*, 'to go.' Here again the initial tenuis *p* is in Low German represented by the aspirate, and *ought* in High German to be the media; but the German is often obstinate in resisting the law. Now let us look at the final consonant: here all is in strict accordance to the law; hence the media in the Sanskrit *pad*, the Greek *pod*, the Latin *ped*, the tenuis in the English *foot*, and the aspirate in the German *fuß* (Old High German *fuoʒ*). Thus we see the offspring of the same parent all preserving the family likeness, or, to use a more scientific expression, the type of the 'species;' but taking by a kind of 'natural selection,' or whatever Mr. Darwin might call it, a particular consonant in particular languages, they form so many 'varieties;' in plain words, that which originally was one language, splits into different dialects.

Now I hope the difference is clear between the task proposed to Descriptive Grammar and that which is left to Scientific Grammar, or, as it is commonly termed, Comparative Grammar; the former stating the facts or the phænomena of a language or languages, the latter explaining these facts, guided always by certain laws. These laws are the result of repeated observation and rigid examination; they have been discovered by exactly the same mental process as all laws of nature. When we treat on Comparative Grammar we have therefore not only to put the grammatical forms of cognate dialects or languages together, but we have also to trace them to their origin and follow them through the different stages of their growth. Comparative Grammar must consequently be historical too. But languages have no history as mankind has its history, taking the word in its limited sense: languages do not act like men, but they grow and live like natural organisms. When therefore we speak of Comparative and Historical Grammar, or Scientific Grammar, we mean the science of the anatomy and physiology of language or of languages. If we treat on language in general, we are dealing with General Grammar; if on a particular language or languages, we are dealing with Specific Grammar. The tribe of Teutonic languages being our special object in this volume, our grammar belongs to the class of the specific.

Now one word as to the terms 'language' and 'dialect.' We speak of Teutonic languages and of Teutonic dialects, of the English language and of English dialects. Dutch, German, English, Gothic, Anglo-Saxon, Old Norse, are, when viewed by themselves, independently of the rest, to be designated each by the term of 'language;' but when considered in their connection and relation to each other and to their common Teutonic mother, then we call them 'dialects.' English, considered as an independent form of speech as distinct from French or German, is a 'language;' but English as seen in the different provincial idioms into which it is split up consists of an aggregate of 'dialects.' The 'literary' language is only one of these dialects, chosen as the medium of thought for the educated classes; such is the Castilian of Spain, the West-Saxon of English, the Highland dialect in German. From all this the reader will easily understand that we often apply the terms 'dialect' and 'language' indiscriminately.

Having to deal chiefly with the Teutonic form of speech, we must devote a short reviewing glance to the different languages which fall within that sphere, consider their relation to each other and to the cognate languages, Greek, Latin, and Sanskrit—all being derived from the same *primitive* tongue, or '*Ursprache.*'

We find the modern Teutonic languages settled in almost exactly the same localities which had been the seat of their mother dialects. Swedish and Danish are the offspring of one of the dialects spoken by the Norsemen, the inhabitants of the Scandinavian peninsula and adjacent islands. Though High German has become the sole literary dialect of Germany, the Low German, or 'Platt-Deutsch,' still holds the ground of its ancestor the Old Saxon, whilst the High German in speech is now, as it was a thousand years ago, confined to the southeast of Germany, Bavaria, Austria, and some adjacent districts. The Modern Frisian dialects still nestle in those dear old 'Halligs' along the coast of the North Sea, between the Weser and the Elbe, and into Holstein and Schleswig. In spite of centuries of humiliation and neglect under the Norman invaders, the Anglo-Saxon language yet holds its ground all over England, and the English of the present day is in its grammatical form quite as Teutonic as the Anglo-Saxon of the tenth century. The West Saxon dialect was destined to become the literary language of England; but the speech of the East Saxons and South Saxons, of the North and the South Angles, continued to flourish, and often had a more luxuriant existence than the literary language which was more than once deposed by foreign intruders. Our numerous dialects are the offspring of those children of nature which in their independent state escaped the mandates of conquerors who attempted to uproot them. As to the modern languages we need not enter into ethnographical discussion when we state that we have to deal with the literary dialects of England, Germany, Holland, Sweden, and Denmark. Their ancient mother dialects will require a more detailed exposition.

The oldest dialect and the most perfect in its inflexional forms is the Gothic. This statement, however, must not be taken without some qualification. When we say Gothic is the oldest dialect we wish this to be understood with reference to literary documents only, which in Gothic reach back to the fourth century[1], while no other dialect possesses any literary

---

[1] *Gospels*, about A.D. 360.

documents which date back further than the sixth century[1]. As we shall point out hereafter more fully, Gothic is not superior to the other dialects throughout; on the contrary, Old High German and Anglo-Saxon possess in several inflexional forms the advantage over Gothic. Hence it will become apparent also that Gothic is not the primitive dialect from which the others were derived, but that all the ancient Teutonic dialects, though closely related, are independent of each other, and, for all we know, equally primitive in their type—venerable old sisters among which Gothic is the most venerable, the eldest sister.

The only literary document which has come down to us in the Gothic dialect is the translation of the Bible by Ulfilas, a Gothic bishop. At the birth of Ulfilas the Gothic occupied the ancient province of Dacia north of the Danube. Though politically they were divided into Ostro-Goths, or East-Goths, and Visi-Goths, or West-Goths, their language was the same. Kindred tribes also, occupying the extreme frontiers of Eastern Germany, such as Vandals, Gepidæ, and others, are supposed to have spoken the Gothic language, though probably in dialects slightly differing from that of Ulfilas. The Gothic language must have become extinct before the final disappearance of East and West Goths from the scene of history; it left no daughter or derivative language behind. Ulfilas was born in A.D. 311. His parents were of Cappadocian origin, and had been carried away from their home as captives about A.D. 267, when the Goths made a raid from Europe to Asia, Galatia, and Cappadocia. From these Christian captives the Goths first received their knowledge of the Gospel. Ulfilas was born among the Goths; Gothic was his native language, though in after life he was able to write and speak both in Greek and Latin. When the Goths were persecuted on account of their Christianity, Ulfilas led them across the Danube into the Roman Empire. As a young man of education, he was sent on an embassy to the Emperor Constantine, who received him with great respect and called him the Moses of his time. Another interview is mentioned between Ulfilas and the Emperor Constantine which occurred in A.D. 348, when Ulfilas had been for seven years bishop among the Goths. Though the exact date of the Gothic exodus is still a disputed point, it is likely that Ulfilas acted as their leader on more than one occasion. Ulfilas never changed his religion, but belonged to the Arian denomination all his life.

[1] *Laws of Ethelbert*, A.D. 597.

He died at Constantinople in A.D. 381[1]. Of his translation, which comprised the whole Bible except the Books of Kings, we still possess the greater part of the Gospels, the Epistles of St. Paul, and small fragments of Esdras and Nehemiah. Besides these portions of the Scriptures there are extant fragments of an exposition in Gothic of the Gospel of St. John, and a fragment of a Gothic calender.

Old High German comprises a number of dialects which were spoken in Upper or South Germany, e. g. the Thüringian, Franconian, Swabian, Alsacian, Swiss and Bavarian (Austrian), and which are embodied in the literary documents of three centuries, dating from the beginning of the eighth to the middle of the eleventh century. We have already observed that none of the Teutonic dialects can be said to have been derived from Gothic. Old High German, therefore, is a sister dialect of the Gothic, of the Anglo-Saxon, and the Old Norse; though, on the other hand, it must be acknowledged that the family likeness between the two former dialects is more intimate and obvious. From the eleventh century a gradual change takes place in the structure of Old High German, the inflexional vowels are gradually worn down or weakened; the full-sounding a is flattened into the thinner vocal sound of e; the vowel of the root itself is more and more affected by the terminational e, so that not only a appears modified into e, but u also into $ü$, o into $ö$.

Thus we see from the Old High German a new dialect gradually developing itself, which stands to the former in the relation of a daughter to a mother. This derivative dialect is called Middle High German. It belonged to Upper Germany in the same manner and to the same extent as its parent tongue. Its literary productions reach over a period of four hundred years, from the beginning of the twelfth to the end of the fifteenth century. Whilst the literary documents in Old High German are far from being abundant, Middle High German has bequeathed to us a literature so various in its details, so clear in its ideas, so grand in its conceptions, so refined and melodious in its diction, that it has rightly been called 'the first *classical* period of German literature.' Exposed, however, to the continued wear and tear of time, the language of the Nibelungen and of the Gudrun, of a Wolfram von Eschenbach and Gottfried von Strassburg, proceeds on its course down the phonetic scale until, in Modern High German, it has almost arrived at zero, the inflexional

---

[1] Max Muller, *Lectures on the Science of Language*, First Series (5th ed.) pp. 199-208.

forms having dwindled down into a few meagre *e* vowels. This modified High German dialect, this daughter of the Middle, and grand-daughter of the Old High German, presents us with its first literary production of note in Luther's translation of the Bible, and reaches its culminating point in the language of Goethe's Iphigenia and Torquato Tasso, the most classical of all works of 'the second *classical* period of German literature.'

The same course which we have attempted to trace in this short sketch will be observed when we turn to the other Teutonic dialects and their modern derivatives. Anglo-Saxon, the literary language, is one of the dialects transplanted into Celtic soil by the invaders who came from the western and north-western districts of Low Germany[1].

The Celtic language was spoken not only by the primitive inhabitants of Britain, but also by the inhabitants of Gaul, Belgium, and part of Spain. No literary documents from that primitive or pre-Roman time have come down to us, probably because the Druids, according to Cæsar's account, shrunk from committing their sacred rites and doctrines to writing. The most ancient Irish documents do not reach back further than to the eighth or ninth century.

The Roman legions brought their language and customs to Britain. The long duration of the Roman occupation, their perennial encampments, the colonies founded by their veteran soldiers, the rise of flourishing cities, the construction of highroads, and other monuments of art and science which are partly extant, show how deeply Roman civilization had struck root in this country. And yet there are no Latin words dating from that time preserved in the language, with the exception of a few compounds, as *colonia*, *coln*, in *Lincoln*, and *castra*, *cestra*, *cester*, in *Chester*, *Winchester*, *Gloucester*, &c. It was only with the introduction of Christianity that a copious Latin vocabulary, chiefly referring to ecclesiastical affairs, found admission into the language of the country. With the scholastic, and subsequently the classical studies, new supplies of Latin terms were introduced into the vernacular; and the mania of latinizing the language in the time of Queen Elizabeth became so general, that Thomas Wilson (died 1581) bitterly complains of the 'strange ink-horn terms' introduced into English. 'Some seek so far for outlandish English, that they forget altogether their

---

[1] There are some who consider the Anglo-Saxon of our ancient documents to be a compound of several dialects which took its rise after the Saxon invasion of England, 'a new speech, resulting from the fusion of many separate elements.' Marsh, *Lectures*, p. 43.

mother's language. And I dare swear this, if some of their mothers were alive, they were not able to tell what they say; and yet these fine English will say they speak in their mother tongue, if a man should charge them with counterfeiting the King's English.' And of Sir Thomas Browne it is asserted, not without reason, that to persons acquainted only with their native tongue, many of his sentences must be nearly unintelligible; and the author is himself of opinion that if the desire after elegancy continued to work in the same direction, it would soon be necessary to learn Latin in order to understand English.

We return to Anglo-Saxon. The four Teutonic tribes that invaded Britain have left no record in the dialect peculiar to each; we therefore have no facts from which to obtain any idea as to the nature of their language. The Jutes who settled in Kent, Hampshire, and the Isle of Wight, may probably have spoken a Low German, that is, a dialect most closely akin to Anglo-Saxon, for we find in those districts no traces whatever which point to the Old Norse dialect. But on the other hand it must be admitted that if their dialect had been Old Norse, it might, from its constant and immediate contact with the overwhelming Saxon element, have gradually become extinct in proportion to the amalgamation of the Jutes with the Saxons. The Angles who came from Western Schleswig settled north of the Saxons, between the Thames and the Wash. Their language must have closely resembled the Saxon dialect. But as to the latter, we have no better evidence. The Saxons who settled in England called themselves simply Saxons in contradistinction to the 'Old Saxons,' that is, those tribes of their nation which had remained behind in the old country. Though the Saxon emigrants and the German Old Saxons must have been most intimately related, it is still doubtful whether they belonged exactly to one and the same tribe. On the contrary, judging from the intimate relation existing between Saxons and Angles, their joint enterprises and settlement in a new country, one might feel inclined to take the English Saxons as belonging to a tribe which occupied the district north of the Elbe, and which is to be distinguished from the Southern Saxons. Still the question remains to be settled, whether their language was identically the same or not.

If we take the degree in which the language of the Anglo-Saxon Beowulf differs from that of the Old Saxon Heliand as the only criterion, we must admit that Anglo-Saxon and Old Saxon were two distinct dialects. This difference however may be accounted for in another way. The Old Saxons who stayed behind in their country were generally stationary, and not exposed to external influences which make themselves keenly felt among emigrants by causing rapid changes in manners, customs, and language. The English Saxons, on the other hand, were eminently exposed to those influences. They found themselves in a new country, in novel scenery and conditions of life; they soon forgot their old country with its songs and sagas; they gradually mingled with the Celtic natives, separated into different parties, and founded seven petty states, which were to a certain extent independent of each other. What wonder that such conditions, differing so materially from those of the German Saxons, should bring about a different course of development in their language, and account for the divergence which we perceive on comparing the Anglo-Saxon and Old Saxon dialects[1].

Under the term of Anglo-Saxon we include all the Teutonic dialects which were spoken in England from the fifth century. The term itself was of a later date, and supplanted the earlier terms of 'Saxon' and 'Anglisc.' Grammarians divide this Anglo-Saxon into two periods, Old and New Anglo-Saxon, or Semi-Saxon. The literary documents in Old Anglo-Saxon extend over a period of almost five hundred years, beginning with Beowulf, a poem which the Anglo-Saxons had imported from their own country, and which is supposed to have been written in the seventh century, although there are no manuscripts that can be referred beyond the tenth century. Old Anglo-Saxon again may be distinguished into two principal dialects, the Saxon and the Anglian, or Southern and Northern dialect. These again were probably subdivided into local dialects, among which that of the West Saxons gained the ascendancy and became the literary language, used in Beowulf, in Caedmon's Metrical Paraphrase, and in the Anglo-Saxon Chronicle. The Northern or Anglian dialect is divided again into the North and South Anglian (Mercia, Anglia—Northumberland), the former being largely tinged with the Danish or Old Norse element. The dialect of Mercia is supposed to have been partly made use of in the composition of the Anglo-Saxon Chronicle, and the Durham Book is written in the dialect of Northumbria.

The first period of Old Anglo-Saxon is characterized by its purely Teutonic elements, its consonants which closely corre-

---

[1] It is true that generally colonization fixes a language, as we learn from the Icelandic for instance; but then the fact is chiefly owing to the isolated position of a people, and want of intercourse with other nations.

spond with the Gothic, its rich and varied vocalism and its inflexional forms, which, though greatly worn and weakened, are still full-sounding vowels. Besides the natural decline and phonetic changes which we have observed in the transition from Old High German to Middle and Modern High German, we find in the English language other agencies at work which combined to give the English language of the present day its diversified aspect, and which therefore deserve some further notice.

The Old Norse dialect, which we shall have especially to mention hereafter, exercised a great influence chiefly upon the language of the north of England, where from A.D. 787 the Norsemen, that is Danes and Norwegians, made repeated inroads and gradually settled in the country. The reign of the Danish Kings too, from A.D. 1002 to 1041, cannot have passed without admitting the Danish element more freely into the language as well as the customs of the Saxons. The Anglo-Saxon vocabulary has consequently adopted a certain stock of Old Norse words, part of which are still preserved in the English of the present day. The northern dialects above all may owe their broad full vowels to Old Norse influences.

Even before the Conquest, Norman-French found entrance into England, chiefly at court. Edward the Confessor, having been educated at the Norman court, had naturally a predilection for the Norman system, which he also imitated by introducing Norman-French as the language of his court. With the Conquest Norman-French found ready entrance among the higher classes. The succession of Norman barons to the confiscated estates of the Saxon nobility, the appointment of the Norman clergy to the higher dignities of the Saxon Church; the erection of convents inhabited by Norman monks and nuns; the intimate connection between the clergy and nobility,—all this tended, in a comparatively short time, to make the Norman tongue the language of rank and education, while Anglo-Saxon continued to be that of the nation at large, that is, the language of the needy and the oppressed. But there is always some intercourse between the upper and lower classes, and where their languages are different, they will of necessity create a mixed tongue, as the occasion requires.

But with the beginning of the thirteenth century, a reaction began. The loss of Normandy by King John suspended further immigrations from that country, and the agreement made between the Kings, Henry III and Louis IX, according to which subjects of one crown could not acquire landed property under the other, put a stop to Norman transmigrations. The despotic aggressions of the English Kings soon joined Normans and Saxons in a common league against their royal oppressors, and in these movements the freedom-loving, honest, Saxon element made itself conspicuous and regained its ascendancy over the Norman-French type. The proud Norman, who heretofore, in order to pronounce dissent or unbelief was wont to exclaim with an oath, 'Then I shall become an Englishman!' or, in order to spurn at an unbecoming proposal, 'Do you take me for an Englishman[1]?'—that same Norman, a hundred years after, was proud of the appellation of Englishman. He in fact gradually lost the consciousness of his Norman-French nationality, so that in 1308 he joined the Saxon in opposing the French favourites whom King Edward had called over, and in compelling the King to dismiss them. These anti-French feelings were still more fostered by the wars with France which commenced in 1339 under Edward III, and which more than anything else tended to amalgamate the Norman and Saxon into one compact nationality—a nationality of which both parties had good reason to be proud. The result of these political changes becomes plainly manifest in the history of the English language. Already in 1258 Henry III ordered the enactments of the Mad Parliament to be published, not only in Latin and French but also in the vernacular; and the victory of the Saxon element was, about a hundred years after, so decided that Edward III in 1363 decreed that henceforth causes pending in courts of law should be conducted in English and registered in Latin, because the French language was too little known. This remarkable document was composed in pure Saxon, unmixed with French[2]. The literary documents of this period in general are characterized by a considerable loss in the inflexional forms, and an important admixture of Norman-French with the Old Anglo-Saxon.

English again is divided into three periods: Old English, Middle English, and Modern English. The period of Old English comprises a hundred years. During this period the old inflexional forms continued their decline, so that the declension of substantives hardly show more than the debris of the old inflexional forms. To the Old English period belong Robert of Gloucester's Chronicle, Peter Langtoft's Chronicle, and the Early English Psalter. To the Middle English period belong the writings of Wycliffe, Chaucer and Sir John Mandeville. The period of Middle English is commonly, and I consider rightly, introduced with Chaucer, 'the father of English poetry,' who undoubtedly had

---

[1] Koch, *Einleitung*, p. 14.   [2] Ibid. p. 15.

a vastly greater influence on the thoughts and on the speech of his countrymen than Wycliffe, whose translation of the Bible was, up to the time of the Reformation, most probably known to none except the learned few. Middle English is characterized by the rapid dilapidation of all inflexional forms, the diminution of strong verbs, and the almost total absence of declensions of substantives as well as adjectives.

Modern English continued the same decline, and has by this time succeeded in stripping itself of all inflexional forms with the exception of the *s* and *st* of the present, the *ed* of the preterite of the verb, the *s* of the genitive, the degrees of comparison of adjectives, and a few pronominal cases. As the first important work in Modern English, we may consider the translation of the Bible under the auspices of King James the First, forming the authorized version up to the present time. It was based upon the Bishop's Bible, and the translations of Coverdale, Tyndale, &c., were to be consulted whenever they were in closer harmony with the original text than the Bishop's Bible. In spite of the drawbacks we have mentioned, the Modern English language has, according to Jacob Grimm, gained in spiritual maturity what it has lost in the more material advantages of inflexional forms; and, according to another authority, it has during the seventeenth and eighteenth centuries been worked out so elaborately that it combines the vigour of the Teutonic with the elegance of the Latin languages, and must be considered completely sufficient for the expression of every thought in poetry or prose.

As to the constituent elements composing modern English the following observations may find their place here. The French element having been engrafted on the German, all inflexions in the English language, such as they are, are German. This is therefore the case with auxiliary verbs and all verbal inflexions, the pronouns, the numerals, conjunctions, and prepositions (with few exceptions). German appellations are preferred for natural objects and phænomena of nature, such as animals, plants and minerals, the parts of the human body, the sky, the weather, and everything connected with them. German are the names which designate articles of dress and weapons; and the farmer characteristically enough uses only German words in the course of his daily occupation; and so, on the whole, does the sailor. The names for articles of food are mixed, some German, others French. Here again it is interesting to observe the characteristic application of French terms for certain kinds of meat, and German for the animals from which the food is derived: the Saxon farmer speaks of *ox* and *cow*, *calf* and *sheep*, out of which the French or Gallicized cook produces *beef*, *veal*, and *mutton*. The French element has decidedly the ascendancy in such appellations as refer to the political organization, the titles, and dignities of the state, to arts and sciences.

Old Norse we call that dialect which in the olden times, and as late as the eleventh century, was spoken and generally understood in Sweden, Norway, Denmark, and the adjacent islands. This language was preserved almost intact in Iceland, while in Denmark and Sweden it grew into two different dialects, the Modern Danish and Swedish. The Icelandic of the present day has a closer affinity to the Old Norse dialects in the literary documents of the ninth century than the Old High German of the eighth shows to the High German of the eleventh century. This stationary existence of the Norse language in Icelandic can be explained partly by its secluded position in an island far out of reach of continental influence, partly by the stereotyped form which it assumed in the old songs and sagas most zealously cultivated by the Icelander of later times. Their island had been known in the ninth century when voyages of discovery were made thither. Even afterwards, when the despotic reign of Harold Haarfagr threatened to reduce the northern freemen to a state of vassalage, many inhabitants of the Scandinavian islands, a number of noblemen amongst them, emigrated to the distant shores of Iceland, while others directed their voyage towards France and England. In Iceland the Northmen established an aristocratic republic, their settlement began to thrive, and they adopted Christianity in the year 1000.

The old poetry which flourished in Norway in the eighth century, and which was cultivated by the Skalds in the ninth, would have been lost in Norway itself had it not been for the jealous care with which it was preserved by the emigrants of Iceland. The most important branch of their traditional poetry was short songs (hliod or Quida) relating the deeds of their gods and heroes. It is impossible to determine their age, but they existed at least previously to the emigration of the Northmen to Iceland, and probably as early as the seventh century. Those ancient songs of the Northmen were collected about the middle of the twelfth century, and are still preserved in the two *Eddas*, of which the elder or poetical Edda contains old mythic poems, the younger or Snorri's Edda gives the ancient myths in prose. Both Eddas were composed in Iceland and form the most valuable part of Old Norse literature[1].

[1] Max Müller, *Lectures*, First Series, p. 211.

INTRODUCTION. 15

From the Old Norse are derived the modern Swedish and Danish languages, although it may reasonably be doubted, whether they have sprung from exactly that form of speech which is preserved in the Old Norse literary documents. It is indeed now taken for granted that Old Norse at a very early date was split into two sister dialects, one, spoken in Norway, being the mother of Old Norwegian or Icelandic, the other the parent of Swedish and Danish. The first germs of Swedish and Danish are considered to have existed long before the eleventh century in the dialects of the numerous clans and tribes of the Scandinavian race. That race is clearly divided into two branches, called by Swedish scholars the East and West Scandinavian. The former would be represented by the old language of Norway and Iceland, the latter by Swedish and Danish. This division of the Scandinavian race had taken place before the Northmen settled in Norway and Sweden[1].

All the dialects spoken in the Lowlands of Germany between the Rhine and the shores of the Baltic are comprised under the term of Low German. Anglo-Saxon is a Low German dialect, and there are belonging to the same category several others which require a passing allusion. On the north coast of Germany between the Rhine and the Elbe, and to the north of the Elbe, extended the Old Frisian dialect. Though it is preserved in literary documents which do not reach back beyond the fourteenth century, and therefore are contemporary with the Middle, not the Old, High German literature, the Old Frisian dialect nevertheless displays a more antique cast and resembles more closely Old, than Middle, High German. 'The political isolation and the noble adhesion of the Frisians to their ancient laws and traditions imparted to their language also a more conservative tendency. For the same reason we see about that time, nay up to the present day, the Icelandic language but slightly deviating from the grammatical forms which are characteristic of the Old Norse dialect. After the fourteenth century the old Frisian forms become rapidly extinct, whilst in the twelfth and thirteenth centuries they were almost on a parallel with the Anglo-Saxon of the ninth and tenth centuries.[2]'

Old Saxon is the dialect which was spoken in the German Lowlands between the Rhine and the Elbe in the districts which lie at the foot of the central plateau of Germany. This language we know from literary productions which date from between the ninth and eleventh centuries, and had their origin in the districts of Munster, Essen and Cleve. The most ancient and most

---

[1] Max Müller, *Lectures*, i. p. 210. [2] Ibid. p. 196.

important document in Old Saxon is the Heliand (the Healer, or Saviour, German *heiland*), a free version of the Gospels, written for the newly converted Saxons about the ninth century. The Old Saxon is the mother of the Middle Low German which is to be distinguished from the Middle German and Middle Netherlandish or Middle Dutch, and the modern derivative of which we find in Modern Low German or 'Platt-Deutsch.' Old Saxon most closely approaches Old High German, whilst the dialect spoken in the districts of Thuringia, Hesse, &c., situated between Upper and Lower Germany, formed a kind of transition between High and Low German. The Dutch language boasts of no such antique documents as we find in English and German, for its literature cannot be traced further back than the sixteenth century. Still it is to the present day a literary and national language, although confined to a small area. Flemish too was in those times the language used in the courts of Flanders and Brabant, but at a later period it had to give way before the official languages of Holland and Belgium, and its use is almost completely confined to the Flemish peasantry.

Having so far sketched the relative position of the different Teutonic languages spread over their respective areas in Europe, we must direct our attention to the degree of relationship in which they stand to each other, and in which they again, taken collectively, stand to other cognate languages. We take for this purpose the Old Teutonic dialects, in which the modern derivative languages will find their illustration at the same time. The six old Teutonic dialects, Gothic, Old High German, Old Norse, Old Frisian, Old Saxon, and Anglo-Saxon, may according to their greater or lesser affinity be classified in three groups: Gothic with its nearest relatives, namely, Anglo-Saxon, Old Saxon, Old Frisian, forming the Low German group; by the side of which we place as a second group Old High German, as a third, Old Norse. All the Teutonic languages however are descended from one common mother which we call the primitive Teutonic (Grundsprache), and the relation of the different groups, ancient and modern, to this primitive tongue will appear from the following diagram.

The Teutonic dialects again, of which the Gothic is our representative, belong to a group which formerly went under the name of 'Indo-European,' now by that of 'Aryan languages[1].' To the same group belong the following classes.

1. The Indian class of languages. Sanskrit, the most important

---

[1] Some German linguists use the term of 'Indo-Germanic.'

language for the student of Comparative Grammar, is the sacred language of the Hindoos. It had ceased to be a spoken language at least three hundred years before Christ. At that time the people of India spoke dialects standing to the ancient Vedic Sanskrit in the relation of Italian to Latin. The dialects, called Prakrit, are known partly from inscriptions which are still preserved, partly from the Pali, the sacred language of Buddhism in Ceylon, and partly from the Prakrit idioms used in later plays and poetical compositions; and we see at last how through a mixture with the languages of the various conquerors of India, and through a concomitant corruption of their grammatical system, they were changed into the modern Hindí, Hindustaní, Mahratti, and Bengali. During all this time, however, Sanskrit continued as the literary language of the Brahmins. Like Latin, it did not die in giving birth to its numerous offspring, and even at the present day an educated Brahmin would write with greater fluency in Sanskrit than in Bengali[1].

2. The Iranic class of languages, among which most closely allied to the Sanskrit is the Zend, or sacred language of the Zoroastrians or worshippers of Ormuzd. To the same class belong Old and Modern Persian, the Kurdic, Armenian, &c.

3. The Greek language, with its derivative, Modern Greek.

4. The Italic class, represented in several dialects—the Umbric, Osk, Sabine, and Latin; and, derived from the latter, the Modern Latin or Romance languages—Italian, Spanish, Portuguese, Provençal, French, and Rumanic.

5. The Slavonic class—Russian, Bulgarian, Polish, Bohemian, and Illyrian.

6. The Lithuanian class, represented by Lettic and Old Prussian (now extinct).

7. The Celtic languages, comprising Welsh, Erse or Gaelic, the Manse, the Breton, and the Cornish (now extinct).

To these different groups or classes of languages we must then refer our Teutonic dialects for the sake of comparison and explanation. But it would be erroneous to suppose that every word or every grammatical form which we meet in Gothic must be preserved in Sanskrit too, or that for every Latin word we can give the parallel in Celtic or Slavonic. Where, however, one class leaves us without a clue, another may step in to supply the defect. If Gothic does not show an analogy to a certain word in Sanskrit, Latin will do so, or Greek. This holds good especially for the etymology of words, while for our grammatical

---

[1] Max Müller, *Lectures*, i. p. 154.

forms, inflexions, and terminations, a reference from the Teutonic to the Latin, Greek, or Sanskrit languages will generally suffice to trace them to their primitive types.

The Aryan languages which we have just enumerated, being again looked upon as the daughters of an older parent stock, are very often reduced to a primitive idiom, called by German grammarians the 'Ursprache.' From the results Comparative Grammar has gained on the field of the cognate languages, science has succeeded in building up the grammar of the primitive language, the mother of the whole Aryan tribe, the 'Ursprache' of German linguists, the language which was spoken by our Aryan ancestors before Sanskrit was Sanskrit, Greek was Greek, or Latin was Latin. It is not without a feeling of wonder and awe that one follows the bold philosopher into those regions of antiquity, in comparison with which the most ancient documents of Greek or even Sanskrit literature are but of yesterday. We shall introduce all the grammatical forms of the 'primitive language' as far as they have been traced, and as far as they may tend to throw light upon the grammatical forms of the Teutonic languages. When we speak of the 'primitive language' we understand of course that language which was the mother of Sanskrit, Greek, Latin, and Gothic; as Latin was the mother of French, Italian, and Spanish. But we do not speak of *the one* primitive language of mankind, because everything tends to prove that there existed *many* primitive languages, some of which became extinct, others gave birth to filial tongues. Looking apart, however, from these questions, which belong to Comparative Grammar in general, we confine ourselves to giving as far as possible the primitive types of all the grammatical forms which the Englishman, Dane, or German, uses in his daily speech. To effect this we have of course to trace our way first to the Old Teutonic dialects, to the cognate languages, and thence to the most ancient form of Aryan speech; or, *vice versa*, placing the primitive form at the head, we follow its course of development in the cognate and Old Teutonic languages, thence through the Middle to the New Teutonic dialects.

The different Aryan languages, though all of them descendants of the same mother, do not stand in exactly the same degree of affinity to their parent, but show more or less family likeness. Thus Sanskrit, for instance, approaches in most cases most nearly the primitive language, while Gothic most widely diverges from it. We may therefore look upon Sanskrit as the eldest, Gothic as the youngest sister of the Aryan family, though it must be well understood that this comparison holds good only to the extent we have pointed out: Sanskrit *looks* older, Gothic younger, in the garment in which we find them dressed up in the most ancient documents. From what we have stated it will also become apparent that there must exist a greater or less affinity of the Aryan languages to each other, in proportion as they have more or less preserved the family likeness to their common mother. This family likeness is greater in the languages of those nations which settled down in the East, it is less in the languages of Western nations; the former contain more of the ancient forms, the latter have more often replaced them by modern formations. From this again it follows that the allied Slavonic and Teutonic tribes first separated from their ancient home and nation and began their migration to the far West; after them the united Greek, Italic, and Celtic tribes emigrated in the same direction, while the tribes that remained behind in their ancient home split again in two, the Iranians (Persians) settling in the southwest, the Indians in the south-east of the plateau of Central Asia, the original home of the Aryan tribes. The divisions of the primitive language into the different Aryan tongues Schleicher has very ingeniously represented in a diagram, given on the following page, where the length of the lines indicates the duration, the divergence of the lines the degree of relationship of these languages.

20   TEUTONIC GRAMMAR.

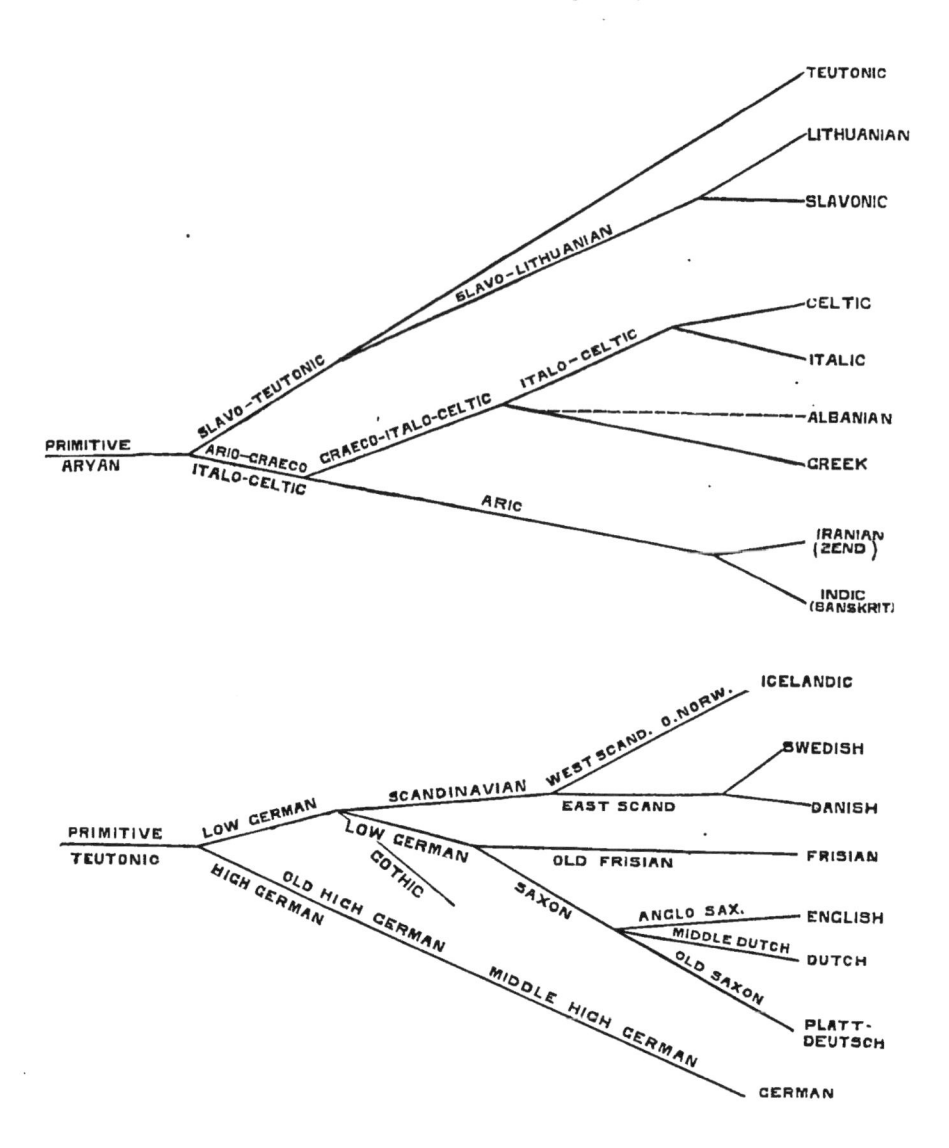

DIAGRAM SHOWING THE RELATION OF THE TEUTONIC LANGUAGES[1].

---

[1] The arrangement I have made in this diagram differs materially from that made by Schleicher in his diagram of the Aryan languages in the pamphlet 'Die Darwinsche Theorie und die Sprachwissenschaft,' Weimar, 1863.

VOWEL SOUNDS.

Vowels are formed by the configuration of the mouth, or the buccal tube; but the pitch or tone inherent to each vowel is determined by the chordae vocales. On emitting the breath from the lungs through the buccal tube in order to pronounce a vowel, we may give the interior of the mouth two extreme positions. In one the lips are rounded and the tongue is drawn down, 'so that the cavity of the mouth assumes the shape of a bottle without a neck,' and we pronounce u. In the other we narrow the lips and draw up the tongue to its utmost, so that the buccal tube represents 'a bottle with a very narrow neck,' and we pronounce i. Intermediate between the u and i, with lips less rounded than in the case of the former, and less narrowed than in the case of the latter, the tongue neither drawn up nor down, and therefore in its natural position, we pronounce a[1]. Between these there is an indefinite variety of vocal sounds, but every language has fixed upon a limited number, just as music, though the number of notes in the octave is unlimited, contents itself with twelve which suffice to give expression to the most wonderful creations of genius. a, i, and u may be considered as the types of all vowels which differ not only in the quality but also in the pitch of the sound. Their relative position will be seen from the following table:—

i—pitch, or inherent tone : D''''
a—pitch, or inherent tone : B'' flat
u—pitch, or inherent tone : F.

From this table it becomes clear that u, as it is the extreme of i in the quality of sound, so it is in its pitch or inherent tone; and that a in both respects occupies an intermediate position. The last-mentioned vowel being equally distant from

[1] Max Müller, *Lectures*, ii. p. 119 sqq.

either extreme, and pronounced while the organs occupy their natural position, it is easily understood that a had every chance of becoming a favourite vowel.

Now if the physiologist may regard the a, i, and u, as the types of all vowels, the linguist will as readily acknowledge that they are the 'primitive' vocal sounds, and that all others owe their origin to a modification of these. From the sounds of the 'primitive language,' the 'Ursprache,' all the sounds in the different Aryan languages have been developed according to certain phonetic laws which we see at work in the vital processes of language; and to these primitive vowels consequently all vowels in the different Aryan languages can be traced as to their common source. The 'primitive language' in its most primitive form was limited to the three typical vowels, which later on, certainly before the first breaking up of the Aryan family, were multiplied by the a entering into combination, first with its own like, and then with the two other vowels. Thus we get the following table of gradations of sounds:—

Primitive.	I. Gradation.	II. Gradation.
1. a	$a + a = aa$	$a + aa = \acute{a}a$
2. i	$a + i = ai$	$a + ai = ai$
3. u	$a + u = au$	$a + au = au$

The combinations aa and $\acute{a}a$ were probably contracted into a at an early period. The vowel a is so characteristically distinct from its two fellows that it may be considered as forming a class of its own in contradistinction to that which comprises the vowels i and u. The latter have in their suit, and are often replaced by, the consonants, or semivowels, j and v, while a never passes into a consonant, and thus displays more energetically its vocalic nature. Each vowel is limited to the combinations mentioned in the table, and these combinations are used as a means of expressing in the root itself its relations in connected speech. The vowels of suffixes also are capable of forming those combinations, because they originally proceeded from independent roots; but the primitive form of a root is always rendered with a primitive, that is, a simple vowel. In a root with two consonants the combinations do not occur, and such a root has always the radical a, never i or u. Thus then the essence of all inflections we find in the system of vowels.

Long vowels being of a secondary formation they did not exist in the primitive language; where nevertheless they occur equally in different Aryan dialects, as Sansk. *pita (rs)*, Greek πατηρ, Goth. *fadar=fathár*, &c. Schleicher supposes them to be of later introduction, perhaps of a period when the different languages had already separated; and he therefore claims for the last-mentioned words in the primitive language the genuine form *patars*.

The Sanskrit has, besides the short vowels *i* and *u*, the lengthened forms *í* and *ú*. The combinations *ai* and *au* are fused into the single vowels *e* and *o*; *e* being the intermediate sound between *a* and *i*, the former ascended, the latter descended to the pitch of *e*, hence twice *e*, or $e+e=e$. In the same manner in the combination *au* the *a* descended, the *u* ascended, to their intermediate pitch *o*, hence for $a+u$ we have $o+o=o$. A peculiar feature in the vital process of vowels is the weakening of a full into a thin vowel, the '*Schwachung*' of German grammarians, a phenomenon which chiefly occurs with the vowel *a*, which may be 'degraded,' as it were, in this scale into *i*, *u*, and *í*, *ú*. Thus then we arrive at the following table:—

	Degradation or weakening.	Primitive.	I. Gradation.	II. Gradation.
1. *a* sounds	*i, u; í, ú*	*a*	*á*	*â*
2. *i* sounds		*i*	*é*	*ai*
3. *u* sounds		*u*	*ó*	*au*

The Teutonic languages, of which Gothic is the most ancient representative, have, with characteristic perseverance, kept each radical vowel in its proper order, and thus guarded the main principle of inflections. The vowel *a* is weakened both into *i* and *u*, and these weakened forms occur quite as regularly as the gradations. The first and second gradations are kept strictly distinct, the former in Gothic being *e*, the latter *o*. The primitive *au* has, in Gothic, weakened the *a* into *i*, and thus the primitive combination is replaced by *iu*; in *ai* the *a* by assimilation to the *i* becomes *e*, and consequently Gothic *ei* stands for the primitive *ai*. *iu* (= primitive *au*) is sometimes represented by *u*. Thus we get the table:—

	II. Degradation.	I. Degradation.	Primitive.	I. Gradation.	II. Gradation.
1. Order *a*	*i*	*u*	*a*	*é*	*ó*
2. Order *i*			*i*	*ei*	*ai*
3. Order *u*			*u*	*iu (ú)*	*au*

In order to give a comprehensive glance over the course of development of vowels in the Old Teutonic languages in general, and the relation of these vowels to those in Gothic, Sanskrit, and the primitive language, I subjoin a table arranged according to the different orders.

1. Order *a*.

	Degradation, or weakening.	Primitive.	I. Gradation	II. Gradation.
Primitive	. . . .	a	aa	âa
Sanskrit	i, u; î, û	a	â	â
Gothic	i; u	a	ê	ô
Old High German	e	a	â	uo
Old Saxon	e	a	a (e)	ô
Anglo-Saxon	ä, o e	a	æ (ä)	ô
Old Frisian	e	a	â	ô
Old Norse	e	a	â	ô

2. Order *i*.

Primitive	. . . . .	i	ai	âi
Sanskrit	. . . . .	i	ê	âi
Gothic	. . . . .	i	ei	ai
Old High German	e	i	î	ei (ê)
Old Saxon	e	i	î	ê
Anglo-Saxon	e	i	î	â (ǽ)
Old Frisian	e	i	î	ê (â)
Old Norse	e	i	î	ei

3 Order *u*.

Primitive	. . . . .	u	au	âu
Sanskrit	. . . . .	u	ô	âu
Gothic	. . . . .	u	iu (u)	au
Old High German	o	u	iu (u)	ou (ô)
Old Saxon	o	u	iu (û)	ô
Anglo-Saxon	o	u	eó (û)	eá (ê)
Old Frisian	o	u	íu (û)	â (ê)
Old Norse	o	u	iu (u)	au

These different vowels of the different languages just enumerated are liable to certain modifications brought about under the influence of other vowels or of consonants. Such modifications taking place according to phonetic laws did not exist in the primitive language. Where two vowels happened to succeed, hiatus probably took place, though it could but rarely occur, because the elision of consonants was not yet known. At a very early period, however, *a*, with a succeeding vowel, may have formed a compound vowel or diphthong, as a and $i = ai$. But in the cognate languages we find various phonetic laws which regulate the changes and modifications of vowels. Of these we have already mentioned the '*gradation*' or 'Steigerung,' according to which the vowel *a* enters into combination with its own kind ($a + a = aa$; $aa + a = áa$), or with *i* and *u* (*ai*, *au*, &c.), combinations which in the cognate languages are often contracted into *one*, and then of course a *long* vowel. The *degradation*, or *weakening*, or 'Schwachung' attacked first of all the most powerful of vowels, the *a*, which in Sanskrit we find weakened into *i* and *u*, in most of the Teutonic dialects weakened into *e*; the latter again often weaken the *u* into *o*, the *i* into *e*.

Vowels in the different Teutonic Dialects[1].

I. OLD TEUTONIC.

SHORT VOWELS.

ă

Gothic. (1) At the beginning of a word:—*alev*, oil; *arja*, I plough (Lat. aro); *arbaidja*, I work (Germ. arbeite); *asneis*, slave; *andeis*, end. (2) In the middle of a word:—*skalks*, servus; *favái*, few; *dal*, valley, dale (Germ. thal); *farja*, I sail (Germ. fahren); *hvar*, where; *þar*, there; *fadar*, father. (3) At the end of a word:—*ba*, both; *fra*, from; *hva*, what; *sa*, he; *sva*, so; *tva*, two; *ja*, indeed, yes (Germ. ja). In Gothic this short *a* is nowhere encroached upon by other vowels. Where in foreign words two *a*'s meet, they are rendered in Gothic either with an intermediate *h* or by one *a* being dropped, e. g. *Abraam*, Goth. *Abraham*; *Isaak*, Goth. *Isak*. In Gothic words however, two *a*'s can only meet where a particle is prefixed to a noun or verb, and in this case they remain intact, e. g. *ga-arbja*, co-heir; *ga-arman* to have pity (Germ. sich erbarmen).

Old High German has adopted the *a* under pretty nearly the same conditions as Gothic; it goes even farther and admits an *a* between liquids, and between liquids and mutes, which in Gothic stoutly refuse the admission of an *a*; as for instance, Gothic *arms*, poor; *akrs*, field); *tagr*, tear;—Old High Germ. *aram* (Germ. arm); *achar* (Germ. acker); *zahar* (Germ. zahre).

But the Old High German *a* is considerably modified by the Umlaut, by the inorganic production *a* (Goth. *ja*, O. H. Germ. *já*); by contraction in the middle of a word, and in a few cases by deviation into *o*, such as *holón* for *halon*, to fetch (Germ. holen); *scol* instead of *scal*, shall (Germ. soll); *joh* for Goth. *jah*, also; and finally in the weak inflexions where Old High German

---

[1] All vowels to be pronounced as in Italian or German, unless directed otherwise.

has *hano*, cock (Germ. hahn); *plinton*, blind, for Goth. *hana*, *blindan*.

The origin of the Umlaut we have already discussed. In Gothic there is no trace of it to be discovered, while in Old High German it appears to have arisen in the sixth or seventh century, and to have gradually developed itself, exposing the *a* to modification into *e*, chiefly before a single consonant followed by *i*. But even in Old High German the Umlaut is not systematically carried out; even the latest writers, as Notker for instance, preferring sometimes the original pure *a* to the Umlaut. Thus we find *alliu*, all, by the side of *hella* ; *angil*, and *engil*, angel (Germ. *engel*); *enti* together with *anti*. As an invariable rule, it must be laid down that the *i* of the termination cannot affect the *a* of the root unless it stands at the beginning of the terminational syllable, as in *enst-i, eng-il*, &c. The position of *a* is exceptional in the gen. and dat. sing. masc. and neut. of the weak declension, where the inflexional *i* has no power over it to create Umlaut. Therefore *hanin* not *henin*, of a cock ; *lamin*, of a lame man ; *scedin* for *scadin* (Germ. schaden), and *nemin* for *namin*, of a name, are exceptions.

Among the Saxon dialects, **Old Saxon** most closely approaches Old High German, and takes a kind of intermediate position between it and Anglo-Saxon. Its vowel *a* is throughout identical with that of Gothic and Old High German, and with the latter it adopts it even between liquids and mutes ; e. g. *sorga* and *soraga*, care (Germ. sorge) ; *bifelhan* and *bifelahan*, to order (Germ. befehlen). It wavers less between *a* and *o* than Old High German, with the exception of a few cases such as *far* and *for*, particle for- (Germ. ver-); *wala* and *wola*, well; *werald* and *werold, weruld, werld*, world. The particles *an* and *af* are turned into *on* and *of*.

The Umlaut is adopted but not generally applied, and the original vowel holds its place before *ht* and *ft*; as in *mahti, mahtig*, mighty (Germ. machtig); *crafti, craftig*, strong (cf. crafty, Germ. kraftig); occasionally also in the 3rd sing. pres. of strong verbs, e. g. *haldid* for *heldid*, he holds (Germ. halt) ; *fallid*, he falls (Germ. fallt); while verbs generally waver between *a* and *e*; e. g. *standid, stendid*, he stands; *slahit, slehit*, he sleeps; *hebbjan* and *habbean*, to have.

Anglo-Saxon has in but very few cases preserved the pure vowel *a*, which is generally weakened into *a* or flattened into *o*. The original *a* keeps its position before a single consonant which is followed by *a, o*, or *u*; e. g. *hwalas*, plur. of *hwäl*, whale ; *dagas, dagum*, nom. and dat. plur. of *dag*, day ; even before *e*, if

VOWEL SOUNDS.

the latter had its origin in *a, o,* or *u* ; chiefly in inflexional forms, as *care*, acc. sing. of *caru*, care. Foreign words always preserve their pure *a* sound, e. g. *Aprelis (Aprilis), aspide (aspis), carcern (carcer)*, &c. Before *m* and *n*, pure *a* may stand or be replaced by *o*, e. g. *wam* and *wom*, stain ; *can* and *con*, to know (Germ. kennen) ; *lamb* and *lomb*, lamb. But *a* is invariably weakened to *ä* in monosyllabic words which end in a single consonant, or in polysyllabic which terminate in *e* preceded by a single consonant. Examples :—(1) *hwäl*, whale ; *gläs*, glass ; *däg*, day ; *bär*, bare, naked ; *äcer, äcre*, field ; *bäcre*, baker ; *fäger*, fair, pretty. (2) Before *f* and *s* followed by another consonant : *cräft, cräftig*, craft, strength (Germ. kraft, kraftig) ; *äfter*, after ; *gäst*, guest (Germ. gast) ; also before a doubled mute or sibilant, e.g. *häbban* and *habban*, to have (Germ. haben); *äppel* and *appel*, apple. (3) In other combinations of consonants which are brought about by the elision of *e*, e. g. *fägres*, gen. of *fäger*, *äpl* for *äppel*. Two consonants beginning with *r* tolerate only the broken vowel *ea* in the preceding syllable, except in cases where *r* succeeds the *a* in transpositions, such as *gärs* for *gräs*, grass ; *bärst* for *bräst*, burst. These rules however do not hold good for all cases ; because in Anglo-Saxon the vowel *a*, unless it is sheltered or supported by a succeeding low-pitched vowel (*a, o,* or *u*), wavers in all directions, so that we cannot look upon its modification in *a* as a strictly fixed law, such as 'Umlaut,' or a systematical weakening of the *a*, but rather as an aberration of the *a* from its original pure sound which it has in Gothic and Old High German. In a few cases the primitive *a* kept its place where one might expect its transition into *ä*, e. g. *blac* for *bläc*, black ; *appel* for *äppel*, *ange* and *onge* for *änge*, narrow (Germ. enge).

As to the orthography of this modified *a*-sound, grammarians are at variance. Grimm writes *ä*, in order to distinguish this short vowel from the long *æ*, a distinction marked out by others spelling *æ* and *ǣ*. I adopt Grimm's mode of spelling, because it keeps the short and long vowels distinct, and, at the same time, runs parallel with the *ä* and *æ* in other Teutonic dialects.

The Anglo-Saxon *e* as Umlaut of *a* must be kept distinct from the modification of the *a* just mentioned. Very often the *i* which brought about the Umlaut is dropped or changed into another vowel, and thus arises the *hidden* Umlaut, e. g. *fen*, fen ; *hel*, hell ; *net*, net ; forms which are used in the place of the geminated *fenn, hell, nett*: these again were introduced instead of *fene, hele, nete*, and the latter stand for Gothic *fani, hali (halja), nati*. Thus we trace the hidden Umlaut to its original conditions, under which alone it could occur.

Old Frisian preserved the vowel *a* before *m* and *n*, whether single, geminated, or combined with a mute, unless it gives way like other dialects to an inclination towards *o*; hence *nama* and *noma*, name; *kampa* and *komp*, fight (Germ. kampf); *man* and *mon*, man. But the vowel *a* can never pass into *o* where Umlaut takes place. Therefore the pure *a* in *framd*, foreign (Germ. fremd); *mantel*, mantle; *manniska*, man (Germ. mensch); *hangst*, horse (Germ. hengst); because by the side of these appear the modified forms, *fremd*, *mentel*, *menska*, *hengst*. The vowels *a* and *u* in the termination preserve the *a* of the penult: *knapa*, boy (Germ. knabe); *fara*, to go (Germ. fahren); *balu*, evil (comp. baleful). Before the double consonants, *a* or *e* may occur, but so that the former appears preferable in the following cases: before *l*, *x* ($=$ks), and geminated mutes, e. g. *falla*, to fall; *balde*, soon (Germ. bald); *salt*, salt; even *kalde*, the cold (Germ. kalte), instead of the Umlaut *kelde*; *sax*, knife, sword; *atta*, father; *katte*, cat.

Old Norse has very largely patronized the pure *a*, after Gothic perhaps more so than any other dialect. This vowel occurs in *gala*, to sing; *snar*, quick; *napr*, cold; *hrafn*, raven; *slag*, blow (Germ. schlag); *vagn*, currus (Germ. wagen).

Where *a* occurs at the end of a word it is always lengthened into *á*; this lengthened form is also adopted by some grammarians and rejected by others, before consonantal combinations with *l* and *n*; *lf*, *lm*, *lp*, *lg*, *lk*, *ls*, *ng*, *nk*.

The Umlaut of *a* into *e* is caused by the occurrence of an *i* in the succeeding syllable, and that of *a* into *ö* by *u* in the same position. Hence the vowels *a*, *e*, and *o* may occur in one and the same word in different cases of the declension according to the terminational vowel; a circumstance which imparts to the Old Norse dialect a peculiar flexibility and softness which we can readily perceive on looking at the different forms of the word *magu*, which declines thus — *mog-r*, *magar*, *megi*, *mog*; plur. *megir*, *maga*, *mogum*, *mogu*. Whenever *i* does not cause the Umlaut of *a* in the preceding syllable, it must be considered inorganic, as for instance in *skari* (Germ. schaar), *Danir* (Danes). The Umlaut *o* is marked differently in different manuscripts and editions of manuscripts, either simply by *o* (hence *hon* and *honum* for *hon*, *honum*); or by the sign ǫ (whence the Danish ø); or by *au* and *av*. The sign *ö*, which is now in general use, is of a far more recent date.

i

This vowel in **Gothic** is, after *a*, the most prominent. Though it is sometimes encroached upon by the 'Brechung' before *h* and *r*, it receives on the other hand a numerical increase by the vocalization of the semi-vowel *j* wherever the latter happens to appear at the end of a word or before a consonant, e. g. *harja*, acc. *hari; nasjan*, preterite *nasida*. A radical *i* followed by another vowel likes to admit the semi-vowel *j*, e. g. *fijan* for *fian*, to hate (cf. fiend).

Old High German preserves the pure Gothic *i* before *m* and *n*, whether geminated or combined with a mute, e. g. *swimman, pintan;* in words which have dropped a final *i* or *u*; in nouns which belong to the themes in *i* and *u*; in the imperative of strong verbs; in the past participles of the fifth conjugational class; in monosyllabic particles. Some prefixes waver between *a* and *i*, e. g. *far-, fir-*, even *for-*, and later on *fer-* (Germ. ver-) ; *ga-, gi- ; za-, zi- ; ar-, ir- ; durah-, durih-*.

In many cases however the pure Gothic *i* is weakened or darkened into *e* by the power of assimilation exercised by an *a* in the succeeding syllable. Hence the rule—'Whenever *i* is followed by *a* in the succeeding syllable it is changed into *e*; before *i* and *u* and in the above-mentioned cases it remains unchanged.' On this rule are based the modifications of the vowels in the two first classes of the strong conjugation; and thus it will be perceived why we read in the sing. pres. *hilfu, hilfis, hilfit; nimu, nimis, nimit;* and in the plural, *helfames, helfat, helfant;* inf. *helfan*, to help; *nemames, nemat, nemant;* inf. *neman*, to take. Monosyllabic words which have dropped the terminational *a*, nevertheless retain the modified vowel *e*, e. g. *wec = wega*, way; *sper = spera*, spear; *ez̧*, it (Goth. *ita*); and others on the contrary which have dropped an *i* or *u* retain, in accordance with our rule, the pure *i* unchanged, e. g. *mist* (Goth. *maihstu*), *lid* (Goth. *lipu*), *list* (Goth. *listi*). How sensitive the Old High German dialect is with respect to the law of assimilation will be perceived from the fact that the modification *e* is always re-exchanged for the original pure *i* whenever it is followed by the adjective termination *in*, e. g. *fell*, skin (Lat. pellis), adjective *fillin*, of skin (Lat. pelliceus); *gersta*, barley, adjective *girstin*, of barley. In several words the *i* has kept its position in spite of the following *a*, such as *fisk = fiska*, fish; *pittar*, bitter, &c.; in others, either *i* or *e* may be used, e. g. *skep* and *skip*, ship; *wiht* and *weht*, thing; *irdin* and *erdin*, earthen (Germ. *irden*, terrenus). Concerning the 'Brechung' of *i* into *e* we shall have to say a few words hereafter.

The rules which we have just mentioned as to the weakening of *i* into *e* in Old High German, will hold good for the Low German dialects as well. Here, however, it is interesting to notice how they more or less apply this rule in proportion to their greater or less affinity to Old High German. **Old Saxon**, the nearest relative to Old High German, from its geographical position as well as its general characteristics, follows the Old High German rule which we have laid down above; but it so far deviates that it retains the unmodified *i* before *m* and *n* where they are geminated or combined with a mute; hence *wind*, wind; *singan*, to sing, &c.

The conjugational forms are affected as in Old High German, but *niman* retains its *i* throughout the present tense. Formations such as *berg*, mountain (Germ. berg), and *gibirgi* (Germ. gebirge); *gersta, girstin*; the fluctuating forms *geba* and *giba*, *fihu* and *fehu*, and the forms remaining unmodified in opposition to the rule, *wiðar*, against; *bittar*, bitter,—all these cases have already received their explanation in Old High German.

The **Anglo-Saxon** dialect has preserved the rule in a very imperfect condition, or it has perhaps never fully adopted it. It is true that *m* and *n* protect the pure *i*, but so do other consonants as well: thus we find *swimman*, to swim; *spinnan*, to spin; and also *gifan*, to give (O. H. Germ. gepan, Germ. geben); *lifer*, liver (O. H. Germ. lepar, Germ. leber); *cniht*, knight, boy, puer (O. H. Germ. cneht, Germ. knecht, servus). In the conjugation of strong verbs the rule is partly preserved. The 1st sing. yields to *e*, but the 2nd and 3rd retain the *i*; hence 1st *helpe* (O. H. Germ. hilfu, Germ. ich helfe), I help; 2nd *hilpst* (O. H. Germ. hilfis, Germ. hilfst), thou helpst; 3rd *hilpð* (O. H. Germ. hilfit, Germ. hilft), he helps.

The **Old Frisian** dialect agrees with Old High German by applying our rule in the following examples: *helm*, helm; *self*, self; *herte*, heart; *helpa*, to help; *werpa*, to throw (Germ. werfen); *berch*, mountain (Germ. berg); *swester*, sister, &c.; but a succeeding *u*, or its representative *o*, has no longer the power of preserving the pure *i*, hence *felo*, many (Germ. viele); *fretho*, peace (Germ. friede); *selover*, silver; and the change between *i* and *e* which we traced in the strong conjugation of Old High German, Old Saxon, and Anglo-Saxon, has altogether disappeared, and the verb is reduced to the monotonous forms, *werpe, werpst, werpth*.

The **Old Norse** dialect in this respect follows the Old High

German more closely than some of the Low German dialects do. It preserves the rule so far as it always admits the modification in *e* whenever succeeded by *a*, and rejects the same before simple *n* and a geminated mute.

Concerning the strong conjugations, we find in the inf. and pres. of the eighth, ninth, and tenth classes the original *i* retained in some roots and before *nn*, *nd*, *rn*, and a geminated media—*finna*, to find; *spinna*, to spin; *binda*, to bind; *vinda*, to wind; *vinna*, to work; *liggia*, to lie, &c., and in the part. pret. of the fifth class; the rest have adopted *e*, which, where it once has entered, keeps its ground throughout as it does in Frisian. In Old Norse, as well as in other dialects, the application of *e* or *i* cannot always be determined by a rule, but must be simply referred to the *usus loquendi*.

ŭ

In Gothic we find this letter, as well as *i*, in its pure sound at the beginning, the middle, and the end of words, in which cases other dialects frequently allow the vowel to be lengthened or weakened. But, like *i*, the letter *u* also is subject to Brechung before the consonants *h* and *r*, in which position it is changed into *au*. More of this phenomenon in its proper place.

Roots ending in *v* vocalize this consonant into *u*, just as roots ending in *j* vocalize this consonant into *i*. Hence the theme þiva forms the nom. þius instead of þivs, servant, voc. þiu: the pret. of *snivan*, to hasten, and þivan, to serve, is *snau*, þau. The opposite case occurs when the vowel *u* is dissolved in the consonant or semi-vowel *v*, especially in the inflexional forms where the hiatus must be avoided, e. g. *hand-ive*, gen. pl. of *handus*, hand; *sun-ive*, gen. pl. of *sunus*, son.

The **Old High German** dialect preserves the pure vowel *u* in many instances; but it modifies it to *o* under the same circumstances under which it changes the *i* into *e*. Hence the rule—'Whenever *u* is followed by *a* in the succeeding syllable, it is darkened or weakened into *o*; but when the succeeding syllable brings *u* or *i* instead of *a*, the original sound *u* regains its position in the root.' Thus will easily be understood forms such as the following: *chlupumes*, we clove, fidimus; *chlupi*, thou clovest, fidisti, and *chlopan*, cloven, fissum; and on the other hand *swummumes*, we swam, part. *swumman*, swum; *sungumes*, part. *sungan*, we sung, sung; in which forms the doubled *m*, and *n* combined with the mute *g*, preserve the *u* from the encroachment of the succeeding *a*.

In **Old Saxon** the vowel *u* is kept intact in many places, as in the words *sculd*, debt (Germ. schuld); *sumar*, summer; *suno*, son; *ubil*, evil. But it allows the Trübung, or darkening, into *o* under the same conditions as Old High German. Fluctuating forms are, *drohtin*, *druhtin*, lord; *drohting*, *druhting*, friend, familiaris; *fohs*, *vusso*, fox; *for*, *fur*, before, fore; *gomo*, *gumo*, man; *corni*, *curni*, corn. The *u* is restored to its position in the root by the influence of the terminational *i*, e. g. *horn*, horn, cornu; adj. *hurnid*, of horn, cornutus; *gold*, gold, aurum; adj. *guldin*, golden, aureus; *fora*, fore, pro, and *furi*.

Anglo-Saxon goes even beyond Old High German in its tendency to preserve the organic *u* in the root, so that it allows *u* before single *m* and *n*, and even before other consonants, whilst Old High German preserves it only before geminated *m* and *n*, or a mute combined with one of these liquids. Examples:— *guma*, man; þ*unor*, thunder; þ*unian*, to thunder; *ful*, full; *fugol*, bird (Germ. vogel); words which have invariably the weakened *o* in Old High German. In the conjugation of the strong verb, especially in the preterite, the vowel *u* is sheltered by a succeeding *m* and *n*, e. g. *swummon*, we swum, natavimus; *swummen*, swum, natum; *clumbon*, we climbed, scandimus; *clumben*, climbed, scansum; *sungon*, we sung, cantavimus; *sungen*, sung, cantatum; but in the past participle, if it is followed by any other consonant than *m* or *n*, it is weakened into *o*, e. g. *multon*, pret. pl. of *meltan*, 'to melt,' part. *molten; wurpon, worpen; budon, boden; curon, coren*, &c.

Peculiar to Anglo-Saxon is the transition of *w* into *u* where it appears in combination with *i*, in which case the latter vowel is often dropped. Thus: *wudu*, wood, for *widu*; *cuman*, to come, for *cwiman*; *suster, swuster*, sister, for *swister*. This *i* preceded by *w* is however safe from encroachment when it is followed by the liquid *m* or *n* combined with another consonant.

In **Old Frisian** the vowel *u* is but rarely preserved, since it has greatly given way to the 'Trübung' in *o*.

Old Norse approaches far more nearly to Old High German in the preservation of the pure Gothic vowels *a*, *i*, and *u*, but in this dialect also the 'Trübung' *o* may take the place of the organic *u* before all consonants, except such as are combined with *m* or *n*. An analogy to the Old High German conjugations we find in the exchange of *u* and *o* in the pret. pl. and part. pret. of the sixth and tenth classes; as, *spurnum, sporninn; spruttum, sprottinn; buðum, boðinn*, &c.

The Umlaut of u *is* y. Old High German, Old Saxon, and Old Frisian reject this Umlaut altogether, whilst in two other

Teutonic dialects we find it more or less developed. Anglo-Saxon shows many examples of this Umlaut: *cyning*, king, from *cunian*, to know; *dyrstig*, daring, from *duran*, to dare; *gyden*, goddess, from *gud*, god. In a few instances the word wavers between the Umlaut *y* and the original *u*, e. g. *wurt*, *wyrt*, wort, herb; *wurm*, *wyrm*, worm, worm; and in others the Umlaut *y* takes place in derivations where the root has the weakened vowel *o* instead of the original *u*, e. g. *gyden* from *god*, *þyrnen* from *þorna*, thorn; *gylden* from *gold*. In Old Norse, which has most widely and persistently developed the system of Umlaut, the *y* occurs regularly for the radical *u*, or its weakened form *o*, under the conditions which we have enumerated above; e. g. *syni*, dat. sing. of *sonr*, son; *kyn*, kin, genus; *fylla*, to fill; *bryggja*, bridge, &c.

ĕ, ŏ, y̆.

These short vowels are altogether unknown in Gothic. Their development and relative position in the other Teutonic dialects we have already had occasion to dwell upon, so that we need hardly do more than sum up our remarks made in the preceding paragraphs. The vowel *e* is of twofold origin, either Umlaut of *a*, or the 'broken' or 'weakened' form of *i*. Old High German, Old Saxon, and Old Norse hardly go beyond this rule in the adoption of the letter *e*, but Anglo-Saxon sometimes, and Old Frisian often, admit *e* instead of the pure *a* in cases which more often show the modification *a* in Anglo-Saxon.

The letter *o* we met either as the 'broken' or 'weakened' form of *u* in all the dialects except Gothic, or as the representative of *a* in cases of assimilation, so much favoured in Old High German.

The vowel *y* has a proper place but in few dialects; the Gothic language uses the sign *v* in Gothic words as a consonant only; but in foreign words this letter represents the Latin vowel *y* as well. In Old High German, Old Saxon, and Old Frisian the Latin form *y* is used in foreign words only, whilst Anglo-Saxon and Old Norse adopt this vowel chiefly for the purpose of expressing the Umlaut of *u*. At the same time, *y* in Anglo-Saxon is often the representative of other vowels; namely of *i*, of *e* where it is the Umlaut of *a*, and of the 'Brechung' *ea* and *eo*.

Brechung.

Gothic: When the consonants *r* and *h* directly succeed the vowel *i* or *u* they affect the purity of the pronunciation in such a manner as to make an *a* to precede the sound of *i* or *u*. The inorganic diphthongs which are thus produced in the Gothic dialect have nevertheless the value of a short vowel, and *ai* and *au* must consequently have sounded in pronunciation similarly to *e* and *o*. In order to distinguish this 'Brechung' from the true diphthongs *ái* and *áu*, modern grammarians have adopted for the former the accentuation *aí* and *aú*. Gothic documents write both Brechung and diphthong perfectly alike; and it was left to the researches of modern philology to point out and prove the difference from corresponding words in the kindred languages which always render the Gothic Brechung by a short vowel, and the Gothic diphthong by a long vowel. Thus Goth. *vaír* is Lat. *vir*; Goth. *tauhum*, Lat. *duximus*; Goth. *faír*, Lat. *per*; Goth. *baíra*, Lat. *fero*, Gr. *phero*; Goth. *taíhun*, Gr. *deka*; Goth. *saíhs*, Gr. *hex*; Goth. *dauhtar*, Gr. *thygater*, O. H. Germ. *tohtar*; Goth. *áins*, Lat. *únus*, O. H. Germ. *ein*, A. S. *an*, O. S. and O. Fris. *en*. Further light is thrown on the pronunciation of the Brechung *aí* and *aú* by the fact of the Goths having rendered the short *e* or *o* in foreign words, without any regard to the succeeding consonants, by the very same letters of the Brechung, certainly because *aí* and *aú* in pronunciation came nearest, or were perfectly alike, to *e* and *o*. Hence they write not only *Teibaírius* = Tiberius, *Faúrtunatus* = Fortunatus, which are in accordance with the Gothic Brechung before the consonant *r*; but also *aípistaule*, epistole; *Naúbaimbaír*, November. By different accentuation of Brechung and diphthong we keep up distinctions which must have been heard in Gothic pronunciation, such as the diphthong *ái* in the singular and the Brechung *aí* in the plural of the verb. Thus Goth. *láihv*, commodavi; O. H. Germ *léh*; A. S. *láh*, pl. *laíhvum*, commodavimus; O. H. Germ, *lihumes*; A. S. *ligon*; Goth. *táuh*, traxi; O. H. Germ. *zoh*; A. S. *teáh*, pl. *tauhum*, traximus; O. H. Germ. *zugumes*; A. S. *tugon*. In very few cases, and then only before the consonants *r* and *h*, it can be doubtful at all whether we have to deal with the Brechung *aí* or the diphthong *ái*, and then comparison with kindred dialects will soon remove the difficulty. Thus *gáiru* requires the diphthong on account of the Old High German *ker*; *haírus* the Brechung on account of the Old Norse *hiörr*. Before any other consonant but *r* and *h* the vowels *ai* and *au* are always true diphthongs. A few exceptional cases have preserved the original vowel intact even before *r* and *h*, e. g. *skura*, shower; *huhrus*, hunger; *hiri*, hear you, audi; *hirjiþ*, hear ye, audite, &c. &c.

Old High German has least of all Teutonic dialects adopted the system of Brechung, since it renders the Gothic Brechung *ai* and *au* by the vowels *e* and *o*, which are quite identical with *e* and *o* the weakened forms of *i* and *u*. We may indeed say that the *e* in *pérgan* and in *sehs* is the Brechung because it stands for *aí* in Goth. *baírgan* and *saíhs;* but this distinction does not avail us much, since the same vowel *e* may occur, not only before *h* and *r*, but before any other consonant as well.

More perfectly perhaps than any other dialect except Gothic has **Anglo-Saxon** developed the system of Brechung. In this dialect the Brechung *ea* for *a* occurs regularly before a combination of consonants beginning with an *l, r,* or *h,* e.g. *beald,* bold; *ceald,* cold (Germ. kalt); *eald,* old (Germ. alt); *eall,* all; *feallan,* to fall; *wearm,* warm; *stearc,* strong (Germ. stark); *eahta,* eight (Germ. acht); *eax* ($x = ks = hs$), axe; *weax,* wax. In such consonantal combinations it may often happen that one or other consonant, perhaps even the *h* itself which caused the 'Brechung' has been dropped, and yet the Brechung continues to exist, e.g. *eal = eall,* all; *mear = mearh,* mare; *ear = earh,* the sea. Sometimes Brechung appears before the single consonant *h,* as in *beneah,* he needs; *gefeah,* he rejoiced: in the verb *slean,* to slay, and *þwean,* to wash, the Brechung continues though *h* has been dropped by the contraction of *sleahan, þweahan*[1]. Even before an *f* and before liquids we sometimes meet with *ea* instead of the usual *a,* e.g. *creaftig = créftig,* strong (Germ. kraftig); *beadu, heaðu,* battle. On the other hand it may occur that the Brechung we should expect before certain consonants has been replaced by the Umlaut *e.*

As *ea* is the Brechung of *a,* so is *eo* the Brechung of *i,* which occurs most frequently before consonantal combinations beginning with an *r,* e.g. *eorl,* earl; *sweord,* sword; *heorte,* heart; *eorðe,* earth; *steorra,* star; *meorc,* dark, murky; *steorfan,* to die (Germ. sterben); *weorpan,* to throw (Germ. werfen). With these examples corresponds the Brechung in Old Norse and Gothic: O. N. *iarl,* earl; Goth. *haírto,* heart; *aírþa,* earth; O. N. *stiarna,* Goth. *staírno,* star; *vaírpan,* to throw. Less frequently it is found before *l,* as in *feola,* much (Germ. viel); *meolc,* milk; *seolfor,* silver: and before *h, leoht,* light; *eoh,* horse: or before mutes, *freoðe,* peace (Germ. friede); *heofon,* heaven. *h* seems to patronize an *i* preceding it, whilst *r, l,* and the mutes prefer the weakened form *e* to the Brechung *eo,* the vowel *e* occurring alternately with the Brechung *eo* in kindred words, e.g. *wer,* man, vir; *weorod,* crowd, turma; *meolc,* milk; *melcan,* to milk; *seolfor,* silver, argentum; *silfren,* of silver,

---

[1] Some write *sleán, þwcán,* as a diphthong, on account of the contraction.

argenteus. In these instances *eo* seems to be sheltered by the *o* in the succeeding syllable, and may consequently be considered an assimilation; as in general, bisyllables with a dark vowel in the last syllable prefer *eo* in the penult. Verbs which admit the Brechung *eo* restore the original *i* in the 2nd and 3rd persons singular, e. g. *weorpan*, to throw, *wirpst*, *wirpð* (Germ. werfen, wirfst, wirft); *steorfan*, to die, *stirfst*, *stirfð* (Germ. sterben, stirbst, stirbt) The close resemblance in the pronunciation of the double vowels *ea* and *eo* may be the cause of an occasional confusion in their application, and of the orthography *eo* instead of *ea*, e. g. *eofor* and *eafor*, boar (Lat. aper, Germ. eber); *beorht* and *bearht*, shining. Another form of the Brechung, though of rare occurrence, is that in *ie*, which however belongs to Old Saxon rather than Anglo-Saxon. It is sometimes used for the Brechung *eo*, *hiere = heore*, of her, ejus; for the weakened *e*, *gield — geld*, money (Germ. geld); for *i*, *siex = six*, six: even for *a*, *giest = gast*, guest.

Old Norse has not the great variety of Brechung we find in Anglo-Saxon, but it is not so capricious either. Wherever *l* or *r* succeed an *i*, this vowel is modified into *ia*. Sometimes a single consonant, or a combination with mutes, may produce the same effect. Examples: — *giald*, money; *stiarna*, star; *biartr*, shining; *iafn*, even, level. The Umlaut of *ia* to *iö* is caused by the letter *u* in the succeeding syllable; but when the inflexional syllable contains an *i* the Brechung is removed altogether, and the radical *i* is, according to the law of assimilation, restored to its place. The influence of these different euphonic laws gives the declension the aspect of a variegated colouring, and imparts to the language a peculiar and melodious softness. Thus compare sing. nom. *hiörtr* (*r = ur*) stag, gen. *hiartar*, dat. *hirti*, acc. *hiört*; pl. nom. *hirtir*, gen. *hiarta*, dat. *hiörtum*, acc. *hiörtu*. Whenever the weakened *e* has taken the place of *i* the Brechung cannot occur. Hence the verbs of the tenth conjugational class have either preserved the original *i*, or they have *e* throughout, with the exception of four verbs, *biarga*, to conceal; *gialla*, to sing; *gialda*, to spend; *ekialfa*, to tremble, which have in the infinitive, imperative and subjunctive present *ia*, in the indicative present *e*.

The other Teutonic dialects have less persistently than Anglo-Saxon and Old Norse carried out the law of Brechung. But with the exception of perhaps Old High German none is altogether without some traces of Brechung. Old Saxon offers the following forms of Brechung: *weard*, ward; *georno* (Germ. gern); *steorro*, star, instead of *ward*, *gerno*, *sterro*—forms which however may be explained by Anglo-Saxon influences which can here and there be traced in Old Saxon. The Brechung *ie* is used instead of the vowels *e, e,* and even *e,* in the following forms: *hieri,* army (Germ. heer); *thieses,* hujus; *thieson,* huic; *thiem,* iis; *kiesur,* emperor (Germ. kaiser). Another *ie* of an altogether different nature seems not so much dependent on succeeding consonants (which is the characteristic feature of every Brechung) as the unsettled nature of the vowel, and which in many instances gradually passed through *ie* into *i.* Thus we find *giuhu,* I confess, for *gihu;* so also *iuhu* for *iiuhu = jiuhu.* Here *iu* must be considered a Brechung. This Brechung in *iu* occurs more regularly in *Old Frisian* whenever *i* precedes the consonants *cht,* e. g. *riucht = richt,* right; *riuchta = richta,* to judge, richten; *kniucht,* servant (cf. Germ. knecht and Eng. knight); *sliucht,* plain (Germ. schlicht); *siucht,* he sees (Germ. sieht and sicht). A few other cases where it seems to occur are *tziurke,* church; *wriust,* wrist; and *tziust,* pellicium.

The only traces of Brechung which we detect in Old High German are in Notker, who has *ie* for *i* before *h* in *jieho, sieho.* The Essen Rotule has twice *thiores holtes* instead of *thurres holtes;* for Old High German *prust* everywhere *briost, breost*—phænomena which we perceive in Old Saxon and Old Frisian as well.

Assimilation.

Words of three and more syllables often show an inclination to assimilate to each other the non-radical vowels in such a manner as to convert the vowel of the preceding into the vowel of the succeeding syllable. Gothic does not yield to this assimilating tendency, but Old High German has developed it most systematically. In words of three syllables the last syllable assimilates the penult, e. g. *sconara* for *sconora; garenem* for *garanem; bitturu* for *bittaru; spíhiri* for *spíhari.* Words of four syllables assimilate either the third to the fourth, as *giholono* for *giholano; irbolgono* for *irbolgano:* or the second to the third, as *hungirita* for *hungarita; wachorota* for *wacharota:* or the second and third to the fourth, as *hungorogon* for *hungaragon.* The assimilated vowels remain short though the assimilating be long, e. g. *pittirí* for *pittarí,* not *pittíri.* Assimilated vowels have the same influence as organic vowels upon the root in causing Umlaut, weakening &c., so that for instance the assimilated *adali* becomes *edili* when the vowel of the penult is assimilated to the final *i,* thus causing the Umlaut of the *a* into *e;* and in *fërahi,* where we perceive the weakening of the radical *i* into *e* on account of the succeeding *a*, the original *i* is restored to its place when the *a* of the penult is assimilated to the final *i*, and thus we get the form *firihi*, vulgus. Thus then we see that the assimilation of vowels took place according to strictly fixed laws, though it was applied in certain authors only and never generally adopted. Since towards the end of the Old High German period the final vowels are more and more flattened and weakened, cases of assimilation become scarcer, and finally disappear altogether.

Old Saxon manifests some traces of assimilation in trisyllables, such as *hélogo* for *hélago*, holy; *mikulun* for *mikilun*, great; *sorogon* for *soragon*, curis; and between liquids and mutes, where, instead of the letter *a*, the vowel of the root finds entrance, e. g. *bereht* for *beraht*, brilliant; *burug* for *burg*, borough, urbs; *wuruhtjo* for *wurohtjo*, workman. Whilst Old Saxon displays scanty traces of assimilation, *Anglo-Saxon* and *Old Frisian* discard it altogether. *Old Norse* again, like *Old High German*, adopts this law and applies it regularly under certain conditions. Thus the trisyllabic plural of the preterite of weak verbs invariably assimilates the letter *a* of the penult to the terminational *u*, e.g. *rituðu* for *ritaðu*, scripserunt; *blotuðu* for *blotaðu*, immolaverunt. This *u* produced by assimilation may cause Umlaut in the root, e. g. *skopuðu*, creaverunt, of *scapa*; *kolluðu*, vocaverunt, of *kalla*. In the same manner are to be explained the feminine forms *gömul* = *gömulu*, *fögur* = *föguru*, *þögul* = *þögulu*, of the adjectives, *gamall*, old; *fagar*, fair; *þagal*, silent. The Brechung *ia* may return to the original *i* by assimilating itself to a succeeding *i*, e. g. *hiörtr*, *hiartar*, *hirti*, mentioned above.

Long Vowels.

â

This vowel is wanting in Gothic. Where therefore it occurs in the cognate dialects its place is taken in Gothic by *e*. Thus we find *a* for Goth. *e* in O. H. Germ. *jar*, Goth. *jer*, year; *mál*, *mel*, time (cf. Germ. ein-mal, zwei-mal, &c.); *wan*, Goth. *vens*, hope (cf. Germ. wahn); *sláfan*, O. S. *slápan*, Goth. *slepan*, to sleep; *dad*, Goth. *déds*, deed; *máno*, Goth. *mena*, moon; O. N. *mál*, Goth. *mel*, time; *máni*, Goth. *mena*, moon; *blása*, Goth. *blesan*, to blow (cf. Germ. blasen). In several dialects the Gothic *e* of the plural preterite of the eighth and ninth conjugational classes is commonly rendered by *á*, thus—

Goth. *nemum*, sumpsimus; O. H. Germ. *námumes*, O. S. *námun*, A. S. *námon*, O. N. *namum*.

Frequently the long *a* has its origin in an inorganic lengthening of the short *a*. Thus then we find for *á* of the Gothic *fáhan*, to catch; *bráhta*, attuli, I brought; *jáh*, yes (Germ. ja), the O. H. Germ. *fáhan*, *práhta*, *já*; O. S. *fáhan*, to catch; *bráhta*, *já*: Goth. pă, then; svă, so, sic, A. S. pa and swá: Goth. să he, is; svă, so, sic, O. N. sá and svá. This production of the Gothic ă into á in the other dialects must invariably take place where two ă's or an *a* and another vowel are contracted into one, or where an elision of consonants occurs. Thus O. H. Germ. *átum* for ăhătum, breath, spiritus; *Wisará* for *Wisarăhă*, Weser; *hán* for *hapen*, to have; *hát* for *hăpet*, he has; O. N. *há*, hay; *tár*, tear; *nátt*, night; *átta*, eight; *ást*, favour, for Goth. hăvi, tăgr, năhts, ăhtau, ănsts. In some dialects we find the Gothic terminational *ó* of the nominative and accusative plural of the declension in -a replaced by *á*, as in O. H. Germ. *viscá*, *kepá* (also *kepo*), for Goth. *fiscos*, *gibos*; and O. S. has besides *fiscos*, *dagos*, also *fiscás*, *dagás*. On the other hand the long *a* passes occasionally into the boundaries of the long *o*, as O. S. *froho* for *fráho*, Goth. *frauja*, lord; *fro*, for *fráh*, joyful (Germ. froh); A. S. *mona* for O. H. Germ. *máno*, Goth. *mena*, moon; *sona* for M. H. Germ. *sán*, soon: and in Old Norse we find a few cases in which the long *a* is even converted into the short *o*, e. g. *quon* for *quán*, Goth. *qens*, wife; *vod* for *vád*, O. H. Germ. *wát*, dress; *von* for *ván*, Goth. *vens*, hope.

In **Anglo-Saxon** the long *a* occurs most frequently as the representative of the Gothic diphthong *ái* (O. H. Germ. *ei*), thus being most probably the condensation, as it were, of a more ancient Anglo-Saxon diphthong *ai*. Examples:—A. S. *ágan*, to have; *tácen*, token; *hláf*, bread; *lare*, doctrine; *scádien*, to separate; *hám*, home, for Goth. *áigan*, *táikns*, *hláifs*, *láiseins*, *skáidan*, *háims*. The same relation to the Gothic *ai* we find in the Old Frisian, e. g. *á*, A. S. *á*, Goth. *ái*, law; *hám*, home; *ága*, to have, &c. In this dialect however the long *á* is most frequently found in the place of the Gothic diphthong *áu*, which in Anglo-Saxon is replaced by *eá*, as we shall have to show hereafter. Hence O. Fris. *áre*, ear; *áge*, eye; *hlápa*, to run; *gá*, region or district (Germ. gau), for Goth. *áuso*, *áugo*, *hláupan*, *gáujans*. In very few cases the Old Norse dialect has, like the Anglo-Saxon condensed *ái* into *á*, as *tá*, toe; *sár*, sore, vulnus; *á*, I have; by the side of which we find, as in Old High German, the diphthong *ei* in *eiga*, to have.

The vowel *æ*, analogous to *e* the Umlaut of ă, appears as the

Umlaut of *a*. In this capacity however we meet it only in Old Norse, and exceptionally in Anglo-Saxon. O. N. *æ* = O. H. Germ. *a*; e. g. *sæll*, happy; *ærr*, year; *væna*, to hope; *sæði*, seed = O. H. Germ. *sálig, jár, wánen, sat:* O. N. *æ* = Goth. *ái*; *æ*, always; *sœ*, lake, sea (Germ. see); *snœ*, snow (Germ. schnee); *lœra*, to teach (Germ. lehren), = Goth. *áiv, sáivs, snáivs, láisjan*.

This same Umlaut appears occasionally in Anglo-Saxon, chiefly in the conjugations, e. g. *hate*, vocor (Germ. ich heiße); *hætst, hæt,* Goth. *háita háitis, háitiþ*. As a rule however the vowel *æ* in Anglo-Saxon has less of the nature of the Umlaut than of that wavering, transitional sound of *a*, which on a former occasion we found encroaching upon the position of the vowel *a*. Thus again *æ* replaces the *á* which undoubtedly in Anglo-Saxon, as in Old High German, was the original vowel, and often indeed preserved its position intact before the consonants *m, v, p, l, t, g,* in the preterite of verbs: in most cases however, yielding to a weakening influence, it was gradually thinned into *æ*. This sound, more nearly than the Old High German *á*, approaches the Gothic sounds of *e* and *ai*, which it has to represent. For O. H. Germ. *á*, Goth. *e*, we meet it in the following words: *sæl*, happiness; *dæd*, deed; *stræt*, street; *wæg*, wave (Germ. woge); and in the preterite plural of the verbs of the eighth and ninth conjugational classes, e. g. *lægon, sæwon, scæwon, tæron,* &c. In this instance, however, the original *á* preserves its place before the consonants which we have just mentioned. Hence we find *lágon* for *lagan, sáwon* for *sœwon*. For Goth. *ai* we meet A. S. *æ* in *sæ*, sea; *dæl*, deal, pars; *clæne*, clean; *hæðen*, heathen; *flæsc*, flesh.

ê

This vowel has in Gothic to fill the place of the long *a*. Examples:—*jer*, year, O. H. Germ. *jár; slepan*, to sleep, O. H. Germ. *sláfan; mena*, moon, O. H. Germ. *máne; mel*, time, O. H. Germ. *mál; rens*, hope, O. H. Germ. *wán:* verbs in the preterite plural of the eighth and ninth conjugational classes, *nemum*, O. H. Germ. *námumes*: terminational in declensions, *dag-e*, of days, dierum.

Very rarely we find the vowel *e* in the other Teutonic dialects correspond in meaning with the Gothic vowel of the same kind, since, as we have already mentioned, the Gothic *e* is commonly replaced by *á* in the other dialects. As rare instances of the Gothic *e* being preserved in its position we may enumerate in Old High German a few derivative forms, such as, *gê-m*, *ge-s*, *ge-t*, *stem*, *stes*, *stet*, from the roots *gá*, *stá* of the verbs *gán*, to go, *stán*, to stand: in Old Saxon the occasional occurrence of the Gothic *e* instead of the typical Old Saxon *a*, as in *jer* instead of *jár*, year; *weg* instead of *wag*, wave (Germ. woge). In Anglo-Saxon also this *é* occurs now and then, especially before the consonants *m* and *n* instead of the organic *æ* = *á*; e. g. *cweman*, to please; *cwen*, queen; *wen*, hope (Goth. *gens*, *rens*, &c.). Old Frisian has its exceptional examples of the same kind: *mel* = *mál*, time; *wepen* = *wápen*, weapon; *weron*, they were; *jevon*, they gave. That this *e* has replaced a more ancient *á* becomes evident from some later forms, where we find the original *á* still preserved in the *ó* of *nómon*, they took, ceperunt, and *komon*, they came, venerunt.

But the proper sphere of the vowel *e* is the representation of the diphthong *ei* (= Gothic *ái*), which it renders in a condensed form when it occurs before the consonants *w*, *h*, and *r*, and in terminations and inflexions. Thus O. H. Germ. *sewes*, Goth. *sáivis*, *snewes*, Goth. *snáivis*, gen. sing. of *seo*, sea; *sneo*, snow; *zeh*, Goth. *táih* (Germ. *zieh*, accusavi); *leran*, Goth. *láisjan*, to teach; *ger*, Goth. *gáiru*, spear. The consonant *w* in the roots *sew*, *snew*, in the mentioned examples, is vocalized when terminational, and thus in the nominative singular it becomes *u*, *o*, or *a*, and later on it is dropped altogether: e. g. *seu*, *seo*, *se* (Germ. *see*, sea, lake); *sneo*, *sne* (Germ. *schnee*, snow). Before *n* the condensed *e* interchanges with *ei*, therefore *en* and *ein*, one; *ben*, *bein*, bone; rarely *peẟo* for *peide*, both, and *escon* for *eiscon*, to ask. In the inflexions *e* is the characteristic vowel of the third weak conjugation: *hapes* = Goth. *habáis*; *hapet* = Goth. *habáiþ*; *hapeta* = Goth. *habáida*, habes, habet, habui; as in general the Gothic inflexional *ái* is represented by *e* in Old High German. The other dialects also yield abundant examples of the condensation of the Gothic *ái* into *e*, such as O. S. *se*, sea; *hem*, home; *era*, honour; *hêl*, heal, salvus; *ewig* (Germ. ewig), eternal; *hetan* (Germ. *heißen*, vocari); *flesc*, flesh; O. Fris. *se*, sea; *sela*, soul; *ger*, spear; *wepen*, weapon; *teken*, token; O. N. *kne* = *kneg* and *kneig* (Germ. *neig-te*, inclinatus sum); *ste* = *steig* (Germ. *stieg*, scandi); *ega* = *eiga*, to have; *meri*, major; *mestr*, maximus.

A very characteristic feature chiefly of the Low German dialects is the reduplicational *e*. In Old High German too we find occasionally the Gothic reduplication preserved in this contracted form: e. g. *fenc* for *fienc*, Goth. *faifah*, pret. of *fahan*, to catch; *slêfun*, Goth. *saislep*, pret. of *slepan*, to sleep; *leʒ* for *lieʒ*, Goth. *lailot*, pret. of *laian*, to scold; *geng*, Goth.

gaigagg; but the pret. form used in Gothic is *iddja* and *gaggida*, pret. of *gaggan*, to go; O.S. *héld*, pret. of *haldan*, to hold; *het*, pret. of *hetan* (Germ. *heiβen*, vocari); *let*, pret. of *látan*, to let; A.S. *geng*, pret. of *gangan*, to go; *let*, pret. of *lætan*, to let; *slép*, pret. of *slæpan*, to sleep; *féng*, pret. of *fŏn=fangan*, to catch; *héng*, pret. of *hangan*, to hang; *het*, pret. of *hátan*, to order; and a few other verbs of a similar form. This preterite *e* is the condensation of the diphthong *eo*, as in Old High German of *ie*, which latter vowel preserved its place in several verbs; in others it is found alternately with *e* : Old Frisian *ble*, preterite of *blá*, to blow, and the preterites *het, held, feng, geng, let*, which correspond in form and meaning with the same verbs in the other dialects already mentioned; and the list may be completed by adding several forms in Old Norse, such as *het, helt, fékk, gekk, let*. In all the mentioned dialects the long *e* is the condensation of diphthongs, as in Old High German of *ia, io, ie*, in Anglo-Saxon of *eo*, or the lengthened forms of short vowels caused by the elision of the reduplicational consonants. Similar productions of the radical vowel by elision of the reduplicational consonants and contraction of the vowels are found in the cognate languages, such as the Latin *jacio, feci=fefici*.

In a few dialects the long *e* has a wider range than we have hitherto mentioned. Thus in Anglo-Saxon and Old Frisian it is used to indicate the Umlaut of *ó*, and in the latter dialect even the Umlaut of *u*, which in Anglo-Saxon is rendered by *y*. Examples in A.S.:—*feran* (Germ. fahren), to go; *wepan*, to weep; *fét*, pl. of *fot*, foot; *meðer*, pl. of *moðer*, mother; *teð*, pl. of *toð*, tooth. O. Fris. Umlaut of *ó—fera, wepan, swet*, sweet, *fét*, feet; Umlaut of *ú—sele* (Germ. *säule*, pillar); *héde*, hide, skin.

The long *e* as the condensation of the Anglo-Saxon *eá* and the Gothic *áu* is also met with in Anglo-Saxon and Old Frisian, e. g. A. S. *néd*, Goth. *náuþs*, need; *heran*, to hear (Goth. *áuso*, ear); *stepan*, to erect, from *steáp*, high, steep; *beg* for *beáh*, ring; *depan*, to dip, and *deápung*, a dipping; and so likewise in O. Fris., *néd*, need; *depa*, to dip, and *skene* (Germ. *schon*, pretty), Goth. *skáuns*.

Not uncommon in Old Frisian and Old Norse is the condensed form of *e* for the Gothic diphthong *iu*=A. S. *eo*, e. g. O. Fris. *kne*, Goth. *kniu*, knee; *pre*=A. S. *preon*, muscle, and O. N. *kne*, knee; *tre*=A. S. *treó*, tree.

For Gothic *ei* we find in a few cases *é* again in O. N., e. g. *se*, A. S. and O. H. Germ. *sí*, sim; *ve*, Goth. *veihs*, temple; *vel*, A. S. *wil*, fraud.

Not uncommon is the production of *e*, or of any short vowel in fact, by the elision of consonants. Thus we have in O. N. *fe* (Germ. *vieh*, pecus, cf. Eng. *fee*, pecunia), Goth. *faíhu; se*, video, Goth. *saihva; ná*, nec, Goth. *nih; rettre*, right, Goth. *raíhts; fletta* (Germ. *flechten*, nectere), Goth. *flaíhtan*.

î

The *i* has in Old High German and most other dialects replaced the Gothic diphthong *ei*. Thus O. H. Germ. *drı*, three; *frí*, free; *huíla*, time; *wın*, wine; *líp*, life; *zít*, time: O. S. *thrı, frí, huíla, wín, líf, líd*: A. S. *hwíl, wín, líf, tíd, wíf*, wife; *tím*, time: O. Fris. *hwíle*, time, delay; *líf*, life; *wíf*, wife; *hwít*, white; *swín*, swine: O. N. *vín, svín, tími, víf, hvítr*, white;—all being nearly identical even to the very words in which they replace by *ı* the Goth. *ei* in þ*reis*, three; *freis*, free; *veila*, time; *vein*, wine, &c. &c.

Sometimes the long *i* is the result of production which takes place in cases of elision where *ı* and *ĭ* meet. Thus we have Old High German *pıht* (Germ. *beicht*, confession), from *pĭgĭht; chít*, dicit, from *chidit*. More frequent is the inorganic production of short *i* at the end of words, and even of syllables, before an inflexional vowel or consonant; e. g. in the Goth. preposition *bi*, apud, O. H. Germ. *pı*; O. S. *bí*, O. H. Germ. *sí, sís, sí-mes, sí-t, sí-n*, for the Gothic *si-au, si-ais*, or *sij-áu, sij-áis*, &c.: and in the same manner *fíant*, enemy, fiend; *fríunt*, friend; Goth. *fij-ands, frij-ands;* where we see in Gothic the semi-vowel *j* introduced in order to preserve the short vowel *i* which precedes it. A few examples of the same kind we have in the O. N. *bí*, a bee; *sía*, to see, Goth. *saíhvan; í*, in; *díar = divar*, gods. Correption takes place—i. e. the organic *ı* (= Goth. *ei*) is replaced by the short *i*—in some forms of the possessive pronouns, as O. H. Germ *mines, dines, mina, dina, sina*, by the side of *mín, dín, sín;* and O. N. *minn, mitt;* þ*inn,* þ*itt; sinn, sitt*, by the side of *mín, sín,* þ*ín*. This correption of the long *i* also occurs in Old Norse where the termination *ið* of the adj. is assimilated to the neutral termination *t*: e. g. *blíðr*, polite; neut. *blĭtt*.

ô

This is a long vowel which in Gothic has, together with *é*, to fill the place of the long *a*. Examples:—*ógan*, to dread; *dóms*, doom; *mods*, mood, mind, courage; *bloma*, Germ. *blume*, bloom, flower; *stols*, seat, stool; *broþar*, brother; *boka*, book.

The Old High German *o* is the condensation of the diphthong *ou*, just as *e* is the condensation of *ei*; and it has therefore the same relation to the Gothic *áu* as *é* has to the Gothic *ái* It appears regularly before *l, n, r, h*, and the linguals *s, d, t, z*. Examples:—*holoht*, a ruptured person, herniosus; *lon* (Germ. lohn), reward; *ror* (Germ. rohr), reed; *hoh*, high; *trost* (Germ. trost), consolation; *ostará* (Germ. ôstern), Easter; *toð* (Germ. tod), death; *not* (Germ. noth); need; *prot* (Germ. brod), bread; *groz* (Germ. groß), great; *ploz* (Germ bloß), bare, nude; *fro*, lord. For this *o* one of the Old High German dialects uses the diphthong *ao*; hence *laon, raor, praot*, &c., instead of *lon, ror, prôt*, &c. The same dialect which replaces *ó* by *ao* makes use of the former vowel in the place of the common O. H. Germ. *uo* = Goth. *ó*, which the Low German dialects also render by *o*. Hence the dialectic *for* = common O. H. Germ. *fuor* (Germ. fuhr), ivi; *plomo* = *pluomo* (Germ. blume), flower, bloom; *hrom* = *hruom* (Germ. ruhm), glory, fame,—forms which are identical with the O. S. *for, blomo, hrom*. The Low German dialects further agree with Old High German in admitting the *ó* for Gothic *áu*, which in Old High German was commonly rendered by *ou*, but then condensed from a diphthong into a single long vowel. The forms *fro, lon, hoh, brod, nod, grot, dod*, are again therefore identical with the Old High German words which we mentioned above.

The Anglo-Saxon *ó* is identical with the Gothic *ó* throughout. Examples:—*bloma*, flower, bloom; *dom*, doom; *for*, ivit; *don*, to do; *mor*, moor; *hróf*, roof; *genoh* (Germ. genug), enough; *boc*, book; *blod*, blood; *flod*, flood; *fot*, foot; *broðer*, brother.

Old Frisian and Old Norse follow the same rule in preserving the original Gothic *ó*. Thus O. Fris. *dom*, doom; *blója*, to bloom; *brother*, brother; *bok*, book; and O. N. *domr*, doom; *bok*, book; *skogr*, forest; *floð*, course. Peculiar to all the Low German dialects is the occasional interchange between *o* and *a* which we have already pointed out. Hence O. S. and A. S. *mona*, moon, *sona*, soon, for *mána* and *sán*; O. Fris. *son* and *sán*, soon; *mona*, moon; *nomon*, ceperunt (Germ. nahmen); *komon* (Germ. kamen), venerunt: and in Old Norse it is preferred to *a* where an assimilation or elision of consonants has taken place; e. g. *sofum* = *sváfum*, dormivimus; *só* = *sva*, sic; *on* = Goth. *auhns*, oven; *drottin* = O. H. Germ. *trohtin*, lord; *dottir* = O. H. Germ. *tohtar*, daughter.

û

This vowel replaces in Old High German and in the Low German dialects three different Gothic vowels; namely, *u, iu, áu*. For Gothic *u* :—O. H. Germ. *dusunt*, thousand ; *runa*, mystery ; *prut* (Germ. braut), bride ; *pruchan* (Germ. brauchen), to use: O. S. *runa*, colloquy ; *brud*, bride ; *brucan*, to make use of, frui : A. S. *run*, mystery ; *bruce*, utor ; *rum*, room, space ; *mur* (Germ. mauer), wall ; *hus*, house : O. Fris. *bruka*, uti ; *hús*, house ; *ful*, foul ; and O N. *full*, run, hus ;—forms which correspond with the *ú* in Gothic *fuls*, foul ; *rums*, room ; *runa*, mystery ; *hus*, house ; *bruþs*, bride ; *brukjan*, uti.

For Gothic *iu* :—O H. Germ. *úf*, upwards, sursum ; *luhhan*, to lock ; *súfan*, to drink (cf. Germ. saufen) ; *sukan* (Germ. sauchen), to suck : O. S. *up*, sursum ; *cusco* (M. H. Germ. *kiusche*), reverenter : A. S. *supe*, bibo ; O. Fris. *frudelf=friudelf*, lover ; *kriose, krus*, cross ; *fliucht, flucht*, fugit : O. N. *luka*, to look ; *suga*, to suck.

For Gothic *au* :—O. H. Germ *puan*, to dwell ; *ka-tru-en* (Germ. ver-trau-en), to trust ; *sul* (Germ. saule), column : O. S. *buan, súl ; clustar* for Latin *claustrum* : O. N. *bua, trua, sul*.

The long vowel *u*, where it occurs at the end of a word, is a later production of the Gothic short *u*. Hence this vowel is, even in Old High German and several Low German dialects, often short or at least doubtful. O. H. Germ. *nu*, now, and *dú*, thou, for the earlier *nu* and *du*, Goth. *nu* and *þu*. The quantity of *nu* and *thu* in Old Saxon is doubtful, whilst in Anglo-Saxon the length of *nú* and *þu* is undoubted. In Old Frisian this vowel is, as in Old Saxon, wavering between short and long, whilst Old Norse gives it undoubted length, since as a rule, in Old Norse all radical vowels suffer production when occurring at the end of a word. Umlaut of *u* occurs in several Low German dialects. The Old High German in its latest documents has occasionally *iu* as Umlaut of *ú*, thus *hús*, house, pl. *hiuser ; chrut*, herb, pl. *chriuter*. In Anglo-Saxon and Old Norse the Umlaut of *u* is *ŷ*.

ŷ

This vowel belongs only to Anglo-Saxon and Old Norse. In Anglo-Saxon it is Umlaut of three vowels :—(1) of *ú*, e. g. *cu*, cow, pl *cŷ*, kine ; *lús*, louse, pl *lŷs*, lice ; *mús*, mouse, pl. *mŷs*, mice ; *brúd*, bride, pl. *brŷd*: ( ) of *eó* (Goth. iu), e.g. *lŷge* (Germ. lüge), a lie ; *cyre*, election : (3) of *eá*, e. g. *hŷran*, to hear ; *gelŷfan*, to believe. In Old Norse ý is Umlaut (1) of ú, e. g. kýr, pl. of kú, cow; mysla, mus femina; lýk, I lock : (2) of iu, or the weakened form io, e. g. fýr, fire; þýr, servant; dýr, animal.

In conclusion of our survey of the long vowels we have to state one more fact which forms a peculiar feature of several Low German dialects, especially Anglo-Saxon and Old Norse, and which consists in the dropping of the consonant *n* before sibilants, and the lengthening of the short vowel, especially *o*, which precedes it. Examples:—A. S. *toð*, O. H. Germ. *zand*, tooth; *gos*, O. H. Germ. *kans*, goose; *sóft*, O. H. Germ. *senfti*, soft. Umlaut of *ó* is *e*, *teð*, *ges*, *séfte* (see above). Analogous forms are, *soð*, sooth, true; *oðer*, Goth. *anþar*, other. Examples of other vowels:—*swið*, strong, Goth. *svinþs*; *fíf*, five, Goth. *fimf*; *user*, our, Goth. *unsar*; *cuðe*, novit; *muð*, mouth, Goth. *munþs*. Some grammarians deny however the length of the vowels in the words *fif*, five; *oðer*, other; *toð*, tooth; *cuð*, notus; *muð*, mouth. In Old Norse the lengthening of the vowel takes place regularly when the consonant *n* suffers elision before the sibilant *s*, not before ð. Hence we read *gas*, goose; *ást*, favour, Goth. *ansts*; while *maðr*, man; *muð*, mouth; *oðrum* (dat. of *annar*, other), preserve the short vowel.

Scandinavian grammarians have moreover proposed to assume the lengthening of the vowels *a, o, u*, before the following combinations of consonants, *lm, lp, lf, lg, lk, ls, ng, nk*, and of the vowel *i* before *ng* and *nk*. It is however considered doubtful whether the Old Norse dialect really had adopted such distinctions, which after all might be the creation of a later period. As to the letter *i* the case appears less doubtful; but the production of *a* and *o* is considered very rare before consonantal combinations with an *l*, especially in the 'Ablaut,' whence forms like *skalf, skolfinn, svalg, svolginn*, preserve the short *a* and *o*. The Umlaut of *a* before *ng* and *nk* is *e* or *o*, both of which are short vowels and must correspond with *a*, not with *a*.

As a rule German grammarians mark the length of a vowel in all the different dialects by the sign ʌ; but some have, in publishing Old Norse and Anglo-Saxon documents, occasionally adopted the mode of Scandinavian and English grammarians, according to which the length is marked by the acute ('). The student will therefore read *toð = tóð* ; *muð = múð* ; *mýs = mýs*.

Diphthongs.

ái

In Gothic this diphthong occurs rather frequently. Examples:
—*sáivs*, sea, lake; *snáivs*, snow; *sáivala*, soul; *dáils*, deal, part; *háima*, home, village; *áins*, one; *stáins*, stone; *bái*, both; *háihs*, blind, caecus; *háils*, heal, whole; *báitrs*, bitter. Always in the reduplication of the verb. Thus *sái-salt, skái-skáid, stái-staut, sái-slep, lái-lo, tái-tok*, are the reduplicated preterita of the verbs *saltan*, to salt; *skáidan*, to separate (Germ. scheiden); *stautan*, to push, beat (Germ. stoßen); *slépan*, to sleep; *laian*, to scold; *tekan*, to touch. This Gothic *ái* is in the other dialects generally rendered by *ei* or its condensation *e* and *i* (vide sub litt. **ei, ê, î**).

ei

This diphthong in its organic nature is met with only in Gothic, Old High German, and Old Norse. In these dialects however it has different tasks to perform. The Gothic *ei* is commonly replaced in Old High German and Old Norse by the long vowel *i*, while the diphthong *ei* in the latter dialects stands for Gothic *ai*. Examples of Gothic *ei*:—*eisarn*, iron; *reisan*, to rise; *tveifls*, doubt (Germ. zweifel); *svein*, swine, pig; *vein*, wine; *meins, þeins, seins* (Germ. mein, dein, sein); compare O. H. Germ. *isaru, rísan, zuível, suuin, win, min, din, sin*. It further occurs in *Gothic* as the termination of substantives of the weak declension, e. g. *aiþei*, mother; *svinþei*, strength.

The *Old High German ei* in *heim*, home; *stein*, stone; *ein*, one; *heil*, heal, whole; *eigan*, to own; *fleisc*, flesh; and the Old Norse *ei* in *eitre*, poison, venom (Germ. eiter); *eir*, iron; *breiðr*, broad; *heill*, heal; *eiga*, to own,—correspond with the Gothic *ái* as we have already mentioned. In Old High German and Old Norse we find the diphthong also in the preterites of the verbs of the fifth class, e. g. *dreif*, pepuli; *hrein*, clamavi; *beit*, **momordi**; **reis**, **surrexi**.

Concerning the condensation of *ei* into *e* we refer to what we have stated sub lit. **e**. The other dialects offer hardly any traces of the diphthong *ei* in its organic nature, that is, coinciding with the Gothic *ái*; but Old Frisian has abundant examples of an inorganic *ei*. Thus we find *ei* originating in contraction of the terminations *eg* and *ag*, e. g. *wei*, way; *dei*, day; *slei*, blow; but pl. *wegar, degar*, where the consonant reappears. As the contraction of *eg* we meet it in *ein=egin*, own, proprius; *heia=hega*, tollere. *ei=e* in *deil*, for *del*, dale; *weisa=wesa*, to be; *ei=ú, iu, ou*; *hei*=O. H. Germ. *hou*, a blow; *beile*=O. H. Germ. *biule*, a tumor (Germ. beule); *breid*=O. H. Germ. *prut*, bride, spouse. In a few words introduced from Old High German the Old Frisian *ei* is identical with the same diphthong in Old High German, such as *keisar*, emperor; *leia*, layman.

iu

This is the only Gothic diphthong which is rendered in its pure and original sound in other dialects as well, though most of them also allow of a weakened form, and Anglo-Saxon replaces it by an altogether different diphthong, namely *eo*. Examples:—Gothic *triu*, tree; *kniu*, knee; *niujis*, new; *jiuleis*, July; *biugan*, to bend (Germ. biegen); *iup*, sursum.

Old High German *iu* coincides with the same diphthong in Gothic, but it is occasionally replaced by *u* or the weakened *io*. The latter stands to *iu* in the same relation as does the vowel *o* to *u*, and consequently it occurs under the same conditions, namely, when the following syllable contains the vowel *a*, while *i* or *u* in the succeeding syllable preserve the pure diphthong *iu*. The same rule holds good for monosyllables which form the theme in *a, i,* or *u*, as well as for the conjugation of the verb. Hence we have the forms *kiuʒu*, fundo; *kiuʒ-is, kiuʒit, kioʒames, kioʒant*; imp. *kiuʒ*; inf. *kioʒan*. So also in the declensions and derivatives of words, as *diota*, people; *diutisk*, popular, vernacular, hence *Deutsch*, German; *lioht*, light; *liuhtjan*, to lighten (Germ. *leuchten*, splendere). The plurals *diopá, stiorá,* or *nium, liutí,* explain forms such as *diop*, thief; *stior*, bull (Germ. stier), or *niun, liut,* people. *Fior*, four, Goth. *fidvor*, has formed the diphthong by the elision of consonants, in the same manner as *diorna*, ancilla, puella (Germ. dirne).

As to the use of the weakened form of *iu*, the Old High German documents differ vastly, so that from the original pure diphthong *iu* we see them pass through the whole scale of vowels, *iu* and *eu*, *io* and *eo*, *ia* and *ea*, and finally *ie*. This variation of sounds is partly owing to dialectic differences, partly to the rapid wearing down of full-sounding vowels, which we observe towards the close of the Old High German period.

Otfrid, where he makes use of 'Schwachung,' chooses *io* for monosyllabic words: in polysyllables he yields to the influence of assimilation; so that he prefers *io* where the following syllable contains an *o, ia* or, rarely, *ie,* where a high-pitched vowel such as *a* or *e* succeeds. Therefore *zioro, thiononti,* and *ziari, liabe, liebes*. But monosyllabic nouns, though they assume a high vowel in the inflexion, nevertheless retain their *io*, hence *thiote, liohtes*; except *ie* in *liedes,* carminis. Later authors, from the time of Tatian, and especially Notker, flatten the *io* still further into *ie*. The *ia* however is peculiar to Otfrid. The more ancient authors down as far as Isidor have a diphthong *eu* for *iu* in ancient proper names, nouns, and pronouns, e.g. *eu*, vobis; *euwih,* vos; *hreunun,* poenitentiam, for *iu, iuwih, hriunun*. Kero and Isidor have *eo* and *ea* for *io* in the inflexions, as *waldend-eo, minn-ea;* ui sometimes instead of *iu*. There occurs another *ia* or *ea* in Kero and Otfrid which corresponds with Goth. *e*, not *iu*; e. g. *mias, meas,* table, Goth. *mes*; *hiar,* here, Goth. *her*.

With this one exception all the vowels mentioned are weakened forms of *iu*. There is however another diphthong *ia* (Otfrid), *ea* (Kero, Isidor), or *ie* (Tatian, Notker), which has its origin in the condensation or contraction of a more ancient reduplication. Thus *hialt, healt,* pret. of *haltan;* blias, *bleas, blies,* pret. of *blasan*. The original reduplication still shows itself unmistakeably in a form *heialt,* used by Kero instead of *hialt,* and which closely approaches the Gothic *haihald,* pret. of *haldan*. The diphthong *io* we find in the preterite of those verbs which have in the present the radical vowel *ou, ó,* or *uo;* e. g. *loufu,* pret. *hof* (Goth. *hlaupan*), pret. *hlaihlaup; stôʒu, stioʒ; wuofu, wiof*.

In Old Saxon the relation between *iu* and *io* is the same as in Old High German, and the same rules are applicable as to the use of *io* where *a*, and of *iu* where *i* or *u* follow in the next syllable. Thus in the conjugation *biudu*, offer; *biudis, biudit;* pl. *biodat;* inf. *biodan*. So also in other words: *hiudu,* hodie (Germ. heute); *thiustri,* darkness; *thiodan,* king; *thiorna,* ancilla (Germ. dirne). Sometimes the distinction of *iu* and *io* denotes words of a different meaning, e.g. *thiu,* ancilla; *thio,* instrum. of *the*; *fiur,* fire; *fior,* four; and occasionally one and the same word wavers between *iu* and *io*, e. g. *fiund, fiond,* enemy, fiend; *diutul, diobol,* diabolus. The weakened *eo* appears not unfrequently for *io: theof,* thief; *brëost,* breast; *theodan,* king. *ie, ia, ea* are rare: *kiesan,* to choose (Germ. kiesen); *thierna,* ancilla; *liaht,* light.

These vowels are in Old Saxon as in Old High German used also to indicate ancient reduplication. Thus *ie* by the side of *e* in the preterite of those verbs which have an *a* in the present— *liet* for *let,* pret. of *látan,* to let; *andried* for *andred*, pret. of *andrádan,* to dread, *io, eo,* or *ie* in the pret. of those verbs which have *ó* in the present—*hliop, hliep,* pret. of *hlopan,* to run (Germ. laufen); *wiop, weop, wiep*, pret. of *wopan*, to weep. Concerning the reduplication in *e*, vide sub lit. e.

Old Frisian is, like Old Saxon, restricted to the sole diphthong *iu*, of which it also admits the weakened form in *io, ia*; so that *iu* and *io* are met where the following syllable contains, or originally contained, *i* or *u*, and *ia* where it contains *a*. Examples:—*hiudega*, hodie; *friund*, friend; *niugun*, nine; *siugun*, seven; and *diore*, dear; *fiower*, four; *liode*, people; *stiora*, to steer. Some words waver between *iu* and *io*, as *fiur* and *fior*, fire; *diure* and *diore*, dear; *liude* and *liode*, people (Germ. leute): *iu* at the end of words, e. g. *thriu*, three; *hiu*, ea; *thiu*, illa; but *diar*, deer, fera; *siak*, sick; *thiade*, people; *kriapa*, to creep; *liaht*, light.

Old Norse also uses the diphthong *iu* as identical with Gothic *iu*. At the end of words:—*niu*, nine; *tiu*, ten; *þriu*, three. Before labials or gutturals:—*diupr*, deep; *biugr*, curved; *hriufr*, sad; *riuka*, to smoke, reek; except þio/r, thief. The weakened form *io* is used before liquids and dentals:—*bior*, beer; *fliot*, river (Germ. fluß); *hiol*, wheel; *kiosa*, to choose (Germ. kiesen). Some words however even here preserve *iu*: examples—*tiurr*, taurus (Germ. stier); *niundi*, nonus; *tiundi*, decimus. As a rule, then, in Old Norse, the use of the pure diphthong *iu*, or its weakened form *io*, does not, as in Old High German, depend on the vowel of the following syllable, but on the nature of the succeeding consonant. The conjugation of the verb does not, as in other dialects, present an alternation between *iu* and *io*, simply because both these diphthongs are in the singular present of the verb replaced by their common Umlaut *y*. *io* also makes occasionally its appearance in the remains of an ancient reduplication: examples—*anða*, gignere, pret. *ioð*; *ansa*, to draw, haurire, pret. *ios*; *bua*, to dwell, pret. *bio*; *hlaupa*, to run (Germ. laufen), pret. *hliop* (Germ. lief). On the reduplication in *e* vide sub lit. e.

eó

This diphthong may be considered as exclusively Anglo-Saxon, and stands to the Gothic *iu* in the same relation as the Old High German *ei*, for instance, does to the Gothic *ái*. It therefore must by no means be regarded as identical with *eo*, or any other Schwachung of *iu* which may occur in the other dialects, but as an independent vowel which in Anglo-Saxon replaces the Gothic *iu* without being a mere Schwachung of this diphthong. In this character it chiefly occurs in the middle of a word: examples—*beor*, beer; *beón*, to be; *deór*, deer, fera; *ceól*, keel, ship; *ceósan*, to choose; *deop*, deep; *leod*, people; *leoht*, light. This *eó* was in later times often replaced by *u*, especially in verbs of the sixth class: *supan* for *seopan*, to drink; *sucan* for *seócan*, to suck; *lúcan* for *leocan*, to lock. More about this *u* vide sub. lit. u.

This diphthong we find in various other places where it has no relation to the Gothic *iu*. It very often appears as the Brechung of *i*, which has its origin in a mistaken analogy to the Brechung of *i* into *eo* before the consonants *h* and *v*. Hence the verbs *wrihan*, to cover; *tihan*, to amuse; *þihan*, to thrive, have been removed into the sixth conjugational class, and thus throwing off the *h*, they appear as *wreón, teon, þeón*, pret. *wreáh, teáh, þeáh*. Of similar formation is *feol*, file, O. H. Germ. *fihila, fila*.

At the end of a word where *j* has been dropped, *i* is replaced by *eo*: examples—*beo*, bee, O. H. Germ. *bi*; *freo*, free, Goth. *freis*, O. H. Germ. *fri*. It appears that a final *i* is repugnant to the nature of the Anglo-Saxon idiom; wherever, therefore, the *i* is preserved in preference of *eo*, it is under the shelter of a following consonant, e.g. *frih, frig,*=*freó*; *sig*, sim, for *seo*; *hig* for *heó*.

So also we see *eó* occur where *i* is followed by *w*, e. g. *sneówan*, to go, Goth. *snivan*; *cneow, cneowes*, Goth. *kniu, knivis*, knee; *treow*, tree, &c. The ancient forms are *cneo* and *treó*, where *eo* appears in its organic character as the representative of the Gothic *iu* in *kniu, triu*.

Similar to *io* and *ie* in other dialects, *eó* is in Anglo-Saxon the contraction of the ancient reduplication which is more commonly represented by the condensed vowel *e* (vide sub lit. e): examples—*geong*, ivi (Germ. gieng); *beón*, jussi; *speon*, junxi; *dreód*, timui; *reórd*, rexi; *leólc*, lusi; *leórt*, sivi: *gangan, bannan, spannan, drædan, rædan, lacan, lætan*, occasionally form their preterites by *eó* instead of the more common *e*.

áu

Gothic. Examples:—*báuan*, to dwell; *sáuil*, sun; *fráuja*, lord; *láubs*, leaf (Germ. laub); *galáubjan*, to believe (Germ. glauben); *hláupan*, to run (Germ. laufen); *áugo*, eye (Germ. auge); *áuso*, ear; *hlauts*, lot, fate.

We have seen before how *j* is transformed into *i*, *v* into *u*, vide sub. lit. u. In the same manner *ij, iv, av* are transformed into *ei, iu, au* when they occur at the end of a word or precede a consonant. Examples:—*eis, ija, ije; freis, frijis, frija; þius, þivis, þiva; naus, navis*, in which the roots *ij, frij, þiv, nav*, before the consonantal termination *s* of the nominative, adopt the corresponding diphthongs *ei, iu, au*. Between *aj* and *ái* such relation does not exist except in the words *bái*, both, *bajoþs; vái, væ, vajamereins*, contumely; but we find *sáian*, to sow; *láian*, to smile; not *sajan, lajan*. The forms *av* and *iv* are also vocalized into *iu* and *au* before the inflexional consonant *j;* where however this consonant itself is vocalized into *i*, the mentioned diphthongs are again dissolved into *iv* and *av*. Hence the nominative *mavi* of the theme *máuja, þiva* of *þáuja*, and the preterite *tavida* of *táujan*, to do (root *tav*).

Among other dialects Old Norse alone has preserved the integrity of the Gothic diphthong *áu*. Examples:—*draumr*, dream; *baun*, bean; *daufr*, deaf; *lauf*, leaf; *hlauf*, a run (Germ. lauf); *auga*, eye (Germ. auge); *glaumr*, clamour, noise. *o* for *au*, vide sub lit. **o**. Very rare is *a* for *au*, as *hár*, high, for *hauhs*. In *far*, few, and *strá*, straw, we have the regular productions of the terminational *ă*. Goth. *fáus*; theme, *java;* also *stravi*, O. H. Germ. *stro*.

Old High German in its most ancient documents has also the Gothic *au* instead of the later *ou;* but as a rule we shall have to look upon *ou* as the Old High German representative of the Gothic *áu*.

Anglo-Saxon has a vowel of its own, the diphthong *eá* taking the place of the Gothic *áu*.

Old Frisian has a diphthong *au*, which however is not the organic vowel representing the Gothic *áu*, but an inorganic diphthong originating in the contraction of *áw*, as *naut* = *náwet*, naught; *auder*, uter (= *ahwedder*); *nauder*, neque (= *nahwedder*).

ou

This is the Old High German representative of the Gothic *áu*. Examples:—*poum*, tree (Germ. baum); *troum*, dream (Germ. traum); *houbit*, head (Germ. haupt); *gilouba*, faith (Germ. glaube); *louf*, a run (Germ. lauf); *ouga*, eye (Germ. auge).

This diphthong is however often encroached upon by the vowel *ô*, into which it is contracted (*o* for *ou*, vide sub lit. **ô**); but the diphthong is invariably preserved before the liquid *m*, before labials and gutturals. Sometimes it is rendered by a Schwachung in *ao, oi, eu;* these forms however are mere dialectic variations, and of very rare occurrence.

VOWEL SOUNDS.

Isidor, one of the Old High German authors, has an Umlaut of *au* in *eu*. Examples:—*freuwidha*, joy; *freuwidih*, laetare; while other documents have *frauwit*, he rejoices; *frauwí*, laetare.

eá

This is the characteristic diphthong of Anglo-Saxon, which has to represent the Gothic *áu*. Examples:—at the end of words = O. H. Germ. *ó* or *ou*: *freá*, lord; *feá*, few. By the elision of the terminational *h*, e. g. *heá=heah*, high; *eá*, water; Goth. *ahva*, O. H. Germ. *aha; neá*, near. This diphthong is very common before the liquids *m* and *n*. Examples:—*beám*, beam; *gleám*, gleam; *seám*, seam; *steám*, steam; *stream*, stream; *teám*, team; *beán*, bean. Before the liquid *r* only in *eáre*, ear, Goth. *áuso; teár*, a tear; *dreárung*, a distilling. Before the liquid *l*, no examples. Preceding other letters: *deáf*, deaf; *heáfod*, head; *leáf*, leaf; *heáp*, heap; *sleáp*, sleep; *eáge*, eye; *breád*, bread; *deád*, dead; *leád*, lead; *neád*, need.

Whilst in Gothic and Old High German the terminal *v* joining *a* is vocalized, and forms the diphthong *au*, it has in Anglo-Saxon a tendency to regain its position after the vocalization has taken place. Thus then a root *dav* would be Goth. *dáu*, and Goth. *dáu* again A. S. *deá:* the consonant *v* however turns up again in its old position and urges upon us the form *deaw*, dew; so also *breáw*, eye-brow; *fcáwa*, few, Goth. *favái; heawan*, to hew, O. H. Germ. *hawan, hauwan*. Sometimes *eá* is contracted in *e:* vide sub lit. e.

uo

This diphthong is peculiar to Old High German, in which it represents a dissolution of a more ancient *ó* into the double vowel or diphthong *uo*. Examples:—*fuoran=foran; tuom=tom; pluomo=plóm; tuon=tón*, &c.

In the inflexions *ó* is preserved throughout. One Old High German dialect, which inclines to the Low German, prefers the *ó*, even in roots, to the common Old High German *uo*: *oa* for *uo* is scarce; *ua* for *uo*, where we meet also *ia, ea*, for *iu*.

ey

Belongs to Old Norse exclusively as Umlaut of *au*: *freyr*, Goth. *fráuja*, lord; *hey*, Goth. *havi*, hay; *dreyma*, to dream, from *drauma*. Sometimes *ey* for *oe*: *beyki*, beech (=*boeki*), Goth. *boka; deya*, to die; *geya*, to rejoice; Umlaut of *au*, pret. *do* and *go*.

II. MIDDLE TEUTONIC.

Short Vowels.

a

Middle High German. Examples:—*al*, all; *gal*, sound; *nahtegal*, nightingale; *mal*, I grind, molo; *swal*, swallow; *tal*, valley, dale; *bar*, naked, bare; *spar*, I spare; *hamer*, hammer; *scham*, shame; *han*, cock; *man*, man; *maget*, maid; *zagel*, tail; *tac*, day; *ahe*, water; *trahen*, tear; *blat*, leaf; *vater*, father; *gras*, grass.

Examples of the pure *a* sound are very numerous, deviations of this sound into that of any other vowel very rare; they occur in almost the identical words which show a fluctuation of sound in Old High German already. Thus *har* = *her*, hither; *wal* = *wol*, well; *sal* = *sol*, shall; *van* = *von*, prefix de, ab; *mahte* = *mohte*, might; *kam* = *kom*, came. *a* is used in the place of *e*, especially where the latter is Umlaut of *a* : thus *schamlick*, adj. of *scham*, shame; *zäglich*, adj. of *zage*, coward; *schädelich*, adj. *schade*, damage. More about this Umlaut sub lit. **e**.

Old and Middle English. The Anglo-Saxon *a* in late Saxon retained its position before syllables with a full vowel, and before *m* and *n*, in which latter case it fluctuates into *o*. Hence we have *fram* and *from; lang*, long; *man*, *mon*; occasionally with a preluding *e*, *heond*, *leond*, &c. The Ablaut of the first strong conjugation is commonly *o*: *bond*, bound; *wond*, wound; *dronc*, drank; *sprong*, sprang; *stong*, stung; more rarely *a*, *swang*, *sprang*; others have always *a* to the exclusion of *o*, *hannd*, *lannd*, *mann*, *cann*. Old English and Middle English keep up the fluctuation of sound before *m* and *n*, e. g. *man*, *mon*; *hand*, *hond*; *sprang*, *sprong*.

Another source of the Middle English *a* is the Anglo-Saxon *ä*. In late Saxon some writers choose a representative in *ä* (*æ*), *a, e*, even *ea*, whilst others strictly adhere to the vowel *a*. Thus we find *brec, bräc, breac*, broke; *spac, spec, späc*, spoke; *queð, quað*, said, quoth; *what, whät, whet; craft, cräft; gras, gräs*. Old English renders the *æ* commonly by *a*, rarely by *e*, as *stal, bare, brak, spak*, or *stel, ber, brec, spec; smal, fader, þat*, *water;* and in the same manner Middle English has *what, craft, gras, raven.*

The third *a* derives its origin from the A. S. *ea,* the Brechung of Gothic *a,* before the consonants *l, r,* and *h.* Even the late Saxon authors reduce the *ea* to *a,* as *al,* A. S. *eall; wal,* A. S. *weal; ale,* A. S. *eale; salt, warm.* Sometimes the sound is wavering between *a, a,* and *e: heard, hard, hard, herd; teares, teres,* tears. The Ablauts in the eighth and tenth conjugations fluctuate between *a, a,* and *e.* Some words even incline to *o: halde, hälden, holde; äld, old; salde, sälde, solde.* These fluctuations become gradually less frequent in Old English until all the different sounds settled down in *a: al, alle, halle; walle, falle;* the Ablaut in the tenth conjugation: *halp, help; dalf, faght; sagh, saw, sau.* Exceptions:—*old, holden, bold.* So also in Middle English *a* has the preference, e. g. *alle, fallen, halle, sharp, harde, harm, arm;* and the Ablaut in the tenth conjugation *faught, faght, half, dalf.* The Umlaut of *a* is as in Anglo-Saxon, though it is in the later Saxon occasionally written *a,* e. g. *hate, hate,* hate; *mate, mat,* meat; *tallen, tällen,* to tell. In Old and Middle English again, the vowel *e* is firmly established, e. g. *hen, fen, men, helle, net, bet, eft, bench, mete, sellen, letten, wenden.*

ĕ

Middle High German. The vowel *e* is by Grimm distinguished into two sounds, one thinner and softer as Umlaut of *a,* and the other marked *e* of a fuller and broader sound as Brechung of *i.* The fact of a difference really existing in the nature of these sounds the same authority proves from the rhymes in Middle High German poetry, where in good classical productions we hardly ever find *e* the Umlaut of *a* rhyming upon *e* the Brechung of *i.* Examples of *e* as Umlaut of *a*:—*her,* army; *bette,* bed; *helle,* hell; *herte,* hard—here the Umlaut is owing to the inflexional *i* which has been dropped—*rede,* speech; *esel,* ass; *glesîn,* vitreus; *elle, ellin,* omnia; *swellen,* to inflate; *brennen,* to burn; *henne,* hen; *steppe,* step. The vowel *a* and its Umlaut *e,* by their frequent exchange, give the inflexional forms a diversified and pleasing modulation. Thus we find often *a* in the singular of the substantive declension replaced by *e* in the plural, e.g. *gast,* guest, pl. *geste; blat,* leaf, pl. *bleter.* Feminine nouns of the second declension preserve *a* in the nom. and acc. sing., but in the gen. and dat. they already replace it by its Umlaut *e,* e. g. *krafte, krefte,* strength; *hand, hende,* hand. The present of the first weak conjugation yields to the

Umlaut *e*, whilst the preterite often preserves the original *a*, e. g. *vellen*, to fell; *wenden*, to turn; pret. *valte, wande*. An interesting contrast is produced by the Umlaut occurring in the adjective, and the original *a* in the adverbial form, as *herte*, hard; *harte*, hardly; *feste*, firm; *faste*, firmly. The Umlaut of *a* has been generally adopted in monosyllabic and bisyllabic words from the thirteenth century, so that we never find *har* for *her*, army; *narn* for *nern*, to preserve; *angel* for *engel*, angel.

Thus then we have the Umlaut of *a* represented by two different letters, *a* and *e*; and what, might be the question, is the meaning of these different signs? It appears that, as far as the intrinsic value of each of these letters or sounds is concerned, they are identical. We therefore find the words which we have enumerated above under the Umlaut *a* quite as often rendered by the Umlaut *e*, so that *schamlich* and *schemlich*, *zäglich* and *zeglich*, *schädelich* and *schedelich* were used without discrimination. If there be any difference at all, it would seem to lie in this, that *a* is used in derivations which were still traceable to their roots, as *schämlich* to *scham*, *zaglich* to *zage*, *schädelich* to *schade*; while the vowel *e* renders that Umlaut which owes its origin to a more ancient modification, such as *her*, from O. H. Germ. *hari*, where the modifying vowel *i* was dropped in the course of time, but the Umlaut kept its place, though the Middle High German author may not have been so conscious of the relation between *her* and O. H. Germ. *hari* as he was of that between *schade* and *schädelich*: *ä* then is the more modern, *e* the more ancient Umlaut. More about this distinction under the chapter of modern German vowels. *e*, the result of Brechung. In the inflexions we meet this *e* chiefly in the plur. pres. ind., and sing. and plur. pres. subj., of several strong verbs; in the substantives of the first strong declension; and, in general, in all those words which have an inflexional *a* after the radical vowel *i*. Thus then in inflexions and derivations *e* exchanges with *i* in the same manner as *e* with *a*; hence *berc, gebirge; velt, gevilde; gerste, girstin; wim, wemen; wirbe, werben*. Compare Old High German *e* and *i*.

The distinction of *e* and *e* is of great importance, since solely by its means we are enabled to keep distinct many words which have the same spelling but a different meaning; e. g. *ber*, berry, *ber*, a bear; *her*, army; *her*, hither; *helle* (Germ. holle), *helle* (Germ. helle); *velt*, cadit, *velt*, ager; *sterben*, caedere, to kill; *sterben*, cadere, to die; *nebelin*, diminutive of *nabele*, umbilicus; *nebelin*, diminutive of *nebel*, nebula. But in spite of all these facts which speak in favour of a distinction between *e* and *e*, it cannot be denied that their sounds even in refined utterance cannot have differed much, since even the most refined poets of the classical period make e and ϵ rhyme occasionally.

Old and Middle English. The Anglo-Saxon e, Schwachung of i, is retained in late Saxon, though subject to many fluctuations. Examples:—*he, me, þe, beren, breken; stelen* and *steolen; self* and *seolf.* Nay, this unsettled fluctuating state of things goes so far as to extinguish all difference between e the Schwachung of i, and e the Umlaut of a, and consequently the letter æ (=ä) is often used for both indiscriminately. Hence *deluen, dälfen; eten, äten; helm, halm;* or both a and eo are substituted for e: *helpen, hälpen, heolpen.* Old English again displays a more settled state of things, and the sound is, as of yore, represented by its legitimate e (rarely i). Middle English already shows a tendency of lengthening the short vowel e into e (=ee), *wee, thee, yee, tere* and *teer, breke* and *breek*.

i

Middle High German. This vowel is used to the same extent as in Old High German, and consequently appears in the nominative of the second and third declensions in the sing. pres. of strong verbs which exchange e and i, and finally in derivations which originally had the vowel i or u. Examples:—*sil*, rope (Germ. seil); *spil*, play (Germ. spiel); *vil*, much; *himel*, heaven; *bin*, sum; *bin*, a bee; *hin*, illuc; *zin*, tin; *siben*, seven; *sige*, victory (Germ. sieg); *michel*, great; *strich*, a line; *smit*, smith; *diz*, this; *siz*, seat; *wil*, I will; *wim*, I take; *bir*, I bear; *gibe*, I give; *briche*, I break; *sihe*, I see; sing. pres. of *wellen, nemen, beren, geben, brechen, sehen.* The vowel i is, however, very limited in the conjugation. Since e rules throughout the pres. subj. as well as in the pl. of the pres. indic., the relation between i and e in the Middle High German is most readily explained by a reference to Old High German, where an a in the following syllable modifies, i or u preserves, the preceding i. Thus *nebel, eben, degen, regen, zehen, swester* = O. H. Germ. *nebal, epan, dekan, rekan, zehan, suestar;* and *himel, michel, birke, kirche* = O. H. Germ. *himil, michil, piricha, chirichá;* and *siben, sicher, videle, witewe* = O. H. Germ. *sibun*, seven; *sichur*, safe; *fidulá*, fiddle; *wituwá*, widow. The i in all adjectives in *in* or *ic* is easily explained; as, *girstin*, adj. of *gerste*, barley; *villin*, adj. of *vel*, skin: and the rule which has been laid down will quite as easily explain the exchange of i and e in the conjugational forms; e. g. pres. sing. *bir, birst, birt;* plur. *bern, bert, bernt*, = O. H. Germ. *piru, piris*, *pirit, peram, perat, perant.* Singular it is to find *i* commonly preceding the consonants *z* and *tz*, and many doubled consonants, apparently for no other reason but the terminational *i* which has been dropped in the course of time; e. g. *spiz, vurwiz,* = O. H. Germ. *spizi, furiwizi.* Several monosyllables of frequent occurrence in daily speech have escaped all modifying influences and preserved the *i* intact, e. g. *ich, mich, dich, vich, mir, dir, bin, bist, ist, in* (*eum, eis* and prep.), *min,* minus, &c.; *er* and *ez* (Goth. *is* and *ita*) yielded to the general decline, but *ir* (Goth. *izos, izái, ize, izo*) pron. possess. has retained its distinctive *i*. Though Grimm is fond of calling the modification of *i* into *e* 'a Brechung,' he at the same time acknowledges that Gothic differs from Middle as well as Old High German Brechung in its essential characteristics, the former changing *i* into *ai* under the influence of succeeding consonants (*r* and *h*), the latter under the influence of succeeding vowels. Being unable to discern any benefit resulting from an adhesion to scientific distinctions which are no longer outborne by facts, we may perhaps discard the term of Brechung for the Middle as well as Old High German *é*, which we consider in all cases as a mere Trübung or Schwachung of the original vowel *i*.

Old and Middle English. The Anglo-Saxon *eo* is rarely retained in the succeeding periods, but late Saxon often replaces it by *e*. Examples:—*heort,* hart; *heorte,* heart; *feole, fele,* many (Germ. vide); *seoluer, seluer,* silver; *sweord, swerd,* sword; *eorðe, erde, earðe,* earth; *heouene, heueue,* heaven. Or by *o*: *weoruld, woreld,* world; *steorre, sterre, storre,* star. In Old and Middle English the Anglo-Saxon *eo* is commonly represented by *e*: *hert,* hart; *herte,* heart; *swerd, erl, heven, erthe, fele, selfe ;—*rarely by *o*: *work, world,* even *hor,* earn; *hour,* iis. A few words return to the original vowel *i*, which even in Anglo-Saxon speech had already been split into *e* and *eo*; and we therefore meet with *silver* and *milk* for the Anglo-Saxon *seolver* and *meolc*. In this instance it may indeed be argued with great plausibility that Anglo-Saxon too allowed the more ancient forms *silver, milc,* by the side of the later breaking in *seolver* and *meolc*.

O

Middle High German. Analagous to the Old High German *o*. Examples:—*hol,* a hole; *ole,* oil; *vol,* full; *wol,* well; *honec,* honey; *kone,* wife; *bischof,* bishop; *oven,* oven, furnace; *vogel,* bird; *herzoge,* duke; *stock,* stick (Germ. stock); *joch,* yoke; *koch,* cook; *worm* and *wurm,* worm; *horn,* horn; *corn,* corn; *dorf,*

VOWEL SOUNDS. 59

village; *sorge*, care; *gebrochen*, broken; *gekrochen*, crept, reptus. This *o* derives its origin sometimes from *a*, sometimes from *u*, of which vowels it is merely a Schwachung or Trübung. Hence *sol* = *scal*, shall; *holn* = *haln*, to fetch; *kom* = *kam*, *von* = *van*, *mohte* = *mahte*, might (Germ. *mochte*, potui). More common is *o* as the Schwachung of *u*, to which class most of the examples which we have given belong: *o* for *e* in *wol*, for *wela*, well; *woche* for *wecha*, week; *kone* for *quena*, wife; *komen* for *quëman*, to come; *koden* for *quedan*, to say (cf. quoth).

The Umlaut of *o* is *o*. This Umlaut however is of rare occurrence; a fact which may be demonstrated *a priori* when we consider that the vowel *o*, of which it is the modification, replaces the original *u*, then only when it is *not* followed by *i*, the vowel which chiefly causes the Umlaut in the root. It is still more interesting to observe that, wherever Umlaut of *o* does occur, it is not this *o* which is modified, but the original *u* for which it stands. Thus then we find by the side of *tor*, door; *vor*, prae, fore; *tür* and *vür*, not *tör* and *vör*—because in Old High German already the organic *u* is sheltered by the *i* in *turi* and *furi*. In the same manner we shall easily explain the Umlaut *ü* in the words *bückîn, dürnîn, güldîn, hülzîn*, adjectives of *boc*, he-goat; *dorn*, thorn; *wolle*, wool; *golt*, gold; *holz*, mood; and by the side of the participles *geworfen, geborgen*, the subjunctives *würfe, bürge*, which are modified forms of the pl. indic. *wurfen, burgen*, infin. *werfen*, to throw; *bergen*, to hide. Exceptional cases are the following:— Old High German nouns passing from the first to the second declension sometimes assumed the plurals in *i* instead of *a*, hence *procchi, frosci* for *poccha, frosca*, he-goats, frogs; whence Middle High German plurals, such as *bocke, frosche, stocke, röcke*, by the side of the formation of the first declension, *bocke, frosche*, &c. In Old High German already we find words fluctuating in the plural between *o* and *u*, e. g. *luchir* and *lochir*, *hulir* and *holir*, which explain the Middle High German plurals *löcher, holer, orter*, &c. Old High German diminutives fluctuating in the same manner, are *luchili* and *lochili*, *puchili* and *pochili*, whence the M. H. Germ. *löchelîn, bockelîn, röckelîn*, not *lüchelîn*, &c.

As to the further development of this Umlaut we have only to observe that it took place in the same way as that of *a* into *e*, namely, under the influence of a succeeding *i*: thus then we find parallel to *semelich*, similar; *gremelich*, irascible—O. H. Germ. *samalih, gramalih*—the forms *götelich*, divine; *löbelich*, laudable— O. H. Germ. *gotalih, lopalih*. The weak preterites *dorfte, mohte, tohte*, have in the subjunctive *dörfte, möhte, töhte; solde* and *wolde* remain unchanged in the subjunctive.

Old and Middle English. The *o* very often takes the place of an original *a*, as it sometimes did in Anglo-Saxon already. Thus Mid. Eng. *mon, lomb, hond, tond, strond*, for *man, lamb*, &c.; exceptionally for A. S. *eo*, as in *world, work*; for A. S. *u—fol, dore, worm, wonder*, &c.

ü

Middle High German. Examples:—*gume*, man; *bruitgum*, bridegroom (Germ. brautigam); *stumb*, dumb; *sumer*, summer; *vrum*, pious (Germ. fromm); *duner*, thunder; *hulde*, favour; *schulde*, guilt, debt; *wurm*, worm; *turn*, tower; *wurz*, wort, herb; *wurzel*, root; *kunst*, art; *luft*, air; *vuhs*, fox; *kum*, venio. Pl. pret. of strong verbs: *schuben*, trusimus; *kluben*, fidimus; *lugen*, mentiti sumus; *trugen*, fefellimus; *vlugen*, volavimus.

u bears the same relation to *o* as does *i* to *e*. As a rule the original vowels *u* and *i* exclude their respective intruders *o* and *e* from any hold upon their position before consonantal combinations, such as *mm, nn, mb, mpf, ng, nk, nd, nz, ns*; the liquids *m* and *n*, fortified by another succeeding consonant affording, it would appear, sufficient shelter to the original vowels *i* and *u*. Where the position is open to both competitors, the original vowel *u* always depends on a succeeding *u* or *i* for its safety, while a succeeding *a* is sure to bring in the intruder *o*. Thus the pl. pret. *kluben, bugen, tugen*, we explain by the O. H. Germ. *chlupun, pugun, tugun*; and the *o* in *honec*, oven, *tohter*, by the O. H. Germ. *honac, ovan, tohtar*.

ü is the Umlaut of *u* brought about by a terminational *i*. Examples:—*hül*, hole, O. H. Germ. *huli*; *vül*, puledrus, O. H. Germ. *fuli*; *kür*, election, O. H. Germ. *churi*; *tür*, door, O. H. Germ. *turi*; *vür*, fore, prae, O. H. Germ. *furi*; *münech*, monk, O. H. Germ. *munih*; *hübesch*, courteous, pretty; *übel*, evil, O. H. Germ. *ubil*. (To these examples may be added those quoted sub lit. **ö**.)

Considering that the radical vowel *u* is exposed to the modifying influences of both *a* and *i*, and that a terminational *u* (which again is scarcer than terminational *i*) alone can save the position of its twin brother in the root, we shall have no difficulty in explaining the preponderance of the Umlaut *ü* over the original vowel *u*—a preponderance which would be still greater if it were not for certain consonantal combinations which reject the Umlaut; as for instance, *ld, lt, ng, nh*, so that the forms *schulde, hulde, schuldic, guldin*, are preferred to *schulde, hülde, schuldic, güldin*.

From these exceptional cases it becomes sufficiently evident that the Umlaut of *u* had pervaded far less generally the vocal

VOWEL SOUNDS.

system of the Middle High German language than the Umlaut of *a* had done; that *ü* is a vowel unknown in Old High German; and that by degrees it developed itself in Middle High German in the same manner as *e*, the Umlaut of *a*, had done in Old High German. Where in Old High German there still remained a fluctuation between the Umlaut *e* and its original *a*, Middle High German decides in favour of the former; and so again Modern High German adopts the Umlaut *ü*, where Middle High German was still wavering between the vowel *u* and its Umlaut *ü*. Grimm places the first transitions from *u* into *u* in the eleventh or twelfth century.

Old and Middle English. The Old English *u* is to a great extent identical with the same letter in Anglo-Saxon. Examples:—*sum, sunne, tunge, wulf, sunde*, sound, healthy (Germ. gesund); but it is not unfrequently replaced by *o*, rarely *ou*; *somer* = *sumer, dombe* = *dumbe, sone* = *sune*, son; *nonne* = *nunne, folle* = *fulle, worm* = *wurm, doust* = *dust*. The pl. Ablaut in the tenth conjugation is often *o*, sometimes *u*. Old English reduces the number of *u* vowels and commonly supersedes them by *o* or *ou*; whence *fol* = *ful, dore* = *dure, som* = *sum, borgh* and *bourgh* = *burgh;* and Middle English makes a kind of compromise between the conflicting elements of sound by engaging in some words the vowel *u*, in others *o*, to the exclusion of the rival vowel. We therefore read *ful, hungre, under, schuldre, lust, dust,* and *worm, wonder, dore, note, nonne*. Still open to the competition of the rivals are *sune, sone,* son; *sunne, sonne*, sun; *sume*, some.

The Anglo-Saxon *u* which, under the influence of a preceding *w*, was developed from the vowel *i*, either retains it place, interchanging sometimes with *o*, as *cumen, comen;* *wude, wode; suster, soster;* þ*us,* þ*os;* or it is reduced to the original vowel *i;* as, *quike, widewe,* widow; *wike*, week. The fluctuation continues in Old and Middle English; we therefore read, *woke, wuke, wyke; to cume, to come; wude, wode, wood; whilk, wuch, wich; swilk, sulk, such.*

y

Middle High German. This vowel is not German, and has therefore in Middle High German no better position than in Old High German. It is looked upon as a foreigner, and solely admitted in words of the Latin and Romance languages. Examples:—*Tyturel, Gynovêr*. German words too which had been Romanized and re-admitted into German literature allowed of the vowel *y*. Examples:—*Tybalt* = *Dietbalt, Ysengrîm* — *Isengrim*. Its sound was no doubt like that of *i*, though occasionally it may, in French words, have had something of the sound of *ü*. In the fourteenth century, and later on still more, the Romance *y* intruded itself into purely German words, and in many cases supplanted the short *i*. Thus then it became customary to write *yot, nymt, yr, yn*; often we find it also in the place of *i*, and in the diphthongs *ay, ey, oy*, for *ai, ei, oi*.

Old and Middle English. *y* is in Anglo-Saxon the Umlaut of *u*. The vowel *u* is often weakened into *o*; hence we find *y* often as the Umlaut of *o*, as in *gold, gylden*, aurum, aureus. In late Saxon this Umlaut *y* is reduced to the original vowel *u*; as, *sunne* for *synne*, *munster* for *mynster*, *umbe* for *ymbe*, *lutel* for *lytel*; or its Trübung *o*: *cume, come*, for *cyme*, arrival; *fulien, follien*, to follow; or, though the sound of the Umlaut is preserved, its characteristic letter is discarded and replaced by the letter *i*, e. g. *king, sinne, kirke, chirche*, kirk, church; *biggen*, to buy; or we find *u* and *i* side by side; e. g. *busi, bisi*, busy; *cuchene, kichene*, kitchen; *wunne, winne*, joy (Germ. wonne); *gulden, gilden*, golden. Though in this manner the sign of the Umlaut has been altered from *y* into *i*, we have every reason to suppose that *y* and *i* were governed exactly alike, and that thus the sound of the Umlaut was kept intact. The letter *y* having thus become super-numerous as it were in native words, it was henceforth assigned to new functions in foreign words, analogous to the *y* in Middle High German, e. g. *Ananyas, Herodyas, Moysæs*. Perhaps the adoption of *y* in Latin words has caused its expulsion from the vernacular. In Old English the application of this vowel is in a state of great confusion, some writers preferring *u*, others *y*, others *i*. Hence we meet *churche, chyrche, kirke; munster, mynster; lutel, lytel: brugge, brigge*. From this confusion of sounds and signs arises also the erroneous form *dude* for *dide*, as well as *pulke, sulue*. This chaotic state continues in Middle English; but in this period the *i* gradually begins to gain the preponderance among the conflicting elements. Hence we read, *king, kin, din, biggen, bie*, to buy; *littel, kisse, birie*; but also, *lyttel, kysse*, and *bury*.

Brechung.

In the Middle Teutonic dialects the system of Brechung is gradually reduced to a few isolated instances which finally disappear altogether. Old High German never had a fully developed system of Brechung like Gothic, Old Norse, and Anglo-Saxon, and it is therefore but natural that Middle High German, its offspring, should be very deficient in the same respect. Still the latter has more frequently adopted the

Brechung *ie*, which, however, must be owing to Low German influences, and may therefore hardly be considered as pure High German. Thus, *viele*, much, A. S. *feolo; hiemel*, heaven; *hienevart*, departure,—comp. A. S. *heona, heonon*, hinc; M. H. Germ. *sieben*, seven, A. S. *seofon*; M. H. Germ. *sien*, to see, A. S. *seon*. Middle High German as well as Old and Middle English have, in fact, gradually disposed of the Brechung by absorbing the broken vowels in one or other of the nearest related simple vowels, thus causing them to return to the sources whence they had started. An attentive examination of the facts we have advanced concerning the course of the different Middle Teutonic vowels, especially in Old and Middle English will sufficiently bear out these views.

LONG VOWELS.

â

Middle High German. In this dialect the vowel *á* corresponds closely to the O. H. Germ. *â*, Goth. *e*. Examples:—*a*, water, in compound names of rivers; *dá*, there; *krá*, crow, gen. *kráwa; klá*, claw, gen. *klawe; zwá*, duo, two; *wa*, where; *ál*, eel; *mál*, sign; *strále*, arrow; *hár*, hair; *jár*, year; *star*, starling; *wár*, true; *krâm*, tavern; *mane*, moon; *wán*, hope; *gábe*, gift; *sláf*, sleep; *strafe*, punishment; *wáfen*, weapons; *gráve*, earl; *rat*, counsel. Very often produced by contraction:—*hán* from *hăben*, to have; *getrán* from *getragen*, borne; *slán* from *slăhen*, to stay; *trán* from *trăhen*, tear; thus also, *gán*, to go; *stan*, to stand; *lán*, to let; *getán*, done. This vowel is frequently met with in foreign words, as *babest*, pope; *tável*, table; especially in the terminations, *Asiâ, Portegâl, Adâm, Afrikán, castellan, capellán, majestát, trinitát*.

Old and Middle English. The Anglo-Saxon *á* is sometimes retained in late Saxon, sometimes inclines to *ó*:—*bá*, both; *wác*, weak; *snaw, snowe*, snow; *hál. hol* (Germ. *heil*), salus; *hálic, holic*, holy; *sár, sor*, pain, sore; *hám, hom*, home; *bán, bon*, bone; *stán, ston*, stone; *brád, brod*, broad; *clád, clod*, cloth; *gást, gost*, ghost (sometimes *æ* as *gæst*, &c.); *gá, go*, to go; *ienawe, ienowe, sáme, some*, &c. Ablaut *á*, or fluctuating between *á, æ, ó*.

Old English preserves the *á*:—*án, stáne, háli*; Ablaut, *dráf, smát, rád;* occasionally also *dróf, smot, rod*. Middle English adopts *ó* for *á*, the length of the *o* sound being marked by a terminational *e* mute, following a single consonant, or by *oo*— *stoon = stone, boon = bone, goost = gost;* Ablaut, *droof = drove, stoove = stove, smoot = smote*, &c.

æ

Middle High German. æ is the Umlaut of *a*. Examples:—
æle, anguillæ, from *ál*; *hærın*, crinalis, from *hár*; *grævinne*, comitissa, from *grave*; *ræte*, consilia, from *rat*; *kræme*, tabernæ, from *krám*.

Old and Middle English. The Anglo-Saxon Umlaut æ of *á* continues to exist in late Saxon—*stán, stænig*; or it wavers between æ and *e*—*læren, leren*; *clæne, clene*. In Old and Middle English it is fixed down as *e* or *ee*—*clene, teche, whete*; except *any* and *lady*.

The Anglo-Saxon æ = Goth. *ái*. Old High German *ei* takes pretty nearly the same course as the Umlaut æ just mentioned.

Anglo-Saxon often represents the *a* by æ, which in sound seems nearly to approach the Umlaut, but in its derivation it must be kept strictly distinct. (Comp. Anglo-Saxon.) This Anglo-Saxon æ, answering to the Gothic *e*, Old and Middle High German *á*, continues to hold its position in Late Saxon: *stræte*, street; *mæl*, meal; *hær*, hair; *spæche*, speech; *dæd*, deed; *wæpon*, weapon; *græf* (M. H. Germ. *gráve*, earl); sometimes it is supplanted by *e*: *sel, nedle, sed*—or wavering between æ, *é* and *a* (especially in the Ablaut of the pl. of the eighth and ninth conjugational class): *æten, seten, quéðen, béren, stálen, bráken, spæken*. In Old and Middle English this doubtful æ sound finally settles down in *e*: *ele, slepe, dede, strete, nedle, mele* (eel, sleep, deed, street, needle, meal).

ê

Middle High German. In this dialect it holds the same position as in Old High German. Examples:—*é*, law; *é*, prius (cf. Germ. eher, Eng. ere); *kle*, clover; *me*, more; *ré*, roe; *sne*, snow, nix, *snewes*, nivis; *se*, sea; *we, wewe* (Germ. *weh*, malum), *sele*, soul; *sér*, dolor (cf. sore). This vowel rarely arises from contractions: *gesché* from *geschehe*, eveniat; *swere* from *swehere*, socero. In manuscripts the different *e* sounds are sometimes a little confused, and can only be kept distinct by strictly referring them to their respective class of *e*, *e*, or *ê*; c. g. *mer*, sea; *mer*, misceo, mix; *mer*, more; *her*, army; *her*, hither: *her*, clarus; *ber*, berry; *bér*, a bear; *ber*, verres. In foreign words not uncommon: *Penelope, Ninive, Michael, ade*, adieu; *cedar*, cedar.

Old and Middle English. The vowel *e* in Old and Middle English derives its origin from divers other vowels, as we had already occasion to point out. (1) From A. S. *æ* (Goth. *e*, O. H. Germ. *a*), *slepe, speche, dede, strete*, &c. (2) From Umlaut of *ó*: *fot, fét, top, tep*, and *to kepe, to fele, to deme*, &c. (see sub lit. ô.) (3) From A. S. *æ* = Goth. *ái*, O. H. Germ. *ei* : *see*, sea ; *delen*, to deal ; *menen*, to mean ; *brede*, bread ; *flehs*, flesh. (4) From A. S. *æ*, Umlaut of *a* : *wete, clene, teche*. (5) From A. S. *eo* : *tre, kne, fle, crepe, dere, thefe, frend, fend*.

î

Middle High German. Examples :—*bî*, by ; *blî*, lead (Germ. blei); *drî*, three (Germ. drei); *sî*, sim, sit ; *vrî*, free ; *bîe*, bee ; *vient* fiend ; *wîle*, time (cf. while and Germ. weile); *swîn*, swine ; *wîn*, wine ; *wîp*, woman ; *zît*, time (cf. tide); *îs*, ice ; *îsen*, iron. Formed by contraction : *gît* = *gibet*, dat. *gelîn* = *geligen*, &c. *ie* occurs where an original *j, g, w*, has been dropped : *snîe* = *snige*, *zwîe* = *zwige*. Often in foreign words : *lîre*, lyra ; *fîn*, fine ; *paradîs, amîe*, and *amîge, arzenîe*, medicine ; *benedîen, maledîen*, benedicere, maledicere. *ı* and *í* distinguish *wine*, friend, and *wine*, wine ; *sige*, victory, and *síge*, trouble, disease ; also pret. and pres. of verbs *kliben*, haesimus, and *klíben*, haeremus.

Old and Middle English. The A. S. *ı*, = Goth. *ei*, continues in late Saxon and in Old and Middle English, the latter dialects using occasionally *y* for *i*, and denoting the length of the vowel by doubling the *i*: *lijf* for *lîf*, *abijde* for *abíde*, *whijle* for *while*, *wyf* for *wîf*.

ô

Middle High German. Examples :—*do*, then ; *hoch*, high ; *ho*, highly ; *vlo*, flea ; *vro*, joyful (Germ. froh); *zwo*, duae ; *mor*, moor ; *ore*, ear; *tor*, fool ; *krone*, crown ; *lon*, reward (Germ. lohn); *schone*, pulchre ; *brot*, bread ; *not*, need ; *tot*, death ; *lôz*, lot. The vowel *ó* stands in the same relation to *ou* as *e* to *ei* ; *o* and *ou* can be traced to Gothic *áu*, *e* and *ei* to Goth *ái*. Foreign are *mor, krone, kloster, Dido, Plato*. Observe the difference between *tor*, door, and *tor*, fool ; *ros*, horse, and *ros*, rose ; *koste*, I taste, gusto, and *koste*, caressed, blanditus sum.

oe is the Umlaut of *o* : *hoere*, I hear ; *ore*, ear ; *moerinne*, fem. of *mor*, moor ; *roemisc*, adj. of *Rom; hoehe*, height, from *hoch*, high ; *toete*, I kill, occido ; and *toetlich*, mortalis, from *tot*, death, mors. The absence of Umlaut in words such as *notec, nótic*, must be explained by the Old High German form *notac*.

Old and Middle English. The *ó* retains its place as in Anglo-Saxon and late Saxon. Thus the late Saxon *dom, boc, blod*, *don, god, fot,* we meet again in Old and Middle English, but commonly in a spelling which endeavours to indicate the length of the vowel *o* by an *e* mute after a single consonant, or by doubling the letter *o*: *shoo, dome* and *doom, boke* and *book, blode* and *blood, done* and *doon, gode* and *good, fote* and *foot.* The Ablaut also in the seventh conjugation retains the *ó.*

û

Middle High German. Examples:—*du,* thou; *nu,* now; *su,* sow; *múl,* mule; *sul,* pillar (Germ. saule); *mur,* wall (Germ. mauer); *schur,* shower; *sur,* sour; *rum,* room (Germ. raum); *schum,* froth (Germ. schaum); *brut,* bride; *hús,* house; *mus,* mouse; *tusent,* thousand. Foreign are *mul, mur,* and *Namur, Neptune, fortune.*

Old and Middle English. The long *u* of Anglo-Saxon is in late Saxon already frequently found alternately with *ou,* as in *ful* and *foul, nu* and *now,* þu and þou, *tun* and *toun, sur* and *sour;* and the intruding *ou* or *ow* becomes predominant in Old and Middle English.

The Umlaut *ŷ* of the Anglo-Saxon *u* disappears already in late Saxon, which lets the sound return to its original *u* or replaces it by *i: hude, brude, rumen, uðe,* and *brid, fir, hiddenn,* &c. In Old and Middle English the fluctuation between *y, u* and *i* is continued, so that we read side by side, *fyr* and *fure, ryme* and *rume, fyl* and *ful, brid* and *brud.*

Diphthongs.

ei

Middle High German *ei* = Old High German *ei,* Gothic *ai.* Examples:—*ei,* egg; *zwei,* duo; *heil,* salus; *seil,* rope; *teil,* part; *heim,* home; *bein,* bone; *stein,* stone; *leip,* bread, loaf; *zeichen,* sign; *kreiʒ,* circle; *geiʒ,* goat, capra; *sweiʒ,* sweat; *greif,* eripui (Germ. griff); *pfeif,* fistulavi (Germ. pfiff); *steic,* scandi (Germ. stieg); *sweic,* tacui (Germ. schwieg); *streit,* pugnavi (Germ. stritt). The diphthong *ei* often originates in the elision of the medial *g* between *a* and a succeeding *i,* e. g. *meist* (Goth. maist) *meil* (Goth. mail)—contractions which are of a very ancient date—*gein* = *gagin,* against (Germ. gegen); *meit* = *magit,* maid; *rein* = *ragin,* counsel; *getreide* = *getregede.* Of foreign origin are *meige, meiger, Keiser, turnei, conterfei, Franzeis, Wáleis, Brituneis.*

Worthy of observation is the difference between *ei* and *i*:—
leim, argilla; *lim*, gluten; *mein*, scelus (cf. Germ. mein in mein-eid); *min*, meus; *schein*, splendui; *schin*, splendor; *swein*, puer; *swin*, sus; *leip*, panis; *lip*, vita. Inaccurate manuscripts show occasionally *ei* for *æ*, even for the short vowels *e* and *e*.

ie

Middle High German *ie* = Old High German *ie*, as well as *ia*, *io* for *iu*. Examples:—*die*, hic; *knie*, knee; *nie*, never; *ie*, ever; *vie*=*vihe*, cattle (Germ. vieh); *kiel*, keel; *bier*, beer; *diet*, people, gens; *liet*, song; *lief*, cucurri: *rief*, vocavi; *slief*, dormivi; *hieʒ*, vocavi; *lieʒ*, sivi. Many of the verbs which formerly had reduplicated preterites, show now the diphthong *ie*. Foreign words:—*tievel*, diabolus; *priester*, presbyter; *spiegel*, speculum; *fieber, fier, banier, revier, soldier, parlieren, formieren, turnieren*.

iu

Middle High German = Old High German. Examples:—*diu*, ancilla; *kniu*, knee; *niu*, new; *getriu*, faithful (Germ. getreu); *iuwer*, vester; *triuwe*, fides; *siule*, column (Germ. saule); *viule*, putresco (Germ. faule); *hiure*, hoc anno (Germ. heuer); *hiute*, hodie (Germ. heute); *tiure*, dear (Germ. teuer); *viur*, fire; *tiufe*, depth (Germ. tiefe); *liuge*, lie (Germ. lüge). The alternate use of *iu* and *ie* we observe chiefly in the verbal forms:—*biute* and *biete*, *biuge* and *biege*, &c.; but *briuwe, kiuwe, bliuwe*, have always *iu*, never *ie*. The transition from *ie* to *iu* may further be traced in the relation between substantives and their respective adjective or verbal forms, e. g. adj. *siech*, subst. *siuch*; adj. *tief*, subst. *tiufe*; *lieht*, lux; *liuhte*, luceo; *diep*, fur; *diubic*, furtivus. The terminational *iu* sometimes adopts the fuller form in *iuwe*, e. g. *niu, getriu*; *niuwe, getriuwe*.

ou

Middle High German = Old High German. Examples:—*ou*, sheep, ovis; *tou*, dew (Germ. tau); *vrow*, woman (German. frau); *ouwe*, water; *boum*, tree (Germ. baum); *stroum*, stream; *troum*, dream (Germ. traum); *loup*, leaf (Germ. laub); *stoup*, dust (Germ. staub); *touf*, baptism (Germ. taufe); *ouge*, eye (Germ. auge); *rouch* (Germ. rauch, fumus). This diphthong has to yield its place to *o* (which may be considered its representative in a more condensed form) whenever the terminational *m* which follows is weakened into *n* as *bon* = *boum*. *ou* is Umlaut of *ou*: *gòu*, pagus (Germ. gau); *hou*, hay (Germ. heu); also *gouwe*, *houwe*; *ouwe*, gen. of *ou*, sheep, ovis; *vrouwin*, femininus, from *vrou*; *loubín*, foliaceus, *louber*, folia, from *loub*, folium; *vröude*, joy (Germ. freude). This Umlaut is comparatively scarce, and seems to have a predilection for a position preceding the *v* sound, as in *ouw*=Gothic *avi*, O. H. Germ. *awi, ewi, ouwi*. Its orthography is unsettled: besides *ou* we find *oi, oy*, and still more frequently *eu*.

uo

Middle High German. Examples:—*druo*, weight, fruit; *kuo*, cow; *ruo*, rest (Germ. ruhe); *schuo*, shoe; *vruo*, early (Germ. frühe); *schuole*, school; *stuol*, chair, stool; *muor*, moor, palus; *bluome*, flower (Germ. blume); *ruom*, glory (Germ. ruhm); *suon*, son (Germ. sohn); *huof*, hoof; *stuofe*, step (Germ. stufe); *pfluoc*, plough; *bruoder*, brother; *bluot*, blood; *guot*, good; *muoter*, mother; *vuoz*, foot; *sluoc*, cecidi; *truoc*, tuli.

ue is the Umlaut of *uo*:—*blüen*, florere; *glüen*, fervere; *grüen*, virere; *müen*, vescare; also *blüejen*, *glüejen*, &c.; *hueve*, hoofs; *büechel*, libellus; *buechín*, fagineus; *blüete*, flores; *gemüete*, animus; *füeze*, feet. The Umlaut in *blüen*, *glüen*, &c., was brought about by a succeeding *i* which has been dropped, but which however is sometimes found as the semivowel *j*, as in *blüe-j-en*, *glüe-j-en*—forms in which the *e* of the infinitive also re-appears, and which in *blüen*, *glüen*, is absorbed by the diphthong of the root.

ai, au, ey, oi, oy

In **Middle High German** these diphthongs appear in foreign words, chiefly such as are imported from the Romance dialects, e. g. *faile*=*velum*, *voile*; *failieren*=*fallere*, *faillir*; *Laurin*, *Kaukasas*; *templeys*, *wáleys*; *boie*, *gloie*, *troie*; *roys*, *poys*, *troys*.

ai, au, eu, öi

Middle High German. These vowels are occasionally used to replace one or other of the organic diphthongs which we have examined in detail. It is therefore hardly necessary to say that they cannot be considered as organic diphthongs, and that they hold a position in dialectic variations, and not in such productions as come up to the standard of good Middle High German. Examples:—*au*=*ou*,*ú*: *haubet*, *gelauhe*, *haus*, *auge*; =*a*: *slauf*, *raut*, *taut*=*sláf*, *rat*, *tat*. This *au* is very harsh and repulsive.

eu=öu: *freude, geuden=fröude, gouden*. This *eu* may be traced to Gothic terminations in *avi*, and thus be considered the direct Umlaut of Goth *au*: *freude* from *frawida*, O. H. Germ.; *streute* from O. H. Germ. *strawita*, Goth. *stravida*. *eu=iu*: *hiute, briute*. *oi* occasionally replaces *ou* the Umlaut of *ou*: *göi=göu*, pagus, shire; *fröide=fröude*, joy; *löiber=löuber*, folia.

ou

Old and Middle English. (1) For Anglo-Saxon *o*, indicating the production of the original vowel, as in *fougten, fought=foogte, fogte*—very rare, because *o* commonly holds its own. (2) For Anglo-Saxon *u*. In late Saxon the long *u* preserves its position, its quantity being denoted by a simple consonant following it, e. g. *ful, þu, dun, rum, sur, ure* (see sub lit. **u**); but even here it must sometimes give way to *ou*: *foule, soure, þou*, &c.

In Old and Middle English, *ou* (*ow*) has gained supremacy over *u*, the latter vowel being apparently applied only to indicate the short *u* sound.

(3) For Anglo-Saxon *eo* we find the diphthong *ou* in Middle English (see sub lit. **eo**).

eó

The Anglo-Saxon *eó* begins in late Saxon already to be supplanted often by simple vowels, especially the long *e*. Thus we find *feond*, fiend; *seoc*, seek; *fleo*, flea; *deor*, door; *deore*, dear; *leof*, leaf; *leom*, gleam; *deop*, deep; *breost*, breast,—by the side of *fle, der, dere, lef, lem, dep, brest*.

Old English rarely retains the diphthong *eo*, as in *heo, deol, eode;* but fills its place indiscriminately, as it were with any other vowel, *e, i, o* or *u*: e. g. *e—kne, tre, fle; o—lese, lose, forlese, forlose, loke*, to lock; *lout; u—aluye; i—lie*.

In Middle English *eo* disappears altogether, being superseded in certain words by a long *e*, in others by the diphthong *ou;* e. g. *e—tree, kne, dere, þe, thefe, frend, fend; ou—foure, youth, to brouke, to loute*.

eá

This Anglo-Saxon diphthong was already abandoned in late Saxon, and its place filled by *æ*, seldom by *a* or *e*; e. g. *ǽ* (A. S. *eá*, water, river), *ære* (A. S. *eáre*, ear), *stræm* (stream), stream; *dæf, læf, bræd*. Old English has occasionally *ea*, as in *gleam, eam*, but commonly *e*, e. g. *streme, depe, chepe, defe;* and Middle English adopts the long *e*, which is sometimes rendered by *ee*, as *need, breed, reed* (Wycliffe). The Anglo-Saxon Ablaut *eá* of the sixth conjugation is also supplanted by *æ* and its cognate vowels *e* and *a*: *scæf, scef, scaf, sæc, soc, læs, les*. Old English, *clef, flet, ches, frese;* Middle English, *cleef, fleet, chees, frees*.

III. NEW TEUTONIC[1].

a

German. In Modern High German this vowel has preserved its original pure sound, and may therefore be considered as perfectly identical with the *a* sound in Old High German, deviating neither towards the higher pitched *e* nor the darker sound of *o*; and this rule holds good not only for cases in which it remains short, but for those also which show it converted into a long vowel. Hence *ab, de, præp; man* (French *on*); *wăld*, forest, contain a sound which is identical with that in *lában*, to refresh; *váter*, father; *háse*, hare; *ságe*, tale, saga; and with the organically long *a* in *gnáde*, grace; *stráße*, street; *fráge*, rogo.

Whilst in Middle and Old High German the sound was often fluctuating between *a* and *o*, Modern German has decided in favour of one or the other, and thus *ohne*, sine; *mond*, moon; *monat*, month, *woge*, wave, for the M. H. Germ. *áne, mane, mánet, wác*; and *monat, bräutigam*, bridegroom; *eidam*, gener; *heimat*, home, for O. H. Germ. *máno, prutigomo, eidum*.

English. The Anglo-Saxon *æ* (for High German *a*) which already in Old and Middle English had been commonly replaced by *a*, finds in Modern English also its expression in the vowel *a*, but it seems still to preserve its original sound wherever the vowel is short. Examples:—*sat, glad, at, that, cat, apple, ash*, &c.

When the vowel is lengthened, the *a* sound is modified in two directions so as to become identical with *e* or *o*, e. g. *whale, grave, ate, late, raven*, and *spoke, broke, stole, bore*. The consonants *ll* at the end, and *w* at the beginning of a word, darken the *a* sound into *a* (*á*), the medium between *a* and *o*, e. g. *small, water, what, was*, &c. The Anglo-Saxon *a*, which often inclines towards *o*, is, in Modern English, either rendered by *o* or has finally adopted the original *a*, which, in pronunciation however, is treated in the same manner as the *a* (= Anglo-Saxon *æ*) which

---

[1] The distinction of organically short and long vowels having all but disappeared, both classes of vowels are treated under the same head.

we have just examined. Thus we read *o* in *long, strong, throng, tong, song, thong;* short *a* in *man, can, camp, thank, and, sand, land, hammer;* long *a* in *name, lame, tame, lane, same; a* sound darkened by preceding *w* in *wan, swan.*

The Anglo-Saxon *ea* is in Modern, just as in Old and Middle, English rendered by *a*, which however under different consonantal influences assumes a different sound. Pure *a* sound before *r*—*harm, farm, yarn, mark, sharp, hard;* darkened into *a* (*a*) before *ll, lt, lk*—*all, hall, fall, malt, halt, talk, walk;* raised towards the higher pitch of *e*—*shall, shadow, ax, wax;* identical with *e* when lengthened—*shame, ale, scale;* supplanted by *e*—*stern, belch.*

Dutch. The distinction between long and short vowels being preserved in this more than in any other Teutonic dialect, we give the examples classified under the heads of short and long.

Short before a single consonant : *dal,* dale, valley ; *smal,* small ; *tam,* tame ; *nam,* cepi (Germ. nahm) ; *gaf,* dedi, gave ; *graf,* grave; *staf,* staff; *dag,* day; *zwak,* weak ; *blad,* leaf; *al,* all ; *stal,* stall ; *zal,* shall ; *kam,* comb ; *lam,* lamb ; *flam,* flame ; *man,* man.

Short before double consonants : *galm,* sound ; *half,* half; *kalf,* calf; *hals,* neck; *arm,* arm; *lang,* long, *zang,* song ; *tand,* tooth ; *gans,* goose ; *arm, warm, damp, hard, band, hand, land,* &c. Geminated consonants : *alle, stallen, mannen,* &c.

The fluctuations of the *a* sound which we have so frequently observed, chiefly in the ancient Low German dialects, is kept alive in Dutch too, the vowel *a* rising into *e* in the words *scherp,* sharp ; *erg,* wicked (Germ. arg) ; *sterk,* strong (Germ. stark) ; and descending to the lower pitch of *o* in the preterite of strong verbs : *ron,* cucurri, ran, run ; *zong,* cecini, sang, sung ; *dronk,* bibi, drank, drunk. Dutch *a* for *e* in *hart,* heart (Germ. herz) ; *smart* (Germ. schmerz) ; *pard,* horse (Germ. pferd) ; *zwárd,* sword (Germ. schwert).

Long *a*, spelt in Dutch *aa*, in Flemish *ae*, is organic in *al*, eel ; *hár,* hair; *jar,* year ; *war,* true ; *gran,* grain, frumentum ; *man,* moon ; *wan,* hope ; *scháp,* sheep ; *sprák,* speech ; *dad,* deed ; long by production in *tál,* language ; *dár,* there ; *war,* where ; *schám,* shame ; *hán,* cock ; *áp,* ape ; *wák,* wake ; *has,* hare ; long by contraction in *blan* foliis (=*bladen*) ; *vár,* father (=*vader*) ; *slán,* slay (=*slahen*) ; *trán,* drag, trahere (=*trahen*) ; *magd,* maid (=*maged*) ; *tragt,* fertis (=*traget*). In the penult before single consonants the Dutch dialect writes simply *a*, whether the vowel is originally long or short, and in this case Grimm recognizes his Middle Dutch 'Schwebelaut,' 'fluctuating sound,' which is neither decidedly long nor short ; as *alen,* anquillæ (=*álen*); *jaren*, anni (=*járen*); *spraken*, linguæ (=*språken*); and *hanen*, galli; *hasen*, lepores; *apen*, simiæ,—in which the *a* was originally short.

Swedish. The vowel *a* has its prototype in the Old Norse vowel of the same quantity, but it remains short only before double consonants: *all*, all; *falla*, to fall; *kalla*, to call; *shall*, shall; *gammal*, old; *hammare*, hammer; *tacka*, to thank; *vatten*, water; *elm*, elm; *half*, half; *barn*, infant; *skarp*, sharp; *salt*, salt; *namn*, name; *hampa*, hamper; *krank*, sick; *hand*, land, &c.

The vowel *a* preceding the combinations *ld*, *rg*, *ng*, is converted into *a*, of which below.

Before single consonants the pure *a* sound is retained, but lengthened in pronunciation: *dal*, dale; *bar*, bare, nude; *bar*, bore, tulit; *skam*, shame; *hane*, cock; *graf*, grave; *dag*, day; *lag*, law; *mat*, meat; *vara*, to be, for *vara*; *qvar*, quiet, for *qvär* (cf. the use of the Dutch *a* for *e*).

The Swedish *a* which stands for the Old Norse *á*, has undoubtedly had its origin in the lengthened *a* or *aa*. Analogous is the frequent decline of the English *a* into the middle sound between *a* and *o* under the influence of certain consonants, as *ll*, *w*, &c.; and still more so the fluctuation between *a* and *o* in some Old Teutonic tongues, as *hond* for *hand*, *holon* for *halon*, *mon* for *man*. Though this vowel is now identical with *o* it must originally have had a middle sound between *a* and *o*, as the English *a* in *wall*, *war*, &c. Examples:—*ål*, eel; *mål*, language; *år*, year; *far*, sheep; *har*, hair; *mane*, moon; *van*, hope; *språk*, speech; *gas*, goose; *a*, river; *gå*, to go; *slå*, slay; *ta*, toe; *sta*, to stand; *strå*, straw; *alder*, age; *gård*, villa (cf. yard and garden); *hard*, hard; *lång*, long; *åtta*, eight; *matte*, might; but *natt*, night (Germ. nacht).

Danish. Before single consonants organically short and long vowels are identical; before double and geminated consonants they are always short. Examples:—*dal*, dale; *gale*, to sing; *bar*, bare, nude; *bar*, bore, tulit; *hare*, hare; *skam*, shame; *hane*, cock; *grav*, grave; *have*, to have; *dag*, day; *blad*, leaf; *had*, hate, odium; *mad*, meat; *alle*, all; *takke*, to thank; *halv*, half; *kalde*, to call; *salt*, salt; *barn*, infant; *skarp*, sharp; *arg*, wicked (Germ. arg); *hamp*, hamper; *vand*, water; *mand*, man; *land*, *sand*, &c.

Transitions into *aa* and *o* are not easily fixed by rules, and sometimes deviate from the Swedish: e. g. *alder*=Sw. *alder*; *folde*, to fold; *holde*, to hold; *volde*, to command; *bold*, *kold*= Sw. *fälla*, *hälla*, *välla*, *käll*; but *falde*, *galde*, *kalde*=Sw. *falla*, *galla*, *kalla*;—*gaard*, yard, *haard*, hard (=Sw. *gård*, *hard*). By the side of *land* we have *baand* and *haand* = Sw. *land, band, hand; lov*, law (= Sw. *lag*).

Danish possesses, like Swedish, the sound *å*, a medium between *a* and *o*, which however most Danish authors, with the exception of Rask and other grammarians, write *aa*, though in its pronunciation it touches very closely on the Swedish *å*. It has chiefly to fill the place of the Old Norse *a*: *aal*, eel; *maal*, language; *aar*, year; *faar*, sheep; *haar*, hair; *saar*, sore; *maane*, moon; *vaaben*, weapon; *daad*, deed; *aa*, river; *daa*, doe; *faa*, few; *gaae*, to go; *graa*, grey; *raa*, raw; *saa*, so; *taa*, toe; *straa*, straw. This vowel, like the Swedish *å*, is chiefly met with before the consonants *ld, nd, rd*, which cannot be preceded by the pure *a* sound. Whilst however the Swedish represents only the Old Norse *a*, the Danish *aa* stands also for Old Norse *o*: *kaare*, to choose, Sw. *kora*; *aaben*, open, O. N. *opinn*; *draabe*, drop, O.N. *dropi*. *aa* = Old Norse *ó*: *raabe*, to shout, Sw. *ropa*, O. N. *hropa*. *aa* = Goth. *au*, O. H. Germ. *ou, ó*: *skaane*, to spare, Sw. *skona*, Germ. *schonen*; *haan*, scorn, Germ. *hohn*; *daab*, Sw. *dop*, baptism, Germ. *taufe*.

a (æ)

German. *a (æ)* is Umlaut of *a (a)*:—*wál*, choice, *wælen*, to choose[1]; *zal*, number, *zælen*, to count; *zám*, tame, *zæmen*, to tame; *hand* (sing.), *hände* (pl.); *gráben*, to dig, *græbt* (3rd pers. sing), *váter, væter; blatt, blätter; grás, græser; arm, ärmer*, poor, poorer; *hart, härter*, hard, harder, &c. From these examples it will be seen that the original *a* is still alive side by side with the Umlaut. Where, on the contrary, the word with the original *a* sound has become extinct, and the Umlaut in the derivative form is no longer felt as such, we find the Umlaut expressed by *e*; e. g. *heer*, army, O. H. Germ. *hari; ende*, end, O. H. Germ. *anti; erbe*, heir; *elle*, ell; *fremd*, foreign; *hemd*, shirt; *engel*, angel; *henne*, hen,—words in which the original *a* is extinct.

Swedish. The vowel *a* in Swedish has superseded five different Old Norse vowels. (1) = O. N. *a*: *grass*, grass (A. S. gras). (2) = O. N. *e*, Umlaut of *a*: *sälja*, to sell; *bar*, berry; *här*, army; *tämja*, to tame; *saga*, to say; *bädd*, bed, *glädja*, to gladden; *nätt*, net; *fälla*, to fell; *ägg*, edge and egg; *drägg*, dreg; *lägga*, to lay; *sätta*, to set; *smälta*, to smelt; *angel*, angel; *äple*, apple; *hast*, horse. (3) = O. N. *e*, Brechung and Trübung of *i*: *väl*, well; *är*, is, est; *bära*, to bear; *väg*, way; *väder*, weather; *äta*, to eat; *svärd*, sword. (4) = O. N. *æ*, whether Umlaut of *a* or

---

[1] *wal, wælen*, commonly spelt *wahl, wahlen*.

contraction of *ai, ei*: *mala*, to talk; *sall* (felix f. A. S. salig), *sad*, seed; *frande*, friend; *ara*, honour (Germ. ehre); *lära*, Germ. *lehren;* *klade*, vestis (Germ. kleid); *mästare*, master (Germ. meister). (5) = O. N. *e*, only at the end of words: *fa*, cattle (Germ. vieh); *knä*, knee; *trä*, wood (cf. tree).

Danish. The Danish *a* stands to the Old Norse in about the same relation as Swedish. Hence Danish *a* (1) = O. N. *a*: *gräs*, grass; *las*, burden. (2) = O. N. *e*: *bar*, berry; *här*, army; *räd*, net; *glade*, gladness; *tämme*, to tame; *sätte*, to set; *sälge*, to sell; *märke*, to mark; *hände*, pl. of *hand*. (3) = O. N. *e*: *bärre*, to bear; *väre*, to be; *väve*, to weave; *äde*, to eat; *väd*, mos (Germ. sitte); *väder*, ram (Germ. widder); *svärd*, sword. (4) = O. N. *æ*: *male*, to talk; *are*, honour; *läre*, to teach; *klade*, vestris; *sad*, seed. (5) = O. N. *e*: *fa*, cattle; *knä*, knee; *trä*, tree.

e

German. This letter can even in Modern German still be traced to the Umlaut of *a*, or to the Brechung or Trübung of *i*. The vowel *e* is Umlaut of *a* in the words *heer, meer, erbe, stellen, hemd, fremd, end*, &c. (Concerning this Umlaut and the Umlaut *a*, see sub lit. a.) The sound *e* as *Trübung* of *i* we find in *regen*, rain; *degen*, sword, which Grimm considers different in pronunciation from *legen* and *bewegen*, where the *e* is caused by Umlaut; but I must plead ignorance of that distinction. The different shades in the pronunciation of the German *e* are owing to consonantal influences (cf. *mehr, meer, sehr, seele, heer, herr, wer, degen, legen, regen, segen, sprechen, stechen*) rather than etymological deductions; nay the 'usus loquendi', the mode of pronunciation, has even corrupted the legitimate spelling of certain words, writing *a* (*æ*) for *e*: *bær*, a bear; *gebæren*, to bear; *rächen*, to revenge; *dämmern*, to dawn, on account of the close analogy to the pronunciation of the modern Umlaut *ä* in *wære, gæbe, læse*.

English. The Anglo-Saxon *e*, as Umlaut of *a*, is retained in the words *den, hen, fen, men, hell, bed, net, better, bench, to sell, to tell*, &c. But the Umlaut has returned to the original *a* in *to bare, to tame, to hate, to quake, angel*. This fact may be explained by the analogy of the adjectives *bare, tame*, which never were subject to the Umlaut.

The Anglo-Saxon *e*, Brechung and Trübung of *i*, on the whole preserves its pronunciation, but not its spelling, in Modern English. Short *e* remains in *well, spell, knell, helm, self, help*, *to fret, weather, to tread, to burst* (=*to berst*), *to burn* (=*to bern*). The sound is lengthened in *to bear, to break*. In *play, way, vain*, the *a* has superseded the *e*, and *y* or *i* takes the place of *g*: *rain* = *rein* = *regen*; *way* = *wey* = *weg*. Lengthened *e* for the A. S. *e* in *he, ye, thee, shield, field, to speak, to eat, to weave, to steal*.

Long *e*, spelt *ee*, is a very favourite vowel in Modern English, which however in pronunciation is identical with the lengthened *i* of the other Teutonic dialects. It stands (1) for A. S. *ǽ*—*eel, sleep, speech, greedy, seed, weed, deed*; but it is supplanted by *ea* (pronounced = *ee*) in *read, meal, deal*, whilst the long *e* sound remains in *hair, were, there, grey, strait*. Short *e* in *weapon*: note *briar* = A. S. *brær*. (2) *ee* = A. S. *e*, Umlaut of *o*: *to feel, heel, to deem, to seem, green, keen, to weep, to seek, to bleed; feet*, pl. of *foot; teeth*, pl. of *tooth; geese*, pl. of *goose*. (3) *ee* = A. S. *eá* and *e*, O. H. Germ. *ou, o*: e. g. *cheek*, A. S. *ceác; leek, reek, need*. But *ea* is more commonly used as the direct representative of the A. S. *ea*, though in pronunciation it is identical with *ee*. (4) *ee* = A. S. *eo*, Goth. *iu*, O. H. Germ. *io*; e. g. *bee*, A. S. *beó; tree*, A. S. *treó; glee*, A. S. *gleó; deep, meek, meed, reed*. (5) *ee* = A. S. *i*: *free, three, peep*.

Dutch. The vowel *e* is rare before single consonants in monosyllables, more common in connection with double consonants. Examples:—*hel*, clear (Germ. hell); *hel*, hell (Germ. holle); *snel*, quick (Germ. schnell); *vel*, skin (Germ. fell); *ster*, star; *ben* (Germ. ich bin), I am; *hen, pen, bed, net, leg*, lay, pono; *weg*, way; *zeg*, say, dico; *helle, snelle, velle, sterren, henne, penne, bedde, leggen, zeggen; melk*, milk; *veld*, field; *werk*, work; *denken*, to think; *enkel*, ankle; *mensch*, homo. The vowel *e* in all these words arises, as in High German, partly from the Umlaut of *a*, partly from the weakening of *i*, but in pronunciation it is the same throughout.

The long *e* is in Dutch, as in English, spelt *ee*. Organic it is in *deel*, deal; *heel*, heal; *meer*, more; *zeer*, sore, pain; *steen*, stone; *week*, weak; *bleef*, mansit; *dreef*, pepulit; *peeg*, inclinavit; *zweeg*, tacuit. Production of *e*: *steel*, steal, furor; *beer*, bear; *beek*, beach; *pleeg*, soleo; *breek*, frango; *steep*, pungo. By syncope of *de*: *vree* = *vrede*, peace (Germ. friede); *veer* = *veder*, feather; *neer* = *neder*, neither. It must be specially remarked that the short *e* placed in the penult before a single consonant is not doubled, though it becomes long by production and rhymes with the long *e* of the words mentioned before; e. g. *hemel*, heaven (Germ. hunnel); *gene*, ille (Germ. jener); *leven*, to live; *geven*, to give; *breken*, to break; *eten*, to eat; *zegel*, sail.

Swedish. *e* represents three ancient vowels: Old Norse *e*, Umlaut of *a*, in which position however it is rare, because Swedish orthography prefers *a* to mark the Umlaut. Examples: —*elf*, O. N. *elfa*, river (Lat. albis); *elg*, alces (O. N. elgr); *enka*, widow (O. N. eckja); *menniska*, homo. This Umlaut is, like the Umlaut *e* in German, no longer felt as such in the vowel-system of the language. *e* = O. N. *e*, rarely rendered by *a*. Examples: —*spel*, play (Germ. spiel); *lem*, limb; *regn*, rain; *ved*, wood; *svett*, sweat; *fred*, peace; *sena*, sinew: this vowel is chiefly met with in the pl. pret. of the strong conjugation (but not in the part. pret.); e. g. *drefvo*, pepulerunt; *sveko*, fefellerunt; *svedo*, doluerunt; *beto*, momorderunt. *e* = O. N. *ei*: *del*, part, deal (Germ. theil); *hel*, heal (Germ. heil); *hem*, home (Germ. heim); *ben*, bone (Germ. bein); *sten*, stone (Germ. stein); *ek*, oak (Germ. eiche). In pronunciation *e* and *a* touch closely upon each other, hence their occasional interchange, as *elf* and *älf*, river; *tvenne* and *tvänne*, bini; yet *e* approaches more nearly the *i*, and *a* the *a*, a circumstance which may be explained from their origin in the Old Norse *i* and *a*.

Danish. The Danish *e* is in its origin identical with the Swedish, though its occurrence may be more or less frequent according to accidental circumstances. *e* = O. N. *e*, commonly before doubled, rarely before single consonants; e. g. *fremmed*, foreign (Germ. fremd); *menneske*, homo; *elv*, river; *elske*, to love; *enke*, widow; *ende*, end; *sende*, to send; *hest*, horse. *e* = O. N. *ei*: *deel, been, steen, eg*, Germ. *theil, bein, stein, ei*.

i

German. This vowel is less frequently used than in the Middle High German, the original *i* being only preserved before double consonants; e. g. *still, nimm*, accipe; *sinn*, sense; *sitte*, mos; *wild, sind*, sunt; *wird*, Lat. fit; whilst before single consonants it is lengthened into *i*: *mir*, mihi; *dir*, tibi; *im*, ei; *in*[1], eum; or it is changed into *ie*. The Middle High German interchange between *e* and *i* in the conjugation of the verb is continued: *werden*, fieri; *wird*, fit; *geben*, dare; *gibt*, dat; *sehen*, videre; *sieht*, videt; *wichsen*, to polish, erroneously for *wechsen* = *wächsen* from *wachs*, wax.

English. Short *i* before single consonants: *him, dim, spin, swim, rib, lip, ship*. For the more ancient *y* in *sin, kin*. Before double consonants: *kill, still, will, stiff, thick, timber, thing, gift*,

---

[1] Commonly spelt *ihm, ihn*.

mist, witch. For the more ancient *y*: *ill, mill, hill, king, kiss, wish, bridge*. Before *r* where it assumes the sound of German *e* or *o*: *sir, fir, bird, birch, girl, mirth*. On comparing *fir, gird, shirt*, with the German *foere, stoeren*, &c., we may find an analogon to the exceptional sound of *i* before *r*, though it will be difficult fully to account for it in the manner in which Grimm traces the verb *to stir* to the A. S. *stŷran*, O. H. Germ. *storan*, Germ. *stoeren*

The long *i* is denoted in English orthography by the *e* mute which follows a single consonant; it has in pronunciation attained the sound of the German diphthong *ei*: *file* (Germ. feile); *while* (Germ. weile); *wine* (Germ. wein); *ripe* (Germ. reif); *side* (Germ. seite); *tide* (Germ. zeit); *drive* (Germ. treiben); *wide* (Germ. *weit*). For the A. S. *ŷ*: *fire*, A. S. *fŷr*, O. H. Germ. *fiur*, Germ. *feuer*; *bride*, A. S. *brŷd*, O. H. Germ. *prut*, Germ. *braut*; *lice*, pl. of *louse*, A. S. *lys*, pl. of *lus*; *mice*, pl. of *mouse*, A. S. *mys*, pl. of *mus*, cf. Germ. *laus, läuse*; *maus, mäuse*. Before *ld* and *nd* the long *i* has replaced the short *i*, as *child, mild, wild, bind, find, grind*; but the short *i* sound is preserved where a second syllable is added: compare the sound in *child* and *children, hind* and *hinder*. The sound of the *i* is fluctuating in the word *wind*. For *y*: *kind*, A. S. *gecynde*; *mind*, A. S. *gemynde*. Before *gh*: *bright*, A. S. *briht* = *byrht* = *beorht*; *to fight*, A. S. *fihtan*; *high*, A. S. *heáh*; *light*, A. S. *leoht*; *thigh*, A. S. *þeóh*.

Dutch. The short *i* is scarce before single, more frequent before double consonants: *stil*, still; *wil*, I will; *min*, love; *zin*, sense; *ik*, I, ego; *lid*, limb (Germ. glied); *smid*, smith; *schip*, ship. This *i* which has commonly been replaced by *e*, is, in pronunciation, an intermediate sound between the German *i* and *e*, so that *min, ik, schip*, are almost identical with *men, ek, schep*; and hence the fact that formerly the orthography was indeed fluctuating between *schep* and *schip, led* and *lid, smed* and *smid*, and that monosyllables in *i* which do not geminate their consonants upon adding another syllable, change the *i* into *e*, e. g. *schip, schepen; lid, leden; smid, smeden*. Before double consonants: *stillen, willen, minne, zinne, schild, wild, vinger, zingen, drinken, blind, wind, kind* (child). It represents a more ancient *ie* in the reduplicational vowel *ging* (=*gieng*), ivit; *hing*, pependit; *ving*, cepit; *vrind* for *vriend*.

The long *i* is spelt *ij*, Flemish *y*. The pronunciation of this vowel is very much like the English *i* in *might*, and the German diphthong *ei*, but so that the *e* element of this diphthong comes more decidedly to the surface; and hence *ij* sounds almost like *e* + *i* pronounced separately but rapidly one after the other. The Dutch diphthong *ei* may be considered identical with the German *ei* in pronunciation as well as derivation, if with Grimm we may consider *ij* the representative of the Gothic *ei*, and the Dutch *ei* of the Gothic diphthong *ái*. Examples of *i* :—*mijn, dijn, zijn*, to be (Germ. sein) ; *wijn*, wine (Germ. wein) ; *rijp*, ripe (Germ. reif) ; *tijd*, tide (Germ. zeit) ; *bijten*, to bite ; *nijd*, envy (Germ. neid) ; *lijf*, life ; *lijk*, body (cf. Germ. leiche) ; *ijs*, ice (Ger. eis).

Swedish. The vowel *i* in this dialect corresponds with the Old Norse *ĭ* as well as *í*. Before single consonants it is scarce, and, just as in Dutch, approaching the *e* in its sound—a fact which here again finds an explanation in the still undecided orthography of some words, as *frid* and *fred*, peace ; further in the pl. pret. and part. pret. of strong verbs, the former adopting, the latter rejecting the *e*, as *drefvo, drifven*. Words retaining the *i* are *til*, to, ad ; *vilja*, to will ; *gifva*, to give ; *mig, dig, sig*, me, te, se ; *frid, kid, vid*. It is the more frequent before double consonants ; e. g. *illa*, ill ; *lille*, little ; *stilla*, quietus (Germ. stille) ; *till*, ad ; *vill*, vult ; *himmel*, heaven ; *svimma*, to swim ; *finna*, to find ; *minne*, memory ; *qvinna*, woman ; *sinne*, mind ; *spinna*, to spin ; *slippa*, to slip ; *ligga*, to lie ; *dricka*, to drink ; *bitter, mild, vild, vinter, blind, fingr, silfver*. *i* = O. N. *í* : *bila*, hatchet (Germ. beil) ; *kil*, wedge (Germ. keil) ; *skir*, pure ; *spira*, spire ; *fin*, fine ; *vin*, wine ; *drifva*, to drive ; *lih*, like ; *spih*, spike ; *rida*, to ride ; *vid*, wide ; *lisa*, leisure. At the end of words : *bi*, bee ; *si*, ecce ; *skri*, clamor (Germ. schrei). *i* for O. N. *e* : *fick* and *gick* for *feck* and *geck*.

Danish. Danish *i* stands to Old Norse in the same relation as Swedish. (1) = O. N. *ĭ* : *spil*, play (Germ. spiel) ; *til*, ad ; *vill*, volo ; *tin, give, skip*, ship ; *mig, dig, sig*, me, te, se ; *kid, himmel*, heaven ; *ligge*, to lie ; *drikke*, to drink ; *bitter, mild, vild, ring, finde, qvinde*, woman ; *sind*, mind (Germ. sinn) ; *spinde*, to spin ; *vinter, fisk*, fish ; *vrist*. (2) = O. N. *í*, before liquids commonly spelt *ü* : *büll*, hatchet (Germ. beil) ; *spür*, spire ; *vün*, wine ; in all other cases spelt *i* : *drive, liv*, life ; *viv*, woman (cf. wife) ; *tid*, tide (Germ. zeit) ; *lig*, like ; *lig*, body (Germ. leiche). At the end of words : *bi*, bee ; *ti*, ten ; *sti*, sty ; *stie*, stem (Germ. stichel).

O

German. Before two consonants it has remained organically short : *voll*, full ; *fromm*, pious ; *sonne*, sun ; *gott*, God ; *gold, wort*. Before a single consonant it is either organically long, as

VOWEL SOUNDS. 79

tod, dead; *rot*[1], red; *zog*, traxit; *lon*, reward; *ror*, read; *or*, ear; *bone*, bean; or it has been lengthened by inorganic production; *son*, son; *lob*, praise; *bogen*, bow; *vogel*, bird; *bote*, messenger.

English. The relation of the *o* sound is rather complicated, since this vowel derives its origin from divers Anglo-Saxon vowels, from *a*, *o*, *u*, *á* and *ó*. (1) *o* organically derived from *u*: *hole*, *borough*, *for*, *fore*, *or*, *nor*, *to come*, *some*, *son*, *love*, *above*, *God*, *gospel*, *folk*, *gold*, *ford*, *short*, *worth*, *fox*, *ox*; strong pret. part. *stolen*, *born*, *shorn*, *torn*, *worn*, *got*, *forgot*, *spoken*. The sound of the short *o* is everywhere preserved except before combinations with *r*, such as *r*, *rm*, *rn*, *rd*, *rt*, where it is pronounced as an intermediate sound between the German *a* and *o*. (2) *o* from *a* chiefly before *ld*, *mq*, *ng*: *bold*, *cold*, *fold*, *hold*, *old*; cf. Germ. *kalt*, *falte*, *halten*, *alt*. Strong pret.: *stole*, *broke*, *trod*, *bore*, *won*; cf. Germ. *stahl*, *brach*, *trat*, *gebahr*, *gewann*; *soft* and *other*, long in Anglo-Saxon, for Germ. *sanft* and *ander*, and identical with the A. S. *o* in *gos* and *toð*, goose, tooth, which latter words have in modern English expressed their length by *oo*, and hence adopted the pronunciation of this vowel as in *tool*, *pool*, &c. In the same manner as we find the organic *o* lengthened into *ó*, we find the long *o* occasionally yielding to correption and becoming short, as in *brother*, *mother*, *bosom*, *blossom*, *Monday* (= Munday, Moonday), &c. (3) *o* = A. S. *a*, in which case it is always long. Example: —*whole*, A. S. *hál* (Germ. heil); *home*, A. S. *ham* (Germ. heim); *bone*, A. S. *ban* (Germ. bein); *both* (Germ. beide); *ghost* (Germ. geist); *most* (Germ. meist). But the Anglo-Saxon *a* is more usually rendered in English by *oa*, of which hereafter. (4) *o* = A. S. *eá* in the pret.: *crope*, repsit. A. S. *creáp*; *chose*, elegit, A. S. *ceás*; *froze*, alsit, A. S. *freás*. (5) The final *o* is of different origin in different words: *so*, A. S. *svá*; *two*, A. S. *twá*; *to do*, A. S. *don*; *to go*, A. S. *gangan*, *gongan*. Contractions are, *lord* from *hlaford*, *woman* from *wíf-man*.

The English long *o* is spelt *oo*, and corresponds to the Anglo-Saxon *ó*, Old High German *uo*, German *u*; with the last it is identical also in pronunciation. Examples:—*cool* (Germ. kuel); *pool* (Germ. pful); *stool* (Germ. stul)[2]; *hoof* (Germ. huf); *book* (Germ. buch); *good* (Germ. gut); *mood* (Germ. mut); *rood* (Germ. rute); *foot* (Germ. fuß); *bloom* (Germ. blume): cf. the Dutch *bloem*, *koel*, &c. To be noted are a few exceptions in the pronunciation of the *oo*, such as the shortening of the vowel in

---

[1] Commonly spelt *roth*, *lohn*, &c., where the *h* is introduced to denote the length of the vowel. See the letter *h*, consonants.
[2] Commonly spelt *kuhl*, *pfuhl*, *stuhl*, &c.

good, *foot*, *look*, and the deviation from the *oo* sound in *blood* (Germ. blut). *ó* (*oo*) for the ancient *a*, which however in Anglo-Saxon is already rendered by *ó*, while in German it is in some words kept alive to the present day: *moon*, A. S. *mona*, M. H. Germ. *mane*, Germ. *mond; soon*, A. S. *sona*, M. H. Germ. *sán; tooth*, A. S. *toð*, M. H. Germ. *zant*, Germ. *zán*. Other and *soft* have preserved the *o* sound. *Choose, lose* (= *loose*) answer to A. S. *ceósan* and *leósan; loose* = *loosen*, to A. S. *lýsan*. The termination *hood* = Germ. *heit* is the A. S. *had; room* is A. S. *rum; door*, A. S. *dor; wood*, A. S. *vudu*.

Dutch. Short *o* occurs before single consonants in monosyllables and before double consonants in trisyllabic words. Examples:—*hol*, hole; *wol*, wool; *dom*, silly (Germ. dumm); *hof*, court (Germ. hof); *lof*, praise (Germ. lob); *zon*, sun; *kop*, head (Germ. kopf); *blos* (blossom); *vos*, fox; *morren, knorren*, to murmur (Germ. murren, knurren); *kommer*, anguish (Germ. kummer); *nonne*, nun; *wolken*, clouds; *golf, wolf, storm, worm, tong*, tongue; *hond*, dog (Germ. hund); *mond*, mouth (Germ. mund); *wond*, wound. *o* = *e* in *worden* = *werden*, fieri. In the preterite of the strong verbs *o* for *a*: *borg, sprong, zong, bond, vond;* cf. Germ. *barg, sprang, sang, band, fand*. *o* for *oe*: *zochte*, Germ. *suchte*, (quæsivit) and the termination *dom*, Eng. *dom*, Germ. *thum*; but *doemen*, to doom. Sometimes *o* before *r* with another consonant is converted into *o*, and thus becomes an inorganic production: *doom*, thorn; *hoorn*, horn; *toorn*, wrath (Germ. zorn); *oord*, place (Germ. ort); *woord*, word.

The long *o* is, as in English, spelt *oo*, but is pronounced like the German *ó* in *thor, lohn*, and the English in *bore, bone*. It occurs organically long in the words *hoor*, audio, hear; *verloor*, perdidi; *moor*, moor; *oor*, ear; *roor*, reed; *boom*, tree (Germ. baum); *stom*, steam; *stroom*, stream; *boon*, bean; *loof*, leaf; *oog*, eye; *dood*, death; *brood*, bread; *nood*, need; *hooren*, audire; *ooren*, aures; *oogen*, oculi, &c. It occurs as production of *o* in *kool*, coal; *zoon*, son; *boog*, bow; *noot*, net; syncope of *de* in *goon* = *goden*, diis; *boon* = *boden*, nuntiis—words which rhyme on *loon, kroon, zoon*. In the following words we have *o* organically short, and yet it is pronounced long so as to rhyme upon the examples with *oo* just mentioned: *geboren*, born; *komen*, to come; *zomer*, summer; *gebroken*, broken, &c.

Swedish. *o* = O. N. *ŏ* or *u*. The sound of *a* which we examined above, being almost identical with *o*, modern orthography has largely adopted the former letter to supply the latter, e. g. *hål, spar, båge, fågel*, for *hol, spor, boge, fogel;* but historically the *o* is preferable. Examples:—*hol*, hole; *kol*, coal; *spor*,

VOWEL SOUNDS.

track (Germ. spuhr); *honung*, honey; *kona*, woman; *son*, son; *hof*, court; *lof*, praise; *boge*, bow; *fogel*, bird; *ok*, yoke; *och*, and; *bod*, messenger. Production is prevented by the gemination of the consonant: *sporre*, spur; *komma*, to come; *sommar*, summer; *droppe*, a drop; *hopp*, hope; *flotta*, fleet; *fox*, *oxe*, ox. Before double consonants: *holm*, island; *orm*, snake; *horn*; *morgon*, early; *ord*, word; *frost*. *o* = O. N. *o*: *sol*, sun; *stol*, stool; *stor*, great; *tondon*, thunder; *dom*, doom; *bog*, bow; *skog*, wood; *bok*, book; *blod*, blood; *broder*, brother; *fot*, foot; *hof*, sustulit; *for*, ivit; *drog*, traxit;—cf. the German preterites *hub*, *fuhr*, *trug*. *o* = Goth. *au*, O. H. Germ. *ou*: *dop*, baptism (Germ. taufe). At the end of words: *bo*, to dwell; *bro*, bridge; *gro*, to grow; *ko*, cow; *ro*, rest; *so*, a sow. Though, as we have stated, *a* is sometimes placed for *o*, it is only for the *o* of the first class, i. e. that which represents the Old Norse *o* or *u*, never for *o* = O. N. *o*; because it would appear that the difference in pronunciation is still great enough to deter a fine ear from rhyming *dam* and *dom*, *tag* and *tog*, *stål* and *stol*.

Danish The rules laid down for Swedish will hold good for this dialect too; wherefore few examples may suffice. *o* = O. N. *ŏ* or *ŭ*: *spor*, track; *spore*, spur; *kone*, woman; *og*, and; *fos*, fox; *holm*, island; *orm*, worm; *torn*, thorn. *o* = *a*: *solde*, *folde*, *holde*; *lov*, law (= O. N. *lag*). *o* = O. N. *ó*: *sol*, sun; *stol*, stool; *dom*, doom; *bog*, book; *blod*, blood; *fod*, foot—preterites of the verb; *for*, *drog*, *slog*, *tog*, &c. *o* = O. N. *a* (compare the Swedish *å* for *o*): *sprog*, language, Germ. *sprache*, Sw. *språk*; *vove*, andere, Germ. *wagen*, Sw. *våga*: cf. Germ. *mond*, *one*[1], for M. H. Germ. *mane*, *áne*. At the end of words: *bo*, dwelling; *bro*, bridge, &c., see **Swedish**.

Ö

German. *o* is Umlaut of *o*: *worter*, pl. of *wort*, word; *sohne*, pl. of *sohn*, son; *loblich*, adj. of *lob*, praise; *vogel*, pl. of *vogel*, bird;—sometimes Umlaut of an original *a*: *hölle*, *schopfer*, *schoffe*, *löffel*, *zwölf*, *lowe*; cf. Goth. *halja*, *tvalif*, &c. In the sixteenth century we even meet *monsch* for *mensch*, *word* for *werd*, island: *monch*, monk, is an inorganic *o* for *münch*; thus also *konig* for *künig*.

English and **Dutch** do not possess this vowel.

Swedish. *o* stands for six different sounds of the Old Norse. *o* = *y*, Umlaut of *o*, or rather *u*; hence Swedish *o* stands to Old Norse *y* in the same relation, as does the German *o* to *ü*. When

---

[1] Common spelling *ohne*.

the Umlaut *y* was no longer distinctly felt, a new Umlaut was created directly from the *o*, just as in German the spirit of the language produced the modern Umlaut *o*, when the more ancient *u* began to die out. Examples:—*bolja*, billow, O. N. *bylgja*; *folja*, to follow, O. N. *fylgja*; *dorr*, door (Germ. thüre); *kon*, kin, A. S. *kyn*; *soner*, filii, Germ. *sohne*; *logn*, lie, Germ. *lüge*; *not*, nut, O. N. *knyt*. Where however *u* keeps its position in the stem of the word, *y* also remains as its Umlaut.   *ö* = *au*, which diphthong at a very early date began to be contracted, first into *o*, then into *œ*: *bola*, mugire, O. N. *baula*; *lordag*, Saturday, O. N. *laugardagr*; *drom*, dream; *strom*, stream; *bona*, bean; *döf*, deaf; *oga*, eye; *lop*, cursus; *brod*, bread;—cf. Germ. *traum, taub, auge, lauf.*   *ö* = *ey*: *do*, to die; *ho*, hay; *mo*, may; *o*, island; *hora*, hear; *ora*, ear; *toga*, to tug; *rök*, reek; *ode*, desertus (Germ. ode).   *ö* = *oe*: *fora*, ducere (Germ. führen); *domma*, to deem, judicare; *bon*, preces; *gron*, green; *hona*, hen; *modrar*, mothers, pl. of *moder*; *fotter*, feet, pl. of *fot*, foot.   *ö* = *io*: *fro*, seed; *sno*, snow; *brost*, breast.   *ö* = *e*, only in the reduplication of the verb: *foll, holl,* = O. N. *fell, held.*

Danish. Though Danish grammarians distinguish two sounds of the vowel *o* = namely one like the French 'eu ferme' in *peu*, and the other like the French 'eu ouvert' in *veuve, cœur*—the former marked ϕ, the latter *o*—we need not keep up this distinction, because it is not warranted by etymology; and we therefore write always *o*.   *o* = O. N. *y*: *son, bon*, where we find the Umlaut in the singular already, while Swedish, with greater nicety and better tact, uses the Umlaut to denote the plural of *son*, and *bon*, bean; *dor*, door, *nod*, nut; *bölge*, billow; *folge*, follow.   *o* = O. N. *i*: *tommer*, O. N. *timbr*; *solv*, O. N. *silfr*.   *ö* = O. N. *o*, Umlaut of *a*: *born*, pl. of *barn*, child.   *ö* = O. N. *au*: *drom*, dream; *ström*, stream; *loverdag*, Saturday; *brod*, bread; *dod*, death; *nod*, need, &c., see **Swedish**.   *o* = O. N. *ey*: *doe*, to die; *ho*, hay; *mo*, maid; *o*, island; *hore*, hear, audire; *ore*, ear; *ror*, reed, &c., cf. **Swedish**. *o* = O. N. *oe*: *fore*, to lead, Germ. *fuhren*; *bon*, preces; *gron*, green; *hone*, hen; *boger*, libri; *domme*, to deem.   *ö* = *œ*: *so*, sea, O. N. *sær*, Sw. *sjo*; *fro*, seed, O. N. *fræ, frio*.

u

German. Before double consonants *u* represents the Old German short vowel: *und*, and; *mund*, mouth; *krumm*, crooked; *kunst*, art; *brust*, breast; *burg*, castle; *huld*, grace. Before a single consonant it is the ancient long vowel: *zug, trug, flug*, *tugend*, or Schwachung of the ancient diphthong *uo*: *rum*[1], glory, = *ruom* ; *klug*, prudent, = *kluog* ; *fuß*, foot, = *fuot* ; *hŭn*, hen ; *blut*, blood ; *fur*, pret. of *fáren* ; *schŭf*, pret. of *schaffen*. Exceptions :—*spur* = M. H. Germ. *spor*, track ; *zuber* = O. H. Germ. *zuipar*, pail.

English. This vowel is not found so frequently as the rest in words of Teutonic origin. Before a single vowel its sound is a medium between the German *o* and *o*, whilst the modern Dutch *u* in pronunciation resembles the French *u*. Examples :—*dun*, *run*, *sun*, *shrub*, *tub*, *up*, *tug*, *hut*, *shut*. In the verb *to bury* it has the sound of the German short *e*; and in the termination *bury*, as *Canterbury*, *Salisbury*, *Tilbury*, it is almost entirely dropped in pronunciation. The tendency in this case of the *u* inclining towards the *e* is already testified by the mediæval mode of spelling *Canterberiensis*, *Saresberiensis*, *Tilberiensis*. (Concerning the sound of *u* in *busy*, vide sub lit. i.) Before double consonants *u* shows the same tendencies in its sound : *summer*, *gulf*, *burden*, *turf*, *hunger*, *thunder*. It assumes a long sound before a consonant followed by the *e* mute; in which case it might be rendered in German by *ju*, e. g. *mule*, *mute*, *duke*, *to mure*, *plume* (mulus, mutus, dux, murus, pluma), and other words of exclusively Latin and French derivation. The same words we find in Middle High German with the vowel *u*—*mŭl*, *mŭr*; in Modern German with the vowel *au*—*maul*, *mauer*; but even the Middle High German dialect admits of a vowel *iu* as the Umlaut of *ú*, e. g. *gemiure*, Germ. *gemäuer*. This phænomenon, according to which *i* and *u* when succeeded by an *e* assume the sounds of *ei* and *iu*, we shall have to consider more closely elsewhere. Words which had the long *u* in Anglo-Saxon already did not preserve that vowel in English, but converted it into *ou*, since the sound of *u* had then yielded to the long *o* = *oo*; hence A. S. *þu*, *mus*, *lŭs*, *hus*, *sur*, *ure*, *cu*, *brun*, Eng. *thou*, *mouse*, *louse*, *house*, *sour*, *our*, *cow*, *brown*.

Dutch. The Dutch *u* in short syllables resembles the English in *gun*, *but*, though it has at the same time a shade of the French *u* in it. It may occur before single and double consonants. Examples :—*dun*, thin ; *druk*, pressure (Germ. druck); *brug*, bridge ; *put*, pit ; *zullen*, debere, shall ; *kunnen*, posse (Germ. konnen); *kussen*, to kiss ; *schuld*, debt ; *zuster*, sister ; *drukken*, premere (Germ. drücken); *rukken*, dimovere (Germ. rucken). It does not occur before the liquids *m*, *n*, *r*. It fluctuates between *o* and *u* in *vollen*, *vullen*.

---

[1] Common spelling *ruhm*, *huhn*, *fuhr*, &c.

The long *u* occurs very rarely, but before *r* exclusively. In Flemish it is spelt *ue*, in Dutch *uu*. Most of the ancient words which contained an *ú* have, in modern Dutch, replaced this vowel by the diphthong *ui* (pronounced like German *eu*, English *oi*), a circumstance which shows here, in the same manner as in the ancient dialects, the fluctuation of sound between *iu, u,* and *u*. The pronunciation of *ú* resembles most nearly that of the French *u*. Examples:—*duur*, dear; *duur*, duro (Germ. dauern); *muur*, murus (Germ. mauer); *uur,* hour (Germ. uhr); *vuur*, fire; *zuur*, sour; *huren*, to hire; *geburen*, rustici (Germ. bauern).

Swedish. *u* stands for the Old Norse short and long vowels of the same sound. (1) O. N. *u* (*o*): *furo*, fir; *gud*, God; *full*, full; *kull*, nest; *kurra*, to murmur, (Germ. knurren, Dutch knorren); *rubba*, to rob (Germ. rauben); *skuld*, guilt (Germ. schuld); *guld*, gold; *rumpa*, tail; *ulf*, wolf; pret. of verbs: *krupo*, crept, repserunt; *klufvo*, cleft, fiderunt; *bruto*, broke, fregerunt; *spunno*, span, neverunt. (2) = O. N. *ú*: *ful*, turpis (cf. foul); *mur*, wall (Germ. mauer); *sur*, sour; *rum*, room; *skum*, scum; *fluga*, fly (Germ. fliege); *brud*, bride; *mus*, mouse; *hus*, house.

Danish. This vowel often keeps its place in Danish where the other dialects weaken it into *o*. It stands for O. N. *u* (*o*): *hul*, hollow; *kul*, coal; *dum*, dumb; *uge*, week (Germ. woche); *gud*, God (Germ. gott); *guld*, gold; *muld*, mould; *fugl*, bird (Germ. vogel); *mund*, mouth. = O. N. *a*: *dug, dugge*, dew; *hugge*, to hew (Germ. hauen). = O. N. *ú*, and spelt *uu* before liquids and *s*: *fuul*, foul; *bruun*, brown; *skuum*, scum; *muur*, wall (Germ. mauer); *brud*, bride (Germ. braut); *hud*, hide (Germ. haut). At the end of words: *drue*, grape (Germ. traube); *bue*, bow; *flue*, fly; *frue*, Germ. frau; *due*, dove (Germ. taube); *lue*, flame (Germ. lohe).

ü (ue), y

German. *ü*, Umlaut of *u*: *krummen* from *krumm*, crooked; *burger* from *burg*, castle; *künstlich*, adj. of *kunst*, art; *huener*[1], pl. of *hun*, hen, &c. The Middle High German *ü* as Umlaut of *o* is dropped and supplanted by *o*, so that the derivative forms of *holz, gold, vogel*, are *holzern, golden, gevogel: gülden*, though occasionally used in poetry, may be considered obsolete. The words *vor* and *fur* (vor-sehung, für-sehung), *tor*, gate, and *tuer*[2], door, are still fluctuating. *hoefisch, hoeflich*[3], courteous, and

---

[1] Common spelling *hühner, huhn.* [2] Common spelling *thor, thür.*
[3] *höfisch, höflich.*

VOWEL SOUNDS. 85

hübsch, pretty, originally expressed the same meaning, both being derived from *hof*, court.

The spelling is fluctuating between *ü* and *i* in the words *hilfe*, *hülfe*, help; *giltig, gültig*, valid; *gebirge, gebürge*, mountain-range; *wirken, würken*, to work; *sprichwort, sprüchwort*, proverb. Grimm decides in favour of *gebirge, hilfe, sprichwort*, and *giltig*, because they are analogous to the Old German forms: *würken* he considers the more preferable orthography on account of the Gothic *vaurkjan*, though in Old High German already *wurchan* and *wirkan* are used indiscriminately. The vowel *y* is in German superfluous; and though it may be used for foreign words, its sound can easily be rendered by *i*. The Romans already wrote and spoke *silva* for *sylva*, and it may therefore be considered as something hyper-classical when German scholars affectedly pronounce *süntax, süstem*, for *syntax, system*. Still more pedantic is the manner in which German authors strive to keep distinct the little monosyllables *sein* (suus) and *seyn* (esse), which are now both rendered by *sein*, since they have the same sound and can be traced to the same form *sin* in Middle High German.

English. This dialect does not know the Umlaut of *u*, and therefore does not require the vowel *ü*. The Umlaut of the Anglo-Saxon *u* was *y*, and this is still preserved in sound at least if not in spelling. Hence A. S. *mus, lus*, pl. *mys, lys;* Eng. *mouse, louse*, pl. *mice, lice*. The letter *y* therefore replaces in the English of the present day Anglo-Saxon vowels of a different kind. *y = i*, originating in the Anglo-Saxon termination *ig: any*, A. S. *ænig; holy*, A. S. *hálig; ivy*, A. S. *ifig; worthy*, A. S. *wyrðig*. *y = í*, German *ei: by*, apud (Germ. bei); *my*, meus (Germ. mein); *thy*, tuus (Germ. dein). *y = y: why*, cur, A S. *hwy*, Goth. *hoe*, O. H. Germ. *huiu*. *y = u : sky*, A. S. *scua*, O. N. *sky*. *y =* A. S. *eo : fly*, volare, A. S. *fleogan*, Germ. *fliegen ; fly*, musca, A. S. *flebge*, Germ. *fliege ; shy*, Germ. *scheu ; sly*, Germ. *schlau*. *y* originating in *g : eye*, A. S. *eáge*, Germ. *auge*.

Dutch does not recognise either the vowels *ü* or *y*.

Swedish. The vowel *y* takes in sound and meaning the place of the German *ü*. It therefore is chiefly used for the Old Norse *y* Umlaut of *u: fylla*, to fill; *gyllen*, golden (cf. Germ. gülden); *mynning*, ostium (Germ. mündung); *bygga*, to build; *rygg*, back (Germ. rücken); *lycka*, luck; *nyckel*, key; *stycke*, piece (Germ. stück); *skyldig*, guilty (Germ. schuldig). *y =* O. N. *y : rymma*, abire (Germ. raumen); *snyte*, snout (Germ. schnauze); *hysa*, domo recipere (Germ. behausen). *y =* O. N. *ý*, contracted from *iu, io : dyr*, dear; *fyr*, four; *krypa*, to creep; *flyga*, to fly; *flyta*, fluere, to float. At the end of words: *bly*, lead (Germ. blei); *fly*, to flee; *hy*, hue; *ny*, new; *sky*, nubes, sky.

Danish *y* appears under the same conditions as the Swedish. *y* = O. N. *y*: *fyr*, fir; *gylden*, golden; *hyld*, alder (Germ. holder); *yngre*, junior (Germ. jünger); *synd*, sin (Germ. sünde); *lykke*, luck; *kysse*, kiss; *bryst*, breast; *dyd* = *dygd*, virtue (Germ. tugend). *y* = *ŷ*, O. N. Umlaut of *u*: *myre*, mere, lake; *syd*, south (Germ. süden). *y* = O. N. *ŷ*, condensed *iu, io*: *syn*, sight; *dyr*, dear; *dyr*, deer (Germ. thier); *fyr*, fire; *flyve*, to fly; *klyve*, to cleave. At the end of words: *bly*, lead (Germ. blei); *by*, town; *ny*, new; *sky*, sky.

Diphthongs.

The different double vowels in English, Dutch and Danish, have already been examined, since we arranged them under the simple vowels *aa, ee, ii, oo, uu*, as identical with *a, e, í, ó, ú*. The diphthongs properly so called are so different in the different modern dialects, and represent ancient vowels so divergent in form and meaning, that we consider it advisable here to abandon our plan of grouping the dialects together under each vowel, and to arrange all the different diphthongs under each dialect respectively.

German.

ai. It is merely an orthographical whim which retains the *ai* in several words, the sound of which might quite as well be rendered by *ei*: *mai*, May; *Main*, the river Mein; *hain*, grove; *saite*, chord; *waise*, orphan; *Kaiser*, Emperor; but *getraide* and *getreide*, corn; *waize* and *weize*, wheat; whence it becomes evident that there is no difference of sound. In *waise*, orphan, and *weise*, a sage; *saite*, chord, and *seite*, side, the different spelling is some help for the eye, and nothing more. *hain* might be justified as originating in the ancient *hagan, hagin*, just as *Rein-hart* from *Regin-hart*, *Mein-fried* from *Megin-fried*.

au. This diphthong represents three different vowels—M. H. Germ. *u, ou, âw*.

au = M. H. Germ. *ú*: *bau*, building; *sau*, a sow; *faul*, foul; *raum*, room; *braun*, brown; *sauer*, sour; *schauer*, shower; *haufe*, heap; *sauge*, suck; *braut*, bride; *haut*, skin, hide; *laut*, loud; *aus*, out; *haus*, house; *laus*, louse; *maus*, mouse. But the M. H. Germ. *du* and *nu*, thou, now, remain *dú* and *nun*.

au = M. H. Germ. *ou* : *baum*, tree, beam ; *saum*, seam ; *traum*, dream ; *laub*, leaf ; *taub*, deaf ; *auge*, eye, A. S. *eáge*, M. H. Germ. *ouge*.

au = M. H. Germ. *a, áw* : *blau*, blue ; *grau*, grey ; *flau*, flaw ; M. H. Germ. *grá, gráwe ; blá, bláwe*, &c.

A reference to the Dutch language will more fully explain the nature of the *au* from *u*, and *au* from *ou*. For the former the Dutch has *ú*, for the latter *ó* ; hence, Dutch *rum*, M. H. Germ. *rum*, Germ. *raum* ; Dutch *drom*, M. H. Germ. *troum*, Germ. *traum* ; cf. *suge, sauge*, and *oge, auge*. Thus, then, German mixes up two different vowels which Dutch still keeps distinct. Even German prefers before certain consonants the vowel *o* to *au* in place of the M. H. Germ. *ou* ; e. g. *lon*[1], reward ; *bone*, bean ; *flog*, flew ; *stro*, straw ; *hoch*, high ; *not*, need, &c.

au is Umlaut of *au*. Examples :—*sau*, a sow, pl. *säue ; raum*, space, room, pl. *räume ; baum*, tree, pl. *bäume ; haus*, house, pl. *häuser ; auge*, eye, diminutive *äuglein*. *äu*, the modern, stands in the same relation to *eu*, the more ancient Umlaut, as does *ä* to *e* (see sub litt. **a, e**).

ei stands for M. H. Germ. *i* and *ei*, Dutch *ij* = *i*, and *ee* = *e* ; as *au* for M. H. Germ. *u* and *ou*.

To test the nature of the German *ei* a reference to the parallel words in Dutch is sometimes sufficient, e. g. *reif*, hoop, Dutch *reep ; reif*, ripe, Dutch *rijp*.

Examples of *ei* = M. H. Germ. *i* : *sei*, sit ; *frei*, free ; *meile*, mile ; *weile*, while ; *mein, dein, sein*, meus, tuus, suus ; *wein*, wine ; *reif*, ripe ; *seide*, silk ; *seite*, side ; *eis*, ice ; *eisen*, iron ; *weise*, wise ; *feind*, fiend ; *reich*, rich.

ei = M. H. Germ. *ei* : *reif*, hoop ; *ei*, egg ; *heil*, heal ; *heim*, home ; *bein*, bone ; *stein*, stone ; *klein*, little ; *eiche*, oak ; *beide*, both ; *geiße*, goat ; *weiß*, white ; *weiß*, novi ; *heiß*, hot.

In some cases the spelling is wavering between *ei* and *eu* (M. H. Germ. *i* and *iu*) : *heirat* and *heurat, heint* and *heunt*. There is indeed a difference in the meaning of *zeigen*, to show, and *zeugen*, to bring forth, gignere ; but it is sometimes difficult to keep them distinct, as in the expression 'Freundschaft bezeigen' and 'bezeugen', which are all but identical. It is however altogether erroneous to write, as is commonly done, *ereignen*, to happen, *ereignis*, event, instead of *eräugnen, eräugnis*, O. H. Germ. *arouenissi*. The fluctuating orthography in *heirat, heurat*, marriage, and *heint, heunt*, hac nocte, we find already in the M. H. Germ. *hírát* and *hiurát, hint* and *hiunt*.

---

[1] *lohn, bohne*, &c.

eu is also adopted in place of two Middle High German vowels, *iu* and *ou*. *eu=iu*: *new*, new (M. H. Germ. *niu*); *heuer*, hoc anno (M. H. Germ. *hiure*); *teufel*, devil; *heute*, hodie (M. H. Germ. *hiute*); *leute*, people; *fleugt, kreucht, fleußt*, for *fliegt, kriecht, fließt*, M. H. Germ. *fliugt, kriucht, fliuzt*.

eu = M. H. Germ. *ou*: *heu*, hay; *streu*, straw; *freuen*, rejoice; *freude*, joy.

ie. We consider this a diphthong, though it is not pronounced like *i-e* but *i*, the English *ee*. Examples:—*dienen*, to serve; *bier*, beer; *dieb*, thief; *frieren*, freeze; *lieb*, dear (cf. lief). Formed by contraction: *priester*, from *presbyter*, *spiegel* from *speculum*, *fieber* from *febris* (French *spiegle, fievre*). For short *i* in *viel*, much; *spiel*, play, &c. For Middle High German *ei* in the preterites *schien, mied, trieb*; *Paradies* for *Paradeis*. Occasionally for *uo, üe*: *mieder*, M. H. Germ. *muoder, liederlich* for *lüederlich*—sometimes *lüderlich*, derived from *luder*. As we see the ancient *i* occasionally lengthened into *ie*, so we find, vice versa, *ie* shortened into *ĭ*: *dirne* for *dierne*, O. H. Germ. *diorna*; *licht, nicht* for *lieht, nieht*; *ging, hing, fing*, for the reduplicated preterites *gieng, hieng, fieng*: the latter mode of spelling is preferable.

iu is no organic diphthong in German, and occurs only in *hui, pfui*, exclamations for M. H. Germ. *hoi, hei—pfi, pfei*.

English.

ai. This diphthong has its origin in the A. S. *äg*: *hail*, A. S. *hägel*, Germ. *hagel*; *tail*, A. S. *tägel*, Germ. *zagel*; *maid*, A. S. *mägð*, Germ. *magd*; *said*, dixit, A.S. *sägde*, Germ. *sagte*; *main*, A. S. *mägen*, M. H. Germ. *megin* (cf. M. H. Germ. *mein, meit, geseit*, for *megin, megit, gesegit*); *daisy*, from A. S. *däges eáge*, day's eye, oculus diei. *ai* represents the A. S. *eg* (both *eg* and *eȝ*) in *sail*, A. S. and Germ *segel*; *lain*, A. S. and Germ. *legen*; *rain*, A.S. and Germ. *regen*; *laid*, A.S. *legde*, Germ. *legte*; *again, against*, A. S. and Germ. *gegen*. In this case the original *e* has been replaced by *a*, so that we read *rain, sail, laid*, instead of *rein, seil, leid*, an occurrence which may be explained by the fact of *ai* answering more closely to the sound of the contracted vowels. *ai*=A. S. *æg* in *stair*, from *stæger*. *ai*=A. S. *á* in *hail*, by the side of *whole* (sanus, salvus), *swain*. *ai*=A. S. *æ* in *hair*, A. S. *hær*; *raise*, A.S. *ræsan*. This diphthong is also often met with in words of Romance origin, where it is derived

VOWEL SOUNDS.

from the Latin *agi*, as the English *ai* is from the A. S. *æg*: *frail*, fragilis.

ay is but a different mode of spelling the same diphthong at the end of words; as *day* from *däg*, *way* from *weg*, *lay* from *legan*, *say* from *segan*.

au. This diphthong is rare and answers to the Anglo-Saxon *o* in a few cases before the consonants *gh*. Examples:—*daughter*, A. S. *dohtor*; *draught*, A. S. *droht*; *aught*, A. S. *áwht*, *áwiht*, O. H. Germ. *iowiht*.

aw. For A. S. *ag, eg, eah, af*: *awe*, A. S. *ege* (cf. Goth. *aggan*); *dawn*, A. S. *dagian*; *draw*, A. S. *dragan*; *hawk*, A. S. *hafoc*, O. N. *haukr*; *law*, A. S. *lag*; *saw* (serra), A. S. *sega*; *saw* (vidit), A. S. *seah*; *raw*, A. S. *hreaw*, O. H. Germ. *hrá*, Germ. *rɔ* [1], rough (from A. S., O. H. Germ. *ruh*, Germ. *rauh* and *rauch*); *strow*, A. S. *straw*, Germ. *stro* [2].

ea. A diphthong of frequent occurrence, and faithful to its traditions, commonly representing the A. S. *eá*. (1) Examples of this kind are,—*beam, dream, gleam, steam, stream, seam, team; ear, hear; bean, lean; cheap, heap, leap; leaf, deaf; bread, head* (heafod), *dead; great, death, east.* (2) *ea* = A. S. *a*: *weak*, A. S. *wác; sweat*, A. S. *swat; sheath*, A. S. *sceáð*. (3) = A. S. *æ*: *deal, heal, tear, year, clean, mean, weapon, ready, thread, wheat.* (4) = A. S. *eo*: *dear, cleave, breast*. In most cases this diphthong has assumed the pronunciation of *ee*; but in certain positions, especially before dentals, it takes the sound of the originally short *ea* in *stead, tread*, as *bread, dread, lead*: exceptions are *great* and *wheat*.

ei. Rare in words of Teutonic origin, and corresponding to the most heterogeneous vowels in A. S.: thus—*their*, A. S. *þara*; *heifer*, A. S. *heahfore, heafre*; *eight*, A. S. *eahta*; *neigh*, A. S. *knægan*; *either*, A. S. *áhwäðer, áwder, auðer*; *neither*, A. S. *náhwäðer, náwðer, nauðer*.

ew is rather frequent, and has the diphthongal pronunciation of *u*, but of *oo* after *l* and *r*. As a rule it answers to the A. S. *eów*, but occasionally to other vowels, such as *o, ea*, &c. Examples:—*to brew*, A. S. *breowan*; *to chew*, A. S. *ceowan*; *ewe*, A. S. *eow*; *dew*, A. S. *deow*; especially in the preterite of strong verbs, e. g. *crew*, A. S. *creów*, cantavit; *grew*, A. S. *greow*, viruit; *knew*, A. S. *cneów*, novit; *blew*, A. S. *bleów*, flavit.

ey. Of rare occurrence, replacing the A. S. *eá* and *æ*, e.g.

---

[1] *roh*.   [2] *stroh*.

eye, A. S. *eáge; grey*, A. S. *græg: prey* is the French *proie*, præda.

ie answers to the A. S. *eo* in *fiend, friend, lief*, and *thief*.

oa stands for A. S. *a* and *æ*: *boar, oar, hoar, foam, loam, groan, moan, broad, goad, toad, goat, oat, oath;* occasionally replaced by *o*, with which it is identical in pronunciation, as *lome* for *loam*: the preterites of the verbs however have regularly *o*, never *oa*, as *shone, smote, drove*, &c. Even the French *o* has been dressed up in the English garb of *oa*: *coach* for *coche, coat* for *cote, broach* for *broche, road* for *rote, toast* for *toste, coast* for *cote = coste*.

oe is no true diphthong, but simply a long vowel, hence pronounced as *o*: *doe*, A. S. *da; foe*, A. S. *fá; roe*, A. S. *rá; toe*, A. S. *táhe, tá; woe*, A. S. *wá*.

In Old High German and Middle High German these words pass from the diphthong *ei* into the simple vowel *e* on account of a following *h, v*, or *s*. (Cf. German *reh, zehe, weh*.)

ou answers in sound and position to the German *au*, and as the latter stands occasionally for Old High German *u*, so also English *ou* stands for Anglo-Saxon *ú* or the production of *u*. *ou* = A. S. *ú: foul, our, sour, loud, out, mouth, south, mouse, louse.* Cf. A. S. *ful, sur, út, múð, mus, lús;* and Germ. *faul, sauer, auß (aus), laus, maus.* *ou* = the production of *u* before *ld* and *nd*: *could, should, would, bound, found, hound, ground, wound*—cases in which German commonly has preserved the short *u*, as *gebunden, gefunden, hund, grund, wunde.* *ou* before *gh* represents divers Anglo-Saxon vowels: *bought*, emi, A. S. *bohte; dough*, A. S. *dáh*, Germ. *teig; though*, A. S. *þeah; through*, A. S. *þurh; soul* from A. S. *sáwel, sáwl, sául; four*, A. S. *feower*.

ow. (1) = Anglo-Saxon *áw*, which is in accordance with the general rule, that A. S. *a* becomes in English *ó*. To this class belong chiefly the strong verbs which have the preterite in *ew*, as *to blow, to grow, to know, to crow, to blow*, A. S. *bláwan, gráwan, cnáwan, cráwan, bláwan.* Exceptions :—*grow*, A. S. *growan; own, ágen* (transition of *g* into *w*). (2) = A. S. *ú*: *bow*, A. S. *búgan; bower*, A. S. *bur; brown*, A. S. *brún; cow*, A. S. *cú; down*, O. N. *dún; how*, A. S. *hú; town*, A. S. *tún; fowl*, A. S. *fugel, fúl*.

ue. Replacing Anglo-Saxon *eo* or *ea* and *i*, but very rare: *hue*, A. S. *hiw; rue*, A. S. *hreow; true*, A. S. *treowe; Tuesday*, A. S. *Tiwesdäg*.

eo, eu, oi, oy occur in Romance words only.

Dutch.

ai. No independent diphthong, but merely a different mode of spelling the vowel *a*, Belgian *ae*, Dutch *aa*, as *hair* for *haer, haar*.

au. This diphthong is softer than its German relative, so that its sound might almost be rendered in German by *a-uw*; but it occurs in few words only, and these mostly of a foreign origin. Examples:—*paus*, pope; *dauw*, dew; *lauwer*, laurel.

ei. The Dutch language has two diphthongs, *ei* and *ij*, resembling the German *ei*, English *i*, in sound, yet neither of the former agreeing quite with the latter, so that their pronunciation offers no slight difficulty to a foreigner. *ei* comes nearest to the German *ei*, and, like the latter, chiefly represents the Gothic diphthong *ái*, whilst *ij*, the doubled *i*, allows the element of the *e* to prevail, and its sound might therefore be rendered by German *e-i* pronounced in rapid succession. In its pronunciation, as well as derivation, it is the representative of the Gothic diphthong *ei*.

Examples:—*heil*, hail, whole (Germ. heil); *rein*, pure (Germ. rein); *weinig*, little (Germ. wenig); *eik*, oak (Germ. eiche); *beide*, both (Germ. beide); *leiden*, to lead (Germ. leiten); *geit*, goat (Germ. geiß). While in some words however, the *ei* has been preserved, it has in others given way to *e*; as for instance in the Ablaut of some strong verbs, as *ned*, led. From the fact that words ending in *heid* form their plural in *heden*, as *dapperheid* (valour), *dapperheden*, it would appear that monosyllabic forms favour the diphthong, while the penult prefers the vowel *e*. In some words this diphthong has, like the English *ai*, and the Middle High German *ei*, its origin in the softened *eg*, as *zeil* for *zegel*, sail; *meid*, maid; *zeide*, said, dixit. For *e*, the Umlaut of *a*, we find it in *heir*, army (Germ. heer); *meir*, sea (Germ. meer); *einde*, end; *peinzen*, to think (Fr. penser).

eu. In pronunciation it approaches the French *eu*, German *o*; as to derivation, it is a doubtful diphthong, replacing *ó* and *e*, even *oe* and *ú*.

eu = o: *deur*, door; *geur*, smell; *keur*, election, choice; *euvel*, evil; *kreupel*, cripple; *jeugd*, youth; *deugen* (Germ. taugen), *deugd* (Germ. tugend).

eu = e: *neus*, nose (Germ. nase). For long vowels: *steunen*, to groan (Germ. stoenen); *treuren*, to mourn (Germ. trauren); *vreugd* (Germ. freude), *beuke*, *bocke*, beech (Germ. buche). Formerly this diphthong was more generally in use, and in Belgium especially, in the place of the Dutch *ó*, as *zeun* for *zoon* (son), *deurpel* for *dorpel*, &c.

ie. A diphthong of frequent occurrence, equivalent to the Middle High German *iu* and *ie*, and the Modern German *ie*. Examples:—*wiel*, wheel; *bier*, beer; *dier*, deer, animal; *tien*, to draw (Germ. ziehen); *vier*, four; *dienen*, to serve; *dief*, thief; *lief*, dear (Germ. lieb); *diep*, deep; *riet*, reed; *siek*, sick; *dier*, dear (M. H. Germ. diur); *vier*, fire (M. H. Germ. viure); *stieren*, to steer (M. H. Germ. stiuren); *vrient*, friend (M. H. Germ. vriunt). In strong verbs, pres. sing.: *biet*, offert (M. H. Germ. biut); *vliet*, fluit (M. H. Germ. vliut); *tiet*, ducit (M. H. Germ. ziut).

oe. In pronunciation and derivation like English *oo*, Germ. *u*, answering to the Gothic *ó*, Middle High German *uo*. Examples:—*stoel*, stool (Germ. stul); *vloer*, floor (Germ. flur); *doen*, to do (Germ. tun); *broek*, brook (Germ. bruch); *broeder*, brother, bruder; *moet*, mood (Germ. mut); *bloet*, blood (Germ. blut); *moeder*, mother (Germ. mutter); *soeken*, to seek (Germ. suchen); *roede*, rod (Germ. rute); *groeten*, to greet (Germ. gruefẓen); *goet*, good (Germ. gut).

ou. This *ou*, like *au*, stands for the German *au*, slightly modified in sound: while the latter is pronounced more deliberately than the German, the former is enounced with greater rapidity, so as to resemble more closely perhaps the English *ou* in *house*. Examples:—*howen*, to hew (Germ. hauen); *vrouw*, lady (Germ. frau); *houden*, to hold; *koud*, cold; *oud*, old; *woud*, wood (Germ. wald); *hout* (Germ. holz); *zout*, salt[1].

ue. Used in Belgium as a different mode of spelling *u*, e. g. *muer* for *muur*, wall.

ui has the sound of the German *eu*, with which it also generally corresponds in derivation, though it often represents the German *au*, Middle High German *ú*. Examples:—*buil*, tumor, bile (Germ. beule); *huilen*, to howl (Germ. heulen); *vuil* (foul (Germ. faul); *zuil* (Germ. säule, column); *ruim*, room (Germ. raum); *schuim*, scum (Germ. schaum); *duif*, dove (Germ. taube); *stuiven* (Germ. stauben); *duivel* (Germ. teufel); *struik*, shrub; *bruid*, bride; *huid*, hide; *kruid*, herb; *luid*, loud; *huis*, house; *muis*, mouse; *luis*, louse. Cf. German *strauch, braut, haut, kraut, laut, haus, maus, laus*.

[1] In these examples the diphthong has its origin in the contraction of the words *halden, kald, ald, wald, zalt*, &c.

Swedish.

This dialect is, strictly speaking, deprived of diphthongs altogether; for the Old Norse *ei* and *au*, are condensed into *e* and *o* and *ju*. The only combination looking like a diphthong concentrates the accent on the *u*, leaving the *i* merely as a preluding sound, resembling herein the English *u* in *tune, June, July*, or the Gothic *ju* in *jus, juk*, the German *juli, juni*; but altogether distinct from the Gothic diphthong *iu* in *iup*, or the Old Norse in *liufr*. The *i* or *j* in this peculiar position participates in the nature of a consonant, half-way at least; whence it is rightly ranked with the semi-vowels. From this fact again may be explained the total suppression in pronunciation of consonants preceding *j* or their combinations in a mixed sound; hence *hjul, ljuf, ljud*—sound, *jul, juf, jud;* whilst in Old Norse we have the diphthong *hiol, liufr, hlioð*. Examples: — *hjul*, wheel; *jul*, Christmas; *djur*, animal (Germ. *thier*, deer; *ljuf*, lief (Germ. lieb); *tjuf*, thief (Germ. dieb); *djup*, deep (Germ. tief); *ljuga*, to lie (Germ. lügen); *skjuda*, to shoot (Germ. schießen). Swedish *ju* is never weakened into *jo*: where this latter form appears it does so by Brechung. *je* is more easily proved by forms such as *tjena*, to serve (Germ. dienen); *tjenst*, service (Germ. dienst), for the Old Norse Schwachung *io* in *þiona, þionust*. Other diphthongs do not exist in Swedish; for *ja, jo, jo*, must be considered as belonging to Brechung.

Danish.

The Old Norse diphthongs *ei* and *au* have in Danish experienced the same fate as in Swedish, dwindling down into the meagre *e* and *o* sounds; and *iu, ou*, are condensed into *y*, rarely replaced by *ju, je*, which can hardly be considered true diphthongs, since the accent is concentrated on the final *u* and *e*. But while ancient diphthongs disappear, new ones spring out of the fertile soil of language, owing their origin, as in English, chiefly to the vocalization of *g* and *v* into *i* and *u*. Thus the Danish language has established three new diphthongs, *au, ei, oi*, which are wanting in Swedish, and impart to the otherwise monotonous vocalism of the Danish language something of a euphonic change. To write and pronounce *av, ej* and *öj*, instead of the true diphthongs, Grimm rightly considers a retrograde movement, depriving the Danish language of one of the few media of variation of sound that are at its disposal.

au. As we have just mentioned, this diphthong is developed out of *av*, especially when occurring before *g* and *s*. Thus Grimm takes the preterite *taug* of the verb *tie*, tacere, as the condensed form of a weak preterite *tagde* (cf. O. N. þagði, þegja), and the adj. *taus*, taciturnus, the contraction of a more ancient *tavse*, *tagse* (cf. Swedish *varse*, *vilse*. &c.); *haug*, pascuum, from *have* (O. N. *hagi*, Sw. *hage*), *laug*, law, for *lav*, *lag* (O. N. *lag*); *faur* from *faver*, *fager* (cf. Eng. *fair* from *fäger*). In many other words the *v* touches very closely on the *u* without however being quite transformed. Examples:—*ave*, discipline; *mave*, stomach (Germ. magen); *ravn*, raven. But, after all, this diphthong must be considered of rare occurrence.

ei. It is more frequent than the preceding diphthong. Examples:—*dei*, dough (Sw. deg, Germ. teig); *sei*, show (Sw. seg); *vei*, way (Sw. vag, Germ. weg); *eie*, to own (Sw. ega, cf. Germ. eigen); *feie*, to polish, Sw. fægja, Germ. fegen); *veie*, to weigh, (Sw. vega, Germ. wiegen); *seil*, sail (O. N. segl, Germ. segel); *leir*, lair (Sw. lager, M. H. Germ. leger). It will be interesting from the preceding examples to observe, that while Danish and English prefer the contraction of *eg* into the diphthong *ei* (*ai*), Swedish and German preserve the old form *eg* in its integrity. On the other hand, Danish retains *eg* in words where English contracts it, as *negl*, nail; *regn*, rain; cf. Germ. *nagel* and *regen*.

oi. This diphthong is historically the same as *ei*, owing its origin to the condensation of *g* and its preceding vowel. The same remarks therefore we have under *ei* will hold good for the diphthong *oi*. Examples:—*floi*, flew (Sw. flog, Germ. flog); *hoi*, high (Sw. hog, Germ. hoch); *öie*, eye (Sw. oga, Germ. auge); *ploie*, to plough (Sw. ploga, Germ. pflügen).

ju stands for Old Norse *iu* in but few words: *hjul* (wheel), *jul* (feast), and *skjul* (latebra)—in all other words *ju* is condensed into *y*, so that for the Swedish *djur*, *tjuf*, *djup*, deer, thief, deep (Germ. thier, dieb, tief), we have in Danish *dyr*, *tyv*, *dyb*. Here again Swedish and German show some analogy on the one, Danish and English on the other hand. Swedish preserves the old diphthong *iu* almost intact, German renders it, at least in spelling, by the Schwachung *ie*, while Danish and English condense it into the *i* sound (= *é*).

ou occurs in but very few words: *broute*, *braute*, to boast; *ploug*, an obsolete mode of spelling for *plov*, plough; *toug*, tow (Sw. tog).

The preceding list of examples will sufficiently tell how in Danish too, since the organic diphthongs of the Old Norse dialect have disappeared, these full sonorous vowel sounds are but exceptionally found; whence Danish vocalism suffers of a certain thinness or spareness which Swedish, though entirely devoid of diphthongs, displays less sensibly, because it has more successfully sheltered the full vowels *a* and *u*, which in Danish again had greatly to yield to the deterioration into *e* and *o*.

TRIPHTHONGS.

These vocalic combinations belong, among Modern Teutonic dialects, to Dutch exclusively. They may be considered as diphthongs having one of the vowels lengthened or doubled. Examples:—*aauw*, pronounced like *au* with a short rest on the vowel *a*, as in *paauw*, pea-cock; *laauw*, luke-warm (Germ. law); *aai*, the diphthong *ai* with *a* lengthened and *i* hardly audible; *kraai*, crow; *fraai*, fair; *eeuw*, in which *e* is lengthened and *w* becomes more audible than in the diphthong *eu*; *leeuw*, lion; *sneeuw*, snow; *ieuw* might in German be rendered by *iüw*, the *i* hardly perceptible: *nieuw*, new; *kieuw*, gill.

The insertion of j in Danish.—The insertion of *j* before a vowel which regularly occurs after the consonants *g*, *k*, *sk*, and occasionally after other consonants, must be kept distinct from the Brechung and the organic diphthongs on which we have already treated. Before *a, aa, o, u,* and *e* in Danish, the consonants *k* and *g* are always hard, as in the English words *cow, gown;* and in order to produce a double sound, as in the English *cure*, a *j* must be inserted, e. g. *skjald,* bard; *kjolo,* coat; *skjule,* to conceal; *gjaldt,* valuit, cost; *gjed,* goat; *gjorde,* made.

Thus then the Old Norse *g, k,* and *sk,* in *gaukr, kaup, skaut,* must have been audible until the gradual modification of the vowel into *ö* influenced the pronunciation of the preceding consonant too. In Swedish this affection of the consonant is marked in its pronunciation, whence the sound of *gok, kop, skot,* might be rendered in German by *tschok, tschop,* and *schot;* while the Danish language adopted a particular mode of spelling and renders a sound almost similar to the Swedish in the forms *gjog, kjob, skjod*. That the whole difference consists in nothing but a different representation of the same sound, may be further concluded from the fact that even in Danish the simple *k* and *g* are preferred before *a, o, y,* and *i*, as *goy, kob, skod,* and *kär, kon, Kobenhaven,* instead of *kjär, kjon, Kjobenhaven;* and that it is acknowledged to be erroneous to insert the *j* when the primitive word has *ka, ko, ga, go,* &c. without *j*: e. g. *kjämbe* for *kämbe,* to fight, would be a fault, because the original word is *kamp;* so also *kjämme* for *kamme*, to comb, from *kam* comb.

Now whether we consider the modification of the vowel owing to the preceding consonant, or the softening of the consonant arising from the modified vowel, thus much is certain, and can be proved by examples from the Old Teutonic dialects,—that certain consonants, and especially the consonants we have mentioned above, exercise a modifying influence on the succeeding vowel. Thus Rask teaches us to pronounce the Icelandic *e* after *g*, *k*, and *sk* = *ie*, and it is a fact that in the sixteenth century already the spelling *ie* for *é* was introduced, e. g. *giefa* for *géfa*, gift; *kiem* for *kem*, come, venio; *skiera* for *skera*, shear. Still more interesting is it to trace this tendency of vocalic modification as far back as Anglo-Saxon, where after *sc* (= *sk*) regularly, and after *g* occasionally, it is optional to write *sceal*, shall, debet, or *scal;* *sceacan*, to shake, or *scacan;* *sceare*, to shear or *scare;* *sceáð* (= sheath) or *scáð;* *sceo* (shoe) and *sco*. (Mark the difference of the double vowels *eá, eo* and the diphthongs *eá, eo*, and that it would be a mistake to write *sceád, sceó*, for *sceád, sceó*.) Here the vowel *e* = *i* was inserted under the influence of the preceding *sc*, as *j* in Danish after *g*, *k*, *sk*; and vice versa, the pronunciation of the softened guttural in the English *shall, shake, share, shoe*, may have arisen under the softening influence of the modified vowel *ea* for *a*, which must be kept altogether distinct from the Anglo-Saxon Brechung *ea* and the diphthong *ea*.

CONSONANTS.

PHYSIOLOGICAL ALPHABET[1].

PLACES.	BREATHS.			CHECKS.		
	Hard.	Soft.	Trilled.	Hard.	Soft.	Nasal.
1. Glottis	‘ hand	’ and				
2. Root of tongue and soft palate . . .	’h loch	’h tage, G.	ṙ	k (kh)	g (gh)	ṅ (ng)
3. Root of tongue and hard palate . . .	ẏ ich, G.	ẏ yea	.	ch (chh)	j (jh)	ñ (ny)
4. Tip of tongue and teeth	s rice	z to rise	l	t (th)	d (dh)	n
5. Tongue reversed and palate	ṣ sharp	ẓ pleasure	r	ṭ (ṭh)	ḍ (ḍh)	ṇ
6. Tongue and edge of teeth	th breath	dh breathe				
7. Lower lip and upper teeth	f life	v live				
8. Upper and lower lips	. .	w quell, G.	.	p (ph)	b (bh)	m
9. Upper and lower lips rounded	ẅ which	ẅ with				
	Continuæ.			Prohibitivæ sive Explosivæ.		

As will appear from the preceding table, consonants may be classified according to the organs which produce them, and according to the duration of the sound. If they are produced by the opening or closing of the organs, their sound will last only while this transaction is taking place and it is incapable of being prolonged: such consonants are called *Checks* or *Mutes* (Prohibitivæ sive Explosivæ). Or they are produced so that the organs do not momentarily open or close, but merely modify their relative position and allow the sound to be prolonged at pleasure: such consonants are called *Breaths* or *Spirants* (Continuæ).

[1] Max Müller, *Lectures*, ii. p. 152.

According to the organs which are chiefly active in producing the different consonants, we classify these as *gutturals, palatals, linguals, dentals*, and *labials*. If produced by a greater effort of the organs, they will be *hard* (tenues); by a less effort, *soft* (mediæ); when accompanied with a breath, tenues and mediæ will make *aspirates*[1].

Spirants again may be guttural, dental, nasal, palatal, labial and lingual (liquids).

Thus a great variety of sounds is produced which but few languages possess in its unlimited richness. Among the Aryan languages Sanskrit has the most complete system of consonants, which we are able to appreciate by comparing the following paradigm of Sanskrit consonants with those of the Primitive and Gothic languages.

Sanskrit.						
Prohibitivæ.				Continuæ.		
Not Aspirated.		Aspirated.				
Tenues.	Mediæ.	Tenues.	Mediæ.	Sibilants.	Nasals.	Liquids.
Gutt. *k*	*g*	*kh*	*gh*	: *ḥ* (χ)	*ṅ*	*h*
Pal. *ch*	*j*	*chh*	*jh*	*ś*	*ñ*	*y*
Ling. *ṭ*	*ḍ*	*ṭh*	*ḍh*	*sh*	*ṇ*	*r*
Dent. *t*	*d*	*th*	*dh*	*s*	*n*	*l*
Lab. *p*	*b*	*ph*	*bh*	: *ḥ* (φ)	*m*	*v*

Primitive[2].						
Prohibitivæ.				Continuæ.		
Not Aspirated.		Aspirated.				
Tenues.	Mediæ.	Tenues.	Mediæ.	Sibilants.	Nasals.	Liquids.
Gutt. *k*	*g*	..	*gh*	..	..	..
Pal. ..	..	..	..	..	..	*y*
Ling. ..	..	..	..	..	..	*r*
Dent. *t*	*d*	..	*dh*	*s*	*n*	..
Lab. *p*	*b*	..	*bh*	..	*m*	*v*

[1] Comp. Max Müller, *Lectures*, ii. p. 130 sqq.
[2] We have arranged in these tables the Primitive and Gothic consonants in accordance with the commonly adopted arrangement of Sanskrit consonants, and this for the sake of uniformity and comparison; but when treating on the Teutonic con-

Gothic.						
Prohibitivæ.				Continuæ.		
Not Aspirated.		Aspirated.				
Tenues.	Mediæ.	Tenues.	Mediæ.	Sibilants.	Nasals.	Liquids.
Gutt. *k*	*g*	..	..	..	*g* (*ng*)	*h*
Pal. ..	..	..	..	..	..	*j*
Ling. ..	..	..	..	..	..	*r*
Dent. *t*	*d*	*th*	*th*	*s z*	*n*	*l*
Lab. *p*	*b*	..	..	*f*	*m*	*v*

Grimm's Law [1].

'If the same roots or the same words exist in Sanskrit, Greek, Latin, Celtic, Slavonic, Lithuanian, Gothic, and High German, then, wherever the Hindus and the Greeks pronounce an aspirate, the Goths and Low Germans generally, the Saxons, Anglo-Saxons, Frisians, &c., pronounce the corresponding soft check, the Old High Germans the corresponding hard check. We thus arrive at the first formula:—

I. (1) Greek and Sanskrit . . . KH   TH   PH
   (2) Gothic, &c. (Low German) . G   D   B
   (3) Old High German . . . K   T   P

'Secondly, if in Greek, Latin, Sanskrit, &c., we find a soft check, then we find a corresponding hard check in Gothic, a corresponding breath in Old High German. This gives us the second formula:—

II. (4) Greek, &c. . . . . G   D   B
    (5) Gothic . . . . K   T   P
    (6) Old High German . . . CH   Z   F(Ph)

'Thirdly, when the six first-named languages show a hard consonant, the Gothic shows the corresponding breath, Old High German the corresponding soft check. In Old High Ger-

sonants specially, we shall keep up the following divisions and discuss them in this order:—Liquids. *l, m, n, r*. Spirants, *v, w, s, z* (=soft *s*), *j* (=*y* in year), *h*. Mutes: (1) *Labials, b, p, f, v, ph, bh*, &c.; (2) *Dentals, d, t, th* (þ), *dh* (ð), *z* (High German aspirated dental, ʓ, soft *z*); and (3) *Gutturals, g, k, c* (=*k*), *ch*, &c.

[1] Max Müller, *Lectures*, ii. p. 199 sqq.

man, however, the law holds good with regard to the dental series only, while in the guttural and labial series the Old High German documents generally exhibit *h* and *f*, instead of the corresponding mediæ *g* and *b*. This gives us the third formula:—

III. (7) Greek, &c. . . . . K   T   P
    (8) Gothic . . . . . H (G, F)   Th (D)   F (B)
    (9) Old High German . H (G, K)   D   F (B,V).'

Proceeding to the illustration of the different formulæ, we begin with the first class, which in Sanskrit shows the aspirate *gh, dh, bh*; Greek χ, θ, φ; Latin fluctuating between soft checks and guttural and labial spiritus. This class must in English, Anglo-Saxon, Gothic, and all Low German dialects be represented by the corresponding mediæ *g, d, b*, whilst High German chooses for the same purpose the tenues *k, t, p*.

I. (1) KH. Greek χ; Sanskrit *gh, h*; Latin *h, f*.
      G.   Gothic *g*; Latin *gv, g, v*.
      K.   Old High German *k*.

Examples[1]:—Engl. *goose*, Goth. *gans*, Germ. *gans*, O. H. Germ. *kans*, Sansk. *hansa*, Gr. χην, Lat. *anser* (=hanser). Engl. *yesterday*, Germ *gestern*, Goth. *gistra*, O. H. Germ. *kestar*, Sansk. *hyas*, Gr. χθές, Lat. *heri*. Engl. *garden*, Germ. *garten*, Goth. *gards*, O. H. Germ. *karto*, Gr. χορτος, Lat. *hortus*. Sansk. *lih*, Gr. λειχω, Lat. *lingo*, Goth. *láigo*, O. H. Germ. *lekom*. Corresponding to *gall* (bile), we find Gr. χολη, Lat. *fel*, instead of *hel*. Engl. *to drag*, Goth. *drag-an*, O. H. Germ. *trak-an*, Lat. *trah-ere*. Gr. εχ-ειν, Goth. *áig-an*, O. H. Germ. *eik-an*.

(2) TH. Greek θ, φ; Sanskrit *dh*; Latin *f*.
      D.   Gothic *d*; Latin *d, b*.
      T.   Old High German *t*.

Examples:—Engl. *daughter*, Goth. *dauhtar*, Germ. *tochter*, O. H. Germ. *tohtar*, Gr. θυγατηρ. Engl. *door*, Goth. *daur*, Germ. and O. H. Germ. *tor*, Gr. θυρα. Engl. *deer*, A. S. *deor*, Goth. *dius*, Germ. *tier*, O. H. Germ. *tior*, Gr. θηρ (φηρ), Lat. *fera* (wild beast). Engl. *to dare*, Goth. *ga-daursan*, O. H. Germ. *tarran*, Gr. θαρσεῖν, Sansk. *dhrish*. To Engl. *doom* (judgment), Goth. *dom-s*, corresponds Gr. θημις (law). Engl. *mid-dle*, Germ. *mit-te*, Goth. *mid-is*, O. H. Germ. *mit-i*, Lat. *med-ius*, Sansk. *madh-ya*. Engl. *rood*, Germ. *rut-e* (virga), A. S. *rod* (crux), O. H. Germ. *ruot-a* (virga), Sansk *ruh* = *rudh* (crescere).

---
[1] The examples are partly taken from Max Muller, l. c., partly from other sources.

(3) PH. Greek φ; Sansk. *bh*; Latin *f*.
B. Gothic *b*; Latin *b*.
P. Old High German *p*.

Examples:—Engl. *to bear*, Goth. *baira*, O. H. Germ. *piru*, Gr. φέρω, Lat. *fero*, Sansk. *bhri*. Engl. *brother*, Goth. *brothar*, O. H. Germ. *pruoder*, Lat. *frater*, Sansk. *bhratri*. Engl. *to break*, Goth. *brikan*, O. H. Germ. *prechan*, Lat. *frangere*, Sansk. *bhanj*. Germ. *bin*, A. S. *beom*, O. H. Germ. *pim*, Gr. φυω, Lat. *fu* (in *fui*), Sansk. *bhavámi*. Engl. *beech*, Goth. *boka*, Lat. *fagus* (cf. Gr. φηγός), O. H. Germ. *puocha*.

The second class comprises examples which, for the mediæ *g, d, b*, in Sanskrit and Greek words, show the corresponding tenues *k, t, p*, in English, Gothic, &c., and the aspirates *kh* (ch), *th* and *ph* in Old High German.

II. (4) G. Sanskrit, Greek, Latin *g*.
K. Gothic *k*.
KH. Old High German *ch*.

Examples:—Engl. *to know*, Germ. *kennen* and *konnen*, A. S. *cneow*, Goth. *kan*, O. H. Germ. *chan*, Lat. *gnosco*, Gr. γνῶμι, Sansk. *jná*. Eng *kin* (relationship), Goth. *kuni*, O. H. Germ. *chuni*, Lat. *genus*, Gr. γένος, Sansk. *játi* (from *jan*, to be born). Engl. *knee*, A. S. *cneo*, Goth. *kniu*, O. H. Germ. *chniu*, Lat. *genu*, Gr. γονυ, Sansk. *jánu*. A. S. *mic-el* (cf. Scotch mickle), Goth. *mih-ils*, O. H Germ. *mih-il*, Lat. *mag-nus*, Gr. μεγ-αλος, Sansk. *mah-at*. Engl. *child*, O. S. *kind*, Gr. γοιος (offspring). Engl. *queen*, Goth. *gino* or *gens*, A. S. *cven*, O. N. *kona*, O. H. Germ. *chena*, Gr. γυνη, Sansk. *jani* (originally meaning 'mother'). Engl. *king*, Germ. *konig*, A. S. *cyning*, O. H. Germ. *chuninc*, Sansk. *janaka* (originally meaning 'father'). Gr. εγω, Lat. *eg-o*, Goth. *ik*, A. S. *ic*, O. N. *ek*, O. H. Germ. *ih*, Germ. *ich*.

(5) D. Sanskrit, Greek, Latin *d*.
T. Gothic *t*.
TH. Old High German *z*.

Examples:—Engl. *foot*, Germ. *fuß*, Lat. *ped-is* (pes), Gr. ποδ-ος (πους), Goth. *fôt-us*, O. H. Germ. *vuoz*, Sansk. *pád-as*. Engl. *wat-er*, Goth. *vat-ó*, Germ. *waß-er*, O. H. Germ. *waz-ar*, Lat. *und-a*, Gr. υδ-ωρ, Sansk. *ud-a*. Engl. *heart*, Goth. *hairt-ó*, Germ. *herz*, O. H. Germ. *hérz-a*, Lat. *cord-is* (cor), Gr. καρδ-ία, Sansk. *hridaya*. Engl. *tear*, A. S. *tear*, Goth. *tagr*, Germ. *zähre*, O. H. Germ. *zahar*, Lat. *lacruma* (= *dacruma*), Gr. δακρυ, Sansk. *asru* (= *dasru*). Engl. *two*, Goth. *tvai*, Germ. *zwei*, O. H. Germ. *zuei*,

Lat. *duo*, Gr. δυω. Engl. *ten*, Goth. *taihun*, Germ. *zehn*, O. H. Germ. *zehan*, Lat. *decem*, Gr. δέκα, Sansk. *dasan*.

(6) B.   Sanskrit *b* or *v*; Greek and Latin *b*.
P.   Gothic *p* (scarce).
PH. Old High German *ph* or *f*.

'There are few really Saxon words beginning with *p*, and there are no words in Gothic beginning with that letter, except foreign words[1].' No suitable examples can therefore be given, except a few where the mentioned consonants occur at the end of the root, e. g. Gk. καυναβ-ις, O. N. *hanp-r*, O. H. Germ. *hanaf*; Engl. *help*, Goth. *hilpa*, Germ. *helfe*, O. H. Germ. *hilfu*.

The third class embraces words which in Sanskrit, Greek and Latin have the tenuis *k*, *t*, or *p*, which in Gothic and the other Low German dialects is replaced by the aspirates *h* (for *ch*, *kh*), *th* and *ph* (*f*) respectively, while Old High German should make use of the media *g*, *d*, *b*. But in the last-mentioned dialect the law breaks down. Instead of the mediæ *b* and *g*, the aspirates *f* and *h* are preferred, and only *d*, the media of the dentals, has been preserved to represent the Gothic *th* and Sanskrit *t*.

III. (7) K.   Sanskrit and Greek *k*; Latin *c*, *qu*.
KH. Gothic *h*, *g* (*f*); Sanskrit *h*.
G.   Old High German *h* (*g*, *k*).

Examples: — Engl. *head*, A. S. *heafod*, Goth. *haubith*, Germ. *haupt*, O. H. Germ. *houpit*, Lat. *caput*, Gr. κεφαλή, Sansk. *kapála*. Engl. *heart*, Goth. *hairto*, Germ. *herz*, O. H. Germ. *herza*, Lat. *cor*, Gr. καρδία, Sansk. *hridaya* (*hrid*, irregular instead of *krid*). Engl. *who*, *what*, A. S. *hwa*, *hwät*, Goth. *hvas*, *hvo*, *hva*, Germ. *wer*, *waß*, O. H. Germ. *wer*. Transliterating this into Sanskrit, we get *kas*, *ká*, *kad*; Lat. *quis*, *quæ*, *quid*; Gr. κος and πος. Engl. *fee*, Germ. *vieh*, A. S. *feo*, Goth. *faihu*, Lat. *pec-us*. A. S. *eág-e* (eye), Germ. *aug-e*, O. H. Germ. *oug-a*, Lat. *oc-ulus*, Gr. ὀκ-ος = ὀπ-ός, gen. from ὄψ.

(8) T.   Sanskrit, Greek, and Latin *t*.
TH. Gothic *th* and *d*.
D.   Old High German *d*.

Examples: — Engl. *thou*, Goth. *thu*, Germ. and O. H. Germ. *du*, Lat. *tu*, Gr. τυ, Sansk. *twam* (nom.). Engl. *the* (cf. *this*, *that*), Goth. *thana*, Germ. *den*, O. H. Germ. *den*, Lat. *is-tum*, Gr. τόν, Sansk. *tam* (acc.). Engl. *three*, Goth. *threis*, Germ. *drei*, O. H. Germ. *drí*, Lat. *tres*, Gr. τρεις, Sansk. *trayas* (n. pl.). Engl.

---

[1] Max Müller, *Lectures*, ii. p 219.

oth-er, A. S. *oð-er*, Goth. *anth-ar*, Germ. *and-er*, O. H. Germ. *and-ar*, Lat. *alt-er*, Gr. ἕτ-ερος, Sansk. *ant ara*. Engl. *tooth*, A. S. *tóth*, Goth. *tunth*, O. H. Germ. *zand*, Lat. *dens*, *dent-is*, Gr. ὀδούς, ὀδόντ-ος, Sansk. *dant-as*.

(9) P.   Sanskrit, Greek, Latin *p*.
    PH. Gothic *f* and *b*.
    B.   Old High German *f* and *v*.

Examples:—Engl. *five*, Goth. *fimf*, Germ. *fünf*, Gr. πεμπε, Sansk. *panchan*. Engl. *full*, Goth. *fulls*, Germ. *voll*, Lat. *plenus*, Gr. πλεος, Sansk. *purna*. Engl. *father*, Goth. *fadar*, Germ. *vater*, O. H. Germ. *vatar*, Lat. *pater*, Gr. πατηρ, Sansk. *pitri*. Engl. *over*, Goth. *ufar*, Germ. *über*, O. H. Germ. *ubar*, Lat. *super*, Gr. υπερ, Sansk. *upari*. The last example is one of the very few within the range of the mute labials in which the law of displacement is strictly carried out in the different dialects.

General Table of Grimm's Law[1].

		I.			II.			III.		
		1.	2.	3.	4.	5.	6.	7.	8.	9.
I.	Sanskrit	gh (h)	dh (h)	bh (h)	g	d	b	k	t	p
	Greek	χ	θ	φ	γ	δ	β	κ	τ	π
	Latin	h, f (g, v)	f (d b)	f (b)	g	d	b	c, qu	t	p
II.	Gothic	g	d	b	k	t	(p)	h, g (f)	th, d	f, b
III.	O. H. Germ.	k	t	p	ch	z	ph (f)	h, g, k	d	f, v

Exceptions to Grimm's Law.

'As in other sciences, so in the science of language, a law is not violated—on the contrary, it is confirmed—by exceptions of which a rational explanation can be given[2].' These exceptions are owing to disturbing influences to which chiefly consonants in the middle and at the end of words are liable and of which we examine a few cases.

A consonant often preserves its position in the different dialects under the shelter of a preceding consonant. Thus, for instance, mutes protect a succeeding *t*, and, whenever the tenuis is preceded at the beginning of words by an *s*, *h*, or *f*, these letters protect the *k*, *t*, *p*, and guard it against the execution of the law. Thus the Sansk. *ashtáu*, Gr. οκτω, Lat. *octo*, is in Goth. *ahtau*, O. H. Germ. *ahto*, where *h* (= Germ. *ch*) preserves the tenuis *t*. A similar case we have in the Sansk. *naktam* (adverbial

---

[1] Compare Max Muller, *Lectures*, ii. p. 222.   [2] Ibid. p. 213.

accusative); Gr. νυξ, νυκτός, Lat. *nox, noctis*, is the Goth. *nahts*, O. H. Germ. *naht*, A. S. *niht* (night). Though Grimm's law is most strictly enforced at the beginning of words, it becomes, even there, powerless under the mentioned conditions. Thus the Sanskrit *stri*, plural *staras* (in the Veda), Latin *stella* (=sterula), is in Gothic *stairno* (star), the tenuis owing its preservation to the preceding *s*.

Since in Gothic and several other Teutonic dialects the guttural aspirate is wanting, it is replaced by the hard breath *h*, sometimes the media *g*, which consonants are both adopted in Old High German; or *g* is displaced by *k*; or the Gothic *g* returns to *h* again. The Gothic aspirate *f* which takes the place of the Sanskrit *p*, should, in Old High German, be represented by the media *b*; but the Old High German dialect makes in this case again rather free with the law, replacing the media by the labial soft breath *v*, and discarding this again in favour of the hard breath *f*, the Gothic representative. Instead of the dental aspirate *th* (þ) the Old High German has its own characteristic consonant *z*, which, according to its position, may be hard (*z*) or soft (*ȥ*).

TEUTONIC CONSONANTS.

Liquids :—l, m, n, r

The Gothic dialect keeps strictly distinct the simple initial liquids *l, n, r*, and their aspirated compounds *hl, hn, hr*; e. g. *luftus*, air (Germ. luft), and *hliftus*, fur, a thief; *reisan*, to rise, and *hrisjan*, to shake; *láif*, mansi, and *hláif*, bread, loaf. This distinction is kept alive in the other Low German dialects, Anglo-Saxon, Old Saxon and Old Frisian, and in Old Norse; while the Old High German, since the beginning of the ninth century renders the initial compounds *hl, hn, hr*, by the single *l, n, r*. The Old Norse *l* and *r* is certainly found for the *wl* and *wr* of the other dialects, but never for *hl* and *hr*.

Gemination, or the doubling, of liquids occurs in Gothic after a short vowel, but it is not there yet developed to a necessary law, whence the single liquid is often retained in the place of the gemination. The liquid *r* especially prefers to lead a single existence. Old High German at a very early stage produces gemination by assimilating more ancient combinations, such as *lj, nj, rj, rz, rn*, &c., to the liquid, and thus forming the combinations *ll, nn, rr*, &c.; e. g. *zellan* from *zaljan, zeljan*; *werran* from *warjan;* *brunna* from *brunja;* *stimma*, voice (Germ. stimme), from an older form *stimna*, Goth. *stibna;* *nennan*, to name (Germ. nennen), from *nemnjan;* *merran*, to impede (Goth. marzjan); *sterro*, star (Germ. stern), Goth. *staírno*. If a geminated liquid should happen to find its place at the end of a word, it is reduced to a simple consonant; e. g. *fal, falles; man, mannes*.

The Low German dialects, Anglo-Saxon and Old Frisian, agree with Old High German in rejecting gemination at the end of a word, while Old Saxon even in this position sometimes retains the doubled liquid. Hence Anglo-Saxon writes like Old High German, *bil, billes; man, mannes; grim, grimmes*.

Peculiar to several Low German dialects is the gemination of the liquid *n* arising from the contraction of two *n*'s, which in consequence of the elision of one or several vowels came into closer contact. Thus Anglo-Saxon has *ánne* for *ánene*, one; *mínne* for *mínene*, mine; Old Frisian *enne* for *enene, mínne* for *mínene, thínne*, &c.

Gemination in the middle of a word is sometimes destroyed by an inflexional syllable being added to the word, e. g. *grimra* instead of *grimmera;* or, under the influence of metathesis (vid. infra), as *horses* for *hrosses* (equi).

Old Norse has in its geminations certain peculiarities of its own which deserve separate enumeration. The gemination *ll* has often its origin in assimilation: (1) *lð—gull* from *gulð*, gold; *villr* from *vilðr*, wild; *ballr* from *balðr*, bold; (2) ðl (of later occurrence), e. g. *milli*, inter, for *miðli; frilla*, pellex, for *friðla, bralla*, quickly, for *braðla;* (3) *l* of the root with *r* of the termination, when in monosyllables preceded by a long vowel or diphthong, in bisyllables after a short vowel as well; e. g. *heill*, heal (Germ. heil), for *heilr; dæll*, sweet, for *dælr* (but *volr*, staff, stick); *gamall=gamalr*, old; *lítill=lítilr*, small, little. But *llr* remains unchanged, as *ballr, villr*. As *lr*, so at a later phase of the language *rl*, also may be converted into *ll*, as *iall* for *iarl*, earl; *kelling* for *kerling* (vetula).

It is a characteristic feature of Old Norse, which distinguishes it from the High as well as the Low German dialects, that *ll*, like every other gemination, is preserved intact at the end of words too, where, besides Old Norse, Old Saxon only allows exceptionally of the gemination.

r

This liquid in **Gothic** is safe from the interchange with the sibilant *s*, while all the other Teutonic dialects have, like the

Greek and Latin, more or less yielded to the inclination of the *s* towards the liquid *r*. This change of *s* into *r* is often called '*Rhotacism.*'

Old High German allows both the sharp and soft Gothic sibilants (*s* and *z*) to be supplanted by *r*: (1) in the inflexion and comparison of the adjectives, e. g. *plinter* (blind), *plintoro*, Goth. *blinds, blindóza;* (2) in roots, e. g. *ror*, Goth. *ráus*, dew (comp. Lat. ros, roris); *ora*, Goth. *áuso*, ear. Especially the Gothic *z* has almost in every instance made room to the liquid *r*, e. g. *rarta*, tongue, language (Goth. razda); *merran*, to impede (Goth. marzjan); *hort*, treasure (comp. Engl. hoard), Goth. *huzd*. The Gothic *z* is however preserved in *fersna*, heel (Germ. ferse), Goth. *faírzna ; asca*, ashes (Germ. asche), Goth. *azgo*. (3) Some strong verbs which in the 1st pers. sing. pret. show a final *s*, convert this *s* into *r* where another inflexional syllable is added, e. g. *kiosan*, eligere; *kôs*, elegi ; *kuri*, elegisti ; *kurumês*, elegimus ; *koranêr*, electus ; thus also, *nas, nári, nárumes, neraner*, of *nesan*, servari, and *lôs, luri, lurumes, loraner* of *liosan*, perdere. The inflexional *s* of the strong declension of the substantive remains intact. So also does the *s* at the beginning of a word, while in the middle or at the end it may or may not pass into the domain of the liquids—a fact for which no rule can be laid down.

Old Saxon has, like Old High German, both the organic *r* and the inorganic *r*, replacing the sibilant *s*. Elision of *r* has taken place in *linon* for *lirnon*, to learn ;—apocope in *he*, is ; *hue*, quis ; *these*, hic; *unca*, ϝωιτερος ; *inca*, σφωίτερος ; *usa*, noster ; *iwa*, vester. Prefix *a=ar*. We have metathesis of the *r* in *frothan* for *forhtan*, to fear.

Anglo-Saxon follows the general rule in replacing *s* by *r*, but still it has often the sibilant preserved where Old High German yields to the *r*; e. g. *baso*, Goth. *basi*, O. H. Germ. *peri*, berry ; *irsgan*, irasci, Goth. *aírzjan*, O. H. Germ. *irran* ; in other words, again, Old High German preserves the *s* where Anglo-Saxon prefers *r*; e. g. O. H. Germ. *haso*, A. S. *hara* (Germ. hase, Engl. hare). Apocope of the *r* sometimes takes place at the end of words, as *we*, we; *ge*, ye ; *me*, mihi ; þe, tibi : *a*, prefix for *ar*: *má*, more, for *már*. The metathesis of the organic *r* is more fully developed than in Old Saxon, this letter being especially fond of taking up its position, whenever possible, immediately before *s*, or the sibilant combinations *st, sc*, e. g. *hors*, horse, instead of *hros* (comp. Germ. ross); *berstan*, to burst, O. S. *brestan ; forst* for *frost*, þerscan for þrescan, to thrash. Other instances of metathesis are—*forma*, primus, Goth. *fruma ; bird* and *brid* (bird), *gars* and *gräs* (grass); *birnan*, to burn, O. H. Germ. *prinnan* (Germ.

brennen); *irnan*, O. H. Germ. *rinnan*, to run; *cerse*, O. H. Germ. *chressa*, cresses.

Old Frisian yields more than any of the preceding dialects to the tendency of replacing *s* by *r*, so that this liquid takes the place of the sibilant even in the plural of the substantive inflexion, e. g. *fiskar, degar*, instead of Goth. *fiskos*, fishes, *dagos*, days. This inflexional *r* is, however, frequently dropped. Metathesis takes place under the same conditions as in Anglo-Saxon, hence the forms *bersta*, to burst; *fersk*, fresh; *hars*, horse; *gers*, grass; *barna*, to burn; *forma*, primus; *warld = wrald* from *werald*. The case is inverted in forms such as *bren* for *bern*, child.

Old Norse, of all Teutonic dialects, has most generally introduced the liquid *r* for the sibilant *s*. As to the verb, the Old Norse so far agrees with the Low German dialects, that it allows rhotacism, or the displacement of *s* by *r* only in the plur. pret. and the part. pret., as *kurum, korinn*, of *kiosa*, to choose; *frorum, frorinn*, of *friosa*, to freeze, except *vera*, to be, which has in the sing. pret. already *var*, I was (comp. Germ. war). *r* is assimilated to its compeer in the combinations *lr, rl, nr, rk*, and sometimes *rs* (vid. sub litt. **l, n, k**). *r* has gained the supremacy in *fiarri = fiarni*, far (comp. Germ. fern), and *verri = versi*, worse.

m, n

Old High German. Since the ninth century the liquid *m* is often weakened into *n*, chiefly in inflexional forms, a case in which the inflexional vowel also is frequently weakened according to the rules indicated above. Thus *wërfames* becomes *wërfan, wërfen; wurfumês, wurfon, wurfen; sagêm, sagên; tagum, tagon; gëbom, gebon; kreftim, kreften*. The consonantal combination *mf* is regularly converted into *nf*, e. g. *funf*, Goth. *fimf*, five; *sanfto* for *samfto*, meek; *kunft* for *kumft*, arrival.

Old Saxon. The termination *m* of the dat. plur. is replaced by *n*, e. g. *wordun* for *wordum*, verbis; *rikiun* for *rikium*, potentibus: the adjectives of the strong declension also change the termination *umu* occasionally into *on*.

It is a characteristic feature of Old Saxon, and the Low German dialects generally, that before certain consonants they drop the liquid *n*. This consonant is omitted (1) before *s*; e. g. *us*, nobis (Germ. uns); *cust*, virtus (Germ. kunst); but retained in *anst*, favour: (2) before ð; e. g. *oðar*, alius, *= andar* (Germ. ander); *cuð*, known; *fiðan* and *findan*, to find; *muð*, mouth (Germ. mund, &c.): (3) before *f*; e. g. *fif*, five (Goth. fimf, Germ. fünf); *safto*, O. H. Germ. *sanfto, = samfto:* (4) before *d* in the terminations of the pres. indic. plur. of all verbs; e. g. *salbód = salbond, hverfad = hverfand, hebbiad = hebbiand.*

Anglo-Saxon. The liquid *m*, which, at the end of words, other dialects weaken into *n*, is retained in Anglo-Saxon.

n occurring in the middle of a word is dropped, (1) before *s — est*, grace, = Goth. *anst*, O. S. *anst; husl*, sacrifice, Goth. *hunsl: canst*, novisti, retains the *u*: (2) before ð—*cuð*, known (cf. Germ. kunde); *muð*, mouth (cf. Germ. mund); *toð*, tooth (cf. Germ. zahn, O. H. Germ. tand); *að = and*, termination of the pres. plur. of the verb: (3) before *f—fíf*, five (Germ. fünf, Goth. fimf); *sófte, sefte*, meek, soft (cf. Germ. sanft, O. H. Germ. senfti).

Old Frisian. The *m*, when occurring in terminations, has throughout been changed into *n*.

n is dropped under the same conditions as in Anglo-Saxon. Compare the following examples with those of Anglo-Saxon given above:—*us*, nobis; *ev-est*, invidia; *fíf*, five; *muth*, mouth; *toth*, tooth; *other*, alius. *n* suffers apocope at the end of the infinitive of the verb: *wertha*, to become (Germ. werden). In the same manner the terminations of the subjunctive of the verb, and of the weak inflexions of the noun, have dropped their final *u*.

Old Norse. The terminational *m* is never weakened into *n*; *mm* in *fimm* is the *mf* of the Goth. *fimf*, five.

The liquid *n* is affected in various ways. It is dropped in roots (1) before *s*: *oss*, nobis; *ást*, favour; (2) before a ð which is followed by *r*: *kuðr*, known; *muðr*, mouth; *maðr*, man; *oðrum* from *annar*, other (By the side of *kuðr* and *muðr* we meet the forms *kunnr* and *munnr*); (3) before *k* which is preceded by a long vowel, e. g. *mukr*, monk; *kanukr*, canonicus; but if a short vowel precedes the *nk*, the gemination *kk* may take place, e. g. *Frakkland*, Frankland, terra Francorum; *akkeri*, anchor; *drekka*, to drink; *okkar, ykkar*, Goth. *uggara, iggara*, νῶν, σφῶν. (4) The terminational *ng* of strong verbs is, in the sing. pret and imperative, converted into *kk*, e. g. *springa*, to spring, imp. *sprikk*, pret. *sprakk*, sprung (Germ. sprang); *hánga*, to hang, imp. *hakk*, pret. *hekk*. In the plur. pret., if followed by a terminational syllable, *ng* preserves its position; hence *sprungum, hengum*, plur. of *sprakk, hekk*. (5) *tt* replaces *nd* in exactly the same manner; hence, *binda*, to bind, imp. *bitt*, pret. *batt; hrinda*, trudere, pret. *hratt;* but the plurals are again *bundum, hrundum*.

The final *n* of the root has been dropped in the particles *i, a. o*, Goth. *-in, -ana, -un*, a circumstance which caused the vowel to become long.

The *n* of the terminations is dropped (1) in the infinitive of verbs; (2) in the weak declension; (3) in the part. pret.; (4) before the neuter termination *t* of the adjectives in *in*; hence *orðit* not *orðint*, neut. of *orðin*, factus (Germ. ge-worden); *gyllit* not *gyllint*, neut. of *gyllin*, golden.

Gemination of *n* is caused (1) in *nð* (if the *n* is not dropped altogether), e. g. *manns*, gen. of *maðr*, man; *finna*, to find; *fðr*, he finds; *nenna*, niti (Goth. nanþjan): (2) in *n-r*, the latter liquid belonging to the inflexion, e. g. *minn*, mine, meus; *sveinn*, boy; *eiginna = eigin-ra*, propriorum.

Spirants:—v, w, s, z, j, h

V, W

Gothic. Much-favoured combinations at the beginning of words are *vr* and *vl*, which in the other dialects are often replaced by the simple *r* and *l*. Examples:—*vláiton*, circumspicere; *vrits*, apex literæ; *vrohjan*, to accuse; *vleits*, vultus. In the middle of a word *v* preserves its position after consonants, e. g. *sparva*, sparrow; *vilvan*, rapere; *bidagva*, beggar; *ufar-skadvjan*, over-shadow;—before a long, and between two short, vowels, e. g. *favái*, few; *havi*, hay; *þivi*, ancilla; *slavan*, silere: but whenever it takes its place at the end of a word, after a short vowel, or before a consonant, it is vocalized (vid. sub lit. **u**). The form *us-skavjiþ izvis* (ἐκνηψατε) is an exception; and so are foreign words and proper names in which the Gothic spelling *av* renders the Byzantine pronunciation of the Greek diphthong *αυ*, as *kavtsgo*, *Pavlus*. At the end of words *v* never occurs except when preceded either by a diphthong or a consonant, e. g. *áiv*, *hráiv*, *valv*, *sahv*.

Old High German. The Gothic *v* in the initial combinations *vr*, *vl*, were, in the oldest forms of Old High German, expressed by *hr*, *hl*, but in later documents represented by the simple *r* and *l*; in the same manner as the more ancient Old High German *hw* is later on replaced by the simple *w*, e. g. *wer* for *hwer*, who; *wedar* for *hwedar*, whether.

The Old High German *w*, which in pronunciation coincides with the English *w*, is rendered in manuscripts by *uu*, *uv*, *vu*, but after a consonant, or before the vowel *u*, simply by *u*.

When it occurs at the end of a word in the combinations *aw* (*ow*), *iw*, it is vocalized into *au* (*ou*), *iu*, but it re-assumes its position when an inflexional syllable is added, hence *tau* (*tou*), genitive *tawes (towes)*; *chniu*, genitive *chniwes*. In these forms, however, a peculiar tendency becomes manifest to retain the diphthong even before the restored *w*, and thus to destroy the short vowel altogether, hence *tau (tou)*, genitive *tauwes (touwes)*; *chniu*, genitive *chniuwes*. From the combination *aw* we get *ew (eu)* by Umlaut, and *ow (ou)* by Schwachung, in the same manner as *eu* and *ou* from *au*; and these again yield the genitive forms *euwes, ouwes*, instead of the simple *ewes, owes*; and in *ouwes* again the *ou* may be replaced by *o* which is a greater favourite to *w*, hence *owes*. Now all these different combinations may be used indiscriminately, just as the different manuscripts prefer the one or the other. Thus then we find *frawjan, frewjan, frowjan, frauwjan, freuwjan, frowjon, frouwjan*, as different modes of spelling one and the same word—the German *freuen*, delectari. Where *ew* is found instead of *iw*, it stands on the same principle of Trübung as does *e* for *i*; and as *iw* becomes *iuw*, so also *ew*, is lengthened into *euw*, e.g. *iwih, iuwih; ewih, euwih*, vobis. Exceptional forms:—*puwen (puen), katruwen (katruen)*, for the Gothic *báuan*, to dwell; *gatráuan*, to trust; where we should expect to find *pawun, ketrawan*, in Old High German. (The former form occurs once, the latter not at all.) In three verbs the original *w* is supposed by some grammarians to have been converted into *r*: *grirumes* for *griwumes, scrirumes* for *scriwumes*, and *pirumés* for *piwumes*, from the verbs *grían*, gannire; *scrían*, clamare. *scriwumes* has actually maintained its position against *scrirumes*. More plausible is the view of others, according to which the *r* has replaced a more ancient *s*, as *scrirumes* for *scrisumes*, &c. See the conjugation of the strong verb.

In the middle of a word the *w* which terminates a root is usually dropped, when between it and the vowel of the root another consonant intervenes, e.g. Goth. *aggvus*, O. H. Germ. *engi*; Goth. *saíhvan*, O. H. Germ. *sëhan*; Goth. *gatvo*, O. H. Germ. *gazza*: in all other cases it retains its position, though at the end of the word it may have been dropped or vocalized; hence *farawa*, colour; *melewes*, farinæ; *garawer*, paratus; *grawer*, grey (Germ. grau). At the end of a word *w* cannot sustain itself, and is therefore vocalized in *u* or *o*, as *garo*, spear; *melo*, flour, meal; *palo*, cædes: where no consonant, but merely a vowel, precedes it, this vocalized *w* may be dropped altogether, as *grá* for *grao*, grey (Germ. grau).

Old Saxon. In this dialect the spirant *w* was probably identical with that of Old High German, and is rendered by *uu, u,* rarely by *v*. Examples:—*dualon*, præstigia; *suart*, swart, black; *huerƀan*, to go; *thuahan*, to wash; *tueho*, doubt. This *w* has been

CONSONANTS. 111

vocalized and has superseded the radical vowel in *cuman* for *cuiman*, to come; *sulic*, such (Goth. svaleiks). The combinations *wl* and *wr* (written *uul* and *uur*), which were extinct in Old High German, retained their position in Old Saxon.

aw and *iw* show, like the same combinations in Old High German, a tendency to lengthen themselves into *auw, iuw*, e. g. *hawan* and *hauwan* (spelt *hauuan* and *hauuuan*), *glawes* and *glauwes, iwar* and *iuwar, fiwar* and *fiuwar*, used alternately. Like Old High German the Old Saxon dialect drops the *w* when, at the end of a root, it is preceded by another consonant, e. g. *sehan*, to see (Goth. saihvan); *engi*, narrow (Germ. enge); also between two vowels, *seola*, soul (Goth. saivala). At the end of a word it is always vocalized in *u* or *o*, e. g. *glau*, prudent; *seo*, sea; *eo*, law; but when an inflexional syllable is added it re-appears again, and hence the genitives *glawes, sewes, ewes*.

Anglo-Saxon. *w*[1] is in Anglo-Saxon as in Gothic the pure spirant which in the manuscripts is rendered by *uu, u*, or by the Runic sign *wen* (ƿ). Where *w* is preceded by another consonant and followed by the vowel *i*, this vowel is dropped and the *w* vocalized in *u*, e. g. *cuman* from *cwiman*, to come; *suster* from *swister*, sister; *hulic* from *hwilic*, which; *uht* from *wiht*, thing. Here again we have something similar to the reappearance of the Old High German *w*, which, though vocalized into *u*, retains its position. So also the Anglo-Saxon *w*, though vocalized in *u*, may yet appear in its original position, e. g. *swuster* for *suster*, from *swister*; *wuht* for *uht*, from *wiht*; *swura* for *sura*, from *swira*, neck. In a few cases the vocalized *w = u* is weakened into *o*, hence the preterite *com, comon*, instead of *cum, cumon*, from *cwam*, veni, *cwâmon*, venimus.

The initial *w* is regularly dropped when the negative particle *ne* enters into a compound with a verb, e. g. *nas = ne was*, non fuit; *næron = ne wæron*, non fuerunt; *nitan = ne witan*, nescire; *nillan = ne willan*, nolle.

The Gothic combinations *av* and *iv* are in a few cases preserved in their integrity, as *slaw*, slow, lazy; *triwen*, wooden, of a tree; but as a rule Anglo-Saxon follows, like Old High German and Old Saxon, the law of vocalization, wherever those combinations occur as final consonants, which consequently are converted into the diphthongs *eá, eo*. But here again, as in Old High German, the *w*, though vocalized, resumes its position before the diphthong to which it gave birth, and in this respect Anglo-Saxon goes further still than Old High German, preserving the

---

[1] German grammarians commonly write *v*.

w even as final consonant. Examples:—The Gothic *favi*, few, we should expect to see rendered in A. S. by *eá*, hence *feá*; *w* however retains its place, and hence we get the declensional form *feáwa*; the same is the case with *heáwan*, to hew; *sceáwan*, to contemplate (Germ. schauen); but even without a final vowel the forms *eáw*, *eów* preserve their position (contrary to the usages of O. H. Germ.), e. g. *cneow*, knee, O. H. Germ. *chniu*; *eow*, vobis, O. H. Germ. *iu*; *gleáw*, prudent, O. H. Germ. *glau*; *deáw*, dew, O. H. Germ. *tou*. Very rarely this final *w* has been dropped. Where a final *w* is preceded by a consonant, it is vocalized into *u* (*o*), but it reappears when an inflexional syllable is added, e. g. *bealu*, evil, gen. *bealwes*; *melo*, meal, flour, gen. *melwes*; or, *w* and its vocalization *u* may occur together, as *bealuwes—bealwes*; the *u* weakened into *e*, *meleves — meluves = melves*,

Old Frisian. The spirant *w* must be kept distinct from the labial aspirate *v*, with which it is occasionally mixed up. *hw*, *kw*, and similar combinations, are, as a rule, strictly preserved from any intermixture with the succeeding vowel; the few cases in which the Anglo-Saxon vocalization is admitted are *suster*, sister, *kuma*, to come; *kom*, came, for *svister*, *kvima*, *kvam*. *wu* is often rendered by a simple *w*, e. g. *wllen* for *wullen*, *wnnen* for *wunnen*, *wrdon* for *wurdon*; *iuw* and *auw* instead of *iw*, *aw*, are to be explained in the same manner as the identical forms in Old High German. Examples:—*fiuwer=fiwer*, four; *triuwe=triwe*, faith (Germ. treue); *hauwan=hawan*, verberatum (Germ. ge-hauen). Instead of a diphthong the *w* has produced a long vowel in *dáwe*, dew, rori; *frowa*. lady (Germ. frau); *strewa*, to strew. At the end of a word the *w* is sometimes preserved, sometimes dropped, e. g. *daw*, dew; *bláw*, livid; *gá*, country (Germ. gau); *a*, law. When it is final, *w* is not vocalized, except perhaps in *kniu* (acc. of *kni*, knee) and *balu-mund*, malus-tutor. Sometimes *w* is dropped in the middle of a word, as *sela*, soul; it is vocalized in *naut=nawet*, naught, nothing, O. S. *niowiht*.

Old Norse. *v* at the beginning of a word is dropped before *u*, before *y* its Umlaut, and *o* its Schwachung, as well as before *ó* and *oe*: it is also rejected from the initial combinations *sv*, *hv*, *þv*; hence *urðum*, *yrði*, *orðinn*, from *verða*, fieri (Germ. werden); *ox*, *oexi*, pret. of *vaxa*, to wax, grow; *Oðinn*, O. H. Germ. *Wuotan*; *sulgum*, *sylgi*, *solginn*, from *svelgia*, glutire (Germ. schwelgen); *sor*, *soeri*, from *sverga*, jurare (Germ. schworen); *hullum*, *hylli*, *hollinn*, from *hvella*, tinnire; *þurrum*, *þyrri*, *þorrinn*, from *þverra*, decrescere. Sometimes *v*, in combination with the vowel *a*, makes *o*, e. g. *on* = *ván*, hope (cf. Germ. wan); *ogum* = *vágum*, interfecimus, from *vega*. Also in the combinations *kv*, *sv*, *tv*, followed by a vowel which is affected by Umlaut or Schwachung, *v* is vocalized; e. g. *koma*, *kom*, for *kvema*, *kvam*; *kona* for *kvana* and *kven*, woman; *sofa* for *svefa*, to sleep; *tuttugu* for *tvintugu*, twenty. At the end of a word, and before the termination *r* of the nominative, *v* is dropped, but in the inflexional or derivative forms it may re-appear; e. g. *sæ-r*, lake (Germ. see, Goth. *sáiv-s*), gen. *sæv-ar*; *há-r*, high, weak form *háv-i*; *dokk-r*, black, acc. *dokkv-an*; *miol*, flour, meal, dat. *miolv-i*. Words with a long vowel in the root have dropped the *v* altogether, as *kló*, claw, gen. *kló-ar*; *frú*, lady (Germ. frau, O. H. Germ. frawe); *ský*, sky; *blár*, blew, &c. At the end of words *v* is never vocalized.

S, Z

Gothic. These letters represent in Gothic, as in modern English, two distinct stages of the sibilant sound, *s* the hard, *z* the soft: the latter, therefore, has nothing in common with the Old and Modern German *z*. Hence they may exchange places, the softer *z* especially taking the place of the hard *s*, when the latter recedes from the end to the middle of a word, e. g. þis, ejus, fem. þizos; *slepan*, pret. *saizlep*; *ans*, trabs, dat. *anza*: so also *fairzna*, heel (Germ. ferse), *azgo*, ashes; *huzd*, hoard, treasure. At the beginning of a word *z* never occurs, but at the end if the following word begins with a vowel. This *z*, or soft *s*, is in the other dialects represented by *r*. In conjugational and derivative forms *s* very often is the result of the dissimilation of dentals; thus *naust* for *naut-t*; *varst* for *varþ-t*; *mosta* for *mot-da*[1]; *blostreis*, worshipper, from *blotan*; *beist*, yeast, from *beitan*. In *ansts*, favour (Germ. gunst), *alabrunsts*, holocaustum, the *s* is inserted between *n* and *t* for euphonic reasons, a case which occurs far more frequently in the other dialects.

Old High German. The Old High German *s* corresponds to the Gothic, but in many cases it has been encroached upon by the letter *r* (rhotacism), of which we have already treated. The combination *sk* which occurs frequently is, towards the end of the Old High German period, worn down to *sch*, chiefly before the vowels *e* and *i*. Gemination is avoided at the end of words, e. g. *ros*—*rosses*.

Old Saxon. Rhotacism of *s* into *r* takes place as in Old High

---

[1] See the conjugation of the strong verb.

German. *s* is inserted for euphonic purposes in *anst*, favour; *cunst*, virtus (Germ. kunst), and in the preterite of verbs, as *con-s-ta, on-s-ta*, &c. *z* seems in Old Saxon to occupy the same relation to *s* as in Gothic, and may often interchange with *s*, e. g. *blidzean*, delectare (A. S. *bledsjan*, to bless); *bezt* = *best* from *betist*, *lazto* and *lezto* = *lasto*, *letisto*.

Anglo-Saxon. A characteristic feature of this dialect is, that the often occurring combination *sc* (cf. O. H. Germ. *sk*) when preceding the vowels *a, a, o, ó*, assumes an *e* immediately after itself, which vowel has the effect of changing the pronunciation into the sound of the English *sh*, e. g. *sceal*, shall; *sceapian*, to create (Germ. schaffen). pret. *sceop*; *sceán*, splendui, shone; *sceo*, shoe; *sceoc*, shook. This combination must be kept altogether distinct from the Brechung *ea, eo*, and the diphthongs *eá, eó*. The insertion of the letter *e* is more common in later documents, and even in these it is occasionally omitted. Peculiar to the Anglo-Saxon dialect is the metathesis or inversion of *s* and *k*, and *s* and *p*, e. g. *froscas*, frogs, and *froxas*; *flascas* and *flaxas*, flasks; *fiscas* and *fixas*, fishes; *cosp* and *cops*, compes; *äspe* and *apse*, tremulus. *z* does not occur in Anglo-Saxon.

Old Frisian. In this dialect the *s* sound is treated as in Old High German and Old Saxon, especially with regard to rhotacism; therefore the *s* is preserved in the pres. and pret. sing. of strong verbs, while the pret. plur. and the part. adopt *r*, e. g. *kiase, kás, keron, keren; wesa, was, weron; urliase, urlás, urleron, urleren*. Metathesis of *sc* and *sp* does not take place. The softening of *sk* into *sch*, which is characteristic of the later Old High German, occurs in Old Frisian as a dialectic variation only, where we find *schet* for *sket*, treasure (Germ. schatz); *scheldech*, guilty (Germ. schuldig); *schel* for *skel*, shall; *schilling*, shilling; and in two cases before *a* and *u*—*schangt* (Germ. schenkt ein) and *schule*, shelter, hut.

Old Norse. This dialect has more thoroughly than any other developed the system of rhotacism; yet the spirant *s* is always preserved at the beginning, and very often in the middle and at the end of words. Geminated *s* (*ss*) occurs often in the middle and at the end of words: it may result from *rs*. The Old Norse *z* has nothing in common with the same letter in Old High German, but it is merely used to supplant certain other consonants and consonantal combinations. Thus, (1) for the *s* of the gen. sing., masc., and neut., e. g. *hestz* = *hests, ordz* = *ords*; also for the *s* which occurs in the formation of the superlative, e. g. *sterkaztr* = *sterkastr, fróðaztr* = *fróðastr*; and on other occasions, as *menzkir* = *menskir*, humani : (2) for *ds* and *ts*, e.g. *lanz* =

lands, helzt=heldst, maxime ; *veizla=veitzla*, convivium : (3) for the inflexional *sk*, the later *st*, of the middle voice, e. g. *reðuz= reðusk, ráðaz=ráðask, beraz=berask:* (4) for the *rs* of a later date, e. g. *veztr—verstr, stoeztr=stverstr*.

j

Gothic. This letter occurs in Gothic only as an initial, never at the end of a syllable, e. g. *jah,* and ; *sun-jus,* filii, sons. Concerning the vocalization of this letter when it is terminational, or when it occurs before consonants, vide supra, sub lit. **i**.

Old High German. This dialect renders *j* by *i*. When however it occurs at the beginning of a word it is rendered by *g* before *ë* and *i*, by *j* before another vowel such as *a* or *á*, e. g. *gëhan*, affirmare ; *gihit,* affirmat ; *jah,* affirmavi ; *jáhumës,* affirmavimus. *j* however occurs before *e* and *i* also in Notker. In the middle of a word *j* is rarely supplanted by *g* even before *e* and *i*, yet we read *eigir*, eggs ; *friger*, ingenuus. In the middle of words *j* often is assimilated to the succeeding consonant, and forms gemination, e. g. *horran* for *horgan, mitter* for *mitjer*. It is vocalized as in Gothic when it stands between two consonants or at the end of a word, e. g. *nerjan,* salvare, *nerita ;* heri, army, gen. *herjes*. Initial *j* is occasionally dropped, as *ener* for *jener* or *gener,* ille ; *ámer* for *jámer,* planctus (Germ. jammer).

Old Saxon. *j* and *i* designate the same sound. At the end of words *j* is always supplanted by *i*, in the same manner as *w* by *u*. This dialect, like Old High German, renders *j* before *e*, and *i* by *g*, whether at the beginning or in the middle of a word, e. g. *ger* for *jar,* year ; *gehan,* affirmare, fateri ; *gi,* ye ; *nigi,* new, Goth. *niujis;* and before other vowels it is often supplanted by *gi,* e. g. *giungaro=jungaro,* disciple (Germ. jünger) ; *giudeo=judeo,* Jew. This *gi* for *j* has nothing to do with the prefix *gi*. The reverse rarely occurs, that is, *j* instead of *g* before a thin vowel (*e* or *i*), a case which is more common in Old Frisian. Before an inflexional *a* it has a tendency to yield its place to the vowel *e*, as *wendean* for *wendjan, bliðean* for *bliðjan,* and before a consonant it is vocalized, e. g. *sáida* from *sájan,* to sow.

Anglo-Saxon. In the more ancient manuscripts *j* is rendered by *g* or *i*, so that before *e* and *i* we find *g*, before other vowels *ge*. (Compare **Old Saxon**). Examples :—*ge,* ye ; *git,* you two ; *gear,* year ; *geoc,* yoke ; *geong,* young. Rarely *i=j : iá, já,* yes ; *ioc, joc,* yoke. The latter consonant is however preferred in the middle of a word : *eardjan*, to dwell, for which we find *eardigean* too. After the liquid *r* the consonant *g* is more commonly used, as *nergan=*

nerjan, wergan = werjan. If *j* at the end of a word is not dropped, it is also replaced by *g*: *sig*, sit, may be (= *si*, Germ. sei); *hig*. they (= *hi*); *frig = fri* and *freo*, free. This *g* which is used for *j* may yield to the spirant *w*, as *buwan* for *buian* or *bugian*, to dwell.

Old Frisian. While the other dialects which we have just examined often supplant *j* by *g*, Old Frisian on the contrary has, besides the organic *j*, used this consonant in the place of *g*. The sibilant *j* is organic in *jer*, year; *jung*, young; *federja*, patruus; *makja*, to make; *sparja*, to spare; *erja*, to honour (Germ. eren). Still, this consonant is rather scarce, because it is commonly vocalized where it forms part of the root, as *nia*, new (Goth. niujis); *frí*, free (Goth. freis, frijis). *g* for *j* is rarely used. *j* once vocalized into *i* is lost altogether from the word; hence *hiri*, army (Germ. heer), has in the dative, not *hirji*, but *hiri*, contrary to the rule followed by the other dialects.

Old Norse. At the beginning of words *j* is dropped throughout, except in *já*, ita, and *jol*, feast; hence Old Norse writes *ar*, *ok*, *ungr*, instead of *jár*, *jok*, *jungr*. In the middle of a derivative word *j* before *i* is dropped, hence *miði* for *miðji*, *siti* for *sitji*. As in Anglo-Saxon, so also in Old Norse, *j* may produce the gemination *gg*. Scandinavian grammarians spell the Brechung *ia, iö*, and the diphthongs *io, iu*, by *ja, jo, jo, ju*. Grimm, however, prefers the former mode of spelling.

h

Gothic. At the beginning of a word it has a soft, in the middle or at the end, a hard sound. It is often produced out of *g* or *k* where these consonants are followed by *t* (vide infra, *Dentals*). Gothic, as well as other Teutonic dialects, is fond of supplying the *h* with the additional spirant *v*, which however must be regarded as merely euphonic and without any etymological value. The cognate languages, with the exception of Latin, render, in accordance with Grimm's law, the Gothic *h* by *k*, as Goth. *hvas*, O. H. Germ. *huer*, Sansk. *kas*; Goth. *hveleiks*, Gr. κηλίκως: while Latin shares the Gothic tendency and says *quis* and *qualis*. The double spirant is avoided at later times, in such a manner that the usurper *v* preserves its place and the original *h* is dropped. Some editors use *w* for the combination *hv*.

When the derivative suffix *ta* follows upon a guttural of the root, the guttural *g* or *k* is changed into *h*, e. g. *mah-ta*, pret. of *mag-an* (posse).

CONSONANTS.

Old High German. This dialect has two distinct sounds which are both represented by the letter *h*; in one case it is the spirant which corresponds to the Gothic *h*, in the other it is the aspirated guttural, answering to the Gothic *k*, and in pronunciation approaching the German *ch*. At the beginning of a word the Old High German *h* is always identical with the Gothic spirant of the same character, e. g. *hano*, cock, Goth. *hana; halz*, halt, claudus, Goth. *halts;* but in the middle and at the end of a word it may be either the spirant or the aspirate. The latter, when occurring in the middle of the word, is rendered by *h, hh*, or *ch*; at the end of the word almost always by *h*. In order therefore to determine whether in a given case we have to deal with the spirant or the aspirate, we must collate the Old High German with the Gothic form, the latter always rendering the Old High German spirant by *h*, the Old High German aspirate by *k*. Thus we have in the words *mihil, zeihan, bráhun*, the aspirate, because they are rendered in Gothic by *mikils, táikns, brékun;* in *slahan, fihu, ziohan*, the spirant, Goth. *slahan, faíhu, tiuhan;* at the end of words, *ih, mih, juh*, the aspirate again, because we find them in Gothic rendered by *ik, mik, juk*, while *sah, zeh, floh*, display the spirant just as the Goth. *sahv, táih, þláuh*.

When occurring in the middle of a word the spirant *h* is often dropped, and then causes the preceding vowel to be lengthened, e. g. *á* = *aha*, water; *bîl* = *bihil*, bipennis. *h* has been dropped before *s* in *mist*, fimus, Goth. *maihstus; zesawer*, dexter, Goth. *taihsva*.

Under the influence of an inflexional *t* the guttural *g* or *k* is changed into *h*, e. g. *mah-ta*, pret. of *magan, mugan*, posse.

In the middle of words spirants can interchange, e. g. *sájan, sáhan, sáwan*, to sow; *fóher, fówer*, few; *cráju, gráwu*, cana.

Old Saxon. The Old Saxon *h* corresponds exactly to the Gothic. The combinations *hl, hr, hn*, &c., are preserved in some documents, in others the *h* is dropped. As in Old High German, an inorganic *h* is produced out of *g* and *k* under the influence of an inflexional *t*, e. g. *sóh-ta*, pret. of *sok-jan*, to seek; *mah-ta*, pret. of *mugan*, posse. *h* is no favourite consonant in the middle of a word, and is, therefore, either dropped or hardened into a guttural; hence *sean* = *sehan*, to see; *gean* = *gehan*, to affirm; *gewîgan* instead of *gewîhan*, to bless (Germ. weihen); and the plur. pret. *logon, slogon*, of *lahan*, to blame, *slahan*, to slay. *h* is occasionally dropped after vowels, e. g. *fera*, anima, for *ferah; frá*, lætus (Germ. froh), for *fráh;* or it is hardened into the media, *ginog* for *ginoh*, enough.

In *sess*, six, and *fuss*, fox, the double *s* takes the place of the spirant combination *hs*.

In the middle of words spirants can, as in Old High German, interchange, e. g. *sáhun, sáwun* (even *sáun* and *ságon*, viderunt), *kneohon* and *kneowon*, dat. plur. of *kneo*, knee; *sájan* and *séhan*, to sow.

Anglo-Saxon. As in other dialects an inorganic *h* is produced out of *g* and *c* (*k*). Where the media *g* occurs at the end of a word it is replaced by *h*, as *burh* (borough), *burge, beah* (ring), *beáges;* but it retains its position after short vowels, hence *dag*, day; *mag*, may, podest; *lag*, law; *mag*, boy; *weg*, way. In the pret. of verbs, *g* yields its place to *h*, e. g. *bealh*, pret. of *belgan; fleáh*, pret. of *fleoge; birhst, birhð*, of *beorgan; fleohst, fleóhð* of *fleogan*. Before the inflexional *t* of the preterite, the guttural *c* (*k*) must, as in other dialects, be changed into *h*, e. g. *secan*, to seek; *sohte*, sought; *recan*, curare, pret. *rohte*. We have interchange of spirants in *geseo=geseohe*, I see, pret. *geseah*, plur. *gesawon*, part. *gesewen* and *gesegen*. *hh=h*.

Old Frisian. The initial *h* is identical with that of the other dialects. The combinations *hl, hr,* and *hw,* are also spelt *lh, rh, wh*. Initial *h* is inorganic in *hága*, to have, Goth. *áigan*. In the middle of a word *h* is either dropped or hardened into *g*, e. g. *sia*, to see; *tian*, ten; *slogon*, plur. pret. of *slá*, to slay; *hlige*, conj. pres. of *hlia*, fateri, O. H. Germ. *jehan;* *hágost*, superl. of *hach*, high (Germ. hoch). The hardened spirant *h* appears as *ch* at the end of a word (unless it is dropped, as in *fia*, pecus, Germ. vich), e. g. *hach*, high; *noch*, yet, adhuc; in the middle of a word always before *t*, e.g. *dochter*, daughter; *achta*, eight; *riucht*, right; and thus every *g* or *k* is changed into *ch* before the inflexional *t*, as *mach-te*, pret. of *meg-a*, may, posse; *sóch-te*, pret. of *sek-a*, to seek. The media *g*, except in the combination *ng* and *eg*, changed into *ei*, always becomes *ch* when it occurs at the end of a word, or before the tenuis *t*, e. g. *berch*, mountain (Germ. berg), gen. *berges;* *orloch*, war, gen. *orloges; fliucht*, volat, of *fliaga*.

Old Norse. The more ancient forms *hl, hn, hr,* drop the *h* in later documents. In the middle and at the end of words *h* has been dropped everywhere: *sía*, to see, O. H. Germ. *sehan;* *ior*, horse (O. S. *ehu*); *líkamr*, body (Germ. leichnam), for *likhamr*. *ht* is changed into *tt*, and by this change the preceding vowel is lengthened, e. g. *rettr*, right, Goth. *raíhts; dróttin*, lord, O. H. Germ. *truhtin*. The combination *kt*, which in the other dialects is converted into *ht*, either remains intact, or is changed into *tt*, e. g. *þoktr* and *þóttr*, part. of *þykja*, videri; *sotti* and *sokti*, pret. of *soekja*, to seek.

Consonants.

Mutes.

1. *Labials:*—b, p, f (ph, v, ƀ)

Gothic. The media *b* occurs frequently at the beginning of words, but in the middle and at the end it is often replaced by the labial aspirate *f*. Before the tenuis *t* the media *b* must invariably be changed into *f*: hence *gróft* from *graban*, *dráift* from *dreiban*. Where the *b* is terminational it can retain its place only after a liquid, as *dumb*, dumb; *þarb*, poor, needy: after any other sound it must yield to *f*, e. g. *gaf*, pret. of *giban*, to give; *gróf*, pret. of *graban*, to dig (Germ. graben); *hláif*, accus. of *hláibs*, bread, loaf. Occasional deviations from this rule occur, so that we find *hláifs* for *hláibs*, and *tvalib* by the side of *tvalif*, twelve. The prepositions *af*, *uf*, *afar* (after), and *ufar* (over), prefer the *f* in every position; but where the interrogative particle *u* follows, the media regains its place, e. g. *abu*, whence, unde.

The tenuis *p* never occurs at the beginning of a native Gothic word, but it is frequent enough at the end and in the middle of words. In the latter case it is before a *t* subject to the same law as the media and must be changed into *f*, e. g. *skapjan*, to create (Germ. schaffen); *scóft*, creavisti; *gaskafts*, creature (Germ. geschopf).

The aspirate *f* has received its explanation in the foregoing remarks.

Old High German. The Gothic media *b* should, in Old High German, according to Grimm's law, always be rendered by the tenuis *p*. This rule is, indeed, followed in the more ancient glossaries, where we read *ipu*, *stap*, *prinkan*, *puah*, for the Gothic *iba*, ne, nonne; *stabs*, element, rudiment; *bringan*, to bring; *boka*, letter (Germ. buchstabe). In other documents we find a less strict adherence to the rule, and though the tenuis is preserved at the beginning and at the end, it is often replaced by the media in the middle of words; hence, *stap*, *puah*, but *ibu* by the side of *lepen*. In other documents again the tenuis keeps its position only where it is terminational, being in every other place superseded by the media, and the final step in this deviation from the true Old High German system is made by replacing the tenuis by the media throughout; so that the Gothic *b* is everywhere rendered in Old High German by *b* as well. The tenuis occurs only in foreign words and after the sibilant *s*, which renders the position of a succeeding tenuis impregnable.

The Old High German aspirate may be expressed by *ph, pf, f,* and *v*: *ph* is found for the Latin *p,* as in *phunt,* Lat. *pondus,* pound, the later *pfunt,* or simply *funt;* or the Latin tenuis remains unaltered, *pun-t.* In the middle of words and at the end *ph* is often used instead of *f,* as *werphan, warph* (Germ. werfen, warf). The initial aspirate is either rendered by *f* or *v,* the former indicating a surd, the latter a soft sound, and either being used according to the propensities of the different dialects in which the different authors have written. As a rule it may be laid down that an *f* which occurs at the end of a word may be changed into *v* when succeeded by another syllable, e. g. *wolf, wolves* (the same in English); *biscof* (bishop), *biscoves.* The media *b* for *v* in the middle of a word is exceptional.

ps does not occur in Old High German, the Latin *psalmus* therefore becomes *salm.* (Compare the pronunciation of *psalm* in English.) O. H. Germ. *fs* = A. S. *sp*: *wefsa, wasp,* wasp.

Since the dialectic variations in the use of the mutes are very complicated in Old High German, we subjoin a table, in which their application by different authors is indicated[1]:—

		Isidor.	Otfried.	Tatian.
Gothic, *b, p, f*; strict O. H. Germ. *p, ph, f*	Initial[2]	*p, f*	*b, ph, f*	*b, ph, f*
	Interior	*b, f, v*	*b, f, f*	*b, ph, v*
	Terminational	*p, ph, f*	*b, f, f*	*b, ph, v*

Old Saxon. Old Saxon labials are rendered by the letters *p, b, ƀ, v, f, ph.*

The tenuis *p,* which is rare at the beginning, occurs frequently in the middle and at the end of words, and is in every respect identical with the Gothic *p.*

The media *b* keeps its position only at the beginning of words, while in the middle and at the end of a word it yields to the aspirate, except in the combinations *mb* and *bb,* as *camb,* comb; *lamb,* lamb; *webbi,* web; *hebbjan,* to have.

There are two aspirates, the softer marked by *ƀ* (= *bh, v*), the surd by *f*; the former is used when a vowel or the media *d* succeeds, the latter before *t, l, n,* and commonly before *r.* Examples:—*clioƀan,* to cleave; *aƀand,* even, evening (Germ. abend); *hoƀid,* head (Germ. haupt, caput); *haƀda,* had, habuit; *liƀda,* lived, vixit; *craft,* vis; *aftar,* after; *efno,* even, pariter: compare further *sueƀan,* somnium, dat. sing. *suefne,* acc. plur. *sueƀanos.* At the end of words we always find *f,* and in one and the same word, therefore, we may find *ƀ* and *f* alternately, as in *clioƀan,*

---

[1] From Heine, *Grammatik der Alt-Germanischen Sprachen,* p. 104.

[2] *Initial,* at the beginning of a word; *Interior,* in the middle; *Terminational,* at the end.

to cleave, pret. *clóf;* *wolf,* gen. *wolƀes;* *hof,* court, yard (Germ. hof), gen. *hoƀes.*

As to the mode of rendering the soft and surd aspirates some confusion exists in documents. The former is marked in the Cottonian text by ƀ (rarely *f*), in the Munich Codex by ƀ and *b*; the Psalms use always *v*, other documents *v* and *f*. For the termination *f* the Heliand has sometimes ƀ (in the Munich Codex *b*), as *liƀ* for *lif*, *wiƀ* for *wif*, &c.

At the beginning of a word the Old Saxon is always identical with the Gothic *f*, which minor documents like to render by *v*: *van=fan*, de; *vohs=fohs*, fox. Noteworthy is the digression of *ft* into *ht*, that is, from the labial aspirate into the guttural spirant, a case more frequent in Dutch, e. g. *craht=craft*, vis; *ahter=after*, post; compare Dutch *cracht* and *achter*, for the Engl. *craft* and *after*. *ph* and *ff* only in foreign words.

Anglo-Saxon. The media *b*, if initial, is always organic; in the middle and at the end of words it occurs only in the combinations *mb* and *bb* (the latter originating in *bj*). Examples:— *lamb, dumb, comb; libban,* to live; *häbban,* to have.

The tenuis *p* is always organic, and never encroached upon by other consonants.

The aspirate *f* also is always organic, and therefore identical with the Gothic, if it occurs at the beginning of a word, while in the middle and at the end its occurrence is far more frequent than in Old High German, even more so than in Gothic, for it often supplants the Gothic *b*, Old High German *p*. The organic *f* we have in the words *wulf,* gen. *wulfes,* Goth. *vulfs,* O. H. Germ. *wolf, wolves,* O. S. *wulf, wulƀes; heofian,* to mourn, Goth. *hiufan,* O. S. *hioƀan.*

The inorganic *f* in the place of the media *b* we find in *seofon,* seven (Goth. *sibun,* O. H. Germ. *sipun,* O. S. *siƀun)*; þeóf*,* thief, gen. þeófes (Goth. þiubs, þiubis, O. H. Germ. *diop, dioƀes,* O. S. *theof, theoƀes*). From these examples it will become evident that the range of the Anglo-Saxon *f* is still further enlarged by the absence in this dialect of a soft labial aspirate like Old High German *v*, Old Saxon ƀ. It is characteristic of Anglo-Saxon that whilst on the one hand it shares the Low German inclination of its sister dialects to convert the labial media, where it is not protected by certain consonants, into the aspirate—first at the end, later on in the middle of words as well, it objects, like the Old Norse, to a modification of the aspirate, and always uses the surd *f*, where Old Saxon and Old Frisian smoothe it down into *v*, and by this means produce a greater variety and elegance of sound.

The gemination *pp* is rare; *ff* occurs in the verb *offrjan*, to offer, and in a few proper names.

Old Frisian. The media *b* is, as in the other dialects, always organic at the beginning of words, and occurs in the middle and at the end only in the combinations *mb* and *bb*, e. g. *dumbe*, stupid (Germ. dumm); *crumb*, crooked (Germ. krumm); *hebba*, to have. In all other cases it yields to the aspirate.

The tenuis *p* is, in its relations, identical with the same letter in the other Low German dialects.

The aspirate *f* is so far identical with the Anglo-Saxon aspirate as it occurs, organic and inorganic, in the place of the media; but it differs from the Anglo-Saxon by admitting a modification of the *f* sound in the soft aspirate *v*, the former being preferred where the aspirate is initial or final, the latter where it stands in the middle of a word. Examples:—*lîf*, life, gen. *lives*; *gref*, grave, gen. *greves*. But a succeeding *t* sound gives shelter to the *f*, hence *efter*, after; *hâfd*, head; *jeftha*, aut.

The gemination *pp* is rare; *ff* only in foreign words, as *offaria*, to offer.

Old Norse. The media is in the same relation as in the Low German dialects; hence it is organic at the beginning of words, and is superseded by the aspirate in the middle and at the end of words, except in the combinations *mb* and *bb*, e. g. *kambr*, comb; *timbr*, building (cf. Engl. timber and Germ. zimmer); *vomb*, womb; *gabba*, to cheat.

As to the tenuis *p*, it is characteristic of the Old Norse dialect that it preserves that consonant in the combinaton *pt* in which the Low German dialects invariably reject it and form the combination *ft*, e. g. *lopt*, air (Germ. luft), Goth. *luftus*; *opt*, often (Germ. oft), Goth. *ufta*; *krapt*, strength, craft (Germ. kraft), A. S. *cräft*. In this respect Old Norse occupies one and the same position with the cognate languages, as O. N. *skript*, a picture, and Lat. *scriptum*, A. S. *scrift* (Germ. schrift). Even where the root ends in *f* it is changed into *p* if a *t* follows it; e. g. *gef-a*, to give; *gip-ta*, in matrimonium dare; *rîf-a*, to tear; *rip-ta*, to cleave. The radical *f* keeps its position before a *t* only in the 2nd pers. sing. of the preterite of the verb, e. g. *rauf-t*, destruxisti, from *riuf-a*. In later documents, however, *pt* is occasionally converted into *ft* in the middle, and into *tt* at the end of words; e. g. *eftir* for *eptir*, after; *ott* for *opt*, oft.

The gemination *pp* has its origin in *mp*, as *kapp*, fight (Germ. kampf), O. Fris. *komp*, *kemp*, O. H. Germ. *kempho*.

The aspirate *f* is organic at the beginning of the word; in the middle and at the end it often represents the media *b*, and, as in

CONSONANTS.

Anglo-Saxon, refuses the modification into *v*, unless we except a few cases where an initial *f* is replaced by *v*.

This dialect in certain words vacillates between the combinations *fn* and *mn*, so that *stafn*, for instance, forms the dative *stamni*, and *iamn* stands for *iafn*; and, vice versa, *safna* for O. H. Germ. *samanon*. The gemination *ff* only in foreign words.

2. *Dentals*:—d, t, đ (dh) þ (th), z, ʒ

Gothic *d, t, þ*. In the dental, as in the labial order, the media and aspirate stand in close relationship, so that the latter in certain positions takes the place of the former. Only the combinations *ld, nd, rd*, where the liquid shelters the media, are organically distinct from *lþ, nþ, rþ*, as *kalds*, cold; *balþs*, bold, which can never become *kalþs* and *balds*; *vinds*, wind; *svinþs*, strong; *vaurd*, word; *vairþs*, worth. If it occurs in any other combination, the media yields its place to the aspirate as soon as it becomes terminational, e. g. *biudan*, pret. *bauþ* (exceptionally *baud*); the nominatives *haubiþ, liuhaþ, vitoþ*, and their genitives, *haubid-is, liuhad-is, vitod-is*. The aspirate may transplant the media even where the terminational *s* of the nominative follows it, as *faheþs* for *faheds*, joy; *mitaþs* for *mitads*. The tendency which manifests itself in the Gothic version of St. Luke's Gospel to restore, or perhaps rather to preserve, the ancient media in preference to the aspirate, is peculiar; hence *nimid*, capit, not *nimiþ*; *sad*, not *saþ*, &c.

The tenuis is in many cases organic, in others it has usurped the place of the media. In the latter capacity we find it chiefly after the spirant *h* in the pret. of anomalous verbs which have dropped the derivative vowel, e. g. *brahta*, brought, for *brahda*; *mahta*, might (Germ. mochte), for *mahda*; *þaurfta* for *þaurfda* (Germ. durfte); *kaupasta = kaupatta = kaupat-da* (*s* from the dissimilation of the *t*, vide sub lit. **s**), from the verb *káupatjan*, colaphizare; further, the anomalous preterite *vissa = vista = vitta = vit-da* from *vit-an*, scire (Germ. wissen[1]).

The aspirate þ is in sound identical with the English *th*, and is sometimes represented by the former, the Runic, sometimes by our modern sign. Where the aspirate belongs to the root it remains unaltered though it recede to the middle of the word, hence *qiþan*, to say, *qaþ, qeþum*; yet we must notice *fraþjan, froþ*, sapere, and *frods*, sapiens.

Old High German *d, t, z, ʒ*. According to Grimm's law the

---

[1] See the strong conjugation of the verb.

Gothic media is in Old High German represented by the tenuis, and this is done in strictly Old High German authors such as Kero and Tatian, whilst in Isidor and Otfried the Gothic media is preserved, so that the former uses the media at the beginning and in the middle, the tenuis always at the end of a word, and therefore writes *dohter*, daughter (Goth. *dauhtar*); *worde*, words (Goth. *vaurda*), but nom. sing. *wort*. The latter leaves the media at the beginning, but he replaces it not only at the end, but often in the middle of a word as well, and therefore writes *dohter*, like Isidor, but *stantan*, to stand, Goth. *standan*; *hant*, hand, Goth. *handus*. In Old High German we should for the Gothic combinations *ld, nd, rd*, expect *lt, nt, rt*, and for the Goth. *lb, nþ, rþ*, O. H. Germ. *ld, nd, rd*; but great confusion prevails in the practice of different authors, so that we find *blinden* instead of *blinten*, *hand* instead of *hant* (Goth. *blindan, handus*), and *munt* instead of *mund* (Goth. *munþs*, mouth).

For the Gothic tenuis Old High German has the aspirate *z*, occasionally rendered by *c*, a sound which occurs in two modifications, as a surd or hard, and as a soft, of which Grimm renders the former by *z*, the latter by *ʒ*, whilst in the Old High German documents *z* is put indiscriminately for both sounds. *z* always occurs as the initial aspirate: in the middle and at the end of a word it is found only when preceded by a liquid, as *welzan*, to revolve (Germ. walzen); *kranz*, garland (Germ. kranz); *wurz*, wort (Germ. wurz), and where it corresponds to a Gothic *tt*, e.g. *scaz*, treasure, Goth. *scatts*; *sizan*, to sit, Goth. *sittan*. The soft aspirate *ʒ* is used only in the middle and at the end of words, and always corresponds to the Gothic *t*, *waʒar*, Goth. *vato*, water (Germ. waßer[1]); *fuoʒ*, Goth. *fotus*, foot (Germ. fuß); *saʒ*, Goth. *sat*, sat (Germ. saß).

The Gothic aspirate is in the strict Old High German replaced by the media; but in many documents this law is much relaxed. Isidor uses for the Gothic þ, in whatever position it may occur, *dh*, which in sound may have resembled the Anglo-Saxon ð (the English soft *th*), e.g. *dhu*, tu; *dher*, is; *werdhan*, fieri; *chindh*, infans (Goth. þu, vairþan, &c.).

Otfried and Tatian use *th* for Gothic þ only at the beginning, and replace it by *d* in the middle and at the end of words.

The gemination *tt* results by assimilation from *tj*, Goth. *dj*, as *bittan*, Goth. *bidjan*, to beg (Germ. bitten). *dd* occurs rarely, and is identical with *tt*: *laddun* (asseres) = *lattun*; but *eddo* is the Goth. *aiþþau*.

---

[1] Commonly spelt *wasser*.

The dentals as applied by different authors yield the following paradigm[1] :—

		Isidor.	Otfried.	Tatian.
Gothic, d, t, þ; strict O. H. Germ. t, z, ʒ, d	Initial	d, z, dh	d, z, th	t, z, th
	Interior	d, zs, dh	t, z, ʒ, d	t, z, ʒ, d
	Terminational	t, zs, dh	t, z, ʒ, d	t, z, ʒ, d

Old Saxon d, t, ð, th. At the beginning of a word the media is used just as in Gothic; so also in the middle and at the end of words, but with the following exceptions :—The O. S. ld, nd, rd, represent the identical Gothic combinations as well as the Goth. lþ, nþ, and rþ, hence Goth. kalds, bindan and balþs, anþar, show in O. S. the media, cald, bindan, bald, andar. When however the n is dropped the aspirate finds its place again, hence fiðan for findan, to find; muð, Goth. munþs, O. H. Germ. munt, mouth (Germ. mund). Old Saxon does not object to the use of the media at the end of words where Gothic replaces it by the aspirate, therefore O. S. god, deus, for Goth. guþs; brud, bride (Germ. braut), Goth. bruþs; so also the termination of the 3rd sing. pres. of verbs : bir-id, ner-id, salb-od. But the Old Saxon terminational media is sometimes affected in another way, so that it yields to the tenuis t (perhaps under Old High German influence) when it occurs at the end of a word, e. g. got for god, but gen. godis again; in the same manner dot, death, gen. dodis; werolt, world, gen. weroldis; behielt, pret. of behaldan, conservare.

The tenuis t, with the exception of the few mentioned cases, preserves its organic character and keeps aloof from any interchange with media and aspirate alike.

The aspirate appears hard in th, soft in ð; but these signs are not always adhered to in the different manuscripts. The Munich Codex has d and ð, rarely th; the Cottonian th and ð indiscriminately; smaller documents commonly th, rarely ð.

Anglo-Saxon d, t, ð, þ. Besides its organic functions the media has frequently to form the substitute of the aspirate, the latter keeping its place after the liquids n and r, but yielding it to the media after l, so that the original distinction between ll and lð is no longer preserved. Hence we find cald, ceald, cold, Goth. kalds; and bald, bold, Goth. balþs. Compare **Old Saxon.**

In the preterite of strong verbs the terminational ð of the root, as soon as it recedes from the end of the word, is replaced by the media, e. g. weorðe, fio; pret. wearð, wurde, wurdon, part. worde; cweðe, dico, cwäð, cwæde, cwædon.

[1] Heine, p. 105.

The tenuis is organic with one exception, which is characteristic of this dialect. Whenever the termination ð in the 3rd sing. of strong verbs follows upon a dental or spirant of the root, *d* + ð, or *s* + ð, make *t*, and thus *bind*-ð, he binds, becomes *bint;* *cys-d* becomes *cýst*, he chooses.

The aspirate is, as in most Low German dialects, modified into hard (þ) and soft (ð), which undoubtedly represent the twofold aspirates still extant in modern English, the soft in *thine* and *soothe*, the hard in *thin* and *sooth*. As to the use of the soft or hard aspirate the manuscripts are so irregular as to render it impossible to form a rule from them, and many editors of manuscripts follow this lawless course. Rask, however, and Grimm after his example, make it a rule to use the hard aspirate þ at the beginning, the soft ð in the middle and at the end of words. Dr. Bosworth places þ where the corresponding word in English has the hard *th*, and ð where we find the soft *th*; hence he always puts þ at the beginning of words *not pronominal*, as þincan, þin, and at the end of radical and inflectional terminations, as *smiþ*, *writaþ*. The soft ð he always uses in the *beginning of pronouns* and in words derived from pronouns, as ðät, and ðätlíc; and also between two vowels, as baðian. Anglo-Saxon words are thus assimilated to modern English.

The connection between *lð* and *ld* has already been mentioned. Gemination of the aspirate is the result of assimilation, as in oððe, or; siððan, since (O. Engl. sith); or of contraction, as in cyððu, home, O. H. Germ. *chundida;* or it is superfluously applied, as in *scäððe* for scaðe, damage (Germ. schaden, cf. Engl. scathe).

Old Frisian *d, t, th*. The Old Frisian dentals occupy very much the same position as the Anglo-Saxon. The media, when initial, is organic. In the middle of a word the combination *nd* remains intact, as in *bindan*, the combination *nth* drops the *n* (compare A. S., &c.), as in *kúth;* *ld* is either organic or it takes the place of *lth*, hence *halda*, to hold, Goth. *haldan*, and *bilde* = *bilthe*, O. S. biliði; *rd* and *rth* are kept distinct, as *gerdel*, girdle; *word;* and *irthe*, earth, *hirth*, hearth. At the end of words the Old Frisian, like the Old Saxon media, remains faithful to its function in the words *breid*, bride; *god;* *háfd*, head; *bed*, asked (Germ. bat, Goth. baþ); but in the terminations of the verb, *d* and *ad* yield, as in Gothic, to the influence of the aspirate, and become *th* and *ath*, as *werp-th*, he throws (Germ. wirft); *salv-ath*, he anoints; Goth. vairp-iþ, salb-oþ, but O. S. *wirp-id, salb-od*.

The tenuis is almost throughout organic. When terminational it is sometimes dropped after a *ch*, as *riuch* for *riucht, fiuch* for *fiucht;* in the 3rd sing. pres. of the verb it replaces exceptionally the *th*, as *nimat* for *nimath*, and in like manner it stands for *dát* = *dáth*, death; *klit* = *kleth*, cloth (Germ. kleid). Other documents place vice versa *th* for *t*, as *weth* for *wet*, A. S. *wät*, wet; *with* for *wit*. This last change, however, seems never to occur where *t* follows upon a mute or a spirant, and *t* therefore always preserves its position in words such as *brust, nacht, aft*.

The aspirate occurs under the sole sign of *th*, yet it is supposed by grammarians to have had a softer sound in the middle and at the end, than at the beginning of words. The aspirate and media interchange occasionally, as *sáda* for *sátha*, cespes, and *steth* for *sted*, stead, place. The gemination *thth* in *aththa*, father, judge, is better replaced by the single aspirate *th*.

Old Norse *d, t,* ð, þ. The media, if initial, keeps always distinct from both tenuis and aspirate. In the middle and at the end of words the combinations *dd, md, nd,* and *ld,* are preserved, while *n*ð and *l*ð are everywhere changed into *nn* and *ll*. In all other cases the aspirate has much encroached on the media in the middle as well as at the end of words.

The tenuis *t* takes the place of the media in the sing. pret. of strong verbs, as *gialda*, valere, *galt*; *halda*, to hold, *helt*; *falda*, to fold, *félt*; compare further *binda, batt; blanda, blett* (vide supra, sub lit. **n**). The gemination *tt* is organic in *skattr*, tribute: it arises from *nt* in *mitt*, meum; þ*itt*, tuum; *sitt*, suum; *hitt*, illud; *eitt*, unum; instead of *mint*, þ*int, sint,* &c.; *tuttugu* = *tvintugu*, twenty. We find caused by assimilation also the gemination in the neuter of adjectives, the roots of which, having dropped a consonant, end in a vowel, e. g. *fá-tt*, paucum, from *fá-r*; *há-tt*, altum, from *há-r*, instead of *fá-t*, *há-t*. For other encroachments on the media, see below.

The aspirate is either hard (þ), or soft (ð), the former being met with only at the beginning of words. The soft aspirate comprises a far wider range than it does in the Saxon dialects. The media which, as we have seen above, can only stand after *l, m, n,* and in the gemination *dd*, is replaced by the aspirate ð, after all the vowels and the consonants *r, f, b, g,* while upon the consonants *p, t, k, s,* the tenuis *t* usurps its place; hence *d* and ð can no longer be distinguished after a vowel or the liquid *r*, as proved by the following examples:—*or*ð, word, Goth. *vaurd*; *ior*ð, earth, Goth. *aír*þ; *ver*ð*a*, to become (Germ. werden), Goth. *vairþan*; *go*ð*r*, good, Goth. *gods*. This rule concerning the replacement of the media by the aspirate or the tenuis in certain positions is of great importance in the formation of the preterite of weak verbs where the termination *da* is to be added, either unaltered or changed either into ð*a* or *ta*, according to the rule just mentioned. Hence we have the preterites *vil-da, fram-da, bren-da, kalla-ða, svaf-ða, glap-ta*, from the verbs *vil-ja, frem-ja, brenn-a, kall-a, svef-ja, glep-ja*. The terminational ð is dropped before the *t* of the neuter gender, and we therefore find *hart* for *harðt*, from *harðr*, bold; *vert* for *verðt*, from *verðr*, worthy; but where this ðt is preceded by a vowel it is assimilated into *tt*, and shortens at the same time the preceding vowel, e. g. *gott*, neut. of *godr*, good; *rautt* from *rauðr*, red.

3. *Gutturals*:—g, c, k, q (kw), ch, h, hh

Gothic *g, k, q*. The media *g* in the middle, as well as at the end of a word, is sometimes replaced by the spirant *h*, a change which cannot be accounted for by any apparent law. Hence *áigands* and *áihands, veigan, váih*. The geminations *gg, gk, gq*, are like the Greek γγ, γκ, nasal, and are therefore rendered in the other Teutonic dialects by *ng, nk*, e. g. Goth. *stiggan*, A. S. *stingan*, Goth. *drigkan*, O. H. Germ. *trinkan*, to drink; Goth. *singqan*, O. S. *sincan*, to sink. *ggk, ggq, = gh, gq*. As the single media, so also has its gemination, a certain relation to the spirant *h*, the latter appearing in derivative forms often in the place of the former, e. g. *gaggan*, to go, *gahts*, gait (Germ. gang); *junggs*, young, comp. *juhiza*.

Whenever the derivative suffix *t* follows upon a radical *g* or *k*, the guttural must be changed into *h*, as *mah-ta*, potui, from *mag-an; váh-tvo* from *vakan*, to wake: but in the 2nd sing. pret. the guttural is preserved before the terminational *t*, as *mag-t*, potes; *vok-t* from *vak-an, sók-t* from *sak-an*, incusare.

q is identical with our *qu=kw*. As in *hv*, so in the combination *q=kw*, the *w* sound seems to be a euphonic addition which has no etymological claim to its position, wherefore *q* is, in the cognate languages represented by the simple guttural, e. g. *qens*, wife, Sansk. *janis*, Gr. γυνη. In later times, however, the usurper occasionally expels the legitimate guttural altogether, as in Goth. *vaurms*, worms, instead of *qaurms*, Sansk. *krimis*. This phenomenon becomes more frequent in O. H. Germ., e. g. *weinon*, to weep (Germ. weinen), which in Gothic still shows the original guttural *qáinon*.

The Greek ξ is rendered by *ks*.

Old High German *g, k, ch (hh, h)*. The media, which in the strict Old High German should be replaced by the tenuis, does indeed, but rarely, occur instead of the legitimate tenuis; but it is frequently used to fill the place of the spirant *j*. But here again, as in the case of the dentals and labials, Old High German

CONSONANTS.

authors differ in the mode of applying the media. Isidor keeps up the Gothic media both at the beginning and at the end of a word, but he applies the tenuis only at the end, hence *got; stigan, steic* (Germ. steigen, stieg). Before a thin vowel, *e* or *i*, he introduces an *h*, which appears to find a place there merely for the sake of preserving the guttural pronunciation of the *g*, as *gheban*, to give, pret. *gab, gheist*, ghost (Germ. geist). Otfried and Tatian use the media quite in the Gothic fashion.

In strict Old High German the Gothic tenuis *k* should be replaced by the aspirate *ch*, as is the case in Isidor, while Otfried and Tatian preserve the Gothic tenuis where it is terminational, but replace it by *ch* in the middle and at the beginning of words, except in the combinations *lk, nk, rk*, which even Isidor likes to retain. The combination *sk* is in Otfried and Tatian already softened into *sg*, which seems to be the transition sound to the later *sch*. Hence *fisg = fisc*, fish (Germ. fisch); *himilisg = himilisc*, heavenly (Germ. himmlisch), by the side of *eiscon, eiscota*.

The aspirate *h, ch* (= *kh*), as we have already seen, replaces the Gothic *k*. In the middle of a word this *ch* is sometimes rendered by *hh*, rarely by *h*, while at the end the latter has the preference. This *h* has of course nothing to do with the spirant *h*, from which it differed etymologically as well as in pronunciation.

qu, answering to the Gothic *q*, is in strict Old High German authors rendered by *chu*; herein also, following Grimm's law, others write *quh*, or *qhu*, or simply *ch*, as *chuedan, quhedan, chedan*, all different modes of spelling one and the same word.

x in Old High German is commonly rendered by *hs*.

The gemination *kk* (*cc*) used by Isidor and others is rendered by *gg* in Otfried and Tatian, and their *kk* is identical with the Gothic gemination of the same kind which in strictly Old High German is often replaced by *cch*.

The list of gutturals as used in the different Old High German authors appears thus[1]:—

		Isidor.	Otfried.	Tatian.
Gothic *g, k*; strict O. H. Germ. *k, ch*	Initial	*g* (*gh*), *ch*	*g, k*	*g, k*
	Interior	*g* (*gh*), *hh*	*g, ch*	*g, hh*
	Terminational	*c, h*	*g, h*	*g, h*

Old Saxon *g, c* (*k*). The media, besides its organic functions, has often to supply the spirants *j* and *h* in certain positions. (Comp. supra, sub litt. **j, h.**)

The gemination has not the nasal sound of the Gothic, but

---

[1] Heine, p. 106.

represents the Old High German *kk*, as in *segg*, man, vir; *wigg*, horse; *seggjan*, to say.

The tenuis is rendered by *c* or *k*, both representing the same guttural sound. In the combination *sc* the *c* has been dropped in the words *sal*, shall, debet; *solun*, debent. *qu = kw*.

The guttural aspirate occurs only exceptionally, and then it is inorganic, as in *ahtodoch*, eighty, by the side of *ahtedeg*. *lichamo* is *lic-hamo*.

Anglo-Saxon *g, c* (= *k*). The media before thin vowels, *e* and *i*, was very likely pronounced like the spirant *j*, whence we find the preterites of *gipan*, to gape; *gifan*, to give; *gitan*, to conceive, to be *geap, geaf, geat*, where the *e* seems to be introduced for the sake of preserving for the *g*, before the preterite *a*, the same soft pronunciation it must have had before the vowel *i* of the present. Even before the full vowels *g* can form alliteration with *ge*, and with the spirant *j* itself. The organic media is in later documents often dropped in consequence of contraction, e. g. *ren*, rain, for *regen* (Germ. regen); *þen*, servant, for *þegen*; *þinen*, maid-servant, for *þignan*. *gn* occurs inverted into *ng* in the forms *fringe, frang, frungon, gefrungen*, instead of *frigne, fragn*, &c. (Concerning the conversion of the terminational *g* to *h*, see sub lit. **h**.) The gemination *gg* in later, *cg* in earlier documents is preserved even at the end of words, where other geminations prefer dissolution, e. g. *ecg*, edge; *vicg*, horse; *secg*, man; *mecg*, man; *lecgan*, to lay (Germ. legen).

The tenuis is commonly rendered by *c*, rarely by *k*, whence *ece, cirm*, sound *eke, kirm*. Before a *t* it must be changed into *h*. *cv = qu*. *x* is frequent, and occurs sometimes for *hs*, as in *feax*, coma, O. S. *fahs*; sometimes as the inversion of *cs*, as *fixas* for *fiscas*; *axe*, ashes, for *asce*, Goth. *azgo*.

The guttural aspirate *ch* occurs only in later documents instead of the tenuis *c*, as *chirche, ich*, for *cyrce, ic*. The words *lichoma* (corpus), *flæschoma* (corpus), *bláchleor* (pale-faced, fair), must be read *lic-homa, flæsc-homa, blác-hleor*.

Old Frisian *g, k*. The initial *g* preceding *e* or *e* may be rendered by the spirant *j*, as *jeva*, to give; *jeld*, money (Germ. geld); *jest*, ghost. The prefixes *g, je, gi*, drop the initial consonant, as *unge*, eat; *ungath*, eunt, for *gunge, gungath*; *iuth*, fundit, from *giata*. When in the middle of a word *g* occurs preceded by *e* and followed by a thin vowel or consonant, it is vocalized, and with its antecedent vowel forms the diphthong *ei*, which occasionally is condensed into *i*; e. g. *rein*, rain, from *regen*; *brein*, brain, from *bregen*; *neil*, nail, from *negel*; further condensed into *brin, nil*, &c. Before full vowels, as *a* and *u*, the media *g* is preserved,

CONSONANTS.

as in the plural forms *degar, degum, wega, wegena; ein,* own (Germ. eigen), for *egin; keia,* key; *heia* for *hegen,* retain the vocalized forms. At the end of a word *g* can only occur in the combinations *ng* and *gg*; in all other cases it is either vocalized, as *wei,* humour, for *weg*; or it is replaced by *ch*. The gemination *gg* is, in the middle of a word, either replaced by the palatal *dz* (vid. infra), as in *sidza* for *sigga, seqqa,* to say; or it has been vocalized, *leia* for O. S. *leggjan,* to lay; but rarely it remains as in *eg,* gen. *egges,* edge.

The tenuis is represented both by *k* and *c,* the latter, however, never occurring before *e* or *i*; *k* preserves its position in the middle and at the end of words, except where it yields to *ch* or the palatal. The gemination of the tenuis occurs rarely, as in *smek,* taste (Germ. geschmack), gen. *smekkes; ekker,* acre; *stok, stokkes,* stick (Germ. stock). *qu = kw. x = hs* in *sax,* knife, sword; *sextich,* sixty.

Change of Gutturals into Palatals.—Peculiar to Old Frisian is the conversion of a guttural into a palatal whenever at the beginning or in the middle of a word it is followed by *i* or its Trübung *e,* even when the vowel is dropped. At the beginning of a word the media *g* is not affected: the tenuis *k* is replaced by a palatal sound, which we find rendered by *sz* and *sth,* whenever it precedes an *i* or *e* which is followed by a single consonant or by a combination which contains a liquid; e. g *sthereke,* church; *szin* for *kin,* chin: *k* remains in *kerva,* findere, to carve; *kersten,* Christian. Owing to a mistaken analogy this change is also effected before *e* where it is Umlaut of *a,* and *e* then is fond of passing into *i,* e. g. *szetel* and *sthitel* by the side of *ketel,* kettle, Goth. *katils; tzilih,* Lat. *calix; tzirl, tzerl,* churl, A. S. *ceorl; szelner,* cellar, Lat. *cellarium.* The tenuis remains in *keda,* chain, Lat. *catena; kempa,* champion, &c.

In the middle of a word *g* is replaced by *dz,* and *k* by *ts, tz, tsz,* under the same conditions as mentioned in the preceding case. The combination *ng* is converted into *nsz, nk* into *nz,* e. g. *ledza,* O. S. *leggjan,* to lay; *lidza,* O. S. *liggian,* to lie; *sedza,* to say; *spretsa* and *spreka,* to speak; *thenzja* and *thanka,* to think. As to the pronunciation of these palatals, *sz, sth, tz,* and *tsz,* may have sounded like the English *ch* in 'church,' *dz* like *g* in 'gentleman.' In West Frisian, where the palatal is far more common than in East Frisian, they adopted a simpler mode of rendering the palatal sounds by the letter *z* or *s*.

The negation *ne* as well as pronouns may, as occasionally in Anglo-Saxon, be joined to the following word, in which case an initial *w, h, th,* is dropped, e. g. *nella = ne willa,* nolle; *nertha =*

ne wertha, non fieri; *nesa — ne wesa*, non esse; *nebba = ne hebba*, non habere; *mát = má hit; thut = thu hit;* mujem for *muqe him*.

Old Norse *g, k.* The terminational *g* in the pret. sing. of strong verbs is often dropped, and in this case a preceding diphthong condensed into a single long vowel; *ng* under the same circumstances becomes *kk*, but a terminational *g* can in this case never become *h*. The gemination *gg* may be (1) = A S. *cg*, O.S. *gg*, as *seggr*, man; *seggja*, to say; *leggja*, to lay, better *segja*, *legja*, as in older manuscripts, since the gemination was the later result of the suppression of the *j*. (2) In the combinations *egg* and *igg* the media *g* is a converted *j* and was, according to Old Norse tendencies, doubled at the end and in the middle of words, thus *egg*, egg (A. S. *üg*, O. H. Germ. *ei*). (3) The combinations *ogg*, *ygg* = Goth. *aggv*, *iggv*, which in Old Norse may, as in other dialects, be also rendered by diphthongs; e. g. *gloggr*, Goth. *glaggvus*, O. H. Germ. *klawer*, *klauwer*, A. S. *gleáv*; *hözgva*, to hew (O. H. Germ. *hauwan*, A. S. *heávan*).

The tenuis *k* is also rendered by *c*, chiefly at the end of words; the gemination is *ck* in earlier, *kk* in later documents. The Old Norse gemination, however, very rarely occurs in cases parallel to the Anglo-Saxon gemination *cc* or the O. S. *kk*, as *rekja*, evolvere, O. S. *rekkjan;* but it commonly takes the place of *ng, nk. kt* is sometimes assimilated into *tt.* $x = hs$ in *lax*, salmon; *uxi*, ox; *vaxa*, to wax, grow. $x = cs$ in *ox*, ax, O. S. *acus; sex*, six — dropped in *setti*, sixth. *qu — kv*.

MIDDLE TEUTONIC.

Liquids.

Middle High German. *l* in some very rare cases supersedes *r*, and is itself superseded by *n*, e. g. *kilche* for *kirche* or *chirche*, church; *knobelouch*, garlic, for O. H. Germ. *chlobilouch :* by the side of *ode, oder*, or, we find frequently *alde*.

The terminational *m* of the inflexions is now throughout (except dat. sing.) weakened into *n*, and even the *m* of the root yields occasionally to *n*, e. g. *hein* for *heim*, home; *ohein* for *oheim*, uncle; *lan* for *lam*, lame; *arn* for *arm*. But whenever this inorganic *n* takes its place again in the middle of the word it must return to *m*: *lein, leimes;* *arn, armes*. In modern German the terminational *m* has in this latter case been replaced. *m* is dropped in *nen* for *nemen*, to take; *kon* for *komen*, to come; *frun* for *frumen*. These, however, are quite isolated forms.

CONSONANTS.

n is, in the middle of words, occasionally dropped: *sint*, since, becomes *sit* (Germ. seit, cf. O. Engl. sith); O. H. Germ. *chuning*, king, becomes *kunic* (Germ. konig).

r suffers apocope in several adverbs: *da*, there (Germ. da); *wá*, where (Germ. wo); *hie*, here (Germ. hier, obs. hie); *sá*, so (Germ. so), for O. H. Germ. *dar*, *huar*, *hiar*, *sar*; but the *r* is preserved in *dar*, thither; *war*, whither; *her*, hither (O. H. Germ. *dara, huara, hiara*). Both *me* and *mer*, more (Germ. mer), are used. The fluctuation between *r* and *s* we shall notice hereafter (vid. sub lit. s). Peculiar to some manuscripts is the inversion of the prefix *er* when preceded by a word ending in a vowel, or *r*, or *n*; e. g. *dorebeizte* = *dó erbeizte*, *wirreslagen* = *wir erslagen*, *unrechant* = *unerchant*. The *r* is dropped in *welt* for *werlt*, world (Germ. welt).

The gemination of liquids is rather frequent: *ll* is organic in the words *all*, all; *vallen*, to fall; *stal*, gen. *stalles*, stall; *vel*, gen. *velles*, skin; *gellen*, to shout; *swellen*, to swell: inorganic *ll* arises chiefly out of *li*, e. g. *helle*, hell; *stellen*, to put; *wille*, will; *hülle*, cover. *mm* is organic in *klimmen*, to climb; *swimmen*, to swim; *brimmen*, to roar; — inorganic for *mb* (*mp*), in *wamme* = *wambe*, womb; *kam* = *kamb*, comb; *zimmer* = *zimber*, timber, building; *amt* = *ambet*, O. H. Germ. *ambaht*, ambitus;—for *mn*, *stimme* = *stimne*, voice; *verdammen* from *damnen*, to damn, condemn. *nn* is organic in *spinnen*, to spin; *gewinnen*, to win; *bannen*, to banish; *tanne*, fir; *minne*, love; *brunne*, fountain; *sunne*, sun; *dünne*, thin;—inorganic from *ni*: *henne*, hen; *künne*, kin; *brunne*, armour, breast-plate;—from *mn*: *nennen*, Goth. *namnjan*. *rr* organic: *werren*, to impede; *kerren*, to grunt; *sperren*, to close; *zerren*, to tear, to tease;—inorganic from *rs*: *irre*, erroneous; *dürre*, dry;—from *rn*: *verre* for *verne*, far (Germ. fern); but *sterre* is only dialectically used for the common *sterne*, star (Germ. stern, Goth. stairno, O. N. stiarna, O. H. Germ. sterno; but O. S. sterro, A. S. steorra).

Old and **Middle English.** *l* in words of Anglo-Saxon origin is commonly preserved; in such of French derivation it is often softened into *u*, e. g. O. Engl. *faus*, false; *assaut*, assault; *caudron*, caldron; *shaffaut*, scaffold[1]. It is dropped in *eche*, each, A. S. *ælc*; *whiche* for *wilke*, A. S. *hwýlic*, which; O. Engl. *swilke*, M. Engl. *swiche*, A. S. *swylic*, such.

m and *n* occupy the same position as in Anglo-Saxon. Where in this dialect they are dropped, they remain so through Old English, Middle English, and New English. *m* is dropped

---

[1] *wode*, wood, lignum, has nothing in common with the Dutch *woud*, forest, silva; the former being the A. S. *wudu*, lignum, the latter the A. S. *weald*, silva.

already in A. S. *fíf* for Goth. *fimf*, five (Germ. fünf); *softe*, O. H. Germ. *samfte*, soft (Germ. sanft). *n* is regularly omitted before *f, s, ð*: A. S. *gos*, goose; *toð*, tooth; *us*, us, for O. H. Germ. *kans*, Goth. *tunþus, unsis;* Germ. *gans, zahn, uns*, where the *n* is preserved: so also *konnte* for Engl. *could*, M. Engl. *coude*, A. S. *cúde*, pret. of *cunnan*. But Old English frequently drops *n* where Anglo-Saxon had retained it, i. e. in inflexions and the terminations of adverbs, e.g. A. S. *æftan, foran, hinan, hwanan, niðan, utan, þanan;* O. Engl. and M. Engl. *afer, after, before, henne, hennes, hens*, hence; *wanne, whennes, whens*, whence, &c.

r occupies the same position as in Anglo-Saxon. The metathesis of *r*, which in Anglo-Saxon already had begun, continues in Old English, as *brid, bridde*, bird; A. S. *brid* and *bird; wrohte*, wrought, worked, A. S. *wohrte, wrohte; frost*, A. S. *frost* and *forst; bernen*, to burn, A. S. *beornan, brinnan* (Germ. brennen); *rennen* and *ernen*, to leak, to run, A. S. *rinnen, irnan* (Germ. rinnen); *kerse*, cress, A. S. *cresse* and *cerse*.

Spirants.

Middle High German. *w* must be kept altogether distinct from the soft aspirate *v*, so that *winden, wand, wunden*, are different words from *vinden, vand, vunden*. In the middle of words this spirant occurs chiefly between two vowels, e. g. *frouwe*, woman (Germ. frau); *riuwe*, repentance (Germ. reue); *senewe*, sinew (Germ. sehne), where the preceding vowel may be dropped, as *melwe* for *melewe*, meal (Germ. mehl); *varwe* for *varewe*, colour (Germ. farbe); so also in *gráwen*, to become grey (Germ. ergrauen); *cláwen*, ungulis (Germ. klauen); *pfáwe*, peacock (Germ. pfau); *klewes*, gen. of *kle*, clover (Germ. klee). While thus the spirant *w* remains in its ancient position after long vowels, it appears that it affects short vowels which precede it, and, in accordance with the general tendency of the development of the language to destroy ancient correptions, changes *ew, iw, uw*, into *euw, iuw, ouw,—iuw* especially being a most favourite combination in the Middle High German dialect, so that it stands not only for *iw*, but even for the organic *iu*, as *fiuwer, tiuwer*, for *fiure*, fire (Germ. feuer); *tiure*, dear (Germ. teuer). By this confusion of *iw* and *iuw* the strong conjugations are materially affected and two classes thrown into one, so that *schríen*, pret. *schrei*, has in the plur. and part. *schriuwen, geschriuwen*, instead of *schriwen, geschriwen;* and *bliuwen*, pret. *blou*, has in the plur. and part. *bliuwen, gebliuwen*, instead of *bluwen, gebluwen*. In all these cases the *w* is not introduced for the sake of euphony, but has been organically developed from the vowel *u*, an origin which plainly shows its nature as a true spirant and its distinctness from the aspirate *v*; and this fact is further illustrated by the interchange of *w* and *h* which existed in Old High German already, as O. H. Germ. *sáhen* for *sáwen*, to sow; *fohe* for *fowe*, few; and M. H. Germ. *schiuwen* for *schiuhen*, vereri (Germ. scheuen).

At the end of words the spirant was preserved in Gothic after long vowels or consonants, as *áiv, valv;* after a short vowel it was vocalized in *u*, as *snau, kniu,* instead of *snav, kniv:* in Old High German the spirant at the end of words was always either vocalized in *u* or *o*, or suffered apocope; in Middle High German it always suffers apocope without being vocalized, where it stands in unaccentuated terminations, as *mel, gar,* O. H. Germ. *melo*, meal, *garo*, ready; also in the accentuated root, when it follows after *á, e, ı, uo, ie*, as *grá*, grey; *brá*, brow; *spí*, spue; *ruo*, quiesce; *hie*, succidit; as also in the terminational *ou, in, eu*, we have apocope of the *w*, e. g. *blou, tou, niu, getriu*, for *blouw*, flagellavit (conf. Engl. blow, ictus); *touw*, dew; *niuw*, new, &c. Even in the middle of words *w* is always dropped where syncope of the terminational *e* takes place, whence *brán* instead of *bráwen*, dat. plur. of *brá*, brow; *fröude* instead of *frouwde*, *toun* instead of *töuwen*.

j at the beginning of words is not very frequent. Examples are *já*, yes; *jár*, year; *jagen*, to chase; *jámer*, grief (Germ. jammer); *jehen*, to say, speak, admit; *junc*, young; *jener*, ille. In the middle of words *j* has commonly been dropped, except in a few words where it kept its position after *l* and *r* by transforming itself into *g*, as *ferge*, ferry, nautus, for *ferje; tilgen*, delere, A. S. *dilgjan;* but immediately after a long vowel the spirant has more frequently been preserved, as *bluejen*, to bloom (Germ. blühen); *bruejen*, Germ. brühen; *gluejen*, to glow (Germ. glühen); *fruege*, early, præcox (Germ. frühe). In all these words the *ue* is the Umlaut of *uo*, caused by the spirant *j*, the remainder of the verbal suffix *ja*: where, therefore, the *j* is dropped the cause of the Umlaut is removed, and the original vowel *uo* resumes its place, as in the contracted infinitives *bluon, bruon, gluon*. The same rule holds good for the combination *æj* in *kræjen*, to crow; *sæjen*, to sow; *mæjen*, to mow, which are contracted into *blán* or *blæn, krán* or *kræn*, &c. After *ue* as well as *æ* the spirant *j* is occasionally replaced in manuscripts by *g*. The contractions we have just mentioned have led to some confusion, because words with the combination *æh* are also contracted into *æ*, as *bæn, dræn,* for *bæhen, dræhen,* just as *schuon* for *schuohen*, calcis, and *ruon* for *ruowen*, quiescere; and when the contraction again was dissolved, it easily happened that *dræn* became *dræjen*, and *kræn* became *krælien*.

s. The simple spirant is preserved in many words. Examples:—*glas*, glass; *gras*, grass; *hase*, hare; *nase*, nose; *esel*, ass; *rîse*, giant; *sus*, thus; *kæse*, cheese; *wîse*, wise (Germ. weis); *spîse*, meat (Germ. speise); *los*, loose; *rose*, rose; *mus*, mouse (Germ. maus); *lús*, louse (Germ. lause); *tusent*, thousand (Germ. tausend). *ros*, horse; *kus*, kiss; *gewis*, certain, take in the middle of the word the gemination. The *s* which in Old High German had been changed into *r* is not replaced again, therefore *ber*, berry; *mer*, more; *ror*, reed, Goth. *basi*, *máis*, *ráus*. On the whole, the spirant *s* shows far more stability than either *w* or *h*, if we except the case of rhotacism we have just mentioned.

h, as an initial, is inorganic in *heischen*, to urge, where the older manuscripts have still the correct form *eischen*: in a similar manner *heidechse* by the side of *eidechse*, lizard. At the end of words *h* is always converted into *ch*. In the middle of words *h* is retained between two vowels, as *slahen*, to slay (Germ. schlagen); *trahen*, a tear (Germ. thrane); *zaher*, a tear (Germ. zahre); *sehen*, to see (Germ. sehen); *vihe*, cattle (Germ. vieh); *zehen*, ten (Germ. zehn); *dáhe*, clay (Germ. thon); *vahen*, to catch (Germ. fangen); *náhen*, near (Germ. nahe). It is interpolated between two vowels, an occurrence which in Gothic and Old High German already is observed, and then tends to preserve the shortness of the preceding vowel. In modern German this object would be obtained by doubling the consonant, while *h* is used just in the opposite case, to lengthen the preceding vowel. Middle High German consequently writes *Dánihel*, *Gábrihel*, in order to avoid the forms *Dániel*, *Gábriel*. *h* is dropped altogether with its succeeding vowel where syncope takes place, as *stál*, *van*, *hán*, for *stahel*, steel (Germ. stahl); *vahen*, to catch (Germ. fangen); *hahen*, to hang (Germ. hangen).

The most important combinations which this spirant forms are *hs* and *ht*. Examples of the combination *hs*:—*wahs*, wax (Germ. wachs); *wahsen*, to wax (Germ. wachsen); *ahsel*, axle (Germ. achsel); *sehs*, six (Germ. sechs); *fuhs*, fox (Germ. fuchs); *ohse*, ox (Germ. ochse); *flahs*, flax (Germ. flachs)—examples all of which are found in Old High German already, and which in Anglo-Saxon and English render the *hs* by *ks* (*x*), and in Modern German by *chs* pronounced like *ks*. *ht* occurs in the words *aht*, eight (Germ. acht); *maht*, might (Germ. macht); *naht*, night (Germ. nacht); *man-slaht*, man-slaughter (cf. Germ. schlacht); *reht*, right (Germ. recht); *fehten*, to fight (Germ. fechten); *tohter*, daughter (Germ. tochter); *lieht*, light (Germ. licht).

With this M. H. Germ. *ht* corresponds A. S. *ht* in the identical words, *ahta, miht, niht*, &c., the former represented by the Modern Germ. *cht*, the latter by the Engl. *ght*. *ht* has arisen from the foreign *ct* in *dihten* (Lat. dictare, Germ. dichten), and in rare instances is used for the German *ct* and *gt*, as in the anomalous preterites, *mohte*, might (Germ. mochte), *suohte*, sought (Germ. suchte), &c., which in O. H. Germ. already had *ht*. *ht* is sometimes used for the organic *cht*, as in *laht, mahte, schahte*.

Old and **Middle English.** The spirant *w* is in Old English sometimes replaced by the aspirate *v*, as *was* and *vas, wende* and *vende*. The Teutonic *w* is rendered in French by *gu*, and many Teutonic words have come back into English in their French garb. Hence it happens that of some words we have in English the German and the French form side by side, as *wile* and *guile, ward* and *guard*, &c. (Compare the same letter under the headings, New Teutonic, English.) *w* is preserved in the middle of words after long vowels, e. g. *blawe, knowe, sowe, grewe*, but it is dropped in O. Engl. *feor, four,* A. S. *feower; saule*, soul, A. S. *sáwel; wheol,* wheel, A. S. *hweowol;* and in compounds, as O. Engl. *oht,* aught, A. S. *áht, áuht, á-wiht*, quædam res; *noht,* naught, A. S. *n-á-wiht. n* is the negation *ne*. The terminational *w* is dropped in O. Engl. *tre* and *kne*, where Anglo-Saxon already writes more frequently *treo* and *cneo* than *treow* and *cneow;* it is vocalized when following *e*, as M. Engl. *blew, grew, sew, threw.* The Anglo-Saxon combination *wl* drops the *w*, but *wr* retains it, as O. Engl. *wraþe*, wrath; *wreken*, to wreak. The Anglo-Saxon *cw* is represented in Old English by *qu*: *quellen*, from which N. Engl. *to quell* and *to kill;* O. Engl *comen*, to come, A. S. *cuman* and *cwiman*. The A. S. *hw* is inverted in *wh*, O. Engl. *whær, whæt, white;* or *w* simply is used, as *wer, wat, wen*. Middle English adopts *wh* exclusively.

j, the Anglo-Saxon spirant, is replaced in Old English by *g* or *y*, as *ge* and *ye, get* and *yet*. Where *j* occurs in the middle of a word, Old English assimilates it to the preceding consonant, and the gemination is preserved in Middle English and New English, e. g. *sellan* for *seljan*. But for the lost Anglo-Saxon spirant letter a new *j* comes into the language with the French spirant *j*, which in Old English is rendered by *g* or *j*, as *gewes* and *Jews, gywel* and *jewel*. In Middle English it becomes more frequent, the greater the number of French words imported, and here also it is sometimes replaced by *g*, sometimes even by *ch*, as *subjettes, suget, sochet*—all standing for the French *sujet; magestee* for *majeste*. From this it would almost appear as if *g, j*, and *ch*, had been very similar if not identical in pronunciation.

s in Anglo-Saxon already yields often to rhotacism, as pret. sing. *ceás*, elegi; *forleás*, amisi; *dreás*, cecidi; plur. *curon, forluron, druron*; part. *coren, forloren, droren*. In Old English the *r* disappears from the preterite, but is preserved in the participle— *ycorn, lorn*; but even in these, Middle English drops the *r* and replaces the *s*—*chosen, lost* (but the Old English form in the M. Engl. and N. Engl. *forlorn*). *s* is preserved by a succeeding *t*, as in *dorst*, durst, dare, A. S. *dearr* = *dears*, Goth. *daurs*. A. S. *sc* becomes in Old English and Middle English *sh* and *sch*, or *sc* and *sk*, e. g. *skam* and *scham*, *ship* and *schip* (sometimes even *ss*).

h before *l, n, r*, where in Anglo-Saxon it was often omitted, is never used in Old English, hence A. S. *hláf*, bread; *hladan*, to lade; *hlud*, loud; *hring*, ring; *hnecca*, neck, are in Old English *loue, laden, lud, ring, necke*. *hw*, as we have already observed, becomes in Old English *wh*, or simply *w*; in Middle English always *wh*. *h* in the middle and at the end of words was, in Anglo-Saxon, already often dropped, as *sleahan, sleán*, to slay; *seohon, seon*, to see; *taher, tær, tear*; *ráh, rá*; *fáh, fá*; *táh, tá*; *feoh, feo*; *sceoh, sceo*; O. Engl. *slen, sen, tere, roe, foe, toe, fe, sho*. Final *h* is often turned in Old English and Middle English into *g*, sometimes *gh*, as A. S. *heah*, O. Engl. *hig, hie*, M. Engl. *hig, heig*, N. Engl. *high*; A. S. *neah*, O. Engl. *nig, nie*, M. Engl. *nig, neig*, N. Engl. *nigh*; A. S. þ*eoh*, O. Engl. þ*egh*, M. Engl. *thigh* and *thie*, N. Engl. *thigh*; A. S. þ*eáh*, O. Engl. þ*ogh*, M. Engl. *tho, though*, N. Engl. *though*. The A. S. *h* in the combination *ht* is rendered in Old English and Middle English by *ht, gt*, or *ght*, the latter remains in New English (vid. New Teutonic, English). The *h* in French words, when initial, was sometimes dropped, sometimes retained, probably never pronounced, as *honour* and *onour*, *homage* and *omage*, *heir* and *eyr*.

MUTES.

1. Labials.

Middle High German. The relation of the tenuis and media of labials, as of mutes in general, is regulated by rules unknown to Old High German, according to which at the end of words only the tenues, in the middle of words only the mediæ, are admissible. If therefore a media happens to occur at the end of a word, it must be changed into the tenuis, and if a tenuis finds its place in the middle of a word, it must be changed into the media, e. g. *geben, gap*, give, gave; *diep*, thief, gen. *diebes*.

The relation of the aspirate is rather complicated, because, as in Old High German already, this class of letters very often evades the application of Grimm's law. The Gothic or Saxon tenuis is in Middle High German in accordance with the rule represented by the aspirate; but the organic *b* of Low German, which in High German should be rendered by *p* (as *d* by *t*), commonly preserves its position in the latter dialect too, and yields to the tenuis *p* only at the end of words. The media, therefore, which in High German properly has to take the place of the Low German aspirate, is already engaged elsewhere, and the aspirate left to shift for itself. Thus then we have two distinct aspirates in High German, one which stands for the Gothic tenuis, the other which runs parallel to the Gothic aspirate. The former occurs as an initial chiefly in words taken from the Latin, where they show the tenuis *p* which Old High German already Germanized into *ph*, *pph*, *pf*, as *pfaffe*, papa; *pfawe*, pavo; *pflanze*, planta; *pfunt*, pondus; *pfilaere*, pilarius. These words consistently retained in Low German the Latin tenuis, as we see on comparing the English words *plant*, *pound*, *pillar*, &c. It indeed appears that all the words beginning with a *pf* are of a foreign origin, though in many cases they are of such ancient date and thorough German type that one feels inclined to seek for a Teutonic descent. But in this we must chiefly inquire whether the word exists in several or in but one Teutonic dialect, whether it has a root in a Teutonic or in a foreign language; if the former is the case, its Teutonic origin is more likely, if the latter, we may put it down as a foreign word. Thus Grimm derives *pfat*, path, O. S. *padh*, from the Gr. πάτος: for if it were German it would use the common aspirate *f* or *v* instead of the *ph*, as does *vuoz*, L. Germ. *fot*, foot, for ποδ-ος. Even *pfluoc*, A. S. *plog*, O. N. *plogr*, plough (Germ. pflug), is set down as foreign; and the verb *pflegen*, solere, which has the essentially Teutonic characteristics of the Ablaut, claims in vain a Teutonic descent, for the existence of its Ablaut, though beyond a doubt in Middle High German, is very uncertain in Old High German, Old Norse and Old Saxon; and in Gothic the word is wanting altogether. In the middle of words this *pf* (instead of *f*) occurs as a favourite combination with the liquid *m*, e. g. *kampf*, fight; *tampf*, vapour (Germ. dampf); *strumpf*, stocking; *stumpf*, truncus, stump: *pf* with *n* occurs only after the prefix *en* for *ent*, O. H. Germ. *anti*, as *enpfähen*, to receive (Germ. empfangen); *enpfinden*, to feel (Germ. empfinden); *enfliehen*, to escape (Germ. entfliehen). This *pf* is very common after short vowels, as *zopf*, cirrus; *apfel*, apple; *zapfe*, tap; *kripfen*, to gripe, rapere; *copfer*, copper; *tropfe*, drop. (But the same words occur with *ff* as well.) After long vowels, however, whether in the middle or at the end of words we find only *f*, never *pf* or *ff*, as *sláf*, *sláfes*, sleep; *grîfen*, *greif*, to gripe; *triefen*, *trouf*, to drop; *f* always after *l*, commonly after *n* and *r*, never after *m*.

The second aspirate, which runs parallel to the aspirate in Low German is sometimes indicated by *v*, sometimes by *f*, which the manuscripts use indiscriminately. Grimm proposes to use *v* in all cases; but editors of manuscripts generally adopt *f* before *u*, and some of them even before *iu*, *l*, and *r*, where others prefer *v*, so that we may in one and the same word find *v* and *f* as the initial, e. g. *vinden*, *vant*, *funden*, find, found, found. In the middle of a word *v* should always be used, never *f*; for in this position it really indicates the soft aspirate and exchanges with *f*, as does *b* with *p*, or *d* with *t*; hence *wolf*, *wolves*, wolf; *zwível*, doubt; *frevel*, crime; *hof*, *hoves*, court: but on the whole examples of this kind are rare in purely Teutonic words. For the opposite reason for which we require *v* in the middle, we put *f* always at the end of words. Foreign words always retain their *f*; but the *v* of foreign words always becomes *f* at the end, as *brief* (Lat. breve), whilst at the beginning it may be rendered by *f* or *v*.

The organic gemination of *p* is very frequent; *ff*, where it occurs, is inorganic, and stands for the terminational *pf*, which is commonly changed into *ff* in the middle of the word. *bb* is found in foreign words only.

Old and Middle English. The tenuis holds the same position as in Anglo-Saxon. It is interpolated in the words, O. Engl. *sempster*, seamster, A. S. *seámestre*; *solempne*, solemn. (Compare New Teutonic, **English**.) The media also, when occurring at the beginning or in the middle of a word, remains intact; but as a final letter it is often dropped, as *lam*, *dum*, *wam*, *clime*, by the side of *lamb*, *dumb*, *wamb* (womb), *climb*. It is interpolated after *m* in M. Engl. *slomber*, to slumber, A. S. *slumerian*; O. Engl. and M. Engl. *limb*, A. S. *lim*. The aspirate *f* is often replaced in Old English by its softer relative *v*, where it is initial, as *vogel*, bird, for *fogel*, *vul* for *ful*, *visc* for *fisc*, fish—in which case New English always replaces the hard aspirate; and frequently in the middle of a word—in which latter case the soft aspirate remains in New English too (see New Teutonic, **English**). *f* is dropped in M. Engl. *hefed*, *hed*, head, A. S. *heafod*, O. Engl. and M. Engl. *wifman*, *wimman*, *womman*, A. S. *wíf-man*. *ph* and *f* are in Old English and Middle English often used indiscriminately, as *Farisee* and *Pharisee*, *Filippe* and *Philippe*, and Middle English replaces *ph* by *f*, as in *fantom*, *fantasie*. Thus we observe in

Old English and Middle English a great inconsistency in the application of the letters *v* and *f, f* and *ph*, until, in New English, the national idiom decides in favour of one or another in each particular word.

The Romance *v* is always adopted with the foreign word, e. g. *veray*, true, very (French *vrai*), *vertew*, *vessell*, &c.

2. *Dentals.*

Middle High German. The general relations between media and tenuis we have touched upon already; as a rule the tenuis always supplants the media at the end of a word, and vice versa, the tenuis, when receding from the end to the middle of a word, must be changed into the media. This rule however must so far be modified, as the roots of strong verbs ending in *id, ied* = Goth. *eiþ, iuþ*, change *d* into *t* not only at the end but in the middle of the word too, if they have a short vowel in the Ablaut. Examples:—*sniden, sneit, snite, gesniten*, to cut (Germ. schneiden, schnitt, geschnitten); *sieden, sot, suten, gesoten*, to seethe, boil (Germ. sieden, sott, gesotten). This process in Middle High German is something parallel to the change of ð into *d* in Anglo-Saxon, e. g. *sniðan, snidon; seoðan, sudon*.

When two words, the former ending in *s*, the latter beginning with *d*, coalesce into one, the *d* is changed into the tenuis *t*, e. g. *bistu, muostu, listu, deste* = *des diu* (= Lat. *quo* and *eo* with the comp.), *lis du* (imp. lege).

As the tenuis supplants the media at the end, in a like manner the media may supersede the tenuis when in the middle of a word it occurs after *l, m*, or *n*. This is chiefly the case with the termination *te* of the weak verb, as *kante* and *kande*, cognovit; *rumte* and *rumde*, excessit; *wolte* and *wolde*, voluit. The combinations *de* and *te* are sometimes dropped by syncope, as *schat* = *schadet, gesmit* = *gesmidet, ermort* = *ermordet, gekleit* = *gekleidet, trit* = *tritet, bit* = *bitet*. This syncope, as we see from the examples, takes place in the 3rd pers. sing. of the present tense, and especially in the pret. part. of weak verbs. It is strange that it does not affect the radical vowel at all, while similar syncope with gutturals lengthens the preceding vowel.

z occurs in two modifications *z* and *ʒ* (see supra, **Old High German**), and the rule for their application is pretty much the same as in Old High German. At the beginning of a word we find always *z*, as also in the middle and at the end of words after the liquids *l, n, r*, and after short vowels; *ʒ*, on the other hand, is rarely used after consonants, but very frequently after vowels.

With consonants it chiefly occurs where syncope has taken place, e.g. *hánʒ=han eʒ, hirʒ=hir eʒ*. When it is used after long vowels we put it both at the end and in the middle of a word; occurring after a short vowel it is single *ʒ* at the end, and *ʒʒ* in the middle of the word, e. g. *aʒ aʒen, beiʒ biʒʒen*. *ʒ* is dropped in the verb *lán, lát, lie*, for *láʒen, laeʒet, lieʒ*, and before the superlative termination *ste*, where *ʒ*, together with its succeeding vowel suffers syncope, as *groeste, beste, leste*, for *groeʒiste, beʒʒiste, leʒʒiste*, greatest, best, last; sometimes with 'rück-Umlaut,' *gröste, baste*.

The gemination *tt* occurs after the vowels *a* and especially *i*; *dd* never. *zz* is commonly rendered by *tz* (sometimes *c* or *cz*), e. g. *katze*, cat; *tatze*, foot, claw; *setzen*, to place, to set; *wetzen*, to wet; *witze*, wit; *switzen*, to sweat; *hitze*, heat. (Compare the *t* in the identical English words and the *tz* in Germ. *katze, tatze*, &c.) *ʒʒ* · *gaʒʒe*, street (Germ. gaße[1]); *waʒʒer*, water (Germ. waßer); *haʒʒen*, to hate (Germ. haßen); *neʒʒel*, nettle (Germ. neßel); *meʒʒer*, knife (Germ. meßer); *eʒʒen*, to eat (Germ. eßen); *wiʒʒen*, to wit, know (Germ. wißen). (Concerning the relation of this *ʒ* to the Modern German ß and the English *t*, see New Teutonic, **German**.)

The combinations into which dentals enter with other consonants remain on the whole the same as in Old High German, so that even *tw* and *dw* are still kept distinct, as in *twerc*, dwarf (Germ. zwerg), and *dwerch*, athwart (Germ. *zwerch*); the latter, however assuming in late Middle High German documents the inorganic form *tw*, which, like the organic *tw*, is in New High German converted into *zw* (see New Teutonic, **German**), while the Middle High German *zw* represents the same combination in Old High German.

Old English and Middle English. The Anglo-Saxon tenuis *t*, in its initial position, is preserved through Old English, Middle English, and New English, and even in the middle and at the end of words, Old English persistently keeps up the Anglo-Saxon tenuis which in Middle English occasionally, and more frequently in New English, had to yield to the encroachment of other consonants. (See New Teutonic, **English**.)

The fluctuation between the media *d* and the soft aspirate ð which had commenced in Anglo-Saxon already, continues in Old English and Middle English, as *hider, wider, weder*, or *wither*, &c., until New English finally decided in favour of the aspirate *hither, whither, weather*. The media is dropped in O. Engl.

---

[1] Commonly spelt *gasse*, &c.

gospell, for A. S. *god-spell;* O. Engl. *answeren*, A. S. *and-swarian*, Germ. *ant-worten*. *d* is interpolated in þ*under*, thunder, A. S. þ*unor*.

Though the distinction of a soft and a hard aspirate, which Anglo-Saxon indicated by the signs ð and þ very probably continued in Old English (as in fact it exists in the English of the present day), the distinction was no longer kept up in writing, and Old English documents commonly rendered both aspirates by þ, Middle English by *th*.

d for *th* in O. Engl. *magde*, maid; *redie*, ready (A. S. *mægeð* and *mægden*, *hræð* and *hræd*); M. Engl. *cude*, could; O. Engl. *quod*, quoth; A. S. *cwæð*.

z, which is no Anglo-Saxon letter, becomes in Old English rather numerous, being imported with French words, and later on assuming an unusual position by supplanting the organic *g*, e. g. *dozter* for *dogter*, daughter, *zeres* for *geres*, *zimmes* for *gimmes*, gems. From this inorganic position, however, *z* soon disappears again, and is restricted to its place in foreign, i. e. non-Teutonic words.

3. *Gutturals.*

Middle High German. The tenuis is commonly rendered by *k*, in some manuscripts by *c*; Grimm puts *c* at the end, *k* at the beginning and the middle of words. The gemination *kk* is expressed by *ck*. Some manuscripts use *ch* in words where the correctness of the tenuis *k* cannot be doubted, and such erroneous spelling must be considered a fanciful innovation of the copyists. This is especially the case at the beginning of words, where High German, instead of following Grimm's law by placing the aspirate *ch* for the Low German tenuis, prefers to adopt the latter and keep it up in spite of rules and laws, while the dentals and labials are more consistent in this case and introduce the regular aspirate, *z* for *t*, and *pf* for *p*. But on the other hand the High German *k* also takes the place of the Gothic *g*, and follows in this the dictates of Grimm's law. Thus then in German words *k* commonly corresponds (1) to the Gothic *k*, chiefly at the beginning of words, which however may be turned into the aspirate in the middle and at the end of words, and (2) to the Gothic media *g* chiefly at the end of words, where Middle High German never tolerates any media whatever, but always converts it into the tenuis. The interchange of the guttural tenuis and media is regulated by the same rules laid down for dentals and labials.

g is a frequently occurring consonant at the beginning and in the middle of words; at the end it is, as we have just stated, always replaced by the tenuis. *g* suffers syncope in *morne* for *morgene*, to-morrow; *pflît*, *lît* for *pfliget*; *ligt*, suescit, jacet. It is vocalized in *i* in the combination *eg*, *e* being the Umlaut of a more ancient *a* in *agi* (the Umlaut produced by the inflexional *i*); and sometimes both the forms *eg* and *ei* are used side by side, e. g. *leite = legte*, laid, posuit; *treit = tregt*, fert; *eise = egese*, fear; *meide = megede*, maid; *gein = gegen*, versus (cf. a-gain, a-gain-st); *getreide = getregede*, corn. Later authors introduce the vocalization *ei* even for *age*, as *meit = maget*, *kleit = klaget*, plangit; *seit = saget*, dicit; *ge-seit = ge-saget*, dictus: the Umlaut *e* in these words is, of course, inorganic, because for *klagt*, *magt*, no forms like *klegt*, *megt* exist. A case opposite to this vocalization of *g* in *i* is the development of *g* from *j* (see sub lit. j).

The media *g* sometimes supplants the *h* in the conjugation of the strong verb, so that (1) the verb *ziehen*, for instance, in the pret. and pret. part. adopts everywhere *g* for *h* when the latter recedes from the end to the middle of the word, as *züge*, traxisti; *zugen*, traxerunt; *gezogen*, tractus: at the end however it must not be changed into the tenuis *zoc, zuoc*; though we find the aspirate in *zoch*, which stands for the original *h* in *zoh*. (2) Some verbs change the final *ch* (which stands for *h*) into *c* (which stands for *g*), e. g. *slahen*, to slay, pret. *sluoc, sluege, sluogen, geslagen*, instead of *sluoh, sluehe*, &c. To the same category belongs the word *genuoc, genuoge*, enough, for Goth. *ganohs, ganoháí*, and the inorganic forms of the verb *sehen*, to see. Such changes of *h* into *c* and *g* in the conjugation of the strong verb occur sometimes in Old High German already, and become still more frequent in New German, where they even affect the forms of the present tense.

ch has two distinct sources from which it derives its origin:—
(1) it stands for the spirant *h*: *noch*, ad huc; *doch*, tamen; *joch*, atque; in the preterites *sach*, saw; *geschach*, happened; *zoch*, drew; *floch*, flew; *nach*, after; *hoch*, high; *schuoch*, shoe; (2) for the Gothic tenuis when preceded by a vowel in the middle or at the end of a word. This *ch* is essentially distinct from the preceding one, inasmuch as it retains its position on receding from the end into the middle of the word, where the first *ch* is replaced again by *h*. Examples:— *ach* (interj.), *bach*, brook; *dach*, roof; *swach*, weak; *wachen*, to wake; *brechen*, to break; *rechen*, to wreak; *ich, mich, dich, sich*, pronouns; *woche*, week; *bleich*, bleak, pale; *eich*, oak; *siech*, sick; *buoch*, book; *suochen*, to seek. (3) When it occurs in combination with *s*, the Gothic

k always becomes *ch,* as *schín,* splendour; *schrift,* writ; *leschin,* to quench. These three different kinds of *ch* are preserved in New High German, whilst all others with few exceptions are replaced again by the tenuis *k*. As we have mentioned before, even in Middle High German the aspirate *ch* does not occur at the beginning of a word. In Middle High German *ch* has occasionally its origin in the conflux of two syllables, as *siecheit = siech-heit,* sickness; *juncherre = junc-herre,* a young nobleman, a *junker.* Where thus *c* and *h* flow together New High German puts *k* instead, as in *junker.* Where *ch* occurs before the termination *t* of the verb, it does not, like the N. H. Germ. *cht,* supplant *ht,* but is owing to contraction, as *bricht = brichet;* N. H. Germ. *cht* is always M. H. Germ. *ht.* The geminations *kk* (*ck*) and *gg* are frequent. (Concerning the combinations *hs* and *ht,* see sub lit. **h**.)

Old and Middle English. The *k* sound of Anglo-Saxon words is commonly preserved before dark vowels and the liquids *l, n, r.* Whilst Anglo-Saxon uses *c* only to indicate the guttural tenuis, Old English and Middle English apply *c* and *k* indiscriminately for the same purpose. Before the thin vowels *e* and *i* we sometimes find in late Anglo-Saxon already *k* changed into *ch,* and this wayward alteration has been kept up to the present moment. Thus in O. Engl. and M. Engl. *kepe, kene, king,* we have the Anglo-Saxon guttural tenuis *cepan, cene, cyning;* but in O. Engl. and M. Engl. *chin, child, chicken,* the Anglo-Saxon tenuis *cin, cild, cicen,* has been converted into the palatal *ch.* In Teutonic words, late Saxon and early Old English authors sometimes used *k* (*c*) and *ch* side by side, as *ic* and *ich,* I; *dic* and *dich,* thee; *benc* and *bench, awaken* and *awachen;* where *ch* no doubt had the *k* sound. Before the A. S. *y,* which is Umlaut of *u,* one would expect to see the guttural tenuis preserved; but even in this case it sometimes yielded to *ch;* thus we find the *k* sound, preserved in O. Engl. and M. Engl. *kin, king,* A. S. *cyn, cyning;* changed into *ch* in O. Engl. and M. Engl. *chirche,* church, for *kirke* (Scotch). Where in Anglo-Saxon *c* precedes *ea, eo, eá,* Old English decides in favour of *ch,* whether the thin vowel or the dark vowel ultimately gained sole possession; e. g. O. Engl. and M. Engl. *chalk, chaff, chester, cherl, chepmon,* merchant (Germ. kaufman), A. S. *cealc, ceaf, ceaster, ceorl, ceápman.* O. Engl. *kerfen* alone preserves the guttural of A. S. *ceafor,* where New English further introduces the guttural *ch, chafer.*

The Anglo-Saxon *g,* in its initial position, commonly remains intact in the succeeding periods of Saxon speech; but in the combination *ge* it is in Old English and Middle English commonly vocalized in *i* or *y*[1], especially in the past participle of the verb, where it represents the augment *ge-* which is still preserved in the German and Dutch verb. Examples are abundant in every Old English and Middle English author, of which we mention a few for the sake of illustration :—*i-seen*, seen (Germ. ge-sehen); *i-cume*, come (Germ. ge-kommen); *i-geten*, eaten (Germ. gegessen); *i-last*, lasted; *i-wiss*, certain (Germ. ge-wiss); *y-wont*, wont, accustomed (Germ. ge-wohnt); *i-armed*, *y-set* (Germ. ge-setzt); *y-done* (Germ. ge-than); *i-nome*, taken (Germ. genommen).

g, in the combination *eg* and *äg*, is vocalized in *i*, which, with the preceding vowel, forms in Old English the diphthong *ei* (N. Engl. *ai*), whilst in German the *g* is preserved; e. g. O. Engl. and M. Engl. *feir* or *fæir*, fair; *neil* or *næil*, nail (Germ. nagel); *twein*, twain; *rein* (Germ. regen); *seil* (Germ. segel); *seide*, said (Germ. sag-te); *wei*, way (Germ. weg),—A. S. *fäger, nagel, twegen, regen, segel, segede, wega.*

g and *w* maintain in Anglo-Saxon already a kind of relationship, by which the spirant *w* sometimes takes the place of the guttural media. This occurs in certain verbal forms, as A. S. *sægon, sáwon, gesegen, gesewen, gesen* (see, saw, seen, &c.); O. Engl. and M. Engl. *drage, drawe, dragen, drawen* (drag and draw); O. Engl. *slogen, slowen, i-slagen, i-slawen* (slay, slew, slain); M. Engl. *slog, slow, slew.*

The Anglo-Saxon final *g* is rarely preserved, but commonly vocalized in *i*, and thus, with the preceding vowel, again forms the diphthong *ei* or *æi* (N. Engl. *ay*), e. g. O. Engl. *dæi*, day; *mæi*, may; *heie*, hay, — A. S. *dag, heg, mag*, Germ. *tag, mag.* The *g* is dropped in O. Engl. *bodi, mani, gredi*, greedy; A S. *bodig, manig, grædig.* The Anglo-Saxon combination *ig* is turned in Old English into *ewe*, and vocalized in the New English *ow*, as, A. S. *sorg* (Germ. sorge), O. Engl. *sorewe*, N. Engl. *sorrow;* A. S. *gealga* (Germ. galgen), M. Engl. *galwe*, N. Engl. *gallows;* A. S. *mearg*, M. Engl. *mereg, merew*, N. Engl. *marrow.*

The Romance *g* has the sound of the guttural media before dark, that of the soft palatal before thin vowels.

ch does not exist in Anglo-Saxon, but has been introduced into late Anglo-Saxon and Old English from the French, where it undoubtedly had, as it still has, the sound of the English sibilant *sh*.

The gemination of the tenuis is frequent in Old English and Middle English, and continues to be marked *ck*. *gg* exists in

---

[1] The transition sound is marked by ȝ which may have had the sound of the English spirant *y*, as in 'year,' and thus partook of the nature of a semi-vowel.

some words, as *egge, slegge,* sledge; *wegge,* wedge,—A.S. *ecge, slecge, wecge;* or it appears side by side with its vocalized form *i,* as O. Engl. *liggen* and *lien,* to lie (A. S. licgan, Germ. liegen); *seggen* and *seien,* to say (A. S. secgan, Germ. sagen); *leggen* and *leien,* to lay (A. S. lecgan, Germ. legen); M. Engl. *biggen* and *bie* (A. S. bycgan), to buy.

NEW TEUTONIC.

Liquids.

German. The Middle High German *n* for *m* at the end of a word is discontinued and the ancient *m* re-admitted to its position, hence never *hein,* but *heim,* home. The Middle High German apocope of the *r* is disused in *hier,* here, *hie* being an obsolete and dialectic form; but apocope is preserved in *da,* there; *wo,* where; while on the other hand the *r* re-appears again in the compounds *dar-in,* there-in; *wor-in,* where-in, &c. The gemination of liquids is frequent.

English. In words of Latin origin, which in Old English and Middle English had, in imitation of the French language, softened the *l* into *u,* the liquid is restored to its position, hence *false, assault, caldron,* for O. Engl. *faus, assaut, caudron;* but the *l,* though written, remains mute in *palm, chalk, psalm,* a fact which by analogy occurs even in Saxon words, as *calf, talk, halser, folk, yolk.* The *l* is dropped altogether in *each,* O. Engl. *eche,* A. S. *ælc;* which, O. Engl. *whilke,* A. S. *hwylíc;* such, O. Engl. *swilke,* A. S. *swylíc.* The Scotch dialect retains the *l* in *whilk* and *ylc,* but drops it in other cases, as *haud* for *hold, gowd* for *gold, hauf* for *half;* and at the end of words, *fa'*=*fall, ca'*=*call, woo'*=*wool.* Metathesis has taken place in *apple,* M. Engl. *appelle,* A. S. *appel;* cattle, M. Engl. *catelle;* marble, M. Engl. *marbelle.* We have the inorganic *l* in *could,* A. S. *cude; principle,* Lat. *principium; myrtle,* Lat. *myrtus; syllable,* Lat. *syllaba.*

m, where once dropped in Anglo-Saxon, never regained its position, hence *five, soft,* for Germ. *funf, sanft,* where *m* is replaced by *n.* After the Anglo-Saxon period great havoc takes place among the inflexions and terminations, in which *m* had been one of the favourite consonants. It is consequently dropped in the adverbial forms *between,* A. S. *betweonum; amid*(*st*), A. S. *middum; while,* A. S. *hwilum*—but in *whilom* the old form is retained.

n has superseded *m* in the words *count*, Lat. *comes*; *noun*, Lat. *nomen*. The intrusion of *p* in the place of *m* is peculiar in words such as *Peg=Meg*, Margaret; *Polly=Molly*, Mary.

n is never again restored in the words where Anglo-Saxon had dropped it, hence we have Engl. *goose, tooth, other, could, mouth, us*, for Germ. *gans, zahn, ander, konnte, mund, uns*. After the Anglo-Saxon period it has been dropped, together with the terminations; e. g. *after, before, hence, out, whence, thence,*—A. S. *äftan, foran, hinan, útan, hwanan, þanan*; while it is preserved in Germ. *vorn, hinnen, außen, wannen, dannen*. In derivations: *waste*, A. S. *westen*; *game*, A. S. *gámen*; *eve*, A. S. *æfen*—while *even* preserves the old form. In compounds: *eleven*, A. S. *endlif*; *Thursday*, A. S. *þunresdäg*; *Oxford*, O. Engl. *Oxenford*, A. S. *Oxnaford*; *Sunday*, O. Engl. *Sonenday*, A. S. *Sunandäg*. *n* is inorganic in *Ned* for *Ed-ward*, *Nancy, Nanny*, for *An-na*; *messenger*, Fr. *messager*; *passenger*, Fr. *passager*. *n* is superseded by *m* in some words, especially where it precedes *p* or *f*, e. g. *hemp*, A. S. *hanep*, Germ. *hanf*; *tempt*, Fr. *tenter*; *comfort*, O. Fr. *confort*; *Cambridge*, A. S. *Canta-brycge*. *n* is mute where it follows upon *m*, as *hymn, solemn, autumn*.

r, with few exceptions, retains the place which it occupied in Anglo-Saxon. It is dropped in *to speak*, A. S. *sprecan*, Germ. *sprechen*; it is inorganically introduced in *groom, bride-groom*, A. S. *guma*, man. Metathesis of the *r* as in Old English and Middle English.

Dutch. Prosthetic *n*, i. e. an inorganic *n* placed before the initial vowel, occurs in *narst = arst*, erst, first; *narm = arm*. (Compare Engl. *Ned, Nanny*, and the dialectic *naunt = aunt*.) We have metathesis of *r* in *borst=brost*, breast; *born=bron*, well, fountain : comp. Germ. *born* and *brunnen*. Interchange of *r* and *s*: *bes* and *ber*, berry; *mes* and *mer*, parus. The Dutch language shows a predilection for the combination *mp* which occurs in very many words. Whenever a terminational *m* of the root is followed by the diminutive particle *je*, a *p* is interpolated, and thus the favourite combination obtained, e. g. *bloem*, bloom, blossom, flower, *bloempje*; *worm, wormpje*: but if the root ends in *l* or *n*, a *t* is preferred as an intermediate letter between the root and the particle, as *vogel*, bird, *vogeltje*; *sten*, stone, *stentje*.

Swedish. Initial *l, n, r*, represent the same consonants of Old Norse, as well as the combinations *hl, hn, hr*, of the latter dialect. Old Norse *vl* is represented by simple *l*; *hv* and *vr* retain their position. Initial as well as terminational *n* remains excluded from words where Old Norse had dropped it. *r* and *s* remain in the same relation in which we found them in Old

CONSONANTS.

Norse, therefore *r* in *ber*, berry; *hare*, hare; *vára*, to be; *vår*, our; *s* in *oss*, us. *gn* is nasal, as *ragn* (rain) = *rängn*; *vagn* (waggon) = *vangn*. Alternation between *ld* and *ll* is to be noticed in *guld*, gold; *gyllen*, golden; *ll* for *lt* in *kall*, cold (Germ. kalt); *hålla*, to hold (Germ. halten). In the same manner occurs *nn* for *nd*, *nn* for *rn*, *mm* for *mb*: thus *lam, kam* = *lamm, kamm* = *lamb, kamb*, lamb, comb. *mn* stands for O. N. *fn*: *hamn* = *hafn*, harbour (Germ. hafen).

Danish. Old Norse *ll, nn,* become *ld, nd*; hence *galde*, gall; *stald*, stall; *kalde*, call; *ilde*, ill; *fuld*, full; *skind*, skin; *kind*, kin; *rinde*, to rin: but we find the O. N. *ll* preserved in *al, alle*, omnis; *stille*, to still; *nenne*, to dare; and *ll* for O. N. *ld* in *heller*, potius. As a rule the O. N. *ld* and *nd* remain in Danish too, as *alder*, age (Germ. alter); *kold*, cold (Germ. kalt); *holde*, to hold (Germ. halten); *haand*, hand; *vinde*, to find; while Swedish prefers the geminations *ll* and *nn*, rejecting the O. N. *d* even in words like *falla*, to fall; *hålla*, to hold; *munn*, mouth (Germ. mund). If Danish has on one hand lost many of the Old Norse geminations *ll* and *nn*, it found, on the other, new inorganic geminations, as *molla*, to mould; *domme*, dumb; *kammen*, the comb; *lammet*, the lamb. O. N. *mp* remains. *Dronning*, queen, has arisen by assimilation of *drottning* (comp. O. H. Germ. *truhtin*, lord).

SPIRANTS.

German. The spirant *w* in Old High German was vocalized if occurring between two vowels, and thus formed diphthongs such as *au* out of *aw*, *eu* out of *ew*; and then at a later stage of the language it re-assumed its place even after the diphthong, so that *frawe* became *fraue*, and *fraue* again *frauwe*. This *w* is preserved still in Middle High German, but modern German has dropped it altogether in the middle as well as at the end of words, hence *frau, treu, blau; mel, meles, schnee, schnees*. After *l* and *r* the labial media has taken the place of the spirant *w*, as *farbe*, colour; *milbe; wittib*, widow, and *witwe;* the *w* remains in *loewe*, lion, and *moewe*, gull.

s is inorganic in many words where ſʒ ought to be used. This is chiefly the case in the neuter pronouns *das* and *was*, and the neuter termination of all the adjectives, *weiſʒes, gutes, schones*, &c. (More about this *s*, see infra, sub lit. ſʒ.) The Middle High German combinations *sl, sm, sn, sw,* turn the *s* into *sch*, as *schlagen* for *slagen, schmecken* for *smeken, schnell* for *snel, schwach* for *swac*; in the combinations *sp* and *st*, however, the *s* remains, but only in writing, while the sound is identical with *sch*, as *stehen, sprechen*, pronounced *schtehen, schprechen*.

j stands as an initial spirant since the most ancient times in words like *ja, jar, jung*, where it is replaced in English only in spelling, not in sound, by *y*: *yes, year, yoke, young*. The spirant *j* is inorganic in *je jetzt*, for *ie, iezt*, which are dialectically still pronounced *í, ízt*, while *ie* has preserved its place in the negative *nie = ne ie*: cf. Engl. *never = ne ever* (*ne* = not). In the middle of a word it is no longer used, but commonly replaced by *h*, as *gluehen*, to glow; *bluehen*, to blossom; *drehen*, to turn; *sæhen (sæen)*, to sow, instead of M. H. Germ. *gluejen, bluejen, dréjen, sæjen*.

h has regained its ancient position in *sáh, gescháh*, instead of the M. H. Germ. *sach, geschach*. It is inorganically used for *j* in *gluehen, bluehen*, &c., as we have just seen; so also in *ruhe* for *ruwe*, and most frequently where it is introduced merely as the mark of the long vowel, as *sehnen, dehnen, mahnen*, for *senen, denen, mánen*. Instead of the more ancient *ht, hs*, we find always *cht, chs*; e. g. *macht*, might; *nacht*, night; *wachsen*, to wax, grow—M. H. Germ. *maht, naht, wahsen*.

English. Where the spirant *w* interchanged in Old English with the labial aspirate *v*, modern English has again established the former; therefore always *to wake, was, wash, wood*, never *vake, vas*, &c. It has become mute in *who, whose, whom*; is dropped in *ooze* (A. S. *wos*, sap); while in *whole* (A. S. *hál*) and its compounds, and in *whoop* it is an inorganic addition. The German spirant *w* is rendered by the French *g, gu*, e. g. A. S. *wile*, O. Fr. *guile*; A. S. *weard*, O. Fr. *guard*; and the words having been re-imported from France, it so happens that in modern English we have both the Saxon and French forms of the same word side by side, e. g. Saxon *warrant, warrantee*, French *guarantee*; Saxon *ward*, French *guard*; Saxon *re-ward*, French *guerd-on*; Saxon *wise*, French *guise*; Saxon *wile, wily*, French *guile*.

Terminational *w* is always mute after dark vowels: *to sow, to mow, saw*; it is vocalized in *hew* (pronounced = *hu*), O. Engl. *hewe*, A. S. *heáwe*; dropped in *four, soul, wheel, aught, naught*; at the end in *tree, knee*, and vocalized in *grew, blew, knew*. The combination *wr* remains, but the *w* is mute: *wrath, wreak, wrestle*. The combination *hw* becomes *wh*, but in pronunciation it is still like the ancient *hw*, as *where, when, why = hwere*, &c.

j. This spirant is replaced in modern English by *y*: *yes, year, yoke, young*. The present English *j* is imported from France, and is therefore chiefly found in words of French derivation, as *jay, joy, just, jest, jaw*—but it has found its way into German

CONSONANTS.

words too, replacing the media *g*, as *jump; jabber*, by the side of *gabble*. In the same manner we still have *j* and *g*, side by side, *jail* and *gaol*, Lat. *caveola, gabiola*, O. Fr. *gaiole, jaiole; jennet* and *gennet*, Lat. *genista*, Fr. *genet; jill* and *gill, jingle* and *gingle*.

s. The Old English *r* for *s* is preserved only in *forlorn*, everywhere else the *s* is replaced: *chose, chosen, lose, lost, froze, frozen*. The *s* is preserved by the succeeding *t* in *durst*. It often cedes its place to *c*, as *mouse, mice*, A. S. *mús, mys; pence*, O. Engl. *pens; ice*, A. S. *ís; twice*, M. Engl. *twies;* so also *thrice, whence, thence, since*, M. Engl. *sithens*, A. S. *siððan*. The Anglo-Saxon combination *sc* is commonly rendered by *sh*: *shame, sharp, sheep, shot, shut, shrub; sc* however is preserved in *scale, scrape, scurf, score, screech*. *st* is preserved throughout. Metathesis of *s* still occurs in dialects: *claps* for *clasp, aps* for *asp, ax* for *ask*.

The French *s* became much modified in English. It has been replaced by *c* in *peace*, O. Fr. *pais; palace*, O. Fr. *paleis;* by *sh* in *finish*, Fr. *finiss-ons* of *finir;* and in the same manner most French verbs in *ir* with the characteristic *ss*. *s* has been dropped both in Saxon and French words: *cherry*, O. Fr. *cherice; riddle*, A. S. *rædelse; alms* (now used as a plural), A. S. *ælmesse; riches*, O. Fr. *richesse; noisome* for *noise-som; exile*, Lat. *exsul*. This spirant has been added inorganically in *smelt* from *melt, squash* from *quash; scratch*, Germ. *kratzen; sneeze*, Germ. *niesen;* and in *island*, A. S. *ealand*, Fr. *isle; aisle*, Fr. *aile*.

We distinguish in English a surd and a soft *s* sound, the former indicated by *s*, the latter by *z*, a distinction we met in the Gothic already. Surd or hard *s* is commonly used at the beginning of words, after short vowels, after liquids, and after gemination or doubled consonants; the soft *s* we usually pronounce between two vowels, after vowels and soft consonants, the inflexional *s*, and *s* as a termination before *e* mute.

h. This letter had in Anglo-Saxon already to represent both the spirant and aspirated guttural. The initial *h* has, after many fluctuations in Old English and Middle English, resumed its position in New English; but the Anglo-Saxon *hit* remains in New English as in Old English *it*. Before the consonants *l, n, r*, the *h* is never replaced, and hence we write as in Old English, *loaf, lade, loud, ring, neck*—A. S. *hláf*, &c. *hw* is inverted into *wh: who, what, while*—A. S. *hwa, hwat, hwíle;* but the ancient sound remains in *what, while*, &c. *h* is dropped in the middle and at the end of words: *wheel, slay, see, tear; roe, foe, doe, fee, shoe*, for A. S. *hweohol, sleahan*, &c., and *rah, fáh*, &c. This letter is preserved and strengthened into *gh*, but the combination is mute, as in *high, nigh, though, thigh*—A. S. *heah, neah,* &c.; and *knight, sight, light, wight, night*—A. S. *cniht, siht,* &c. So also with the *h* which has its origin in *c* or *g*, as *right*, A. S. *riht*, from *recian*; *sought*, A. S. *sohte*, from *secan*; *might*, A. S. *meaht*, from *mäg*; *bought*, A. S. *bohte*, from *bycgan*. This *gh* makes everywhere the preceding vowel long, even in French words, *spright*, Fr. *esprit*; but in *delight*, and the obsolete *extraught, distraught*, it more probably renders the Latin *c* in *delicium, extractum, distractum*. In a few instances the *h* is strengthened into *gh*, and the combination pronounced = *f*, e. g. *draught* and *draft*, A. S. *droht*, O. Engl. *draht*; *enough* (rarely *enow*), A. S. *genoh*, O. Engl. *inoh*; *to laugh*, A. S. *hleahhan*, O. Engl. *lahhgen*; *tough*, A. S. *toh*, O. E. *toge*. The initial *h* in Romance words which Old English and Middle English had often dropped, as in *onour, omage*, is replaced in New English, but it remains mute, as in *honour, homage*, Lat. *honor, homagium*. In the word *inveigh*, Lat. *invehere*, the *h* follows the Saxon course, while in *convey*, Lat. *convehere*, it is dropped after the French fashion.

Dutch. As to the spirant *w* we have only to observe that it preserved its position where New High German has rejected it, i. e. after the diphthongs which have been formed by the vocalization of the ancient *w*. Hence, where we read in New High German *frau, bauen*, Dutch continues the forms *vrouw*, woman; *bouwen*, to build; *kouw*, cold; *laauw*, lukewarm (Germ. lau); *paauw*, peacock (Germ. pfau).

j corresponds to the same spirant in German and the semivowel *y* in English, e. g. *ja, jaar, jong*, Germ. *ja, jahr, jung*, Engl. *yes, year, young*.

The Dutch language has, like the English, two letters for the *s* sound, i. e. *s* indicating the hard, *z* the soft sibilant, of which the latter never occurs at the end of a word or syllable, but commonly finds its place in the middle and at the beginning before vowels, while the former is commonly used at the end of words and at the beginning before most consonants, e. g. *zon*, son; *zoeken*, to seek; *zouten*, to salt; *zalf*, ointment (Germ. salbe); *zwaard*, sword; *slim*, bad (Germ. schlimm); *snel*, quick (Germ. schnell); *sprong*, leap (Germ. sprung); *stelen*, to steal; *spreken*, to speak (Germ. sprechen); *slaen*, to slay; *ons*, us (Germ. uns); *was*, was; *is*, is. The combinations *sl, sn*, &c., are never changed as in German into *schl, schn*, nor do *st* and *sp* ever adopt the broad pronunciation as in the German *stechen, sprechen*.

h, which in Middle Dutch was subject to many irregular influences, resumes again its organic position, chiefly at the beginning of words. Remarkable, however, is the fact of this spirant being supplanted, in some words, by the media *d*, e. g. *naader*, nearer (Germ. naher); *vlieden*, to flee (Germ. fliehen); *geschieden*, to happen (Germ. geschehen)—forms which are used in the place of the more common *vlien, geschien*.

Swedish. The spirant *s* remains on the whole as in Old Norse. It is of frequent occurrence in derivative forms of nouns and verbs, as *gumse*, ram; *rensa*, to rinse; *gramsa*, rapere, by contraction of *gumise*, &c.; but especially in adjectives, e. g. *armse*, angry; *ense*, concors; *sorgse*, anxious.

The spirant *j* is a very favourite letter in Swedish. Its relation to the gutturals will be examined later on: it is organic in *já*, yes; *jága*, to hunt (Germ. jagen); and in the combinations *ja, je, jo, jä, jö, ju*, where it is, of course, consonantal, like the German *j* and the English semi-vowel *y* in *yes, year*, &c. The combination *sj* sounds like the English *sh*, as *sjette, sju, sjael,= shette*, &c.

h occurs only at the beginning of words, and is pronounced as in the other Teutonic dialects; but before *j* and *v* it is mute, hence *hvete*, wheat; *hjerta*, heart,=*vete, jerta*.

Danish. The spirants of this dialect are identical with those of the Swedish. As peculiar to Danish we may mention the frequent omission of the initial *j*, as *aar*, year, for *jaar*. *j* commonly represents the Old Norse *i*, in the combinations *io, ia, iö*, &c., as *björn*, bear; *kjoel*, keel. Where a guttural precedes a thin vowel, *j* is interpolated between them, probably in order to indicate a softer pronunciation of the guttural, e. g. *kjende, kjoebe, gjest* for *kende*, &c.

h never occurs at the beginning or the end of words.

MUTES.

1. *Labials*.

German. Though there are two different letters to denote the aspirated labial, yet both *f* and *v* now express one and the same sound. The former is used at the beginning of a word before *u, ei, eu, l, r*, and in foreign words; in all other cases *v* stands as the initial labial, e. g. *futter*, fodder; *fein*, fine; *feuer*, fire; *flucht*, flight; *freund*, friend: but *viel*, much; *voll*, full; *vogel*, bird; *väter*, father; *vor*, fore; and the prefix *ver*. In many cases, however, the original *v* has been supplanted by *f*: *folgen*, to follow; *fangen*, to catch; *befehlen*, to command; always in the middle of a word, hence *gráfen*, earls; *zweifel*, doubts; *wolfe*, wolves; which words in Middle High German always had *v* : *frevel*, crime, alone preserves the *v* in the middle of a word.

English. In a few cases the media takes the place of the tenuis, as *lobster*, A. S. *loppestre; slab*, A. S. *slapp*. The tenuis *p* is interpolated occasionally between *m* and *t*, or *m* and *s*, e. g. *empty*, O. Engl. *emti; glimpse*, A. S. *gleam;* in other cases again New English omits this *p* where Old English had interpolated it, as O. Engl. *sempster*, A. S. *seámestre*, N. Engl. *seamster;* O. Engl. *solempne*, N. Engl. *solemn*.

The media *b* is still written in English, though not pronounced, at the end of words after *m*, where other modern Teutonic dialects have dropped it altogether, e. g. *lamb, dumb, womb, climb*—words in which Old English too used to drop the *b*. English also restores the *b*, though it leaves it mute again, in Latin words which had lost the media in French, as *debt*, Fr. *dette*, Lat. *debita; doubt*, Fr. *douter*, Lat. *dubitare*. In the words *slumber*, A. S. *slumerian; limb*, A. S. *lim; thumb*, A. S. *þuma; crumb*, A. S. *cruma; humble*, Lat. *humilis; number*, Lat. *numerus*, the media has been interpolated. A peculiar and isolated case is the transition of the media *b* into *m* in the word *summerset*, Fr. *soubresaut*.

The aspirated labial is represented by two letters, *f* and *v*; the former of which denotes the hard, the latter the soft aspirate. Initial *f* of Anglo-Saxon words is always restored in New English where Old English used occasionally to replace it by *v*; while at the end and in the middle of words the soft aspirate gains the better over its harder twin, hence *five*, A. S. *fíf; silver*, A. S. *seolfor; devil*, A. S. *deofol; give*, A. S. *gifan; even*, A. S. *éfen; raven*, A. S. *hráfen*. The transition already observed in Old English, of the final *f* into *v* when it recedes into the middle of a word is continued in New English, as *wife, wives; calf, calves*— a transition which must have arisen first at a time when the plurals where still pronounced as bi-syllables, *calves*, &c. The *f* is dropped in *head, woman*, A. S. *heafod, wífman* (see **Old English**).

ph, which properly belongs to foreign words only, is partly preserved in New English, partly replaced by *f*, as *fancy, fantom, frenzy*, and *phenomenon, phrase, pheasant*. In the word *nephew*, the *ph* stands for the *f* of the A. S. *nefa*, O. Fr. and O. Engl. *neuew*.

The use of the soft aspirate *v* in words of Saxon derivation we have already mentioned; far more extensively, however, it is found in words of Latin origin, examples of which will occur to any one. We have only to point out a few extraordinary modifications and changes of the soft aspirates, as for example the transition of *v* into *w* in the word *periwinkle*, Fr. *pervenche*, Lat. *perivinca* ; of *v* into *m*, *malmsey*, O. Engl. *malvesie*, Fr. *malvoisie*: in the word *sennight* = *seven-night*, elision of the *v* and contraction has taken place.

Dutch. Like English the Dutch language very often softens the more ancient hard aspirate *f* into the softer *v*, in which case it corresponds to the German media *b*, e. g. *leven*, to live (Germ. leben); *geven*, to give (Germ, geben); *nevel*, mist (Germ. nebel); *seven*, seven (Germ. sieben). Peculiar to Dutch is the conversion of *ft* into *cht*, as *kracht* for Engl. *craft*, Germ. *kraft*; *achter*, Engl. *after*; fluctuating between *ft* and *cht* is *schaft* and *schacht*, Engl. *shaft*, Germ. *schacht*.

Gemination of the labials, as *pp*, *bb*, *ff*, is very frequent in Dutch. In the word *effen* the *ff* is inorganic for *v* : Engl. *even*, Germ. *eben* ; *neffens*, juxta, Germ. *neben*.

Swedish. The labials hold very much the same positions as in Old Norse. The terminational *f*, when followed by a vowel, becomes *fv*, which indicates a softer sound of the aspirate, as *hafva*, to have ; *léfva*, to live ; the same modification takes place between liquids and vowels, e. g. *sperf*, sparrow (Germ. sperber), *sperfven* ; *ulf*, wolf; *ulfven*, wolves. This *fv* answers in sound to the English *v*, and perhaps the O. S. *ƀ* (*bh*) and O. H. Germ. *v*.

Organic geminations of the labials are frequent. *ff* occasionally stands inorganically in words imported from German : *träffa*, to hit (Germ. treffen); *straffa*, to punish (Germ. strafen); *skaffa*, curare (Germ. schaffen); but the same words occur in their Scandinavian form and with a different meaning : *dräpa*, to strike ; *skapa*, to create. The old aspirate *v* is still preserved before *r* in the words *vrak*, wreck, ejecta maris; *vræka*, to cast out, ejicere ; *vrång*, wrong.

ft stands for O. N. *pt* ; *mn* for O. N. *fn*.

Danish. This dialect, like Swedish, preserves the labials on the whole in their ancient position. But quite peculiar to Danish is the introduction after vowels of the media for the tenuis, which we have already mentioned. Thus *skib*, *gribe*, for the Sw. *skep*, *grípa*, Engl. *ship*, *gripe*. Exceptional is the gemination *pp* in *skipper* (Engl. skipper and shipper).

The aspirate *f*, after vowels and the liquids *l* and *r*, is changed into *v*, e. g. *háv*, pelagus (Germ. hafen); *give*, *gav*, for O. N. *gëfa*, *gaf*, Sw. *gifva*, *gaf*; *solv*, silver. The *f* remains only in the combination *ft*. The soft aspirate *v* is a favourite sound of the soft Danish language, and occurs in all different positions. It is in pronunciation neither exactly like the English *v* nor the

German *w*, but somewhat between the two, so that it might as well be mentioned under the head of spirants, by which it is indeed rendered in the cognate dialects; as, *vaaben*, weapons (Germ. waffen); *vand*, water (Germ. wasser). It is inorganic for the media *g* in *lav*, low; *máve*, stomach (Germ. magen); vocalized in *plou = plov = plog* (Germ. pflug), *hau = have = hage*, where the *g* occasionally reappears, as in *ploug*, *háug*.

The gemination of labials is frequent.

2. *Dentals.*

German. *th*, which had disappeared in Middle High German, reappears again in New German, but it is, wherever it is used, inorganic and objectionable, because it is both in sound and derivation nothing else but the Old High German tenuis, corresponding to the media in English and Low German generally. Examples:—*thal*, dale, valley; *thun*, to do; *thau*, dew; *theil*, deal; *noth*, need; *muth*, mood, courage; *roth*, red. The *h* after the tenuis has probably been introduced in order to mark out and preserve the length of the radical vowel; but if this is the case, it has been put in the wrong position, and it would have been more to the purpose to have written *tahl*, *tuhn*, &c. This misapplication of the *h* was in the sixteenth and seventeenth centuries far more frequent than it is now. Modern writers discard it altogether in *flut*, flood; *brut*, breed; but very inconsistently keep it up in *roth* and *muth*; those only who follow the teachings of historical grammar reject it in all cases where it is used merely for the sake of indicating a long vowel. Perfectly absurd is the attempt to distinguish certain homophonous words of different meaning by the introduction of the letter *h*, as *hut*, hat, and *huth*, pascuum; *ton*, sound, and *thon*, clay; while we are obliged to look for some other criterion than that of spelling, if we wish to know, whether in a given case the word *thor* is used to indicate a *gate* or a *fool*.

The relation between tenuis and media continues, as it was in Middle High German already, rather complicated, nay, it becomes more so by the interchange of *d* and *tt*, as in *schneiden*, to cut, pret. *schnitt*; *sieden*, to seethe, boil, pret. *sott*; but *meiden*, to shun, a verb of the same conjugational class, forms the pret. *mied*. The preterite termination of the weak conjugation is in New German always *te* instead of *de*. In the word *des-to* the tenuis instead of the media in the second syllable is kept up by the preceding *s*.

z occurs, as in Old High German and Middle High German,

as a hard and as a soft sibilant; but while the former has preserved its ancient pronunciation of *ts*, the latter, instead of preserving the sound *ds*, has been flattened into *s*, and is written ß. The German *z* then corresponds to Middle High German *z*, and German ß to Middle High German ʒ. Examples:—*fuß*, foot; *groß*, great; *daß*, that; *aß*, ate; *iß*, eat, imper.; *laß*, let, imper. The inorganic change of long and short vowels in the same word, as *eßen*, to eat, *aß*, ate; *meßen*, to measure, *maß*, is as inconsistent as the change of ß into the gemination *ss* in *essen, messen.* It is an arbitrary rule that ß, when succeeding a long vowel, is allowed to stand at the end or in the middle of a word, but that it must be changed into *ss* in the middle of the word after a short vowel. The old grammarians therefore write *fuß*, plur. *füße*, but *faß*, barrel, plur. *fässer*; *essen*, pret. *aß*; *messen*, pret. *maß*; always *wasser*, not *waßer*. As to pronunciation, this letter is perfectly identical with *s*, and might therefore be rendered by the latter, since *fús* and *gros* would sound like *fuß* and *groß*. This change has actually been effected where the Middle High German ʒ was the termination of the neuter adjective or pronoun, as *és*, it; *das*, that; *was*, what; *gutes*, bonum; M. H. Germ. *eʒ*, *daʒ*, *waʒ*, *guoteʒ*. An absurd mode of spelling has been invented for the distinction of the pronoun and conjunction, the former being spelled *das*, the latter *daß*; though both were originally one and the same word and should therefore be uniformly spelled, just as well as *that*, their English equivalent, both as a pronoun and as a conjunction.

Historical grammar teaches us to use ß in all cases where Middle High German applied the organic ʒ, and this rule is now frequently obeyed by German authors even in works which have no direct bearing upon grammar and which are written for the public at large. It will therefore be well to lay down the rule so as to render it intelligible to those who are not versed in Middle High German. It may be stated as a safe guide in most cases, that in words where the German *s* sound is rendered in English or Dutch by *t*, High German should write ß, e. g. *waßer*, not *wasser*, because of the Dutch and Engl. *water*; *laßen*, not *lassen*, Engl. *to let*, Dutch *laten*; *haßen*, not *hassen*, Engl. *to hate*, Dutch *haten*.

zw represents three ancient combinations, i. e. *dw*, *tw*, and *zw*, which are organically quite distinct; e. g. *zwerg, zwerch, zwei.*

English. The tenuis *t*, when initial, remains as in Old English and Anglo-Saxon. It is changed into the media in *proud*, O. Engl. *prout*, A. S. *prut*; *diamond*, Fr. *diamant*; and into the aspirate *th* in *Thames* (but pronounced *t*), A. S. *Temese*; *author*,

Lat. *autor*. We have *s* instead of *t* in the words *must*, *mos-te* = *mot-te* = *mot-de*, debui; *wist*, A. S. *wis-te* = *wit-te* (comp. A. S. sub lit. s); *glisten*, A. S. *glisian* = *glitian*. *t* is often mute when it occurs between two consonants, as *Christ-mas*, *chest-nut*, *castle*, *mistletoe*. It is dropped in the words *best*, A. S. *betest*, *betst*, *best*; *Essex*, O. Engl. *Est-sex*; *Wessex*, O. Engl. *West-sex*; *dandelion*, Fr. *dent-de-lion*. A *t* is added after *s*, especially after the *s* of the genitive, and in the particles *amids-t*, *amongs-t*, *whils-t*, *agains-t*, &c.; and in the words *behest*, A. S. *behæs*; *thwart*, A. S. þweorh; *tyrant*, Lat. *tyrannus*; *ancient*, O. Fr. *ancien*; *parchment*, O. Fr. *parchemin*.

The media *d* on the whole occupies the same position as in Anglo-Saxon. It is changed into *t* in the words *abbot*, A. S. *abbad*; *partrige*, Fr. *perdrix* (a change more frequent in various dialects). The media *d* and the soft aspirate ð, which in Anglo-Saxon are often fluctuating, in New English finally settle into *th*, as *whether*, *together*, *father*, *mother*, A. S. *hwäder*, *togädere*, *fader*, *modor*. *d* is dropped in *gospel*, A. S. *god-spell*; *to answer*, A. S. *and-swärian*; *wood-bine*, A. S. *vudu-bind* (dialectically even *vine*, *mine*, for *find*, *mind*). The media is interpolated in *gander*, A. S. *gandra*, masc. of *gos*; *alder*, A. S. *alor*; *gender*, Lat. *genus*; *jaundice*, Fr. *jaunisse*. In the termination *ed* of the weak conjugation the *d*, when following upon *p*, *f*, *k*, *ch*, &c., has the pronunciation of the tenuis, as *plucked*, *whipped*, *marked* = *pluckt*, *whipt*, *markt*,—a pronunciation with which the spelling formerly harmonized.

th. In Anglo-Saxon the soft *th* or ð is occasionally replaced by the media *d*, or both are used indiscriminately in certain words. This wavering between the two sounds ceases, however, in Old English already which adopts either one or the other, e. g. A. S. *hræð* and *hræd*, O. Engl. *redie* and *rather*, N. Engl. *ready* and *rather*; A. S. *mägeð* and *mägden*, O. Engl. *mayde*, N. Engl. *maid*; A. S. *lið* and *lid*, N. Engl. *lithe*; but A. S. *burðen* and *burden*, N. Engl. *burthen* and *burden*. The media has been adopted for the aspirate in *murderer*, A. S. *myrðra*; *could*, A. S. *cuðe*, O. Engl. *coupe*, M. Engl. *cude*; *fiddle*, A. S. *fiðele*; *deck* and *thatch*, A. S. þeccan, to cover. For O. Engl. *quod*, N. Engl. reassumes the aspirate, and writes *quoth*, A. S. *cwäð*. The aspirate is replaced by the tenuis, chiefly after the consonants *f*, *h*, *s*, *r*, as *theft*, A. S. þeofð; *height*, A. S. *heahðo*; *dart*, A. S. *darað*. *th* is dropped in *Norwich* for *North-wich*, A. S. *Norðwic*; *Norman* for *North-man*, A. S. *Norðman*; *worship* for *worthship*, A. S. *weorðscipe*.

z is not an Anglo-Saxon letter, but in Old English, where it was chiefly imported with French words, it is rather frequent. It is very peculiar that in Old English this letter occasionally replaces *g* (or *ʒ*), as *dozter* for *dogter*, *zeres* for *geres*; but from this position it soon disappears again, and the letter is limited to foreign words. In New English it continues to occupy its place in foreign words, and frequently encroaches upon the range of the sibilants *s* and *c*, as *to freeze*, A. S. *freosan*; *hazel*, A. S. *häsel*; *hazard*, Fr. *hasard*; *to seize*, Fr. *saisir*; *lizard*, Lat. *lacerta*. Very strange is the word *ginger* for Lat. *zinziber*, the inversion of the case of Old English which places the *z* for the *g* in *dozter = dogter*. *s* and *z* we have side by side in *glass* and *glaze*, *gloss* and *gloze*.

Dutch. The media is terminational again, hence the preterite of the weak verbs ends in *d* instead of the Middle Dutch *t*. The *th* in *thans* is caused by the contraction of *te-hans*, at hand (Germ. zur hand). The use of the media *d* in the place of *h* is peculiar, as *náder*, nearer (Germ. naher); *vlieden*, to flee (Germ. flichen), *geschieden*, to happen (Germ. geschehen), used instead of the more common *vlien*, *geschien*. Dutch has a great facility in slipping over the media *d* and its succeeding *e*, thus forming a contraction and lengthening the vowel of the root, e. g. *vár = vader*, father; *ár = ader*, vein (Germ. ader); *bo = bode*, messenger, (Germ. bote); *blán = bladen*, foliis; *gon = goden*, diis; *woen = woeden*, to rage (Germ. wüthen); *bien = bieden*, to offer (Germ. bieten); *ner = neder*, nether (Germ. nieder). The Dutch way of writing these contractions is, *vaár*, *neer*, *goon*, &c. Just the opposite course is followed in the case of *l*, *n*, *r* being succeeded by *er*, where always a *d* slips in between them; as *minder*, minor (Germ. minder); *merder*, more (Germ. mehr); *kleinder*, smaller (Germ. kleiner); *helder*, lighter (Germ. heller); *schonder*, prettier (Germ. schoner). (As to the relation between *z* and *s*, see sub lit. **s.**)

Swedish. The Old Norse aspirate disappears; where it was initial it is replaced by the tenuis, as *tunga*, tongue; *tung*, heavy; hence the Swedish *t* stands for German *d* (or *z*), and English *th*, e. g. Sw. *ting*, Germ. *ding*, Engl. *thing*; *tistel*, Germ. *distel*, Engl. *thistle*. The tenuis and media retain the same position as in Old Norse. The gemination *tt* is very frequent in Swedish; it stands (1) = O. N. *tt*, as in *skatt* (treasure), *hatt*; (2) = O. N. *ht* in *natt* (night); (3) = O. N. *nt* in *mitt* (meum), *ditt* (tuum), *sitt* (suum). The combination *dt* is of frequent occurrence as the neuter termination of the adjectives in *d*.

Danish. In this dialect also the aspirate gives way, sometimes to the tenuis, sometimes to the media (as in the pronouns *den*, *de*, *der*, &c.), whence a great confusion prevails in this class of mutes. When *d* is terminational, and follows upon a vowel, it is almost pronounced like the soft English *th* (O. N. *dh*), so that in *ved*, with, it sounds *veth*. In the middle of a word it is hardly heard at all, and the word *manden*, therefore, almost sounds *mannen*. The media is, as in Dutch, often dropped between vowels, e. g. *fáer, moer, broer, lær, véjr,* for *fader,* father; *moder,* mother; *broder,* brother; *læder,* leather; *veder,* weather. The geminations *dd* and *tt* are of frequent occurrence.

3. *Gutturals.*

German. The guttural tenuis is represented by *k* and *ck*, and in foreign words by *c*. The media may occur at the end of a word where in Middle High German it was always replaced by the tenuis. *ch* represents different ancient letters; it stands (1) for the spirant *h*: *doch,* yet; *hoch,* high; *noch,* still; *nacht,* night; *wachsen,* to wax, to grow; but the spirant is replaced in the preterite of the strong verbs: *sáh,* vidi; *gescháh,* accidit; *floh,* fugi, instead of Middle High German *sach, geschach,* &c.; (2)= Gothic *k,* where we still use *k* in English, e. g. *schwach,* weak; *machen,* to make; *wachen,* to wake; *brechen,* to break; *eiche,* oak; *siech,* sick.

The Gothic *sk* is always rendered in German by *sch*, Engl. *sh,* e. g. Goth. *skadus,* Germ. *schatten,* Engl. *shade;* Goth. *skaban,* Germ. *schaben,* Engl. *to shave;* Goth. *skildus,* Germ. *schild,* Engl. *shield;* Goth. *skilliggs,* Germ. *schilling,* Engl. *shilling;* Goth. *skohs,* Germ. *schuh,* Engl. *shoe. ch* had in Old High German and Middle High German a much wider range than it has in New High German, for, with the exception of the different cases just mentioned, it is now commonly replaced by the tenuis *k*, e. g. M. H. Germ. *dechen,* N. H. Germ. *decken,* to deck, cover; M. H. Germ. *chindiske,* N. H. Germ. *kindisch,* childish; M. H. Germ. *chirche,* N. H. Germ. *kirche,* church.

English. The tenuis *k* answers to the Anglo-Saxon tenuis *c*. In Old and Middle English *c* and *k* are used indiscriminately; New English decides for the initial *k,* where it is mute, and for *c* where it is pronounced, and then the *c* always preserves the Anglo-Saxon *k* sound before dark vowels and the liquids *l, n, r,* e. g. *to know, knee, knot, knife; to creep, craft, clean, cloth.* Before the thin vowels *e* and *i,* the *c* is in Anglo-Saxon already sometimes replaced by *ch*; Old English adopted either one or the other for each particular word, and the adopted letter has been preserved to the present day; e. g. *to keep,* A. S. *cepan; cheese,* A. S. *cese; keen,* A. S. *cene; chin,* A. S. *cin; child,* A. S.

cild; chicken, A. S. *cicen*. (See **Old English** and **Middle English**.)

Before the Anglo Saxon *y*, which is the Umlaut of *u*, one would expect to see the *k* sound preserved, but it yields even here sometimes to *ch*, e. g. *kin*, A. S. *cyn; king*, A. S. *cyning; kitchen*, A. S. *cycene; church* (Scotch *kirke*), A. S. *cyrice*. Where in Anglo-Saxon a *c* precedes *ea, eo, eu*, Old English already decided in favour of *ch*, which in New English has been kept up, e. g. *chalk*, A. S. *cealc; chester*, A. S. *ceaster; churl*, A. S. *ceorl; chapman* (still in vogue as a proper name, meaning 'merchant,' Germ. kaufmann), A. S. *ceápman*; except *care*, A. S. *cearu; keel*, A. S. *ceol*. A. S. *cw* is N. Engl. *qu*.

In the middle of words *c* is replaced either by *k* or *ch*, as *acre*, A. S. *äcer; fickle*, A. S. *ficol; wreak*, A. S. *wrecan; sink*, A. S. *sincan; to seek* and *beseech*, A. S. *secan; to teach*, A. S. *tæcan; to reach*, A. S. *ræcan*. The *k* sound is commonly preserved at the end of words: *ark, rank, clerk, folk*, A. S. *arc, ranc, clerc, folc*. *c* is dropped in the 1st sing. of the personal pronoun: A. S. *ic*, N. Engl. *I*, Germ. *ich*, Dutch *ik*, and in the suffix *lic*, N. Engl. *ly*, Germ. *lich*. It appears that in late Anglo-Saxon already the *c* before thin vowels, as *e* and *i*, assumed the sound of the sibilant *s*, and hence the interchange between *c, s*, and *z*, which we have already dwelt upon (see sub lit. **s**). The Romance *c* takes in English a somewhat different course from that in French. (1) It preserves its *k* sound as in French before dark vowels and before *l* and *r*, e. g. *captain, court, cousin, cross, clear*. (2) It has the *k* sound in English, though it is sibilant in French, e. g. *carpenter*, Fr. *charpentier; carrion*, O. Fr. *charoigne*, Lat. *caro; kennel*, Fr. *chenil*, Lat. *canile*. Or (3) the French sibilant is introduced in English too, e. g. *chapel*, Lat. *capella; chair*, Lat. *cathedra; to challenge*, O. Fr. *chalonge*, Lat. *calumniari; chamber*, Lat. *camera*. Or (4) we have both sounds side by side, as *candle* and *chandler*, A. S. *candel*, Lat. *candela; carnal* and *charnel-house*, from Lat. *caro; cattle* and *chattel*, O. Fr. *catel, chatel*, Lat. *capitalis*.

The Romance *c* before *e* and *i* (*y*) either remains and is sibilant as in French *city, cignet*, or it is replaced by *s, succory*, Lat. *cichorium; search*, O. Fr. *cercher;* or it is thickened into *ch, sh, cherry*, Fr. *cerise; shingle*, O. Fr. *cengle*, Lat. *cingulum*. It takes the same course in the middle of a word. At the end, however, it has the *k* sound when it is terminational, and the *s* sound when it is followed by *e* mute, e. g. *public, lilac; pumice, chalice*. Before a *t* it is converted into *h*, as *delight*, Lat. *delectari; straight*, Lat. *strictus*.

The media *g* commonly remains unaltered where it is initial; but in the words *guest* and *ghost* (A. S. *gäst*, *gást*) the *g* is unnecessarily sheltered against sibilation by the addition of *u* and *h*. The vocalization of *g* takes place on a very large scale in Old English. We have remnants of this vocalization still preserved in *hand-i-work* (A. S. *hand-ge-weorc*), *hand-i-craft*, *hand-y-stroke*. Initial *g* is dropped in *if*, A. S. *gif*; *icicle*, A. S. *is-gicel*. *g*, if in the middle of a word it occurred in the combinations *eg*, *äg*, has been vocalized into *i*, and thus forms a diphthong, N. Engl. *ai* (O. Engl. and M. Engl. *ei*), as *fair*, *hail*, *maiden*, *nail*, *sail*, &c., A. S. *fäger*, *hägel*, *mägden*, *nägel*, *segel*. In the combination *orchard*, A. S. *ort-geard*, fruit-garden, the media *g* is converted into the hard palatal *ch*. Anglo-Saxon already allows of a transition of the media *g* into the spirant *w*, chiefly in verbal forms, which in New English are still preserved, as A. S. *sægon*, we see; *sáwon*, we saw; *gesegen*, *gesewen*, *gesen*, seen; so also are to be explained, *to drag* and *to draw*, *dragged* and *drew*, *dragged* and *drawn*; *slew* and *slain*: further, the words *law*, A. S. *lag*; *to gnaw*, A. S. *gnagan*; *to dawn*, A. S. *dagian*, from *dag*, day; *fowl*, A. S. *fugol*; *morrow*, A. S. *morgen*. Compare Germ. *nagen*, *tagen*, *vogel*, *morgen*.

g when terminational is rarely preserved, as in *twig*, *egg*, A. S. *twig*, *äg*; but it is commonly vocalized into *i* (*y*), forming with the radical vowel the diphthong *ey* or *ay*, e. g. *grey* and *gray*, *hay*, *may*, *lay*, *day*, A. S. *græg*, *heg*, *mag*, *läg*, *däg*. It is dropped in the suffix *ig*, N. Engl. *y*, as *holy*, Germ. *heilig*; *body*, A. S. *bodig*; *many*, A. S. *manig*; *greedy*, A. S. *grædig* (O. Engl. and M. Engl. *i*). The A. S. *ig* is in Old English converted into *w*, *ewe*, N. Engl. *ow*, in the words *sallow*, *sorrow*, *marrow*, *gallows*, A. S. *salig*, *sorg*, *mearg*, *gealg*. *g* is mute and the preceding vowel long in *foreign*, Lat. *forensis*; *feign*, Fr. *feindre*; *sovereign*, Fr. *souverain*.

In Anglo-Saxon the media *g* is sometimes replaced by *j*, and later on is altogether converted into the spirant *y*. In New English it occurs both with the sound of the guttural media and that of the spirant, or rather the soft palatal, in Saxon words, as well as in such of Latin origin. We have the media in *garden*, *get*, *go*, *give*, *geese*, of Saxon origin; and in *gain*, *gust*, *guttural*, *glory*, *grace*, of French derivation; the soft palatal in the Saxon *singe*, *cringe*, *angel*, and in the French *gem*, *giant*, *elegy*, *deluge*, *refuge*, and always before *e* and *i*. Even the Teutonic gemination *gg* is rendered by *dg*, as *edge*, *bridge*, *hedge*, instead of *egge*, &c. It must have been at a comparatively recent period of the language that the German element was infected with the French pronunciation, since terminational *g* is commonly doubled at the end; and this doubling or gemination of the media preserves it from being converted into the palatal. The French sound of sibilant *g* is a soft *sh*, and thus we find in Middle English too *oblishen* instead of *oblidge*. The transition is supposed to have taken place towards the end of the fourteenth century[1].

g is mute before *n*: *gnash, gnarl, gnaw, foreign, sign, impugn, poignant.* The letter *u* is sometimes added to *g* in order to indicate the sound of the guttural media, first of all in French words, e. g. *guide, guise, guile*—then, though unnecessarily, in Saxon words, e. g. *guest, guild,* while we use the simple *g* in *get, give.* In the words *distinguish*, Lat. *distinguere ; extinguish*, Lat. *extinguere ; anguish*, Lat. *anguus,* we pronounce *g* and *u* distinctly, because the *u* is not euphonic but belongs to the root.

gh is in different words of different origin and sound. (1) It is the Italian way of writing the guttural media, identical to the French *gu*, e. g. *Ghent*, and even *ghost*. (2) It is derived from *h*, strengthened into *k*: *hough, shough*. (3) It is derived from the guttural, but the strengthened form has the sound of *f*, a circumstance which may originate in the fact of the *w* having sometimes taken the place of the guttural *h* and *g* (see sub lit. w), e. g. *cough, trough, tough, laugh.* (4) It is derived from the Saxon guttural *h*, but in this case *gh* is always mute, e. g. *fight, right, might, night,* A. S. *riht, miht, niht,* while Scotch, like German, still preserves the guttural: *fecht, recht, mecht,* Germ. *nacht, macht.*

ch. This letter was foreign to Anglo-Saxon and imported with French words. Later on it found its way into words of Teutonic origin. As to the development of this letter in Old English and Middle English, vide supra. It is now used as a palatal aspirate in many words of German and French origin, as *child, chin, church, cheese, chester*—and *chamber, chapel, chief, chapter; choose* is the A. S. *ceosan; choice,* the French *choix*. In some French words it preserves the French sibilant, as *machine, moustache, charade, chandelier.* *ch = k* in Greek words: *chaos, chemist, chord, chyle.* It is mute in *drachm* and *schism.*

As to gemination we have only to remark that *ck* as the gemination of *k* continues to exist; the gemination of *g* is commonly dropped, but remains in *egg*; it becomes a soft palatal aspirate in *sledge, edge, bridge,* for *slegge,* &c.

Dutch. The distinction of M. Dutch *ch* and *gh* is lost, hence for M. Dutch *dach, daghen,* N. Dutch writes *dag, dágen*. In

[1] Koch, i. p. 139.

many cases the old *ch* is superseded by the media *g*, as *nagt*, night; *vlugt*, flight; where certainly the other mode of spelling *nacht*, *vlucht*, is preferable, as *ch* generally is a favourite letter before *t*. The M. Dutch *cht* for Germ. and Engl. *ft* remains in N. Dutch, as *lucht*, air (Germ. luft); *cracht*, strength, craft (Germ. kraft). The *ch* in *zich* (se) is inorganic for *k*: compare Goth. *ik*, *mik*, *sik*, Germ. *ich*, *mich*, *sich*, Dutch *ik*, *mî*, *zich*; from which we see that while all the German forms have their organic *ch* = Goth. *k* (see Grimm's Law), in Dutch the 1st person only has its organic *k*; in the 2nd person the *k* suffers apocope as the *k* in Engl. *I*, A. S. *ic*; and the 3rd person adopts inorganic *ch* for *k*. The combinations *ck*, *qu*, *x*, are now rendered by *kk*, *kw*, *ks*.

Swedish. Peculiar to this dialect is the transition of the guttural *k* into the sound of the palatal *ch* or *j*, similar to the course A. S. *c* (*k*) takes in English before all thin vowels and vowels preceded by *j*. As to the pronunciation grammarians differ, some preferring the sound of the English *j*, others that of *ch* (Rask), the latter undoubtedly being preferable, because it is more general among the natives and more agreeable to etymology. Thus, then, the words *kek* (maxilla), *kil*, wedge (Germ. keil); *kyss*, kiss; *kaer*, dear; *koen*, chin, are to be pronounced *jek*, *jil*, &c., or better, with Rask, *chek*, *chil*, &c. Before the dark vowels *a*, *o*, *u*, the guttural remains, and may therefore in one and the same word alternate with the palatal, as *kam*, comb (Germ. kamm); *kämma* = *chämma*, to comb (Germ. kammen). But in the middle and at the end of words *k* retains its pure guttural sound. In some cases it is indeed replaced by the media, as *jag*, ego; *mig*, me; *dig*, te; *sig*, se; instead of the organic *k* in O. N. *jak*, *mik*, *dik*, *sik*.

The sound of the media *g* is changed into the soft palatal *j* before the same vowels where the *k* must be changed into *ch*, e. g. *get* (goat) = *jet*; *gälla* (to sound) = *jalla*, *goek* (cuckoo) = *joek*; but before the combinations *je*, *jä*, *jo*, *ju*, the media is not heard at all, and the words *gjärn*, *gjoerna*, *gjuta*, sound like *järn*, *joerna*, *juta*. As *k* and *ch*, so also *g* and *j*—that is, guttural and palatal—may alternately be heard in different forms of the same word, as *gifva* (to give) = *jiva*, and *gaf*, gave; *guld*, gold, and *gyllen* = *jyllen*, golden. In the middle and at the end of words *g* retains the pure sound of the guttural media, except after *l* and *r*, where again it changes its pronunciation into *j*; and the neuter of adjectives in *lig*, where before *t* it is pronounced like *k*, as *heligt* = *helikt*.

ch occurs only in the particles *ach* and *och*, pronounced *ack* and *ock*.

The geminations *gg* and *kk* (*ck*) are frequent. *qv*=*kv*. *x*=*ks*. The use of *gt* and *kt* is unsettled. The M. H. Germ. *ht* (A. S. *ht*. Engl *ght*) should everywhere be rendered by *tt*. But by the side of *natt*, night (A. S. niht, M. H. Germ. naht, Germ. nacht); *rett*, right; *lett*, light, we read *makt*, might; *rigtig*, right; *vigt*, weight.

Danish. The gutturals *g* and *k* have before thin vowels a softer pronunciation, approaching in fact the palatal modification of the Swedish guttural, which is indicated by a *j* interpolated between the guttural and the vowel, as *kjende, kjoebe, gjest*. (This *j* is to be kept distinct from the *j* answering to the O. N. *i* in *io, ia*, &c.: see sub lit. j.) Before hard vowels the full guttural sound is retained. In the middle and at the end of words the tenuis *k* makes place to the media *g*. We find organic *g* changed into *v* after vowels in liquids, e. g. *voven* for *vogen*, waggon (Germ. wagen); after soft vowels into *j*, e. g. *lejr*, camp (Germ. lager); *regn* pronounced *rejn*. *g* is dropped after *u* and *i*, as *stie*, stairs (Germ. stiege); *due*, valere (Germ. taugen, O. N. *düga*).

ch occurs only in foreign words.

The geminations *gg* and *kk* at the end of words are not written but pronounced, as *tyk* (thick)=*tykk* or *tyck*, *äg*, egg. For the O. N, *ht* we should, as in Swedish, expect *tt*, which in fact does occur in *natt*, night; *aatte*, eight; but *gt* instead of the gemination we find in *magt*, might; *frugt*, fruit.

ROOTS AND THEMES[1].

THE most ancient and primitive constituents of words in the Aryan languages are the roots. A root is the syllable which is the bearer of the meaning or signification of a given word; as for instance, the primitive *as*, to be, is the root of the words *as-mi*, I am; *as-ti*, he is. But the suffixes also which are used for the formation of themes and words were originally nothing but roots joined to the principal root or root of signification, relinquishing thereby their independence, and becoming, as it were, roots of relation, that is, expressing a certain meaning, not for its own sake, but for the purpose of defining, limiting, directing, the sense of the principal root. Then the consciousness of their formerly independent position was gradually lost, and they became mere suffixes, appendages to the principal root, without which they did not appear capable of any signification and existence of their own. It forms one of the most important tasks of the science of language to restore these suffixed roots to their primitive independence, to show them in their original shape and signification. Thus we have for instance in the word *as-mi* the root *as*, meaning 'to be,' and the root *ma*, which is weakened into *mi* and expresses the relation of the principal root to the 1st person. As an independent root *ma* means 'to measure,' 'to think,' 'man' (homo), 'I' (ego); *as-mi* then means *be-I = I am*. *As-ti*, again, contains the principal root *as* and the root *ta*, weakened into *ti*, expressing the relation of the principal root to the 3rd person. The original meaning of *ta* is 'this' (hic, hæc, hoc), 'he' (is, ea, id); *as-ti*, then means *be-he = he is*. Hence the Sansk. *as-mi*, Gr. εἰμι (= ἐσ-μι), Lat. *sum*, Goth. *im*, Engl. *am*; and Sansk. *as-ti*, Gr. ἐσ-τι, Lat. *est*, Goth. *ist*, Engl. *is*, originally mean nothing else but simply 'be-I,' 'be-he,' i.e. 'I am,' 'he is'. Again, the primitive *vak-s*, speech (nom. sing.), consists of the principal root *vak*, speech, and the root *sa*, shortened into *s*, and meaning 'this,' 'the'; so that *vak-s* originally means 'speech-the,' and is a formation similar to that caused by the suffixed article in the Scandinavian languages.

[1] Bopp, i. pp. 96-123. Schleicher, pp. 341-479.

ROOTS AND THEMES.

To get at the root (*the* root, the principal root) of a word in its original shape, we must divest it of all syllables and letters which are used merely to express certain relations, and of all modifications which may have been caused by suffixes and terminations; so that the radical vowel especially, where it is lengthened or otherwise modified, is always reduced to its primitive form: e. g. of the primitive *da-dá-mi*, I give, *da* is the root; of *vaks*, speech, *vak*; of *daiv-a-s*, shining, heavenly, god, *div*; of *dyau-s*, heaven, *dyu*, = *div*; of *su-nu-s*, son, *su*, to beget, to bear.

All roots in the Aryan languages are monosyllables. They may occur in the following combinations of letters:—

1. A single vowel, or rather a combination of 'spiritus lenis' and a vowel; as, *a* (demonst. pron.), *i*, to go; *u*, to rejoice.
2. One consonant + one vowel, e. g. *da*, to give; *bhu*, to become.
3. One vowel + one consonant, e. g. *ad*, to eat; *us*, to burn.
4. One consonant + one vowel + one consonant, e. g. *pat*, to fly, to fall; *vid*, to see; *bhug*, to bend.
5. Two consonants + one vowel, e. g. *sta*, to stand; *kru*, to hear; *pri*, to love.
6. One vowel + two consonants, e. g. *ardh*, to grow; *ark*, to shine, to lighten.
7. Two consonants + one vowel + one consonant, e. g. *star*, to scatter; *stigh*, to mount, to ascend (Germ. steigen).
8. One consonant + one vowel + two consonants, e. g. *dark*, to see; *vart*, to turn.
9. Two consonants + one vowel + two consonants, e. g. *skand*, scandere.

Out of roots our languages formed *themes*. A theme is that part of the word which remains after we have removed from it all the terminations which declensions or conjugations require. The simple root, therefore, may be a theme as well. Thus in *as-mi* and *as-ti*, *as-* (to be) is the root as well as the theme of the present tense; in *dyau-s*, heaven, *dyu* (= *div*) is the nominal theme as well as the root.

Another mode of forming themes we observe in the addition of suffixes to the simple or reduplicated root with its vowel lengthened, or, as we called it, gradated[1]; e. g. *daiv-a-*, nom. sing. *daiva-s*, divus, deus, where the root is *div*, out of which we form the theme by the gradation of the radical vowel, hence *daiv-*, and adding the suffix *a* (demonst. pron.), hence the theme *daiva-*, which in the nom. sing. assumes the inflexional termination *-s*, and thus becomes the word *daiva-s*. Themes formed directly

[1] Vide p. 22, sqq.

from the root we call 'primary,' and the suffixes used '*primary* suffixes'; themes formed from other themes we call 'secondary,' and the suffixes used '*secondary* suffixes.' One and the same suffix may be used to form a theme from the root, or from another theme; one and the same suffix therefore may in one position be primary, in another secondary.

SUFFIXES USED IN THE FORMATION OF THEMES.

1. VERBAL THEMES.—(Derivative[1].)

ya (a-ya)

The radical vowel takes gradation, forming chiefly causative and transitive, but also derivative and intransitive verbs. *a-ya* consists of *a*, the final vowel of the verbal or nominal theme, and *ya*, a suffix frequently used in the formation of themes. (Compare the pronominal root *ya*, relative and demonstrative.)

Examples :—

Sanskrit. *bhára-ya-ti*, 3rd pers. sing. pres. of the causative verb, from the root *bhar*, nominal theme *bhára*, burden, or the verbal theme *bhara-* (*bhara-ti*, he bears).

Greek. *a-ya* becomes †*a-ye*, †*e-ye*, *o-ye* (*y* dropped), e. g. τιμα, he honours, = τιμαει = †τιμαγε-τι, from the theme τιμη, honour.

Latin. (1) *aya* is contracted into *a*, as *seda-t*, he causes to sit, = †*sedá-t* = †*sedayi-t*, root *sed* (*sed-eo*, I sit). (2) *aya* contracted into *e*, as *mone-mus* = †*moneyi-mus*, root *mon* = *man*, to think; *mon-eo*, I remind. (3) *aya* contracted into *i*, e. g. *sopio*, to cause to sleep, = *sopiyo*, *iyo* = *aya*, hence *sópiyó* = prim. *svápayá* = *svá-payá-mi*, root *svap*, sleep.

Gothic. (1) *aya* contracted into *ó* (= prim. *á*), e. g. 1st sing. *ga-leiko*, 3rd sing. *ga-leikó-þ*, 1st plur. *galeiko-m*, = prim. †*leika-yá-mi*, *leika-ya-ti*, †*leika-yá-masi*; perf. *ga-leiko-da*; from *ga-leik-s*, theme *leika-*, like, similar. (2) *aya* becomes *ai*, parallel to the Latin *e*, e. g. *veihai-* = †*veiha-ya*, to consecrate (Germ. weihen), theme *veiha-*, nom. sing. *veih-s*, holy. (3) *aya* becomes *ya*, hence *yi* (*ji*), hence *ei*, corresponding to the Latin *i*; e. g. from the verbal theme *sita-*, *siti-*, prim. *sada-*, to sit, we have the 3rd pers. sing. pres. *siti-þ*, prim. *sada-ti*; from the theme *satja*, *satji*, to set, to cause to sit, 3rd sing. pres. *satji-þ*, prim. *sáda-ya-ti*.

[1] These form the verbs which in our Teutonic conjugations we call 'Weak.'

ROOTS AND THEMES. 169

We frequently find nominal themes without any alteration used as verbal themes, occasionally with the addition of the suffix *ya*.

2. NOMINAL THEMES[1].

a

This suffix is used very frequently; the root preceding it has the radical vowel sometimes lengthened, sometimes in its primitive form.

Examples: —

Sanskrit. *bhav-a-*, masc. being, origin, root *bhu*, to be; *bhar-a-*, masc. burden, root *bhar*, to bear; *bodh-a*, masc. knowledge, root *budh*, to know.

Greek. Ϝέργ-ο-(ν), neut. work, root Ϝεργ- (ἐργ-άζο-μαι, I work); φορ-ό-, adj. bearing, φόρ-ο-, tribute, φορ-ά, offer, root φερ, to bear; φυγ-ή, fem. flight, root φυγ (φευγ-ω, ἔ-φυγ ον, to flee).

Latin. *vad-o-*, neut. *vadum*, a ford, root *vad*, to go; *div-o-*, divine; *deo-*, God, from †*dev-o-*, †*deiv-o-*, root prim. *div*, to shine.

Gothic. *vig-a-*, masc., nom. sing. *vigs*, way, root *vag*, *vig-an*, to move (Germ. be-wegen); *vulf-a*, masc., nom. *vulfs*, wolf, root prim. *vark*, to tear; *gib-a*, fem., nom. sing. *giba*, gift (Germ. gabe), root *gab*, *gib-an*, to give; *staig-a*, path, root *stig*, *steigan*, to mount, to ascend (Germ steigen, comp. Engl. to sty).

i

Primitive. *ak-i*, eye (A.S. eage, Germ. auge), root *ak*, to have an edge, to be sharp, to see.

Sanskrit. *lip-i-*, writing, root *lip*, to smear; *bodh-i*, wise, root *budh*, to know.

Greek. ὀκ-ι-, neut. eye; preserved in the dual οσσε = οκψε, οκιε, root prim. *ak*, to have an edge, to see; τρόχ-ι-, masc. runner, root τρεχ, τρέχω, I run.

Latin. *ovi-*, *ovis*, sheep (comp. Greek ὄϝ-ι-ς, Sansk. *av-i-s*), root *u*, *av*, perhaps in the sense of 'to clothe.'

Gothic. *mat-i-*, nom. sing. *mats*, meat, root *mat*, *mat-jan*, to eat; *qen* = *kven-i-*, fem. woman, prim. *gán-i*, root *gan*, to bear, bring forth.

---

[1] Many of these suffixes are also used in the formation of verbs belonging to the 'Strong' conjugation. In this respect they are treated under the chapter of Strong Conjugations, Formation of the Present and Perfect Themes.

u

Sanskrit. *prath-u, prth-u*, broad, root *prath*, to be extended; *pur-u*, much, = †*par-u*, root *par*, to fill; *svad-u*, sweet, root *svad*, to taste.

Greek. πλατ-υ, broad, = Sansk. *prthu*, root Sansk. *prath*, prim. *prat*; πολ-υ, much, = Sansk. *pur-u*, prim. *par-u*; ηδ-υ, sweet, = Sansk. *svadu*, root *svad*.

Latin. Themes in *u* have passed into the declension in *i*, whence the *u* is always followed by *i*. Examples: — *tenu-i-*, *tenuis*, thin, from †*ten-u-*, prim. *tan-u-*, root *tan*, to extend, to stretch; *suáv-i-*, sweet, for †*suádu-i*, from *svád-u-* (comp. Gr. ηδ-υ-, Sansk. *svád-u-*). The form in *u* is preserved in *ac-u-, acus*, fem. needle, root *ak*, to have an edge, to be sharp, and several others.

Gothic. *fot-u-, fotus*, foot, root prim. *pad*, to go; *hand-u-, handus*, hand; *faih-u*, cattle, wealth. But adjectives have the form in *u* in the nom. only, in the other cases they follow the themes in *ya*, e.g. þaurs-u-, nom. sing. masc. þaursu-s, neut. þaursu, dry, acc. sing. masc. þaurs-ja-na, &c., &c.

ya

This suffix is used very frequently in all Aryan languages.

Sanskrit. *vid-yá*, fem. knowledge, root *vid*, to know; *vák-ya*, neut. speech, root *vach*; *che-ya*, root *chi*, to gather; *pák-ya*, root *pach*, to cook. Chiefly used to form the participium necessitatis.

Greek. αγ-ιο-, holy, prim. *yag-ya-*, Sansk. *yaj-ya-*, venerandus, root *yaj*, to revere; πάγ-ιο-, fast, firm, root παγ, πηγ-νυμι, I fasten.

Latin. *ad-ag-io-, adagium*, adage, saying, proverb, root *ag*, to say (comp. *ajo* = *ag-yo*); *exim-io-, eximius*, excellent, root *im, ex-im-o*, I take out; *conjug-io-, conjugium*, marriage, root *jug*, to join (comp. *jung-o, jug-um*); *fluv-io-, fluvius*, river, root *flu, fluere*, to flow. The suffix *io-ni-* seems an extension of *io* by means of *ni*, e.g. *leg-ioni-* = *leg-io-ni-*, root *leg*, leg-ere; *reg-ion-, reg-ioni-*, root *reg*, reg-ere.

Gothic. *band-ja-*, fem. nom. sing. *bandi*, band, bandage; *ga-bund-ja-*, fem. nom. sing. *ga-bundi*, Germ. *ge-bund*, Engl. *bund-le*, root *band, bind-an*, to bind; *kun-ya-*, neut. nom. sing. *kuni*, genus, gens, root *kan*, prim. *gan*, to beget. Adjectives: — *un-qeþ-ja-*, nom. sing. *un-qeþ-s*, inexpressible, root *qaþ, qiþ-an*, to speak; *anda-nem-ja-*, nom. sing. *anda-nem-s*, agreeable (comp. Germ. *ange-nehm*), root *nam, nim-an*, to take (Germ. nehmen).

Gothic, like all Teutonic languages, frequently extends the suffix *ja* by adding *n*, originally perhaps *ni*. With adjectives this *n* has the function to impart to the adjective a certain relation or direction; hence *anda-nem-jan* by the side of *anda-nem-ja*; *band-jan*, masc. nom. sing. *band-ja*, a prisoner, root *band*, *bind-an*, to bind; *gasinþ-jan*, companion, root *sanþ*, to go (comp. *sinþ-s*, path, way; *sand-jan*, to send).

ya also occurs as a secondary suffix in all Aryan languages. Examples in Gothic are:—*haírd-ja-*, masc. nom. sing. *haírd-eis*, shep-*herd*, Germ. *hirt-e*, from *hairda*, herd; *anda-vaúrd-ja*, neut. answer (comp. Germ. *ant-wort*), from *vaurda-*, word (Germ. wort). These also are extended by *n*, as *fisk-jan-*, fisher, fisher-man, from *fiska-*, nom. sing. *fisk-s*, fish; *manag-ein-* for *manag-jan-*, nom. sing. *managei*, multitude, many, from *managa-*, adj. much.

va; related to it, van

Sanskrit. *pad-va*, masc. way, root *pad*, to go; *pak-va-*, adj. cooked, root *pach*, to cook; *e-va*, masc. *itus*, walk, root *i*, to go; so also *pad-van-*, way (comp. *pad-va-*).

Greek. It is difficult to recognise the suffix *va* on account of the total disappearance of the letter *v* from this dialect. Examples are: — ιπ-ο-, horse for †ικ-Fο-, = Lat. *equo-*, prim. *ak-va-*; πολλο (= πολυ), from †πολ-Fο, prim. *parva*, root *par*, to fill. The suffix *van* we have in αιων, time, time of life (= αι-Fων-), prim. *ai-van-* (comp. Lat. *æ-vo-*, Gr. *ai-va-*, Sansk. *e-va-*), root *i*, to go.

Latin. *eq-vo-*, horse; *æ-vo-* (see Greek); *ar-vo-*, ploughed, *arvu-m*, field, root *ar*, *ar-are*, to plough; *vac-uo-*, empty, root *vac*, *vac-are*, to be empty; *al-vo-*, fem. belly, root *al*, *alere*, to feed. Also formations in *ivo*, as *noci-vo-*, *vaci-vo-* for *noc-uo*, &c.

Gothic. *ai-va-*, masc., nom. sing. *aivs*, time, root *i*, to go (comp. Sanskrit, Greek, Latin); O. S. *ehu-*, horse, requires a Gothic *aih-va-* for a more ancient *ih-va-*, prim. *ak-va*.

vant, used to form a part. pret. active, probably a compound of *va + nt* (= *ant*), in the same manner as *yant = ya + nt* (*ant*) (see the comparative), and *mant = ma + nt* (*ant*), and *ant = a + nt* (*ant*); so that we get the orders *ant*, *vant*, *yant*, *mant*, by the side of *an*, *yan*, *van*, *man*, and *a*, *ya*, *va*, *ma*, consisting of one, two, and three, component elements. It frequently occurs that suffixes of the second order may be used for those of the first, and suffixes of the third order may replace those of the second.

vant does not occur in the Teutonic languages, unless we except the nom. plur. masc. Goth. *berusjos*, parents, which is supposed to stand for a more ancient *beransjá-s* = *babar-ansya-s*, root *bar*, Sansk. *bhar*, to bear, to beget.

ma and man (= ma + an)

Sanskrit. *jan-man*, neut. birth, root *jan*, gignere; *ná-man-*, neut. name, = †*gná-man-*, root *gna-gan*, to know; *ush-man-*, summer, root *ush*, to burn.

Greek. θερ-μό-, adj. hot, θέρ-μη, fem. heat, root θερ, θερ-ομαι, to grow hot; γνω-μη, opinion, root γνο, prim. *gan*, to know; αν-ε-μο-, wind, prim. root *an*, to breathe; γνω-μον-, masc., nom. sing. γνω-μων, one who knows, root γνο, prim. *gan*.

Latin. *an-i-mo-*, nom. sing. *animus*, mind, root *an* (see Greek); *al-mo-*, almus, nourishing, root *al*, alere; *fá-ma*, report, root *fa*, *fa-ri*, to say.

Gothic. The suffix *ma* is rarely used except in the superlative (see below). Examples:—*var-ma-*, adj., nom. sing. *varm-s*, warm; O. H. Germ. *tou-m*, smoke, Sansk. *dhu-ma-*, Lat. *fu-mo-*, root *dhu*, to move. More frequent in Gothic is the suffix *man*, e. g. *mal-man-*, masc., nom. sing. *mal-ma*, sand, root *mal*, *mal-an*, Germ. *ma-len*, to grind; *na-man-*, neut., nom. sing. *namo*, name (comp. Sansk. *ná-man*). This suffix appears in an extended form with *ya* and with its vowel *a* weakened into *u*, as *lauh-munja-*, nom. sing. *lauh-mani*, lightning, prim. *ruk-manya*, root *luh* = prim. *ruk*, to shine, to lighten.

ra (la)

Sanskrit. *dip-ra-*, shining, root *díp*, to shine; *aj-ra-*, a plain, floor, root *aj*, to go, to drive; *an-i-la*, wind, air, root *an*, to breathe.

Greek. ἐρυθ-ρό-, red; ακ-ρο-, topmost, highest; ἄκ-ρα, top, root prim. *ak*, to have an edge, to be sharp; δῶ-ρο-, gift, root δο, to give; πτε-ρο-, neut. wing, root πετ, = Sansk. *pat*, to fly; μεγ-άλο-, great, strictly 'grown', root prim. *mag* or *magh*, to grow; στή-λη, column, root στα, to stand.

Latin. *rub-ro-*, red, root *rub*, prim. *rudh*; *gna-ro-*, experienced, root *gna* = *gan*, to know; *ple-ro-*, much, root *ple* = *pra* = *par*, to fill; *sella*, chair, = *sed-la-*, root *sed*, *sedere*, to sit; *cande-la*, candle, light, root *cande-*, *candere*, to glow, to be white.

Gothic. *bait-ra*, bitter, O. H. Germ. *bittar*, bitter, root *bit*, *beitan*, to bite; *mik-ila-*, great, = Gr. μεγαλο-, prim. root *mag* or *magh*, to grow; *sit-la*, seat, nest, root *sat*, to sit.

an

Sanskrit. *rā́j-an-*, nom. sing. *raj-a*, king, root *raj*, to shine; *sneh-an*, friend, root *snih*, to love; *ud-an-*, neut. water, root *ud*, to moisten.

Greek. τερ-εν-, nom. sing. masc. τέρ-ην, tender, root τερ, τεί-ρω, I rub; εἰκ-όν-, fem., nom. εἰκ-ων, image (comp. ἐ-οι-κα, perf. I resemble); λειχ-ην, lichen, root λιχ, λείχω, I lick; κλυδ-ων, billow, root κλυδ, κλυζω, I wash.

Latin. *com-pag-en-*, nom. sing. *compago*, fixture, root *pag*, *pango*, I fasten; *pect-en*, neut. comb, *pecto*, I comb; *ed-on-*, glutton, root *ed*, *edo*, I eat.

Gothic. *liub-a-*, nom. sing. masc. *liub-s*, Germ. *lieb*, dear, in an indefinite sense; *liub-an-*, nom. sing. masc. *liub-a*, dear, in a definite sense, root *lub*, Sansk. *lubh*; *raud-a-*, red, indef.; *raud-an-*, red, def., root prim. *rudh*, to be red.

ana

Used chiefly in the formation of themes which occur as infinitives; further, nomina actionis and nomina agentis.

Sanskrit. *gam-ana-*, to go, root *gam*, to go; *bhar-ana-*, to bear, root *bhar*; *nay-ana-*, neut. eye, 'that which guides,' root *ni*, to guide; *vad-ana-*, mouth, 'that which speaks,' root *vad*, to speak; *vah-ana-*, waggon, 'that which conveys,' root *vah*, to fare, to convey.

Greek. δρέπ-ανο-, sickle, root δρεπ, δρεπ-ομαι, I cut off; τυμπ-ανο-, neut. drum, root τυπ, τυπτω, I beat; ὄχ-ανο-, handle, root εχ, ἔχω, I have, hold.

Latin. *pāg-ina*, fem., leaf, page, root *pag*, to join, fix; *dom-ino-*, master, fem. *dom-ina*, mistress, root *dom*, *domo*, to overcome, to tame.

Gothic. Infinitives: *bair-an*, to bear, theme prim. *bhar-ana-*, pres. theme Goth. *baíra-*, root *bar*, Sansk. *bhar*; *it-an*, to eat, pres. theme *ita-*, root *at*, prim. *ad*; *sit-an*, to sit, pres. theme *sita-*, root *sat*, prim. *sad*.

na

Themes with *na* are frequently used as part. pret. passive, identical in meaning to those in *ta*.

Sanskrit. *svap-na-*, sleep, root *svap*, to sleep; *anna*, food, = †*ad-na*, root *ad*, to eat; part. pret. pass. *pur-na-*, root *par*, to fill; *stīr-na-* = †*star-na*, root *star*, sternere, to scatter.

Greek. Adjectives: σεμνό- = †σεβ-ρο-, revered, root σεβ, σεβ-ομαι, I revere; αγ-νο-, revered, sanctified, root αγ, αζ-ομαι, I revere.

Latin. *ple-no-*, filled, full, root *ple = pla = pra = par*, to fill; *mag-no-*, great, literally 'grown,' root *mag*, Sansk. *mah*, to grow.

Gothic. Part. pret. passive: *baura-na*, pres. theme *baira*, root *bar*, to bear; *viga-na*, pres. theme *viga-*, root *vag*, to move; *buga-na*, root *bug*, to bend (Germ. biegen); *bar-na-*, nom. sing. *barn*, child, 'that which has been born,' root *bar*.

na, ná (Gothic), used in the formation of passive intransitive verbal forms, as *ga-hail-ni-þ*, he is healed, from *heil-s*, heal, theme *haila-* (comp. *hail-ja-n*, to heal); *veih-ni-þ*, he is sanctified, he becomes holy, from *veih-s* holy, theme *veiha-*.

ni

Compare **ti**. Orders of similar meaning are *na, ni, nu,* and *ta, ti, tu*.

Sanskrit. *glá-ni-*, fatigue, root *gla*, to lose strength; *há-ni*, abandon, abandonment, root *ha*, to abandon.

Greek. μῆ-νι-, μῆνις, wrath, root prim. *ma*, to think.

Latin. *ig-ni-*, fire, Sansk. *ag-ni-*; *pa-ni-*, bread, root *pa* (comp. *pa-sco*, to feed).

Gothic. *hausei-ni-*, hearing, = *hausja-ni*, verbal theme *hausja*, to hear; *golei-ni-*, greeting, verbal theme *golja-*, to greet; *libai-ni-*, life, verbal theme *libai-*, to live.

nu

Sanskrit. *ta-nu-*, thin, root *ta, tan*, to stretch; *su-nu-*, born, son, root *su*, to beget, to bear (comp. Goth. *barn*, son, root *bar*); *bha-nu*, sun, root *bha*, to shine.

Greek. θρῆ-νο-, stool, root θρα, θρῆ-σασθαι, to sit down, θρᾶ-νος, seat, root prim. *dhra, dhar*, to hold, support.

Latin. *te-nu-i-*, thin (comp. Sansk. *ta-nu-*); perhaps also *ma-nu-*, hand, prim. root *ma*, to measure, to form.

Gothic. *su-nu-*, son (comp. Sansk.); as to *kinnu-*, it is doubtful whether it is formed by the suffix *nu*.

ta

Compare the pronominal root *ta*. This suffix is frequently used to form the part. perf. passive, the 3rd person of the verb, perhaps also the abl. sing. of the noun.

Sanskrit. *ma-ta-*, root *ma, man*, to think; *bhr-ta-*, root *bhar*, to bear; *yuk-ta-*, root *yuj*, to join.

Greek. κλι-τό-, root κλυ, to hear; σπαρ-το-, root σπερ, to sow; στα-το-, root στα, to stand.

Latin. *da-to-*, root *da*, to give; *sta-to-*, root *sta*, to stand; *di-ru-to-*, root *ru*, to fall down; *passo-* = †*pas-to* = †*pat-to*, root *pat*, to suffer.

Gothic. *sati-da-* of *satjan*, root *sat*, to set; *veihai-da-*; *mah-ta-* for *mag-da-*, from the perf. theme *mag*, I am able, may; þah-ta for þak-da-, root þak, to think; brah-ta for brag-da, root brag, to bring. (On the change of the final *g* of the root into *h* before the dental, see the letters **h** and **g**, pp. 116, 128.)

tar, tra

The suffix *-tar* is used to form nomina agentis, and the part. fut. active; *-tra*, nomina which denote an instrument and the like. The origin of these suffixes is obscure; perhaps they both are derived from *tara*, a compound of *ta + ra*, in the same manner as *man* and *mna* from *mana = ma + na*. Formations with these suffixes are traced to the primitive language, especially those in *-tar-*, used as family terms; e. g. *ma-tar-*, genitrix, mother, root *ma*, gignere, to produce, to bear; *pa-tar-*, father, root *pa*, to protect, to govern; *bhrá-tar-*, brother, root *bhar*, *bhra*, to bear, to support; *da-tar-*, giver, root *da*, to give; *su-tar-*, woman, root *su*, to beget, to bear, hence *sva-star = sva-sutar-*, sister; *gan-tar-*, genitor, begetter, root *gan*, to beget. Instrumental nouns in *-tra*, as *dak-tra-*, tooth, root *dak*, to bite; *gá-tra-*, limb, root *ga*, to go, to move; *krau-tra-*, ear, root *kru*, to hear.

Sanskrit. *pi-tar-*, father; *má-tar*, mother; *bhrá-tar*, brother; *svasar-* (sister) for †*sva-star* = †*sva-sutar-*; *kar-tar*, root *kar*, to make; *pak-tar-*, root *pach*, to cook, &c.; *da-tar*, fem. nom. sing. *da-tri – da-tryá*, the feminine being formed by the addition of the secondary suffix *ya*, except in family terms where both the masculine and feminine may end in *tar* (comp. *má-tar*, mother). Suffix *-tra*: *gá-tra*, limb, root *ga*, to go; *vas-tra-*, vestis, clothes, root *vas*, to clothe; *vak-tra*, mouth, root *vach*, to speak.

Greek. -τερ, -τηρ, -τορ, for the primitive *-tar*, e. g. πα-τερ-, father; μη-τερ-, mother; δο-τηρ- or δω-τηρ, giver; ρή-τορ-, orator, root ρε = ϵρ, to speak; Ϝισ-τορ-, ἴστωρ, one who knows, who bears witness, root Ϝιδ, to know; -τυρ only in μάρ-τυρ-, witness, root *smar*, to remember. The primitive *-tra* becomes in Greek -τρο, -θρο (neut.), -τρα, -θρα (fem.). Examples:—αρο-τρο-, plough, from the verbal theme αρο-, to plough, root αρ; ἰά-τρο-, physician, verbal theme ἰα, 'ια-ομαι, to heal; βα-θρο-, ground, bottom, root βα = prim. ga, to go; κοιμή-θρα, sleeping place, dormitory, verbal theme κοιμα-, κοιμαω, to cause to sleep.

Latin. The family terms end in *ter*, *tr*, the nomina agentis in *tor*, for the primitive *tar*; e. g. *pa-ter, má-ter, frá-ter* (but *soror-* from †*sosór-*, †*sos-tor*, †*sva-s-tar*, †*sva-su-tar*); *vic-tor-*, root *vic*; *censór-* = *cens-tor*, root *cens*, censeo. Future participles: *da-turo-*, *vic-turo-*; the fem. *tura* forms nomina actionis, e. g. *sepul-tura* (comp. *sepul-tus*), sepelio, to bury. *tro* = prim. *tra*, e. g. *ros-tro-*, *rostrum*, beak, = †*rod-tro*, root *rod*, *rodare*, to gnaw; *claus-tro* = †*claud-tro*, root *claud*, *claudere*, to lock. We have an extension of the suffix *tra* by the addition of the suffix *ya* in the terminations *-trio-*, and *-torio-*, as *pa-tr-io-*, *audi-tor-io*, &c.; *tric*, by the addition of *ic*, as *vic-tr-ic-*; *trina*, by the addition of *ina*, as *doc-tr-ina*, root *doc*.

Gothic. The suffix *tar* is preserved in family terms only, e. g. *fa-dar*, father; *bro-þar*, brother; *dauh-tar*, daughter; *svis-tar*, sister. Suffix *tra* forms neuter nouns, as *maur-þra*, nom. sing. *maur-þr*, murder, prim. root *mar*, to die; O. H. Germ. *hla-tar*, laughter, root *hlah*, Goth. *hlah-jan*, to laugh; O. H. Germ. *ruo-dar*, rudder, oar (Germ. ruder), root *ra* = *ar* (comp. *ar-are*, &c.).

ti

Sanskrit. *ma-ti-*, opinion, root *ma, man*, to think; *uk-ti*, speech, root *vach*, to speak; *yuk-ti*, junction, root *yuj*, to join; *pá-ti-*, lord, root *pa*, to protect.

Greek. τι or σι: μῆ-τι-, prudence, root *ma*, to think; φά-τι-, saying, report, root φα, to say; φυ-σι, nature, root φυ, to grow.

Latin. *do-ti-*, *dos*, dowry, root *da*, to give; *men-ti*, *mens*, mind, root *men* = *man, ma*, to think; *ves-ti-*, root prim. *vas*, to clothe. An extension of *ti* is *tio*, *tia* = *ti* + *o* (*a*, perhaps for *ya*): *in-i-tio-*, beginning, root *i*, to go; *justi-tia-* from *justo*, &c.

Gothic has *-di* and *-thi* for the primitive *-ti*, e. g. *kno-di-*, genus, gens, prim. root *gna* = *gan*, gignere; *mah-ti-*, might, power = †*mag-ti*, root *mag*, to be able; *ga-mun-di-*, remembrance, root *mun* = *man, ma*, to think; *an-s-ti-* favour, root *an*, to favour; *fa-di-*, nom. sing. *faþ-s*, lord, prim. root *pa*, to protect (comp. Sansk. *pa-ti-*).

tu

Used in the formation of verbal nouns.

Sanskrit. *da-tu-m*, root *da*, to give; *stha-tu-m*, root *stha*, to stand; *vet-tu-m*, root *vid*, to know; *kar-tu-m*, root *kar*, to make.

Greek. βρω-τυ-, meat, root βρο (comp. βι-βρω-σκω); ἐδη-τυ-, meat, root ἐδ, to eat; ἄσ-τυ = Ϝάσ-τυ, town, prim. root ϝας, to dwell. Secondary suffix is -συνη = †-τυνη, e.g. δικαιο-συνη from δίκαιο-, just; μνημο-συνη, remembrance, theme μνημον-, mindful, root μεν = man, ma, to think.

Latin. sta-tu-, nom. sing, status, root sta, to stand; dic-tu-, root dic, to say; vic-tu-, root vig, viv, viv-o, to live, &c., &c. Secondary suffixes used in the formation of abstracts are tu-ti-, tu-don-, and tu-din-, as servi-tuti-, alti-tudin-.

Gothic. dau-þu-, death, root dau, div, du, to die; vrato-du-, journey, theme vrato, to go; vahs-tu-, root vahs, to grow. The suffix -dva (= Sansk. -tva, Lat. -tuo) forms secondary themes, as þiva-dva-, servitude, from þiva-, þius, servant.

ant, nt

Used chiefly in the formation of the participle active out of the theme of the present tense.

Sanskrit. ad-ant, root and theme of the present ad, to eat; tuda-nt, root tud, to push, to strike; fem. ad-atí, neut. ad-at, &c.

Greek. -οντ, -ντ, fem. †-οντya, †-ντya, which becomes -οντσα, -ουσα, e.g. φέρο-ντ-, fem. φερουσα = †φερο-νσα = †φερο-ντya, root φερ, to bear; τιθέ-ντ-, root θε, to set; δεδο-ντ-, root δο, to give, so also the 2nd aor. θέ-ντ-, δο-ντ-.

Latin. -ent, ancient -ont, -unt: vehe-nt-, root veh, to fare, to convey; vol-ent-, ancient vol-ont-, vol-unt-, root vol, to will. (præ)-s-ent- = es-ent, root and pres. theme es, Sansk. as, to be; i-ent-, e-unt- = †e-ont-, root i, to go. Secondary formations are the abstracts in antia, entia, antium, entium, = ant, ent + ia, io, prim. ya, e.g. silent-iu-m, licent-ia, abundant-ia.

Gothic. bairands, pres. part. = bira-nd(a)-s, root bar, to bear; giba-nd-, root gab, pres. theme giba-. Other Teutonic dialects show with these participles an extension of the theme by means of adding the suffix ya, as O.S. helpandja-, helping, definite form helpandjan.

as

The themes in -as are commonly used as neuter nomina actionis, rarely as nomina agentis.

Sanskrit. jan-as, genus, root jan, gignere; man-as, sense, root man, to think; vach-as, speech, root vach, to speak; ap-as, work, root ap.

Greek. μέν-ος, sense, courage, wrath, gen. μέν-εσ-ος, μένεος, μενους, root μεν = man, to think; γέν-ος, gen. γέν-εσ-ος, γενους;

ἐπ-ος = Ϝεπ-ος, Ϝέπ-εσ-, word, root Ϝεπ, prim. *rak*, Sansk. *vach*, to speak ; μηκ-ος, μῆκ-εσ-, length, root μακ, μακ-ρο-, long.

Latin. *gen-us*, ancient †*gen-os*, Sansk. *jan-as*, root *gen*, gignere ; *op-us*, work, old form †*op-os*, Sansk. *ap-as ; foed-us*, old form *foid-os*, root *fid*, fido ; *corp-us*, Sansk. root *karp ; jus*, right, old form *jov-os*, root *ju*, to join ; *pus*, old form *pov-os*, root *pu*, to rot. The masculines in *or* = *os*, e. g. *arb-or* = *arb-os ; sop-or*, prim. root *svap*, to sleep.

Gothic expresses the primitive *as* by -*isa*, as if it came from an ancient -*asa*, theme in *a*. Examples :—*hat-isa*-, nom. sing. *hatis*, hate, root *hat, hat-a*, I hate ; *ag-isa-*, nom. sing. *ag-is*, fear, root *ag, og*, I fear. In Old High German the suffix prim. *as*, Goth. -*isa*, O. H. Germ. -*ira*, is used in the plural only, while the suffix *a* forms the singular, e. g. sing. *grab*, grave, from a primitive *graba-m*, plur. nom. *grab-ir*, = ancient †*grab-isa*, more ancient †*grab-asá*. (Concerning the formation of the plural in *ir, er*, see the Teutonic Declensions of the Noun.)

ka

Sanskrit. This suffix is rarely used in primary, but more frequently in secondary themes, as *putra-ka*, little son, from *putra*, son.

Greek, secondary suffix in φυσι-κο-, theme φυσι- ; θηλυ-κό, θηλυ- ; καρδια-κό-, καρδία.

Latin, secondary suffix in *civi-co-*, theme *civi- ; urbi-co-*, theme *urbi- ; belli-co-*, theme *belli-*.

Gothic, primary suffix in O. H. Germ. *fol-ca*, neut. folk (comp. Slavonic *plu-ku*, multitude, army), prim. *par-ka*, root *par*, to fill. Secondary suffix in *anda-ga*, beatus, theme *anda-*, happiness ; *handu-ga*, wise, skilful, theme *handu-*, hand ; *staina-ha-*, petreus, theme *staina-*, stone (Germ. stein). The suffix -*iska* is used for derivative adjectives which correspond to those ending in -*ika* in Greek and Latin, as *barn-iska-*, childish, from the theme *barna-*, neut. *child*.

Note.—All other suffixes will be explained in their proper places, when we treat on the *Comparisons, Numerals*, &c., &c.

PRONOUNS.

PERSONAL PRONOUNS.

TABLE OF PERSONAL PRONOUNS IN THE COGNATE LANGUAGES.

1st and 2nd Person.

SINGULAR.

	Sanskrit.	Greek.	Latin.	Gothic.
Nom.	aham	ἐγώ	ego	ik
	tvam	σύ	tu	þu
Accus.	mâm, mâ	ἐμέ, μέ	mē	mik
	tvâm, tvâ	σέ, τέ	tē	þuk
Instr.	mayâ	. . .	. . .	. . .
	trayâ	. . .	. . .	. . .
Dat.	mahyam	ἐμίν	mihi	mis
	mê	. . .	. . .	. . .
	tubhyam	τείν, τίν	tibi	þus
	tvê, tê	. . .	. . .	. . .
Abl.	mat	. . .	me(d)	. . .
	mattas	. . .	. . .	. . .
	tvat	. . .	te(d)	. . .
	tvattas	. . .	. . .	. . .
Gen.	mama	ἐμου, μοῦ	mei	meina
	mê	. . .	. . .	. . .
	tava	σοῦ	tui	þeina
	tê	. . .	. . .	. . .
Loc.	mayi	ἐμοί, μοί	mei	mis
	tvayi	σοί	tui	þus

DUAL.

	Sanskrit.	Greek.	Latin.	Gothic.
Nom.	âvâm	νώ, νῶι		vit
	yuvâm	σφώ, σφῶι		†yut
Accus.	âvâm	νώ, νῶι		ugkis
	nau	. . .		. . .
	yuvâm	σφώ, σφῶι		igqis
	vâm	. . .		. . .
Instr.	âvâbhyâm	. . .		. . .
	yuvâbhyâm	. . .		. . .
Dat.	âvâbhyâm	νῶιν, νῷν		ugkis
	nâu	. . .		. . .
	yuvâbhyâm	σφῶιν, σφῷν		igqis
	vâm	. . .		. . .
Abl.	âvâbhyâm	. . .		. . .
	yuvâ'hyâm	. . .		. . .
Gen.	âvayôs	. . .		†ugkara
	nâu	. . .		. . .
	yuvayôs	. . .		†igqara
	vâm	. . .		. . .
Loc.	âvayôs	. . .		. . .
	yuvayôs	. . .		. . .

PLURAL.

	Sanskrit.	Greek.	Latin.	Gothic.
Nom.	vayam	ἄμμες, ἡμεῖς	nos	veis
	asmê	. . .	. . .	. . .
	yûyam	ὔμμες, ὑμεῖς	vos	yus
	yushmê	. . .	. . .	. . .
Accus.	asmân	ἄμμε, ἡμᾶς	nos	unsis
	naḥ	. . .	. . .	. . .
	yushmân	ὔμμε, ὑμᾶς	vos	izvis
	vaḥ	. . .	. . .	. . .
Instr.	asmâbhiḥ	. . .	nobis	. . .
	yushmâbhiḥ	. . .	vobis	. . .
Dat.	asmabhyam	ἄμμιν, ἡμῖν	nobis	unsis
	naḥ	. . .	. . .	. . .
	yushmabhyam	ὔμμιν, ὑμῖν	vobis	izvis
	vaḥ	. . .	. . .	. . .
Abl.	asmat	. . .	nobis	. . .
	yushmat	. . .	vobis	. . .
Gen.	asmâkam	ἀμμέων, ἡμῶν	nostri	unsara
	naḥ	. . .	. . .	. . .
	yushmâkam	ὑμμέων, ὑμῶν	vestri	izvara
	vaḥ	. . .	. . .	. . .
Loc.	asmâsu	. . .	. . .	. . .
	yushmâsu	. . .	. . .	. . .

3rd Person.

SINGULAR[1].

	Prâk.		Latin	Gothic
Accusative	. .	ἕ, ἑέ	se	sih
Instrumental	. .	. . .	. . .	. . .
Dative	sê	ἕιν, ἵν	sibi	sis
Genitive	sê	εἷο, οὗ	sui	seina
Locative	. .	ἑοῖ, οἷ	. . .	. . .

REMARKS ON THE PERSONAL PRONOUNS OF THE COGNATE LANGUAGES.

From the personal terminations of the verb, as well as from the different cases of the pronoun itself, the primitive root of the 1st singular appears as *ma*, of the 2nd singular as *tu* or *tva*. Schleicher considers this *ma*, 'ego,' identical with the verbal root *ma*, 'to measure, to think,' a root from which is also derived 'man,' Sansk. *ma-nu-*, Goth. *ma-n-*, i. e. the being that 'thinks'; a very appropriate term for individual self-assertion, quite as

[1] The singular supplies, except in Greek, the place of the plural.

distinct as, and far more concise than, the well known 'cogito, ergo sum' of the scholastic school. The derivation of the root *tva* is obscure.

1st Person Nominative Singular.

Primitive (Ursprache) *agam* or *agham*. Whether *ag*, *agh* is the root and *-am* a termination, which occurs in Sanskrit too not unfrequently, or the initial *a* is the remainder of the root *ma*, and *agham* stands for *ma-gha-m*, is not decided. The primitive *ag-am* is represented in Sanskrit by *ah-ám*, Gr. εγ-ω, Æol. εγ-ων, Lat. *eg-o*, Goth. *ik*.

2nd Person Nominative Singular.

The primitive *tu-am* is in Sanskrit represented by *tvám* (= *tu-am*), Gr. συ for the more ancient and Doric τυ, Dor. and Ep. τυν-η, Bœot. τουν, where the final ν is considered the last remnant of the termination *am*, of the primitive *tu-am*, just as in εγων for *agam*. The Latin *tu* and the Gothic þu are the weakened forms of *tva*.

Accusative Singular.

In this, as well as in the remaining cases of the singular, the proper bases of these pronouns become distinctly apparent, i. e. (1) *ma*, (2) *tva*, (3) *sva*. The primitive language probably used for the accusatives (1) *ma-m*, (2) *tva-m*, (3) *sva-m*; so also in Sanskrit the roots *ma*, *tva*, are treated as bases in *a* and form the accusatives (1) *má-m*, (2) *tvá-m* (enclit. *má*, *tvá*). Greek (1) ἐ-μέ, με, (2) σε, Dor. τε for τϝέ, (3) ε, Æol. ϝέ = σϝε, Hom. εε, probably for σεϝε. Characteristic of all these Greek accusatives is the loss of the accusative termination *m*. The Latin accusatives (1) *me*, (2) *te*, (3) *se*, for *me-m*, *te-m*, *tve-m*, *se-m*, *sve-m*, seem to lead us to an original *mi-m*, *tvi-m*, *svi-m*, where we have the bases *mi*, *tvi* and *svi*, instead of the primitive *ma*, *tva* and *sva*, as they distinctly appear in the datives *ti-bi*, *si-bi*, and in the Umbr. *ti-om* for *tu-om*, Osc. *si-om* for *su-om*. The Gothic also shows the base †*mi* for †*ma* = †*ma-m* in the accus. (1) *mi-k*, where the *k* corresponds to the primitive *ga*, Sansk. *gha*, *ha*, Gr. γε, a particle of emphatic force, so that *mi-k* would be represented by a primitive †*ma-m-ga*, Gr. †με-γε. In the same manner the accus. (2) þu-k would be rendered by a primitive †*tu-m-ga*, (3) *si-k*, *sva-m-ga*.

Locative Singular.

The locative case in the Ursprache is formed by adding the termination *i* to the root, (1) *ma-i*, (2) *tva-i*, (3) *sva-i*. These are rendered in Sanskrit, (1) *má-y-i*, (2) *tvá-y-i;* a more ancient form was (1) *me*, (2) *te*, *tve*, which though originally a locative came to be chiefly employed as an enclitic form to express the relations of the genitive and dative. Gr. (1) ἐ-μο-ι, μο-ί; (2) σο-ί = σϝο-ί = τϝο-ι, (3) οἶ, ἑοι, primitive form *sava-i*. In Latin wanting. The form which in Gothic expresses the relations of the dative is supposed to have originally been a locative, so that the words (1) *mi-s*, (2) þu-*s*, (3) *si-s*, are the relics of locatives, i. e. *ma-smin, tu-smin, sva-smin*.

Dative Singular.

Primitive (1) *ma-bhiam*, (2) *tu-bhiam*, (3) *sva-bhiam*. The suffix *bhiam* which we find added to the root is one of the extensions of the simpler form *bhi*, a form which in various modifications is applied to perform the functions of the locative and the dative, in nouns as well as pronouns. The Sansk. (1) *ma-hyam* for †*ma-bhyam*, (2) *tu-bhyam;* Gr. (1) Dor. ἐμίν, (2) Hom. τε-ιν, Dor. τίν, (3) ἑΐν (korinna), contracted ἵν, probably derived from the more ancient forms †ἐμε-φῖν, †τε-φιν, †ἑ-φιν, †-φιν, being a true dative suffix in the place of the primitive *bhiam*, and altogether distinct from the locative *bhi*. The Latin (1) *mi-hi = mi-bi = mi-bei;* (2) *ti-bi = ti-bei*, (3) *si-bi = si-bei*, show the bases *mi*, *ti = tvi*, and *si = svi*, which are the weakened forms of the primitive *ma, tva, sva*, the inflexional suffix *bi, bii*, from the primitive *bhiam* (comp. Sansk. above), which gradually declined to *bei(m), bei, bi(m)* (comp. *sit* for *siet, seit*). In Gothic the dative is supplied by the locative.

Ablative Singular.

Primitive (1) *ma-t, mama-t*, (2) *tva-t*, (3) *sva-t*. The Sanskrit forms are identical with these: (1) *ma-t*, (2) *tva-t*, followed by the ablative termination *tas* (1) *mat-tas*, (2) *tvat-tas* (comp. *i-tas, a-tas*, from here, from there). In Greek it is wanting: the termination -θεν in ἐμέ-θεν, σε-θεν, ἐ-θεν,— οἶκο-θεν is not the Sanskrit *tas*, but *dhas*, as in *a-dhas*, down from. Latin (1) *me-d*, (2) *te-d = tve-d*, (3) *se-d = sve-d*, which forms are considered regular ablatives (for †*mei-d*, †*tei-d*, †*sei-d*) of the Latin bases *mi, ti, si*. Gothic wanting.

Genitive Singular.

The primitive language is supposed to have at an early period formed this case by means of the reduplication of the root, (1) *ma-s, mama-s*, (2) *tva-s, tvatva-s*. The Sanskrit drops the case termination: (1) *mama*, (2) *tava*. Greek (1) ἐ-με-ῖο = *ma-sya*, with the usual case suffix *sya*, whence ἐ-μέο by dropping the sibilant, and then by contraction: ἐ-μευ, μευ, ἐ-μου, μου; (2) τεο-ῖο = *tava-sya*, root *tava*, Gr. τεϝο; from †τϝε-ιο it became σέο, σευ, σου; (3) ἐ-ιο = *sva-sya*, hence εο, ευ, ου. The Doric forms, such as ἐμέος, ἐμεῦς, ἐμους, add the genitive termination *s* to the old genitive. The genuine genitive is wanting in Latin, and its functions are performed by the genitive of the possessive pronouns *mei, tui, sui,* for †*me-io,* †*tovo,* †*sovo,* = primitive *ma-ya, ta-va, sa-va*. (Compare the Latin *tuus* = †*tovo-s,* †*tevo-s* with the Greek τεϝό-ς, *suus* = †*sovo-s,* †*sevo-s*, Gr. ἐϝος.) The Gothic forms (1) *meina*, (2) *þeina*, (3) *seina* are considered of a more recent formation, having no connexion with the primitive *mana, mama*, but originating perhaps in the plural genitive of an adjective base. (Compare Latin *mei*, &c.)

Instrumental Singular.

Its existence in the Ursprache is uncertain, the Sanskrit forms are (1) *ma-ya*, (2) *tva-ya*. The Greek, Latin, and Gothic languages are devoid of these forms.

Plural.

The base of the plural pronouns is in its origin perhaps nothing but a compound of the bases for the pronouns of the 1st and 2nd singular with the suffix *sma*: (1) *ma-sma*, (2) *tva-sma* (*ma-sma*, 'I and he,' *tva-sma*, 'thou and he'). As to the terminations, it is doubtful whether to these bases were joined the usual case suffixes of the plural, or those of the pronominal declension, or those of the singular; and on the whole the terminations are of minor importance in the formation of the plural of the personal pronoun where the modifications of the root imprint a peculiar character on the different languages: Sansk. (1) *a-sma*, (2) *yu-shma*, where the *a* and *yu* are considered to be the remains of the primitive *ma* and *tva*. The case suffixes are partly those of the plural, partly of the singular.

In Greek all the plural bases are treated as themes in *i*; they are (1) primitive *asma-*, hence ἀσμι, from which by assimilation the Æol. αμμε-, αμμι, and the usual form ἡμι- for aἡμι; (2) primitive *yu-sma-*, whence *yusmi-*, Æol. υμμε-, υμμι-, and the common υμι-, where the vowel is lengthened on account of the elision of *s* (comp. ειμι for †εσμι), and the spirant *y* is replaced by *h*. The nominatives (1) ἡμεῖς, (2) ὑμεῖς, (3) σφεις, are regular formations of themes in *i*, while the Æol. αμμες, Dor. αμες, &c., show the same termination with the vowel shortened, i. e. ες instead of εες, εις. The accusatives ἡμας, &c., are the contracted forms of ἡμέας, &c., and regular themes in *i* (primitive †*asmay-ans*). The Æol. ἄμμε, &c., is formed analogously to the sing. εμε. The dat. Æol. αμμι(ν) and the common ἡμιν are in analogy to the dat. sing. εμίν, primitive *asmi-bhyam*, whence †αμμι-φιν, &c. σφι-σι(ν) is of course the common locative dative. The genitives Æol. αμμέ-ων, ἡμεί-ων, ἡμέ-ων, are regular transformations of the primitive *asmay-am*. The bases of the 2nd and 3rd persons follow a similar course.

The Lat. (1) *nos*, (2) *vos*, seem to have introduced an inorganic *ó* in place of a more ancient *nos, vos*, which would strictly correspond to the Sansk. *nas* and *vas*. The datives and ablatives (1) *nobis*, (2) *vobis*, have the plural in *bi*, like *tibi*, where *bi = bei* stands for the primitive *bhyam-s; vo* and *no* for *vos, vo-s*, and *nos, no-s* (comp. *nos-ter, vos-ter*), and these are the remains of *no-smo, vo-smo;* so that *no-bi-s, vo-bi-s*, stand for the more ancient †*nos-bei-is*, †*vos-bei-is* (*s* dropped before *b* and compensated for by the production of the vowel), primitive †*ma-sma-bhyam-s*, †*tva-sma-bhyam-s*. The genitives (1) *nos-tru-m, nos-tri*, (2) *vos-tru-m, vos-tri*, are pronominal adjectives in *tero*, the primitive suffix *tara*, chiefly used in the formation of comparatives; the genitives in *i* have the singular, those in *um* the *plural* termination, the latter being sometimes replaced in Plautus by *orum*, e. g. *nostrorum* for *nostrum*, primitive forms †*ma-sma-taram*, †*tva-sma-taram*.

Goth. nom. (1) *veis*, plural of a base in *i*, *vi-*, perhaps for *mi, ma*, (2) *jus*. The accus. and dat. (1) *unsi-s*, *uns* (abbreviated form), (2) *izvi-s*, where *s* seems to stand in analogy to that of the dat. sing., and the themes (1) *unsi*, (2) *izvi*, are considered inversions of the original (1) *ma-sma*, (2) *tva-sma*. The genitives (1) *unsara*, (2) *izvara*, are adjective stems in the same inflexional case as the sing. *meina*, &c., that is, most likely, the genitive plural.

The Dual.

Sanskrit (1) base, *áva-*, (2) base, *yuva-*, which are treated as if they were feminine. These bases are thought to be the mutilated forms of the more primitive †*ma-dva-*, †*tva-dva-;* the *a* and *yu* at the beginning of the dual bases would then be the remains of the pronouns *ma* and *tvá*, and *va* might very likely be the mutilated numeral *dva* (two). Greek (1) nom. and accus. νώ, from a base νο-: νῶι seems to be formed in analogy to the dative. (2) σφω, probably from a more ancient †τϝω, with σφωι, seems to be an analogon to (3) σφωε, which consists of σφω-, as the base, and -ε a new dual termination, as we find with the substantives. In the dat. and gen. (1) νῶ-ιν, (2) σφῶ-ιν, (3) σφω-ίν, we have the termination -ιν = -φιν, corresponding to the Sanskrit *bhyám*, base *bhi*. In Latin the dual is wanting.

Gothic nom. (1) *vi-t*; *vi-* is the pronominal base (comp. nom. plur. *vei-s*), and the *-t* is the relic of the numeral *tva* (two); (2) does not occur in the documents, but in analogy to the Old Norse it may have been *i-t = ju-t*, which would be formed similarly to the 1st person, the *-t* being the numeral *tva*, and the *i-* the remnant of the pronoun *ju-* (comp. 2nd plur. *ju-s*). In the dat. and accus. (1) *ugki-s*, (2) *igk-vis*, the *-s* is the same termination as in the dat. sing. and plur. The origin of the bases *ugki-*, *igkvi-* is obscure; they are considered as being of a more recent formation. Gen. (1) *ugka-ra*, (2) *igkva-ra* have the same termination as the plur. (1) *unsa-ra*, (2) *izva-ra*. From this similarity between the dual and plural forms it will appear that the former is not organic, but merely an inflexional modification of the plural, since, according to Bopp, the dual and plural bases are the mutilated remains of one and the same suffix which was originally used in the plural only, and later on came to be applied to express the dual, i. e. *sma*, which by metathesis becomes in the plural *msa* = Teut. *nsi*, and in the dual *mha* = Teut. *nki*.

We cannot more aptly conclude this chapter than by quoting a remark made by Schleicher with regard to these pronouns:— 'On reviewing,' he says, 'the bases of the personal pronouns which differ so widely in the various languages, it becomes evident that here we have not to deal with changes occurring in accordance with phonetic laws, but with more or less arbitrary commutations. It appears as though the different languages had avoided the distinct expression of the bases of the 1st and 2nd persons, a fact in which we may perhaps recognise a kind of euphemism such as is often manifested in languages by a squeamishness which shrinks from pronouncing the 'ego' and 'tu.' (Schleicher, p. 657. Anm.)

TABLE OF THE OLD TEUTONIC PERSONAL PRONOUNS.

1st Person.

SINGULAR.

	1. Gothic.	2. A.S.	3. O.S.	4. O. Fris.	5. O. H. Germ.	6. O. Norse.
Nom.	ik	ic	ic	ik	ih (ihha)	ek
Gen.	meina	mín	mîn	mîn	mîn	mîn
Dat.	mis	me	mi	mi	mir	mer
Accus.	mik	mec, me	mic, mi	mi	mih	mik

DUAL.

Nom.	vit	wit	wit	. . .	†wiz	vit
Gen.	ugkara	uncer	uncero	. . .	unchar	okkar
Dat.	ugkis	unc	unc	. . .	†unch	okkr
Accus.	ugkis	uncit, unc	unc	. . .	†unch	okkr

PLURAL.

Nom.	veis	we	wi, we	wi	wir	ver
Gen.	unsara	user (úre)	user	user	unsar	vâr (vôr)
Dat.	unsis, uns	us	us	us	uns	oss
Accus.	unsis, uns	usic, ús	ûs	ûs	unsih	oss

2nd Person.

SINGULAR.

Nom.	þu	þu	thu	thu	du, dú	þû
Gen.	þeina	þin	thin	thin	din	þin
Dat.	þis	þe	thi	thi	dir	þer
Accus.	þik	þec, þe	thic, thi	thi	dih	þik

DUAL.

Nom.	†jut	git	git	. . .	†jiz, iz	it, þit
Gen.	igqara	incer	†incero	. . .	†inchar	ykkar
Dat.	igqis	inc	inc	. . .	†inch	ykkr
Accus.	igqis	incit, inc	inc	. . .	†inch	ykkr

PLURAL.

Nom.	jus	ge	gi, ge	i, gi	ier, ir	er, þer
Gen.	izvara	eówer	iwar	iuwer	iwar	yðar
Dat.	izvis	eów	iu	iu, io	iu	yðr
Accus.	izvis	eówic, eów	iu	iu, io	iwih	yðr

3rd Person.

SINGULAR.

	1. Gothic.	2. A.S.	3. Old Saxon.	4. O. Fris.	5. O. H. Germ.	6. O. Norse.
Nom.	. . .	wanting.	. . .	. . .	. . .	. . .
Gen.	*seina*		. . .	*sin*	*sin*	*sin*
Dat.	*sis*		(*sig, sih, sic*)	. . .	. . .	*ser*
Accus.	*sik*		(*sig, sih, sic*)	. . .	*sik*	*sik*

Dual wanting.

PLURAL.

Nom.	. . .		. . .	. . .	. . .	. . .
Gen.	*seina*		. . .	. . .	. . .	*sin*
Dat.	*sis*		(*sih, sig, sic*)	. . .	. . .	*ser*
Accus.	*sik*		(*sih, sig, sic*)	. . .	*sih*	*sik*

REMARKS ON THE PRONOUNS IN THE OLD TEUTONIC LANGUAGES.

Concerning the primitive forms of the Teutonic pronouns, and the relation of the latter to the pronouns of the cognate languages, we must refer to the remarks we advanced on the proper occasion. (See p. 180 sqq.) Here we have to add a few words only in explanation of some unusual forms which occur in the ancient Teutonic dialects.

Gothic. The nom. dual 2nd person, which does not occur in the documents, has been set down as *jut* in analogy to the plur. *jus*, as we find nom. dual 1st person *vit* analogous to the plur. *veis*. *ju-* in *jut, jus* is the softening of the sing. base þu, and *veis* the extension of the root *vi*; the *t* in *jut, vit* is the dual termination from *tva* (Sansk. *dva*), two. The accus. plur. 1st and 2nd persons are anomalous, which, instead of selecting the forms identical with the dative, should, in analogy to the A.S. *usic, eowic*, and the O. H. Germ. *unsih, iwih*, be in Goth. *unsik, izvik*.

Old High German. *wîr* and *îr* are sometimes marked as long on account of the corresponding *veis* and *jus* in Gothic; but in later Old High German the *i* of the nom. plur. *wir, ir* is short. The gen. plur. and dual ends in *er* as well as *ar*. Instead of *iwer, iwih*, there occurs *iuwer, iuwih*, and again for *iu* and *iuwih* we find *eu, euwih*. The dual forms, with the exception of *unchar*, which alone occurs in the documents, are Grimm's constructions.

Anglo-Saxon. The most ancient documents only have the accusatives *mec, þec, usic, eowic;* in later times the accus. is identical with the dat. *me, þe,* &c. Very remarkable is the accus. dual (2) *incit*, which occurs in Cædmon, and according to which we may presume an accus. dual (1) *uncit*. The forms *user, us,* of Anglo-Saxon and other Low German dialects come from *unser, uns*, with elision of the *n* before *s*. (Concerning the elision in Anglo-Saxon of the *n* before ð, *f*, and *s*, see the respective letters.) And for the more ancient *user* we find in later Anglo-Saxon *ure*, with transition of *s* into *r*. The Gothic spirant *j* in *jut* is hardened into the media *g* in the Saxon *git;* but in the oblique cases, in Gothic as well as in Saxon, the *j* is vocalized into *i*, and in *eówic* the *i* is lengthened into the diphthong *eó*. From what we have stated it will become evident that Anglo-Saxon has in some cases of the pronoun more ancient forms than even the Gothic.

Old Norse. The *vár, vor, or,* of the gen. plur. 1st pers. stand in the same relation to a more ancient *ossar* or *osar*, as the A. S. *ure* to *user*. In *okkar, ykkar,* &c., the *n* preceding the *k*, as in Goth. *ugkar*, A. S. *uncer*, O. H. Germ. *unchar*, is assimilated to the *k*, and thus forms the gemination *kk*.

All other modifications in the various dialects will easily be explained by a reference to the Phonetic Laws.

TABLE OF PERSONAL PRONOUNS IN THE MIDDLE AND NEW TEUTONIC LANGUAGES.

1st Person.

SINGULAR.

	1. M. H. Germ.	2. N. H. G.	3. O. E.	4. N. E.	5. M. D.	6. Dutch.	7. Swed.	8. Danish.
Nom.	*ich*	*ich*	*ich*	*I*	*ic*	*ik*	*jag*	*jeg*
Gen.	*min*	*mein*	*min*	*mine*	*mîns*	*mijns*	..	..
Dat.	*mir*	*mir*	*me*	*me*	*mî*	*mij*	*mig*	*mig (me)*
Accus.	*mich*	*mich*	*me*	*me*	*mî*	*mij*	*mig*	*mig (me)*

PLURAL.

	1.	2.	3.	4.	5.	6.	7.	8.
Nom.	*wir*	*wir*	*we*	*we*	*wî*	*wij*	*vi*	*vi*
Gen.	*unser*	*unser*	*ours*	*ours*	*onser*	*onzer*	..	*vores*
Dat.	*uns*	*uns*	*us*	*us*	*ons*	*ons*	*oss*	*os*
Accus.	*unsich (uns)*	*uns*	*us*	*us*	*ons*	*ons*	*oss*	*os*

PRONOUNS.

2nd Person.

SINGULAR.

	1. M.H.G.	2. N.H.G.	3. O.E.	4. N.E.	5. M.D.	6. Dutch.	7. Swed.	8. Danish.
Nom.	du	du	þou	thou	du	singular wanting, plur. used in its place.	du	du
Gen.	din	dein	þin	thine	dins		..	..
Dat.	dir	dir	þe	thee	di		dig	dig
Accus.	dich	dich	þe	thee	dî		dig	dig

PLURAL.

Nom.	ir	îr	yhe	ye, you	ghi	gij	î	î
Gen.	iuwer	euer	yhours	yours	hûwer	uwer	..	eders
Dat.	iu	euch	yhou	you	hû	u	êder, êr	eder (jer)
Accus.	iuch	euch	yhou	you	hû	u	êder, êr	eder (jer)

3rd Person.

SINGULAR.

Nom.	..	..		..	..	..	..
Gen.	sin	sein	wanting.	sins	zijns	..	..
Dat.	..	sich		..	zich	sig	sig
Accus.	sich	sich		..	zich	sig	sih

PLURAL.

Nom.	..	..		..	..	..	..
Gen.	..	..	wanting.	..	..	..	..
Dat.	..	sich		..	..	sig	sig
Accus.	sih	sich		..	zich	sig	sig

Note.—The personal pronouns display more tenacity in the preservation of their ancient inflexional forms than any other species of words. This is a phenomenon which we observe among other tribes of languages also. The Romance tongues, which have greatly mutilated and mostly dropped the inflexional forms of their ancient mother, the Latin, in the declension of the noun, were far more conservative in the sphere of the pronoun, where many of the inflexional forms were retained. One of the main characteristics of the modern Teutonic, especially German forms, is the lengthening of the vowels in some of the oblique cases, as *mır, wır,* for the ancient *mır, wır;* the dropping of final consonants, as the English *I* for *ic* (Germ. *ich*), *me* for *mec* (Germ. *mich*), both forms being used in Anglo-Saxon already. For the ancient genitive form *mine, thine,* modern English prefers the new formation *of me,* &c.; German uses the inorganic formation *meiner* by the side of *mein,* the latter occurring rarely, except in poetry. The English *me, thee,* has lost its force as a dative, and consequently designates that relation by means of the preposition *to, to me, to thee.* All other peculiarities the student will be able to explain by applying to the phonetic laws of vowels and consonants.

ADJECTIVE PRONOUNS.

Pronominal Bases.

Sansk. *ta,* fem. *tá* (he, this, that), Goth. *tha,* fem. *tho.* From the same base are derived the Lat. *talis, tantus, tot;* further *is-te* for *is-to-s,* Gk. αυ-το-ς, οι-το-ς. The Sanskrit demonstratives *sa, sá, tat,* Goth. *sa, so,* þata, Gk. ὁ, η, το, where in the masculine and feminine the root *ta* is replaced by a pronominal root *sa,* which is used in no other case. *sa* stands for *sa-s,* as Gr. ὁ for ὁ-ς, the case-sign of the nom. sing. being easily dropped. (Comp. Lat. *iste* for *isto-s, ipse* for *ipso-s, qui* and *qui-s.*)

Sansk. *sya = tya = ta-ya,* consisting of *ta* and a relative base *ya* and occurring only in the nom. sing., Goth. *si,* O. H. Germ. *siu.* This base is of greater importance for Old High German, which derives its definite article from it (*diu* from *tya*), while Gothic uses the base *ta* for that purpose. The O. H. Germ. *der, des,* &c., Bopp considers to come from the older forms *dyar, dyas.* Remnants in Old High German of the base *ta* we have perhaps in *daʒ* (hoc) and *de* for *die* = Sansk. *te,* Goth. *thai.*

The base *i* is used in Latin to form the pronoun of the 3rd pers. sing. *is* (he), and in Sanskrit for the demonstrative *this,* and adverbs only, as *itas* (from here). This base is in Latin lengthened by an inorganic *o* or *u,* and weakened into *e,* and consequently passes from the third into the second declension, using the forms *eum, eo, eorum,* instead of *im, i, ium,* while in Gothic it remains intact, as accus. sing. Goth. *ina,* Lat. *eum;* accus. plur. Goth. *ins,* Lat. *eos.* As in Sanskrit *a* so is *o* in Gothic 'the fulcrum of the feminine base' (Bopp), and the base *i* is thus extended into fem. *ijo* (= *i* + *o*), accus. *ija,* plur. nom. and accus. *ijôs.*

Deserving of special mention is the combination of the radical base *i* with the radical base *ta,* both having the force of demonstrative pronouns. The pronominal root *ta* we have met already in the Sansk. *ta-t,* the neuter of the demonstrative *sa;* Goth. þa-*ta,* the neuter of *sa,* and Gr. το (= †τό-τ), the neuter of ὁ.

This neuter root, if we may use the term, is employed in most pronouns for the formation of the neuter gender (comp. Lat. *i-s, i-d, qui-s, qui-d, aliu-d, istu-d, quo-d*). In Gothic this neuter *t* has been sheltered as it were by the adoption of the final vowel *a*, as þa-*t-a*=prim. *ta-t*; *i-t-a*=*i-t*. (The *t* is dropped in *hva*, quod, =prim. *ka-t*). The importance of this fact will become more evident when we treat on the declension of the substantives. The Gothic relative particle *ei* is by Grimm derived direct from the base *i*, by Bopp from the relative particle Sansk. *ya*, though the latter too admits that the Sansk. relative base *ya* is to be traced to the demonstrative base *i*. (Concerning the application in Gothic of this relative suffix *ei*, see Relative Pronouns.)

The demonstrative base *ana* with the comparative suffix *tara* we have in the Sansk. *antara* (alius), Goth. *anþara* (alius, alter, secundus), as well as in the Lat. *al-ter* and *al-ius* (where the liquid *l* replaces the liquid *n*).

The relative root *ya* we find in the Sansk. *yas, yá, yat*, Gr. ος, η, ο, the Gothic adjective suffix *jis, ja, jata*[1], and, as mentioned already, probably in the Gothic *ei* too.

As interrogative bases we may mention three: *ka, ku, ki*—the two latter owing their existence to the modification of the vowel *a* of the first. The root *ka* appears in the prim. *ka-s*, neut. *ka-t* (*quis, quid; qui, quod*); in Greek under the form πο, Ionic κο, as πο-τε = κό-τε, πως = κω-s, ποι-ος = κοι-ος; Lat. *quo, quo-d*, &c. The Gothic form shows, in accordance to Grimm's law, initial *h* for the prim. *k*, hence Goth. *hva* (quod). (Comp. O. S. *hua-t*, O. H. Germ. *hua-ʒ*.)

The root *ku* may be recognised in the Sanskrit adverbs *ku-tra*, where; *ku-tas*, whence; perhaps too in the Latin *cu-jus, cu-i*, if these forms are considered as ancient as *quo-ius, quo-i*; but it is more likely that *cu* is a later modification of *quo*, in the same manner as *cunde, cubi* (ubi), in *ali-cunde, ali-cubi* of an earlier *quonde, quobi*.

The base *ki* is easily discovered in the Sansk. *ki-m* (what), the Lat. *qui-s, qui-d*, and *hí-c* (-*c* is the enclitic particle of emphasis *ce*=Gr. γε), where the primitive *k* has been supplanted by the spirant *h*, a fact which occurs even in Sanskrit. This base *ki*, modified according to Grimm's law into *hi*, appears also in the Gothic *himma, hina*, adv. *hita*, but only in certain combinations, as *himma daga* (hoc die, to-day), whilst Anglo-Saxon and Old Frisian use it regularly in the formation of the demonstrative

---

[1] For the declension of this demonstrative suffix see under the strong declension of the adjective in Gothic.

pronoun (see below). In Old High German its application is restricted to certain combinations where it appears as the instrumental *hiu*, e. g. *hiu-jaru* (M.H. Germ. hiure, N. Germ. heuer), this year, hoc-anno; *hiu-tagu* (M. H. Germ. hiute, Germ. heute), to-day (comp. *hoc-die, hodie*); *hiu-naht* (M. H. Germ. hiunte, Germ. heunt), this night, hac-nocte.

As to the declension of these pronouns in the cognate languages few words must suffice, their inflexional changes in the Teutonic languages receiving special attention hereafter.

The nom. sing. takes -*s*, which is the termination of the same case in the declension of nouns. (Concerning the derivation of this inflexional -*s*, see the declension of nouns.) Thus Sansk. *ka-s*, who, *sa-s* (and *sa*), is, ipse. The case-sign *s* is dropped in Greek and Gothic : o = σο, Goth. *sa*, for σος, Goth. *sas*. In Latin also the case-sign is wanting in *is-te* for †*is-to-s* and in several other pronouns. The accus. sing. has the nominal termination *am*, except in Gothic, where the *m* has been changed into *n*, which is preserved from elision by a final *a* it has adopted, hence þa-*n*-*a* from †þa-*n*, and this from the primitive *ta-m*. The nom. and accus. neut. are formed by the suffix *t = ta*, a demonstrative root. Examples:— Sansk. *ta-t* (id), *ka-t* (quid); in Gr. το for †το-τ it has been dropped. In the Lat. *is-tu-d, i-d, qui-d, quo-d*, the *d* stands for the primitive *t*; and in the Goth. þa-*t*-*a*, *i-t-a*, the *t* has been preserved by the addition of the vowel *a*.

The termination of the nom. plur. in its primitive form was †*ta-i*, which may be the remnant only of a full form †*ta-i-sas* (*ta*, the demonstrative root, *sas* the plur. termination as in the declension of nouns). The primitive termination is preserved in its original form only in the Goth. þai, whilst in the Sansk. *te*, the Lat. *qui, hi = quei, hei = queis*, the Gr. τοί (later οί) it appears in weakened and otherwise modified forms. The nom. and accus. dual have the same inflexions as the nom., so also the accus. plur. The ablative sing., as well as the locative sing. and dative sing., is formed by joining to the stem the suffix *sma*, which probably arose from the demonstrative †*sa-ma*, a base in -*ma*- from the pronominal root *sa* (hic). The gen. sing. masc. and neut. originally had the same termination as the noun, that is, Sansk. and prim. *tasya*, Gr. τοιο from †τοσιο, Goth. þis : the *sy* is the remnant of *smi = sma* (vid. supra).

The gen. plur. has the full termination *sám*, Sansk. *teshám*; Greek and Latin the same as the noun; Gothic masc. and neut. þi-*ze*, fem. þi-*zo*, i. e. †*ti-sám*. Dat. sing. prim. and Sansk. *tásmái*, from the base *tasma-* (= *ta + sma*, vid. supra), which appears also in the Gothic masc. þamma = *tasmái*, fem. þizai = *ti-smy-ái*.

PRONOUNS.

The dative and ablative plur. have the same inflexions as the noun, but Gothic increases the stem by adding *i* (which in Sanskrit is always added in this case to the nominal stems in *a* masc. and neut.), hence Goth. *thai-m*.

TABLE OF OLD TEUTONIC PRONOUNS OF THE 3rd PERSON.

Masculine.

SINGULAR.

	Gothic.	Anglo-Saxon.	Old Saxon.	Old Frisian.	O.H.Germ.	Old Norse.
Nom.	*is*	*he*	*hi, he, hie*	*hi, he*	*ir, ër*	*hann*
Gen.	*is*	*his*	*is*	— (*sîn*)	— (*sîn*)	*hans*
Dat.	*imma*	*him (heom)*	*imu-o*	*him*	*imu (-o)*	*hanum, honum*
Accus.	*ina*	*hine*	*ina*	*hini, -e, -a*	*inan, in*	*hann*

PLURAL.

Nom.	*eis*	*hi (hig)*	*siâ*	*hia, sê*	*sia, siê*	
Gen.	*ize*	*hira*	*irô*	*hira, hiara*	*irô*	wanting.
Dat.	*im*	*him*	*im*	*him, hiam*	*im, in*	
Accus.	*ins*	*hi (hig)*	*siâ*	*hia, sê*	*siê*	

Feminine.

SINGULAR.

Nom.	*si*	*heó*	*siu*	*hiu, sê*	*siu (sie, sî)*	*hon, hun*
Gen.	*izós*	*hire*	*ira*	*hiri*	*irâ, irô*	*hennar*
Dat.	*izai*	*hire*	*iru*	*hiri*	*iru, irô*	*henni*
Accus.	*ija*	*hi, (heo, hig)*	*sia*	*hia, sê*	*sia, sie, si*	*hans*

PLURAL.

Nom.	†*ijôs*	*hi (hig)*	*siâ*	*hia, sê*	*siô, sie*	
Gen.	*izo*	*hira*	*irô*	*hira, hiara*	*irô*	wanting.
Dat.	*im*	*him*	*im*	*him, hiam*	*im, in*	
Accus.	*ijos*	*hi (hig)*	*siâ*	*hia, sê*	*sio, sie*	

Neuter.

SINGULAR.

Nom.	*ita*	*hit*	*it*	*hit*	*iȝ, ëȝ*	
Gen.	*is*	*his*	*is*	— (*sîn*)	*is, ës*	wanting.
Dat.	*imma*	*him (heom)*	*imu(-o)*	*him*	*imu (-o)*	
Accus.	*ita*	*hit*	*it*	*hit*	*iȝ, ëȝ*	

PLURAL.

Nom.	*ija*	*heó*	*siu*	*hia, sê*	*siu, sie, si*	
Gen.	†*izê*	*hira*	*irô*	*hira, hiara*	*irô*	wanting.
Dat.	*im*	*him*	*im*	*him, hiam*	*im, in*	
Accus.	†*ija*	*heó*	*siu*	*hia, sê*	*siu*	

REMARKS ON THE PRONOUNS OF THE 3rd PERSON.

From the preceding table it will become evident that the different dialects vary considerably in the formation of these pronouns. This variation is owing to the different choice the dialects have made out of the various demonstrative bases which we have just examined. The Gothic chose for all cases, with the exception of one, the demonstrative base *i*, which it occasionally lengthened into *ija*; the *simple* forms in *i* it has in common with Old High German and Old Saxon, but instead of the lengthened base *ija* the latter dialects use an altogether different base, the demonstrative *si* (comp. Sansk. *sa, sá,* Goth. *sa, so,* A. S. *se, seo,* &c.), which occurs, though in a rather mutilated form, in Gothic too, *si*, fem. of *is*. But in Old High German and Old Saxon out of this base all the cases are formed which Gothic deduces from *ija*, the lengthened form of the base *i*; hence O. H. Germ., O. S. fem. *siu*, plur. *sio, siá*. &c. The Anglo-Saxon and Old Frisian again have a base of their own out of which they construe their pronouns of the 3rd person. Their base is the demonstrative *hi*, which, as we have seen before, stands for the prim. *ki, ka*, and yields in Latin the demonstrative pronoun *hi(c), hæ(c), ho(c)*. Old Saxon also makes use of it in the nom. sing. masc. of the 3rd person, whilst Gothic and Old High German use it in but few isolated cases which we have mentioned already. From these forms deviates the Old Norse *han-* again, which however is used only in the sing. masc. *hann,* and fem. *hon*, while all other cases are wanting. Old Frisian and Old High German supply the genitive by the genitive of the pers. pron. of the 3rd pers. *sin*, whilst, vice versa, we see in later dialects the demonstrative of the 3rd pers. supplying the pers. pronoun of the 3rd person. The word *man* in Gothic is used merely in the sense of 'homo', but in all other dialects we find it already in the sense of the German 'man', French 'on'.

To recapitulate then, we have in Gothic the demonstrative base *i*, except in the nom. sing. fem. the demonstrative *si*.

In Old High German the demonstrative base *i* occurs in all those cases which have in Gothic the simple base *i*, but *si* in all those cases which in Gothic show the lengthened form *ija* of the base *i*. The Old High German gen. sing. masc. is supplied by the gen. of the 3rd pers. pron. *sin*.

Old Saxon uses the base *i* in the same cases as Old High German, except the nom. sing. masc. where it prefers the

PRONOUNS.

demonstrative *hi*; the base *si* is employed as in Old High German.

Anglo-Saxon makes use of the demonstrative *hi* throughout.

Old Frisian the same as Anglo-Saxon, except in the gen. sing. masc. and neut., where it uses the gen. of the 3rd pers. pron. *sîn*, like Old High German; in the nom. plur. throughout, and in the nom. sing. fem., we find by the side of *hi* the base *si* as well.

Old Norse stands isolated in its pronominal forms *hann*, fem. *hon* (*hun*).

TABLE OF MIDDLE AND NEW TEUTONIC PRONOUNS OF THE 3rd PERSON.

Masculine.

SINGULAR.

	1. M.H.G.	2. N.H.G.	3. Old Engl.	4. N.E.	5. M. Du.	6. Dutch.	7. Swed.	8. Danish.
Nom.	ěr	êr	he	he	hi	hij	han	han
Gen.	..	..	..	..	..	..	hans	hans
Dat.	im	îm[1]	him	him	hem	hem	honom	ham (hannem)
Accus.	in	în[1]	him	him	hem	hem	honom	ham

PLURAL.

	1.	2.	3.	4.	5.	6.	7. & 8.
Nom.	sie	sie	heo, hi, þei	they	si	zij	
Gen.	ir	îrer[1]	hir	..	haer	hunner	
Dat.	in	înen	hem, þam	them	hen	hun	wanting.
Accus.	sie	sie	hem, þo, þam	them	si	zig	

Feminine.

SINGULAR.

	1.	2.	3.	4.	5.	6.	7.	8.
Nom.	sie	sie	heo (scho)	she	soe	zig	hôn	hun
Gen.	ir	îrer	..	..	haer	hârs	hennes	hendes
Dat.	ir	îr	hire (hir)	her	haer	hâr	henne	hende
Accus.	sie	sie	hire (hir)	her	si	hâr	henne	hende

PLURAL.

	1.	2.	3.	4.	5.	6.	7. & 8.
Nom.	sie	sie	heo, hi, þet	they	si	zij	
Gen.	ir	îrer	hir	..	haer	hârer	
Dat.	in	înen	hem, þam	them	hen	hâr	wanting.
Accus.	sie	sie	hem, þo, þam	them	si	zij	

[1] Common spelling, *ihm, ihn, ihrer*, &c.

Neuter.

SINGULAR.

	1. M.H.G.	2. N.H.G.	3. Old Engl.	4. N.E.	5. M.D.	6. Dutch.	7. Swed.	8. Danish.
Nom.	ëӡ	es	it	it	..	het		
Gen.	es	..	..	..	..	..	wanting.	
Dat.	im	îm	him	..	hem	hem		
Accus.	ëӡ	es	it	it	het	het		

PLURAL.

	1. M.H.G.	2. N.H.G.	3. Old Engl.	4. N.E.	5. M.D.	6. Dutch.	7. Swed.	8. Danish.
Nom.	sie	sie	heo, hi, þei	they	soe	zij		
Gen.	ir	îrer	hir	..	haer	hunner	wanting.	
Dat.	in	înen	hem, þam	them	hen	hun		
Accus.	sie	sie	hem, þo, þam	them	soe	zij		

REMARKS ON THE MIDDLE AND NEW TEUTONIC PRONOUNS OF THE 3rd PERSON.

In Old and New English the Anglo-Saxon *he* (*hi*) remains throughout; but in Old English we find by the side of the Anglo-Saxon *heo* a feminine *scho*, which may have been introduced into English through the Old Saxon *siá*, or the Old Norse *su*, and which gains the supremacy over *heo* in the Middle English *sche*, New English *she*. The Anglo-Saxon genitives of the sing. *his, hire*, disappear in Old English. The dative and accusative (*him, hine*, &c.) begin already in late Anglo-Saxon to be mixed up, and in Old English the dative has expelled the accusative and usurped its place. In order then to distinguish between *him*, the accusative, and *him*, the dative, it became necessary to introduce a new sign for the dative which presented itself in the preposition *to*. Old English however continued to use *him* for the dative neuter until New English did away with this dative also and supplanted it by the accusative joined to the dative sign *to*. The plur. *hi* and its derivative cases have been supplanted in late Anglo-Saxon already by the demonstrative *se* (*þe*).

The Middle High German pronoun is the regular derivative of the Old High German, no other changes having taken place than the weakening or apocope of final vowels, as *sie*, M. H. Germ. fem. nom. sing. for O. H. Germ. *siu* (*siu* rare in M. H. Germ.), *ir* M. H. Germ. gen. plur. for O. H. Germ. *iro*. These pronominal forms have been more seriously affected in their transition into New High German. All organically short vowels have been lengthened, hence *er, îm (ihm), in (ihn)*, for M. H. Germ. *er, im, in*. The dat. plur. N. H. Germ. *inen (ihnen)* is an inorganic form for the M. H. Germ. *in*, O. H. Germ. *im, in*, with which it has no affinity, but it reminds one rather of the O. H. Germ. accus. sing. *inan*. In the neut. sing. nom. and accus. we write erroneously *s* for ß, in the place of the M. H. Germ. and O. H. Germ. ʒ. The gen. sing. neut. M. H. Germ. *es*, O. H. Germ. *is, es*, has disappeared altogether and is, like the gen. sing. masc., replaced by the 3rd pers. pron. or reflective, *sein, seiner*.

The Middle Dutch dat. plur. *hen* is still used in New Dutch in the place of the inorganic *hun*, and gen. plur. *haarer* instead of *hunner*.

The Swedish and Danish forms are the direct and organic representatives of the Old Norse.

TABLE OF OLD TEUTONIC POSSESSIVE PRONOUNS.

	Gothic.			Old High German.			Old Norse.		
	Masc.	Fem.	Neut.	Masc.	Fem.	Neut.	Masc.	Fem.	Neut.
Sing.									
1st	*meins*	*meina*	*meinata*	*minêr*	*minu*	*minaʒ*	*minn*	*min*	*mitt*
2nd	*þeins*	*þeina*	*þeinata*	*dinêr*	*dinu*	*dinaʒ*	*þinn*	*þin*	*þitt*
3rd	*seins*	*seina*	*seinata*	*sinêr*	*sînu*	*sînaʒ*	*sinn*	*sin*	*sitt*
Dual.									
1st	*ugkar*	*ugkara*	*ugkar*		wanting.		*okkar*	*okkur*	*okkart*
2nd	*iggar*	*iggara*	*iggar*				*ykkar*	*ykkur*	*ykkart*
Plur.									
1st	*unsar*	*unsara*	*unsar*	*unsarêr*	*unsaru*	*unsaraʒ*	*var*	*varr*	*vart*
2nd		wanting.		*iwarêr*	*iwaru*	*iwaraʒ*	*yoarr*	*your*	*yoart*

Note.—The Old High German dialect already in the neut. sing. prefers the undeclined to the declined forms, hence *mîn, dîn, sîn*, and these undeclined forms are used in all the dialects except those already mentioned. Hence we have to complete our table as follows:—

	Old Saxon.			Anglo-Saxon.			Old Frisian.		
	1st	2nd	3rd	1st	2nd	3rd	1st	2nd	3rd
Sing.	*min*	*thin*	*sin*	*min*	*þin*	*sin*	*min*	*thin*	*sin*
Dual	*unca*	*inca*	..	*uncer*	*incer*	..	\{ *unser (úse)*	*iuwer*	..
Plur.	*úsa*	*iwa*	..	*úser (úre)*	*eówer*	..	\{ (*onse*)	*iuwer*	..

TABLE OF MIDDLE AND NEW TEUTONIC POSSESSIVE PRONOUNS.

	M. H. Germ.			N. H. Germ.			Old English.		
	1st	2nd	3rd	1st	2nd	3rd	1st	2nd	3rd
Sing.	mîn	dîn	sîn	mein	dein	sein	min	þin	his, hire, his
Plur.	unser	iuwer	..	unser	euer	..	our	yhoure	þer, þair

	New English.			Middle Dutch.		
	1st	2nd	3rd	1st	2nd	3rd
Sing.	mine (my)	thine (thy)	his, her(s), its	mîn	dîn	sîn
Plur.	our(s)	your(s)	(their(s))	ons	hû	..

	New Dutch.			Swedish.			Danish.		
	1st	2nd	3rd	1st	2nd	3rd	1st	2nd	3rd
Sing.	mijn	..	sijn (haar, heur)	mîn	dîn	sîn	mîn	dîn	sîn
Plur.	onze	uw	(hun, haar)	vår	eder	..	vôr	eder (jer)	..

The form *ure* by the side of *user* appears to be the genitive of the pers. pron. which encroached upon the original possessive. When *sr* precedes several consonants, as *rr*, *rn*, it suffers elision, e. g. *urne* for *userne*, *úrre* for *userre*. In the most ancient period of Anglo-Saxon we find the possess. *sîn* which later on is replaced by the genitive of the pron. of the 3rd pers. (*his, hire*, &c.) Old Norse shortens the radical vowel of these possessives whenever the final *n* assimilates the succeeding consonant, hence masc. *minn* = *min-r*, neut. *mitt* = *min-t*. Instead of *vár* we find also *vorr, orr*, and in the oldest documents *oss*, as *ossum* (nostro), *ossir* (nostri), &c.

The possessive *sin* having originally the signification of the reflective, it gradually lost its possessive signification and was replaced by the genitive of the pronoun of the 3rd person, hence the A. S. *his, hire*, Engl. *his, her*, instead of the more ancient *sín;* and in the same manner the Dutch *haar* (her) from the gen. *hars;* further the M. H. Germ. *ir, iriu, irʒ*, plur. *ire*, N. H. Germ. *ír* and *íre* (her and their), from the gen. sing. fem. and gen. plur. O. H. Germ. *iro*. In late Anglo-Saxon already we find in the place of the plur. *heore, here*, the genitive of the demonstrative *þeggre*, whence the New English possessive *their* (s); *min*, *þin* (mine, thine), are shortened into *mi, þi* (my, thy), but the complete forms are preserved before a word beginning with a vowel, or when they follow after the noun, a rule which may be considered still in force in the poetical style of Modern English. For the neuter form *his* Modern English introduced *its*, first spelt *it's*, as a neuter possessive genitive analogous to the possessive genitive *his* of *he*.

The Swedish and Danish possessives require no further explanation when we state that they are the direct derivatives of the Old Norse possessive pronouns. Their genders also, Sw. *min, mina, mitt*, Dan. *min, mine, mit*, will be easily accounted for by a reference to the O. N. *minn* (= *min-r*) and *mitt* (= *min-t*), which we have just examined. In Danish the neuter gender of the 3rd person, as also its plural in all genders, are supplied by the demonstrative pronoun *den, det*, plur. *de*.

The New Teutonic pronouns take the inflexions of the strong declension of the adjective, where they are used as possessive adjectives, as Germ. *mein, meine, mein*, gen. *meines, meiner, meines;* Dutch *mijn, mijne, mijn*, gen. *mijns, mijner, mijns;* and in the same manner Sw. *min, mina, mitt*, Dan. *min, mine, mit*. But where they are used as substantives, and then preceded by the article, they take the inflexions of the weak declension, as Germ. *der meine*, or *meinige*, Dutch *de mijne*, &c., &c.

DEMONSTRATIVE PRONOUNS.

First Demonstrative (is).

Masculine.

SINGULAR.

	1. Sanskr.	2. Gothic.	3. Ang.-Sax.	4. O. N.	5. Old Saxon.	6. O. Fris.	7. O. H. Germ.
Nom.	*sah*	*sa*	*se*	*sa*	*thie, the, se*	*thi*	*dër, dë, thie*
Gen.	*tasya*	*þis*	*þäs*	*þess*	*thies thes*	*thes*	*dës*
Dat.	*tasmai*	*þamma*	*þam*	*þeim*	*themu, thiem*	*tham, tha*	*dëmu*
Accus.	*tam*	*þana*	*þone*	*þann*	*thana, than*	*thene*	*den*
Instr.	*têna*	*þê*	*þý, þê*	..	*the, thiu*	..	*diu, du*

PLURAL.

Nom.	*tê*	*þai*	*þa*	*þeir*	*thia, thie, the*	*tha*	*die dia, de*
Gen.	*têshâm*	*þizê*	*þara, þära*	*þeirra*	*thero*	*thera*	
Dat.	*têbhyaḥ*	*þaim*	*þâm, þæm*	*þeim*	*thiem, them*	*tham, tha*	*diem, dem*
Accus.	*tân*	*þans*	*þa* ..	*þa* .	*thia, thie*	*tha* .	*die, dia, de*

TEUTONIC GRAMMAR.

Feminine.

SINGULAR.

	1. Sanskr.	2. Gothic.	3. A. S.	4. O. N.	5. Old Saxon.	6. O. Fris.	7. O. H. Germ.
Nom.	sâ	só	seó	sû	thiu, the	thiu	diu, deo, de
Gen.	tasyah	þizôs	þäre	þeirrar	thera, -u	there	děra, děru
Dat.	tasyai	þizai	þäre	þeirri	thera, -u	there	děru, děra
Accus.	tâm	þô	þa	þa	thia, the	tha	dia, die, de

PLURAL.

Nom.	tâḥ	þôs	þa	þær	thia, the	tha	dio, dia, de
Gen.	tasam	þizô	þara	þeirra	thero	thera	děro
Dat.	tâbhyah	þaim	þâm	þeim	them	tham, tha	diem, dêm
Accus.	tâṇ	þôs	þa	þær	thia	tha	diô, dia, de

Neuter.

SINGULAR.

Nom.	tat	þata	þät	þat	that, the	thet	daz
Gen.	tasya	þis	þäs	þess	thas	thes	dës
Dat.	tasmai	þamma	þam	þvî	themu, theim	tham, tha	děmu
Accus.	tat	þata	þät	þat	that	thet	daz
Instr.	têna	þê	þý, þê	..	thiu, thio	thiu	diu, du

PLURAL.

Nom.	tâni	þô	þa	þau	thiu, thia	tha	diu, die
Gen.	teshâm	þizê	þara	þeirra	thero	thera	děro
Dat.	têbhyah	þaim	þâm	þeim	them	thâm, tha	diem, dêm
Accus.	tâni	þô	þa	þau	thiu, thia	tha	diu, die

We have to deal with three demonstratives which, according to their meaning, answer to the Lat. *is, hic,* and *ille,* Gr. αυτος, ουτος, and εκεινος. The first of these is derived from the demonstrative base *ta,* concerning which we must refer the student to preceding paragraphs. The Gothic *sa, so,* þata, and its declension will, after our previous remarks, offer no difficulties to the student. As to the corresponding forms in O. H. Germ. *der, diu, daz,* the masc. *de-r* might be explained so that *de* represents the primitive *ta* (O. H. Germ. *d* for Sansk. *t* according to Grimm's law, and *e* the weakening of *a*), and *r* is the terminational *s,* so that the analogous form of O. H. Germ. *der* would be Goth. þis. But as to the O. H. Germ. fem. *diu* we are inclined with Bopp to refer it to the double base, Sansk. *sya = tya = ta-ya,* consisting of the demonstrative *ta* and the relative base *ya,* so that the O. H. Germ. *diu* stands for an ancient *tya.* The O. H.

Germ. neut. *da-ʒ* is the organic representative of the Goth. *þa-t(a)*. Anglo-Saxon closely follows the Gothic in the formation of this pronoun, using the base *sa* for the nom. sing. masc. and fem., and the base *ta* for all other cases, while the other Low German dialects, like Old High German, prefer the root *ta* for the nom. sing. masc. and fem. as well, so that O. S. *thie*, O. Fris. *thi*, fem. *thiu* correspond to the O. H. Germ. *de-r*, *diu*, the analogon to which in Gothic would be *þis*, fem. *þija*. Old Norse again goes with Gothic and Anglo-Saxon and forms the nom. sing. masc. and fem. *sá* and *su* respectively; but in the most ancient documents we find *siá* in both genders. Peculiar to Old Norse is the use of the instrumental *þvi* in the dat. sing. neut. instead of *beim*, which would be analogous to the dative used in the other dialects; further the dat. sing. masc. *þeim*, the fem. gen. sing. *þeirrar*, dat. sing. *þeirri*, gen. plur. *þeirra*, where the *ei* and the gemination *rr* make the Old Norse dialect deviate from the rest.

In the Old Teutonic dialects already this demonstrative is used as the definite article.

TABLE OF DEMONSTRATIVE PRONOUNS IN THE MIDDLE AND NEW TEUTONIC DIALECTS.

Masculine,

SINGULAR.

	1. M.H.G.	2. N. H Ger.	3. O.E.	4. N. Engl.	5. M.Du.	6. New Dutch.	7. Swedish.	8. Danish.
Nom	der	der	þe, þat	the, that	die	de, die	den	den
Gen.	des	des, dessen	..	..	des	des, diens	dens	dens
Dat.	dem	dem	..	..	den	den, dien	den	den
Accus.	den	den	..	..	den	de, dien	den	den

PLURAL.

	1. M.H.G.	2. N. H Ger.	3. O.E.	4. N. Engl.	5. M.Du.	6. New Dutch.	7. Swedish.	8. Danish.
Nom.	die	die	..	..	die	de, die	de	de
Gen.	der	der, deren	..	..	der	der, dier	déras	déres
Dat.	den	den	..	..	den	den, dien	dem	dem
Accus.	die	die	..	..	die	de, die	de	de

Feminine.

SINGULAR.

	1. M.H.G.	2. N. H Ger.	3. O.E.	4. N. Engl.	5. M.Du.	6. New Dutch.	7. Swedish.	8. Danish.
Nom.	diu	die	..	..	die	de, die	den	den
Gen.	der	der, deren	..	..	der	der, dier	dens	dens
Dat.	der	der	..	..	der	der, dier	den	den
Accus.	die	die	..	..	die	de, die	den	den

PLURAL.

	1. M.H.G.	2. N.H.Ger.	3. O.E.	4. N. Engl.	5 M.Du.	6. New Dutch.	7. Swedish.	8. Danish.
Nom.	die	die	þe, þat	the, that	die	de, die	de	de
Gen.	der	der, deren	..	..	der	der, dier	dêras	dêres
Dat.	den	den	..	..	den	den, dien	dem	dem
Accus.	die	die	..	..	die	de, die	de	de

Neuter.
SINGULAR.

	1. M.H.G.	2. N.H.Ger.	3. O.E.	4. N. Engl.	5 M.Du.	6. New Dutch.	7. Swedish.	8. Danish.
Nom.	daʒ	das	..	..	dat	(het) dat	det	det
Gen.	des	des, dessen	..	..	des	des, diens	dets, dess	dets
Dat.	dem	dem	..	..	den	den, dien	det	det
Accus.	daʒ	das	..	..	dat	(het) dat	det	det

PLURAL.

	1. M.H.G.	2. N.H.Ger.	3. O.E.	4. N. Engl.	5 M.Du.	6. New Dutch.	7. Swedish.	8. Danish.
Nom.	diu	die	..	..	die	de, die	de	de
Gen.	der	der, deren	..	..	der	der, dier	dêras	dêres
Dat.	den	den	..	..	den	den, dien	dem	dem
Accus.	diu	die	..	..	die	de, die	de	de

REMARKS ON THE NEW TEUTONIC DEMONSTRATIVES.

This demonstrative in the Middle and New Teutonic dialects continues to be used as the definite article. But New High German and New Dutch develope different forms, where it has a demonstrative force. Dutch indeed has a separate declension for the article and the demonstrative pronoun, though both are equally derived from the Middle Dutch *die, die, dat,* so that the Dutch article is *de, de* (*het*), the demonstrative proper *die, die, dat.* The article being without a neuter, this gender had to be supplied by the neuter (*het*) of the personal pronoun. In German the article and the demonstrative pronoun have the same forms throughout, with the exception of the genitives, where the demonstrative assumes masc. and neut. *dessen* by the side of *des*, fem. and plur. *deren* by the side of *der*. The article, moreover, is unaccented, while the demonstrative always has an emphatic accent. But all these distinctions are rather arbitrary, and we might designate the article and the demonstrative pronoun as identical.

As to the Danish and Swedish article we shall have to devote to this subject a separate chapter hereafter.

The fate of the Anglo-Saxon demonstrative on its course through Old English and New English deserves a more detailed notice. In late Anglo-Saxon the nominatives *se* and *seo* disappear, and the use of the pronoun as definite article assists much in weakening and destroying its inflexional forms. In order to give a notion of the gradual dissolution of the declen-

PRONOUNS.

sion we subjoin the different inflexional forms in late Anglo-Saxon[1].

SINGULAR.

	Masculine.	Feminine.	Neuter.
Nom.	þe, þa	þeo, þa, þe	þat, þæt, þet, þe
Gen.	þæs, þas, þes, þeos, þıs, þe	þare, þære, þere, þe	Gen. and Dat. = Masc.
Dat.	þan, þon, þane, þone, þoune, þeoune, þen, þe	þare, þære, þere, þe	
Accus.	þene, þane, þæne, þen, þaune, þon, þe	þa, þeo, þe	
Instr.	be		

PLURAL.

Nom.	þaie, þæie, þo, þe
Gen.	þare, þere
Dat.	þan, þon, þen, þane, þærn, þeon
Accus.	þaie, þo, þe

From this table it will become evident how the undeclinable *þe* invaded the declension and gradually supplanted all the inflexional forms; but it was in Old English that the final break up took place, and the havoc which at that period was made in all the grammatical forms of the language can nowhere be better observed than in the case of this pronoun. The plural nom. *þai*, *þei*, and accus. *þaim*, *þem*, are detached altogether from the demonstrative to which they belonged, and enlisted among the personal pronouns. The sing. *þe*, *þat*, plur. *þa*, *þo*, retain their position as demonstratives, so that in combination with prepositions they are used to supply all cases, e. g. *of þo*, *of þa* (eorum), *to þo*, *to þa* (iis). When used as the definite article this pronoun in Old English simply sounds *þe*, and this *þe* is undeclinable. Though we find occasionally inflexional forms of this *þe*, as for instance the accus. *þen*, the total absence of all consciousness of its inflexional value is proved by the fact that this accusative form is used for the nominative case. The instrumental *þe* finds its place before comparatives.

The Middle English preserves the Old English forms, so that *thei* and *them* are personal pronouns; the sing. *that* and the plur. *tho* remain demonstrative; the undeclinable article is *the*, and the instrumental *the* keeps its position before comparatives.

The same relation we find in New English: *they* and *them* are personal pronouns, *that* and *those* remain demonstrative, the latter being derived from *tho* by the addition of the plural *s* and final *e* to indicate the length of the radical vowel. The undeclinable article is *the*, and the instrumental *the* continues to be used before comparatives, as '*the* sooner *the* better.'

[1] Koch, i. p. 475.

Second Demonstrative (hic).

Masculine.

SINGULAR.

	1. A. S.	2. Old Saxon.	3. Old Frisian.	4. Old Norse.	5. O. H. Germ.
Nom.	þe-s	thë-se	thi-s, the-s	þes-si	di ser
Gen.	þises	thësas	thisses	þessa	dĭsses
Dat.	þisum	thesumu	thissa	þessum	desemu
Accus.	þisne	thësan	[thisne, thesne]	þenna	disan

PLURAL.

Nom.	þâs	thësa	thisse, thesse	þessir	disê (desê)
Gen.	þissa	thesaro	thessera	þessara	desero (dirro)
Dat.	þisum	thësun	thisse, thesse	þessum	desêm
Accus.	þâs	thësa	thisse	þessa	desê (disê)

Feminine.

SINGULAR.

Nom.	þeó-s	thësu (thius)	thiu-s	þes-si	di-su (di-siu)
Gen.	þisse	thësara	thisse	þessarar (þessar)	desera
Dat.	þisse	thësaru	thisse	þessari (þessi)	deseru
Accus.	þas	thësa	thisse	þessa	disa

PLURAL.

Nom.	þâs	thësa	thisse	þessar	dise (desô)
Gen.	þissa	thësaro	thessera	þessara	desero (dĭrro)
Dat.	þisum	thësun	thisse	þessum	desêm
Accus.	þas	thësa	thisse	þessar	desô (dise)

Neuter.

SINGULAR.

Nom.	þĭ-s	thi-t	thi-t	þet-ta	di-z (di-tzi)
Gen.	þises	thësas	thisses	þessa	disses
Dat.	þisum	thesumu	thissa	þessu	desemu
Accus.	þis	thĭt	thit	þetta	diz (di-tzi)
Inst.	þeós	thius	..	..	desju

PLURAL.

Nom.	þâs	thius	thisse	þessi	disiu
Gen.	þissa	thësaro	thessera	þessara	desero
Dat.	þisum	thësun	thisse	þessum	desêm
Accus.	þâs	thius	thisse	þessi	disiu

The demonstrative in Gothic receives emphatic force by adding to the simple pronouns *sa, so, bata,* the suffix *uh,* which drops its vowel after monosyllabic forms or such as end in a long vowel; which however retains its *u* and absorbs the preceding vowel, if it follows upon bi-syllabic forms ending in a short vowel: hence Goth. *sa-h* (=*sa-uh*), *só-h*, *þat-uh* (hic, hæc, hoc), gen. *þiz-uh*, *þizóz-uh*, *þiz-uh*, &c. In the other dialects this demonstrative is formed out of two distinct bases, *tya*, the extension of the demonstrative root *ta*, and its relative base *sya*, so that *tya-sya* would answer to O. H. Germ. *di-ser*, *di-su*, *di-z*, A. S. *þe-s*, *þeo-s*, *þi-s*, O. N. *þessi*, *þetta*. In O. N. *þe-t*, the *t* is organic for O. H. Germ. *z* in *di-z*; the O. H. Germ. *d* organic for the low Germ. *th*. The A. S. gen. sing. fem. and gen. plur. *þisse* and *þissa* are inorganic forms standing for *þisre*, *þisra* (*r* assimilated to the preceding *s*). The weak forms *þessi*, *þessa*, in Old Norse nom. and gen. sing. are unexpected, as are also the terminations -*arar*, -*ari*, -*ara*, for -*rar*, -*ri*, -*ra*. This demonstrative assumes in the Middle and New Teutonic dialects the following forms:—

	M. H. Germ.			N. H. Germ.			O. Eng.	N. Eng.	Middle Dutch.		
	Masc.	Fem.	Neut.	Masc.	Fem.	Neut.			Masc.	Fem.	Neut.
SING.											
Nom.	*dirre*	*disiu*	*diz*	*diser*[1]	*dise*[1]	*dises*[1]	*þis*, *þes*	*this*	*dese*	*dese*	*dit* (*ditte*)
Gen.	*dises*	*dirre*	*dises*	*dises*	*diser*	*dises*	..	..	*deses*	*desre*	*deses*
Dat.	*diseme*	*dirre*	*diseme*	*disem*	*diser*	*disem*	..	..	*desen*	*desre*	*desen*
Acc.	*disen*	*dise*	*diz*	*disen*	*dise*	*dises*	..	..	*desen*	*dese*	*dit*
PLUR.											
Nom.	*dise*	*dise*	*disiu*		*dise*		*þise*, *þese*	*these*		*dese*	
Gen.	*dirre*	*dirre*	*dirre*		*diser*		..	..		*desre*	
Dat.	*disen*	*disen*	*disen*		*disen*		..	..		*desen*	
Acc.	*dise*	*dise*	*disiu*		*dise*		..	..		*dese*	

	New Dutch.			Swedish.			Danish.		
	Masc.	Fem.	Neut.	Masc.	Fem.	Neut.	Masc.	Fem.	Neut.
SING.									
Nom	*deze*	*deze*	*dit*	*denna*	*denna*	*detta*	*denne*	*denne*	*dette*
Gen.	*dezes*	*dezer*	*dezes*	*dennas*	*dennas*	*dettas*	*dennes*	*dennes*	*dettes*
Dat.	*dezen*	*dezer*	*dezen*	*denna*	*denna*	*detta*	*denne*	*denne*	*dette*
Acc.	*dezen*	*deze*	*dit*	*denna*	*denna*	*detta*	*denne*	*denne*	*dette*
PLUR.									
Nom.		*deze*		*desse*	*dessa*	*desse*		*disse*	
Gen.		*dezer*		*desses*	*dessas*	*desses*		*disses*	
Dat.		*dezen*		*dessa*	*dessa*	*dessa*		*disse*	
Acc.		*deze*		*dessa*	*dessa*	*desse*		*disse*	

[1] Common spelling, *dieser*, *diese*, &c.

Concerning the German and Dutch pronouns which are regularly derived from Old High German and Middle Dutch we have no special remarks to make. The Swedish and Danish pronouns however in the singular of the masculine and feminine are inorganic forms, probably derived from the simple pronoun *den*, whilst the neuter *detta*, *dette*, may be traced to the O. N. *þetta*, or also to the simple pronoun *det*. The plural is regularly formed after the O. N. *þessi*.

The Anglo-Saxon demonstrative is in Old English already stripped of all inflexions, and the only remains of the old declension are the singular forms *þis*, and the plural *þes*, *þise*, *þese*, which in Middle English are sing. *this*, plur. *thise*, *these*, *thes*, *theise*. The genitive singular occurring in Wycliffe is remarkable: *þisis fader*, pater ejus; N. Engl. *this*, plur. *these*.

Third Demonstrative (ille).

This demonstrative is represented only in Gothic, High German, and Old Norse, while the Saxon and the Frisian dialects are deprived of it. In Gothic and Old High German this pronoun is declined after the strong adjective declension, in Old Norse it follows the declension of the numeral *einn, ein, eitt*; hence Goth. *jain-s, jain-a, jain ata*, O. H. Germ. *gen-er, gen-u, gen-aʒ*, M. H. Germ. *jener, jeniu, jeneʒ*, N. H. Germ. *jener, jene, jenes*, Dutch *gene* (commonly weak declension *de gene*); from it we have the Anglo-Saxon adverb *geond* (illic, illuc), whence the Engl. *yon, yond, yonder*. The Old Norse forms are:—

	Singular.				Plural.		
	Masc.	Fem.	Neut.		Masc.	Fem.	Neut.
Nom.	*in-n* (= *in-r*)	*in*	*it-t* (*in* = *it*)	Nom.	*in-ir*	*in-ar*,	*in*
Gen.	*in-s*,	*in-nar*,	*in-s*.	Gen.	*in-na*,	*in-na*,	*inna*
	&c.	&c.			&c.	&c.	

Instead of *inn, in, itt*, we also meet *enn, en, ett*, and in later documents always *hinn, hin, hitt*. From this pronoun are derived the Swed. and Dan. *hin, hin, hint*, plur. *hine*, which are used in the nominative only. When employed as pronominal adjectives, they take, like other demonstratives, the genitive sign *s*. It is very peculiar that the modern Scandinavian dialects here reject the Old Norse gemination (*hitt*) which in other words they commonly adopt, and render the neuter in its primitive form (*hin-t*).

The Suffixed Article in the Scandinavian Languages.

This Old Norse pronoun is of more than common interest, because it has first been used as the suffixed article, which is a characteristic feature of the Scandinavian languages up to the present day. The pronoun *inn, in, itt,* in its function as article may precede the noun or follow after it—form an appendage or suffix to it. In the latter case both the noun and pronoun are declined, and the *i* or *u* of the suffixed pronoun is incapable of causing Umlaut. In this combination the following rules are obeyed: (1) the declension of the noun remains unaltered, except that in the dative plural *-um* with *-inum* becomes *-unum* (not *-uminum*); (2) the radical vowel of the pronoun is always absorbed by the final vowel of the noun, but it remains where the noun ends in a consonant, except nom. plur. masc., and nom. and accus. plur. fem., where the pronominal vowel is also dropped, as *dagarnir* for *dagar-inir, giafarnar* for *giafar-inar*. We subjoin some examples for the sake of illustrating our remarks.

	Without the Article.			*With the Article*	
	SING.	PLUR.		SING.	PLUR.
Nom.	fat-	föt-	Nom.	fat-it	föt-in
Gen.	fat-s	fat-a	Gen.	fats-ins	fata-nna
Dat.	fat-i	föt-um	Dat.	fati-nu	fötu-num
Accus.	fat-	fot	Accus.	fat-it	föt-in

Weak Declension.

Theme: *hanan* (cock).

	Without the Article.			*With the Article.*	
	SING.			SING.	PLUR.
Gen.			Gen.	hani-nn	hanar-nir
				hana-ns	hana-nna
				hana-num	hönu-num
Accus.	han-a	han-a	Accus.	hana-nn	hana-na

Strong Declension.

Theme: *giafa* (gift).

	Without the Article.			*With the Article.*	
	SING.	PLUR.		SING.	PLUR.
Nom.	giöf-	giaf-ar	Nom.	giöf-in	giafar-nar
Gen.	giaf-ar	giaf-a	Gen.	giafar-innar	giafa-nna
Dat.	giöf-u	giöf-um	Dat.	giöf-inni	giöfu-num
Accus.	giöf	giaf-ar	Accus.	giöf-inna	giafar-nar.

In the same manner the modern Scandinavian languages suffix the definite article to its respective noun, Swedish and

Danish *en* for the masculine and feminine gender, *et* for the neuter; plural Swed. *na* or *ne* (for *ena, ene*) Dan. *ne* (for *ene*). The genitives are *ens, ets, nas, nes*; all other cases are like the nominatives. *en* is of course the O. N. *inn, in;* *et* the O. N. *it.* A few examples may suffice :—

Swedish.

Singular.	Plural.
N. D. A. *konung-en*, the king	*konungar-na*, the kings
Gen. *konungens*, of the king	*konungar-nas*, of the kings
N. D. A. *bord-et*, the table	*bord-en*, the tables
Gen. *bordets*, of the table	*bord-ens*, of the tables
N. D. A. *stjern-an*, the star	*stjernor-na*, the stars
Gen. *stjernans*, of the star	*stjernor-nas*, of the stars.

Danish.

Singular.	Plural.
N. D. A. *kong-en*, the king	*konger-ne*, the kings
Gen. *kongens*, of the king	*konger-nes*, of the kings
N. D. A. *hjaert-et*, the heart	*hjaerter-ne*, the hearts
Gen. *hjaertets*, of the heart	*hjaerter-nes*, of the hearts.

Other Demonstratives.

Another demonstrative which we have already noticed is the base *hi*, occurring in the Latin *hic* and in several Teutonic forms. Most of the Low German dialects have used this base to make up the whole (Anglo-Saxon) or part (Old Saxon, Old Frisian) of their pronominal cases of the 3rd person, while Gothic and Old High German show merely a few cases formed of this base, and these even are used merely with reference to *time:* as dat. masc. and neut. *himma*, e. g. *himma daga*, (on) this day, to-day; *fram himma (nu)*, from now, henceforth; accus. masc. *hina*, e. g. *und hina dag*, unto this day; accus. neut. *hita*, e. g. *und hita (nu)*, until now. Old High German has besides a mutilated form of the accusative in *hi-naht*, from *hia naht*, this night, to-night (whence the M. H. Germ. *hinte*, N. H. Germ. *heunt*, to-night), preserved only the instrumental *hiu* in the following adverbial compounds: *hiu-tu* or *hiu-to*, from *hiu tagu*, this day, to-day; whence the M. H. Germ. *hiute*, N. H. Germ. *heute*, to-day; *hiu-ru* or *hiu-ro*, from *hiu jaru*, this year; whence the M. H. Germ. *hiure*, N. H. Germ. *heuer*—forms which are partly preserved in the Saxon dialects too, as A. S. *heodäg*, this day, to-day, O. S. *hiu-du*, &c.

The Goth. *sama*, fem. *samo*, neut. *samo*, theme *saman* (ipse, o αυτος), follows the weak declension; so does the Old High German *samo*, fem. *sama*, neut. *sama*, which rarely occurs (hence N. H. Germ. *samt*, together, *zu-sammen*, &c.), and the O. N. *sami*, fem. *sama*, neut. *sama*; the latter however may also be inflected after the strong declension *sam-r*, *son*, *sant* (hence Sw. *samma*, Dan. *samme*, gen. *sammes*, the same). The Anglo-Saxon dialect does not possess this word, except as an adverb *same*, together (whence the Engl. *same*), and its place as a pronoun is supplied by *ylca*, fem. and neut. *ylce*, which occurs in combination with the demonstrative *se*, *seo*, þæt, as *se ylca*, *þæt ylce* (the same). Compounds of this are þylic (such) and *swilc* (such), only the latter being preserved in English, for it is from this pronoun that we have the O. Engl. *swilk*, M. Engl. *swiche, suche*, N. Engl. *such*.

The Goth. *silba*, fem. and neut. *silbo*, theme *silban* (ipse, αυτος), goes after the weak declension; the Old High German may be strong or weak, *selper, selpiu, selpaȝ*, and *selpo, selpa, selpa*; in Old Saxon the weak form *selbo, selba, selba*, is more common than the strong *self*, while, vice versa, in Anglo-Saxon the strong *self* is more frequent than the weak *selfa*; Old Norse may be strong, *sialf-r, sialf, sialf-t*, or weak, *sialfi, sialfa, sialfa*. From these are derived the M. H. Germ. *selp*, gen. *selbes* (ipse) and the N. H. Germ. *der selbe*, which go after the weak declension and the undeclinable *selbst*, the O. Engl. and M. Engl. *silf, silue, selue, self*, N. Engl. *self*, Sw. *sjelfva, sjelf*.

INTERROGATIVE PRONOUNS.

There are different interrogative pronouns for the different questions (1) *quis?* (2) *uter?* (3) *quis eorum?* (4) *qualis?* or, to express (1) a question after a person or thing in general; (2) after one out of two persons or things; (3) after one out of several or many persons or things; (4) after the kind or quality of a person or thing.

TABLE OF INTERROGATIVE PRONOUNS.

1. *Quis?* (Sansk. *kas.*)

i. Old Teutonic.

SINGULAR.

	Gothic.			Ang.-Sax.		Old Saxon.	
	Masc.	Fem.	Neut.	Masc.	Neut.	Masc.	Neut.
Nom.	hva-s	hvô	hva	hva	hvät	hue	huot
Gen.	hvis	†hvaizôs	hvis	hväs	hväs	huës	huës
Dat.	hvamma	†hvai	hvamma	hvam	hvam	huemu	huemu
Accus.	hvana	hvô	hva	hvone	hvät	huena, huane	huat
Intr.	..	..	hvê	..	hvý	..	huiu

	Old Frisian.		O. H. Germ.		Old Norse.	
	Masc.	Neut.	Masc.	Neut.	Masc.	Neut.
Nom.	hwa	hwet	hwe-r	hwaʒ	hva-r	hvat
Gen.	hwammes	hwammes	hwës	hwës	hvess	hvess
Dat.	hwam	hwam	hwemu	hwemu	hveim	hvî
Accus.	hwane, hwene	hwet	hwenan, hwen	hwaʒ	hvann	hvat
Intr.	..	..	..	hwiu	..	..

PLURAL *deest.*

ii. Middle and New Teutonic.

SINGULAR.

	M. H. Germ.		N. H. Germ.		Old English.		N. Engl.	
	Masc.	Neut.	Masc.	Neut.	Masc.	Neut.	Masc.	Neut.
Nom.	wer	waʒ	wer	was	wha, who	what, wat	who	what
Gen.	wes	wes	wessen	wessen	whos, wos	..	whose	..
Dat.	wem	wem	wem	wem	wham, whom (to)	..	whom (to)	..
Accus.	wen	waʒ	wen	was	wham, whom	what	whom	what
Intr.	..	wiu	..	..	..	..	whom	..

Middle Dutch.		New Dutch.			Swedish.		Danish.	
Masc.	Neut.	Masc.	Fem.	Neut.	Masc.	Neut.	Masc.	Neut.

	Masc.	Neut.	Masc.	Fem.	Neut.	Masc.	Neut.	Masc.	Neut.
Nom.	wie	wat	wie	wie	wat	(hô) hvem	hvad	(hvô) hvem	hvad
Gen.	wies	wies	wiens	wier	wiens	(hvars) hvems	..	(hvis)hvems	..
Dat.	wien	wien	wien	wier	wien	hvem	..	hvem	..
Accus.	wien	wat	wien	wie	wat	hrem	hvad	hvem	hvad

Note.—The New High German genitive *wessen* is an inorganic extension of the old *wes*.

In Old English the dative and accusative become identical, and the former therefore adopts the dative sign *to*.

The New Dutch fem. form *wie, wier,* is a very remarkable sign of grammatical vitality in a modern language, this form being altogether wanting in Middle Dutch. The gen. *wiens* also for the Middle Dutch *wies* is an inorganic form developed out of the accus. *wien* with the genitive sign *s*.

The Swedish and Danish dialects have rejected the organic forms of the nom. gen. sing. masc., and instead of these have adopted the accus. *hvem* as nominative, and out of this formed the genitive by the case-sign *s*.

2. *Uter?*

In Gothic there occurs only the nom. masc. and neut. *hvaþar;* O. H. Germ. *hwedarer, hwedaru, hwedaraʒ,* is declined like an adjective, as well as the O. S. *hueðar,* A. S. *hväðer.* Old Norse has nom. *hvar-r, hvár, hvar-t,* gen. *hvár-s, hvár-rar, hvár-s,* &c. Later on we find the form *hvorr, hvort,* for the same pronoun. The German and English *weder, wether,* are used only as conjunctions, and of course undeclinable.

3. *Quis eorum?* (who out of many?)

The Goth. *hvarjis, hvarjata,* is declined as an adjective. No other dialect possesses the same word except Old Norse, where it shows the forms, nom. *hver-r, hver, hver-t,* gen. *hvers, hverrar, hvers,* &c., &c. It appears that from this gen. *hvers* is derived the obsolete Sw. gen. *hvars*.

4. *Qualis?*

Goth. *hveleiks, hveleika, hvelaikata;* O. H. Germ. *hwiolihh-er, hwelihher (weler),* fem. *-iu,* neut. *-aʒ;* O. S. *huilíc,* A. S. *hwilc (hwylc),* O. N. *hvílik-r,* Fris. *hwelk (hwek),* M. H. Germ. *welcher (wel,* gen. *wels,* accus. *weln,* &c.), N. H. Germ. *welcher,* M. Dutch *welke,* N. Dutch *welke,* O. Engl. *whylc, whilke, wuch, woch, wich,* M. Engl. *whiche,* N. Engl. *which* (Scotch *whilk*), Sw. and Dan. *hvilken*.

Note.—All these are declined as adjectives.

RELATIVE PRONOUNS.

There is in none of the Teutonic languages, ancient or modern, a relative pronoun properly so called, but the relative connexion is expressed (1) by the first demonstrative pronoun, Goth. *sa, so,* þata, A. S. *se, seo,* þät, Engl. *that,* O. H. Germ. *der, diu, daȝ,* Germ. *der, die, das,* Dutch *die, dat,* &c., &c. (see the Demonstrative); (2) by the first and fourth interrogative *quis* and *qualis,* hence Engl. *who, what,* Dutch *wie, wat,* Germ. *wer, was,* Sw. Dan. *hvem, hvad,* like the Lat. *qui, quæ, quod,* used in a relative sense. The most frequently occurring relatives in the modern Teutonic languages are the forms answering to the Lat. *qualis,* as Germ. *welcher, welche, welches,* Engl. *which,* Dutch *welke, welk,* Sw. and Dan. *hvilken, hvilket;* (3) by a mere particle, or (4) by a particle added to one of the just-mentioned pronouns.

The cases stated under 3 and 4 occur in the ancient Teutonic dialects. In Gothic the particle *ei* is used as a relative suffix and very probably derived from the same pronominal base as the demonstrative *is,* plur. *eis*[1]. It may be appended to personal or demonstrative pronouns, and, if added, imparts to these pronouns a relative force; e. g. *ik-ei,* ego qui, I who; þu-ei, tu qui, thou who; þuz-ei, tibi cui; þuk-ei, te quem; *iz-ei,* is qui, he who; *s-ei = si-ei,* ea quæ, she who. Most frequently this enclitic particle occurs with the demonstrative *sa, so,* þata, which thus becomes a relative, e. g. nom. *sa-ei, so-ei,* þat-ei (qui, quæ, quod), gen. þiz-ei, þizóz-ei, þiz-ei (cujus), and so on through all cases of the singular and plural.

In Old High German this particle has disappeared from the pers. pron. altogether, and with the demonstrative it occurs very rarely, as *der-i,* he who; *daȝ-i,* that which. But the Old High German dialect has another relative particle in the demonstrative adverb *dar,* or its weakened form *dir, der,* e. g. *ih dir,* I who, ego qui; *wir dir,* nos qui; *thaȝ ther,* id quod.

In the Saxon dialects also we find a particle used in a relative sense, namely O. S. *the,* A. S. þe, the undeclinable form of the demonstrative pronoun *se, seo,* þat; hence A. S. *ik* þe, I who, ego qui; þu þe, tu qui. Frequently we find this particle joined to the demonstrative pronoun, and like the Gothic *ei* imparting to it a relative force, as þam þe, cui, to which; *se* þe, qui, &c.

[1] Comp. p. 191.

In the same manner the Frisian dialect uses the particles *ther* and *the;* the Old Norse, the particle *er,* later on *sem* as well, which may express all cases except the genitive; e. g. þ*ann er,* quem; þ*eim er,* cui; *sa er,* qui: a mere *s* also added to the demonstrative *sa, su,* þ*ata,* may express relative connexion, e. g. *sa-s,* qui; *su-s,* quæ; þ*az=*þ*at-s,* quod; þ*ann-s,* quem; þ*eim-s,* cui. This *s* is nothing but the remainder of the particle *er* in its more ancient form *es.*

INDEFINITE PRONOUNS.

1. Goth. *sum-s, sum-a, sum-ata (sum),* answers to the Greek indefinite τίς, τι; it may or may not be combined with the particle *uh* without altering its sense. O. H. Germ. *sumer, sumiu, sumaʒ,* O. S. *sum,* A. S. *sum,* O. Fris. *sum,* O. N. *sum-r,* O Engl. *sum, summe, som, some,* N. Engl. *some;* Dan. *somt,* plur. *somme,* some people; Dutch *sommige,* several. It goes throughout after the strong declension of the adjectives. The meaning in the Low German dialects of this pronoun added to cardinal numerals is explained under the chapter of Numerals.

2. The Goth. *man,* which is used only in the sense of 'homo,' acquires, when preceded by the negation *ni,* and sometimes followed by the suffix *hun,* the negative sense of 'nemo' (= *ne homo*), e. g. *ni manna,* or *ni manna-hun* (nemo), gen. *ni mans-hun,* &c. The O. H. Germ. *eo-man, ie-man,* is formed with the adverbial accusative *io, éo,* answering to the Goth. *áiv* from *áivs* (time), as *áiv* (ever), *ni aiv* (never); *eo-man* then would mean 'ever a man,' and *ni* or *ne-eoman,* 'never a man;' M. H. Germ. *iaman, iemen; niaman, niemen;* N. H. Germ. *je-mand* (*d* inorganic, *j* inorganic for *i*) and *nie-mand,* ullus and nullus.

In the modern Teutonic dialects *man* is of frequent use as an indefinite pronoun of the 3rd person, in its sense answering to the French 'on'. Thus the Germ. *man sagt* (on dit), Sw. *man sade så* (on l'a dit). (Swedish may use *De* instead of *man: De sade så*). Dan. *man taler meget derom,* on parle beaucoup de cela. It is used only in the nominative, the oblique cases being supplied in German by *eines, einem, ein,* in Swedish and Danish by *En,* gen. *Ens.*

3. Goth. *ains* is not used as an indefinite pronoun, but when the suffix *hun* is added to it, it assumes the meaning 'ullus,' as *ains-hun,* fem. *aino-hun,* neut. *ain-hun,* gen. *ainis-hun, ainaizós-hun,* dat. *ainumme-hun,* &c. In Old High German *einer, einiu, einaʒ,* is used in the sense of 'quidam'; derived from this is

einigér-u-aʒ, aliquis; *dih-ein, doh-ein*, ullus; *nih-ein, noh-ein*, nullus. So also O. S. *nig-en, neg-én, ni-en*, nullus; A. S. *an*, ullus, one; *n-án*, nullus, none; A. S. *ænig*, ullus; *n-ænig*, nullus; O. N. *ein-n*, ullus; *n-ein-n*, nullus. Compare the Germ. *ein, k-ein, n-ein*, the Engl. *one, n-one*; and from A. S. *ænig*, the O. E. and M. E. *ony, any*, N. Eng. *any*. The Old Norse suffix *gi* also has a negative force like the particle *ni, ne*, hence O. N. *ein-gi*, nullus, and in the same manner *svá-gi*, ita non; *ulfr*, wolf; *úlf-gi*, no wolf; *sialf*, ipsa; *sialf-gi*, ipsa non. With verbs Old Norse used the suffix *-a, -at*, or *-t*, as *skal-a*, he shall not; *verðr-at* (Germ. er wird nicht), *em-k-at* for *ek am at*, I am not.

4. The Old High German as well as Low German *wiht* (thing, res), with the prefix *eo*, is used in the sense of 'aliquid,' *eo-wiht* (quelquechose, something), and with the negation *neowiht, ni-wiht* (nothing, nihil). Hence the M. H. Germ. *iht* (something), negative *niht*, N. H. Germ. *icht* (obs.) *nicht* (not), and *nichts* (nothing); O. S. *io-wiht* (aliquid), *nio-wiht* (nihil); A. S. *á-wiht* (aliquid), *n-á-wiht* (nihil). Hence the Anglo-Saxon vocalized forms *auht, nauht, aht, naht*, the O. Engl. *ouht, nouht, oʒt, noʒt*, M. Engl. *ought, nought, ouʒt, nouʒt*, N. Engl. *aught, naught*.

Many indefinite pronouns are compounds of pronouns (chiefly the interrogatives) with particles or other words. Thus we have with the Goth. *leik*, O. H. Germ. *líh*, A. S. *líc* (original meaning 'flesh,' 'body'; hence 'stature', 'form', shape' &c.) the compounds, Goth. *sva-leiks*, O. H. Germ. *sulíh, solíh*, A.S. *þý-líc* and *swilc* (=*swi-líc, swa-líc*), and O. N. *þvilíkr, s-líkr* (=*svá-líkr*). Compare Germ. *solch-er, -e, -es*, O. Engl. *swilk, such*, M. Engl. *swiche, suche*, N. Engl. *such* (Scotch *sic, sicken*, &c.). All other compounds, ancient and modern, find their explanation in the respective dictionaries.

NUMERALS.

CARDINALS.

TABLE OF CARDINAL NUMERALS IN THE COGNATE LANGUAGES.

No.	1. Primitive.	2. Sanskrit.	3. Greek.	4. Latin.	5. Gothic.
1	ai-na-	êka-	εἷς, ἕν, f. μία	ū-no, Old oi-no-	ai-na
2	dua-, dva-	dva-	δύο-	duo	tva-
3	tri-	tri-	τρι- (τρεῖς, τρία)	tri-	thri-
4	katvar-	chatvár, chatúr	τετταρ-, τεσσαρ-ες	quatuor-	fidvôr-
5	kankan	pánchan	πέντε (πέμπε)	quinque	fimf
6	ksvaks	shash	ἕξ (Ϝέξ)	sex	saihs
7	saptan-	sáptan-	ἑπτά	septem	sibun
8	aktu	ashṭan-	ὀκτώ	octo	ahtau
9	navan-	návan-	ἐννέα	novem	niun
10	dakan-	dáśan	δέκα	decem	taihun
11		êkâ-daśan	ἕν-δεκα	un-decim	ain-lif
12	duá dakan	dvâ-daśan	δώ-δεκα	duo-decim	tva-lif
14		chátur-daśan	τεσσαρες-καί-δεκα	quatuor-decim	fidvôr-taihun
20		viśáti	εἴκοσι	viginti	tvai-tigjus
40		chatvâriśát	τετταράκοντα	quadraginta	
60		shashṭí	ἑξήκοντα	sexaginta	saihs-tigu-
70		saptatí	ἑβδομήκοντα	septuaginta	sibun-tehund
100	kan-ta-(m)	śatá	ἑκατό-(ν)	centum	hunda-
200		dve śate (dviśa-tam)	διακόσιο(ι)	ducenti	tva-hunda
300		triṇi satâni (tri śatam)	τριακόσιο(ι)	trecenti	trija-hunda
400		chatvâri śatâni (chatukṣatam)	τετρακόσιο(ι)	quadringenti	(?)
500		pañchaśatâni (pañchaśatam)	πεντακόσιο(ι)	quingenti	fimf-hunda
1000		daśa śatâni (da-śaśatî)	χιλίο(ι)	mille	thusundja- (N.i)

REMARKS ON THE CARDINAL NUMERALS IN THE COGNATE LANGUAGES.

one

There is in the different Aryan languages a great variety of stems for the number 'one,' but all are formed from the root *i*, which in the primitive language may have been represented by the word *ai-na-*. In Sanskrit the word *éka-* shows the pronominal root *i* and the suffix or pronominal root *ká*. The Greek εἷς (= ἐν-s), neut. ἐν, gen. ἐν-ός, fem. μία, has the base ἐν- from the primitive form *san-* = *sam* (comp. Lat. sim-plex, sem-el, sin-guli), contained in the Sansk. *sama* (similis; a superlative of the demonstrative pronominal base *sa-*). This view is corroborated by the feminine form μία (for ʽμια = *sm-yá* = *smyá*, a feminine base in *ya*) which presupposes a base *sa-mya*, as ἐν-, a base *sa-n-* from one and the same root *sa*. Latin, in its more ancient form *oi-no*, the later *u-no-* shows clearly the primitive form *ai-na-*, and is, in the same manner as the Sanskrit pronominal base *e-na-*, formed from the pronominal root *i* with the suffix *na*. The Teutonic dialects have cultivated a form which is identical with the Latin, Engl. *one*, Germ. *ein*, A. S. *an* being represented by the Goth. *ains*, the theme of which is *Ai-na-*.

The expression of the number 'one' in the following Teutonic words is peculiar:—Goth. *haihs*, one-eyed; *hanfs*, one-handed; *halts*, halt, one-footed, lame; *halbs*, half. In all these words the number 'one' is expressed by *ha*, and this *ha* answers to the Sansk. *ka* in *e-ka*; *iha*, the second half of the word *haihs*, theme *ha-iha*, is the Sansk. *ashi*, eye. The Latin *cæcus* = *ca-ico* is formed on the same principle. In *hanfs*, theme *ha-nfa* we have again the pronominal root *ha* and *nifa*, a transposition of the Sansk. *páni*, hand. (*f* for *p* harmonizes with Grimm's law.) *halts*, theme *ha-lta*, consists of two roots, the pronominal *ha* and the verbal root *lith*, to go, from which also is derived *lithus*, limb, i.e. that which is moved; hence *ha-litha*, *halta*, *halts*, halt = one-limbed, one-footed: *halbs*, theme *ha-lba* from *ha* and *leiba*, remnant, part; hence *haliba*, *halbs*, half = one part of a whole that has been divided.

two

The Sansk. base *dva*, Gr. δυο-, Lat. *duo*, Goth. *tva-* all point to a primitive form *dua-* or *dva-*. The Latin prefix *bi* and adverb *bis*, Gr. δις, seem to have arisen from the same form, the initial *d* being dropped and *v* hardened into *b*. The same prefix we have in the A. S. *tvi* (Gr. and Lat. *d* is, according to Grimm's law, in Low German *t*, and in High German *z*) and O. H. Germ. *zui*, e. g. A. S. *tvi-finger*, two fingers long; *tvi-hive*, bicolor; O. H. Germ. *zui-beine*, bipes; *zui-falt*, duplex. The English adverb *twice*, O. H. Germ. *zuiro*, more fully *zuiror*, O. N. *tvis-var*, again contains the prefix *tvi* (bis, δις) and *var*, Sansk. *vara*, time; hence *twice = two times*, &c. (This *var* also appears in the Latin *ber* in *Septem-ber*, i. e. the seventh time, or part, of the year.)

three

In Sanskrit, Greek, and Latin, the theme or base is *tri*, in Goth. *thri*, O. H. Germ. *dri*, the displacement of the initial dentals being in strict accordance with Grimm's law. It is considered a shortened form of a more ancient *tar-i* or *tra-i*; the Sanskrit fem. form is *ti-sar-* which Bopp takes for a reduplication, *ti-tar-*.

four

As the primitive form is laid down *katvar-*, which in Sanskrit is represented by *chatvár-*, base *chatur*, theme of the feminine *chatasar-*. This word is strictly formed after the analogy of 'three,' Sansk. fem. theme *ti-sar-*, and *cha = ka*, one (comp. *e-ka* above), hence *cha-tasar* = 1 + 3. The Gr. τετταρ-, τεσσαρ-, stand for †τετϝαρ-, κετϝαρ-, Dor. τετορ-, †τετϝορ, Bœot. πετταρ-, Hom. and Æol. πίσυρ-, where we find τ or π in the place of the primitive κ. In the Lat. *quatuor*, the *q* stands for the primitive *k*, and the *u* (= *w*) is a favourite sound in Latin after the tenuis *k*, just as in Gothic the aspirate *h* at the beginning of a word. (Comp. Gr. τις, Lat. *quis*, Goth. *hvas*.) The Gothic *fidur* (with *f* = *p* = *k*) is the simple theme of *fidvor*, analogous to the Sansk. *chatur* for *chatwár-*.

five

The primitive form laid down by Schleicher as *kan-kan-* is evidently a reduplication, where in Sanskrit *p* crept in for the first *k* in the theme *panchan-*; but Bopp derives the word from *pa + ka* (the *n* in the middle considered a later addition, and the final consonant euphonic), and thus he gives it the meaning 'and one,' i. e. one in addition to the preceding number four. Gr. πέντε puts first π for κ, and next τ for κ (both dislocations occur under 4), Æol. πεμπε; while the Lat. *quinque* preserves the primitive *k* sound, and the Goth. *fimf=fimfi* (from a primitive *kanki-*) has *f=p* and *p* for *k*. (Comp. **4, 11, 12,** &c.)

six

The primitive form is supposed to have been *ksva-ksva*, again a reduplication, from which the Sansk. *shash* may be explained by an intermediate form *kshaksh*, which again stood for *ksaks*. Gr. ἑξ, Dor. Ϝεξ, Lat. *sex*, presuppose a more primitive *svex=sve-c-s*, the Greek spiritus asper answering here as elsewhere to the original *s*. Goth. *sai-h-s* is formed on the same principle as the Lat. *sex*, Gothic *h* being the representative of the Latin *k* (see Grimm's law).

seven

The primitive form was probably, like the Sansk. base, *saptan-*, which is rendered by the Gr. ἑπτά (a=an), Lat. *septem* for *septim*, Goth. *sibun*. (Gr. *h* again for *s*.) Bopp thinks that the *m* in *septem* has crept in from the ordinal *septim-o*, an opinion which is contradicted by Schleicher upon the evidence of the analogous forms in the other Aryan languages.

eight

A primitive base *aktu* must have given origin to the Sansk. *ashtan, ashtu, ashtáu* (probably from *aktáv-as*), Gr. ὀκτω, Lat. *octo*, Goth. *ahtau, ahtu*. Sanskrit, Greek, and Latin, are apparently dual forms. The primitive form of the theme *aktu* is quite distinct in the ordinals *octav-o*, †ογδοϜ-ο: the same base is apparent in the Goth. *ahtau*, theme *ahtavi-* (comp. *sunau*, loc. sing. *sunavi*); so also in the Gothic ordinal *ahtu-da-n, ahtu=aktu* (Goth. *h=*Sansk. *k*, Grimm's law) we trace the primitive base again.

nine

The primitive and Sansk. *navan* appears in Greek as ἐννέα for †νεϜα(ν), with the favourite prelude ε introduced, and ν dropped; Lat. *novem* instead of *novim*; Goth. *niun*, theme *niuni*, from †*nivani=*†*navani*.

ten

Primitive *dakan*, Sanskrit base *daśan*, Gr. δέκα=ʼδεκαν, Lat. *decem=decim;* Goth. *taihun*, theme *tihuni*, O. H. Germ. *zehan*. (Observe Grimm's law: Sansk. *d*, Goth. *t*, O. H. Germ. *z*.) The Sansk. *dasan*, or rather its primitive form *dakan*, stands for *dra-kan; dra = two, kan* for *kankan, panchan=five,* and hence *daśan,* our *ten,* means 'two times five.'

11, 12

For these numbers the primitive language had distinct words, as *duá dakan* (12), &c.; so also in Sansk. *eka-daśan* (11), *dvá-dasan* (12), Gr. ἐν-δεκα, δω-δεκα, Lat. *un-decim = uni-decim, duo-decim.* Goth. *ain-lif* (11), *tva-lif* (12), are the nominatives of *ain-libi, tva-libi*. The bases *ain* and *tva* have been treated on above; the second part of the compounds, *libi,* is derived from the *dakan* (10) of the Ursprache, which in Gothic may first have assumed the form *tigi,* substituting, according to Grimm's law, *t* for the Sansk. *d*, and, instead of proceeding according to the same law from the Sanskrit guttural to the aspirate, returning into the media *g*. This guttural media was then exchanged for the labial media *b,* an occurrence which is not without a parallel in other words. The further exchange of the initial dental for the liquid *l* is without a parallel in Gothic, but not unknown in the cognate languages. The Lat. *lacruma* is the same word as the Gr. δακρυ, *l* taking the place in the Latin which *d* holds in the Greek word. The replacement of the *d* by *l* in *dakan,* or rather its Gothic form *tigi, tibi,* may have been facilitated by the close resemblance between this word and the Gothic verb *leib-an,* to remain, leave, pret. *laif,* plur. *libum;* so that finally the two words of different origin become phonetically the same. Our *eleven, twelve,* therefore mean 1+10, 2+10 respectively.

13—19

These numerals are in Sanskrit compounds of *dasan* and the respective unit, as *trayo-dasan* (13), *chatur-daśan* (14): the corresponding Greek words are merely joined by the copulative καί, as τρεις-και-δέκα (13), τέσσαρες-και-δεκα (14), whilst Latin forms, like Sanskrit, compounds, as *tre-decim, quin-decim* (15), *se-decim* (16), and on the same principle are formed the Goth. *fidvor-taihun* (14), *fimf-taihun* (15).

20—90

We have to consider the 'tens' only; the intermediate members, i. e. their combination with 'units' require no explanation, because in none of the languages here considered do they form compounds, but are merely put together, occasionally joined by the copula 'and.'

In the manner of forming these numerals the South-European differ from the North-European or Slavono-Teutonic languages: the former express the 'tens' by an agglutination of the units with a substantive derived from *dakan* (10), which, by means of abbreviation or other modifications, has dwindled down into a mere termination; while the latter express the 'tens' and 'units' by distinct words, which however may form compounds.

Sanskrit originally expressed the 'tens' by *daśa-ti*, *daśa-ta*, of which nothing remained but *śati*, or only *ti*, or *śat*, as *ví-sati* (20) for †*dvi-daśati*, *shash-ti* (60) = *shash-daśati*, *pancha-sat* (50) = = *pancha-sata*. In the Gr. εικοσι- the first syllable shows the base ἑν (one); κο-σι is the primitive *daka-ti*, or rather, dropping the first syllable, *ka-ti*. The κον-τα of the other 'tens' is perhaps derived from a neuter plural base *kan-ta* for *dakan-ta*. The Latin *vi-ginti* presents in its first syllable *vi* the base *dvi* (two), and *vi-ginti* stands for a form †*dvi-ginti* in the same manner as the Sansk. *visati* for a †*dviśati*; and *ginti* stands for †*deginti* = †*decinti*, from a primitive form *dakan-ti*, so that the full form of *triginta* would be †*tria-decinta*.

Gothic, our representative of the North-European or Slavono-Teutonic tribe, forms the 'tens' from 10 to 60 by putting two distinct words together, expressing the 'tens' by *tigu*, a base in *u* for *daku*, derived from *dakan* (10), hence *trai-tiggu-s* (20); the 'tens' from 70 to 90 are formed by *dakan* with the suffix *ta*, in the Gothic garb reading *tehun-d*, e. g. *sibun-tehund* (70).

100

The genitive base used to indicate this number appears to be *kanta*, an abbreviation of *dakan-dakan-ta*, a form which in English might be rendered by an analogous compound, namely *ten-ty* = ten times ten, in the same manner as we say *nine-ty* = ten times nine, and in Greek and Latin the compounds would be †δεκηκοντα, †*centaginta*. The *n* of the primitive *kanta* is preserved in Latin and Gothic, *cent-um*, *hund-a*; but it is dropped in Sanskrit and Greek, *sata*, ἑ-κατο (ἑ = ἑν). The Gothic language has, besides the word *hunda*, a more modern form to denote the same number, *taíhun-taíhun-d*, which is composed exactly on the principle of the *dakan-dakan-ta*, ten times ten (compare *sibuntehund*, seventy).

200—900

The primitive language undoubtedly applied two words to express the foregoing figures; Sanskrit also uses two distinct words, or contracts them into one, e. g. *dve-śate* or *dvisata* (200), *sata* being of course the base *kanta* again. The Greek forms are κατο, κοτο, with the derivative suffix *ya*—κατιο, κοτιο, later form κοσιο; compare τρια-κατιο-, a Doric form, and the Attic τρια-κοσιο-. The Latin base *cento* is used as an adjective in the plural, *tre-centi* (300) for *tre-cento*, *quin-genti* for *quin-cento* (700), where the *c* after *n* is softened into the media *g*; and in the same manner *septin-genti*, where the *septin* answers exactly to the primitive *saptan*. (See above, sub **7**.) Gothic never forms compounds by agglutination, like Greek and Latin, but it simply puts the two words together, e. g. *tva-hunda* (200).

1000

A word for this number does not seem to have existed in the primitive language. The Sanskrit *sahasra*, Gr. χίλιοι. †χηλιοι (leading to a primitive †χελιο=gharya), the Latin *mili-*, *milli-*, are all of an obscure origin. The Gothic word is *thusundja* (thousand), in which Schleicher finds the number 'ten times hundred' expressed, namely, *daka* (10) in the initial syllable *thu* (=*tu*), *kantya*, *kanti* (100) in the form *sundi*, *sundja*; and this would yield as the result *daka-kant-t* (10 × 100).

TABLE OF CARDINALS IN THE OLD TEUTONIC LANGUAGES.

Masculine.

No.	1. Gothic.	2. Anglo-Saxon.	3. Old Saxon.	4. Old Frisian.	5. O. Norse.	6. O. H. Germ.
1	ains	ân	ên	ên	[ein-n]	ein
2	tvai	tvegen	tuêna	twêne	tveir	zwênê
3	†þreis	þrî	thria	thrê	þrîr	drî
4	fidvôr	feóver	fiwar	fiuer	fiorir	vior
5	fimf	fîf	fîf	fîf	fimm	fimf
6	saihs	six	sehs	sex	sex	sëhs
7	sibun	seofon	siðun	sigun	siau	sibun
8	ahtáu	ahta	ahtô	achta	âtta	ahtô
9	niun	nigon	nigun	nigun	nîu	niun
10	taihun	tin	tehan	tian	tîu	gëhan
11	ain-lif	end-leofan and el-lefan	†êl-lif	and-lova, el-leva	ellifu	ein-lif
12	tva-lif	twelf	tue-lif	twi-lif	tôlf	zwe-lif
13	†þrija-taihun	þreó-teon (týne)	..	†thrêtine	þrettian	dri-zëhan
14	fidvôr-taihun	feóver-teon.	..	fiuwer-tine	fior-tian	fior-zëhan
15	fimf-taihun	fîf-teon	..	fîf-tine	fim-tian	finf-zëhan
16	†saihs-taihun	six-teon	..	sex-tine	sex-tian	sëhs-zëhan
17	†sibun-taihun	seofen-teon	..	siugun-tine	siau-tian	sibun-zëhan
18	†ahtáu-taihun	eaht-teon	..	achta-tine	âttian	ahtô-zëhan
19	†niun-taihun	nigon-teon	..	niugen-tine	nîtian	niun-zëhan
20	tvai tigjus	twen-tig	tuên-tig	twint-ich	tut-tugu	zwein-zug
30	þreis tigjus	þrí-tig	thrî-tig	thrî-tich	þria-tigi	drî-zug
40	fidvor tigjus	feóver-tig	fiwar-tig	fiuwer-tich	fior-tîu	fior-zug
50	fimf tigjus	fîf-tig	fîf-tech	fîf-tech	fimm-tîu	fimf-zug
60	saihs tigjus	six-tig	sehs-tig	sex-tich	sex-tîu	sëhs-zug
70	sibun-têhund	seofen-tig	ant-sibun-ta	siugun-tich	sió-tigi	sibun-zô
80	ahtau-têhund	eaht-tig	ant-ahtô-da	achtan-tich	âtta-tigi	ahto-zô
90	niun-têhund	nigon-tig	†ant-nigun-da?	nigon-tich	nîu-tigir	niun-zô
100	taihun-têhund	teon-tig	hund	hundred	hundrad	zëhan-zô

TABLE OF CARDINALS IN THE MIDDLE TEUTONIC LANGUAGES.

No.	Old and Middle English.	Middle High German.
1	an, on, oon	ein(er), (f. einiu, n. einez)
2	twey, twi, twein, twe, two	zwêne (f. zevô, zwei)
3	þre, three	drî (drî, driu)
4	four	vier(e) (viere, vieriu)
5	five	vunf (vünve, vünviu)
6	sixe	sehs
7	seuen	siben (sibeniu)
8	eigte, aught	aht (ëhte, ahtiu)
9	nyne, nye	niun (niune, niuniu)
10	ten	zëhen
11	elleuen, elleue	einlif, einlef, einleve
12	twelue	zwelef, zwelf, zweleve

NUMERALS.

No.	Old and Middle English.	Middle High German.
13	þrottene, þrittene	dri-zëhen, drizên
14	four-tene	vier-zëhen, -zên
15	fíf-tene	vunf-zëhen
16	sixtene	sehszëhen
17	seuentene	sibenzëhen
18	eigtetene, eigtene, auhtene	ahtzëhen
19	ninetene	niunzëhen
20	tuen-ti	zwein-zec, zweinzich.
30	thri-tti	drî-zec, -zich
40	(fourti?)	vierzec
50	fyfti	vunfzec
60	sixti	sehszec
70	seuenti	sibenzec
80	eigteti	ahtzec
90	nienti	niunzec
100	hundred	zëhen-zec, zehenzich, hunt, hundert
1000	þousend	túsent

TABLE OF CARDINAL IN THE NEW TEUTONIC LANGUAGES.

No.	German.	English.	Dutch.	Swedish.	Danish.
1	ein	one	één	en (N. ett)	een (eet)
2	zwei	two	twee	två	to
3	drei	three	drie	tre	tre
4	vier	four	vier	fyra	fire
5	fünf	five	vijf	fem	fêm
6	sechs	six	zes	sex	sex
7	sieben	seven	zeven	sju	syv
8	acht	eight	acht	åtta	aatte
9	neun	nine	negen	niô	ni
10	zehn	ten	tien	tiô	ti
11	elf	eleven	elf	elfva	èlleve
12	zwölf	twelve	twaalf	tolf	tolv
13	drei-zehn	thir-teen	der-tien	tre-tton	tre-tten
14	vier-zehn	four-teen	veer-tien	fjòr-ton	fjòr-ten
15	fünfzehn	fifteen	vijftien	femton	femten
16	sechzehn	sixteen	zestien	sexton	sejsten (sexten)
17	siebenzehn	seventeen	zeventien	sjutton	sytten
18	achtzehn	eighteen	achttien	aderton	atten
19	neunzehn	nineteen	negentien	nitton	nitten
20	zwan-zig	twen-ty	twin-tig	tjugu (-ô -ê)	tyve
30	drei-ßig	thir-ty	der-tig	tre-ttiô (-e)	trè-dive
40	vier-zig	for-ty	veer-tig	fyr-tiô (-e)	fyrre-tyve
50	fünfzig	fifty	vijftig	femtiô	halvtrés (indstyve)
60	sechzig	sixty	zestig	sextiô	tres (tresindstyve)
70	siebenzig	serenty	seventig	sguttiô	halvfjèrs (indstyve)
80	achtzig	eighty	tachtig	åttatiô	firs (firsindstyve)
90	neunzig	ninety	negentig	nittiô	halvfèms (indstyve)
100	hundert	hundred	honderd	hundrade (hundra)	hundrede
200	zwei hun ert	two hundred	twee honderd	två hundrade	to hundrede
1000	tausend	thousand	duizend	tusende (tusen)	tusinde.

REMARKS ON THE TEUTONIC CARDINALS.

one

We find the primitive base *aina-* for the number 'one' in all Teutonic languages, ancient and modern, modified of course in accordance with the phonetic character of each dialect, as O. H. Germ. *ein*, A. S. *an*, Germ. *ein*, Dutch *een*, O. Engl. *on*, Engl. *one*, &c.[1]

two

The Goth. *tvái* is not the base from which the Anglo-Saxon and Old High German forms are derived, but rather the distributive *tveihnai*, which in Old High German has dropped the *h* (*zwene*) and hardened it in Anglo-Saxon into *g = twegen*. The Gothic gen. *tvaddje* also cannot result from the nom. *tvái*, but requires a base *tvaddja*, which Bopp brings into connection with the Sanskrit ordinal *dvitíya*.

In the other Low German dialects, O. S. *tuena*, O. Fris. *twene*, the *h* again suffers elision, and in the Modern Engl. *two*, Dutch *twee*, Dan. *to*, Swed. *två*, contraction has taken place. Very ancient forms are preserved in the Old Norse datives *tvei-mr* and *þri-mr* for *tvei-ms* and *þri-ms*, where the case-sign of the dative plural is found in a completeness unparalleled in the Teutonic languages. This numeral is especially noteworthy for its strict adhesion to Grimm's law, according to which we have the media *d* in the cognate languages, *dva, duo;* the tenuis *t* in the Low German dialects, Goth. *tvai*, A. S. *twegen*, O. S. *tuena*, O. N. *tveir;* and the aspirate *z* in the O. H. Germ. *zwene*. The law continues to be observed in the O. Engl. *twey* and M. H. Germ. *zwene;* even in the N. H. Germ. *zwei* for the Low German forms with *t*, as Engl. *two*, Dutch *twee*, Dan. *to*, Swed. *tva*. The O. N. *r* in *tvei-r* has usurped the place of the Goth. *s*.

three

The Goth. *þri-* (in *þrija, þreis*) harmonizes with the *tri-* in the cognate languages by using the aspirate *th* in place of the tenuis, a submission to law which is equally practised by all the Old Low German dialects (A. S. *þrí*, O. N. *þrir*, &c.), whilst Old High German adopted, as by law it was directed, the media *d*. As to the modern dialects we observe that Middle and New

---

[1] Concerning the radicals, Goth. *ai*, A.S. *a*, Germ. *ei*, see the table of gradations, Order *i*, p. 24.

High German follow the course of their ancient mother by preserving the media; but among the Low German it is English alone that keeps up the ancient lawful *th*, while the Dutch and the Old Norse dialects yield to intruders, the former adopting the media (probably under High German pressure), the latter hardening the aspirate into the tenuis for the simple reason that they have expelled the aspirate altogether from their domain.

four

The Gothic *fid-vor* (*fidur*) which renders fully the Sansk. *chatvár* (*chatur*), primitive *kat-var*, replaces the guttural tenuis by the labial aspirate, a change which equally occurs in all the Teutonic dialects, ancient as well as modern, with this modification only, that the High German dialects (and Dutch following their example) supplant the *f* by *v*, a distinction however which is merely graphical, the sound of H. Germ. *v* and *f* at the beginning of a word being identical. But the Gothic *fid-vor* appears in a more mutilated form in the other Teutonic dialects, the *d* being dropped in all, and in Old High German the *w* as well, which latter consonant is vocalized in the modern dialects. This numeral has thus mostly become monosyllabic, as Engl. *four*, Dutch and Germ. *vier*.

five

In this numeral all the Teutonic dialects adopt, like Gothic, and in accordance with Grimm's law, the labial aspirate *f* in the place of the tenuis *p* which occurs in the cognate languages, the only exception being Middle High German and New Dutch, where the letter *v* is used to denote the same sound as *f*. The *m* however of the Goth. *fimf*, which stands for the primitive *n*, has been subject to divers modifying influences. In the H. Germ. *fünf* we see the original *n* restored in its place. The Norse dialects to the present day preserve the *m* and dismiss the final *f* (hence O. N. *fimm*, Dan. and Swed. *fem*), while the Low German dialects, which never tolerate an *n* before *f* or ð (see sub lit. **n**), preserve the *f* and dismiss the *n* (*m*) instead: A. S. *fíf*, Engl. *five*, &c., compared to Germ. *fünf*, Dan. *fem*.

six

The Gothic *h* in *saíh-s* duly represents the *k* of the cognate languages, as Latin *sex = sec-s*. This guttural *h*, which must not be confounded with the sibilant marked by the same letter, is found in Old Saxon according to the rule, and in Old and Middle High German in spite of it. All the other Teutonic dialects have hardened the *hs* into *ks*, *cs*, *x*, as A. S., Engl. *six*, Scandinavian *sex*, &c. Exceptional forms are the Dutch *zes* and the Germ. *sechs*, the former having dropped the guttural altogether and softened *s* into *z*, the latter having developed the Old and Middle German *h*, into *ch*, a change which occurs in all words which in Old German ended in *hs* or *ht*.

seven

The Goth. *sibun*, which renders the primitive *saptan* in a greatly modified and rather irregular form, is still further modified according to the spirit of each dialect. Thus the High German dialects have the *b* in common with the Gothic contrary to the rule, but so far only as Gothic is here in the wrong and High German in the right, because the *p* of the cognate languages should be represented in Gothic by the aspirate (*ph*, *f*), and consequently in Old High German by the media *b*. If therefore we put for instance the A. S. *seofon* as the representative of the Low German class, we find Grimm's law strictly applied in the order P, PH, B. The Old Saxon dialect replaces the media by the soft aspirate *b̄* = *v*, a course which is followed in most of the modern Teutonic languages, as Engl. *seven*, Dutch *zeven*, Dan. *syv*, while German remains faithful to the H. Germ. *b*, *si(e)ben*: the *e* is an inorganic addition. Peculiar is the vocalization of *v* for the Gothic *b* in the O. N. *siau* for *siav*, which yields the Swedish *sju*, and the completely isolated case of the O. Fris. *sigun*, where the guttural replaces the labial media.

eight

The Goth. *ahtáu* is a regular rendering of the primitive *aktu*, the *k* of the cognate languages being in Gothic supplanted by the guttural aspirate *h*, and the *t* preserved by the preceding *h*, which like *f*, suffers no other letter but the tenuis after it. In the other Teutonic dialects, however, the guttural has experienced divers vicissitudes. Anglo-Saxon and Old Saxon adopted, like Gothic and according to law, the guttural aspirate *h*, and Old High German adapted itself here again to Low German usage, while Old Frisian, in advance of its sister dialects, developed the *h* into the hard guttural *ch*, a course which was followed later on by modern dialects, the German and Dutch having *acht* for *aht*, while the English developed out of the Anglo-Saxon *h* the combination *gh*, *eight*—for which Old English *eiȝt* and *aught*. The O. N. *átta* has assimilated the guttural to the succeeding *t*, whereby gemination is produced with the lengthening of the preceding vowel. The form is strictly preserved in the Dan. *aatte* and the Swed. *åtta*.

nine

The Goth. *niun* shows the primitive *navan* in a contracted form, with which the O. H. Germ. *niun* is identical; and Old Norse would be, but for the *n* it has dropped, *níu*. From the O. H. Germ. and M. H. Germ. *niun* we have the German *neun* (*eu* for *iu* according to the rule), and from the O. N. *niu* the Danish *ni*, giving preponderance to the first of the two vowels to the loss of the second, the Swedish patronising the latter in *nio*. But far more noteworthy is the Anglo-Saxon, Old Saxon, and Old Frisian guttural media *g* in the place of the primitive *v* in *navan*, so that the A. S. *nigon*, O. S. *nigun*, O. Fris. *nigun = nijun*, correspond to the Goth. *niu-n = nivu-n*. Here again Gothic is far outdone in point of antiquity and primitive characteristics by its Low German sister-tongues. The modern dialects followed the course commenced in Gothic already, and dropping the middle consonant, contracted the two syllables into one, hence the Engl. *nine*, O. Engl. still *nye*, *nyne*, probably bisyllabic, from A. S. *nigon*, or perhaps rather O. N. *níu*, Germ. *neun* from *niun*; Dutch alone has preserved the full Low German form in *negen*.

ten

Grimm's law is strictly carried out by the Goth. *taíhun* and all its Low German representatives rendering the primitive media *d* by the tenuis *t*, and the High German using, also according to law, the aspirate *z*. But the middle guttural of the primitive *dak-an* is greatly modified not only in the Teutonic but in the cognate dialects as well. It is preserved in the Gr. δέκ-α, the Lat. *dec-em* and the Goth. *taih-un* (*h* in Gothic being the lawful representative of the primitive *k*), while the Sanskrit has adopted the sibilant *s* in *daś-an*. Among the Teutonic languages Old Saxon and High German have preserved the *h*, O. S. *tehan*, O. H. Germ. *zëhan*, M. H. Germ. *zëhen* (and contracted *zen*), N. H. Germ. *zehen*, *zehn*. The other old Teutonic dialects and their modern derivatives drop the middle guttural and contract the word into a monosyllable, as A. S. *tin*, Engl. *ten*, Dutch *tien*, O. N. *tíu*, Dan. *ti*, Swed. *tio*.

11, 12

Concerning the formation of these numerals we have seen above how the Goth. *lif* in *ain-lif*, *tva-lif*, corresponds to the Lat. *decem*, Gr. δεκα and Sansk. *dasan*, and that consequently our words *eleven, twelve*, simply mean 10 + 1 and 10 + 2 respectively. The same compound of numeral and suffix occurs in the other Teutonic dialects too, but in forms greatly modified by elisions and contractions. The suffix *lif* we find fully preserved in Old Saxon, Old Frisian, and Old High German; Middle High German modified the *lif* into *lef*, and Anglo-Saxon and Old Norse drop the vowel altogether, leaving simply *lf* to represent the suffix. This *lf* occurs in all the modern Teutonic dialects except in English and Danish, where the ancient *f* is rendered by *v* its softer twin aspirate. Very strange is the occurrence of the inorganic *d* in the A. S. *end-leofan*, O. Fris. *and-lova*, the unit in the former language being *an*, in the latter *en*. The Old High German and Middle High German preserve the numeral 'one' intact in the word *ein-lif*, *ein-lef*, whilst Old Norse drops the vowel and assimilates the *n* to the succeeding *l*, hence *el-lifu*; thus also in O. Engl. *elleue*, Dan. *elleve*. Most mutilated are the German and Dutch *elf*, Engl. *eleven*, where the numeral is represented merely by *e*. The numeral *tva* in *tva-lif* (12) is preserved in the different dialects with a modification of the vowel, as *twi, twe*, H. Germ. *zwe*; the Scandinavian dialects, however, vocalize the *va* into *ó*, O. N. *to-lf*, Swed. *tolf*, Dan. *tolv*.

13—19

All these numerals are in the different Teutonic languages, just as in Gothic, compounds of the 'units' with the word 'ten,' so that the O. N. *tian*, A. S. *teon* (*tin, týn*), O. H. Germ. *zehan*, bear their explanation in themselves, and the terminations of these numerals in the modern Teutonic dialects are easily explained as derivatives of the ancient forms.

20—90

The *tigjus* of the Goth. *tvai-tigjus* (20) having been explained already, we may confine ourselves to a short review of the corresponding forms and their peculiarities in the other Teutonic languages.

The O. N. *tigi* in þria-tigi and þiu in fior-tiu are modifications of the fuller form *tugu* in *tu-ttugu*, which, like the O. H. Germ. *zug* in *zwein-zug*, represent the Goth. *tigjus*, a base in *u*, *daku* from *dakan* (10); and quite as readily will be perceived the relation of A. S., O. S. *tig*, O. Fris. *tich*. The final consonant is dropped in the O. Engl. *tuen-ti*, N. Engl. *twen-ty*, with the usual change of the final *i* into *y*. The Swed. *tio* is the direct descendant of the O. N. *tiu*, while the Dan. *dive* undoubtedly owes its origin to some other source. Very characteristic in this form is the use of the labial aspirate for the guttural media, *dive* = *dige*, which is the reverse of the O. Fris. *sigun* for A. S. *seofon*, O. S. *siƀun* (7), and the A. S. *nigon*, O. Fris., O. S. *nigun* for the Goth. *niun* = *niv-un*, primitive *nav-an*.

For the formation of the 'tens' from 'seventy' upwards, most of the Old Teutonic dialects use a word differing from *tigjus* in form and, to a certain extent, in derivation, though not in meaning. The Goth. *tehun-d*, which is used in *sibun-tehund* (70), &c., pre-supposes, as we have explained before, a primitive *dakan-ta*, and answers in meaning to the Gr. δεκας. This *tehund* we meet in the other dialects in more or less modified forms. The whole form we find contracted in the O. H. Germ. *zô*, *sibun-zo*. The most ancient mode of forming the numerals 'seventy,' &c., in Anglo-Saxon was to place the undeclinable *hund*, shortened from *tehund*, and expressing the 'tens,' side by side with the respective unit of the ordinals, e. g. *hundeseofoðe* (70), *hundeahtoðe* (80), *hundnigoðe* (90); in a like manner the O. S. *ant* is used (though its identity with the A. S. *hund* is not proved), and forms the 'tens' by entering into a combination with the ordinals, e. g. *antsibunda* (70), *antahtoda* (80), *antnigunda* (90), forms which may be rendered in Latin by *decas septima*, *decas octava*, *decas nona*. But in later times the Anglo-Saxon suffix *tig* (= Goth. *tigjus*), which had been used for the numerals from 10 to 60 only, found entrance also in the higher numbers, as *seofontig* (70) (in the same manner as in late Old High German we find *sibunzug* for *sibunzo*), although the ancient prefix *hund* did not yield its place at once; and thus it happened that in forms like *hundseofontig* (70), *hundeahtatig* (80), &c., the 'ten' is expressed twice, by the suffix *tig* and the prefix *hund*. The same pleonasm occurs in the O. Fris. *t-achtich* (80), *t-niogentich* (90), and the last trace is in the Modern Dutch of the present day, where the *t* in *tachtig* (80), is as in Old Frisian the mutilated form of a word like O. S. *ant*, expressing the 'decas,' which is repeated in the suffix *tich*, *tig*.

From this circumstance may perhaps be explained a peculiar mode of reckoning from 70 upwards, which was adopted in

Old English by the side of the regular one mentioned in our tables, and according to which the numbers were expressed by the numeral 'sixty' and its respective addition, e. g. *sixti and sixtene* (76), *sixti and þrittene* (73), in the same manner as now the French say *soixante seize*, *soixante treize*. From 'eighty' upwards the term *score* was used, as *four score and nien* (89), identical with the French *quatre-vingt-neuf*; *six score and on* (121). It would appear as if, with the suffix *hund*, which was dropped in the course of time, the numeral itself had, though only for a period and in certain localities, fallen into disuse.

Among the ancient Teutonic tribes the reckoning by 'decades' did not stop below the 'hundred,' but the latter number itself, and the numbers up to 120 were expressed like their predecessors below hundred. Hence the Gothic *taihun-tēhund*, A. S. *hund-teontig*, O. N. *tíu-tíu*, which we could imitate in English if we were allowed to say *ten-ty* as well as *nine-ty* or *twen-ty*. This mode of reckoning was indeed preserved so late as the period of Middle High German, where we find *zehen-zich* used by the side of *hundert* (100). The different forms in the Teutonic dialects for the word 'hundred' have their prototype in the Gothic *hund-a*, which, like the Latin *cent-um*, may be traced to a primi-

No.	Engl.	Old Engl.	Ang.Sax.	Dutch.	Old Sax.	O. Fris.	Danish.	Swedish.	O. N.
1	one	an, on	án	één	én	én	een (eet)	en (ett)	ein
2	two	twey, tuo	twegen	twee	tuéna	twéne	to	tvä	tveir
3	three	þre	þrí	drie	thria	thré	tre	tre	þrír
4	four	four	feóver	vier	fiwar	fiwer	fire	fyra	fiowr
5	five	five	fíf	vijf	fíf	fíf	fém	fem	fimm
6	six	sixe	six	zes	sehs	sex	sex	sex	sex
7	seven	seuen	seofon	zeven	sibun	sigun	syv	sju	siau
8	eight	eigte, aught	ahta	acht	ahtó	achta	aatte	åtta	átta
9	nine	nyne, nye	nigon	negen	nigun	nigun	ni	nió	ntu
10	ten	ten	tin	tien	tehan	tian	ti	tió	tiu
11	eleven	elleuen	end-leofan	elf	(el-lif)	and-lova	élleve	elfva	ellifu
12	twelve	twelue	twelf	twaalf	tue-lif	twi-lif	tolv	tolf	tólf
13	thirteen	þrottene, þrittene	preo-téon	der-tien	(?)	(thré-tine)	tretten	tretton	þrettian
20	twenty	tuenti	twen-tig	twin-tig	tuén-tig	twin-tich	tyve	tjugu	tut-tugu
30	thirty	thritti	þri-tig	der-tig	thrí-tig	thri-tich	tredive	trettió	þriatigi
70	seventy	seuenti	seofen-tig	seven-tig	ant-sibunda	siugun-tich	halvfjèrs	sjuttió	siötigi
100	hundred	hundred	teon-tig } hundred	honderd	hund	hundred	hundrede	hundrade	hundrad
1000	thousand	þousend	þúsend	duizend	thuseud	thusend	tusinde	tusende	..

NUMERALS.

tive *dakan-ta* for *dakan-dakan-ta* (10 × 10), and the ancient word 'hundred' would consequently be identical in meaning and in formation with the more modern *taihun-tehund* = ten times ten.
As to the modern Teutonic languages none give occasion to any special notice except the Danish. The compounds *tresindstyve* (60), *firsindstyve* (80), *femsindstyve* (100), the latter not used in this form, express the meaning 'three times twenty,' 'four times twenty,' 'five times twenty,' and form an analogon to the French *quatre-vingt*. They contain (1) the cardinals *tres, fir, fem*, (3, 4, 5), (2) the word *sinds* = Goth. *sinþs* or neut. *sinþ*, O. H. Germ. *sind*, A. S. *sið* (meaning 'a walk,' 'a turn'), which were used to form adverbial numerals, e. g. Goth. *ainamma sinþa*, ἅπαξ, *tvaim sinþam*, δις, &c.; A S. *feower siðum* (quater), *seofon siðum* (septies), &c., where we say *five times, seven times*, &c. (3) The numeral *tyve* (20). The forms *halvtresindstyve* (50), *halvfjersindstyve* (70), *halvfemsindstyve* (90), prefix the adverbial noun *halv* (half) to indicate that half the amount of twenty is reckoned, hence *halvtresindstyve* is *tresindstyve*, i. e. 'sixty,' but half the amount of *tyve* or twenty is taken off the sixty, hence it means 'fifty;' *femsindstyve*, for 'hundred,' is not used, but *halvfemsindstyve* to express the number 'ninety.'

Gothic.	Germ.	M. H. Germ.	O. H. G.	Latin.	Greek.	Sanskrit.	Primitive.	No.
ain(s)	ein(s)	ein	ein	un-us	εἶς, ἔν-	ékă-	aina-	1
tvai	zwei	zwéne(ei)	zwéné	duo	δύο	dva	dua, dva	2
(þreis)	drei	drî	drî	tres	τρεῖς, τρι	tri-	tri-	3
fidvor	vier	vier	vior	quatuor	τέτταρες	chatúr	katvar	4
fimf	fünf	vunf	fimf	quinque	πέντε	pánchan	kankan	5
saihs	sechs	sehs	sëhs	sex	ἕξ (Fέξ)	shash	ksvaks	6
siun	si(e)ben	siben	sibun	septem	ἑπτά	sáptan	saptan	7
ahtdu	acht	aht	ahtó	octo	ὀκτώ	ashṭau	aktu	8
niun	neun	niun	niun	novem	ἐννέα	nádvan	navan	9
taihun	zehn	zëhen	zëhan	decem	δέκα	dáśan	dakan	10
ain-lif	elf	einlif	ein-lif	un-decim	ἕν-δεκα	ékă-daśan	aina-dakan	11
tva-lif	zwölf	zwelf	zwé-lif	duo-decim	δώ-δεκα	dva-daśan	dud-dakan	12
(þria-taihun)	dreizehn	drizén	dri-zëhan	tre-decim	τρεῖς-καὶ-δέκα	..	..	13
tvai tigjus	zwanzig	zweinzec(zich)	zweinzug	viginti	εἴκοσι	viśátí	..	20
þreis tigjus	dreiβig	drizec	drizug	triginta	τριάκοντα	..	..	30
sibun-téhund	siebenzig	sibenzec	sibunzó	septuaginta	ἑβδομή-κοντα	saptati	..	70
taihun-téhund	hundert	zehenzec hundert	zëhanzó	centum	ἑκατόν	śatá	kanta	100
..	tausend	tûsent	..	mille	χιλίοι	daśaśati	..	1000

DECLENSION OF CARDINALS.

OLD TEUTONIC LANGUAGES.

In Gothic the numerals 'one' to 'three' only have a complete declension through all cases and genders; the other numerals are of *common* gender and uninflected, or, extending the theme by *i*, they form a few isolated cases. The same remark holds good for the other Low German dialects, while in the Old High German we find the distinction of genders, and sometimes the complete declension, with the numerals above 'three,' the inflexion being brought about as in Gothic by the addition of the thematic *i*.

one

	Gothic.			Anglo-Saxon.	Old Saxon.
	Masc.	Fem.	Neut.	The A.S. masc. *ám*, fem. *án*, neut. *án*, and the O.S. masc. *ên*, fem. *ên*, neut. *ên*, take the inflexions of the strong adjective declension.	
Nom.	*ains*	*ain-a*	*ain, ain-ata*		
Gen.	*ain-is*	*ain-aizôs*	*ain-is*		
Dat.	*ain-amma*	*ain-ai*	*ain-amma*		
Accus.	*ain-ana*	*ain-a*	*ain, ain-ata*		

	Old Frisian.			Old Norse.			O. H. Germ.
	Masc.	Fem.	Neut.	Masc.	Fem.	Neut.	Masc. *ein, ein-êr*, fem. *ein, ein-ju*, neut. *ein, ein-aʒ*, have the inflexions of the adjective.
Nom.	*ên, ân*	*ên, ân*	*ên, ân*	*ein-n*	*ein*	*eit-t*	
Gen.	*ênes, ânes*	*ênere*	*ênes*	*ein-s*	*ein-nar*	*ein-s*	
Dat.	*êna*	*ênere*	*êna*	*ein-um*	*ein-ni*	*ein-u*	
Accus.	*ênne, ânne*	*êne*	*ên*	*ein-n*	*ein-a*	*eit-t*	

Note.—This numeral is in several Old Teutonic dialects used in the singular feminine also, and then it assumes the meaning of *sola;* this is the case in Gothic, Old High German, Old Frisian (which in this case supplies the prefix *al* before the numeral), and Anglo-Saxon, where the masculine also may be applied in the sense of 'solus.'

The plural also occurs, and renders in Gothic the meaning of μονοι, in Old High German and Old Norse of 'quidam,' in Anglo-Saxon of 'singuli,' 'nonnulli.' (Compare the French *les uns, quelques uns*, and the Spanish *unos* in the sense of 'quidam,' 'nonnulli.')

NUMERALS. 233

two

	Gothic.			Anglo-Saxon.		
	Masc.	Fem.	Neut.	Masc.	Fem.	Neut.
Nom.	tvai	tvôs	tva	twegen	twâ	twâ, twig
Gen.	tvaddj-ê	†tvaddj-ô	†tvaddj-ê	..	twegra, twega	..
Dat.	tvaim	tvaim	tvaim	..	twâ	..
Accus.	tvans	tvôs	tva	twegen	twâm	twâ, twig

	Old Saxon.			Old Frisian.		
	Masc.	Fem.	Neut.	Masc.	Fem.	Neut.
Nom.	tuêna, tuêne	tuâ, tuô	tuê	twêne	twâ	twâ
Gen.	..	tuêjô	..	..	twira	..
Dat.	..	tuêm	..	..	twâm	..
Accus.	tuêna, tuene	tuâ, tuô	tuê	twêne	twâ	twâ

	Old Norse.			Old High German.		
	Masc.	Fem.	Neut.	Masc.	Fem.	Neut.
Nom.	tveir	tvoer	tvau, tvö	zwênê	zwô, zwâ	zwei
Gen.	..	tveggja	..	..	zweiô, zweierô	..
Dat.	..	tveimr, tveim	..	..	zweim, zwêm	..
Accus.	tvâ	tvoer	tvau, tvö	zwênê	zwô, zwâ	zwei

three

	Gothic.			Anglo-Saxon.		
	Masc.	Fem.	Neut.	Masc.	Fem.	Neut.
Nom.	†þreis	†þreis, þrijos	þrija	þrî	þreó	þreó
Gen.	þrijê	†þrijô	þrijê	..	þreóra	..
Dat.	þrim	þrim	þrim	..	þrîm	..
Accus.	þrins	†þrins, þrijôs	þrija	þrî	þreó	þreó

	Old Saxon.			Old Frisian.		
	Masc.	Fem.	Neut.	Masc.	Fem.	Neut.
Nom.	thria(ea, ie)	thria(ea, ie)	thriu	thrê	thria	thriu
Gen.	..	†thrijô, thrîjeró	..	..	thrîra	..
Dat.	..	thrim	..	..	thrium	thrim
Accus.	thria(ea, ie)	thria(ea, ie)	thriu	thrê	thria	thriu

	Old Norse.			Old High German.		
	Masc.	Fem.	Neut.	Masc.	Fem.	Neut.
Nom.	þrîr	þriar	þriu	drî, driê	driô	driu
Gen.	..	þriggja	..	..	driô, drierô	..
Dat.	..	þrimr	þrim	..	drim	..
Accus.	þria	þriar	þriu	drî, driê	driô	driu

Note.—Besides the regular declension of the first three numerals which we have given in the foregoing tables, we have to add a few remarks concerning the declension of the following numerals. Where the latter are declined at all, they take as a rule the termination of the numeral 'two' and 'three,' that is:—

	Goth.	A. S.	O. N.	O. H. G.
Gen.	ê	a	a	ô
Dat.	m(im)	m(um)	m(um)	im

Examples:—Goth. *niun* (9), gen. *niune;* *tva-lif* (12), gen. *tvalib-e,* dat. *tvalibi-m.* A. S. *nigon, nigene* (9), gen. *nigen-a,* dat. *nigen-um;* *twelf* (12), *twelfe,* gen. *twelf-a,* dat. *twelf-um.* O. H. Germ. *niuni* (9), gen. *niuno;* *zwelif, zwelivi* (12), gen. *zwelf-ô,* dat. *zwelif-in* ($n = m$). The numeral *fiorir* (4) in Old Norse is declined throughout, showing in the nom. masc. *fiorir,* fem. *fiorar,* neut. *fiogur,* gen. and dat. of all genders *fiögra* and *fiögrum* respectively.

Where the Gothic termination *tigjus*, used in the formation of the 'tens,' is declined, it takes in the genitive *e*, dat. *m*, accus. *ns*. In the same manner we find in the most ancient documents of the Old Norse dialect the nom. sing. *tug-r* (decas), plur. *tigir,* gen. *tega,* dat. *togum.* The other dialects very rarely have any inflexions in the numerals formed by the 'tens,' the O. H. Germ. *zweinzuge,* accus. of *zweinzug* (20) being an almost isolated exception.

The expressions for 'hundred' and 'thousand' are the same in the ancient and modern Teutonic languages. Whatever can be said concerning their origin we have advanced on a former occasion, to which we must here refer.

Middle and New Teutonic Languages.

As to the declension of the cardinals in these languages we may briefly state, that, as in the ancient dialects, it is identical with the strong declension of the adjectives, and that therefore a tabular view of their nominative forms in the different genders may here suffice:—

one

	Masc.	Fem.	Neut.
M. H. Germ.	einer	einiu	einez
N. H. Germ.	einer	eine	eines(ß)
Old English.	an (on, a)	an	an
New English.	one (an, a)	one	one
Swedish.	ên	ên	êtt
Danish.	ên	ên	êt
Middle Dutch.	ên	ên	ên
New Dutch.	ên	ên	ên

Note.—We have observed before that in several Old Teutonic dialects the numeral 'one' was used in the sense of 'quidam;' hence it came to be used as the indefinite article in the Middle and New Teutonic languages, in exactly the same manner in which the Italian, Spanish and French languages derived their indefinite article from the Latin numeral *un-us*. Becoming a regular link in the structure of the language, it gradually lost its numeric distinctiveness, just as the definite article, originally a demonstrative pronoun, lost much of its demonstrative force, and consequently it dwindled down in Modern English to the single vowel *a*, while before vowels *an* reappears, and *one* was chosen to express the number. In Modern German, where both the numeral and the article are rendered by *ein*, this word has, where it is used in its numeric force, more emphasis than in its position as indefinite article, where it is very slightly accented in conversation, and in dialects becomes scarcely audible; so that it has some sound similar to the English *an* or *a*. The Middle High German preserved the full accent or tone on the word *ein*, whether article or numeral, and used it even in rhymes, but the wear and tear of time and circumstances can be observed already in the license it gave to shorten the nominative and accusative forms, *einer, einiu, einez—einen, eine, einez*, into the simple *ein*. In this respect the Modern German is superior to its mother dialect, as it allows no abbreviation except in the nominative masculine and neuter.

The entire loss of inflexional forms, which dates back as far as the period of Old English, may coincide with the conversion of the numeral into the indefinite article; in Layamon (thirteenth century), at any rate, we find full inflexions still preserved, as nom. *an, a*; gen. masc. *anes, œnnes, ones;* fem. *œre:* dat. masc. *ane, anne;* fem. *are:* acc. masc. *œnne,* fem. *ane, œne.* In High German the numeral appears to have first been used as the indefinite article by Otfried (ninth century).

This numeral has, whether used as such or as the indefinite article, abandoned its plural form, unless we reckon as such the modern German *die einen* (Fr. *les uns*), where it occupies the position of a substantive. A similar plural we observe in modern Swedish, where the 'tens' may be turned into substantives by connecting them with the definite or indefinite article, e. g. *en etta,* a number consisting of one; *ettan, the* number consisting of one; *ettor-na,* the numbers consisting of one; *två-an,* the number consisting of two; *tvåor-na,* the numbers consisting of two. (Compare the Dutch *eene zes,* a number of six; *drie zessen,* three numbers of six.) These may be rendered by the Lat. *singuli, bini,* &c.

The English *one* preserves the genitive *s* where it is used as a substantive, *one's.*

two

	Masc.	Fem.	Neut.	
M. H. Germ.	*zwene*	*zwo*	*zwei*	Gen. *zweier, zweiger;* dat. *zwein*
N. H. Germ.	*zwei*	*zwei*	*zwei*	Gen. *zweier;* dat. *zwein*

three

	Masc.	Fem.	Neut.	
M. H. Germ.	*drî*	*drî*	*driu*	Gen. *drîer;* dat. *drîn*
N. H. Germ.	*drei*	*drei*	*drei*	Gen. *dreier;* dat. *dreien*

Note.—In the other modern dialects these numerals have lost their inflexions altogether; where old inflexional forms are preserved, they have lost their old inflexional meaning, as N. Germ. *zwei* and *zwo,* N. Engl. *two* and *twain* (Shakesp.), Swed. *tva, tu, tvennes* (2); *tre, trenne* (3); which latter forms do not indicate inflexional modifications, but render different shades of meaning, and are therefore used in different combinations.

ORDINALS.

The ordinal numerals are, with the exception of two, superlatives, though in certain peculiarities they differ from the superlatives of adjectives.

TABLE OF ORDINALS IN THE COGNATE LANGUAGES.

No.	Sanskrit.	Greek.	Latin.	Gothic.
1st	pra-thama-	πρώ-το-(s)	pri-mo-(s)	fru-ma-n-
2nd	dvi-ti-ya-	δεύ-τερο-(s)	sec-undo-(s)	an-thara
3rd	tṛi-tíya	τρί-το-(s)	ter-tio-(s)	thri-dja-n-
4th	chatur-tha (turya)	τέταρ-το-(s)	quar-to-(s)	(fidur-tha-n)
5th	(pancha-tha) pancha-ma	πέμπ-το-(s)	quin(c)-to-(s)	(fimf-ta-n)
6th	shash-tha-	ἕκ-το-(s)	sex-to-(s)	saihs-ta-n-
7th	sapta-ma-	ἑβδό-μο-(s)	septi-mo-(s)	(sibun-da-n-)
8th	ashṭa-ma	ὀγδό-ο- (ὀγδό-ϝο-)-(s)	octa-vo-(s)	ahtu-da-n-
9th	nava-ma-	ἕνα-το-(s)	no-no-(s)	niun-da-n-
10th	daśa-ma-	δέκα-το-(s)	deci-mo-(s)	taihun-da-n-
11th	eká-naśa-	ἕν-δεκα-το-(s)	un-deci-mo-(s)	..
15th	pañcha-daśa-	πέπ-τος καὶ δέκατος	quintus decimus	fimfta taihunda-n-
20th	viṁśati-tama (viṁśa)	εἰκοσ-τό-(s)	vi-cesi-mo-(s)	wanting.
100th	śata-tama	ἑκατο-σ-τό-(s)	cent-esimo-(s)	wanting.

one—ten

The Sanskrit term for 'first' is *pra-thama*, which consists of the preposition *pra* (fore, before), and *thama = tama*; and of analogous formation is the Gr. πρω-το-, Dor. πρα-το-, showing the preposition and the suffix *ta*. The Lat. *pri-mo-* stands for *pro-imo-*, and this for *pro-timo-* (compare the Sanskrit suffix *thama*); and the Goth. *fru-ma-n-* for *pra-ma-n-* (for Sansk. *p*, Grimm's law), where we find the suffix *ma* instead of *ta*[1].

The Sansk. *dvi-ti-ya* (second), *dvi-tya* is derived from *dvi* (2) and the suffix *ta*; the Gr. δεύτερο- is a comparative of δευ = dva (2); the Lat. *secundo-* from the root *sec, seq* (sequi). The Northern languages form their term from a base *An-tara-*, as Goth. *anthara* (the other, the second), which is the comparative of the demonstrative pronominal base *ana*.

The term 'third' may be derived from a primitive *tar-tya* or *tra-tya* ('three,' and the base *ta* in its extended form *tya*); in the Sansk. *tṛ-tíya* we have in the form *tṛ = tra, tar*, the number

---
[1] Compare the chapter on the formation of the Superlative of Adjectives.

three. In Greek all the ordinals (with the exception of 7th and 8th) are formed from the cardinals, to which το (=ta), the suffix of the superlative, is added, e. g. τρί-το. The Lat. ter-tio and the Goth. thri-dja-n- are formed in analogy to the Sanskrit with the suffix tya.

The ordinal 'fourth' may in the Ursprache have been katvar-ta; Sansk. chatur-tha (tha=ta) or tur-ya=chatur-ya. The two suffixes ta and ya may occur in the combination tya, or each may form a superlative independently of the other. Gr. τέταρτο= τετFαρ-το, Lat. quarto = quatuor-to, parallel to which we may assume a Goth. fidur-tha—the suffix ta throughout.

five

Ursprache kakan-ta- or kank-ta, Sansk. panch-a-ma, Ved. pancha-tha, Gr. πέμπ-το-, Lat. quin(c)-to, Goth. fimf-ta.

six

The suffix ta throughout. Ursprache ksvaks-ta, Sansk. shash-tha, Gr. ἔκ-το for ἕξ-το, Lat. sex-to, Goth. saíhs-ta-n.

seven

Ursprache sapta-ma or sapta-ta, Sansk. sapta-ma, Gr. εβδο-μο for †έπτο-μο (comp. the old and poet. εβδο-ματο), Lat. septimo, Goth. sibun-da-n.

eight

Ursprache aktu-ma, Sansk. ashta-ma, Gr. ὄγδοο-=†ὀγδοFο-= †οκτοFο-, Lat. octavo-, probably from a primitive aktáv-a, where the suffix a only is added to the stem aktu, which appears very distinctly in the Goth. ahtu-da-n.

nine

Ursprache nava-ma or nava-ta, Sansk. nava-ma, Gr. ἔνα-το, ἐννα-το=†ἐνεFα-το, Lat. no-no-=†nov-no- =†novi-no, Goth. niun-da-n.

ten

The Sansk. daśa-ma and the Lat. deci-mo are compounds of the cardinal with the suffix ma, the Gr. δέκα-το, Goth. taihun-da-n with the suffix ta.

11—19

The Sanskrit uses the compound of 'units' and 'tens' of the cardinal numbers, but *daśan* (10) drops its *n*, and thus the final *a* is treated as the suffix, e. g. *ekā-dasa* (11th), *dva-dasa* (12th). The Latin language adopted the suffix *ma*, as *un-deci-mo-*, &c., the Greek and Gothic again the suffix *ta*, e. g. ἐν-δέκα-το (11th), Goth. *fimf-ta-taihun-da-n*; compare Lat. *quintus decimus*, where, as in Gothic, both the 'unit' and the 'ten' take the ordinal suffix.

20—90

The Sanskrit numerals of this class assume either the suffix *tama*, as *vimsati-tama* (20th), or they drop the terminational *ti* (*t*) of *vinsati* (20), and then put the final *a* as in the termination, just like the ordinals 11–19, e. g. *vimśa* (20th). In Greek the suffix το (*ta*) is added to the termination κοτι, κοιτο of the cardinal numerals, which, after dropping the final vowel, yield the form κότ-το, from which arises κοσ-το, as τριακοστο (30th). The Latin suffix of ordinal numerals is *timo*, old form *tumo* ($=ta+ma$?), which is added to *cinti, cinta* after the latter has dropped the final vowel, and thus we get the form *cent-tumo*, and from this *cesumo, cesimo, gesimo*, as *vi-cesi-mo* (20th), *quadra-gesi-mo* (40th). In Gothic these ordinals are wanting, but in Old High German they are formed by adding the termination of the adjective superlative *osta-n* to the cardinals, as *fior-zug-osta-n* (40th)[1].

100—1000

Sansk. *sata-tama* (100th) adds the suffixes *ta* and *ma* to the cardinal *śata*, Gr. στο-=ισ-το; ισ corresponds to the primitive *yans*, a comparative, and το=*ta*, the superlative termination, e. g. ἑκατο-στο. The Latin word *cent-esimo* is irregularly formed, as if the termination were *esimo*, whilst after the analogy of the 'tens' it should be expected to be *censesimo* from *cent-tesimo*. In Gothic these ordinals are wanting.

The words we have just mentioned, and which express the ordinal of 100 in the different languages are further used together with the units to form the compounds which denote the ordinals from 200 to 900.

1000

Sansk. *sahasra-tama*, Gr. χιλιο-στο, Lat. *mill-esimo*, Gothic wanting.

---

[1] Compare the chapter on the formation of the Superlative.

No.	Gothic.	Anglo-Saxon.	Old English.	English.	Old Frisian.	Old Saxon.	Dutch.	Old Norse.	Swedish.	Danish.	O. H. Germ.	M. H. G.	G.
1st	fruma	fruma, forma, ærësta	forma, fîrste, wurste verste	first(-arst)	forma, ërosta	formo, ëristo	eerste	fyr-st-r	fö-ta	fôrste	êr-ist-ër, vur-ist-ér	êrist-	ersti
2nd	anthara	ôđer	ôđer (secunde) other	(second) other	other, ôr	andar, ôđar	twee de	annar-r	an·ra	ani·n'et	andar	ander	zwei
3 d	thri-dja	þri-dda	þridde	thi·d	thre-dda	thri-ddi	der-'e	þri-di	tr··dje	tre·ie	dri-tto	dritte	dri
4th	(fidur-tha)	feover-đa	ferđe	four-th	feuwer-da	fior-đo	vier le	fior-đi	sjer-de	sjer-de	fio·-do	vier-de	vier
5th	(finf-ta)	fîf-ta	fîfđe	fif-th	fîf-ta	fîf-to	vijf-le	fim-ti	fem-te	fem-te	fimf-to	fünfte	fün
6th	sahsta	six-ta	sixđe	six-th	sex-ta	sehs-to	zes-e	set-ti	sex·te	sjet-te	sëhs-to	sehs-te	sec
7th	(sibun-da)	seofo-đa	sueđe	seven-th	sigun-da	sibun-do	zeven-de	staun-di, sibn-di	sju·a-de	syvn-de	sibun-do	siben-de	stet
8 h	ahtu-da	eahto-đa	e3teđe	eight-th	achtun-da	ahto-do	acht ste	at-ti	ått·-de	atten-de	ahto-do	ah(t)-te	ach
9 h	niun-da	nigo-đa	niyđe	nine-th	niugun-da	nigun-do	negen-de	niun-di	nio-de	nien-de	niun-to	niun-de	neu
10 h	taihun-da	teo-đa	tio·i	ten-th	tian-da	tehan-do	tien-de	thun-di	tion de	ten-de	zëhan-to	zehen-de	zeh
15 h	fimfta tai-hun-da	fîfteo-đa	vyfteđe	fifteen-th	fîftîn-da		vijftien-de	fimtan-di	fem-tom-de	fim-ten-de	fimfto zëhanto	fünfta-zehen-de(?)	für
20th	wanting.	twentig-o-đa	twentiğđe	twenti-e-th	twintig-osta		twintig-ste	tuttug-a·i	thygom-de	tyven de	zweinzic-ôsto	zweinzig-este	zwi
30th	..	þrittigo-đa	þryttið:	thirti-e-th	thrittig-osta		dertig-ste	þrituɡ as -i	trettion-de	tredti de	dr·i-ôsto	drîstig-est	dre
00th	..	hund-teontigo-đa	..	hundred-th	honder-ta	..	honderd-ste	id-ast-i	hundrade	hund-rede	zëhanzug-ôsto	zëhenzig-ist	hur

REMARKS ON THE TEUTONIC ORDINALS.

We have had occasion already to remark that the ordinals in the cognate languages, as well as in Gothic, are superlatives. The other Teutonic ordinals agree on the whole with the Gothic, and differ from it only in a few peculiarities which we are about to discuss.

one

The Gothic *fruma-n* has already been explained as an ancient superlative, to which would answer a primitive *pra-ma-n* (Goth. *f* for Sansk. *p*, Grimm's law), consisting of the preposition *pra* (fore, before, pro) and the superlative suffix *ma*. This *fruma* again undergoes another superlative inflexion by adding the comparative termination *is* (primitive *yans*[1]), and the superlative suffix *ta*, *frum-is-ta*. This, no doubt, is a later formation, and originated at a time when the consciousness of the superlative force of *fruma* itself was lost. In the other Low German dialects the Gothic form is sometimes preserved, as in the A. S. *fruma*, or the *u* is weakened into *o*, or metathesis of the *r* takes place; hence A. S., O. S., and O. Fris. *forma*. Then we further find the more recent superlative termination with it, and thence we have, corresponding to the Gothic *frumista*, the A. S. *fyrmesta*, where *y* is the Umlaut of *u*, which is caused by the succeeding *i* in the termination *ist*, here weakened into *est*: *fyrmesta* again is contracted into *fyrsta*. The Frisian superlative *form-est*, the Old High German superlative *vur-ist-er*, and the O. N. *fyr-st-r*, are formed on the same principle. We might also explain the forms *vur-ist-er*, &c., as being directly derived from the preposition O. H. Germ. *fora*, Goth. *faura*, the Teutonic garb in which the preposition *pra*, Gr. προ commonly appears. Besides the ordinal *fruma* and its derivative forms we meet another word in the Teutonic tongues, exclusive of Gothic, in the shape of the A. S. *ær-est-a*, O. H. Germ. *er-ist-er*, which is formed of the adverb A. S. *ær* (Engl. ere), O. H. Germ. *er* (Germ. ehe, eh-er), meaning 'fore,' 'before,' and the suffix *ist*, *est* (= *is-ta*), a form which undoubtedly is of a much later formation, since it is represented neither in Gothic nor the cognate languages.

From these Old Teutonic words their Middle and New Teutonic representatives will easily be explained, where mostly preposition and suffix are still clearly traceable, as O. Engl. *form-est-e*, *vor-ste*, *fir-st-e*, M. H. Germ. *vür-est-e*, and *er-st-e*, Engl.

---

[1] About these suffixes see the chapter on Comparison, p. 248 sqq.

fir-st, er-st, Germ. *er-st,* Dutch *eer-st,* Swed. *for-st-a,* Dan. *for-st-e,* some of the modern tongues adopting both terms, others selecting one of the two.

two

The Gothic *anthara,* second, derives its origin from the demonstrative pronominal base *ana* and the comparative suffix *tara,* which consistently with Grimm's law is *thara* in Gothic. The Low German *th* is duely represented in the O. Fris. *other,* and in its softened form in the A. S. and O. S. ð. These dialects, however, do not tolerate an *n* preceding the aspirate *th,* and therefore drop it regularly, hence A. S. *oðer,* O. S. *oðar* (by the side of O. H. Germ. *andar*). The Old Norse dialect, in its propensity for geminated forms, assimilates the *d* (for *th*) from *andar* into *annar,* whilst Old High German preserves the Gothic form most completely, and at the same time carries out the law of the mutation of sound, rendering the Goth. *th* by the media *d,* hence *andar.*

Few remarks will suffice with reference to the history of this form in the later Teutonic dialects. Old English and New English preserve the Anglo-Saxon form in the words *oðer* and *other;* but in Old English already it yields its ancient position to the Latin form *secunde,* which, as the N. Engl. *second,* supplants the Teutonic word altogether, the latter being exclusively used in the sense of *alter, alius,* a fate which also befalls the Germ. *ander,* replaced by *zwei-te,* Dutch *twee-de.* The Swedish and Danish languages alone not only preserve the ancient forms in their original position, but in retaining the media *d,* surpass in correctness even the Old Norse dialect — Swed. *andra,* Dan. *anden.*

three

The Goth. *thri-dja* shows, like the same form in Sanskrit, the suffix *tya,* an extension of the superlative base *ta.* In the other Old Teutonic dialects we find the sibilant *j* of the base *dja* assimilated to the preceding *d,* hence the A. S. þri-dda, O. Fris. *thre-dda,* O. S. *thri-ddi,* O. H. Germ. *dri-tto* (*d* for Goth. *th,* and *t* for *d,* Grimm's law).

Old English preserves the A. S. þri-dde, which in New English introduces metathesis of the *r* in *thir-d,* so also Dutch *der-de.* The O. N. þri-di is surpassed in correctness of form by the Swed. *tre-dje,* Dan. *tre-die.* The Germ. *dri-tte* remains faithful to its Old High German source.

4–19

The other Teutonic ordinals up to 'nineteen' are formed by the superlative suffix *ta*, the *t* of which in Gothic and the other Teutonic dialects ought to be rendered in Low German by *th*, Old High German by *d*, which, however, appears as *t*, *d*, and *th*, in the Old Teutonic dialects, either of these dentals being chosen agreeably to the preceding consonant. Thus, for example, it is a law common to all the ancient Teutonic languages that no other dental but the tenuis can follow upon the aspirate *f*; hence Goth. *fimf-ta*, A. S. *fif-ta*, O. Fris. *fif-ta*, O. S. *fif-to*, O. H. Germ. *fimf-to*. The omission of the *m* in the Low German dialects is analogous to the omission of the *n* before ð which we have just mentioned. The O. N. *fem-te* drops the *f*. The same rule holds good for the Gothic *saíhs-ta*, A. S. *six-ta*, O. H. Germ. *sehs-to*, &c. As to the other numerals, it is Anglo-Saxon exclusively which adopts the aspirate, the regular representative in Low German of the tenuis in the cognate languages, A. S. ð, O. Engl. þ, N. Engl. *th*, as A. S. *seof-ða*, O. Engl. *seue-þe*, N. Engl. *seven-th*; while the other Low German dialects, like Gothic, prefer the media; so that Old High German also gets into a confusion, adopting the regular media *d* in *fior-do* (4th), *sibun-do* (7th), and *ahto-do* (8th) only, in the remaining ordinals *to*.

The modern languages follow the footsteps of their mothers, but so that they introduce the favourite dental throughout, hence Engl. *fifth* for A. S. *fif-ta*; Germ. *vier-te* (4th) for O. H. Germ. *fior-do*, *sieben-te* (7th) for *sibun-do*. In the Swed. and Dan. *fem-te* (5th), *sjet-te* (6th) only, we find the Old Teutonic tenuis of the O. N. *fim-ti*, *set-ti* preserved.

20–1000

From 'twenty' upwards the ordinals are wanting in Gothic, whilst in the other Teutonic dialects, Anglo-Saxon excepted, they are formed by the common superlative suffix *ost-*, *ast-*, e. g. O. H. Germ. *drízug-osto* (30th), O. Fris. *thrítig-osta*, O. N. *þritug-asti*. Anglo-Saxon, on the other hand, forms the ordinals above like those below twenty, i. e. with the suffix ða, which is added to the cardinal by means of the connective vowel *ó*. The Modern Teutonic dialects followed various courses; the High German remained faithful to its traditions, and adopted the O. H. Germ. *ost* in the weakened form *est*, contracted *st*, which is also preserved in Dutch. The Scandinavian languages abandoned the *ast* of Old Norse and continued the ordinals above 'twenty' with the suffix *de*. Old English and New English preserve the A. S. ða, as A. S. þrittig-o-ða, O. Engl. þrytti-þe, N. Engl. *thirti-(e)th*.

OTHER NUMERALS.

Old Teutonic Languages.

In all the Teutonic dialects we have, besides the cardinal *two*, the numeral *both*, answering to the Gr. ἀμφοτεροι, Lat. *ambo*. It appears in Gothic as *bai*, O. S. *beðja*, O. N. *baðir*, O. Fris. *bethe*, A. S. *begen* (*bá*, *bu*). The declension, it will be seen, is very defective in Gothic.

	Gothic.			Anglo-Saxon.			Old Saxon.		
	Masc.	Fem.	Neut.	Masc.	Fem.	Neut.	Masc.	Fem.	Neut.
Nom.	bai / bajôþ-s	wanting.	ba	bêgen	bâ	bu	bêðja	bêðja	bêðju
Gen.	..	..	..	bega, begra			bêðerô		
Dat.	baim / bajôþ-um	..	..	bâm, bœm			bêðjun		
Accus.	bans	..	ba	bêgen	bâ	bu	bêðja	bêðja	bêðju

	Old Frisian.			Old Norse.			O. H. Germ.		
	Masc.	Fem.	Neut.	Masc.	Fem.	Neut.	Masc.	Fem.	Neut.
Nom.	bêthe	bêthe	bêtha	bâðir	bâðar	bæði	pêdê	pêdô	pêdiu
Gen.		bêthera			beggja			pêdêrô	
Dat.		bêtha			bâðum			pêdêm	
Accus.	bêthe	bethe	betha	bâða	bâðar	bæði	pede	pedo	pediu

In Anglo-Saxon some forms of this word combine occasionally with the numeral 'two,' e. g. *bátwá = bá* (both) + *twá* (two), neut. *butu;* they occur also declined, e. g. dat. *bám twám*.

Distributive numerals we have in the Goth. *tveinaih*, occurring in the accus. fem. *tveihnos;* O. H. Germ. *zwene*, which was adopted to supply the cardinal numeral 'two' — O. N. *einn*, *tvennr, þrennr, fern:* plur. of *tvennr, þrennr,* is *tvennir, tvennar, tvenn,* &c.; they may be used in a distributive or multiplicative signification, so that *tvennr* may mean binus and duplus, *þrennr* =trinus and triplex.

Multiplicatives are formed in Gothic by *falþ-s* (fold), fem. *falþa,* neut. *falþ.* This Gothic *falþ* is in Anglo-Saxon *feald,* Old Saxon and Old Frisian *fald,* Old Norse *fald-r,* Old High German *falt.* Examples:—Goth. *ain-falþ-s,* one-fold, simple; A. S. *án-feald,* O. S. and O. Fris. *en-fald,* O. N. *ein-fald-r,* O. H. Germ. *ein-falt-er,* Goth. *fidur-falþ-s,* four-fold; A. S. *twi-feald,* two-fold; O. S. *tehin-fald,* ten-fold; O. Fris. *thri-fald,* three-fold; O. N. *fimm-fald-r,* five-fold; O. H. Germ. *dri-falt,* three-fold.

Numeral adverbs answering to the question *quoties?* how often? are not met with in Gothic, but some occur in the other old dialects.

Examples:—

	SEMEL.	BIS.	TER.
O. H. Ger.	*eines, einest*	*zwiror, zwiro, zwiron*	*driror*
Ang.-Sax.	*æne (anes)*	*twiwa*	*þriwa*
Old Saxon	*enes*	*twiwa*	*thrijo, thriwo*
Old Frisian	*enis, enes (ense)*	*twira*	*thria*
Old Norse	*einna*	*tysvar*	*þrysvar*

To supply the wanting numeral adverbs, the Low German languages, Gothic included, use the dative of the word *sinþ-*, meaning way, turn, time, punctum temporis, Goth. *sinþa,* A. S. and O. S. *síþ* (*n* dropped on account of the succeeding aspirate ð), O. Fris. *seth* (for *síth, sinth*), O. N. *sinn* (the final ð assimilated to the preceding *n*), while Old High German uses for the same purpose the substantive *stunta, stunt* (punctum temporis, hour, comp. Germ. stunde), a word which is occasionally used in Old Frisian too. Examples:— Goth. *ainamma sinþa,* one time, once; *anþaramma sinþa,* a second time; *tváim sinþam,* two times, twice. A. S. *on ænne síð,* once; *eahtoðan síðe,* for the eighth time; *eahta síðon,* eight times. O. S. *sibun síðun,* seven times; *tehan síðun,* ten times. O. Fris. *tian sethen* or *tian stunda,* ten times. O. N. *átta sinnum,* eight times; *tuttugu sinnum,* twenty times. O. H. Germ. *fior-stunt,* four times; *zehan-stunt,* ten times, and *drim stuntom, drio stunto,* three times.

There is another kind of numeral adverbs in the Teutonic languages, which express companionship of as many persons as are indicated by the numeral. For this purpose the Anglo-Saxon language makes use of the indefinite pronoun *sum,* which it adds to the respective cardinals, e. g. *eode eahta-sum,* we went eight together, including myself: *eahta-sum* can be rendered in German by one word, *selb-achter*. This Germ. *selb* (meaning 'self') has its forerunner in the O. H. Germ. *selp, selb*, e. g. *selp-andar* (Germ. *selb-ander*, i. e. we were two together, I was the second); *selp-dritto, selb-dritt*, we were three together, I was the third. In Frisian and Old Saxon *sum* is used as in Anglo-Saxon.

The Old Norse has some forms answering to the Latin numeral adjectives in *-arius*, e. g. þrítug-r, tricenarius; *sextug-r*, sexagenarius.

Middle and Modern Teutonic Languages.

The root *ba* is preserved in the modern dialects, and appears in the Engl. *both*, from O. E. *beiþe, boþe* for *bege, bo*, A. S. *begen, bá, bu*. The Germ. *beide*, M. H. Germ. *beide* (for *béde*), are derived from the Old High German neuter form *beidiu* (for *bédiu*); the Swed. *bade*, Dan. *baade*, from the O. N. *báðir*; Dutch *beede*, O. S. *béðja*.

The distributive numerals answering to the question 'how often?' have disappeared from all Modern Teutonic languages except the English, where they are preserved in the forms *once, twice, thrice*. The word *once* is derived from the O. Engl. *oones* (exchanging the sibilant *c* for *s*), A. S. *ánes, áne, æne; twice* from O. Engl. *twies, twie*, with which corresponds the A. S. *twíwa*; but still more so the O. Fris. *twira = twisa* and the O. N. *tysvar*, from which it becomes sufficiently evident that the full form must have been *twiswa*, the *s* of which was dropped in Anglo-Saxon, but restored in Old English from some other source, perhaps Old Frisian or Old Norse. The same case we have in *thrice*, O. Engl. *thries* for *thrie*, A. S. þriwa, O. N. þrysvar.

The Modern Teutonic languages being deprived of these numeral adverbs have to supply them by circumscriptive forms, an expedient adopted already in Old Teutonic dialects; but the word *sinþa, sinð, sinn*, has disappeared, and others have taken its place in the different modern tongues. (The Old Norse *sinn* in the Danish cardinals, see above.) The English makes use of the word 'time': *three times, four times, five times*, &c. The equivalents in the German and Dutch languages are *mal, maal* respectively, as *ein-mal, een-maal; zwei-mal, twee-maal; drei-maal, drie-maal*, &c. The word *mál* which occurs in Old High German already, and in the Goth. *mel*, means 'punctum,' a point, and hence 'punctum temporis,' a point of time, or moment—a meaning which corresponds to that of the words *sinþa* and *stunt* used in the Old Teutonic dialects. It is certain that this form was adopted in High German before Luther's time; but in Middle High German the O. H. Germ. *stunt* is used for the same purpose.

The Scandinavian languages employ for the same purpose the word *gang*, which originally means *walk, step, turn*, and hence *time*; e. g. Swed. *engång, två ganger, tre ganger*; Dan. *engang, to gange, tre gange*.

The A. S. *sum*, mentioned above, is no longer used in English with its peculiar meaning when in combination with cardinals; and in German too the O. H. Germ. *selb* has disappeared altogether, except in the term *selbander*, we two together: *selb-dritt*, &c., are out of fashion.

Multiplicatives are formed in the modern as well as in the ancient dialects by the termination *fold*, Germ. *falt, fältig*, Dutch *voudig*; e. g. *three-fold, drei-fältig, drie-voudig; six-fold, sechs-fältig, zes-voudig*.

Fractions are rendered either by the ordinals, as in English and Dutch—e. g. *a fourth, een vierde; a twelfth, een twaalfde*—or by adding the word *deal* to the cardinal, as is done in the Germ. *tel = theil*, and the Danish and Swedish *deel, del*, e. g. Germ. *vier-tel = vier-theil*, Dan. *en fjerde-deel*, Swed. *en fjerde-del*.

COMPARISONS.

THE COGNATE LANGUAGES.

Comparative Bases.

1. *Formations with the suffix* **-yans**.

The primitive suffix *yans* is perhaps the modification of a still more ancient *yant*, and related to the suffixes *ant, mant, vant*. In the last of the three just mentioned it also occurs that the *t* is replaced by *s*, and so it may be in *yans* for *yant*. This suffix is always joined directly to the root and limited to certain roots, as *nav-a*, new, comp. *nav-yans*; *svad-u*, sweet, *svad-yans*.

In Sanskrit the primitive *yans* becomes *yás* or *íyás*, e. g. *nava*, new, comp. *nav-yás*; *bhu-ri*, much, *bhu-yás*; *yuvan*, young, *yav-íyás*; *mah*, great, *mah-iyás*.

The Greek language drops the *s* of *yans*, changes *y* into *i*, or combines it with the preceding consonant into σσ or ζ; e. g. κακ-ό-, bad, comp. κακ-ιον-, κακιων; ἐλαχ-υ, light, levis, ελασσον, for †ελαχ-ιον-; μεγ-as, μεγ-άλος, great, μειζων for μεγ-ιον; πολ-υ-, much, πλειον-, primitive form *pra-yans* from *par-u*; root *pra = par*, to fill; με-ιον-, less, primitive form *ma-yans* from a root *ma*, commonly weakened to *mi* (comp. Lat. *mi-nus*).

In Latin the primitive *yans* became *yons*, *-ions*, *-ios*, the final *s* yielding later on to rhotacism which produced the form *-ior*; but the original *s* was always preserved in the neuter *-ius = yus* (comp. Sansk. *yás*). Examples:—*mag-no-*, great, comp. *má-jor*, for †*mag-ior*, neut. *ma-jus =* †*mag-ius*; *plus*, more, from *plous =* †*plo-ius* (comp. πλε-ῖον) primitive *pra-yans*, root *pra = par*, to fill; *plures = pleores =* †*ple-ior-es*, comp. of *ple-ro-*, *plerus*. *ple-no-*, full, root *ple = plo = pra = par*, to fill; *minor*, less, *= min-ior*, *min-us = min-ius*, root *min = man, ma*; *facil-ior* comp. of *facil-i-*, root *fac*.

The Gothic comparative terminations are *-is*, *-ós*, both derived from *yans*: *is = yas* (*i = ya*) *ós = a-as* (Goth. *ó = a + a) = a-yas = a-yans*. To these comparative bases is added the termination *an* in the masculine, *jan* (*= yan*) in the feminine form of the adjective, so that the comparative suffix in Gothic is *izan*, fem. *izjan*, *izein* (final *s* is softened into *z* in the middle of the word), *-ōzan*, fem. *-ozjan*, *-ōzein*. Examples:—*manag-izan-*, nom. sing. masc. *managiza*, neut. *managizo* (*o*=*an*), fem. *managizei*, theme *manega*, nom. sing. *manegs*, (much, many); *maizan-* = *mak-izan* (compare Lat. *mag-is*, *major*, *mag-ior*, Gr. μεγ-ιον-), comparative of theme *mik-ila-*, nom. sing. *mikils*, great, root *mik*, Lat. *mag*, Gr. μεγ, Sansk. *mah*, primitive *mag*, great. In the adverbial form of this word the case termination has disappeared, and it therefore ends in *s*: *mais* = Lat. *mag-is*; *hauh-is*, comparative *hauh-izan-*, theme *hauha-*, nom. sing. *hauhs*, high; even the *i* of *is* is sometimes dropped: *min-s*, adverbial comparative of *minn-iza*, less (comp. Lat. *min-us* for *min-ius*).

2. *Formations with the suffixes* -tara *and* -ra.

These suffixes are chiefly used in Sanskrit and Greek for the formation of the comparative; *-tara* is probably a compound of the frequently occurring suffixes *ta* and *ra*. The latter by itself expresses comparison, e. g. Sansk. *ava-ra*, inferior, comp. of the preposition *ava*, de, of, from; *apa-ra*, after, of prep. *apa*, ab, of, from. Compare with these examples the Latin *sup-eru-s* (*sup-er*), *inf-eru-s* (*inf-er*), which have the ancient comparative suffix *ra*. The consciousness however of the comparative force of the termination *er* being lost, the common comparative suffix *ior* was superadded, so that in the Latin *superior, inferior*, we have in fact double comparatives.

tara forms in the Ursprache the very old stem *an-tara*, interior, from the demonstrative base *ana-*, root *an*; and *ka-tara*, uter, from the interrogative base and root *ka*.

This suffix appears in Sanskrit as the masculine termination *-taras*, fem. *-tara*, and is simply added to the nominal stem, e. g. *punya-tara*, comp. of *punya*, pure; *ka-tara* (uter) of *ka*, quis; *ya-tara* (uter) of the relative *ya*, qui; *i-tara*, other, from demonstrative *i*, is; *an-tara*, exterior.

The comparative base *tara* is rendered in Greek by -τερο, e. g. πο-τερο- = κο-τερο-, uter, root πο, κο, = Sansk. *ka;* κουφό-τερο-, comp. of κουφο-, light, levis; σοφώ-τερο- (ω on account of the preceding short syllable). The termination εσ-τερο seems to have been adopted from the adjectives ending in εσ, as in σαφεσ-τερο- of σαφης, to other adjectives as the combining syllable between the root and the termination, e. g. ευδαιμον-έσ-τερο- of ευδαί-μων. The form ισ-τερο must be kept distinct altogether from the preceding, it being a compound of ισ, the shortest contracted form of *yans*, and τερο = *tara*, e. g. λαλ-ίσ-τερο-, comparative of λάλο-, talkative.

In Latin the suffix *tara* is very rare. It occurs in *u-tero* = *cu-tero*, *quo-tero*, root *ku*, *ko*, Gr. πο, κο, Sansk. *ka*; *u-ter*, fem. *u-tra*, neut. *u-tro-m* (elision of *e*); *in-ter*, *dex-ter*. Further examples are:—*min-is-tero-*, minor, minister, servant, from the root *min*, small; *mag-is-tero-*, major, master, from the root *mag*, great; *sin-is-tero-*, left,—examples where we find, as in the Greek λαλ-ίσ-τερο, the suffixes *yans* + *tara*.

In Gothic the suffix *tara* does not occur frequently. It is used in the following words:—*an-thara-*, nom. sing. *an-thar*, other, second, where the Gothic *th* represents the Sansk. *t* (see Grimm's law); *hva-thara*, nom. sing. *hva-thar*, uter, whether, *h* for Sansk. *k* (Grimm's law), *v* introduced after *h* (see the respective letters); *hin-dar*, hinder, posterior; *af-tra*, after, retro, prep. *af*, of; *hva-thro*, whither, theme *hva-thra-* = primitive *ka-tara*, *tha-thro*, thither, primitive *ta-tara*; *hva-dre*, whither; *hi-dre*, hither, primitive *ki-tara*.

Superlative Bases.

1. *Formations with the suffix* -ta.

The regular suffixes used in the formation of the superlative are *ta* and *ma* (which have other functions besides this), and their combinations *tama*, *mata*, *tata*, which, as secondary suffixes are sometimes added to the comparative.

ta is used chiefly in the formation of ordinals[1]. It forms superlatives by joining the comparative suffix *yans*. The reduplicated *ta* = *tata* is in Greek the regular termination of the superlative by the side of the comparative in *tara*.

The primitive language either used the full form in *yans-ta*, as *magh-yans-ta* (μεγιστος), *ak-yans-ta* (ωκιστος), or the shortened form of *yans*, i. e. *is*, e. g. *magh-is-ta*, *ak-is-ta*. Schleicher decides in favour of the former.

In Sanskrit the superlative suffix *ta* is joined to the comparative *yás*, -*iyás*-, shortened in *is*, and the combination *is-ta* becomes *ish-tha*, e. g. *mah-ishtha*, greatest, of root *mah*; *gar-ishtha*, superl. of *guru*, heavy.

The Greek language joins the superlative το (= *ta*) to the comparative base ισ (*yans*), e. g. κάκ-ισ-το-, ἥδ-ισ-το-, μέγ-ισ-το-, πλε-ισ-το-. The reduplicated form *tata*, Gr. τατο, of this suffix,

---

[1] See the respective chapter, p. 237 sqq.

COMPARISONS.

forms the regular superlative to the comparatives in *tara*, Gr. τερο, e. g. κουφό-τατο-, σοφώ-τατο-, εὐδαιμον-έσ-τατο-, λαλ-ίσ-τατο-.

The Latin renders the suffix *ta* by *to*, *tu*, but it is not used in the superlative, where *mo* (Sansk. *ma*), and *simo*, *timo* (the primitive *ta-ma*) have the preference, e. g. *long-is-simo-*, *brev-is-simo-*, *op-ti-mo-* (see below).

The primitive *ta* is rendered in Gothic by *da-n*, the *n* being an addition peculiar to the Teutonic tongues, and *d* standing irregularly for *th*, which should represent the Sansk. *t* (see Grimm's law). Here again the superlative is added to the comparative case *-is*, *-ós*, and the *d* of *da* is then replaced by *t*, on account of the preceding *s* (see the chapter on Consonants), e. g. *manag-is-ta*, *hauh-is-ta*, *minn-is-ta*, *ma-is-ta*, *arm-ós-ta*.

2. *Formations with the suffix* -ma.

It occurs in :—the Sansk. *ava-má*, lowest, last, from prep. *áva*, of a demonstrative base ; *madhya-má*, medius ; *para-má*, furthest ; *ádi-ma*, first, from *ádi*, beginning ; and in many ordinals.

In Greek it is very rare ; it occurs in ἑβδο-ματο- (combined *ma + ta*, and with the remarkable change of πτ into βδ) and in πυ-ματο-, last.

ma is the favourite suffix in the Latin superlative, where it appears as *mo*, e.g. *sum-mo-* = *sup-mo-*, like the comparative *sup-er*, from *sup* (*sub*) ; *infi-mo-*, comp. *inf-ero-* ; *mini-mo-*, comp. *min-or* ; *pluri-mo-*, old form *plusi-mo-* = *plo-is-umo-*, where we have again the primitive *yans + ma*. Perhaps it may come from a primitive Latin form *plo-yus-u-mo-*, as *plus* = *plous* = *plo-yus*, and *min-us* = *min-yus*.

It occurs rarely in Gothic, and where it does it is accompanied by the Teutonic final *n*, e.g. *innu-ma-n*, intimus, inmost ; *fru-ma-n*, foremost, first, and with an additional superlative suffix in *fru-m-is-ta*, an example which shows that the consciousness of the superlative force of the suffix *ma* must have been lost at an early time.

3. *Formations with the suffix* ta-ma.

It is in Sanskrit the regular superlative termination by the side of the comparative in *tara*, as *ka-tamá*, which out of many, interrogative ; *ya-tamá*, which out of many, relative.

In Greek it is wanting.

The Latin language uses it as the regular superlative termination, where the primitive *tama* is rendered by *simo*, *sumo*, =

timo, tumo, and commonly added to the comparative suffix *is* (primitive *yans*), e. g. *long-is-simo-, brev-is-simo-, op-timo-, op-tumo-; ul-timo-, in-timo-, maximo-=†mag-simo-=†mag-timo-*. Adjectives which have dropped their final vowel and end in *r* or *l* join the suffix *timo, simo,* immediately to the root, as *veter-rimo-* for †*veter-simo-,* †*veter-timo-,* stem *veter; pulcher-rimo-,* stem *pulchero-, facil-limo-* for †*facil-simo-,* †*facil-timo-*. But these superlatives may be explained in another manner, so as to derive them from a form *veter-is-timo, vetersimo-, veterrimo-,* &c.

The suffix *tama* appears in Gothic under the form *du-ma-n* (compare Lat. *tumo* in *op-tumo-*), where we find *d* inorganic in the place of *th* to represent the Sansk. *t* and the final *n* superadded, e. g. *af-tu-ma-n,* aft-most, last, to which a further superlative suffix is added in *af-tu-m-is-ta-n,* a double superlative containing four suffixes which are added to the preposition *af,* namely, *tama-yans-ta;* thus also *hin-du-ma-n,* hindmost, latest, last, and *hin-du-m-is-ta-n, if-tu-ma-n,* the next, following.

OLD TEUTONIC LANGUAGES.

1. THE COMPARATIVE.

As we have already stated, the Gothic comparative of the adjectives is formed by the terminations *is* and *ós,* which answer to the Sanskrit suffix *yás,* primitive *yans,* the final *s* being softened into *z* when the comparative suffix is followed by a termination, hence *izan, ozan,* of which either one or the other is used, the selection being made perhaps on euphonic rather than grammatical grounds. While the termination for the masc. and neut. is *an,* the fem. adopts *jan,* hence *ein.*

Examples:—

manags, much, many, theme *manega;* comparative *manag-izan-,* nom. sing. masc. *managiza,* fem. *managizei,* neut. *managizo* (*ó =an*).

blinds, blind, theme *blinda;* comparative *blind-ozan-,* nom. sing. masc. *blindoza,* fem. *blindozei,* neut. *blindozo.*

azets, light, easy, theme *azeta;* comparative *azet-izan-,* nom. sing. masc. *azetiza,* fem. *azetizei,* neut. *azetizo.*

frobs, prudent, wise, theme *froda;* comparative *frod-ozan-,* nom. sing. masc. *frodoza,* fem. *frodozei,* neut. *frodozo.*

In the other Teutonic dialects rhotacism has taken place throughout, that is, the *s* of the terminations *is* and *ós* has been supplanted by *r*, so that the comparative suffixes are in Old High German *ir* and *ór*, in Old Saxon *ir* and *or*, in Old Frisian *ir* and *or*, whilst Anglo-Saxon has dropped the vowel altogether and merely puts *r*. But we can prove that this dialect also originally used both *ir* and *or*, because, wherever the former occurred, it caused the Umlaut of its adjective, which Umlaut remained after the *i* of *ir* had been dropped; the termination *or*, on the other hand, never caused Umlaut. Similar is the case in Old Norse, where *ar* stands for *or*, Goth. *ós*, and *r* for *ir*, Goth. *is*, the latter being always distinct by the Umlaut which the *i* of the suffix *r*, originally *ir*, had caused.

Examples:—

Goth.   *blinds, blinda,*   comp. *blind-oz-a, blind-oz-ei, blind-oz-ó.*
O. H. G. *plint*   . . .   ,,   *plint-or-o, plint-or-a, plint-ór-a.*
O. S.   *blind*   . . .   ,,   *blind-or-o, blind-ór-a, blind-or-a.*
A. S.   *blind*   . . .   ,,   *blind-r-a,* &c.
O. Fris. *blind*   . . .   ,,   *blind-or-a,* or *blind-er-a,* or *blind-r-a.*
O. N.   *blindr*   . . .   ,,   *blind-ar-i, blind-ar-í, blind-ar-a.*

REMARKS ON THE COMPARATIVE FORM IN THE DIFFERENT DIALECTS.

1. Old High German allows of the assimilation of the vowel in the suffixes *or* and *ir* to the vowel of the succeeding termination, e. g. *plintara* for *plintora*, *ríchoro* for *ríchiro*, where *o* has been assimilated to the succeeding *a*, and *i* to the succeeding *o*. The *i* of *ir* may cause the Umlaut of the vowel in the preceding syllable.

2. Old Saxon may, like Anglo-Saxon, drop the *i* of *ir* altogether, or weaken it into *e*, and weaken the *o* of *or* into *a*; e. g. *bet-er-a* for *bet-ir-a, ald-r-o* for *ald-ir-o, jung-ar-o* for *jung-ór-o*, for which we even find *jung-r-o*, so that it would appear, as if by the side of *jung-or-o*, a comparative *jung-ir-o* had been in use. It is a peculiarity of the Old Saxon dialect that it likes to preserve the derivative spirant *j* even before the terminations, so that from the word *suoti*, theme *suotja*, sweet, we have the comparative *suótj-er-a* and *suot-er-a, wóðj-er-a* and *woð-er-a* from *woði, woðja*, joyful. Gothic and Old High German never allow this derivative spirant to appear before the comparative suffixes.

3. Anglo-Saxon comparatives in *ir* are—*yld-r-a* from *eald*, old; *leng-r-a* from *lang*, long: in *or*—*earm-r-a* from *earm*, poor (Germ. arm); *brád-r-a* from *brad*, broad; the former causing the Umlaut (on account of the *i*), the latter not.

4. Old Frisian often weakens the forms *ir* and *or* into *er*, the former being always recognizable by the Umlaut it causes in the preceding syllable, e. g. *alt*, old, comp. *eld-er-a;* sometimes nothing but the consonant of the suffix remained, as *fir*, far, comp. *fer-r-a; hach*, high, comp. *hag-r-a* for *hag-er-a*.

5. Old Norse also drops the *i* of *ir*, which however, just as in the other dialects, leaves the traces of its original presence behind by the Umlaut it has caused in the preceding syllable; e. g. *full-r*, full, comp. *fyll-r-i; diup-r*, deep, comp. *dýp-r-i*.

6. All the comparatives in all the dialects have the inflections of the weak declension.

2. The Superlative.

In the Teutonic dialects the superlative is formed just as in Gothic and some of the cognate languages, by adding the superlative suffix *ta* to the comparative suffix *yans*, and this primitive *yans-ta* (Sansk. *is-ta*) appears in Gothic as *is-ta* or *ós-ta* (*s* reinstated for *z* on account of the following *t*, and *t* instead of the regular *d*, or rather *th*, on account of the preceding *s*), and these combined suffixes *ista, osta*, appear in all the Teutonic dialects with modifications similar to those which affect the comparative terminations, i. e. the *i* of *ist* being often weakened into *e* or dropped altogether, and the *o* of *ost* weakened into *a*. From what we have just stated it will be self-evident that the superlative in *ist* answers to the comparative in *ir*, and the superlative in *ost* to the comparative in *or*. Concerning the different Teutonic dialects our remarks may be brief. In Anglo-Saxon the superlative terminations resume their ancient vowels in *est* (= *ist*) and *ost*, while the comparative suffix *r* had dropped both *i* and *o*; e. g. *leng-est*, sup. of *lang; earm-ost*, sup. of *earm*. But on the other hand, Anglo-Saxon does not strictly keep apart the terminations *ist* and *ost* for the comparatives *ir* and *or* respectively, but frequently uses one for the other, as *geong-ost* for *gyng-est*, and vice versa *leóf-est* for *leóf-ost*. In Old Frisian the vowel of the superlative suffix is rarely dropped, but it may appear in various modifications as *ist*, and *est*, and *ast*. Old Norse is the only dialect which regularly drops the vowel of the suffix *ist*, while it changes *ost* into *ast;* e. g. *sæl-l*, happy, sup. *sæl-st-r; full-r*, full, sup. *fyl-st-r; fróð-r*, prudent, sup. *fróð-ast-r*.

Where *i* in the comparative causes Umlaut, it does the same in the superlative; e. g. O. N. *full-r*, comp. *fyll-r-i*, sup. *fyl-st-r;* A. S. *eald, eld-r-a, eld-est*.

The superlative may follow both the weak and strong declensions.

TABLE OF COMPARISONS.

		Positive.	Comparative.	Superlative.
Gothic		*hauhs*, high	*hauh-iz-an-*	*hauh-ist-a-*
		blinds, blind	*blind-ôz-an-*	*blind-ôst-a-*
O. H. G.		*guot*, good	*peʒ-ir-o-*	*peʒʒ-ist-o-*
		plint, blind	*plint-ôr-o-*	*plint-ôst-o-*
O. Sax.		*ald*, old	*ald-ir-o-*, *ald-r-o-*	*ald-ist-o-*
		skôni, fair	*scônj-or-o-*	*scônj-ôst-*
A. S.		*eald*, old	*yld-r-a*	*yld-est*
		earm, poor	*earm-r-a*	*earm-ost*
O. Fris.		*hâch*, high	*hâg-er-a*, *hâg-r-a*	*hâg-ist*
		skêne, fair	*skên-r-a (or-a)*	*skên-ast*
O. Norse		*fullr*, full	*fyll-r-i*	*fyl-st-r*
		frôð-r, prudent	*frôð-ar-i*	*frôð-ast-r*.

3. ANOMALOUS FORMS.

We have had an opportunity already to mention that there are various suffixes for the comparative as well as superlative, out of which the different cognate languages select one or another. Thus the Teutonic dialects prefer the suffix *yans* for the formation of the regular comparative, while Greek chooses the suffix *tara* (τερο-); the former use the suffix *ta* added to *yans* in order to form the superlative, whilst Latin, for the same purpose, selects the suffix *tama (tumo, timo)* added to *is = yans*, hence *issimo-*. But by the side of the common forms of comparatives and superlatives ending in the usual suffixes, the Teutonic languages make, like all others, occasional use of other suffixes for the formation of comparatives and superlatives.

The comparative suffix *tara* we meet in the Goth. *an-thara-, an-thar*, other, which is modified in the O. H. Germ. *an-dar*, Germ. *an-der*, A. S. *oðer*, Engl. *other;* Goth. *hva-thar*, uter, whether, A. S. *hwäðer*, Engl. *whether;* Goth. *hva-thro*, A. S. *hwäder*, Engl. *whither;* Goth. *tha-thro*, A. S. *thider*, Engl. *thither;* Goth. *hin-dar*, A.S. *hinder; aftra (af* preposition *of*, ab, de, retro), A. S. *after*, Engl. *after*.

Far more common are superlatives formed not by the regular suffix *yans + ta*, but by the suffix *ma* simply, or by the suffixes *ta-ma*.

The simple suffix *ma* we have in the Goth. *fru-ma-* (compare *fru* with the Sansk. preposition *pra*, Lat. *pro*), A. S. *for-m-a*, O. Fris. *for-m-a*, first (compare Lat. *pri-mo-*); Goth. *innu-ma-*, A. S. *inne-ma*, intimus; Goth. *auhu-ma-*, superus. The suffix *tama* occurs in the Goth. *if-tuma* (proximus, sequens), *af-tuma* (ultimus), *hin-duma-* (postremus); and in the A. S. *hin-dema* (ultimus), and *ut-ema* (extimus), *síð-ema* (novissimus, ultimus), *lät-ema* (ultimus) *nið-ema* (infimus), which very probably have dropped the *d* in the suffix *dema* (= *tama*) because it followed a dental. These combinations do not occur in the other Teutonic dialects. They take the inflexions of the weak declension. In Gothic already the superlative force of these suffixes must have been lost at an early date, whence it occurs that these superlatives assume the regular terminations of comparison as well; e.g. Goth. *fruman*, comp. *frum-oz-a*, sup. *frum-ist-s*; *aftuman, aftumists*; *hinduman, hindumists*. In the same manner are formed the Anglo-Saxon superlatives *formest* or *fyrmest* from *forma*; *medema* (medius), comp. *medemra*, sup. *medemest*; *utema*, sup. *utemest* or *ytemest*; *niðema*, sup. *niðemast*. It is in general a characteristic feature of Teutonic comparison to double its suffixes, in order perhaps to create greater emphasis. Such double comparatives we have in the Goth. *vairsiza* (which ought to be *vairiza*), A. S. *vyrsa*, worse, where *vyr* already is a comparative, and *sa* the ancient comparative *s* of *iza*. (Compare O. N. *ver-ri* where the suffix *s* has submitted to rhotacism.) Thus, again, we find in O. H. Germ. *bezeroro* for the simple comp. *bezir*, and *meroro* for simple *mero*, which sounds, as if we said *betterer, morer*, and as some do say *lesser, worser*.

Deserving of special notice are the Anglo-Saxon double superlatives which are derived by adding the superlative suffix *est* or *ost* to the old superlative ending in *ma, dema*, e. g. *hin-dem-est* from *hin-dema*, *ut-em-est* from *ut-ema*, *lät-em-est* from *lät-ema*, *síð-em-est* from *síð-ema*. Compare the English *hindmost, utmost, foremost*, &c., superlatives which are no compounds with *most* (maximus), but have gradually grown out of the *m-est* of the foregoing Anglo-Saxon superlatives.

4. Defective Comparisons.

	Gothic.	O. H. G.	O. S.	Anglo-Saxon.	Old Frisian.	O. N.
Bonus.						
Pos.	*gôd-s*	*guot*	*gôd*	*god*	*gôd*	*gôd*
Comp.	*bat-iza*	*peziro*	*betiro*	*betera (betra)*	*betera*	*betri*
Sup.	*bat-ist-s*	*pezzist-êr*	*best*	*betost (betst)*	*best*	*beztr*
Malus.						
Pos.	*ubil-s*	*ubil*	*ubil*	*yfel*	*evel*	*illr* / *vándr*
Comp.	*vair-s-iza*	*wirsiro*	*wirso*	*wyrsa*	*wirra (werra)*	*verri*
Sup.	*vair-s-ist-s*	*wirsist-êr*	*wirsist*	*wyrst*	..	*verstr*

	Gothic.	O. H. G.	O. Sax.	A. S.	Old Frisian.	O. N.
Parvus.						
Pos.	leitil-s	luzil	luttil	lytel	litik	litill
Comp.	minn-iza	minniro	..	lässa	lessa (minnira)	minni
Sup.	minn-ist-s	minnist-êr	minnist	läst	litekest (leist) / lerest	minstr
Magnus (multus).						
Pos.	mikil-s	mihhil	mikil	mycel	.. (grât)	mikill
Comp.	maiza	mêro	mêro	mâra	mâra	meiri
Sup.	maist-s	meist-êr	mêst	mæst	mast	meistr

In the Gothic *máiza* (= *mak-iza*), *máists*, the *k* of the root *mik* in *mik-il-s* has been dropped, and the primitive *a* reappeared[1] (comp. Lat. root *mag*, Sansk. *mah*). The other dialects still more modify the Gothic *máiza* by contractions, &c., as O. H. Germ. *mero*, A. S. *mara*, where the *s* suffers rhotacism and the Gothic diphthong is represented by the long *e* and *á*[2]. The O. S. *lat*, late (comp. *latoro*), has contracted the superlative into *last*, *lezt* (= *let-ist-o*). The Anglo-Saxon comparative *lassa* of *lytel* stands for *minra*, which is wanting in this dialect. This comparative may be explained by the Goth. *lasiv-óz-a* (infirmior), comp. of *lasiv-s* (infirmus).

The O. Fris. *mara* (more, greater) is deprived of the positive *mikel* which we find in the other dialects. There is in this dialect a form *let*, which in the positive signifies piger, tardus; in the comp. *letera*, tardior, posterior; in the sup. *letast*, contracted *lest*, tardissimus, ultimus. The comparative *fer-r-a* (dexter) and the superlative *fer-ost*, *fer-est* are derived from the preposition *fora* (prae, pro). The Old Norse has a few other comparisons for which we find no analogies in the other dialects. These are, *margr* (multus), comp. *fleiri*, sup. *fleistr*; *gamall* (old), comp. *eldri*, sup. *elztr*; *ungr* (young), comp. *yngri*, sup. *nystr*, from *nyr*.

The explanation of the defective comparisons, commonly called irregular, is the same as that which we give of the defective comparisons in Greek and Latin. There are certain adjectives which only occur in the positive, without being able to form a comparative or superlative; there are others which have a comparative, or superlative, or both, but are devoid of a positive, which, though we may still be able to trace to its probable form, has become obsolete or fallen out of use altogether. We

---

[1] Grimm assumes that the positive may have been *mag-s*.
[2] Compare the Table of Gradations, p. 24.

have a positive of the adjective *good*, but a comparative and superlative of it are wanting. We therefore lay hold of the comparative *better* and the superlative *best* to supply the meaning of a 'gooder' and 'goodest' which are forbidden forms. But on the other hand the positive *good* returns the compliment and supplies that in which the forms *better* and *best* are deficient, namely a positive. There is nothing irregular in all this; *better* and *best* are regular forms, and *good* is a regular form, but both parties are defective in their comparison and must therefore supply each other wherein they are wanting.

The Goth. *gód-s, batiza, batists* (good, better, best), has its equivalent and analogous forms in all other Teutonic dialects, as will be seen from our Table of Defective Comparisons. These comparative and superlative forms would require a positive which might be in Goth. †*bat-s*, O. H. Germ. †*paʒ* (comp. *peʒir*), and this positive would be a relation to the Gothic verb *batan*, pret. *bot*, which signifies 'to be useful,' 'to be good.'

The Goth. *ubils, vaírsiza, vairsists* (evil, worse, worst) is also represented in the other Teutonic dialects. As the base of this comparative form there must have been some word which was related to the M. H. Germ. verb *werren*, to disturb, to molest, to do evil, and the A. S. *werian*, to weary, to molest.

The Goth. *leitil-s* (little) forms the comparative *minn-iza* and the superlative *minn-ist-s*. These forms occur in all the other dialects except Anglo-Saxon. The comparative *minn-iza* (adverbial *min-s*) is derived from the same root as the Lat. *min-us, min-or* (for *min-ius, min-ior*). This form is supplanted in Anglo-Saxon by *lässa*, and in Old Frisian too we have a comparative *lessa* by the side of *minnira*. The A. S. *lässa* is the same as the Gothic comparative *lasivoza* of *lasivs* (infirmus), and may perhaps be an assimilation of *r* to *s*, hence *lässa* for *läsra*; or the more primitive *s* of the comparative termination, as in the case of *vyrsa* (worse), may have resisted the transition into *r*. The same rules apply to the superlative: Goth. *minnists*, A. S. *läst*, O. Fris. *minnist* and *lerest*, where the *s* of the root submits to rhotacism[1].

---

[1] The A. S. *lässa* (minor), *last* (minimus), must be kept well distinct from *latora* (posterior), and *latost* (postremus).

5. Comparison of the Adverbs.

Only the 'Adverbia qualitatis' are at all capable of taking the degrees of comparison; these degrees, however, are no independent adverbial forms, developed out of the adverbial positive, but they are mere modifications of the degrees of comparison of their corresponding adjectives. The formation of the adverbial degrees may take place in two different ways, either the accusative neuter is, as in the positive, used as an adverb, or a distinct form is developed. As to the superlative there is only the former mode put into practice; it never has a form of its own, and must always be considered as an accusative of the adjective. Examples:—Goth. *frumist* (πρῶτον); O. H. Germ. *erist* (primum), *meist* (maxime), *beʒʒest* (optime), *gernost* (lubentissime); A. S. *ærest* (primum), *mæst* (maxime), *geornost* (lubentissime); *latost* (ultimum). O. N. *best* (optime); *optast* (saepissime), *vídast* (latissime).

The comparative of the adverb may either be expressed by the accus. neut. of the adjective, or it developes a form of its own. To the former belong the adverbial comparatives: Goth. *managizo* (plus), *minnizo* (minus), *frumozo* (prius); O. H. Germ. *mera* (plus), *minnira* (minus).

Adverbial comparatives of the latter class may be formed either in *is* or *ós*, like the adjectives. In *is* we have the Goth. *máis* (magis) from *máiza* (major), O. H. Germ. *mer*, O. S. *mer* and *merr*, A. S. *má*, O. Fris. *mar* and *má*, O. N. *meir*; Goth. *mins* or *minz* (minus) from *minniza* (minor), O. H. Germ. *min*, O. S. (*min*?), A. S. *läs*, O. Fris. *min*, O. N. *minnr* or *miðr*; Goth. *bats* (melius) from *batiza* (melior), O. H. Germ. *paʒ*, O. S. *bet*, A. S. *bet*, O. Fris. *bet*, O. N. *betr*; Goth. *vairs* (pejus), O. H. Germ. *wirs*, O. S. *wirs*, A. S. *wyrs* (adj. *wyrsa*), O. N. *verr*.

In *os*:—Goth. *raíhtos* (rectius), *svinþos* (fortius); O. H. Germ. *gernór* (lubentius), *leidor*[1] (proh dolor, Germ. leider), *oftor* (saepius); O. S. *diopor* (profundus), *suithor* (fortius); A. S. *smalor* (tenuius), adj. *smälra* (tenuior); *sparor* (parcius), adj. *spärra* (parcior); O. N. *breidar* (latius), *vídar* (amplius). A list of the anomalous or defective comparisons of the adverbs may conclude our remarks on this subject.

---

[1] This comparative with positive signification serves to express the interjection 'alas!'

		Gothic.	O. H. Germ.	O. S.	Ang.-Sax.	O. Fris.	Old Norse.
Bene.							
	Pos.	vaila	wela	wèl	wèl	wèl	vel
	Comp.	bats	paʒ	bet	bet (sel)	bet	betr (skarr)
	Sup.	batist	peʒist	best	best	best	bezt (skast)
Male.							
	Pos.	ubilabɔ	upilo	..	yfele	..	illa
	Comp.	vairs	wirs	..	wyrs	..	verr
Multum.							
	Pos.	†miku	sero †mihhu	..	sore †mycu	..	miök
	Comp.	máis	mer	mêr	mâ	mâr, mâ	meir
	Sup.	máist	meist	..	mœst	..	meist
Parve.							
	Pos.	leitil, leitl	luzil, luzilo	..	lytel	..	litt, litit
	Comp.	mins	min	min	läs	..	min, siðr
	Sup.	minnist	minnist	minnist	läst	..	{ minnst, sîzt (=siðst)

MIDDLE AND NEW TEUTONIC LANGUAGES.

In the Middle and New Teutonic languages the ancient suffixes *ir, ist,* and *or, ost* are mixed up and usually represented by *er, est,* or simply *r, st*. The only criterion by which we can trace a comparative to the form in *ir* is the Umlaut. Wherever we have to deal with an adjective which has taken Umlaut in the comparative, we may be certain that this adjective took the suffix *ir* in the comparative. But this rule is necessarily very limited in its application, because there are adjectives which have Umlaut in the positive already, or they have a vowel in the root which cannot take Umlaut, such as *e* and *i*, and then it is impossible to tell whether the comparative belongs to the formation in *ir* or *or*.

Formations in ir.

In Old English there prevails some confusion as to the application of the suffixes *ir (er)* and *or,* the latter being sometimes used where undoubtedly *er* should be expected, i. e. after Umlaut; e. g. *strong, strengor* for *strenger; eldost* for *eldest*. The terminations *or* and *ost* have altogether disappeared in Middle English, but the Umlaut with comparatives in *ir* sometimes continues, e. g. *long, lenger; strong, strenger, strengest; old, elder, eldest;* but also *longer, stronger, older*. New English has rejected the formations with the Umlaut, and thus obliterated all distinction between the comparison in *ir* and that in *or*, the only example left being the comparative *elder* and superlative *eldest* of the adjective *old*, which however uses the modern forms *older* and *oldest* as well, though in a slightly different sense.

Middle High German has, like Old English, occasionally retained the formations in *o*, but in most cases it was like *i* converted into *e*, and thus the regular terminations were *er*, *est*. But the Umlaut having in High German more than in any other language preserved its ancient position, we can tell with tolerable accuracy where we have to deal with a comparative in *ir*. Such examples are *herte*, hard, *herter*; *kalt*, cold, *kelter*; *krank*, sick, *krenker*; *schoene*, fair, *schoener*; *senfte*, gentle, *senfter*; *strang*, severe, *strenger*; *veste*, fast, firm, *vester*. Some of these, *herte*, *schoene*, &c. have the Umlaut in the positive already, and then retain it of course in the comparative and superlative. New High German on the whole follows the same rule as its predecessor, the formation in *i* causing Umlaut wherever Umlaut is possible (*a*, *o*, *u*); e. g. *schmal*, narrow, *schmaler*, *schmälest*; *arm*, poor, *ärmer*, *ärmest*; *warm*, *warmer*, *warmest*; *fromm*, pious, *frommer*, *frömmest*; *gesund*, healthy, *gesünder*, *gesündest*. Those adjectives which have the Umlaut in the positive already retain it throughout the degrees.

The Scandinavian languages also have in a few adjectives retained the Umlaut and therewith the distinctive feature of the formation in *ir*; e. g. Swed. *lag*, low, humble, *lägre*, *lägst*; *lång*, long, *längre*, *längst*; Dan. *lang*, *längere*, *längst*; Swed. *stor*, great, *större*, *storst*; Dan. *stor*, *storre*, *storst*; Swed. *ung*, young, *yngre*, *yngst*; Dan. *ung*, *yngre*, *yngst*; Swed. *tung*, heavy, *tyngre*, *tyngst*; Dan. *tung*, *tyngere*, *tyngest*; Swed. *små*, small, little, **smärre, smärst**.

Middle and New Dutch, which reject the Umlaut and adopt *er* and *est* for the formation of the degrees throughout, know no longer any distinction between the comparison in *i* and that in *o*. The only trace of Umlaut left in Dutch are the anomalous forms *beter*, *best*, of which hereafter.

Formations in or.

In Old English the fluctuations between *er* and *or*, *est* and *ost* make it difficult to assign any adjective to the formation in *i* or *o*, for we read *faire*, *fairor* and *fairest*, by the side of *vayrost*; *holy*, *holyor*; *feblor*, feebler; *poueror*, poorer, and, as we have already mentioned, even after an Umlaut *eldost* for *eldest*; but in Middle English *er* and *est* become more and more settled, and in

New English they must be considered the regular suffixes of the degrees of comparison which unite in them the ancient formations in *i* and *o*.

In Middle High German there are many adjectives which reject the Umlaut, and thus indicate the ancient formation in *o*; e. g. *alt*, old, *alder, aldest; lang*, long, *langer, langest; zart*, tender, gentle, dear, *zarter, zartest; lam,* lame, *lamre.* Local adjectives even retain the *o* in the superlative (not in the comparative), as *vorderost,* foremost; *oberost,* topmost; *niderôst,* lowest.

New High German forms the degrees in most cases by rejecting the Umlaut, and leaving the root of the adjective unaltered; nay, it has removed the Umlaut from words which used it in Middle High German, as for instance in *sanft,* soft, *sanfter, sanftest;* and in the literary language this removal of the ancient Umlaut continues to be attempted, as in *frommer* for *frömmer* (*fromm,* pious); *gesunder* for *gesünder* (*gesund,* healthy), whilst the language of the people favours the Umlaut and introduces it in words where the literary language rejects it, where it was wanting even in Middle High German, e. g. *zärter* for *zarter* (*zart,* gentle), *flächer* for *flacher* (*flach,* flat). These facts undoubtedly prove the higher antiquity of the forms with the Umlaut, or, what is identical, of the formation in *i*. Comparisons without the Umlaut are very numerous; we give a few examples: *blank, blanker, blankest; klar,* clear, *klarer, klarest; zart,* gentle, *zarter, zartest; matt,* weak, *matter, mattest; voll,* full, *voller, vollst; stolz,* proud, *stolzer, stolzest; bunt,* variegated, *bunter, buntest; blau,* blew, *blauer, blauest.* To these belong all adjectives ending in *sam, bar, haft, el, en, er,* and adjectives ending in *ig,* if their positive has no Umlaut, and the adjectives indicating a locality, which however use the superlative only, as *oberst,* topmost; *unterst,* lowest; *vorderst,* foremost.

In the Scandinavian languages all adjectives, except those mentioned under *ir,* are formed by the suffix *or,* which in Swedish is rendered, as in Old Norse, by *ar* and *ast,* in Danish by the modern *er* and *est.* Umlaut is in these adjectives impossible. Examples: — Swed. *varm,* warm, *varmare, varmast;* Dan. *varm, varmere, varmest;* Swed. *stark,* strong, *starkare, starkast;* Dan. *stark, starkere, starkest;* Swed. *rik,* rich, *rikare, rikast;* Dan. *rig, rigere, rigest;* Swed. *mägtig, mägtigare, mägtigst*[1]*;* Dan. *mägtig, magtigere, mägtigst.*

---

[1] In adjectives ending in *ig* the inflexional vowel suffers syncope before *st* in the superlative.

Anomalous and Defective Comparisons.

		M. H. Germ.	N. H. G.	O. Engl.	N. Engl.	Dutch.	Swedish.	Danish.
Bonus.								
Pos.	Adj.	guot	gut	god	good	goed	gôd (bra)	god
	Adv.	wol	wohl	wel	well	..	väl	vel
Comp.		beʒʒer (adv. baʒ)	beßer	better (betur)	better	beter	bättre	bedre
Sup.		best	best	best	best	best	bäst	bedst
Malus.								
Pos.		..	..	uvel	evil (bad)	..	(elak, ônd)	(ond, slem)
Comp.		..	..	wors, wers	worse	..	värre	vaerre
Sup.		..	..	worst, werst	worst	..	värrst	vaerst
Multus.								
Pos.	Adj.	michel	(viel)	muchel	..	..	mycken	megen
	Adv.	..	..	muche	much	..	..	..
Comp.		mërre	†mere	more	more	meer	mera	mere
Sup.		meist	†meist	moste	most	meest	mest	meest
Parvus.								
Pos.		lützel	(klein)	litel	little	..	liten	liden
Comp.		minner	minder	less	less	minder	mindre	mindre
Sup.		minnest	mindest	leest	least	minst	minst	mindst.

Besides these there are various other defective comparisons in the different dialects, such as the Engl. *many*, Germ. *viele*, which adopt the comparative and superlative of M. H. Germ. *michel*, O. Engl. *muchel*, whilst Danish has preserved the true Old Norse comparison of *many*—Dan. *mange, flere, fleest; few,* Dan. *faa, faerre, faerrest.* The Swed. *nara*, near, *närmare, närmast;* Dan. *naer, naermere, naermest*, are derived from the ancient superlative *närma*. The Engl. *next* by the side of *nearest*, *last* by the side of *latest*, are contractions, the former of which stands for A. S. *nehst*, the regular superlative of *neah*, nigh, of which *nearre*, our *near*, is the comparative. The comparative *further, farther*, used for the positive *far*, was originally the comparative of *for(th)*.

The comparatives in *ther*, A. S. þer, Goth. þar, as *other, whither, hither, thither, nether, whether*• Germ. *ander, nieder, weder,* &c., will find their explanation by a reference to the Old Teutonic forms[1].

The superlatives *utmost, hindmost, inmost,* &c., are no compounds of *most* (maxime), but a superlative termination *est* converted into *ost*, and combined with the preceding *m*, which is the remainder of an ancient superlative termination. (See Anglo-Saxon, p. 256.)

[1] See pp. 250, 255.

All modern Teutonic dialects allow of a comparison effected by the addition of the adverbs *more* and *most*, instead of terminations. In English we use this mode of comparison with most adjectives that are not monosyllables, hence we say *beautiful, more, most beautiful*. This form is used in German where two qualities are compared, e. g. *mehr klug als tapfer*, more prudent than brave, prudent rather than brave. Participles never take the terminations in Swedish, Danish and Dutch, but always form their comparisons by *mera, mest, meer, meest;* e. g. Swed. *mera alskat*, Dan. *meer elsket,* more beloved; *meest godgjorende*, most charitable; Dutch *meer doordrongen, meest doordrongen*, more penetrated, &c.

DECLENSIONS.

THE COGNATE LANGUAGES.

NUMBERS, CASES, GENDERS.

Roots and themes (stems) are not yet words, parts of a phrase or sentence. In the Aryan languages every real word, every part of a phrase, is either a verb or a noun. (Interjections are no words, but mere sounds; adverbs, particles, prepositions, &c., were originally nominal or verbal forms.) Themes of themselves are neither one nor the other; they may become such or such under the influence of a case-suffix of the noun, or a personal termination of the verb. Case-suffixes, therefore, and personal terminations in the Aryan languages are the agents chiefly at work in the formation of words, in contradistinction to the elements which constitute themes or stems. The suffixes employed in the formation of words are easily recognised as the primary elements of pronouns, which at an earlier period of Aryan life were still independent roots.

Since verbs and nouns are in such relation to each other as to constitute the defined forms of heretofore undefined elements of speech, the former cannot occur without the latter. A language either distinguishes the forms of nouns from those of verbs, or it possesses neither of the two. We cannot, therefore, speak of the priority of either: the noun and the verb started into existence at one and the same time.

The inflexional elements of the noun belong to two distinct spheres—the cases and numbers. In the Aryan languages we distinguish *three* numbers, the *Singular*, *Dual*, and *Plural*; the dual, however, is rightly considered a mere modification of the plural; it is a number therefore which easily disappears again from a language. The Latin is altogether devoid of it, and the ancient Teutonic languages miss the dual form in the declensions of the noun; Gothic alone has a dual of the verb, all have the dual of certain pronouns. Our modern languages have lost the dual altogether.

The Aryan languages had originally *eight* cases, namely the *Nominative, Accusative, Locative, Dative, Ablative, Genitive*, and two *Instrumentals*, which however coalesced into one at a very early date. The vocative is no case, not even a word; it is the simple theme or stem used as an interjection. The eight cases together with the vocative are, even by the most ancient representatives of the Aryan tribe, distinguished in the singular only. The locative and dative, the ablative and genitive of the singular are closely related. The plural partly possesses case-suffixes which differ from those of the singular, partly it joins two cases into one, as the dative and ablative, to which the instrumental bears a close resemblance. The dual has but three cases: (1) nominative and accusative; (2) dative, ablative, and instrumental; (3) genitive and locative. At a very early period our Aryan languages began to drop one and another of the case-signs, and consequently cases which originally were distinct coalesced into one. Thus in Greek the ablative was lost in the genitive; the instrumental begins to disappear even in the most ancient form of the language; the dative and locative are joined in one. A similar course is followed by the Latin language. As to our Teutonic languages, in their ancient constitution they are as perfect, or as mutilated, as either Greek or Latin in the declension of cases; but in their further development through the periods of the Middle and New Teutonic they were gradually stripped of most inflexional forms, so that now it is only German (and partly Dutch) which show anything like a declension of the substantive or adjective through the first four cases (as commonly arranged), while English and the Scandinavian dialects have preserved but one case, namely the genitive or possessive in *'s*; all other cases, the nominative, dative, and accusative, being identical with the theme or stem of the word.

The Aryan languages distinguish *three* genders, while other languages do not at all take them into account, or others again form more numerous distinctions than ours. A particular inflexional sign for the distinction of the genders does not exist in the Aryan languages, and it is perfectly evident that at an early stage the primitive Aryan language knew no discrimination of genders, which in the course of time was gradually developed and marked out by secondary inflexional forms. We mention a few only of the means which our languages apply for the expression of the different genders. (1) The themes which end in consonants or the vowels *i* and *u* do not pay any regard to gender,

DECLENSIONS.

while the themes in *a* mark out the feminine by the production of the thematic *a* into *a*, a process however which is not to be considered exclusively characteristic of the feminine. (Comp. the Greek κριτη-ς, πολίτη-ς.) (2) The gender is distinguished by case-suffixes which are adopted only in certain genders, e g. Lat. masc. *qui-s*, neut. *qui-d = qui-t*. (3) The gender is marked out in the theme itself by the application of particular suffixes. Thus, for instance, the themes in *ya* (*yá*), e. g. Sansk. *deví* (goddess) = *dev-yá*, theme *dev-ya-*, while the masc. is not *dev-ya-s*, but the ancient *dev-as;* Sansk. *dátri* (datrix, she who gives) = *dátr-yá*, theme *dátr-ya* from *dátar-ya*, for the more ancient *datar* which was common to all genders; thus also the Gr. δοτειρα = †δοτερ(y)α, along with which there does not exist a masc. δότειρο-ς, primitive *datarya-s*, because in the masc. form the more ancient δο-τηρ-, Sansk. *dá-tar-* was preferred; Sansk. *svádví* (sweet) = *svádv-yá*, Gr. ηδεια (adjective of three terminations) = Sansk. *svádav-ya*, by the side of the more ancient forms Sansk. *svádu-s*, Gr. ἡδύ-ς, which were used for the feminine as well; thus also the Latin theme *vic-tric-* for the feminine only by the side of the masc. *vic-tor*. (4) Of a comparatively recent introduction is the mode of distinguishing the genders by a phonetic change in terminational forms which at first were identically the same; e. g. Sansk. *patí-n* (fem.) for *pati-ms;* Gr. ιπποτη-ς (masc.), ἀρετη (fem.); Old Lat. abl. sing. masc. *novó-d*, fem. *nová-d*, the primitive form of both *nová-t;* Gothic gen. plur. masc. and neut. *-e*, fem. in several themes *-ó*, both *-e* and *-ó* standing for an original *-ám*.

THE TERMINATIONS OF NOMINAL THEMES.

The termination of a nominal theme has a decisive influence on the declension, because the theme is the changeable element of the noun, while the case-terminations are for all nouns and declensions ever the same. We might therefore speak of different themes rather than of different declensions. The themes deserve special arrangement and examination, for it is with them that the case-suffixes enter into an alliance, and by them that they, according to their nature, are differently affected and modified. Themes are either *consonantal* or *vocalic*, that is, ending in a consonant or a vowel. The former easily disappear from languages because they have a tendency to follow the analogy of the latter. The consonantal themes, moreover, may modify their final consonant and lengthen or shorten their final syllable before certain case-suffixes, or they remain the same throughout. They therefore are divided into *mutable* and *immutable* themes. The vowels nearest related to the consonants are *u* and *i*, for they may easily go over into the semi-vowels or consonants *v* and *j* respectively. Next then to the consonantal we place the themes ending in a diphthong, as *áu* or *áv*, and those in *u* and *i* (long or short). The themes in *a* (the most frequent in our languages) are peculiar in this respect, that *a* never can pass into a consonant (that is, follow the analogy of a consonantal theme), a fact which imparts to them certain characteristic features distinct from anything we find with the rest.

1. Consonantal Themes.

(1) Immutable themes. The final consonant of the root is also the termination of the theme; e. g. Sansk. *vách*, speech, Gr. οπ-, Lat. *voc-*, Goth. *man-*, homo. Some of these follow the analogy of vocalic themes.

(2) Themes in *-as*, the thematic suffix of which is changed by the phonetic influence of the case-suffix added to it, as Lat. *cinis-*, *ciner-*, *arbos-*, *arbor-*, *genos-*, *gener-*, *vetus-*, *veter-*.

(3) Themes in *-n*. These are subject to considerable modifications, as Gr. ποιμέν-, shepherd, μελαν-, black; Lat. *homen-*, man, *sermon-*, speech; Goth. *hanan-*, cock; fem. *tuggon-*, tongue; *managein-* = *managjan-*, many, multitude; neut. Lat. *nomen-*, Goth. *naman-*, name.

(4) Themes in *-ant-*, *-ans-*, occurring in active participles and comparatives. These are subject to great changes; they may drop the *n* and exchange *t* and *s*, using the latter before vowels, the former before consonants; as in the part. active, pres. and fut., e. g. Sansk. *bharant-*, Gr. φέροντ-, Lat. *ferent-*, bearing, Goth. *fijand-* (hating, enemy, fiend); the part. pret. active, e. g. Sansk. *vidvant-* (for primitive *vidvid-vant-*), Gr. εἰδότ- (for Ϝειδ-Ϝοτ-).

(5) Themes in *-r*. Sansk. *dátar-*, giver; *bhrátar-*, brother; *mátar-*, mother; Gr. δοτηρ-, giver; πατέρ-, father; μητερ-, mother; Lat. *dator-*, *pater-*, *mater-*; Goth. *brothar-*, brother; *daúhtar-*, daughter.

2. Vocalic Themes.

(6) Themes ending in a diphthong; e. g. Sansk. *nau-*, ship; Gr. ναυ-.

(7) Themes in *u* and *i*: they are no primitive forms, as little as the long vowels upon which they are based; Sansk. *bhru-*, brow, for the primitive *bhru-*, Gr. ὀφρυ-; Lat. *su-*, sow, pig; before vowels *su*.

(8) Themes in -*u*. Sansk. *sunu-*, son, fem. *hanu-*, cheek; Gr. γένυ-, chin, γλυκυ-, sweet; Lat. *fructu-*, fruit; Goth. *sunu-*, son, fem. *handu-*, hand : neut. Sansk. *madhu-*, honey, Gr. μεδυ- ; Lat. *pecu-*, cattle; Goth. *faihu-*, possession, wealth (comp. Germ. vieh. Engl. fee).

(9) Themes in -*i*. Sansk. *avi-* (masc. and fem.), sheep; Gr. φυσι-, nature; Lat. *ovi-*, sheep; Goth. *mahti-*, might, power: masc. Sansk. *pati-*, lord ; Gr. ποσι-, husband ; Lat. *hosti-*, enemy; Goth. *gasti-*, guest : neut. Sansk. *vári-*, water; Lat. *mari-*, sea.

(10) Themes in *a*. Masc. primitive *akva-*, horse; Gr. ἱππυ-, Lat. *equo-* ; Goth. *vulfa-*, wolf : neut. Sansk. *yuga-*, yoke; Gr. ζυγό-, Lat. *jugo-*, Goth. *juka-* : fem. (commonly with lengthened *a*), Gr. χωρα-, χώρᾱ-, Lat. *equa-*, Goth. *giba-*, gift.

The themes in *ya* have in several languages certain peculiarities which are the result of their respective phonetic laws : as in Sanskrit where the feminines in -*yá* contract this suffix into *í*, e. g. *bharantí-* (φερουσα). Compare Gothic masc. *harja*, army (Germ. heer); *hairdja*, shepherd (Germ. hirte) ; neut. *kunja*, kin, kind, genus ; fem. *bandja*, band, bandage.

FORMATION OF THE CASES.

NOMINATIVE SINGULAR.

Masculine and feminine nouns add the case-sign *s* to the termination of the theme; neuter nouns supply the nominative by the accusative. The *s* of the nominative is undoubtedly the remainder of the pronominal root *sa*, which is used in a demonstrative sense in Sanskrit and Gothic, and appears also in the Greek article ὁ = *so* = *sa*. (See Demonstrative Pronouns.) The neuter of *sa* is in Sanskrit *tat*, Goth. þa-*ta*. Gr. το. The *t* in *ta-t* and *tha-ta* is the remainder of the root *ta* which is used to indicate the neuter gender in the pronominal declension, as Sansk. masc. and fem. *ki-s*, neut. *ki-t*, Lat. *qui-s*, *qui-t* (*qui-d*). Here we find *s* and *t* representing the genders in the same manner as in the independent pronouns *sa* and *ta*, and we therefore conclude that in the pronominal as well as nominal declension we have to deal with the same pronouns, applied as case-suffixes. This fact again is a proof that the inflexional terminations in the Aryan languages were originally nothing but independent roots added to the simple noun—that our declensions were simply 'post-positions.'

The addition of the nominative sign *s* to the theme must of course take place in accordance with the phonetic laws adopted in each of the Aryan languages. What changes must hereby necessarily occur will best be seen from a selection of examples which we give, numbered according to the number of the theme to which they belong, and which is to be found by reference to the preceding paragraph.

Examples :—

Sanskrit. (1) *vák* for *rách-s* (no *ch* final); *bharan, bharās.* (5) *dátá, bhrátá, mátá,* with loss of *-r-s* and lengthening of the final vowel; (6) *nau-s,* (7) *bhru-s,* (8) *sunu-s, hánu-s,* (9) *ávi-s, páti-s.* (10) *vrkí-s* for †*vrkyá-s,* she-wolf; *sihí-s,* lioness, for *sihyá-s ; gna-* and *gná-s,* woman, goddess.

Greek. The loss of the case-suffix *s* causes the lengthening of the preceding vowel. Examples :—(1) οπ-ς (οψ), (3) ποιμην from †ποιμεν-ς, τεκτων from †τεκτον-ς, but μελας for †μελαν-ς ; (4) φερων from †φεροντ-ς, but τιθεις, ιστάς, δεικνος for †τιθεντ-ς, †ισταντ-ς, †δεικνυντ-ς ; ειδως from †Fειδϝοτ-ς: (5) δοτηρ from δοτηρ-ς ; πατηρ, μητηρ for †πατερ-ς, †μητερ-ς : (6) ναυ-ς, (7) οφρυ-ς, (8) γενυ-ς, (9) φυσι-ς, (10) ιππο-ς.

Latin. (1) *vóc-s,* vox ; *pes* for *ped-s ; miles* (later on *mīles*) for *milet-s ;* (2) *arbos* for *arbos-s, cinis-* for *cinis-s ;* (3) *homo* for *homen-s,* but *tubicen* for *tubicen-s ;* (4) *feren(t)-s ;* (5) *pater, máter, dator,* as in Greek (the short vowel of the second syllable is of later origin); (6) *bó-s* (originally *bou-s,* like Gr. βοι-ς); (7) *su-s,* (8) *fructu-s,* (9) *ovi-s ;* but *mor-s* for *mort-s* for *morti-s,* root *mar,* suffix *ti ; ars* for *art-s,* for *arti-s ; ácer* and *ácri-s,* vigil and *vigili-s :* (10) *equo-s,* but *puer* for *puero-s, vir* for *viro-s.*

Gothic. Nos. 3 and 5 lengthen the final vowel if the nom. case-suffix is dropped: *hana* for †*haná* from †*hanan-s ;* fem. *tuggo* from †*tuggan-s ; managei* for †*managjan-s ;* (4) *fijand-s;* (5) *brothar, dauhtar,* for *brothár* from *brothar-s,* &c.; (8) *sunu-s, handu-s ;* (9) *maht-s, gast-s* for *mahti-s, gasti-s,* (10) *vulf-s* for †*vulfa-s, giba* for †*giba, harji-s* for *harja-s, haírdei-s* for *haírdja-s;* fem. *bandi* for *bandjá.*

Nominative Plural.

In addition to the termination *s* (*sa*) of the nominative singular, the nominative plural takes the plural sign *s,* which again appears to be the abbreviation of *sa,* so that the original termination of the nom. plur. may have been *-sasa,* thence *sas,* which, dropping the first *s* for the sake of euphony, became *as.*

DECLENSIONS.

Examples:—

Sanskrit. (1) *rách-as*, (4) *bharant-as*, (5) *dátár-as, mátar-as*, (6) *náv-as*, (8) *sunav-as*.

Greek. The primitive suffix is represented by -ες; the themes in *a* have a formation analogous to that of the pronouns. Examples:—(1) οπ-ες, (2) δυσμενεῖς = †-μενέ-ες = †-μενεσ-ες, (3) τέκτον-ες, (4) φέροντ-ες, εἰδότ-ες, (5) δοτηρ-ες, πατερ-ες, μητερ-ες, (6) ραϝ-ες, νηϝ-ες, (7) οφρυ-ες, (8) νέκυ-ες, γλυκεις = γλυκέϝ-ες. (10) ιπποι and ζευκταί are formed on the same principle as οι and αι, more ancient τοι and ται, perhaps from *ta-y-as*, fem. *tá-y-as*. The loss of the final *s* may partly have been caused from an attempt to dissimilate the nominative -οις, -αις from the locative forms -οις, -αις for -οισι, -αισι. (See the Declension of the Pronouns.)

Latin. All the consonantal themes have adopted the form of the themes in *i*, hence *voc-es, bov-es, su-es* from *voceis, boveis, sueis*, in the same manner as *oves* from *oveis* (theme in *i*); (8) *fructus*, probably from †*fructous, fructov-os, fructev-es*, as πηχεις from †πηχεϝ-ες; or it may be derived from †*fructu-es* (comp. ἰχθυ-ες), so that the primitive form of both the Greek and Latin would be *-u-as*. (10) *equi*, more ancient *equei, equeis, equoe*, †*equoi*, †*equois*. The *s* dropped as in Greek, a rather frequent occurrence in Latin. (Compare *pote* and *potis, mage* and *magis, amare* and *amaris; hi, hei* for *heis; magistri, magistrei* for *magistreis*.)

Gothic. All vocal themes put *-s* directly to the lengthened final vowel. (1) *man-s* from †*man-as*), (3) *hanan-s* from †*hanan-as*, (4) *fijand-s* (= †*fijand-as*), (5) *brothrju-s* (a theme in *r* follows the analogy of the themes in *u*, under 8); (8) *sunj-us* from †*suniv-s*, †*suniv-as*, †*sunav-as*; (9) *mahtei-s, gastei-s*, from †*mahtej-s, mahtag-as*; (10) *vulfo-s*, primitive *varka-s(as)*; fem. *gibo-s*, primitive, *gibá-s(as)*.

NOMINATIVE DUAL.

The dual forms of the noun being wanting in the Teutonic languages, we omit examining them.

ACCUSATIVE SINGULAR.

The case-sign with a consonantal theme is *-am*, with a vocalic theme *-m*, very probably the abbreviation of *-am*. The neuter themes in *a* adopt this form for the nominative too, all other neuters have in the accus. and nom. no suffix whatever. This *-am, -m* seems to be related to the *-m* which is frequently used in the formation of themes, and it must be derived from a pronominal base, the principal part of which is *m*: this we might find in the Sansk. *ama-* (hic), *amu-s, ami-s* (ille), perhaps from a pronominal root *am*.

Examples:—

Sanskrit. (1) *vách-am*, (4) *bharant-am*, (5) *bhrátar-am, mátaram, datar-am;* (6) *náv-am*, (7) *bhruv-am*, (8) *sunu-m, sunv-am;* (9) *avi-m*, (10) *juga-m*.

Greek. According to the phonetic laws, Greek adopts *n* (ν) for *m*; with a consonantal theme ν is dropped and simple *a* used in the accusative: (1) οπ-α, (3) ποιμέν-α, (4) φέροντ-α, ειδοτ-α, (5) πατέρ-α, μητερ-α, δοτῆρ-α, (6) ὀφρυ-ν, (7) ναυ-ν, Hom. νῆF-α, prim. *náv-am;* (8) γλυκυ-ν, (9) ποσι-ν, φυσι-ν; (10) ἱππο-ν, ζυγο-ν, ζευκτή-ν, χώρα-ν.

Latin. The consonantal themes follow the analogy of themes in *i*; hence they have, instead of the regular *-om* or *-um* which they should use for the primitive *-am*, the termination *-em* = †*im*, with the weakened *e* for *i*, adopted also by the themes in *i*: (1) *voc-em;* (2) *ciner-em*, neut. *genus;* (3) *homin-em*, neut. *nomen;* (4) *ferent-em*, (5) *patr-em, mátr-em;* (6) *bov-em*, (7) *su-em*, (8) *fructu-m*, neut. *cornu;* (9) *navi-m, nave-m*, neut. *mare* for †*mari;* (10) *equo-m*, neut. *jugu-m*.

Gothic. The terminational *m*, which in Gothic, as in Greek, was replaced by *n* (as we still see in the declension of the pronoun), was dropped, together with the short vowel preceding it; and consequently in themes in *i* and *a* the accus. sing. became identical with the nominative: (3) *hanan* = †*hanan-an*, neut. *namo* = *nam-on* = *nam-an;* (4) *fijand*(*-an*), (5) *bróthar*(*-an*), *dauhtar*(*-an*); (8) *sunu*(*-n*), fem. *handu*(*-n*), neut. *faihu;* (9) *maht*(*-in*), *gast*(*-in*); (10) *vulf*(*-a-n*), neut. *juk*(*-a-n*), fem. *giba* from †*gibá-n*. Themes in *ja*: *hari* = *harja-n*, neut. *kuni* = *kunja-n*, fem. *bandja* = *bandja-n*.

Accusative Plural.

Masculine and feminine nouns add the plural sign *s* to the termination of the accusative singular, so that the primitive case-sign of the accus. plur. may have been *-ams*, which became *-ans* (in most languages the *n* is preferred to the *m* before *s*), and dropping the *a*, *-ns*. This *ns* in Sanskrit was again dissected into *-n* and *-s*, the former being used with the masculine, and the latter with the feminine vocalic themes which end in a long vowel. But the original *-ms* is preserved with masculine vocalic themes before *t* and *ch*, and all the consonantal themes have *-as*.

DECLENSIONS.

Neuters end in *i* (weakened *a*). The Greek and Latin languages reject the *n* altogether, and thus we have the terminations *ās, as, os*, while Gothic alone preserves the primitive form of the case-sign, using always -*ns* in the accus. plur. with vocalic themes, which with consonantal themes is replaced by -*as*. The neuter ends throughout in *a* which is also used in the nom. plur.

Examples:—

Sanskrit. (1) *vach-as*, (3) neut. *naman-i*, (4) *bharat-as*, neut. *bharant-i*; (5) *dátr-n (datr̃-s)*, neut. *dátr̃-n-i, bhrátr̃-n, mátr-s*; (6) *nav-as*, (7) *bhruv-as*, (8) *sunu-n, sunv-as*, fem. *hanu-s*; (9) *patí-n*, fem. *aví s*; (10) *asvá-n*, fem. *asva-s*, neut. *yuga-ni*.

Greek. (1) οπ-ας = †Ϝοπ-ᾶς = †Ϝοπ-αυς, (3) τέκτον-ας, neut. ταλαν-α; (4) φέροντ-ας, neut. φεροντ-α; (5) πατερ-ας, (6) νῆϜ-ας, ναῦς. (7) οφρυ-ας, ὀφρυ-ς; (8) †γλυκέϜ-ας, γλυκεις; ιχθύ-ας, ιχθῦς, γενι-ας, γενύ-ς. (9) †πολεγ-ας, πολεις; (10) ιππους = †ἱππο-νς, neut. ζυγ-ά.

Latin. (2) *gener-a* (= †*ganas-á*), (3) *nomin-a*, (4) *ferenti-a* (as theme in *i*); (8) *fructu-s* = †*fructu-ns*, neut. *cornu-a*; (9) *oveis, ovis, orés* (comp. Gr. πολεις and πολις), from †*ovi-ns*, neut. *mari-a* (comp. ἴδρι-α). (10) *equo-s* = †*equo-ns*, fem. *equá-s* = †*equa-ns*.

Gothic. (1) *man-s* (= †*man-as*), (3) *hanan-s* (= †*hanan-as*), neut. *namn-a* (prim. *náman-á*); in neuter themes the termination -*an*- is changed into -*on*-, if the theme is bisyllabic, or -*an*- succeeds two consonants, e. g. *hairton-a*, theme *hairtan-*; (4) *fijand-s* (= *fijand-as*). (:) *brothru-ns* follows the analogy of themes in *u*. (8) *sunu-ns, handu-ns*; (9) *mahti-ns, gastin-s*; (10) *vulfan-s*, neut. *juka* (= †*juká*), fem. *gibô-s*.

Ablative Singular.

This case is formed by the termination -*at*, or its abbreviated form -*t*, which is a frequently occurring element in the formation of themes, and may be identical with the pronominal demonstrative root *ta*, in an inverted form *at*. This case being lost in the Teutonic languages we abstain from examining it any further.

Genitive Singular.

The case-suffix of the genitive singular is -*as*, -*s*, which is added to the theme in the same manner as -*at*, -*t*, in the ablative, both suffixes being nearly related with regard to form as well as function. The masc. and neut. themes in *a* do not take -*s* but -*sya*, also of pronominal origin, probably = *sa* + *ya*. (Compare the demonstratives *sa*- and *ta*-, *sya* and *tya*.)

Examples:—

Sanskrit. (1) *vách-as*, (2), *manas-as*, (3) *namn-as*, (4) *bharat-as*, (5) *dátu-s*, *bhrátu-s*, *mátu-s* (ved. *pitr-as*, the more ancient form) from *dátr-s*, *mátr-s* = *dátr-as*, *mátr-as*, prim. *dátar-as*, *mátar-as*. (6) *náv-as*, (7) *bhrur-as*, (8) *suno-s;* fem. *hano-s* or *hanv-ás*, neut. *madhu-n-as*, *madv-as*, *madh-os*. (9) *pate-s*, also *paty-us* = *paty-as:* fem. *avé-s* = *avy-as*, neut. *vari-n-as;* neut. *yuga-sya*.

Greek. Case-suffix $os =$ prim. *as*; sometimes lengthened in ως. The themes in *a* masc and neut. have †-σyο = prim. -*sya;* the fem. in *a* have the common case-suffix prim. -*as*, the *a* of which is absorbed by the final vowel of the theme. Examples: —(1) Fοπ-ος, (3) τέκτον-ος, (4) φεροντ-ος, εἰδοτ-ος; (5) πατρ-ος, μητρ-ος, for πατερ-ος, μητερ-ος, which also occur; (6) ναF-ός, νηF-ός. (7) συ-ος, (8) γέννυ-ος, perhaps for γεν-υF-ος; (9) Ion. πολι-ος, πολε-ως. (10) †ιππο-σyο, ἵππο-ιο, ἵππο ο, ιππου; neut. ζυγοῖο, ζυγου; fem. χώορα-ς, τιμῆ-ς; masc. πολίτου, from πολιτ-αο (αο Hom.) = †πολιτ-αyο = †πολιτ-α-σyο.

Latin. Suffix *-os* as in Greek, later *-us, -is*. Examples:—(1) *vóc-os* (as preserved in *senatu-os, domu-os*, &c.; perhaps for *-uv-os, -ov-os*, comp. Gr. γλυκεF-ος), hence *voc-us* (as preserved in *vener-us, honor-us, part-us*), hence *voc-is*. It is the same with all other consonantal themes. (2) †*genes-os, gener-is;* (3) *homin-is* = †*homen-os, nómin-is* = †*nómen-os;* (4) *ferent-is* = †*ferent-os*, (5) *patr-is* = †*patr-os*, (6) *bov-is* = †*bov-os*, (7) *su-is* = *su-os;* (8) *fructú-s* = †*fructu-os* = *fructov-os* (comp. γλυκεF-ος), like *suus* from *soros*, or *fructus* from *fructu-is* (comp. *senatu-is*). Sometimes after the analogy of themes in *a*: *senati, sumpti, quæsti;* (9) *ovi-s*, probably = †*ovi-s* = *oveis*, †*ove-is*, †*ovi-is;* by the shortening of *-is* the consonantal are mixed up with the themes in *i*. (10) Masc. neut. *equei, equi; jugei, jugi*, probably †*equeis* = *equois* the more ancient form. (As we have already observed, the loss of the final *s* is of rather frequent occurrence in the Latin language.) This †*equeis*, †*equois*, in its primitive shape might be †*akvay-as*. Feminine, *familiá-s, terrá-s, viá-s, deivá-s* = χωρα-ς, Goth. *gibô-s;* or, *Dianaes, Octaviaes, dimidiaes, suaes;* *-aes* = *-ais* = prim. *-áyas*, as masc. *-ois* for *ayas*, in both genders an extension of the termination *-as* having taken place. To this *-ais* will also lead forms like *fameliai, vitai, Romai*, and the common *-æ* = *-ae* which replaced the more ancient *-ai*. The themes in *ya* masc. and neut. in the more ancient form contract *-ii* into *-i*, as *fili, consili*.

Gothic. Suffix *-s* for the primitive *-as*; the themes in *i* and *u* lengthen their final vowel and take *-as*; the masc. and neut. themes in *a* shorten much their termination: (1) *man-s* (= †*man-*

as), (3) *hanin-s*, neut. *namin-s* = †*hanin-is*, †*namin-is*, primitive *náman-as*. (4) *fijandis* (like 10), (5) *brothr-s* (= prim. *bhrátar-as*), *dauhtr-s*. (8) *sunau-s*, *handau-s*, *faihau-s*; this *-au-s* points to a more ancient †*sunav-is*, prim. *sunav-as*, from which Goth. †*sunav-s*, *sunau-s*. (9) *gastis* (masc. like 10), fem. *mahtai-s*, the *-ai-s* pointing to a more ancient *mahtay-is*, prim. *mahtay-as*. (10) *vulfi-s*, *dagi-s*, like Old Saxon *daga-s* from a primitive *-asya*, with the loss of the final *ya*; fem. *gibó-s*.

Genitive Plural.

The genitive plural ends in *-ám* and *-sám*, the latter suffix being almost exclusively used in the pronominal declension. It appears that *-ám* has its origin in *-sám*, as the nom. plur. *-as* in *-sas*. Perhaps this *-sám* is a fuller or lengthened form of the original genitive suffix which seems to have lost the sign of the plural. This sign being supplied and the lengthened form reduced, we shall get -†*sams* as the primitive form. With this we may compare the dat. dual *-bhyám* from *-bhyáms*, by the side of the dat. plur. *-bhyas* from *-bhyam-s*. In the same manner as we find the form *bhy-am* by the side of the case-suffix *-bhi*, so we have together with the suffix *-s*, *-as*, the form *-s-am*. With this *-sam* must originally have been joined the plural sign *-s*, hence *-sam-s*, as we have already stated.

Sanskrit. The suffix *-ám* is joined to the shortest form of mutable themes; vocalic themes increase themselves by adopting *n*, before which they lengthen the vowel of the theme; the *ar* of themes in *ar* is weakened into *r*, and this *r* treated as a vowel. Examples:— (1) *vách-ám*, (2) *manas-ám*, (3) *námn-ám*, (4) *bharat-ám*, (5) *dátr̥-n-ám*, *bhátr̥-n-ám*; ved. *nar-ám* (*nar-*, man), *svasr-ám* (*svasar-*, sister); (6) *náv-ám*, (7) *bhruv-ám*, (8) *sunu-n-ám*, (9) *avî-n-ám*, (10) *asvá-n-ám*, neut. *yugá-n-ám*.

Greek. The case-suffix is -ων = *-am*. (1) ϝοπ-ων, (2) μεν-ῶν = †μενεσ-ων; (3) τεκτον-ων, (4) φερόντ-ων, εἰδοτ-ων; (5) δοτηρ-ων, μητερ-ων; (6) ναϝ-ων, βοϝ-ῶν; (7) συ-ῶν, (8) γενυ-ων, (9) Ion. πολι-ων, πολε-ων = †πολεy-ων. (10) λυκ-ων, fem. χωρῶν = †χωρα-(σ)-ων; -σων = prim. *-sám*.

Latin. Suffix *-om*, *-um* = prim. *-ám*; with themes in *a* it is *-rom*, *-rum*, from *-som* = prim. *-sám*. Examples:— (1) *vóc-um* = †*voc-om*; *gener-um* = *genes-om*; (3) *nomin-um*, (4) *parent-um*, *sapient-um*, or after the analogy of the themes in *i*, *sapienti-um*; (5) *dator-um*, *patr-um*; (6) *bo-um* = †*bov-um*; (8) *fructu-um*, perhaps from †*fructov-óm*; (9) *ovi-um*, (10) *equum*, *equo-rum*; fem. *equa-rum* (comp. Gr. χωρά-σων, *r = s*).

Gothic. The primitive suffix *ám* was in Gothic reduced to *e*. The feminines of 3 and 10 change the primitive *a* of *ám* into *ô*. Examples: — (3) *hanan-e auhsn-e* (theme *auhsan-*, ox), neut. *hairtan-e, namn-e*, fem. *tuggon-o*; (4) *fijand-e* (like 10); (5) *brothr-e, dauhtr-e*; (8) *suniv-e*, fem. *handiv-e* (*-iv-e'*= prim. *-av-ám*); (9) *gast-e*, fem. *anst-e* (like 10). (10) Masc. *vulfe*, neut. *juke*, prim. *vulfám, jugám*; fem. *gib-o*.

Locative Singular.

With nominal themes *i* is the case termination, but in the pronominal declension the locative takes the suffix *in*, probably the weakened form of *an* which may be derived from the pronominal demonstrative base *ana-* (to which belongs the preposition *in*, Lat. *in*, Gr. ἐν, Goth. *ana*). The locative is preserved as an independent case in Sanskrit and several other Aryan languages, but in the Teutonic as well as Latin, Greek and Celtic tongues, it has become identical with the dative, to which it originally bore a close relationship.

Sanskrit. The suffix *i* is in mutable themes joined to the shortest thematic form. Vocalic feminines in *î, û, á*, have *-ám* as case-suffix, which is joined to *a* (10) by means of the spirant *y*. The themes in *u* have lost the case-suffix and terminate in *-au*, which stands for a more ancient *-av-i;* themes in *i* follow this analogy; neuters in *i* and *u* extend the theme by *n*. Examples: —(1) *vách-i*, (2) *manas-i*, (3) *náman-i* and *námn-i*; (4) *bharat-i*, (5) *dátar-i, mátar-i*; (6) *náv-i*, (7) *bhruv-i* and *bhruv-ám*; (8) *sunáu, hanáu*, ved. *sunav-i, hanv-i*, neut. *madhu-n-i*; (9) *aváu*, fem. *avy-am;* (10) masc. *aśvé* = †*aśva-i*, neut. *jugé*, fem. *aśva-y-ám*.

Greek. The locative has the functions of the dative; the masc. and neut. themes in *a* (10) have both cases, locative and dative, the former however is not used as a regular case of the noun, but as an adverb. Examples:—(1) οπ-ι, (2) μένει = †μένεσ-ι; (3) τέκτον-ι, (4) φεροντ-ι, εἰδοτ-ι; (5) δοτηρ-ι, μητρ-ί; (6) νηϝ-ί, (7) συ-ί, (8) γλυκεῖ = †γλυκεϝ-ι; (9) πολει = †πολεy-ι; (10) οικο-ι, ποῖ, οἶ, fem. χαμα-ι (humi, theme χαμα-).

Latin. Locatives proper are the following forms of the themes in *a: humí, domí, bellí, Corinthí; í = ei = oi* (comp. οικοι); fem. *Romae* = †*Romai* (comp. χαμαί); (*ruri*, or *rure*, is a common ablative, no locative.) As to the rest the locative has the functions of the dative.

Gothic. The locative has the functions of the dative; only the themes in *a* have the form of the dative proper; the case-suffix *i* is dropped throughout; themes in *u* and *i* (feminine) lengthen the final vowel. Examples:—(1) *mann(-i)*, (3) *hanin-(-i)*, (4) *fijand(-i)* (5) *brothr-(i)*, *dauhtr(-i)*; (8) *sunau* = †*sunav(i-)*, fem. *handau* = †*handav(-i)*. (9) fem. *mahtai* = *mahtaj(-i)*; masc. *gasta* (dative like 10). (10) Masc. and neut. form a dative; the fem. *gibai* may be taken as the dative or the locative.

Dative Singular. (See Locative.)

Sanskrit. The dative suffix is *-e* for *-ai*, of which the former may be the weakened form; *ai* is perhaps the lengthened form of the locative *i*. Examples:—(1) *vách-e*, (2) *manas-e*, (4) *bharat-e*, *dátr-e*, *mátr-e*, (6) *náv-é*, (7) *bhruv-é*, (8) *sunav-e*, (9) *patay-e*, (10) *asvaya*, *á-y-a* = †*á-y-ai*.

Greek. The true dative with the themes in *a* (10), as ἵππῳ = ιππωι, prim. *akvai* = *akva-ai*; χωρα, τιμῇ, a, η = *ái* = *á-ai*.

Latin. As in Greek the true dative with the themes in *a* only (10), as *equó* = *equói*; thus *populoi*, *romanoi*, *quoi*; fem. *equae* = *equái*.

Gothic. The same as with Greek and Latin. Themes in *a* (10): *vulfa* = †*vulfá* = *vulfái*; fem. *gibai* = *gibái*.

Locative Plural.

The suffix of this case is prim. *-sva* (comp. the pronominal root *sva*, relative and reflective), Sansk. *-su*, Gr. σσι = σϕι (used for the dative). In the Teutonic languages this case is lost.

1st Instrumental Singular.

The instrumental singular is rendered by two distinct suffixes, where it has been conjectured that originally there must have been two distinct instrumentals. The case-suffix of the first instrumental is *a* (a demonstrative base frequently occurring in the formation of themes or stems); it is exclusively used in Sanskrit, while in Greek and Gothic we find it in adverbial forms only, or by the side of the second instrumental suffix in certain nominal themes.

Examples:—

Sanskrit. (1) *vách-á*, (2) *manas-á*, (3) *námn-á*, (4) *bharat-á*, (5) *bhrátr-á*, *dátr-á*; (6) *náv-á*, (7) *bhruv-á*, (8) *sunu-n-á*, (9) *pati-n-á*, (10) *asvená*, *yugena*.

Greek. Probably the adverbs in η and α, as πάντη, Dor. παντ-α, τάχ-α, ἄμ-α, perhaps ἷ-ν-α.

Gothic (see below).

Old High German in feminine themes in *a*, as '*mit ercnâ ewâ*' certa lege; *zwifaldâ lera*, duplici doctrina.

2nd Instrumental Singular.

Case-suffix *bhi*, of doubtful origin, but frequently occurring in the formation of cases; with the plural sign *s* (-*bhi-s*) it forms the plural instrumental; it is used moreover to discharge the functions of the dative and ablative (*tu-bhi-am*, tibi; *ma-bhi-am*, mihi); in the dative and abl. plur. it appears again in the form -*bhi-am-s*. This suffix -*bhi* forms the instrumental singular in the Teutonic and other languages, by the side of the suffix -*â* (see 1st Instr.) used with feminine themes in *a*.

Greek very scarce: Hom. suffix φι = *bhi*; it is not limited to the instrumental, but may express locative and ablative relations as well. Examples:—Hom. ἧφι βίηφι; κρατερῆφι βίηφι; στήθεσ-φιν, Ἰλιό-φιν, δεξιό-φιν, &c.

Gothic has this case but in few examples; in **Old High German**, on the contrary, we meet it as a regularly occurring formation, where, with themes in *a*, it ends in -*u*, -*u* (later *o*) This -*u*, -*u*, is derived from -*am*, -*ami*, or rather -*âmi*, e. g. *wolfu*, *wortu*, *plintu*; *wolfu* from †*wolfam*, *wolfâ-mi*. With pronouns this case is commonly found after the analogy of themes in *ya*, as *hwiu*, theme *hwa-* (interrog.) from *hwyâ-mi*; feminines in *a* use the first instrumental sing. (See 1st Instr. above.)

The Gothic language has this case only in *the* (after prepositions, and as particle before the comparative) of the demonstrative *tha-*; *hve* (as *du hve*, wherefore, why) of the pronominal theme *hva-*; *sve* (how) of the pronoun *sva-*[1].

Instrumental Plural.

This case is wanting in the Teutonic languages.

---

[1] **Old Saxon** and **Anglo-Saxon** also have an instrumental in the declension of nouns and adjectives, the former using, like Old High German, the termination *u*, the latter the termination *e*, like Gothic. **Old Norse** possesses no instrumental, and the only instance where it occurs in **Old Frisian** is the form *thiu* of the demonstrative pronoun. (Comp. the Declension of Pronouns, p. 199 sqq.)

Dative and Ablative Plural.

The suffix *bhi* with -*am* forms the dative singular of the personal pronouns. This dat. sing. suffix -*bhyam*, to which was added the plural sign *s*, yields the suffix -*bhyam-s* for the formation of the dative and ablative plural. These cases occur in all Aryan languages except the Greek, which uses the locative instead of the dative, and the genitive instead of the ablative.

Sanskrit. Suffix *bhya-s* for *bhyam-s*, which is added to the theme in the same manner as the instrumental suffix -*bhis*. Examples:—(1) *vag-bhyas*, (2) *mans-bhyas*, (3) *nâma-bhyas*, (4) *bharad-bhyas*, (5) *bhrâtr-bhyas*, (6) *nâu-bhyas*, (7) *bhru-bhyas*, (8) *sunu-bhyas*, (9) *pati-bhyas*, (10) *asve-bhyas*, neut. *juge-bhyas*.

Latin. Suffix -*bos*, -*bus*, for a more ancient †-*bios*, †-*bius* (comp. *minus* for *minius*); a different development in the pronouns *vo-bi-s* = *vo-bei-s* (as *ti-bi* for *ti-bei*); themes in *a* reject the *b*; consonantal themes follow those in *i*. Examples:—(1) *voci-bus*, (3) *nomini-bus*, (5) *mâtri-bus*, (8) *acu-bus;* but themes in *u* also usually follow those in *i*, as *fructi-bus*: (9) *ovi-bus*, (10) *ambo-bus*, *duo-bus*, exceptional forms which strictly follow the rule. Forms such as *parvi-bus*, *amici-bus*, *dii-bus*, prove how in compounds the final *o* of the theme was weakened into *i*. The usual dat. and abl. suffix -*is* seems to pre-suppose an ancient -*bios*, or -*fios* for the prim. *bhyams*, Sansk. *bhyas*, as for instance, †*equo-fios*, whence *equo-hios*, whence *equo-ios*, whence *equo-is*, whence *eque-is*, whence *equis*. Feminine themes in *a* have frequently preserved the primitive form, as *equâ-bus*, *deâ-bus*, *filiâ-bus;* the usual *is* which has rejected the *b* must be derived from *ais*, as *mensis* from †*mensais*, †*mensa-bios*.

Gothic. Of the primitive suffix *bhyam-s* nothing remained but the simple -*m*, while in Old Norse, where we find *thri-mr* (tribus) by the side of *thri-m*, the primitive *s* also is represented of a form †*thri-mas* or †*thri-mus* = *tri-bhyams* (*r* for *s*). Themes in *n* take occasionally, as themes in *a* always do, *am* instead of -*m*. Examples:—(3) *hana-m*, neut. *hairta-m*, fem. *tuggo-m*, from †*hanan-m*, &c.; but *abn-am*, theme *aban-*, man; (4) *fijandam* (like 10), (5) *brothru-m* (like 8); (8) *sunu-m*, (9) *mahti-m*, *gasti-m*. (10) masc. *vulfa-m*, neut. *juka-m*, fem. *gibo-m*.

Vocative.

The vocative, as we have said before, is no case, not even a word, but the noun in the form of an interjection, devoid therefore of a case-suffix. Only the singular has a vocative, whilst dual and plural supply it by the nominative, a fact which often occurs in the singular too.

Sanskrit. The accent always on the first syllable; consonantal themes appear in the simple thematic form; masc. and fem. of themes in *i* and *u* lengthen the final vowel; feminine themes in *â* (10) weaken the *a* into *e*; themes ending in a diphthong or a long vowel do not form a vocative, but supply it by the nominative. Examples:—(1) *vak*, (2) *manas*, (3) *nâman*, (4) *bharan* for †*bharant*; (5) *mâtar*, (6) *nâus*, (7) *bhrus*, (8) *sunó*, (9) *pate, ave*; (10) *asva*, neut. *yuga*.

Greek. Consonantal themes commonly use the nominative for the vocative. Examples:—(1) παῖ for †παιδ; (3) δαιμον (but ηγεμων, nom.); (4) γέρον (but φερων part. nom.); (5) σῶτερ, ῥῆτορ, πατερ. (6) ῥαυ, (7) συς, (8) γλυκυ, (9) πόσι, πολι; (10) ἱππε, neut. ζυγόν; fem. χώρᾱ, γλῶσσα.

Latin. A vocative with masc. themes under No. 10 only, as *eque* (=ιππε), prim. *akva*; themes in *ya*, as *fili* for *filie*.

Gothic. The vocal themes only form a vocative (3=nom.; 4 *giband*, like 10; 5=nom.); (8) *sunau, handau*, but also *sunu*. (9) *gast* for *gasti*, fem. *anst*; (10) *vulf*=†*vulfa*, fem. *giba*; themes in *ya: hari, hairdi*=†*harja*, †*hirdja*.

THE OLD TEUTONIC LANGUAGES.

STRONG DECLENSION.

All the ancient Teutonic dialects preserve in the declensions the distinction of themes in **a, i,** and **u**; and these thematic vowels giving the declension a peculiar colouring, we may well arrange all nouns under three declensions: viz. the declension in **a,** that in **i,** and that in **u**. The declension of themes ending in a consonant we shall treat under a separate head hereafter[1].

Though we find the themes in **a, i, u,** in all the different Teutonic dialects, we must not omit to notice that it is in Gothic only where they appear altogether distinct; though even here the thematic vowels are frequently dropped or weakened and the case-terminations much mutilated.

The thematic vowel of the declension in **a** is in Gothic distinctly preserved only in the dative singular and the dative

[1] Comp. pp. 169, 170, and pp. 268, 269.

and accusative plural, while we find it in a lengthened form in the nominative and vocative plural. The feminines of this declension lengthen the thematic vowel *a* into *ó*, except in the nom. accus. and voc. sing. where the *a* remains. The neuter nom. and accus. sing. drop the thematic vowel as well as the case-sign.

While the declension in a comprises all three genders, the declension in i has only substantives of the masculine and feminine. The feminine, always showing an inclination to full and lengthy forms, which, as already mentioned, changed in the first declension the thematic vowel *a* into *ó*, follows its natural propensities in the second declension also and takes 'gradation,' or what Sanskrit grammarians call 'guna,' by introducing an *a* before the thematic vowel *i*[1].

The declension in u shelters its thematic vowel most persistently, so that we find the *u* preserved before the case-sign *s* of the nom. masc. and fem. as well as in the nom. neut., where the other two declensions have dropped their thematic vowels.

In the other Teutonic dialects also the three delensions in a, i, and u, can be traced; but it is the first only which is in a flourishing condition, uncorrupted by the influence of the other declensions and comprising the three genders. The declension in u is in most dialects in a dilapidated condition or encroached upon by the other declensions. In Old Norse however the declensions are in their fullest vigour, in some respects more so than in Gothic, while Old High German, though it has preserved some ancient case-signs which are lost in Gothic, has suffered great losses with the dilapidation of its declension in u, the plural of which has transgressed into the declension in i. In the same manner the Low German dialects, Anglo-Saxon, Old Frisian, and Old Saxon appear greatly mutilated, though in some respects they too show more ancient forms than we find in the Gothic dialect.

As to the case-terminations in the different Teutonic dialects we must let them pass a short review in order to compare them with the primitive case-signs which we have eliminated above.

Nominative Singular.

The primitive case-sign -*s*, from the demonstrative root *sa*, has been dropped in all the Teutonic dialects except the Gothic and Old Norse, the latter however following its propensity to

---

[1] Comp. pp. 22-25.

rhotacize, that is, to convert the sibilant *s* into *r*. But Gothic and Old Norse too, like all the other Teutonic tongues, have lost the thematic vowel in the nom. sing., so that for the O. H. Germ., A. S., O. S., O. Fris. *fisk (visk* or *fisc)*, we find in Gothic *fisk-s*, in Old Norse *fisk-r*. An exception to this rule is found in the u declension, which retains its thematic vowel in all the dialects but Old Norse, and in Gothic yields the full termination *us*, as in nom. sing. Goth. *sunu-s* (son), O. H. Germ., A. S., O. S., O. Fris. *sunu*, O. N. *son-r*. The feminine nouns retain the thematic vowel in the a and u declensions, as Goth. *giba*, O. H. Germ., O. S. *geba*, A. S. *gifu* (*a* darkened into *u*), O. Fris. *jeve;* but O. N. *giöf*. Neuter nouns dispense with the thematic vowel as well as the termination. Even in the cognate languages the accusative is used to supply the nominative case; compare Goth. *vaurd*, O. H. Germ. *wort*, A. S., O. S., O. Fris. *word*, O. N. *orð*, Lat. *verbum*.

Nominative Plural.

The primitive case-sign -*as* (for *sas = sa-sa*) is most completely preserved in Anglo-Saxon and Old Saxon, where the theme *fiska*- with the case termination -*as* yields the legitimate form *fiskás*, whilst in Gothic the combination of *a + a* results in the long vowel *o*, and hence the nom. plur. *fiskos*. Old Frisian and Old Norse rhotacize the case-sign -*s* and join the final -*r* directly to the theme, so that their nom. plur. is *fiskar*. Old High German preserves the long *a* which is the product of the combined *a* of the theme and *a* of the termination, but the final *s* is dropped, hence nom. plur. *viská*. In the feminine gender the Gothic and Old Norse alone retain the case-sign *s* (O. N. *r*), while the other dialects either use the simple thematic vowel (A. S. *gifa*, O. Fris. *jeva*), or its lengthened form (O. S. *gibá*, O. H. Germ. *gibá* or *gibó*); but Goth. *gibos*, O. N. *giafar*. The neuter rejects the thematic vowels as well as the case-sign, except in Gothic, where we find in the nom. plur. the termination *a*.

Accusative Singular.

The primitive case-sign -*am* after consonants, -*m* after vowels, from the demonstrative root *am* (comp. Sansk. *ama-*, hic), is altogether lost in the Teutonic strong declensions (themes in a, i, u), but preserved in the weak declension (consonantal themes in n)[1], where it is converted into *n* (compare the accus. sing. Lat. -*m*,

---

[1] Weak Declension, see below.

Gr. -ν); wherefore the accus. sing. of the theme *hanan-* is in O. H. Germ. and O. S. *hanun*, Goth. and A. S. *hanan*; but the *n* is dropped in O. Fris. *hona*, O. N. *hana*. Very remarkable in Old High German is the preservation of the ancient case-sign -*n* in the masculine, chiefly of proper nouns in a, where even Gothic has completely lost the case-sign; e. g. O. H. Germ. *got* (deus), acc. sing. *gota-n*.

Accusative Plural.

The primitive -*ams* (= *am*, the case-sign of the accus. sing. + *s*, the termination of the plural) appears in Gothic as -*ans*, -*ns*, *n* being preferred to *m* before the sibilant *s*; hence *fiskans* (a), *balgins* (i), *sununs* (u), in the strong, and *hanans* (n), in the weak declension; so again the feminine *anstins* (i), *handuns* (u), *tuggons* (n), but *gibos* for *gibans* (a). Next to Gothic the Anglo-Saxon and Old Saxon dialects most faithfully render the ancient case-sign, but suppress the consonant *n* in the same manner as the Gothic feminine in a, which elision causes the preceding vowel to be lengthened, hence A. S. *fiscás*, O. S. *fiskás* and *fiskos*. Old High German drops the case-sign altogether and lengthens the thematic vowel, hence accus. like nom. plur. *viská*; and Old Frisian rhotacizes the final *s*, hence the accus. like the nom. plur. *fiskar*. Old Norse drops the case-sign altogether and uses the simple thematic vowel as its accusative termination. This example is followed by the other dialects in the fem. accus. plur., as in the A. S. *gifa*, O. Fris. *jeva*, while Old High German and Old Saxon lengthen the thematic vowel in *gébo*, *gébá*.

Genitive Singular.

The primitive termination -*as*, -*s*, is found in all the Teutonic dialects; even Old Norse, which on other occasions so frequently supplants the sibilant by the liquid *r*, preserves the original case-sign of the genitive singular, at least in the declension in a, while those in i and u admit rhotacism. The thematic vowel preceding the case-sign is variously modified. The Gothic has gradation of the thematic *u* into *au*, and yields the thematic *a* for *i* in the genitive *fiski-s*, where the Old Saxon dialect still owns the more ancient form *fiska-s*. But in the latter as well as in the other dialects, High and Low German, the thematic *a* is usually weakened into *i* or *e*, hence the genitive forms O. H. Germ. *viskes*, A. S. *fisces*, O. Fris. *fiskes*; while Old Norse, rejecting the thematic vowel altogether in the a declension, has *fisks*.

In the fem. the thematic vowel is in most dialects lengthened, whether it be succeeded by the case-sign or not; hence Gothic *gibos*, O. H. Germ. *gebo*, O. S. *gebá*, but A. S. *gife*, O. Fris. *jeve* (a); Goth. *anstais* (gradation of *i* into *ái*), O. H. Germ. *ensti*, but O. S. *ensti* (i). The genitive forms in Old Norse are peculiar, where the masculine in a alone has the regular ancient case-sign, while the masculines in i and u, and the feminines in a and i adopt the liquid *r*, which is preceded throughout by the vowel *a*.

Genitive Plural.

The ancient case-sign -*ám*, the probable derivation of which we have given above, is in Gothic reduced to the simple vowel *e*, feminine *ó*; hence the genitives *fiske, gibo*. The other Teutonic dialects also have the lengthened *ó* or *á*, or simply *a* as the genitive termination, as O. H. Germ. *visko*, O. S. *fiskó* or *fiská*, A. S. *fiscá*, but O. Fris. and O. N. *fiska*. The same terminations are used for the genitive plural feminine in the declensions i and u, but in the a declension the genitive feminine has in Old High German and Old Saxon the extended termination *ó-n-ó*, A. S. and O. Fris. *e-n-a*, which seems to have been formed in analogy to the weak declension, where it occurs as the regular termination. Though Gothic has the simple *ó* in *gibo* for the O. H. Germ. *gebono*, the introduction of the liquid *n* must be of very ancient date, since it occurs in the Indian dialects too. (Comp. the gen. plur. fem. in a, Sansk. *ásva-n-am* for *ásvam*, where the Sanskrit termination *a-n-am* corresponds to the O. H. Germ. *ó-n-ó*, A. S. *e-n-a*.)

Dative Singular.

A dative proper we have only in the masculine of the declension in a and of that in i, the latter having adopted the thematic vowel of the former. Thus we find in Gothic the dative *fiska*, O. H. Germ. *viska*, O. S. *fiska*, or weakened into *fiske*, A. S. *fisce*, O. Fris. *fiska*, or *fiski*, or *fiske*, O. N. *fiski* (a). The same terminations occur in the dative singular of the declension in i, e. g. Goth. *balga*, O. H. Germ. *palka*, O. S. *gasta*. The case-sign *e* or *i* is throughout the weakened form of *a*, wherefore the *i* cannot cause Umlaut. But in all declensions and genders other than those just mentioned the Teutonic languages are deprived of a true dative, and consequently use the locative singular to perform its functions. The termination of this locative is *i*, the origin of which we have mentioned before. It is generally

DECLENSIONS.

dropped, and the thematic vowel then has gradation, as in *mahtai* (**i**) for *mahtaj(-i)*, *handau* (**u** fem.) for *handar(-i)*; *sunau* (**u** masc.) for *sunav(-i)*; *hanin* for *hanin(-i)* (**n**). The dative feminine *gibai* (**a**) may be considered a locative or a true dative.

DATIVE PLURAL.

The primitive suffix *bhyams* has in the Teutonic languages dwindled down to the simple *-m*, e. g. Goth. *fiska-m* (masc.), *gibo-m* (fem.) (**a**); *balgi-m, ansti-m* (**i**); *sunu-m, handu-m* (**u**); *hana-m, tuggo-m* (**n**). Gothic only preserves the thematic vowels distinct in the terminations *-am, -im, -um*; Old High German puts *um* for *am* in the **a** declension, and all the other dialects prefer in all declensions the darkened form *um* in the different genders, though it must be mentioned that we meet also, chiefly in Old Frisian, with weakened forms such as *em* and *on*. This leads us to notice another change, namely, of *m* into *n*, which already occurs in late Old High German, sometimes in Frisian and almost regularly in Old Saxon, a change which moreover is accompanied by a weakening of the thematic vowel from *u* into *o*; hence the termination of dat. plur. *on*. Deserving of special notice is a form in Old Norse *thri-m-r* by the side of *thrim* (tribus), *tveim-m-r* for *tveim* (duobus), in which, besides the *m*, the *s* of the original case-sign is preserved, changed of course into *r* according to the phonetic laws of the Old Norse dialect, so that *thri-mr* stands for *thri-ms* = *thri-mas* = primitive *tri-bhjams*.

INSTRUMENTAL.

There were originally two distinct suffixes for the instrumental singular, and therefore probably two distinct instrumentals with different functions, a distinction however which at an early period was obliterated. The first instrumental was formed with the demonstrative suffix *a*, rudiments of which we have in Old High German in one or two examples of feminine nouns in **a**[1]. The second instrumental is formed with the suffix *bhi*, which is also frequently used to form the dative. (Comp. the declension of the Latin pronoun, e. g. *ti-bi* = *tu-bhi-am*, &c.) In the north European languages, both Slavonic and Germanic, the suffix *bhi* appears in the form of *mi*, probably in the combination *-am* for *-ami*, out of which the termination *ú* or *u* of the instrumental in Old High German and Old Saxon are explained, so that the

[1] Comp. p. 278.

O. H. Germ. *wolfu* would come from †*wolfam* and this from *wolfa-mi*. The Gothic has this instrumental in but few adverbial pronominal forms, such as *the* (comparative particle) from the pronominal theme *tha-*; *hve* (as *du hve*, why), from the pronominal base *hva-*; *sve* (as) from *sva-*. If these instrumental forms were the first instrumental with the suffix *a*, they would appear as *tha-a*, *hva-a*, &c., and these as *thô*, *hvô*, rather than *the*, *hve*. This instrumental *e* then originates like the Old High German *û* or *u* in the primitive *a-mi*, Teutonic for *a-bhi*. What we have said with regard to the instrumental *é* in Gothic holds good for the *é* of the instrumental in Anglo-Saxon, where it is used as the regular case-sign with all nouns that are capable of forming the mentioned case.

The Plural Neuter with the Suffix ir.

Several Teutonic dialects apply the suffix *-ir* (or its modified form *-er* or *-r*, or even *-ar*) in the formation of the plur. neut. of the declension in **a**. In Old High German we find this suffix often used with those neuter nouns which have lost their ancient termination *-a*. Thus, for example, *kalp* (calf) has the nom. plur. *kelb-ir* (the *i* of the suffix *ir* causes the Umlaut of *a* into *e*), and to this form are added the respective case-signs of the other cases, as in the gen. plur. *kelb-ir-ô*. The use of this suffix is more limited in Old Saxon, where we find but few forms, such as the genitives plur. *ei-er-o*, *hon-er-o* of *ei*, egg. *hon*, hen. Anglo-Saxon too does not patronize this suffix very largely, and in the few words where it does occur it is always followed by the ancient case-sign *-u* of the nom. plur. as well, e. g. *äg*, egg, nom. *ag-r-u*; *cealf*, calf, nom. plur. *cealf-r-u*; *cild*, child, nom. plur. *cild-r-u*; *lamb*, lamb, nom. plur. *lamb-r-u*. For the plural *hryð-er-u*, armenta, there is no singular *hryð*, but *hryðer*, the suffix *-er* having been adopted in the singular too. In Old Frisian the suffix *-ir*, in the modification *-ar*, or *-er*, is used in the formation of the plural of the following words: *kind*, child, plur. *kind-er-a* or *kind-er*, or the ancient form *kinda*; *klath*, cloth, dress, plur. *kláth-er-a*, or *kláth-ar*, or *klátha*; *horn*, horn, plur. *horn-ar*; *bon*, mandatum, plur. *bonn-ar*, *bonna* and *bon*. *hrither* (Germ. rind), has, as in Anglo-Saxon, the suffix in the singular also.

The Umlaut in the Old Teutonic Declensions.

The reader will do well first to refer to our remarks concerning the formation of Umlaut in general, in our chapter on Old

Teutonic vowels[1]. In no Teutonic language have the inflexional forms so wide a range of influence upon the vowel of the stem of the word as in the Old Norse, where both *i* and *u*, vowels which very frequently occur in the terminations, may cause Umlaut, while in the other Teutonic languages this prerogative is restricted to the vowel *i*, and the Gothic dialect is deprived of Umlaut altogether. The frequent occurrence of the Umlaut in the declensions of the Old Norse imparts to this language a degree of softness and richness of sound for which we might hardly find a parallel in any other Teutonic tongue, ancient or modern. In order to illustrate this remark we need only quote the different cases of the declension of the theme: *magu-*, son; sing. *mogr, magr, megi, mog*; plur. *megir, maga, mogum, mogu*. The reader will be able to account for these different changes or modifications of the vowel, if he will apply to this particular instance the laws and rules which regulate the occurrence of the Umlaut in general. We may therefore here restrict ourselves to certain phenomena of Umlaut which are peculiar to particular declensions and particular dialects.

Declension in **a**.—In Old High German this declension shows no Umlaut except in the neuter plural, where it may be effected by the suffix *-ir*, as in *kalp*, plur. *kelbir*. The Old Saxon, Anglo-Saxon, and Old Frisian languages have no Umlaut in the declension in **a**, because the case-signs lack the element which begets the Umlaut. In Old Norse, on the contrary, it is of frequent occurrence, as a reference to the paradigms will teach. A few cases require special explanation. The feminine nouns have in the nom. sing. dropped an *u*, the weakened form of an original *a*, the effect of which *u* is still perceptible in the Umlaut of the *a* of the stem into *o*. The same Umlaut occurs in the dat sing., where the *u* was dropped at a later period of the language, but its effect, the Umlaut, remained. Examples: —theme *giafa*, gift, nom. sing. *giöf* (for *giöfu*), dat. *giöf(u)*. Neuter nouns originally had in the nom. and accus. plur. the termination *-u*, which, though dropped, left the Umlaut of *a* into *o* behind, e. g. *fat*, vessel, plur. *fot* for *fotu*.

Declension in **i**.—All the Teutonic dialects (Gothic of course excepted) show Umlaut in this declension.

Old High German. Umlaut of *a* into *e*, caused by the *i* of the termination, takes place in the plural throughout, as well as in the gen. and dat. sing. of the feminine (unless the fem. is

---

[1] See pp. 26 28.

reduced to the simple stem of the word). Examples:—*palc*, hide, plur. *pelki; anst*, gen. *ensti*, plur. *ensti*. In the gen. plur. the *j* (from the thematic *i*) is often dropped, but the Umlaut remains, as *pelko, ensto*, for *pelkjo, enstjó*.

Old Saxon. The Umlaut of *a* into *e may* occur in the plural, and in the feminine in the gen. and dat. sing. as well, but it is not of *general* occurrence. Examples:—*gast*, guest, plur. *gesti* (or *gasti*); *anst*, favour, plur. *ensti* (or *ansti*).

Anglo-Saxon. The termination *i* of the dat. sing. and of the nom. and accus. plur., which in the course of time was dropped, caused Umlaut, which remained, e. g. masc. nom. sing. *fót*, dat. *fet* for *feti*, from *foti*; nom. accus. plur. *fét*, fem. nom. sing. *mus*, dat. *mýs*, nom. accus. plur. *mýs*, &c.

Old Frisian. The masculine gender has two words where Umlaut remained after the terminational *i* had been dropped, namely *fót*, nom. accus. plur *fet*; *tóth*, nom. accus. plur. *teth*; but there is no Umlaut either in the dat. sing of the masculine or in any case of the feminine gender.

Old Norse. Some of the masculine nouns of this declension adopt a *j* before the vowels *a* and *u* of the terminations, which *j*, whether retained or dropped, causes Umlaut of the preceding syllable, as in *belgr, belgjar*, where the *j* appears in certain cases, and *gestr, gestar*, where it is dropped throughout and yet its Umlaut remains. In the feminine nouns *gas, mús, lus* and *brun*, the terminations *ir* and *i*, dropped later on, caused the Umlaut in *ges, mýs, lys, bryn*.

Declension in **u.**—This declension shows no Umlaut in any dialect except in Old Norse, where, just in this declension, the Umlaut is most richly developed. (See the paradigms in **u.**) It requires but few explanations. The nom. *mogr* of the theme *magu-* (son) owes its Umlaut to an earlier *mogur* for *magur*, Goth. *magus*. The dat. sing. fem. *tonn* of the theme *tannu-* (tooth), owes its Umlaut to the ancient case-sign *u*, which was dropped at a later period.

Note.—The weak declension has Umlaut in no dialect except Old Norse, where the terminational *u* converts the *a* of the stem into *ö*.

PARADIGMS.

VOCAL THEMES (STRONG DECLENSIONS).

THEMES IN a.

Gothic.

Themes:—*fiska-*, *gibo-*, *vaurda-*.

	MASCULINE.		FEMININE.		NEUTER.	
	Sing.	Plur.	Sing.	Plur.	Sing.	Plur.
Nom.	*fisk-s* (fish)	*fiskô-s*	*giba* (gift)	*gibô-s*	*vaúrd* (word)	*vaúrda*
Gen.	*fiski-s*	*fisk-ê*	*gibô-s*	*gib-ô*	*vaúrdi-s*	*vaúrd-ê*
Dat.	*fiska*	*fiska-m*	*gibai*	*gibô-m*	*vaúrda*	*vaúrda-m*
Accus.	*fisk*	*fiska-ns*	*giba*	*gibô-s*	*vaúrd*	*vaúrda*
Voc.	*fisk*	*fiskô-s*	*giba*	*gibô-s*	*vaúrd*	*vaúrda*

Old High German.

Themes:—*viska-*, *gebô-* (for *kepo-*), *worta-*.

	MASCULINE.			FEMININE.	
	Sing.	Plur.	Sing.	Sing.	Plur.
Nom.	*visk* (fish)	*viskâ*	*got* (god)	*geba* (gift)	*gëbô*, *gëbâ*
Gen.	*viske-s*	*visk-ô*	..	*gëbô*, *gëbâ*	*gëbô-n-ô*
Dat.	*viska*	*visku-m*	..	*gëbô*, *gëbu*	*gëbô-m*
Accus.	*visk*	*viskâ*	*gota-n*	*gëba*	*gëbô*, *gëbâ*
Instr.	*visk-u*	..	..	..	..

	NEUTER.			
	Sing.	Plur.	Sing.	Plur.
Nom.	*wort* (word)	*wort*	*kalp* (calf)	*kelb-ir*
Gen.	*worte-s*	*wort-ô*	*kalbe-s*	*kelb-ir-ô*
Dat.	*worta*	*wortu-m*	*kalba*	*kelb-iru-m*
Accus.	*wort*	*wort*	*kalp*	*kelb-ir*
Instr.	*wort-u*	..	*kalb-u*	..

Old Saxon.

Themes:—*fisca-, gebó-, worda-*.

	MASCULINE.		FEMININE.	
	Sing.	Plur.	Sing.	Plur.
Nom.	fisc (fish)	fisco-s, fisca-s	geba (gift)	geba
Gen.	fisca-s, fisce-s	fisc-ô, fisc-a	geba, gebô	gebo-n-o
Dat.	fisca, fisce	fiscu-n, fisco-n	gebu, gebo	gebu-n, gebo-n
Accus.	fisc	fiscô-s, fisca-s	geba	geba
Instr.	fisc-u	..	..	..

	NEUTER.			
	Sing.	Plur.	Sing.	Plur.
Nom.	word	word	bac (back)	bacu
Gen.	worda-s, worde-s	word-ô	baca-s, bace-s	bac-ô
Dat.	worda, worde	wordu-n	baca, bace	bacu-n
Acc.	word	word	bac	bacu
Instr.	word-u	..	bac-u	..

Anglo-Saxon.

Themes:—*fisca-, daga-, gifa-, worda-, fata-*.

	MASCULINE.		FEMININE.	
	Sing.	Plur.	Sing.	Plur.
Nom.	fisc (fish)	fiscâ-s	gifu (gift)	gifa
Gen.	fisce-s	fisc-â	gife	gife-n-a
Dat.	fisce	fiscu-m	gife	gifu-m
Accus.	fisk	fiscâ-s	gife	gifa
Instr.	fisk-ê	..	..	..

	NEUTER.			
	Sing.	Plur.	Sing.	Plur.
Nom.	word	word	fät (vat)	fatu
Gen.	worde-s	word-â	fäte-s	fat-â
Dat.	worde	wordu-m	fäte	fatu-m
Accus.	word	word	fät	fatu
Instr.	word-ê	..	fät-ê	..

Old Frisian.

Themes:—*fiska-, jeva-, worda-, skipa-*.

	MASCULINE.		FEMININE.	
	Sing.	Plur.	Sing.	Plur.
Nom.	fisk (fish)	fiska-r, fiska	jeve (gift)	jeva
Gen.	fiski-s, fiske-s	fisk-a	jeve	jeve-n-a
Dat.	fiska, -i, -e	fisku-m, -on, -em	jeve	jevu-m, -on
Accus.	fisk	fiska-r, fiska	jeve	jeva

	NEUTER.			
	Sing.	Plur.	Sing.	Plur.
Nom.	word (word)	word(a)	skip (ship)	skipu, -o
Gen.	wordis, -es	word-a	skipi-s, -es	skip-a
Dat.	worda, -e	wordu-m, -on	skipa, -e	skipu-m, -on
Accus.	word	worda	skip	skipu, -o

Old Norse.

Themes:—*fiska-, arma-, giafa-, orða-, fata-*.

	MASCULINE.				FEMININE.	
	Sing.	Plur.	Sing.	Plur.	Sing.	Plur.
Nom.	fisk-r (fish)	fiska-r	arm-r (arm)	arma-r	giöf (gift)	giafa-r
Gen.	fisk-s	fisk-a	arm-s	arm-a	giafa-r	giaf-a
Dat.	fiski	fisku-m, -om	armi	örmu-m	giöf(u)	giöfu-m, om
Accus.	fisk	fiska	arm	arma	giöf	giafa-r

	NEUTER.			
	Sing.	Plur.	Sing.	Plur,
Nom.	orð (word)	orð	fat (vat)	föt
Gen.	orð-s	orð-a	fat-s	fat-a
Dat.	orði	orðu-m	fati	fötu-m, -om
Accus.	orð	orð	fat	föt

Notes to the Declension in a.

Gothic.

1. The following words belong to the declension in a.

MASC. áiþs, oath (Germ. eid); asts, branch (Germ. ast); bagms, tree (Germ. baum, cf. beam); dags, day (Germ. tag); hunds, dog (Germ. hund, cf. hound); hláibs, bread, cf. loaf; láubs, leaf (Germ. laub); stains, stone (Germ. stein); raír, man, cf. Lat. vir; vigs, way (Germ. weg); vulfs, wolf; þiubs, thief; sáivs, sea (Germ. see); snáivs, snow (Germ. schnee); fugls, bird (Germ. vogel, cf. fowl); sitls, seat (Germ. sessel); svibls, sulphur (Germ. schwefel); þiudans, king; himins, heaven (Germ himmel); akrs, field (Germ. acker, cf. acre); figgrs, finger; tagrs, tear (Germ. zähre).

FEM. aírþa, earth; boka, book; faþa, path (Germ. pfad); gaírda, girdle (Germ. gurte); giba, gift (Germ. gabe); haírda, herd (Germ heerde); hveila, hour, cf. while (Germ. weile = time); rasta, rest (Germ. rast); saurga, care (Germ. sorge); stáiga, path (Germ. steig); ramba, womb; þiuda, people, gens; nepla, needle, nadel; sairala, soul (Germ. seele); stibna, voice (Germ. stimme); gáitsa, goat (Germ. geiß); ahva, water; diupiþa, depth; sunja, truth.

NEUT barn, child: baurd, plank (Germ. bord); blóþ, blood (Gem. blut); daur, door (Germ. thür); hus, house (Germ. haus); jer, year (Germ. jahr); juk, yoke (Germ. joch); kaurn, corn; lamb, lamb (Germ. lamm); land, land (Germ. land); leik, body (cf. Germ. leiche, Engl. like); mel (time, cf. Germ. mal); mes, month; salt, salt (Germ. salz); skip, ship; vaurd, word; tagl, hair (cf. Engl. tail, Germ. zagel); áigin, property (cf. Germ. eigen, Engl. own); maurþr, murder (Germ. mord); silubr, silver (Germ. silber); eisarn, iron (Germ. eisen); hatis, hatred, hate (Germ. haß); háubiþ, head (cf. Germ. haupt); kniu, knee (Germ. knie); triu, tree.

2. Words of the masculine gender which have no plural may belong to the declension in a or i, because both are in the singular alike; and those of which the nominative singular is lost may belong to the masculine or neuter gender.

3. Themes ending in sa reject the s of the nominative singular after the s of the stem, in order to avoid the harsh succession of two identical sibilants, hence hals, neck (Germ. hals), instead of hals-s from the theme halsa-. The genitive is of course

halzi-s, &c. Themes ending in *ra* also suppress the case-sign *s* if the *r* is preceded by a vowel, hence *vair*, vir, nom. sing. of the theme *vaira*; but if a consonant precedes the *r*, the regular formation takes place, as *akr-s*, &c.

4. Words of the feminine gender which occur in the dat. sing. only might belong to the declension in **a** or **i**; those of which we know the nom. plur. only might be masculine or feminine.

5. Neuter nouns which show the gen. sing. only may be considered masculine or neuter.

Old High German.

1. The following words belong to the Declension in **a**.

MASC. *diop*, thief (Germ. dieb); *dorn*, thorn (Germ. dorn); *eid*, oath (Germ. eid); *hals*, neck (Germ. hals); *hleip*, bread; *hund*, dog (Germ. hund); *hof*, court-yard (Germ. hof); *keist*, spirit (Germ. geist, cf. goast); *muot*, animus (Germ. muth, cf. mood); *mund*, mouth (Germ. mund); *nid*, envy (Germ. neid); *poum*, tree (Germ. baum, cf. beam); *scaz*, treasure (Germ. schatz); *stap*, staff (Germ. stab); *stein*, stone (Germ. stein); *visk*, fish; *vokal*, bird (Germ. vogel); *aram*, arm; *fadum*, thread (Germ. faden); *rekan*, rain (Germ. regen); *achar*, field (Germ. acker); *vinkar*, finger; *mánod*, month (Germ. monat).

FEM. *aha*, water; *ea, ewa*, law; *erda*, earth (Germ. erde); *huîla*, mora (Germ. weile); *kepa*, gift (Germ. gabe); *lera*, doctrine (Germ. lehre); *sela*, soul (Germ. seele); *stimna*, voice (Germ. stimme); *stunta*, hour (Germ. stunde); *straza*, street (Germ. straße); *wampa*, womb.

NEUT. *chint*, child (Germ. kind); *chorn*, corn; *chrut*, herb (Germ. kraut); *dinc*, thing (Germ. ding); *hros*, horse (Germ. ross); *jar*, year (Germ. jahr); *joh*, joke (Germ. joch); *lamp*, lamb (Germ. lamm); *loup*, leaf (Germ. laub); *parn*, child; *pein*, bone (Germ. bein); *scif*, ship (Germ. schiff); *scâf*, sheep (Germ. schaf); *isarn*, iron (Germ. eisen); *silapar*, silver (Germ. silber); *wazar*, water (Germ. waßer); *houpit*, head (Germ. haupt).

2. In Old High German also the singular of nouns masculine is the same in the declensions in **a** and **i**, and it therefore is sometimes difficult to say to which declension they belong, especially since such words often form their plural in a different manner, either in **a** or **i**, in different documents.

Old Saxon.

1. The following words belong to the declension in **a**.

MASC. *bom*, tree (Germ. baum); *dag*, day (Germ. tag); *del*, deal (Germ. theil); *drom*, dream (Germ. traum); *fisk*, fish; *hund*, dog; *kuss*, kiss; *muth*, mouth; *slap*, sleep (Germ. schlaf); *sten*, stone (Germ. stein); *thiob*, thief; *stróm*, stream; *thorn*, thorn; *weg*, way (Germ. weg); *wer*, vir, man; *engil*, angel; *fugl*, bird; *himil*, heaven; *erl*, earl; *heban*, heaven; *fingar*, finger; *cuning*, king (Germ. konig); *berag*, mountain (Germ. berg); *séo*, sea; *sneo*, snow.

FEM. *aha*, water; *ertha*, earth; *geba*, gift; *helpa*, help; *huila*, time, while (Germ. weile); *lera*, doctrine; *seola*, soul; *sorga*, care (Germ. sorge); *strata*, street; *stemna*, voice (Germ. stimme); *wahta*, watch (Germ. wacht); *minnea*, love (Germ. minne).

NEUT. *bac*, back; *blad*, leaf (Germ. blatt); *barn*, child; *fat*, vessel, vat (Germ. faß); *fiur*, fire; *folc*, folk, people; *gold*, gold; *hus*, house; *jar*, year; *kind*, proles; *corn*, corn; *crud*, herb (Germ. kraut); *lioht*, light; *segal*, sail (Germ. segel); *tecan*, token; *silubar*, silver; *watar*, water; *wedar*, weather (Germ. wetter); *hobid*, head (Germ. haupt); *kneo*, knee; *treo*, tree.

2. The two different forms of the nom. and accus. plur. neut. deserve special notice; they are not applied, one or the other, at random, but as it would appear in accordance with the following rules:—All words consisting of a short syllable have preserved the ancient termination *u*, as *bac, bacu; blad, bladu; grab, grabu; tal, talu;* while words with a long syllable reject the termination; whence *barn, crud, thing, wib, word*, remain unchanged in the nominative and accusative plural.

Anglo-Saxon.

1. The following words belong to the declension in **a**.

MASC. *beorg*, mountain (Germ. berg); *ceol*, keel; *copp*, cup *craft*, craft; *dag*, day (Germ. tag); *dæl*, deal; *dom*, doom; *eard* soil; *feld*, field; *fisc*, fish; *gäst*, guest; *gást*, ghost; *heap*, heap *hring*, ring; *mor*, marsh; *múð*, mouth; *rap*, rope; *secg*, vir *stäf*, staff; *stán*, stone; *stream*, stream; *tear*, tear; *wæg*, wave *weg*, way; *weard*, warden, guard; *wind*, wind; *wulf*, wolf; *wyrm* worm; *nägel*, nail; *heofon*, heaven; *hrafn*, raven; *segn*, sign *finger*, finger; *þunor*, thunder; *cyning*, king; *monað*, month *hláford*, lord.

FEM. *duru*, door; *gifu*, gift; *lufu*, love; *sceamu*, shame; *scolu*, school; *-waru*, complexus incolarum; *land-waru*, province; *burh-waru*, civitas; *ceaster-waru*, arx.

NEUT. *äg*, egg; *bäc*, back; *bán*, bone; *bearn*, child; *cealf*, calf; *cild*, child; *fat*, vessel (cf. vat, Germ. faß); *geat*, gate; *gläs*, glass; *gräs*, grass; *hors*, horse; *lamb*, lamb; *leaf*, leaf; *leoht*, light; *sweord*, sword; *weorc*, work; *wíf*, woman (cf. wife); *word*, word; *yfel*, evil; *cicen*, chicken; *mæden*, maiden; *tácen*, token; *wästen*, waste, desert.

2. In Anglo-Saxon we have, as in Old Saxon, two forms for the nom. and accus. plur. neut., the termination *u* being preserved in words consisting of a short syllable, and rejected after long syllables and in words consisting of more than one syllable.

Old Frisian.

1. The following words belong to the declension in **a**.

MASC. *bâm*, tree (Germ. baum), *búr*, villager (Germ. bauer); *del*, deal; *erm*, arm; *eth*, oath; *fisk*, fish; *hap*, heap; *kláth*, coat, cloth; *stef*, staff; *tusk*, tooth, tusk; *wei*, way; *dëgan*, man, vir; *finger*, finger; *monath*, month (Germ. monat).

FEM. *ierde*, earth (Germ. erde); *nose*, nose; *sele*, soul (Germ. seele); *sine*, sinew, nerve; *spreke*, speech (Germ. sprache); *dêd*, deed; *ned*, need; *tid*, time, tide; *wrald*, world.

NEUT. *ben*, bone; *bern*, child; *her*, hair; *hus*, house; *kind*, child; *láf*, leaf; *muth*, mouth; *haved*, head; *ríke*, kingdom (Germ. reich).

2. In documents of a later period the plural of the masculine takes in the nominative, and especially in the accusative, *a* or *á*, instead of *ar*, and in the dative *on* for *um*.

3. The feminine nouns of this declension are not easily distinguished from those of the declension in **i**, because the nom. sing, and the gen. plur. only have distinctive terminations.

4. The plural of the neuter has the two forms of the nominative as in the Saxon dialects, one preserving the case-sign *u*, the other rejecting it and forming the nom. plur. like the nom. sing.

Old Norse.

1. The following words belong to the declension in **a**.

MASC. *armr*, arm; *brunnr*, fountain, well (Germ. brunnen); *dagr*, day (Germ tag); *dómr*, doom; *draumr*, dream (Germ.

traum); *fiskr*, fish; *haukr*, hawk; *heimr*, world; *hestr*, horse; *hringr*, ring; *móðr*, mind, mood; *stockr*, wood; *vindr*, wind; *steinn*[1], stone; *þraell*, slave; *ver*, vir, man; *mur*, wall (Germ. mauer); *háls*, neck (Germ. hals); *ís*, ice; *engill*, angel; *fugl*, bird (Germ. vogel); *iarl*, earl; *þiodan*, king; *himin*, heaven; *hrafn*, raven; *hamar*, hammer; *akur*, field (Germ. acker); *sigur*, victory (Germ. sieg); *konungr*, rex.

FEM. *giöf*, gift; *giorð*, girdle; *gröf*, grave (Germ. grab); *holl*, hall; *iorð*, earth; *mon*, mane; *nos*, nose; *ros*, rest; *sin*, sinew; *seil*, rope (Germ. seil); *skomm*, shame; *vomb*, womb; *fiöður*, feather.

NEUT. *bak*, back, tergum; *barn*, child; *blað*, leaf (Germ. blatt); *fat*, vessel, vat (Germ. faß); *glas*, glass; *gras*, grass; *hross*, horse (Germ. ross); *lamb*, lamb; *mál*, time; *rum*, room, space; *orð*, word; *sax*, knife; *skip*, ship; *tal*, speech, tale; *hagl*, hail (Germ. hagel); *tagl*, tail (Germ. zagel); *vín*, wine; *þak*, roof (Germ. dach); *nafn*, name; *vatn*, water; *sumar*, summer; *fóðr*, fodder; *silfr*, silver.

2. The case-sign *-i* of the dative sing. masc. is sometimes dropped in monosyllabic words with a long radical vowel, as in *hring*, *ís*, &c.; on the whole this termination seems to be inorganic, because it never causes Umlaut (except in *degi*, dative of *dagr*, day, which however seems to pass into the declension in u, as do many other words which sometimes form the whole plural after the latter declension).

3. Some words adopt forms from the declension in i, others form their plural both in a and i, as *vegr*, way, plur. *vegar* and *vëgir*.

4. Most words of the feminine in a incline to the declension in i, after which they in later times regularly form their plural, as *giöf*, gift, plur. *giafar*, later on *giafir*. These words also form their dative singular sometimes in *-u*, as *giöfu* for *giöf*; the latter seems to be the more recent form.

5. The case-sign *-i* of the dative sing. neuter, like that of the masculine, does not cause Umlaut.

---

[1] The case-sign *-r* of the nominative singular is assimilated to the preceding consonant, hence, *steinn*, *þraell*, for *stein-r*, &c.; in *hals*, *iarl*, *himin*, &c., it is dropped altogether.

Themes in ja (ya).

Gothic.

Themes: — *harja-*, army (Germ. heer); *hairdja-*, herdsman (Germ. hirte); *sunjo-*, truth; *þiujó*, servant; *kunja-*, genus, kin; *andbahtja*, ministerium (Germ. amt).

	Masculine.		Feminine.		Neuter.	
Sing.						
Nom.	*harjis* (army)	(*hairdeis* (herdsman)	*sunja* (truth)	*þivi*	*kuni*	*andbahti*
Gen.	*harjis*	*hairdeis*	*sunjos*	*þiujôs*	*kunjis*	*andbahteis*
Dat.	*harja*	*hairdja*	*sunjai*	*þiujai*	*kunja*	*andbahtja*
Accus.	*hari*	*hairdi*	*sunja*	*þiuja*	*kuni*	*andbahti*
Voc.	*hari*	*hairdi*	*sunja*	*þivi*	*kuni*	*andbahti*
Plur.						
Nom.	*harjos* &c.	*hairdjos* &c.	*sunjôs* &c.	*þiujos* &c.	*kunja* &c.	*andbahtja* &c.

Old High German.

	Masculine.		Feminine.	
	Sing.	Plur.	Sing.	Plur.
Nom.	*hirti* (herdsman)	*hirt-â*	*sippja, sippa* (peace)	*sippjô, sippô(-â)*
Gen.	*hirte-s*	*hirt-ô*	*sippjô, sippô*	*sippjô-n-ô, sippônô*
Dat.	*hirta*	*hirtu-m*	*sippjô, sippô(-u)*	*sippjô-m, sippôm*
Accus.	*hirti*	*hirtâ*	*sippja, sippa*	*sippjô, sippô*
Inrtr.	*hirt-u*	..	..	..

	Neuter.	
	Sing.	Plur.
Nom.	*kunni*	*kunni*
Gen.	*kunnje-s, kunnes*	*kunnj-o, kunnô*
Dat.	*kunnje, kunne*	*kunnju-m, kunnum*
Accus.	*kunni*	*kunni*
Instr.	*kunnju, kunnu*	..

Old Saxon.

	Masculine		Neuter	
	Sing.	Plur.	Sing.	Plur.
Nom.	*hirdi*	*hirdjôs*	*cunni* (kin)	*cunni*
Gen.	*hirdjes*, *-eas*	*hirdjo*, *-eô*	*cunnjes*, *-eas*	*cunnjô*, *-eô*
Dat.	*hirdje*, *-ea*	*hirdjun*	*cunnje*, *-ea*	*cunnjun*
Accus.	*hirdi*	*hirdjôs*	*cunni*	*cunni*
Instr.	*hirdju*	..	*cunnju*	..

Anglo-Saxon.

	Masculine		Neuter	
	Sing.	Plur.	Sing.	Plur.
Nom.	*hirde*	*hirdâs*	*rîce* (regnum)	*rîcu*
Gen.	*hirdes*	*hirdâ*	*rîces*	*ricâ*
Dat.	*hirde*	*hirdum*	*rîce*	*rîcum*
Accus.	*hirde*	*hirdâs*	*rîce*	*rîcu*
Instr.	.	..	*rîcê*	..

Old Norse.

Themes: — *herja-*, army; *hirðja-*, herdsman; *eggja-* edge; *festja-*, fetter, chain; *kynja-*, kin; *rikja-*, regnum.

	Masculine				Feminine			
	Sing.	Plur.	Sing.	Plur.	Sing.	Plur.	Sing.	Plur.
Nom.	*her-r*	*herja-r*	*hirði r*	*hirða-r*	*egg*	*eggja-r*	*festi*	*festa-r*
Gen.	*her-s*	*herj-a*	*hirði-s*	*hirð-a*	*eggja-r*	*eggj-a*	*festa-r*	*fest-a*
Dat.	*her(-i)*	*herju-m*	*hirði*	*hirðu-m*	*egg(-ju)*	*eggju-m*	*festi*	*festu-m*
Accus.	*her*	*herja*	*hirði*	*hirða*	*egg*	*eggja-r*	*festi*	*festa-r*

	Neuter			
	Sing.	Plur.	Sing.	Plur.
Nom.	*kyn*	*kyn*	*riki*	*riki*
Gen.	*kyn-s*	*kynj-a*	*riki-s*	*rikj-a(-a)*
Dat.	*kyni*	*kynju-m*	*riki*	*rikju-m(-um)*
Accus.	*kyn*	*kyn*	*riki*	*riki*

DECLENSIONS.

Notes to the Declension in ja.

Gothic.

1. The following words belong to the declension in ja.

MASC. *harjis*, army (Germ. heer); *niþjis*, relative, cognatus; *andastaþjis*, adversary; *andeis*, end; *hairdeis*, herdsman (Germ. hirte); *háiteis*, wheat; *leikeis*, physician; *sipóneis*, disciple; *bokareis*, scribe; *láisareis*, teacher, doctor.

FEM. *þivi*, ancilla; *mavi*, virgin; *þusundi*, thousand; *lauhmóni*, lightning; *aquizi*, ax, hatchet; *vundusni*, wound (Germ. wunde); *frijondi*, friend, amica.

NEUT. *arbi*, inheritance (Germ. das erbe); *badi*, bed; *basi*, berry (Germ. beere); *havi*, hay (Germ. heu); *háili*, health (Germ. heil); *kuni*, kin; *nati*, net; *andanahti*, evening, = 'before night;' *reiki*, kingdom (Germ. reich); *gavaurki*, gain; *andavaurþi*, answer; *hauhisti*, height.

2. The *j* which is introduced before the thematic vowel belongs of course to the theme, not to the case-sign. It has the effect in nouns masculine to preserve the thematic vowel in the nom. sing., though in a weakened form as *i*, hence nom. sing. *harji-s* of the theme *harja*. Where a syllable with a vowel which is long by nature or position, or several syllables, precede, the combination *ji* appears as *ei* in the nom. as well as gen. sing., hence *hairdeis* for *hairdjis*.

3. Feminine nouns in *ja* which contain a long syllable, or more than one syllable, before the thematic vowel, drop the *a* in the nom. and voc. sing. and vocalize the *j* into *i*, which again causes the preceding *u* to take the consonantal form in *v*, hence the nom. sing. of the theme *þiujó* (ancilla) is *þivi*. The themes with a short syllable are declined regularly after the declension in **a**.

4. The neuter nouns which regularly drop the thematic vowel in the nom. and accus. sing. must of necessity vocalize the *j* into *i*; but in the gen. sing. they follow the rule laid down for nouns masc., that is, after short syllables they have *jis*, after long syllables *eis*.

Old High German.

1. The following words belong to the declension in ja.

MASC. *heri*, army (Germ. heer); *enti*, end (Germ. ende); *hirti*, herdsman (Germ. hirte); *hrucki*, back (Germ. rücken); *hueizi*, wheat (Germ. waizen); *láhhi*, physician; *risi*, giant (Germ. riese); *wini*, friend; and all words with the ending *-are, -ere* (*-ari*), Goth. *-areis.*

FEM. *alti*, old age (Germ. alter); *chundi* (Germ. kunde, notitia); *heri*, glory; *heili* (Germ. heil, salus); *huldí*, favour (Germ. huld); *mihhili*, magnitude (Germ. große); *náhi*, proximity (Germ. nahe); *tiufí*, depth (Germ. tiefe); *sconi*, beauty (Germ. schoue); *toufí*, baptism (Germ. taufe).

NEUT. *arpi*, inheritance (Germ. erbe); *ampahti*, office (Germ. amt); *chruci*, cross; *chunni*, kin; *hirni*, brain (Germ. hirn); *antlutti*, face (Germ. antlitz); *chwini*, corn; *enti*, end; *heri*, army (Germ. heer); *nezzi*, net (Germ. netz); *oli*, oil; *peri*, berry; *petti*, bed (Germ. bett); *ríhhi*, empire (Germ. reich); *antwurti*, answer; *steinili*, calculus; *vingiri*, annulus; *heiminki*, home (Germ. heimat, patria); *arunti*, messenger; *einóti*, solitude (Germ. einode); *kiwáti*, dress, vestitus.

2. The masculine and neuter in *ja* vocalize the *j* in the nom. and accus. sing. into *i*, if it occurs at the end of a word, as *hirti* from the theme *hirtja*, *chunni* theme *chunnja*; in the other cases the *j* is usually dropped. More frequently the thematic *j* is preserved in the feminine, though weakened into *e*.

Old Saxon.

1. The following words belong to the declension in **ja**.

MASC. *hirdi*, custos (Germ. hirte); *meti*, meat; *wini*, friend; *slegi*, homicidia; *maki*, sword; words ending in *ári*, *eri*.

FEM. *bendi*, bandage (Germ. binde); *eldi*, age; *heri*[1], army; *huldi*, favour; *meri*, sea (Germ. meer); *menniski*, humanitas.

NEUT. *arbedi*, labour (Germ. arbeit); *arundi*, messenger; *bilidi*, picture (Germ bild); *endi*, end; *kunni*, kin; *curni*, corn; *urlagi*, war; *riki*, empire (Germ. reich); *giwádi*, dress; *giwirki*, work; *bed*, bed; *inwid* (dolus) for *beddi, inwiddi*, gen. *beddjer, inwiddjes.*

2. The *j* of the themes in *ja* is preserved, except in the nom. and accus. sing. masc. and neut., and in the nom. and accus. plur. neut, because these cases have no case-signs, and consequently the *j* is vocalized into *i*, as *hirdi, cunni*. But if in the case-terminations the original *a* is preserved, then the *j* is commonly weakened into *e*, as accus. sing. *hirdea* for *hirdja* (compare the dative *hirdje*): the same weakening process also occurs before the case-vowel *ó*.

[1] More frequently of the masculine and neuter gender.

Anglo-Saxon.

1. The following words may be considered belonging to the declension in **ja**.

MASC. *bere*, hordeum; *bryne*, conflagration; *ele*, oil; *ende*, end; *here*, army (Germ. heer); *hyge*, friend; *hwæte*, wheat; *læce*, physician; *lige*, flame; *mece*, sword; *mere*, lake; *mete*, meat; *sige*, victory; words ending in *-ere*, as *fiscere*, fisher; *huntere*, hunter.

FEM. *brædo*, breadth; *hælo*, health; *hyldo*, favour; *menigo*, multitude; *yldo*, old age.

NEUT. *inne*, house, cf. inn; *yrfe*, inheritance; *rice*, empire (Germ. reich); *gemære*, boundary; *getimbre*, building; *gelæte*, exitus (Germ. geleite).

2. Masculine nouns in *ja* weaken the *j* into *e*, in the nom. and accus. sing., and frequently drop it in all other cases. Sometimes the *j* is preserved before the case-terminations in the weakened form *e*. The neuter nouns which have retained the *j* in the nom. and accus. sing. in the weakened form *e* take in the nom. and accus. plur. the termination *u*. Such however are few, because most of them have entirely lost the characteristic semi-vowel of the thematic *ja*.

Old Frisian.

Of the the themes in **ja** no trace is left except the termination *-e* in the nom. sing. of masc. and neuter nouns, e. g. *hodere* (hat-bearer), gen *hoderes*; *hiskthe* (family), neut., gen. *hiskthes*. Words derived from Latin frequently drop this *-e*, the weakened form of *j*; e. g. *abbit* for *abbete*, abbot; *alter* for *altáre*, altar; *prester* for *prestere*, priest. But *i* (for *j* vocalized) in *biti* (bite), gen. *bites*; *hiri* (army), gen. *hires*.

Old Norse.

1. The following words belong to the declension in **ja**.

MASC. *hirdir*, herdsman (Germ. hirte); *einir*, juniper; *endir*, end; *fylkir*, dux; *hellir*, antrum (Germ. hohle); *laekner*, physician; *maekir*, sword; *stillir*, king; *styrir*, emperor; *viðir*, willow (Germ. weide); *oegir*, sea.

FEM. *byrði*, burden (Germ. bürde); *elfi*, river; *festi*, chain; *lygi*, lie; *meri*, water; *myri*, pool; *aefi*, aevum; *elli*, old age; *mildi*, lenity (Germ. milde).

NEUT. *egg*, egg; *kyn*, kin; *nef*, nose; *net*, net; *býli*, dwelling;

engi, meadow; *epli,* apple; *fylik,* province; *klaeði,* dress (Germ. kleid); *merki,* mark, sign.

2. Words with a short syllable preserve the *j* of *ja* then only when it is followed by the thematic vowel or by a case-sign; words with a long syllable, on the contrary, drop the *j* before a terminational vowel, but they preserve it in the vocalized form *i* before the case-sign *r* of the nominative, and *s* of the genitive singular, and in all those cases which have lost the termination altogether, i. e. dat. and accus. sing., nom. sing., and nom. and accus. plur. of the neuter.

Themes in va.

Gothic.

Themes :— *þiva-,* servant, famulus; *kniva-,* knee; *sáiva-,* sea.

	Singular.		
Nom.	*þiu-s*	*sáiv-s*	*kniu*
Gen.	*þivi-s*	*sáivi-s*	*knivi-s*
Dat.	*þiva*	*sáiva*	*kniva*
Accus.	*þiu*	*sáiv*	*kniu*
Voc.	*þiu*	*sáiv*	*kniu*

Old High German.

Themes :—*snewa-,* snow; *kniwa-,* knee.

	Singular.	
Nom.	*snêo* (snow)	*kniu, knëo*
Gen.	*snêwe-s*	*kniwe-s, knëwe-s*
Dat.	*snêwa*	*kniwe, knëwe*
Accus.	*snêo*	*kniu, knëo*
Instr.	*snêw-u*	*kniw-u, knew-u*

Old Saxon.

Themes :—*snewa-,* snow; *trewa-,* tree.

	Singular.	
Nom.	*snêu, snêo*	*trëu, trëo*
Gen.	*snêwa-s*	*trëwa-s*
Dat.	*snêwa*	*trëwa*
Accus.	*snêo, snêu*	*trëu, trëo*
Instr.	*snêw-u*	*trëw-u*

Old Norse.

Themes:—*hiarva*, sword; *doggva-*, dew; *fiörva-*, life.

Masculine.		Feminine.		Neuter.	
Sing.	Plur.	Sing.	Plur.	Sing.	Plur.
Nom. *hiör*	*hiörva-r*	*dögg*	*döggva-r*	*fiör*	*fiör*
Gen. *hiör-s*	*hiörv-a*	*döggva-r*	*döggv-a*	*fiör-s*	*fiörv-a*
Dat. *hiörvi*	*hiör(v)u-m*	*dögg(vu)*	*döggvu-m*	*fiörvi*	*fiörvu-m*
Accus. *hiör*	*hiörva*	*dögg*	*döggva-r*	*fiör*	*fiör*

Notes to the Declension in va.

Gothic.

Themes in *va*, preceded by a short syllable, vocalize the *v* when it is followed by the case-sign *s* of the nom. sing., and when it occurs at the end of the word; hence of the theme *þiva* (famulus) the nom. sing. is *þius*, the accus. and voc. *þiu;* of the neut. theme *kniva* (knee) the nom. and accus. *kniu*. But when *v* is preceded by a long vowel it remains unaltered, e. g. theme *sáiva*, sea, nom. *sáivs*, accus. *sáiv*.

Old High German.

Themes in *va* (*wa*) are confined to the masculine and neuter. The nom. and accus. sing. always vocalize the *w*, while the oblique cases of the singular and all cases of the plural preserve it; e. g. *sneo*, snow, gen. *snewes; kniu*, knee, gen. *kniwes*.

Old Saxon.

The *v* before the thematic vowel is vocalized into *u* or *o* when it occurs at the end of a word; hence the masc. themes *sewa*, sea; *ewa*, law; *snewa*, snow, have in the nom. and accus. sing. *seu* or *zeo, eu* or *éo, sneu* or *sneo;* the neuter themes *trewa*, tree; *hrewa*, corpse, in the nom. and accus. sing. and plur. *treu, treo; hreu, hreo*. But occasionally the *w* is dropped altogether, e. g. *se*, sea, dat. sing. *see;* or the vocalized *w* causes the thematic vowel or case-sign to be dropped, e. g. *eo*, law, dat. sing. *eo* by the side of *ewa*. The feminine theme *thiwo* (ancilla) drops the thematic vowel altogether and vocalizes the *w*, hence nom. and accus. sing. *thiu*. The nom. *thiwi* which occurs in but one instance may be explained from a theme *thiujo*.

Anglo-Saxon.

The feminine nouns *sæ* (sea), *eá* (river), are indeclinable in the singular; occasionally we find the genitive *sæ-s*, *eá-s* (Goth. *sáivi-s*, *ahvô-s*); nom. plur. *sæ-s*, *eá-s*; dat. plur. *sæ-m*, *eá-m*.

Old Frisian.

The masculine and neuter themes drop the *w* altogether, e.g. *se*, sea, dat. and accus. *se;* *kni*, *kne*, dat. *kní*, *kne*, accus. *kni*, *kniu*.

Old Norse.

In all genders *v* is preserved when followed by a terminational vowel; where it has disappeared the Umlaut which it has caused still remains.

Encroaching forms of the declension in i we have in the masc. *lit-r*, colour; *log-r*, sea, lake; *kiolr*, ship; *siðr*, mos, which in the dat. sing. drop the *i*, and in the accus. plur. adopt *i* for *u*. Forms of the declension in a we find in *hior*, sword. The dat. sing. of the feminine *hönd* is *hendi*. The forms of the neuter *fé* (pecus) are altogether irregular.

Themes in i.

Gothic.

Themes:—*balgi-* (Germ. balg), *anstai-*, favour.

	Masculine.		Feminine.	
	Sing.	Plur.	Sing.	Plur.
Nom.	*balg-s*	*balgei-s*	*anst-s*	*anstei-s*
Gen.	*balgi-s*	*balg-ê*	*anstai-s*	*anst-ê*
Dat.	*balga*	*balgi-m*	*anstai*	*ansti-m*
Accus.	*balg*	*balgi-ns*	*anst*	*ansti-ns*
Voc.	*balg*	*balgei-s*	*anst*(?)	*anstei-s*

DECLENSIONS.

Old High German.

Themes:—*palki-*, pellis; *ansti-*, favour.

	MASCULINE.		FEMININE.	
	Sing.	Plur.	Sing.	Plur.
Nom.	palc	pelki	anst	ensti
Gen.	palke-s	pelkj-ô (-ëo)	ensti, anst	enstj-o (eo)
Dat.	palk-a	pelki-m	ensti, anst	ensti-m
Accus.	palc	pelki	anst	ensti
Instr.	palk-u	..	..	..

Old Saxon.

Themes:—*gasti-*, guest; *ansti-*, favour.

	MASCULINE.		FEMININE.	
	Sing.	Plur.	Sing.	Plur.
Nom	gast	gasti, gestî	anst	ansti, ensti
Gen.	gasta-s, -es	gastj-ô, geste-ô	ansti, ensti	anstj-ô, enste-ô
Dat.	gast-a, -e	gastju-n, gestju-n	ansti, ensti	anstju-n, enstju-n
Accus.	gast	gasti, gesti	anst	ansti, ensti
Instr.	gast-u	..	..	..

Anglo-Saxon.

Themes:— *buri-*, son, barn; *fôti-*, foot; *dædi*, deed; *musi-*, mouse.

	MASCULINE.				FEMININE.			
	Sing.	Plur.	Sing.	Plur.	Sing.	Plur.	Sing.	Plur.
Nom.	byre	byre	fôt	fêt	dæd	dæda	mûs	mŷs
Gen.	†byre-s	byr-â	fôte-s	fôt-â	dæde	dæd-â	mûse	mûs-a
Dat.	†byre	byru-m	fêt	fôtu-m	dæde	œdu-m	mŷs	mûsu-m
Accus.	byre	byre	fôt	fêt	dæd(e)	dæda	mûs	mŷs
Instr.	†byr-ê	..	fôt-ê	..	..	..	..	..

Old Frisian.

Themes:—*liodi-*, song (Germ. lied); *fôti-*, foot; *nedi-*, need.

	MASCULINE.				FEMININE.	
	Sing.	Plur.	Sing.	Plur.	Sing.	Plur.
Nom.	wanting.	liode	fôt	fet	ned	neda
Gen.		liod-a	fote-s	fôt-a	nede	ned-a
Dat.		liode-m -um, -on	fot-(e)	fote-m, -on	nede	nedi-m (-em, -um, -on)
Accus.		liode	fôt	fet	nede	nêda

Old Norse.

Themes:—*bragi-*, carmen; *belgji-*, follis; *ásti-*, amor; *musi-*, mouse.

	MASCULINE.				FEMININE.			
	Sing.	Plur.	Sing.	Plur.	Sing.	Plur.	Sing.	Plur.
Nom.	brag-r	bragi-r	belg-r	belgi-r	âst	âsti-r	mûs	mŷs
Gen.	braga-r	brag-a	belgja-r	belgj-a	âsta-r	âst-a	mûsa-r	mûs-a
Dat.	brag	brögu-m	belg	belgju-m	âst(u)	âstu-m	mûs(u)	mûsu-m
Accus.	brag	bragi	belg	belgi	âst	âsti	mûs	mŷs

Examples and Remarks to Themes in **i**.

Gothic.

1. The following words belong to the declension in **i**.

MASC. *áivs*, aevum; *arms*, arm; *baurs*, genitus; *gadrauhts*, soldier; *faþs*, dux; *gards*, house; *gasts*, stranger, guest (Germ. gast); *láuþs*, homo; *mats*, meat; *saggvs*, song; *stads*, place (cf. stead); *vegs*, wave (Germ. woge).

FEM. *alds*, age; *ansts*, favour; *deds*, deed; *mahts*, might; *quens, queins*, woman, wife; *vaihts*, thing (cf. Engl. wight, Germ. wicht); *vaurts*, root, wort; *gabaurþs*, birth (Germ. geburt); *gamáinþs*, ἐκκλησία, congregation (Germ. gemeinde).

2. Words which in their simple stem end in *s* or *r* reject, like those of the first declension, the case-sign of the nom. sing.; hence of the theme *baúri* the nom. is *baúr*; of *garunsai* (fem.) the nom. is *garuns*. The theme *vaurtsai* preserves its *s* in the singular and drops it in the plural, e. g. gen. sing. *vaurtsais*, nom. plur. **vaúrteis**.

3. The theme *navi* (mortuus) vocalizes the *v* before the case-sign *-s* of the nom. sing. *nau-s*, and in its terminational position in the accus. and voc. sing. *nau*.

4. Feminine nouns derived from verbs, and formed with the derivative suffix *-ein*, substitute in the plural the theme *-eino* for the theme *-einai*: e. g. the theme *laiseinai*, doctrine, from the verb *laisjan*, to teach, has the sing. nom. *laiseins*, gen. *laiseinais*, &c.; plur. nom. *laiseinos*, gen. *laiseino*, dat. *-einóm*, accus. *-einós*. But the dative and accusative occasionally occur also in *-einim*, *-einins*. In a similar manner the theme *haimai*, vicus (cf. home), in the plural adopts forms in **a**, as *haimós, haimo*, &c.

DECLENSIONS.

Old High German.

1. The following words belong to the declension in **i**.

MASC. Sing. *arn*, plur. *erní*, eagle (Germ. aar); *ast, estí*, ramus; *chás, chási*, cheese; *halm, helmi*, reed, stalk (Germ. halm); *heit, heití*, person; *cast, kesti*, guest; *lid, lidi*, limb (Germ. glied); *palc, pelki*, skin; *scilt, scilti*, shield; *sun, suni*, son; *tisk, tiski*, table (Germ. tisch); *vuoʒ, vuoʒí*, foot (Germ. fuß); *zand, zendí*, tooth; *zahar, zahari*, tear (Germ. zahre); *vuhs, vuhsi*, fox; *luft, lufti*, air (Germ. luft); *scaft, sceftí*, shaft, spear; *sunft, sunftí*, pool (Germ. sumpf).

FEM. *ankunst*, anxiety (Germ. angst); *anst*, favour; *arapeit*, labour (Germ. arbeit); *arm*, harvest (Germ. ernte); *chraft*, strength (Germ. kraft, cf. Engl. craft); *chuo, chuoí*, cow; *diu, diwí*, serva; *eih*, oak (Germ. eiche); *hant*, hand; *hut*, skin (Germ. haut); *kans*, goose (Germ. gans); *keiʒ*, goat (Germ. geiß); *kift*, gift; *last*, burden (Germ. last); *lust*, desire (Germ. lust); *makad*, maid; *naht*, night (Germ. nacht); *not*, need; *prust*, breast; *prut*, bride (Germ. braut).

2. Before the termination *ó* of the genitive plural the *j* which stands for the thematic vowel *i* is often weakened into *e*, or dropped altogether, as *pelkj-o*, or *pelke-o*, or *pelk-ó*; *enstj-ó, enste-ó*, or *enst-ó*.

3. The feminine nouns, and partly the masculine too, of the Gothic declension in **u** have in Old High German adopted the declension in **i**, such as *hant, vuoʒ, sun*, &c. A trace of an ancient Old High German declension in **u** is left in the dat. plur. *hantu-m*, and in its weakened form *hanto-n*.

Old Saxon.

1. The following words belong to the declension in **i**.

MASC. *liudi*, homines (Germ. leute); *fot*, foot; *segg*, vir; *scild*, shield; *gast*, guest; plur. *trahní*, gender? lacrymæ (Germ. thräne).

FEM. *bank, benkí*, bench; *buok*, book; *burg*, arx (Germ. burg, cf. borough); *brud*, bride, wife; *dad*, deed; *fard*, journey (Germ. fartb); *hand*, hand; *anst*, favour; *idis*, woman; *maht*, might; *nod*, need; *juguð*, youth; *craft*, power; *list*, knowledge; *magad*, maid; *werold*, world; *wiht*, thing; *wurt*, root, wort.

2. In the dative plural the termination *-jan* of the first declension (**a**) has found its way into the second declension (**i**) as well,

and expelled the legitimate termination -*in*, the only trace of which is left in the dat. plur. *trahnin*, by the side of *trahnjun*, *trahnun*, thence *trahni*, tear (Germ. thrane).

3. Some feminine nouns have a genitive in -*es* by the side of -*i*, as theme *weroldi*-, world, nom. *werold*, gen. *weroldes* and *weroldi*; theme *custi*-, choice, nom. *cust*, gen. *custes* and *custi*. This -*es* may be considered the weakened form of the ancient -*i-s*, which in Gothic we find lengthened into -*áis*, as *anstáis*, gen. of *ansts*.

4. The feminine nouns of the declension in **u** have adopted the declension in **i**: a trace of the former we find, as in Old High German, in the dat. plur *handun*, *handon*, manibus, by the side of nom. accus. *handi*, *hendí*.

Anglo-Saxon.

1. The following words belong to the declension in **i**.

MASC. In the singular the word *byre* (son) only; in the plural *leóde*, homines; the national appellatives *Dene*, Danes; *Engle*, Angles; and compounds of -*vare*, incolæ, as *burh-vare*, cives; *cant-vare*, cantium habitantes, inhabitants of Kent: but even these may have the plur. in -*as* (**a**) by the side of -*e* (**i**), as *byrás* and *byre*, *varás* and *vare*;—*fót*, *fét*, foot, feet; *toð*, *teð*, tooth, teeth; *turf*, *tyrf*, turf.

FEM. *ár*, honour (Germ. ehre); *ben*, wound; *ben*, prayer; *bend*, band; *blis*, joy; *breost*, breast; *brýd*, bride; *dǽd*, deed; *dun*, hill (cf. downs); *ecg*, edge; *heal*, hall; *hen*, hen; *lár*, doctrine (Germ. lehre); *mag*, maid; *mearc*, mark; *mèd*, meed; *miht*, might; *niht*, night; *ród*, cross, rood; *sprǽc*, speech (Germ. sprache); *strǽt*, street; *syn*, sin; *tíd*, time (cf. tide); *womb*, womb; *woruld*, world; *wund*, wound; *wyn*, joy; *ýð*, wave; *byrðen*, burden, burthen; *ellen*, strength; *gyden*, goddess; *stëfen*, voice; *ceaster*, arx, castra; *ides*, woman; *meoloc*, milk; *duguð*, virtue (Germ. tugend); *yrmð*, poverty (Germ. armuth);—*boc*, *bec*, book; *broc*, *brec*, bracca; *gos*, *ges*, goose, geese; *cu*, *cý*, cow, kine; *lús*, *lýs*, louse, lice; *mús*, *mýs*, mouse, mice; *burh*, *byrig*, arx, borough.

2. As we see under No. 1, the masculine nouns in **i** very frequently pass into the declension in **a**.

3. *Fot*, *tóð*, &c., have in Anglo-Saxon, as in other dialects, migrated from the third declension (**u**) into the second (**i**).

DECLENSIONS.

4. On the whole the declension in **i** is in Anglo-Saxon much mutilated, and appears in mere fragments, either as the termination *e*, the weakened form of the ancient thematic *i*, or in the Umlaut which was caused by an ancient terminational *i*, and which continued to exist after the final vowel had been dropped. But in both instances the forms in **a** have much encroached upon those in **i**, especially in the plural.

Old Frisian.

1. In Old Frisian, as in Anglo-Saxon, we find but few remnants of the declension in **i**. These remnants may either be the thematic *i* weakened into *e*, or the Umlaut, which continued to exist after its cause, the final *i*, had been removed. To the former class belong but two substantives, *liode* (homines), and *rumere* (romipeta); to the second, *fot* (foot) and *toth* (tooth), which, as in the other dialects, originally belonged to the third declension (**u**), Goth. *fotu-s, tunþu-s*. The forms of the first declension (**a**) have here again much encroached upon those of the second (**i**); but still Old Frisian is so far superior to Anglo-Saxon, as in the dative plural of the feminine we find occasionally the original vowel *i* instead of the ususper *a* or its weakened form *u*.

2. The -*e* of the oblique cases is gradually admitted into the nominative too, so that there exists no longer a distinction between the nom. sing. *dede* (for *dêd*) and the dat. sing. *dede*.

3. The feminine nouns *bok* (book), *kû* (cow), have not, as in Anglo-Saxon, the Umlaut.

Old Norse.

1. The following words belong to the declension in **i**.

Masc. (1) Words interpolating *j* in the genitive singular, and genitive and dative plural:—*beckr*, scamnum; *belgr*, follis; *bylr*, turbo; *drengr*, vir; *dryckr*, drink; *her*, army; *hryggr*, back (Germ. rücken); *hyr*, fire; *laekr*, rivus; *leggr*, crus; *reykr*, reek, smoke; *seggr*, vir; *seckr*, sack; *verkr*, grief; *boer*, town; *beðr*, bed. (2) Words which do not interpolate the *j*:—*bolr*, trunk; *bragr*, poem, song; *bur*, son; *dalr*, dale; *gestr*, guest; *gramr*, hero; *hamr*, skin; *hagr*, condition; *hlutr*, thing; *hugr*, mind; *hvalr*, whale; *lyðr*, nation; *mar*, horse; *matr*, meat; *réfr*, fox; *rettr*, right; *salr*, hall (Germ. saal); *staðr*, place, stead; *stafr*, staff; *vegr*, way; *vinr*, friend.

FEM. *ást,* favour, love; *braut,* way; *dáð,* deed, ill-deed; *dros,* maid; *ferð,* journey (Germ. farth); *grund,* ground; *hiálp,* help; *ið,* business; *krás,* meat; *leið,* way; *nauð,* need; *sol,* sun; *tið,* time (cf. tide); *sul,* pillar (Germ. saule); *und,* wound; *unn,* wave; *váð,* dress; *auðn,* desertum; *eign,* property; *höfn,* haven; *dygð,* virtue (Germ. tugend); *aett,* genus; *ambott,* ancilla; *vaett,* weight; *gás,* goose; *mus,* mouse; *lus,* louse; *brun,* brow.

2. We have just enumerated certain masculine nouns which interpolate the semi-vowel *j* throughout all cases. Though this letter does not come to appearance except in the genitive singular, and the genitive and dative plural, its presence at a more ancient stage of the language is certified by the Umlaut which runs throughout all cases in the mentioned words. On the other hand it is curious to observe that the masculine nouns enumerated under No. (2), and which do not interpolate the semi-vowel *j*, never have an Umlaut caused by the final *i*, not even in the nominative and accusative plural, where *i* is the thematic vowel. In the same manner most feminine nouns reject the Umlaut, except *gás, mus, lús, brun,* which have the plural *ges, mýs, lýs, brýn,* and the plur. neut. *dyr,* valvae, gen. *dura,* &c.— an Umlaut which was effected by the plural terminations nom. *ir,* accus. *i,* and which continued to exist after these terminations had been dropped.

3. There are a few words which have the Umlaut though they reject the interpolation of *j,* as *gestr,* guest; *brestr,* defect; *lýðr,* nation, &c., where the Umlaut is of course considered inorganic.

4. The nominatives *bur, mar, byr,* &c., stand for *burr, marr,* &c.

5. The feminine nouns *bruðr,* bride; *hildr,* war; and the proper nouns *Boðvildr, Borgvildr,* retain the case-sign *-r* of the nominative singular, and have commonly the termination *i* in the dative and accusative singular.

THEMES IN U

Gothic.

Themes: — *sunu-*, son; *handau-*, hand; *faíhu-*, cattle (Germ. vieh; comp. Engl. fee).

	MASCULINE.		FEMININE.		NEUTER.	
	Sing.	Plur.	Sing.	Plur.	Sing.	Plur.
Nom.	sunu-s	sunju-s	handu-s	handju-s	faíhu	wanting.
Gen.	sunau-s	suniv-ê	handau-s	handiv-ê	faíhau-s	
Dat.	sunau	sunu-m	handau	handu-m	faíhau	
Accus.	sunu	sunu-ns	handu	handu-ns	faíhu	
Voc.	sunau	sunju-s	handau	handju-s	faíhau	

Old High German.

Themes:—*sunu*, son; *fihu-*, cattle.

	MASCULINE.		NEUTER.	
	Sing.	Plur.	Sing.	Plur.
Nom.	sunu (-o)	suni	fihu (-o)	fihju (-u, -o)
Gen.	sune-s	sunj-ô	fihe-s	fihj-ô (-ô)
Dat.	sunju (-u)	suni-m (-um)	†fihju	†fihi-m
Accus.	sunu (-o)	suni (-u)	fihu (-o)	fihju (-u, -o)
Instr.	sunj-u (-u)	..	†fihj-u	..

Old Saxon.

Themes:—*sunu-*, son; *fëhu-*. pecus.

	MASCULINE.		NEUTER.	
	Sing.	Plur.	Sing.	Plur.
Nom.	sunu (-o)	sunî, sunjôs	fëhu (-o)	wanting.
Gen.	sunu (-o), sunje-s	†sunj-ô, -eô	fëha-s (-es)	
Dat.	sunu (-o), sunje	sunju-n (-un)	fëha, -e	
Accus.	sunu (-o)	sunî, sunjôs	fëhu (-o)	
Instr.	†sunj-u	..	fëhu (-o)	

Anglo-Saxon.

Theme:—*sunu-*, son.

	MASCULINE.	
	Sing.	Plur.
Nom.	*sunu*	*suna*
Gen.	*sun-a*	*sun-a*
Dat.	*sun-a*	*sunu-m*
Accus.	*sunu*	*suna*
Instr.	†*sun-ê?*	..

Old Frisian.

Themes:—*sunu-*, son; *fihu-*, pecus.

	MASCULINE.		NEUTER.	
	Sing.	Plur.	Sing.	Plur.
Nom.	*sunu* (-o)	*suna-r* (-a)	*fia*	wanting.
Gen.	*suna*	*sun-a*	*fia-s*	
Dat.	*sun-a*	*sunu-m*	*fia*	
Accus.	*sunu*	*suna-r* (-a)	*fia*	

Old Norse.

Themes:—*sonu-*, son; *magu-*, son; *tannu-*, tooth; *fihu-*, pecus.

	MASCULINE.				FEMININE.		NEUTER.	
	Sing.	Plur.	Sing.	Plur.	Sing.	Plur.	Sing.	Plur.
Nom.	*son-r*	*syni-r*	*mög-r*	*megi-r*	*tönn*	*tenn-r*	*fê*	wanting.
Gen.	*sona-r*	*son-a*	*maga-r*	*mag-a*	*tanna-r*	*tann-a*	*fiâ-r*	
Dat.	*syni*	*sonu-m*	*meg-i*	*mögu-m*	*tönn-u*	*tönnu-m*	*fê*	
Accus.	*son*	*sonu*	*mög*	*mögu*	*tönn*	*tenn-r*	*fê*	

Notes to the Declension in u.

Gothic.

1. The following words belong to the declension in u.
MASC. *aírus*, messenger; *daúpus*, death; *flodus*, river (Germ. fluß, cf. flood); *fotus*, foot; *hairus*, sword; *lipus*, limb (Germ. glied); *lustus*, lust; *magus*, boy; *sakkus*, sac; *skadus*, shade; *stubjus*, dust (Germ. staub); *sunus*, son; *tigus*, decas; *tunþus*,

tooth; *vintrus,* winter; *vulpus,* glory; *þaurnus,* thorn; *asilus,* ass; *diabaulus,* diabolus; *praúfetus,* propheta; *apaustaulus,* apostolus.

FEM. *handus,* hand; *asilus,* she-ass; *vaddjus,* vale; *kinnus,* maxilla; *vritus,* herd, flock.

NEUT. *faíhu,* pecunia (cf. Germ. vieh and Engl. fee).

2. This declension has more fully than any other preserved the ancient case-signs, as well as the thematic vowel which precedes them, and which in several cases is strengthened by the gradation (guna) of *u* into *áu.*

3. It occurs in later documents that the ancient use of the gradation is abandoned and the simple thematic vowel adopted, as gen. sing. *sunus,* dat. and voc. *sunu,* for the organic forms *sunáus* and *sunáu.*

4. A few substantives have the derivative *j* before the thematic vowel, but the case-signs remain unaltered; hence *stubjus,* gen. *stubjáus ; vaddjus,* gen. *vaddjáus.*

Old High German.

1. The following words belong to the declension in **u**.

MASC. *haru,* linum; *huku,* mind; *siku,* victory (Germ. sieg); *situ,* mos (Germ. sitte); *sunu,* son; *vridu,* peace (Germ. friede); perhaps also *maku,* boy; *eru,* messenger; *heru,* sword; *apostolu,* apostle; *mágu,* magus, sapiens.

NEUT. *vihu,* pecus (Germ. vieh); *witu,* wood.

2. The declension in **u** is, in Old High German, as already observed, nearly extinct, few words only belonging to it, and most of these forming the plural almost regularly after the declension in **i**. We find a few remnants of the declension in **u** in the dative and accusative plural.

3. In later documents *sunu* appears in the nominative singular as *sun,* and follows the declension in **a**; so does likewise *vuoȝ,* foot, Goth. *fotus* (**u**).

4. The number of neuter nouns is limited to two, and these do not occur in all the different cases.

Old Saxon.

1. The following words belong to the declension in **u**.

MASC. *friðu,* peace (Germ. friede); *heru,* sword; *lagu,* water; *magu,* boy; *sidu,* mos (Germ. sitte); *sunu,* son; *wísu,* princeps; *ehu,* horse; *eru,* messenger.

NEUT. *fihu*, pecus; *widu*, wood.

2. The declension has adopted not only forms in **i** (chiefly in the plural), but also in **a**, especially in the neuter singular.

Anglo-Saxon.

The few nouns masculine which in the nom. sing. have preserved the thematic *u* (sometimes weakened to *o*) hardly occur in any other cases than the nom. and accus. sing., *sunu*, son, only being an exception (see the Paradigm). The dat. sing. in *a* is found with several other masc. nouns, namely, *winter*, winter; *sumer*, summer; *feld*, field; *ford*, ford, as well as with the fem. nouns *hand*, hand, and *duru*, door. The masc. *wudu*, wood, has the gen. and dat. sing. *wudu*, but also the gen. sing. *wudes*, nom. plur. *wudás*, following the declension in **a**.

Old Frisian.

We find a few remnants of this declension in the masc. *sunu*, son, and *fretho*, peace, and the neut. *fia*, pecus. Perhaps the dative *honda* of the feminine *hond*, hand, may also be mentioned as a remnant of this declension.

Old Norse.

1. The following nouns belong to the declension in **u**.

MASC. *örn*, eagle (Germ. aar); *biorn*, bear; *borkr*, bark; *bogr*, armus (Germ. bug); *féldr*, hide (Germ. fell); *fiörðr*, sinus, bay, gulf; *friðr*, peace (Germ. friede); *háttr*, mos; *hiörtr*, stag (Germ. hirsch, cf. hart); *kiolr*, ship (cf. keel); *liðr*, limb (Germ. glied); *limr*, limb; *logr*, water; *máttr*, might (Germ. macht); *siðr*, mos (Germ. sitte); *skiöldr*, shield; *sonr*, son; *viðr*, wood; *vollr*, vale; *volr*, stick; *vondr*, wand; *vorðr*, warden; *þráðr*, thread.

FEM. *ond*, mind, soul; *bok*, book; *eik*, oak (Germ. eiche); *geit*, goat (Germ. geiß); *hond*, hand; *hind*, cerva; *kinn*, maxilla; *miolk*, milk; *not*, sagina; *nyt*, nut; *rönd*, margin (Germ. rand); *rot*, root; *steik*, caro frixa, steak (?); *strönd*, shore (Germ. strand); *tong*, tongs (Germ. zange); *tonn*, tooth (Germ. zahn).

NEUT. *fë*, fihu, pecus.

2. Concerning the Umlaut, which is particularly developed in this declension, we have already given the necessary explanations.

3. As to the influence of a final *i* in neutralizing the preceding Brechung *ia*, see p. 36.

DECLENSIONS.

4. The integrity of this declension is in Old Norse too affected by encroaching forms of other declensions, as in the dative singular and nominative plural of the masculine, which follow the declension in i.

5. The nom. sing. *mogr*, of the theme *magu-*, must have arisen from an earlier *magur*, Goth. *magus*; the accus. plur. *mogu* would correspond to a primitive *mogu-ns*, the case-sign being dropped, and the dat. plur. *mogu-m* may be taken as the organic form.

6. The dative in *u* of the feminine may be considered the primitive case-sign of the declension in u, or a weakened form of the case-sign *a* of the declension in a, and from the latter point of view it would be inorganic.

7. The nominative and accusative plural of the feminine have adopted the vowel *i* instead of the thematic *u*, and thus follow the declension in i. Though the adopted vowel was dropped again in the course of time, the Umlaut which it had caused remained, and thus bears witness to its former existence.

CONSONANTAL THEMES (WEAK DECLENSION).

THEMES IN n.

Gothic.

Themes:—*hanan-*, cock (Germ. hahn); *tuggôn-*, tongue; *managein-*, multitude, many; *haírtan-*, heart.

	Masculine.		Feminine.			
	Sing.	Plur.	Sing.	Plur.	Sing.	Plur.
Nom.	*hana*	*hanan-s*	*tuggô*	*tuggon-s*	*managei*	*managein-s*
Gen.	*hanin-s*	*hanan-ê*	*tuggôn-s*	*tuggôn-ô*	*managein-s*	*managein-ô*
Dat.	*hanin*	*hana-m*	*tuggôn*	*tuggô-m*	*managein*	*managei-m*
Accus.	*hanan*	*hanan-s*	*tuggôn*	*tuggôn-s*	*managein*	*managein-s*
Voc.	*hana*	*hanan-s*	*tuggô*	*tuggôn-s*	*managei*	*managein-s*

	Neuter.	
	Sing.	Plur.
Nom.	*haírtô*	*haírtôn-a*
Gen.	*haírtin-s*	*haírtan-ê*
Dat.	*haírtin*	*haírta-m*
Accus.	*haírtô*	*haírtôn-a*
Voc.	*haírtô*	*haírtôn-a*

Old High German.

Themes:—*hanan-*, cock; *zungan-*, tongue (Germ. zunge); *hèrza-*, heart (Germ. herz); *managín-*, multitude.

	Masculine.		Feminine.		Neuter.			
	Sing.	Plur.	Sing.	Plur.	Sing.	Plur.	Sing.	Plur.
Nom.	*hano*	*hanun*	*zunga*	*zungûn*	*managîn*	*managîn*	*hërza*	*hërzûn*
Gen.	*hanin*	*hanôn-ô*	*zungûn*	*zungôn-ô*	*managîn*	*managîn-ô*	*hërzin*	*hërzôn-ô*
Dat.	*hanin*	*hanô-m*	*zungûn*	*zungô-m*	*managîn*	*managîm*	*hërzin*	*hërzô-m*
Accus.	*hanun*	*hanun*	*zungûn*	*zungûn*	*managîn*	*managîn*	*hërza*	*hërzûn*

Old Saxon.

Themes:—*hanan-*, cock; *tungan-*, tongue; *hertan-*, heart.

	Masculine.		Feminine.		Neuter.	
	Sing.	Plur.	Sing.	Plur.	Sing.	Plur.
Nom.	*hano*	*hanun*	*tunga*	*tungun*	*hërta*	*hërtun*
Gen.	*hanun*	*hanôn-ô*	*tungun*	*tungôn-ô*	*hërtun*	*hërtôn-ô*
Dat.	*hanun*	*hanu-n*	*tungun*	*tungu-n*	*hërtun*	*hërtu-n*
Accus.	*hanun*	*hanun*	*tungun*	*tungun*	*hërta*	*hërtun*

Anglo-Saxon.

Themes:—*hanan-*, cock; *tungan-*, tongue; *eágan-*, eye.

	Masculine.		Feminine.		Neuter.	
	Sing.	Plur.	Sing.	Plur.	Sing.	Plur.
Nom.	*hana*	*hanan*	*tunge*	*tungan*	*eáge*	*eágan*
Gen.	*hanan*	*hanen-â*	*tungan*	*tungen-â*	*eágan*	*eágen-a*
Dat.	*hanan*	*hanu-m*	*tungan*	*tungu-m*	*eágan*	*eágu-m*
Accus.	*hanan*	*hanan*	*tungan*	*tungan*	*eáge*	*eágan*

Old Frisian.

Themes:—*honan-*, cock; *tungan-*, tongue; *ágan-*, eye; *áran-*, ear.

	Masculine.		Feminine.		Neuter.			
	Sing.	Plur.	Sing.	Plur.	Sing.	Plur.	Sing.	Plur.
Nom.	*hona*	*hona*	*tunge*	*tunga*	*âge*	*âgon*	*âre*	*âra*
Gen.	*hona*	*honan-a (-ona)*	*tunga*	*tungan-a*	*âga*	†*âgen-a*	*âra*	*âren-a*
Dat.	*hona*	*honu-m*	*tunga*	*tungu-m*	*âga*	*âgen-um, âgu-m*	*âra*	*âru-m*
Accus.	*hona*	*hona*	*tunga*	*tunga*	*âge*	*âgon, âgene*	*âre*	*âra*

Old Norse.

Themes:—*guman-*, man, homo; *hanan-*, cock; *tungan-*, tongue; *harpan-*, harp; *hiartan-*, heart.

	Masculine.				Feminine.			
	Sing.	Plur.	Sing.	Plur.	Sing.	Plur.	Sing.	Plur.
Nom.	gumi	gumna-r	hani	hana-r	tunga	tungu-r	harpa	hörpu-r
Gen.	guma	gumn-a	hana	han-a	tungu	tungn-a	hörpu	harpn-a
Dat.	guma	gumnu-m	hana	hönu-m	tungu	tungu-m	hörpu	hörpu-m
Accus.	guma	gumna	hana	hana	tungu	tungu-r	hörpu	hörpu-r

	Neuter.	
	Sing.	Plur.
Nom.	hiarta	hiörtu
Gen.	hiarta	hiartn-a
Dat.	hiarta	hiörtu-m
Accus.	hiarta	hiörtu

REMARKS ON THE WEAK DECLENSIONS.

Gothic.

1. The weak declension has added to the thematic vowels *a, i, ja*, the suffix *-n*, which consonant is the characteristic termination of the themes of this declension.

2. The thematic *-n* is dropped in the nom. and voc., and in the neut. accus. of the singular, and in the dative plural, where the case-sign *-m* has expelled its fellow liquid. Masculine and neuter nouns in the gen. and dat. sing. have weakened the vowel *a* into *i*, and the latter lengthen it in the nom. and accus. sing. and plur. into *ó* (= *a + a*). The feminine nouns which, as we have already mentioned, show a predilection for full-sounding forms, have the second gradation before the thematic *n*, so that *a* appears as *o, i* as *ei*[1]. In the same manner as the masculine they drop the *n* in the nom. and voc. singular.

3. The masculine themes *aban* (vir), *auhsan* (ox), and the neuter *naman* (name), *vatan* (water), suffer syncope in several cases, as gen. plur. *abne, auhsne*, dat. plur. *abnam;* nom. accus. plur. *namna, vatna*, gen. *namne, vatne*, dat. *namnam, vatnam*.

[1] See p. 24.

Old High German.

1. The *a* preceding the thematic *-n* is variously modified, or weakened, into *i, o, u*. The feminine shows here, as in Gothic, lengthened forms, *an* appearing as *un*, *in* as *ín*. With respect to the latter termination they follow a different course in different words, the *-n* being admitted in the nom. sing. and then preserved in all other cases, or rejected in the nom. sing. and then rejected in all other cases, so that the word appears without any inflexional forms; e. g. *guatí*, which remains unaltered throughout. The plural of the feminines in *in* passes sometimes into the strong declension in **a**, so that of *managín* we have the weak form of the nom. plur. in *managín*, and the strong form in *managíná*.

2. Some feminines in *-an* adopt forms of strong declension of the feminines in **a**, both declensions being indeed closely related.

3. The terminational *i* of the gen. and dat. sing. masc. and neut. does not cause Umlaut. The forms *nemin* and *scedin* for *namin* (nominis) and *scadin* (damno) are exceptions.

Old Saxon.

1. The pure vowel of the themes in *-an* is rarely met, its representative being *-un*, which often is weakened into *on* and *en*.

2. Feminine nouns of the strong declension in **a** frequently adopt forms of the weak declension, as for instance *erða* (earth), *stemna* (voice), &c.

3. Feminine nouns which originally ended in *-ín* have dropped the thematic vowel, and are consequently without any inflexional forms, unless they adopt, as they sometimes do in the plural, forms of the strong declension in **i**.

Anglo-Saxon.

1. Two masculine nouns originally terminating in the spirants *j* and *h* drop the terminational vowel, but adopt the case-sign *-n* of the weak declension: these are *freá* (lord) for *freá'-a*, Goth. *frauj-a* and *tveo* (doubt) for *tveo'-a*, O. S. *tveh-o*, which have in the gen. *freán, tveon*. Analogous are the forms of the feminine nouns *tá* (toe) for *tá'-e*, O. H. Germ. *zéh-a*, gen. *tán*, nom. plur. *tan*, &c., and *beó* (bee), plur. *beón*.

DECLENSIONS.

2. As in Old High German and Old Saxon we have feminine nouns in *in* which drop the thematic consonant and then remain unaltered in all cases, so we meet in Anglo-Saxon corresponding feminine nouns ending in *-u*, *-o*, later on weakened to *-e*, which also reject inflexional forms; e. g. *menigo*, multitude; *äðelu* or *äðelo*, nobility; *yldo*, old age, &c. If they form a plural at all, they follow in this the strong declension.

Old Frisian.

1. The masculine and feminine nouns have lost the thematic *-n* throughout; but in the neuter plural we find, on the other hand, the very ancient form *agon*, nom. plur. of *age* (eye), which approaches very near the Goth. *augona;* and in the dat. plur. *ágenu-m*, where, as in the Gothic *vatnam*, &c., the thematic consonant *-n* has been preserved before the case-sign *-m*.

2. In this, as in the preceding dialects, there are feminine nouns of the weak declension which have dropped the thematic vowel and appear with the termination *-e*; e. g. *kelde*, cold; *hrene*, smell, &c., used in the sing. only.

3. Several documents still show in the nom. and accus. of the masc. and fem. the case-sign *-n*, which usually was dropped in the mentioned cases; e. g. *fona*, vexillum (Germ. fahne), accus. plur. *fonan; frowe*, woman (Germ. frau), *frowan*.

Old Norse.

1. The weak declension has in the Old Norse tongue many peculiarities which will be appeciated upon a comparison of the paradigms we have given above. The nominative singular of the masculine has generally weakened the original *a* to *i*, two words only preserving the ancient *a*, namely *herra*, herus (Germ. herr), and *sîra*, lord.

2. The thematic *-n* is but rarely preserved in the plural of masculine nouns, to which exception belong *gumnar*, homines; *bragnar*, soldiers; *gotnar*, horses; *skatnar*, kings; *oxnar*, oxen, &c.; but these words also show the plural without *n*, as *gumar*, *bragar*, &c.

3. Feminine nouns terminating in *-n*, suppress the thematic *n* before the case-sign *n* of the genitive plural, as *kona*, wife, gen. plur. *kona*, instead of *kon-n-a*. The same process takes place in feminine themes ending in *-jan*, unless this termination is preceded by a guttural; hence *lilja*, lily, gen. plur. *lilja* (the

thematic *n* dropped); *kirkja,* church, gen. plur. *kirkna* (the thematic *n* preserved).

4. There are in Old Norse also feminine nouns which have dropped the *n* of the thematic termination *-in* and reject all inflexional forms; such are *aefi,* aevum; *elli,* old age; *mildi,* mildness; they have no plural.

WORDS FORMING THEIR THEMES IN n (BELONGING TO THE WEAK DECLENSION).

The following words belong to the weak declension.

Gothic.

MASC. *aba,* husband; *aha,* mens; *ara,* eagle (Germ. aar); *atta,* father; *bloma,* flower (Germ. blume, cf. bloom); *brunna,* fountain (Germ. brunnen); *funa,* fire; *hoha,* plough; *hana,* cock; *manna,* man, homo; *mena,* moon; *sunna,* sun; *ahma,* spiritus; *sparva,* sparrow; *broþraha,* brother; *aípistula,* epistle; *vilja,* will; *arbja,* heir (Germ. erbe); *bandja,* band, bandage; *fiskja,* fisher; *fráuja,* lord; *maurþrja,* murderer; *timrja,* carpenter; *vardja,* warden.

FEM. *aglo,* molestia; *azgo,* ashes; *dauro,* door; *dubo,* dove (Germ. taube); *fauho,* fox; *qino,* wife; *staírno,* star; *sunno,* sun; *tuggo,* tongue; *aíkklesjo,* ecclesia; *aívaggeljo,* evangelium; *heþjo,* cubiculum; *mitaþjo,* mensura; *raþjo,* reason, ratio; *agláitei,* lasciviousness; *bleiþei,* mercy; *faurhtei,* fear (Germ. furcht); *frodei,* wisdom; *managei,* multitude; *mikilei,* magnitude; *áiþei,* mother; *gabei,* possession; *magaþei,* virginity.

NEUT. *áugo,* eye (Germ. auge); *áuso,* ear; *haírto,* heart; *kaurno,* corn; *namo,* name; *vato,* water; *ubilo,* evil; *barnilo,* infant.

Old High German.

MASC. *ano,* grandfather (cf. Germ. ahne); *aro,* eagle (Germ. aar); *cherno,* corn; *chnapo,* boy (Germ. knabe); *cholo,* coal; *disco,* disciple; *dumo,* thumb (Germ. daume); *erpo,* heir (Germ. erbe); *hano,* cock (Germ. hahn); *haso,* hare (Germ. hase); *herro,* lord (Germ. herr); *húfo,* heap (Germ. haufe); *karto,* garden; *komo,* homo, man; *krávo,* earl (Germ. graf); *mako,* stomach (Germ. magen); *máno,* moon; *namo,* name; *narro,* fool (Germ. narr); *sámo,* seed (Germ. samen); *scado,* damage (Germ. schaden); *snepho,* snipe (Germ. schnepfe); *sparo,* sparrow; *sporo,* spur (Germ. sporn); *sterno,* star (Germ. stern); *trubo,* grape (Germ.

DECLENSIONS.

traube); *willo, willjo, willeo,* will; *verjo,* remex; *arpeo,* heir (Germ. erbe); *murdreo,* murderer (Germ. morder); *stapheo,* step.

FEM. *alpa,* mountain; *asca,* ashes; *chrusta,* crust; *herra,* lady, mistress; *lúta,* voice; *nálda,* needle; *pluoma,* flower (Germ. blume); *phifa,* pipe; *phlanza,* plant (Germ. pflanze); *repa,* vine (Germ. rebe); *seha,* sight; *smerza,* pain (Germ. schmerz); *stunta,* hour (Germ. stunde); *tuba,* dove (Germ. taube); *zunga,* tongue (Germ. zunge); *winja,* amica; *lectja,* lectio; *redja,* ratio; *huldın,* favour, grace (Germ. huld); *managín,* multitude; *keilín,* pride; *siochín,* sickness; *mendın,* joy.

NEUT. *herza,* heart (Germ. herz); *ouga,* eye (Germ. auge); *óra,* ear (Germ. ohr).

Old Saxon.

MASC. *bano,* murderer; *bodo,* messenger (Germ. bote); *froho,* lord; *gumo,* vir; *hano,* cock; *herro,* master, lord; *máno,* moon; *namo,* name; *stuopo,* step (Germ. stufe); *gilobo,* faith (Germ. glaube); *gigado,* husband (Germ. gatte); *brunnjo,* fountain (Germ. brunnen); *wrekkjo,* exsul; *willeo,* will.

FEM. *dubha,* dove (Germ. taube); *erða,* earth; *quena,* woman; *rasta,* rest; *ruoda,* cross, rood; *sunna,* sun; *stemna,* voice (Germ. stimme); *strata,* street; *thiorna,* maiden (Germ. dirne); *wanga,* cheek (Germ. wange); *hellja,* hell; *sundja,* sin; *uðja,* wave, unda.

NEUT. *herta,* heart; *oga,* eye (Germ. auge); *óra,* ear (Germ. ohr).

Anglo-Saxon.

MASC. *bana,* death; *broga,* terror; *guma,* vir; *hana,* cock; *lichoma,* corpse (Germ. leichnam); *maga,* relative; *mona,* moon; *muða,* mouth, i. e. of a river; *nama,* name; *nëfa,* nephew (Germ. neffe); *oxa,* ox; *plega,* play; *steorra,* star; *tıma,* time; *wiga,* warrior; *willa,* will; *freá,* lord.

FEM. *byrne,* lorica; *eorðe,* earth; *heorte,* heart; *mage,* relative, cognata; *myre,* mare; *sunne,* sun; *tunge,* tongue; *wuce,* week; *þrote,* throat; *fǽmne,* woman, femina; *cycene,* coquina; *swalewe,* swallow; *wuduwe,* widow.

NEUT. *eáge,* eye (Germ. auge); *eáre,* ear (Germ. ohr).

Old Frisian.

MASC. *boda*, messenger (Germ. bote); *frána*, judge; *greva*, earl (Germ. graf); *hona*, cock (Germ. hahn); *hera*, lord (Germ. herr); *knapa*, servus (cf. Germ. knabe and knappe); *maga*, stomach (Germ. magen); *mutha*, mouth, i. e. of a river; *neva*, nepos; *noma*, name; *omma*, spiritus; *thuma*, thumb; *willa*, will; *menniska*, homo (Germ. mensch).

FEM. *fovne*, woman; *herte*, heart; *lunge*, lungs; *sunne*, sun; *swarde*, skin; *táne*, toe; *tunge*, tongue.

NEUT. *age*, eye; *are*, ear.

Old Norse.

MASC. *andi*, animus; *api*, ape; *ari*, eagle; *arfi*, heir; *bani*, murderer; *bogi*, bow; *dauði*, death; *dropi*, drop; *gumi*, homo; *hani*, cock; *máni*, moon; *nefi*, brother; *skati*, king; *skuggi*, shade; *uxi*, ox; *þánki*, mens; *vili=vilji*, will; *tiggi*, king.

FEM. *aska*, ashes; *bara*, wave; *egda*, eagle, fem.; *dúfa*, dove; *gánga*, iter; *harpa*, lyra; *pípa*, pipe; *saga*, tale; *staka*, verse; *tala*, speech (cf. tale); *tunga*, tongue; *vika*, week; *bylgja*, billow; *dryckja*, drink; *gyðja*, goddess; *kirkja*, church; *manneskja*, homo (Germ. mensch).

NEUT. *auga*, eye (Germ. auge); *eyra*, ear; *hiarta*, heart; *lúnga*, lungs.

OTHER CONSONANTAL THEMES.

THEME: PRIMITIVE -tara, -tar.

Gothic.

The primitive suffix *-tar*, *-tara*, was employed to form nouns expressive of family connections. On the whole these nouns are the same in all the cognate languages with regard to the suffix as well as the respective root of which they are formed. (Concerning the origin and derivation of these words, see the chapter on Roots and Themes under the respective suffixes.) To these themes in *-r* belong in Gothic the words *fadar*, father; *broþar*, brother; *dauhtar*, daughter; *svistar*, sister. Where a case-sign is added to these words they drop the vowel of the suffix *-tar* (þar or dar), so that *broþar*, for example, has in the sing. nom. accus. and voc. *broþar*, and in the gen. *broþr-s*, dat. *bróþr*; plur.

nom. and voc. *broþr-ju-s*, gen. *brobr-e*, dat. *broþr-u-m*, accus. *broþr-u-ns*. The plural evidently follows the strong declension in **u**.

Old High German.

The masc. nouns. in -*r* either have in the singular no inflexions at all, or they take those of the strong declension in **a**; but their accus. is formed in -*an*, as *fatar* (pater), *fatar-an* (patrem), *pruodar* (frater), *pruodar-an* (fratrem). The fem. nouns *muotar* (mother), *swester* (sister), *tohtar* (daughter), have in the sing. no inflexions, and *muotar* and *swestar* remain unchanged in the nom. and accus. plur. as well, but the latter by the side of the uninflected form *swester*, also shows *swestera* in the nom. and accus. plur. The plural of *tohtar* is declined both strong and weak, as nom. *tohterá* or *tohterun*, gen. *tohtero* or *tohterono*, dat. *tohterum* or *tohterom*, accus. *tohterá* or *tohterun*.

Old Saxon.

The words *fadar* (father), *broðar* (brother), *modar* (mother), *dohtar* (daughter), *suestar* (sister), are undeclined in the singular, and in the nom. and accus. plur. There occurs of *broðar* the dat. plur. *broðrun*; of other cases we have no examples; the genitive might be *fadaró* or *fadro*, &c.

Anglo-Saxon.

fader (father) is in the singular uninflected; the genitive *fäderes* is of rare occurrence. In the plural it has adopted the terminations of the strong declension in **a**, hence nom. accus. *fäderás*, gen. *fäderá*, dat. *fäderum*. The word *broðor* (brother) has in the dat. sing. the Umlaut; and in the nom. plur. the theme is, as in Gothic, enlarged into *broðru*. It is in the sing., nom., gen., accus. *broðor*, dat. *breðer*; plur. nom. and accus. *broðru* or *broðor*, gen. *brodrá*, dat. *broðrum*. In the same manner are declined *modor* (mother), *dohtor* (daughter), *sveoster* (sister).

Old Frisian.

The masculine themes in -*r*, *feder* (father), *brother* (brother), are either undeclined in the singular, or they take -*s* in the gen. and -*e* in the dat. as *feder-s*, *brother-s*; *feder-e*, *brother-e*; the plural has the nom. *federa*, gen. *feder-a*, dat. *federu-m*, accus. *federa*; nom. *brothera*, &c. The feminine nouns *moder* (mother), *swester* (sister), and *dochter* (daughter), are declined in the same manner, but in the gen. sing. they may also take the termination *-e*; hence the gen. sing. of *moder* for instance may be *moder*, or *moders*, or *modere*.

Old Norse.

faðir (father), *broðir* (brother), *moðir* (mother), *dóttir* (daughter), *systir* (sister), take in all cases of the sing. *ur*; hence gen. *foður*, *broður*, &c. (exceptionally *feðr*.) In the plural the nom. and accus. are *feðr*, *broeðr*, gen. *feðra*, *broeðra*, dat. *feðrum*, *broeðrum*. The *i* in the termination *ir* of the nom. sing. does not cause Umlaut, because it stands inorganic for a more ancient *ar*; while, on the other hand, the Umlaut of the plural is caused by the *i* of the termination *ir* which has been dropped, so that *feðr* stands for *feðir*(=*faðir*), and the gen. may have been *feðira*, dat. *feðirum*, wherefore we see the Umlaut *e* of *a*, caused by *i*, preserved in the gen. and dat. plur. instead of the forms *faðra*, *foðrum*, which we should expect in accordance with the vowels *a* and *u* of the terminations.

Themes in -nd.

Gothic.

The themes in *-nd* comprise present participles declined as substantives. In the gen. sing. and dat. plur. they adopt the forms of the strong declension in a. The word *nasjands* (saviour), for example, has in the singular, gen. *nasjandi-s*, dat. accus. voc. *nasjand*; in the plural, nom. accus. voc. *nasjand-s*, gen. *nasjand-e*, dat. *nasjanda-m*. In the same manner goes *menóþ* (month), but dat. plur. *menoþu-m*.

Old High German.

The themes in *-nt*, as *friunt* (friend), may follow the strong declension in a by the side of the following forms which are more common: sing. nom. dat. accus. *friunt*, gen. *friunte-s*; plur. nom. accus. *friunt*, gen. *friunt-o*, dat. *friuntu-m*. In the same manner *mánod*, month.

Old Saxon.

The participial themes in *-nd*, as *friund* (friend), may in the oblique cases adopt the forms of the strong declension in a. The common declension is sing. nom. accus. *friund*, gen. *friunde-s*, dat. *friunde*; plur. nom. accus. *friund*, gen. *friund-o*, dat. *friundu-n*. In Old Saxon however this declension is limited to certain words, as *friund*, friend; *fiond*, enemy (cf. fiend); *lerjand*, teacher; *heljand*, saviour, and a few others.

Anglo-Saxon.

Among participial themes in *-nd*, *freond* (friend) and *feond* (enemy, fiend), have adopted the strong declension in a, hence plur. *freondas, feondas*; but by the side of these we also find the plurals *freond, feond*, or, with Umlaut, *frŷnd, fŷnd*. Other themes of this kind either have the nom. plur. like the nom. sing., or they form the nom. plur. after the strong declension in a.

Old Frisian.

Participial themes in *-nd*: *friund*, friend; nom. accus. sing. *friund*, gen. *friunde-s*, dat. *friund* or *friunde*; plur. nom. accus. *friund*, gen. *friund-a* or *friunda-n-e*, dat. *friund-um*. In the same manner is declined *fiand*, enemy; also the masc. *monath*, month, which later on however has the strong plural *monatha-r* as well; *wigand* (miles, filius) and *werand* (autor) are doubtful.

Old Norse.

The participial themes in *-nd* have in the singular adopted the weak declension; the plural in *-r* has the Umlaut, so that the plural sign *-r* appears to have its origin in the suffix *-ir*. Examples:—*frændi*, friend, gen. dat. accus. *frænda*; plur. nom. accus. *frænd-r*, gen. *frænd-a*, dat. *frændu-m*. In the same manner are declined *fiandi*, enemy; *bondi*, ruricola, plur. *boend-r*.

THEMES ENDING IN A GUTTURAL OR DENTAL.

Gothic.

Theme *baurg*, borough, nom. gen. *baurg-s*; dat. accus. voc. *baurg*; plur. nom. accus. voc. *baurg-s*, gen. *baùrg-e*, dat. *baurgi-m*. In the same manner are declined *nahts*, night, with the dat. plur. *nahta-m*; *miluks*, milk; *vaíhts*, thing; *brusts*, breast; *dulþs*, feast: *dulþ* and *vaiht* also follow the strong declension in i from the themes *dulþai, vaihtai*.

Old High German.

In this dialect the mentioned themes have adopted the strong declension in **i**, such as *prust*, breast (dat. plur. has also *prustum*); *purc*, borough; *miluk*, milk; *naht*, night. The last-mentioned has, however, preserved some traces of the ancient declension: sing. nom. accus. *naht*, gen. *nahte-s*, dat. *nahte;* plur. nom. accus. *naht*, gen. *naht-ó*, dat. *nahtu-m, nahto-n.*

Old Saxon.

Most of the themes have passed into the strong declension in **i**; *naht*, night, has preserved more of the ancient forms: sing. nom. dat. accus. *naht* (dat. once *nahta*), gen. *nahte-s*; plur. nom. accus. *naht*, gen. *naht-ó*, dat. *nahtu-n;* *burg*, borough, which follows the declension in **i** has the exceptional gen. *burge-s*, and rarely the dat. *burg* for *burgi*; *magað*, maid, dat. accus. sing. and accus. plur. *magað*.

Anglo-Saxon.

Some traces of the ancient declension of these themes we find in the words *niht*, night; *viht, vuht*, thing; plur. nom. *niht, viht, vuht;* *burh*, castle, borough, which follows the declension in **i**, has the gen. sing. *byrg, byrig*, by the side of *burge*.

Old Frisian.

naht, night: sing. nom. accus. *naht*, dat. *naht* and *nahte*, gen. *nahte-s;* plur. nom. and accus. *naht* and *nahta*, gen. †*naht-a*, dat. *nahtu-m*. *burch*, castle, dat. sing. *burch*, nom. plur. *burga*.

Old Norse.

nátt for *naht*, night: nom. dat. acc. *nátt*, gen. *náttu-r;* plur. nom. accus. *naet-r*, gen. *nátta*, dat. *náttum*. *nott*, for *nátt*, has the gen. *noet-r*, dat. accus. *nott;* plur. *noet-r*, gen. *nott-a*, dat. *nottum*.

ANOMALOUS DECLENSIONS.

Gothic.

1. The consonantal theme, *man* (homo) is in some forms enlarged into *mannan-*, and then follows the weak declension; hence sing. nom. *manna*, gen. *man-s*, dat. *mann*, accus. *mannan*, voc. *manna;* plur. nom. *man-s, mannan-s,* gen. *mann-e*, dat. *manna-m*, accus. *man-s, mannan-s,* voc. *man-s, mannan-s.*

2. *fadrein* (status parentis) is, strictly speaking, a neuter noun, but in the nom. and accus. plur. it is used as a masculine, *þai fadrein, þans fadrein* (parentes), otherwise regular. When used as a feminine theme in **i**, as gen. sing. *fadreinais*, it means 'family.'

3. *fôn* (fire) an indeclinable neuter, substitutes in the gen. and dat. sing. the masculine theme *funan-*, without the plural.

Old High German.

man, homo, forms its cases in the singular in a twofold manner, namely, either *man* throughout, or nom. *man*, gen. *mannis*, dat. *manne*, accus. *mannan;* plur. nom. *man*, gen. *manno*, dat. *mannum*, accus. *man*.

Old Saxon.

1. *man*, in a similar manner as in Old High German, has the singular indeclinable, or nom. *man*, gen. *manna-s, -es*, dat. *manna, -e*, accus. *man;* plur, nom. *man*, gen. *mann-ó*, dat. *mannu-n*, accus. *man*.

2. The feminine strong theme *helljo*, infernus, nom. *hellja*, is sometimes supplanted by a masc. theme *hella*, nom. *hell* or *hel*. *thiodo* (gens) is often superseded by the fem. theme *thiodi*, nom. *thiod*.

Anglo-Saxon.

1. *man*, gen. *mannes*, dat. *men*, accus. *man;* plur. nom. *men*, gen. *manna*, dat. *mannum*, accus. *men*.

2. The feminines *sæ* (sea), *æ* (law), *eá* (river), are in the singular indeclinable; but occasionally there occur the genitives *sæ-s*, Goth. *saivi-s; eá-s*, Goth. *ahvo-s;* the nom. plur. also is *sæ-s, eá-s* : dat. plur. *sæ-m. eá-m.*

3. *drŷ*, magus, has the nom. plur. *drŷás*, but the gen. *drŷ-r-á*.

Old Frisian.

mon (vir), gen. *monnes*, dat. *mon, monne*, accus. *mon;* plur. nom. *mon*, gen. *monna*, dat. *monnum*, accus. *mon*.

Old Norse.

1. *maðr* (homo), gen. *mann-s*, dat. *mann-i*, accus. *mann;* plur. nom. *menn* (also *með-r*), gen. *mann-a*, dat. *monnu-m*, accus. *men*. Both forms *maðr* and *mann*, according to Old Norse phonetic laws, spring from a more ancient *manðr* (see p. 108).
2. Corresponding to the Goth. *sáiv-s*, A. S. *sǽ*, sea, lake, the Old Norse has in the singular a variety of forms, as nom. *sǽ-r*, gen. *sǽvar*, dat. *sǽ*, accus. *sǽ;* or *sior, sios, sio, sio;* or *siar, sioar* (*siofar, siavar*), *sia, sia;* plur. *sǽvar, sǽva, sǽm* (*siam*), *sǽva*. In the same manner, corresponding to the Goth. *snáiv-s*, snow, the O. N. *snǽr, snior, sniar*.
3. *fingr, fingur* (finger), gen. *fingr-s*, follows the declension in **a**, but in the nom. accus. plur. it has *fingr* for *fingrar, fingra;* in the same manner *vetr, vetur* (declension in **u**), has in the nom. accus. plur. *vetr* for *vetrir, vetru*.
4. *fotr* (foot), follows the declension in **u**; gen. *fotar* (or *fots*, **a**), dat. *foeti* (or *foti*, **a**); nom. plur. *foetr* for *foetir*.
5. Monosyllabic words ending in a vowel, which in other dialects follow the declensions in **a** or **u**, never have a thematic vowel in Old Norse; hence they are declined, e. g., masc. *ná-r* (corpse), gen. *ná-s*, dat. *ná*, accus. *ná;* plur. *ná-r*, gen. *ná-a*, dat. *ná-m*, accus. *ná*. Fem. *spa* (vaticinium), gen. *spá-r*, dat. *spá*, accus. *spá;* plur. nom. *spá-r*, gen. *spá-a*, dat. *spá-m*, accus. *spá-r*. To this declension belong masc. *ŷ-r* (arcus), *skó-r* (shoe), *io-r* (horse); fem. *á* (river), *brá* (brow). *mey* (maid), *ey* (island), þý (serva), have *j* before the thematic vowel by which the latter is preserved; hence the gen. *meyjar, eyjar*, &c., plur. nom. the same; plur. dat. *meyjum, eyjum;* neut. (which decline like masc. except nom. plur.) *bu* (rus, country), dat. sing. *bui*, dat. plur. *buum; kne* (knee), *tré* (tree), dat. plur. *knia-m, tria-m; vé* (temple), gen. plur. *ve-a*, dat. *veu-m*. Forms in analogy to the declension in **u** we have in *tá* (toe), gen. *tá-r*, plur. nom. *tǽ-r*, gen. *tá-a*. Words with *u* have the vowel *a* before the case-sign; e. g. *brú* (bridge), gen. *bruar*. The secondary form *ky-r* for *kú* (cow) has the case-sign *-r* of the nom. sing. preserved; compare *ǽ-r* (sheep), *mǽ-r* (maid).

DECLENSION OF PROPER NAMES.

Gothic.

Of Gothic proper names no examples occur in Ulfilas; foreign ones he uses either undeclined, or with their Greek inflexions, or also adapted to one of the Gothic declensions. A few proper names, as *Aíleisabaiþ, Magdalene, Beþlahaim*, are indeclinable. We have Greek inflexions in the nom. *Annas*, accus. *Teitaum*, gen. *Judaias*, nom. plur. *Israelitai*. More frequently we find them follow the Gothic declensions, so that all Greek proper names ending in a consonant (except those in *os* and *as*) are declined after the Gothic in **a**, as *Adam*, gen. *Adamis*, dat. *Adama*. After the Gothic in **i** go the names of nations, of which we have chiefly the plural nom. in *eis*, as *Rumoneis, Makidoneis*. After that in **u** the proper names ending in *-ius, -us, -aius*, the last two having in the nom. gen. plur. always *-eis, -e*, the first mentioned remaining unaltered in the nom. plur. All the masculine names in *-a, -ó, -on*, and *-as*, and the feminines in *-a*, follow the weak declension, as *Marja*, gen. *Marjins; Iaíreikó, Iaireikons; Aharon, Aharons*,

Old High German.

Proper names, whether native or foreign, follow the strong declension in **a**, commonly forming the accus. sing. in *-an*, as *Hludwíg*, accus. *Hludwígan* and *Hludwíg; Swap*, Suevus, accus. *Swapan*, plur. *Swapá, Swapo, Swapum*. The strong declension in **i** we find in *Hun*, plur. *Huni;* but no examples of the declension in **u**. After the weak declension go the names *Bruno, Kero; Franko, Sahso*, Saxon. Feminine proper names follow the strong declension in **a**, as *Hiltiruna, Roma*, or the declension in **i** (especially those ending in *-lind, -rat, -gund, -trut*), or the weak declension, as *Marja*, gen. *Marjun*. The strong neutral declension is used in some names of cities, as in *Betlehem, Sion*, gen. *Betlemes, Siones*.

Old Saxon.

Masculine names follow the strong declension in **a**. In this dialect there appears, as in Old High German, the ancient accusative termination *-an*, as *Lazarus*, accus. *Lazarusan* and *Lazarus*. The feminine names *Ruma, Bethania, Galilea*, follow the strong declension in **a**, *Maria* the weak declension. The masc. *Judeo* is weak. Some masculine nouns decline strong or weak according to different stages of the language and different documents. Some are indeclinable.

Anglo-Saxon.

All masculine names which decline strong follow the declension in a; so do the words *Swæf, Finn,* Þ*yring*, plur. *Swæfas,* &c. Feminine names in a occur very rarely. After the declension in i go the words *Dene, Engle,* and those ending in *-vare* (as already mentioned); to these may be added *Grece* (Greek), *Surpe* (Sorbi), and a few others. Many names, especially feminine, follow the weak declension, as *Marie,* gen. *Marian, Eve,* gen. *Evan;* the names of nations, *Seaxan,* Saxons; *Frisan,* Frisians, &c.: *Judeás,* Jews, is strong. Foreign proper nouns often appear with their respective foreign declensions.

Old Frisian.

The native names follow the strong declension; foreign ones may have the strong Frisian, or their own foreign declension, as *Peder, Pederes,* or *Petrus, Petri;* or some are indeclinable, as *Leo,* the pope. Of names of nations some decline strong, others weak: *Riostring,* plur. *Riostringa,* is strong; *Fresa,* Frisian, *Saxa,* Saxon, &c., are weak. Names of towns, such as *Breme, Colene, Rume,* which are feminine, may decline strong in a, or weak. *Marie* is, as in the other dialects, weak; *Eva* is indeclinable.

Old Norse.

Some of the masculine proper nouns follow the strong, others the weak declension; the former commonly have the thematic *-a,* as *Gunnar,* gen. *Gunnars,* dat. *Gunnari; Askr, Alfr,* &c. Such as *Grípir, Brímir,* &c., follow the declension of *hirðir,* that is, the themes in *-ja*. The declension in u is frequently followed by proper names, especially those ending in *-mundr, -undr, hiortr, -biorn, -vindr, -viðr;* as *Saemundr, Volundr, Arn-biorn,* &c. Some decline weak, as *Bragi, Loki*. Feminine nouns which decline strong may be attributed either to the declension in a or i, because both are identical in the singular. The words *Edda, Nanna,* &c., are weak. Names of nations, such as *Alfr, Finnr, Svafr,* and those in *-ungr,* follow the declension in a; *Danr,* plur. *Danir, Grikr,* plur. *Grikir,* the declension in i; *Saxi, Goti, Judi,* decline weak. *Ás* has in the sing. gen. *As-s,* plur. *Aesir,* gen. *Asa,* dat. *Ásum,* accus. *Ásu,* thus showing forms in a and u mixed. Names of towns (which are no compounds of *borg* or *staðr*) ending in a consonant, follow the declension in a or i, as *Paris*, gen. *Parísar;* those ending in the vowel *-a* have the weak declension, as *Troja*, gen. *Troju*.

DECLENSION OF ADJECTIVES.

Adjectives in the Teutonic languages show a greater flexibility than those of the cognate tongues, such as Greek and Latin; for not only do they display special inflexional forms for the three different genders, but they follow moreover two distinct declensions, commonly known as the *strong* and *weak* declension. The former is produced by a demonstrative pronoun which is suffixed to the adjective root, and which by its various inflexional forms yields the case-signs to the declension of the adjective; the latter assumes the case-signs of the weak declension of the noun, and consequently stands on a parallel with the adjective declensions in the cognate languages. The former might be more properly called the *pronominal*, the latter the *nominal*, declension of adjectives. In the strong, or pronominal, declension the adjective adopts a form which is analogous to a suffixed article; this declension therefore is chiefly used where the adjective is *not* preceded by the article or a pronoun supplying it.

STRONG DECLENSION.

The thematic vowels *a, i, u,* which yielded us three strong declensions of the noun, are not all adopted by the adjectives; themes in a are most frequent, themes in ja still appear distinctly in the Gothic, but in the other Teutonic dialects merely in a few remnants; themes in u we find in Gothic only, while such in i do not appear in any of the Teutonic languages.

The terminations or case-signs of the strong declension are, as we have already stated, derived from the different inflexional forms of a demonstrative pronoun. This pronoun occurs in Sanskrit as a relative under the forms *yas, yá, yad*, while in the Germanic tongues, where it assumed a demonstrative force, its most ancient forms will appear from the following table.

	Singular.			Plural.		
	Masc.	Fem.	Neut.	Masc.	Fem.	Neut.
Nom.	jis	ja	jata	jai	jôs	ja
Gen.	jis	jaizôs	jis	jaizê	jaizô	jaizê
Dat.	jamma	jizai	jamma	jaim	jaim	jaim
Accus.	jana	ja	jata	jans	jôs	ja

These pronominal forms however, when suffixed to the adjective, do not always appear in their full integrity, but are in the different dialects more or less modified. The following paradigms may suffice to convey an idea of these modifications.

Theme in u.

Gothic.

	Singular.			Plural.		
	Masc.	Fem.	Neut.	Masc.	Fem.	Neut.
Nom.	hardu-s (hard)	hardu-s	hardu, hard-jata	hard-jai	hard-jôs	hard-ja
Gen.	hard-jis	hard-jaizôs	hard-jis	hard-jaizê	hard-jaizô	hard-jaizê
Dat.	hard-jamma	hard-jai	hard-jamma	hard-jaim	hard-jaim	hard-jaim
	&c.	&c.	&c.	&c.	&c.	&c.

All the remaining cases are formed regularly by the suffixed pronoun as it appears in the paradigm above.

Themes in a.

	Singular.			Plural.		
	Masc.	Fem.	Neut.	Masc.	Fem.	Neut.
Nom.	blind-s	blind-a	blind-ata	blind-ai	blind-ôs	blind-a
Gen.	blind-is	blind-aizos	blind-is	blind-aizê	blind-aizô	blind-aizê
Dat.	blind-amma	blind-ai	blind-amma	blind-aim	blind-aim	blind-aim
Accus.	blind-ana	blind-a	blind-ata	blind-ans	blind-ôs	blind-a

Old High German.

	Singular.			Plural.		
	Masc.	Fem.	Neut.	Masc.	Fem.	Neut.
Nom.	plint-êr	plint-ju, u	plint-aʒ	plint-ê, -â	plint-ô	plint-ju, -u
Gen.	plint-es	plint-êrâ	plint-es	plint-êro	plint-êrô	plint-êrô
Dat.	plint-emu	plint-êru	plint-emu	plint-êm	plint-êm	plint-êm
Accus.	plint-an	plint-a	plint-aʒ	plint-ê	plint-ô	plint-ju, -u
Instr.	plint-u	..	plint-u	..	..	..

Old Saxon.

	SINGULAR.			PLURAL.		
	Masc.	Fem.	Neut.	Masc.	Fem.	Neut.
Nom.	blind	blind	blind	blind-a, -e	blind-â, e	blind-a, u (blind)
Gen.	blind-as	blind-aro	blind-as	blind-arô	blind-arô	blind-arô
Dat.	blind-umu	blind-aro	blind-umu	blind-un	blind-un	blind-un
Accus.	blind-an, -ana	blind-a	blind	blind-a, -e	blind-a, -e	blind-a, -u (blind)
Instr.	blind-u	..	..	..	..	..

Anglo-Saxon.

	SINGULAR.			PLURAL.		
	Masc.	Fem.	Neut.	Masc.	Fem.	Neut.
Nom.	blind	blind(u)	blind	blind-e	blind-e	blind-u
Gen.	blind-es	blind-re	blind-es	blind-ra	blind-ra	blind-ra
Dat.	blind-um	blind-re	blind-um	blind-um	blind-um	blind-um
Accus.	blind-ne	blind-e	blind	blind-e	blind-e	blind-u
Instr.	blind-ê	..	blind-ê	..	..	..

Old Frisian.

	SINGULAR.			PLURAL.
	Masc.	Fem.	Neut.	Masc. Fem. Neut.
Nom.	blind	blind-e	blind	blind-a, -e
Gen.	blind-es	blind-ere, -re	blind-es	blind-era, -ra
Dat.	blind-a, -e	blind-ere, -re	blind-a, -e	blind-a, -e
Accus.	blind-ene, -ne, -en	blind-e	blind	blind-a, -e

Old Norse.

	SINGULAR.			PLURAL.		
	Masc.	Fem.	Neut.	Masc.	Fem.	Neut.
Nom.	lang-r	löng	lang-t	lang-ir	lang-ar	löng
Gen.	lang-s	lang-rar	lang-s	lang-ra	lang-ra	lang-ra
Dat.	löng-um	lang-ri	löng-u	löng-um	löng-um	löng-um
Accus.	lang-an	lang-a	lang-t	lang-a	lang-ar	löng

Remarks on the above Paradigms.

Gothic.

1. Adjectives preserve the thematic vowel *u* in the nom. sing. of the three genders; in the oblique cases however they drop this thematic vowel and suffix the pronoun *jis* in its full integrity, as *hardu-s, hard-jis,* &c.

2. Themes ending in *a* drop the thematic vowel as well as the *j* of the suffix *jis* throughout all cases, as *blind-s, blind-is,* &c.

3. Adjectives with the theme in *ja* display four different modes of the nom. sing. masc.; namely, (1) If the thematic *ja* is preceded by a vowel or a short syllable ending in a single consonant, the nom. has the termination *jis=ja-s*, the *a* being weakened to *i*, e. g. *sak-ji-s*, rixosus; *mid-ji-s*, medius; *fullato-ji-s*, perfect; *niu-ji-s*, new. Where the thematic termination *ja* is preceded by a long syllable ending in a consonant, three different modes of formation occur, namely, (2) *ja* is contracted into *ei*, e. g. *vilþ-ei-s*, verus; *alþ-ei-s*, old; or (3) *ja* is contracted into *i*, e. g. *sut-i-s* (ἀνεκτός), *aírkn-i-s* (ὅσιος); or (4) *ja* is dropped altogether, e. g. *blaiþ-s*, mitis; *hrain-s*, clean, pure (Germ. rein). But under all circumstances the *j* of *ja* re-appears in the oblique cases, except with the adjectives in *ei-s* which preserve this contracted form in the gen. sing. masc. and fem., as the following examples will suffice to show: (1) *sakjis*, gen. *sakjis*, dat. *sakjamma*, &c.; (2) *vilþeis*, gen. *vilþeis*, dat. *vilþjamma*, &c.; (3) *sutis*, gen. *sutjis*, dat. *sutjamma*, &c.; (4) *hrains*, gen. *hrainjis*, dat. *hrainjamma*, &c.

4. Themes in *ja* which suppress this thematic termination in the nom. sing. masc, form sometimes the feminine in the same manner, as masc. fem. *bruk-s*, useful; *skeir-s*, clear; *sel-s*, benign; the neuter is probably without any termination, as *bruk, skeir, sel*.

5. Adjectives, the stem of which ends in *s*, do not adopt the case-sign *-s* in the nom. sing.; as *sves*, proprius, gen. *svesis:* in the same manner the nom. *anþar*, other: but all other adjectives ending in *r* take the termination *-s* in the nom., as *sver-s*, honoratus; *gaür s*, moestus.

Old High German.

1. In Old High German, as well as in all other dialects which we shall yet mention, every *s* which occurs between two vowels, and which in this position in Gothic already had been converted into *z*, is changed into *r*. This change occurs in Old High German in the nom. sing. masc. too, hence *plint-er*, Goth. *blind-s*.

2. Old High German, as well as the other dialects, drops the *j* of the pronominal suffix throughout, with the exception of the Old High German nom. sing. fem. ending in *ju*; but in other respects the pronominal suffix is sometimes more intact than even in Gothic. Thus the nom. sing. masc. *plint-er* may, according to Bopp, be a contraction of *plinta-ir*, *ir* the suffix answering to Gothic *is = jis*.

3. The case-termination is often dropped, so that *plint* stands for the nom. sing. masc. *plint-er*, fem. *plint-ju*, neut. *plint-az*.

4. For the termination *ju* we find in the nom. sing. fem. *u* only; and the gen. and dat. fem. may take *ero-* for *-era*, *-eru*, respectively; the dat. sing. masc. *-emo* for *-emu*.

5. The plural has sometimes in the nom. accus. *a* for *e*, and, in later documents, *en* for *em* in the dative.

6. The *j* of the thematic *ja* is either dropped or assimilated to the preceding consonant, as in *mitt-er* for *mitj-er*. But where the stem is uninflected, the *j* remains, hardened in *i*, as *miti*, medius; *kleini*, subtilis; *hreini*, pure; *wildi*, wild. The adjective *fri* preserves the thematic *j*, as *friger, friju, frijaz*, or contracted *frier, friu, friaz*.

7. The spirant *w*, at the end of the stem, is in the uninflected nom. vocalized into *o*, as nom. *plawer*, lividus, uninflected *pláo*.

Old Saxon.

1. The full inflexional vowels are frequently weakened; thus the genitive terminations *-as, -aro*, are replaced by *-es, -ero*, or *-eru*; the dative *-umu, -aro*, by *-emu, -um, -on*, and *-eru, -uru*. But the accusative suffix is sometimes preserved in its completeness, especially in compound or polysyllabic adjectives, as *langsam*, slow; *unsundig*, unhealthy; accus. *langsam-ana, unsundig-ana*; or, dropping the first *a*, it is shortened into *-na*, as *máhtig*, mighty, acc. *máhtig-na*. This *-na* is, later on, weakened into *-ne*.

2. The nom. plur. neut. has more frequently the weakened *-u*

instead of the original -*a*; and the dat. plur. -*un* is often weakened into -*on*.

3. Themes in -*ja* vocalize the *j* into *i* in the uninflected, but preserve the *j* in the inflected cases or weaken it into *e*, e.g. *middi*, medius, gen. masc. *middj-es*, or *midde-as*, fem. *middj-aro*, &c. But occasionally it occurs that the *j* is dropped altogether, e.g. *derni*, occultus, gen. plur. *dern'-ero*.

4. A stem ending in *w* commonly vocalizes this *w* in the uninflected nominative, as *glau*, prudent, gen. *glaw-es*.

Anglo-Saxon.

1. The termination -*u* of the nom. sing. fem. is preserved after monosyllabic adjectives with a short vowel, as *hvatu*; polysyllabic words weaken it into -*e*, and adjectives with a long radical vowel drop it altogether.

2. Monosyllabic adjectives with the short radical *a* weaken this vowel into *a*, unless it is sustained by a terminational vowel, e.g. nom. sing. masc. *hvät*, acer, fem. *hvat-u*; nom. plur. *hrat-e*, gen. *hvät-ra*. Other adjectives of this kind are, *bar*, naked; *bläc*, black; *hrað*, quick; *lät*, late; *spär*, spare, &c.

3. A double consonant ending a stem is shortened into a single one before terminations beginning with a consonant, as *grim*, gen. masc. *grimm-es*, gen. fem. *grim-re*.

4. Themes in *ja* show a remnant of the thematic *j* in the terminational *e* of the uninflected nominative and in the Umlaut of the radical vowel, as *bliðe*, blithe; *grene*, green (O. H. Germ. *gruoni*); but the inflected cases drop this *e* throughout, hence *blið-re*, *grēn-re*, &c.

Old Frisian.

The terminational vowels are generally weakened, and the dative of the masc. and neut. sing. and plur. has dropped the final *m*, so that this form is identical with the nom. and accus. plur. of the three genders.

Themes in *ja* have only in the nom. sing. preserved a trace of the ancient *j* in the termination *e*, as *diore*, dear; *grene*, green; *ríke*, rich, &c.

Old Norse.

Peculiar is the dat. sing. neut. in *-u*, which bears no analogy to the case-sign *-um*, derived from the pronominal suffix *-amma*, in the other dialects; and the nom. plur. masc. in *-ir*, from *-is*. It appears that in the first-mentioned case the instrumental case-sign *-u* has expelled the termination of the dative and usurped its place; in the latter the nominative case-sign of the substantive seems to have found admission into the declension of the adjective.

Concerning the assimilation, or omission of the *r* in the nom. sing. as well as in the case-suffixes *-rar*, *-ri*, *-ra*, the same rules hold good which are observed in the declension of the substantive. The *-r* therefore is dropped if the stem terminates in *r*, *rr*, *s*, or *n*, which is preceded by a consonant, e. g. *snar*, quick, gen. fem. *snar-ar; vis*, wise, *vis-ar; iafn*, even, *iafn-ar*. It is assimilated to *l* and *n* final of long or polysyllabic stems, as *sael-l*, happy, for *sael-r*, gen. fem. *sael-lar* for *sael-rar; brun-n*, brown, for *brun-r*, gen. fem. *brun-nar* for *brun-rar*. But the *r* remains unassimilated after *ll* and *nn* ending the stem, e. g. *all-r*, all, gen. *all-rar*, &c.; and after single *l* and *n* which are preceded by a short vowel, as *hol-r*, hollow, gen. fem. *hol-rar*.

The suffix *-t* of the nom. sing. neut. assimilates a preceding ð which follows upon a vowel; if this vowel is long it becomes short under the mentioned circumstance; hence neut. *glat-t* from masc. *glað-r*, *got-t* from *goð-r*, good. If a stem terminates in *nd*, *rð*, *st*, the dental is dropped before the neuter suffix, as *blin-t* for *blind-t*, from masc. *blind-r; har-t* for *harð-t*, from *harð-r*, hard. The gemination of *l, m, n, r, s, t*, is reduced to the single consonant, e. g. *snial-t* for *sniall-t*. A preceding *r* is dropped in *anna-t* from *annar*, other.

Adjectives which, in consequence of having dropped a final spirant, end in a long vowel, double the case-sign of the neuter; e. g. *blá-r*, blew, O. H. Germ. *pláo*, *pláw-er*, has in the neuter *blá-tt; ny-r*, new, Goth. *niujis*, has the neuter *nӱ-tt;* so that apparently the spirant has been assimilated to the neuter suffix *-t*. For the same reason the initial consonants of the suffixes *-rar*, *-ri*, *-ra*, may be doubled; e. g. *hárrar*, *nyrrar*, by the side of **hárar, nӱrar.**

Derivative adjectives in *-in* have in the neut. *i-t* for *in-t*, and in the masc. accus. *in-n* for *in-an;* e. g. *steinin-n*, lapideus, has the neut. *steini-t*, accus. masc. *steinin-n*.

litil-l (little) and *mikil-l* (great) have the neut. *liti-t*, *miki-t* for *litil-t*, *mikil-t;* accus. sing. masc. *litin-n*, *mikin-n* : *litil-l* moreover shortens the radical vowel, if, before an inflexional vowel, elision of the vowel in the derivative syllable takes place; e. g. dat. sing. *litl-um, litl-u,* plur. *litl-ir;* but gen. sing. *litil-s,* &c

The vowel *i*, where it occurs in the pronominal suffix, does not cause Umlaut; but *u* does, even in the nom. sing. fem. and in the nom. and accus. plur. neut., where it has been dropped; hence the form *long* in the mentioned cases. The process which occurs in adjectives ending in *al* and *ar* is remarkable. In the cases just mentioned, where the case-sign *u* is dropped, they supplant the *a* of those syllables by the vowel *u*, which then causes Umlaut of the preceding vowel; e. g. *gamal-l*, old, fem. *gömul* for *gamal*(*-u*); *fagar*, fair, fem. *fögur* for *fagar*(*-u*). Elision of the vowel in the derivative syllables *al* and *ar* always takes place when the case-sign begins with a vowel, as *gaml-an* for *gamal-an*.

The adjective *annar*, other, Goth. *anþar*, forms some cases with the stem *ann*, others with the stem *að*, both standing for the more ancient *anð*.

The declension runs thus :—

	Singular.			Plural.		
	Masc.	Fem.	Neut.	Masc.	Fem.	Neut.
Nom.	annar	önnur	annat	aðrir	aðrar	önnur
Gen.	annars	annarar	annars	annarra	annarra	annarra
Dat.	öðrum	annarri	öðru	öðrum	öðrum	öðrum
Accus.	annan	aðra	annat	aðra	aðrar	önnur

Themes in *ja* have generally dropped the *j*, except in the adjectives *miðr* (medius), *ny-r* (new), *rík-r* (rich), where it is often preserved before the case-sign beginning with the vowel *a* or *u*, as *midj-um, nyj-an, rikj-u;* but where it is dropped it has caused the Umlaut of the preceding vowels, as *groenn*, green, O. H. Germ. *groni*, A. S. *grene;* *dyr*, dear.

The spirant *v* at the end of a stem, though dropped, has often caused the Umlaut of the preceding *a* into *o*, as *dokk-r*, dark, black; *gorr*, done (comp. Germ. gar). It frequently reappears before case-signs beginning with a vowel, as *dokkv-am, dokkv-an*, &c.; sometimes hardened into *f*, as *há-r*, celsus (Germ. hehr), accus. *háv-an* and *háf-an;* but disappears generally in later documents, hence *há-ir* for *háv-ir; há-um, há-m* for *háv-um*.

WEAK DECLENSION OF ADJECTIVES.

Paradigms.

Gothic.

	SINGULAR.			PLURAL.		
	Masc.	Fem.	Neut.	Masc.	Fem.	Neut.
Nom.	*blinda*	*blindô*	*blindô*	*blindans*	*blindôns*	*blindôna*
Gen.	*blindins*	*blindôns*	*blindins*	*blindanê*	*blindônô*	*blindanê*
Dat.	*blindin*	*blindôn*	*blindin*	*blindam*	*blindôm*	*blindam*
Accus.	*blindan*	*blindôn*	*blindô*	*blindans*	*blindôn*	*blindôna*

Old High German.

	SINGULAR.			PLURAL.		
	Masc.	Fem.	Neut.	Masc.	Fem.	Neut.
Nom.	*plinto*	*plintâ*	*plinta*	*plintun*	*plintûn*	*plintûn*
Gen.	*plintin*	*plintûn*	*plintin*	*plintônô*	*plintônô*	*plintônô*
Dat.	*plintin*	*plintân*	*plintin*	*plintôm*	*plintôm*	*plintôm*
Accus.	*plintun*	*plintûn*	*plinta*	*plintun*	*plintûn*	*plintûn*

Old Saxon.

	SINGULAR.			PLURAL.		
	Masc.	Fem.	Neut.	Masc. Fem. Neut.		
Nom.	*blindo(-a)*	*blinda*	*blinda*	*blindu*		
Gen.	*blindun*	*blindun*	*blindun*	*blindônô*		
Dat.	*blindun*	*blindun*	*blindun*	*blindun*		
Accus.	*blindun*	*blindun*	*blinda*	*blindun*		

Anglo-Saxon.

	SINGULAR.			PLURAL.		
	Masc.	Fem.	Neut.	Masc. Fem. Neut.		
Nom.	*blinda*	*blinde*	*blinde*	*blindan*		
Gen.	*blindan*	*blindan*	*blindan*	*blindena*		
Dat.	*blindan*	*blindan*	*blindan*	*blindum*		
Accus.	*blindan*	*blindan*	*blinde*	*blindan*		

Old Frisian.

	Singular.			Plural.		
	Masc.	Fem.	Neut.	Masc.	Fem.	Neut.
Nom.	blinda	blinde	blinde	blinda		
Gen.	blinda	blinda	blinda	blindena		
Dat.	blinda	blinda	blinda	blindum		
Accus.	blinda	blinda	blinde	blinda		

Old Norse.

	Singular.			Plural.		
	Masc.	Fem.	Neut.	Masc.	Fem.	Neut.
Nom.	langi	langa	langa	löngu		
Gen.	langa	löngu	langa	löngu		
Dat.	langa	löngu	langa	löngu		
Accus.	langa	löngu	langa	löngu		

Remarks on the Paradigms.

As we have already stated, and as will readily be seen from the preceding paradigms, the weak declension of the adjectives is, with regard to its case-signs or terminations, in all Teutonic dialects perfectly identical with the weak declension of the noun. A few peculiarities in the different dialects deserve a short notice.

In Gothic the *a* of the thematic termination -*an* is, in the feminine, lengthened into *o*, hence the lengthened theme -*on*. Adjectives in *ja* preserve the thematic *ja* in the weak declension, though the *j* may have been dropped in the strong declension, e. g. *hrainja*, gen. *hrainjins*, dat. *hrainjin*, &c. (strong, *hrain-s*, &c.) Themes in u adopt the forms in *ja*, hence *hardja, hardjins*, &c. (strong, *hardus*, &c.) The weak adjective *ainaha*, solus (Germ. einiger), has the fem. *ainohô*.

Old High German and Old Saxon have preserved the Gothic feminine theme in *on* in the darkened form *un*, which in Old Saxon however may rather be the shortened -*un*. Anglo-Saxon adopts the theme in -*an* for the singular of all genders, with the exception of the nominative feminine and neuter and accusative neuter. The plural is, in Old Saxon and Anglo-Saxon, identically the same for all genders.

Old Frisian and Old Norse reject in the singular of the adjective as well as of the substantive declension the thematic -*n*, and allow the word to end in the bare vowel *a*, or its modification in

DECLENSIONS. 341

i or *u*. In Old Norse, moreover, it is the singular only which has preserved the terminations of the weak declension of the noun, while the plural, rejecting whatever case-signs the noun has preserved, adopted the neuter termination *u* for all cases and all genders.

The Old Norse themes in *jan* and *van* preserve their respective spirant throughout, except that the nom. *-ji* is commonly rendered by *i*, as *ríki, ríkja; dokkvi, dokkva*. Some adjectives have the weak declension only, e. g. *lami*, lame; *faxi*, jubatus; *fulltíði*, full-grown, or they adopt in all genders the indeclinable termination *-a*, as *lama*.

DECLENSION OF THE PARTICIPLES.

Present Participle.

These participles have in all Teutonic dialects a substantive as well as an adjective declension; as to the former we refer to the proper place[1]. The adjective declension of the present participle again may be strong or weak.

The Gothic dialect uses the strong form in the nom. masc. only; in the weak declension the feminine is not formed after the analogy of the adjectives in *-on*, but by a more ancient theme in *-ein*, hence the fem. of *hilpanda*, helping (Germ. helfend), is *hilpandei*, gen. *hilpandeins*[2], &c.

Old High German declines the adjective form of the participle regularly after the analogy of the strong and weak declensions of the adjective; hence strong, *gebanter, gebantju, gebantaz*; weak, *gebanto, gebantá, gebanta*.

Old Saxon is fond of introducing the spirant *j* before the case-signs; as to the rest it follows the strong and weak declensions of the adjectives; e. g. strong, *helpandi, helpandi, helpandi*, gen. *helpandjes, helpandjero, helpandjes*, &c. From this example it will appear that the *j* in the nominative (as in all indeclinable cases) is vocalized into *i*. Such an *i* we find in Old High German too where the cases of the strong declension of the participle adopt the indeclinable form, as *gebanti* in all genders instead of *gebanter, gebantju, gebantaz*. This *i* must of course, like that in Old Saxon, have its origin in an ancient *j*, which in the participle declension was commonly preserved before the case-signs by the Old Norse, but rejected by the Old High German dialect.

---
[1] See the declension of the themes in *-nd*, p. 324.
[2] Compare the weak noun *managei, manageins*.

Anglo-Saxon hardly differs at all from the preceding dialects in the declension of the participle present. Like them it follows the strong and weak declension of the adjective, and like them it shows the trace of an ancient *j* before the case-signs in the termination *e* of the uninflected cases of the strong declension, as nom. *gifende*, gen. *gifendes;* weak, masc. *gifenda*, fem. neut. *gifende*.

Old Frisian follows in every respect the rules laid down for Anglo-Saxon.

Old Norse has, like Gothic, preserved in the feminine the ancient termination *i* (Goth. *ei*), which has been lost in all the other dialects. This fem. *i* has in the plural usurped the position of all other terminations; hence sing. masc. *gefandi*, *gefandi*, *gefanda*, gen. *gefanda*, *gefandi*, *gefanda*, &c. like the adjective; plur. *gefandi* in all cases and genders. But by the side of this indeclinable plural the masculine has the strong substantive forms in -*r* (from *ir*, therefore causing Umlaut), as nom. *gefend-r*, gen. *gefanda*, &c.

Preterite Participle

It follows in Gothic and all other Teutonic dialects the strong and weak declensions of the adjective.

With regard to Old High German we have however to observe that the pret. part. of the weak conjugation drops the characteristic vowel *i* (*ja*), from which cause 'Rück-Umlaut' may be produced; e.g. *gi-nant-er*, named (Germ. ge-nannt), instead of *gi-nennit-er;* but where the participle is uninflected the characteristic vowel remains, hence *gi-nennit*.

Old Norse displays a peculiarity in forming the pret. part. of weak verbs with a short radical in -*iðr* instead of -*ðr*. The forms in *iðr* may exchange the *ðr* for *nn*, an exchange we have often observed with *nð* and *nn*; hence we have the forms *taliðr*, *talið*, *talið*, *talit*, and *talinn*, *talin*(?), *talit;* and from both forms may be derived oblique cases, as gen. masc. *talið-s*, (*talin-s*?), gen. fem. *talin-nar*, plur. fem. nom. *tald-ar*, gen. *talin-na:* from which examples it would appear that case-signs beginning with a consonant prefer the form in -*n* to precede them.

Declension of the Infinitive.

The Teutonic dialects, with the exception of the Gothic and the Old Norse, possess a declension of the infinitive which is analogous to the strong declension of the noun. In Old High

German the infinitive, though in itself it is but the accusative of a verbal noun, developes a new theme in -*a*, from which it forms two new cases, a genitive and a dative; e. g. *helfan*, to help, gen. *helfannes*, dat. *helfanne*; *nerjan*, servare, gen. *nerjannes*, dat. *nerjanne*. In the same manner proceeds the Old Saxon infinitive; e g. *helpan*, gen. *helpannas(-es)*, dat. *helpanna(-e)*; *nerjan*, *nerjannas*, *nerjanna*. Here too we occasionally find the derivative *j* before the thematic vowel. Anglo-Saxon and Old Frisian have only the dative, which however occurs pretty frequently; e. g. A. S. *faranne, etenne*; O. Fris. *farane gungane*. As to the latter we observe that the *n* of the infinitive, which is usually dropped, in this case reappears.

MIDDLE TEUTONIC DECLENSIONS.

In the Middle Teutonic dialects the declensions undergo great changes, and in consequence thereof can no longer be brought under the same classification which we adopted in the Old Teutonic languages. The terminational vowels are each and all weakened into *e*, so that in the singular the declension in a can no longer be kept distinct from that in i, both *i* and *a* being rendered by *e*. The declension in u disappears altogether; and thus it happens that a distinction of three strong declensions, characterized by three different thematic vowels, becomes all but impossible. But on the other hand there continues to exist the distinction between the strong and the weak declensions—a distinction which in some dialects has been preserved up to the present day. We further observe the continuation of the different inflectional forms of the different genders, and we therefore arrange the declensions of the Middle and New Teutonic languages under the heads of Strong and Weak, and then again sub-divide according to the different genders, always indicating the thematic vowel as far as it can be traced. Features of development which are peculiar to one or the other of the Middle Teutonic dialects will be delineated in their proper places.

The weakening down of the different thematic and terminational vowels into the one flat-sounding *e* deprived the Teutonic languages of their finest phonetic ornament, and the inflectional forms, where such still continue to exist, have a wearisome sameness about them, so that it is almost difficult to say which serves the highest praise and admiration:—New High German, for its fidelity to ancient inflexional forms, though they be ever so mutilated, flat, and unmusical; or Modern English for having, with wonderful discrimination, eliminated from its system the shattered remains of inflexional forms which, their functions being performed by other means, have often become mere cumbersome ballast.

Old and Middle English.

Among late Anglo-Saxon authors Layamon alone distinguishes three declensions for the three different genders. The masculine follows, on the whole, the Anglo-Saxon declension in a, so that the genitive singular commonly shows *es*, the dative *e*, the latter being sometimes replaced by *en*. The instrumental is lost. In the plural we find *es* and *en* side by side, the latter having perhaps found its way from the dative into other cases, or being formed in analogy to the weak declension in n. The genitive plural has the termination *ene* (A. S. *ena*), besides *es* and *en*; the dative plural *en* (A. S. *um*, *on*). Nouns which in Anglo-Saxon already had the Umlaut, preserve it in the plural (though not always), and drop it in the dative singular. Examples:— sing. nom. *dai* (day)=A. S. *dǣg*; gen. *daʒes, daʒes;* dat. *daʒe, daye*. The dative is formed with *en* in *cnihten, kingen*. The nom. plur. has *es* or *en*, e. g. *dæges, dawen* (=*dagen*); *sones, sonen;* the gen. plur. *en, es, ena, ene,* as *dægen, kinges* or *kingena, eorlene;* the dat. *en*, e. g. *daʒen, dawen* (=*dagen*)[1]. The Umlaut is preserved in *fet, fæt,* by the side of which occurs also the plur. *fote* (feet); *man* has the plur. *men* and *monnen; wifman, wiman, womman* (woman), plur. *wifmen, wimen*.

The feminine nouns follow chiefly the Anglo-Saxon declension in i. In the genitive and dative singular they have the termination *e*; but in the genitive the termination *es* begins to encroach upon the legitimate *e*, so that in this case the feminine form becomes identical with the masculine and neuter. The plural shows in the nominative the terminations *es* and *en*, gen. *e*, dat. *en*, accus. *e*. But *es* often assumes the place of all other terminations in the different cases of the plural. Umlaut is preserved only in *boc*, plur. *bæc*, by the side of *boc* and *bokes*. Examples:—*burh* (borough, castle), gen. *burʒe*, dat. *burʒe*, plur. nom. *burʒes*, gen. *burʒe*, dat. *burʒen*, accus. *burʒe*.

The neuter has the regular terminations in analogy to the Anglo-Saxon declension in a, gen. *es*, dat. *e*; but in the latter, as in the dative singular masculine, we find also *en*, as *londe, londen,* dat. of *lond* (land). The plural nominative preserves the

---

[1] Concerning the relation of the consonants ʒ, *w*, *g*, to one another, and to the semi-vowel *y*, see the respective sections on Old English consonants, pp. 146 and 162.

ancient uninflected forms, e. g. *bern, scep, hors;* but also *en— scipen, leoten; childe* has the plur. *childre* and *children;* even *es* is introduced—*scipes.* The genitive plural has sometimes *ene* for *e,* as *scipene.*

The weak declension in **n** begins to be broken up since the *n* was no longer considered as an inherent part of the theme, but as an inflexional form. Consequently the *n* is often dropped or superseded by the termination *es;* but, on the other hand the *n* encroaches upon the nominative too, where *e* (rarely *a*) occupies the place of the Anglo-Saxon *a.* So again in the genitive plural, *n* is added to the ancient termination *ene* (A. S. *ena*). Examples:—sing. nom. *noma, nome; swiken;* gen. *draken, drakes;* dat. *monen, mone* (moon); plur. nom. *draken, drakes;* gen. *gumene, gumenen;* dat. *sterren, storre;* accus. *teonen, teone; namen, names.* The feminine is subject to the same fluctuations; as gen. sing. *churche* and *churches;* dat. *sunne* and *sunnen* (sun); accus. *eorben* and *eorþe;* plur. nom. *heorten* and *heortes;* gen. *wikene;* dat. accus. *wiken* and *wike;* accus. *chirchen* and *chirches.* Neut *eȝe* (eye), plur. nom. accus. *eȝene;* dat. *eȝan, eȝenen.* The themes in -*r,* such as *fæder* (father), *moder* (mother), &c., are in the singular indeclinable; in the plural we find *en, es,* and *s,* side by side; the genitive is sometimes uninflected, sometimes with the termination *ne,* as *dohter* and *dohterne* (filiarum).

The forms we have just enumerated, and which, as we have already stated, most frequently occur in Layamon, are far more extensively modified by other authors. We may limit ourselves to pointing out the most important modification, which consists in the introduction of the case-sign *es,* or *ess,* in the genitive singular and in the plural of all genders.

Old English abandons the grammatical gender, or identifies it with the sexes, and the distinction therefore of the genders in the declension is discontinued. Inflexional forms are limited to the genitive singular, the plural, and some remnants of the dative.

The PLURAL is commonly formed by the termination -*s* (-*es,* -*is,* -*ys*), as *dayes, kinges, townes;* rarely by -*e,* as *erle, monke, monþe;* more frequently by *en* or *n,* e. g. *clerken, applen, oxen, chirchen, honden* (hands), *eyen;* by -*er*—*childer, childir,* to which is added a second plural termination, *child-er-en.* The Umlaut indicates the plural in—*fot, fet; toþ, teþ; man, men; wommann, wymmen; gos, gese; kou, kie.*

With regard to the chief plural signs *en* and *es,* it must be observed that they do not in Old English represent the Anglo-Saxon plurals, the former of the weak declension in -*an,* the latter of the strong in -as, but that one or the other was adopted quite arbitrarily; hence we find O. Engl. *dayes, leuedys, riches,* for A. S. *dagas, hlæfdigan, ricu;* and O. Engl. *clereken, honden, oxen,* and *heuenden* for A. S. *clericas, hundas, oxan,* and *heafod.*

Concerning the CASES, none but the genitives and isolated traces of the dative are preserved.

The genitive singular commonly has the case-sign *-ys, -es, -'s,* as *kynges, Gode's, ȝere's* (anni); in the phrase 'kyng Kenulf ys fader,' it is doubtful whether *ys* must be taken as the genitive case-sign, or the possessive pronoun. (Koch, i. p. 415.) Sometimes it is dropped altogether, as 'for his broþer deþ,' 'þe quene fader,' 'my fader name.' Observe 'þe name of þe fadere' (Koch, loc. cit.) as the first appearance of the preposition *of* for the indication of the genitive.

The genitive plural remains where the plural sign is *es,* uninflected, as 'þe Danes king'; but if the plural does not end in *s* already, the genitive adopts the case-sign *es,* as *men, mennes;* the old case-sign *ene* is rarely met, e. g. *monkene, clerkene.*

Traces of the dative are considered to be left in the following phrases: *ys owne honde,* with his own hand; *Gode next,* nearest to God.

Middle English. The inflexional forms of the dative disappear, and the declension is limited to the formation of the plural and of the genitive case.

The PLURAL is formed by the termination *s* (*es, is, ys,* rarely *us*), e. g. *thornes, thornys, sones, folkis, thingis, thingus, hondis, hondus;* sometimes *z* for *s* in Romance words, as *citez* and *citees.* After *v* the *s* is always preceded by *e,* as *wives, knives, theves.*

The plural in *en* must be considered an exceptional mode of formation. Examples are—*kneen, shoon, oxen, ashen, eyen, sustren* (sisters), *daughtren, kien, bretheren.* We have two plural terminations, *er* and *en,* in the words *child-er-en, calv-er-en, lamb-r-en; ey-r-en* (comp. Germ. eier), by the side of the regular plural *egges* (eggs).

The plural is indicated by the ancient Umlaut in the following words: *fete, feet,* but we find also *fote; goos, gees; lous, lys; mous, mys, mees; man, men; womman, wommen, wemmen, wymmen; tooth, teeth; brother, bretheren*[1].

Some words, which in Anglo-Saxon were neuter, appear without the plural sign *s,* and consequently seem to follow the analogy of the ancient uninflected forms, e. g. *hors, scheep, swyne, thing, frut* (fruit), but also *horses, thinges, frutes; peny* has *penyes* and

---

[1] About the irregularities in the phonetic system of Old and Middle English, the student will find explanations in the chapters on Vowels and Consonants.

pens; the measures *span* and *fadme* (fathom) occur without *s*; *degrees, furlonges,* with the plural sign *s*.

The genitive singular is formed by *-s, -is, -ys* (Wycliffe), *-s, -es* (Chaucer); e. g. *Goddis, chykenys* and *cockis; widewes* (of a widow), *stones* (of a stone); *swynes flessche* (pork).

The genitive plural is not indicated after words which have the plural case-sign *s*; but where the plural is formed by other means, *es* serves to indicate the genitive case, as *mennes wittes,* men's wits. The old genitive form *ene* (A. S. *ena*) is preserved in the words *childrene* (of children), *clerkene, kyngene.*

The words of relationship, as *father, mother*, are sometimes used without, more often with, the genitive case-sign; hence 'the mother love'; but 'thi fathris brother,' 'the kinges moderes court.' Observe 'the brother of his fader' (Koch, i. p. 417).

Middle High German.

All the different terminational vowels are weakened into *e*; the features of the thematic declensions are therefore in this, as in the other Middle Teutonic dialects, greatly mutilated, sometimes hardly traceable. This circumstance causes a confusion between the declension in **a** and that in **i**, the singular of both being perfectly alike, a defect which in Old High German already becomes apparent. The plurals of both declensions are often kept strictly apart by means of the Umlaut which takes place in words with the theme in **i**. But then again there are many words that, from the nature of the radical vowel cannot have the Umlaut, as *tisch*, &c. These then can no longer be distinguished from the declension in **a**, the word *tisch* (in **i**) declining exactly like *visch* (in **a**). Words in **a**, on the other hand, sometimes adopt an inorganic Umlaut, and thus transgress upon the declension in **i**. The original cause of the Umlaut in general being no longer perceived, Umlaut is formed on blind analogy, and we thus meet with the plural *böcke, frösche* (in **i**), instead of *bocke, frosche* (in **a**). But as a rule, masculine nouns, the stem of which ends with a geminated consonant, preserve the plural in **a**, and consequently reject Umlaut, e. g. *kus* (kiss), plur. *kusse;* but in the fourteenth century already there occurs the inorganic Umlaut, plur. *küsse.*

A peculiar feature of the Middle High German declensions is the frequent elision of the *e* in the terminations. Thus in masculine monosyllabic words which end in a single consonant preceded by a short vowel, the *e* is dropped; e. g. *kil, man,* gen. *kil-s, man-s.* The same phenomenon we observe in the feminine in **a**, as *schar,* gen. plur. *scharn.* Feminine words in **i** may drop the terminational *e* of the genitive and dative, and then the word is uninflected in the singular. The neuter performs the elision of the *e* under the same conditions as the masculine; hence *sper*, gen. *sper-s; tal*, plur. *telr* for *teler*. If neuter nouns which originally belonged to the declension in **ja** drop the *e*, as they do sometimes, they may be ranked under the declension in **a**, as *ber* (for *bere*), gen. *ber-s*.

Concerning the Umlaut in the plural of the words in **i** no strict rule can be laid down, further than the remark that certain combinations of consonants seem to favour its occurrence. Some neuter nouns take in the plural the termination *er* (comp. O. H. Germ. *ir*), which termination causes Umlaut, e. g. *kalp, kelber; ort, örter; loch, locher;* most of which may also have the old uninflected plural without *er*. While some nouns always adopt this termination, others never do so.

Neuter nouns in **ja** always adopt the Umlaut, wherever this modification of the radical vowel can take place.

The weak declension adopts the same rules for the elision of the terminational *e* which we have just pointed out in the strong declension; e. g. *kol, koln; ar, arn*.

We subjoin the paradigms of the different declensions, indicating the thematic vowels as far as they can be traced.

	a		**ja**		**i**	
	Sing.	Plur.	Sing.	Plur.	Sing.	Plur.
MASCULINE.						
Nom.	*visch*	*vische*	*hirte*	*hirte*	*balc*	*belge*
Gen.	*visches*	*vische*	*hirtes*	*hirte*	*balges*	*belge*
Dat.	*vische*	*vischen*	*hirte*	*hirten*	*balge*	*belgen*
Accus.	*visch*	*vische*	*hirte*	*hirte*	*balc*	*belge*
FEMININE.						
Nom.	*gebe*	*gebe*	..	..	*kraft*	*krefte*
Gen.	*gebe*	*geben*	..	..	*krefte*	*krefte*
Dat.	*gebe*	*geben*	..	..	*krefe*	*kreften*
Accus.	*gebe*	*gebe*	..	..	*kraft*	*krefte*
NEUTER.						
Nom.	*wort*	*wort*	*künne*	*künne*	..	..
Gen.	*wortes*	*worte*	*künnes*	*künne*	..	..
Dat.	*worte*	*worten*	*künne*	*künnen*	..	..
Accus.	*wort*	*wort*	*künne*	*künne*	..	..

As to the declension in **a** the paradigms will show it to be the only one traceable in all three genders; the declension in **ja** is

DECLENSIONS.

lost in the feminine and becomes identical with that in **a**, because Old High German *i* (*—ja*) and *a* both become *e*. The neuter never had a declension in **i**. We omitted giving examples of the declension in **u**, because there are but few remnants of it left, and these are doubtful. Among these Grimm reckons such words as end in *e* without causing Umlaut, a circumstance from which he concludes that the *e* stands for the ancient *u*, e. g. *schate* (never *schete*), damage. He further takes to the declension in **u** the words *sige* (victory), *wite* (wood), *site* (manner), *vride* (peace); but in the thirteenth century all, except *vride*, drop the *e* and go after the declension in **a**. Among the ancient class in **u** may also count the neuter *vihe*, cattle; *wite* is sometimes neuter, commonly masculine.

Middle Dutch.

Masc. (**a**) *vissch, -es, -e, vissch*; plur. *vissche, -e, -en, -e*.
Fem. (**a**) sing. *miede*, plur. *mieden* throughout all cases (**i**) sing. *daet* throughout; plur. *dade, -e, -en, -e*.
Neut. (**a**) *wort, word-es, -e, wort*; plur. *wort, -e, -en, wort*. Ancient themes in **ja** end in *e* and go after the weak declension.

The Weak Declension is for the masculine, feminine, and neuter alike, e. g. *hane, -en, -en, -e*; plur. *-en* throughout.

MODERN TEUTONIC DECLENSIONS.

English.

All the case-signs of the ancient declensions have disappeared with the exception of the *'s* of the genitive singular, and the *-s* (or *-es*) which all nouns have adopted for the formation of the plural. A few remnants of the ancient forms are still extant, especially in words which indicate the plural by Umlaut; these are *brother, brether-en* (Umlaut and ancient termination *en*); *man, men; foot, feet; goose, geese; tooth, teeth; mouse, mice; louse, lice; cow, kine;—ox, ox-en*, preserves the ancient plural sign *en*, and *child, child-r-en*, has two plural terminations, *r = er* (O. H. Germ. *ir*) and *en*: the old plural *egren*, of *egg*, is disused in the modern language.

The foreign plural forms which have been adopted in English together with the foreign word—such as French *beau, beaux;* Latin *index, indices;* Greek *phenomenon, phenomena;* Hebrew *seraph, seraphim* – may still be considered as foreign, and therefore hardly to fall within the range of Teutonic grammar. The circumscriptive case-formation with the prepositions *of* and *to*, which occasionally occurs in Old English already, came more and more into use, the more the ancient case-signs disappeared.

German.

MASCULINE.

	Declension in a.			Declension in i.	
	Sing.	Plur.		Sing.	Plur.
Nom.	*fisch*	*fische*	Nom.	*balg*	*balge*
Gen.	*fisches*	*fische*	Gen.	*balges*	*balge*
Dat.	*fische*	*fischen*	Dat.	*balge*	*bälgen*
Accus.	*fisch*	*fische*	Accus.	*balg*	*balge*

The declension in **u** is extinct; the declension in **ja** is represented by one word, *kaese*, cheese, gen. *kaeses*, &c., whilst all those words which of old belonged to this declension have become weak, e. g. *hirte*, shepherd, gen. *hirten*.

Many words in **a** also have passed from the strong into the weak declension; others have done so partly, that is, forming their singular after the strong, their plural after the weak declension, as *mast*, gen. *mastes*, plur. *masten*; *stachel* (sting), gen. *stachels*, plur. *stacheln*.

The Umlaut is more extensively adopted in the plural of words in **a**; and the presence or absence of Umlaut being the only distinctive feature between the declension in **a** and that in **i**, these words may be considered as having passed into the declension in **i**. This is the case with all those words which are capable of Umlaut, i. e. having *a, o, u*, or *au* in the root, with the exception of about nine that reject the Umlaut and consequently remain faithful to the declension in **a**; e. g. *aal*, eel, plur. *aale*; *tag*, day, plur. *tage*; *hund*, dog, plur. *hunde*; *schuh*, plur. *schuhe*.

FEMININE.

	Declension in a.			Declension in i.	
	Sing.	Plur.		Sing.	Plur.
Nom.	*gabe*	*gaben*	Nom.	*kraft*	*kräfte*
Gen.	*gabe*	*gaben*	Gen.	*kraft*	*kräfte*
Dat.	*gabe*	*gaben*	Dat.	*kraft*	*kräften*
Accus.	*gabe*	*gaben*	Accus.	*kraft*	*kräfte*

The declensions in **ja** and **u** are extinct.

The singular has dropped all inflectional forms.

Words in **i** which cannot have the Umlaut, follow the declension in **a** and take in the plural the termination *en*, e. g. *arbeit*,

DECLENSIONS.

work, labour, plur. *arbeiten;* the same course is pursued by some words which are capable of Umlaut, as *burg* (castle), *geburt* (birth), *that* (deed), *jugend* (youth), *tugend* (virtue), plur. *burgen*, &c. Some pass altogether into the declension in **a**, and consequently adopt the *e* (the representative of the ancient *a*) in the singular, e. g. *eiche* (oak), *geschichte* (history, story), *bluete*, (blossom); M. H. Germ. *eich, geschiht, bluot*, plur. *eiche, geschihte*, &c. From this old plural form the *e* probably penetrated into the modern singular.

NEUTER. Declension in **a**: *wort*, gen. *wortes*, is declined like the masc. *fisch*.

The plural in *er* is more frequent, and causes Umlaut; e. g. *buch* (book), *bücher, dach* (roof), *dächer*.

Words in **ja**, which on the earlier stage of Modern German ended in *e*, as *bette, bilde, glücke*, have now dropped the *e* and go after the declension in **a**, as *bett*, gen. *bettes*.

Weak Declension.

To this declension belong all words which in the nominative singular end in *e*; they have the termination *en* through all other cases of the singular and plural; e. g. *hase*, hare, gen. *hasen*.

Some drop the final *e* of the nominative singular, as *baer*, bear; *fürst*, prince; *graf*, earl; *herr*, lord, master; *mensch*, man, homo. This apocope has perhaps been caused by a tendency in the mentioned words towards the strong declension. The same course towards the strong declension, though from a different starting-point, we observe in words such as *bogen*, bow, gen. *bogens*, for the M. H. Germ. *boge, bogen*—words in which the inflexional *en* seems to have been mistaken for a derivative termination, and then were supplied with the genitive case-sign -*s* of the strong declension. To this class belong *gräben*, ditch; *brunnen*, well; *glauben*, faith; *haufen*, heap; *kuchen*, cake; *namen*, name; *willen*, will; *frieden*, peace; *schatten*, shade. Some of them preserve the ancient *e* by the side of *en*, as *friede, schatte, glaube, wille*. Their origin in the weak declension is further recognized by the fact of their having no Umlaut, which always occurs with originally strong nouns in *en*, as *wágen*, carriage, *waegen; boden*, floor, *boeden*. In but few instances, and then erroneously, have such words as were originally of weak declension taken the Umlaut, e. g. *garten*, garden, *garten; gräben*, ditch, *graeben; mágen*, stomach, *maegen; krágen*, collar, *kraegen*.

The M. H. Germ. *spor* (spur), *sporn*, ought, in New High German, to have become *spore, sporen*, or (like *bogen*) *sporen, sporens*; but it adopted a mixed form, i. e. the singular of the strong and the plur. of the weak declension, *sporn*, gen. *spornes*, plur. *spornen*.

The following words pass altogether from the weak into the strong declension: *ár* and *adler* (eagle), *mond* (moon), *keim*, (germ), *stern* (star), declension in **a**; *hán* (cock), *salm* (salmon), *schwán* (swan), *herzog* (duke), declension in **i**.

We find digression from the strong (in **a**) into the weak declension in the words *held*, hero; *rábe*, gen. *raben*, for the old *raben, rabens*,—which shows the case of *bogen*, &c., inverted: from the strong in **ja**, *hirte* (shepherd), *rücke* (back), *weize* (wheat); but the latter again follow the analogy of *löge, bogen*, and return into the strong declension in the forms *rücken, weizen*, gen. **rückens, weizens**.

The feminine of the weak declension is identical with the feminine of the strong declension in **a**.

The weak neuter nouns *herz* (heart), *auge* (eye), *or* (ear), have adopted a strong singular, gen. *herzens, auges, ores;* but the plural continues to follow the weak declension.

Of the anomalous forms, *vater* (father) and *schwager* (brother-in-law) now follow the declension in **i**; *mutter* (mother) and *tochter* (daughter) are in the singular unchangeable, in the plural they take the Umlaut, *mütter, töchter;* *schwester* (sister) and *schwíger* (mother-in-law) are in the singular indeclinable, in the plural weak. *mann* has the plural *mannen* and *männer*.

Examples:—

STRONG. Masculine in **a** :—*ál*, eel ; *berg*, mountain ; *biß*, bite ; *dieb*, thief ; *fisch*, fish ; *freund*, friend ; *feind*, enemy ; *geist*, spirit (cf. ghost); *hirsch*, stag ; *hund*, dog, hound ; *krieg*, war ; *leib*, body ; *pfeil*, arrow ; *stein*, stone ; *sper*, spear ; *tág*, day ; *theil*, deal ; *tisch*, table ; *weg*, way ; *wein*, wine ; *zwerg*, dwarf ; *zweig*, twig. In **i** :—*ast*, branch ; *bach*, brook ; *balg*, skin, hide ; *baum*, tree ; *fluß*, river ; *frosch*, frog ; *fuß*, foot ; *fuchs*, fox ; *grund*, ground ; *hóf*, court, yard ; *koch*, cook ; *mund*, mouth ; *pfád*, path ; *pflug*, plough ; *wolf*.

Feminine in **a** :—*amme*, nurse ; *bere*, berry ; *bitte*, prayer ; *blume*, flower (cf. bloom); *ere*, honour ; *henne*, hen ; *fliege*, fly ; *minne*, love ; *náse*, nose ; *quelle*, fountain ; *rute*, rod ; *sage*, tale, saga ; *schwalbe*, swallow ; *sonne*, sun ; *straße*, street ; *woche*, week ; *zunge*, tongue. In **i** :—*angst*, fear, anxiety ; *bank*, bench ; *brust*, breast ; *faust*, fist ; *gans*, goose ; *hand ;* *kraft*, strength (cf. craft) ; *kunst*, art ; *luft*, air ; *macht*, power, might ; *nacht*, night.

Neuter in **a** :—*beil*, hatchet ; *brot*, bread ; *ding*, thing ; *eis* ice ; *fleisch*, flesh ; *gold* ; *hár*, hair ; *heu*, hay ; *jar*, year ; *knie*, knee ; *maß*, measure ; *pferd*, horse ; *roß*, horse, steed ; *scháf*, sheep ; *schiff*, ship ; *schwert*, sword ; *thier*, animal ; *vih*, pecus ; *werk*, work ; *wort*, word.

WEAK. Masculine :—*affe*, ape ; *búbe*, boy ; *drache*, dragon ; *falke*, falcon ; *gotze*, idol ; *hase*, hare ; *junge*, youth ; *knábe*, boy ; *laie*, layman ; *lowe*, lion ; *ochse*, ox ; *rise*, giant ; *waise*, orphan ; *zeuge*, witness.

Concerning feminine and neuter nouns, see above.

Dutch.

This dialect no longer distinguishes between strong and weak declensions.

All nouns may, instead of the inflexional forms of the genitive and dative, use the circumscriptive cases formed by the prepositions *van* (of) and *aan* = *án* (to) ; e. g. *van den vader, aan den vader ; van de vaders, aan de vaders ; van de moeder, aan de moeder ; van de moeders, aan de moeders ; van het boek, aan het boek ; van de boeken, aan de boeken*, just as English *of the father, to the father, of the book*, &c.

MASC. All nouns have in the genitive singular the case-sign -*s* (after ft, cht, st, sch, -*es*), in the plural -*en* throughout ; or in other words, they follow the strong declension in the singular, the weak in the plural ; hence *sten* (stone), formerly of the strong declension, has in the genitive *stens*, in the plural *stenen* ; and *han* (cock), formerly weak, has likewise *hans* in the genitive singular, *hanen* in the plural. The genitive and dative singular, as a rule, show no inflexional forms, though occasionally the dative singular still preserves the ancient case-sign -*e*, especially where it is preceded by the article, as *den vosse*, vulpi.

Nouns ending in *el, em, er, ár*, may form the plural with *s* ; e. g. *vader*, father, plur. *vaders* ; *wágen*, carriage, *wágens* ; *dienár*, servant, *dienárs* ; but the weak forms *vaderen*, &c. also occur, especially in the higher style of writing ; words in *en* only take always *s*.

Sometimes we meet in the nominative singular with the termination *e* which is the remnant of the ancient termination or of the weak declension, as in *vrede*, peace ; *rugge*, back ; *yonge*, youth ; *ewe*, heir ; *name*, name.

The word *veulen*, foal, gen. *veulens*, passes from the weak into the strong declension, analogous to the Germ. *bogen, bogens*, &c. (vide supra, p. 351.)

The weak genitives in *en* are exceptional, as *heren* (domini), *graven* (comitis), *menschen* (hominis), *hertogen* (ducis), which in High German are the regular forms, *herren, grafen, menschen;* but *herzogs.*

FEM. The feminine nouns take in the genitive and dative singular the case-sign *e*, in the plural *en* through all cases, the former being derived from the strong, the latter from the weak declension. Hence *kracht*, power (Germ. kraft, cf. craft), gen. *krachte,* dat. *krachte;* plur. *krachten* (formerly of the strong declension), and *tong*, tongue, gen. *tonge*, dat. *tonge*, plur. *tongen* (formerly of the weak declension).

As in the masculine, nouns in *el, en, er,* may form the plural in *-s*, as *netels, splinters.*

Feminine nouns which originally ended in *ja* or *a*, or belonged to the weak declension, sometimes preserve the *e*, the weakened form of the ancient termination, and then all the cases of the singular are alike; e. g. *árde*, earth; *béde*, prayer; *duive*, dove; *henne*, hen; *koude*, cold; *stemme*, voice, or simply *stem, hen*, &c.

The declension of the NEUTER coincides with that of the masculine.

Here also the plural in *-s* may occur, as *waters, bloempjes,* &c.

The ancient plural form of the neuter in *er* is in the refined style followed by the plural sign *-en*, in the common language by *-s*, e. g. *ben*, bone; *benderen, benders;* *blád*, leaf (Germ. blatt); *ey*, egg; *kind*, child; *lam*, lamb; plur. *kinderen, lammeren.* But these words may also have the regular plural in *-en*, as *blád, bláden;* so that consequently certain words may adopt three different forms, as *blád*, plur. *bláden,* or *bláderen,* or *bláders.*

The old termination *-e* occurs occasionally in the nominative singular, as *herte* (heart), *bedde* (bed), for *hert, bed.*

Examples:—

MASC. *árd*, kind; *arm; ber*, bear; *bom*, tree; *dag*, day; *dief*, thief; *disch*, table (Germ. tisch); *dod*, death; *gast*, guest; *gest*, ghost; *grond*, ground; *hond*, dog (Germ. hund, cf. hound); *kus*, kiss; *mond*, mouth; *slap*, sleep; *smid*, smith; *sten*, stone (Germ. stein); *visch*, fish; *vloed*, flood; *vos*, fox; *vriend*, friend; *wolf; worm; weg*, way.

FEM. *ár*, ear of corn (Germ. aere); *bruid*, bride; *dad*, deed; *deugd*, virtue; *deur*, door; *er*, honour (Germ. ere); *gans*, goose; *geit*, goat (Germ. geiß); *jeugd*, youth; *kracht*, power (Germ. kraft, cf. craft); *lucht*, air (Germ. luft); *mágd* and *meid*, maid; *min*, love; *muis*, mouse; *stad*, town; *tál*, language; *vrouw*, wife

(Germ. frau); *wereld*, world; *wik*, vicus; *zák*, thing (Germ. sache, cf. sake); *ziel*, soul (Germ. sele).

NEUT. *bed*; *blád*, leaf (Germ. blatt); *bloed*, blood; *dal*, dale; *del*, deal; *ding*, thing; *goud*, gold; *hár*, hair; *hófd*, head; *huis*, house; *jar*, year; *kruis*, cross; *lid*, limb; *lod*, lead; *mel*, meal; *scháp*, sheep; *werk*, work; *word*, word; *zout*, salt; *zwerd*, sword.

Swedish.

	MASCULINE IN a		IN ja		IN i		IN u	
	Sing.	Plur.	Sing.	Plur.	Sing.	Plur.	Sing.	Plur.
Nom.	*fisk*	*fiskar*	*fiskare*	*fiskare*	*vaen*	*vänner*	*sôn*	*soener*
Gen.	*fisks*	*fiskars*	*fiskares*	*fiskares*	*vaens*	*vänners*	*sôns*	*soeners*
Dat.	*fisk*	*fiskar*	*fiskare*	*fiskares*	*vaen*	*vänner*	*sôn*	*soener*
Accus.	*fisk*	*fiskar*	*fiskare*	*fiskare*	*vaen*	*vänner*	*sôn*	*soener*

The declension in ja shows the singular and plural perfectly alike. It comprises many words ending in *are* (Engl. and Germ. *er*; comp. *fiskare* with Engl. *fisher*, Germ. *fischer*).

Most Old Norse nouns in u have passed into the declension in a: some preserve the Umlaut; as *örn*, eagle; *biorn*, bear, plur. *ornar*, *biornar*; others drop it, as *vall*, valley, *tråd*, thread, plur. *vallar*, *trädar*.

	FEMININE IN a		IN ja	IN i		IN u	
	Sing.	Plur.		Sing.	Plur.	Sing.	Plur.
Nom.	*sôl*	*sôlar*	wanting.	*kraft*	*krafter*	*tand*	*tänder*
Gen.	*sôls*	*sôlars*		*krafts*	*krafters*	*tands*	*tänder*
Dat.	*sôl*	*sôlar*		*kraft*	*krafter*	*tand*	*tänder*
Accus.	*sôl*	*sôlar*		*kraft*	*krafter*	*tand*	*tänder*

The criterion of the declension in u is, in the feminine as in the masculine, the Umlaut; the declension in i is recognized by the absence of the Umlaut.

	NEUTER IN a		IN ja	
	Sing.	Plur.	Sing.	Plur.
Nom.	*ord*	*ord*	*kynne*	*kynne*
Gen.	*ords*	*ords*	*kynnes*	*kynnes*
Dat.	*ord*	*ord*	*kynne*	*kynne*
Accus.	*ord*	*ord*	*kynne*	*kynne*

The singular and plural of the neuter declensions are identical. The plural sometimes shows the case-sign -*r*, as *klaede*, *klaeder*, and *lander, stander, viner,* by the side of the regular plural *land, stand, vin.* They are commonly used with the suffixed article, e. g. *kynnen, riken.*

Weak Declension.

	Masculine.		Feminine.	
	Sing.	Plur.	Sing.	Plur.
Nom.	*hane*	*hânar*	*tunga*	*tungor*
Gen.	*hanes* (-as)	*hânars*	*tungas* (-os)	*tungor*
Dat.	*hane* (-a)	*hânar* (-om)	*tunga* (-o)	*tungor* (-om)
Accus.	*hane* (-a)	*hânar*	*tunga* (-o)	*tungor*

	Neuter.			
	Sing.	Plur.	Sing.	Plur.
Nom.	*hierta*	*hiertan*	*oega*	*oegon*
Gen.	*hiertas*	*hiertans*	*oegas*	*oegons*
Dat.	*hierta*	*hiertan*	*oega*	*oegon*
Accus.	*hierta*	*hiertan*	*oega*	*oegon*

The terminations given in parentheses are used in old documents.

Feminine nouns occur in the singular without the *a*, as *rós*, rose; *våg*, wave (Germ. woge).

Anomalous.

fader, broder, form the plural *faedar, broedar,* or *faedrar, broedrar; moder, moedrar; dotter, dottrar; man, manner,* in compounds *man.*

The feminine nouns *gas,* goose; *lús,* louse; *mús,* mouse, have the plural *gäss, loss, moss.*

Monosyllabic stems ending in a vowel commonly are inflected regularly, but sometimes they drop the inflexional vowel.

Examples:—

STRONG. Masculine in **a**:—*arm; dag,* day; *dâl,* dale; *fisk,* fish; *häst,* horse; *hund,* dog; *hoeg,* hill (Germ. hügel); *lag,* law; *orm,* worm; *sten,* stone; *stol,* chair; *ulf,* wolf. In **ja**:— words ending in *are;* e. g. *älskare,* lover; *fiskare,* fisher, &c. In **i**:—*balk,* beam (Germ. balken); *ed,* oath; *gast,* guest; *led,* limb; *rätt,* right; *sed,* mos (Germ. sitte); *skald,* poet; *sven,* boy, swain; *vaen,* friend. In **u**:—*fot,* plur. *fötter; stâd,* plur. *staeder; son, soener.*

Feminine in a:—*aln*, all; *boek*, beech; *ek*, oak; *húd*, skin (Germ. haut); *jord*, earth; *mân*, mane; *sjael*, soul; *skâm*, shame; *sol*, sun; *varld*, world. In i:—*boen*, prayer; *hielp*, help; *hind*, hind; *kraft*, power; *loen*, reward (Germ. lon); *mín*, mien; *noed*, need; *ort*, wort; *sak*, cause; *tíd*, time, tide. In u:—*bok*, book, plur. *boeker*; *hand*, hand, *händer*; *nat*, night, *natter*; *rot*, root, *rotter*; *tand*, tooth, *tänder*.

Neuter in a:—*år*, year; *barn*, child; *ben*, bone; *berg*, mountain; *blád*, leaf; *diur*, animal (Germ. thier); *folk*, people, folk; *glás*, glass; *haf* sea; *har*, hair; *lamb*; *land*; *lius*, light; *ord*, word; *sar*, wound, sore; *svärd*, sword; *tágel*, horse-tail; *namn*, name; *vatten*, water; *hufvud*, head. In ja:—*aerende*, message; *apple*, apple; *hvete*, wheat; *klaede*, dress; *kynne*, kin; *minne*, memory; *näste*, nest; *värde*, worth.

WEAK. Masculine:—*ande*, spirit; *biälke*, beam; *boge*, bow (Germ. bogen); *hare*, hare; *háne*, cock; *lunge*, lung; *mâne*, moon; *oxe*, ox.

Feminine:—*aska*, ashes; *boena*, bean; *hoena*, hen; *manniska*, man (Germ. mensch); *naesa*, nose; *qvinna*, woman; *stierna*, star.

Neuter:—*hierta*, heart; *nysta*, glomus; *oega*, eye (Germ. auge); *oera*, ear.

Danish.

MASCULINE IN a		IN ja		IN i		IN u	
Sing.	Plur.	Sing.	Plur.	Sing.	Plur.	Sing.	Plur.
Nom. *fisk*	*fiske*	*fisker*	*fiskere*	*vên*	*venner*	*fôd*	*födder*
Gen. *fisks*	*fiskes*	*fiskers*	*fiskeres*	*vêns*	*venners*	*fôds*	*födders*
Dat. *fisk*	*fiske*	*fisker*	*fiskere*	*vên*	*venner*	*fôd*	*födder*
Accus. *fisk*	*fiske*	*fisker*	*fiskere*	*vên*	*venner*	*fôd*	*födder*

Some words in a suffer syncope in the plural, as *finger*, plur. *fingre*, whilst those in ja always preserve all syllables intact, and thus keep their declension distinct from that in a, hence *fisker*, plur. always *fiskere*, not *fiskre*.

The declension in i is characterized by its rejection of the Umlaut, that in u for introducing it in the plural.

FEMININE IN a		IN i		IN u	
Sing.	Plur.	Sing.	Plur.	Sing.	Plur.
Nom. *sôl*	*sôle*	*sâg*	*sâger*	*tand*	*tänder*
Gen. *sôls*	*sôles*	*sâgs*	*sâgers*	*tands*	*tänder*
Dat. *sôl*	*sôle*	*sâg*	*sâger*	*tand*	*tänder*
Accus. *sôl*	*sôle*	*sâg*	*sâger*	*tand*	*tänder*

	Sing.	Plur.	Sing.	Plur.
			Neuter in a	
Nom.	ord	ord	fâd	fâde
Gen.	ords	ords	fâds	fâdes
Dat.	ord	ord	fâd	fâde
Accus.	ord	ord	fâd	fâde

The termination *e* is chiefly used in the plural of words which *originally* had a short radical, though this radical may now be long. This *e* is remarkable as being the representative of the ancient termination *u*, and still more striking is the Umlaut in *barn*, child, plur. *börn*, an Umlaut which was originally caused by the termination *u*, and which was preserved after the ending vowel had been dropped.

The plural in *er* occurs in the nouns *bryst*, breast, *brýster*; *hoved*, head, *hoveder*; *sted*, place, *steder*, &c.

Nouns in **ja** have frequently passed into the declension in **a**; those which remained faithful to their declension have, as in Swedish, the singular in *e*, and in the plural, if they form it at all, *er*, or the suffixed article; e. g. *klaede*, dress; plur. *klaeder*.

Weak Declension.

	Masculine.		Feminine.	Neuter.	
	Sing.	Plur.		Sing.	Plur.
Nom.	hâne	hâner	Like Masculine.	hierte	hierten
Gen.	hânes	hâners		hiertes	hierten
Dat.	hâne	hâner		hierte	hierten
Accus.	hâne	hâner		hierte	hierten

Some weak nouns suffer apocope of the *e* in the singular, as *aand*, spirit; *oxe*, ox, has the plural *oxene*, *oxne*, not *oxer*, perhaps from a singular *oxen* of the strong declension.

Examples:—

STRONG. Masculine in **a**:—*biorn*, bear; *dag*, day; *dâl*, dale; *dom*, doom; *droem*, dream; *fisk*, fish; *hest*, horse; *örn*, eagle; *skov*, wood, grove; *himmel*, heaven (Germ. himmel); *engel*, angel (Germ. engel); *finger*; *fugl*, bird (Germ. vogel); *ravn*, raven. In **ja**:—words ending in *er*: *fisker*, fisher, &c. In **i**:—*balg*, hide; *ed*, oath; *flod*, river, flood; *giest*, guest; *lem*, limb; *ret*, right.

Feminine in **a**:—*boeg*, beech; *borg*, castle; *brud*, bride; *eg*, oak; *hiord*, flock; *skam*, shame; *siael*, soul; *sol*, sun. In **i**:—

art, kind, genus; *boen,* prayer; *dyd,* virtue; *ged,* goat; *hov,* hoof; *hud,* skin, hide (Germ. haut); *jord,* earth; *sag,* cause (cf. sake); *tid,* time.

Neuter in a:—*aar,* year; *aeg,* egg; *bierg,* mountain; *dŷr,* animal; *fad,* vessel; *led,* limb; *haar,* hair; *liv,* life; *lys,* light; *ord,* word; *saar,* wound, sore.

WEAK. Masculine:—*åbe,* ape; *bue,* bow; *hane,* cock; *hare,* hare; *aand,* spirit.

Feminine:—*due,* dove; *kone,* woman; *pige,* girl; *qvinde,* wife; *tunge,* tongue.

Neuter:—*hierte,* heart; *oeje,* eye; *oere,* ear.

DECLENSION OF THE ADJECTIVE IN THE MIDDLE AND NEW TEUTONIC DIALECTS.

Old and Middle English.

Among late Anglo-Saxon authors, Layamon still declines the adjective with as much completeness as Modern German at least. He keeps up the distinction of the strong and weak form, of the genders and numbers. The paradigm of his strong declension looks as follows:—

	SINGULAR.			PLURAL.
	Masc.	Fem.	Neut.	Masc. Fem. Neut.
Nom.	*blind*	*blinde*	*blind*	*blinde*
Gen.	*blindes*	*blindre*	*blindes*	*blindere*
Dat.	*blinde(n)*	*blindre*	*blinde(n)*	*blinden*
Accus.	*blinde*	*blinde*	*blind*	*blinde*

In the Ormulum the declension of the adjective has nearly disappeared altogether. Old English has only *e* to indicate the plural, a form made up in Middle English with the adjective used as a substantive.

Middle High German.

Strong Declension.

	MASCULINE.		FEMININE.	
	Sing.	Plur.	Sing.	Plur.
Nom.	blind-er	blind-e	blind-iu	blind-e
Gen.	blind-es	blind-er (ere)	blind-er (ere)	blind-er (ere)
Dat.	blind-em (eme)	blind-en	blind-er (ere)	blind-en
Accus.	blind-en	blind-e	blind-e	blind-e

	NEUTER.	
	Sing.	Plur.
Nom.	blind-eʒ	blind-iu
Gen.	blind-es	blind-er (ere)
Dat.	blind-em (eme)	blind-en
Accus.	blind-eʒ	blind-iu

The terminations *may* be dropped in all genders and cases.

The Umlaut before the inflexional *iu* (which stands for the Old High German *ju*) does not occur in the more ancient manuscripts.

Syncope and apocope of the *e* mute occur in the same manner as with the substantive. As to the terminations which have two vowels, as *eme, ere*, &c., the following general rule may be laid down: monosyllabic adjectives with a long radical preserve the first inflexional vowel and reject the second; those with a short radical preserve the second and reject the first after the consonants *l, m, r,* e. g. dat. sing. *-eme, blind-em;* but *hol-me, bar-me, lam-me;* fem. *-ere, blind-er,* but *hol-re, bar-re, lam-re.*

The thematic *ja* shows some trace of its existence in nom. *-e,* as *boese,* bad; *enge,* narrow; *mitte,* medius; *naehe,* near, &c. All adjectives of this kind have Umlaut if the radical is capable of it.

Weak Declension.

Masc., fem., and neut.:—*blind-e, blind-en,* &c., the same as the weak declension of the noun. The rules applying to *e* mute are also the same.

Some adjectives are used only in the weak form.

The ancient suffix *ja*[1] is preserved in the *e* of the nom. *herte,* hard, never *harte;* its inflexions are regular, and the Umlaut keeps its place throughout.

---
[1] Compare the Old Teutonic adjective, p. 331 sqq.

Middle Dutch.

Strong Declension.

	MASCULINE.		FEMININE.		NEUTER.	
	Sing.	Plur.	Sing.	Plur.	Sing.	Plur.
Nom.	blint	blind-e	blint	blind-e	blint	blint
Gen.	blind-es	blind-re	blind-re	blind-re	blind-es	blind-re
Dat.	blind-en	blind-en	blind-re	blind-en	blind-en	blind-en
Accus.	blind-en	blind-e	blind-e	blind-e	blint	blint

The nominative singular is without any inflexion; all other cases of the three genders *may* be used without such.

The genitive and dative feminine and the genitive plural may end in -*er*, or -*re* (from *ere*); but the use of one or the other of these terminations does not, as in Middle High German, depend on the nature of the radical vowel, but on the consonant preceding the termination; thus *re* always after *n*, *nd*; *er* after *d*, *t*, *g*, *k*, &c.

The suffix *ja* is preserved in the nominative termination *e*; as *dinne*, thin; *clene*, small (Germ. klein).

Weak Declension.

The terminations of the weak declension are, sing. -*e*, *en*, -*en*, *en*; plur. -*e*, -*en*, -*en*, -*e*, for the three genders.

These terminations differ from the Middle Dutch weak noun by using accus. sing. *en* for *e*, and nom. accus. plur. *e* for *en*; but they are identical with the terminations of the weak noun and adjective in Middle High German.

English.

The adjective has no inflectional forms.

German.

Strong Declension.

	MASCULINE.		FEMININE.		NEUTER.	
	Sing.	Plur.	Sing.	Plur.	Sing.	Plur.
Nom.	blind-er	blind-e	blind-e	blind-e	blind-es	blind-e
Gen.	blind-es	blind-er	blind-er	blind-er	blind-es	blind-er
Dat.	blind-em	blind-en	blind-er	blind-er	blind-em	blind-en
Accus.	blind-en	blind-e	blind-e	blind-e	blind-es	blind-e

In the nominative and accusative singular and plural of all genders the uninflected form *blind* may be used.

The Middle High German *iu* is lost. The Middle High German neuter termination -*eʒ* first was rendered by *eß*, next passed into -*es*, so that now the nominative and accusative neuter have the same case-sign as the genitive.

The genitive and dative singular feminine, and the genitive plural have always simply *er* for the Middle High German *ere, re, er*.

The rule of syncope is no longer of any great consequence. All polysyllabic adjectives should have syncope like nouns; e. g. nouns, gen. *engels, fingers, regens*; adjectives, gen. *dunkels, heiters, elends*; but the *e* is always preserved, hence *dunkeles*, &c. But the accusative singular masculine and the dative plural *may* have syncope, as *dunkeln* for *dunkelen*. Instead of the terminational *e*, however, they prefer to throw off the derivative *e*, as *dunkler, heitrer, dunklen*; the accusative singular masculine and dative plural have better *dunkeln* than *dunklen*.

ja. Many adjectives have dropped its last remnant, the nominative termination *e*, as *mild, dürr, schoen*, for *milde*, &c. In some adjectives it is preserved in the uninflected form, e. g. *irre, enge, boese*.

Dutch.

The strong and weak declensions are identical. (Grimm.)

	Masculine.		Feminine.		Neuter.	
	Sing.	Plur.	Sing.	Plur.	Sing.	Plur.
Nom.	blind-e	blind-e	blind-e	blind-e	blind-e	blind-e
Gen.	blind-en	blind-en	blind-e	blind-en	blind-en	blind-en
Dat.	blind-en	blind-en	blind-e	blind-en	blind-en	blind-en
Accus.	blind-en	blind-e	blind-e	blind-e	blind-e	blind-e

When without the article, the nominative and accusative masculine have the termination *e*, the neuter *r*, as *goede wijn, witte wol, helder water*. Is this *r* the representative of an ancient *s*?

The genitive forms of the above paradigm are hardly ever used, this case being commonly circumscribed with the preposition *van*. In the higher style of writing there is the old genitive preserved, namely masc. *blind-es*, fem. *blind-er*, neut. *blindes*, plur. **blind-er**.

Sometimes the nominative singular occurs uninflected: *blind*.

Swedish.

Strong Declension.

In the singular the inflexions have disappeared, with the exception of the neuter termination -*t*, which is added to the preceding consonant of the stem; but it is omitted after the combinations *tt, et, nt, st, ms, rs*. Adjectives ending in a vowel take in the neuter *tt*; e. g. *blå-tt*, blew; *fri-tt*, free; *ra-tt*, raw. Those in *n* drop this consonant before the neuter *t*; e. g. *liten*, little, *litet*; *egen*, own (Germ. eigen), *eget*.

The plural has the weak forms throughout.

Weak Declension.

In the singular the masculine has in all cases the *e*, the feminine and neuter have *a*; in the plural all cases of the three genders have the termination *a*. Exceptionally, for instance when the adjective is used as a substantive, the old genitive singular still appears, e. g. masc. *blindes*, plur. *blindas*.

Syncope occurs in polysyllabic adjectives, as *gamle, gamla*, for *gammale, gammala*.

The declension of the adjective in **Old Swedish** is deserving of special notice, as it is commonly used in the translation of the Bible.

Strong Declension.

	Masculine.		Feminine.		Neuter.	
	Sing.	Plur.	Sing.	Plur.	Sing.	Plur.
Nom.	*blind-er*	*blind-e*	*blind*	*blind-a*	*blind-t*	*blind-t*
Gen.	*blind-s*	*blind-es*	*blind-s*	*blind-as*	*blind-s*	*blind-es*
Dat.	*blind-om*	*blind-om*	*blind-e*	*blind-om*	*blind-o*	*blind-om*
Accus.	*blind-an*	*blind-e*	*blind-a*	*blind-a*	*blind-t*	*blind-t*

Weak Declension.

	Singular.		Plural.
	Masc.	Fem. and Neut.	Masc. Fem. Neut.
Nom.	*blind-e*	*blind-a*	*blind-a*
Gen.	*blind-es*	*blind-as*	*blind-as*
Dat.	*blind-e*	*blind-a*	*blind-a*
Accus.	*blind-e*	*blind-a*	*blind-a*

Danish.

The singular of the strong declension as in Swedish. The neuter -*t* is dropped after *t* (=*tt*), *st, es;* *d* and *sk* sometimes retain, sometimes drop it. Vowels take *t* (= *tt* Swed.), e. g. *blaa-t,* blew; *nig-t,* new: some refuse it. Adjectives in *en* drop the *n* before *t.*

The plural takes the weak declension in *e.* Syncope as in Swedish, e. g. *gamle.* In Old Danish there are traces of perfect inflexions, masc. nom. sing. *-er,* gen. *-s,* accus. *-en.*

The weak declension has *e* throughout.

THE VERB.

Verbs are either of primary or secondary formation; that is, the verbal theme is formed directly from the root, or it is derived from a nominal or another verbal theme. Verbs belonging to the former class are commonly called primary verbs or stem-verbs, those of the latter, derivative verbs. Thus the Gothic *baíran*, our English *to bear*, are primary or stem-verbs, because the Gothic theme or stem *baír-a-*, for †*bir-a-*, is formed directly from the root *bar*; but the Gothic *saltan*, our English *to salt*, are derivative verbs, because the Gothic theme or stem *salt-a-* is originally a nominal theme, the base of the Gothic and English noun *salt*, from which the verb is derived.

The root is the first element of words, verbs as well as nouns: but a root is not a verb; to become such it must be provided with personal terminations, which are as indispensable to a verb as the case-signs are to a noun. The terminations of the persons may be added to the root immediately, or by means of one or more connective letters; in the former case the root itself is the verbal theme, in the latter the theme must be formed by means of a suffix. Thus, for instance, take the root *as* (to be) and the termination of the 1st pers. sing. *ma*, weakened to *mi*, and you will derive from these two elements the Sansk. *as-mi*, the Gr. $\epsilon\mathrm{i}\mu\iota = \epsilon\sigma\text{-}\mu\iota$, the Lat. *sum* = *es-u-m*, the Goth. *i-m*, the A. S. *eo-m*, the English *a-m*. But given the root *bhar* (to bear) and the termination of the 1st pers. sing. *mi*, we require a connective in order to join the latter to the former; and this connective we find in the suffix -*a*- which we add to the root *bhar*, and thus form the theme *bhar-a-*, and from this, by means of the personal termination, the 1st pers. sing. *bhar-á-mi*, I bear. In the same manner the Gr. $\phi\epsilon\rho\text{-}o\text{-}\mu\epsilon\nu$ (we bear) is formed from the theme $\phi\epsilon\rho\text{-}o\text{-}$ ($o = a$), root $\phi\epsilon\rho$ (to bear), the Lat. *veh-i-mus* (we convey), from the theme *veh-i-* ($\iota = a$), root *veh*, and the Goth. *baíra* (I bear), dropping the personal termination, from the theme *baír-a-* = †*bir-a*, root *bar*.

By means of the personal terminations we distinguish the three grammatical persons in three numbers, the singular, dual, and plural; so that the Aryan languages, in their most primitive type known to us, required nine personal terminations. These terminations are the roots of the respective personal pronouns, added to the root or theme of the verb, a formation which we might imitate by compounding the verb and our personal pronouns, as *love-I, love-thou, love-he*, &c.

Another element in the formation of the verb which craves attention in proportion as it modifies the form of the verb, is the mood or modus. Let us take again the roots *as* (to be) and *bhar* (to bear). Of these roots we got the indicative by adding the personal terminations directly to the root or the theme developed from it. Now if we wish to express with the same roots the relations of any other mood, the optative for instance, we require a distinct suffix for this purpose. The root *as* and the termination *mi*, when joined, yield the 1st sing. indic. *as-mi*: in order to obtain the optative the Aryan languages avail themselves of the suffix *-ya-*, which they very properly place between the root or theme and the personal termination. Thus then we have the root *as*, the theme *bhar-a-*, and the personal termination *mi*, typical forms which may be modified but never suppressed. The suffix expressing the modus of the action takes its place between them, and thus we get the optative primitive *as-ya-m* (*m* for *mi*), Sansk. *s-ya-m;* Gr. εἴην = ἐσ-γη-μ, Lat. *sim* = *s-ié-m* = ᵀ*es-ié-m* ; and of the theme primitive *bhara-* we get *bhara-i-m* ($i=ya$), Sansk. *bibhr-íy-a*, theme *bibhar-*, Gr. διδο-ίη-ν, theme διδο-, Goth. pres. tense *bairau* = ᵗ*bira-i-u* = ᵗ*bira-i-m*, prim. *bhara-i-m*, theme *baíra-*, prim. *bhara-* ; perf. tense *ber-ja-u*, prim. *bhabhar-yá-m*, theme *ber*, prim. *bhabhár-*. As the optative by *-ya-*, so the subjunctive is formed by means of the suffix *-a-*, while the indicative has no mood suffix at all, and the imperative is merely the theme with the personal termination in the vocative, and may rightly be called a verbal interjection.

A third function to be performed by the verb is that of expressing relations of time; the modified forms assumed by the verb for this purpose we call the tempora or tenses. The modifications thus assumed may consist in the reduplication of the root, or in the gradation of the radical, or in the addition of suffixes. As to our Teutonic languages the tenses which require special notice are the present and the perfect, the formation of which will be submitted to an examination in detail. But we may at once remind the reader how strongly the mode of forming the perfect characterizes our Teutonic verbs, which we

THE VERB.

classify according to this formation in Gothic as well as in the languages of the present day. The English *steal, stole, stolen,* the German *stele, stal, stolen,* are as expressive of their type, as the Anglo-Saxon *stele, stäl, stælon,* and the Gothic *stila, stal, stelum, stulans*—all being examples of the perfect formed by the modification of the radical; while in the English *love, I lov-ed,* the German *lieben, ich lieb-et-e,* the Anglo-Saxon *nerian, ner-e-de,* the Gothic *nasjan, nas-i-da,* we have examples of the perfect formed by means of composition, an auxiliary verb being added to the root. Verbs belonging to the former class we call 'simple,' or with Grimm 'strong;' those of the latter 'compound,' or with Grimm 'weak[1].'

Thus then we have to consider three elements which enter into the formation of every verb,—the Persons, the Moods, and the Tenses. Though the signs which originally expressed these different relations may in our modern Teutonic languages be partly or wholly obliterated, they are nevertheless of such supreme importance for the right understanding of the Teutonic verb as to render a detailed exposition absolutely necessary.

FORMATION OF THE PERSONS.

1st Person Singular.

The 1st person singular is formed by the suffix *-ma,* which is the base used in Sanskrit in the declension of *aham* (ego), the 1st person singular of the personal pronoun, where we find the ablative *ma-t,* the genitive *ma-ma.* In the perfect tense the *a* only remained; and as secondary suffix, in the optative for instance, it appears merely as *-m.* Hence we get of the root *bhar* (to bear), the primitive present tense *babhár-a,* perf. *babhár-a.* But at a very early period the *a* of *ma* was weakened into *i,* so that *mi* appears as the regular primary suffix, e. g. *as-mi* (sum, I am); the secondary suffix *-m* we have in *as-ya-m* (sim = sie-m). In the same manner are formed the Sansk. *as-mi,* and optative pres. *sya-m;* the Gr. $\epsilon \check{\iota}$-$\mu\iota$ = $^{\dagger}\check{\epsilon}\sigma$-$\mu\iota$ and $\epsilon \check{\iota}\eta\nu$ = $^{\dagger}\epsilon\sigma$-$y\eta$-μ; the Lat. *sum* = †*es-μ-m* = †*es-mi* = *as-mi, sim* = *sie-m* = *s-ya-m* = *as-ya-m.* The last-mentioned language does not distinguish between primary and secondary suffix, but applies *-m* in all examples. This *-m* we find everywhere in the present subjunctive, as *veha-m,*

---

[1] The active and the passive voice do not form distinct themes, but express their different relations merely by different modifications of the personal terminations.

and in the imperfect in *-ba-m*. The Gothic has the *-m* only in *im* = †*is-mi* = *as-mi*; everywhere else it has dropped the termination of the 1st person singular.

1st Person Plural.

As suffix of the 1st person plural the Ursprache used *-masi*, secondary form *-mas*, e. g. pres. indic. *as-masi* (we are), optative *as-yá-mas*. In this termination grammarians see two pronominal roots *ma* + *si* combined. The former, as we have already stated, is the root of the 1st pers. sing.; *si* stands for *ti*, and *ti* is held to be derived from *tva* the base of the 2nd pers. sing. of the personal pronoun; and *-masi* consequently means 'I-thou,' 'I and thou,' hence 'we.' But the plurality of the 1st person may also include the ideas of 'I and he,' 'I and ye,' &c., combinations for which the primitive language no doubt had its special forms, which however in the course of time were lost, and of the different words expressing the different kinds of 'we' only one remained and took the place of the other forms as well. In Sanskrit the primary suffix is *-mas*, Ved. *-masi*, as *i-masi*, *i-mas* (imus), *vahá-masi*, *vahá-mas* (vehimus); the secondary suffix, *-ma*, the shortened form of *-masi*, as *vahe-ma*. The corresponding form in Greek is $-\mu\epsilon\nu$, that is, $\mu\epsilon$ with ν ephelkysticon, which succeeded in establishing itself for good; e. g. ἴ-μεν = prim. *i-masi*. More primitive is the Doric $-\mu\epsilon s$ = primary *-masi*, secondary *-mas*, and is closely allied to the Latin *-mus*, more ancient *-mos*, as *i-mus*, *vehi-mus*. The Gothic has preserved nothing of this suffix but the *m*, e. g. *viga-m* (movemus) = prim. *vagha-masi;* the secondary suffix in Gothic is *-m-a*, that is, *-m* which was preserved from destruction by the final *a* supporting it[1], e. g. *vigai-ma* (moveamus) for †*vigai-m*, prim. *vaghai-mas*.

1st Person Dual.

The plural *m* was modified into *v*, hence prim. *vasi*, Sansk. *vas*, perf. *-va*; e. g. pres. *vahá-vas*, impf. *a-vahá-va*. In Greek and Latin this form is wanting; the Gothic drops the *v* of the primitive *-vas*, *-vasi*, and thus forms *vigos* = †*viga-as* = *viga-vas*, prim. *vaghá-vasi*. The perfect has lost the termination and ends in the connective vowel, as *vegu* for *veguv*, from prim. *vavagh-vas*. The secondary *-va* corresponds to the plur. *-ma*, as *vigai-va*, optative pres. for *vigai-v*, from prim. *vaghai-vas*.

---

[1] Scherer does away with the auxiliary *a* by contending that this *a* is the remainder of an ancient termination *-am*, = Gr. ἄν, Sansk. *u*; in the pronoun also, e. g. *hvata*, he takes it as the remainder of an ancient *am*, as in Sansk. *idám*.

2nd Person Singular.

The primitive theme of the 2nd person singular of the personal pronoun is *tva*, as we find it in the Sansk. *tvat, tvam*, &c. As a termination we meet it in its completest form in the suffix *-ta* of the perfect and the *-dhi* of the imperative. But as a rule *si* is put for *ti = tva*, perhaps in order to keep the *ti = tva* of the 2nd person distinct from the *ti = ta* of the 3rd person. The perfect termination of the Sanskrit is *-tha*, e. g. *chakar-tha* (fecisti), root *kar* (facere), *vet-tha* (vidisti, οἶσθα) = *vaid-tha*, root *vid* (to see, to know). The imperative ends in *-dhi*.

The Greek *-θa* after σ is the oldest Greek form of the primitive *ta*, e. g. οισ-θα = Ϝοῖσ-θα = Sansk. *vet-tha*. The termination *-σθα*, as in the subjunctive βαλη-σθα, optative βαλοι-σθα, indicative τίθη-σθα, seems to be so formed that to the usual termination *s* (as in ἔχει-ς) there was added the suffix *-ta*, the *t* of which following the spirant *s* was changed into the aspirate θ. The Greek language is rather fond of the termination *-σθα* in the conjugation of verbs; but the commonly used suffix is *s = σι*, as we find it in the termination *-εις* of the indicative, and *-ης* of the subjunctive, e. g. φέρεις = †φερε-σι, φέρης = †φερη-σι ; the secondary suffix always *-s*, as in ἔ-φερε-ς, φέροι-ς.

The Latin perfect has *-ti* for *-ta*; the *s* preceding it belongs not to the termination but to the theme of the perfect. The *i* probably stands for an older *ei*, as *tutudis-ti = tutudis-tei*. The length of the *i* was perhaps adopted in analogy to the long *i* of the 1st person (vide infra). The imperative in *-dhi* is lost, but the emphatic imperative in *-to(d)*, Ved. *-tat*, preserves the original *ta* in a very primitive form. In Latin, as in Greek, the common suffix is *-s = -si*, e. g. *es = †es-s* and †*ed-s*, prim. *as-si*, root *as* (to be) and *ad-si*, root *ad* (to eat), *vehi-s*, prim. *vagha-si*; optative present *sie-s*, prim. *as-yá-s*.

The Gothic has *-t* for *-ta*, e. g. *váis-t*, prim. *viváid-ta*; simple perfect *nam-t*, root *nam* (to take), prim. *nanám-ta*. But the common primary suffix is, as in Greek and Latin, *-s* = prim. *-si*, e. g. *vigi-s*, prim. *vagha-si*; *is* (thou art) = *is-s*, prim. *as-si*; also in the compound perfect, as *nas-i-de-s, hab-ai-de-s, salb-ó-de-s*. The secondary suffix is *-s* = prim. *-s*, e. g. *vigai-s*, prim. *vaghai-s*. Specially to be noticed is the rule according to which in Gothic a dental (*d, t, th*) which precedes the terminational *-t* of the 2nd pers. sing. of the perfect is changed into the sibilant *-s*, e. g. *váis-t* for *váit-t* (οἶσθα), *mos-t* for *mót-t* (debes), *qas-t* for *qaþ-t*, perf. of *qiþan* (to say). Thus the *st* gradually came to be considered the termination of the 2nd person, and invaded other verbs, e. g.

B b

the Gothic *sai-so-st* instead of a regular †*sai-só-t*, root *sa* (to sow,) and finally it usurped the position of the older -*s* and -*t* in both the present and the perfect tense in all Teutonic languages, a fact we shall have to notice hereafter. This perfect in *st* may well be taken as an analogy to the Greek perfect in -σθα.

2nd Person Plural.

The primitive suffix is -*tasi*, which consists of two roots, namely *ta* = *tva* and *si* = *ti* = *tva* ; whence -*tasi* = *tva* + *tva*, and means 'thou and thou,' that is, 'ye.' In Sanskrit it is represented by the primary -*tha* and the secondary -*ta*, e. g. present indic. *bhara-tha*, imperf. *a-bhara-ta*. The perfect has lost the consonant of the termination ; hence *babhra* for *babhar-a*, for *babhar-ta*, for *babhar-tasi*. The Greek verb has -τε throughout, as φερε-τε, ἐσ-τε, φέροι-τε ; the Latin -*tis* = *tisi* = *tasi*, e. g. *es-tis*, *ama-tis*, *amaba-tis*, *tetigis-tis*. The imperative in -*tote* contains more distinctly even than the Ved. -*tat* twice the pronominal base *tva ;* the imperative in -*te* is, like the Greek -τε and the Sanskrit -*ta*, a shortened form. The Gothic has -*th* throughout, which is the remainder of an older -*tha* = -*ta*, e. g. present indicative *vigai-th*, optative *vigai-th*, perfect indicative *vegu-th*, root *vag* (to move).

2nd Person Dual.

The suffix in Sanskrit is -*thas*, perf. -*athus* (-*thus* a weakened form of -*thas ?*); secondary suffix -*tam ;* which in Greek are represented by -τον, in Gothic by -*ts* (*t* preceding *s* resists Grimm's law), e. g. present indic. *baíra-ts*, optative *baírai-ts*, perf. indic. *beru-ts*, optative *berei-ts*. The -*ts* = prim. -*tas*, -*tasi*.

3rd Person Singular.

The primitive -*ta* is a demonstrative root ; as a verbal termination we find it weakened into -*ti*, secondary -*t*, e. g. present indic. *as-ti* (est), *vagha-ti* (vchit), optative *as-yá-t* (siet, sit), *vaghai-t* (vehat). The imperative suffix is *tata*, whence the Ved. *tát*, the Lat. *to(d)*, and the Gr. τω(τ). The Sanskrit perfect suffix is -*a* for -*ta*, as *babhar-a* for †*babhar-ta ;* the primary suffix -*ti* in *as-ti*, *bhara-ti ;* the secondary -*t* in *bhare-t*, *syá-t*. The Ved. imperative ends in *tát* = *ta-ta*. Greek has in the perf. ε = Sanskrit *a* for -*ta*, e. g. λέλοιπ-ε = *riráik-a* for *riráik-ta*. But the primary suffix -τι = -*ta* is preserved in εσ-τι, and in the Dor. τίθη-τι ; σι for τι in τίθη-σι and the Homeric subjunctive ἔχη-σι, λάβη-σι. But the *s* of σι is commonly dropped after the thematic vowel, as φερει, φερη for †φερεσι, †φερη-σι. The secondary -τ is dropped everywhere, as in ε-φερε-(τ), φεροι-(τ). The imperative suffix -τω = †τω-τ = ta-ta. The Latin has -t for -ti throughout, e. g. -es-t, era-t, dedi-t. The to of the imperative is like the Greek for to-d, prim. ta-ta, as vehi-to, Sansk. vaha-tát. The primary suffix in Gothic is -th = -ti, e. g. vigi-th, prim. vagha-ti; -t only in is-t (est), where the t is preserved on account of the preceding s; the secondary suffix -t is always dropped, hence optative vigai, prim. vaghai-t. The perfect has lost its primitive final a which stood for ta, as in bar for bára, prim. babhar-(t)a.

3rd Person Plural.

The primitive suffix an-ti, after vowels -n-ti, secondary -ant, after vowels -nt, contains two roots, ti = ta, a demonstrative which we have already met in the formation of the 3rd person singular, and an, a demonstrative root from which is derived the pronominal base ana- (comp. the comparative an-tara, Goth. an-thar, Germ. an-der, our other). The termination anti, therefore, means 'this and this,' 'that and that,' 'he and he,' that is, 'they.' Sansk. -anti, -nti, e. g. s-anti (sunt), bhara-nti (ferunt); secondary -ant, -nt, which according to Sanskrit phonetic laws may appear as -an and -us. Imperative -antu, -ntu, emphatic Ved. -ntát. Gr. -αντι, -ντι, e. g. ε-ᾱσι (Ion.), that is, as-anti, root εσ = as (to be); φερουσι = φερο-ντι (Dor.); perf. λελοιπ-ᾱσι, prim. riráikanti. Secondary suffix -εν, -ν, prim. -ant, -nt, as optative φεροι-εν; imperf. ε-φερ-ον; imperative -ντω-ν, Dor. -ντω = Ved. n-tát. The final ν is an inorganic addition. More primitive in its form is the Latin -nt = -nti, e. g. vehu-nt, old form †veho-nti, prim. vagha-nti; but in sunt = †es-onti, prim. as-anti, the suffix -anti comes once to appearance. The imperative in -nto, as vehu-nto, prim. vagha-ntát. In Gothic the primary suffix is -ind = anti, -nd = -nti, e. g. s-ind (sunt) = †s-anti, prim. as-anti; viga-nd (vehunt), prim. vagha-nti; the secondary suffix -n for -nt, and even the n must be supported by a final a, e. g. optative present vigai-n-a[1] for vigai-n from vaghai-nt.

3rd Person Dual.

Like the 2nd person it has as primary suffix -tasi, as secondary -tas; but on account of its total absence in Gothic and the other Teutonic languages it requires no further notice on our part.

---

[1] Scherer's view of this point has already been mentioned, p. 368, foot-note.

THE PERSONS OF THE VERB IN THE TEUTONIC LANGUAGES.

1st Person Singular.

The suffix *mi — ma* of the primitive language is, as in Gothic, preserved in the termination *-m* in the Old Teutonic, and as *-n* in some of the Modern Teutonic languages; among the latter, English alone shows the primitive *-m*. It occurs chiefly in the various forms of the verb 'to be;' thus from the root *as* (to be) we have the Goth. *i-m* (= †*is-mi* = *as-mi*), the O. N. *e-m* (=†*er-m* =†*is-mi*=*as-mi*), the A. S. *eo-m* (=†*eor-m*=†*is-mi*=*as-mi*), whence the Engl. *am*; from the root *bu*=prim. *bhu* (to be) there is the O. H. Germ. *pi-m* (comp. Sansk. *bhav-á-mi*), the O. S. *biu-m*, the O. Fris. *be-m*, the A. S. *beo-m*, M. Dutch *be-m*, but Middle and New High Germ. *bi-n*, and following their analogy N. Dutch *be-n*. These are the only forms in which all the Teutonic languages have preserved the primitive suffix; but there are a few other words with the termination *-m* in which Old High German appears more primitive than Gothic, namely *tuo-m* (I do), also in the O. S. *dó-m*, *do-n*; *gá-m* (I go), *stá-m* (I stand)[1]. The derivative themes in *e* and *o*, perhaps following the analogy of the mentioned verbs, also take in Old High German the suffix *-m* in the 1st sing., as *hape-m*, *salbo-m*.

1st Person Plural.

The primitive suffix *-masi* appears in its completest form in the Old High German *-mes*, while Gothic and Old Norse have reduced it to a single *-m*, which *m* the Middle and New High German and Dutch have converted into *n*, while the Saxon dialects have dropped this termination altogether and put in its stead, Old Saxon that of the 3rd, Anglo-Saxon that of the 2nd person plural; e. g. O. H. Germ. *find-a-mes*, Goth. *finþ-a-m*, O. N. *finn-u-m*, Germ. *find-e-n*, O. S. *find-a-d*, A. S. *find-a-ð*, by the side of which we have the uninflected plural in the Engl. *we find*. In the preterite and subjunctive the Saxon dialects adopt for the 1st person the termination *-n* of the 3rd person plural, e. g. Old Saxon subjunctive *find-a-n*, preterite *fund-u-n*, Anglo-Saxon subjunctive *find-e-n*, preterite *fund-o-n*. From this fact we may perhaps explain a curious phenomenon which we observe in Early English. It is this,—that in Layamon we find the plural throughout formed with the termination *-th*, in the Ormulum

[1] Compare *gedo-m*, *do-am*, *gesea-m*, *geseo-m* (I see) in the Durham Book.

commonly with the termination -*en*, or -*n*[1], while in Old English again the former, in Middle English the latter predominates, until New English discards them both, though at the dawn of our modern period -*en* was still in favour. The form in -*th* and that in -*n* were kept distinct in Anglo-Saxon; but both were often dropped when the pronoun succeeded the verb, as ' ne *gá* ge' for *gáð*, ' hwat *ete* we' for *eten*. The subjunctive rarely had any termination in Old English, and even the indicative drops the ending not unfrequently, as ' we *kalle*' for *kalleth*, ' thei *luf*' for *lufeth*. From all this it becomes evident that at an early period a confusion set in, which was finally solved by the total dismissal of all terminations in the subjunctive as well as in the indicative plural.

2nd PERSON SINGULAR.

The primitive suffix -*ti* and its representative -*si* appear in the Old Teutonic languages in the present tense originally as -*s*, in the perfect as -*t*. Thus in the present tense Old High German has, like Gothic, -*s*; e. g. O. H. Germ., O. S., and Goth. *hilp-i-s*, Goth. *hab-ai-s*, O. H. Germ. *hap-e-s*, even A. S. *häfe-s* (thou hast), though in the last-mentioned dialect this form is rare, and occurs chiefly when the verb is succeeded by a pronoun, as *spreces þu* (loqueris), *leornas þu* (discis), and in contractions between verb and pronoun as *gesiistu* (vides), *cueðestu* (dicis). The Old Norse, and Swedish and Danish also, have the termination -*s*, but in the favourite shape of *r*. In a few words, however, all the Teutonic languages prefer the still more ancient suffix -*t* to its modified form -*s*. This takes place chiefly in the verbs commonly called Præterito-Præsentia, which have the form of the perfect though the meaning of the present (comp. Gr. οιδα, Lat. *memini*). Thus Goth. *kan-t* (potes), *þarf-t* (eges), *skal-t* (debes), *mag-t* (potes), &c.; O. H. Germ. *darf-t*, *scal-t*, *mag-t*, but *can-st* for †*can-t* (vide infra); O. S. *tharf-t*, *scal-t*, *mah-t*, but *can-st*, *far-man-st*; A. S. *þearf-t*, but *can-st*, *ge-man-st*, *dear-st*; O. Fris. *skila*, *skal-t*. Though the verb 'will' often ends in a vowel in the 2nd singular, it also has the form *wil-t* in the Old Teutonic dialects: M. H. Germ. *sol-t*, *darf-t*, *wil-t*. Among the Modern Teutonic dialects English has preserved the ancient forms *shal-t*, *wil-t*, while Modern German has given way to the corruption into *st*, *kann-st*, *will-st*, *soll-st*, &c. The regular suffix of the perfect 2nd singular was -*t*, which however we find intact only in Gothic and Old Norse, while Old High German, Old Saxon, Anglo-Saxon, and Old Frisian

---

[1] The Ormulum has *christnepþ* and *christnenn*.

have the vocalic termination *i*, or weakened *e*. Some grammarians consider this *i* or *e* as having come over together with the plural Ablaut from the subjunctive, others take it as the connective vowel which remained behind after the termination had been dropped. This termination is greatly modified by a law which we have already mentioned under Gothic, and according to which the stem of a verb ending in a dental changed this dental into *s* before the termination -*t* of the perfect. Thus the Gothic *gas-t* for *gaþ-t*, and in the præterito-præsentia *mos-t* for *mot-t*, *vais-t* for *vait-t*. Now in imitation of these forms Old High German has already the form *can-s-t*, where the stem does not end in a dental, but the *s* has simply been interpolated, and thus the present tense, following the analogy of the præterito-præsentia, adopted *st* as its regular termination in Anglo-Saxon, Old Frisian, and all the Middle and New Teutonic dialects (only Middle Dutch has commonly *s*). While in Gothic and Old High German the compound perfect ends in the 2nd singular as the present in -*s*, the other dialects, such as Anglo-Saxon and Old Saxon, which adopted a vocalic termination for the simple perfect, imported the termination -*st* in the compound perfect too, and finally this termination was generally adopted in the 2nd sing. present and perfect, indicative and subjunctive.

2nd Person Plural.

The primitive suffix -*tasi* has been curtailed in the same manner as the primitive termination of the 1st plural. It appears in Gothic, Anglo-Saxon, Old Frisian, and Old Norse, as -*th*, in Old High German as -*t*, in Old Saxon as -*d*. In Early English it either reigns supreme, invading all the persons of the plural, or yields, together with the 1st, to the usurpation of the termination -*n* of the 3rd person. (Compare the 1st and 3rd person plural.) It is peculiar that this -*n* is still preserved in the 2nd pers. plur. of the Swedish verb, while it has been dropped in the 3rd pers. to which it originally belonged.

3rd Person Singular.

Corresponding to the primitive suffix -*ta*, Gothic -*th*, we find -*th* in the Anglo-Saxon and Frisian dialects, -*d* in the Old Saxon, and -*t* in the High German and Dutch. The root *as* (to be) forms the 3rd person everywhere by means of the ancient -*t*, which is protected by the preceding *s*, hence Gothic *is-t*, Germ. *is-t* (he is); the Engl. *is* — *as* has dropped the terminations and is reduced to the simple root. We have irregular forms in the Norse and English languages. The Old Norse, and, following it, Swedish and Danish, have -*r* in the 3rd pers. sing., a termination which stands in no relation whatever to the legitimate suffix which undoubtedly in Old Norse too was originally -*th*, perhaps in the form of -ð. This suffix, however, was at a very early period expelled and its place taken by that of the 2nd pers. sing., where we find, in accordance to Old Norse phonetic laws, -*r* for -*s*, which -*r* took possession of the 3rd pers. sing. as well.

A peculiar course was adopted in Modern English, where the primitive -*th* (though still used in poetry) had to give way to a new comer in the shape of -*s*. This *s* has no legitimate claim whatever to its position, and it is very difficult to account for its introduction. It makes its appearance in the Durham Book already, where we find forms such as *forgefes, does, singes, geheres;* Layamon and the Ormulum refuse it admittance. In Old English it is used side by side with -*th*; Chaucer himself applies -*th* exclusively, but the scribes of the Northern Strother he makes to use the form in *s*, as *it gas, falles, has*. In Modern English Ben Jonson still prefers the -*th*, but Shakespeare the -*s*, while Spenser uses either one or the other on rhythmical and euphonic grounds. Some suppose this *s* to be the result of Norse influence and the representative of the Old Norse -*r* in the 3rd (or 2nd) pers. sing., others take it to be merely a corruption of the original Anglo-Saxon termination -*th*. The former opinion can hardly be maintained when we consider that Old Norse forms, where they are imported at the expense of native elements, are taken in 'ready made,' not in their primitive shape. When the Norsemen came into contact with the Saxons they had no doubt lost all consciousness of the fact that the -*r* of the 3rd person of their verb was originally *s*, converted according to the law of rhotacism[1]. We consider it far more likely that the terminational *s* originated in a corruption of the legitimate *th*, first in pronunciation. It is a well-known fact that foreigners who have not made themselves masters of English orthoepy always pronounce the *th*, especially at the end of words, more or less like *s*, and it is not unreasonable to suppose that the introduction of *s* was a kind of accommodation the natives made to foreign weakness, *s* being the nearest approximation which a Norman, for instance, could make to the sound of *th*[2].

---

[1] Concerning the conversion of *s* into *r* (Rhotacism), see the phonetic laws under the respective consonants.
[2] Marsh, *The Origin and History of the English Language*, &c., p. 216.

3rd Person Plural.

The primitive *-anti, -nti,* appears only in the Gothic *-ind, -nd,* and the Old and Middle High German *-nt*; in all the other dialects it has been lost. But the secondary suffix *-n,* which in Gothic and Old High German already was used for the present subjunctive and the perfect indicative and subjunctive, we find again in all the other dialects, not only for the 3rd person, but forming the plural throughout. In Early English it often contested the place with the legitimate *th* in the present indicative, and so successfully that at the dawn of our modern period it resisted the levelling tendencies of the age, until it shared the fate of most inflexions and disappeared together with the other terminations of the plural. Modern German supplanted the primitive *-nt,* which was still used in Middle High German by the secondary suffix *-n,* which we find also in Modern Dutch; Swedish and Danish have, like English, dropped the termination, which in Old Norse had already been vocalized, in the present indicative into *a,* perfect *u,* subjunctive *i.*

The Dual.

The different persons of the dual do not claim any further exposition here, because they appear in Gothic only, and have so far already received our attention elsewhere.

THE PERSONS OF THE MEDIUM OR MIDDLE VOICE.

The primitive medial forms we find in none of the Teutonic languages, save the Gothic, and we shall therefore consider them so far only as they occur in the mentioned language. The personal terminations of the medium arose from the respective pronominal root being twice added to the verbal theme. These compound terminations were, for the singular 1st *-mámi,* 2nd *-sási,* 3rd *-táti;* 3rd plur. *-ntanti.* Derived from these primitive forms were *-mai, -sai, -tai, -ntai,* as preserved in the Sanskrit subjunctive, and the Greek terminations -μαι, -σαι, -ται, -νται.

1st Singular.

This form is wanting in Gothic, and is replaced by that of the 3rd person, a defect which shows that at the time when Ulfila translated the Bible the medial form had in Gothic also begun to collapse.

THE VERB.

2nd Singular.

Primary suffix *-za* for *-sai*, e. g. *baira-za* = Gr. φέρε-σαι, Sansk. *bhara-se*, prim. *bhara-sa(s)i*. Secondary *-zau*, e. g. *baírai-zau*. The latter suffix seems to stand for a more ancient *sám*, in the same manner as 1st sing. optative perfect *ber-jau* for a more ancient *bar-yam*, so that *sám* comes from *sa*, as Sansk. *-tám* (3rd sing. imperative medial) from *ta*.

3rd Singular.

Primary suffix *-da* = *-tai*, e. g. *baira-da* = Gr. φερε-ται; prim. *bhara-ta(t)i*. Secondary *-dau* = *tám* (comp. 2nd sing. *zau* = *sám*), e. g. optative *baírai-dau*, prim. *bharai-tám*; imperative *baira-dau*, Sansk. *bhara-tám*.

3rd Plural.

Primary suffix *-nda* = *-ntai*, e. g. *baíra-nda* = Gr. φέρο-νται, Sansk. *bhara-nte*, prim. *bhara-nta(nt)i*. Secondary *-ndau* = *-ntám* (comp. 2nd and 3rd sing.), e. g. optative present *baírai-ndau*, prim. *bharai-ntám*; imperative *baíra-ndau*, Sansk. *bhara-ntám*.

1st and 2nd Plural.

Wanting in Gothic, and replaced by the 3rd plural which we have just examined.

FORMATION OF THE MODI (MOODS).

The mood-suffix is placed between the verbal theme and the personal termination. The indicative and imperative have no mood-suffix, and are therefore, strictly speaking, no modi. The imperative is only the vocative form of the personal termination.

The Subjunctive Mood.

The theme of the subjunctive mood is formed by means of the demonstrative suffix *-a-*, which, where an *a* belonging to the temporal theme precedes, is contracted with it into *á*; e. g. prim. present theme *bhara-*, subjunctive theme *bhara-a-* = *bhará-*. Thus Latin *vehá-m*, *vehá-s*, *vehá-t* for †*veha-a-m*, &c. (the short vowel of the Latin subjunctive is a correption of a later date); Gr. φέρω, φερῃ-s = φερη-σι, φέρη = φερη-τι. The subjunctive mood being totally absent in the North-European languages (Teutonic and Slavonic), we need not submit it to a detailed discussion.

The Optative Mood.

The theme of the optative mood is formed with the suffix -*ya*-, commonly gradated into -*yá*-, which also yields the base of the relative pronoun. If it succeeds upon a temporal theme ending in *a*, the suffix is weakened into *i*. The optative throughout has the secondary personal suffixes. Examples: — Primitive theme *as*, Sansk. *as*, Gr. ἐσ, Lat. *es*, Goth. *is*—hence present optative 1st sing. prim. *as-yá-m*, Sansk. *s-yá-m*, Gr. εἴην = †ἐσ-yη-μ, Lat. *sim* = *s-ie-m*, Goth. *sijau* = †*s-ija-m* = †*is-ija-m*. The primitive theme *as-ya-* is in Gothic extended into *as-iy-a-*, hence *sija-*, which form is treated as a theme in *a* and assumes the usual personal terminations of the optative, as 2nd pers. *sijais*, 3rd *sijai*. 1st plur. prim. *as-yá-mas*, Sansk. *s-yá-ma*, Goth. *sij-u-m*. Theme prim. *bhara-*, Sansk. *bhara-*, Gr. φερε-, Goth. *baíra-*; hence present optative 1st sing. prim. *bhara-i-m*, Sansk. *bhare-ya-m*, Gr. φερο-ι-μι(ν), Goth. *baírau* = †*bira-ı-m*. 2nd sing. prim. *bhara-i-s*, Sansk. *bhare-s*, Gr. φέρο-ι-s, Goth. *baıra-i-s*. Thus then we have in the Gothic optative present the optative form in *i*, because the present theme ends in *a*; but the perfect theme ending in the final of the root, the optative perfect is formed by means of the suffix -*ya*-; e. g. perfect theme *ber* (of *bar*, to bear), perfect optative 1st sing. *ber-ja-u*, prim. *bhabhár-yá-m*, 2nd sing. *ber-ei-s*, prim. *bhabhár-yá-s*.

THE MODI IN THE TEUTONIC LANGUAGES.

The optative in the Teutonic languages, which is commonly called conjunctive or subjunctive, is formed on the same rules as the Gothic, or, we had perhaps better say, derived from a primitive Teutonic form to which the Gothic bears the closest resemblance. It is, in most of the Teutonic dialects, ancient and modern, and in its greatest integrity, preserved in the root *as* (to be), which invariably supplies the present subjunctive, except in the Modern Norse languages, and in Early and Modern English. The subjunctive theme or stem is in Old High German and all the Low German dialects *sí*, in Old Frisian and Old Norse *se*, which may be explained by reference to the Gothic. The *u* of the Gothic *sijau* being dropped, the remainder appears in a contracted form in the *sí* and *se* of the other dialects, the former presupposing perhaps the vocalization of the Gothic *sij* into *siu* and hence *si*, and the latter the elision of the *j* in Gothic *sija*, thus producing *sia* and hence *se*. Thus then we have in the 1st and 3rd sing. of the present subjunctive the O. H. Germ., O. S., A S., M. H. Germ., M. Dutch, N. Dutch *sî*; the O. Fris. and O. N. *se*; the N. H. Germ. *sei* (N. H. Germ. *ei*= M. H. Germ. *î*), the other persons being only modified by the personal terminations in several of the dialects mentioned. In late Saxon (Layamon and the Ormulum) the subjunctive *si* is gradually supplanted by the subjunctive *beo* of the root *bhu*, which existed in Anglo-Saxon already, and which in the shape of *be* became the sole form of the present subjunctive in Old English, and remained so in Middle English and New English.

The subjunctive of other verbs forms its theme in the present tense by means of *e* (Old Saxon *â*), in the perfect by means of *i*. These thematic vowels may again be explained by a reference to the Gothic. Take the Gothic present theme *baíra-* which in the optative yields the form *baírau* = †*bira-i-m*, 2nd *baíra-i-s*, the suffix *ya* being weakened to *i* on account of the preceding *a* of the theme. The thematic *a* and the suffixed *i* combine in Old High German and other dialects to produce the form *e*, e.g. 2nd sing. *ber-e-s*, a contraction which corresponds to that in the Sanskrit *bhar-e-s* compared to the prim. *bhara-i-s*. The Old Saxon *a* which stands in the place of the *e* was undoubtedly originally long, a length which was lost in the course of time, just as it was in Anglo-Saxon, Old Frisian, Old Norse, and the New Teutonic dialects, where it can no longer be distinguished from the thematic *e*; so that in the Anglo-Saxon, Old Frisian, *find-e*, the Old Norse *find-i*, we may simply see the thematic form (*a* weakened to *e* or *i*), or the *e* (*i*) may be considered as the correption of the optative *e* (= *a* + *i*) which we still find in Old High German. Thus again in Middle High German the subjunctive and indicative forms are identical; in New High German a distinction is kept up in so far as the *e* in the subjunctive termination may not suffer syncope, as indicative *du sag-st*, but subjunctive *du sage-st*, where the thematic *e* (= *a*) is preserved.

The vowel of the perfect subjunctive theme is *i* in Old High German, Old Saxon, and Old Norse, the length being preserved only in the former two dialects; the *i* is flattened to *e* in Anglo-Saxon and Old Frisian as well as in the Modern Teutonic dialects, if they have preserved any vowel at all. The Old High German *í* corresponds to the Gothic *ei*[1], and the Gothic *ei* to the primitive -*ya*-; hence we have for the Gothic 2nd sing. *funth-ei-s*, the O. H. Germ. *fund-î-s*, O. S. *fund-î-s*, O. N. *fynn-i-r*,

---

[1] Compare the Table of Gradations, p. 24.

A. S. and O. Fris. *fund-e*, N. H. Germ. *fünd-e-st*. In these forms of the preterite the *i* or *e* cannot be considered to be the weakened thematic *a*, because all the Old Teutonic dialects rejected the *a* of the present theme in the perfect, as Gothic present *stila, baira, hilpa, finda*, perf. *stal, bar, halp, fand*, a practice kept up in the Modern Germ. *stele, helfe, finde*, perf. *stál, half, fand*. The vowel then which is added in the perfect subjunctive in ancient and modern dialects must be the representative of the primitive optative suffix *-ya*.

TEMPORA (TENSES).

Formation of the Present Theme.

What we call the Present Tense in the Aryan languages comprises a number of formations morphologically distinct one from another. These different forms must originally have had different significations as well; for, as Schleicher rightly observes, a difference of form without a difference in the meaning is altogether inconceivable. We find, moreover, in the extant languages occasionally different functions performed by the different themes of the present tense, though it is true that this variety of functions has mostly disappeared, while a variety of formations remained.

The personal terminations are added to the theme in such a manner that the indicative and subjunctive assume primary, the optative secondary, suffixes[1].

In the subsequent list we enumerate those themes only which Gothic has in common with the cognate languages.

I. *The theme consists of the simple pure root.*

The personal terminations are suffixed directly to the root without any connective vowel, or consonant, or combination of such.

Primitive. Root *as* (to be), 1st sing. *as-mi*, 2nd *as-si*, 3rd *as-ti*; 1st plur. *as-masi*; subjunctive 1st sing. *as-â-mi*; optative 1st sing. *as-ya-m*.

Sanskrit. 3rd sing. *as-ti*, 1st plur. *s-masi* for †*as-masi*. Root *ad* (to eat), 1st sing. *ad-mi*, 2nd *at-si* = *ad-si*; 1st plur. *ad-masi*.

Greek. Root ἐσ (to be), 1st sing. εἰ-μί = ἐσ-μι, 3rd sing. ἐσ-τι; 1st plur. ἔσ-μεν.

Latin. Root *es* (to be), 1st sing. *sum* = †*es-u-m* = †*es-mi*, 3rd

---

[1] See the chapter on Roots and Themes, p. 166 sqq.

THE VERB.

sing. *es-t;* 2nd plur. *es-tis,* 1st. plur. *s-u-mus,*=†*es-u-mus*=†*es-mus,* prim. *as-masi.*

Root *ed* (to eat), 3rd sing. *es-t* from *ed-(t)i;* in the same manner *es-tis,* &c. But *edo, edimus* belong to the themes of Class II. In their extant form *sta-t* and *da-t* belong to Class I, though originally to Class IV. (Comp. Sanskrit and Greek, Class IV.)

II. *To the simple pure root is added the suffix -a-.*

This formation probably occurs only with roots which have the radical *a*. The suffix *a* of the theme, that is, the final, *a* has gradation in the 1st singular and plural[1].

Primitive. Root *bhar* (to bear); present theme *bhar-a,* 1st sing. *bhar-á-mi,* 2nd *bhar-a-si;* 1st subjunctive *bhar-a-á-mi,* hence *bhar-á-mi;* optative 1st *bhara-i-m.* In the same manner are formed the present themes *pat-a-,* root *pat* (to fly, to fall); *vart-a-,* root *vart* (to turn). To this formation belong most of the derivative verbal themes, especially those in *-aya-,* e. g. theme *viad-aya-* (to make known), root *vid* (to know), 1st sing. *vaid-ayá-mi.*

Sanskrit. Root *tud* (to strike), present theme *tudá-,* 1st sing. *tudá-mi,* 1st plur. *tudá-masi.* Root *bhar,* present theme *bhará-,* 1st sing. *bhará-mi.* Derivative verbs in *-aya-,* e. g. root *vid,* present theme *védaya-* (to make known), 1st sing. *védayá-mi.*

Greek. Root φέρ (to bear), present theme φερε-, φερο-, 1st sing. φερ-ω(-μι), 1st plur. φερ-ο-μεν. Derivative verbs in *-aya-*: nominal theme φορο-, verbal theme φορ-εyo-, 1st plur. φερουμεν =†φορ-εyo-μεν, prim. *bhar-aya-masi;* nominal theme τιμή, verbal theme τιμ-αyo-, 1st plur. τιμῶμεν=τιμαyo-μεν.

Latin. Root *veh,* prim. *vagh* (to move, convey), theme *veh-i-,* 1st sing. *veho*=†*veho-mi,* prim. *vaghá-mi; vehi-t,* prim. *vagha-ti,* 1st plur. *vehi-mus,* prim. *vaghá-masi.* (Conjugation in *-ere.*) In Latin and Greek the 1st plur. differs from that of the preceding languages in not having the gradation of the suffix *-a-.* The derivative suffix *-aya-* is represented by *e, í, á,* as *monetis,* †*moneitis* =†*mon-eyi-tis,* prim. *mán-aya-tasi.* (Conjugations in *-are, -ere, -ire.*)

Gothic. The formations in *-a-* are very frequent in Gothic, chiefly with primary themes[2]. The radical *a* is with few exceptions weakened to *i*. It is not weakened in 1st sing. *fara*=*fará,* prim. *fará-mi,* root *far* (to go); *graba-,* root *grab* (to dig); *slaha-,* root *slah* (to slay); *valda-,* root *vald* (to govern). It is weakened

---

[1] Gradation of vowels, p. 22 sqq.
[2] Concerning *primary* and *secondary* themes, see pp. 167, 168.

to *i* in *giba-*, root *gab* (to give); *brika-*, root *brak* (to break); *hilpa-*, root *halp* (to help);—weakened to *u* in *truda-* (perf. *traþ*, plur. *tre-dum*), root *trad* (to kick). To the themes in *-a-* belong also the verbs with gradated radical (commonly second gradation, and the gradation remaining throughout), e. g. *háita-*, to be called (O. Engl. to hight, Germ. heißen); *hvopa-*, to boast; *leta-*, to let; *slepa-*, to sleep; *stáuta-*, percutere (Germ. stoßen). The final *a* of the theme is treated according to the primitive law; so that corresponding to the *a* in the primitive language we have *a* in Gothic, corresponding to the short *a* in the primitive we have the weakened form *i* in the Gothic language: e. g. 1st sing. *viga* for †*vigá*, prim. *vaghá-mi*; 2nd *vigis* for †*vigi-si*, prim. *vagha-si*; 1st plur. *vigam* for *vigá-mas*(?), prim. *vaghá-masi*; 2nd *vigith* for †*vigi-þis*(?), prim. *vagha-tasi*; 3rd *viga-nd* for *viga-ndi*, prim. *vagha-nti*. In the 3rd plural the *a* is preserved by two succeeding consonants of the termination. The 1st dual *vigos* arises from *vigaas*, *viga-vas* (Goth. *a + a = o*), prim. *vaghá-vasi*; the 2nd dual *viga-ts* seems as if it were derived from a more primitive form with the thematic vowel gradated or lengthened.

The primitive *-aya-*, used for the formation of derivative verbs, appears in Gothic in three distinct forms: (1) the first *a* dropped, *ja*; (2) the *y* of *aya* dropped, makes *a + a = ó*; (3) the final *a* dropped, *ai*.

1. The verbs in *ya* (corresponding to the Latin in *i*) form the present theme in *ja*, *ji*, or *ei*, and all other themes in *i*; e. g. present theme *nasja-*, *nasji-* (to save), perf. theme *nasi-*, hence present 1st sing. *nasja*, 2nd *nasjis*, 1st plur. *nasjam*, &c., perf. 1st sing. *nasida*. Instead of *ji* we have *ei* after a long radical, e. g. theme *sokja-*, 2nd sing. *sokeis*, but the combination *ja* always remains intact, as 1st sing. *sokja*, 1st plur. *sokjam*.

2. Verbs in *ó* (= prim. *a*) can easily be traced to nominal themes from which they are derived; thus from theme *leika-*, adj. *ga-leiks* (similar, like), we get 1st sing. *ga-leiko* (compare Germ. ver-gleiche), 3rd sing. *ga-leikoþ*, 1st plur. *ga-leikom* for †*leika-já-mi*, †*leika-ja-ti*, †*leika-já-masi*; from *fiska-*, *fisks* (fish), 3rd sing. *fiskóþ* (piscatur). In *leikajámi* the *j* was dropped first, and *a + a* make *ó*.

3. The verbs in *ai* (= Latin *e*, Greek εε) for the primitive *-aya-* have this derivative form only in the 2nd and 3rd sing. and 2nd plur., and in the perfect; but in all other persons of the present, and in the optative of the present throughout, they assume the form of primary themes, so that they have always two themes, one for the former, another for the latter forms; e. g. the theme *habai-*, of the root *hab* (to have), makes 2nd sing. *habai-s*, 3rd *habai-þ*,

2nd plur. *habai-þ*, perf. *habai-da;* the theme *haba-* forms 1st plur. *haba-m*, 3rd *haba-nd*.

III. *The root has first gradation and takes the suffix -a-*.

Primitive. Root *dik* (to show), present theme *daika;* root *bhug* (to bend), *bhauga-;* root *sru* (to flow), *srava-*.

Sanskrit. Root *budh* (to know), 3rd sing. *bodha-ti*, 1st plur. *ó͡dhá̱-mas*.

Greek. This formation very frequent. Root φυγ (to flee), present theme φευγ-ε, φευγ-ο-, plur. φευγ-ο-μεν, φευγ-ε-τε; root λιπ (to leave), theme λειπ-ε, λειπ-ο, plur. λείπ-ο-μεν, λειπ-ε-τε; root λαθ (to be hid), theme ληθ-ο-, 1st plur. ληθο-μεν.

Latin. Root *duc* (to lead), theme *duc-ī = douc-ĭ-*, prim. *dauk-a-*, 3rd sing. *douc-i-t*. Thus also *dīc-i-t = deic-i-t*, root *dic* (to say); *fīd-i-t = feid-i-t*, root *fid* (to trust).

Gothic. This formation occurs regularly with primary themes, containing the radical *i* or *u*, e.g. root *gut* (to pour), 1st sing. *giuta*, 2nd *giuti-s;* part. pret. pass. *gut-ans;* root *grip* (to seize, gripe), 1st sing. *greipa*, 2nd *greipi-s*, part. pret. pass. *grip-ans*.

IV. *The root is reduplicated, and, if ending in a vowel, assumes first gradation.* The gradation is subject to the same rules as under II.

Primitive. Root *da*, present theme *da-dá*, 1st sing. *da-dá-mi*, 2nd *da-dá-si*, 1st plur. *da-dá-masi*, subjunctive 1st sing. *da-da-á-mi*, optative *da-da-yá-m;* root *dha* (to put, to set, to do), present theme *dha-dhá-;* root *ga* (to go), present theme *ga-gá-*.

Sanskrit. Root *bhi* (to fear), 1st sing. *bi-bhê-mi;* root *da* (to give), 1st sing. *da-dá-mi*, 1st plur. *da-d-mas;* root *dha* (to put), 1st sing. *da-dhá-mi*, 1st plur. *da-dh-mas*. Peculiar to the two last-mentioned verbs is the loss of the thematic *a* in the ungradated forms.

Greek. The vowel of the reduplication is ι; the plural has no gradation. Root δο (to give), theme δι-δο-, 1st sing. δι-δω-μι, 1st plur. δι-δο-μεν; root στα (to stand), theme ἰ-στα- for *si-sta-*, 1st sing. ἵ-στη-μι, 1st plur. ἵ-στα-μεν; root θε (to put), theme τι-θε-, 1st sing. τι-θη-μι, 1st plur. τί-θε-μεν; root πλα (to fill), 1st sing. πί-μ-πλη-μι; root πρα (to burn), 1st sing. πί-μ-πρη-μι (comp. πλήσω, πλήθω and πρησω, πρηθω). The two last-mentioned verbs add a nasal to the reduplication, and thus connect the themes under V with those under IV.

Latin. This formation is rare, and recognizable in but few fragments, and even in these not without the suffix *-a-;* e. g. *gignit* for †*gi-gen-i-t*, prim. *ga-gan-a-ti* (comp. γιγ(ε)νο-μαι); root *gan* (to beget); *sistit*, i. e. *si-sti-t*, prim. *si-sta-ti*, root *sta* (to stand); *serit*, i. e. †*si-si-t*, prim. *si-sa-ti*, root *sa* (to sow); *bi-bi-t*, root *bi*, prim. *pi, pa* (to drink).

Gothic. This formation is, strictly speaking, wanting in Gothic; for the only fragment this language possesses is a theme with the suffix -*a*-, in which, moreover, the reduplicational syllable is nasalized: 1st sing. *gagga*, 3rd *gaggi-th*, from a prim. 1st *ga-n-g-á-mi*, 3rd *ga-n-g-a-ti*, root *ga* (to go). In Old High German we find a few more remains of this formation; namely from the root *ga* (to go), 1st sing. *gá-m*, prim. *ga-gá-mi*, 2nd *gá-s*, 3rd *gá-t*, 1st plur. *gá-mes*; from the root *sta* (to stand), 1st sing. *stá-m*, prim. *sta-stá-mi*, 2nd *stá-s*, &c.; root *ta* (to do), 1st sing. *tuo-m*, prim. *dha-dhá-mi*; but these again have lost the reduplication, and the gradation crept into the plural too; in their extant form therefore they more properly belong to Class I.

V. *To the root is added the suffix -na- and the vowel of the suffix gradated in the 1st sing.*

Primitive. Root *star* (to scatter, to strew), 1st sing. *star-ná-mi*, 1st plur. *star-na-masi*. This suffix, as well as -*nu*-, are demonstrative roots, and occur frequently in the formation of nominal themes.

Sanskrit. Root *grabh, grah* (to seize), 3rd sing. med. *grh-na-te, grh-ní-te*; root *yu* (to join, jungere), 1st sing. *yu-ná-mi*, 1st plur. *yu-ní-mas*. *na* in the ungradated forms is weakened to -*ni*.

Greek. Root δαμ (to tame), theme δάμ-να-, 1st sing. δάμ-νη-μι, 1st plur. δάμ-να-μεν; root πέρ (to sell), 1st sing. πέρ-νη-μι. This form often occurs in combination with the suffix -*ya*- (Gr. -*o*-), as ἰκ-νέ-ο-μαι, I come. The *a* of *na* is treated in the same manner as the final of the themes in -*a*-, e. g. root πί (to drink), theme πί-νε-, πί-νο-, 1st sing. πί-νω, 2nd πί-νε-ις, 1st plur. πί-νο-μεν. Almost exclusively peculiar to Greek is the formation of the present theme with the suffix -ανε-, -ανο-, prim. *ana*, e. g. root ἰκ (to come), theme ἰκ-άνο-, 1st plur. ἰκ-άνο-μεν; root αυγ, αυξ (to increase) αυξ-άνο-μεν. If the radical is short, the nasal *m* is inserted between it and the final of the root; e. g. λαβ (to take), theme λα-μ-β-άνο-, 1st plur. λα-μ-β-άνο-μεν.

Latin. The *a* of the suffix -*na*- is treated as the final of the themes in -*a*-. This formation occurs chiefly after vowels and roots ending in *r*, e. g. root *li* (to smear), 3rd sing. *li-ni-t*; root *si* (to let), *si-ni-t*; root *cre, cer* (to separate), *cer-ni-t*; root *spre, sper* (to despise), *sper-ni-t*. On a more ancient stage of the language we find *da-n-unt*, root *da* (to give), *prodi-n-unt*, &c.

THE VERB.

Gothic. The *a* of the suffix -*na*-[1] is treated as in the cognate languages. Exclusively belonging to the present, we find -*na*- only in the theme †*fraih-na-* from the root *frah*, to ask (Germ. fragen), in which the *a* of the root is weakened to *i*; 1st sing. *fraih-na*, 2nd *fraih-ni-s*, 1st plur. *fraih-na-m*, perf. sing. *frah*, plur. *freh-n-u-m*. From these present themes there has been developed in Gothic a class of derivative verbal themes (with passive functions) which gradate this *na* into *no* in the perfect tense, so that we have a theme in -*na*- for the present, a theme in -*no*- for the perfect, which moreover follows the system of the weak conjugation; e. g. present theme *veihna-* (to be sanctified), from *veih(a)s* (holy). Present sing. 1st *veih-na*, 2nd *veih-ni-s*, 3rd *veih-ni-th*, 1st plur. *veih-na-m*, &c., going exactly as *fraihna* (Latin *cerno*); but the second theme is *veih-no-*, whence the perfect *veih-no-da*; thus also *fullnan* (to be filled), from *fulljan* (to fill); *andbundnan* (to be loosened), from *andbindan* (to loosen); *usluknan* (to be opened), from *uslukan* (to open); *af-dumbna* (to be dumb, to be silent), from *dumba* (dumb).

VI. *The demonstrative -na- or its shortened form -n- is infixed to the root itself before the final consonant.*

Primitive. It is difficult to decide whether this infix occurred in the primitive language, though from its occurrence in all the cognate languages it would appear that it did. The pronominal root -*na*-, which first was used as a suffix, seems to have gradually crept into the root itself and to have become the infix of which we now treat, so that to the Latin *ju-n-g-i-t* (root *jug*, Sansk. *yuj*, to join) corresponds a primitive *yu-n-g-a-ti*, which originally may have been *yug-na-ti*. This infix also occurs in nominal themes, as the Gr. τυ-μ-π-ανο-ν, root τυπ (to strike); Goth. *du-m-b-s* (dumb), root *dub*, from which also *daub-s* (deaf). Compare also the Goth. *ma-na-g-a* (many), root *mag*, prim. *magh* (to grow) with the Lat. *mag-nu-s*, from a primitive *magh-na-*, as the Gothic from a primitive *ma-na-gha-*.

Sanskrit. Root *yuj* (to join), present theme *yu-na-j-*, *yu-n'-j-*, 1st sing. *yu-na-j-mi*, 1st plur. *yu-n'-j-mas*; root *much* (to loosen), present theme *mu-n'-cha-*, 1st sing. *mu-n-ch-á-mi*.

Greek. This formation is very rare: one example we have in σφίγγω, root σφιγ (to squeeze), comp. σφίγ-μα, σφιγ-μός.

---

[1] A near relation to this is the suffix -*nu*- which Schleicher discards from the Teutonic languages; but Delbrueck (in Deutsche Lautverschiebung, Zacher's Zeitschrift für Deutsche Philologie, i. p. 13) recognizes it in Goth. *brinnan* (to burn), where he takes *nn* as the assimilation of *nv*, and this *nv* for *nu*; *bri*, the root corresponding to a Sansk. *bhar*.

Latin. Chiefly with roots ending in a consonant; e. g. root *tag* (to touch), *ta-n-g-i-t*; *pag* (to fasten), *pa-n-g-i-t*; *fig* (to form), *fi-n-g-i-t*; *fud* (to pour), *fu-n-d-i-t*; *rup* (to break), *ru-m-p-i-t*.

Gothic. 1st sing. *sta-n-da*, root *stath*, *stad*, an extension of the simple root *sta* (to stand); perf. *stoth*. The form *gagga* also might be mentioned here, if we assume a compound root *gag*, formed by means of reduplication from the simple *ga* (to go). But the explanation given under IV is preferable, because we find nasalized roots in Greek and Sanskrit also. To this formation belong the following verbs, though they form their perfect like the derivative verbs by means of composition; 1st sing. *brigga*, I bring (Goth. $gg = ng$, $gk = nk$; comp. the Greek), perf. *brah-ta*, root *brag* (the radical is weakened to *i* in the present); *thagkja*, I think (comp. A. S. thencan, Germ. denken), and *thugkja*, I opine (comp. A. S. thincan, Germ. dünken, Engl. me-think-s), perf. *thah-ta*, *thuh-ta*, root *thak*, *thuk*. In the present they have both besides the infix *-n-* the suffix *-ya*. (See II.)

VII. *To the root is added the suffix -ya-, the a of which is treated like that of the themes in -a-.*

Primitive. Root *svid* (to sweat), theme *svid-ya-*, 1st sing. *svid-yá-mi*, 2nd *svid-ya-si*, &c., like *bhar-á-mi*.

Sanskrit. Root *nah* (to bind), pres. theme *nah-ya-*, 3rd sing. *nah-ya-ti*; root *mad* (to be intoxicated), 3rd sing. *mád-ya-ti* (with the radical gradated).

Greek. A favourite formation; the *ya* occurs in various modifications. (1) The *y* of *ya* remains as *i*; root δα (to divide), theme δα-ιε-, prim. *da-ya-*, 1st sing. δα-ίο-μαι; root φυ (to beget), Æol. φυ-ιω. (2) The *y* is transplanted as *i* into the preceding syllable, that is, into the root, e. g. root τεν (to stretch), 1st sing. τείνω for †τεν-yω; root βα, prim. *ga* (to go), theme βα-ν-yo-, 1st sing. βαίνω for †βα-ν-yω; root φα, prim. *bha* (to shine), hence with the suffix *-n* the root φαν (to appear, to show), 1st sing. φαίνω for †φαν-yω. In the last two cases we have the suffixes *n* and *ya*, that is, Class II and V combined. (3) The *y* joins the final of the root, and this combination appears in the form of ζ or σσ; but if the final consonant of the root is λ, the *y* is assimilated to it; e. g. root οδ (to smell), 1st sing. οζω for †οδ-yω; thus also φυλάσσω = †φυλακ-yω, τάσσω = †τακ-yω, λίσσομαι = †λιτ-yομαι, root λιτ (to implore), κορυσσω = †κορυθ-yω; but στελλω = †στελ-yω. (4) The *y* disappears between two vowels, as, φυ-ω, comp. Æol. φυ-ίω, in which the spirant *y* is vocalized into *i*.

Latin. The *y* of the suffix *ya* is vocalized into *i*, but dropped where another *i* succeeds, e. g. root *cap* (to take), 1st sing. *cap-io*, 1st plur. *cap-i-mus* for †*cap-yi-mus*; in the same manner *fug-io*, root *fug* (to flee), *aio* = †*ag-yo*, root *ag* (to say). *ero* for †*eso*, †*es-io*; *erunt* for †*es-unt*, *es-iunt*, have dropped the *i* of the primitive *-ya-* before the *o* and *u*. The last two forms assumed in Latin, as in other Aryan languages, the meaning of the future— a phenomenon which we observe also in the form *-bo*, used as the termination of the future, which stands for a more ancient †*bio*, *bu-io* (comp. Æol. φυ-ιω), root *bu*, *fu*, prim. *bhu* (to be). The suffix *-ya-* occurs in derivative verbs, as *statuo* for †*statuio*, from a prim. *statu-yá-mi*, in the same manner as the Gr. μεθυω for †μεθυιω, prim. *madhu-yá-mi*; *moneo*, prim. *mana-yá-mi*.

Gothic. Root *frath* (to understand), present theme *frath-ja-*, 1st sing. *frath-ja*, 2nd *frath-ji-s*, 1st plur. *frath-ja-m*; perf. *froth*; thus also 1st sing. *hlahja* from the root *hlah* (to laugh). If the root ends with *a*, *ya* is changed into *ia*, e. g. root *sa* (to sow). 1st sing. *sa-ia*, 3rd *sa-ii-th*, 1st plur. *sa-ia-m*; prim. 1st sing. *sa-yá-mi*, 3rd *sa-ya-ti*, 1st plur. *sa-yá-masi*; in the same manner *vaia*, root *va* (to breathe, to blow, Germ. wehen), *laia*, root *la* (to scold). Perf. of *sa* is *sái-so*, of *va*, *vái-vó*, of *la*, *lái-ló*. All these are stem-verbs and to be kept distinct from the derivative verbs in *-aya-*. (See Class II.)

VIII. *To the root is added the suffix -ta-.*

Sanskrit, and very likely the Primitive language too, did not make use of this suffix.

Greek. A frequent formation; the suffix *ta* occurs as -τε-, -το-, chiefly after labials, e. g. root τυπ (to strike), 1st plur. τυπ-το-μεν; ράφ (to sow), ράπ-το-μεν; πεκ (to comb), πέκ-το-μεν.

Latin. This formation occurs in but few cases, chiefly where the root ends with a guttural; e. g. *nec-ti-t* (*necto*, I bind), Sanskrit root *nah* (nectere); thus also *pec-ti-t*, *flec-ti-t*, *plec-ti-t*.

Gothic. One single trace of this formation is found in the Old High German root *flaht*, to weave (Germ. flechten).

THE FORMATION OF THE PRESENT THEME IN THE TEUTONIC LANGUAGES.

I. *The theme consists of the simple, pure root.*

To this formation belong, as in Gothic, the present themes of the root *as*, to be, which take the personal terminations without any thematic or connective vowel; e. g. A. S. *eo-m* = †*eor-m*, O. N. *e-m* = †*er-m*, Goth. *i-m* = †*is-m* = †*is-mi*, prim. *as-mi*, Engl. *a-m*; Goth. *is-t*, prim. *as-ti*, Germ. *is-t*; Goth., A. S., Germ., *s-ind* (they are) = '*is-ind*, prim. *as-anti*; O. H. Germ., O. S., *si-s*, Goth. *si-jai-s*, prim. *as-ya-s*, optative present of *as*, to be. In the same manner the root *bu*, prim. *bhu*, to be, forms in Anglo-Saxon the present 1st *beo-m*, 2nd *bi-st*, 3rd *bi-ð*, O. S. *biu-m*, *bi-st*, O. Fris. *be-m*, *bi-st*, O. H. Germ. *pi-m*, *pi-s*, Germ. *bi-n*, *bi-st*, A. S. *bu*, to dwell, inf. *buan*, 2nd *bý-st*, 3rd *by-ð*. To these belong also the O. H. Germ. *gá-m*, *stá-m*, *tuo-m*, A. S. 1st *ga*, 2nd *gæ-st*, 3rd *gæ-ð*; 1st *do-m*, 2nd *dæ-st*, &c. (See IV.)

II. *To the simple pure root is added the suffix -a-.*

This formation is one of the most frequent in the Teutonic languages, occurring in almost all the stem-verbs. As in Gothic it weakens the radical *a* to *i*; but the pure radical is preserved chiefly in those verbs which gradate the *a* into *ó* in the perfect; hence the root *far*, to go, has, for its present theme, *far-a-* (perf. *for*); thus also the present themes *scap-a-*, create; *grab-a-*, dig; *stand-a-*, stand; *svar-a-*, swear. The radical is weakened to *i* in the present themes, Goth. *gib-a-*, *stil-a*, *hilp-a*; and again the *i* is weakened to *e* in the A. S. *stel-e-*, *hèlp-e-*, and in all modern dialects, e. g. Germ. *stel-e-*, *helf-e-*, Dutch *stel-e-*, *help-e-*. Other modifications of the radical in the different ancient and modern dialects are discussed in the chapter which treats on the strong conjugations; but as to the *a* of the theme we have to mention that, as in Gothic, it is preserved in the 1st sing. and 1st and 3rd plural; weakened into *i* in the 2nd and 3rd singular. But while Gothic weakens it also in the 2nd plur. the other dialects preserve the *a* intact. In the Anglo-Saxon, Old Frisian, and in the modern dialects, the *i* is further weakened into *e*, and in the latter the thematic *a*, where it occurs at all, is represented by the weakened form *e*.

The themes in *-aya-* which occur chiefly with the derivative or so-called weak verbs may appear in three distinct forms, or as three distinct conjugations in Old High German as in Gothic,

THE VERB.

so that we find themes in *ja*, *ô*, and *ai*. In Old High German moreover the theme in *ai* forms all the persons of the present, while in Gothic it is supplanted by the theme in *a* in the 1st sing. and 1st and 3rd plur. Thus then for Goth. *haba, hab-a-m, hab-a-nd*, we have O. H. Germ. *hap-e-m*, &c., corresponding to a Gothic †*hab-ai-m*, &c. All the other dialects preserve merely the two former themes, and the modern Teutonic languages render the three forms by the single *e* or drop the thematic vowel altogether. The combination *ja* is kept up in most of the old dialects, but *ji* (of the 1st and 2nd sing.) is vocalized into *i*. We give a few forms in the following paradigm for the sake of illustration.

1. In ja.

	Gothic.		O. H. Ger.	O. Sax.	A. S.	O. Fris.	O. N.
PRES. Sing. 1st	*nas-ja*	*sôk-ja*	*ner-ju*	*ner-ju*	*ner-je*	*ner-e*	*kenni*
2nd	*nas-ji-s*	*sôk-ei-s*	*ner-i-s*	*ner-i-s*	*ner-e-st*	*ner-i-st*	*kenn-i-r*
3rd	*nas-ji-þ*	*sôk-ei-þ*	*ner-i-t*	*ner-i-d(t)*	*ner-e-ð*	*ner-i-ð*	*kenn-i-r*
Plur. 1st	*nas-ja-m*	*sôk-ja-m*	*ner-ja-mês*	*ner-ja-d*	*ner-ja-ð*	*ner-a-ð*	*tel-ju-m*
SUBJ. Sing. 1st	*nas-ja-u*	*sôk-ja-u*	*ner-je*	*ner-ja*	*ner-je*	*ner-i*	*tel-i*
PERF. Sing. 1st	*nas-i-da*	*sôk-i-da*	*ner-i-ta*	*ner-i-da*	*ner-e-de*	*ner-e-de*	*tel-da*

2. In ô.

	Gothic.	O. H. Ger.	O. Saxon.	Anglo-Saxon.	O. Fris.	O. N.
PRES. Sing. 1st	*salbô*	*salp-ô-m*	*scaw-ô-n*	*sealf-je (-ige)*	*salv-je*	*kalla*
2nd	*salb-ô-s*	*salp-ô-s*	*scaw-ô-s*	*sealf-a-st*	*salv-a-st*	*kall-a-r*
3rd	*salb-ô-þ*	*salp-ô-t*	*scaw-ô-d*	*sealf-a-ð*	*salv-a-th*	*kall-a-r*
Plur. 1st	*salb-ô-m*	*salp-ô-mês*	*scaw-ô-d*	*sealf-ja-ð (igea-ð)*	*salv-ja-th*	*köll-u-m*
SUBJ. Sing. 1st	*salb-ô*	*salp-ô-e*	*scaw-ô*	*sealf-je (-ige)*	*salv-je*	*kall-i*
PERF. Sing. 1st	*salb-ô-da*	*salp-ô-ta*	*scaw-ô-da*	*sealf-ô-de*	*salv-a-de*	*kall-a-ða*

3. In ai.

	Gothic.	O. H. Ger.
PRES. Sing. 1st	*hab-a*	*hap-ê-m*
2nd	*hab-ai-s*	*hap-ê-s*
3rd	*hab-ai-þ*	*hap-ê-t*
Plur. 1st	*hab-a-m*	*hap-ê-mês*
SUBJ. Sing. 1st	*hab-au*	*hap-ê-e*
PERF. Sing. 1st	*hab-ai-da*	*hap-ê-ta*

III. *The root has the first gradation, and takes the suffix -a-.*

To this class belong, in the Teutonic languages, all stem-verbs which have the radical *i* or *u*; e. g. Gothic root *skin* (to shine), present 1st sing. *skeina*, O. H. Germ. *scinu*, O. S. *skínu*, A. S. *scine;* root *grip* (to seize, gripe), Goth. *greipa*, O. H. Germ. *krífu*, O. S. *grípu*, A. S. *grípe*, O. Fris. *grípe*, O. N. *gríp;* root *gut* (to pour out, fundere), Goth. *giuta*, O. H. Germ. *kiuzu*, O. S. *giutu*, A. S. *geote;* root *kus* (to choose), Goth. *kiusa*, O. H. Germ. *chiusu*, O. S. *kiusu*, A. S. *ceose*, O. Fris. *kiuse*.

IV. *The root is reduplicated and, if ending in a vowel, assumes the first gradation.*

We have already remarked that this formation is almost totally wanting in Gothic, and we may now add that none of the ancient Teutonic dialects has anything more than mere rudiments or fragments of themes of this class. To these belong the O. H. Germ. *gá-m, stá-m,* and *tuo-m,* of the roots *ga* (to go), *sta* (to stand), *ta* (to do), which yield the forms 1st sing. *gá-m, stá-m, tuo-m,* from the prim. *ga-gá-mi, sta-stá-mi, dha-dhá-mi,* 2nd sing. *gá-s, stá-s, tuo-s,* 1st plur. *gá-mes, stá-mes, tuo-mes,* for the prim. *ga-ga-masi, sta-sta-masi, dha-dha-masi,* the long vowel having crept irregularly into the plural too. Here we must also mention the A. S. *gá, gæ-st, gæ-ð,* plur. *gá-ð;* do-*m, de-st, de-ð,* plur. *do-ð*. But, as we said before, these verbs as they now are before us belong more properly to Class I.

V. *To the root is added the suffix -na-.*

It occurs in Old High German and the other dialects, except Gothic, only in one particular form, e. g. O. H. Germ. *gifregin' ih* (tando accipio), O. S. *fregnan* (tando accipere).

VI. *The demonstrative -na- or its shortened form -n- is infixed in the root itself before the final consonant.*

To this class belongs, through extension of the root, the verb to *stand* as it occurs in the different dialects, derived from the primary root *sta*, a secondary root *stath, stad,* which, with the infix, becomes *sta-n-d;* Goth. *standa*, perf. *stóþ;* O. H. Germ. *stantu, stuont;* O. S. *standu, stod;* A. S. *stande, stod;* Engl. *I stand, I stood*. In the same manner we derive from the simple root *ga*, by means of reduplication, the compound root *gag*, which, with the infix -*n*-, forms the present theme *ga-n-g-a* in the different dialects; from the root *brag* (to bring) the present theme *bri-n-g-a-* (with the weakening of the radical into *i*), infinitive O. H. Germ., A. S. *bringan*, O. S. *brengjan*, O. Fris. *brenga*. Thus we have, by the side of the Goth. *fahan* (to catch), and *hahan* (to hang), in O. H. Germ. and A. S. *fa-n-g-an*, *ha-n-g-an*; from the root *þak*, *dak*, the Goth. *þagkjan* = †*þa-n-k-jan*, O. H. Germ. *de-n-k-an*, O. S. *the-n-k-jan*, A. S. *þe-n-c-an*, O. N. *þe-n-k-ja*, O. Fris. *tha-n-k-a* or *the-n-zja*, Germ. *de-n-k-en*, Engl. *thi-n-k*; from the root *thuk*, *duk*. Goth. *þugkjan* = †*þu-n-k-jan*, O. H. Germ. *du-n-k-an*, O. S. *thu-n-k-jan*, A. S. *þy-n-c-an*, O. Fris. *thi-n-szja*, Germ. *dü-n-k-en*; but O. N. *þykkja* (in *nk* the *n* assimilated to the *k*).

VII. *To the root is added the suffix ja, prim. ya.*

Verbs belonging to this class are stem-verbs, and must not be confounded with the derivative verbs in *ja*, prim. *aya*. They can easily be kept distinct, because the former take the suffix *ja* only in the present and form the perfect like other stem-verbs, the latter preserve the derivative suffix throughout the conjugation. In the present tense, of course, both classes are inflected alike, so that at first sight it would appear as if the strong verbs in *ja* had adopted something of the weak verbs in *ja*, wherefore Grimm considers them of a mixed character. In Gothic we have already mentioned *fraþjan* (to understand, to know), *hlahjan* (to laugh); we may add *hafjan*, to lift (Germ. heben); *raþjan*, to reckon; *skapjan*, to create; *skaþjan*, to damage, to scathe (Germ. schaden), which make the perf. in *ó*, as *fróþ*, *hlóh*, *hóf*, &c.;—*bidjan* (to ask, to bid), has the perf. *baþ*, *beþum*, perf. part. *bidans*. In Old High German we have to mention *bittan*, to ask (Germ. bitten); *sizzan*, to sit (Germ. sitzen); *liggan* to lie (Germ. ligen); *heffan*, to lift (Germ. heben); *seffan*, to understand; *swerran*, to swear. The doubling of the final consonant of the root is the result of the assimilated *j*, as *bittan* for *bitjan*, &c., the *j* being still preserved in some forms such as *bitju*, *pitju*, *swerju*; *heffjan*, *swerjan*; imperative *piti*, *sizi*, &c. In the verbs *pittan*, *liggan*, *sizzan*, it is owing to the influence of the *j* that the radical *i* was not weakened into *e*, and to the same influence must be ascribed the Umlaut of *a* into *e* in the verbs *swerran*, *seffan*, *heffan*. Old Saxon has *biddjan*, *liggjan*, *sittjan*, *hebbjan*, *suerjan*, *af-sebbjan*, animadvertere. The gemination which occurs in most of them is not, as in Old High German, organic, that is, caused by the assimilation of the *j* to the final consonant; it is dropped in the 2nd and 3rd sing. present and in the imperative; e. g. *biddjan*, 2nd sing. *bidis*, 3rd *bidid*, imperative *bidi*, &c. In the perfect they make, *bad*, *bádun*, *lag*, *lágun*, &c. Anglo-Saxon has, like Old High German, commonly assimilated the *j* to the final consonant of the root; hence *biddan, sittan, licgan, hliccan,* reprehendere; *þicgan,* to touch; *hebban, swerjan.* They are in the present inflected like the weak verbs in *ja*; except *swerjan,* which has not assimilated the thematic *ja,* makes in the 1st pers. *swer-ie* (*-ige*), 2nd *swer-a-st,* 3rd *swer-a-ð,* 1st plur. *swer-ja-ð;* imperative *swera.* O. Fris. *bidda, bidja; lidza, lidzja,* to lie (A. S. licgan); *sitta,* to sit; *swerja,* to swear. In the 3rd sing. of *lidzja* the gemination is dropped; hence *leith, lith;* O. N. *swelgja,* to riot, glutire (Germ. schwelgen); *erja,* to plough, arare; *biðja, liggja, sitja, þiggja,* to get; *blíkju* and *blíka,* to glitter; *svíkja,* to deceive; *víkja,* to yield (Germ. weichen); *syngja,* to sing; *slýngja,* to sling, projicere; *tyggja,* to chew; *geyja,* to bark; *deyja,* to die; *hefja, hnefja,* to squeeze; *hhæja,* to laugh; *kefja,* to suppress; *sverja,* to swear; *skekja* and *skaka,* to shake. The present throughout is conjugated in the fashion of the weak verbs.

VIII. *To the root is added the suffix -ta-.*

As we had occasion to observe before, there is no sign of this formation in Gothic; the only trace we find in the Old High German root *flaht = flah-t,* to weave (Germ. flechten); present 1st sing. *flihtu,* 2nd *flihti-s,* 1st plur. *fleht-a-mes,* perf. *flaht.* Compared with *plec-to,* Gr. πλέκ-ω, the compound character of *flah-t* becomes soon apparent, the suffix *t = ta* having crept into the root itself. (The *t* not affected by Grimm's law on account of the preceding *h.*)

FORMATION OF THE PERFECT THEME.

As long as the primitive Aryan language preserved its most simple character, roots kept the place of words; roots consequently were used as verbs or verbal themes, whether present or perfect. On this stage the language possessed no other means to express the various relations of an action, but that of repetition, that is, the repetition of the root, called Reduplication. Thus then all temporal relations also were originally expressed by means of the reduplication of the root. In order to form the perfect of the root *vid,* to see, the root was reduplicated into *vid vid;* to the perfect theme thus formed were added the personal pronouns, and thus was obtained the 1st sing. *vid vid ma,* vidi; 3rd sing. *vid vid ta,* vidit. On the secondary stage of the development of the language the three roots were agglutinated into one word, hence 1st *vidvidma*, 3rd *vidvidta*, and *then* only the first 'vid' might rightly be called the reduplication, and 'ma' and 'ta' terminations. The language having thus passed through the first, or radical, and second, or agglutinative, to the third, or inflexional, stage, further changes and modifications took place which tended more emphatically to distinguish the primary root, as the bearer of the meaning or sense of the word, from the secondary roots, expressing merely the relations of the former. This distinction the language brought about by means inherent in itself, that is, by strengthening the primary root, and by curtailing and weakening the secondary roots. The former was strengthened by the gradation[1] of the radical vowel, *i*, *o*, or *u*, which gave rise to the following scale:—

Primitive radical.	I. Gradation.	II. Gradation.
a	aa	áa
i	ai	ái
u	au	áu

This gradation always took place in the perfect theme, except where the root ended in two consonants succeeding *a*, and it is a peculiar phenomenon that as a rule the second gradation was applied. Thus then the root *vid*, to see, appears in the perfect as *váid*; *kru*, to hear, as *kráu*; *ruk*, to shine, as *rátuk*; *da*, to give, as *da*; *sta*, to stand, as *stá*; *ad*, to eat, as *ád*. The secondary roots, on the other hand, were curtailed in various ways. The reduplicational root commonly lost the final consonant (except when the primary root consisted of but one consonant and one vowel), so that the reduplicated perfect of the root *vid* was *viváid*, of *ruk*, *ruráuk*, but of *da*, *dadá*, of *sta*, *stasta*, of *ad*, *adád*. The perfect theme being thus completed, all now required was the personal termination. The terminations, as we have seen before, were supplied in the demonstrative roots added to the theme as suffixes. These suffixes also, when the language had entered on the inflexional stage, were gradually more and more curtailed and weakened down, until, in the course of time, their original character was hardly perceptible. In the primitive language however these modifications were not yet so great as to obliterate the radical character of the personal suffixes; nay, in one instance the suffixed pronoun gained the better over the primary root. This remarkable phenomenon occurs in the perfect plural, where the long bisyllabic termination resisted all change and

---

[1] Concerning the gradation of vowels, see p. 22 sqq.

even prevented the gradation of the primary root. It must have existed in the primitive language, before Goths, Greeks, and Indians had separated, for we observe it equally in the different languages of the Aryan tribe. The following facts will sufficiently illustrate the phenomenon to which we refer. The primitive and Sanskrit root *vid*, to see, appears in Greek as Ϝιδ, and if the root itself occurred in Gothic it would be *vit*. We meet it in the form of the perfect, but with the meaning of the present, 'I know,' a meaning which it has acquired in Sanskrit, Greek, and Gothic alike. The perfect theme of this root, according to the rules mentioned before, must be in the primitive *vivaíd-*, which in Sanskrit we find as *ved-*, in Greek οἰδ- = Ϝοιδ-, in Gothic *váit-*. Its course through the different persons will appear from the following paradigm.

		Primitive.	Sanskrit.	Greek.	Gothic.
Sing.	1st	*vivaíd-(m)a*	*véd-a*	οἶδ-α for Ϝοιδα	*váit*
	2nd	*vivaíd-ta*	*véd-tha*	οἶσ-θα	*váis-t* for *vait-t*
	3rd	*vivaíd-(t)a*	*véd-a*	οἶδ-ε	*váit*
Plur.	1st	*vivid-masi*	*vid-ma*	ἴσ-μεν for Ϝιδ-μεν	*vit-u-m*
	2nd	*vivid-tasi*	*vid-a*	ἴσ-τε	*vit-u-th*
	3rd	*vivid-anti*	*vid-us*	ἴσ-ασι	*vit-u-n*

Though it lies beyond the limits of this book to enter upon a detailed exposition of the reduplicated perfect in the cognate languages, a short sketch will nevertheless be necessary in order to make us more fully to appreciate this part of grammar, which is of such high importance in the Teutonic languages also. The laws of reduplication, which in the primitive language were no doubt very simple, became in the different cognate dialects more numerous and complicated; but our sketch shall comprise merely those most important for our purpose.

Sanskrit.

The first syllable of a root (i. e. that portion of it which ends with a vowel) is repeated, e. g. *budh* (to perceive), *bu-budh;* but *bhu* (to be), *ba-bhu*. Aspirated letters are represented in reduplication by their corresponding unaspirated letters; e. g. *bhid* (to cut), *bi-bhid; dhu* (to shake), *du-dhu*. Gutturals are represented in reduplication by their corresponding palatals, *h* by *j;* e. g. *kut* (to sever), *chu-kut; gam* (to go), *ja-gam; has* (to laugh), *ja-has*. If a root begins with more than one consonant, the first only is reduplicated, e. g. *krus* (to shout), *chu-krus; kship* (to throw), *chi-kshıp*. If a root begins with a sibilant, followed by a tenuis or aspirated tenuis, the tenuis only is reduplicated; e. g. *stu* (to praise), *tu-shtu*; *stan* (to sound), *ta-stan*; *sthá* (to stand), *ta-sthá*¹.

The reduplicated perfect theme has commonly the first gradation of the radical vowel, e. g. *tud* (to strike), *tu-tod-*; *kar* (to make), *cha-kár*; *bhid* (to cleave), *bi-bhéd-*. Final vowels may have first or second gradation, e. g. *dha* (to place), *da-dhá-*; *stu* (to praise), *tu-shtáu-*; *hri* (to be ashamed), *ji-hraı-*. In the plural and dual active, and in the medium, the gradation does not take place. Roots in *a* sometimes drop the radical, as *tan* (to stretch), *ta-tnire-*. Roots in *a* in the 1st and 3rd pers. sing. have *au*, ved. commonly *a*, e. g. *da, da-dáa*, ved. *da-dá*.

Greek.

The reduplicational syllable does not repeat the radical, but supplants it by ε, probably in analogy to the great number of roots with the radical η = prim. *á*. Of two consonants only one is admitted in the reduplication, e. g. πλαγ (to beat), πέ-πληγ-α; φαν (to show), πέ-φην-α. This also happens in a few archaisms, as μνη = *man* (to think, remember), μέ-μνη-μαι. But as a rule the reduplicational syllable repudiates a combination of two initial consonants, as κτεν (to kill), ε-κτον-α.

The Attic reduplication is either the doubling or repetition of the whole root, as ὀδ (to smell), οδ-ωδ-α; οπ (to see), οπ-ωπ-α; or, in analogy to the preceding case, the doubling of the first part of the root, as αλειφ (pres. αλειφω, I anoint; a primitive root with α prefixed), ἀλ-ηλιφ-α.

The radical vowel has either the first or the second gradation. First gradation: λαθ (to be hid), λε-ληθ-α, λε-λᾱθ-α; Ϝαγ (to break), Ϝέ-Ϝᾱγ; Ϝεργ (to do, to make), Ϝέ-Ϝοργ-α; φυγ (to flee), πέ-φευγ-α. Second gradation: Ϝραγ (to break), ερρωγα =⁺ε-Ϝρωγ-α; λιπ (to leave), λέ-λοιπ-α; ἐλυθ (to come), ειλ-ηλουθ-α. The gradation does not take place in the plural, just as in Sanskrit; compare οιδα, plur. ἴσ-μεν = ⁺Ϝιδ-μεν with Sansk. *véda*, plur. *vid-ma*; πιθ (to trust), πέ-ποιθ-α, 1st plur. pluperf. ἐ-πέ-πιθ-μεν; τλα (to suffer), τε-τλη-κα, plur. τε-τλα-μεν; βα (to go), βε-βη-κα, plur. βε-βα-μεν; δι (to fear), δε-δοι-κα, plur. δε-δι-μεν. This law however is perceptible only in a few old formations; as a rule most verbs follow a new formation which has grown up in analogy to the compound aorist, and thus assumed for the perfect theme a final *a* which

Max Müller, *Sanskrit Grammar*, p. 145.

originally was foreign to it. Thus then we get the so-called regular forms: e. g. sing. 1st λέλοιπα-(μ) for †λελοιπ-(μ)a, 2nd λελοιπα-s for †λελοιπ-τα; 1st plur. λελοίπα-μεν for †λελιπ-μεν, &c. There are in general many new formations in the Greek perfect, of which we mention one more, that which contains inorganic aspiration, known in grammar as Perfectum Primum, e. g. δακ (to bite), δε-δηχ-α; φυλακ (to guard, watch), πε-φυλαχ-α; βλαβ (to hurt, injure), βε-βλαφ-α. Thus however only the gutturals and labials, not the dentals are aspirated.

Another phenomenon must be mentioned, which very likely originated in a very remote period, because we shall observe the same in Latin and even in some of the Teutonic languages; we mean the perfect in -s-. Vocalic themes have not rarely in the perfect med. an increase of the root by an additional -s, e. g. πλυ (to sail), πέ-πλευ-σ-ται.

Latin.

The final of the perfect stem is preserved in but few obsolete forms, as *faxo* = †*fac-so* = †*fe-fac-so*, and also *faxim-*†*fac-sim* = †*fe-fac-sim*. In all other forms it takes an *i* as the final vowel of the perfect theme, which *i* is obscure in its origin, as *fece-rim* = †*feci-sim* = †*fefici-siem* = †*fefaci-siem*. In the 1st sing. perf. we often read *ei* for *i* which very likely is the remainder of a more ancient -*eim*; in the 3rd sing. *it, et* = *eit*, as *dedet, fuet, fuit, dedeit, rediet*. Both the 1st and 3rd sing. as well as the 1st plur. are based upon the theme in *i*; e. g. 1st sing. *tu-tud-ei*, 3rd *tu-tud-ei-t*, 1st plur. *tu-tud-i-mus*, perfect theme *tu-tud-i-*, root *tud*, to strike; but in the 2nd sing. and plur. we have a perfect theme in -*is*- (comp. the Greek perf. in -*s*-, as πλυ, πεπλευ-σ-ται, and the perf. in -*s*- in Old High German and Old Norse); e. g. 2nd sing. *tu-tud-is-ti*[1], plur. *tu-tud-is-tis*. In the termination -*erunt* of the 3rd pers. plur. the long *e* is of later origin; the more ancient form was -*erunt*, as †*fec-er-unt* = †*fec-is-onti*, with the theme in -*is*-, which also occurs in the perfect infinitive *fec-is-se*, and in the optative pluperf. *fec-is-sem*. Final *a* disappears before the *i* or *is* of the perf. theme; as root *da*, perf. theme *de-d-i-, ded-is-*; root *sta*, perf. theme *ste-t-i-, ste-t-is-*.

The perfect in Latin has commonly lost the gradation of the root, and even replaced it by the weakened form of the radical vowel. The reduplication is mostly dropped; but where it appears it does so in a very primitive form. Fragments of the

---

[1] The spelling -*etsti* depends on a false conception of the length of the *i*, which is position, not nature; for the short *i* we have a proof in the contractions *scripsti* for *scripsisti*, *duxti* for *duxisti*.

ancient gradation we possess in *scábi* for †*sce-scáb-i*; *fugi* for *fu-fug-i*; *fui*, from a more ancient †*fuvi* = †*fu-fouvi*; thus also *plúi*, *rúi*, &c.; *tu-tud-i* (in Priscianus), for *tu-toud-i*, root *tud*, to strike. At an early epoch of the language, therefore, there may have been in Latin, as in Sanskrit, Greek, and Gothic, the regular alternation of long and short vowels in the singular and plural, as 3rd sing. *tu-toud-ei-t*, 1st plur. *tu-tud-i-mus*. Later on the short vowel penetrated, just as it did in the Teutonic languages, from the plural into the singular.

After what we have stated we may arrange all the different phenomena we observe in the formation of the perfect in Latin under three heads: namely, we find either (1) the reduplication preserved, or (2) the reduplication simply dropped, or (3) the initial of the root lost and then the vowel of the reduplication contracted with that of the root. (The vowel thus formed is of course always long.)

1. Reduplication preserved.

The laws of reduplication are very simple in Latin, because very primitive in their origin, and may be brought under two distinct heads. (1) The initial consonants are unaltered in the reduplicational syllable, even the combinations *st*, *sp*, and *sc*; but in these the root itself when reduplicated loses the spirant *s*, e. g. *spond* (to vow), *spo-pond-i*; *scid* (to cleave), *sci-cid-i*; *sta* (to stand), *ste-t-i*, for *spo-spond-i*, *sci-scid-i*, *ste-st-i*. (Comp. Gr. ἵ-στη-μι = *si-sta-mi*, and Sansk. *ti-shthá-mi*.) (2) The reduplicational syllable preserves the radical vowel; but roots in *a* have always the reduplication with *e*, e. g. *can* (to sing), *ce-cin-i*; *tag* (to touch), *te-tig-i*; *pag* (to fasten) *pe-pig-i*; *man* (to think), *me-min-i*; *parc* (to spare), *pe-perc-i*. The radical *o* always remains in the reduplication, e. g. Sansk. root *mard*, to rule, Latin present *mord-eo* (I bite), *mo-mord-i*; *posc*, to demand (=*porsc*, Sansk. *prachh* = *prask*), *po-posc-i*. In the more ancient style (Nonius, Gellius) also *me-mord-i*, *pe-posc-i*. Radical *i* remains in the reduplication, e. g. *scid* (to cleave), *sci-cidi*; *bi-bo* (I drink, root *pi* = *pa*), *bi-bi*: radical *u* remains, e. g. *tud* (to strike), *tu-tud-i*; *pug* (to sting), *pu-pug-i*; *curro* (I run, root probably *kar*), *cu-curr-i*; archaic (Gellius) *pe-pug-i*, *ce-curr-i*.

2. Reduplication dropped.

Examples:—*tuli* = †*te-tuli*; *scidi* = *sci-scid-i* (not for the later *sci-cidi*), *fidi* = †*fi-fidi*. The loss of the reduplicational syllable chiefly occurs in composition, e. g. *con-cidi*, *ex-puli*, but *ce-cidi*, *pe-puli*. Further examples are *fugi* = *fu-fugi*, *rupi*, *fudi*, *vídi* = †*vi-veid-i*, prim. *vi-váid-a*, *víci*, *scábi*. But these cases are often doubtful, and might belong to those to be mentioned under No. 3. We must also consider the reduplication to have been lost in all those verbs which have the theme of the perfect identical with that of the present, as *defendo*, *defendi*; *scando*, *scandi*; *verto*, *verti* = *ve-vert-i*, &c.; also the themes in *u*, e. g. *fu-i* = *fuvi* = †*fu-fou-vi*, and in the same manner *plui*, *rui*, *solui*; and the derivative themes in *u*, as *tribu-i*, *statu-i*, present *tribu(y)o*, *statu(y)o*; perhaps also *júvi* (present juvo), *cávi* (present caveo), *fávi*, *lávi*, *pávi*, *móvi* (mŏveo), *vóvi*.

3. The initial of the root lost, and the vowel of the reduplication contracted with that of the root.

Examples:—*feci* — †*fe-fici* = †*fa-fac-i* (comp. Osc. *fe-fak-ust*), *fregi* = †*fre-frigi* (or rather *fra-fagi*? comp. *spo-pondi*); and in the same manner *jeci*, *cepi*, *egi*, *legi*, *veni* = †*vevini* (comp. *tetini* of *teneo*). This formation seems to be limited in Latin to roots with the radical *a*, as *fac*, *jac*, *cap*, *ag*, &c.; but it deserves the greater attention the more frequently it occurs in the Teutonic languages, where for instance the German perfect *hielt* (of *halten*, to hold) must be referred to the O. H. Germ. *hialt* = †*hei-halt*, by the side of the Gothic reduplicated form *hái-hald*; Germ. *stieβ* (of *stoβen*, to push, to butt), to O. H. Germ. *stioʒ* = †*stei-stoʒ*, by the side of the Gothic reduplicated form *stái-stáut*, and numerous other examples which we shall mention hereafter both in the ancient and modern Teutonic dialects. The loss of the reduplication in these verbs may perhaps be ascribed to a tendency of languages in general to suppress one of two succeeding elements which are either similar or identical in form. The Latin language under such circumstances is fond of suppressing at least one consonant of the root where it begins with two, as *ste-ti*, *spo-pondi*, †*fra-fagi*, i. e. *frêgi*,

Gothic.

Only the stem-verbs and a few derivative verbs which are analogous to them (as *saltan* from *salt*) form a simple perfect; the perfect of the derivative verbs is always compound. In the Gothic perfect their remained, as a rule, either the reduplication or the gradation of the radical. The former we find chiefly with verbal themes which do not allow of gradation, namely such as have the radical *a* followed by two consonants, or take the highest gradation in the present theme already; we rarely find reduplication along with gradation of the radical *a* into *ó*, *e* into *ó*.

In the reduplicational syllable the vowel *ai* has supplanted the vowel of the root, which no doubt originally occurred in the reduplication too.

The more primitive mode of reduplicating is preserved in the O. H. Germ. *te-ta = ta-ta*, root *ta* (to do), which in Gothic would be *di-da = da-da*, and which answers to the Sansk. *dadháu*, prim. *dhadhá*. Of two consonants the initial only remains in the reduplication, except the combinations *hv, sk*, and *st*, which remain entire, e. g. *slepa* (I sleep), *sái-zlep; greta* (to weep), *gái-grot;* but *hláupa*, I run (Germ. laufe), *hlái-hláup; stauta*, percutio (Germ. stoße), *stái-stáut; skáida*, I separate (Germ. scheide), *skái-skáid*. According to the laws of reduplication and gradation we have to distinguish three forms of the Gothic perfect, which are produced by reduplication and gradation combined, by reduplication without gradation, and by gradation without reduplication.

1. Reduplication and gradation combined.

In all verbs coming under this head the radical is either *a* or *e*, gradated in the perfect into *o*. (1) The radical *a* (the present tense formed with the suffix *-ya-*): 1st sing. present *vaia*, = prim. *va-ya-mi*, root *va*, flare (Germ. wehen), perf. *vai-vo*. Thus also the roots *la*, to scold, *sa*, to sow. (2) The radical *e*: infinitive present *letan*, to let, perf. *lai-lot*. The long *e* in the present tense is explained by some to be the effect of a nasal consonant having been dropped after the radical *a*, which nasal is still preserved in the cognate languages, e. g. Goth. *tek-a*, Lat. *tango;* Goth. *flek-a*, Lat. *plang-o*, Goth. *gret-a*, Sansk. *krand-ámi*.

2. Reduplication without gradation.

According to the rule laid down before, all the verbs falling under this head should be (1) such as have the radical *a* followed by two consonants, or (2) such as have the highest gradation in the present theme already. To the former belong *halda* (I hold), *hái-hald; valda*, I govern (Germ. walte), *vái-vald:* but *fahan*, to catch (Germ. faugen), and *hahan*, to hang (Germ. hangen), though they end with but one consonant, make by analogy *fai-fah* and *hái-hah* in the perfect. To the class under (2) belong *hvopan* (to boast) *hvái-hvop; skáidan*, to separate (Germ. scheiden), *skái-skáid; stautan*, percutere (Germ. stoßen), *stái-stáut;* because we have in these verbs the highest gradation in the present tense, namely *o* being the highest or second gradation of *a*, *ái* of *i*, and *áu* of *u*. But *slepan*, to sleep, following the analogy of these verbs, also makes *sái-zlep*, though its *e* is only the first gradation of *a*.

3. Gradation without reduplication.

(A) In the verbs belonging to the sub-class (A) the singular of the perfect has the second (or highest) gradation, while the plural, the dual, and the optative present the simple radical i or u. Thus of the root *vit*, prim. *vid* (to know), we have the perf. sing. 1st *váit*, 2nd *váis-t* = †*váit-t*, 3rd *váit*, plur. 1st *vit-u-m*, &c. Comp. prim. 1st sing. *viváida*, 1st plur. *vivid-masi* as well as the corresponding forms in Sanskrit and Greek, p. 394.

In the same manner we have of the root *grip* (infinitive *greipan*, to gripe; Germ. greifen), the perf. *gráip, grip-um;* root *stig*, infinitive *steigan*, ascendere (Germ. steigen), *stáig, stig-um;* root *thih*, theiha, cresco (Germ. ge-deihe), *tháih, tháih-um—aí* for *i* on account of the succeeding *h;* root *gut* (infinitive *giutan*, to pour; Germ. gießen), *gáut, gut-um;* root *tuh* (infinitive *tiuhan*, to draw, to pull; Germ. ziehen), *táuh, tauh-um—au* for *u* on account of the succeeding *h*.

(B) The radical is *a* in the perfect gradated to *ó*, which gradation remains in the plural, dual, and optative also; e. g. *far-an*, to go, present prim. *fa-fara*, perf. *for*, plur. *fór-um*, prim. *fa-fára, fa-fár-masi; slah-an*, to slay, perf. *sloh, slóh-um; mal-an*, molere (Germ. malen), *mol, mol-um; haf-ja-n*, to lift (Germ. heben), *hóf, hóf-um;* root *stath, stad*, infinitive *sta-n-d-an*, to stand, perf. *stoth*. These verbs seem to have preserved the radical *a* intact in the present, under the shelter of an ancient reduplication, as *fara-* = *fá-fara*, *sta(n)da-*, from a reduplicated form *sta-sta-*.

(C) The singular of the perfect has weakened the original *á* into *a*, while the plural preserved it in the form of *e*, e. g. root *vag*, to move (Germ. be-weg-en), perf. sing. *vag*, prim. *va-vágh-a*, plur. *veg-um*, prim. *vavágh-masi*. In the present tense *vig-a* the radical *a* is weakened into *i*. Thus we have of the root *at* (to eat), present *it-a*, perf. sing. *at*, perf. plur. *et-um*; *stal* (to steal), *stila, stal, stelum; sat* (to sit), *sita, sat, setum; vas* (to be), *visa, vas, vesum*. The radical of the perfect may have resisted the weakening into *i* under the influence of its ancient reduplication, hence *nam* = *na-nam*, *vag* = *va-vag*.

(D) The singular of the perfect has the radical *a*, but the plural the weakening of *a* into *u*, while in the present tense again the *a* is, as in the preceding case, weakened to i[1]. To this class belong chiefly verbs which have the radical *a* succeeded by two

---

[1] 'In the preterite the reduplication which the Gothic but sparingly preserved, has been torn away in the course of time; but the strong vowel placed behind was sheltered, and where it was weakened it was not degraded to the weakest form (*i*), but to an intermediate degree (*u*), hence *bundum* (we bound), by the side of *bindam* (we bind).' Bopp, *Vocalismus*, p. 215.

consonants; e. g. root *rann,* to leak (Germ. rinnen), present *rinna,* perf. *rann,* plur. *runn-um;* prim. *rarann-a,* plur. *rarann-masi:* in the same manner, *hilpan* (to help), *halp, hulpum; bindan* (to bind), *band, bundum; sviltan* (to die), *svalt, svultum; siggvan* (to sing), *saggv, suggvum; singgqan = siggkvan* (to sink), *saggq, suggqum.* In this class there are many secondary roots; the root *rann* (to leak), for instance, is formed as a present theme by means of the suffix *-na-* from the primitive root *ar,* to go; *band* (to bind) has an inorganic *n*; *saggv* and *saggq* also are unprimitive in their final element.

Perfect in -s-.

In Old High German and in Old Norse there are remains of a perfect formed with *s,* as the Latin 2nd sing and plur. in *is* (*-is-ti, -is-tis*); e. g. Old Norse root *sa,* to sow, perf. *se-ra, se-ri,* for †*se-sa,* †*se-si;* root *gra,* vivere, perf. *gre-ri;* root, *ar, ra,* to row, perf. *re-ri.* Old High German root *scri,* to shriek, 1st plur. perf. *scri-r-u-mes,* from a primitive *skri-s-masi* (*u* is the connective vowel); root *pi, pu,* prim. *bhu,* to be, 1st plur. perf. *pi-r-u-mes,* prim. *bhu-s-masi,* 2nd *pi-r-u-t,* prim. *bhu-s-tasi.* (Compare the consonants *w* and *r, s* and *r.*)

The Compound (Weak) Perfect in the Teutonic Dialects.

The compound perfect is formed by the addition of the preterite of the verb 'to do' to the verbal theme. This formation we might imitate by coining new compounds, such as 'I love-did,' 'thou love-didst,' &c. It is not found in the cognate languages, but was produced in the Teutonic primitive language after the separation from its Aryan sisters; it is therefore often called the New Perfect, and by Grimm the Weak Form, because it does not affect the radical vowel. Our English *do, did,* the German *thu, that,* Old High German *tuó-m,* and the Gothic noun *de-d-s* (deed) may be referred to a Gothic root *da,* prim. *dha,* from which we get the 1st sing. pres. *da-dhá-mi.* Now in the Gothic compound the reduplication of the original †*dida =* †*da-da* is lost in the singular, but preserved in the plural and in the optative, and the *a* is, in the last-mentioned forms, gradated to *e = á,* following the analogy of the frequently occurring perf. themes, as *sat,* plur. *set.* The reduplicated *da,* however, in the form of †*dad-,* plur. *déd-,* appeared then in the form of a true verbal theme.

Where it occurs in the composition of the perfect this word is considerably modified, as will appear from the following. 1st pers. sing. the termination of the perf. is -*da* for †*dida* (O. H. Germ. teta), from an older *dada*, prim. *dha-dha*. 2nd -*des* for *dides*, older *dades*, with the personal suffix -*s* which we do not find elsewhere in the Teutonic perfect. Of the assumed perfect theme †*dad*, the 2nd pers. would be *das-t*—†*dad-t*. 3rd pers. has *da* again for †*dida* or *dad*. Plural 1st *déd-u-m*, dual *dédu*, prim. *dhádh-masi*, &c., like the other forms in analogy to the common strong perfect. 2nd *déd-u-th*, dual *dédu-ts*. 3rd *déd-u-n*. Optative -*déd-jau*, -*déd-eis*, prim. *dhadh-yám*, *dhadh-yás*. Thus then the perfect of the theme *nasja-*, *nasi-*, is in the 1st sing. *nasi-da*, 1st plur. *nasi-dédum*; of the theme *salbo-*, 1st sing. *salbo-da*, plur. *salbô-dédum*.

The perfect themes with present signification (præterito præsentia) form in this manner a new perfect; e. g. 1st sing. *mah-ta* for †*mag-da*. (Mutes or checks before dentals are changed into the spirants of the same organ, and every dental must be rendered by the tenuis *t*.) 2nd *mah-te-s*, 1st plur. *mah-téd-um*, root *mag*, possum; *vissa* for †*vis-ta* for †*vit-da*, of *váit*, root *vit*, to know; *skul-da* of *skal*, shall, debeo. Besides these there are few examples of this formation, such as *thah-ta* for †*thak-da*, I thought, present *tagkja*, I think.

In the Teutonic dialects generally the compound perfect is formed as in Gothic, the suffix 'did' assuming the following modifications in the different dialects.

	Gothic.	O. H. G.	O. S.	A. S.	O. Fris.	O. N.
Sing. 1st	*da*	*ta*	*da*	*de*	*de*	*da*
2nd	*des*	*tôs*	*dôs*	*dest*[1]	*dest*[1]	*dir*
3rd	*da*	*ta*	*da*	*de*	*de*	*di*
Plur. 1st	*dêdum*	*tumês*	*dun*	*don*	*don*	*dum*
2nd	*dêduth*	*tut*	*dun*	*don*	*don*	*duð*
3rd	*dêdun*	*tun*	*dun*	*don*	*don*	*du*
Dual 1st	*dêdu*	..	..	..	..	..
2nd	*dêduts*	..	..	..	..	..

These modified forms are added to the theme of the derivative verbs in *aya*, which again appears in three modifications: (1) The first *a* dropped, as *ja, ji*, in the present and -*i*- (-*e*-) in the perfect; e. g. Goth. *nasja*, *nasjis*, perf. *nas-i-da*, O. H. Germ. *ner-i-ta*, O. S. *ner-i-da*, A. S. *ner-e-de*, O. Fris. *ner-e-de*, O. N. (without

---

[1] The -*st* in Anglo-Saxon, and Old Frisian -*dest*, would answer to a Gothic †*dast* = *dad-t*, and is more correct than the -*s* in the termination of the other dialects.

THE VERB. 403

the derivative suffix) *ken-da*. (2) The *y* of *aya* being dropped *a* + *a* appears as *o*, e. g. Goth. *salb-ó, salb-ó-s*, perf. *salb-ó-da*, O. H. Germ. *salp-ó-ta*, O. S. *scaw-o-da* (1st sing. pres. *scaw-o-n*, 2nd *scaw-o-s*); A. S. *sealf-ó-de* (1st sing. *sealf-je*, 2nd *sealf-a-st*); O. Fris. *salv-a-de*, O. N. *kall-a-ða*. (3) The last *a* of *aya* disappears, and the derivative suffix is *ai*, e. g. Goth. 1st sing. present indicative *haba*, 2nd *hab-ai-s*, perf. *hab-ai-da*, O. H. Germ. *hap-e-ta*. Thus Gothic and Old High German have three, the other dialects only two conjugations of the weak form. Concerning the details, see the Conjugations. The modern dialects either drop the thematic suffix altogether and join the termination directly to the root, or the suffix always appears in the weakened form *e*.

THE INFINITIVE.

The suffix *-ana-* is used in Sanskrit, Greek, and the Teutonic languages, to form themes which are used as infinitives, which therefore must have belonged to the primitive language.

In Sanskrit the dative and locative singular of abstracts in *-ana- (-anáya, -ane)* have the function of the infinitive, e. g. dative *gam-anáya*, locative *gam-ane*, theme *gam-ana-*, nom. sing. *gam-ana-m* (neuter noun), root *gam*, to go; *ás-aná*, root *ás*, to sit.

The Greek language forms with the suffix *ana* the infinitive in -εναι, which Schleicher looks upon as the locative of feminine themes. Thus λελοιπ-έναι refers us to a primitive theme *riráik-ana-*, i. e. a nomen agentis derived from the perfect theme by means of the suffix *-ana-*. Themes which end with a vowel commonly take *-na* instead of *-ana*, hence διδο-ναι, ἱστάναι, δεικνυναι; but θειναι = ⁺θε-εναι, δουναι = ⁺δο-εναι. -ειν, Dor. -εν, are shortened forms of -εναι.

The Gothic infinitive has lost the case-sign of the noun as well as the final *a* of the theme-suffix *ana*, and it consequently always ends with *an*. This suffix however is so added as to suppress the final *a* of the theme, or we might say, vice versa, the final *a* of the theme is also the initial of the suffix, e. g. theme *baíra-*, prim. *bhara-*, infinitive *baír-an*, prim. *bhar-ana-*, root *bar*, prim. *bhar*, to bear; thus also *it-an*, to eat; prim. *ad-ana-*, pres. theme *ita-*, prim. *ada-*, root *at*, prim. *ad*; *steig-an*, to ascend (Germ. steigen), prim. *staigh-ana-*; *satjan*, prim. *saday-ana-*.

As in Gothic so in the Teutonic dialects generally *-an* is adopted as the termination of the infinitive, which in Old Frisian and Old Norse is curtailed to *a*, as *faran*, O. Fris. and O. N. *fara*.

This *an* appears in the Middle and New Teutonic dialects as *en*, e. g. Germ. *lieb-en*, Dutch *be-minn-en*. The English language also preserved the termination of the infinitive as late as to the times of Spenser and Shakespeare, though we find also in Layamon already forms where the *n* is dropped, and the force of the infinitive imparted to the verb by the preposition 'to.' Swedish and Danish follow their Old Norse mother, the former rendering the infinitive by the termination *a*, the latter weakening it to *e*.

PARTICIPLES.

PRESENT PARTICIPLE ACTIVE.

The suffix *-ant, -nt*, which occurs in all the Aryan languages, is chiefly employed in the formation of the present participle.

Primitive. Root *bhar*, to bear, present theme *bhara-*, present part. *bhara-nt-*; root *star*, to strew, present theme *star-na-*, present part. *star-na-nt-*.

Sanskrit. Root and present theme *ad-*, to eat, part. *ad-ant-*; root and present theme *as-*, to be, part. *as-ant-*; root *tud*, to strike, present theme *tuda-*, present part. *tuda-nt*; root *yu*, to join, present theme *yuna-*, present part. *yuna-nt-*.

Greek. The suffix appears in the shape of *-οντ, -ντ*, fem. *-ουσα*=†*-ονσα*=†*οντγα*. Root φερ, to bear, theme φερο-, part. φέρο-ντ-, fem. φέρουσα; root δο, to give, theme διδο-, part. διδο-ντ-; root θε, to set, theme τιθε-, part. τιθε-ντ; root στα, to stand, theme ιστα-, part. ιστα-ντ.

Latin. Suffix *-ent, -nt*, in a more ancient form *-unt,* †*-ont*; e. g. root *veh*, to move, theme *vehe-*, part. *vehe-nt-*; root *i*, to go, present theme *ī=ei*, part. *i-ent-, e-unt-*=†*e-ont-*.

Gothic. The form of the suffix is *-nd, -nda*. Root *bar*, to bear, present theme *baira-* for *bira-*, part nom. sing. masc. *baira-nd-s*, from a primitive *bhara-nt-s* or *bhara-nt(a)-s*; very likely the latter, because it is treated as a theme in *-a* in all the other cases. Under these circumstances the form of the theme *-nda, -ndja*, is extended by the addition of the suffix *-an*, fem. *-jan*, so that we arrive at the thematic suffix *-ndan-, -ndjan-*, which forms are treated like the themes in *-n* of the definite adjective; e. g. accus. sing. masc. *baira-ndan*, from a prim. *bhara-ntan-am;* loc (dat.) *baira-ndiu*, from a prim. *bhara-ntan-i*; nom. sing. fem. *baira-ndei*, from a prim. *bhara-ntyán-s*; gen. *baira-ndein-s*, prim. *bhara-ntyán-as*.

THE VERB.

But when these participles are used as substantives, they still show the older consonantal theme in -*and*, -*nd*, in several cases, e. g. nom. sing. *giba-nd-s*, one giving, a giver, theme *giba*, root *gab*; *bi-sita-nd-s*, one sitting near, a neighbour, theme *sita-*, root *sat*. These nominatives may fairly be considered true consonantal themes, because they are supported by the consonantal character of the locatives (datives), e. g. *giband*, *bisitand*, from a primitive locative *sadant-i*, &c. Thus also the plural *sitand-s* from a prim. *sadant-as*[1].

The other Teutonic dialects also have preserved the participial suffix, and some of them to the present day. It occurs, as in Gothic, in the form -*nd*, respectively -*nt*, which is joined to the vowel of the theme. The participle is in the ancient dialects treated in the same manner as the definite adjective, in the modern, as any other adjective, definite or indefinite, as the case may be. The different forms will easily be understood from the following paradigm.

Gothic.	O. H. Germ.	Old Saxon.	Anglo-Saxon.	O. Fris.	Old Norse.
finth-a-nd-s, finding	*find-a-nt-êr*	*find-a-nd*	*find-e-nd-e*	*find-a-nd*	*finn-a-nd-i*
nas-ja-nd-s, saving	*ner-ja-nt-êr*	*ner-ja-nd*	*ner-je-nd-e*	*ner-a-nd*	*tel-ja-nd-i*, telling
hab-a-nd-s, having	*hap-ê-nt-êr*	*scaw-ô-nd*, looking	*sêc-e-nd-e*, seeking	*sec-a-nd*	*kenn-a-nd-i*, knowing

In the Middle and New Teutonic dialects the *e* of the termination -*e-nd* is no longer felt as the thematic vowel, but treated as belonging to the participial termination, so that in Late Saxon we have *inde*, *ande*, instead of the original *ende*. On the other hand, in Modern English, the whole form is supplanted by the verbal substantive in -*ing*, a fact which occasionally occurs in Layamon already, while in Old English and Middle English we find the participial form in *end*, *ind*, *ynd*, *and*, side by side with the verbal substantive in *ing*, *inge*, *ynge*, performing the functions of the participle. New English discarded the legitimate form altogether to the benefit of the intruder, so that now the participle and the verbal substantive are identical. Some of the modern dialects however have preserved the participle in *end*, as we see in the German *find-end*, *lieb-end*, *hab-end*, &c., where the Old High German *t* has yielded to the influence of the Low German *d*.

---

[1] On the declension of the participle, see Themes in -*nd*, p. 324.

Perfect Participle Passive of Stem-Verbs.

Suffix -na.

This form occurs in Sanskrit in very few examples, such as *púr-na-* for †*par-na-*, root *par*, to fill; *bugh-na-*, root *bhug*, to bend; in Greek and Latin also it is only fragmentary, chiefly in adjectives; but in Gothic all stem-verbs form their perfect participle in -*na*, which, combined with the thematic *a* and the case-sign *s*, yields the terminations for the nominative singular masculine *an-s*, fem. *ana*, neut. *an*, from the primitive forms masc. -*ana-s*, fem. -*aná*, neut. -*ana-m*; e. g. *salta* (salio), perf. part. *saltan-s, saltana, saltan; haita* (voco), *haitan-s; giba* (I give), *giban-s; stila* (I steal), *stulan-s*; or, if we take the thematic vowel separately, *salt-a-n-s, háit-a-n-s*, &c. At any rate we may say that the theme of this participle ends in Gothic with -*an-*.

The same termination is taken up by the other Teutonic dialects ancient and modern, the latter weakening it to -*en*, a form which even Modern English has preserved among the few grammatical fragments handed down from its Anglo-Saxon mother. The suffix -*an*, -*en*, is used only with stem-verbs, which form their perfect by modifying the radical, and belong to Grimm's strong conjugation. One example may suffice for the sake of illustration. The Gothic *stilan* (to steal), perf. *stal*, plur. *stelum*, makes the perfect participle *stulan-s*[1], O. H. Germ. -*stolan-er*[2], O. S. *stolan*, A. S. *stolen*, O. Fris. *stolen*, O. N. *stolinn*, M. H. Germ. *stoln*, M. Dutch *stolen*, Late Sax. *stolenn*[3], O. Engl. *stolen*, M. Engl. *stoln*, N. Engl. *stolen* and *stoln*, N. H. Germ. -*stolen*, N. Dutch *stolen*, Swed. *stulen*, Dan. *stiaalen*.

Perfect Participle Passive of Derivative Verbs.

The primitive suffix is -*ta*, which in the masculine assumes the case-sign -*s*, in the neuter -*m*, in the feminine gradates the final vowel; so that the terminations are, masc. *a-s*, fem. *a*, neut. *a-m*; Greek suffix -το-, terminations ο-s, η, ο-ν; Latin suffix -*tu*- for -*to*-, terminations *u-s* (for †*o-s*), *a* (for *a*), *u-m* (for †*o-m*).

---

[1] Concerning the modification of the radical, see the Formation of the Perfect Theme in Gothic, p. 398 sqq.

[2] Where we prefix the hyphen to the participial form, it indicates the augment *ge*, Old High German *ga*, which precedes the verb.

[3] Layamon has in this word dropped the *n*, and makes the participle *stole*; but he has *cumen, toren, broken*, &c.

THE VERB.

Primitive. Participles *da-ta-*, *kru-ta-*, *kak-ta-*, *sádaya-ta-*, of the roots *da* (to give), *kru* (to hear), *kak* (to cook), *sad* (to sit).

Sanskrit. Participles *ma-ta-*, *bhr-ta*, *bad-dha-* for †*bad-ta-*, of the roots *man* (to think), *bhar* (to bear), *badh*, *bandh* (to bind).

Greek. Participles κλυ-το-, φευκ-το-, στα-το-, θε-το-, γνω-το, of the roots κλυ (to hear), φυγ (to flee), στα (to stand), θε (to set), γνο (to know).

Latin. Participles *da-to-*, *sta-to*, *i-to-*, *coc-to-*, of the roots *da* (to give), *sta* (to stand), *i* (to go) *coc* (to cook).

Gothic. The suffix in the form of *-da*, nom. sing. masc. *-th-s* for †*da-s*, neut. *-th* for †*da-m*, fem. *-da*. These terminations are added to the theme of derivative verbs; e. g. theme *soki-*, part. masc. *soki-th-s*, neut. *soki-th*, fem. *sóki-da*; theme *fisko-*, part. masc *fisko-th-s*, neut. *fisko-th*, fem. *fiskó-da*. This suffix is also used in all those verbs which apply the perfect theme for the functions of the present (Præterito-Præsentia) and their analogues, such as *mah-ta*, *thah-ta*, *brah-ta*, of the roots *mag* (to be able), *thak* (to think), *brag* (to bring).

The other Teutonic dialects apply the same suffix in the form of *-d*, or *-t*, respectively, which they add to the thematic vowel of the derivative or weak verb; e. g. O. H. Germ. *-ner-i-t-er*, O. S. *-ner-i-d*, A. S. *ner-e-d*, O. Fris. *ner-i-d*, Goth. *nas-i-th-s* for †*nas-i-da-s*, from *nasjan*, to save; thus also the O. N. *tal-d-r* for an older †*tal-i-da-s* from *taljan*, to count, to tell; O. H. Germ. *salp-o-t-er*, Goth. *salb-ó-th-s* for *salb-ó-da-s*; compare O. N, *kall-a-ð-r* for †*kall-a-da-s*; O. S. *scáw-o-d*, looked; A. S. *-sealf-o-d*; Late Saxon *makode* and *makede*, *ascode* and *askede*; O. Engl. *thanked* and *thankid*; N. Engl. *thanked*, N. H. Germ. *-dankt*. In the Middle and New Teutonic languages the distinction of different weak conjugations, that is, of different themes formed by the derivative suffix *aya*, is, with few exceptions, lost; hence the thematic or connective vowel is always *e*, and the participial termination *-ed*, *-et*, respectively; or, dropping the thematic *e* altogether, *-d*, *-t*. On the whole the thematic *e* and the suffixed participial *d* are treated in the same manner as the perfect termination and its preceding thematic vowel, and we shall therefore leave the details of their various modifications for the section on Weak Conjugations.

THE PERFECT IN THE TEUTONIC LANGUAGES.

REDUPLICATION (ABLAUT). CLASSIFICATION OF STRONG VERBS.

Reduplication was in the Teutonic, as in the other Aryan languages, the most primitive mode of forming the perfect. This fact must always be borne in mind if we wish to arrive at something like order and system in a subject which is rather complicated in its nature because often obscure in its origin and development. Many phenomena in the Ablaut of Teutonic verbs can only be explained by the influence of a reduplicational syllable upon the radical, the effect of which remained even when the cause had ceased to exist. Several examples of the kind in Gothic we had already occasion to notice. As to the other Teutonic languages our rule is of the same importance. Though the reduplication has completely disappeared from the verb, it has left an indelible impression on the system of Ablaut. Under 'Ablaut' Teutonic grammarians understand a modification of the radical which takes place in the perfect tense and the perfect participle. This modification consisted originally in the gradation of the root in the perfect singular, gradation or weakening in the present tense, weakening in the perfect participle; and it was a phonetic change of secondary importance, concomitant with the reduplication, but not necessary for the formation of the perfect, far less sufficient of itself to denote that tense. The more however the ancient mode of reduplication was abandoned, the more important became the modification of the radical in the formation of the tenses, until finally it was the only means of expressing the temporal relations of the verb. Still it would be impossible to deny the influence of reduplication on the Ablaut, not merely in the ancient Teutonic verb, but in verbal forms of the present day. This point we are about to examine. Reduplication, in its original form, must have contained the vowel of the root; the perfect of the verb *haldan* must have been *ha-hald* in the primitive Teutonic. Now we find that in the Gothic, such as it is in extant documents, the radical is everywhere replaced by the vowel *ai* in the reduplicational syllable. This change may have occurred before the separation of the different Teutonic tribes took place, and must therefore have affected all the dialects. Thus then the Old High

German would use *hei-halt* for *ha-halt*, the Low German *hí-hald* or *hi-hald*, Anglo-Saxon probably *heo-heald*. (*eo* for *i*, see Anglo-Saxon Brechung of the vowel *i*.)

The loss of the reduplication seems to date from a period when the Teutonic nation had lost the centre of unity, and had separated into tribes independent of one another. While Gothic has preserved the reduplication in many verbs, the other dialects have lost it altogether—all of them, however, show traces of the ancient grammatical form. We have seen how in Latin, through a process of contraction, forms arose such as *cepi* from †*ca-capi*, *feci* from †*fa-faci*, *fregi*, from †*fra-fragi* or rather †*fra-fagi*. A similar inclination to combine the reduplicational and the radical syllable came upon the Teutonic languages, and a like effect was produced in the contraction of the vowels; hence O. H. Germ. *hialt*, O. S. *held* for the Goth. *hai-hald*. In the first-mentioned dialect the diphthong still represents the bisyllabic nature of the ancient perfect, while in the Low German they were more closely amalgamated into *e*. This process of contraction becomes clearly apparent from two examples left in Old High German. One we find in the perfect *pi-hei-alt*, used by Kero (eighth century), which is but one step from the primitive form *hei-halt*, the reduplicated perfect of *halt-an*. From this example it would appear, that the initial consonant of the root was lost first, and that then the vowels were more and more closely contracted, so that from *heialt* we arrive in later documents at the forms *hialt*, *hialt*, *hielt*, until in Modern German it is pronounced *hilt*, though still spelt as a diphthong in *hielt*. The closest contraction took place in the ancient Low German dialects, which passed through the diphthongal form to *held*, *hild*. Another example we have in the O. H. Germ. *ana-steroʒ* (impingebat), which stands for *ana-stésoʒ*, the *s* of the original form being changed into *r*, and the *e* being the weakened form of *i*, the remainder of the original reduplicational vowel *ei*, so that we arrive next at *stestoʒ* and finally at *stei-stoʒ*, the parallel to the Gothic *stai-stáut*, perfect of *stáutan*, O. H. Germ. *stoʒan*, percutere. In the same manner was formed *pleruʒ* for †*ple-tuz* (the second *l* dissimilated) for †*plei-ploʒ*, perfect of *pluoʒan*, to sacrifice. The usual form of the perfect of *stoʒan* is *stioʒ* (*stiaz* and *stieʒ* are peculiarities of special dialects) with *io*, because of the dark full radical O. H. Germ. *o*, Goth. *áu*, in which case the Low German dialects also have the diphthongal form *io* or *eo*; but of *haldan*, *heiʒan*, it is *hiald*, *hiaʒ* (never *hiold*, *hioʒ*), Low Germ. *held* (A. S. *heold*), *hét*, *ia*, *e*, on account of the high-sounding radicals *a*, *ei* = Goth. *a*, *ái*. A few fragments of reduplication are preserved in Anglo-Saxon too in the words *leolc* = ⁺*leo-lác*, perfect of *lácan*, to jump; *héht* (more ancient instead of *hét*), perfect of *hátan*, to be called; *leort* = ⁺*leolt* = *leo-lǽt*, perfect of *lǽtan*, to let; and in a similar manner *reord*, perfect of *rǽdan*, to advise; *ondreard*, perfect of *ondrǽdan*, to fear. It is peculiar to all these forms that they have dropped the radical, the reduplication being preserved at the expense of the root, a case which may be compared to the loss of a consonant in a similar way in the Latin *ste-ti*, *spo-pondi*. In later documents the contraction proceeds, *leolc* becomes *leoc*, then *lec*, *leort*, *leot*, *let*, *ondreord*, *ondreíd*, so that finally they arrive at the closest contraction in *e*.

From this then it may be clear how the Ablaut, or modification of the radical, in the perfect tense, was affected in the Teutonic dialects by the reduplication, or rather the loss of the reduplication, and we therefore feel justified in arranging the different Teutonic verbs in the same manner as we did in Gothic.

We shall now take the Ablaut of the perfect participle also into account, because it is one of the chief characteristics in the conjugation of the strong verb in the modern Teutonic dialects, and because it gives the beginner one criterion more to direct him in the examination and study of that subject in the ancient Teutonic languages.

We first proceed to the classification of the Old Teutonic strong verbs.

I.

Under this head we consider to fall all those verbs which in Gothic have reduplication and gradation combined. The radical is either *a* or *e*; where the former occurs, the present theme is formed with the suffix *-ya-*, that is, *ai*; in the perfect singular and plural we have the second gradation *o*; the perfect participle has the radical of the present. In the other Teutonic languages the *e* of the Gothic present is represented by their respective vowels of the first gradation; e. g. Old High German *a*, Anglo-Saxon *ǽ*, &c.[1] The radical of the perfect is of course modified by the reduplication. Thus we get the vocalic system of—

---

[1] The Table of Gradations should always be consulted (p. 24).

THE VERB.

Class I. (Grimm IV, V, VI.)

Radical *a, ê*:—

	Pres.	Perf. Sing.	Perf. Plur.	Perf. Part.
Gothic	ai (a) ê	ô	ô	ai, ê
O. H. Germ.	â	ia	ia	â
Old Saxon	â	ê, ie	ê, ie	â
Anglo-Saxon	æ	ê	ê	æ
Old Frisian	ê	î, ê	î, ê	ê
Old Norse	á	ê	ê	á

Examples:—

Gothic	saia	sai-sô	sai-sôum	saians
,,	lêta	lai-lôt	lai-lôtum	lêtans
O. H. Germ.	lâʒu	liaʒ	liaʒumes	lâʒanêr
Old Saxon	lâtu	let	lêtum	lâtan
Anglo-Saxon	læte	let	lêton	læten
Old Frisian	lêta[1]	lit	liton	lêten
Old Norse	láta	let	lêtum	látinn

Verbs belonging to this Class.

Gothic. *saia*, sow (Germ. sæe; sero); *laia*, scold, irrideo; *vaia*, breathe, blow (Germ. wehe; flo); *greta*, cry, weep, ploro; *fleka*, complain, plango; *leta*, let (Germ. laße; sino); *teka*, touch, tango. *slepa*, sleep (Germ. schlafe; dormio), makes the perf. *saizlep*, avoiding the second gradation.

Old High German. *slâfu*, sleep (Germ. schlafe); *râtu*, advise (Germ. rate; consulo); *lâʒu*, let (Germ. laße; sino). *hâhu*, hang (Germ. hange; suspendo), and *fâhu*, catch (Germ. fange; capio), take the perfect of *hankan*, *vankan*. (Class II.)

Old Saxon. *slâpu*[2], *râdu*, *lâtu*, *ondrâdu*, fear, dread, metuo. *hâhu* and *fâhu* make their perfect after Class II.

Anglo-Saxon. *slæpe, græte, læte, ondræde. sáwe*, sero = Goth. *saia*, follows the analogy of Class III.

Old Frisian. *slepa, reda, leta, wepa*, weep; plorare.

Old Norse. *gráta, láta, ráða, blása*, breathe, spirare. *fá* (catch, capere) makes the present *fæ*, perf. sing. *feck*, plur. *fengum*, perf. part. *fenginn*.

---

[1] Of Old Frisian and Old Norse we give the infinitive instead of the 1st singular present indicative.

[2] Where no translation is given, the meaning of the word may be seen from the parallels in the preceding cognate dialects.

II.

Under this head we group in Gothic all those verbs which have reduplication without gradation. They have either the radical *a* followed by two consonants (commonly liquid with mute), or highest gradation in the present theme already; the radical of the present remains throughout. In the other Teutonic languages the radical *a* is preserved in the present, and in the perfect participle; in the perfect it is changed under the influence of the reduplication. The verbs with the second gradation have either *ai* (second gradation of *i*) or *au* (second gradation of *u*) in the present tense, which gradation is rendered in the other Teutonic languages by the corresponding vowels.

Thus we get three classes, of which we give the vocalic system in the following.

Class II. (Grimm I.)

Radical *a*:—

	Pres.	Perf. Sing.	Perf. Plur.	Perf. Part.
Gothic	a	a	a	a
O. H. Germ.	a	ia	ia	a
Old Saxon	a	ê, ie	ê, ie	a
Anglo-Saxon	a, ea	ê, eó	ê, eó	a, ea
Old Frisian	a	î, ê	î, ê	a
Old Norse	a	ê	ê	a

Examples:—

Gothic	halda	hai-hald	hai-haldum	haldans
O. H. Germ.	haltu	hialt	hialtumês	haltanêr
Old Saxon	haldu	hêld	hêldun	haldan
Anglo-Saxon	heulde	heóld	heóldon	healden
,,	spanne	spên	spênon	spannen
Old Frisian	halda	hilt	hildon	halden
Old Norse	halda	hêlt	hêldum	haldinn

Verbs belonging to this Class.

Gothic. *salta*, salt (Germ. salze; salio); *halda*, guard, pasco; *walda*, rule, command (Germ. walte; impero); *falþa*, fold (Germ. falte; plico); *faha*, catch (Germ. fange; capio); *haha*, hang (Germ. hange; suspendo).

Old High German. *vallu*, fall (Germ. falle; cado); *haltu*, hold (Germ. halte; teneo); *spaltu*, cleave (Germ. spalte; scindo); *valdu*, fold (Germ. falte; plico); *salzu*, salt (Germ. salze; salio); *kanku*, *gangu*, go, eo; *fangu*, receive (Germ. em(p)fange; suscipio); *hanku*, *hangu*, hang (Germ. hange; suspendo); *aru*, plough, aro.

THE VERB.

Old Saxon. *fallu, haldu, waldu, fangu, gangu; blandu*, mix, blend, misceo.

Anglo-Saxon. *fealle, healde, fange, hange*, occur in the perfect only; *spanne*, span (Germ. spannen; tendo), *wealde*, rule, command, dominor.

Old Frisian. *halde, valde*, impero.

Old Norse. *falla, halda, valda, blanda, ganga; hangi*, pendeo; *falda*, plicare. As to the irregularities of this class, see our remarks below.

Class III. (Grimm II.)

Radical *ai* (*i*):—

	Pres.	Perf. Sing.	Perf. Plur.	Perf. Part.
Gothic	*ai*	*ai*	*ai*	*ai*
O. H. Germ.	*ei*	*ia*	*ia*	*ei*
Old Saxon	*ê*	*ê, ie*	*ê, ie*	*ê*
Anglo-Saxon	*a*	*ê, eó*	*ê, eó*	*â*
Old Frisian	*e*	*î, ê*	*î, ê*	*ê*
Old Norse	*ei*	*ê*	*ê*	*ei*

Examples:—

Gothic	*skaida*	*skai-skaid*	*skai-skaidum*	*skaidans*
,,	*haita*	*hai-hait*	*hai-haitum*	*haitans*
O. H. Germ.	*skeidu*	*skiad*	*skiadumês*	*skeidanêr*
Old Saxon	*skêdu*	*skêd*	*skêdun*	*skêdan*
Anglo-Saxon	*scâde*	*sceód*	*sceódon*	*scâden*
,,	*hâte*	*hêt*	*hêton*	*haten*
Old Frisian	*hête*	*hît*	*hîton*	*hêten*
Old Norse	*heita*	*hêt*	*hêtum*	*heitinn*

Verbs belonging to this Class.

Gothic. *haita*, am called (Germ. heiße, O. Engl. hight; vocor); *maita*, cut off, abscido; *skaida*, separate (Germ. scheide; separo); *fraisa*, tempt, tento; *af-aika*, deny, nego; *laika*, leap, jump, rejoice, ludo.

Old High German. *heiʒu, skeidu, meiʒu, zeisu*, carpo.

Old Saxon. *hetu, skedu, suepu*, verro.

Anglo-Saxon. *hate, scâde, swápe, lace.*

Old Frisian. *hete, skethe.*

Old Norse. *heita, leika, sweipa.*

Class IV. (Grimm III.)

Radical *au* (*u*):—

	Pres.	Perf. Sing.	Perf. Plur.	Perf. Part.
Gothic	au	au	au	au
O. H. Germ.	ou, ô	io, ia	io, ia	ou, ô
Old Saxon	ô	io, ie	io, ie	ô
Anglo-Saxon	eá	eó	eó	eá
Old Frisian	â	î, io	î, io	a, ê
Old Norse	au	io, ê	io, ê	au

Examples:—

Gothic	hlaupa	hlai-hlaup	hlai-hlaupum	hlaupans
O. H. Germ.	hloufu	hliaf	hliafumês	hloufanêr
Old Saxon	hlôpu	hliop	hliopun	hlopan
Anglo-Saxon	hleápe	hleóp	hleópon	hleápen
Old Frisian	hlápa	[hliop	hliopon]	hlápen
Old Norse	hlápa	hliop	hliopum	hlapinn

Class IV a.

Radical *ó* (*a*):—

	Gothic	O. H. Germ.	Old Saxon	Anglo-Saxon	Old Frisian	Old Norse
Pres.	ô	uo	ô, uo	ô, ê	ô, ê	ô
Perf. Sing.	?	io, ia	io, ie	eó	î, io	ê
Perf. Plur.	?	io	io, ie	eó	î, io	ê
Perf. Part.	?	uo	ô, uo	ô, ê	ô, ê	ô

Examples:—

Gothic	blôta	bai-blôt?	bai-blôtum?	blôtans?
O. H. Germ.	pluoʒu	pliaʒ?	pliaʒumês?	pluoʒanêr
,,	hruofu	hriof	hriofumês	hruofanêr
Old Saxon	hrôpu	hriop	hriopun	hrôpan
Anglo-Saxon	blôte	bleót	bleóton	blôten
,,	hrêpan	hreóp	hreópon	hrêpen
Old Frisian	flôka	fliok	fliokon	flôken
,,	wêpa	wiop	wiopon	wêpen
Old Norse	blôta	blêt	blêtum	blôtinn

Verbs belonging to this Class.

IV. **Gothic.** *hlaupa*, run (Germ. laufe; curro); *stauta*, strike, butt (Germ. stoße; percutio); *ana-auka*, add, join, addo.

Old High German. *hloufu*; *houwu*, cut, hew (Germ. haue; cædo); *scrotu*, cut (Germ. schrote; seco); *stóʒu* = Goth. *stauta*.

Old Saxon. *hlopu*, *ôcan*, perf. part. of *ôku*, augeo; †*odan*, perf. part. of †*odu*, gigno; *gihauwan*, perf. part. of †*hauwan*.

Anglo-Saxon. *hleápe*; *heáwe*; *beate*, beat, verbero; part. *eáden* genitus; *eácen*, auctus, from †*eáde*, †*eod*; †*eáce*, †*eóc*.

THE VERB.

Old Frisian. *hlepe* = Goth. *hlaupa; stete* = Goth. *stauta*.
Old Norse. *hlaupa; auðinn*, genitum, perf. part. of †*eyð; ausa*, haurire; *auka*, augere; *bua*, dwell, habitare; *spna*, spit (Germ. speien; spuere); *hoggva*, to cut, strike, cædere = O. H. Germ. *houwu*, A. S. *heáwe*.

IV a. **Gothic.** *blota?* revere, deum colo; *hvopa?* boast, glorior.

Old High German. *hruofu*, call (Germ. rufe; clamo); *pluoʒu*, sacrifice, libo; *wuofu*, weep, groan, ululo, plango, ejulo; *vluohhu*, curse, maledico = Goth. *fleka* (Class I).
Old Saxon. *hropu; wopu*, weep; *flocan*, maledictus, perf. part.
Anglo-Saxon. *hrepe, wepe; rowe*, row, remigo.
Old Frisian. *hrepa, wepa; floka*, maledicere.
Old Norse. *blóta*, sacrifice.

III.

Under this head we enumerate verbs which in the perfect take gradation without reduplication. These again may be divided into different classes. Some have in the perfect singular second gradation, but in the plural the simple pure root, in accordance with the primitive rule of gradation. The perfect participle has, like the perfect plural, the short radical; the present tense commonly raises the radical to the first gradation. This class again may be subdivided into such as have the radical *i*, and others with the radical *u*. As to the mode of gradation in the present and the perfect singular, compare the Table of Gradations. Where the radical is *u*, it is in all the dialects, except Gothic, weakened to *o* in the perfect participle; Old Frisian weakens it to *e* in the perfect plural and the perfect participle.

CLASS V. (Grimm VIII.)

Radical *i*:—

	Pres.	Perf. Sing.	Perf. Plur.	Perf. Part.
Gothic	*ei*	*ai*	*i*	*i*
O. H. Germ.	*î*	*ei, ê*	*i*	*i*
Old Saxon	*î*	*ê*	*i*	*i*
Anglo-Saxon	*î*	*á*	*i*	*i*
Old Frisian	*î*	*ê*	*i*	*i*
Old Norse	*î*	*ei*	*i*	*i*

Examples:—

	Pres.	Perf. Sing.	Perf. Plur.	Perf. Part.
Gothic	greipa	graip	gripum	gripans
„ •	leihva	láihv	laihvum	laihvans
O. H. Germ.	krîfu	kreif	krîfum	krîfans
Old Saxon	grîpu	grep	gripun	gripan
Anglo-Saxon	grîpe	grâp	gripon	gripen
Old Frisian	grîpa	grep	gripon	gripen
Old Norse	gripa	greip	gripum	gripinn

Verbs belonging to this Class.

Gothic. *keina,* germ (Germ. keime; germino); *skeina,* shine (Germ. scheine; luceo); *greipa,* seize, gripe (Germ. greife; rapio); *dreiba,* drive (Germ. treibe; pello); *sveiba,* cease, desino; *hneiva,* bow (Germ. neige; inclino); *speiva,* spit (Germ. speie; spuo); *smeita,* smite, smear (Germ. schmeiße, schmiere; illino); *in-veita,* adore; *beida,* expect, abide; *leiþa,* go, eo; *sneiþ-a,* cut (Germ. schneide; seco); *ur-reisa,* rise, surgo; *steiga,* ascend (Germ. steigen); *ga-teiha,* announce (Germ. an-zeige, zeihe, αναγγέλλω); *þeiha,* grow (Germ. ge-deihe; cresco).

Old High German. *chînu,* germino; *scînu,* luceo; *krîfu,* rapio; *trîpu,* pello; *knîhu,* inclino; *stîkû,* scando; *dîhu,* cresco, proficio; *zîhu,* annuntio, accuso; *scrîpu,* write (Germ. schreibe, scribo); *spîwu,* spuere; *mîdu,* avoid (Germ. meiden; evito); *snîdu,* seco; *pîtu,* expecto; *rîtu,* ride (Germ. reiten; equo vehor); *wizu,* know (Germ. weiß; imputo); *grîu,* gannio; *scrîu,* shriek (Germ. schreie; clamo), perf. plur. *grirumes, scrirumes,* see Perfect in -s-, p. 401.

Old Saxon. *kinu,* germino; *skînu,* luceo; *grîpu,* arripio; *drîbu,* pello; *spîwu,* spuo; *wrîtu,* scribo; *bidu,* expecto; *mîðu,* evito; *snîðu,* seco; *stîgu,* scando.

Anglo-Saxon. *scine,* fulgeo; *grîpe,* arripio; *drîfe,* pello; *spîwe,* spuo; *smîte,* percutio; *bîde,* expecto; *lîðe,* proficiscor; *hnîge,* inclino; *stîge,* scando; *tîhe,* arguo; *pîhe,* proficio.

Old Frisian. *grîpa,* prehendere; *drîfa,* pellere; *snîtha,* secare; *hnîga,* flectere; *stîga,* scandere, perf. *stêch.*

Old Norse. *skîn,* luceo; *grîp,* prehendo; *drîf,* pello; *zvîf,* moveor; *bît,* bite, mordeo; *lîð,* proficiscor; *qvîð,* metuo; *rîð,* equito; *snîð,* seco; *swîð,* doleo; *rîs,* surgo; *vîk,* yield (Germ. weiche; cedo); *hnîg,* inclino.

THE VERB.

CLASS VI. (Grimm IX.)
Radical *u* :—

	Pres.	Perf. Sing.	Perf. Plur.	Perf. Part.
Gothic	iu	au	u	u
O. H. Germ.	iu, io, û	ou, ô[1]	u	o
Old Saxon	iu, io, u	o	u	o
Anglo-Saxon	eó, û	eá	u	o
Old Frisian	íu, ia, u	â	e	e
Old Norse	iu, io, ú	au	u	o

Examples :—

Gothic	giuta	gaut	gutum	gutans
,,	kiusa	kaus	kusum	kusans
O. H. Germ.	kiuʒu	kôʒ	kuʒumês	koʒanêr
,,	chiusu	chôs	churumês	choranêr
,,	triufu	trouf	trufumês	trofanêr
Old Saxon	giutu	gôt	gutun	gotan
,,	kiusu	kôs	kurun	koran
Anglo-Saxon	geóte	geát	guton	goten
,,	ceóse	ceás	curon	coren
Old Frisian	kiusa	kâs	keron	keren
Old Norse	kiosa	kaus	kusum	kosinn

Verbs belonging to this Class.

Gothic. *dis-hniupa*, break, dirumpo; *hiufa*, weep, fleo; *sniva*, hasten, go, come, verto, vado, for †*sniua*, perf. sing. *snau*, plur. *snivum*, *snevum* for *snuum*, perf. part. *snivans* for †*snuans*; *giuta*, pour out (Germ. gieße; fundo); *biuda*, offer (Germ. biete); *driusa*, fall, cado; *kiusa*, choose (Germ. kiese; eligo); *fra-liusa*, loose (Germ. ver-liere; perdo); *biuga*, bend (Germ. biege; flecto); *liuga*, lie (Germ. luege; mentior); *ga-lúka*, lock, claudo; *tiuah*, tug, pull (Germ. ziehe, traho).

Old High German. *chliupu*, cleave, findo; *súfu*, drink (Germ. saufe; bibo); *triufu*, drop (Germ. traufe; stillo); *chiuwu*, chew (Germ. kaue; mando); *piutu*, offero; *siudu*, seethe (Germ. siede; coquo); *kiuʒu*, pour out (Germ. gieße; fundo); *chiusu*, choose (Germ. kiese; eligo); *vliuʒu*, flow (Germ. fließe, fluo); *sliuʒu*, lock (Germ. schließe; claudo); *liusu*, loose (Germ. ver-liere; perdo); *vriusu*, freeze (Germ. friere; gelo); *piuku*, flecto; *vliuku*, fly (Germ. fliege; volo); *vliuhu*, flee (Germ. fliehe; fugio); *ziuhu*, traho; *liuku*, mentior.

Old Saxon. *hiufu*, ploro; *cliufu*, findo; *giutu*, fundo; *niutu*, enjoy (Germ. ge-nieße; fruor); *biudu*, offero; *driusu*, cado; *kiusu*, eligo; *far-liusu*, perdo; *liugu*, mentior; *lúku*, claudo; *riuku*, reek (Germ. rauche; fumo); *tiuhu*, traho.

---

[1] ô chiefly before dentals and sibilants.

Anglo-Saxon. *creope*, creep, repo; *deófe*, mergo (Germ. taufe); *sceófe*, trudo; *reófe*, rumpo; *breówe*, brew (Germ. brauc); *ceowe*, chew (Germ. kaue, manduco); *hreowe*, rue (Germ. reuc; pœnitet me); *breote*, break, frango; *geote*, pour out, fundo; *neote*, enjoy, fruor (Germ. ge-nieße); *sceote*, shoot (Germ. schieße; jaculor); *beode*, offero (Germ. biete); *seoðe*, seethe, boil (Germ. siede; coquo); *ceose*, choose (Germ. kiese; eligo); *freose*, freeze, gelo; *for-leose*, loose, perdo; *lúce*, lock, claudo; *suce*, sugo (Germ. sauge); *reoce*, exhalo, reek (Germ. rauche); *smeoce*, fumo, smoke (Germ. schmauche); *beoge*, bend (Germ. biege; flecto); *dreóge*, ago; *fleoge*, volo, fly (Germ. fliege); *leóge*, mentior, lie (Germ. luege); *fleohe*, flee (Germ. fliehe; fugio); *teohe*, traho, tug (Germ. ziehe); *seo*, colo; *teo*, arguo; *þeó*, proficio; *wreo*, proficio, perf. *seah, teah, þeáh, wreáh*, plur. *sugon, tugon, þugon, wrugon*.

Old Frisian. *driupe*, stillo; *kriapa*, repere; *niata*, uti; *skiata*, jaculari; *stúta*, claudere; *biada*, offerre; *kiasa*, eligere; *liasa*, perdere; *liaka*, claudere.

Old Norse. *briota*, frangi; *fliuga*, volare; *luka*, claudere; *kiosa*, eligere; *driupa*, stillare; *fliota*, fluere; *niota*, frui; *luga*, mentiri.

Some of the verbs which apply the gradation without reduplication have the radical *a* which, under various circumstances, was variously affected in the different tenses[1]. Where the radical was protected by an ancient reduplication, it is still preserved in the present tense, as in *fara*, from an ancient *fa-fara*; these verbs have the perfect in *ó*, as *fór*, probably from a primitive *fa-fára*. In those verbs in which the radical *a* was not sheltered in the present tense by reduplication, it was weakened into *i*, as *giba, stila, hilpa*, probably from a more ancient *gaba, stala, halpa*; in the perfect singular the pure short radical is preserved, perhaps also under the influence of reduplication, as *halp, stal, gab*, from a more ancient *ha-halp, sta-stal, ga-gab*. In the plural perfect some have *e*, the first gradation of *a*, others weaken the radical *a* to *u*. The verbs which gradate the radical to *é* in the plural, weaken it to *i* or to *u* in the perfect participle. Thus then the different modifications of the radical give rise to four more classes, the vocalic system of which is as follows.

---

[1] Compare pp. 400 403, A, B, C, and D.

Class VII. (Grimm VII.)

Radical *a* :—

	Pres.	Perf. Sing.	Perf. Plur.	Perf. Part.
Gothic	a	ô	ô	a
O. H. Germ.	a	uo	uo	a
Old Saxon	a	ô, uo	ô, uo	a
Anglo-Saxon	a, ea	ô	ô	a
Old Frisian	a, e	ô	ô	a, e
Old Norse	a	ô	ô	a, e

Examples :—

Gothic	fara	fôr	forum	farans
O. H. Germ.	varu	vuor	vuorumês	varanêr
Old Saxon	faru	for	fôrun	faran
Anglo-Saxon	fare	for	fôron	faren
Old Frisian	fara	for	fôron	faren
Old Norse	fara	for	forum	farinn

Verbs belonging to this Class.

Gothic. *us-ana*, expire; *standa*, stand, sto, perf. *stoþ*; *fara*, go, travel (Germ. fare; proficiscor); *svara*, swear (Germ. schwoere; juro); *graba*, dig (Germ. grabe; fodio); *hafja*, lift (Germ. hebe; tollo); *fraþja*, understand, know, sapio; *skapa*, create (Germ. schaffe; creo); *raþja*, count, reckon, numero; *skaþja*, damage, scathe (Germ. schade; noceo); *saka*, scold, increpo; *hlahja*, laugh (Germ. lache; rideo); *slaha*, slay (Germ. schlage; percutio); *rahsja*, grow, wax (Germ. wachsen; cresco).

Old High German. *stantu*, sto; *varu*, vehor; *suerju*, juro; *krapu*, fodio; *skafu*, creo; *heffu*, tollo; *wasku*, wash (Germ. wasche; lavo); *traku*, bear (Germ. trage; porto); *slahu*, percutio; *hlahhu*, rideo; *wahsu*, cresco.

Old Saxon. *standu, faru, skapu, grabu; hebbju*, tollo; *skaku*, shake, quatior; *dragu*, porto; *hlahu*, rideo; *slahu*, cædo; *wahsu*, cresco.

Anglo-Saxon. *gale*, sing, cano; *stande*, sto; *fare*, eo; *swerige*, juro; *scape*, creo; *hebbe*, elevo; *grafe*, fodio; *wasce*, lavo; *scace*, shake, quatio; *bace*, bake, pinso; *tace*, take, prehendo; *drage*, porto, drag; *sleahe*, slay, cædo; *hleahhe*, laugh, rideo; *weaxe*, grow, wax, cresco.

Old Frisian. *fara, skapa, vaxa, draga, slaga*, perf. *sloch*.

Old Norse. *gala*, canere; *standa*, stare; *fara*, proficisci; *svara*, jurare; *skapa*, creare; *grafa*, fodere; *hafa*, tollere; *vaða*, ire, perf. *oð*; *vaxa*, crescere, perf. *ox*; *skaka*, concutere; *taka*, capere; *draga*, ferre—all these have the pres. in *e*; *deya*, die, moriri, perf. *do*, part. *dáinn*; *geya*, latrare; *flá*, from *flaga*, flay, excorire, pres. *flæ*, perf. sing. *flo*, plur. *flogum*, part. *fleginn*: in the same manner *hlæja*, laugh, ridere; *slá* from *slaha*, slay, percutere.

Class VIII. (Grimm X.)

Radical *a* :—

	Pres.	Perf. Sing.	Perf. Plur.	Perf. Part.
Gothic	*i*	*a*	*ê*	*i*
O. H. Germ.	*i, ë*	*a*	*â*	*ë*
Old Saxon	*i, e*	*a*	*â*	*ë*
Anglo-Saxon	*i, e*	*a, ä*	*â, œ*	*i, e*
Old Frisian	*i, e*	*a, e*	*â, ê*	*i, e*
Old Norse	*i, e*	*a*	*â*	*e*

Examples :—

Gothic	*giba*	*gab*	*gêbum*	*gibans*
O. H. Germ.	*kipu*	*kap*	*kâpumês*	*këpanêr*
Old Saxon	*gibu*	*gaf*	*gâbun*	*gëban*
Anglo-Saxon	*gife*	*geaf*	*geâfon*	*gifen*
,,	*ëte*	*at*	*œton*	*ëten*
Old Frisian	*jëfa*	*jef*	*jêfon*	*jëfen*
Old Norse	*gëfa*	*gaf*	*gâfum*	*gëfinn*

Verbs belonging to this Class.

Gothic. *giba*, give (Germ. gebe; do); *bi-gita*, find, get, invenio; *frita*, devour (Germ. freβe; voro); *ita*, eat (Germ. eβe; edo); *sita*, sit (Germ. sitze; sedeo); *bidja*, pray (Germ. bitte; oro); *truda*, tread (Germ. trete; calco); *mita*, measure (Germ. meβe; metior); *in-vida*, deny, abnego; *qviþa*, say, dico; *lisa*, colligo (Germ. lese); *ga-nisa*, recover (Germ. ge-nese; sanor); *visa*, am, remain, maneo; *ga-brika*, break (Germ. breche; frango); *liga*, lie (Germ. lîge; jaceo); *viga*, move (Germ. be-wege; moveo, veho); *fraíha*, ask (Germ. frage; interrogo); *saíhva*, see (Germ. sehe; video).

Old High German. *kipu*, dono; *pittu*, rogo; *tritu*, calco; *quidu*, dico; *iʒu*, edo; *vriʒu;* voro; *miʒu*, metior; *sizu*, sedeo; *wiṣu*, sum, existo; *liku*, jaceo; *sihu*, video.

Old Saxon. *gibu, itu, bi-gitu*, consequor; *sittu, biddu, quithu, lisu, wisu, liggu, sihu*, perf. plur. *sâhun* and *sâwun*, part. *sewan*.

Anglo-Saxon. *gife; wëfe*, weave (Germ. webe; texo); *ete, frete, mete; on-gite*, intelligo; *sitte, trede, bidde, cweðe, lese, genese, wese; wrece*, wreak, ulciscor; *licge; geseo*, see (Germ. sehe; video), perf. sing. *geseah*, plur. *gesáwon*, part. *gesewen, gesegen*, plur. *gesëne = gesewene*.

Old Norse. *gëfa, eta; geta*, acquirere; *sita; biða*, petere; *lesa*, legere; *vera*, only in the perf. *var* for *vas;* *leka*, leak, stillare;

frega, interrogare, perf. sing. *frá* for *frag*, plur. *frágum*: in the same manner *vega*, interficere; *ligga*, jacere; *þigga*, obtinere; *sia*, see, videre, = *siha, sihva*, pres. *sê* for *se*, plur. *seum*, perf. *sá*, plur. *sáum*, perf. part. weak *seðr; troða*, calcare, pres. *treð*, perf. *trað; sofa*, to sleep, = *svëfa*, pres. *séf* for *svéf*, perf. *svaf*, plur. *sváfum*, part. *sofinn* for *svefinn; vëfa*, to weave, texere, perf. plur. *váfum* and *ófum*, part. *ofinn* for *vëfinn;* compare the analogous form *koma = qvema*, Class XI.

Class IX. (Grimm XI.)
Radical *a*:—

	Pres.	Perf. Sing.	Perf. Plur.	Perf. Part.
Gothic	*i*	*a*	*ê*	*u*
O. H. Germ.	*i, ë*	*a*	*â*	*o*
Old Saxon	*i, ë*	*a*	*â*	*u, o*
Anglo-Saxon	*i, e*	*a, ä*	*â, œ*	*u, o*
Old Frisian	*i, e*	*a, e*	*â, ê*	*i, e*
Old Norse	*i, e*	*a*	*â*	*u, o*

Examples:—

		Pres.	Perf. Sing.	Perf. Plur.	Perf. Part.
Gothic		*stila*	*stal*	*stêlum*	*stulans*
,,		*qvima*	*qvam*	*qvêmum*	*qvumans*
,,		*baira*	*bar*	*bêrum*	*baúrans*
O. H. Germ.		*stila*	*stal*	*stâlumês*	*stolanêr*
Old Saxon		*stila*	*stal*	*stâlun*	*stolan*
,,		*cumu*	*quam*	*quâmum*	*cuman*
Anglo-Saxon		*stële*	*stäl*	*stælon*	*stolen*
,,		*cume*	*com, cwom*	*cômon*	*cumen*
Old Frisian		*stëla*	*stel*	*stêlon*	*stëlen*
Old Norse		*stëla*	*stal*	*stâlum*	*stolinn*
,,		*koma*	*kom, kvam*	*kvâmum*	*kominn*

Verbs belonging to this Class.

Gothic. *stila*, steal (Germ. stele; furor); *nima*, take (Germ. nême; sumo); *qvima*, come (Germ. komme; venio); *ga-timan*, decere (Germ. ge-zîmen); *baíra*, bear, fero; *ga-taira*, tear, destroy, destruo.

Old High German. *stilu, nimu, quimu, ziman, piru*, fero; *ziru*, consumo; *sciru*, shear (Germ. scheere, tondeo); *rihhu*, wreak (Germ. rache; ulciscor); *prihhu*, break (Germ. breche; frango); *sprihhu*, speak (Germ. spreche; loquor); *stihhu*, sting, prick (Germ. steche; pungo); *vihtu*, fight (Germ. fechte; certo); *vlihtu*, weave (Germ. flechte; plecto).

Old Saxon. *stilu, nimu, cumu* (venio), *biru, briku, stiku* (pungo), *briku, spriku, wriku* (persequor).

Anglo-Saxon. *stele, nime, cume, bere, scere* (tondeo), *tere* (scindo), *brëce, sprëce*.

Old Frisian. Classes VIII and IX are identical, because the perfect participle has in both the weakened radical *e* : *bira, stela, nima, jëfa* (dare), *wesa* (esse), *breka, spreka*.

Old Norse. *stela, nema, koma* for *kvema* (venire), *bera, skera,* tondeo; *svëma* (natare), *svam, swaminn*; *erja* (arare), *ar, arinn*.

Class X. (Grimm. XII.)

Radical *a* :—

	Pres.	Perf. Sing.	Perf. Plur.	Perf. Part.
Gothic	*i*	*a*	*u*	*u*
O. H. Germ.	*i, ë*	*a*	*u*	*u, o*
Old Saxon	*i, ë*	*a*	*u*	*u, o*
Anglo-Saxon	*i, e, eo*	*a, a, ea*	*u*	*u, o*
Old Frisian	*i, e*	*a*	*u*	*u*
Old Norse	*i, e, ia*	*a*	*u*	*o, u*

Examples :—

Gothic	*hilpa*	*halp*	*hulpum*	*hulpans*
,,	*vairpa*	*varp*	*vaúrpum*	*vaúrpans*
O. H. Germ.	*hilfu*	*half*	*hulfumês*	*holpanêr*
,,	*rinnu*	*rann*	*runnumês*	*runnanêr*
Old Saxon	*hilpu*	*halp*	*hulpun*	*holpan*
,,	*rinnu*	*rann*	*runnun*	*runnan*
Anglo-Saxon	*hëlpe*	*healp*	*hulpon*	*holpen*
,,	*irne*	*arn*	*urnon*	*urnen*
,,	*weorpe*	*wearp*	*wurpon*	*worpen*
Old Frisian	*helpa*	*halp*	*hulpon*	*hulpen*
,,	*winna*	*wann*	*wunnon*	*wunnen*
Old Norse	*rinna*	*rann*	*runnum*	*runninn*
,,	*skella*	*skall*	*skullum*	*skollinn*

Verbs belonging to this Class.

Gothic. *hilpa*, help (Germ. helfe; adjuvo); *vilva*, seize, rob, rapio; *svilta*, die, morior; *gilda*, am worth (Germ. gelte; rependo); *brinna*, burn (Germ. brenne; ardeo); *du-ginna*, be-gin (Germ. be-ginne; incipio); *rinna*, flow, run (Germ. rinne.; fluo); *spinna*, spin (Germ. spinne; neo); *vinna*, suffer, patior; *binda*, bind (Germ. binde; necto); *bi-vinda*, wind (Germ. winde; circumdo); *finþa*, find (Germ. finde; invenio); *drigka*, drink (Germ. trinke; bibo); *bliggva*, cut, kill, cædo; *siggva*, sing, read (Germ. singe; cano, lego); *sigkva*, sink, fall (Germ. sinke; cado); *vairpa*, throw (Germ. werfe; jacio); *hvairba*, walk, turn about, verto; *gairda*, gird (Germ. gürte; cingo); *vairþa*, become (Germ. werde; fio).

Old High German. *hilfu*; *tilfu*, delf, fodio; *kiltu*, rependo; *sciltu*, scold (Germ. schelte; increpo); *smilzu*, smelt (Germ. schmelze; liquefio); *suimmu*, swim (Germ. schwimme; nato);

prinnu, ardeo; *rinnu,* fluo; *spinnu,* neo; *winnu,* laboro; *pintu,* necto; *suintu,* evanesco (Germ. schwinde); *vindu,* invenio; *sinku,* cano; *sinhu,* cado; *stinhu,* stink (Germ. stinke; oleo, odorem spargo); *trinhu,* bibo; *huirpu,* revertor; *stirphu,* die (Germ. sterbe; morior); *wirfu,* jacio; *wirdu,* fio.

Old Saxon. *hilpu, dilbu, suiltu* (morior), *gildu, brinnu, biginnu, winnu, bindu, findu, singu, drinku, wirpu, huirbu, wirthu* (fio).

Anglo-Saxon. *helpe, delfe, melte, swelte, gilde,* perf. *healp,* &c.; *on-ginne,* incipio, perf. *on-gan; spinne, winne, birne = brinne,* perf. *barn; irne = rinne,* perf. *ran; binde,* perf. *band;* in the same manner *grinde,* grind, molo; *swinde,* tabesco (Germ. schwinde); *winde,* wind (Germ. winde; plecto); *drince; swince,* laboro; *stince,* oleo; *bringe; singe; springe,* salio; *meorne,* mourn, curo, angor, perf. *mearn;* in the same manner *speorne,* spurn (Germ. sporne; calcitro); *weorpe,* jacio; *hweorfe,* revertor; *weorðe,* fio.

Old Frisian. *hilpa, binda, finda, winna, berna* (ardere), *werpa, wertha.*

Old Norse. *gialla,* sing, shout, resonare; *svelta,* esurire; *velta,* roll, turn, volvere; *gialda,* expendere; *brenna,* ardere; *renna,* fluere; *spinna,* nere; *vinna,* laborare; *finna,* invenire; *binda,* ligare, perf. *batt; winda,* torquere; *drecka,* bibere, perf. *drack; springa,* salire, *sprack; verpa,* jacere; *verða,* fieri.

CONJUGATION.

General Remarks.

Conjugation teaches us to combine the various elements which we observed in the formation of the verb, so as to express correctly the different relations of a certain action. The action independent of all relations is expressed in the root. The verb, however, is not merely the expression of an action, but it renders at the same time an exact account as to the person by whom, the time when, the modus or condition under which, that action took place. In order to express those various relations of persons, time, modus, activeness, or passiveness—in short, to make the root a verb, it is necessary that secondary roots, or suffixes, be added to the primary root, and thus force it out of its indefiniteness, and impart to it life and individuality. A condition without which a verb is inconceivable is that of personality: without the personal suffixes or terminations a verbal root or base can as little become a verb, as a nominal root or theme a substantive or adjective without the case-signs. If then the personal terminations are the most essential of the verbal elements, they are in a few instances alone sufficient to create a verb out of a root, as we have seen above with the roots *as* (to be), *bhu* (to be). But in most cases the root requires a connective, a binding vowel or a suffix to enable it to enter into communication with the personal termination. This connective vowel or suffix we called thematic, and the form which the root acquired by adopting it we called the theme or stem—the verbal theme, as on another occasion we spoke of nominal themes. The root *bhar* requires the suffix -*a*- to enter into combination with the personal termination -*ti* and to form the 3rd pers. sing. pres. ind. *bhar-a-ti*. Where we speak of an absolute fact, uninfluenced by, and independent of, circumstances and conditions, that is, in the indicative mood, we join the personal terminations immediately to the root or theme, so that out of *as* we make *as-ti*, out of *bhar-a-*, *bhar-a-ti;* but where we make the action dependent on certain conditions and circumstances, that is, in the optative and subjunctive (conjunctive), we require the aid of another suffix, which we place between the theme and the personal terminations. If then in the indicative the primitive language used simply *as-ti*, *bhar-a-ti*, it put in the optative *as-ya-t*, *bhar-a-ya-t ;* in the subjunctive *as-a-t*, *bhar-a-a-t*, hence *bhar-á-t*. But the same action may appear in different relations of time; it may be present or past: we therefore must have a present theme and a perfect theme—the former is *bhar-a-*, the latter was formed by reduplication, and thence resulted *bha-bhar-a-*. Take the Gothic root *bar*, which in the present weakens the radical into *i*, hence the theme †*bir-a*, *baír-a-* ; in the perfect it will take the first gradation of its radical and form *ber-*, dropping the thematic vowel of the present; the optative suffix is *ja*, hence *ber-ja-* ; added to this the personal suffix -*m* would be *ber-ja-m*, but appears as *ber-jau ;* or, to follow the opposite, or analytical course, given the Gothic present subjunctive 1st plural *vigaima* = *vig-a-i-m-a*, in which the final *a* is an inorganic addition to support the preceding *m*, the latter is the personal termination of the 1st plural, $i = ya$ the suffix of the optative mood, *a* the final of the present theme *vig-a-*, *vig* the weakened form of the root *vag*, primitive *vagh*, to move.

Though we may recognize all these different elements in the Teutonic, and chiefly the Old Teutonic verb, they are not all of equal importance. We might indeed divide verbs into such as have the thematic suffix, and others that have not: but the latter are so very few, as to render such classification impracticable. There are many ways to form the present theme, but out of the many the Teutonic languages have chosen a few, and these few became part and parcel of the inflexions or the conjugation, so that we cannot attempt to erect anything like the conjugational classes, as in Sanskrit for instance. That element however which truly and most distinctly characterizes the Teutonic verb, and places it in contraposition to the verb in all other Aryan languages, is the formation of the perfect. Though the sister-languages also have the gradation of the root, though most of them have the reduplicational system far more complete, yet nowhere do we find this element to enter so deeply into the whole organization of the language. We therefore unhesitatingly follow former grammarians and divide the whole conjugational system, according to the formation of the perfect, into two great classes. To the first conjugational class belong all those verbs which form the perfect by modifying the vowel of the root (mostly stem-verbs), to the second those which form the perfect by assuming an auxiliary suffix-verb (derivative verbs). The former, which the Teutonic languages have, partly at least, in common with their cognate sisters, we may fairly call the 'Old Form,' because it must have existed before the separation of the Aryan tribes; the latter the 'New Form,' because it is peculiar to the Teutonic languages, and must have been created after the Aryan separation. The verbs of the old form have a *simple* perfect, consisting of but one word; those of the new form have a *compound* perfect, consisting of the verb and its suffixed auxiliary verb. Grimm calls the former the 'Strong Conjugation,' because the verbs belonging to it form their perfect by means lying in the root itself, gradation, &c.; the latter 'Weak Conjugation,' because its verbs form the perfect with the assistance of an auxiliary. We do not see any cause why we should not follow the last-mentioned terms, which have been applied by the father of Teutonic philology, which, moreover, are sufficient to keep up the distinction and serve the purpose quite as well as any other terms as yet proposed.

I. PARADIGM TO THE STRONG CONJUGATION.

Present Indicative.

	Gothic.	O. H. Germ.	Old Saxon.	Ang.-Sax.	O. Fris.	Old Norse.
Sing.						
1st	finþ-a	find-u	find-u	find-e	find-e	finn
2nd	finþ-i-s	find-i-s	find-is	find-e-st	find-e-st	finn-r
3rd	finþ-i-þ	find-i-t	find-i-d	find-e-ð	find-e-th	finn-r
Plur.						
1st	finþ-a-m	find-a-mes	find-a-d	find-a-ð	find-a-th	finn-u-m
2nd	finþ-i-þ	find-a-t	find-a-d	find-a-ð	find-a-th	finn-i-ð
3rd	finþ-a-nd	find-a-nt	find-a-d	find-a-ð	find-a-th	finn-a
Dual.						
1st	finþ-os	..	..	..	..	..
2nd	finþ-a-ts	..	..	..	..	..

Present Subjunctive.

	Gothic.	O. H. Germ.	Old Saxon.	Ang.-Sax.	O. Fris.	Old Norse.
Sing.						
1st	finþ-au	finde	find-a (e)	find-e	find-e	finn-i
2nd	finþ-ai-s	find-e-s	find-a-s (es)	find-e	find-e	finn-i-r
3rd	finþ-ai	find-e	find-a (e)	find-e	find-e	finn-i
Plur.						
1st	finþ-ai-m-a	find-e-mes	find-a-n (en)	find-e-n	find-e	finn-i-m
2nd	finþ-ai-þ	find-e-t	find-a-n	find-e-n	find-e	finn-i-ð
3rd	finþ-ai-n-a	find-e-n	find-a-n	find-e-n	find-e	finn-i
Dual.						
1st	finþ-ai-v-a	..	..	..	..	..
2nd	finþ-ai-ts	..	..	..	..	..

Present Passive.

Gothic.

	Indicative.	Subjunctive.
Sing. 1st	finþ-a-da	finþ-ai-dau
2nd	finþ-a-za	finþ-ai-zau
3rd	finþ-a-da	finþ-ai-dau
Plur. 1st	finþ-a-n a	finþ-ai-ndau
2nd	finþ-a-nda	finþ-ai-ndau
3rd	finþ-a-nda	finþ-ai-ndau

THE VERB.

IMPERATIVE.

	Gothic.	O. H. Germ.	Old Saxon.	Anglo-Sax.	Old Frisian.	Old Norse.
SING. 2nd	finþ	find	find	find	find	finn
PLUR. 1st	finþ-a-m	..	..	..	..	..
2nd	finþ-i-þ	find-a-t	find-ad	find-a-ð	find-a-th	finn-i-ð
DUAL. 2nd	finþ-a-ts	..	..	..	..	..

INFINITIVE.

SING. 2nd	finþ-a-n	find-a-n	find-a-n	find-a-n	find-a	finn-a
PLUR. 2nd	finþ-a-nd-s	find-a-nt-êr	find-a-nd	find-e-nd-e	find-a-nd	finn-a-nd-i

PRETERITE INDICATIVE.

SING.						
1st	fanþ	fand	fand	fand	fand	fann
2nd	fans-t	fund-i	fund-i	fund-e	†fund-e	fann-t
3rd	fanþ	fand	fand	fand	fand	fann
PLUR.						
1st	funþ-u-m	fund-u-mês	fund-u-n	fund-o-n	fund-o-n	funn-u-m
2nd	funþ-u-þ	fund-u-t	fund-u-n	fund-o-n	fund-o-n	funn-u-ð
3rd	funþ-u-n	fund-u-n	fund-u-n	fund-o-n	fund-o-n	funn-u
DUAL.						
1st	funþ-u	..	..	..	..	..
2nd	funþ-u-ts	..	..	..	..	..

PRETERITE SUBJUNCTIVE.

SING.						
1st	funþ-jau	fund-i	fund-i	fund-e	fund-e	fynn-i
2nd	funþ-ei-s	fund-i-s	fund-i-s	fund-e	fund-e	fynn-i-r
3rd	funþ-i	fund-i	fund-i	fund-e	fund-e	fynn-i
PLUR.						
1st	funþ-ei-m-a	fund-î-mês	fund-î-n	fund-e-n	fund-e-n	fynn-i-m
2nd	funþ-ei-þ	fund-î-t	fund-î-n	fund-e-n	fund-e-n	fynn-i-ð
3rd	funþ-ei-n-a	fund-î-n	fund-î-n	fund-e-n	fund-e-n	fynn-i
DUAL.						
1st	funþ-ei-v-a	..	..	..	..	..
2nd	funþ-ei-ts	..	..	..	..	..

PRETERITE PARTICIPLE.

	funþ-a-n-s	ga-fund-a-n-er	fund-a-n	fund-e-n	fund-en	funn-i-nn

II. PARADIGM TO THE STRONG CONJUGATION.

Present Indicative.

	O. H. Germ.	Old Saxon.	Anglo-Sax.	Old Frisian.	Old Norse.	
Sing.						
1st	hilf-u	hilp-u	help-e	kias-e	kýs	tek
2nd	hilf-i-s	hilp-i-s	hilp-e-st	kios-e-st	kýs	·tek-r
3rd	hilf-i-t	hilp-i-d	hilp-e-ð	kios-e-th	kýs	tek-r
Plur.						
1st	hëlf-a-mes	hëlp-a-d	help-a-ð	kias-a-th	kios-u-m	tŏk-u-m
2nd	hëlf-a-t	hëlp a-d	help-a-ð	kias-a-th	kios-i-ð	tak-i-ð
3rd	hëlf-a-nt	hëlp-a-d	help-a-ð	kias-a-th	kios-a	tak-a

Present Subjunctive.

	O. H. Germ.	Old Saxon.	Anglo-Sax.	Old Frisian.	Old Norse.	
Sing.						
1st	hëlf-e	help-a	help-e	kias-e	kios-i	taki
2nd	hëlf-ê-s	help-a-s	help-e	kias-e	kios-i-r	tak-i-r
3rd	hëlf-e	help-a	help-e	kias-e	kios-i	tak-i
Plur.						
1st	hëlf-ê-mês	help-a-n	help-e-n	kias-e	kios-i-m	tak-i-m
2nd	hëlf-ê-t	help-a-n	help-e-n	kias-e	kios-i-ð	tak-i-ð
3rd	hëlf-ê-n	help-a-n	help-e-n	kias-e	kios-i	tak-i

Imperative.

	O. H. Germ.	Old Saxon.	Anglo-Sax.	Old Frisian.	Old Norse.	
Sing.						
2nd	hilf	hilp	help	kios	kios	tak
Plur.						
2nd	helf-a-t	help-a-d	help-a-ð	kias-a-th	kias-a-ð	tak-i-ð

Infinitive.

	O. H. Germ.	Old Saxon.	Anglo-Sax.	Old Frisian.	Old Norse.	
Sing.						
2nd	hëlf-a-n	help-a-n	help-a-n	kias-a	kios-a	tak-a

Present Participle.

helf-a-nt-êr	help-a-nd	help-e-nd-e	kias-a-nd	kios-a-nd-i	tak-a-nd-i

Preterite Indicative.

	O. H. Germ.	Old Saxon.	Anglo-Sax.	Old Frisian.	Old Norse.	
Sing.						
1st	half	halp	healp	kâs	kaus	tôk
2nd	hulf-i	hulp-i	hulp-e	†kere	kaus-t	tôk-t
3rd	half	halp	healp	kâs	kaus	tôk
Plur.						
1st	hulf-u-mês	hulp-u-n	hulp-o-n	ker-o-n	kus-u-m	tôk-u-m
2nd	hulf-u-t	hulp-u-n	hulp-o-n	ker-o-n	kus-u-ð	tôk-u-ð
3rd	hulf-u-n	hulp-u-n	hulp-o-n	ker-o-n	kus-u	tôk-u

THE VERB.

PRETERITE SUBJUNCTIVE.

	O. H. Germ.	Old Saxon.	Anglo-Sax.	O. Fris.	Old Norse.	
SING.						
1st	*hulf-i*	*hulp-i*	*hulp-e*	*ker-e*	*kys-i*	*toek-i*
2nd	*hulf î-s*	*hulp-î-s*	*hulp-e*	*ker-e*	*kys-i-r*	*toek-i-r*
3rd	*hulf-i*	*hulp-i*	*hulp-e*	*ker-e*	*kys-i*	*toek-i*
PLUR.						
1st	*hulf î-mês*	*hulp-î-n*	*hulp-e-n*	*ker-e*	*kys-i-m*	*toek-i-m*
2nd	*hulf-i-t*	*hulp-î-n*	*hulp-e-n*	*ker-e*	*kys-i-ð*	*toek-i-ð*
3rd	*hulf-î-n*	*hulp-i-n*	*hulp-e-n*	*ker-e*	*kys-i*	*toek-i*

PRETERITE PARTICIPLE.

ga-holf-a-n-êr | *holp-a-n* | *holp-e-n* | *ker-en* | *kos-i-nn* *tek-i-nn*

REMARKS ON THE STRONG CONJUGATION.

I. The vowels of the Ablaut.

1. In **Old High German** the reduplicational vowel is rendered in different documents according to dialectic differences. Isidor (eighth century) uses *ea, eo*; Tatian (ninth) *ie, io*, Otfried (ninth) *ia* for *io*, as *ua* for *uo*; Notker (tenth) *ie, io*; the Vienna Gospel of St. Matthew (eighth) *e, io*.

Old Saxon uses as reduplicational vowel *e*, where the root itself has the high-sounding *a* or *e*; in Class IV, where the radical is the dark-sounding *ó* or *uo*, we find the diphthongal preterite *io*, weakened to *ie*.

Anglo-Saxon has, as reduplicational vowel of the preterite, *é*, or *eo*, the former chiefly in verbs which have *n* or *l* after the radical *a*.

Old Frisian uses the contractions *e* and *í*, the former exclusively in Class I if the radical is followed by a consonantal combination with *n*; in all other cases the reduplicational vowel is *í*. It is doubtful whether in Class IV the vowel of the preterite was the diphthongal *io*.

Old Norse, on the whole, follows the analogy of the Low German dialects.

2. There is in most Teutonic languages in the present singular of Classes VIII, IX, and X of the strong conjugation an alternation of *i* and *e* as vowels of the root, which the student will easily explain on referring to the phonetic laws mentioned under the respective letters.

Thus we find in **Old High German** *hilfu, nimu, hilfis, nimis*, because the vowel of the root is followed by *i* or *u* of the pre-preceding syllable — but *hëlfames, nemames, helfat, nemat*, &c., because the vowel of the root is followed by *a* in the succeeding syllable. The same alternation of sound takes place in the preterite participle of Class IX between *u* and *o*, directed by the same law as that of *i* and *e*, and in the present tense of Class VI, between *iu* and its weakened form *io*. (See the diphthong *iu*.) Of these changes nothing is observed in Gothic.

Old Saxon submits to the same laws as Old High German, but where a contraction takes place, the original *u* is preserved in the participle preterite of Class IX, as *cuman* from *cviman*.

Anglo-Saxon, which in its phonetic changes is far more capricious than any other dialect, follows in this also a few rules of its own. The vowels *i* of the present, *a* of the preterite singular, *u* of the preterite plural remain intact in but few instances, that is, if followed by doubled *m* or *n*, or by either of the two combined with a mute, where *a* however is found to turn into *o*. But *e, eo*, are used in the present; *a, ea* in the preterite singular, and *o* in the preterite participle. In Classes VIII and IX those verbs only preserve the *i* of the present which end in *m*, besides a few others, such as *hipan* (hiare), *gifan* (to give), *gitan* (to get), &c., and the strong verbs which form the present theme in *ja*, as *biddan*, to bid, beg, &c. The preterite shows the regular vowels *a, a* = Goth. *a, e*, only in *nime, nam, námon,* þ*icge,* þ*ah;* but plur. þ*ægon; licge,* preterite sing. *lag*, but plur. *lágon* and *lægon; geseo, geseah, gesávon*. All others have *a* in the singular, *æ* in the plural of the preterite. In the present of Classes VIII, IX and X, *i* and *e, eo*, interchange in the same manner and after the same rules as in Old High German and Old Saxon, except that the 1st sing. indicative and the 2nd sing. imperative have always *e, eo*, the weakened form of *i*, as *helpe, hilpst, hilp*ð, plur. *helpa*ð, imperative *help; steorfe, stirfst, stirf*ð, plural *steorfa*ð, imperative *steorf*. An interchange between *iu* and *io* in the present of Class VI cannot take place, because the diphthong *iu* occurs regularly in the weakened form *eo*.

Old Frisian preserves the *i* of the present, Class X, before double *n*, or *n* with a mute. The preterite participle has always the original *u*; but once *worpen* for *wurpen*. The *i* of the present, Classes VIII and IX is kept up in verbs which form the present theme in *ja*, before *m* in *nima*, and in verbs which end in a vowel; e.g. *sia* (to see), *skia* (to happen); but *ia* (to confess) has *e* in the present. The same classes have the *a* of the singular and *á* of the plural preterite before *m*; but they may pass into *o, ó*, respectively. (See letter *a, o,* Old Frisian.) The preterite participle of the verbs of Class IX having rejected the radical *o* (*u*), and adopted that of the present, a distinction between the Classes VIII and IX no longer exists, and they may be considered as identical.

The alternation or interchange of *i* and *e* in different persons of the present is unknown in Old Frisian, the vowel adopted in the infinitive keeping its place throughout the present tense. But Class VI uses the interchange of *io* (*iu*) and *ia* on the same conditions as the other dialects already mentioned; but, like Anglo-Saxon, it has the weakened form too in the 1st sing. present. Old Norse shows the *i* in the present of Class X if a verb ends in *n,* or *n* combined with a mute; also in the verb *spirna,* to spurn; but *e* we find in *brenna,* to burn, and *renna,* to run. The verbs *gialla* (to shout, sing), *gialda* (rependere), and *skialfa* (to tremble), retain the *ia* in the infinitive, plural indicative, and throughout the subjunctive. In the preterite participle all verbs ending with *n,* or *n* with a mute, have *u; brenna* and *renna* also take *u;* all others, *spirna* too, have *o*. In Classes VIII and IX we find the *i* of the present only with strong verbs which form the present theme in *ja;* also in *svima* (to swim), which occurs side by side with *svema*. An interchange or alternation between *i* and *e,* or *iu* and *io,* in different persons of the present, does not take place.

3. Some verbs of Class VI have condensed the *iu* of the present into *u,* as Gothic. O H. Germ. *súfu,* bibo (Germ. saufe); *súku,* suck (Germ. sauge; sugo); *luhhu,* lock, claudo. O. S. *lúcan,* to lock. A. S. *brucan,* to use; *hrútan,* to fall; *supan,* to drink; *sucan,* to suck; *stúnan,* strepere; *strútan,* populari; *lúcan,* to lock. O. Fris. *lúka,* to lock; *skúva,* protrudere; *sluta,* to lock (O. H. Germ. sliuzu); *spruta,* to sprout. O. N. *luca, supa* and *sиpa,* sorbere; *súga* and *siuga,* to suck.

4. The preterites of Classes V and VI, in Old High German, condense their diphthongs *ei, ou,* into the long vowels *e, ó,* respectively, the former before *w, h,* the latter before *h, r, s,* and dental mutes; in Anglo-Saxon, on the contrary, the *a* of the present and *ó* of the preterite are dissolved into two vowels, namely *ea* and *eo,* e. g. *sceapan, sceop, sleahan, sleoh.*

5. Verbs of Class VII in Old Norse, which end with a guttural (*k, g*), have in the preterite participle *e* instead of *a*.

6. Umlaut affects the verbal stem more or less in the conjugation of the Old Teutonic verb.

Gothic of course repudiates this as well as any other Umlaut.

In **Old High German** the Umlaut of *a* into *e* may take place in the present of Class II (reduplicated verbs) and Class VII, if an *i* follows in the second syllable, e. g. *wallu*, 2nd *wallis* or *wellis; varu*, 2nd *varis* or *veris*. As in general, so also in the verb, old documents preserve the original *a*, more recent ones adopt more largely the Umlaut.

Old Saxon favours occasionally this modification of sound in the 2nd and 3rd sing. present of Classes II and III, just like Old High German; e. g. *waldu*, 2nd *weldis*, 3rd *weldid*.

Anglo-Saxon admits of Umlaut in the 2nd and 3rd sing. present, even if the final vowel which caused the Umlaut has suffered syncope. In this manner *a* is modified into *e* (*a*); *a* into *æ*; *eó, ea, ú,* into *y*; *ó* into *e*; e. g. *hate*, 3rd sing. pres. *hæt, blote*, 3rd sing. *blete, sceote*, 3rd sing. *scýt; fare*, 3rd sing. *ferð, färð*.

Old Frisian seems to do without the Umlaut in its verbal inflexions. Though forms occur such as 1st *fere*, 2nd *ferest*, 3rd *fereth*, plur. *farath*, it would no doubt be preferable to explain the *e* as a weakening rather than Umlaut of the *a*, for the *e* occurs in the preterite participle *ferin* too, where it is no Umlaut, but the inorganic representative of an original *a*; thus also the infinitive *drega* and the participle *dregin*.

Old Norse, which favours Umlaut in every possible position, makes use of it largely in the conjugation of the verb throughout the singular of the present indicative and the whole of the preterite subjunctive. We find it therefore in all reduplicated verbs (except Class III, of course), and in all the remaining classes, except V, because the *ei* of Class III and the *í* of Class V are not capable of Umlaut. Verbs of Class VII, which in consequence of dropping an *h*, end in *a*, have in the singular present the Umlaut *æ*, as *slá* (to strike, slay) from *slaha*, present *slæ; fla* (to flay), present *flæ; hlá* (to laugh), present *hlæ*. Umlaut of *a* into *o* occurs with verbs of Classes II and VII in the 1st plur. present; with the former only if they have *ia* in the infinitive, as *gialla*, 1st plur. *giöllum; gialda, gioldum:* but *skiálfa* makes *skiálfum*.

II. The consonants affected by the inflexions.

1. The consonants of the theme or stem are variously affected in the different dialects by the terminations of the persons. We have already seen that in Gothic, before the *t* of the personal termination of the 2nd sing. preterite, a dental of the stem preceding it must be changed into *s*.

In **Anglo-Saxon** the connective (thematic) vowel almost regularly suffers syncope in the 2nd and 3rd sing. present indicative, and the consonants of the termination and those of the stem or theme are joined directly, the former influencing the latter to a certain degree. As to the 2nd person we have to notice the following facts. Before the termination -*st* no dental can keep its position except *t*; *d* and ð are dropped; the combination *nd* is changed into *nt*. Hence *hladan, blotan, cweðan, standan*, make the 2nd sing. *hle-st, blet-st, cwi-st, stent-st*. In the same manner a final *s* or *st* of the stem is dropped before the *st* of the termination; e. g. *cy-st* from *ceosan, bir-st* from *berstan*. As to the 3rd person the following rule must be observed: The ð of the personal termination is dropped after a *t* or *st* of the stem, e. g. *blet* for *blet-ð, birst* for *birst-ð*; the terminational ð following *d*, both are rendered by *t*, as *hlet* for *hledð, stent* for *stend-ð*; ð preceded by *s*, both make *st*, as *cýst* for *cys-ð*; a ð of the stem is dropped before ð of the termination, e. g. *cwi-ð* for *cwið-ð*.

Old Frisian. As to the 2nd person the same rules hold good, that is, no dental but *t* remains before the termination *st*; -*d-st*, -*th-st*, -*s-st*, -*st-st*, are all contracted into *st*; hence *halda, halst; finda, finst: xst* becomes *xt*, as *wext* from *wax-a*. In the 3rd person the termination *th* is contracted with a preceding *d* into *t*, as *halt, fint;* with a preceding *t* into *t*; with a preceding *th* into *th*; with a preceding *s* or *st*, to *st*; with a preceding *x* to *xt*.

Old Norse. The *r* of the 2nd sing. is assimilated to a preceding *l* or *n* of the stem; it remains after *ll* and *nn*. If the stem ends with an *s, r, rr*, it is dropped altogether, and the 2nd and 3rd persons become identical in form with the 1st. In the 2nd sing. preterite before the personal termination *t* a final dental of the stem is changed into *z*, e. g. *lez-t* from *lát-a, galz-t* from *gialda, quaz-t* from *queð-a;* but the 2nd of the preterite, *stod* (from *standan*) is *stott*. A preterital form which after dropping an *h* or *g*, ends in a long vowel, has also *tt* in the 2nd sing., e. g. *slo* for *sloh* (from *slahan*), 2nd preterite *slott*.

2. RHOTACISM greatly affects the terminational *s* of the stem in the bisyllabic or polysyllabic forms of the plural preterite, especially in verbs belonging to Classes V and VI, where the change seems to be less obstructed by the preceding short vowel than it is in the singular by the long radical; e. g. *vriosan* (to freeze), preterite plur. *vrurumes*, part. *vroraner; kiosan* (to choose), preterite sing. *kos*, 2nd *kuri*, 3rd *kos*, plur. *kurumes*, part. *koraner;*

rısan (decidere), present sing. *reis*, 2nd *riri*, 3rd *reis*, plur. *rirumes*, part. *riraner;* *wĕsan* (to be), *was, warumes,* part. *wesaner*, and a few others.

In **Old Saxon** we have only one instance of rhotacism in Class VIII, i. e. *wesan* (to be), *was, wárun, wesan;* several of Class VI, i. e. *kiosan, kos, kuri, kos,* plur. *kurun,* part. *koran,* and *for-liosan,* to loose.

Anglo-Saxon offers but few examples, namely *wesan, was, wære, was,* plur. *wæron,* part. *wesan; ceosan, ceás, cure, ceás,* plur. *curon,* part *coren;* thus also *freosan* (to freeze), *for-leosan* (to loose), *hreosan* (ruere).

Old Frisian adopted rhotacism in the plural preterite, e. g. *wesa, was, weron, wesen; kiasa, kás, keron, keren;* in the same manner *ur-liusa,* to loose.

Old Norse. Rhotacism throughout in *vera* (to be), *var, varum, verinn* by the side of the Gothic *visa, vas, resum, visans;* it may also occur in *friosa* (to freeze) and *kiosa* (to choose), which have the preterite plur. *frurum, kurum,* part. *frerinn, kerinn,* by the side of *frusum, kusum, frosinn, kosinn.*

3. GEMINATION, or a double consonant occurring in the middle of a word, is dissolved into the single consonant at the end of the word, and after a long radical, e. g. **Old High German** *spinnan, span; wallan, wialumes.*

Old Saxon *rinnan, ran, thrinnan, thran;* reduplicated verbs may have the single consonant or its gemination, e. g. *fallan,* pret. *fēl* and *fēll.*

The same law holds good for **Anglo-Saxon** and **Old Frisian**, where gemination, moreover, is dissolved into the single consonant before the consonants of the termination.

Old Norse does not obey this law. Gemination is, on the contrary, produced in Old Norse in the singular preterite and in the imperative, where *ng* is changed into *kk*, and *nd* into *tt*; e. g. *fanga* (to catch), preterite sing. *fekk,* imperative *fakk; springa* (to jump), preterite *sprakk,* imperative *sprikk;* except *sýnga, slýnga,* which make *saung, slaung; blanda* (to mix, blend), present *bletl,* imperative *blatt; hrinda* (trudere), preterite *hratt,* imperative *hritt.*

4. The media, when final, is often exchanged for the tenuis, especially in the preterite singular, often in the plural too; e. g. **Old High German** *quĕdan* (to say), preterite singular *quat,* plural *quátumes* and *quádumes; snídan* (to cut), preterite *sneit,* plural *snitumes,* participle *snitaner.*

THE VERB.

Thus also in **Old Norse** *ld*, when at the end of the monosyllabic preterite, is converted into *lt*, e.g. *falda, felt; gialda, galt*.

5. The spirant *h* and the media *g* are in close relationship in many verbs.

In **Old High German** an *h* belonging to the root is replaced by *g* in the preterite plural (rarely in the singular) and in the preterite participle; e.g. *slahan* (to slay), pret. sing. *sluoh*, or *sluog*, plur. *sluogumes*, part. *slaganer; zihan* (to accuse), pret. *zeh*, plur. *zigumes*, part. *ziganer*.

In **Old Saxon** the *g* is used regularly in the preterite singular too; e.g. *slahan, slog, slogum*, but the part. *slahan*.

Anglo-Saxon makes, like Old High German, *sleahan*, 1st *sloh*, 2nd *sloge*, 3rd *sloh*, plur. *slogon*, part. *slagen*, where the media creeps into the 2nd singular.

In **Old Norse** the *h* of the root has commonly been dropped, but reappears again in the form of *g* in the bisyllabic forms of the preterite; e.g. *slá* (to slay) for *slaha*, plur. preterite *slogum* (also *sloum*), preterite part. *sleginn;* thus also *klæa* (fricare), and *hlæa* (to laugh).

6. The occurrence of both the spirants *h* and *w* in the **Old Saxon** preterites *sáhun* and *sáwun*, and *farliwi* from *farlíhan* (concedere), may be explained by the Gothic forms *saihvan, leihvan*, from which **Anglo-Saxon** adopted either one or the other of the spirants. A similar exchange we observe in the A.S. *seon* (to see) for *seohan*, preterite 1st *seah*, 2nd *sáwe*, 3rd *seah*, plur. *sáwon*.

7. Syncope of *h* is frequent in the present and infinitive of **Anglo-Saxon** verbs, where it is dropped together with the thematic vowel; e.g. *slean, þwean, seon* for *sleahan, þweahan, seohan*. Some write *sleán, seon*, &c., considering the case one of contraction rather than of syncope.

8. The reverse of the case we have considered under 5 is given in **Anglo-Saxon** verbs, the radical of which is followed by *g*. Wherever the media has to take its position at the end of the word or before the inflexional consonants, it is changed into *h*; e.g. *stíge*, ascend, 2nd *stih-st*, 3rd *stíh-ð*, plur. *stígað*, pret. *stáh;* plur. *stigon; belge, bilhst, bilhð*, pret. *bealh*, plur. *bulgon*. In the combination *ng* the *g* remains intact.

9. The relation between *ð* and *d* is this, that the former is replaced by the latter in the bisyllabic forms of the preterite, e.g. *cweðan*, to say, pret. *cwäð*, 2nd *cwæde*, 3rd *cwäð*, plur. *cwædon*, part. *cweden*.

10. In **Old Norse** the *g* is often dropped in the preterite, and if so, the *ei* is condensed into *e*, and *au* into *o*, and the Ablaut of the singular remains in the plural too. Thus *hniga* may have the preterite *hneig, hnigum,* or *hne, hnegum; smiuga,* may have *smaug, smugum,* or *smo, smoum.* The combination *gð* is dropped in the sing. preterite. *bra* of *bregða,* and the plural again is *brugðum.* The verb *hoggva* (to hew, cut) has the sing. preterite *hio;* in all other instances the *gg* of this verb is preserved, but the *v* is dropped, and yet the Umlaut it has caused remains; hence the forms—pres. indic. *hogg, hogg-r, hogg-r,* plur. *hoggum, hoggvið, hoggva,* pres. subj. *hoggvi,* pret. indic. *hio,* pret. subj. *hioggvi,* imper. *hogg,* plur. *hoggvið.* *Spua* (to spit) makes the preterite *spio,* plur. *spioggum;* thus also *búa* (to inhabit), *bio, bioggum.*

III. Isolated changes.

1. The Gothic language changes the vowel *i* into *aí* before *h* and *r*, the vowel *u* into *au*; this phenomenon is known as Brechung, 'a break[1].' It occurs in verbs too; hence the forms *baírga* for †*birga, baurgum* for †*burgum, laíhvum* for *lihvum,* þ*lauhans* for þ*luhans;* and vocalic systems such as *baira, bar, berum, baurans,* and *leihva, laihv, laíhvum, laíhvans,* will be easily understood.

2. The thematic vowel is, as a rule, preserved in the present, but dropped in the preterite. All the ancient dialects, except Old Norse, have it intact in the 1st and 3rd plural, and (except Gothic and Old Norse) in the 2nd plural present indicative; all weaken it to *i,* or still further to *e,* in the 2nd and 3rd singular, Gothic also in the 2nd plural. The 1st sing. present indicative ends in the thematic *a* in Gothic, while Old High German and Old Saxon weaken it to *u,* Anglo-Saxon and Old Frisian to *e*; Old Norse drops it altogether. The last-mentioned dialect drops it in the 2nd and 3rd sing. also, and joins the personal termination *r = s* directly to the root. In the 1st pers. plur. Old Norse weakens the thematic *a* to *u*. The preterite in all the dialects drops the thematic *a* and adds the termination of the 2nd sing. directly to the root, or rather the perfect theme. In the plural the personal terminations join the perfect theme by means of the connective vowel *u,* which has nothing to do with the thematic *a.* The connective *u* is in Anglo-Saxon and Old Frisian regularly, in the other dialects occasionally, weakened to *o.*

3. The Gothic verb *trudan* (to tread, calcare), of Class VIII,

---

[1] See p. 33.

has in the present the radical *u* instead of *i*. Bopp considers this to be the weakened form of *a*, while Grimm adopts for this verb an Ablaut of its own, namely *truda, trad, tródum, trudans*. We follow Bopp by inserting it among the regular verbs of Class VIII.

4. Verbs in *-na* are inflected after the strong conjugation in the present, and after the weak in the perfect tense. In the former the *a* of the suffix *na* is treated like the thematic *a* mentioned above; in the perfect it is gradated to *ó*, and thus is formed the suffix *no* which acts as connective between the root and the weak terminations. Of this formation we have only fragments left in the other Teutonic languages. (See Formation of the Present Suffix *-na-*.) The most common verbs of this class are, *af-hvapnan*, extingui; *af-dóbnan*, obmutescere; *af-lifnan*, super-esse; *dis-hnaupnan*, rumpi; *dis-skritnan*, findi; *fra-gistnan*, feriri; *ga-hailan*, sanari; *ga-staúrknan*, rigescere; *ga-nipnan*, moerere; *ga-qiunan*, revivescere; *ga-þaúrsnan*, arescere; *ga-plasnan*, turbari.

5. Concerning the strong verbs in *-ja* we have only to mention that in their conjugation they differ in nothing from other strong verbs; in the present they treat the *a* of *ja* in the same manner as the thematic *a*. As to the contraction of the thematic *ja* in some of the Teutonic languages and other points in connexion with this formation, see p. 391.

6. The verb *snivan* (to go) for †*sniuan*, Sanskrit root *snu*, has the preterite singular of Class VI, *snáu;* but the plur. *snevum* by the side of the regular *snivum:* in the same manner *divan*, to die, mori.

7. *standan* (stare), root *stath, stad*, from *sta*, drops the infix *-n-* in the preterite and makes *stoþ, stóþum* for †*stodum*. The forms in the other Teutonic languages follow the analogy of the Gothic, as Old Saxon, Anglo-Saxon, Old Frisian, *stod*, plur. *stod-un, stod-on;* Old Norse *stoð*, plur. *stoðum;* but Old High German preserves the infix *-n-* in the preterite *stuont*, plur. *stuontumes*.

8. The Gothic *gaggan* (to go) ought to have the preterite *gaigagg*, but it takes the weak form *gaggida;* the preterite *iddja, iddjes, iddja*, plur. *iddjedum*, is commonly used, formed irregularly from the root *i* (to go). This verb in the other Teutonic dialects goes regularly like the other strong verbs with lost reduplication after Class II.

9. The Gothic verb *briggan* has not the strong preterite *bragg*, but the weak *brahta;* Old High German has both strong and weak forms, hence *brang, brungumes*, and *brahta, bráhtumes;* the

Old Saxon *brengjan* has only the weak preterite *bráhta*. Anglo-Saxon follows the analogy of Old High German in forming both a strong and a weak preterite of the verb *bringan*, namely *brang*, *brungon*, and *broht*, *brohton*. We have also strong and weak forms side by side in the Old Norse *erja* (to plough, arare), perf. *ar* and *arða*; *quíða* (to fear), perf. *queith* and *quidda*; *hanga* (to hang), perf. *hekk* and *hangða*; *blota* (to sacrifice), perf. *blet* and *blotaða*, part. *blotinn* and *blotaðr*.

10. The Gothic *fahan* (to catch), and *hahan* (to hang), which form their perfect regularly with reduplication after Class II, cannot preserve their short radical in the other Teutonic dialects, they therefore must take the infix -*n*- and make the present themes *fanga-*, *hanga-*, or they adopt the inorganic length of the vowel, as O. H. Germ., O. S. *fáhan*, *háhan*; or thirdly they are contracted into *fan*, *hán*, A. S. *fon*, *hón*, O. Fris. *fá*, *hua*. The Anglo-Saxon declines 1st *fo*, 2nd *fest*, *fæst*, *fæhst*, 3rd *feð*, *fæð*, *fæhð*, plur. *fo-ð*; in the same manner *ho*, &c.; O. Fris. 3rd *feth*, plur. *fáth*, subjunctive *fé*. But the preterite is in all dialects always the regular perfect of the infinitive *fangan*, *hangan*, after Class II. In Old Frisian however the preterite participle occurs, as *fangen*, *fenszen*, *fén*, *fán*, *finsen*; *húen*, *huendzen*, *hinsen*.

11. The verb *brída* (trahere), Old Frisian for *bregda*, has in the 3rd sing. *breith*, *bríth*, preterite participle *bruden*, *brugden*. A similar inclination to get rid of the media we find in the Anglo-Saxon *bregdan* (nectere), which thus passes from Class X to IX and forms *brad*, *brædon*, *broden*.

12. As in the Anglo-Saxon *bregdan*, so we observe in other verbs an inclination to pass from one conjugational class to another. Thus the Anglo-Saxon *þihan* (proficere), *síhan* (colere), *tíhan* (arguere), *wríhan* (operire), pass from Class V to VI by changing the *í*, which is succeeded by an *h*, into *eo* (wrongly following the analogy of Brechung of *i* into *eo*), the preterite *á* into *ea*, and thus adopting the forms *þeón*, *seon*, &c., preterite sing. *þeáh*, *seáh*, &c., plur. *þugon*, *sugon*, &c., for *þigon*, *sigon*, &c. The Old Norse verbs *syngja* (to sing) and *slyngja* (to sling, jactare) have passed from Class X into VI, and have the forms *saung*, *sungum*, *súnginn*, &c.

13. There is in Old Norse a number of verbs ending in a vowel which have in some forms passed from the strong to the weak declension. They make the preterite weak, the preterite participle commonly strong; e.g. *gnua* (fricare), present *gny*, plur. *gnuum*, preterite *gnúða*, preterite part. *gnuinn*; *ná* (concepi), present *næ*, plur. *náum*, preterite *náða*, part. *náinn*; *knua*

(cogere), present *knŷ*, plur. *knuum*, preterite *knuða*, part. *knuinn;* *ské* (fieri), *ske, skeum, skeða, skeinn;* *strá* (spargere), *strái, stráum, straða, strainn;* *trua* (fidem habere), *trúi, truum, trúða, truinn* and *truðr*, &c. The verb *sía* (to see) has lost the strong participle, and has the following forms: present *se*, preterite *sá*, plur. *sáum*, part. *seðr; valda* (to command) has in the preterite *olli, ollum* (from *valdi, valdum*) instead of *velt, veldum*.

14. There are in Old High German and Old Norse remains of a preterite formed with -*s*-, like the Latin perfect, 2nd sing. and plur. (in -*is-ti*, -*is-tis*[1]). Such are in O. H. Germ. *scri-r-u-mes*, root *scri*, to shriek; *pi-r-u-mes*, 2nd *pi-r-u-t*, root *pi* for *pu*, prim. *bhu*, to be; *spi-r-u-mes*, root *spiv*, to spit; *gri-r-u-mes*, root *gri*, gannire. They belong to Class V, and form their perfect as follows: e. g. sing *screi, scriri, screi;* plur. *scrirumes;* part. *scriraner*. In these examples *r* stands for *s*, and *u* is the connective vowel of the plural. Some consider this *r* to have arisen from an original *w*, a view which they support by a form *scri-w-u-mes*, which occurs by the side of *scri-r-u-mes*. But the former opinion is strengthened by a number of similar formations which occur in Old Norse. Thus of the root *gra*, prim. *ghra* (virere) the infinitive is *groa*, present *groe*, plur. *groum*, preterite *greri*, part. *groinn; gre-r-i =* †*gre-s-i =* †*gre-s-a;* in the same manner *nua* (fricare), preterite *neri; roa*, to row, *reri; snua*, torquere, *sneri; soa*, to sow, *seri*.

15. The Old High German preterites *steroȝ, pleruȝ*, have nothing to do with the perfect formation in -*s*-, but find their explanation in an ancient reduplication[2].

MIDDLE AND NEW TEUTONIC LANGUAGES.

The Middle and New Teutonic languages continue their progress on the road their predecessors had taken. In the conjugation the system of Ablaut gained absolute sway, and the ancient reduplication was no longer felt, though it had left indelible traces in the modifications of the radical which it had caused. The Ablaut itself did not remain stationary, but developed itself in the different dialects more or less in accordance with the phonetic laws of each. Thus the transition from Old High German to Middle High German, and again to New High German, is extremely regular and simple, and the different conjugational

---

[1] See the Formation of the Perfect in the Cognate Languages.
[2] See the Formation of the Perfect in the Teutonic Languages.

classes of the German of the present day, are, as far as the vocalic system is concerned, not very far distant from those of the German of a thousand years ago. In English, on the other hand, where the phonetic system was so often and so violently disturbed since the Anglo-Saxon times under the influence of foreign intruders, we find in almost every successive century a great change in the vowels of the Ablaut, and often in two contemporaneous writers two altogether different systems adopted; nay, one and the same writer seems often perfectly at a loss in the application of the Ablaut-vowels and to use them indiscriminately so long as he contrives to keep distinct the different parts of the verb with which the Ablaut is connected, the preterite from the present, the plural preterite from the singular. Now this much has been done successfully in all the Middle Teutonic languages. Whatever the confusion of vowels may have been in some of them at various periods, the characteristic feature of the Teutonic verb was never obliterated; the Ablaut was always handled with a consciousness of its nature, its meaning and its importance in the structure of the Teutonic languages. No modern language has passed through so many and so great changes as the English; and yet read but over a table of its strong verbs and compare them with those of Modern German and you will find a resemblance which often appears identity, and which will strike you with wonder and astonishment when you consider how great the divergence of these two languages now is, and how great the distance back to their starting-point in the Primitive Teutonic language, which even Old High German and Anglo-Saxon already had left a good long way behind.

The Middle Teutonic languages followed their mother dialects in obeying the law which demanded that the perfect tense should be kept distinct from the present, and the perfect plural from the perfect singular by means of the Ablaut. The modern languages made a considerable alteration in this law handed down from their ancestors. Instead of allowing the perfect plural a radical of its own, they imposed upon it the radical of the singular, or in some cases the radical of the preterite participle. Thus the German of five and of ten centuries ago made of *stilu* (I steal) the perf. *stal*, the plural of which was *stulumes, stulen;* the German of to-day says in the present tense *stele*, in the preterite sing. *stâl*, and in the preterite plur. *stâlen*, so that plural and singular have the same Ablaut; but the perfect participle has the special Ablaut *o*, O. H. Germ. *stolaner*, M. H. Germ. and N. H. Germ. *stolen*. The Dutchman of five centuries ago, said, like his High German cousin, *stele, stal, stulen,* part. *stolen;* the Dutchman of to-day has *stele, stal, stolen,* part. *stolen,* importing the vowel *o* from the preterite participle into the plural of the perfect tense. In this manner all the Teutonic languages of modern times have abolished the special Ablaut of the preterite plural, the only exception occuring in Swedish, where, as we shall see, the distinction is still kept up in some conjugational classes. Before we proceed to survey these classes we examine as shortly as possible the different modifications of the Ablaut which took place in the Middle and New Teutonic languages.

The Middle High German is in some respects hardly distinct from its Old High German parent; the vocalic systems of both are almost identical. It needs little demonstration to show that the Ablaut of the conjugational classes is essentially the same in both dialects; a glance at the succeeding tables will suffice to prove this. We therefore may confine ourselves to examine the few points in which they really differ. The reduplicational Ablaut (i. e. the Ablaut formed by the amalgamation of the reduplicational vowel and the radical) was in Old High German *ia* for verbs having a high-sounding radical in the present, *io* for those which had the dark radical *ó* or *ou*. The latter (*io*) however was often rendered by *ia* also, and both were in Old High German already occasionally weakened to *ie*. In this weakened form the Ablaut always occurs in Middle High German, so that there is no longer any difference in the preterite of our first four classes, its radical being always *ie*. Further changes do not occur in Middle High German, unless we mention the weakening of the Old High German *u* of the preterite participle, Classes IX and X, into *o* in Middle High German, a form which occurred in Old High German already side by side with the original *u*. But in Modern German the vocalic system experienced a few modifications which make themselves felt of course in the Ablaut too. First of all we have to mention the inorganic production, or lengthening of the radical vowel, which was not dictated by any discernible causes. In all the different classes the radical has become long, unless it was protected in its original character by its position. Thus we have for the Middle High German *gibe, gab,* the New High German *gebe, gab*[1]; the nice distinction between the sing. *gab* and the plur. *gáben* disappears, of course, and with it that richness and variety of

---

[1] To make these observations more useful, the student should always compare the tables of the conjugational classes of the ancient dialects which precede, and of the modern dialects which follow below.

modulation of the voice so peculiar to our ancient dialects. A further change for the worse we find in the weakening of the *i* to *e* wherever it may occur in the 1st singular of the present tense or in the preterite participle; hence we always meet for the M. H. Germ. *gibe, hilfe,* the N. H. Germ. *gebe, helfe.* The reduplicational preterite is in New High German as in Middle High German always *ie* for the O. H. Germ. *ia, io.* The M. H. Germ. *ou* (like O. H. Germ. *ou* = Goth. *áu,* second gradation of *u*) is rendered by the N. H. Germ. *au*; hence Goth. *hlaupan,* O. H. Germ. *hloufan,* M. H. Germ. *loufen,* N. H. Germ. *laufen.* The M. H. Germ. *i* (*like* O. H. Germ. *i* = Goth. *ei,* first gradation of *i*) we find in New High German as *ei,* e. g. Goth. *greipa,* O. H. Germ. *krífu,* M. H. Germ. *grífe,* N. H. Germ. *greife;* and, vice versa, the M. H. Germ. *ei* (like O. H. Germ. *ei* = Goth. *ai,* second gradation of *i*) is represented in New High German by *i* (spelt *ie,* which is not to be confounded with the *ie* of the reduplication verbs); hence Middle High German present *schide,* preterite *scheit,* is in New High German *scheide, schíd (schied).* The *iu* of the present tense of our Class VI, which in Gothic, Old High German, and Middle High German is used as the first gradation of *u,* we find in New High German again in the weakened form *ie,* while the *ou* of the preterite is rendered in New High German by *o* or *o* instead of the corresponding diphthong *au.* Corresponding to the Middle High German preterite in *uo* of Class VII, New High German has *ú.* All other vowels are, in sound at least, in both languages the same, though they may differ in quantity.

Modern Dutch has, like Modern German, lengthened all originally short vowels, except in certain positions. The reduplicational preterite is in Middle Dutch and New Dutch *ie* throughout. Here we may take occasion to notice that Middle Dutch and Middle High German, and New Dutch and New High German, following their example, are, in certain important points of grammar more primitive than several of the Old Teutonic languages of far greater antiquity. The Goth. *ái* (O. H. Germ. and M. H. Germ. *ei*), as the second gradation of *i* in the present of Class III, is in Middle Dutch and New Dutch rendered, as in Old Saxon, by *e*; the Goth. *áu* (O H. Germ. and M. H. Germ. *ou,* N. H. Germ. *au*), second gradation of *u,* is given in Middle Dutch and New Dutch, as in Old Saxon, by *o*; in the same manner the Dutch *í* of the present, Class V, answers to the O. H. Germ. and M. H. Germ. *í,* N. H. Germ. *ei,* Goth. *ei,* while in the preterite of the same class we have again, as above, *e* = Goth. *ái.* In Class VI we have for the Goth. *iu,* first gradation of *u* in Middle Dutch as in N. H. Germ. *ie,* but in New Dutch *ui*, a diphthong which in sound corresponds to the German *eu*, the frequent representative of an ancient *iu*, and even preserved in some verbal forms, as *kreucht, fleucht*, for the ancient *fliuht*, &c. The preterite of the same class has for the Goth. *áu* (O. H. Germ. and M. H. Germ. *ou*) the *o* which we find in Old Saxon already. The Gothic *o* of the preterite, Class VII, which in Old High German and Middle High German has the diphthong *uo*, takes in Dutch the diphthong *oe*, which in sound is identical with the New High German *ú* of the preterite of the same class. All other vowels need no further explanatory remarks.

As to the development of the vocalic system from Anglo-Saxon to Modern English we have already stated that its deviations are so multifarious, as to make it sometimes difficult to recognize any system whatever. But we may at any rate notice a few leading points which will help us more easily to survey the following table of the conjugational classes and the list of words belonging to each class, to which we must refer the student for further details. The reduplicational preterite, which in Anglo-Saxon had the radical *eo*, or its more condensed form *é*, we find in the writers since Layamon rendered in two ways, either as a diphthong, *eo*, or its occasional substitute *ea*, or as a simple vowel, *e*, or its cognate in sound, *æ*. Sometimes we meet with *o* in the preterite, which may be explained as the substitute of *a*, the latter again having taken the place of the original *e*. In the Ablaut verbs there was not so much room for an arbitrary choice of vowels, because its peculiar character was too deeply impressed on each vowel to render it liable to so great changes as its confreres in the reduplicational class. Still the deviations from the original form are many, a few of which may be mentioned.

The most stable of all vowels is *i*, which, through all periods, is either preserved in its original state or rendered by the weakened form *e*. The vowel *a*, the most stable, energetic, and persistent of vowels in other languages, such as German, is exposed to considerable modifications; it may be darkened into *o*, or weakened to *e*. The vowels *æ* and *e*, perhaps identical in sound, seem to have been interchangeable in most periods of Early English. The ancient *u*, chiefly in the preterite participle, is regularly rendered by *o*, as in other Teutonic languages. The Anglo-Saxon *á* we find either as *a* or *o*; *o* commonly as *o, oo*, or *ou*; the Anglo-Saxon *a* commonly returns to its original form, *a*; the long vowel *æ* occurs in Late Saxon, but in Early English it is already supplanted by *a* or its neighbours *o* and *e*. On the whole we find the Anglo-Saxon system of the Ablaut most consistently applied in the *Ormulum*, where in general licence and arbitrary changes are repudiated, and a strict grammatical system is strictly carried out. There we find not only the ancient distinction between the singular and preterite plural kept up by different vowels, but even the original quantity often preserved; as in Class VIII, Anglo-Saxon present *i, e*, pret. sing. *a*, plur. *æ*, pret. part. *i, e*; Ormulum, pres. *i, e*, pret. sing. *a*, plur. *æ*, pret. part. *i, e*. Layamon, on the other hand, allows himself a vast range of vowels to make up his system of Ablaut. But both agree in keeping up the ancient distinction between the radical of the singular and that of the plural of the preterite. Even in Old English and Middle English it is occasionally preserved, though its gradual disappearance in the latter dialects cannot be overlooked.

The Scandinavian languages of the present day, though not the direct descendants of Old Norse, have nevertheless much in common with the ancient dialect. As peculiar to the Swedish alone among all the modern languages of the Teutonic tribe, we must mention the nice distinction it makes between the Ablaut of the preterite singular and the preterite plural of verbs belonging to the Ablaut class; e.g. Class VIII, O.N. *i...a...a...e* (Goth. *i...a...e...i*), Swed. *ı...a...a...ı*; Class X, O.N. *ı...a...u...u* (Goth. *i...a...u...u*), Swed. *ä...a...u...u*. Danish makes the plural and singular always alike. As to the vowels of the Ablaut a few observations may suffice. Old Norse already renders the reduplicated perfect by the most condensed form of the vowels of the root and the reduplication, applying, instead of the diphthong, the long vowel *e*, with the exception of Class IV, where the Gothic *au* gives rise to the diphthong *io*, though even this is often replaced by *e*. Swedish and Danish follow the analogy of their Old Norse relative, so that in Class I they make the preterite *æ* = O. N. *é*; in Class II, Swed. *o*, Dan. *a* (*o*) = O. N. *e*; in Class III both *e* = O. N. *e*; in Class IV, Swed. *o, o*, Dan. *oe, u* = O. N. *io* (*e*). It is peculiar to the Danish language that in the reduplicational classes the vowel of the preterite becomes the radical of the present too, or vice versa, that the vowel of the present is preserved in the other tenses as well, so that in this case we can hardly speak of any Ablaut at all. Swedish follows more closely the analogy of Old Norse. The radical of the present, Class I, O. N. *a* = Goth. *é*, is rendered in Swedish by *a*; in the same manner O. N. *a* = Goth. *a* in Class II. The O. N. *ei*, in the present of Class III, is identical with the *ei* in High German, and corresponds to the Goth. *ái*; it is in Danish condensed into *e*. The O. N. *au* = Goth. *áu* of Class IV,

THE VERB.

Swedish and Danish render by *oe* or *u*. In the Ablaut classes the analogy between Old Norse and Swedish is still greater, the only disadvantage of the latter being the total absence of diphthongs in the Modern Scandinavian languages. In Class V we find in Swedish and Danish, as in Old Norse, *i* in the present for the O. H. Germ. *i* and the Goth. *ei*. The Gothic preterite *ái* is in Old Norse *ei*, which in Swedish and Danish is again condensed into *e*. The Gothic and Old Norse *iu* of the present in Class VI remains the same in Swedish; but occasionally it is rendered as in Danish by *y*, the representative (Umlaut?) of a more ancient *u*. In Class VII Old Norse and Swedish are identical. This identity might be observed in the last three classes also, if Swedish had preserved the ancient shortness of the vowels; but like its modern sisters it has in most cases given way to inorganic production. Still, if not by different quantities, it does keep up the distinction of singular and plural preterite by difference of sound, putting for the Old Norse *a* and *a* (Gothic *a* and *e*) *a* and *a* respectively.

The distinction in Class X· is perfect. The details may be further examined in the vocalic system of the classes and the examples which we give in the following.

Class I.

	Pres.	Pret.	Part.
O. H. Germ.	â	ia	â
M. H. Germ.	â	ie	â
N. H. Germ.	a	ie	â
Old Saxon	â	ie, e	â
Middle Dutch	â	ie	â
New Dutch	â	ie	â
Old Norse	á	ê	â
Swedish	á	œ	á
Danish	œ	œ	(œ)
Anglo-Saxon	œ	eo, ê	œ
Layamon	œ, e	œ, e, ea	e, a
Ormulum	œ	e	œ, e
Old English	e	e	e, a
Middle English	e	e	e
New English	e	e	e

Verbs belonging to this Class.

Middle High German[1]. *sláfe, slief, sláfen*, to sleep; *bráten*, to roast; *ráten*, to advise; *lázen*, to let; *blásen*, to blow; *háhe, hie*, to hang; *váhe, vie*, to catch.

---

[1] For examples in the Old Teutonic languages, see above, p. 411 sqq.

New High German. *schláfe, schlief, schláfen*[1]; *ráten, laβen, bläsen.*
Middle Dutch. *slape, sliep, slapen; laten*, to let; *raden, blasen.*
New Dutch. *slap, sliep, slápen; laten, ráden, brádden, blázen.*
Swedish. *grater, græt, gråten*, to weep; *later, læt, låten.*
Danish. *græder, græd, græd*, to weep; *láder* follows Class VII.
Layamon. Pres. *slæpe*, pret. *slæp (sleap)*, sleep; pres. *læte (lete)*, pret. *lette (lætte, leatte)*, part. *ilete; drede*, I dread, part. *adredde, adrád.*
Ormulum. *slæpe, slepte* (weak); *læte (lete), let, letenn (lætenn); dræde*, pret. *dredde.*
Old English. *slepe*, pret. *slep; lete (late)*, pret. *let (lete, lette)*, part. *ilete (ilate, laten); drede*, pret. *dred.*
Middle English. *slepe*, pret. *slep (sleep, slepte)*, part. *slept* (weak); *lete (lat)*, pret. *leot (lete, lette)*, part. *letun (lete); drede (dreede)*, pret. *dred (dredde, dradde)*, part. *adred, adrad.*
New English. *sleep* (weak); *let; dread* (weak).

Class II.

	Pres.	Pret.	Part.
O. H. Germ.	a	ie	a
M. H. Germ.	a	ie	a
N. H. Germ.	a	ie	a
Old Saxon	a	ie, ê	a
Middle Dutch	a	ie, e, i	a
New Dutch	a	ie	a
Old Norse	a	ê	a
Swedish	å	ö	å
Danish	a, o	a, o	a, o
Anglo-Saxon	a, ea	eo, ê	a, ea
Layamon	a, o	e, eo, a	a, o
Ormulum	a	e	a
Old English	a	e, o	a, o
Middle English	a, e, o	e	o, e
New English	a, o	e, u	e, u

Verbs belonging to this Class.

Middle High German. *valle, viel, vallen*, to fall; *halten*, to hold; *schalten*, to rule; *spalten*, to cleave; *walten*, to command; *salzen*, to salt; *bannen*, to banish, interdicere.

New High German. *falle, fiel, fallen; halten; hange, hieng, hangen*, to hang; *fange, fieng, fangen*, to catch; *gange* (obsolete), *gieng, gangen*, to go.

[1] I give the perfect participle without the augment *ge-*, though in Modern German it is essential in the formation of the past participle, while its use was optional in Old High German.

Middle Dutch. *valle, vel, vallen; houde* (=*halte*[1]) *helt* (*hilt*), *houden*, to hold; *soude, selt* (*silt*), *souden; banne, ben, bannen; ganghe, ghinc, ganghen*, to go; *vanghe, vinc, vanghen*, to catch (comp. *gaen, faen*); *heffe, hief, heven*, to lift, from Class VII.

New Dutch. *val, viel, vallen; houd', hield, houden; hang, hing, hangen; vang* (usually *vá*), *ving, vangen; gá* (*gange*, obsolete), *ging, gangen; hef, hief, hêven*.

Swedish. *faller, föll, fallen*, to fall; *haller, holl, hållen*, to hold; *far, fick*, plur. *finge, fången*, infin. *få*, to catch; *gar, gick, ginge, gangen*, infin. *gå*, to go.

Danish. *falder, faldt, falden*, to fall; *holder, holdt, holten*, to hold; *faaer, fik, fangen*, to catch; *gaaer, gik, gangen*, to go.

Layamon. *halde* (*hælde, holde*), pret. *heold* (*held, hæld, huld*), part. *ihalden, iholden; falde, feold*, to fall; *walde* (*wælde, welde*), pret. *walde* (*welde*), part. *awald; fo*, pret. *ifeng*, part. *ifongen* (*ifon*); *hange, heong* (*heng*), *hongen* (*hon*); *ga*, go; part. *igan* (*igon*).

Ormulum. *falle, fell, fallenn; halde, held, haldenn; fange* (*fo*), *feng; hange, heng, hangenn; gange* (*ga*), *ȝede*[2], *gan*.

Old English. *falle, fel, fallen; halde, held* (*huld*), *yholde; fange, fong* (*feng*) (*fanged* weak), part. *fanged; hange* (*honge*), part. *hong* (*honge*) (*hanged* weak); *go* (*ga*), *ȝede, ȝeode, ȝode*, part. *go, gon, gone, gane*.

Middle English. *fonge, feng, fongen; honge* (*hange*), *henge* (*heeng*) (*hangide, hongede*, weak), *heng* (*hanged, hongid*, weak); *goon* (*gon, go, goo*), *ȝede* (*wente*), *goon* (*gon, go, ygo*).

New English. *fall, fell, fallen; hold, held, held; hang, hung, hung; go* (*went*), *gone*.

Class III.

	Pres.	Pret.	Part.
O. H. Germ.	*ei*	*ia*	*ei*
M. H. Germ.	*ei*	*ie*	*ei*
N. H. Germ.	*ei*	*ie*	*ei*
Old Saxon	*ê*	*ê, ie*	*ê*
Middle Dutch	*ê*	*ie*	*ê*
New Dutch	*ê*	*ie*	*ê*
Old Norse	*ei*	*ê*	*ei*
Swedish	*ê*	*ê*	*ê*
Danish	*ê*	*ê*	*ê*
Anglo-Saxon	*â*	*eo, ê*	*â*
Layamon	*a, æ, o*	*e, eo, æ*	*a, o*
Ormulum	*a, æ*	*a, æ, e, eo*	*a*
Old English	*a, e, o*	*e*	*a, o*
Middle English	*o*	*e*	*o*
New English	*o*	*e*	*o*

---

[1] *al* vocalized in *ou*; see the phonetic laws of New Dutch.   [2] A. S. *eóde*.

Verbs belonging to this Class.

Middle High German. *scheide, schiet, scheiden,* to separate; *eischen,* to demand; *heizen,* to command, to be called; *sweifen,* vibrate.

New High German. *heiße, hieß, heißen; scheide* follows the analogy of Class VIII.

Middle Dutch. *hete, hiet, heten,* to order, to be called; *scede, sciet, sceden,* to separate; *vresche, vriesch, vreschen,* to demand.

New Dutch. *het, hiet, heten; eisch, esch, eischen.*

Layamon. *hate (hæte, hote),* pret. *hahte (hehte),* part. *bihæten (ihote), blawe (blæwe, blowe,* &c.), pret. *bleou (bleu),* part. *iblowen; cnawe (cnowe), cneow (cnew), cnawen (cnowe); sawe (sowe),* pret. *seow; mawe (mowe), meow (mew).*

Ormulum. *hate, het, hatenn; blawe,* part. *blawen; cnawe, cnew (cneow); sawe,* part. *sawenn.*

Old English. *hote, het,* part. *hatte (yhote); blowe (blawe), blewe; knowe (knawe), knew, knowen (knawen); sowe, sewe (seu).*

Middle English. *hote,* pret. *behote,* part. *bihoten; blowe, blew, blowun (blowen); knowe, knew (knewʒ, kneʒ, knowide), knowen (know); sowe (sewe),* pret. *sewe (sowide* weak), *sowen (sowid).*

New English. *blow, blew, blown; know, knew, known; crow, crew, crown* (obs. for *crowed*); *throw, threw, thrown.*

Class IV.

	Pres.	Pret.	Part.
O. H. Germ.	*ou, ô, uo*	*io*	*ou, ô, uo*
M. H. Germ.	*ou, ô, uo*	*ie*	*ou, ô, uo*
N. H. Germ.	*au, ô*	*ie*	*au, ô*
Old Saxon	*ô, uo*	*io, ie*	*ô, uo*
Middle Dutch	*ô*	*ie*	*ô*
New Dutch	*ô, oe*	*ie*	*ô, oe*
Old Norse	*au, ô*	*io, ê*	*au, ô*
Swedish	*oe, u*	*o, ö*	*oe, u*
Danish	*oe, u*	*oe, u*	*oe, u*
Anglo-Saxon	*ea, ô, ê*	*eo, e*	*ea, ô, ê*
Layamon	*æ, e*	*eo, e*	*eo, ea, e*
Ormulum	*æ, o*	?	*æ, o*
Old English	*e, o*	*e, o*	*e*
Middle English	*e, o*	*e, o*	*e, o*
New English	*ô*	*e*	*ô*

Verbs belonging to this Class.

Middle High German. *loufe, lief, loufen,* to run; *houwe, hiu,* plur. *hiuwen,* part. *houwen,* to hew, cut; *stoze, stiez, stozen,* to

THE VERB.

butt, strike; *schróte, schriet, schroten,* to cut; *ruofe, rief, ruofen,* to call.

New High German. *haue, hieb, hauen,* cut, strike; *laufe, lief, laufen; stoβe, stieβ, stoβen; schrote, schriet, schroten; rúfe, rief, rúfen,* to call.

Middle Dutch. *lope, liep, lopen,* to run; *howe, hieu,* plur. *houwen; stote,* to strike, butt, *stiet, stoten; roepe, riep, roepen.*

New Dutch. *lop, liep, lopen; houw, hieuw, houwen; roep, riep, roepen,* to call.

Layamon. *læpe (lepe),* pret. *leop (lep, leup, leoup, ileope),* plur. *lupon, leopen; wepe (weope),* pret. *weop (wep); hewe (hæuwe),* pret. *hewe (heowe),* part. *heawen (heouwen, hewen); rowe (rouwe),* part. *rowen; growe,* pret. *greu (greowen, growe).*

Ormulum. *læpe,* pret. *lupe; hæwe,* part. *hæwenn; bæte,* part. *bætenn.*

Old English. *lepe,* pret. *lepe (lept,* weak*); wepe,* pret. *wep (wepe* and *wepte, weped,* weak*); hewe,* pret. *hew (hewe),* part. *hewen; growe (grewe),* pret. *grew (greu).*

Middle English. *lepe,* pret. *lepe (leep* and *lepte, leppide,* weak), part. *lopen (leppid, lept* weak*); hewe, heew (hew* and *hewide* weak), part. *hewun (hewen* and *hewid* weak*); growe,* pret. *grew* (and *growide* weak), part. *growun (growen).*

New English. *hew,* part. *hewn; grow, grew, grown; weep, wept, wept* (weak); *leap, leapt, leapt* (weak); *beat,* part. *beaten.* Externally some verbs of Classes III and IV are identical in form; their different origin will be seen on reference to Classes III and IV in Anglo-Saxon.

Class V.

	Pres.	Pret. Sing.	Plur.	Part.
O. H. Germ.	î	ei	i	i
M. H. Germ.	î	ei	i	i
N. H. Germ.	ei	î, i		i, i
Old Saxon	î	ê	i	i
Middle Dutch	î	ê	ë	ë
New Dutch	î	ê		ê
Old Norse	î	ei	i	i
Swedish	î	ê		î
Danish	î	ê		î
Anglo-Saxon	î	â	i	i
Layamon	i	a, æ	i	i
Ormulum	i	a	i	i
Old English	i	a, o	i, o	i
Middle English	i	o, oo	i	i
New English	i	o, i		o, i

Verbs belonging to this Class.

Middle High German. *grīfe, greif, griffen, griffen,* to seize; *pfīfen,* to whistle; *bīten,* to bite; *rīten,* to ride; *līden,* to suffer; *mīden,* to avoid; *snīten,* to cut; *glīʒen,* to glitter; *stīgen,* to ascend; *swīgen,* to be silent; *nīgen,* to bend down, bow; *wīchen,* to yield; *krīgen,* to get; *rīse,* pret. *reis,* plur. *rirn,* part. *rirn* for ᵀ*risn;* *glīe,* ganmo, *schrīe,* clamo, *spīe,* spuo, pret. *glei, schrei, spei,* and *gle, schre, spe;* plur. of *schrei, schrirn* (comp. O. H. Germ. *scri-r-u-mes*), part. *geschrirn;* also *schriuwen, geschriuwen.*

New High German. *greife,* pret. *griff,* part. *griffen; pfeifen, beißen, reiten, leiden, schneiden, gleißen, weichen; meiden,* pret. *mied,* part. *mieden:* in the same manner *steigen, schweigen, schreien, scheiden* (to separate), *scheinen* (shine), *bleiben* (to remain).

Middle Dutch. *scīne, scen, scenen, scenen,* to shine; *grīpen,* to seize; *blīve, bléf, bleven, bleven,* to remain; *scriven,* to write; *smiten,* to smite; *splīte,* to slit; *lide,* transeo, pret. *let,* plur. *leden,* part. *leden.*

New Dutch. *schīn,* pret. *schen,* part. *schenen; blīf, bléf, bleven; driven,* to drive; *blīven,* to remain; *grīpen,* to seize; *krīten,* to cry; *smīten,* to smite; *līden,* to suffer; *risen,* to rise; *stīgen,* to ascend; *belīden,* to confess; *prīsen,* to praise.

Swedish. *skīner,* pret. *sken,* part. *skīnen; grīpa,* to seize; *blifva,* to remain; *rida,* to ride; *skrifva,* to write; *bīta,* to bite; *skrīka,* to shriek.

Danish. *blīver,* pret. *blév,* part. *bleven; grībe,* to dig; *drīve,* to drive; *rīde,* to ride; *stīge,* to ascend; *svīge,* to be silent.

Layamon. *scine,* pret. *scæn (scean); gripe,* pret. *grap,* plur. *gripen,* part. *gripen; driue, draf, drifen,* part. *driuen; bite, bat, biten, biten; smite, smat, smiten,* part. *ismite:* thus also, *write, abide, ride, arise.*

Ormulum. *shine, shan,* plur. *shinenn,* part. *shinenn; gripe, grap, gripenn, gripenn:* in the same manner, *drife, write, bite, rise; strike, strac, strikenn, strikenn.*

Old English. *schīne, schon,* plur. *schinen,* part. *schinen; gripe,* pret. *gripte* (weak), part. *gripen; drife, draf,* plur. *driue,* part. *driuen; bite, bate,* plur. *biten,* part. *biten; smite, smate (smot),* plur. *smitton (smiten),* part. *smiten; ride, rad, (rode),* plur. *rade (rode),* part. *riden; rise, ras (rose),* plur. *risen,* part. *risen.*

Middle English. *shyne, shone (schoon),* plur. *shinen,* part. *shinen; dryue, drof, dryuen, dryuen; shryue, shrof, shryuen, shryuen; thrive, throf, thriuen, thriuen; byte, boot, biten, to-bite; smyte, smoot, smyten, smyten; wryte, wroote, writen, writen; rede, rood, riden, riden; rise, roos, risen, risen.*

THE VERB.

New English. *shine, shone,* part. *shone; drive, drove, driven:* thus also, *shrive, thrive; bite, bit, bitten; smite, smote, smitten; abide, abode, abode; ride, rode, ridden; rise, rose, risen; strike, struck, struck (stricken).*

Class VI.

	Pres.	Pret. Sing.	Plur.	Part.
O. H. Germ.	*iu*	*ou*	*u*	*o*
M. H. Germ.	*iu*	*ou*	*u*	*o*
N. H. Germ.	*ie*	*ô, o*		*ô, o*
Old Saxon	*iu, io, û*	*ô*	*u*	*o*
Middle Dutch	*ie, u*	*ô*	*o*	*o*
New Dutch	*ui*	*ô*		*ô*
Old Norse	*iu, io, ú*	*au*	*u*	*o*
Swedish	*iu, g*	*oe*	*û*	*u*
Danish	*g*	*oe*		*û*
Anglo-Saxon	*eo*	*ea*	*u*	*o*
Layamon	*eo, e*	*œ, a*	*u, o*	*o*
Ormulum	*eo, e*	*œ*	*u*	*o*
Old English	*e*	*e*	*o*	*o*
Middle English	*e*	*e, o*		*o*
New English	*e, o*	*o*		*o, e*

Verbs belonging to this Class.

Middle High German. *schiube, schoup, schuben, schoben,* to push; *kliube, kloup, kluben,* to adhere, stick; *stiuben,* to move; *sliufen,* to glide; *triufen,* to drop; *briuwen,* to brew; *riuwen,* to rue, repent: *giuʒe, goʒ, guʒʒen, goʒʒen,* in the same manner, *biuten,* to offer; *siuden,* to boil; *kiuse, kos, kurn, korn,* to choose; *verliuse, verlôs, verlurn, verlorn; vriuse, vros, vrurn, vrorn,* to freeze; *suge, souc, sugen, sogen,* to suck; *ziuhe, zoch, zugen, zogen,* to pull.

New High German. *triefe, troff, troffen,* to drop; *siede, sott, sotten,* to boil; also, *riechen,* to smell; *kriechen,* to creep; *schlieβen,* to lock; *schieβen,* to shoot; *schiebe, schob, schoben,* to push; *schnaube, schnob, schnoben,* anhelare; *erkiese, erkor, erkoren,* to choose: thus also *verliere,* to loose; *friere,* to freeze; *biegen,* to bend; *luegen,* to lie, mentiri; *saugen, sog, sogen,* to suck; *fliehe, floh, flohen,* to flee; *fliege, flôg, flôgen,* to fly; *ziehen, zog, zogen,* to pull.

Middle Dutch. *drupe, drop, dropen, dropen,* to drop; *crupen,* to creep; *slupen,* to glide; *scuven; giete, got, goten, goten:* thus also, *verdrieten,* to offend; *scieten,* to shoot; *verliese, verlos, verloren, verloren:* thus also, *kiesen,* to choose; *vriesen,* to freeze; *luke, lôc, loken, loken,* to lock; *bughen,* to bend; *vlieghen,* to fly; *vlien,* to flee.

New Dutch. *druip, drop, dropen,* to drop ; thus also, *kruipen,* to creep ; *sluipen,* to glide ; *kluifen,* to cleave ; *schuifen,* to push ; *giet, got, goten,* to pour out : thus also, *verdrieten,* to offend ; *vluiten,* to flow ; *sluiten,* to lock ; *bied, bod, boden ; kies, kós* and *kor, kozen* and *koren,* to choose ; *vries, vros* and *vror, vrozen* and *vroren,* to freeze.

Swedish. *drŷner, droep, drupe, drupen,* to drop : also *krŷpa,* to creep ; *brŷta,* to break ; *giuta,* to pour out ; *sluta,* to lock ; *biuda,* to bid ; *liuga,* mentiri ; *snŷta,* to cut.

Danish. *kryber, kroeb, kroebe, kroeben,* to creep : also, *byde,* to bid ; *skyde,* to shoot ; *snŷde,* to cut ; *gŷse,* to pour out ; *kyser, koes, kysen,* to choose ; *flyger (flyver), floei, floejen,* to fly ; *lyger (lŷven), loei, loejen,* to lie.

Layamon. *crepe,* pret. *crap,* plur. *crupon,* part. *-cropen ; cleouie, clæf, cluuen, clouen ; geote, gæt, geoten, -goten,* to pour out ; *sceote, sceat (scæt), scuten, -scoten ; beode (bede), bad (bæd, bed), budon (biden), -boden, -beden ; cheose, chæs, curon (ichose), icoren (ichosen) ; leose, læs (lees, losede* weak) ; *iloren (ilosed* weak) ; *fleo, flæh (fleh), fluȝen (fluwen), fluȝen (floȝe),* to fly ; *fleo, flæh (fleh, fleih, flei), flluȝen, fluwen, ifloȝen (iflowe),* to flee.

Ormulum. *clefe, clæf, clufenn, clofenn ; gete, gæt, gutenn, gotenn ; bidde (bede), badd (bæd), budenn, beodenn ; chees, chæs, curenn? chosen ; forlese, forlæse, forlurenn, forrlorenn ; leȝhe, læh, luȝhenn, loȝhenn ; fleȝhe, flæh, fluȝhenn, floȝhenn,* to fly ; *fle(o), flæh, fluȝhen, floȝhen.*

Old English. *cleve, clef, clouen, ycloue ; brewe, brew, browen ; schete, schet,* plur. *schot,* part. *schotten ; ȝhete,* pret. plur. *ȝhotten,* part. *ȝhoten, ȝet ; bede, bed, boden, boden ; chese, ches,* plur. *chosen,* part. *ycorn,* chosen ; *lie (liȝhe), liȝhed ; fle,* pret. *flegh,* plur. *flowen,* part. *yflowe,* to fly ; *fle, flew (fley, fled),* plur. *flowen (fled),* part. *fled.*

Middle English. *crepe, crope,* plur. *cropen,* part. *cropen ; bede, bad (beede),* plur. *beden,* part. *boden (beden) ; ȝeete, gotte (ȝetide),* part. *ȝotun ; schete, schotte (schete),* plur. *schete,* part. *schott ; chese, chees (cheside),* plur. *chosen (chesen),* part. *chosen ; liȝe (lie) ; leiȝh (liede),* plur. *lieden,* part. *leiȝed (lowen, lyed) ; flee (fleȝe, fliege), flew (fleiȝ),* plur. *flewen* (to fly) ; *flee, fleiȝ (fledde),* plur. *flowen (fledden),* part. *fled,* to flee.

New English. *creep, crept* (weak) ; *cleave, clove (clave, cleft* weak), part. *cloven (cleft* weak) ; *seethe, sod (seethed* weak), *sodden (seethed* weak) ; *shoot, shot, shotten, shot ; choose, chose, chosen ; freeze, froze, frozen ; fly, flew, flown ; flee, fled, fled.*

Class VII.

	Pres.	Pret. Sing.	Plur.	Part.
O. H. Germ.	a	uo	uo	a
M. H. Germ.	a	uo	uo	a
N. H. Germ.	a	ú		ú
Old Saxon	a	ô (uo)	ô (uo)	a
Middle Dutch	a	oe	oe	a
New Dutch	a	oe	oe	a
Old Norse	a	ó	ó	a, e
Swedish	å	ó	ó	å
Danish	å	oe, ó	oe, ó	å
Anglo-Saxon	a	ó	ó	a
Layamon	o, a, e	o, ea, eo	o	a, o
Ormulum	a	o	o	a
Old English	a, e, o	o, ou, a, e	o, ou	a, o
Middle English	a, o, e	o, oo	o, oo	a, o
New English	a, ea	o, oo		a, o

Verbs belonging to this Class.

Middle High German. *mal, muol, maln,* to grind, molere; *var, vuor, varn,* to go, drive, convey; *grabe, gruop, graben,* to dig : also, *schaben,* to scrape; *schaffen,* to work, create; *heben,* to lift; *waschen,* to wash; *tragen,* to bear, carry; *bache,* to bake; *slahe, sluoc, sluogen, slagen,* to strike, slay.

New High German. *fare, fur, fáren; grábe, grub, gráben; schaffe, schúf, schaffen; wasche, wusch, waschen; tragen, schlagen,* to strike, slay; *backen,* to bake; *wachsen,* to grow.

Middle Dutch. *male, moel, malen; vare, voer, varen; grave, groef, graven :* also, *draghen,* to bear; *waden,* transire; *scapen,* to make, create; *slaghe, sloech,* plur. *sloeghen,* part. *sleghen,* to strike, slay.

New Dutch. *vár, voer, váren; gráf, groef, grácen,* to dig; *slá, sloeg, slágen,* to strike, slay : also, *stá, stond, gestán,* to stand.

Swedish. *far, for, fáren; står, stod, ståden,* infin. *stå,* to stand; *skáper, skop, skápen :* also *græfva,* to dig; *hæfva,* to lift up; *drága,* to move, drag, bear; *væfva,* to weave; *slar, slog, slágen,* to strike, slay.

Danish. *fárer, foer, fáren; staaer, stod, standen :* also *gráve,* to dig; *láde,* to let; *dráge,* to bear; *slaaer, slog, slágen.*

Layamon. *fare, for, foren, ifaren; stonde, stod, istonden,* to stand; *swerie, swor, isworen,* to swear; *sceke, scoc,* plur. *scæken,* part. *asceken,* to shake; *take, toc, token, itaken; draʒe, droh,* plur. *droʒen (drowen), idraʒen (idrawen); sle (slæ), sloh (slæh), sloʒen (slowen), islagen (islawen); waxe, weox (wax, wex),* plur. *weoxen (wuxen),* part. *iwaxen (iwox, iwoxen).*

Ormulum. *fare, for,* plur. *forenn,* part. *farenn:* also, *stannden,* to stand; *forsaken, waken, taken; draʒhe, droh,* plur. *droʒhenn,* part. *draʒhen; sla, sloh,* plur. *sloʒhenn,* part. *slagenn; waxe, wex,* plur. *wexenn,* part. *waxenn.*

Old English. *fare, fore, faren; stonde, stod, standen; swere, swor, sworn; schake, schok, schaken; take, tok, taken; wake, woke; drawe, drowe (drewe, drouh), drawen (drauhen); sle (slo), slow (slogh, slouh, slou);* part. *slawe,* slain; *lıʒhe, low (lowʒ),* plur. *louʒh; waxe (wexe), wex (wax),* part. *waxen (ywox).*
Middle English. *fare,* pret. *fared* (weak), part. *faren (fore); stonde, stood (stod),* part. *stonden; sweer, swoor,* plur. *sworen (sweren),* part. *sworen; forsake, forsoke, forsaken; schake, schook (schoke, schakide,* weak), part. *schakun; take, tok(e),* plur. *token,* part. *taken; wake, wook,* plur. *woken,* part. *waken: drawe, drow (drew),* part. *drawen; sle (sle, slea),* pret. *sloʒ (slow, slew),* part. *slain (slawen, slawe); wexe (waxe), woxe (wax, wex),* part. *woxen (waxen, wexen).*
New English. stand, stood; swear, swore (sware), sworn; heave, hove, hoven (also weak); forsake, forsook, forsaken; wake, woke; draw, drew, drawn; slay, slew, slain; wax, part. waxen (else weak).

Class VIII.

	Pres.	Pret. Sing.	Plur.	Part.
O. H. Germ.	i	a	á	e
M. H. Germ.	i	a	á	e
N. H. Germ.	ê	á		ê
Old Saxon	i, ë	a	á	ë
Middle Dutch	e	a	a	ë
New Dutch	é	á		ê
Old Norse	i, e	a	á	e
Swedish	î	á	á	i
Danish	î, œ	á	œ	i, œ
Anglo-Saxon	i, e	ä	œ	i, e
Layamon	i, e	œ, a	œ, e	e, i
Ormulum	i, e	a	œ	e, i
Old English	e, i	a, e	a, o, e	o, e
Middle English	e, i	a	a, o, e	o, e
New English	e, i	a, o		o, i

Verbs belonging to this Class.

Middle High German. *gibe, gap, gáben, geben,* to give; *biten,* to ask, beg; *triten,* to tread; *lisen,* to read; *ligen,* to lie, jacere; *pfligen,* to be accustomed; *wigen,* to move; *iʒʒe, aʒ, áʒʒen, eʒʒen,* to eat; *vergiʒʒen,* to forget; *miʒʒen,* to measure; *sihe, sach, sáhen, sehen,* to see; *geschihe, geschach, gescháhen, geschehen;* wise, *was, wáren, wesen,* to be.

THE VERB.

New High German. *gebe, gab, geben; bitte, bat, beten*: also, *tréten, lésen, liegen, pflégen, eßen, vergeßen, meßen; séhe, sah, séhen; geschéhe, geschàh, geschéhen; sitze, sáß, seßen; (wése) wár, waren, wesen*, to be.

Middle Dutch. *gheve, gaf, gaven, gheven; cleven,* to adhere, stick; *weven,* to weave; *ete, at, aten, eten,* to eat; *mete, mat, maten, meten,* to measure; *bidde, bat, baden, beden,* to ask, beg; *terden* (=*treden*), tread; *lesen,* to read; *wese, was, waren, wesen,* to be; *breken,* to break; *sprèken,* to speak.

New Dutch. *géf, gáf, gáven, geven; et, at, áten, geten; siten,* to sit; *bidden,* to ask, beg; *lesen; liggen,* jacere; *wes, wás* (rarely *war*), plur. *wáren*, part. *wezen*.

Swedish. *gífver, gáf, gáfve, gífven; æter, at, ate, æten; for-gæter, forgát, forgåte, forgæten,* to forget; *mæter, mat, mate, mæten; sitter, satt, sate, seten* (*sutten*); *fræter, fråt, frate, fræten,* to eat voraciously (Germ. freßen, fraß); *qvæder, qvád, qvváde, qvæden,* to say; *ligger, lag, lag, legen; ser, sag, sage, sedt* (weak), to see.

Danish. *give, gáv, given; æder, aad; træder, traad; kvæder, kráder, kvæden,* to say; *sidder, sad,* plur. *sadde, sidden; ligger, laae, liggen; ser, saae, sen,* to see; (*være*), *vár, væren,* to be.

Layamon. ʒife, ʒaf, ʒeuen, ʒiuen; ete, æt, æten, ieten; ʒite, ʒæt, ʒeten, ʒeten; frete, fræt, freten, freten; sitte, sæt, seten, iseten; queðe, quæð, queðen, iqueðen, to say; ligge, læi, læien, to lie, jacere; iseo (se), sæh, iseʒen, iseʒen.

Ormulum. ʒife, ʒaff, ʒæfenn, ʒifenn; ete, ett, etenn, eten; bi-ʒette, -ʒatt, -ʒætenn, -ʒetenn; sitte, satt, sæten; eweþe, cwaþþ, cwæþenn, cweþenn; lie, laʒʒ, læʒhenn, leʒhenn; seo (se), sahh, sæʒhenn, seghenn (sene), to see.

Old English. *giue, gaf* (*gef*), plur. *gafe*, part. ʒyuen (ʒouen); *ete, et,* plur. *ete,* part. *eten*; ʒete, ʒat (ʒet), plur. ʒet (ʒot), part. ʒeten; *queðe, quoð* (*quað*); *ligge* (*lie*), *lai,* plur. *laye,* part. *ileye, iliggen; se* (*iseye*), *say* (*sagh, sau, saw*), plur. *yseye* (*sauh*), part. *seue, seie*.

Middle English. ʒife (ʒefe), ʒaf (ʒaue), plur. ʒauen (ʒaun, ʒiuen), part. ʒiuen (ʒeuen, ʒouen); *ete, ete* (*eet*), plur. *eten* (*eeten*), part. *etun* (*etyn*); ʒete, *gat* (*geet*), plur. *geeten* (*goten*), part. *geten* (*gotun*); *sitte, sat* (*sate*), plur. *saten* (*seeten*), part. *sitten* (*sete*); *ligge* (*lie*), *lay* (*leye*), plur. *laien* (*lien*), part. *leyen* (*ileye*).

New English. *give, gave, given; weave, wove, woven* (*wove*); *eat, ate, eaten; sit, sat, sat; get, got* (*gat*) *gotten* (*got*); *tread, trod, trodden* (*trod*); *bid, bade* (*bid*), *bidden* (*bid*); *see, saw, seen; lie, lay, lain;* (*wese*), *was, were*.

Class IX.

	Pres.	Pret. Sing.	Plur.	Part.
O. H. Germ.	i, ë	a	â	o
M. H. Germ.	i	a	â	o
N. H. Germ.	ê	â (o)		ô
Old Saxon	i, ë	a	â	u, o
Middle Dutch	e	a	a	o
New Dutch	ê	â		ô
Old Norse	i, e	a	â	u, o
Swedish	æ	â	å	û
Danish	æ	â		aa
Anglo-Saxon	i	ä, a	æ, â	o
Layamon	e i	a, o	a o. e	o, u
Ormulum	e, i	a, o	æ. o	o, u
Old English	e, i	a, o	a, o, e	o, u
Middle English	e, i	a, o	a, o, e	o u
New English	éa, eá	a, o		o

Verbs belonging to this Class.

Middle High German. *stil, stal, stâlen, stoln,* to steal; *nim, nam, nâmen, nomen,* to take; *kome* (=*quime*), *kam* (*kom, quam*), *kâmen* (*komen*), *komen:* also, *stimen,* cohibere; *zimen,* decere; *biren,* to bear; *swiren,* to swear; *triffen,* to hit; *drischen,* to thrash; *sprichen,* to speak; *stichen,* to prick, to sting; *brichen,* to break; *erschricke, erschrac, erschrâken, erschrocken;* *vihten,* to fight; *vlihten,* to weave.

New High German. *stele, stâl, stolen;* *neme, nâm, nommen;* *komme, kâm, kommen;* *gebære, gebâr, gebôren;* *treffe, trâf, troffen:* also, *dreschen, sprechen, stechen, brechen, erschrecken.*

Middle Dutch. *stele, stal, stalen, stolen:* also, *nemen,* to take; *beren,* to bear; *sceren,* to shear; *breken,* to break; *come, quam, quamen, comen,* to come.

New Dutch. *stel, stâl, stolen:* also, *nemen,* to take; *breken, spreken;* *plege, plâg,* part. *plâgen* for *plogen;* *kom, quâm, komen.*

Swedish. *stiæler, stâl, stale, stulen;* *bær, bâr, bare, buren;* *skær, skâr, skåre, skuren,* to shear; *kom, komme, kommen.*

Danish. *stiæler, stiâl, stiaalen;* *bær, bâr, baaren;* *skiær, skâr, skaaren.*

Layamon. *stele, stal, stalen, stole;* *nime, nam (nom, nam), nomen (namen, numen), nomen (numen);* *kume (come), com, comen, comen (cumen);* *bere, bær (bar), beren, boren (iborne);* *breke, brac (bræc, breac), brecon (braken) broken;* *speke (spæke), spac (spæc), spæken (speken), ispecen.*

Ormulum. *stele, stall, stælenn, stolenn;* *nime, namm, næmenn, numenn;* *cume, comm, comenn, cumenn;* *bere, barr, bærenn, borenn;* *breke, bracc, brǽcen, brokenn;* *speke, spacc, spǽkenn.*

THE VERB. 457

Old English. *stele, stel,* plur. *stal,* part. *stolen; nime, nam (nom),* plur. *nam (nomen),* part. *nomen (ynome); come, cam (com),* plur. *cam (comen),* part. *comen (ycome); bere, ber (bare),* plur. *bere (bare),* part. *ybore (born, yborne); schere, schare,* plur. *schere;* part. *schorn; breke, brac (brek),* plur. *braken (breke)* part. *broken; speke, spac (spec),* plur. *speke,* part. *spoken (speke).*

Middle English. *stele, stal (staal),* plur. *stolen,* part. *stolen (stoln); nyme, nam, nomen (nemen), nomen; cume (com), cam (com),* plur. *camen (comen),* part. *comen (cummen); schere, schar, scharen, schorun (schor); breke (breek), brak (bracke),* plur. *braken (breeken),* part. *broken (broke); speke, spac (spake),* plur. *spaken (speken),* part. *spoken.*

New English. *steal, stole, stolen; come, came, come; bear, bore (bare), born, borne; shear, shore, shorn; tear, tore, torn; speak, spoke (spake), spoken.*

Class X.

	Pres.	Pret. Sing.	Plur.	Part.
O. H. Germ.	i, e	a	u	u
M. H. Germ.	i	a	u	o
N. H. Germ.	e	a		o
Old Saxon	i, e	a	u	u, o
Middle Dutch	e	a	o	o
New Dutch	e	o		o
Old Norse	i, e, ia	a	u	u, o
Swedish	ä	a	u	u
Danish	ä	a	a	u
Anglo-Saxon	i, e eo	a ea, ä	u	u, o
Layamon	i, e, eo	a, œ, o	u, o	u, o
Ormulum	e, i	a	u	u, o
Old English	e, i	a, o	a, o, ou	o, ou, u
Middle English	e, i	a, o, oo	a, o, oo, ou	u, o
New English	e, i, u	a, u, o, ou		o, u, ou

Verbs belonging to this Class.

Middle High German. *hilfe, half, hulfen, holfen,* to help: also, *gilten,* to be worth; *schilten,* to scold; *milken,* to milk; *swilgen,* to riot, glutire; *klimmen,* to climb; *brinnen,* to burn; *rinnen,* to run, to flow, to leak; *spinnen,* to spin; *sinnen,* to cogitate; *binden,* to bind; *vinden,* to find; *schinden,* to flay; *trinken,* to drink; *dringen,* to urge; *singen,* to sing; *springen,* to leap; *stirben,* to die, moriri; *wirfen,* to throw; *wirden,* to become.

New High German. *helfe, half,* plur. *halfen,* part. *holfen:* also, *gelten, melken, molk, molken; klimme, klomm, klommen; brenne, brannte, gebrannt* (see the Anomalous Verbs); *rinne, rann,* *ronnen:* also, *spinnen*; *binden, band, bunden:* also, *schinden, finden, trinken, dringen, singen; springe, sprang, gesprungen; sterbe, starb, storben; werfe, warf, worfen; werde, ward (wurde), wurden, worden.*

Middle Dutch. *helpe, halp, holpen:* also, *delven,* to delve, dig; *smelte, smout* (= *smalt*), *smouten; climme, clam, clommen; beghinne, began, begonnen, begonnen:* also, *rinnen, spinnen, binden, vinden, drinken, sinken, werpen, sterven; werde, wært,* plur. *worden,* part. *worden.*

New Dutch. *help, holp, holpen:* also, *melken, schelden, klimmen, beginnen, rinnen, binden, vinden, drinken, springen, werpen, sterven, treffen, vechten.* But *helpen, werpen, sterven,* commonly make the preterite *hielp, wierf, stierf.*

Swedish. *hialper, halp, hulpe, hulpen; svälter, svalt, svulte, svulten,* to die: also, *nimma,* to take; *brinna,* to burn; *finna,* to find; *binda,* to bind; *siunga,* to sing; *hänga,* to hang; *värpa,* to throw; *värfva* (Germ. werben); *dricker,* to drink.

Danish. *hiälper, hialp, hiulpen:* also, *giälde, binde, finde, synke, hange, springe, träffe, drikke.*

Layamon. *helpe, halp,* plur. *heolpen; delue,* pret. plur. *dulfen,* part. *idoluen; swimme, swomm,* plur. *swummen; climbe, clomb,* plur. *clumben,* part. *iclumben; aginne, agon, gunnen, gunnen; irne (eorne), orn (ran),* plur. *urnen,* to run; *beorne, born,* plur. *burnen,* to burn; *binde, bond, bunden, ibunden; finde, fond, funden, ifunden; weorpe, warp, wurpen, iworpen; kerfe, carf (cærf), curuen, coruen; fehte, faht (feaht), fuhten, iuohten.*

Ormulum. *hellpe, hallp, hulpenn, hollpenn; dellfe, dallf? dullfenn? dollfenn? biginne, gann, gunnenn, bigunnenn; erne (eorne), rann,* part. *runnenn,* to flow, leak; *binde, band, bunden; finde, fand, fundenn, fundenn; drinnke, dranke, drunnkenn, drunnkenn; werrpe, warrp, wurrpenn? worrpenn.*

Old English. *helpe, halp (help),* plur. *holpe,* part. *yholpe (helped* weak); *delue, dalf, dolue, doluen; clim(b), clam, clommpe, yclombe; swim, swam,* plur. *swam; ginne, gan,* plur. *gonne,* part. *gun; binde, bond (band),* plur. *bonde (bounde),* part. *bonden (ybounde); finde, fond (fand),* plur. *fonde (founde),* part. *funden (yfonde); drinke, drank (dronk),* plur. *dronke (drunken),* part. *drunk (ydronke); werpe, warp; berste, barst,* plur. *borste,* part. *yborste.*

Middle English. *helpe, halp (helped* weak), plur. *holpen (helpeden* weak), part. *holpen (helped* weak); *delue, dalf (deluide), doluen (delueden), doluen (deluen); swimme, swam,* plur. *swommen?* part. *swommen? climbe, clamb (clomb), clamben (clomben),* part. *clomben; beginne, began, bigunnen (gonnen),* part. *bigunnen (bi-*

THE VERB.

gonne); renne, ran (rennede), runnen (ronnen), part. ronnen; binde, bonde (bounde), plur. bounden, part. bounden (ybound); finde, fond (foond), fonden (foonden, founden), part. founden; drinke, drank (dronk), plur. dronken, part. drunken (dronken); sterue, starf, storven, ystorven, to die; fiʒte (feiʒt), faʒt (fauʒte, fauʒt), plur. foʒten, (fouʒten, foughten), part. fooʒte (fouʒten, foughten).

New English. help, holp (helped weak), holpen (helped weak); melt, molt (melted weak), molten (melted weak); swim, swum (swam), swum (swam); climb, clomb (climbed weak), clomb (climbed weak); begin, begun (began), begun; run, ran, run; bind, bound, bound; find, found, found; burst, burst, burst; fight, fought, fought.

PARADIGMS TO THE MIDDLE AND NEW TEUTONIC STRONG CONJUGATION.

High German.

	PRESENT INDICATIVE.			PRESENT SUBJUNCTIVE.		
	O. H. Ger.	M. H. Ger.	N. H. Ger.	O. H. Ger.	M. H. Ger.	N. H. Ger.
Sing. 1st	hilf-u	hilf-e	helf-e	hëlf-e	helf-e	helf-e
2nd	hilf-i-s	hilf-e-st	hilf-(e)-st	hëlf-ê-s	helf-e-st	helf-e-st
3rd	hilf-i-t	hilf-e-t	hilf-(e)-t	hëlf-e	helf-e	helf-e
Plur. 1st	hëlf-a-mês	helf-e-n	helf-e-n	hëlf-ê-mês	helf-e-n	helf-e-n
2nd	hëlf-a-t	helf-e-t	helf-(e)-t	hëlf-ê-t	helf-e-t	helf-e-t
3rd	hëlf-a-nt	helf-e-nt	helf-e-n	hëlf-ê-n	helf-e-n	helf-e-n

	PRETERITE INDICATIVE.			PRETERITE SUBJUNCTIVE.		
Sing. 1st	half	half	half	hulf-i	hulf-e	hulf-e
2nd	hulf-i	hulf-e	half-(e)-st	hulf-i-s	hulf-e-st	hulf-e-st
3rd	half	half	half	hulf-i	hulf-e	hulf-e
Plur. 1st	hulf-u-mes	hulf-e-n	half-e-n	hulf-i-mes	hulf-e-n	hulf-e-n
2nd	hulf-u-t	hulf-e-t	half-e-t	hulf-i-t	hulf-e-t	hulf-e-t
3rd	hulf-u-n	hulf-e-n	half-e-n	hulf-i-n	hulf-e-n	hulf-e-n

	IMPERATIVE.		
	O. H. Ger.	M. H. Ger.	N. H. Ger.
Sing. 2nd	hilf	hilf	hilf
Plur. 2nd	helf-a-t	helf-e-t	helf-(e)-t

Present Participle.

O. H. Germ.	M. H. Germ.	N. H. Germ.
helf-a-nt-er	*helf-e-nd-e*	*helf-e-nd*

Preterite Participle.

ga-holf-an-er	*ge-holf-en*	*ge-holf-en*

English.

Present Indicative.

		Ang.-Sax.	Lay.	Orm.	O. Eng.	M. Eng.	N. Eng.
Sing.	1st	*ber-e*	*ber-e*	*ber-e*	*ber(e)*	*ber(e)*	*bear*
	2nd	*ber-e-st* (*bir-st*)	*ber-est*	*ber-esst*	*ber-est*	*ber-est*	*bear-est*
	3rd	*ber-e-ð* (*bir-ð*)	*ber-eð*	*ber-eþþ*	*ber-eþ*	*ber-eþ*	*bear-s*
Plur.		*ber-að*	*ber-eð*	*ber-enn*	*ber-eþ*	*ber-en*	*bear*

Present Subjunctive.

		Ang.-Sax.	Lay. Orm.	O. Eng. M. Eng.	N. Eng.
Sing.	1st	*ber-e*	*ber-e*	*ber(e)*	*bear*
	2nd	*ber-e*	*ber-e*	*ber(e)*	*bear*
	3rd	*ber-e*	*ber-e*	*ber(e)*	*bear*
Plur.		*ber-en*	*ber-e(n)*	*ber(e)*	*bear*

Imperative.

ber	*ber*	*ber*	*bear*
ber-að	*ber-eþ*	*ber-eþ*	*bear*

Preterite Indicative.

		Ang.-Sax.	Lay. Orm.	O. Eng.	M. Eng.	N. Eng.
Sing.	1st	*bär*	*bar*	*bar(e)*	*bar-e*	*bore*
	2nd	*bær-e*	*ber-e*	*bar-e*	*bar-e*	*bore-st*
	3rd	*bär*	*bar*	*bar(e)*	*bar-e*	*bore*
Plur.		*bær-on*	*ber-en*	*bar-e*	*bar-en*	*bore*

THE VERB.

PRETERITE SUBJUNCTIVE.

	Ang.-Sax.	Lay. Orm.	O. Eng. M. Eng.	N. Eng.
Sing. 1st	bær-e	ber-e	bare	bore
2nd	bær-e	ber-e	bare	bore
3rd	bær-e	ber-e	bare	bore
Plur.	bær-en	ber-e(n)	bare	bore

INFINITIVE	ber-an		ber-en	bear
PRES. PARTICIPLE	ber-ende		ber-ende	bearing
PRET. PARTICIPLE	boren		boren	born(e)

Dutch.

PRES. INDICATIVE.		PRES. SUBJUNCTIVE.	
M. Dutch.	N. Dutch.	M. Dutch.	N. Dutch.
Sing. 1st help-e	help	help-e	help-e
2nd help-e-s	(2nd pl.)	help-e-s	(2nd pl.)
3rd help-e-t	help-e-t	help-e	help-e
Plur. 1st help-e-n	help-e-n	help-e-n	help-e-n
2nd help-e-t	help-e-t	help-e-t	help-e-t
3rd help-e-n	help-e-n	help-e-n	help-e-n

PRET. INDICATIVE.		PRET. SUBJUNCTIVE.	
Sing. 1st halp	halp	holp-e	holp-e
2nd halp-e-s	(2nd pl.)	holp-e-s	(2nd pl.)
3rd halp	halp	holp-e	holp-e
Plur. 1st holp-e-n	holp-e-n	holp-e-n	holp-e-n
2nd holp-e-t	holp-e-t	holp-e-t	holp-e-t
3rd holp-e-n	holp-e-n	holp-e-n	holp-e-n

M. and N. Dutch.

IMPERATIVE	helpe, helpet
INFINITIVE	help-en
PRES. PARTICIPLE	help-end
PRET. PARTICIPLE	holp-en

Scandinavian.

	PRES. INDICATIVE.		PRES. SUBJUNCTIVE.	
	Swedish.	Danish.	Swedish.	Danish.
Sing. 1st	hiälp-e-r	hiälp-e-r	hiälp-e	hiälp-e
2nd	hiälp-e-r	hiälp-e-r	hiälp-e	hiälp-e
3rd	hiälp-e-r	hiälp-e-r	hiälp-e	hiälp-e
Plur. 1st	hiälp-a	hiälp-e	hiälp-e	hiälp-e
2nd	hiälp-e-n	hiälp-e	hiälp-e-n	hiälp-e-n
3rd	hiälp-a	hiälp-e	hialp-e	hiälp-e

	PRET. INDICATIVE.		PRET. SUBJUNCTIVE.	
Sing. 1st	halp	hialp	hulp-e	hiulp-e
2nd	halp	hialp	hulp-e	hiulp-e
3rd	halp	hialp	hulp-e	hiulp-e
Plur. 1st	hulp-o	hialp-e	hulp-e	hiulp-e
2nd	hulp-e-n	hialp-e	hulp-e-n	hiulp-e
3rd	hulp-o	hialp-e	hulp-e	hiulp-e

	Swedish.	Danish.
IMPERATIVE	{ hiälp { mælpen	hiälp hiälper
INFINITIVE	hiälpa	hiälpe
PRES. PARTICIPLE	hiälpande	hiälpende
PRET. PARTICIPLE	hulpit	hulpet(en)

REMARKS ON THE CONJUGATION IN MIDDLE AND NEW TEUTONIC.

English.

REDUPLICATIONAL CLASSES (I—IV.) It is a peculiarity of the Anglo-Saxon language and its daughters to treat the radical vowel in a very arbitrary manner: a glance at our tables will sufficiently illustrate the fact. This vacillation in the choice of vowels seems to have increased since Anglo-Saxon ceased to be the literary language of educated writers, and was handed down through the channels of the various dialects spoken by the Anglo-Saxon populace. When therefore native writers resumed the vernacular language for literary purposes, they must have been at a loss as to the choice they had to make out of a great variety of forms, chiefly in the vocalic system, where great confusion apparently prevailed. Layamon, as we see from the conjugational tables, availed himself largely of the abundance of vowels, and often renders one and the same form of a verb by four or five different radicals in different places; his language mastered him, not he his language. The writer of the Ormulum, on the contrary, is commonly content with one or two vowels in one and the same verbal form, and he goes often so far as to surpass many Anglo-Saxon writers in this wise economy of choosing his material out of a heap of matter. In this tasteful choice, it would appear, he had Anglo-Saxon writers of the older and better period as models before him; his own unaided power of discrimination would hardly have been a safe guide through so intricate a subject. It is interesting to observe how in many instances the special forms he selects approach not only the purest Anglo-Saxon, but are often more in harmony with the laws that directed Teutonic speech in general, than those of many an Anglo-Saxon author before him.

It would lead us too far to follow **Layamon** with an endeavour to systematize the prolixity of radicals he uses in his conjugation. So far as they can be judged by the standard of phonetic laws, the student will find some direction for their explanation in previous paragraphs. (See the chapters on Vowels and Consonants.) Here we shall limit ourselves to mention a few of his peculiarities. Before a *w* he likes to introduce a *u*, e. g. *hæuwen* for *hæwen*, A. S. *heáwan*. He has preserved some fragments of the ancient reduplication in the forms *hehte* (he called, appellavit) and *hepte* (he ordered, præcepit); but he had no idea of the force of this reduplicated form, for he used it in the present as well, *hæhte*, *hahte* (appello, præcipio). Where a *w* succeeds the radical *eo*, it often converts this diphthong into *eu*, as *heuwen* for *heowen*, *bleuwen* and *blewen* for *bleowen*. Not unfrequently this *w* is vocalized into *u*, hence forms such as *greu* for *grewe*, *growe*, *bleu* for *blewe*, *cneou* for *cnewe*, *cneowe*. Verbs which in Anglo-Saxon always followed the strong conjugation occasionally assumed weak forms in Layamon, as *leop* and *leopt*, pret. of *læpen* (to leap). The preterite of *gan*, *gon* (to go), *eode*, *ȝeode*, finds its explanation in the A. S. *eóde* = Goth. *iddja* (preterite of *gangan*).

The writer of the **Ormulum** has a peculiarity which, like several others, reminds one of Old Frisian and Old Norse influence; the Anglo-Saxon vowel *eo* of the preterite he uses only before *w*, while in every other position he renders it by *é*, the favourite form of the Northern dialects. In **Old English** the *w* is frequently vocalized into *u*, and the forms *greu, seu, þreu,* occur side by side with *knewe, blewe, þrewe.* More and more strong verbs assume weak forms, as *weeped* and *wept* for *wep.* The verb *go, gan,* has, besides the preterite *yede, yode, ȝede,* the form *wende, went.* In **Middle English** the radicals begin to be established; out of the great number used in the older language one is fixed upon for a certain form of the verb; and the more the English language approached a settled condition, the more the vowels of the verb also became subject again to rules and liable to systematic arrangement. The particle commonly has the radical of the present, but sometimes it is occupied by that of the preterite as in *held, heng.* The preterite takes the vowel *e,* or rather *é,* which is rendered by *ee,* as in *leep, beet, heew, creew, heeng,* or by *e,* the length of the vowel being indicated by the mute final *e,* as *lepe, bete,* &c. *yede, ȝede,* and *wente* are used as in Old English; in the participle we find *gon, goon, gone, ygo, go,* in the infinitive *goon, go.* **New English** has lost many strong verbs altogether which had existed in Anglo-Saxon and Early English, such as *lǽcan* (to leap, play), *wealdan* (to rule), *hrepan* (to call), *fangen* (to catch), &c., which are partly still preserved in German, as *walten, rufen, fangen,* &c. The different forms of the Anglo-Saxon *hátan* (to be called) have become obsolete; but Spenser has 'he hight' (he is called), pret. 'hot;' and Byron uses the part. 'hight' (called); 'behight,' 'behott.' Some verbs of the reduplicational class have become weak, as *to walk, to row, to low, to fold, to leap, to sleep,* &c. The *o* in the Modern English *hold, blow, sow,* and the other verbs of this class arises either from Anglo-Saxon *ea* (as *healdan*), or Anglo-Saxon *a* (as *bláwan, sáwan*); in the same manner *go* from *gan, gá*: but the *o* of *grow* was already in Anglo-Saxon, *growan.* The distinction of a strong and a weak preterite of the verb *hang,* we find in the Anglo-Saxon verbs *hangan* and *hangjan* already, and ever since in all the different periods of the English language; but the distinction in the meaning, i.e. one with transitive the other with intransitive signification was then a general rule as little as now. The participle *holden* is now used only in the court and law style, the preterite from *held* having invaded the participle too. The preterites *grew, blew, knew, threw,* though preserving the consonant *w* in writing, have vocalized it into *u* in pronunciation.

In ABLAUT VERBS (Classes V to X) the radical was less exposed to change, because it had too deeply taken root to yield easily to external influences. We observe therefore in these verbs a more regular course of the Ablaut through all periods of the English language. For the direction of the student it may suffice to refer to the respective tables of the conjugational classes and our remarks which precede them.

Class V. **Layamon** admits here as elsewhere a variety of vowels, while the writer of the **Ormulum** leaves the Anglo-Saxon Ablaut unchanged. As to the latter we have moreover to notice that he does not mark the shortness of the vowel in the preterite plural, whilst everywhere else he strictly adheres to this rule. Perhaps the fact may be explained from a change in the quantity of the radical in the preterite plural A clearly Old Norse form he has in þrifann, part. of þrifen (to prosper). In **Old English** already it happens that the *i* of the preterite plural is lost and the Ablaut of the singular adopted for the plural as well. We find in the Ablaut of the preterite some difference in the radical according to the locality of the dialect; Northern authors use in the preterite *a*, while in the south *o* is the favourite vowel. **Middle English** is, in some respects, more Anglo-Saxon than Old English, for the plural *i* of the preterite is commonly preserved in the former, while the latter usually adopts the radical of the singular in the plural also. Wycliffe renders the *o* (= A. S. *a*) commonly by *oo*, while Chaucer and Maundeville designate the length of the vowel by the *e* mute, hence Wycliffe *smoot*, Chaucer and Maundeville *smote*. **New English** has lost many verbs of this class which were in use in Anglo-Saxon and Early English; others have passed over into the weak declension. In the participle we often find the vowel *i* of the present and *o* of the preterite side by side, as *rode* and *ridden*, *smote* and *smitten*. Ben Jonson has some similar participial forms of his own, e. g. *ris*, *rose*, and in the same manner of *smite, write, bite, ride*, &c. Some verbs have adopted the plural *i* of the preterite in the singular too, as *bite, bit, bitten; chide, chid, chidden*.

Class VI. **Layamon** renders the Ablaut of the plural preterite in several ways, while the writer of the **Ormulum** preserves the ancient *u*, and renders the Anglo-Saxon *eá* by *æ* in the preterite singular. **Old English** condensed this *æ* to *e*, so that the radicals of the present and preterite singular are identical; sometimes it replaced it by other vowels, so as to make a general rule impossible. But the preterite plural commonly has the ancient *u* in its weakened form *o*; exceptionally it has taken the Ablaut of the singular. **Middle English** adopted the Ablaut of the preterite singular almost generally for the plural; the ancient *o* (for *u*) is preserved in but few forms, such as *crope, gotte*. The preterite singular condensed the ancient *æ* (= A. S. *eá*) into *e*, and weakened the radical *i* of the present into *e*, so that both tenses

H h

became identical. In order then to have some distinction for these tenses, the weak conjugation became more and more general in verbs of this class, hence *rewide, brewed, sethede, fresede,* for the A. S. *hreáw, breáw, seáð,* &c. In the preterite plural there exists a great vacillation between the vowel *e* of the present and *o*, the original vowel of the plural; e. g. *chosen* and *chesen, flowen* and *flewen;* but also weak, *chesiden*. **New English** has lost altogether some verbs of this class, for others it has adopted the weak form, as *creep, crept; cleave, cleft; flee, fled; shoot, shot.* But by the side of these we find the strong preterite preserved in *clave,* the strong participle in *cloven, shotten.* Many verbs, on the other hand, which in Anglo-Saxon were weak, follow in New English the strong conjugation of this class, as *wear, stick, betide, spit, dig, show,* from the Anglo-Saxon weak verbs *werjan, sticjan, tidjan, spittan, dicjan, sceáwjan;* but the strong forms *spat* and *spitten* have become obsolete.

Class VII. The vowels of this class are perhaps less than those of any other subject to the fluctuation of sound, the original Anglo-Saxon Ablaut being preserved through all periods up to Modern English. **Layamon** uses *stonden* for the A. S. *standen,* and *færren* by the side of *faren;* but on the whole the *a* of the present is left intact. In the preterite the original *o* is used almost without exception (*swar* for *swor; stop,* plur. *stepen*), though weak forms are occasionally introduced, as *ferde, takede, wakeden;* in the participle Layamon has been uncommonly strict and persistent in the application of the original vowel *a* which but rarely passes into the neighbouring sounds of *o* and *e*. The writer of the **Ormulum** displays his usual tact and sagacity in the application of the Ablaut. The present retains its pure *a,* except in *swere* and *hefe* (lift), where it has Umlaut; the only exception is *wessh, wax, wex,* in which the preterite however shows the legitimate *ó*; the preterite participle has but once *ó,* in *hófen,* in all other words the ancient *a,* which in *ladenn* and *stanndenn* is marked short, in all other participles long. **Old English** also preserves the *a* of the present except in *stonde;* the preterite *o* is sometimes replaced by *a* or *e,* but in most words it retains its position. The participle keeps its ancient *a* in most words; occasionally it passes into *o, e, a,* as *isuore, up-hoven* and *heven, forsake* and *forseke*. **Middle English** retains the *a* of the present (except *stonde*), but commonly marks it long, as *schaak* and *shake, taak, aak* and *ake;* the *e* in *swere, heue, sle* is of more ancient date. The preterite *o* is commonly preserved; but where the *o* is followed by *w* it is frequently replaced by *e,* hence the new preterites *slew, drew,* for the more ancient *slow, drow,* = *sloȝ, droȝ,*

A. S. *slóh, dróh,* plur. *slog-on, drog-on.* The participle has the ancient *a,* except in some cases where it is invaded by the *o* of the preterite, e. g. *sworne, stopen* (of *stepen,* to step), and *woxen* by the side of *waxen* and *wexen.* Weak forms are introduced in the preterite *shapide* for *shop, waschide* for *wosshe, wesshe,* and the participle *shapid* for *shapen, graued* for *grauen,* &c. The weak verb *quake* has in Chaucer a strong preterite *quoke.* **New English** follows the ancient forms in showing an inclination to preserve the Ablaut of this class in its integrity. It has, almost without any exception, the ancient *a* in the present (though commonly assuming the German *e*-sound, as in *bake ;* once the *o*-sound, *wash*); the ancient *ó* is rendered either by *oo,* or the *o* denoted as long by the final *e* mute, as *shook, took ;* but *hove, woke.* The Anglo-Saxon *stande,* which in Old English and Middle English had taken the radical *o, stonde,* resumes its original vowel in the English *stand.* The participle commonly takes the legitimate *a,* except in *stood, awoke,* where the vowel of the preterite encroaches upon it. Some of the verbs of this class have grown weak in New English, as they have strong and weak forms side by side, especially in the participle, as *shaved* and *shaven, loaded* and *loaden, laded* and *laden, graved* and *graven.*

Class VIII. **Layamon** commonly weakens the present *i* to *e,* and replaces the latter by *æ* ; the preterite singular Anglo-Saxon *a* he renders with *æ, e, a,* even *ea,* and the plural with *e* or *æ* ; the participle retains *e,* rarely *i.* In the **Ormulum** the present tense has the vowels of the Anglo-Saxon. The distinction between the plural and the singular preterite is kept up in the sound as well as the quantity of the vowels, as *gaff, gafenn; gatt, gæten,* &c. The participle has *e,* except *ȝifenn.* **Old English.** While Southern writers (as Robert of Gloucester) apply several vowels in the preterite (*e, o, a*), Northern authors (as in the Psalms) retain here as elsewhere the ancient *a* ; participle *e,* rarely *i.* **Middle English** also has a great variety of vowels in the preterite singular and plural, which may be seen from our examples to Class VIII (see p. 455). **New English** preserves the ancient forms in *give, gave, given ; bid, bade, bidden ;* but in most cases it allows the vowel of the preterite, *a* or *o,* to encroach upon the participle, as *get, got, got ; sit, sat, sat,* &c. Some verbs have become weak, as *mete, wreak,* &c. The termination *en* of the participle has frequently been dropped in this as in other classes.

Class IX. **Layamon's** vowels are subject to the usual fluctuations, while the **Ormulum** displays a strict vocalic system or Ablaut conformable to that of Anglo-Saxon. In the present we find the Anglo-Saxon vowels; in the preterite singular Anglo-Saxon *a*, supplanted by the primitive *a*; in the preterite plural the Anglo-Saxon *æ* again, and in the participle the ancient *o* or *u*.

Old English. The distinction between the Ablaut of the singular and that of the plural preterite has almost disappeared, except in the different quantity. Southern writers (as Robert of Gloucester) prefer *e* as the Ablaut of the preterite, the Northern (as in the Psalms) adhere to the ancient *a*; the former have *stel, ber, brek*, the latter *stal, nam, cam*, &c. The participle has *o* throughout. **Middle English** preserves the ancient vowels of the present, but the quantity seems to be altered in Wycliffe's *teere, breek*, perhaps also in *stele, bere*, and the like. The plural and singular of the preterite are rarely distinguished by the Ablaut; perhaps the distinction of quantity remained, as in *bracke*, plur. *braken, breeken;* but also *beer*, plur. *beeren*. The participle has *o;* but in its termination *en*, either the *e* or the *n* is sometimes dropped, e. g. *stoln* for *stolen, come* for *comen*. **New English.** The verb, *come, came, come*, appears to deviate from the forms of this class; but it will soon be understood if we bear in mind that its present is a contracted form, as the Anglo-Saxon *cuman* for an ancient *quiman, qviman;* the participle has the same vowel *o*, originating in the same contraction. The preterite *a* is commonly replaced by *o*, which has taken possession of the participle too; *torn, born*, have dropped the *e, come* the *n* of the participle termination *en*.

Class X. **Layamon** has the *i* of the present usually before *m* and *n*, sometimes the weakened form *e;* in other verbs he uses *e*, or *eo*, or *æ*, or even *u*. The Ablaut *a* and *ea* of the preterite singular still occurs, the former being replaced by *o* before *m* and *n*. The Anglo-Saxon Brechung *ea* is rendered with *e, æ*, or *a*. The *u* of the plural preterite is weakened to *o*, and thus the singular and plural Ablaut are in many cases identical, and every distinction between the two gradually disappears. In the participle *u* is usually kept before *m* and *n*, in all other positions *o*. We find some weak forms already in use side by side with the strong, as *barnde* and *born, rongen* and *ringeden, clemde* and *clumben*. The **Ormulum** also has *i* in the present before *m* and *n*, elsewhere *e*. Metathesis, as in Layamon, is used in the verbs *erne, eorne=irne*, Goth. *rinna*. The Ablaut of the preterite singular never fluctuates from the Anglo-Saxon and primitive *a*. The shortness of the *a* is everywhere marked by the gemination of the following consonant; but *n* followed by a media is never doubled. What we stated with regard to the singular Ablaut, holds good for the plural Ablaut *u*. Participles have *u* before *m* and *n*, in every other case *o*. **Old English.** The present is treated as in the preceding dialects. In the singular preterite, Southern writers prefer *o*, Northern the original *a*. The plural Ablaut *u*, or its weakened form *o*, is sometimes preserved, but it often gives way to singular *a*, as in *swan*, *gan*, *ran*, *fand*, and the like, used both in the singular and plural. The participle has commonly *o*, rarely *u*. **Middle English** has in the present tense the same radicals as the preceding dialects. It is a remarkable fact that Wycliffe makes the radical of the preterite long before *n* with a media, as *foonde*, *soong*, *bounde*. May we bring this fact to bear on the omission of gemination in the Ormulum under the same circumstances, and draw the conclusion that the writer of the Ormulum considers the radical long in the position just mentioned? The plural Ablaut *u* is sometimes preserved, or changed into *o*, often however replaced by the Ablaut of the singular. The participle as in Old English. **New English.** Many verbs of this class have been lost, others have turned weak; others again use strong and weak forms, as *climbed* and *clomb*, *melted* and *molten*, &c. The *i* is commonly preserved in the present, though often lengthened into the diphthongal sound (= Germ. *ei*). The preterite singular has retained the original *a* in some, but adopted the plural *u*, or its lengthened form *ou* in far more verbs; the Ablaut of the participle is identical with that of the present. Distinguish between *to wind* (spirare, canere), and *to wind* (torquere); the latter is strong, the former, derived from *wind*, should be weak. Sir Walter Scott has 'again his horn he *wound*' in the Lady of the Lake; but 'he *winded* his horn' in Ivanhoe.

High German.

Middle High German. The thematic or connective vowel is everywhere weakened to *e*, while the radical of the present theme remains the same as in Old High German, and in some cases where the radical is *i* it is unchanged in verbs in which Old High German had weakened it to *e*. Concerning the thematic or connective *e* which precedes the personal terminations, we have a few remarks to make as to the manner in which it is affected by the latter. It is a rule generally observed in Middle High German that the unaccented *e* is mute if preceded by a short vowel with a simple consonant, and that this *e* mute is dropped altogether. With regard to the verb we have to consider the following cases. Where the thematic *e* is final and preceded by *l* or *r*, apocope must take place, as *mal, var, bir, stil*, for *male, vare, bire, stile*. Apocope according to this rule must occur in the 1st sing. present indicative, and 1st and 2nd sing. present subjunctive of verbs of Classes VII and IX, in the 2nd sing. preterite of Classes V and VI, &c. If the thematic *e* is followed by the personal terminations *-st, -t, -n, -nt*, and the infinitive *-n*, it suffers syncope in all those verbs where it is subject to apocope when final; hence *melst* (molis) for *mel-e-st, stilt* (volat), *maln* (molamus), *malt* (molitis), *helt* (celatis), *rirn* (ceciderunt), *kurt* (eligistis), *kürt* (eligeretis), *maln* (molere), *heln* (celare), *steln* (volare), &c. This syncope may take place also after *m* and *n*, though the rule is not generally observed, and before an *-n* or *-nt* of the termination syncope must be avoided; hence *nemen, nement*, not *nemn, nemnt*. But in this position both the *e* and the termination are dropped together, as in *man* (to remind) for *manen*. Syncope may further occur after *s* and *h*, if the thematic *e* is followed by the terminations *-st, -t*, as *list* (legis) for *lis-e-st* (*lis-st* is of course contracted into *list*), *list* (legit) for *lis-e-t*, *sihst* (vides), *siht* (videt). Syncope may take place after the media *b* or *g* if the thematic *e* is followed by the terminations *-st* or *-t*, as *gibt* (dat), *ligt* (jacet). Though after *t* no syncope is admitted, it may happen that where a *t* of the root is followed by a *t* of the termination, the latter, together with the thematic vowel may be dropped, as *git* (evellit) for *gitet*. (Compare *man* for *manen*, mentioned above.) The unaccented *e* may not be omitted where it is not mute or silent, that is, if preceded by a long vowel in the root or by two consonants. Peculiar to some Middle High German dialects is the tendency to drop the infinitive termination *n*, sometimes together with the thematic *e*, as *sehe, valle, man, var*, for *sehen, vallen, manen, varen*, a tendency which has its parallel in Anglo-Saxon already, while what there was an exception becomes, since the period of Old English, the general rule. Not to be mixed up with this loss of the infinitive termination is the occasional disappearance of the personal terminations under the influence of a succeeding or suffixed pronoun, a phenomenon which is known as inclination. Such takes place in Middle High German in the 1st plur., as *heiʒe-wir* (appellamur), *neme-wir* (capimus), for *heiʒen, nemen*. It is difficult to account for the termination *a* which is added occasionally to the singular imperative, as in *láʒa, rata*, for *láz, rat*. Grimm considers it as a new suffixed particle and not the old thematic *a*.

Concerning the manner in which the radical is affected by the inflexions a few remarks may suffice. There is an alternation of

THE VERB.

the radicals *iu* and *ie* in Middle High German, as of *iu* and *io* in Old High German; thus, sing. *giuze, giuzest, giuzet,* plur. *giezen, giezet, giezen.* About the original cause of this alternation of sound compare p. 430. UMLAUT takes place in Classes II and VII, where *a* is converted into *e*, as *valle, vellest, vellet; var, vert; grabe, grebt;* except before *-lt, -lk*, where the radical *a* remains, as *walte, waltest, waltet.* Umlaut of *á* into *æ* takes place in Class I, e. g. *rate, rætet; láze, lœzet.* In the 2nd sing. preterite indicative and throughout the preterite subjunctive we find the Umlaut of *uo* into *ue*, of *u* into *ü*, of *a* into *æ*, as *vuoren, vuere, kurn, kür, lásen, læse.*

The consonants of the root, especially if final, are also variously affected by the inflexions. Gemination is always reduced to the simple consonant when at the end of the word, or in any position after a long vowel; e.g. *izze, az, ázen; triffe, traf, tráfen.* A media, when final, is converted into the respective tenuis, as, *tribe, treip, sige, seie;* in the same manner *h* converted into *ch*, as, *sihe, sach* (see, saw). Where syncope takes place it is often accompanied by a vocalization of the preceding consonant, thus *tregest* by syncope becomes *tregst (tre-g-st)*, and then *treist (tre-i-st), tregt, treit, gibst, gist, ligt, lit.* The relation between *g* and *h* and *ch* respectively has been slightly modified since Old High German times. There are still the forms *slahe, twahe, giwahe*, in the present, but in the singular preterite we find *sluoc, twuoc, gewuoc*, while according to Middle High German phonetic laws we should expect *sluoch* for Old High German *sluoh.* The exceptional form *sluoc*, &c., may be explained as the representative of Otfried's Old High German sing. preterite *sluog;* the imperative however is *slach, twach, gewach.* A similar relation of the mentioned consonants we find in Classes V, VI, VIII, as *lihe, lech; vliuhe, vloch; sihe, sach*, the *ch* being used in the imperative also; but in the preterite plural and participle some verbs retain the spirant, others replace it by the guttural media, as *sáhen, lihen, vluhen;* but *sluogen, twuogen, gewuogen, zigen, rigen,* &c. RHOTACISM occurs in the forms *rirn* (Class V); *kurn, verlurn, vrurn* (Class VI); *wáren,* and sometimes *náren, láren* (Class VIII); *gir, gar, gáren, gorn* (Class IX).

The strong verbs with the suffix *ja*, as *swern* (to swear), *heben* (to lift), *entseben* (to taste, *sapere*), *biten* (to ask, pray), *sitzen* (to sit), are, as in Old High German, weak in the present only, strong in all other forms.

New High German. The short radical being everywhere lengthened, the Middle High German rule concerning the apocope of the *e* mute is of course no longer in force. Syncope of the thematic *e* can never take place except before the termination -*st* of the 2nd sing. and the -*t* of the 3rd sing., while before the -*t* of the 2nd plur. syncope is rather avoided, though it is not incorrect to use it. But in the positions just mentioned syncope may never take place if the thematic *e* is preceded by a simple *d* or *t*, and the vowel of the root is unmodified; we therefore say, *nimmst, wirfst, nimmt, wirft, hältst, halt* (for *hält-et*) *ræthst, ræth* (for *ræth-et*), *heißt* (for *heiß-est* and *heißet*), but *waltest, waltet, bietest, bietet, reitest, reitet, meidest, meidet*. In the subjunctive syncope is avoided, as *nemest, haltest, rathest;* 2nd plur. *heißet, w ltet, bietet,* &c.

The radical is in various ways affected by the inflexions. The vowel *i* of the present has yielded its position in the 1st sing. to the weakened form *e*, but in the 2nd and 3rd sing. the original *i* is preserved, while in the plur. again *e* finds place in the root, just as in Middle High German and Old High German. The Middle High German *iu* is, in New High German, commonly rendered with *ie*, but where an alternation of vowels occurs in the present tense, as between the Old High German *iu* and *io*, Middle High German *iu* and *ie*, the former is occasionally given with *eu*, the latter always *ie*; e. g. 1st *fliege* (not *fleuge*, because New High German has converted the radical *i* into *e*, and *iu* into *ie* in the 1st sing.; if Middle High German conditions still prevailed it would certainly be *fleuge*), 2nd *fleugst*, 3rd *fleugt;* plur. *fliegen*, &c., with *ie* throughout; in the same manner of *gießen*, 2nd and 3rd *geußt*, of *fließen, fleußt*, of *kriechen, kreuchst, kreucht*. But these forms with *eu* are used only in the poetic style, when we sing of 'Alles was kreucht und fleugt,' but simple prose prefers *kriecht, fliegt*, all persons of the present formed with the radical *ie*. UMLAUT occurs in the 2nd and 3rd sing. of Classes I, II, VII, where *a* is converted into *a*, *a* into *æ*, as *falle, fällt, schláfe, schlæft, fáre, fært*. The *au* and *ú* of Class IV avoid the Umlaut, but *o* accepts the Umlaut *oe*, as *haue, haut, rúfe, rúft;* but *stoße, stoeßt*. The preterite subjunctive has Umlaut of *a* into *a*, *a* into *æ*, *u* into *ü*, *o* into *o*, *ó* into *oe*, e. g. *wir banden, ich bände, gáben, gæbe, wurden, würde, stunden, stünde*[1], *furen, fuere, troffen, tröffe, boten, boete*.

The consonants are less frequently affected by the inflexions than in Middle High German. Gemination or any other combination of consonants remains unchanged, whether it occur at the end or in the middle of a word. But inorganic gemination

---

[1] The new formations *stande, träfe*, from the plurals *standen, trafen*, had better be avoided.

THE VERB.

sometimes takes place and then protects the original shortness of the vowel, as *neme, nimmst, nimmt,* but the plur. again *nemen,* &c.; *kommen, kommst, kommt,* plur. *kommen,* &c. The inorganic correption of the radical of the preterite singular is often accompanied with gemination, as *reiten,* pret. *ritt,* plur. *ritten,* by the side of M. H. Germ. *ride,* pret. *reit,* plur. *riden.* The consonants *h* and *g* have settled their mutual relations to the effect that *g* occupies the only verb *schlágen* (M. H. Germ. *slahen,* O. H. Germ. *slahan,* to slay), while *h* takes possession of all the rest, as *leihen* (to lend), *zeihen* (to accuse), *fliehen* (to flee), *geschehen* (to happen); but they share the possession of one verb, *ziehen* (to draw, pull), pret. *zog.* Where syncope is admitted in the 3rd sing. a *t, d,* or *th* of the root absorbs the *t* of the termination; e. g. *ræth* for *ráth-et, halt* for *halt-et, læd* for *lád-et.*

RHOTACISM. The *r* for *s* which first appeared in the pret. plur. forms *wáren, froren, koren, verloren,* penetrated from there into the pret. sing. *war, fror, kor, verlor,* and then again into the New High German pres. *friere, verliere;* but the pres. of *kor* is still *kiese,* not *kiere.*

Strong verbs originally formed with the suffix *ja,* namely *schwoeren* (for *schweren,* to swear), *heben* (to lift), *bitten* (to beg), *sitzen* (to sit), are still inflected strong except in the present, where they are weak, as we see from the imperative, *schwoere, hébe, bitte, sitze.*

Dutch.

Middle Dutch. The alternation of *i* and *e* does not occur, but a few verbs have *i,* most of them *e,* throughout the present tense; as *bidden, sitten, ligghen,* but *gheven, helpen,* &c.

Concerning the manner in which the vowels are affected by the inflexions, we have chiefly to mention the change of *a* into *ae* before *rp, rf, rt,* which resembles the Brechung in the Old Teutonic languages, as *waerp, staerf, waert.* The contraction of *-old* (= *ald*) into *-oud* is one of the most characteristic features of the Dutch languages; e. g. *houden* for *holden, halden; gouden* for *golden,* M. H. Germ. *gulten.* The conjugation is greatly disturbed by the inorganic production or correption of the radical under the influence of the succeeding inflexional vowels; thus *varet, wevet,* become *vært, wéft;* thus also by inclination, as *wæft,* for *waf het.*

Consonants are not considerably affected by the inflexions. Gemination is reduced to the simple consonant at the end of a word, as *vel* from *vallen.* The consonants *d, gh, v,* can never hold a final position, but are changed into their corresponding tenues, so that as final consonants there occur only *p, t, c, f, ch*. Where syncope is admitted, a *t* or *d* of the root and the *t* of the termination appear as one, as *het* (vocatur), *rit* (equitat), *læt* (sinit), *biet* (offert), *bit* (rogat), *wæt* (transit), for *hetet, ritet, latet, biedet, biddet, wadet*. (Comp. M. H. Germ. and N. H. Germ. pp. 470, 471.) The *h* is dropped in *slaen, dwaen, sien, vlien*, but appears as *ch* in the pret. *sloech, dwoech, sach*, plur. *sloeghen, dwoeghen, saghen*. RHOTACISM takes place in *verloren*, part. of *verliesen, verlos;* the same in *koren, vroren*, part. of *kiesen, vriesen*.

The strong verbs in *ja*, namely *sweren, heffen, beseffen, bidden, sitten*, make the present weak.

New Dutch. The *e* for *i* in the present tense is almost general even before *m* and *n*. Transitions from one class into another are frequent, as from Class VII to II, so from X to IV; e. g. *hief, wies*, where *ie* (Class II) stands for *oe* (Class VII); but *wierp* and *kierf* may be considered the result of the *r* in *rp, rf*, like the Brechung in the Anglo-Saxon *wearp, cearf*, and perhaps the Middle Dutch *waerp, caerf*. It is very remarkable that New Dutch dissolves again the combination *-oud* which Middle Dutch had produced of *-old*, and thus makes *smolt, smolten, gold, golden*, for the Middle Dutch *smout, smouten, gout, gouden*. Inflexional accuracy, says Grimm[1], gained the better of phonetic nicety. The only form *houden* was preserved by the side of the preterite *hield*. Gemination is reduced to the simple consonant, if final; *v* and *z* at the end of a word turn *f* and *s*; *d* and *g* may be final. The dentals *d* and *t* are dropped before the *t* of the termination, as *sluit* (claudit) for *sluitet*.

Scandinavian.

Swedish. The Old Norse Umlaut finds no place in this New Scandinavian dialect. The occurrence of *ÿ, iu (ju)* and *u* in the present of Class VI is independent of the law that directed the use of one or the other of those vowels in Old Norse. All geminations, except *mm, nn*, remain at the end of the word. Syncope takes place occasionally in the present singular as *bær* for *bærer, blir* for *blifver*.

The strong verbs in *ja* retain the ancient Umlaut and the gemination of the consonant, and re-introduce the *j*, as *sværja, hæfja, bedja, sittja, ligga;* and added to these *le* (for *leja*), *doe* (for *doeja*).

[1] *Grammar*, i. p. 992.

THE VERB.

Danish. The present *faldt, holdt, bandt, fandt*, have no Ablaut. Roots ending with *ld, nd,* of Classes II and X are changed into *ldt, ndt,* in the preterite, as *faidt, bandt*. The plural preterite not only loses its own Ablaut, but even its termination *e,* and is perfectly identical with the present; necessarily so after a combination of consonants in Classes II and X, optionally after a single consonant. We have the reverse of the case in *saae* and *laae* for *saa* and *laa,* where the plural *e* has penetrated into the singular.

The strong verbs in *ja* with weak present may be recognized, as in Swedish, by the Umlaut, gemination, and the *j* of the derivation; they are—*hedder* (O. N. *heitir*), *svärger, ler, doer, sidder, ligger,* some of ancient, some of more modern formation.

Strong and weak preterites occur side by side in *fárede, foer, jágede, jog, grínte, gren,* &c. Some verbs have assumed a weak preterite chiefly in Classes V and VI.

WEAK CONJUGATIONS [1].

PARADIGMS [2].

FIRST CONJUGATION (Connective ja).

Present Indicative.

	Gothic.		Old High German.		Old Saxon.	
Sing. 1st	nas-ja	sôk-ja	ner-ju	send-u	ner-ju	send-ju
2nd	nas-ji-s	sôk-ei-s	ner-i-s	send-i-s	ner-i-s	send-i-s
Plur. 1st	nas-ja-m	sôk-ja-m	ner-ja-mês	send-a-mês	ner-ja-d	send-ja-n
Dual 1st	nas-jo-s	sôk-jô-s	..	..	..	..

	Anglo-Saxon.		Old Frisian.		Old Norse.	
Sing. 1st	ner-je	sêc-e	ner-e	sêk-e	tel	kenn-i
2nd	ner-e-st	sêc-e-st	ner-i-st (ner-st)	sêk-i-st (sêk-st)	tel-r	kenn-i-r
Plur. 1st	ner-ja-ð	sec-a-ð	ner-a-th	sêk-a-th	tel-ju-m	kenn-u-m

[1] Concerning the three conjugations of derivative verbs, the three modes of adding the suffix *aya,* the formation of the weak preterite, the use of personal terminations, &c., compare pp. 366, 382, 388, 389.

[2] Only the 1st and 2nd singular, 1st dual, and 1st plural, are given in the paradigms; the student who has mastered the strong conjugations will easily make out the rest for himself. Peculiarities of the different weak conjugations will be noticed in our Remarks following upon the Paradigms.

Present Subjunctive.

	Gothic.		Old High German.		Old Saxon.	
Sing. 1st	nas-jau	sok-jau	ner-je	send-e	ner-ja(e)	send-ja
2nd	nas-jai-s	sok-jai-s	ner-je-s	send-e-s	ner-ja-s(jes)	send-ja-s
Plur. 1st	nas-jai-ma	sok-jai-ma	ner-je-mes	send-e-mes	ner-ja-n	send-ja-n
Dual 1st	nas-jai-va	sok-jai-va	..	..	..	..

	Anglo-Saxon.		Old Frisian.		Old Norse.	
Sing. 1st	ner-je	sec-e	ner-i(e)	sek-i(e)	tel-i	kenn-i
2nd	ner-je	sec-e	ner-i	sek-i	tel-i-r	kenn-i-r
Plur. 1st	ner-je-n	sec-e-n	ner-i(e)	sek-i(e)	tel-i-m	kenn-i-m

Imperative.

	Gothic.		Old High German.		Old Saxon.	
Sing. 2nd	nas-ei	sok-ei	ner-i	send-i	ner-i	send-i
Plur. 2nd	nas-ji-þ	sok-ei-þ	ner-ja-t	send-a-t	ner-ja-d	send-ja-d
1st	nas-ja-m	sôk-ja-m	..	..	..	..
Dual 2nd	nas-ja-ts	sok-ja-ts	..	..	..	..

	Anglo-Saxon.		Old Frisian.		Old Norse.	
Sing. 2nd	ner-e	sec	ner-e	sec-e	tel	kenn
Plur. 2nd	ner-ja-ð	sec-a-d	ner-a-th	sec-a-th	tel-i-ð	kenn-i-ð

Infinitive.

Gothic.	O. H. Germ.	Old Saxon.	Ang.-Sax.	O. Fris.	Old Norse.
nas-ja-n	ner-ja-n	ner-ja-n	ner-ja-n	ner-a	tel-ja
sôk-ja-n	send-a-n	send-a-n	sêc-a-n	sêk-a	kenn-a

Present Participle.

nas-ja nd-s	ner-ja-nt-er	ner-ja-nd	ner-je-nd-e	ner-a-nd	tel-ja-nd-i
sôk-ja-nd-s	send-a-nt-er	send-ja-nd	sec-e-nd-e	sek-a-nd	kenn-a-nd-i

Preterite Indicative.

	Gothic.		Old High German.		Old Saxon.	
Sing. 1st	nas-i-da[1]	sok-i-da	ner-i-ta	san-ta	ner-i-da	san-da
2nd	nas-i-de-s	sok-i-de-s	ner-i-tô-s	san-to-s	ner-i-dô-s	san-do-s
Plur. 1st	nas-i-ded-u-m	sok-i-ded-u-m	ner-i-tu-mes	san-tu-mes	ner-i-du-n	san-du-n
Dual 1st	nas-i-ded-u	sok-i-ded-u	..	..	..	..

[1] The suffix of the weak preterite is the preterite of a Gothic verb, the forms of

THE VERB.

PRETERITE INDICATIVE (continued).

	Anglo-Saxon.		Old Frisian.		Old Norse.	
Sing. 1st	ner-e-de	sôh-te	ner-e-de (ner-de)	sôch-te	tal-da	ken-da
2nd	ner-e-de-st	sôh-te-st	ner-e-de-st	sôch-te-st	tal-di-r	ken-di-r
Plur. 1st	ner-e-do-n	sôh-to-n	ner-e-do-n (ner-don)	sôch-to-n	töl-du-m	ken-du-m

PRETERITE SUBJUNCTIVE.

	Gothic.		Old High German.		Old Saxon.	
Sing. 1st	nas-i-ded-jau	sôk-i-dêd-jau	ner-i-ti	san-ti	ner-i-di	san-di
2nd	nas-i-ded-ei-s	sôk-i-dêd-ei-s	ner-i-tî-s	san-tî-s	ner-i-di-s	san-di-s
Plur. 1st	nas-i-ded-u-m	sok-i-ded-ei-ma	ner-i-tî-mês	san-tî-mês	ner-i-di-n	san-di-n
Dual 1st	ne ei-va	sok-i-ded-ei-va	..	..	..	..

	Anglo-Saxon.		Old Frisian.		Old Norse.	
Sing. 1st	ner-e-de	sôh-te	ner-de	sôch-te	tel-di	ken-di
2nd	ner-e-de	sôh-te	ner-de	sôch-te	tel-di-r	ken-di-r
Plur. 1st	ner-e-de-n	sôh-te-n	ner-de	soch-te	tel-di-m	ken-di-m

PRETERITE PARTICIPLE.

Gothic.	O. H. Ger.	Old Sax.	A.S.	O. Fris.	O. N.
nas-i-þ-s	ga-ner-i-t	ner-i-d	ner-ed	ner-i-d	..
sôk-i-þ-s	ga-send-i-t (ga-san-t)	send-i-d	s-ôh-t	sôch-t	..

PASSIVE PRESENT.

Gothic.

	Indicative.	Subjunctive.
Sing. 1st	nas-ja-da	nas-jai-dau
2nd	nas-ja-za	nas-jai-zau
3rd	nas-ja-da	nas-jai-dau
Plur.	nas-ja-nda	nas-jai-ndau

which would be *didan, dad, dedum, didans* (to do); the terminations *da, des, da,* stand for an original *dad, dast, dad;* the rest are the regular forms of a strong verb.

SECOND CONJUGATION (Connective ô).

Present Indicative.

		Gothic.	O. H. Germ.	Old Saxon.	Anglo-Saxon.	Old Frisian.	Old Norse.
Sing.	1st	salb-ô	salp-ô-m	scaw-ô-n	sealf-je (sealf-ige)	salv-je	kall-a
	2nd	salb-ô-s	salp-ô-s	scaw-ô-s	sealf-a-st	salv-a-st	kall-a-r
Plur.	1st	salb-ô-m	salp-ô-mês	scaw-ô-d (scaw-ô-ja-d)	sealf-ja-ð (sealf-igea-ð)	salv-ja-th	köll-u-m
Dual	1st	salb-ô-s	..	..	..	..	..

Present Subjunctive.

		Gothic	O.H.G.	Old Saxon	Anglo-Saxon	Old Frisian	Old Norse
Sing.	1st	salb-ô	salp-ô-e	scaw-ô (scaw-ôgea)	sealf-je (sealf-ige)	salv-je	kall-i
	2nd	salb-ô-s	salp-ô-ê-s	scaw-o-s (saw-ôjes)	sealf-je	salv-je	kall-i-r
Plur.	1st	salb-ô-m	salp-ô-ê-mês	scaw-ô-n	sealf-je-n (sealf-ige-n)	salv-je	kall-i-m
Dual	1st	salb-ô-s	..	..	..	..	..

Infinitive.

salb-ô-n	salp-o-n	scaw-ô-n (scaw-ôgean) (scaw-ôjan)	sealf-ja-n (sealf-iga-n) (scalf-igea-n)	salv-ja	kalla

Imperative.

		Gothic	O.H.G.	Old Saxon	Anglo-Saxon	Old Frisian	Old Norse
Sing.	2nd	salb-ô	salp-ô	scaw-ô	sealf-a	salv-a	kall-a
Plur.	2nd	salb-ô-þ	salp-ô-t	scaw-ô-d	sealf-ja-ð (sealf-igea-ð)	salv-ja-th	kall-i-ð
Plur.	1st	salb-ô-m	..	..	..	..	..
Dual	1st	salb-ô-ts	..	..	..	..	..

Present Participle.

salb-ô-nds	salp-ô-nt-er	scaw-ô-nd (scaw-ô-gea-nd)	sealf-je-nd-e (sealf-ige-nd-e)	salv-ja-nd	kall-a-nd-i

Preterite Indicative.

		Gothic	O.H.G.	Old Saxon	Anglo-Saxon	Old Frisian	Old Norse
Sing.	1st	salb-ô-da	salp-ô-ta	scaw-ô-da	sealf-o-de	salv-a de	kall-a-ða
	2nd	salb-ô-de-s	salp-o-to-s	scaw-ô-dô-s	sealf-ô-de-st	salv-a-de-st	kall-a-ði-r
Plur.	1st	salb-o-ded-u-m	salp-ô-tu-mes	scaw-ô-du-n	sealf-ô-do-n	salv-a-do-n	köll-u-ðu-m
Dual	1st	salb-ô-ded-u	..	..	..	..	..

THE VERB.

Preterite Subjunctive.

	Gothic.	O. H. Germ.	Old Saxon.	Anglo-Saxon.	Old Frisian.	Old Norse.
Sing. 1st	salb-ô-dêd-jau	salp-ô-ti	scaw-ô-da	sealf-ô-de	salv-a-de	kall-a-ði
2nd	salb-ô-dêd-ei-s	salp-ô-tî-s	scaw-ô-dô-s	sealf-ô-de	salv-a-de	kall-a-ði-r
Plur. 1st	salb-ô-dêd-ei-ma	salp-ô-tî-mês	scaw-ô-du-n	sealf-ô-de-n	salv-a-de	kall-a-ði-m

Preterite Participle.

| salb-ó-þ-s | salp-o-t-er | scaw-ô-d | sealf-o-d | salv-a-d | kall-a-ð-r |

THIRD CONJUGATION (Connective ai).

Present Indicative.

	Gothic.	O. H. Germ.
Sing. 1st	hab-ai	hap-e-m
2nd	hab-ai-s	hap-e-s
Plur. 1st	hab-a-m	hap-e-mes
Dual 1st	hab-ô-s	..

Pres. Subjunctive.

	Gothic.	O. H. Germ.
Sing. 1st	hab-au	hap-e-e
2nd	hab-ai-s	hap-e-e-s
Plur. 1st	hab-ai-ma	hap-e-e-mes
Dual 1st	..	..

Preterite Indicative.

	Gothic.	O. H. Germ.
Sing. 1st	hab-ai-da	hap-e-ta
2nd	hab-ai-de-s	hap-e-tô-s
Plur. 1st	hab-ai-ded-u-m	hap-e-tu-mes
Dual 1st	hab-ai-ded-u	..

Pret. Subjunctive.

	Gothic.	O. H. Germ.
Sing. 1st	hab-ai-dedjau	hap-e-ti
2nd	hab-ai-dedeis	hap-e-tî-s
Plur. 1st	hab-ai-dedeima	hap-e-tî-mês
Dual 1st	..	..

	Gothic.	O. H. Germ.
Imperative	hab-ai	hap-e
	hab-ai-þ	hap-ê-t
	hab-a-m	
	hab-a-ts	
Infinitive	hab-a-n	hap-ê-n
Pres. Participle	hab-a-nds	hap-e-nt-êr
Pret. Participle	hab-ai-þ-s	hap-e-t-êr

REMARKS.

1. In all the dialects there are verbs conjugated after the first and second; the third conjugation is limited to the Gothic and Old High German. Parallel verbs in the other dialects, which in the latter belonged to the third, must follow either the first or the second conjugation.

2. The personal terminations are the same as in the strong conjugations; the few exceptions are mentioned in the chapter on personal terminations in the Teutonic languages.

FIRST CONJUGATION.

Gothic. The radical is either short or long; if the former, the suffix *ja* is treated in the same manner as the suffix *-a* in strong verbs, hence it is changed into *ji* in the 2nd and 3rd singular and 2nd plural. After a long radical the suffix *ja*, or rather *ji*, is, in the persons just mentioned, changed into *ei*; e. g. *nas-ji-s, nas-ji-þ; sok-ei-s, sók-ei-þ*. In the preterite, all verbs of this class change the suffix *ja, ji*, into the connective vowel *i*, as *nas-i-da, sók-i-da*.

Old High German also makes a distinction between verbs with a short or long radical. The former condense the *ja* or rather *ji* of the 2nd and 3rd singular into *i*, and in the preterite into *i* again; hence *ner-ju* (*a* of *ja* weakened to *u*, like the *a* of strong verbs), 2nd *ner-i-s*, &c., preterite *ner-i-ta*. Sometimes the *j* of the suffix appears as *g*, as *nergan* for *nerjan*, *nerige* for *ner-ju*, or it is assimilated to a preceding *r*, as in *nerran;* but where *ja* is already condensed into *i* gemination cannot take place, hence *neris, nerit*.

Those verbs which have the radical long by nature or position retain only the vowel *a* and drop the *j* of the combination *ja*, except where it is already condensed in *i*, e. g. *sendu, sendames;* but *sendis, sendit;* in the preterite the connective *i* is usually dropped altogether, and if so, Rück-Umlaut takes place; as *san-ta*, preterite of *sendan*, rarely *send-i-ta*. In this case the preterite suffix *ta*, if preceded by *d* or *t*, in combination with another consonant, causes these dentals to be dropped; as *san-ta* for *sand-ta, heft-an, haf-ta;* and if preceded by a gemination, resolves it into the simple consonant, e. g. *nenn-an, nan-ta;* but the simple dental is retained, e. g. *huot-an, huot-ta, plíd-an, plíd-ta*. Several authors, chiefly Isidor (eighth century), and Tatian (ninth century), join the suffix *da* to the root by means of the connective *i*, forming the preterite quite after the analogy of the Gothic, so that a difference in the treatment of the long and short radicals does not exist. Other writers, on the contrary, go far to annihilate the short forms altogether, and to treat all the verbs of this class as those with a long radical. This is brought about by the assimilation of the *j* of *ja* to the preceding consonant and the gemination thus produced; e. g. *zellan* for *zeljan*, makes *zellu*, *zellis*, *zellit*, pret. *zal-ta*—an example where the verb is treated as if its gemination was organic, the *j* is dropped altogether, the preterite suffix joined to the root without the connective *i*, and Rück-Umlaut takes place. In the course of time this transition of verbs with a short radical into the rank of those with a long radical, become more and more frequent in this as well as in the other dialects.

Old Saxon keeps up the distinction between verbs with a long or a short radical, but it frequently mixes the two classes so as to deprive certain verbs of their original character. Thus it uses the connective *i* after long radicals on one hand, and, on the other, renders short radicals long by inorganic gemination and makes them drop the connective *i* in the preterite. We had therefore better classify all these verbs into such as take the connective *i* and such as do not. Verbs with the preterite in *-ida* are (1) the few which still have a short radical followed by a simple consonant, as *ferjan* (remigare), *nerjan* (servare), *queljan* (cruciare). Like these are sometimes treated those which dissolve their inorganic gemination into the simple consonant in the preterite, e. g. *quelljan* (necare), pret. *quelida*. (2) Verbs which join the thematic *ja* directly to the long vowel of the root, as *sájan* (to sow), *strójan* (to strew). (3) Verbs in which the suffix *ja* is preceded by a combination of consonants one of which is a liquid, or by the combination *sk*; e. g. *mahljan*, to speak; *drenkjan*, potare (Germ. tranken); *wernjan*, recusare; *naðjan*[1], niti; *nemnjan*, to name; *leskjan*, to extinguish. (4) Verbs which have a long radical followed by a single consonant, *may* take the preterite in *-ida*, or in *-da*, e. g. *dopjan* (to baptize), pret. *dópida* and *dópta*; *heljan* (to heal), *helida* and *helda*. All other verbs which do not belong to one of the classes just enumerated, must make their preterite in *-da*, that is, without the connective vowel *i*. Verbs of the latter class *may* have Rück-Umlaut in the preterite, about which however no rule can be fixed upon. Examples are *hebbjan* (to have), pret. *habda*; *leggjan* (to lay), *lagda* and *legda*; *seggjan* (to say), *sagda*; *selljan* (to give, sell), *salda*; *tell-*

---

[1] ð = *nd*, vid. sub litt. *n* and ð.

jan (to tell), *talda;* *settjan* (to set), *satta* and *setta;* *wekkjan* (to waken), *wahta* and *wekida;* *sendjan* (to send), *sanda* and *senda*. The regular preterite suffix *da* is changed into *ta* if preceded by a tenuis or double *s;* as *dopjan, dopta; botjan, botta; cussjan* (to kiss), *custa* (where one *s* must be dropped); *wekkjan, wahta, sokjan, sohta* (where the guttural tenuis is changed into *h*.) If the suffix *da (ta)* is preceded by a combination of consonants the last of which is a dental, this dental is absorbed, as in Old High German, e. g. *send-jan*, pret. *san-da*. Organic gemination is preserved in the 2nd and 3rd sing. pres. and 2nd imperative; inorganic gemination is dissolved in the mentioned persons, as *fulljan, fullis, fullid, cussjan, cussis, cussid;* but *telljan, telis, telit; fremnjan, fremis, fremit.* Those which belong to the latter class take Rück-Umlaut if possible, e. g. *seggjan, sajis, sagid,* imper. *sag-i*.

Anglo-Saxon follows the analogy of the preceding dialects in keeping up the distinction between verbs with a short, and verbs with a long radical, though of the former there are but few. The *ja* or *ji* of the 2nd and 3rd singular present is vocalized in *e* (Old High German *i*). The *j*, when following upon an *r*, is often rendered with *g* or *ig,* as *nergan, nerge, nerige,* for *nerjan, nerje;* but when preceded by *l, m, f, s,* it is assimilated to its precedent and forms inorganic gemination, which gemination must be dissolved again into the simple consonant in all those forms which have the *ja* vocalized in *e*, that is, in the 2nd and 3rd sing. pres. indic. and 2nd imperf., and in the preterite; e. g. *fremman* (=*fremjan*), 2nd *fremest,* 3rd *fremeð*. As in Old Saxon, so it often happens in Anglo-Saxon, that verbs with the inorganic gemination *(ll, dd, cg, cc,* for *lj, dj, cj)*, make this gemination their own as if it were organic, and are then treated like verbs with a long radical, i. e. they drop the *j* of the combination *ja* and the weakened *e* (=*i*=*ja*), and, if possible have Rück-Umlaut. But it is noteworthy that they preserve the final *e* in the imperative. Verbs with a long radical are treated as in Old High German and Old Saxon, suppressing the *j* in the present and the connective in the preterite. Organic gemination is preserved as in Old Saxon, provided that the derivative or thematic vowel (*e* = O. H. Germ. *i* = *ja*) is not dropped; but where this takes place every gemination must be dissolved into the simple consonant, which then enters into such combination with the consonant of the personal termination as is presented by phonetic laws for weak as well as strong verbs. (See Remarks on the Strong Conjugation.) It is peculiar to weak verbs with a long radical that they form the imperative like strong verbs without the derivative *e*, as *sec*, 2nd sing. imper. of *secan, secjan*, to seek. The preterite suffix *de* is changed into *te*, if preceded by a tenuis or the spirants *s, h*, single or double; in this case the guttural tenuis *k* must be changed into *h* (except in the combination *nc*), e. g. *sec-e. sóh-te*. As in Old Saxon, a dental, if the last letter in a combination of consonants which precede the suffix *de* or *te*, must be dropped, *mn* must give up the *n* and every gemination must be dissolved; e. g. *send-an, sen-de; häft-an, häf-te; nemn-an, nem-de; cyss-an, cys-te*.

The Rück-Umlaut is limited to the following:—*e* returns to *a*, and *e* to *o*, in all those verbs of which the stem ends in *l* or *c*; e. g. *fellan* (to fell), pret. *fealde; á-stellan* (statuere), *á-steald; reccan* (to count, exponere), *reahte; secan* (to seek), *sohte; recan* (to care), *rohte*.

Old Frisian. Short and long as in the preceding dialects. Short verbs also dismiss the *j* of the derivative suffix. They are very few in number: *bera* (decere), *era* (arare), *nera* (servare), *wera* (defendere), *lema* (debilitare), *spera* (investigare). These may add the preterite suffix by means of the connective *e* ($=i=ja$), though very rarely they make use of it. There is a great number of short verbs which by means of inorganic gemination have become long, as *sella* ($=selja$, tradere); *setta*, to set; *tella*, to number; *segga*, to say, &c., which in the same manner as verbs with organic gemination, add the suffix *da* without the connective. In this case *de* or *te* may be the form to be chosen according to the nature of the preceding consonant. (See Old Saxon.) The participle preterite also has *d* (*id, ed*, in verbs with short radical) or *t*, as the preterite takes *de* or *te*; e. g. *sell-a, sel-de, sel-d; wisa, wís-de, wís-d*; but *kess-a, kes-te, kes-t; acht-a, ach-te, ach-t*. Rück-Umlaut occurs in the preterite only where the stem had a final *k* or its gemination, as *sek-a, sóch-te; thekka, thach-te*. Where syncope of the derivative or connective vowel takes place, the consonants of the root and of the personal terminations are liable to the same modifications as in the strong conjugation. (See p. 429 sqq.)

Old Norse. Long or short radical. The present of those with a short radical has lost in the singular the derivative *ja*, except in *segja* (to say) and *þegja* (to be silent), where the derivative suffix appears, as in those with a long radical, condensed into *i*; as *segi, segir*, &c. In the plural the *ja* always reappears, but under divers modifications. The *j* of the suffix *ja* is assimilated to the preceding consonant only in the case of *gj*, and forms the inorganic gemination *gg*; but nevertheless the *j* is not lost, but finds its place again behind the gemination it has caused, hence *seggja* for *segja*. The suffix *ja* preceded by the consonants *l, m, n, r*, never assimilates its *j*, and therefore never causes gemination in these positions. Contrary to the rule obeyed in Old High German the Old Norse dialect admits of Rück-Umlaut in verbs with a short, not in those with a long radical. But *setja* (to set) and *selja* (to deliver, to give), though of short radical, make pret. *setta, selda*, not *satta, salda*. Under any circumstance the suffix of the preterite joins the verb without the connective *i*, except in the participle *lag-i-ð-r*, occurring in the Edda, for *lag-ð-r*. The verbs with a long radical have dropped the *j* of the suffix *ja*, but preserved the *a* variously modified. Only those verbs in which *g* or *k* precedes the suffix *ja* we find the spirant *j* preserved, as in Old High German, whenever in the combination *ja* or *ju*; but in *ji* the vocalization in *i* takes place, as *hengja*, sing. *heng-i, heng-i-r* (for †*heng-ji*, †*heng-ji-r*), plur. *heng-ju-m, heng-i-ð, heng-ja*; in the same manner *merk-ja*. The suffix of the preterite appears as *da* after *l, m, n*; as *ða* upon *r, f, b, g*, and upon a vowel; as *ta* when succeeding a *p, t, k*, or *s*. As in the other dialects, gemination is dissolved before the preterite suffix, except the combination *kk*. The dentals *d* and *t* preceding the preterite suffix are dropped; *ð* is assimilated to the *d* of the suffix and they thus make the geminations -*dda*, as *queðja*, pret. *quadda*.

SECOND AND THIRD CONJUGATIONS.

Gothic. Some forms fluctuate between the third and first conjugations, as *hatan* and *hatjan*, to hate. The strong verb *báuan*, to build (Germ. bauen), has in the 3rd sing. pres. *báuiþ* and *báuaiþ*. The modus-suffix *i* disappears where it comes in direct contact with the thematic or connective vowels *ó* of the second, and *ai* of the third conjugation.

Old High German. Two Old High German writers, Tatian and Otfried (both ninth century) throw out the modus-suffix *e* (= *i* = *ya*) in the subjunctive present of the third and fourth conjugations, and join the personal terminations immediately to the thematic *ó*, or *e*, as *salpo, salpos, salpo, salpomes; hape, hapes, hape, hapemes*; for *salpoe, salpoes, hapee, hapees*, &c. Fluctuations between the second and third conjugations are not unfrequent, e.g. *haȝen, haȝon*, to hate; *fagen, fagon*, exhilarate; or, between the third and first conjugation, as *hapen, hebjan; lepen, libjan*, to live; between the third, second and first, as *dolen, dolon, doljan*, to suffer. Some verbs take in the preterite the

THE VERB.

Ablaut, as well as the suffix *ta*, and therefore are commonly designated as belonging to the mixed form of conjugation, as *denkan*, to think; *dunkan*, videri, which make the preterite *dáhta*, *duhta*. More about these under the chapter of Anomalous Verbs. *hapen*, which makes some forms after the first conjugation, we find in the late Old High German often contracted in the 1st and 3rd pers. sing., e. g. *hán*, *hat*, for *hapem*, *habem*, *hapet*, *habet*.

Old Saxon shows in the second conjugation a peculiar tendency of adding the suffix *ja* twice to the root, which, for instance, appears in the infinitive termination *ójan*, or *-ogean* (*ge* = *j*), where we have the second *ja* unchanged, and the first primitive *ja* converted into *o*. Thus we find for the infinitive *fragon* (to ask), the forms *fragójan* or *fragogean*. We meet sometimes *a* for the derivative *o*, as *hatan* for *haton*, to hate; *giwisadin* for *giwisodin*, instruerent. Fluctuations between the second and first conjugations are not rare; examples are *nemnjan*, *namon*, to name; *loson*, *losjan*, to loosen, set free; *minnjon*, *minnjan*, to love. Verbs of the mixed conjugation as in Old High German.

Anglo-Saxon. As in Old Saxon we meet sometimes *a* in the singular, and moreover *e* in the plural of the preterite, for the derivative *ó*. The use of this derivative suffix has further been limited by the encroachments of the suffix *ja* which has taken possession of the present tense to the exclusion of the forms in *o*; hence it happens that the verbs in *ó* have divers forms in common with those in *ja*, and the two conjugations are no longer kept strictly distinct. The terminations *-ige*, *-igan*, *-igean*, for the infinitive termination *jan*, and the pres. 1st sing. *je*, have their origin in the ancient mode of spelling the sound of *j* by *ge*, as *bryttigean*, *bryttigan* for *bryttian* = †*bryttjan*, largiri; *lufige* for †*lufje*, *lufigom*; *lufigean* for *lufjan*, *lufian*, to love. There is no doubt that in the spelling of *lufigean* instead of *lufjan*, *lufian*, one thing is superfluous, either the *i* or the *ge*, so that in these forms we have perhaps twice the suffix *ja*. Comp. O. S. *ogean*. Transitions from one conjugation into the other we find rather frequently, so that some forms of the verb are derived from a theme of the first, others from a theme of the second conjugation; e. g. *leofjan*, *libban*, to live; first pres. *leofige* or *libbe*, second *leofast*, third *leofað*, plur. *libbað*; imper. *leofa*, plur. *libbað*; pret. *leofode*; *habban*, *häbban*, to have; first *habbe*, second *hafast*, *häfst*, third *hafað*, *häfð*, plur. *habbað*, imper. *hafa*, pret *häfðe*. In the same manner *hycgan* and *hogjan*, to think; *tellan* and *taljan*, to speak, tell; *secgan* and *sagjan*, to say; the first-mentioned themes following the first conjugation, the last-mentioned, the second conjugation: different forms of the verb are derived from the one or the other. Mixed Verbs see under Anomalous.

Old Frisian. While in Old Saxon the vowel *a* but occasionally replaces the thematic *ó*, this change becomes the rule in Old Frisian. As in Anglo-Saxon we meet the enlarged spelling *-igia, -egia* for *ja*; *-ige, -ege, -igi* for *je*; *skathigia* for *skathja*, to damage, to scathe; *rávege* for *rávje*, subjunctive of *rávja*, to rob. Perhaps these extended themes contain twice the suffix *ja* as the Old Saxon themes in *-ó-gea-—*†*-ó-ja*. Sometimes the first part *ig* of the suffixed *igea* is mistaken for a part of the root or stem and therefore treated as such in the formation of the preterite; e. g. *nédigia*, to urge, oblige, pret. *nédigade*, part. *nédgad*. The fluctuation of certain verbs between themes of the first and such of the second conjugation occurs as in the other dialects. Such themes are *achtja* and *echta*, to condemn; *fullja* and *fella*, to fill; *talja* and *tella*, to number (Germ. zælen); *rávja* and *ráva*, to rob. 'To live' is represented by the themes *libba* and *levja* or *livja*; hence 3rd sing. *lev-a-th, liv-a-th*, plur. *libbath*, subj. *libbe*, pret. *liv-a-de* and *lif-de*. Contractions of the verb *hebba, habba*, are frequent: 1st sing. *hebbe, habbe*; 2nd *hest, hást*; 3rd *heth, hát*; plur. *hebbath*; subj. *hebbe, habbe*; pret. *héde*; pret. part. *heved, hevd*. Mixed verbs as in the other dialects.

Old Norse. The derivative suffix *ó* is, as in Old Frisian, always rendered by *a*. This *a* in the preterite plural is changed into *u*, under the influence, probably, of the *u* in the preterite suffix. Under these circumstances the derivative *u* (= *a*) causes the Umlaut of the *a* of the root into *o*; e. g. *kall-a*, pret. sing. 1st *kall-a-ða*, pres. plur. 1st *koll-u-ðum*. The connective *u* of the present 1st plural also causes the Umlaut of *a* into *o*, hence *kall-a*, plur. *koll-u-m*. The modus-suffix *i* of the subjunctive never causes Umlaut. It is peculiar to this class that it comprises verbs which in the present theme have no Umlaut, while the verbs of the first conjugation have Umlaut in the present theme already, or do not modify the vowel at all. Among the former there are a few which have extended the present theme by the addition of *j*, which spirant has caused Umlaut; e. g. *eggja* (acuere), *emja* (ululare). Such verbs keep the *j* everywhere before the derivative vowel.

There occur in Old Norse, as in the other dialects, verbs which derive their different forms partly from themes of the first, partly from such of the second; e. g. *lifa*, to live; *spara*, to spare, save; *trua*, to trust; *þola*, to suffer; *vaka*, to watch, wake; *vara*, to beware, which form their present after the first conjugation, as *lifi, spari, trui*, without taking Umlaut; the preterite after the first or second conjugation, as *lifða, sparða, truða*, or *lif-a-ða, spar-a-ða, tru-a-ð*; pret. part. *lifaðr, sparaðr, truaðr*. *hafa*, to have, has in the present first *hefi*, second *hefir*, third *hefir*, plur. first. *höfum, hafið, hafa*, pret. *hafða*.

Verbs belonging to the First Weak Conjugation.

Gothic. (1) Radical short. *aljan*, to feed, saginare, alere; *raljan*, to choose (Germ. wælen), eligere; *arjan*, to plough, arare; *farjan*, to sail, navigare; *varjan*, to defend (Germ. weren); *matjan*, to eat (comp. Engl. meat); *satjan*, to set, ponere; *rakjan*, to rack, extendere; *lagjan*, to lay, ponere; *hugjan*, to think, cogitare; *stráujan*, to strew, spread (Germ. streuen), sternere, pret. *stravida*; *stójan*, to judge, judicare.

(2) Radical long. *valvjan*, to turn, volvere; *namnjan*, to name, nominare; *brannjan*, to burn, urere; *sandjan*, to send, mittere; *vandjan*, to turn (Germ. wenden), vertere; *draggkjan*, to cause to drink (Germ. tranken), potare, potum præbere; *varmjan*, to warm, calefacere; *andbahtjan*, to serve, officiate, ministrare; *timrjan*, to timber, to fabricate, to build; *gablindjan*, to make blind (Germ. verblenden), occœcare; *fulljan*, to fill (Germ. füllen), implere; *huggrjan*, to hunger (Germ. hungern), esurire; *þugkjan*, to seem (Germ. dünken), videri; *maurþrjan*, to murder (Germ. morden), occidere; *gavaurkjan*, to work, operari; *faurhtjan*, to fear (Germ. fürchten), timere; *meljan*, to write, scribere; *venjan*, to hope, sperare (comp. Germ. wænen); *domjan*, to judge, judicare (comp. to deem, doom); *dáiljan*, to deal (Germ. teilen), partiri; *hailjan*, to heal (Germ. heilen), sanare; *stáinjan*, to stone (Germ. steinigen), lapidare; *arbáidjan*, to work (Germ. arbeiten), laborare; *kisáuljan*, to soil, contaminare; *daupjan*, to baptize (Germ. taufen); *hausjan*, to hear (Germ. horen), audire; *lausjan*, to loosen (Germ. lösen), solvere; *skeirjan*, to interpret; *kukjan*, to kiss, osculari; *liuhtjan*, to give light (Germ. leuchten), lucere.

Old High German. (1) Radical short. *queljan*, to kill, necare; *seljan*, to make over, sell, tradere; *weljan*, to choose (Germ. wælen); *denjan*, to stretch (Germ. denen); *nerjan*, to save, preserve, servare; *werjan*, to defend (Germ. weren); *strewjan*, to strew (Germ. streuen); *lckjan*, to lay (Germ. legen), ponere; *sekjan*, to say (Germ. sagen), dicere; *spurjan*, investigare (Germ. spuren).

(2) Radical long. *stellan*, to put (Germ. stellen), collocare; *vellan*, to fell (Germ. fallen); *nennan*, to call, to name (Germ. nennen); *prennan*, to burn (Germ. brennen); *rennan*, to run;

sendan, to send; *senchan*, to sink, to lower (Germ. senken), inclinare; *werman*, to warm (Germ. warmen); *sezan*, to set (Germ. setzen); *decchan*, to cover (Germ. decken); *strecchan*, to stretch (Germ. strecken); *miltan*, misereri; *vullan*, to fill; *antwurtan*, to answer (Germ. antworten), respondere; *hôran*, to hear (Germ. hoeren); *losan*, to loosen (Germ. losen); *teilan*, to deal (Germ. teilen); *heilan*, to heal (Germ. heilen); *spreitan*, to spread (Germ. spreizen); *liuhtan* (Germ. leuchten), lucere; *tuoman*, to doom.

Old Saxon. (1) Radical short. *queljan*, *frumjan*, *fremjan*, efficere; *nerjan*, *werjan*, *rekjan*, to relate; *wekjan*, to waken.

(2) Radical long. *dopjan*, to baptize; *losjan*, to loosen; *selljan*, to sell; *telljan*, to tell; *hebbjan*, to have; *seggjan*, to say; *leggjan*, to lay; *sendjan*, to send; *endjan*, to end; *ledjan*, to lend; *grotjan*, to greet; *cussjan*, to kiss; *sokjan*, to seek; *fulljan*, to fill; *deljan*, to deal; *foljan*, to feel; *domjan*, to doom; *quelmjan*, to kill; *brennjan*, to burn; *horjan*, to hear.

Anglo-Saxon. (1) Radical short. *cweljan*, to kill, to quell; *seljan*, to sell; *teljan*, to tell: also *cwellan*, *sellan*, *tellan* long; *erjan*, to ear, to plough, arare; *werjan*, to prohibit, defend; *nerjan*, to save, preserve; *smyrjan*, to smear.

(2) Radical long. *cwellan*, *sellan*, *tellan*; *fellan*, to fell; *nemnan*, to name; *sendan*, to send; *drencan*, potare; *sencan*, to sink, mergere; *streccan*, to stretch; *reccan*, exponere; *weccan*, to waken; *leccjan*, to lay; *fyllan*, to fill; *cyssan*, to kiss; *dælan*, to deal; *hælan*, to heal; *stænan*, to stone, lapidare; *lædan*, to lead; *tæcan*, to teach, pret. *tæhte*; *deman*, to judge, to deem, to doom; *gretan*, to greet; *metan*, to meet; *spedan*, to speed; *fedan*, to feed; *secan*, to seek; *hýran*, to hear; *lýsan*, to loosen, solvere.

Old Frisian. (1) Radical short. *wera*, to defend; *era*, to ear, to plough, arare; *bera*, to behove, decere; *lema*, to weaken, debilitare; *nera*, to save; *spera*, to investigate, search.

(2) Radical long. *sella*, to sell, tradere; *setta*, to set; *thekka*, to cover (Germ. decken); *strekka*, to stretch; *tella*, to number; *segga* and *sedza*, to say.

Old Norse. (1) Radical short. *dvelja*, to stay, to dwell, morari; *qvelja*, to torture (Germ. quælen), cruciari; *telja*, to number; *temja*, to tame; *þenja*, to stretch (Germ. denen); *yrja*, to ear, plough, arare; *smyrja*, to smear; *setja*, to set; *wekja*, to waken; *leggja*, to lay; *hyggja*, to think.

(2) Radical long. *mæla*, to speak; *fella*, to fell; *fylla*, to fill; *doema*, to judge, doom, deem; *dreyma*, to dream; *brenna*, to burn; *læra*, to teach; *leifa*, to leave; *leiða*, to lead; *foeða*, to feed; *reisa*, to raise, rouse, excitare; *girða*, to gird; *byggja*, to build; *fylgja*, to follow (Germ. folgen).

THE VERB.

Verbs belonging to the Second and Third Conjugations.

Gothic. SECOND CONJUGATION. þiudanon, to reign, regnare; fráujinón, to command; gudjinon, sacerdotio fungi; raginón, to reign, regnare; reikinon, to govern; skalkinon, to serve; salbon, to anoint (Germ. salben), ungere; fiskon, to fish, piscari; vundon, to wound, vulnerare; kaupon, to buy, to cheap (Germ. kaufen), emere; raubon, to rob (Germ. rauben), spoliare; liuþón, to sing, canere; frijón, to love.

THIRD CONJUGATION. skaman, to be ashamed (Germ. schæmen), pudere; haban, to have, hold, tenere; hahan, to hang, pendere; þahan, tacere; silan, silere, to be silent; liban, to live; vitan, to observe; gakunnan, to observe; maurnan, to mourn, moerere; hvopan, to boast, gloriari; blotan, deum colere, pret. blotaida (weak ?) or bai-blot (strong ?); aistan, to revere; báuan, to build (Germ. bauen); ga-hveilan, to stay, delay, morari; galeikan, to please; veihan, to sanctify (Germ. weihen); fijan, to hate.

Old High German. SECOND CONJUGATION. halon, to fetch (Germ. holen); namon, to name, nominare; manon, to admonish (Germ. manen), monere; scawon, to behold (Germ. schauen), contemplari; ladon, to invite (Germ. laden); scadón, to damage (Germ. schaden); spilon, to play (Germ. spîlen); peton, to pray (Germ. beten); damnon, damnare; danchon, to thank (Germ. danken); haʒon, to hate (Germ. haßen); minnon, to love (Germ. minnen); irron, to err (Germ. irren); wunton, to wound (Germ. ver-wunden); málon, to paint (Germ. malen); steinon, to stone, lapidare; and all derivatives from substantives and adjectives ending in -sam, -al, -il, -ol, -an, -in, -ar, -id, -ód, -ik, -ah, aht.

THIRD CONJUGATION. skamen, to blush (Germ. schæmen), erubescere; sparen, to spare (Germ. sparen), parcere; saken, to say (Germ. sagen), dicere; lepen, to live (Germ. leben), vivere; hanken, to hang (Germ. hangen), pendere; haʒen, to hate (Germ. haßen), odisse; lahhen, to laugh (Germ. lachen), ridere; lernen, to learn (Germ. lernen), discere; ar-stummen, to grow dumb or silent, obmutescere (Germ. ver-stummen); vraken, vrahen, to ask, (Germ. fragen), interrogare; truren, to mourn (Germ. trauren), moerere: also derivatives in -al, -am, -an, -ar, &c., though not so frequent as in the second conjugation.

Old Saxon. SECOND CONJUGATION. truon, to trust (Germ. trauen), credere; spilon, to play; fullon, to fill; folgon, to follow (Germ. folgen); manon, monere (Germ. manen); endon, to end; hangon, pendere; eron, to honour (Germ. eren); ardon, to dwell; wardon, to guard; copon, to buy; scawon, to behold

(Germ. schauen), contemplare; *haton*, to hate; *bedon*, to pray; *wison*, to visit; *wacon*, to wake, to watch, vigilare; *frágon*, to ask; *suígon*, to be silent (Germ. schweigen); *minneon*, to love; *gibáreon*, to behave (Germ. ge-bæren), gestire; *merkjon*, signare (Germ. merken).

Anglo-Saxon. SECOND CONJUGATION. *taljan*, to tell, loqui; *tiljan*, to till, colere; *sealfjan*, to anoint, ungere; *folgjan*, to follow, sequi; *monjan*, monere; *wunjan*, to dwell (Germ. wonen), habitare; *endjan*, to end, finish; *þancjan*, to thank; *árjan*, to honour; *leornjan*, to learn; *mearcjan*, to mark, notare; *clýpjan*, to call, vocare; *reáfjan*, to rob; *leofjan, lúfjan*, to love; *ebbjan*, to ebb, recedere; *niwjan*, to renew; *þeowjan*, to serve; *þrowjan*, to suffer; *hatjan*, to hate; *bodjan*, to bode, announce (comp. fore-bode); *wisjan*, visitare; *licjan*, to please (comp. to like); *plegjan*, to play; *pluccjan*, to pluck; *hogjan*, to think, meditate. Derivatives in -*el*, -*en*, -*er*, -*l*, -*n*, -*r*, as *micljan*, magnificare; *segljan*, to sail; *tácnjan*, signare; *tácen*, a token, sign; *þegnjan, þenjan*, to serve; *geregnjan, gerenjan*, to adorn; *hleodrjan*, personare; *wuldrjan*, to glorify. Derivatives in -*w*, -*s*, -*g*, e. g. *scadwjan*, to shade, umbrare; *bletsjan, bledsjan, blessjan*, to bless; *ricsjan*, to reign; *syngjan*, to sin; *blodgjan*, to bleed (Germ. bluten), sanguinare. Derivatives in -*sum*: *gehyrsumjan*, to obey (Germ. gehorchen), obedire.

Old Frisian. SECOND CONJUGATION. *cápja*, to buy; *makja*, to make; *halja*, to fetch; *nomja*, to name, call; *rávja*, to rob; *endgja*, to end, finish; *folgja*, to follow; *áskja*, to ask, to demand; *klagja*, to complain, to accuse (Germ. klagen); *radja*, to speak (Germ. reden); *skathja, skathigia*, to damage (Germ. schaden, comp. to scathe); *wardja*, to guard (comp. ward).

Old Norse. SECOND CONJUGATION. *tala*, to speak, tell; *kalla*, to call; *mana*, provocare; *banna*, interdicere; *kanna*, scrutari; *svara*, to answer, respondere; *vara*, to beware; *marka*, to mark; *skapa*, to create (comp. to shape); *hata*, to hate; *fasta*, to fast; *hasta*, to hasten; *baka*, to bake; *rita*, to write; *líka*, to please; *hropa*, to shout; *blota*, to sacrifice (also strong *blota*, pret. *blet*) *biona*, to serve (Germ. dienen); *hlioða*, to sound. Derivatives in -*l*, -*n*, -*r*: as *hamla*, to impede; *sagla*, to lock; *sofna*, to fall asleep; *klifra*, to ascend. Derivatives in -*t*, -*d*, -*s*: *neita*, to deny (Germ. ver-neinen), negare; *gáta*, to assert, affirmare (Germ. be-jaen); *hreinsa*, to cleanse (Germ. reinigen). Derivatives in -*k*, -*g*: as *elska*, to love; *minka*, minuere, to diminish; *syndga*, to sin. Verbs which insert *j* before the termination of the infinitive: *emja*, ululare; *synja*, to deny, negare; *herja*, debellare; *skepja*, ordinare; *lifja*, sanare; *eggja*, acuere.

THE WEAK CONJUGATION IN THE MIDDLE AND NEW TEUTONIC LANGUAGES.

English.

It will be well to remind the student that the verbs of the weak conjugation form their preterite and past participle by means of a suffix, while those of the strong conjugation attain the same end by means of the Ablaut, the modification of the radical. Verbs of the former class are derivative, those of the latter primitive, or stem verbs. The derivative suffix of the weak verbs is *aya*, which in Gothic appears as *i*, *ai*, and *o*, vowels which enter as connectives between the root and the terminations, and according to which we distinguish three weak conjugations. The suffix of the preterite is *did*, the preterite of the verb *to do*, which is added to the connective. The personal terminations are the same as in the strong conjugations. In the Middle and New Teutonic dialects the connective is weakened to *e*, and of the suffix *did* nothing is left but the consonant *d*, followed by the personal terminations; hence the weak preterite ends in English, for example, in *ed*, in German in *et-e* (German *t* = English *d*, see the phonetic laws). Compare pp. 2, 366, 382, 388, 389, 477 (foot-note).

In late Saxon already the two conjugations are mixed up, because the connective *o* is commonly weakened to *e*, and thus becomes identical with that of the first conjugation. Though Layamon still has *makode* by the side of *makede*, and Old English *ascode*, *robbode*, and even the Romance word *destruiode*, these forms are nevertheless exceptional; even Layamon has *e* for both conjugations, and the writer of the Ormulum rejects the connective *o* altogether. We therefore distinguish no longer different conjugations characterized by the thematic, or connective, vowel, but arrange all verbs in two classes, those with a short, and others with a long radical.

I. RADICAL SHORT. The connective *e* is retained in the preterite and participle, its short character is clearly indicated by the spelling *-edd* in the Ormulum; e. g. *sweuen* (to sleep), pret. *sweu-e-de*, part. *i-sweu-ed*[1]; *þankien* (to thank), *þank-e-de*, *iþank-ed*.

---

[1] *i-*, or *y-*, the early English form of the Anglo-Saxon augment *ge-*, German *ge-*, Old High German *ga-*. The ancient dialects admitted the augment in the past participle; modern German requires it, and modern English has dropped it altogether.

Old English uses -*e-d*, or -*i-d* in the preterite and participle, as *end-i-d*, *command-i-d*, and *end-e-d*, *command-e-d*. **Middle English** has the same terminations: e. g. *thanke*, pret. *thank-e-de*, *thank-i-de*, part. *thank-e-d*, *thank-i-d*, and **New English** confines itself to -*e-d* for the preterite and participle, as *thank*, *thank-e-d*, *thank-e-d*, where *e* is the thematic or connective vowel and represents the primitive suffix *ya*; the *d* of the preterite stands for the suffixed auxiliary verb 'did', and the *d* of the participle is the remnant of the participial suffix -*da*-, Greek and Latin -*to*-. The termination -*ed* however has nowhere preserved full pronunciation except where following upon a dental of the stem, as *guard-ed*, *reward-ed*, *wett-ed*; in every other position the *e*, though preserved in writing is dropped in pronunciation, and *loved*, *praised*, are pronounced as *lov'd*, *prais'd*. Though such forms with syncope occur in Old English and Middle English documents, the interchange between *e* and *i* seems to prove that it was not the rule then to slur over the vowel of the termination. Modern poets leave or drop the *e*, often merely guided by reasons of metrical conveniance or euphonic predilections[1]. There are a few phonetic changes in New English brought about by the addition of the termination -*ed* which deserve a passing notice. Single *y* before -*ed* is changed into *i*; a verb with a short vowel and simple consonant doubles the latter; e. g. *carry*, *carried*, but *convey*, *conveyed*; *beg*, *begg-ed*, *wet*, *wett-ed*, *wed*, *wedd-ed*. The *ed* of the termination is changed into *t* after verbs with final gemination or any combination of consonants, e. g. *smell*, *smelt*, *spill*, *spilt*; *past*, *burnt*, are obsolete. Formerly the change also occurred upon *p* and *k*, as *whipt*, *dropt*, *knockt*, which are still pronounced in this fashion though spelled *whipped*, &c.

II. RADICAL LONG. (1) The preterite and participle suffix -*d* is added immediately to the stem of the verb, as **Layamon**, *dem-en*, *dem-de*, *idem-ed*; *lenen*, *len-de*, *ilen-ed*, to lean; *læden*, *læd-de*, *ledd*; *fedenn*, *fed-de*, *fedd*. **Ormulum**. *demenn*, *demenn*, *demm-de*[2], *dem-edd*; *ræfenn*, *ræf-de*, *bi-ræf-ed*, to rob; *ledenn*, *led-de*, *ledd*, to lead; *fedenn*, *fed-de*, *fedd*, to feed. **Old English**. *dele*, *delde*, *deled*; *deme*, *demde*; *fede*, *fedde*, *fed*. **Middle English**. *here*, *herde*, *herd*, to hear; *fede*, *fedde*, *fed*; *drede*, *dredde*, *drad*, to dread.

(2) Where the suffixed *d* follows upon *ld*, *nd* (*dd*), the *d* of the combination is dropped; after the tenuis *t* the suffixed *d* is lost.

---

[1] For some interesting details concerning the use of the termination -*ed* in Spenser and Shakespeare, see Koch, i. p. 309.

[2] The spelling in the Ormulum shows that the radical becomes short in the preterite.

THE VERB.

Examples: — **Layamon.** *senden, sende, isend; wenden, wende, iwent* and *iwend; resten, reste, irǽste; casten, cast, icast.* **Ormulum.** *senndenn, sennde, sennd; reddenn, redde, redd* (to save); *setten, sette, sett.* In verbs of this class Layamon often replaces *d* by *t*, as *wenden, went, iwent.* **Old English.** *bulde, bulde* (to build); *bende, bende; sende, sende* and *send, send, send; caste, caste, cast; sette, sette, yset.* The change of *d* into *t* becomes more frequent, chiefly among northern writers, e.g. *sende, sent; wende, went, mende, ment,* &c. **Middle English** regularly converts the *d* into *t*; e.g. *blende, blent, blent, blent; sende, sente, sent; wende, wente, went; schende, schente, schent.* The suffix *d* is dropped altogether after a combination of consonants with the tenuis *t*, e.g. *casten, caste, cast; renten, rent, yrent; resten, reste, reste.*

(3) The suffix -*d* is changed into -*t* after *p, ch, cch, ss,* and *t*; *ch* must then become *h, nch* becomes *ng,* or is vocalized. E.g. **Layamon.** *drenchen,* pret. *drengte* and *dreinte* (to water); *tæchen, tahhte, tahht; kepen, kepte, kept.* **Ormulum.** *kepenn, keppte, keppt; lacchenn, lahhte? lahht* (to seize). **Old English.** *kepen, kepte, kept; meten, mette; lefen, left* (to leave); *cache, caȝte, caȝt* (to catch). **Middle English.** *kepen, kepte* and *kepide, kepte* and *kept; leve, leeve,* pret. *lefte* and *laft,* part. *left* and *laft; greten, grette, gret; pliechen, plight, plight* (to pluck); *quenchen, queinte, queinte; drenchen, dreint, dreint.*

(4) Rück-Umlaut occurs throughout all the periods of the English language, though it is no longer felt as such, and might be mistaken for Ablaut. Examples:—**Layamon.** *sechen, isohte, isoht; tellen, talde, itald* and *itold; seollen, sǽlde* and *solde, isǽlde.* **Ormulum.** *sekenn, sohhte, sohht; tæchenn, tahhte, tahht; tellen, talde, tald.* **Old English.** *seche, soȝte, soȝt; teche, taght* and *tauht; telle, tolde* and *tald; selle, solde, sold.* **Middle English.** *telle, tolde, told; selle, soold* and *selde, solde* and *seeld; seche, sought, ysought; biggen, bouȝte, bouȝte; teche, touȝte, touȝt* and *tauȝt.* **New English.** *tell, told, told; seek, sought, sought; teach, taught, taught; reach, raught, raught; catch, caught, caught; buy, bought, bought.* There are a few peculiarities in Modern English in the treatment of the suffixed *d* which deserve a separate notice. (a) The *d* remains and the radical is shortened, as in *hear, hear-d, hear-d, flee, fle-d, fle-d.* (b) The suffixed *d* is dropped after a *d* (*t*) of the stem, and the radical, if long, is shortened; e.g. *lead, led, led; read, read, read; speed, sped, sped; feed, fed, fed; spread, spread, spread.* (c) *t* has replaced *d,* probably for the sake of indicating the short radical in *feel, felt, felt; deal, dealt, dealt;* also after gemination and

certain combinations of liquids, as *smell, smelt, smelt; spell, spelt* and *spelled; burn, burnt* and *burned; learn, learnt* and *learned.* (d) We find *t* and *d* side by side, e. g. *mean, meant* and *meaned, meant* and *meaned; dream, dreamt* and *dreamed, dreamt* and *dreamed.* (e) *t* has replaced *d* after *p, f, s,* and the radical is shortened, e. g. *sleep, slept, slept; creep, crept, crept; weep, wept, wept; cleave, cleft, cleft.* (f) Verbs ending with *ld, nd, rd,* change the *d* into *t* in the preterite and participle without adding the suffix, e. g. *build, built, built; blend, blent, blent; gild, gilt, gilt.* (g) The preterite suffix is simply dropped after *d, t,* and the combinations *st, rt, ft,* the present, preterite, and participle being thus identical in form; e. g. *to put, to set, to rid, to spread.* Some of these have regular forms, as *quit, quitted; to light* and *to alight* have *lighted* and *lit, alighted* and *alit.*

Middle High German.

The thematic vowel has become *e* throughout, taking the place of the different forms of the derivative suffix, O. H. Germ. *i* (*ja*) in the first, *ó* in the second, and *e* in the third conjugation. The only distinction we might draw between the first and second conjugation is this, that in the former the derivative *e* is commonly dropped, and almost as regularly preserved in the latter; it being in one case the representative of the thin vowel *i*, in the other of the full-sounding *ó*. The derivative or connective vowels *ó* and *e* (of the second and third conjugation) appear only in few isolated cases, as *volgot, manot,* &c., chiefly in the participle. But here again so many exceptions occur, where the derivative *e* is dropped also, that the two conjugations continually meet on common ground, and that therefore a distinction of several weak conjugations is no longer practically advisable. From the standpoint of historical grammar, however, some advantage may result from the endeavour to keep still separate the two conjugations in Middle High German, until in New High German they have with few exceptions lost all the characteristic features of former days, all weak verbs following the same conjugation.

Both the first and the second conjugation contain verbs with a short, and verbs with a long radical. To distinguish the short verbs of the first from those of the second, we have to bear in mind that short verbs of the first conjugation necessarily have Umlaut in the present theme, while those of the second are devoid of it. (Exceptions occur, as in *hern, herte.*) The long verbs have several characteristics of their own, by means of which the student may know the verbs of the first from those of the second conjugation. Those of the first conjugation are commonly intransitive in meaning; they have Umlaut in the present, and Rück-Umlaut in the preterite, where such is possible; hence in the present only the vowels *e, u, æ, oe, iu, ue,* may occur, but in the preterite *a, u, a, o, u, uo*—that is, vowels which from the modified return to their original form—a phenomenon we call Rück-Umlaut: they suffer syncope of the derivative *e* in the preterite. Long verbs of the second conjugation follow in everything the opposite course; the meaning attached to them is commonly intransive; they have neither Umlaut nor Rück-Umlaut; they do not suffer syncope in the preterite. Useful as these rules may be in a general way, they admit so many exceptions as to be no sufficiently safe guides in certain cases, and the student will often have to recur to Old High German in order to determine the conjugation to which a given verb in Middle High German originally belonged.

Verbs of the first conjugation were originally short, as *queln* (to torture), *nern* (to save, preserve), *ern* (to plough, arare), *legen* (to lay), *zeln* (to count); but many of this class have adopted inorganic gemination and are therefore treated as long verbs, though they are no longer traceable, as in Old High German, to the assimilated *j* of the suffix; e. g. *zellen, zalte, twellen, twalte,* the short forms of which are *zeln, tweln,* not *zeljen, tweljen.* One verb only occurs with the suffix *j*, namely *werjen* for *wern* (the M. H. Germ. *j* almost identical with *g*). These verbs always allow the syncope of *e* in the preterite, as *ner-te, leg-te,* for *nerete, legete,* and in the present necessarily after *l* and *r*, and usually after *m, n, t, b, g.* The vowel of the root is *e* or *ü* which never makes Rück-Umlaut in the preterite.

Verbs of the first conjugation which have a long radical reject the *e* (= *i*) in the preterite and have Rück-Umlaut. In this respect they not only follow the analogy of Old High German, but go beyond it by admitting Rück-Umlaut of *iu* into *u*, though the former is organic, not the Umlaut of *u*. A dental preceding the *t* of the preterite suffix is usually dropped; every gemination is, under the same circumstance, resolved to the simple consonant, and a media converted into the corresponding tenuis; *c* and *ch* preceding the *t* of the preterite are sometimes preserved, sometimes changed into *h*. Examples to these rules are:— *brenn-en* (to burn), *bran-te; send-en* (to send), *san-te; engen* (to narrow), *ancte; decken* (to cover), *dacte* and *dahte; suochen, suochte* and *suohte.* There are some exceptions with regard to the Umlaut which may be noticed here. The Umlaut is rejected by all verbs of this class which end in *-uld, -ung,* the verbs in *-ou,* and some in *-uo* ; the Rück-Umlaut is not adopted by those in *-elt, -ert, -ürt, -end, -erb, -ett, -est.* Only those verbs which have no Rück-Umlaut in the indicative of the preterite, take Umlaut in the subjunctive. Though the vowel of the derivative suffix ($e = i = ja$) suffers syncope in the preterite, it may keep its place in the participle of the preterite; e. g. *brennen,* pret. *bran-te,* part. *ge-bran-t,* and *ge-brennet; erkennen,* pret. *erkant,* part. *erkant* and *erkennet.*

Verbs of the second conjugation drop the *n* or *en* (= O. H. Germ. *on*) in the sing. pres., e. g. *lebe* for *leben, dol* for *dolen.* The *e* mute (that is, *e* following upon a short radical and a single consonant) is always dropped after *l* and *r*, in which case the second and first conjugation become identical; but *e* preceded by *m* or *n* and followed by *n* or *nt* keeps its position; e. g. *zal, zalte, hol, holte, spar, sparte, zaln, holn, sparn;* but *manen, manent, wonen, wonent.* After *b, d, g,* the *e may* be retained, as *lobe, lobete,* rarely *lobte.* Where syncope takes place the *t* of the termination sometimes absorbs a preceding dental, as *schat* for *schad-et, reist* for *redest, gereit* for *geredet.* A lengthening of the radical by contraction of the radical and the terminational syllables, as in the preceding example, we find also in *seist, geseit* for *sagest, gesaget.* Verbs with a long radical preserve the thematic or derivative *e* in the present, as *male, málest, minne, minnet;* they also keep it in the preterite, but the *e* of the suffix as termination, *te, test,* &c., becomes often mute, as *minnet, rinnet* for *minnete, rinnete;* sometimes the derivative *e* is dropped, as *erte* for *erete;* but more often the full form is preserved, as *málete, dankete, minnete,* &c.

New High German.

The distinction of the different conjugations is lost altogether, with the exception of a few traces of the ancient types. Thus we still find the preterites *kannte, nannte, brannte, sandte, wandte,* which we noticed as peculiar to verbs with long radical in the first conjugation; but by the side of these we have *nennte, brennte, sendete, wendete* (not *kennte*); then again the inorganic forms *rannte, trannte,* which should always be replaced by *rennte, trennte.* The preterites with Rück-Umlaut resume their *e* in the subjunctive, hence *kennte, nennte, sendete,* not *kännte,* &c. The *d* in *sandte, wandte* was introduced at a time when the ancient forms *sante,* &c., were no longer understood. With the general production of vowels in New High German the short radical has everywhere turned long. The preterite of weak verbs suffers syncope, to whatever conjugation they may have belonged; as *næren, nærte, legen, legte, salben, salbte, minnen, minnte:* but if the *t* of the preterite is preceded by a dental the *e* must necessarily be retained; hence, *wáten, wátete, hueten, huetete, reden, redete, retten, rettete, tödten, todtete.* The preterite of the weak conjugation has never Umlaut, hence *wátete, bádete, tobte, raufte;* while verbs of the strong conjugation take Umlaut, as *hülfe, würde, gæbe, goβe,* subj. of *half* (plur. *halfen* for *hulfen*), *wurde, gáb, goβ.* Derivatives in *-el, -em, -en, -er, -ig,* suffer syncope, so that those in *-el, -er,* drop the thematic or connective *e*; e.g. *sickeln, wundern, sichelte, wunderte: sichlen, wundren,* is wrong. But those in *em, en,* drop the *e* of the nominal, and preserve that of the verbal theme; e.g. *áthem* (breath), *áthmen* (to breathe); *regen* (rain), *regnen* (to rain); *áthmete, regnete* in the preterite.

Middle Dutch.

The characteristic features of the different conjugations are more effaced than in Middle High German, both admitting the syncope of the *e* in the preterite, and the first having lost the consciousness of its Umlaut and the use of Rück-Umlaut. As a practical guide we may follow Grimm's rule, that most verbs with the radical *e* (that is, Umlaut) belong to the first, and those with the radical *a* to the second conjugation. It is a peculiarity of the Middle Dutch to turn the radical *a,* followed by a single consonant, into *ae* before the termination of the preterite; e.g. *maken, maecte, wanen, waende.* Before the termination *d* the consonants *v* and *gh* become *f* and *ch,* as *scraven, scræfde, vraghen, vrachde, sorghen, sorchde;* but *minghen, mincte.* The terminational *d,* on the other hand, must be changed into *t* after the tenues *p, t, c,* and *s* (from *ss*); e.g. *dropen, dropte, vágen, væcte, haten, hætte, cussen, custe.*

New Dutch.

The derivative or connective *e,* is dropped throughout, even in those words which in Middle Dutch still had *ede* as the preterite termination. The use of *de* or *te* is continued in accordance with the nature of the preceding consonant; *-de* is put in most cases, *-te* after *p, t, k, f* (from *ff*), *ch, s* (from *ss*); *f* and *s* take the suffix *-de* if they are derived, the former from *v,* the latter from *z.* Every gemination is dissolved into the single consonant.

Examples:—*horen, hórde*[1]; *beminnen, beminde; sturen*[1], *sturde; léven, léfde*[1]; *drukken, drukte; schaffen, schafte; höpen, höpte; beslissen, besliste*. Contractions are *leit* for *legt* (ponit), *leide* for *legde* (posuit), *zeit* (dicit), *zeide* for *zegde* (dixit); *kopen* has *kocht = koft*, for *kopte*[2]. Derivatives in *-el, -em, -en, -er, -ig*, drop the thematic or derivative *e* in the preterite; e. g. *sneuvelen, regenen, wonderen,* pret. *sneuvelde, regende, wonderde*. Compare Germ. *regnete;* but also *wunderte*.

Swedish.

The distinction of the first and second conjugation is still very accurate, the former conjugation showing *je, ja* in the present, and *de* ($=e\text{-}de$) in the preterite, the latter the connective *a* in the present, and the termination *-a-de* (O. N. *-a-da* = Goth. *-ó-da*) in the preterite. The first conjugation always drops the thematic or connective vowel *e* before the termination of the preterite; as *täljer, tálde, bränner, brände*. The *j* of *följa, följde, förja, förjde,* has its origin in an original *g* of the stem, and has nothing to do with the derivative *ja*. The regular termination of the preterite is *-de,* but after *p, t, k,* it uses *te;* gemination is always dissolved, as *bränna, brände*. Those which originally had the radical short, have often preserved the thematic *j* and the Rück-Umlaut in the preterite; e. g. *tælja, tálde; doelja, dolde; tæmja, támde; spoerja, sporde*. Verbs which originally had a long radical have neither the *j* in the present, nor the Rück-Umlaut in the preterite; e. g. *bränna, brände; fyla, fylde; droema, droemde*. On comparison with the Old Teutonic dialects it will be seen that this rule is in accordance with the one observed in Old Norse, but just the opposite of that followed in Old High German and other dialects. Though the characteristic forms of the second conjugation are preserved, the spirit of the language tends more and more to assimilate them to those of the first conjugation, first by allowing the syncope of the derivative *a* in the preterite, as *nekte* for *nekade, tálte* for *tálade,* and then by weakening the present termination *ar* into *er,* as *neker* for *nekar, tiener* for *tienar*. Very few verbs, on the contrary, have passed from the first into the second conjugation; as *dela, délade; boerja, boerjade*.

---

[1] Spelt *hoorde, stuurde, leefde,* &c., to keep the length of the vowel before two consonants.

[2] The spirant *f* instead of the tenuis *p* before another tenuis; the use of *ch* for *f*, a peculiarity of the Dutch language. See p. 163.

Danish.

This dialect has nothing of the ancient distinction of the two conjugations left, but the syncope of the *e* in the preterite termination -*e-de* in the first, and its preservation in the -*e-de* = -*a-de* of the second conjugation. The termination *de* of the first conjugation is preserved only after vowels, and a simple *b, v, g*; it is changed to -*te* in all other cases, especially after dentals and the spirant *s*; e. g. *valgte, strakte, tänkte, viste*, which modern writers, contrary to grammatical tradition, sometimes spell *valgde, strakde, tankde, visde*. The original verbs with short vowel may still be recognized in the gemination, as *tälle, skille, smorre, rakke*, for O. N. *telja, skilja, smyrja, rekja*; or in the media *g* into which the *j* of the derivative *ja* was hardened, as *välge, dolge*, for O. N. *velja, dylja*. Rück-Umlaut also we still find in the preterite of some verbs of this class, e g. *tálte, rakte, smurte* of *tälle, smolle, räkke*. Those verbs which originally had a long radical reject gemination, the hardening of *j* into *g*, and the Rück-Umlaut; only few exceptions to this rule occur. The second weak conjugation takes always -*ede* in the preterite. Derivatives in *l, m, n, r*, dismiss the *e* of the nominal theme, as *samle, tumle, roedme, elske*. The connective *e* of the preterite is sometimes dropped, as in *elskte* for *elskede*. The *d* of the preterite termination is changed into *t* under the same circumstances as in Swedish.

ANOMALOUS VERBS.

Under this head we range all those verbs which in their inflexional forms show certain peculiarities so as to require separate treatment as a class of their own. We avoid the term irregular, for it is high time that this designation, which cannot but convey erroneous notions, should disappear from the terminology of grammarians. There is nothing irregular in these verbs, and nothing irregular in language generally. Every phenomenon is founded upon a law; it is not the product of hap-hazard or of an arbitrary will. Where the law has not yet been discovered, it remains the noblest task of linguists to strive after its discovery and elucidation. What as yet evades explanation may be left standing over as a fact which is sure to find some day sufficient illustration from other corollary facts grouped around. But we must do away once and for all with notions of irregularity, and therefore drop the term which keeps such notions alive. The verbs which we arrange under the head of Anomalous (a term, if not much differing in meaning from that of 'irregular,' is at least not fraught with preconceived ideas) may be divided into two classes. One comprises all those verbs which form the present theme by adding the personal terminations directly, without a connective vowel, to the root—a class which may have mustered many verbs in the most primitive times; which however in our Teutonic languages, ancient and modern, is reduced to a few isolated forms, most verbs forming the present theme with the suffix -*a* (strong), or with the suffix -*ya* (weak). The other class embraces verbs which use the perfect theme to supply the meaning of the present, and, in order to render the meaning of the participle, form a new out of the ancient perfect by adding to it the suffix -*da* of the weak preterite. These are commonly designated by grammarians as Præterito-Præsentia, a term which, for the sake of convenience, we adopt.

VERBS WITHOUT A CONNECTIVE OR THEMATIC VOWEL.

There are only few roots in the Teutonic languages which may take the personal terminations without a connecting suffix, binding the root and termination together. As we mentioned on a former occasion, these roots are *da*, prim. *dha* (to do), *ga* (to go), *sta* (to stand), and *as* (to be); to which may be added in the Teutonic languages *bu*, prim. *bhu* (to be), though in Sanskrit it forms the present theme in -*a*. This formation we find in its most perfect state in Old High German, while in Gothic it is limited to the root *as*, and in the other Teutonic dialects shows few traces besides the present themes of the roots *as* and *da*. But even in Old High German this formation does not pass beyond the present theme, the perfect being derived from a root and theme of its own. Concerning the manner in which the terminations of the persons are joined to the root we need not enter into further details after the remarks we had occasion to make in previous chapters. As to the root itself we find it quite intact in the O. H. Germ. *gá-m*, *stá-m*, *tuo-m*, where the primitive gradation is preserved but the reduplication has been dropped, prim. *ga-gá-mi*, *sta-stá-mi*, *dha-dhá-mi*. It is altogether different with the roots *as* and *bu*, which have been greatly modified under the addition of the personal termination so as to be sometimes hardly recognizable. Thus the prim. 1st sing. *as-mi* appears as the Gothic *i-m* for †*is-mi*, the prim. 3rd plur. *as-anti*, as the Goth. *s-ind*, where nothing is retained of the root but its consonant. Similar modifications of the root *as* occur in the other Teutonic dialects. The root *bu*, prim. *bhu*, takes the terminations without a connective in several of the Teutonic languages, while in Sanskrit and in the primitive language it forms the theme in -*a*, and gradates the root from *bhu* to *bhau*, changing under the influence of a succeeding vowel the final *u* in *v*; hence the pres. tense *bhav-á-mi*. The gradated condition of the root may perhaps still be recognized in the O. S. *biu-*, the A. S. *beo*, while the O. H. Germ. *pi-* is a weakened form of *pu* = prim. *bhu*. Whether the *r* in the plur. *pi-r-u-mes* took the place of *w* in *pi-w-u-mes* and would thus correspond to the *v* in the prim. *bha-v-á-masi*, or represents the *s* of the ancient formation of the perfect[1], is a question unsettled as yet. Further details about the modifications of the mentioned roots in the different Teutonic dialects may be gathered from the paradigms as well as the remarks following upon them. For the sake of comparison we give the different roots with their inflexions as they appear in the primitive language, before we lay before the student the paradigms in the different Teutonic dialects.

	I.	II.	III.
	Root **dha**, to do.	*Root* **ga**, to go.	*Root* **sta**, to stand.
Sing. 1st	*dha-dhâ-mi*	*ga-gâ-mi*	*sta-stâ-mi*
2nd	*dha-dha-si*	*ga-ga-si*	*sta-sta-si*
3rd	*dha-dha-ti*	*ga-ga-ti*	*sta-sta-ti*
Plur. 1st	*dha-dhâ-masi*	*ga-gâ-masi*	*sta-stâ-masi*
2nd	*dha-dha-tasi*	*ga-ga-tasi*	*sta-sta-tasi*
3rd	*dha-dha-nti*	*ga-ga-nti*	*sta-sta-nti*

	IV.	V.
	Root **as**, to be.	*Root* **bhu**, to be.
Sing. 1st	*as-mi*	*bhav-â-mi*
2nd	*as-si*	*bhav-a-si*
3rd	*as-ti*	*bhav-a-ti*
Plur. 1st	*as-masi*	*bhav-â-masi*
2nd	*as-tasi*	*bhav-a-tasi*
3rd	*as-anti*	*bhav-a-nti*

The paradigms of the Teutonic languages follow in the same order; but the roots *as* and *bu* must be treated conjointly, because in different Teutonic dialects some forms of the present are derived from the root *as*, others from the root *bu*. The preterite is formed with a different root altogether, namely *vas*, which is

---

[1] About the perfect in -*s*-, see p. 491.

the preterite of the verb *visan* (manere). Though it has nothing in common with the roots now under discussion, we nevertheless introduce it into the paradigm, in order to give the verb 'to be' complete.

Root **da, ta.**

PRESENT AND PRETERITE INDICATIVE.

O. H. G.	M. H. G.	N. H. G.	Old Sax.	A.-Sax.	Lay.	Orm.	O. E.	M. E.	N. Eng.
tuo-m	*tuo-n*	*tû(e)*	*dô-m*	*dô-m*	*do*	*do*	*do(e)*	*do(e)*	*do*
tuo-s	*tuo-st*	*tû-st*	*dô-s*	*dê-st*	*de-st* (*do-st*)	*do-(s)st*	*de-st* (*do-s*)	*dost* (*doost*) (*doist*)	*do-st* (*do-est*)
tuo-t	*tuo-t*	*tû-t*	*dô-d*	*dê-ð*	*de-ð* (*do-ð*)	*do-ð*	*de-þ* (*do-s*)	*do-th* (*does*)	*do-th* (*do-es*)
tuo-mês	*tuo-n*	*tû-n*	*dô-d* (*du-a-d*)	*dô-ð*	*do-ð*	*do-n*	*do-þ*	*do-n* (*do-en*) (*do-ith*)	*do*
tuo-t	*tuo-t*	*tû-t*	*dô-d*	*dô-ð*	*do-ð*	*do-n*	*do-þ*	..	..
tuo-nt	*tuo-nt*	*tû-n*	*dô-d*	*dô-ð*	*do-ð*	*do-n*	*do-þ*	..	..
tëta	*tëte*	*tât*	*dëda*	*dide*	*dide*		*dide*		*did*
tâti	*tæte*	*tât-st*	*dëdôs* (*dâdi*)	*didest*	*didest*		*didest*		*didst*
tëta	*tëte*	*tât*	*dëda*	*dide*	*dide*		*dide*		*did*
tâtu-mês	*tâten*	*tâten*	*dëdun* (*dâdun*)	*didon* (*dædon*)	*diden* (*dide*)		*dide*		*did*
tât-ut	*tâtet*	*tâtet*	*dëdun*	*didon*	..		..		..
tât-u-n	*tâten*	*tâten*	*dëdun*	*didon*	..		..		..

PRESENT AND PRETERITE SUBJUNCTIVE.

O. H. G.	M. H. G.	N. H. G.	Old Sax.	A.-Sax.	Orm. Lay.	O. E. M. E.	N. E.
tuo-e	*tuo*	*tûe*	*dua*	*dô*	*do(e)*	*do*	*do*
tuo-ês	*tuost*	*tûest*	*dua*	*dô*	*do(e)*	*do*	*do*
tuo-e	*tuo*	*tûe*	*dua*	*dô*	*do(e)*	*do*	*do*
tuo-ê-mês	*tuon*	*tûen*	*du-an*	*dô-n*	*do(en)*	*don*	*do*
tuo-ê-t	*tuot*	*tûet*	*du-an*	..	..	..	..
tuo-ê-n	*tuon*	*tûen*	*du-an*	..	..	..	..
tât-i	*tæte*	*tæte*	*dëdi* (*dâdi*)	*dide*	*dide*	*dide*	*did*
tât-î-s	*tætest*	*tæte*	*dëdîs* (*dâdîs*)	*dide*	*dide*	*dide*	..
tat-î	*tæte*	*tæte*	*dëdi* (*dâdi*)	*dide*	*dide*	*dide*	..
tât-î-mês	*tæten*	*tæten*	*dëdîn* (*dâdin*)	*diden*	*dide(n)*	*dide*	..
tat-î-t	*tætet*	*tæten*	..	..	..	..	..
tât-î-n	*tæten*	*tæten*	..	..	..	..	..

THE VERB.

Root ga.

PRESENT INDICATIVE.

Prim. Teut.	O. H. G.	M. H. G.	A. S.	Layamon.	Orm.	Old Engl.	M. E.	N. E.
gâ-mi	gâ-m	gâ-n	gâ	ga, go	ga	go	go	go
gâ-si	gâ-s	gâ-st	gœ-st	gœ-st	ga-st	go-st	go-st	go-est
gâ-ti	gâ-t	gâ-t	gœ-ð	geð, goð	ga-þ	go-þ	go-th	go-es
gâ-masi	gâ-mês	gâ-n	gâ-ð	gað, ga, go	ga-n	go-þ, go-n	go-n	go
gâ-tasi	gâ-t	gâ-t	gâ-ð	gað, ga, go	ga-n	go-þ, go-n	go-n	go
gâ-nti	gâ-nt	gâ-nt	gâ-ð	gað, ga, go	ga-n	go-þ, go-n	go-n	go

PRESENT SUBJUNCTIVE.

gâ-i-m	gê	gê	gâ-(e)	go ga	go, ga	go	go(e)	go
gâ-i-s	ge-s	ge-st	gâ-(e)	..	..	..	..	..
gâ-i-t	gê	gê	gâ-(e)	..	..	..	..	..
gâ-i-mas	gê-mes	ge-n	gâ-(en)	..	..	..	..	..
gâ-i-tas	ge-t	ge-t	gâ-(en)	..	..	..	..	.
gâ-i-n?	ge-n	ge-n	gâ-(en)	..	..	..	..	..

IMPERATIVE, O. H. Germ. 2nd plur. *get*.   INFINITIVE, O. H. Germ. *gan, gen*.
PARTICIPLE, O. H. Germ. *gánter, genter*.

Root sta.

PRESENT INDICATIVE.

O. H. Germ.	M. H. G.	Old Saxon.	O. Fris.
stâ-m (stê-m)	stâ-n	..	..
stâ-s (stê-s)	stâ-st	stê-s	..
stâ-t (stê-t)	stâ-t	stêd (stâd)	stêt
stâ-mês (stê-mês)	stâ-n	..	..
stâ-t (stê-t)	stâ-t	..	.
stâ-nt (stê-nt)	stâ-nt	stâd	..

SUBJUNCTIVE, O. H. Germ. 1st sing. *ste*.
IMPERATIVE, O. H. Germ. 2nd plur. *sta-t (ste-t)*
INFINITIVE, O. H. G. *stâ-n (ste-n)*.   M. H. G., O. S., O. Fris. *stâ-n*.
PARTICIPLE, O. H. Germ. *stánter (stenter)*.

THE VERB 'TO BE.'

Roots **as, bû, vas.**

PRESENT INDICATIVE.

Gothic.	Old High German.		Old Saxon.		Anglo-Saxon.		O. Fris.		Old Norse.	
as.	as.	bû.	as.	bû.	as.	bû.	as.	bû.	as.	bû.
i-m	..	pi-m	..	biu-m	ëo-m	beo-(m)	..	be-m	e-m	..
i-s	..	pi-s(st)	..	bi-st	ear-t	bi-st	..	bi st	er-t	..
is-t	is, is-t	..	is, is-t	..	is	bi-ð	is-t	..	er	..
sij-u-m	..	{ pi-r-u-mes / pi-r-u-n / pi-r-n }	s-ind	..	{ ar-on / s-ind(-on) } beo-ð		s-end	..	er-u-m	..
sij-u-þ	..	{ pi-r-u-t / pi-r-t }	s-ind	..	{ ar-on / s-ind(-on) } beo-ð		s-end	..	er-u-ð	..
s-ind	s-ind	pi-r-u-n	s-ind(-un)	..	{ ar-on / s-ind(-on) } beo-ð		s-end	..	er-u	..

PRESENT SUBJUNCTIVE.

Gothic.	O.H.G.	Old Saxon.		Anglo-Saxon.			O. Fris.	Old Norse.	
as.	as.	as.	vas.	as.	bû.	vas.	as.	as.	vas.
si-jau	s-î	s-î	..	s-î	beo	wës-e	s-ê	s-ê	ver-i
sij-ai-s	s-î-s	s-î-s	..	s-î	beo	wës-e	s-ê	s-ê-r	ver-i-r
sij-ai	s-î	s-î	(wësa)	s-î	beo	wës-e	s-ê	s-ê	ver-i
sij-ai-ma	s-î-mês	s-î-n	..	s-î-n	beo-n	wës-e-n	s-ê	s-êi-m	ver-i-m
sij-ai-þ	s-î-t	s-î-n	..	s-î-n	beo-n	wës-e-n	s-ê	s-êi-þ	ver-i-þ
sij-ai-na	s-î-n	s-î-n	..	s-î-n	beo-n	wës-e-n	s-ê	s-êi`	ver-i

IMPERATIVE.

	O. H. Germ.		Anglo-Saxon.		O. Fris.	O. Norse.
	bû.	vas.	vas.	bû.	vas.	vas.
Sing. 2nd	pi-s	wis	wes	beo	wes-e	ver
Plur. 2nd	(si-t)	wës-at	wës-a-ð	beo-ð	wes-a-th	ver-i-ð

THE VERB.

Root **vas**.

Preterite Indicative.

		Gothic.	O. H. Germ.	Old Sax.	Ang.-Sax.	O. Fris.	O. Norse.
Sing.	1st	vas	was	was	wäs	was	var
	2nd	vas-t	wâr-i	wâr-i	wære	wêre	var-t
	3rd	vas	was	was	wäs	was	var
Plur.	1st	vês-u-m	wâr-u-mês	wâr-un	wær-on	wêr-on	vâr-u-m (vor-um
	2nd	vês-u-þ	wâr-u-t	wâr-un	wær-on	wêr-on	vâr-u-ð (vor-uð
	3rd	vês-u-n	wâr-u-n	wâr-un	wær-on	wêr-on	vâr-u (vor-u)

Preterite Subjunctive.

Sing.	1st	ves-ja-u	wâr-i	wâr-i	wær-e	wêr-e	vær-i
	2nd	ves-ei-s	wâr-i-s	wâr-i-s	wær-e	wêr-e	vær-i-r
	3rd	ves-i	wâr-i	wâr-i	wær-e	wêr-e	vær-i
Plur.	1st	ves-ei-ma	wâr-i-mes	wâr-i-n	wær-e-n	wêr-e	vær-i-m
	2nd	ves-ei-þ	wâr-i-t	wâr-i-n	wær-e-n	wêr-e	vær-i-ð
	3rd	ves-ei-na	wâr-i-n	wâr-i-n	wær-e-n	wêr-e	vær-i

Infinitive.

vis-an	wës-an / sî-n	..	wes-an / beo-n	wes-a	ver-a

Present Participle.

vis-a-nd-s	wes-a-nt-er	..	wes-e-nd-e	wes-a-nd	ver-a-nd-i

Preterite Participle.

vis-a-n-s	wes-a-n-er	wes-a-n	ge-wesen	wesen	ver-i-nn.

MIDDLE AND NEW TEUTONIC LANGUAGES.

Present Indicative.

		Layamon.	Ormulum.	Old English.	Mid. Engl.	N. Engl.	M.H.Ger.	N.H.G.	M. Dutch.	N. Dutch.	Swedish.	Dan
Sing.	1st	am, æm beon	amm	am be	a i be	am	b'n	bin	b'm	ben	ær	er
	2nd	ært, art, eart beost, bist	arrt best	art, ert is	art best	art	b_st	bist	b st	..	ær	er
	3rd	is beoð, beð, bið	iss beoþ, beþ	is, es beþ	is bes	is	ist	ist	es, is	is	ær	er
Plur.	1st	sunden beoð, beð, bið	sinndenn arrn, (e), ben	are, ere, er beþ, ben, be	arn, are beþ, ben, be	are be	sin birn sit birt	sind scit	s'n sit	z'n b'n n m z t bent	ære(o)	er
	2nd	..	..	..	..	..					æren	er
	3rd	..	..	..	..	..	sint	sind	s'n	z n b'n n m	æro	er

Present Subjunctive.

		Layamon.	Ormulum.	Old English.	Mid. Engl.	N. Engl.	M.H.Ger.	N.H.G.	M. Dutch.	N. Dutch.	Swedish.
Sing.	1st	beo si	beo, be si	be	be	be	si	sci	si	zi	vare
	2nd	..	..	..	..	..	sist si	scst sci	sis si	..	vare
	3rd	..	..	..	..	..				zi	vare
Plur.	1st	beon sion	beon?	be	be	be	sin	scien	sin	zin	vare
	2nd	..	..	..	..	..	sit	sciet	sit	zit	varen
	3rd	..	..	..	..	..	sin	scien	sin	zin	vare

PRETERITE INDICATIVE.

st	was, wors, wes	wass	was, wes	was	was	wâr	was	vâr
nd	..	was	wære, was	was, wast	were	wûrdest	..	vâr
rd	was, wæs, wes	wass	was	was	was	wâr	was	vâr
st	weren	..	were, ware	were(n)	wære	wâren	wâren	vôren
nd	..	..	..	..	wâret	wâret	wârt	vôre
rd	..	..	..	..	wâren	wâren	wâren	vôro

PRETERITE SUBJUNCTIVE.

st	were	were	were	were	ware	wære	wâre	vôre
nd	..	..	..	..	..	wærest	wâre	..
rl	..	..	..	..	..	wære	wâren	..
si	weren	wæren	were	were	wæren	wæren	wâret	vôre
nd	..	..	..	..	..	wâret	wâret	vôren
rl	..	..	..	..	..	wæren	wâren	vore

IMPERATIVE.

nd	beo, be	beo, be	be	be	bis	sei	wes	var
nd	wes, seo beoð	beþ	beþ, bes	beoth, beth	sit (?)	sei(e)t	wêst, zit	3 sing. vare varen 1 pl. varom

INFINITIVE.

| beon | beon, ben | ben, bin
beo, be | ben, be | be | wêsen, sîn | sein | wêsen, sîn | vara |

PRESENT PARTICIPLE.

| .. | .. | .. | beende | being | wesende(?) | seiend | wesende
stnde | varande |

PRETERITE PARTICIPLE.

| íbeo
beon | beon
ben
ibe | bene
bien | ben | been | ge-wesen
ge-sîn | ge-wesen | geweaen
gewêst
gesîn | varit |

REMARKS ON THE PARADIGMS.

The root **da** (to do); O. H. Germ. *ta*; Prim. *dha*.

Gothic. This root never appears except in the preterite terminations of the weak conjugation, considered above, and in the noun *dèds* (deed).

Old High German. The diphthongal form of the present corresponds to the second gradation *dhá* of the Sanskrit and Primitive; the preterite *tëta* is one of the few traces of complete reduplication in Old High German, and stands for a more ancient *tita = tata*. The lengthened form in 2nd sing. *táti* is the contraction of †*ta-ta-ti* (*-ti* is personal termination), prim. *dha-dha-ti*; and in the same manner the plural *tát-u-mes = ta-ta-mes*, prim. *dha-dhá-masi*. A conjugation somewhat differing from that in the paradigm we find in Otfried's *dua-n, dua-s (dui-s), dua-t (dui-t)*; 1st plur. *duen*, 3rd *duant, duent*.

Old Saxon. The *ó* corresponds to the second gradation *uo* in Old High German, *á* in Sanskrit and Primitive. The short forms *du-a-d* by the side of *do-d* in the plural of the present, and the lengthened radical in *dádi, dádun* by the side of *dedos, dedun* in the preterite, indicate a tendency to leave the ancient mode of conjugating this verb and to assimilate it to that of the verbs in *a*.

Anglo-Saxon admits Umlaut of *ó* into *e* in the 2nd and 3rd sing. present. The plur. *dæd-u-n* by the side of *did-o-n* corresponds to the O. S. *dád-u-n* by the side of *ded-u-n*, the O. H. Germ. *tät-u-mës*.

Old Frisian has the principal forms of this verb left: pres. 1st *due*, 3rd *de-th*, plur. *du-a-th*; subj. *du-e*, pret. *dede*, plur. *dedon*; pret. part. *de-n, dá-n*. The forms will show of themselves how they approach certain peculiarities in the preceding dialects.

Old Norse has as little as Gothic any of the verbal forms of the root *da*.

The roots **ga** (to go); O. H. Germ. *gá, ká*. **sta** (to stand).

Gothic possesses this root in its extended form *gaggan*, but never makes any verbal forms out of the simple root *ga*. The root *sta* also occurs in no other but the extended form *sta-n-d-an*.

Old High German has by the side of the forms *stám, stás, stát; gam, gas, gat*: also *stem, stes, stet; gem, ges, get*, and even *geist, geit, steist, steit*. The extended roots *ga-n-g-an, sta-n-t-an*, formed by means of reduplication and the infix -*n*- are used too side by side with the simple forms in the present, and in the preterite exclusively, because the latter do not form this tense; hence *giang, stuont:* the preterites of *gangu, stantu,* belong also to *gam* and *stám*.

Old Saxon has but few fragments of the verb *gán*, namely 3rd sing. pres. *ge-d*, and the infin. *te-gán-de*. In the Heliand no trace is found, the whole verb being replaced by the extended form *gangan*. Of the verb *stán* are found the 2nd sing. *stes*, 3rd *stád, sted, steid,* 3rd plur. *stád,* infin. *stán*. All other forms are replaced by those of *standan*.

Anglo-Saxon has all the principal forms: 1st sing. *gá*, 2nd *gæst, gæð*[1]; subj. sing. 3rd. *gá*, imper. *gá*, plur. *gá-ð*, infin. *gán*, part. *ge-gán;* but those of *gangan* occur side by side with them: the preterite is *gieng, geong, geng* of *gangan,* or *eode,* like the Gothic *iddja,* derived from the root *i* (to go), with the suffix of the weak preterite. The verb *stán* does not occur, but only the extended form *standan,* pret. *stód, stodon*.

Old Frisian has of the root *ga* only 3rd sing. *gáth, geith,* plur. *gá-th;* pret. part. *gen;* all other forms supplied by *gunga,* pret. *geng, gengon,* part. *gangen, gengen, gendzen*. Of the root *sta* we find only the infin. *stán* and 3rd sing. *stet;* everywhere else **stonda, stôd, stôdon, stenden** (*stinsen*).

Old Norse has no forms of the roots *ga* and *sta*, which are supplied by *ganga, gekk, gengam, genginn,* and *standa, stoð, stóðum, staðinn*.

The Middle and New Teutonic Languages.

German.

Middle High German and New High German develop the different forms of the verb *tuom* from the Old High German according to the phonetic laws. The diphthong *uo* is preserved in Middle High German, but replaced by *u* in New High German; as to the personal terminations they are subject to the same rules here as in the strong conjugation. The forms of *gán* and *stán* are the same as in Old High German, and may, as in the latter dialect interchange with *sten, stest, stet, gen, gest, get,* and even *geist, geit, steist, steit*. New High German has apparently lost these forms unless we derive *geh-e, geh-st, geh-t,* from *ge, ge-st, ge-t,* &c., which would correspond to the Old High

---

[1] The Umlaut is no doubt owing to the fact that *gæst* and *gæð* were considered to have arisen by syncope of *gangest, gangeð*.

German *gá-m, gá-st, gá-t; geh-en=gá-n*. The preterite is of course both in Middle High German and Old High German *gienc, gieng*, from an obsolete *gangen*. The N. H. Germ. *stehe, stehst* for *ste, ste-st*, infin. *steh-en* for *sten* stands in the same relation to O. H. Germ. *stá-m, stá-s*, infin. *stá-n*. The pret. *stand*, plur. M. H. Germ. *stunden*, N. H. Germ. *standen*, belongs to an obsolete infinitive *standen*. The result therefore with regard to Modern German would be this: the forms of the present, including the infinitive and participle are derived from the simple roots *ga* and *sta*, those of the preterite including the participles from the extended roots in the lost infinitives *gangen, standen*.

English.

The different forms of the Anglo-Saxon *don* are preserved in the different periods; but in late Saxon already the 1st singular present loses the personal termination -*m*, while the *st* of the 2nd, the ð of the 3rd, and the *n* of the plural are still found in Middle English. New English has dropped the plural termination and replaced the *th* of the 3rd singular by *s*. The forms of the simple root *ga* have gained the better over the extended *gangan*, which at an early date disappeared from English altogether. Layamon has, as in *de-st, de-ð*, thus also in *gæst, geð*, preserved the Anglo-Saxon Umlaut. The writer of the Ormulum returns to the original vowels *o* and *a* in *do-st, ga-st*, &c. Old English has still the Umlaut in *de-st, de-þ*, but rejects it in *ga*, where it darkens the original *a* into *go, gost, go-þ*, forms which were adopted in all subsequent periods to the present day. The simple root *sta*, on the other hand, has disappeared from English since the late Saxon times, Layamon and the Ormulum already using the extended form *standen*, darkened into *stonden*, instead of it, which forms run side by side in Old English and Middle English and settle down into the New English *stand*.

Dutch.

The different forms of the verb 'to do' are mostly preserved in the Middle Dutch infinitive *doen*: pres. *doe, does, doet*, plur. *doen*; pret. *dede, dades, dede*, plur. *daden*; subj. *dade*; pret. part, *daen*. New Dutch has the infin. *doen*, pres. 1st *doe*, 3rd *doet*, plur. *doen*; pret. *déd*, plur. *déden*; part. *ge-dan*, Germ. *ge-tán*. *gaen* and *staen* have several forms in the present besides the infinitive just mentioned: 3rd sing. *gaet, staet*; occasionally *ghét, stet*; 1st sing. *gae, stae*. The forms of the preterite are derived from *gangen* and *standen*. The New Dutch infinitives *gán (gaan)* and *stán*

THE VERB.

(*staan*) may scarcely be considered the forms of the simple root, but rather contractions of the extended infinitives *gangen, standen*, in the same manner as 1st sing. *sta, ga*, seem to be used for *stande, gange, gestan* for *gestanden*. The preterites are regularly *ging* and *stond* of *gangen* and *standen*.

Scandinavian.

Swedish and Danish have no verbal forms derived from the root *da*. The Swedish infin. *gå*, pres. *gar* may be taken as the representatives of the simple root *ga* or as contractions of *ganga, ganger*; the pret. *gick, ginga*, will find its explanation in the Old Norse *gekk, gengum*. In a similar manner must be viewed the forms *star, stod, ståden*, infin. *stå*. Analagous to the Swedish are the Danish forms *gaaer, gik, gangen*, infin. *gaae;* and *staaer, stod, standen*, infin. *staae*.

The roots **as, bu, vas** (to be).

Gothic makes all the forms of the present out of the root *as*, all the forms of the preterite out of the root *vas*. Concerning the other Old Teutonic languages we may lay down as a general rule that *as* and *bu* are used in the formation of the present tense, *vas* in the formation of the preterite. The latter is the preterite of an infinitive *visan* (manere), which follows our eighth conjugational class, *visa, vas, vesum, visans*. This fact will suffice for our guidance in explaining the different forms of this root used to supply certain forms of the verb 'to be.' As to the first-mentioned roots a few remarks will not be out of place here. We leave it for the student to compare the paradigm of the present tense in the Teutonic languages with that of *as-mi* in the primitive language, and to trace the modifications to which the root as well as the personal terminations are liable: our remarks are intended to direct his attention to a few important points.

ROOT **as**. The primitive radical *a* is in the Teutonic languages weakened to *i*; but this *i* appears in Anglo-Saxon as *eo*, which must be looked upon as the Brechung of *i*. The Brechung was most likely caused by a succeeding *r*, which would stand for the primitive *s* of the root *as*; hence *as-mi* is modified into the Gothic $i(s)$-$m(i)$, this again by rhotacism into $i(r)$-$m(i)$, whence the A. S. $eo(r)$-$m(i)$, the O. N. $e(r)$-$m(i)$, i. e. *eom, em* = Goth. *im*. By the side of *eom* we find in some of the northern Saxon dialects *eam, am*, forms in which the English *am* will find its explanation. The 2nd person, where the Goth. i-$s = i(s)$-$s(i)$ represents the prim. *as-si*, the A. S. *eart*, must be considered an analogous form to *eom*, so that the Sanskrit *asi*=*as-si*, for a still more ancient *as-ti*=*as-tva*, appears in Anglo-Saxon with the most primitive termination, *-t*, which as a rule we find only in the 2nd singular preterite. The 3rd person of the Goth. and H. Germ. *is-t*=†*is-ti* approaches closely the primitive form *as-ti* = *as-ta* (to be kept distinct from *as-si*, *as-ti* = *as-tva* of the 2nd). Anglo-Saxon however, and its English descendants, drop the terminational *-t* and put the mere root *is*=*as*. The 3rd plur. of Goth., O. H. Germ., and Modern Germ. *s-ind*=*is-ind* has the personal suffix of the prim. *as-anti* almost intact. This form was in the course of time no longer understood in its plural capacity, wherefore the Anglo-Saxons superadded the plural termination (*on* = *um* of the preterite) in *sindon*, Old Saxon *sindun*. Modern German introduced the form *sind* into the 1st plural as well, which in analogy to Middle High German ought to be *sein* instead of *sind*. The double plural form in Anglo-Saxon is peculiar, where, by the side of *sindon*, we have from the same root the plur. *aron*. This *ar-on* refers to the O. N. *er-u-m*, and is sometimes replaced by *earun*. From this and the Old Norse form we may be warranted to take the *a* as the representative of the Brechung *ea*, and the latter to have arisen from the fact of the vowel *i* of the root *is*=*as* being under the influence of a succeeding *r* into which the ancient *s* was converted, so that the course would be from *as-masi* to †*is-m*, and, the two succeeding consonants requiring a connective vowel, *is-u-m*, *ir-u-m*, O. N. *er-u-m*, A. S. *ear-u-n*, *ar-o-n*, whence the English *we are*, &c. The Gothic 1st and 2nd plural as well as the subjunctive having lost the vowel of the root *as*, and dropped everything of the termination except the consonant, would be reduced to nothing but two consonants, e. g. 1st plur. *s-m* for prim. *as-masi*. A vowel being necessary for the sake of pronunciation it adopted the theme of the subjunctive for the plural as well. Now the subjunctive theme is formed, not like the primitive *as-y-m* by bringing the *s* of the root and the suffix *ja* in direct contact, which would make *s-ja-*, but, by supporting the radical *s* by *i*, Gothic makes the subjunctive as if it were from a theme *sija-*, hence the subj. *sijau*. This theme then was adopted too as the theme of the 1st and 2nd plural, and after the manner of perfect themes it took the connective *u*, hence *sij-u-m*. A similar tendency to make present forms after the analogy of the preterite has already been observed in the O. N. *er-u-m*, A. S. *ar-o-n*, and we shall observe it again in the O. H. Germ. *pi-r-u-mes*. The Middle High German 1st plur. *sîn*, 2nd *sît*, Dutch *zîn*, *zît*, Germ. *seit*, are analogous to the Gothic theme *sija*- in a contracted state. Thus also we explain the subjunctives *si* or *se*, often *sio*, *sie*, Germ. *sei*, as the contracted form of the theme *sija*- of the Goth. subj. *sijau*, *sij-ai-s*, &c.

ROOT bu. It appears in Old Saxon as *biu*, in Anglo-Saxon as *beo*, in Old High German in the weakened form *pi*. Anglo-Saxon alone derives from this root forms for all the persons of the present tense, indicative as well as subjunctive; so that in the mentioned dialect we have two, sometimes three, forms for each person side by side in the present tense. Old High German, Old Saxon, and Old Frisian, use the root *bu* in the 1st and 2nd singular, and Old High German throughout the plural. Compare O. H. Germ. *pim*, O. S. *bium*, A. S. *beom*, O. Fris. *bem*; 2nd O. H. Germ. *pi-s* or *pi-st*, O. S. *bi-st*, A. S. *bi-st*, O. Fris. *bi-st*. Derived from these are the M. H. Germ. and N. H. Germ. *bin*, *bist*, M. Dutch *bem*, *best*, N. Dutch *ben*; *m* changed to *n* according to the phonetic laws. In the 3rd singular and the plural of the indicative, and throughout the subjunctive, Anglo-Saxon alone derives its forms from the root *bu*, which through Late Saxon and Old and Middle English run side by side with forms derived from the root *as*, and even in Modern English *be* is sometimes used dialectically for *are* in the plural. The Old High German plural *pi-r-u-mes*, &c., has been formed in analogy to the ancient perfect themes in *s*. Some consider this *r* to stand in place of an original *w*, hence *pi-r-u-mes* for *pi-w-u-mes*, primitive *bha-v-á-mas*; but I incline to the view of those who refer the *r* to a more ancient *s*, because this view is borne out by the analogy of the Old Norse perfect forms, *seri*, *greri*, &c. (See p. 401.) In later documents *pirumes* is shortened to *pirun*, then *pirn*, *pirut* to *pirt*, forms which still appear in Middle High German as *birn* and *birt*. There is also in Middle High German a form *bint* in the 2nd plural which must originally have come from the 3rd plural, and is formed with the root *bu*, *bi*, as *sint* with the root *as*, the former perhaps in analogy to the latter. The formations of the present subjunctive, as far as they are derived from the root *as*, have already been touched upon. Anglo-Saxon however makes its subjunctive out of three different roots, *as*, *bu* and *vas*. Later English dialects have selected out of these the root *bu*, *beo*, which, since Old English times, assumes the form *be* for the present subjunctive; for the infinitive, the present and preterite participle, N. Engl. *to be*, *being*, *been*. The modern Scandinavian dialects adopted the form of the 3rd person (Swed. *ær*, Dan. *er*) for the 1st and 2nd as well, and in the plural use the same root with the usual termination. Their subjunctive, if subjunctive they have, is formed by means of the root *rar* = *vas*. Thus then we might sum up, to the effect that the English dialects form their subjunctive with the root *bu*, High German and Dutch with the root *as*, the Scandinavian languages with the root *vas*. (Old Norse has *as* and *vas* side by side, e. g. 1st sing. *s-é* and *ver-i*.)

ROOT **vas**. It is used in all the Teutonic dialects, ancient and modern, to form the preterite of the verb 'to be.' It is one of the verbs of Class VIII, and treated as such; its Ablaut therefore is Goth. *visa, vas, vesum, visans*; O H. Germ. *wisu, was, wárumes, wesaner*; A. S. *wese, was, wæron, wesen*. We need therefore hardly point out the manner in which it forms its plural and subjunctive, the former being conditioned by the conjugational class to which the verb belongs, the latter being dependent on the form of the plural. As to the 2nd pers. sing. it follows the analogy of other strong verbs, that is, in Gothic and Old Norse it has the form of the singular with the termination *-t*, in the other dialects it takes the form of the plural with the vocalic termination *i* or *e*. The *s* of the root *vas* is intact in Gothic, while in Old Norse it submits to rhotacism throughout; in Old High German and the other dialects (Middle High German included) the *s* remains in the 1st and 3rd sing., but yields to rhotacism in the plural and all forms dependent on it. The Modern High German and Scandinavian languages have *r* throughout; the English, early and modern, as well as the Modern Dutch, keep the *s* in the singular and submit to rhotacism in the plural and the subjunctive which is dependent on it. The infinitive, the participles, and the imperative, avail themselves of different roots in different languages, the details of which formations, to gather from the paradigm, may be left as an interesting and profitable task to the student.

A few hints about the forms of Modern English must conclude our remarks. The present indicative is formed exclusively with the root *as*, where Scandinavian forms have gained the ascendancy, chiefly in the plural. The root *beo* (*bu*) is used for the formation of the present subjunctive, the infinitive, the participles and the imperative. The preterite indicative and subjunctive are formed with the root *vas*, which still presents the ancient Ablaut between the radicals of the sing. and plur. *was, were*. The 2nd sing. indic. instead of the A. S. *were*, makes the form *wast*, which occurs in Gothic already, though in the Saxon tongue it does not reach back beyond Middle English; by its side we find *wert*, which is formed after the analogy of *shalt* and *wilt* with the primitive suffix *-t* of the 2nd sing. It is against grammar to use this *wert* for the 2nd sing. subjunctive, which should always have *were*.

PRÆTERITO-PRÆSENTIA.

There are in the Teutonic as well as in other languages verbs which, after having lost their present, express the meaning of the lost tense by means of the preterite. Well known among these are the Latin verbs *odi, coepi, memini,* the Greek οιδα. Verbs of this class in the Teutonic languages have, moreover, the peculiarity to substitute a new preterite form in the place of that which has undertaken the functions of the present. This new preterite is formed by means of the suffix *-da* of weak verbs, which is added to the plural of the original strong preterite. It results from this as a matter of course that the preterite of this class of verbs shows both the Ablaut of the strong and the tense-suffix of the weak conjugation.

In considering the meaning of the verbs of this class we examine first those which occur in Gothic and the other Teutonic dialects equally, and then a few which are not found in Gothic; it will be convenient to interpret them by their Latin equivalents: *kann* (novi) has its origin in a verb *kinnan* (gignere) with which we may compare the root in the O. H. Germ. *chind*, Germ. *kind* (proles); *kann*, the preterite of *kinnan* therefore originally was identical in meaning with the Latin *genui.* Þarf (egeo) is the preterite of a lost infinitive Þaırban (agere, facere, operari), and must originally have been an expression used in religious rites, with the signification 'I have spent, offered,' 'I am without a sacrifice and wait for another.' *Dars* (audeo), from *daırsan*, perhaps with the original signification 'I have fought.' *Skal* (debeo) must come from a present *skila*, which meant 'I kill,' and with which we may compare *skilja* (butcher); *skal*, therefore, meant 'I have killed,' 'I must pay penance, wergeld;' hence 'I am under an obligation,' 'I am obliged,' 'I must.' *Man* refers us to a present form *mina* (cogito), and has the signification of the Latin *memini*, 'I have thought over,' therefore 'I remember.' *Mag* (possum) is the preterite of an ancient verb *migan* (crescere, gignere), and thus originally expresses the meaning 'I have begotten, produced,' hence 'I am able.' *Nah* (sufficere), from an infinitive *naíhan*, is considered to have been of the same signification as the preceding verb. *Aih* (habeo) comes from an infinitive *eıgan* (to labour, to work), whence the preterite would mean 'I have worked,' 'I have earned,' therefore 'I possess.' *Lais* (didici, οιδα) comes from a lost present *leisa* (calce, pede premo), which strictly means 'I have traced,' 'I am on the track,' and may be compared with the O. H. Germ. *leisa*, a track, vestigium. *Váit* (scio) comes from the root *vit* and requires a present form *veitan* (videre), which is in reality preserved in the compounds *in-veitan* (adorare), *fraveitan* (ulcisci); *váit* therefore originally meant 'I have seen,' hence 'I know.' Compare the Gr. οἶδα, Sansk *veda*, both from the same root *vid* (to see), and with the meaning 'I know.' *Daug* (prosum, valeo) from a present *diugan*, probably with the meaning of 'gignere,' 'to beget.' *Mot* (locum habeo) from a present *mata*, which is obscure in its origin and signification. *Og* (timeo) comes from a present *aga* (tremo) of which the present participle is preserved in *unagands* (without fear, fearless[1]). *An* (faveo), which does not occur in Gothic, but is preserved in Old High German and some other dialects, must come from an infinitive *innan*. *Kná* (possum), which occurs in Old Norse only, is no doubt related to the O. H. Germ. *knuot* (natura), the Goth. *knoda* (γενος), and the Sanskrit root *jan* (gignere). The Old Norse *muna* (recordari) and *munu* (μέλλειν) are no doubt of the same origin, as they are much alike in meaning: the difference of the infinitive forms is remarkable, the former being the present infinitive, the latter very likely a remnant of the ancient preterite infinitive in Old Norse.

PARADIGM.

	Pres. Sing.	Pres. Plur.	Preterite.	Infinitive.	
O. H. Germ.	an	unnumês	onda, onsta	unnan	favere
Old Saxon	[an]	[unnun]	onsta	[unnan]	,,
Anglo-Saxon	an	unnon	úðe	unnan	,,
Old Norse	ann	unnum	unna	unna	,,
Gothic	kann	kunnum	kunþa	kunnan	nosse
O. H. Germ.	kan	kunnumês	kunda, kunsta	kunnan	novisse
Old Saxon	can	cunnun	consta	cunnan	,,
Anglo-Saxon	can	cunnon	cúðe	cunnan	,,
Old Frisian	kan	kunnon	kunda	kunna	,,
Old Norse	kann	kunnum	kunna	kunna	,,
Gothic	þarf	þaúrbum	þaúrfta	þaúrban	egere
O. H. Germ.	darf	durfumês	dorfta	durfan	opus habere
Old Saxon	tharf	thurbun	thorfta	thurban	,, ,,
Anglo-Saxon	þarf, þearf	þurfon	þorfte	þurfan	,, ,,
Old Frisian	thurf	thurvon		thurva	,, ,,
Old Norse	þarf	þurfum	þurfta	þurfta	indigere

[1] Grimm's *Geschichte der Deut. Sprache*, p. 901.

THE VERB.

	Pres. Sing.	Pres. Plur.	Preterite.	Infinitive.	
Gothic	dars	daúrsum	daúrsta	daúrsan	audere
O. H. Germ.	tar	turrumês	torsta	turran	,,
Old Saxon	gi-dar	[-durrun]	-dorsta	-durran	,,
Anglo-Saxon	dar	durron	dorste	durran	,,
Old Frisian	thur-dur	thuron	thorste	thura	,,
Gothic	skal	skulum	skulda	skulan	debere
O. H. Germ.	scal	sculumês	scolta	sculan	,,
Old Saxon	scal	sculun	scolda	sculan	,,
Anglo-Saxon	sceal	sculon	sceolde	sculan	,,
Old Frisian	skil	skilu(n)	skolde	skila	,,
Old Norse	skal	skulum	{ skulda / skylda }	skulu	,,
Gothic	man	munum	munda	munan	meminisse
Old Saxon	far-man	munun	{ -munsta / -monsta }	-munan	contemnere
Anglo-Saxon	ge-mon	munon	-munde	-munan	meminisse
Old Norse	man	munum	{ munna / munda }	muna	recordari
Gothic	mag	magum	mahta	magan	posse
O. H. Germ.	mac	{ magumês, mugu-mês }	mahta / mohta	magan / mugan	,,
Old Saxon	mag	mugun	{ mahta / mohta }	[mugan]	,,
Anglo-Saxon	mäg	mâgon	meahte	magan	,,
Old Frisian	mei, mî	mugu(n)	machte	[mega]	,,
Old Norse	mâ	megum	mâtta	mega	,,
Gothic	nah	nauhum	nauhta	nauhan	sufficere
Anglo-Saxon	neáh	nugon	nohte	nugan	,,
Gothic	áih	áigum	áihta	{ áigan / áihan }	habere
O. H. Germ.	. . .	eigumês	. . .	eigan	,,
Old Saxon	[éh]	êgun	êhta	êgan	,,
Anglo-Saxon	áh	ágon	áhte	ágan	,,
Old Frisian	âch	âgon	âchte	âga, hâga	,,
Old Norse	â	eigum	âtta	eiga	,,
Gothic	láis	lisum	lista	lisan	didicisse
Gothic	vâit	vitum	vissa	vitan	scire
O. H. Germ.	weiʒ	wiʒumês	{ wissa / wista }	wiʒan	,,
Old Saxon	wêt	witun	wissa	witan	,,
Anglo-Saxon	wât	witon	{ wiste / wisse }	witan	,,
Old Frisian	wêt, wit	. . .	. . .	wita	,,
Old Norse	veit	vitum	vissa	vita	,,
Gothic	dáug	dugum	daúhta	dugan	valere
O. H. Germ.	touc	tugun	tohta	tugan	,,
Old Saxon	dôg	dugun	. . .	dugan	,,
Anglo-Saxon	deáh	dugon	duhte	dugan	,,
Old Frisian	duch	. . .	. . .	duga	,,

	Pres. Sing.	Pres. Plur.	Preterite.	Infinitive.	
Gothic	mot . .	. . môtum . .	môsta . .	môtan . .	locum habere
O. H. Germ.	muoʒ . .	muoʒumês .	{ muosa { muosta }	muoʒan . .	,, ,,
Old Saxon	mot . .	. môtun . .	môsta . .	môtan . .	,, ,,
Anglo-Saxon	mot . .	. môton . .	môste . .	môtan . .	,, ,,
Old Frisian	mot . .	. môton . .	môste . .	môta . . .	,, ,,
Gothic	ôg . . .	ôgum . .	ôhta . . .	ôgan . . .	timere
Old Norse	mun, man .	munum . .	munda . .	{ munu } { mundu }	μέλλειν
Old Norse	kna . . .	knegum . .	knatta . .	knêya . .	posse

REMARKS ON THE PARADIGM OF PRÆTERITO-PRÆSENTIA.

Gothic. The inflexions are the same as those of the strong preterites in general; the 2nd singular therefore of the present (the ancient preterite) has -*t,* the 1st plural -*u-m,* &c. The preterite suffix -*da* is inflected as in weak verbs and added directly to the preterite theme without a connective vowel, so that the consonant of the termination *da* and the preceding consonant of the preterite theme often modify one the other; hence the pret. of *kann, kunþa,* of *þarf,* plur. þaurbum, pret. þaurfta[1]; *mag,* pret. *mahta*[1]; *váit,* plur. *vitum,* pret. *vissa* for †*vis-ta*[2], †*vit-ta;* mot, pret. *mosta*[2] for *mot-ta*—modifications which are strictly in accordance with Gothic phonetic laws. As to the Ablaut, it is to be noticed how the radical of the present (ancient pret.) plural is changed in *skulum* for †*skelum, munum* for †*menum,* while the plur. *mágum* retains the *a* of the preterite singular instead of the common plural in *e*. The infinitive has always the radical of the present (ancient pret.) plural. The verb *ogan* has a 2nd sing. imper. *ogs;* may we thence infer an imper. *mots, dugs?* With regard to *kunnan, munan, vitan,* it may be observed that their confreres *munan* (mente agitare, velle, μέλλειν), *vitan* (observare), and *ga-kunnan* (observare) follow the third weak conjugation.

Old High German. The inflexions are the same as with the strong conjugation in general; only in the 2nd sing. pres. (ancient pret.) the ancient termination -*t* is preserved, which in the 2nd pret. of all other strong verbs has been lost. An *s* is added to the *t* in the verb *chan, chan-st.* This -*st* probably arose in analogy to the *s-t* in *vais-t* for *vait-t,* where the Gothic phonetic law requires the change of a dental into *s* before the termination *t.* How this termination -*st* gradually crept into the 2nd person of

---

[1] *f* and *h* owing to the succeeding *t*.   [2] Dental before dental changed into *s*.

the present and preterite we have observed elsewhere[1], as well as the persistency with which the ancient -*t* keeps its place in some of the præterito-præsentia up to the present day. *an* forms the pret. *onda* and *onsta*; *kann*, pret. *konda*, *konsta*, *kunda*, *kunsta*; and *bi-ginnan*, following their analogy, makes, by the side of its regular pret. *bi-gan*, also *bigonda*, *bi-gansta*.

Old Saxon. The termination of the 2nd singular is -*t*, except in *can-st* and *far-manst: biginnan* has, besides the regular pret. *began*, the form *begonsta*.

Anglo-Saxon. The 2nd singular had originally the termination -*t*, but the vocalic ending of the common preterite of strong verbs gradually replaced the ancient termination; hence *an*, *unne*, *can*, *cunne*, þ*earf*, þ*urfe*, &c.; but *dear* has by the side of *durre* the more ancient *dearst:* besides this there are preserved *canst*, *gemanst*, *áhst*—all having interpolated the *s* before the ending -*t*. *cuðe*, with ð for *nd* (comp. the letters *n* and ð).

Old Frisian. The 2nd singular occurs only once, of the verb *skila*, 2nd *skalt*. *skilu* and *mugu* appear to be dual forms used in the signification of the plural. Some of the præterito-præsentia in this dialect adopt forms of the weak conjugation; thus, for example, *wet* (of *wita*) has sometimes the weak form *wit*, plur. *witath*; of *duga* there occurs the 3rd sing. *ducht*; plur. in late Frisian *dáged*; of *ága* we find a 3rd sing. *acht*. *bijenna* has, by the side of the regular preterite, also *bigunde*, *bigonste*.

Old Norse. The 2nd singular ends in -*t*, as the preterite of strong verbs generally. Under the influence of this terminational *t* consonants are affected in the same manner as we showed above with regard to strong verbs. þ*ora* (andere) and *duga* (valere) make the pres. þ*ori*, *dugi*, pret. þ*orða*, *dugða*; *oga* (metuere) follows the second weak conjugation.

The infinitives *skulu* and *munu* are considered by Grimm as remnants of an ancient formation of a preterite infinitive in Old Norse. As such Grimm mentions also *foru* (ivisse), *stoðu* (stetisse); there occur also *skyldu*, *myndu*, and *bendu*, preterite infinitive of *benda*.

VERBS FOLLOWING THE ANALOGY OF PRÆTERITO-PRÆSENTIA.

There are a few verbs in the Teutonic languages which in the formation of their preterite follow the analogy of the præterito-præsentia, that is, they take both the Ablaut of the strong, and

[1] See p. 369.

the preterite suffix of the weak conjugation, the latter without the connective vowel. To these belong:—

Gothic þagkjan (to think, cogitare), root þak, pret. þahta; þugkjan (videri, Germ. dünken), þuhta[1]; brukjan (uti, Germ. brauchen), brúhta; bugjan (to buy), bauhta (bought); vaurkjan (operari, to work), vaurhta (wrought); káupatjan (colaphizare), pret. káupasta.

Old High German. denkan (to think, Germ. denken), pret. dáhta. part. dáht; dunkan (videri, Germ. dünken, to seem, appear), pret. duhta; wurkan, wirkan (to work), pret. worhta, wurhta, worahta, warahta, part. worht, wurht, woraht; furhtan (to fear, Germ. fürchten), pret. forhta, forahta, part. forht, foraht, furhtit. bringan (to bring) has, by the side of the strong preterite brang, brungumes, the anomalous forms bráhta, bráhtumes.

Old Saxon. thenkjan (to think), pret. tháhta, thunkjan (videri, Germ. dünken) thuhta; wirkjan (operari), warhta; buggjan (to buy) has only the part. gi-boht; brengjan (to bring), pret. bráhta.

Anglo-Saxon. þencan (to think), pret. þohte (thought); þyncan (videri), pret. þuhte; weorcan, wircan, wyrcan (to work), pret. worhte, weorhte; bycyan (to buy), pret. bohte (bought). bringan has, by the side of the strong preterite brang, brungon, the anomalous forms brohte, broht.

Old Frisian. werka (laborare), pret. wrochte[2] (wrought); branga, brendza (to bring), brochte; thanka, thenzja (to think), thochte; thinszja, the West-Frisian pret. tuchte for thuchte; bijenna (to begin) has the strong preterite and the anomalous forms bigunde, bigonste.

Old Norse. þynkja (videri), pret. þótta[3], but þenkja (to think) has þenk-ta, not þátta.

Besides the verbs just mentioned there is in all Teutonic languages the verb 'to will,' Goth. viljan, which also follows the analogy of præterito-præsentia, and has moreover a few peculiarities of its own which deserve special mention. The **Gothic** viljau (I will) has in the present only this subjunctive form which originally belonged to the preterite. By the side of this there must have been an ancient indicative preterite sing. váil, plur. vilum, and a present sing. veila (Class V). The preterite subjunctive is used to supply the forms of the present indicative, and the new anomalous preterite vilda is formed out of the plural form vilum. The present, being originally the subjunctive of the preterite, is inflected, as this form usually is, in the strong

---

[1] As to the infix n in þagkjan, þugkjan, of the roots þak, and þuk see **Formation of the Present.**
[2] Metathesis.   [3] tt = ht, see the respective letters.

conjugation, as *viljau, vileis, vili,* &c.; the new preterite makes the indicative *vilda, vildes,* &c., and the subjunctive *vildedjau,* &c., after the manner of weak verbs in general. **Old High German.** The verb *wellan* strives after indicative forms in the present tense, and the conjugation is therefore subject to considerable anomalies. Thus we have true preterite subjunctive forms in *wili, wilis, wili;* but present subjunctive forms in the plur. *wëllémes,* &c. An endeavour to assume indicative forms we see in the 2nd sing. *wilt,* a form analogous to the præterito-præsentia; and in the 3rd plur. *wollent, wellent, wellant* for *wellen,* &c.; 3rd sing. *wilt* for *wili.* The preterite indicative is always in imitation of the præterito-præsentia *wolta,* rarely *welta,* subj. *wolti.* **Old Saxon** has, more decidedly than Old High German, acquired indicative forms for the verb *willjan,* so that we find in the present an indicative and subjunctive kept strictly distinct, as indic. *willju, wili* or *wilt, wili, wil,* or *wilit,* plur. *willjad;* subj. *willje (-ea), willjes (-eas),* plur. *willjen (-ean);* pres. *welda, wolda;* subj. *weldi, woldi.* **Anglo-Saxon** takes a similar course: pres. sing. *wille, wilt, wille;* plur. *willað,* pret. *wolde.* **Old Frisian** pres. sing. *wille, wilt, wille* (also *wilt, wil,* &c.); plur. *willath;* pret. *welde, wolde.* **Old Norse** *vilja, velle,* has the following forms: pres. sing. *vil, vill* and *vilt, vill* (for *vil-r*), plur. *viljum, vilið, vilja;* subj. *vili,* pret. *vilda.*

MIDDLE AND NEW TEUTONIC LANGUAGES.

English.

The Goth. *kann,* A. S. *can (con)* we find throughout all the periods of the English language. It takes *-st* in the 2nd, hence *canst;* in the plural we find the Ablaut *u* down to Middle English, hence, *cunnen, kunnen;* New English makes the plural and singular alike. The *n* of the Gothic pret. *kunba* was dropped in the A. S. *cuðe,* Orm. *cuþe,* O. Engl. *couþe,* M. Engl. *coude;* N. Eng. *could,* perhaps in analogy of *would* and *should.*

The Goth. *þarf,* A. S. *þearf,* appears in the Late Saxon plur. *þurfen,* pret. *þurfte,* O. Engl. *tharf;* it is lost in New English.

The Goth. *dars,* A. S. *dear,* is preserved in the *der, dar* of Early and *dare* of Modern English. The 2nd sing. *-st* throughout. The 3rd sing. (as all the præterito-præsentia) like the 1st; but New English introduced *dares* by the side of *dare,* plur. Late Saxon *durren,* O. Engl. *durre,* M. Engl. *durn,* N. Engl. *dare.*

The preterite Goth. *daursta*, A. S. *dorste*, we find in the late Saxon *durste*, O. Engl. and M. Engl. *dorste*, N. Engl. *durst*.

The A. S. *gemunan* is only in the Ormulum subjunc. *mune*, pret. *munde*, &c.

The A. S. *unnan* we find in Layamon as *on*, plur. *i-unnen*, pret. *uðe*, Crm. *uþe*, and in the Old English pres. sing. and infin. *an*.

Goth. *skal*, A. S. *sceal*, Orm. *shall*, O. Engl. and M. Engl. *schall*, N. Engl. *shall*; 2nd, *-t* throughout; plur. A. S. *sculon*, Lay. *sculen*, Orm. *shulenn*, O. Engl. *schulleþ*, M. Engl. *schullen*, New Engl. *shall*; pret. Goth. *skulda*, A. S. *sceolde*, Lay. *scolde*, Orm. *shollde*, O. Engl. and M. Engl. *schulde*, N. Engl. *should*, the *l* suppressed in pronunciation, perhaps in analogy to *could* M. Engl. *coude*.

The A. S. *deah* occurs only in the 3rd sing. *dæh* of the Ormulum and O. Engl. *degh*.

Goth. *mag*, A. S. *mæg*, Lay. *mæi*, Orm. *maʒʒ*, O. Eng., M. Engl. and N. Engl. *may;* 2nd, A. S. *meaht*, O. Engl. *miht, miʒt*, &c., M. Engl. *maist*, N. Engl. *mayst;* subj., A. S. *mage*, O. Engl. *mowe;* pret., A. S. *meahte*, O. Engl. *mihte, myʒte*, &c., N. Engl. *might*.

Goth. *váit*, A. S. *wat*, Late Sax. *wat*, O. Engl. and M. Engl. *wot(e)*, N. Engl. *wot*; 2nd, *wast, wost* throughout, lost in N. Engl.; plur. *witon, witen* throughout, lost in N. Engl.; pret. A. S. *wiste*, Lay. *wuste*, Orm. *wisste*, O. Engl. and M. Engl. *wiste*, N. Engl. *wist;* infin., A. S. *witan*, Late Sax. *witen*, O. Engl. and M. Engl. *witen, wite*, N. Engl. *to wit*.

Goth. *áih*, A. S. *ah*, Late Sax. *ah*, O. Engl. *auh, ouh*, M. Engl. *awe, owe*, N. Engl. *owe;* 2nd sing., *-est*, or *-ist*; plur. *-en;* pret. Goth. *áihta*, A. S. *áhte*, Late Sax. *ahte, ahhte*, O. Engl. *aʒte*, M. Engl. *owʒte*, N. Engl. *ought*. Layamon already applies this verb in the two distinct senses of possession and duty; the latter we find in phrases such as 'he ah to don' = 'he has to do,' 'he ought.' In connection with this sense it developed the meaning of being in debt, 'to owe,' which verb follows the weak conjugation, *ought* being quite reserved for the expression of moral obligation. The meaning of possession is, in Modern English, attached to the verb 'to own,' which seems to have arisen from the part. *ágen, awen, owen*, or from the A. S. *ágnjan* (to possess).

The A. S. *mot* we find with slight variations throughout all periods; the present is lost in New English; pret. Goth. *mosta*, A. S. *moste* we find in Early English as *moste*, N. Engl. *must*.

The A. S. *wille* appears as *wille, wolle, wulle* in the different Early English periods, N. Engl. *will;* 2nd sing. *wilt* (or *wolt, wult* in Early English); plur. *willeþ, wulleþ*, &c., or *wilen, wolen*, N. Engl. *will;* pret. A. S. *wolde*, Early Engl. *wolde, walde*, N. Engl. *would, l* not pronounced, perhaps in analogy to *could*, M. Engl. *coude*.

German.

M. H. Germ. 1st *muoz*, 2nd *muost*, plur. *muezen*, pret. *muoste* (also *muosa, muese*); N. H. Germ. *muß, mußt, müßen, mußte*. M. H. Germ. *weiʒ, weist, wiʒʒen, wiste (weste, wisse* [1], *wesse*); N. H. Germ. *weiß, weißt, wißen, wußte*. M. H. Germ. *touc, toht, tügen, tohte;* N. H. Germ. *tauge* (weak). M. H. Germ. *mac, maht, mügen, mohte (mahte);* N. H. Germ. *mag, magst, moegen, mochte*. M. H. Germ. *sol, solt, süln, solte;* N. H. Germ. *soll* (weak). M. H. Germ. *gan, ganst, günnen, gunde;* N. H. Germ. *gonne* (weak). M. H. Germ. *kan, kanst, künnen, kunde;* N. H. Germ. *kann, kannst, konnen, konnte*. M. H. Germ. *tar, tarst, türren, torste;* N. H. Germ. lost. M. H. Germ. *darf, darft, dürfen, dorfte;* N. H. Germ. *darf, darfst, dürfen, durfte*. M. H. Germ. *wil (welle), wil (wellest, wellen, wolte);* N. H. Germ. *will, willst, wollen, wollte*. Inorganic Umlaut is, in the present indicative plural and in the infinitive, both in Middle High German and New High German. But perhaps we may suppose in Middle High German the infinitives *muozen, tugen, kunnen, durfen*, &c., by the side of *muezen, tügen, kunnen, durfen*. The preterite subjunctive which has never Umlaut in weak verbs (e. g. *brennen*, pret, subj. M. H. Germ. *brante*, N. H. Germ. *brannte*, not *brente, brännte*).

Dutch.

M. Dutch 1st *moet*, 2nd *moetes*, plur. *moeten*, pret. *moeste;* N. Dutch 1st *moet*, plur. *mocten*, pret. *moest*, part. *gemoeten*. M. Dutch *doch, doghes, doghen, dochte;* N. Dutch *deug, deugen, docht*. M. Dutch *mach, moghes, moghen, mochte;* N. Dutch *mag, mogen, mocht, gemocht*. M. Dutch *sal, sules, sulen, sulde (soude* [1]); N. Dutch *zal, zullen, zoude* [1] *(zou)*. M. Dutch *an, onnes, onnen, onste;* N. Dutch lost. M. Dutch *can, connes, connen, conste;* N. Dutch *kan, konnen, konde (kon, kost), gekonnen (gekost)*. M. Dutch *dar, dorres, dorren, dorste;* N. Dutch *derr* (weak). M. Dutch *dærf, dorves, dorven [dorfte];* N. Dutch *durf, durven, dorst* (this preterite originally belonged to *der*). M. Dutch *wille, willes, willen, wilde (woude);* N. Dutch *wil, willen, wilde* (vulg.

---

[1] Compare Goth. *vissa*.   [2] The contraction *ou* for *old, ald*.

woude, won), gewilt. M. Dutch *wet, wetes, weten, wiste;* N. Dutch *wet, weten, wist, geweten.*

Scandinavian.

Swed. *vet,* plur. *vete,* pres. *viste;* Dan. *ved, vide, vidste.* Swed. *ma, mage, matte;* Dan. *maa, maae, maatte.* Swed. *skal, skole, skulle;* Dan. *skal, skulle, skulde.* Swed. *kan, kunne, kunde;* Dan. *kan, kunne, kunde.* Swed. *æger* (habeo, weak); Dan. *ejer* (weak). Swed. *tors* (passive), pret. *torde;* Dan. *toer, turde.* Swedish pres. and pret. *maste* (debui and debeo). O. Swed. *månde,* O. Dan. *mon, monne* (comp. O. N. *man, mundi*). Swed. *vill, vilja,* pret. *ville;* Dan. *vil, ville, vilde.*

VERBS FOLLOWING THE ANALOGY OF PRÆTERITO-PRÆSENTIA.

English.

The A. S. *bringan, brohte,* O. Engl. and M. Engl. *broȝte, brouhte,* N. Engl. *brought;* A. S. *bycgan, bohte,* O. Engl. and M. Engl. *boȝte, bouhte,* N. Engl. *bought;* A. S. *þencean, þohte,* O. Engl. *þoȝte,* M. Engl. *thoȝte, thouht,* N. Engl. *thought;* A. S. *þyncð, þuhte,* Lay. *þunceð, þuhte,* Orm. *þincheþþ, þuhte,* O. Engl. *þyncþ, þoȝte,* M. E. *thinketh, thoȝt (thouȝt),* N. E. *thinks (me-thinks), thought;* A. S. *wyrcean, worhte,* Lay. *wurchen, worhte,* Orm. *wirrkenn, wrohhte* (metathesis), O. Engl. *wyrce, wroȝte, wroht,* M. Engl. *worche (wyrke), wroȝte (wrouhte),* N. Engl. *work, wrought* and *worked.* Other anomalous formations in English are: A. S. *cláðjan, cláð-ode,* which makes in O. Engl. *cloþien,* pret. *cloþ-ed* and *cladde,* N. Engl. *clothed* and *clad;* A. S. *makjan, mac-ode,* O. Engl. *maked* and *made,* N. Engl. *made;* A. S. *sagjan, secgan* (to say), pret. *sägde* and *sæde,* O. Engl. and M. Engl. *seide,* N. Engl. *said;* A. S. *lagjan* and *lecgan,* pret. *lagode, legede, lede,* O. Engl. *leide,* N. Engl. *laid.*

German.

M. H. Germ. *bringen, bráhte,* N. H. Germ. *brachte;* M. H. Germ. *denken, dáhte,* N. H. Germ. *dachte;* M. H. Germ. *dunken, duhte,* N. H. Germ. *dunken, dauchte (däuchte); däucht* for *dünkt* in the pres. is wrong. M. H. Germ. *würken (wirken), worhte; vurhten, vorhte;* N. H. Germ. *wirken, furchten* (weak).

Dutch.

M. Dutch *bringhen, brochte;* N. Dutch *brengen, brocht.* M. Dutch *denken (dinken), dachte (dochte)*; N. Dutch *denken, docht.* M. Dutch *dunken, dochte;* N. Dutch *dunken, docht.* M. Dutch *werken, wrochte;* N. Dutch *werken, wrocht; vruchten* (metathesis; comp. M. H. Germ. *vurhten*), *vrochte; duchten* (to fear), *dochte.*

Scandinavian.

Swed. *bringe, bragte;* Dan. *bringe, bragte.* Swed. *tänka, tycka* (weak); Dan. *tänke, tykkes* (passive; weak).

APPENDIX.

The reader is requested to compare with these notes the Tables of Possessive Pronouns on pp. 197 and 198, where they ought to have been inserted.

REMARKS ON THE POSSESSIVE PRONOUNS.

The possessive pronouns are in close relationship to the genitives of the personal pronouns, the theme of both being identical.

They take the inflexions of the strong declension of adjectives; the weak inflexions, as they occur in Old High German alone, are quite isolated.

In Gothic the nom. sing. and plur. of *seins, seina, seinata,* is not used, but the gen. of the demonst. pron. of the 3rd person. (Gen. masc. *is,* fem. *izo,* neut. *is;* plur. *ize, izo, ize;* compare the use in Greek of the genitive of the personal instead of the possessive pronoun.)

The O. H. Germ. *unsarer, iwarer,* occur in a shortened form *unsêr, iwêr.*

The A. S. *user* has a parallel form in *ure.* *Úser,* whenever *s* and *r* (after the elision of *e*) meet in the inflexions, assimilates the *r* to the *s* and thus produces the gemination *ss.*

The declension, therefore, of the A. S. *user* and *ure* is as follows:—

	SINGULAR							
	Masculine.			Feminine.			Neuter.	
Nom.	ûser,	ûre	..	ûser,	ûre		ûser,	ûre
Gen.	..	ûseres,	ûsses	ûserre,	ûsse,	ûrre	ûres	..
Dat.	..	ûserum,	ûssum	ûserre,	ûsse,	ûrre	ûrum	..
Accus.	ûserne,	ûrne	..	ûsere,	ûsse,	ûre	ûser,	ûre

	PLURAL.			
	Masculine.			Neuter.
Nom.	ûsere,	ûsse,	ûre	ûser, ûre
Gen.	..	ûsera,	ûssa	ûre
Dat.	..	ûserum,	ûssum	ûrum
Accus.	ûsere,	ûsse,	ûre	ûser, ûre

University of Toronto Library

**DO NOT
REMOVE
THE
CARD
FROM
THIS
POCKET**